THE HISTORY OF
CANADA

Clio Bibliography Series No. 10

Gail Schlachter, Editor
Pamela R. Byrne, Executive Editor

Users of the Clio Bibliography Series may refer to current issues of
America: History and Life *and* Historical Abstracts
*for continuous bibliographic coverage of the subject areas
treated by each individual volume in the series.*

1.
The American Political Process
Dwight L. Smith and Lloyd W. Garrison
1972   LC 72-77549   ISBN 0-87436-090-0

2.
Afro-American History
Dwight L. Smith
1974   LC 73-87155   ISBN 0-87436-123-0

3.
Indians of the United States and Canada
Dwight L. Smith
1974   LC 73-87156   ISBN 0-87436-124-9

4.
Era of the American Revolution
Dwight L. Smith
1975   LC 74-14194   ISBN 0-87436-178-8

5.
Women in American History
Cynthia E. Harrison
1979   LC 78-26194   ISBN 0-87436-260-1

6.
The American and Canadian West
Dwight L. Smith
1979   LC 78-24478   ISBN 0-87436-272-5

7.
**European Immigration and Ethnicity
in the United States and Canada**
David L. Brye
1983   LC 82-24306   ISBN 0-87436-258-X

8.
Afro-American History Volume II
Dwight L. Smith
1981   ISBN 0-87436-314-4

9.
**Indians of the United States and Canada
Volume II**
Dwight L. Smith
1983   LC 73-87156   ISBN 0-87436-149-4

10.
The History of Canada
Dwight L. Smith
1983   LC 82-24307   ISBN 0-87436-047-1

11.
Urban America
Neil L. Shumsky and Timothy Crimmins
1983   LC 82-24292   ISBN 0-87436-038-2

12.
Religion and Society in North America
Robert de V. Brunkow
1983   LC 82-24304   ISBN 0-87436-042-0

THE HISTORY OF
CANADA

AN ANNOTATED BIBLIOGRAPHY

Dwight L. Smith

Editor

Alan H. MacDonald

Introduction

ABC-Clio Information Services
Santa Barbara, California
Oxford, England

Library of Congress Cataloging in Publication Data
Main entry under title:

The History of Canada.

    (Clio bibliography series; no. 10)
    Includes index.
    1. Canada—History—Bibliography. 2. Indians of
North America—Canada—History—Bibliography.
I. Smith, Dwight La Vern, 1918-   . II. Series.
Z1382.H57 1983 [F1026] 016.971 82-24307
ISBN 0-87436-047-1

© 1983 by ABC-Clio, Inc.

All rights reserved. No part of this publication may be reproduced, stored in a retrieval
system, or transmitted, in any form or by any means, electronic, mechanical, photo-copying,
recording, or otherwise, without the prior written permission of ABC-Clio, Inc.

REF.

Z
1382
, H57
1983

The History of Can-
ada

36,618

American Bibliographical Center—Clio Press, Inc.
2040 Alameda Padre Serra
Santa Barbara, California

European Bibliographical Center—Clio Press
55 St. Thomas Street
Oxford OX1 1JG, England

Design by Lance Klass
Printed and bound in the United States of America.

TABLE OF CONTENTS

PREFACE. vii
INTRODUCTION. ix
ABSTRACTS. 1
SUBJECT INDEX 223
AUTHOR INDEX 316
LIST OF PERIODICALS. 323
LIST OF ABSTRACTERS. 326
LIST OF ABBREVIATIONS. 327

---

1. GENERAL CANADIAN HISTORY. 1

2. THE NATURAL SETTING. 18

3. THE NATIVE PEOPLES
   General 19
   Pre-Columbian History 19
   Inuit (Eskimo). 21
   Indian 23

4. PRE-COLUMBIAN EXPLORATION
   AND EXPLOITATION
   The Norse Venture 33
   European Exploration 33

5. NEW FRANCE, 16TH CENTURY-1763
   General 34
   Exploration 35
   Colonization and Settlement 35
   Indian Relations 36
   Society 36
   The Church 38
   The Government 39
   Fish, Furs, and Farming 39
   Continental Penetration 40
   Decline and Fall 41

6. BRITISH NORTH AMERICA, 1763-1867
   General 44
   Accommodation to the French 49
   The American Revolution 51
   Loyalist Influx 53
   The War of 1812 54

Settlement and Economic Growth. 55
The Rebellions of 1837 58
Responsible Government and
   Self-Government 59
Mid-Century Developments 60
Confederation 64

7. EMERGENT NATIONALISM, 1867-1914
   General 66
   Western Expansion. 69
   The Conservative Years, 1867-1896. 75
   The Laurier Years, 1896-1911 78

8. ACHIEVEMENT OF NATIONHOOD,
   1914-1945
   General 82
   World War I 84
   The Twenties 85
   The Great Depression. 87
   World War II 89

9. THE CONTEMPORARY SCENE, SINCE 1945
   General 92
   The Domestic Scene. 93
      General 93
      Society and Culture. 96
      Economic Matters 107
      Government and Politics 114
   International Posture 120
   Canadian-American Relations 133
   Constitutional Crisis. 140

10 CANADA: REGIONS
   General 144
   The Atlantic Provinces 146
      General 146
      Newfoundland. 147
      Prince Edward Island 150
      Nova Scotia 150
      New Brunswick 159
   Quebec. 162
      General 162
      Society and Culture. 165

CAMROSE LUTHERAN COLLEGE
LIBRARY

Economic Matters 174
Separatism and Nationalism 179
Ontario 183
The Western Provinces 193
General 193
Manitoba 198
Saskatchewan 202

Alberta 206
British Columbia 210
The Territories 216
General 216
Arctic Exploration 218
Yukon Territory 219
Northwest Territories 220

PREFACE

The History of Canada is the tenth volume in the Clio Bibliography Series. Three of the previous volumes in the series, those concerned with the West, Indians, and European immigration and ethnicity, encompass Canada and the United States in their titles and contents. Those which deal with Afro-Americans, women, and the American Revolution include sections devoted to Canada. Because Canadian history is a unique and important subject of study, because Canadian-American relations are a major factor in North American history, and because of Canada's increasing role in the international scene, it is eminently appropriate to devote a volume exclusively to scholarship on Canada.

The History of Canada is an annotated bibliography of the periodical literature relating to Canadian history and life, and is based on the data base of *America: History and Life*. The bibliography, consequently, consists of annotated citations to the relevant literature appearing in approximately 2,000 serial publications published in some forty-two languages. This volume focuses on articles which appeared from 1973 through 1978.

From the data base of over 36,000 abstract entries I selected 3,362 for this bibliography. My selection was designed to include any entries related to Canadian history in any way, or which support or add a bit of information to the total picture. One concerning French Canadian workers in Massachusetts, for example, may well interest a student of the social, economic, or demographic history of French Canada.

The History of Canada ranges from prehistory to the present and reflects the amount of periodical literature dealing with each era. The plethora to paucity range of coverage from category to category means simply that this bibliography represents what was published in those years as recorded in *America: History and Life*. I organized the entries so as to highlight the history of Canada on a chronological basis or by geographical location. While a given item may not fit under the rubric itself, it may be placed there either because of its chronological or geographical context. Precisely where to locate or assign an entry, however, is often a difficult matter. In each instance I classified according to the principal emphasis within the scheme of the volume. When an entry straddled two or more sections, the one most prominent determined ultimate location. I used one of the general categories if the emphasis was not clear or if it was equally distributed over two or more divisions.

Entries which could logically be located in two or more places presented another classification problem. One concerned with Indians in Saskatchewan, for instance, might be put under "Indians, 1492- ," "Western expansion," or "Saskatchewan." For that matter, Indian-related items are scattered throughout the volume as well as under the regular Indian sections.

These classification difficulties point up the exceedingly important nature of the index. When the user of this bibliography pursues a topic that is more specific than the arrangement provided for by the organizational scheme or when the search is concerned with a subject that moves across chronological or geographical lines, the index is essential as an analytical guide to the contents of the entries. The Subject Profile Index used herein is especially suited as an in-depth device to enhance the utility and value of this bibliography. More comprehensive than conventional indexes, ABC-SPIndex is uniquely designed to increase access to the bibliographic entries. The subjects of each entry are indexed as a set of terms (an index string) that provides a complete profile of the subject matter, location and inclusive dates of the cited article—in effect giving the user an abstract of the abstract. I urge users to read the brief explanatory note at the beginning of the index to appreciate the full potential that it offers.

Finally, historical bibliographies sometimes have special sections devoted to such things as historiography, methods, bibliographies, and other research aids. Rather than add specific chapter designations for these categories, I have included them within the most appropriate subject matter headings.

Actually, *The History of Canada* is the product of the efforts of a large number of specialists, scholars and historians throughout the world who prepared the abstracts of the periodical literature represented in this volume. Attribution is indicated with each entry and a list of abstracters appears in the back of the volume.

In a very real sense, it is impossible to describe discrete roles for the individuals who coordinated their several specialties to bring this volume to publication. In varying degrees, we were all involved in every aspect of its production. I assumed the responsibility as the bibliographer and editor for *The History of Canada* while serving as consultant to the American Bibliographical Center in Santa Barbara during the summers of 1980 and 1981 and for other, briefer periods in Ohio.

The intellectual involvement of the bibliographer and editors on the one hand and the technical contributions of the systems analyst and data processing specialists on the other are closely related. With skillful editorial management and patient good humor, Pamela R. Byrne, executive editor of the Clio Bibliography Series, coordinated this complicated team effort from data selection to publication. She and her staff, particularly Suzanne Robitaille Ontiveros, Paula May Cohen, Lance Klass, Shirley A. Matulich, and David J. Valiulis edited the entries, prepared the index, and readied the book for publication. The intellectually demanding and tedious

aspects of production are reflected especially in the sophisticated Subject Profile Index.

Kenneth H. Baser, director of data processing services, and Deborah A. Looker, production supervisor, retrieved the abstracts from the data base of *America: History and Life,* carried out the complex correction processes, and performed other technical services. Their ready cooperation and advice facilitated the coordination that brought the text to the form necessary for publication.

It is our good fortune that Alan H. MacDonald, director of libraries at the University of Calgary, has written the introductory essay for *The History of Canada.* His excellent survey places the contents of this bibliography of recent periodical literature concerned with the history of Canada into a meaningful context.

Dwight L. Smith
Miami University
Oxford, Ohio

INTRODUCTION

Francois-Xavier Garneau's *Histoire du Canada* (1845) is traditionally considered the first major survey work in Canadian historiography. Like Garneau, most 19th century writers of Canadian history were not professionally-trained historians. Not until 1895 were separate chairs of history established at Toronto and McGill, while lectures on Canadian history were offered for the first time at McGill, Queen's and Toronto during that decade. The emphasis in the fledgling departments was on the teaching of English and American history. Up to the end of World War I, English-Canadian writers participated in several major cooperative ventures: *Makers of Canada* (20 vols., 1903-1908); *Chronicles of Canada* (32 vols., 1914-1916); *Canada and its Provinces* (23 vols., 1914-1917). Although the methodology and styles varied appreciably and many of the volumes would be found lacking by the standards of contemporary scholarship, these works remain the foundation of English language historical writing.

It is appropriately Canadian that the major landmarks in the development of history as a domestic discipline are reports, one a Royal Commission and the other a private report. The publication of the *Report of the Royal Commission on National Development in the Arts, Letters and Sciences* (1951) was the first occasion that the Canadian public was made aware of the state of Canadian historical scholarship. Chaired by Vincent Massey, Chancellor of the University of Toronto and subsequently the first Canadian-born Governor General, the Commission investigated all aspects of Canadian culture. Major recommendations were made regarding the care of historic sites and monuments, of public records and the strengthening of the Public Archives of Canada. Of equal importance to the *Report* itself was the auxiliary volume of essays entitled *Royal Commission Studies*. Essays were published by four leading historians on English national history, French national history, Canadian archives, and historical societies and museums. Hilda Neatby's analytical essay on English national history surveyed twentieth century developments. Although the writing of Canadian history had become increasingly "professionalized" and much excellent work had been published on constitutional and economic history during the interwar years, she lamented the lack of scholarship by Canadian historians in the fields of historical biography and foreign history. Secondly, although she noted a "renewed" interest in Canadian history at the universities, good textbooks for schools were lacking. Sadly she concluded that "we have as yet no national history, and no genuine national consciousness of the past." (p. 216)

Sixteen years after the publication of the Massey Report, Canada celebrated its Centennial year. Neatby might have argued that Canadians still had no national history, but no one would deny the awakening of the mass of Canadians to a consciousness of their country—a pride in its present and a feeling for its past. Witnessing Expo '67 in Montreal or participating in any of the hundreds of Centennial projects and events throughout the country helped to make Canadians more aware of both their regional differences and common bonds. During the sixties, the impact of the postwar "baby boom" resulted in the founding of new universities and a phenomenal growth of established institutions. The healthy domestic economy of the mid-sixties heightened Canadians' collective confidence in their nation. Not surprisingly, the President of the Canadian Historical Association in his annual address for 1967 sounded an optimistic note and echoed sentiments which rapidly became cliche in Centennial year: "a nation is a venture in history, that through an understanding of its history it knows itself, finds confidence to be true to itself, and guidance for the future." (p.8)

Within five years, however, it was once again felt necessary to scrutinize aspects of Canadian culture with a second major study. This time the initiative was taken by the Association of Universities and Colleges of Canada. The AUCC commissioned Professor Thomas H. B. Symons, founding President of Trent University, to investigate all aspects of the teaching and research of Canadiana in Canadian universities. The report was published in 1975 as *To Know Ourselves: The Report of the Commission on Canadian Studies*. The commissioners noted the expansion of the teaching of Canadian history at the universities and concluded that more Canadian material was found in the course descriptions of history departments than any other discipline. However, an analysis of the curricula across the country suggested that more work should be done in other areas such as urban, economic, business, labour, social, military, ethnic, biographical, and intellectual history. It was strongly recommended that a "substantial" introductory course in Canadian history be available for all freshman undergraduates, regardless of faculty.

In its reply to the Symons Report, the Canadian Historical Association's Committee on the Historical Profession considered the expansionist recommendations of Symons unrealistic. The unprecedented growth of the universities in the 1960's—expanding student enrollment, doubling of the number of Canadian historians in academic positions, more doctoral theses written on Canadian history since the mid-sixties than during the whole period prior to 1965—was indeed past history. The outlook for the foreseeable future suggested restraint at best. Any expansion of the teaching and research of Canadian history would result in a consequent reduction in areas of non-Canadian history. The committee also noted the phenomenal outpouring of monographs and new serial titles (both general and specialized) relating to Canadian history. What another Canadian historian has referred to as the "golden age" of Canadian historical writing, c.1965-1976, was clearly past, however temporarily.

Possibly the final word on the state of Canadian historiography should come from an outsider. Writing in the *Canadian Historical Review* (1977), H. J. Hanham of England noted three major recent trends in Canadian historiography: the results of changes in the universities; a greater emphasis on social and economic history; a growing interest among English-Canadian historians to write for an international community. Hanham concludes by stating that the problem facing the next generation of Canadian historians is "to write about Canadians without being constantly preoccupied with the mystery of what is Canada." (p.22)

An historical overview of the bibliographic control of periodical literature pertaining to Canadian history should probably begin with the *Review of Historical Publications Relating to Canada.* Published annually from 1886-1917/18 under the editorship of George Wrong, the *Review* lists English and French language monographic and serial literature, 1895-1918. Because of the "increasing volume of publications dealing with Canada that have issued from the press in recent years," the members of the Canadian Historical Association founded the *Canadian Historical Review (CHR)* in 1920. The *Review* was published quarterly and was enlarged to a forum for the publication of articles on any aspect of Canadian history.

The "Recent Publications Relating to Canada" section of the *CHR* remains one of the premier sources for accessing periodical literature of Canadian history. For Canadian periodical literature, in general, bibliographic control can be traced to the work of Agnes Lancefield and Angus Mowat at Windsor Public Library and the founding of the *Canadian Periodical Index* in 1928. With one break (1933-37), *CPI* has been published continuously, having been taken over permanently by the

Canadian Library Association in 1949. *CPI* is now a monthly indexing service covering one hundred forty-five Canadian periodicals of all types.

Since 1967, *Revue d'Histoire de l'Amerique Francaise* has published a quarterly section "Bibliographie d'Histoire de l'Amerique Francaise," a bibliography of works, including journal articles, on Laurentiana or the history of French-speaking Canadians. The *Revue* itself, published since 1947, is indexed in *CPI*. Access to Laurentiana can be difficult for anglophones; however, *Bibliographia Canadiana*, edited by Claude Thibault, is the most comprehensive source for periodical and other forms of historical literature covering all aspects of Canadiana from earliest times to 1969. Thibault indexes both French and English language journals and the bibliography is an efficient tool for accessing the periodical literature. Other bibliographies like *Western Canada Since 1870: A Select Bibliography and Guide* by Alan Artibise and *Bibliography of Ontario History, 1867-1976: Cultural, Economic, Political, Social* edited by Olga Bishop have been published within the past five years and index periodical literature, among other forms. The proliferation of such regional and provincial bibliographies, to say nothing of the provision of a variety of subject bibliographies in Canadian history, has understandably vastly improved our access to periodical literature. Even Thibault's work, regarded by many bibliographers as a pioneering effort, was published only a decade ago.

If politics is present history, then one cannot ignore access to Canadian newspapers. *Index de l'Actualite* has indexed *Le Devoir* since the inception of the indexing service in 1966; *La Press* and *Le Soleil* were added in 1972. Not until 1977 was an attempt made to index articles in the English language press. Through most of its life, *Canadian News Index* has had as its purpose the indexing of English language dailies—four Western and three Eastern. Although historians and political scientists will continue to debate where the line between the study of the two disciplines should be drawn, newspaper indexes will prove, if they have not already done so, a significant tool for gaining access to journalistic literature as a means of sampling the tone of an era.

With the commencement of publication of *America: History and Life* (v. 1, 1964/65-), yet another means was devised for controlling the publication of periodical literature relating to Canadian history. The 3,362 abstracts in this bibliography have been selected from Part A (Article Abstracts and Citations) of volumes 11-16 of *America: History and Life,* covering 1973-78. Approximately 75 Canadian serials are fully covered in *AHL,* in addition to almost 2,000 originating in the United States and elsewhere. The variety of non-Canadian journals represented in the abstracts is indicative of both the growing interest in Canada and its history among scholars in other countries and the degree to which Canadian scholars have obtained access to non-Canadian journals.

Because of this breadth of coverage, the abstracts reach beyond the traditional boundaries of the discipline of history, covering not only the specialized areas identified by the Symons Report such as urban, social, economic, religious, military, ethnic and intellectual history but also many contiguous areas of a social and political nature that have influence Canadian "history."

The full range of traditional historical topics covered include the explorations and conquests of the Europeans, the establishment of the British hegemony, the American Revolution and the coming of the Loyalists, the Rebellions of 1837, the movements for representative and responsible government, Confederation, the railroad and western development, the overseas wars, and the issues of French Canada.

In addition, abstracts are included on an almost endless range of topics of import to Canadian life varying from business, art, fisheries, and journalism to the native people, sport, archaeology, and law. The long and difficult history of US-Canada relationships is represented by the usual diplomatic and political topics as well as less usual topics such as the 20th century military planning of both countries for war—with each other.

As one should expect, there is a good representation of French-language items, mainly in the sections on New France and Quebec but in many other sections as well.

There are few aspects of the complex nature of this enormous, lightly populated country that are not represented in this collection of abstracts. The work is structured according to a mixed chronological and geographic structure. As can be expected in any work of this type, one could debate the choice of headings and structure used in the table of contents but the real value to the user of the work is in the comprehensive index and good quality abstracts which will readily serve pursuit of most topics in Canadian history and allied areas from almost any perspective.

It was one of the thrusts of the Symons Report that there should be an increased effort to develop the tools to permit scholars and students of the Canadian condition to gain access to the existing resources of our "history" in order to facilitate the growth of scholarship and greater understanding of our identity. This work is a useful response to that thrust and should well serve the cause of Canadian scholarship.

Alan H. MacDonald
Director of Libraries
University of Calgary

1. GENERAL CANADIAN HISTORY

1. Albrecht-Carrie, Rene. COMMENTARY: THE CANADIAN DILEMMA. *J. of Can. Studies 1974 9(1): 53-62.* The historic trend to the identification of the nation and the state may not apply everywhere. Bilingualism would give Canada an identity separate from the United States and demonstrate that the "Second Hundred Years' War" has ended in North America as it has in Europe. Secondary works; 8 notes.
G. E. Panting

2. Angrave, James. WILLIAM DAWSON, GEORGE GRANT AND THE LEGACY OF SCOTTISH HIGHER EDUCATION. *Queen's Q. [Canada] 1975 82(1): 77-91.* Discusses the careers of two Nova Scotians, John William Dawson and George Monro Grant, both of whom studied in Scotland and subsequently made notable contributions to higher education in Canada. The nature of these men's studies at the University of Edinburgh and the way their curriculum influenced their own teaching are discussed in detail. Both became principals of major Canadian universities and stand among the foremost of the country's 19th-century educators. Based on printed and manuscript sources; 40 notes.
J. A. Casada

3. Arès, Richard. L'INFLUENCE DE L'ESPACE SUR L'ÉVANGÉLISATION DU PAYS [The influence of space on the evangelization of the country]. *Tr. of the Royal Soc. of Can. [Canada] 1976 14: 163-172.* Defines space and evangelization. Notes negative influences such as the great distance required to cross the Atlantic. Once in Canada, one found an immense territory and nomadic indigenous tribes. Great spaces allowed expansion. Priests were among the early explorers, and there was regional development of the Catholic Church. In 1820 British authorities allowed the development of four dioceses: in the Maritimes, at Montreal, at Kingston, and at the Red River. Earlier there had been one diocese of Quebec. Other dioceses were created later. 11 notes.
J. D. Neville

4. Armitage, Christopher M. "FEAST OF STEVENSON": THE LIONEL STEVENSON COLLECTION OF DUKE UNIVERSITY. *Am. Rev. of Can. Studies 1977 7(2): 51-59.* Duke University has two significant collections relating to Canadian critic and scholar Lionel Stevenson. One collection, dating back to the 1860's, consists of about 600 Canadian works of poetry, fiction, criticism, essays, travel, and history, many rare, that were collected by Stevenson. Included are several sets and series and much material relating to western Canada. The second collection is of letters (ca 1920-70) received by Stevenson, many from significant literary figures including Duncan Campbell Scott, Bliss Carman, and Robert Service. A guide to the latter collection is in preparation.
G. A. Patzwald.

5. Arnon, Ruth Soulé. THE CHRISTIAN COLLEGE. *Hist. of Educ. Q. 1974 14(2): 235-249.* Review article prompted by Ira Jerry Burnstein's *The American Movement to Develop Protestant Colleges for Men in Japan, 1868-1912* (Ann Arbor, Michigan: U. of Michigan School of Education, 1967), Richard P. N. Dickinson's *The Christian College in Developing India: a Sociological Inquiry* (London: Oxford U. Pr., 1971), Rao H. Lindsay's *Nineteenth Century American Schools in the Levant: A Study of Purposes* (Ann Arbor, Michigan: U. of Michigan School of Education, 1965), Jessie Gregory Lutz's *China and The Christian Colleges, 1850-1950* (Ithaca: Cornell U. Pr., 1971), and D. C. Masters' *Protestant Church Colleges in Canada: A History* (Toronto: U. of Toronto Pr., 1966). Most find that conflict between secular education and the colleges declined in the face of nationalism.
L. C. Smith

6. Baboyant, Marie. THE MELZACK COLLECTION. *Can. Lib. J. 1974 31(5): 380-385.* The Melzack Collection of Canadiana at the University of Montreal has more than 3,500 books, hundreds of manuscripts, and a number of engravings, mostly from the 18th and early 19th century; it is now open to researchers.
S

7. Bain, George Sayers and Elsheikh, Farouk. TRADE UNION GROWTH IN CANADA: A COMMENT. *Industrial Relations [Canada] 1976 31(3): 482-490.* In a recent paper in this journal, Swidinsky developed an econometric model of union growth in Canada between 1911 and 1970. The purpose of this note is to evaluate his model and to demonstrate that some of the conclusions which he derives from it need to be revised.
J

8. Baird, Ron. CANADIAN FICTION COLLECTION AT THE GREATER VICTORIA PUBLIC LIBRARY. *Can. Lib. J. 1968 25(3): 238.*

9. Bakan, David. PSYCHOANALYSIS IN NORTH AMERICA. *Modernist Studies [Canada] 1977 2(3): 29-36.* Psychoanalysis became a major philosophy because it articulated the profound changes in relationships after World War I and provided scientific license for examining inner life in an ultrarational society.

10. Baker, Donald G. IDENTITY, POWER AND PSYCHOLOGICAL NEEDS: WHITE RESPONSES TO NON-WHITES. *J. of Ethnic Studies 1974 1(4): 16-44.* White attitudes in the United States and Canada towards non-whites (defined to include Africans, Asians, and Amerindians) need to be seen as a product of a complex set of factors, all of which must be examined to achieve a comprehensive understanding of the present racial situation. To simply label white response as "racism" adds little to the analysis. Study of the distinct components and causes of racism, including identity issues, power relationships, and psychocultural needs of white society is necessary. Identity is how white society defines itself and other groups in relationship to itself. The central identity of white Canada and America is "White Anglo" and all other groups have to meet the qualifications of being white and culturally anglicized. The power factor is a complex notion centering around the idea that inferior power means subjugation, subjugation becomes a definition of inferiority, and by extension, the means of perpetuating inferiority. Among the features of the psychocultural factor is the argument that white response to non-whites is partly the result of stresses within white society created out of conflict between New World environment and Old World norms. Based on secondary sources; 90 notes.
T. W. Smith

11. Balthazar, Louis. CULTURE AND HISTORY SHAPE APPROACHES TO FOREIGN POLICY: SINGLE SOURCES BUT DIFFERENT CHANNELS. *Int. Perspectives [Canada] 1976 (Special Issue): 18-21.* Examines how separate historical and cultural traditions have influenced a spirit of flamboyancy in American foreign policy and an attitude of conciliation in Canadian foreign policy from the 18th to 20th centuries; considers aspects of national self-image.

12. Barkley, Murray. RECENT PUBLICATIONS RELATING TO CANADA. *Can. Hist. Rev. [Canada] 1975 56(4): 521-534.* Lists published materials relating to Canadian history and culture. Includes both periodical articles and monographs. Organized alphabetically by author under the following topics: Canada's Commonwealth and International Relations since 1867, the History of Canada, Provincial and Local History, Economic History, Social, Cultural and Intellectual History, Bibliography and Historiography, and Genealogy. Omitted sections will be included in later issues.
R. V. Ritter

13. Barral, Pierre and Tavernier, Yves. MOUVEMENTS PAYSANS VISANT À ADAPTER L'AGRICULTURE À L'ECONOMIE [Peasant movements concerning the adaptation of agriculture to the market economy]. *Cahiers Int. d'Hist. Écon. et Sociale [Italy] 1976 6: 36-51.* Synthesizes reports at the International Colloquium (Naples, 1969) on peasant movements in the industrialized societies of Europe and North America in the late 19th and 20th centuries. The evolution of "capitalistic agriculture" added to the old peasant struggle for land, new problems created by salaried employees, technical equipment, and transport. World War II brought the peasant into direct encounter with the technical revolution of the 19th century and thereby altered the history of peasants. Peasant movements developed from pressure groups to political parties, and peasant voters forced all political groups to formulate policies for agricultural problems.
F. X. Hartigan

14. Benson, J. BRITISH NATIONAL CHARACTER IN NORTH AMERICAN SCHOOL HISTORIES, 1880-1930. *J. of Educ. Administration and Hist. [Great Britain] 1975 7(2): 1-8.* Analyzes British national characteristics as exemplified in history books used in schools in Canada and the USA, and asserts that in general they presented a favorable interpretation.

15. Bogina, Sh. A.; Kozlov, V. I.; Nitoburg, E. L.; and Fursova, L. N. NATSIONAL'NYE PROTSESSY I NATSIONAL'NYE OTNO-SHENIIA V STRANAKH ZAPADNOI EVROPY I SEVERNOI AMERIKI [National processes and ethnic relations in developed capitalist countries of Europe and North America]. *Sovetskaia Etnografiia [USSR] 1975 5: 3-16.* In a number of developed European countries ethnic consolidation may be regarded as completed but in some of them acute inter-ethnic situations are developing both between their long established peoples (e.g. in Belgium and Spain), and through the rise of a considerable immigrant population (e.g. in France and England). The aggravation of inter-ethnic situations is due to economic causes called forth by the revolution in science and technology. In North America inter-ethnic consolidation is not as yet complete. The American nation, a young ethnic formation, comprises a number of structural elements formed by immigrant ethnic groups. These have reached different stages of assimilation. While inter-ethnic integration in the various aspects of human activity is far advanced, the ethnic components of the U.S. population have of late shown more active ethnocentrism; this received its stimulus from the rise of the Negro movement. In this movement, with its dominant tendency towards integration, there exists also a separatist, nationalist tendency. Canada owes the aggravation of its national contradictions mainly to the French Canadian problem but also to the presence of a large number of immigrant groups and to the discrimination against the Indian and Eskimo population. An all-Canadian problem is the drive towards liberation from U.S. monopolies. This aggravation of the nationalities problem may in part be explained by: the influence of colonial liberation movements; the increasing inequalities between different nationalities due to the technological revolution; a reaction against the monotony of mass culture.   J

16. Bonenfant, Jean-Charles. LA FÉODALITÉ A DÉFINITIVE-MENT VÉCU... [The feudal system is definitely dead...]. *Rev. de l'U. d'Ottawa [Canada] 1977 47(1-2): 14-26.* French feudalism, which had been brought into Quebec with some changes and confirmed by the *Acte de Québec* (1774), was abolished by the *Acte pour l'abolition des Droits et Devoirs féodaux dans le Bas-Canada* (1854), but rental duties remained in effect with possibility of redemption. After subsequent laws gradually improved the procedure, these duties became extinct in 1971. The Canadian feudal system was then, definitely ended. Primary and secondary sources; 39 notes.   G. P. Cleyet

17. Bonin, Bernard. LES FACTEURS ÉCONOMIQUES DE LA POLITIQUE ÉTRANGÈRE DU CANADA [Economic factors in foreign policy in Canada]. *Pol. Étrangère [France] 1973 38(2): 149-178.* Describes the important roles of the United States and Great Britain in the Canadian economy during the last century, notably in restricting diversification of economic relations with the rest of the world, in acting as principal investors, and in monopolizing Canadian imports and exports.

18. Bothwell, Robert. MINISTER OF EVERYTHING. *Int. J. [Canada] 1976 31(4): 692-702.* Assesses the public career of Clarence Decatur Howe (1886-1960), an important Canadian cabinet minister from 1935-57. He was an engineer in a political system composed mostly of lawyers. Based on primary materials; 9 notes.   R. V. Kubicek

19. Buggey, Susan. RESEARCHING CANADIAN BUILDINGS: SOME HISTORICAL SOURCES. *Social Hist. [Canada] 1977 10(20): 409-426.* Until recently little has been written about Canadian architectural history, but there is relevant information in regional and local histories, travel accounts, and city directories. Government records (federal, provincial, and municipal), such as deeds, census records, and building permits, are also helpful. Private buildings are not as well-documented, but for commercial buildings there are business publications, newspapers, and trade journals. Iconographic sources of value include urban maps, artistic representations, line drawings, and photographs. 7 illus., 31 notes.   D. F. Chard

20. Burley, Kevin H. CANADA AND THE IMPERIAL SHIPPING COMMITTEE. *J. of Imperial and Commonwealth Hist. [Great Britain] 1975 3(3): 349-368.* Due to a national independence and highly critical opinions regarding the economic worth of Great Britain's Imperial Shipping Committee, Canada proved to be of major concern to the Committee during its 1918-63 jurisdiction.

21. Bush, Edward F. BEACON LIGHTS ON CANADIAN SHORES. *Can. Geographical J. 1975 90(2): 22-29.* Pictorial essay on lighthouses of Canada.   S

22. Bush, Edward F. THE CANADIAN LIGHTHOUSE. *Can. Historic Sites 1974 (9): 5-107.* This study traces the evolution of the Canadian lighthouse from the first structure at Louisbourg to the latest developments in lighthouse design and technology within the past decade. The treatment is regional, with emphasis on the older extant structures. An appendix lists data on individual lighthouses within regional agencies.   J

23. Calam, John. A LETTER FROM QUESNEL: THE TEACHER IN HISTORY, AND OTHER FABLES. *Hist. of Educ. Q. 1975 15(2): 131-146.* Historiographical treatment of teachers and teaching in Canada during the 19th-20th centuries, including philosophical treatises, autobiographical accounts, and chronicles of persons and institutions who serve as models for present-day educators.

24. Calton, Jerry M. BEAVERBROOK'S SPLIT IMPERIAL PERSONALITY: CANADA, BRITAIN, AND THE EMPIRE FREE TRADE MOVEMENT. *Historian 1974 37(1): 26-45.* His multifarious concerns and his erratic political behavior cause difficulties for biographers of Canadian-born William Max Aitkin, first Baron of Beaverbrook, who became a British newspaper and magazine magnate and member of the House of Lords, and who dedicated his life to the theme of success. His role in the imperial free trade campaign is the key to understanding the press lord's personality, because it demonstrates that he had no home base to give direction to his activities—neither in the Canada he left in 1910, nor among the British upper classes whose ways he imitated and whose government he sought to dominate. 73 notes.   N. W. Moen

25. Carlson, Alvar W. BIBLIOGRAPHY ON BARNS IN THE UNITED STATES AND CANADA. *Pioneer Am. 1978 10(1): 65-71.* Lists 120 sources, mostly from books and periodicals, on barns in the United States, with a few entries exclusively devoted to Canada. Most entries are dated 1940's-present. Those from periodicals are evenly divided between well-known professional journals and lesser-known publications. Based on state and provincial historical societies' libraries; 120 notes.   C. R. Gunter, Jr.

26. Caulais, Jacques. LE CANADA ET L'UTOPIE [Canada and Utopia]. *L'Année Pol. et Écon. [France] 1975 47(242): 338-351.* Reports on problems of thought-instinct duality, human alienation, and the degradation of civilization in Canada—especially Quebec—due to population growth and industrialization of society in modern times, commenting on the quest for utopia concept in popular Canadian consciousness.

27. Chaison, Gary N. and Rose, Joseph B. AN ANALYSIS OF ANNUAL TURNOVER RATES FOR CANADIAN UNION PRESIDENTS. *Industrial Relations [Canada] 1977 32(4): 547-563.* This paper re-examines the common views that presidential turnover occurs infrequently, is often the result of political forces and provides an adequate measure of union democracy. Moreover, the authors try to determine to what extent environmental factors influence annual presidential turnover rates among Canadian national unions.   J

28. Chichekian, Garo. ARMENIAN IMMIGRANTS IN CANADA AND THEIR DISTRIBUTION IN MONTREAL. *Cahiers de Géographie de Québec [Canada] 1977 21(52): 65-82.* Using census data and information from Canada's Immigration Department, chronicles the immigration pattern of Armenians into Canada, 1900-66.

29. Clifford, N. K. THE INTERPRETERS OF THE UNITED CHURCH OF CANADA. *Church Hist. 1977 46(2): 203-214.* Discusses the historiography of the church union movement and the United Church of Canada. Notes the unionists' and dissidents' differences and

explains the union movement and its opposition in terms of their responses to religious and social change. Arthur S. Morton laid the foundations for the environmentalist interpretation. C. E. Silcox modified the environmentalists' interpretations, and set the stage for revisionist interpretations. John W. Grant saw the implications of this shift in relation to United Church of Canada history. His concern with consensus and the church's impact on Canadian culture not only marked a transition from environmentalism to consensus but also reflected a shift in emphasis from external to internal factors. 24 notes.   M. D. Dibert

30. Cody, Howard. THE EVOLUTION OF FEDERAL-PROVINCIAL RELATIONS IN CANADA: SOME REFLECTIONS. *Am. Rev. of Can. Studies 1977 7(1): 55-83.* The strong centralized federation envisioned at the time of Canadian Confederation has never materialized because of the absence of a sense of national allegiance, constitutional allocation of significant responsibilities to the provinces, the disproportionate strength of Ontario and Quebec, and Quebec's cultural individuality. An initial period of provincial ascendancy ended about 1910 when fiscal difficulties forced the provinces to accept federal aid and accompanying federal ccntrol over provincial programs. Since 1960, the increasing importance of certain provincial responsibilities, such as natural resources has fostered a system under which national policy is negotiated through federal-provincial conferences. Based on government publications and secondary sources; 58 notes.   G. A. Patzwald

31. Comstock, Betsy. PRESERVING CANADA'S ART AND ARTIFACTS. *Can. Geographic [Canada] 1978 97(1): 30-35.* The Canadian Conservation Institute, located in Ottawa, is responsible for the restoration and preservation of art pieces and ethnographic artifacts from all over Canada.

32. Cook, Terry. THE CANADIAN CONSERVATIVE TRADITION: AN HISTORICAL PERSPECTIVE. *J. of Can. Studies 1973 8(4): 31-39.* Chronicles Canada's tradition of conservatism, 1850-1970.

33. Corry, J. A. NOTES TO ENGLISH CANADIANS. *J. of Can. Studies [Canada] 1977 12(3): 33-38.* English Canadians need to be more tolerant and understanding of the position of the Québécois. The cultural community that is Quebec has a history of 300 plus years along the banks of the St. Lawrence, and must be respected. If equality of the two cultures in Canada were guaranteed, in reality as well as in word, and if much wider autonomy were given the government of Quebec, and other Canadian provincial governments, the wind might be taken out of the sails of the Parti Québécois. By cherishing and cultivating their diversity, Canadians would find a larger, more spacious unity than they had before.
J. C. Billigmeier

34. Cowley, George A. THE EMERGENCE OF CULTURE AS A FACET OF FOREIGN POLICY. *Int. Perspectives [Canada] 1976 (5): 27-32.* Discusses the role of cultural relations as a means of promoting international understanding in the diplomacy and foreign policy of Western European nations, the United States, and Canada since the mid-19th century; considers possible conflicts that could arise from sending intellectuals as cultural ambassadors.

35. Cox, Robert W. and Jamieson, Stuart M. CANADIAN LABOR IN THE CONTINENTAL PERSPECTIVE. *Internat. Organization 1974 28(4): 803-826.* Analyzes Canada's position in the North American labor market system (1880's-1974).

36. Cutler, Maurice. ARE WE ALIENATING TOO MUCH RECREATIONAL LAND AND TOO MUCH OF OUR BEST AGRICULTURAL LAND? *Can. Geographical J. 1975 90(5): 18-33.* Discusses alien ownership of property in Canada.

37. Deschênes, Gaston. ASSOCIATIONS COOPÉRATIVES ET INSTITUTIONS SIMILAIRES AU XIX⁰ SIÈCLE [Cooperative associations and similar institutions in the 19th century]. *Rev. d'Hist. de l'Amérique Française [Canada] 1976 29(4): 539-554.* Agricultural, mutual aid, fire protection, and construction cooperatives were first started by English Canadians during the 19th century. They were subsequently adopted and often transformed by the French Canadians. There was a minimum of cooperation among and continuity between cooperatives. Based on newspapers, published government documents, and monographic studies; 87 notes.   L. B. Chan

38. Dewar, Kenneth C. TECHNOLOGY AND THE PASTORAL IDEAL IN FREDERICK PHILLIP GROVE. *J. of Can. Studies 1973 8(1): 19-28.* Discusses the imagery of technology contrasted with that of the Canadian pastoral past as they appear in Grove's literature.

39. Dick, Ernest J. RESOURCES ON MENNONITE HISTORY IN THE PUBLIC ARCHIVES OF CANADA. *Mennonite Life 1975 30(4): 26-28, 1976 31(1): 19-22.* Covers research tools since the 19th century. In two parts.

40. Dickey, John Sloan. BOTH SIDES OF THE BORDER: PERSPECTIVES ON TWO CENTURIES OF CANADIAN-AMERICAN RELATIONS. *Vermont Hist. 1976 44(2): 65-70.* Canadians, "a border people," learned from events of the American Revolution, reinforced in the War of 1812 and by sporadic annexationism since, to fear and resist US absorption. 7 notes.   T. D. S. Bassett

41. Doerksen, A. D. "Tony." THE HISTORY OF THANKSGIVING. *Manitoba Pageant 1975 21(1): 1-8.* Canada and Manitoba each have a long history of celebrating Thanksgiving. The dates for the celebration have varied, and there have been years with no celebration.
B. J. LaBue

42. Donneur, André P. LES RELATIONS FRANCO-CANADIENNES: BILAN ET PERSPECTIVES [Franco-Canadian relations: Outline and perspective]. *Pol. Étrangère [France] 1973 38(2): 179-200.* Describes the scanty bilateral relations between France and Canada, from the earliest diplomatic contact (1882) to the normalization of relations in 1972, with some views on the future evolution of their foreign policy.

43. Dornfield, A. A. STEAMSHIPS AFTER 1871. *Chicago Hist. 1977 6(1): 12-22.* Discusses the evolution of steamships, 1871-1976 and their importance in shipping on the Great Lakes as they virtually put schooners out of business.

44. Doyle, James. FROM CONSERVATIVE ALTERNATIVE TO VANISHING FRONTIER: CANADA IN AMERICAN TRAVEL NARRATIVES, 1799-1899. *Can. R. of Am. Studies 1974 5(1): 26-35.* Analyzes books and magazine articles by noted American writers and visitors to Canada. American commentators first expressed the greatest interest in Canada's French populace, its governance, and its position in the British empire. By the 1890's writers stressed Canadian expansion on its western frontiers. Based on first-hand travel accounts; 31 notes.
H. T. Lovin

45. Drache, Daniel. REDISCOVERING CANADIAN POLITICAL ECONOMY. *J. of Can. Studies [Canada] 1976 11(3): 3-18.* Political economy is the study of the laws and relations of capitalist development. Out of it a Canadian perspective was established for the critical and independent study of Canadian society. After considering the seven phases of its history, the conclusion is that this tradition was overwhelmed by American social sciences in the universities during the 1950's. As a result, the nationalist dimension, unique to Canadian social science, was submerged. Secondary sources; 64 notes.
G. E. Panting

46. Duly, Leslie C.; Robb, Andrew; and Spira, Thomas, eds. ANNOTATED BIBLIOGRAPHY OF WORKS ON NATIONALISM: A REGIONAL SELECTION. *Can. Rev. of Studies in Nationalism [Canada] 1974 1(supplement): 1-144; 1975 2(supplement): 1-231; 1976 3(supplement): 1-152.* Part I. Reviews articles, monographs, and general studies on nationalism, 1970-74. Part II. Bibliography on nationalism, 1970-75, including articles and monographs on Africa, Europe, the Caribbean, Canada, the United States, and Latin America. Part III. Bibliography of articles, monographs, and general studies in nationalism, 1974-76, covering the United States, Arab Middle East, Australia, Quebec, Brazil, and Hungary, 1949-76.

47. Dunton, Davidson. RECOGNIZED, EQUITABLE DUALITY. *J. of Can. Studies [Canada] 1977 12(3): 106-108.* The attitudes of English-speaking Canadians have much to do with the rise of Québécois nationalism. Anglophones have tended to consider Canada as an English-speaking country, with a small, quaint pocket of French in Quebec. Tolerated there, the French language was actively discouraged elsewhere.

Maybe it is too late, but Canadians from coast to coast should make a real effort to put French on an equal level with English at the provincial level. Rather than talking of Canadian unity, we might speak of Canadian duality—recognized, equitable duality from which could come immense strength and quality. J. C. Billigmeier

48. Edson, William D. LOCOMOTIVE ROSTERS FOR MAJOR RAILROADS. *Railroad Hist. 1978 (139): 78-85.* Provides an alphabetical listing of major US, Canadian, and Mexican railroads whose locomotives rosters have been published; includes information on sources, 1911-29 and degree of completion, 1921-78.

49. Eichler, Margrit. SOCIOLOGY OF FEMINIST RESEARCH IN CANADA. *Signs 1977 3(2): 409-422.* Canadian feminist researchers share not only the dependency of women on men, but the dependency of their nation on the United States. They occupy marginal positions, lack power as members of both groups, and are searching for a new identity. Recent research attempts to identify the major issues confronting Canadian women, including cultural and ideological dependency, economic dependency, physiological and psychic dependency in the treatment of their bodies and minds, and states of double dependencies for female members of marginal groups. Based on recent feminist literature published since 1974; 46 notes. J. K. Gammage

50. Ellis, William Donohue. NAMES ON THE LAND. *Inland Seas 1974 30(4): 242-265.* An address to the Great Lakes Historical Society 19 October 1974, sketching some of the historical background, as well as later mutations, of various place-names in the Great Lakes region. K. J. Bauer

51. Ervin, Linda and Bogusis, Ruth. COLLECTIONS OF ETHNIC CANADIANA AT THE NATIONAL LIBRARY OF CANADA: THE ETHNIC SERIALS PROJECT. *Serials Librarian 1977 1(4): 331-336.* The Ethnic Serials Project was undertaken by the National Library of Canada to preserve and make available all ethnic newspapers and to promote national appreciation and knowledge of ethnic groups in Canada, 18c-20c.

52. Fairweather, Gordon L. et al. CIVIL VIOLENCE AND CIVIL RIGHTS: A COMPARATIVE APPROACH TO LAW, ORDER, AND REFORM. *Am. Soc. of Int. Law Pro. 1974 68: 156-169.* Discusses the sources of violence in the US, Canada, and Mexico since the 18th century and the general problem of legally curbing violence while protecting civil rights.

53. Falcone, David. MINORITY GOVERNMENT IN CANADA: JEUX PARLIAMENTAIRES. *Round Table [Great Britain] 1974 (255): 259-276.* Outlines the development of the Canadian parliamentary system. Describes its British orientation in the 90 years before 1957 and the subsequent trend toward minority government. Examines the implications of minority government for Canada's parliamentary system, and its relationship to consensus politics. Although the character of the government has not affected governmental allocation of resources in Canada, the fact that legislatures must mobilize support for the political system has meant that minority government may damage the efficiency of Parliament. Presents a table showing percentage distribution of seats in the Canadian House of Commons during 1953-74. 31 notes. C. Anstey

54. Faucher, Albert. LES POLITIQUES NATIONALES ET L'ESPACE TRANSCONTINENTAL DANS L'HISTOIRE CANADIENNE [National politics and transcontinental space in the history of Canada]. *Tr. of the Royal Soc. of Can. [Canada] 1976 14: 149-161.* Discusses the influence of space on the development of Canada and notes the effect of transcontinental railroads, Britain, the United States, the Hudson's Bay Company, and canals on Canada. Canada, once part of Europe, is now more influenced by the United States. American canals drained commerce away from the St. Lawrence River and toward American ports. Some railroads also did so; yet, railroads allowed the unification of Canada. Also discusses the relationship between provincial governments and the federal government. 4 notes. J. D. Neville

55. Ferres, John. FROM SURVIVAL TO AFFIRMATION: NEW PERSPECTIVES ON CANADIAN LITERARY CRITICISM. *Am. Rev. of Can. Studies 1973 3(1): 122-134.* Examines 20th-century Canadian literature and analyzes major themes; popular acceptance of Canadian literature has been slowed by overshadowing of publishing industries and population in the US and because few Canadian writers were willing to concentrate on those things uniquely Canadian in exchange for appeal to international audiences.

56. Filion, Gérard. L'INFLUENCE DE L'ESPACE SUR LA VIE CANADIENNE: QUELQUES OBSERVATIONS ET CONCLUSIONS [The influence of space on Canadian life: some observations and conclusions]. *Tr. of the Royal Soc. of Can. [Canada] 1976 14: 173-176.* The first European explorers were overwhelmed by the size of Canada, its rivers, lakes, and mountains. Later generations were not astonished; yet, they were greatly influenced by the size of Canada. It changed their language as well as their mental attitudes. In less than a century after the American Revolution, the British government built in North America a new country 20 times larger than the 13 rebellious colonies. J. D. Neville

57. Flaherty, David H. ACCESS TO HISTORIC CENSUS DATA IN CANADA: A COMPARATIVE ANALYSIS. *Can. Public Administration [Canada] 1977 20(3): 481-498.* Calls for measures to ensure the right to privacy for census participants, so that historical research may be conducted on materials gathered 1918-77; a model used by the US National Archives is good.

58. Fleming, Roy F. SHIPWRECKS OF LAKE ONTARIO. *Inland Seas 1976 32(3): 213-220.* Lake Ontario is the least dangerous of the Great Lakes for navigation, although in November 1780 the British naval sloop *Ontario* sank with the loss of 350 lives. The worst storm occurred on Thanksgiving Day 1842. Details the wrecks of the *Sweden* (1877), *Norway* (1882), *Bavaria* (1889), and *Jessie A. Breck* (1890). K. J. Bauer

59. Forbes, Ernest R. IN SEARCH OF A POST-CONFEDERATION MARITIME HISTORIOGRAPHY, 1900-1967. *Acadiensis [Canada] 1978 8(1): 3-21.* Early in the 20th century interest in imperial conflicts encouraged numerous works on the Acadians, and interest in Canadian constitutional development encouraged exploration of related Maritime topics. Subsequent shifts to Canadian-US relations and the frontier ignored the Maritimes. Little attention was paid to the vigorous Maritime Rights movement and active labour and suffrage movements. Stereotypes and accumulated ignorance finally broke down with the expansion of Maritime universities and the hiring of regional specialists interested in the modern period. 52 notes. D. F. Chard

60. Forsey, Eugene. CONSTITUTIONAL ASPECTS OF THE CANADIAN ECONOMY. *Pro. of the Acad. of Pol. Sci. 1976 32(2): 53-62.* Canada's constitution gives virtually all economic power to the central government, but the courts, using simple reinterpretation, have undone this. The provinces now enjoy considerable freedom in economic affairs, though the government can step in during times of emergency. The tendency in recent years has been to strengthen the federal government. The provinces control minerals in the ground but not offshore resources. The trend is mild, and even the central government's emergency powers must pass a validity test if the question arises. V. L. Human

61. Frye, Northrop. NATIONAL CONSCIOUSNESS IN CANADIAN CULTURE. *Tr. of the Royal Soc. of Can. [Canada] 1976 14: 57-69.* American influence on Canadian culture is at least as great as that of the British. But the United States is a highly protectionist country and is reluctant to import Canadian culture. Canada is "culturally descended from the Tory opposition to the Whig triumph at the time of the Revolutionary War." In the United States, which has a great revolutionary tradition, there is the assumption that violence pays. Canadian culture rejects revolution and has as its symbol the mountie. Here violence has been mainly repressive violence, rarely getting beyond the individual or his family. Canada has had no leaders such as George Washington, Thomas Jefferson, or Benjamin Franklin. Its history is more like that of the United States if the United States had started with the Civil War rather than the Revolutionary War. Canadians deal with a large, scantily populated country. In their literature one sees allusions to great amounts

of space. And, unlike the Americans who pushed westward to the Pacific, Canadians were part of a world empire, a link between Europe and the Orient.   J. D. Neville

62. Gear, James L. FACTORS INFLUENCING THE DEVELOP-MENT OF GOVERNMENT SPONSORED PHYSICAL FITNESS PROGRAMMES IN CANADA FROM 1850 TO 1972. *Can. J. of Hist. of Sport and Physical Educ. 1973 4(2): 1-25.* A few government officials advocated physical training in the mid-1800's, but the U.S. Civil War and the threat of annexation of Canada prompted Parliament to promote military training. A trust fund of $500,000 from Lord Strathcona in 1909 stimulated physical and military training. World Wars I and II stimulated military drill in the schools. The federal government supported Provincial-Recreation Programmes in the 1930's, and a National Physical Fitness Act during World War II. In 1961 the government passed legisla-tion to enhance amateur sport and national prestige. In the 1970's there was a strong move to encourage physical fitness to help keep down the cost of government medical services. The government has used physical fitness to accomplish various societal ends. Based on primary and second-ary sources; 80 notes.   R. A. Smith

63. Genest, Jean. LE PROCÈS DE M. CASTONGUAY [The trial of M. Castonguay]. *Action Natl. [Canada] 1974 63(5): 353-375.* The views of Claude Castonguay, minister of social welfare, regarding Cana-dian federalism versus Quebec nationalism are blind to the long history of Ottawan dominance over the provincial autonomy of Quebec. Based on Michel Roy's interview of Castonguay in *Le Devoir*, 20 November 1973.

64. Gersman, Elinor Mondale. HISTORIOGRAPHY AND BIBLI-OGRAPHY. *Hist. of Educ. Q. 1975 15(2): 227-249.* Bibliography of materials printed 1973-74 pertaining to education, 17th-20th centuries, with special sections for historiography and bibliography, women, family and youth, and professionalism, as well as geographic delineations: Africa, Asia, Australia, Canada, Europe, Great Britain, Latin America, and the United States.

65. Gibbens, R. G. HOW HYDRO POWER BROUGHT ALUMI-NUM TO CANADA. *Can. Geographical J. 1976 93(1): 18-27.* Chroni-cles the 75-year history of the aluminum industry in Canada made possible by the country's abundance of hydroelectric power.

66. Gibson, James A. ECHOES FROM FAR SHORES: REMINIS-CENCES OF GOVERNORS-GENERAL. *Dalhousie R. [Canada] 1972/73 52(4): 535-552.* Personal reminiscences of the Governors-Gen-eral of Canada from 1915 to the present. Emphasizes the qualities of character, manner, and conduct which have made them worthy represen-tatives of the English throne.   R. V. Ritter

67. Godfrey, William G. SOME THOUGHTS ON THE *DICTIO-NARY OF CANADIAN BIOGRAPHY* AND MARITIME HIS-TORIOGRAPHY. *Acadiensis [Canada] 1978 7(2): 107-115.* Volumes I, II, and III, covering the period 1000 to 1770, provide "a blend of gentle revision and polite reconciliation." They say little about Indian leader-ship, but effectively discuss French missionaries, and offer illuminating glimpses of Acadia's relationship to France and New France. Volumes IX and X deemphasize Acadians and Indians, and devote much attention to Maritime politics, in Prince Edward Island and New Brunswick, as con-tests between elites. The treatment of Maritime economic and intellectual development suggests that the legendary mid-19th-century Golden Age was only a veneer. 4 notes.   D. F. Chard

68. Goheen, Peter G. INTERPRETING THE AMERICAN CITY: SOME HISTORICAL PERSPECTIVES. *Geographical J. 1974 64(3): 362-384.* "Social scientists have examined the historical experience of cities in the United States and in Canada from two different perspectives. They have regarded the city as a laboratory in which a new culture evolves in response to economic change and social pressure. The work of Robert E. Park has given theoretical orientation to this large body of writing, in which many themes of change have been examined. Social scientists have also thought of the city as historically significant for the impact that ideas and institutions developing there have had on the national social and political scene. Both of these approaches have proven inadequate to the task of developing an historically sensitive theory of the

American city. One formulation is proposed as a way of contributing to such an understanding."   J

69. Goldberg, Steve. CANADIAN "CIVIL WAR": SEPARATISM VS. FEDERALISM IN MODERN CANADA. *Strategy and Tactics 1977 (64): 25-35.* Summarizes Canadian history, providing background on the possible separation of Quebec; combines an analysis of political and military factors, concluding that Canadian union deserves preservation.

70. Gonick, Cy. DISCOVERING INDUSTRIAL DEMOCRACY. *Can. Dimension [Canada] 1977 12(3): 25-30.* Discusses 20th-century industry, the growing demands of the labor force, the incompatibility of industrial democracy to the capitalist system, and the discovery of work-er's control as a means of transforming worker-employer relationships and society.

71. Gorham, Deborah. MARXISM, FEMINISM, WOMEN AND WORK. *Queen's Q. [Canada] 1976 83(2): 299-304.* Review article prompted by Charnie Guettel, *Marxism and Feminism,* and Janice Acton et al. (eds.), *Women at Work: Ontario 1850-1930.* Both works are prod-ucts of the Canadian Women's Educational Press, and are welcome addi-tions to the mushrooming field of women's history in Canada.
                                    J. A. Casada

72. Gorham, Deborah. "SINGING UP THE HILL." *Can. Dimen-sion 1975 10(8): 26-38.* Discusses the significance of the British North America Act of 1929 by which Canadian women were declared to be legally "persons," and traces the suffragist movement and equal rights advocates in Canada from the late 19th through the early 20th century.
                                    S

73. Goyder, John C. and Curtis, James E. OCCUPATIONAL MO-BILITY IN CANADA OVER FOUR GENERATIONS. *Can. Rev. of Sociol. and Anthrop. [Canada] 1977 14(3): 303-319.* Occupational mobil-ity over three and four generations is examined in order to provide addi-tional perspective on Canada's mobility processes and especially to test hypotheses of cumulative family ascription. Data are provided by male respondents' reports, in a recent national sample survey, of their own occupations plus those of their fathers, grandfathers, and eldest sons. Results using correlational, regression, and matrix analyses are com-pared. Direct links between occupational status scores over three genera-tions are found but, as would be expected, the effects here are relatively low compared to those between fathers and sons. Perhaps surprisingly the occupations of great-grandfathers and great-grandsons are found to show no association. Among other findings, there is some evidence of a status consistency effect (for family status in two earlier generations) on respon-dents' status attainments. White-collar respondents with white-collar fa-thers and grandfathers are more numerous than would be expected according to a simple additive model. Results also suggest that the effect of grandfather's status on occupation in the third generation is channelled through the grandson's education. Implications of the findings for inter-pretations of the level of ascription vs. achievement in Canadian society are discussed.   J

74. Graff, Harvey J. CRIME AND PUNISHMENT IN THE NINE-TEENTH CENTURY: A NEW LOOK AT THE CRIMINAL. *J. of Interdisciplinary Hist. 1977 7(3): 477-491.* Important source mate-rial, largely untapped, exists for the investigation of significant quantita-tive questions about the patterns of crime and about the criminal in the 19th and early 20th centuries. The most important sources are the jail registers of municipal sanctuaries. The use of such evidence is illustrated through the records of Middlesex County, Ontario. Data from Middlesex County, Ontario records; 2 tables, 13 notes.   R. Howell

75. Gutteridge, Don. TEACHING THE CANADIAN MYTHOL-OGY: A POET'S VIEW. *J. of Can. Studies 1973 8(1): 28-33.* Discusses the author's (and in the broadest sense, all of Canada's) poetry as myth-making to promote expression of national character.

76. Hagan, John and Leon, Jeffrey. REDISCOVERING DELIN-QUENCY: SOCIAL HISTORY, POLITICAL IDEOLOGY AND THE SOCIOLOGY OF LAW. *Am. Sociol. Rev. 1977 42(4): 587-598.* This paper examines a Marxian social historical approach to the study of legal evolution. The emergence of the Marxian perspective and the logic of its

premises are reviewed. Using Canadian delinquency legislation as an historical example, it is found that the Marxian perspective assumes a great deal that is unconfirmed (e.g., that this legislation serves the teleologically inferred "basic interests" of an ambiguously identified "ruling class"), asserts other things that are wrong or misleading (that this legislation increased imprisonment, "invented" new categories of youthful misbehavior, created a "specialized labor market" and increased "industrial discipline"), and ignores much that an organizational analysis helps to reveal (that the emergence of probation work as an organizational concern was the prime factor in the development of Canadian delinquency legislation). Implications of these findings are considered.   J

77. Hamilton, William B. SOME HISTORICAL OBSERVATIONS ON THE "DOWN EAST" ROUTE. *Am. Rev. of Can. Studies 1975 5(1): 3-16.* Examines present strains in Canada and New England's "good neighbor policy" due to jurisdictional disputes, American recreational land ownership, and environmental problems, 1850's-1970's.

78. Hanham, H. J. CANADIAN HISTORY IN THE 1970'S. *Can. Hist. Rev. [Canada] 1977 58(1): 1-22.* Surveys recent literature about the history of Canada, especially major works published during 1970-76 in French or English. Emphasizes the growing preoccupation with economic and social history, and the special strengths of French-Canadian historiography. Suggests areas for further research in Canadian-American relations, the history of the Catholic Church in Quebec, economic, labor, and urban history.   A

79. Hanham, Harold J. THE MATURING OF FRINGE CULTURES. *Tr. of the Royal Soc. of Can. [Canada] 1976 14: 111-119.* Discusses the cultural development of the United States and Canada and notes that neither has achieved its cultural potential. The Founding Fathers believed that the United States, then on the fringe of European culture, would someday be a cultural leader; yet, today Canada seems a better candidate for such a position because of an American reluctance to spend money for cultural things. Another US obstacle is a "desire for a superficial national unity" giving rise to a fear that cultural development will center on ethnic groups and their diverse interests. Note.
                J. D. Neville

80. Hanrahan, James. A CURRENT BIBLIOGRAPHY OF CANADIAN CHURCH HISTORY. *Study Sessions: Can. Catholic Hist. Assoc. 1973 40: 69-93.*

81. Hardisty, A. Pamela. SOME ASPECTS OF CANADIAN OFFICIAL PUBLISHING. *Government Publ. Rev. 1973 1(1): 7-18.* Reviews Canadian official publishing since 1791, types of Canadian government publications, availability of catalogues and indexes, and describes current methods of distribution.

82. Hardy, Allison Taylor. WOMEN: ALWAYS DIPLOMATIC AND MORE RECENTLY DIPLOMATS. *Int. Perspectives [Canada] 1976 (4): 26-32.* Examines the increased number of women to serve as diplomats and ambassadors in Canada's Department of External Affairs from 1909-75 due to recent equal employment regulations.

83. Harney, Robert F. THE COMMERCE OF MIGRATION. *Can. Ethnic Studies [Canada] 1977 9(1): 42-53.* Southern Italians who wished to come to Canada and the United States encountered bewildering emigration procedures in which cash payments were expected by middle-class "brokers," from the village mayor to loan financiers to travel and steamship agents. It was commercially advantageous to these "go-betweens" to allow and encourage emigration. Upon arrival in North America these immigrants once again found themselves indebted to similar bourgeois agents. The system continues today. The profit motive made and makes migration possible.   K. S. McDorman

84. Hayball, Gwen. HISTORIC LOBSTICKS AND OTHERS. *Can. Geographical J. 1973 86(2): 62-66.* A peculiar type of monument.
                S

85. Hayes, Alan L. INTRODUCTION. *J. of the Can. Church Hist. Soc. [Canada] 1977 19(1-2): 2-5.* Summarizes a series of papers presented to meetings of the Canadian Methodist Historical Society during 1975-76. Until its 1925 merger into the United Church of Canada, Methodism

constituted the largest single Protestant denomination in Canada. Representing a strongly evangelistic faith, Methodist missionaries from both Great Britain and the United States went into many areas of Canada as early as 1765 and were very successful in their efforts at conversion. Eventually Methodism lost its evangelical character and became thoroughly established and institutionalized. Its original character was so strong, however, that there remained some evangelical elements, and a new social reform movement emerged. Canadian Methodism has made significant contributions both to the beliefs of the United Church of Canada and to the development of the secular culture of English Canada. This issue is *J. of the Can. Church Hist. Soc.* 1977 19(1-2) and *Bull. of the United Church of Can.* 1977 26.   J. A. Kicklighter

86. Hayward, Robert J. SOURCES OF URBAN HISTORICAL RESEARCH: INSURANCE PLANS AND LAND USE ATLASES. *Urban Hist. Rev. [Canada] 1973 (1): 2-9.* Explores information available to urban historians through building plans of insurance agencies and land use atlases of Canada, 1696-1973.

87. Hébert, Gérard. MANAGEMENT AND WORK ACCIDENT PREVENTION. *Industrial Relations [Canada] 1976 31(1): 28-31.* Reviews work accident and job safety in relation to management theories; mentions accident prevention and responsibilities in the 20th century.

88. Henderson, M. Carole. FOLKLORE SCHOLARSHIP AND THE SOCIOPOLITICAL MILIEU IN CANADA. *J. of the Folklore Inst. 1973 10(1/2): 97-107.* Canada's folklore studies have been overly selective in concentrating on Anglo regional subculture studies, French, Indian, and ethnic traditions, and oral tradition, and have been influenced more by social, political, and economic factors than by scholarship.

89. Heron, Craig and Palmer, Bryan D. THROUGH THE PRISM OF THE STRIKE: INDUSTRIAL CONFLICT IN SOUTHERN ONTARIO, 1901-14. *Can. Hist. Rev. [Canada] 1977 58(4): 423-458.* Based on previously unused federal department of labour records for the 1920's and on prime ministers' correspondence. Examines the first federal involvement with labour exchanges, unemployment insurance and relief between 1918 and 1921 and the abandonment of this initiative during the first Mackenzie King administration. Threat of social unrest following World War I demobilization prompted original federal involvement with unemployment. Agrarian and business demands for low-cost, mobile labour forced an abandonment of the policy after 1922 leaving the country unprepared for the Depression.   A

90. Hershberg, Theodore, et al. OCCUPATION AND ETHNICITY IN FIVE NINETEENTH-CENTURY CITIES: A COLLABORATIVE INQUIRY. *Hist. Methods Newsletter 1974 7(3): 174-216.* Examines employment and ethnicity in Philadelphia, Pennsylvania; Hamilton, Ontario; Kingston, New York; Buffalo, New York; and Poughkeepsie, New York, and concludes that property ownership was related to class considerations, but was substantially modified by ethnicity and culture. Based on primary and secondary sources; tables, graphs, and charts.
                D. K. Pickens

91. Hogan, Brian F. A CURRENT BIBLIOGRAPHY OF CANADIAN CHURCH HISTORY. *Study Sessions: Can. Catholic Hist. Assoc. [Canada] 1976 43: 91-119.* Groups work on Canadian church history according to the following categories: guides, church history, the communions, general works, regional history, institutions, individual biography and biographical material, religious practice and pastoral care, missions, and special problems.

92. Hogan, Brian F. A CURRENT BIBLIOGRAPHY OF CANADIAN CHURCH HISTORY. *Study Sessions: Can. Catholic Hist. Assoc. [Canada] 1977 44: 111-144.* Alphabetical listing of articles, books, and general sources, published during 1970-77.

93. Holmes, John W. DIVIDED WE STAND. *Int. J. [Canada] 1976 31(3): 385-398.* Explores the divisiveness in Canada's relations with the US; the negative effects of those Canadian attitudes are built on a misplaced sense of grievance. 4 notes.   R. V. Kubicek

94. Hopkinson, Marvin W. CATALOGUE: THE BEATRICE HITCHINS MEMORIAL COLLECTION OF AVIATION HISTORY.

Hopkinson, Marvin W. *Library Bulletin No. 9.* (London, Ont.: D. B. Weldon Library, University of Western Ontario, 1976): 1-73. Organizes and lists, by author or title, the world aviation history collection of historian and aviator Fred H. Hitchins (1904-72). Part One of the collection includes writings by Hitchins, research sources, correspondence, illustrations, card files, rough notes, and original drafts. Part Two includes books, periodicals, pamphlets, and magazine articles and clippings. The D. B. Weldon Library at the University of Western Ontario houses the collection.　　　　　　　　　　　　　　　　S

95. Hubbard, R. H. AMPLE MANSIONS: THE PRE-CONFEDERATION GOVERNMENT HOUSES OF THE PROVINCES. *Tr. of the Royal Soc. of Can. [Canada] 1977 15: 263-285.* Studies pre-Confederate government houses in the Canadian provinces beginning with the first French settlements in Acadia. Describes government houses in Quebec, Newfoundland, Nova Scotia, Prince Edward Island, New Brunswick, Ontario, and British Columbia. Omits post-Confederation houses of Manitoba, Saskatchewan, and Alberta. 17 fig., 58 notes.
J. D. Neville

96. Hughes, Helen McGill. WASP/WOMAN/SOCIOLOGIST. *Society 1977 14(5): 69-80.* The author discusses her careers as mother and sociologist, in Canada and the United States, 1916-77.

97. Jackson, C. I. FUR AND FOOTNOTES: THE HUDSON'S BAY RECORD SOCIETY. *J. of Imperial and Commonwealth Hist. [Great Britain] 1976 5(1): 111-115.* Reviews four books published in the 1970's on the Hudson's Bay Company's fur trading in British North America during 1670-1870.

98. Jackson, Robin. DEVELOPMENT OF THE MULTICULTURAL POLICY IN CANADA, A BIBLIOGRAPHY. *Can. Lib. J. [Canada] 1976 33(3): 237-243.* This annotated bibliography lists works published during 1967-76 that trace the development of Canadian multicultural policy, government programs, provincial initiatives, and non-governmental evaluations of the policy.　　　　L. F. Johnson

99. Jenness, R. A. CANADIAN MIGRATION AND IMMIGRATION PATTERNS AND GOVERNMENT POLICY. *Internat. Migration R. 1974 8(1): 5-22.*

100. Johnston, Richard and Ballantyne, Janet. GEOGRAPHY AND THE ELECTORAL SYSTEM. *Can. J. of Pol. Sci. [Canada] 1977 10(4): 857-866.* Tests the proposition that Canada's electoral system gives seats in disproportionate numbers to parties whose votes are concentrated geographically. Covers 1921-74. 20 notes.　　　R. V. Kubicek

101. Karr, Clarence. WHAT IS CANADIAN INTELLECTUAL HISTORY? *Dalhousie R. [Canada] 1975 55(3): 431-448.* States the difficulties of developing a definition of intellectual history, and discusses three approaches to Canadian intellectual history: 1) Traditional history of ideas, 2) The history of historiography, 3) Culture. Discusses Lawrence Fallis, Jr., Jack Bumsted, S. F. Wise, Carl Berger, Richard Allen, Arthur Lower, Stanley Ryerson, Ramsay Cook, and others. In addition to the three more or less distinct approaches mentioned there is also the cross-fertilization between the three branches. 41 notes.　　C. Held

102. Kattan, Naim. LA DIMENSION CULTURELLE DES DEUX SOLITUDES [The cultural dimension of the two solitudes]. *Études Int. [Canada] 1977 8(2): 337-341.* Discusses the parallel development of the British and French cultures in Canada, noting especially the dissimilarities in their historical origins, religious orientation, and cosmology.
J. F. Harrington, Jr.

103. Kealey, Gregory S. THE WORKING CLASS IN RECENT CANADIAN HISTORICAL WRITING. *Acadiensis [Canada] 1978 7(2): 116-135.* Canadian historians had no concept of social class before the mid-1960's. The mass university and numerous successful revolutions then renewed social scientists' interest in history. Small presses, the labor movement, and radical groups published numerous works, but few of the comprehensive labor histories are better than Charles Lipton's *The Trade Union Movement in Canada.* Oral history works are more important, along with memoirs such as Tim Buck's, but sociological works are slight in quantity and quality, and most journalistic endeavours are weak. 27 notes.　　　　　　　　　　　　　　　D. F. Chard

104. Keane, Patrick. LIBRARY POLICIES AND EARLY CANADIAN ADULT EDUCATION. *Humanities Assoc. Rev. [Canada] 1978 29(1): 1-20.* Mechanics' and apprentices' libraries, the forerunners of Canada's public library service, in the 19th century disseminated reading material supportive of the economic, social, and political status quo to assimilate the working classes into the middle classes.

105. Keane, Patrick. THE WORK/LEISURE ETHIC IN ADULT EDUCATION. *Dalhousie Rev. [Canada] 1977 57(1): 28-46.* A history of the evolving struggle between technical and liberal education, which now centers on adult education. Discusses the English and Canadian evolution of adult education from the early mechanics' institutes to the YMCA programs of the late 19th century, and the struggle between the "useful" and "recreational" within these programs. 66 notes.
C. Held

106. Kelly, Nora. THE EVOLUTION OF THE R.C.M.P. *Can. Geographical J. 1973 86(5): 168-181.* The Royal Canadian Mounted Police has modernized and expanded.　　　　　　　　　S

107. Kendall, John C. A CANADIAN CONSTRUCTION OF REALITY: NORTHERN IMAGES OF THE UNITED STATES. *Am. Rev. of Can. Studies 1974 4(1): 20-36.* Gives a brief synopsis of Canada's feelings about the United States, 18th-20th centuries, highlighting the constant anti-Americanism expressed by Canadians as well as the resentment felt by many Canadians that Americans regard the country as a second-best America. 25 notes.

108. Kenn, John M. THE SAINT CLAIR RIVER RAILROAD TUNNEL. *Inland Seas 1975 31(3): 175-185, 212-213.* Although train ferry service between Port Huron, Michigan, and Sarnia, Ontario, began in 1872 it was not entirely satisfactory. During 1884-91, therefore, the Saint Clair Frontier Tunnel Company, with support from the Grant Trunk Railroad and the Canadian government, built a railroad tunnel under the Saint Clair River to connect the two cities. The tunnel was the target of abortive sabotage efforts in both World Wars. Despite the loss of passenger service and its inability to handle some of the larger modern cars, the tunnel remains in service. Based primarily on newspapers; illus., 15 notes.　　　　　　　　　　　　　　K. J. Bauer

109. Kenney, Alice P. and Workman, Leslie J. VOLUMES OF HOMAGE: FESTSCHRIFTEN IN AMERICA. *N. Y. Hist. 1974 55(4): 459-481.* The authors present a historical review of the homage volume in Europe and America, and discuss four recent examples. The scholars honored by festschriften publications are Fred B. Kniffen of Louisiana State University, Bernard Mayo of the University of Virginia, Richard B. Morris of Columbia University and James J. Talman of the University of Western Ontario. Based on historical essays; 25 notes.
A. C. Aimone

110. Killam, G. D. AFRICAN LITERATURE AND CANADA. *Dalhousie U. [Canada] 1973/74 53(4): 672-687.* Suggests comparisons between Canada and African countries in terms of Literature studies. One of 10 papers read at the Conference on African Literature, Dalhousie University, 1973.　　　　　　　　　　　　　　　　S

111. Kirk-Greene, Anthony H. M. THE GOVERNORS-GENERAL OF CANADA, 1867-1952: A COLLECTIVE PROFILE. *J. of Can. Studies [Canada] 1977 12(4): 35-57.* Discusses 17 governors-general of Canada. The governor-general, representative of the crown in Canada, was appointed by the sovereign on the advice of the British cabinet until 1926 and since then on the advice of the Canadian government. His duties, like those of the British monarch, are largely ceremonial. His term varies from five to seven years. Of the governors-general discussed, all were peers whose educational background included Eton or Harrow and Oxford, Cambridge, or Sandhurst. Several were military men, half were at one time members of parliament or ministers, and one was a popular novelist. Half had had prior experience of Canada, yet none ever returned there. Four were later viceroy of India. Secondary sources; 17 photos, table, 106 notes.　　　　　　　　　　L. W. Van Wyk

112. Kirschbaum, J. M. SLOVAK AMERICAN ORGANIZATIONS IN CANADA. *Jednota Ann. Furdek 1977 16: 233-238.* Discusses Slovak American organizations which were transplanted to

Canada with immigration; discusses the labor, political, and community organizing aspects of these immigrant associations, 1890-1964.

113. Kirschbaum, J. M. SLOVAKS IN CANADA. *Jednota Ann. Furdek 1977 16: 97-101.* Of the three waves of immigration of Slovaks to Canada, the first two were for economic reasons, the last for political ones; describes settlement and acculturation.

114. Kirschbaum, J. M. SOME OF CANADA'S SLOVAK PARISHES. *Jednota Ann. Furdek 1977 16: 114-117.* Discusses 10 Catholic parishes having a majority of Slovakian parishioners.

115. Kleinschmidt, Martha. TIDAL POWER AT PASSAMAQ-UODDY BAY: IS IT A VIABLE ENERGY ALTERNATIVE? *Synthesis 1975 3(2): 35-50.* Chronicles the proposal to produce electric power from tides in the Bay of Fundy, from its suggestion by Dexter Cooper in 1919 through the New Deal and the Kennedy era into the mid-1960's. Concludes that the project cannot produce electricity as cheaply as conventional or nuclear power plants. 44 notes.

M. M. Vance

116. Knight, David B. and Taylor, John H. "CANADA'S URBAN PAST": A REPORT ON THE CANADIAN URBAN HISTORY CONFERENCE. *Urban Hist. Rev. [Canada] 1977 (2): 72-86.* Describes the Canadian Urban History Conference held at the University of Guelph, 12-14 May 1977. Analyzes the papers presented along with important comments from the audience. C. A. Watson

117. Knight, David B. and Clark, John. SOME REFLECTIONS ON A CONFERENCE ON THE HISTORICAL URBANIZATION OF NORTH AMERICA. *Urban Hist. Rev. [Canada] 1973 (1): 10-14.* Discusses the proceedings and papers delivered at the Conference on the Historical Urbanization of North America; topics included sources and methodology of urban history research, role of the city in 19th-century North America, internal relationships in urban situations, urbanization in the colonial era, regional variations in urbanization, and residential change in North America.

118. Kuruvilla, P. K. COLLECTIVE BARGAINING IN THE CANADIAN PUBLIC SERVICE. *Philippine J. of Public Administration [Philippines] 1974 18(4): 279-296.* Canadian public servants began to press for their right to collective bargaining in the 1920's. The Federal government responded initially by creating a National Joint Council of the Public Service of Canada to handle employee grievances. Later, the Public Service Staff Relations Act was enacted in March, 1967. This law granted the public servants the status of trade unions with the right to collective bargaining, conciliation and the right to stage a strike. However, the government employees were dissatisfied with the law, since it levies to them the right to negotiate on basic matters such as job security and classification. Consequently, Prime Minister Trudeau formed the Bryden Committee to amend the law. Other reforms are needed. In the Canadian public service, a sound and viable collective bargaining system must include all the terms and conditions of employment and must proceed in an atmosphere of goodwill among the government, public servants and the public. J

119. Kydd, Ronald. H. C. SWEET: CANADIAN CHURCHMAN. *J. of the Can. Church Hist. Soc. [Canada] 1978 20(1-2): 19-30.* In many ways Dr. H. C. Sweet demonstrated his unique character. First, as missionary, minister, and professor, he served several Christian denominations. Second, he was well-educated and maintained his intellectual curiosity all his life; he obtained the doctorate in theology at the age of 61. Third, he carried out his Christian commitment in a variety of ways. In his early years he was a missionary to Indians in Saskatchewan. Later he served as pastor to a black congregation in Winnipeg. He also devoted a number of years to Christian education through his teaching at two theological institutions. Beloved and respected, H. C. Sweet had such diversity in his career that he merits special attention among Canadian clergy. Primary and secondary sources; 89 notes.

J. A. Kicklighter

120. Lamonde, Yvan. LES ARCHIVES DE L'INSTITUT CANADIEN DE MONTRÉAL (1844-1900)—HISTORIQUE ET INVENTAIRE [The archives of the Canadian Institute of Montreal (1844-

1900)—a history and an inventory]. *Rev. d'Hist. de l'Amérique Française [Canada] 1974 28(1): 77-94.* Gives a history of the archives of the Canadian Institute of Montreal in terms of documents destroyed and preserved, and its locations, methods, and ideological and financial crises.

121. Lamontagne, Maurice. SCIENTIFIC RESEARCH AND CANADIAN ECONOMIC VIABILITY. *Am. Rev. of Can. Studies 1973 3(1): 164-172.* Examines Canadian-US relations in terms of economic viability 1900's-70's; relates these to technological advances experienced over the 20th century and concludes that growing dependence of the USA on foreign natural resources will provide a wider market for Canada, as well as a stronger bargaining position in world affairs.

122. Laver, A. Bryan. THE HISTORIOGRAPHY OF PSYCHOLOGY IN CANADA. *J. of the Hist. of the Behavioral Sci. 1977 13(3): 243-251.* Brief but comprehensive in scope, the author covers everything from history programs, undergraduate and graduate, to recent surveys and publishing outlets. 36 notes. D. K. Pickens

123. LaViolette, Forrest E. THE CANADIAN JAPANESE: A NEW LOOK. *Pacific Affairs [Canada] 1977 50(1): 107-111.* Review article prompted by Ken Adachi's *The Enemy That Never Was: A History of the Japanese Canadians.* The first Japanese immigrants came to Canada in 1877. Their acceptance in frontier Canada was restricted, racially biased, and feared. Vigorous measures by the Canadian government during World War II, which included concentration camps, were the most flagrant examples of the unfair and unjust treatment of persons of Japanese ancestry. Primary and secondary sources; 10 notes.

S. H. Frank

124. Lederman, W. R. DIFFERENCES IN TIME EXPLAIN DIFFERENT CONSTITUTIONAL FORMS. *Int. Perspectives [Canada] 1976 (Special Issue): 24-27.* Examines British influences in the evolution of the legal systems of the United States and Canada from the 18th to 20th centuries; compares the separation of powers concept in American constitutional principles with union of powers in Canada's cabinet government.

125. Lederman, W. R. THE SUPREME COURT OF CANADA AND THE CANADIAN JUDICIAL SYSTEM. *Tr. of the Royal Soc. of Can. 1975 13: 209-225.* Commemorates the centennial of the foundation of the Canadian Supreme Court by asking questions about the court and its origins in English constitutional history. "The unitary character of the Canadian judicial system" is an advantage to the subject who in court cases and appeals is in one judicial system whether involving federal or provincial statutes in comparison with the United States with its dual system of state and federal courts. However, in the United States the systems are not as separate as many people think. Until given the power by the Canadian Parliament to restrict cases it hears, the Supreme Court was greatly overworked. Explains how one appeals a case to the Supreme Court. 22 notes. J. D. Neville

126. Lefebvre, Jean-Jacques. LA LIGNÉE CANADIENNE DE L'HISTORIEN SIR THOMAS CHAPAIS (1946) [The Canadian line of the historian Sir Thomas Chapais (1946)]. *Tr. of the Royal Soc. of Can. 1975 13: 151-168.* Studies the family of the historian Sir Thomas Chapais, beginning with a discussion of the lack of genealogical information in many biographical dictionaries. Notes Sir Thomas' father, Jean-Charles Chapais, one of the "Fathers of the Confederation." Discusses the members of Sir Thomas' family from the 17th through the 19th centuries and shows, for the most part, their marriages, descendants, occupations, etc. Concludes with Sir Thomas' marriage to Miss Hectorine Langevin in 1884. She died in 1934 and he in 1946 without issue. 42 notes.

J. D. Neville

127. Lemon, James T. APPROACHES TO THE STUDY OF THE URBAN PAST: GEOGRAPHY. *Urban Hist. Rev. [Canada] 1973 (2): 13-19.* Examines geographical studies concerning city planning and settlement in both the United States and Canada, 19th-20th centuries.

128. Lipset, Seymour Martin. RADICALISM IN NORTH AMERICA: A COMPARATIVE VIEW OF THE PARTY SYSTEMS IN CANADA AND THE UNITED STATES. *Tr. of the Royal Soc. of Can. [Canada] 1976 14: 19-55.* Compares the United States and Canada, with emphasis on why socialism developed in Canada and not in the

United States. Some scholars see the cause to be the counterrevolutionary background of the creation of Canada and the egalitarian traditions of the United States which left little basis for the development of a socialist party. According to H. G. Wells, the United States lacked not only a socialist party, but also a tory party. Louis Hartz sees all Americans as liberals. Canada, on the other hand, had a Conservative Party and a tradition of government intervention in economic and local political matters. Canadian unions, although affiliated with American unions, are ideologically influenced by British Trade Unionism. The United States, according to Hartz, Marx, Engels, and Lenin, is "a pure bourgeois, pure liberal, born-modern society;" hence, it is "too socialist for socialism." More important is the difference in electoral systems. Canada has a parliamentary system which encourages the development of third parties. In the United States, the two-party system is almost impossible to change. Voters feel that to vote for a third-party candidate is to throw one's vote away. The Democratic Party has a close relationship with labor but is not a socialist party. The Canadian socialist party remains small. 98 notes.
J. D. Neville

129. Long, Janet E. SURVEYOR'S MARKERS AS HISTORIC MONUMENTS. *Can. Geographic [Canada] 1978 97(2): 66-71.* Surveyor's markers, some dating back to 1765, were collected when resurveying and remarking was done, 1960-70, and gathered together in a collection at the National Museum of Science and Technology in Ottawa.

130. Lucas, Glenn. CANADIAN PROTESTANT CHURCH HISTORY TO 1973. *Bull. of the United Church of Can. [Canada] 1974 (23): 5-50.* Outlines the history of the Methodist, Presbyterian, Anglican, Baptist, Congregational, and Lutheran churches in Canada and the United Church of Canada since 1825; includes bibliographies and historiography.

131. Lucas, John. ANOMALIES OF HUMAN PHYSICAL ACHIEVEMENT. *Can. J. of Hist. of Sport and Physical Educ. [Canada] 1977 8(2): 1-9.* Discusses sports feats, 1740-1975, by Americans, Canadians, and Europeans.

132. Lund, Rolf T. SKIING IN CANADA: THE EARLY YEARS. *Beaver [Canada] 1977 308(3): 48-53.* The first printed reference to skiing in Canada appeared in 1879. Skiing was the result of Norwegian and Finnish influence and developed in Canada on a regional basis. In the east the sport became formalized in 1904 with the founding of the Montreal Ski Club. In the west, mining engineer Olaus Jeldness, a Norwegian, won the first downhill event at Red Mountain, British Columbia, in 1897. In most places in Canada, ski-jumping became popular before racing. The friction between groups from eastern and western Canada was quieted somewhat in 1920 with the founding of the Canadian Amateur Ski Association, but only in 1935 was the association representative of all clubs in the country. 8 illus.
D. Chaput

133. Lunt, Richard. THE ST. LAWRENCE RIVER SKIFF AND THE FOLKLORE OF BOATS. *New York Folklore Q. 1973 29(4): 254-268.*

134. MacDonald, L. R. MERCHANTS AGAINST INDUSTRY: AN IDEA AND ITS ORIGINS. *Can. Hist. R. 1975 56(3): 263-281.* Outlines and examines an interpretation of Canadian history presented in the works of radical historians based on the principle that the excessive power of merchant interests in 19th-century Canada obstructed the growth of indigenous manufacturing. Test against primary and secondary sources this interpretation is shown to face serious problems in empirical verification and theoretical plausibility. A regionalist response to metropolitanist historical interpretations, the idea is traced to a convergence of radical and nationalist themes over a century of Canadian economic thought.
A

135. Maloof, George. CLAUDE HENRI GRIGNON A LA DEFENSE DE LA LANGUE CANADIENNE-FRANCAISE [Claude Henri Grignon in defense of Canadian-French language]. *Rev. de Louisiane 1977 6(1): 77-85.* Discusses French Canadians in the 20th century, especially the Anglicization of the French language; that is, incorporation of English words, with the addition of accent and verb endings.

136. Manning, Frank E. THE BIG BROTHER: CANADIAN CULTURAL SYMBOLISM AND BERMUDIAN POLITICAL THOUGHT. *Rev. Interamericana [Puerto Rico] 1977 7(1): 60-72.* Canadian presence in Bermuda has been particularly strong in the fields of religion and education. This presence is likely to expand soon to other areas. As ties with Great Britain are slowly loosened, many Bermuda citizens favor an official political tie with Canada. 3 notes, biblio.
J. A. Lewis

137. Marsh, John. THE CHANGING SKIING SCENE IN CANADA. *Can. Geographical J. 1975 90(2): 4-13.*

138. Marshall, John U. GEOGRAPHY'S CONTRIBUTION TO THE HISTORICAL STUDY OF URBAN CANADA. *Urban Hist. Rev. [Canada] 1973 (1): 15-23.* Surveys major literature in the field of Canadian urban studies, ca 1900-73.

139. Martin, Anita Shilton. WOMEN AND IMPERIALISM. *Can. Dimension 1975 10(8): 19-25.* Socialist women in Canada systematically analyze how women have been affected by the operation of capitalism on a world scale, from the late 19th century to the present.

140. Martyn, Howe. PAST IS FUTURE FOR THE MULTINATIONAL FIRM. *Dalhousie R. [Canada] 1974 54(1): 103-111.* The term multinational firm became a general one following the introduction of a course on the multinational firm at American University in 1961. One of the conditions leading to the acceptance of this type of firm was the encouragement received in Canada under the national policy of industrialization in 1879. Another condition was the acceptance in the United States of the wholly owned subsidiary abroad. Canada has been the proving ground of the multinational firm. Because of the efforts of Senator Gerald Nye in the United States to discourage American firms from cooperating with foreign firms, the development of the wholly owned subsidiary became an important fact. The future of such firms is conditioned by developments around the world and involves such items and persons as "colonialism," "nationalization," Senator Hartke, Representative Burke, AFL-CIO, and Peter G. Peterson. 15 notes.
C. Held

141. McCook, James. "GREAT GUNS." *Beaver [Canada] 1974 305(3): 18-23.* Surveys the cannons used in military actions and at fur trade posts throughout Canada. Specific examples selected from Nova Scotia, Quebec, Hudson's Bay, and British Columbia. Examines problems of weight, transportation, and safe gunpowder. 7 illus.
D. Chaput

142. McDonald, Virginia. PARTICIPATION IN THE CANADIAN CONTEXT. *Queen's Q. [Canada] 1977 84(3): 457-475.* Examines the concept of participatory democracy for Canada, particularly how it "is conducive to the well-being of people." Mentions historical developments in Canada and expresses concern about tendencies toward big government, elitism, and resultant nonparticipation. There is a need for more openness in government and for greater opportunities for individual voters to have real knowledge. Based on printed sources; 12 notes.
J. A. Casada

143. McGavin, Robert James. WATER, WATER EVERYWHERE: BUT SHORTAGES ARE COMING. *Int. Perspectives [Canada] 1978 (July-Aug.): 27-31.* Four schemes already exist to divert Canadian water to the United States. As water supply becomes more critical, Americans will increase their demands. Unfortunately, Canada cannot supply this need. Good relations with the United States require that Canada communicate the following facts to the American public: Canada has limited water resources; the provinces, rather than the federal government, control the water flow; and the preservation of the environment requires that no water be diverted from the country. Map.
E. S. Palais

144. McKechnie, R. N. SHIPS, COLONIES, AND COMMERCE. *Naut. Res. J. 1975 21(3): 115-125.* Discusses the construction and operation of wooden square-rig ships in Canada in the 19th century, emphasizing their role in Canadian commerce and colonization.

145. McKillop, A. B. NATIONALISM, IDENTITY AND CANADIAN INTELLECTUAL HISTORY. *Queen's Q. [Canada] 1974 81(4): 533-550.* Discusses the recent rise in Canadian self-awareness as evidenced by growing interest among historians in Canada's intellectual

heritage. In relation to other aspects of the Canadian past, intellectual history has been neglected. One explanation is the persisting problem of national identity. Canadians must put aside concerns regarding nationalism and be more concerned with a world view in order to make progress in intellectual spheres. Secondary sources; 27 notes.
J. A. Casada

146. McMillan, Keith. CANADIAN MUSIC. *Am. Rev. of Can. Studies 1975 5(2): 66-81.* Covers the 20th century.

147. McNaught, Kenneth. THE AMERICAN IMPACT UPON CANADA. *Can. Geographical J. 1976 92(1): 4-13.* Explains why Canada has remained independent of the US.

148. McNaught, Kenneth. WHAT'S LEFT. *Int. J. [Canada] 1976 31(3): 434-441.* Accounts for the lack of socialist political parties in the United States and their existence in Canada despite the revolutionary tradition in the United States and the evolutionary process in Canada. 4 notes.
R. V. Kubicek

149. McPherson, Hugo. VERNACULAR ART: CANADIAN AND AMERICAN. *Can. Rev. of Am. Studies [Canada] 1976 7(2): 187-192.* Reviews and contrasts American and Canadian folk art as described in *A People's Art: Primitive, Naive, and Folk Painting in Canada* (Toronto, 1974) by Russell Harper, and *The Flowering of American Folk Art: 1776-1876* (New York, 1974) by Jean Lipman and Alice Winchester. Although some similarities are discerned, the art reflects differences between American and Canadian ways of "seeing and feeling." 2 photos.
H. T. Lovin

150. McQuillan, D. Aidan. FARM SIZE AND WORK ETHIC: MEASURING THE SUCCESS OF IMMIGRANT FARMERS ON THE AMERICAN GRASSLANDS, 1875-1925. *J. of Hist. Geography 1978 4(1): 57-76.* In America farm size is often seen as an indicator of farming success. To test this assumption, colonies of French Canadians, Mennonites, and Swedish Americans were studied in Kansas. Although the Swedish farms were largest, they were the least productive, while the Mennonites with the smallest farms were the most productive because they were the most labor-intensive farmers of the three groups. The poor reputation of French Canadian farmers in Canada was not repeated in Kansas. Based on Kansas township records and on secondary sources; map, 3 tables, 6 graphs, 32 notes.
F. N. Egerton

151. McRoberts, Kenneth. QUEBEC AND THE CANADIAN POLITICAL CRISIS. *Ann. of the Am. Acad. of Pol. and Social Sci. 1977 433: 19-31.* For the first 90 years of Canada's existence, political conflict between the French-Canadian minority and the English-Canadian majority embraced electoral politics, government policies, and federal-provincial relations, but there was no major challenge to the Canadian political community itself. At the same time, there was only limited accommodation of French Canadians in federal institutions and virtually none in provinces other than Quebec. Apparently, the existence of a Quebec provincial government sufficed to prevent the rise of a strong secessionist movement. With the modernization of Quebec, however, such a movement has now emerged. The large difference in size between the English-speaking majority and the French-speaking minority appears to preclude mutual veto arrangements or general parity of representation in federal institutions. It has even hindered the attainment of proportional representation in federal power structures. Attempts to reinforce the French-Canadian presence outside Quebec have also been frustrated by demographic factors. Meanwhile, intensification of ethnic conflict within Quebec and preference for French-Canadian controlled institutions have strengthened demands by French Canadians to make Quebec their primary political community.
J

152. Mealing, F. M. PORTRAITS OF DOUKHOBORS: PREFACE AND CHRONOLOGY. *Sound Heritage [Canada] 1977 6(4): 1-11.* Discusses the social structure, economic conditions, values, and religious beliefs of the Christian Community of Universal Brotherhood, or Dukhobors, a communalistic religious sect which migrated from Russia to Saskatchewan and eventually settled in British Columbia; includes a chronology, 1652-1976.

153. Metcalfe, Alan. SPORT AND ATHLETICS: A CASE STUDY OF LACROSSE IN CANADA, 1840-1889. *J. of Sport Hist. 1976 3(1): 1-19.* Examines the history of lacrosse in Canada and throws light on the concepts of "sport" and "athletics." The first recorded lacrosse game between whites and Indians was held in 1843. In 1856 the Montreal lacrosse club was established, and in the 1860's teams were formed in eastern Ontario. In 1867 the National Lacrosse Association was organized. In the early 1880's it spread from coast to coast, and over the years the sport developed from a game for a select group into a highly developed spectator sport. Early in the sport's history there was concern over the rough and violent play, and over the standard of officiating. A lengthy analysis indicates that lacrosse and any other game holds potentiality for "sport" or "athletics." In the 1860's players, administrators, and spectators espoused the ideal of "muscular Christianity," but when lower class players and spectators became interested, and when the game became better organized, it became athletics, emphasizing winning at all costs. 58 notes.
M. Kaufman

154. Miller, J. R. UNITY/DIVERSITY: THE CANADIAN EXPERIENCE. *Dalhousie R. [Canada] 1975 55(1): 63-82.* Reviews the ideas behind the Canadian union as expressed by such men as George-Etienne Cartier, Donald Creighton, and Arthur Lower. Discusses the formula "Unity for diversity" used by the Fathers of Confederation, and terms such as dualism, biculturalism, centralization, disallowance, and bilingual. Early unity was based upon pursuit of common economic goals, which began to erode in the 1880's. New ideas focusing national unity on language and culture by such men as D'Alton McCarthy and Goldwin Smith, and massive immigration from Europe in the 1890's meant trouble for the doctrine of diversity. The solution proposed by Protestant Anglo-Saxons, "a good English education," met with French opposition. The most recent facet of the problem is the Trudeau government's move toward multiculturalism in 1971. 46 notes.
C. Held

155. Minville, Esdras. QUELQUES ASPECTS D'UN GRAND PROBLÈME [Several aspects of a major problem]. *Action Natl. [Canada] 1978 67(9): 779-787.* At the time of Confederation, Ontario and Quebec formed a geological and topographic unity, as did Nova Scotia and New Brunswick. The social and political fact of ethnic contrasts, however, prevents the two central provinces from sharing common interests. As additional Anglo-Canadian provinces were created, Quebec became the sole defense for a threatened minority. A true confederation, a union of sovereign provinces, coordinated rather than ruled by a central power, is the only guarantee of a fruitful association. Reprinted from *L'Actualité économique,* November 1937.
A. W. Novitsky

156. Monet, Jacques. LA COURONNE DU CANADA [The crown in Canada]. *J. of Can. Studies [Canada] 1976 11(4): 27-32.* Frank MacKinnon's *The Crown in Canada* (Glenbow-Alberta Inst., McClelland and Stewart West, 1967) deals with the effects of the British crown in Canada during the 19th and 20th centuries.

157. Morse, Eric W. RECREATIONAL CANOEING: ITS HISTORY AND ITS HAZARDS. *Can. Geographical J. [Canada] 1977 95(1): 18-25.* Discusses canoeing in Canada in regard to Indians, fur traders, and 20th-century exploratory and recreational canoeing.

158. Nelles, H. V. and Armstrong, Christopher. "THE GREAT FIGHT FOR CLEAN GOVERNMENT." *Urban Hist. Rev. [Canada] 1976 76(2): 50-66.* Questions the current theory of motivation of Canadian urban reformers (1890-1920) which ascribes reform to the businessmen's and professionals' self-interest in bringing order and efficiency to city government. Urban reform in Toronto and St. John, New Brunswick, are examples of democratic rather than elitist reform movements. Experienced politicians reasserted their influence by adapting to the reforms. Historians should concentrate more on events and less on the ideas and rhetoric of the time. Based on primary and secondary sources and on newspapers; 46 notes.
C. A. Watson

159. Nelson, J. G. CANADA'S NATIONAL PARKS: PAST, PRESENT, FUTURE. *Can. Geographical J. 1973 86(3): 68-89.*

160. Neutell, Walter. NATIONAL ETHNIC ARCHIVES. *Can. Lib. J. [Canada] 1976 33(5): 435-436.* Canada's archival repositories have largely neglected ethnic records. The 1971 multiculturalism policy placed

increased emphasis on ethnic archives and initiated a project to collect records and papers from organizations and persons of other than English or French backgrounds who have had broad impact on their communities or on Canadian society.   L. F. Johnson

161. Niosi, Jorge. LA LAURENTIDE (1887-1928): PIONNIÈRE DU PAPIER JOURNAL AU CANADA [The Laurentide (1887-1928): pioneer of newsprint in Canada]. *R. d'hist. de l'Amérique française [Canada] 1975 29(3): 375-415.* Presents the history of the Laurentide Company, the largest Canadian producer of newsprint during the first two decades of the 20th century. The firm was launched by American and Canadian forestry capitalists. The members of the Montreal bourgeoisie who invested in the company were identified with the Canadian Pacific, the Bank of Montreal, and associated capitalist interests. Based on company records and secondary sources; diagram, 31 notes.
                                                                 L. B. Chan

162. Noel, S. J. R. CANADA AND THE AMERICA QUESTION. *J. of Commonwealth and Comparative Pol. [Great Britain] 1975 13(1): 87-92.* Describes the Canadian fear of Americanization, and its treatment by the Canadian press and by Canadian historians and political scientists, in particular Samuel E. Moffett. Examines the influence of Moffett's early 20th-century publications on the treatment of the American issue by historians today. 4 notes.   C. Anstey

163. Orfila, Alejandro. HUMAN RIGHTS IN THE AMERICAS. *Américas [Organization of American States] 1977 29(5): 18-20.* Covers the 19th and 20th centuries.

164. Ostry, Bernard. THE ILLUSION OF UNDERSTANDING: MAKING THE AMBIGUOUS INTELLIGIBLE. *Oral Hist. Rev. 1977 (2): 7-16.* Audio and video tapes lend an added dimension of understanding to history, by providing an insight into the personalities who create history. Reviews the work of the Canadian Museum of Man and of the War Museum, and concludes that the ultimate value of oral and video history is the opportunity they give to common men to express their story, which supplements academic history. 10 notes.
                                                              D. A. Yanchisin

165. Ouellet, Fernand. HISTORIOGRAPHIE CANADIENNE ET NATIONALISME [Canadian historiography and nationalism]. *Tr. of the Royal Soc. of Can. 1975 13: 25-39.* Discusses the development of Canadian historiography and the influence of nationalism on it ever since J. Viger, the first mayor of Montreal, began to accumulate historical sources (1810). Notes Ramsay Cook's study of historians and nationalism and discusses the effect of historians on attitudes in both English-speaking and French-speaking Canada. Deals first with nationalism and narrative history, discussing the effect of such historians as Garneau, David, Chapais, Groulx, McMullen, Christie, Innis, Creighton, Lower, Burton, Landon, Underhill, and Morton. Discusses the development of history departments at the universities of Laval and Montreal, and the varying interrelation of Canadian history as seen by the different schools of thought.   J. D. Neville

166. Ouellet, Fernand. L'HISTOIRE SOCIO-CULTURELLE: COLLOQUE EXPLORATOIRE [Socio-cultural history: exploratory symposium]. *Social Hist. [Canada] 1976 9(17): 5-10.* A September 1975 conference at the University of Ottawa explored sociocultural history, a field not yet well developed in Canada. Cultural history has focused on the national level, rather than on the primary agents of socialization, while social historians are beginning to incorporate culture in their analyses. The work of sociologists, anthropologists, and folklorists can provide useful models and data. Papers at the conference explored the relationships between culture and class structure and between culture and ethnicity. 2 notes.   W. K. Hobson

167. Painchaud, Paul. TERRITORIALIZATION AND INTERNATIONALISM: THE CASE OF QUEBEC. *Publius 1977 7(4): 161-175.* Describes the historical existence and development of a French political identity within the Canadian population. The present conflict developed slowly because of Canadian nationalism and a widely spread French population. Quebec maintains that its development requires access to the international system. Predicts that other individual territorial components will wish to share sovereignty on both the internal and

external levels. Canadians and Quebecois are creating a new type of federalism, "diplomatic federalism" and suggests that it may "provide a solution to the growing problems posed by the polyethnic character of liberal and industrialized societies." 10 notes.   R. S. Barnard

168. Palmer, Howard. MOSAIC VERSUS MELTING POT?: IMMIGRATION AND ETHNICITY IN CANADA AND THE UNITED STATES. *Int. J. [Canada] 1976 31(3): 488-528.* Stresses the similarities rather than the differences in immigration policy and attitudes to immigrants in the two countries. 2 tables, 81 notes.   R. V. Kubicek

169. Panting, Gerald E. LITERATURBERICHT ÜBER DIE GESCHICHTE KANADAS: VERÖFFENTLICHUNGEN 1945-1969 [Report on writings on the history of Canada: Publications appearing between 1945 and 1969]. *Hist. Zeitschrift [West Germany] 1973 5(special issue): 629-654.* Discusses persons, works, and issues in Canadian historiography, including 131 works in general Canadian history, reference works, source collections, and political, religious, constitutional, economic, social, intellectual, and military history.   G. H. Davis

170. Pearse, Charles R. COAL COMES BACK: ITS PROMISE AND CHALLENGE. *Can. Geographical J. [Canada] 1978 96(2): 70-75.* Examines the development of Canada's bituminous coal industry, 1892-1978, and the recent resurgence of interest in coal as a major source of energy.

171. Pearson, Samuel C., Jr. CHRISTIANITY IN BRITISH NORTH AMERICA. *Encounter 1978 39(1): 85-91.* In Robert T. Handy's *A History of the Churches in the United States and Canada* (New York, 1977), the author ably presents the view that while the United States and Canada have some similar attitudes toward religion (e.g., neither country has been comfortable with an image of itself as a secular nation), differences in their histories (e.g., US guilt feelings about slavery, and loyalist feelings among 18th-century "English" Canadians) have made Canada less concerned than the United States with rigid separation of church and state.

172. Pichette, Robert and Lussier, Jean Jacques. ARMORIAL DES CHEVALIERS DE MALTE FRANÇAIS EN TERRE D'AMERIQUE [The Heraldry of the French Knight of Malta in America]. *Rev. de l'U. d'Ottawa [Canada] 1976 46(1): 40-67.* The Knights of Malta were involved in the founding, development, and defense of the French colonies in America and in the American Revolution. Although the Canadian order of Malta was not founded until 1950, its roots are deep in both America and Canada. Lists some of the more important knights and provides a history of their coat of arms. Primary and secondary sources; biblio.   M. L. Frey

173. Piédalue, Gilles. LES GROUPES FINANCIERS AU CANADA 1900-1930—ÉTUDE PRÉLIMINAIRE [The financial groups of Canada, 1900-30: A preliminary study]. *Rev. d'Hist. de l'Am. Française [Canada] 1976 30(1): 3-34.* During 1900-30, Canadian economic activity was divided into four major sectors: financial, industrial, mining, and public services. The administrators of companies in these sectors formed an economic elite. Few of the men were self-made. Most were born in Quebec or Ontario, English-speaking, very well-educated, and from successful business families. They began their careers as managers or company lawyers. Based on published statistics and secondary works; 15 tables, 8 figs., 35 notes.   L. B. Chan

174. Plumb, Louise. HOW WE BEGAN DRIVING ON THE RIGHT. *Can. Geographical J. 1974 89(3): 14-16.* The left-hand drive design of the Conestoga wagon train was in part responsible for the custom of driving on the right.   S

175. Polisenský, Josef. PROBLEMÁTICA DE LAS RELACIONES RUSO-LATINOAMERICANAS EN LA COSTA PACÍFICA DEL CONTINENTE AMERICANO [Problems of Russo-Latin American relations on the American continent's Pacific coast]. *Archív Orientální [Czechoslovakia] 1977 45(2): 122-131.* America's West Coast attracted considerable attention in Bohemia and Slovakia during the 16th to 19th centuries. The Czech public followed English seafaring attempts to discover the Northwest Passage to Japan and China, and followed Russian expansion to the east. Prague was visited by the future author of the

Araucana, Alonso Ercilla y Zúñiga; Chile and Peru were considered, along with Flanders and Bohemia, as borderlands of the vast Spanish Empire. Princess Elizabeth of England's son, Rupert of the Palatinate, gave his name permanently to Canadian maps. The US-Mexican border became a new home for dozens of Bohemian Jesuit missionaries. Also discusses Czech scholarly interest in the American Southwest and Czech immigration to California.   J/S

176.   Powles, Cyril.   E. H. NORMAN AS A HISTORIAN: A CANADIAN PERSPECTIVE: A REVIEW ARTICLE.   *Pacific Affairs [Canada] 1977-78 50(4): 660-667.* Examines the debate among Japanese and Western historians regarding the scholarship of E. Herbert Norman. In the summer of 1977, George Akita, writing in the *Journal of Japanese Studies,* detailed the most serious negative criticisms of Norman's writings. Norman earned the respect of virtually all scholars and students of the history of Japan for his work, *Japan's Emergence as a Modern State.* Even 20 years after his death Norman the diplomat and scholar was the subject of considerable critical investigation. Charles Taylor believes that Norman's perspectives and writings were molded by his Canadian upbringing. Based on secondary sources; 30 notes.   S. H. Frank

177.   Presser, Carolynne.   CODOC: A COMPUTER-BASED PROCESSING AND RETRIEVAL SYSTEM FOR GOVERNMENT DOCUMENTS.   *Coll. and Res. Lib. 1978 39(2): 94-98.* Much has been written in the literature recently concerning the application of machine technology to complex library operations. This paper describes a computerized system specifically designed to provide a quick and economical method of in-depth access to individual publications within a government documents collection. The system, CODOC (COoperative DOCuments), is currently operated in a network configuration in Ontario and Quebec and independently by several other libraries in Canada and the United States.   J

178.   Preston, Richard A.   TWO CENTURIES IN THE SHADOW OF BEHEMOTH: THE EFFECT ON THE CANADIAN PSYCHE. *Int. J. [Canada] 1976 31(3): 413-433.* Examines 19th-century and early 20th-century public attitudes and secret military planning concerning a possible US invasion of Canada. Also looks at the effect on Canada's present military stance of its proximity to the armed might of the United States. 32 notes.   R. V. Kubicek

179.   Qualter, Terence H.   THE REGULATION OF THE NATIONAL FRANCHISE: A PROBLEM IN FEDERAL POLITIES. *J. of Commonwealth and Comparative Pol. [Great Britain] 1975 13(1): 65-78.* Examines the problems of establishing the legal bounds of the right to vote in a Federal system, particularly in regard to election to the national legislature, in Australia, Canada, and the United States. Australia (since 1900) and Canada (since 1920) have had distinct national and state and provincial authorities for defining electoral laws. In the United States the states insisted on retaining legal control of franchise laws for all elections, but in practice the options open to the states have been steadily narrowed, producing a national and state franchise quite as uniform as Australia's or Canada's. Based on material from the Reports of the Subcommittee on Constitutional Rights, and secondary works; 33 notes.   C. Anstey

180.   Randall, Stephen J.   THE DEVELOPMENT OF CANADIAN BUSINESS IN PUERTO RICO.   *Revista/Review Interamericana [Puerto Rico] 1977 7(1): 5-20.* The Canadian economic interest in Puerto Rico has been remarkably consistent over the last century and a half. Canada has always imported Puerto Rican agricultural products, and her investments on the island traditionally have been confined to banking (Royal Bank of Canada and the Bank of Nova Scotia) and to public services (Puerto Rico Railway, Light and Power Company). Based on primary and secondary sources; 52 notes.   J. A. Lewis

181.   Rannie, William F.   OLD, BIG, COLOURFUL: CANADA'S DISTILLING INDUSTRY.   *Can. Geographical J. 1976/77 93(3): 20-27.* Discusses the Canadian distilling industry, primarily whiskey, 1668-1976.

182.   Reaburn, Pauline and Reaburn, Ronald.   FENCE PATTERNS ON OLD CANADIAN FARMS.   *Can. Geographical J. [Canada] 1977 95(1): 36-41.* Discusses methods of wood, stone, iron, and wire fence construction on Canada's farms, 17th-19th centuries.

183.   Reaburn, Pauline.   POWER FROM THE OLD MILL STREAMS.   *Can. Geographical J. 1975 90(3): 22-27.* Looks at Canada's pioneer heritage of water-powered mills (1607-1975).   S

184.   Redekop, Calvin and Hostetler, John A.   THE PLAIN PEOPLE: AN INTERPRETATION.   *Mennonite Q. Rev. 1977 51(4): 266-277.* An analysis of the nature and causes of the Plain People, who include Amish, Hutterites, Mennonites, Molokans, and Dukhobors. The Plain People perceive that religion has failed to integrate larger communities, but have faith that it can integrate small communities. Plain People are not interested in joining the larger majority, a policy which separates them from so-called minority groups. They simply want to be left alone to deal with people on a person-to-person basis. All Plain People groups have a religious bond, almost invariably Protestant. Their major concerns at present are perpetuation of their society in the face of technological change and the acquisition of new lands to support expanding communities. 4 notes.   V. L. Human

185.   Redekop, John H.   A REINTERPRETATION OF CANADIAN-AMERICAN RELATIONS.   *Can. J. of Pol. Sci. [Canada] 1976 9(2): 227-243.* Reviews and finds wanting analyses premised on conventional bi-national relations between autonomous states. Argues instead that the major components of Canadian-American affairs consist of the workings of mainly nongovernmental, continental subsystems. 71 notes.   R. V. Kubicek

186.   Resnick, Philip.   THE POLITICAL THEORY OF EXTRA-PARLIAMENTARISM.   *Can. J. of Pol. Sci. 1973 6(1): 65-88.* Extraparliamentarism is opposition to participation in parliamentary politics. Sees it as "a critique of the class-based, anti-participatory character of bourgeois political institutions" and a challenge as well to social democracy and orthodox communism which "have seemingly made their peace with capitalism . . . . " 110 notes.   R. V. Kubicek

187.   Rich, E. E.   THE FUR TRADERS: THEIR DIET AND DRUGS.   *Beaver [Canada] 1976 307(1): 42-53.* Discusses the differences in the food of the Montreal-based traders and those of the Hudson's Bay Company. Both groups found it necessary to use the Indian remedy for scurvy, spruce beer. Discusses the diet changes in all far-flung trade outposts, and the function of post personnel in providing fish, meat, vegetables, and medicines, and shows the interdependence of traders and Indians. Based on archives of the Hudson's Bay Co.; 10 illus.
                                                         D. Chaput

188.   Robinson, Willard B.   NORTH AMERICAN MARTELLO TOWERS.   *J. of the Soc. of Architectural Historians 1974 33(2): 158-164.* Reviews Martello towers built in the United States and Canada in the 19th century for military fortifications.

189.   Rose, Frances.   CANADIAN GOVERNMENT PUBLICATIONS.   *Government Publ. Rev. 1977 4(1): 71-76.* Semiannual column aimed at aiding librarians and researchers in the identification and acquisition of government publications; includes recent publications of the Canadian government.

190.   Ross, David and Summers, Jack L.   BEGINNING A CENTURY OF SERVICE: THE ROYAL CANADIAN MOUNTED POLICE 1873-1973.   *Military Collector & Historian 1973 25(4): 178-185.* Emphasizes the early evolution of the uniform of the Royal Canadian Mounted Police.   S

191.   Rouslin, Virginia Watson.   THE INTELLIGENT WOMAN'S GUIDE TO PIONEERING IN CANADA.   *Dalhousie Rev. [Canada] 1976 56(2): 319-335.* Discusses the feminine experience of 19th-century pioneering in Canada and argues for reexamining our heroes of the period. Quotes the writings of Susanna Strickland Moodie (1804-85), Catherine Parr Traill (1802-99), Anna Brownell Jameson (1794-1860), and Mary Gapper O'Brien (1798-1876) at length, and examines unique feminine experiences. 39 notes.   C. Held

192.   Rowe, P. A.   THE EVOLUTION OF THE CANADIAN WINE INDUSTRY.   *Can. Geographical J. 1977 94(3): 36-41.* Covers 1867-1976.

193. Roxborough, Henry. THE BEGINNING OF ORGANIZED SPORT IN CANADA. *Canada 1975 2(3): 30-43.* Traces the roots of organized Canadian sport 1770-1900 from its various local cultural origins, e.g., horseracing at the British military garrisons, curling in the Scottish communities, ice hockey, and lacrosse among the Indians. Notes the rise of athlete heroes, especially the Canadian scullers who won several international championships. Questions the appropriateness of modern, highly organized and promoted national sports. 10 photos, biblio., note.   W. W. Elison

194. Ruggle, Richard. "BETTER NO BREAD THAN HALF A LOAF," OR "CRUMBS FROM THE HISTORIC EPISCOPATE TABLE": HERBERT SYMONDS AND CHRISTIAN UNITY. *J. of the Can. Church Hist. Soc. 1976 18(2-3): 53-84.* In the first part of this century, an Anglican clergyman, Herbert Symonds, initiated, participated in, and furthered all efforts to involve Anglicans in Canadian church unification. Such efforts led him to suggest that the Church permit non-Anglican clergy to preach in its churches and non-Anglicans to receive communion there as well. Some liberals outside the church derided the proposal in such slogans as "better no bread than half a loaf." But Symonds faced great opposition within the church, even against the ideas of the educational organizations he helped found: the Canadian Society of Church Unity (1898) and the Church Unity League (1913). Symonds and his associates did create some interest in unity, but they were never able to convince the churchmen who were dedicated to the maintenance of the historic episcopate. Nevertheless, by the time of Symonds' death (1921), a General Synod did support the right of bishops to permit Anglican and non-Anglican clergy to preach in each other's churches. Based on primary and secondary sources; 103 notes.
J. A. Kicklighter

195. Russell, Loris S. THE FIRST CANADIAN COOKING STOVE. *Canada 1975 3(2): 34-35.* Discusses the introduction of cast-iron cooking stoves in Canada 1820-80's, emphasizing the patent design of Joseph Van Norman.

196. Samaroo, Brinsley. THE POLITICS OF DISHARMONY: THE DEBATE ON THE POLITICAL UNION OF THE BRITISH WEST INDIES AND CANADA, 1884-1921. *Revista/Review Interamericana [Puerto Rico] 1977 7(1): 46-59.* Ever since 1884, a number of groups representing Canadian imperialists or hoping for certain economic benefits have proposed political union of Canada and the British West Indies. These proposals never have had widespread popular appeal in Canada and the Caribbean and always have had to confront the problem of Canadian racism. 71 notes.   J. A. Lewis

197. Sanderson, Lilian. THE SUDAN INTERIOR MISSION AND THE CONDOMINIUM SUDAN, 1937-1955. *J. of Religion in Africa [Netherlands] 1976 8(1): 13-40.* The Sudan Interior Mission (SIM), headquartered in Canada, had worked in Nigeria and Ethiopia before entering the Sudan in 1937. Provides a year-by-year account of the SIM's activities, including its difficulties with the British government. Of particular importance to the SIM was the development of schools and the role of the British government in the education of Africans. The areas where SIM went were peopled by Africans who had little interest in missionaries or their schools. 116 notes.   H. G. Soff

198. Saunders, Ivan J. A HISTORY OF MARTELLO TOWERS IN THE DEFENSE OF BRITISH NORTH AMERICA, 1796-1871 *Can. Historic Sites 1976 15: 5-169.* Martello towers were a distinctive and popular form of light permanent artillery defense in British North America from 1796 to 1846, where sixteen of them were built in that time. After 1848 their value diminished in the face of a variety of changing political and technological conditions until they were finally rendered obsolete by major advances in ordnance technology in the 1860's. This type of tower originated largely by accident, but it quickly found a wide and enduring acceptance in British North America because it met a great variety of political, military and economic needs. Martello towers often offered the only practical means of beginning or augmenting the permanent defenses of important colonial centers. Throughout the whole era of the construction of masonry fortifications in British North America, Martello towers were a substitute for larger and more desirable but financially impracticable works of defense.   J

199. Scheinberg, Stephen. INVITATION TO EMPIRE: TARIFFS AND AMERICAN ECONOMIC EXPANSION IN CANADA. *Business Hist. R. 1973 47(2): 218-238.* Argues against the proposition that American economic domination of Canada was only the result of geographic proximity and not conscious policy. Sees a "continuing active role of United States businessmen and their government . . . to secure Canada for American economic control." Secondary sources; 72 notes.
C. J. Pusateri

200. Schrodt, Barbara. SABBATARIANISM AND SPORT IN CANADIAN SOCIETY. *J. of Sport Hist. 1977 4(1): 22-33.* Parliament passed the Lord's Day Act (1906), but stated that a provincial act could allow specific activities prohibited by the federal law. In areas where Sunday professional sports were well established, the activities continued. The Lord's Day Alliance tried to force a strict enforcement of the act, repressing amateur and recreational as well as professional athletics. After World War I, attitudes began to change, Sunday became a day of leisure as well as church worship, and pressures grew for sport on Sunday. The automobile made society more mobile, and Sunday became the ideal time for family leisure activities away from home. Also, increased affluence encouraged the growth of popular Sunday sports such as golf. As time passed, the religious restraints were weakened, and sports gained in influence. Now, the Lord's Day Act no longer prevents Canadians from enjoying sports on Sundays, and Canadian sport is healthier and stronger than ever. 38 notes.   M. Kaufman

201. Schroeter, Gerd. IN SEARCH OF ETHNICITY: MULTICULTURALISM IN CANADA. *J. of Ethnic Studies 1978 6(1): 98-107.* Discusses the historiography of the "new ethnicity' and problems of definition, while viewing the "policy" of multiculturalism in Canada today as fraught with contradictions. Reviews the first three volumes of the federally commissioned *Generations: A History of Canada's Peoples,* viz., Anderson and Higgs's *A Future to Inherit: The Portuguese Communities of Canada,* Radecki's *A Member of a Distinguished Family: The Polish Group in Canada,* and W. Stanford Reid, ed., *The Scottish Tradition in Canada.* All are valuable contributions which will remain standard sources, and all point to the conclusion, "there is no indication that a neo-ethnicity, of the sort described by Novak or Glazer and Moynihan, is developing in Canada." Schroeter suggests ethnicity may be largely a statistical artifact arising from censuses, or merely the exploitation of government support for "cultural" programs. Secondary sources; 30 notes.
G. J. Bobango

202. Scott, Anthony. THE REVOLUTIONARY TRADITION IN CANADIAN AND AMERICAN SOCIETY: ECONOMIC ASPECTS. *Tr. of the Royal Soc. of Can. [Canada] 1976 14: 97-110.* Discusses the economic influence of the American Revolution on Canada and suggests that Canada developed nationalistic policies as a defensive measure against the booming United States. Most of Canada's economic ideas were European rather than American. In government, however, Canadians were influenced by the federal system as created in the United States. 7 notes.   J. D. Neville

203. Sealock, Richard B. and Powell, Margaret S. PLACE-NAME LITERATURE, UNITED STATES AND CANADA, 1975. *Names 1975 23(4): 296-299.* Presents a state-by-state bibliography of 1964-75 books and studies dealing with onomastics and place-names.

204. Segal, Beryl. THE EDUCATION OF AN IMMIGRANT. *Rhode Island Jewish Hist. Notes 1976 7(2): 277-293.* Reminiscences of Russia before World War I and of the immigration of a Jewish family to Canada and the United States, 1900-70's.

205. Shaw, Edward C. THE KENNEDYS—AN UNUSUAL WESTERN FAMILY. *Trans. of the Hist. and Sci. Soc. of Manitoba [Canada] 1972/73 Series 3(29): 69-79.* Traces the origins of the Kennedy family from their Scottish ancestry and devotes considerable attention to the activities of those who settled in Canada in the late 18th and early 19th centuries. 2 charts.   J. A. Casada

206. Shugg, Roger W. *CUI BONO? Scholarly Publ. [Canada] 1978 10(1): 3-16.* Offers a history of scholarly publishing as exemplified by university presses in North America, 1920's-70's; discusses specific examples and draws contrasts with other publishing modes.

207. Sims, A. G. CANADIAN AIRMEN ON THE MAP. *Can. Geographical J. 1975 91(5): 28-33.* Discusses the history of Canadian aviation in the 20th century.

208. Skinner, Brian J. CYCLES IN MINING AND THE MAGNITUDE OF MINERAL PRODUCTION. *Tr. of the Royal Soc. of Can. [Canada] 1977 15: 13-27.* Notes that in the history of discovery and exploitation of metallic mineral resources in industrial countries there is a consistent pattern of growth followed by decline. Similar patterns also exist in the amount of mineral smelting and processing in a country, in the exportation of metals, in the development of the industries making use of the metals, and eventually in the importation of supplies as production falls below demand. Suggests that we rely on ore minerals for our metal supplies. A finite quantity of these minerals are recoverable; thus, the aforementioned cycles are inevitable. Concludes that the United States and Canada are well into their productive cycles. Table, 12 fig., biblio.
J. D. Neville

209. Smiley, Donald V. CANADA AND THE QUEST FOR A NATIONAL POLICY. *Can. J. of Pol. Sci. 1975 8(1): 40-62.* Examines the continuing complex of policies undertaken by successive Canadian governments to establish and sustain a national economy. 103 notes.
R. V. Kubicek

210. Smith, Allan. THE CONTINENTAL DIMENSION IN THE EVOLUTION OF THE ENGLISH-CANADIAN MIND. *Int. J. [Canada] 1976 31(3): 442-469.* Traces the origins and characteristics of the cultural environment which disposes English Canadians to see themselves as joint participants with their southern neighbors in the development of the North American continent. 79 notes. R. V. Kubicek

211. Smith, David and Tepperman, Lorne. CHANGES IN THE CANADIAN BUSINESS AND LEGAL ELITES, 1870-1970. *Can. R. of Sociol. and Anthrop. 1974 11(2): 97-109.* "This paper examines the social origins and activities of two Canadian elites, those of business and law, in the nineteenth and twentieth centuries. It attempts a provisional explanation of the changes in access to wealth, authority, prominence, and influence that have occurred in the last hundred years. As an explanatory study, this paper suggests the need for an approach to the history of stratification in Canada that has not received much attention heretofore; namely, the historical analysis of stratifying institutions." J

212. Smith, David E. PROVINCIAL REPRESENTATION ABROAD: THE OFFICE OF AGENT GENERAL IN LONDON. *Dalhousie Rev. [Canada] 1975 55(2): 315-327.* Recapitulates the growth of the office of agent general through its various titles from the late 18th century through the 1970's. The friction between federal and provincial jurisdictions is noted. The main break in the evolution of the agencies is World War II. Since then the roles of the provincial agents have proliferated and the relationships with the federal high commissioners have been harmonious. 27 notes. C. Held

213. Smith, Janet. EQUAL OPPORTUNITY IN THE PUBLIC SERVICE. *Can. Labour 1975 20(2): 13-15, 24.* Notes sex discrimination in Canada's public service since 1870. S

214. Smith, Roger S. LAND PRICES AND TAX POLICY: AN HISTORICAL REVIEW. *Am. J. of Econ. and Sociol. 1977 36(4): 337-350.* Surveys use of tax measures to control land prices and concludes that most of the current measures were developed 1890-1920; examines the attempt to control land prices through fiscal controls of public policy; discusses Germany, Great Britain and Canada.

215. Smith, W. I. ARCHIVES AND CULTURE: AN ESSAY. *Cultures [France] 1977 4(2): 51-68.* Discusses the increasingly important role of archives as cultural agents, focusing on the growth of their educational services to the public in Canada, the United States, and France.

216. Snyder, David. EARLY NORTH AMERICAN STRIKES: A REINTERPRETATION. *Industrial and Labor Relations Rev. 1977 30(3): 325-341.* Most studies of aggregate strike activity in the United States and Canada have stressed the importance of economic determinants such as the stage of the business cycle and the rate of change in real wages. This study tests the hypothesis that such economic models are most appropriate for explaining fluctuations in strike activity during the post-World War II period, when bargaining was well established in both countries, but an expanded model—including measures of the political environment and of labor's organizational strength—is necessary to explain strike behavior in the years prior to 1948. This hypothesis is supported by an analysis of data for 1900-71 for the United States and for 1912-71 for Canada. J

217. Soward, F. H. INSIDE A CANADIAN TRIANGLE: THE UNIVERSITY, THE CIIA, AND THE DEPARTMENT OF EXTERNAL AFFAIRS. *Int. J. [Canada] 1977-78 33(1): 66-87.* An academic describes his past assignments with the government and his involvement with the Canadian Institute of International Affairs (CIIA). 14 notes.
R. V. Kubicek

218. Spigelman, Martin S. SURVIVAL: NEW VIEWS ON THE FRANCOPHONE MINORITIES IN CANADA. *Acadiensis [Canada] 1978 7(2): 141-150.* Many recent works on French minorities outside Quebec suggest that their assimilation is inevitable. Richard Joy's *Language in Conflict* (1972) reveals continued language loss while Thomas R. Maxwell's *The Invisible French, the French in Metropolitan Toronto* reveals divisions among Toronto's French, and a general acceptance of assimilation. Similarly, Robert Choquette's work explores divisions between Ontario's French and Irish. These and other works suggest that lessening self-consciousness, not Anglo-Protestant pressure, has weakened French culture outside Quebec. 4 notes. D. F. Chard

219. Sproule-Jones, Mark. AN ANALYSIS OF CANADIAN FEDERALISM. *Publius 1974 4(4): 109-136.* Analyzes the constitutional and institutional arrangements for the provision of collective goods and services by Canadian federal and provincial governments, and evaluates Canadian federalism in the light of the public choice theory of federalism. Contrasts assumptions of hierarchic structure and omnicompetence in Canada with the polycentrism of public choice theory. Criticizes the functioning of the Canadian political system, in which the collaboration of authority among federal and provincial governments predominates over local government and nongovernment interests. Based on government studies and secondary sources; table, 87 notes.
J. B. Street

220. Stelter, Gilbert A. CANADA'S URBAN PAST: CANADIAN URBAN HISTORY CONFERENCE. *Urban Hist. Rev. [Canada] 1977 (1): 3-32.* Discusses the Canadian Urban History Conference held at the University of Guelph, 12-14 May 1977, and presents abstracts of the papers presented. The program emphasized the city-building process within which these topics were discussed: 1) the factors involved in urban growth, 2) the role of planners, developers, and builders in the shaping of cities, and 3) the place of government, especially provincial and municipal, in determining urban form. C. A. Watson

221. Stelter, Gilbert A. CURRENT RESEARCH IN CANADIAN URBAN HISTORY. *Urban Hist. Rev. [Canada] 1975 (3): 27-36.* Discusses and presents a bibliography of recent research in Canadian urban history covering the 19th and 20th centuries.

222. Stelter, Gilbert A. THE HISTORIAN'S APPROACH TO CANADA'S URBAN PAST. *Social Hist. [Canada] 1974 7(13): 5-22.* Two main approaches characterize Canadian urban history. The most common are studies dealing with anything that has happened in cities, without concern for what is "urban" in the subject. Less common are studies which focus on the processes of urbanization and the problems such processes generate. An increasing methodological sophistication and a genuine interest in interdisciplinary communication characterize recent work. Based on secondary sources. 58 notes. W. K. Hobson

223. Stelter, Gilbert A. INTRODUCTION. *Urban Hist. Rev. [Canada] 1975 75(1): 2-6.* Introduces eight papers in this issue on the Canadian city in the 19th century; examines economic growth, metropolitan development, population, social organization, and environment. Papers are those to be presented at the 1975 Canadian Historical Association meeting.

224. Stelter, Gilbert. A SENSE OF TIME AND PLACE: THE HISTORIAN'S APPROACH TO THE URBAN PAST. *Urban Hist. Rev.*

[Canada] 1973 (2): 20-22. Examines methodology of urban historians in studying urban history in Canada, 1960's-70's.

225. Strong-Boag, Veronica. THE ROOTS OF MODERN CANADIAN FEMINISM: THE NATIONAL COUNCIL OF WOMEN, 1893-1929. *Canada 1975 3(2): 22-33.* Discusses the evolution of the National Council of Women of Canada and its role in the federation of social and political women's organizations in Canada 1893-1929.

226. Swanson, Roger Frank. CANADIAN CONSULAR REPRESENTATION IN THE UNITED STATES. *Can. Public Administration [Canada] 1977 20(2): 342-369.* Discusses the functions, responsibilities, and staffing policies of Canadian consulates in the United States, 1833-1977.

227. Swidinsky, R. TRADE UNION GROWTH IN CANADA: 1911-1970. *Industrial Relations [Canada] 1974 29(3): 435-449.* This paper is primarily an attempt to isolate the determinants of trade union membership growth in Canada over the past six decades. J

228. Taylor, Mimi Cazort. HENRY A. C. JACKSON: AMATEUR CANADIAN NATURALIST. *Beaver [Canada] 1978 309(1): 30-35.* Henry A. C. Jackson, born in Montreal in the 1870's, taught himself art and worked for Montreal commercial art firms. He enjoyed nature walks and became adept at painting mushrooms. Over the decades he became well known for his paintings of mushrooms and was an expert on the subject, acknowledged in Canada and in the United States. He recorded diaries during 1931-54, good for detail on his nature walks and approaches used in his work. Includes six color reproductions from originals in the National Gallery of Canada. D. Chaput

229. Thompson, Katheryn M. THE ARCHIVE SYSTEMS OF THE UNITED STATES OF AMERICA AND CANADA. *J. of the Soc. of Archivists [Great Britain] 1977 5(8) 534-537.* A brief, general account of US national, presidential, state, city, and local archives, and of Canadian archives. L. A. Knafla

230. Tiblin, Mariann and Welsch, Erwin K., ed. AMERICAN-SCANDINAVIAN BIBLIOGRAPHY FOR 1972. *Scandinavian Studies 1973 45(4): 324-375.* Classifications include: General Bibliography, Language, Literature, Social Sciences, History, and a subdivision, Scandinavians in the US. Arrangement within each class is by country. Mostly unannotated references are provided for books published in Scandinavia. Includes books, parts of books, periodical articles, book reviews, and dissertations published in the United States and Canada, and a few English publications published abroad. E. P. Stickney

231. Torrance, Judy. THE RESPONSE OF CANADIAN GOVERNMENTS TO VIOLENCE. *Can. J. of Pol. Sci. [Canada] 1977 10(3): 473-496.* Examines the federal government's handling of the five most serious challenges to its authority before 1970: the Red River rising, the Northwest Rebellion, the Quebec city riots, the Winnipeg strike, and the Regina riot. Primary material; 46 notes. R. V. Kubicek

232. Trépanier, Pierre. LE CANADA ANGLAIS ET SES HISTORIENS [English Canada and its historians]. *Action Natl. [Canada] 1977 67(1): 75-78.* Reviews Carl Berger's *The Writing of Canadian History: Aspects of English-Canadian Historical Writing: 1900-1970* (Toronto: Oxford U. Pr., 1976). Historians Wrong, Shortt, Morton, Innis, Lower, Underhill, Creighton, and Morton are nationalists. Their nationalism is imperial, representing Canadian history as distinct from American history, and continental, emphasizing the nation's independence from Great Britain. English-Canadian intellectuals, including historians, have been preoccupied with the assertion and definition of a distinct Canadian culture. English-Canadian historiography has evolved in four stages: 1) constitutional history emphasizing the conquest of responsible government and autonomy; 2) analysis of geo-economic forces; 3) biographical studies; and 4) metropolitanism and regionalism. Note. A. W. Novitsky

233. Unsigned. THE ARCHIVAL ORGANIZATION OF THE UNITED CHURCH OF CANADA. *Bulletin of the United Church of Can. 1973 (22): 5-15.* Briefly traces the history of the collection and housing of archival material by the Methodist and Presbyterian churches

prior to 1925, and by the United Church of Canada since that time. Brief notes on the Central Archives, presently housed at Victoria University in Toronto, and on the regional archives in St. John's, Halifax, Montreal, Hamilton, London, Winnipeg, Saskatoon, Edmonton and Vancouver. Photos. B. D. Tennyson

234. Urquhart, G. M. CANADIAN DEFENCE POLICY. *J. of the Royal United Services Inst. for Defence Studies [Great Britain] 1977 122(2): 29-34.* Surveys the defense policy of the Canadian Co-operative Commonwealth Federation and the New Democratic Party (NDP) since 1932. Analyzes the factors which produced an isolationist policy, 1932-46, unconditional internationalism, 1946-52, and selective internationalism, 1952-70. In the 1970's, NDP criticism of Canadian involvement in the North American Air Defense system declined as a result of a shift toward political pragmatism by the party and its views on defense came closer to those of the Liberal and Progressive Conservative Parties. 115 notes. D. H. Murdoch

235. Vachon, G.-André. NAISSANCE D'UNE ÉCRITURE [Birth of a kind of writing]. *Études Françaises [Canada] 1973 9(3): 191-196.* Highlights the course of political and social writing by the Canadian Democrats in the 19th century. Based on primary and secondary sources; illus., 2 notes. G. J. Rossi

236. VanNus, W. THE FATE OF CITY BEAUTIFUL THOUGHT IN CANADA, 1893-1930. *Can. Hist. Assoc. Hist. Papers [Canada] 1975: 191-210.* After the Chicago World's Fair in 1893, city planners called for curved streets, parks, parkways and civic centers in order to make cities beautiful. Advocates of better workers' housing called for suburbs in the name of health and humanity. By the 1920's, city planning meant the efficient provision of suburban housing. Therefore, orderliness from efficient zoning was all that was left of a city beautiful movement that became identified with the irresponsible use of public money. Based on government reports, proceedings of architectural associations, and secondary sources; 98 notes. G. E. Panting

237. Van Nus, Walter. SOURCES FOR THE HISTORY OF URBAN PLANNING IN CANADA, 1890-1939. *Urban Hist. Rev. [Canada] 1976 76(1): 6-9.* Surveys urban planning in Canada since 1912. Reviews the sources for the history of urban planning, listing the journals and most important city planning reports of the period. Urges further historical study of urban planning and suggests possible research topics, particularly case studies of individual cities. 11 notes. C. A. Watson

238. Vaughan, Frederick. PRECEDENT AND NATIONALISM IN THE SUPREME COURT OF CANADA. *Am. Rev. of Can. Studies 1976 6(1): 3-31.* Reviews the history of the Supreme Court of Canada's efforts to interpret the Canadian Constitution with the aid of US Supreme Court precedents and in the face of nationalist criticism.

239. Velez, Claudio. THE SURROGATE AMERICANS. *J. of Interamerican Studies and World Affairs 1977 19(3): 419-427.* Reviews J. C. M. Ogelsby's *Gringos From The Far North: Essays in the History of Canadian-Latin American Relations 1866-1968* (Toronto: 1976) and P. V. Lyon and T. Y. Ismael, eds., *Canada And The Third World* (Toronto: 1976). Discusses Canadian relations with developing nations. Canada cannot break away from its geographical proximity to the United States. Canada's reputation for fairness and impartiality may stem from its inability to define a decisive foreign policy. Sadly, Canada may be on the verge of seeking a more active, moralistic role in world affairs. ? notes, ref. T. D. Schoonover

240. Vellathottam, T. George and Jones, Kevin G. HIGHLIGHTS IN THE DEVELOPMENT OF CANADIAN LACROSSE TO 1931. *Can. J. of Hist. of Sport and Physical Educ. 1974 5(2): 31-47.* The game of lacrosse is described from the Indian game of "baggataway" to the introduction of box-lacrosse as the official Canadian game in 1931. The conflict between amateurs and professionals, rule changes, championships, and the eventual decline of lacrosse after World War I are included. Based on primary and secondary works; 118 notes. R. A. Smith

241. Vézina, Raymond. ARCHIVISTES, HISTORIENS D'ART ET DOCUMENTS ORAUX [Archivists, art historians, and oral docu-

ments]. *Can. Oral Hist. Assoc. J. [Canada] 1976-77 2: 36-45.* Examines art history in Canada 1800-1930, focusing on Napoléon Bourassa, who attempted to compile personal oral histories of painters, 1856-1916.

242. Ward, Norman. [POLITICAL LEADERSHIP IN CANADA]. *Can. Hist. Rev. [Canada] 1974 55(3): 307-312.* Reviews *Mike: The Memoirs of the Rt. Hon. Lester B. Pearson. II: 1948-1957* (Toronto: University of Toronto Press, 1973), edited by John A. Munro and Alex I. Inglis; *I Chose Canada: The Memoirs of the Honourable Joseph R. "Joey" Smallwood* (Toronto: Macmillan of Canada, 1973); Denis Smith's *Gentle Patriot: A Political Biography of Walter Gordon* (Edmonton: Hurtig, 1973); and Geoffrey Stevens' *Stanfield* (Toronto: McClelland and Stewart, 1973). Pearson's memoirs cover his decade as Secretary of State for External Affairs—a chronicle of almost unbroken success. Joey Smallwood's autobiography, "unencumbered by false modesty," is a vivid account by a father of Confederation. Denis Smith's *Gentle Patriot* describes the life of a lovable man unprepared for his rise to cabinet status. Geoffrey Stevens' biography of Stanfield is an honest, affectionate contribution to understanding the roles and problems of a Leader of the Opposition.   W. R. Hively

243. Weaver, John C. INTRODUCTION: APPROACHES TO THE HISTORY OF URBAN REFORM. *Urban Hist. Rev. [Canada] 1976 76(2): 3-11.* Introduces an issue on the history of urban reform. Compares recent Canadian interest in urban reform to earlier US interest. Combines a bibliographic approach to the history of Canadian urban reform with a historical overview of the subject. Raises questions about the definition of urban reform and notes that urban changes are not necessarily urban reforms. 16 notes.   C. A. Watson

244. Wees, Ian. THE NATIONAL LIBRARY OF CANADA: THE FIRST QUARTER-CENTURY. *Can. Lib. J. [Canada] 1978 35(3): 153-163.* The National Library of Canada was founded in 1953. Relates problems, achievements, and failures of the Library, along with suggestions for improvements, particularly catalog automation, system coordination with Canadian research libraries, creation of service for the handicapped, separation from housing in the Public Archives, and completion of a retrospective bibliography of Canadiana. Reviews accomplishments, particularly in the extension of special services; publications; acquisitions of special collections; creation of special divisions for music, rare books, and children's literature; international cooperative efforts, such as a serials data system; and a cataloging-in-publication program. 9 photos.   D. J. Mycue

245. Whitfield, Carol. SIR SAM HUGHES (1853-1921). *Can. Historic Sites 1975 (13): 143-155.* Samuel Hughes (1853-1921), as MP for Lindsay and later for Victoria and Haliburton from 1892 to 1921, epitomized the strong pro-imperialist sentiment which characterized central Ontario in the late 19th and early 20th centuries. As Borden's Minister of Militia from 1911 to 1916, Hughes played a major role in the creation of the modern Canadian army. His handling of the Canadian Expeditionary Force during the war at once contributed to the growth of Canadian autonomy and exacerbated Anglo-French divisions within Canada. His often abrasive personality led to frequent clashes with colleagues, superiors and subordinates, and Hughes was forced to resign from the government in 1916.   J

246. Whyte, John H. THE CATHOLIC FACTOR IN THE POLITICS OF DEMOCRATIC STATES. *Am. Behavioral Scientist 1974 17(6): 798-812.* The Roman Catholic Church is an important political factor in many democratic states in North America and Western Europe (1870-1974).   S

247. Wills, Morris W. SEQUENTIAL FRONTIERS: THE CALIFORNIAN AND VICTORIAN EXPERIENCE, 1850-1900. *Western Historical Q. 1978 9(4): 483-494.* A regional approach to the study of the frontier, utilizing Frederick Jackson Turner's dual concept of the frontier as an area and as a process, holds promise for fruitful research in comparative topics. This is especially true for regions of the American West, Australia, New Zealand, and British settlements of Canada. Suggests a case study comparing the region of Victoria in Australia with northern California. This lends itself well to a "metropolitan-maritime" interpretation. 55 notes.   D. L. Smith

248. Wilson, J. Donald and Jones, David Charles. THE "NEW" HISTORY OF CANADIAN EDUCATION. *Hist. of Educ. Q. 1976 16(3): 367-376.* Review article prompted by Paul H. Mattingly and Michael B. Katz, eds., *Education and Social Change: Themes from Ontario's Past* (New York U. Pr., 1975) and Alison L. Prentice and Susan E. Houston, eds., *Family, School and Society in Nineteenth Century Canada* (Toronto: Oxford U. Pr., 1975).

249. Wilson, Marion C. *CANADIANA:* CHANGES IN THE NATIONAL BIBLIOGRAPHY. *Can. Lib. J. [Canada] 1977 34(6): 417-419, 421.* Reviews the origins, growth, and expected future of *Canadiana,* the national bibliography of Canada since 1950. Published by the National Library of Canada, the bibliographical effort recently has undergone an intensive review, the results of which, including recommendations for improvement, comprise the core of this article. Proposes a thorough revamping of the effort, to expand its services by: presenting the information on magnetic tapes, microforms, and print; increasing the comprehensiveness of its coverage; adhering to international bibliographical standards; and automating the catalog. 2 notes.   D. J. Mycue

250. Wittlinger, Carlton O. THE ORIGIN OF THE BRETHREN IN CHRIST. *Mennonite Q. R. 1974 48(1): 55-72.* Discusses the 1775-80 founding of the Brethren in Christ in Lancaster County, Pennsylvania, by Jacob Engel (1753-83), the nature of their belief, and disputes between the United States and Canadian branches over the organization's name.   S

251. Woodcock, George. THE LURE OF THE PRIMITIVE. *Am. Scholar 1976 45(3): 387-404.* Studies the return to an enhanced interest in the primitive in several segments of the contemporary cultural world, its ancestry, and present expressions of it. It can be seen in the work of the Canadian artist Jack Shadbolt, the Canadian literary critic Northrop Frye, and the French anthropologist Claude Levi-Strauss. In the Western world the lure of the primitive appears "in a pointless nostalgia for peoples and ways of existence that our greed for land and resources has destroyed; ... and in a positive desire to find what is common to all societies, what illuminates our modern selves with light from pasts and distances we shall never visit."   R. V. Ritter

252. Woolfson, Peter. A QUESTION OF IDENTITY: A REVIEW OF RECENT WORK ON BLACKS IN CANADA. *Am. Rev. of Can. Studies 1977 7(1): 84-100.* Recent literature on the Canadian black experience indicates that Canadian blacks have fared no better than their counterparts in the United States. Selective immigration policies, inferior schools, segregated housing, and discrimination in employment have all worked against the black Canadian. Several scholars believe that historical, geographical, economic, and social diversity among Canadian blacks have delayed their unification into groups that could press for equal opportunities. Recently, under the influence of the American civil rights movement, black Canadians have begun to organize for change and to develop the pride and sense of identity characteristic of other Canadian ethnic groups.   G. A. Patzwald

253. Wright, Gerald. THE USES OF HISTORY IN CANADIAN-AMERICAN RELATIONS. *Can. Rev. of Am. Studies 1976 7(2): 215-219.* Review article prompted by *Canada's War: The Policies of the Mackenzie King Government, 1939-1945* (Toronto, 1975) by J. L. Granatstein, *Canadian-American Relations in Wartime: From the Great War to the Cold War* (Toronto, 1975) by R. D. Cuff and J. L. Granatstein, and *Canadian-American Summit Diplomacy, 1923-1973: Selected Speeches and Documents* (Toronto, 1975), edited by Roger Frank Swanson. These writers assess American influence on the decisions and policies of Canadian governments. Some regard American influence as excessive; the others rate it less pervasive.   H. T. Lovin

254. Wright, Gerald. VIVISECTING INDEPENDENCE: GOALS AND STRATEGIES OF CANADIAN FOREIGN POLICY. *Am. Rev. of Can. Studies 1973 3(1): 192-209.* Against a background 1891-1911 when Canada accepted independence, the author defines independence in terms of status, freedom of action, and maintenance of political community, and then reviews Canadian foreign policy 1950's-70's, offering proposals for Canada's assumption of broader responsibility in international affairs in the future.

255. Yaffe, Phyllis. FEMINIST PUBLISHING IN CANADA. *Serials Librarian 1977 1(4): 337-340.* Annotated bibliography of feminist publishing in Canada during 1968-76; includes publishing houses and periodicals or catalogs available.

256. Yoder, Don. INTRODUCTORY BIBLIOGRAPHY ON FOLK RELIGION. *Western Folklore 1974 33(1): 16-34.* A "preliminary bibliography . . .constructed to illustrate the extent of research in the subject areas of folk religion and folk belief." Centers on Europe and North America and includes 271 entries from primary, secondary, and periodical sources. S. L. Myres

257. Yonge, C. M. THE SEA-OTTER AND HISTORY. *Hist. Today [Great Britain] 1978 28(3): 171-177.* Gives a history of human interaction with sea otters, 18th-20th centuries, throughout Pacific coastal areas in the United States, Canada, and Japan; highlights present endangered status of the animals and their former importance in the fur trade.

258. Young, R. S. MINERALS AND THE FUR TRADE. *Alberta Hist. 1976 24(3): 20-24.* Extensive records of the Hudson's Bay Company reveal that the company had little impact on mineral discoveries. Examines reasons for this, such as little native knowledge and use of metals, company interests in immediate riches from fur trade, and personnel from Scotland, rather than from the mineral-rich regions of Cornwall and Wales. Even when some minerals were found and identified, there was no use for them until the 20th century. Based on Hudson's Bay Co. records; 2 illus. D. Chaput

259. Zezulka, J. M. THE PASTORAL VISION IN NINETEENTH-CENTURY CANADA. *Dalhousie Rev. [Canada] 1977 57(2): 224-241.* Poetic visions of North America before 1800 are discussed through the works of Thomas Cary, Stephen Parmenius, Sir William Vaughn, John Guy, Robert Hayman, and J. MacKay. The 19th-century pastoral authors are represented by Susanna Moodie, Cornwall Bayley, the Canadian Oliver Goldsmith, Joseph Howe, Alexander MacLachlan, Isabella Valancy Crawford, and Archibald Lampman. 35 notes. C. H. Held

260. Zureik, Elia T. and Frizzell, Alan. VALUES IN CANADIAN MAGAZINE FICTION: A TEST OF THE SOCIAL CONTROL THESIS. *J. of Popular Culture 1976 10(2): 359-376.* Quantitative content analysis of seven English-Canadian and French-Canadian periodicals covering 1930's, 60's-70's. Tests the "social control" thesis of imaginative literature—that literature acts to maintain the accepted social order. The results of the analysis support the hypothesis. Primary and secondary sources; 9 tables, 25 notes. D. G. Nielson

261. —. CANADA. *Américas (Organization of Am. States) 1974 26(11-12): Supplement 1-32.* Overview of the history, geography, cities, customs, agriculture, industry, ethnic groups, and government of Canada, prehistory-1974.

262. —. ENTENTE CORDIALE? BILATERAL COMMISSIONS AND INTERNATIONAL LEGAL METHODS OF ADJUSTMENT. *Am. Soc. of Int. Law Pro. 1974 68: 226-250.*
Jordan, David Herrera. THE UNITED STATES-MEXICAN INTERNATIONAL BOUNDARY AND WATER COMMISSION, *pp. 226-229.*
Ross, Charles R. THE INTERNATIONAL JOINT COMMISSION, UNITED STATES-CANADA, *pp. 229-236.*
Cohen, Maxwell. THE INTERNATIONAL JOINT COMMISSION, UNITED STATES-CANADA, *pp. 236-239.*
Brower, Charles N. THE CASE FOR CROSS BORDER LITIGATION: THE CONTINENT THAT SUES TOGETHER HEWS TOGETHER, *pp. 239-243.*
Friedkin, Joseph F. COMMENTS, *pp. 244.*
Bourne, Charles S. COMMENTS, *pp. 244-246.*
Christenson, Gordon. COMMENTS, *pp. 246-247.*
Ohly, D. Christopher. DISCUSSION, *pp. 247-250.* Discusses the use of international judicial organizations and bilateral commissions such as the US-Mexican International Boundary and Water Commission and the US-Canadian International Joint Commission for solving disputes between the US, Canada, and Mexico, 19th century-1974.

263. —. SUMMARIES OF DOCTORAL DISSERTATIONS. *J. of Econ. Hist. 1978 38(1): 268-300.* Presents short dissertation reports from the 37th annual meeting of the Economic History Association, 1977. The nine topics consider labor markets and the early stages of industrialization in the United States and Canada; Germany under the Zollverein; the Habsburg Empire, 1841-65; Lancashire' 1815-50; and Japan, 1920-60. Comments by Louis P. Cain and Knick Harley. C. W. Olson

2. THE NATURAL SETTING

264. Altmeyer, George. THREE IDEAS OF NATURE IN CANADA, 1893-1914. *J. of Can. Studies [Canada] 1976 11(3): 21-36.* An integral part of the Canadian experience is the interaction between man and his natural environment. A menacing continent led to psychological dependence upon England, but the unsettling tendencies of modern society produced a more positive approach to nature. From the mid-1890's to 1914, nature was seen as a source of therapy, as a finite storehouse to be husbanded, and as a temple providing for a redefiniation of man's relationship to God. 123 notes.   G. E. Panting

265. Barsness, Larry. THE BISON IN ART AND HISTORY. *Am. West 1977 14(2): 10-21.* Traces the coming of the buffalo to North America, its dispersion to virtually all parts of the continent and into Central America, and its use, abuse, near-extinction, and recovery. 12 illus.   D. L. Smith

266. Birrell, Andrew J. CLASSIC SURVEY PHOTOS OF THE EARLY WEST. *Can. Geographical J. 1975 91(4): 12-19.* Discusses 19th-century photographic methods and their application to geological and surveying efforts in Canada's western provinces, 1858-97.   S

267. Bonenfant, Claude. RESURGENCE OF THE CARIBOU IN QUEBEC. *Can. Geographical J. 1974 89(1/2): 48-51.*

268. Campbell, Robert. THE INTERACTION OF TWO GREAT RIVERS HELPS SUSTAIN THE EARTH'S VITAL BIOSPHERE. *Smithsonian 1977 8(6): 38-51, (7): 100-111.* Part I. The Mackenzie and Amazon River Valleys, 6,000 miles apart, are tied together through "flows of air and water, regulating climate; determining the number and extent of species; eroding and depositing soil; distributing minerals and contaminants; influencing the flux of deserts and the retreat or advance of glaciers; altering planetary reflectivity and atmospheric conductance." When these river currents shift, whether naturally or due to man's increasing industrial activity, the impact on atmospheric, oceanic, and biological links in both hemispheres is incalculable. 16 illus., map. Part II. Deals exclusively with the Amazon.   S. R. Quéripel

269. Camu, Pierre. GEOGRAPHICAL REALITIES. *Am. Rev. of Can. Studies 1973 3(1): 20-25.* Examines the geographical perspective in Canadian life and foreign relations, particularly with the USA; explores the differences which weather and natural features have made in the development of the Canadian national character since the 19th century.

270. Clark, Arthur Hill. THE CONCEPTIONS OF "EMPIRES" OF THE ST. LAWRENCE AND THE MISSISSIPPI: AN HISTORICO-GEOGRAPHICAL VIEW WITH SOME QUIZZICAL COMMENTS ON ENVIRONMENTAL DETERMINISM. *Am. Rev. of Can. Studies 1975 5(2): 4-27.* Examines the opportunities of entrance into North America afforded by the St. Lawrence River and the Mississippi River; touches on explorers and users of the natural resources found, as well as the environmental aspects of discovery and exploration, 17th-19th centuries.

271. Classen, H. George. ICE CAPS: CLIMATIC RECORDS OF AGES PAST. *Can. Geographic [Canada] 1978 97(1): 50-55.* Core samples taken from Canada's ice caps, 1954-77, give clues to climate changes of the earth during the last 125,000 years.

272. Ellis, William Donohue. MIDCONTINENT IN TRANSITION: THE GREAT LAKES REGION. *Am. West 1974 11(5): 40-47, 61-63.* Traces the geological history of the Great Lakes which constitute "the largest inland sea" on earth. Satellite views of central North America help to establish the centrality of the Great Lakes as one of the three principal drainage basins of the continent. In geologic terms, the Great Lakes are still young and their geologic evolution is dramatic and observable. Adapted from a forthcoming book. 7 illus., 3 maps.   D. L. Smith

273. Folinsbee, Robert E. SHIFTS IN THE BALANCE OF CANADA'S RESOURCE ENDOWMENTS. *Tr. of the Royal Soc. of Can. [Canada] 1977 15: 11-12.* Discusses the westward movement of the balance of Canada's natural resources and notes that, although boosters of Alberta proclaim its benefits, others suggest that changes in climate will reduce its agricultural potential. Also notes the decline of resources of the Cordillera Mountains and the Canadian Shield.   J. D. Neville

274. Gourd, Benoît-Beaudry. LA COLONISATION DES CLAY BELTS DU NORD-OUEST QUÉBÉCOIS ET DU NORD-EST ONTARIEN [Colonization of the Clay Belts of northwestern Quebec and northeastern Ontario]. *R. d'Hist. de l'Amérique Française [Canada] 1973 27(2): 235-256.* A comparative study of the efforts of the governments of Quebec and Ontario to propagandize through their official publications the Great Clay Belt that joins the two provinces to the north.

275. Kelly, Kenneth. DAMAGED AND EFFICIENT LANDSCAPE IN RURAL AND SOUTHERN ONTARIO. *Ontario Hist. [Canada] 1974 66(1): 1-.* In the late 19th century, awareness of ecology and ecological damage to the land from deforestation and the effects of agricultural development began to grow in Ontario. Discusses this problem and proposed solutions. 3 maps, 41 notes.   W. B. Whitham

276. Parks, J. G. M. and Day, J. C. THE HAZARD OF SENSITIVE CLAYS: A CASE STUDY OF THE OTTAWA-HULL AREA. *Geographical R. 1975 65(2): 198-213.* "Awareness of and adjustment to the potential natural hazard presented by sensitive clays in the Ottawa-Hull region are examined. The analysis is primarily concerned with the spatial variation of the flow-side potential, with the accuracy of the perception of this hazard by individuals, private companies, and public agencies, and with the structural and nonstructural measures used to minimize the potential danger of clay movement. Some tentative guidelines for implementing development control are suggested in clay areas designated as potentially unsafe. It is contended that programs such as public-hazard information schemes, land-use planning, zoning, differential insurance rates, or the imposition of mandatory notification of landslide risk when hazard-zone structures are sold could produce long-term shifts in development patterns to minimize risk."   J

277. Schneer, Cecil J. THE GREAT TACONIC CONTROVERSY. *Isis 1978 69(247): 173-191.* In 1839-42 Ebenezer Emmons, working on the New York Geological Survey, concluded that the Taconic Mountains of eastern New York were made up of some of the oldest sedimentary rocks in the world, strata deposited on the primary crystalline crust of the earth. Not all of his colleagues on the Survey agreed, and from their disagreement arose "a controversy which lasted for the remainder of the century and affected the lives and careers of every prominent geologist in the United States and Canada." Traces the argument and summarizes the positions taken by many of the participants. 4 illus., 52 notes.   M. M. Vance

278. Tennyson, B. D. EARTHQUAKES IN CAPE BRETON. *Nova Scotia Hist. Q. [Canada] 1978 8(2): 147-151.* Cape Breton is located in the former Appalachian geosyncline which extended from Newfoundland through Cape Breton and the eastern United States to Alabama. Three earthquakes have been recorded on the island: a minor one on New Year's Eve 1882, another on 20 December 1909 which was more severe, and most famous on 18 November 1929. The 1929 earthquake was the most severe of the three and resulted in an eight foot tidal wave which broke transatlantic submarine cables and overturned boats. Secondary sources; 19 notes.   H. M. Evans

279. Woods, John G. THE NATURAL WORLD IN THE THOUSAND ISLANDS. *Can. Geographical J. [Canada] 1977 95(1): 26-31.* Discusses the Thousand Islands area of the St. Lawrence Seaway, 19th-20th centuries, including early habitation, strategic importance, and its current significance as a natural reserve and national park.

3. THE NATIVE PEOPLES

General

280. Ames, Michael M. A NOTE ON THE CONTRIBUTIONS OF WILSON DUFF TO NORTHWEST COAST ETHNOLOGY AND ART. *BC Studies [Canada] 1976 (31): 3-11.* Wilson Duff (1925-76) was a pioneer in the development of anthropology in the Pacific Northwest. He chaired the British Columbia Archaeological Sites Advisory Board, was editor of *Anthropology in British Columbia*, was consultant for the Kitwancool Indians, was a founder and president of the British Columbia Museums Association, and taught at the University of British Columbia. Duff was interested in Northwest Coast art as both "high art" and as a subject for "deep analysis." Biblio.   D. L. Smith

281. Armstrong, Terence E. ETHICAL PROBLEMS OF NORTHERN DEVELOPMENT. *Polar Record [Great Britain] 1978 19(118): 3-10.* Speculates on population growth in Alaska, Canada, Greenland, and Scandinavia, assessing the impact of increased economic activity and of military and educational facilities on native peoples.

282. Cole, Douglas. THE ORIGINS OF CANADIAN ANTHROPOLOGY, 1850-1910. *J. of Can. Studies 1973 8(1): 33-45.* Canadian anthropological studies began in the 1850's with the work of Daniel Wilson, continued by Horatio Hale and Franz Boas, and eventually led to the 1910 establishment of the Anthropology Division of the Geological Survey of Canada under Edward Sapir.

283. Dagg, Michael A. SOURCES OF MATERIALS ON THE NATIVE PEOPLES OF CANADA. *Can. Lib. J. 1975 32(2): 122-126.* Bibliography of publications and list of national organizations representing native peoples of Canada. Indicates ways to acquire materials reflecting Indian, Métis, and Eskimo (Inuit) viewpoints.   L. F. Johnson

284. Elliott, Jean Leonard. NATIVE MINORITIES AND ETHNIC CONFLICT IN CANADA. *Current Hist. 1974 66(392): 177-181, 183, 192.* Examines the sociological problems that the Cree Indians and Eskimos are facing with the rapid development of the Canadian North.   S

285. Faust, Richard. NATIVE PEOPLES OF THE PACIFIC BASIN: AN ETHNOGRAPHIC SETTING. *J. of the West 1976 15(2): 15-32.* Divides the Pacific Basin into four culture areas: Eskimos and Aleuts of western Alaska, Indians of the Pacific Northwest, Indians of the California coast, and Polynesians of the Hawaiian Archipelago. Discusses language, commerce, housing, sexual customs, religious practices, and the effects of contacts with Europeans.   R. Alvis

286. Hickerson, Harold. FUR TRADE COLONIALISM AND THE NORTH AMERICAN INDIANS. *J. of Ethnic Studies 1973 1(2): 15-44.* In the Archaic Era egalitarian systems of production and exchange characterized the Indian cultural system and peaceful intertribal relations prevailed. The introduction of the fur trade disrupted the intratribal systems of both production and exchange (and thereby their social systems). Caught up in the exploitive clutches of fur trade colonialism, tribes and individuals adopted similar practices in an attempt to control fur bearing areas, maintain middle man positions, and secure other advantages. The result was the destruction of Indian cultural unity. Primary and secondary sources. 39 notes.   T. W. Smith

287. Hobler, Philip M. A CACHE OF ABORIGINAL FISHING GEAR FROM THE QUEEN CHARLOTTE ISLANDS. *BC Studies [Canada] 1978 (37): 37-47.* Describes a cache of 70 wooden hooks and a few other objects found in a small rock-shelter in the Queen Charlotte Islands off British Columbia. These Haida Indian black cod hooks are from a late prehistoric or early historic date. 6 illus., table, biblio.   D. L. Smith

288. Jackman, Albert H. ALASKA NATIVE LAND SETTLEMENTS AND SIMILAR MOVEMENTS IN CANADA. *Michigan Academician 1977 10(2): 207-214.* Examines land claims and land use of Indians and Eskimos in Alaska and Canada during 1958-77; the natives' traditional life-style will be affected by progress in terms of land use, social organization, and economic development.

289. Kennedy, Dorothy I. D. and Bouchard, Randy. THE LILLOOET PEOPLE AND LILLOOET STORIES. *Sound Heritage [Canada] 1977 6(1): 1-9.* The Lillooet Indians of southwestern British Columbia use storytelling as a major part of their oral tradition about tribal history, social values, and world view, prehistory-1976.

290. Upton, Leslie F. S. THE BEOTHUCKS: QUESTIONS AND ANSWERS. *Acadiensis [Canada] 1978 7(2): 150-155.* Recent studies of Newfoundland's indigenous people surpass both numerous romantic works and the more authoritative *The Beothucks or Red Indians*, by J. P. Howley. Recent archaeological work and F. W. Rowe's *Extinction: The Beothucks of Newfoundland* (Toronto, 1977) are informative and balanced. Rowe denies that Europeans frequently indulged in mass slaughter. Instead he suggests that, as in Tasmania, European seizure of native women reduced native numbers. Manuscripts still coming to light may answer some of the questions Rowe raises. 12 notes.   D. F. Chard

291. —. STORIES. *Sound Heritage [Canada] 1977 6(1): 10-78.* Recounts part of the oral tradition of the Lillooet Indians of southwestern British Columbia; stories include tribal history, moral and practical instruction, world view, and social values, prehistory-1976.

Pre-Columbian History

292. Borden, Charles E. WILSON DUFF (1925-1976): HIS CONTRIBUTIONS TO THE GROWTH OF ARCHAEOLOGY IN BRITISH COLUMBIA. *BC Studies [Canada] 1977 (33): 3-12.* Wilson Duff (1925-76), trained in anthropology and archaeology at the Universities of British Columbia and Washington, established himself as an active and trusted friend of the Pacific Northwest Indians. As Curator of Anthropology at the British Columbia Provincial Museum and in other capacities, he worked for legislation to protect the province's archaeological resources and to promote systematic studies in ways that benefited Indians. Biblio.   D. L. Smith

293. Clegg, Legrand H., II. WHO WERE THE FIRST AMERICANS? *Black Scholar 1975 7(1): 33-41.* Argues from anthropological evidence that the first inhabitants of the Americas were Africoids rather than Mongoloids.

294. Coulton, Richard L. PRESERVED ABORIGINAL CANOES IN WESTERN CANADA. *Mariner's Mirror [Great Britain] 1977 63(3): 248-252.* Suggests that a knowledge of the development of canoes could illuminate the early development of ships. Presents a list of specimens of American aboriginal canoes available for study, giving construction, size, origin, use, and current location. Illus., 22 notes.   W. B. Whitham

295. Eyman, C. E. and Forbis, R. G. THE DE WINTON BURIAL: A TRAGEDY ACROSS THE YEARS. *Plains Anthropologist 1976 21(72): 119-130.* A human burial was discovered during house-building operations in the community of De Winton, a few miles south of Calgary, Alberta, Canada. The fragmentary remains consist of an immature aborigine of uncertain chronological and cultural assignment. The remains are described and forensically evaluated. Floral and faunal remains in presumed association with the burial are also described and evaluated. All materials are then interpreted with relevance to some anthropological literature and to each other.   J

296. Harington, C. R.; Bonnichsen, Robson; and Morlan, Richard E. BONES SAY MAN LIVED IN YUKON 27,000 YEARS AGO. *Can. Geographical J. 1975 91(1/2): 42-48.*

297. Inglis, Richard I. and MacDonald, George F. FIVE THOUSAND YEARS OF HISTORY ON THE WEST COAST. *Can. Geographical J. 1975 91(6): 32-37.* Discusses archaeological findings about the Tsimshian Indians who lived 5,000 years ago in the Prince Rupert area of British Columbia.

298. Jacobs, Wilbur R. THE TIP OF AN ICEBERG: PRE-COLUMBIAN INDIAN DEMOGRAPHY AND SOME IMPLICATIONS FOR REVISIONISM. *William and Mary Q. 1974 31(1): 123-132.* Recent literature on Indian demography shows that the American wilderness was more densely populated than historians have assumed. In the 15th century the Western Hemisphere may have been more densely populated than Western Europe. The catalyst for Indian depopulation was the European invasion, but this cannot fully explain the tremendous and rapid depopulation. A comparison of the findings of various researchers (chiefly Shelburne F. Cook, Woodrow Borah, and Henry F. Dobyns) with the author's own fieldwork in Australia and elsewhere suggests that a large native population did exist and that Europeans triggered the immediate decline. Based on primary and secondary sources and field work; 29 notes.
H. M. Ward

299. Johnson, Ann M. THE DUNE BUGGY SITE, 24RV1, AND NORTHWESTERN PLAINS CERAMICS. *Plains Anthropologist 1977 22(75): 37-49.* The study of ceramics in the northwestern Plains has lagged since Wissler included "the lack of pottery"as one of the core Plains traits. In recent years, however, the poor development in ceramic studies is due to the lack of reported sites rather than a real void. The first part of this paper describes the Dune Buggy site [in Montana] and its large ceramic collection. In the second party, the pottery is identified as belonging to a non-Middle Missouri tradition and related to sites in northeastern Montana, Southeastern Saskatchewan, Southwestern Manitoba, and northwestern North Dakota. The combinations of profile, designs, and decoration appear to be heterogeneous, and an analogy is drawn to the historic period for the area to suggest an explanation for the apparent mixing. Specific problems include the lack of absolute dates and stratigraphic relationships, unpublished data, and potentially mixed components.
J

300. Matthews, Barry. ARCHAEOLOGICAL SITES IN THE LABRADOR-UNGAVA PENINSULA: CULTURAL ORIGIN AND CLIMATIC SIGNIFICANCE. *Arctic [Canada] 1975 28(4): 245-262.* Examines apparent Eskimo sites occupied *ca.* 400-1800, but especially 600-700 years ago; from evidence of carved and nailed artifacts, contact with Europeans is believed to have occurred.

301. McMillan, Alan D. and St. Claire, Denis E. ARCHAEOLOGICAL INVESTIGATIONS IN THE ALBERNI VALLEY. *BC Studies [Canada] 1975 (25): 32-77.* After describing the ethnography and site description of archaeological research near Port Alberni, British Columbia (1973), lists and describes the artifacts found. Primary and secondary sources; 9 tables, 7 figs., 4 notes.
W. L. Marr

302. Miller, Virginia P. ABORIGINAL MICMAC POPULATION: A REVIEW OF THE EVIDENCE. *Ethnohistory 1976 23(2): 117-128.* Twentieth century anthropologists have almost uniformly estimated the aboriginal population of the Micmac Indians of Eastern Canada at about 3,500. Evidence on population taken from the earliest historical accounts of the seventeenth century shows that this figure is unrealistically low and results from accepting as aboriginal an estimate of Micmac population made in 1616, when a significant decline in Micmac numbers had already taken place. This decline was the result of endemic diseases brought on by dietary changes following sixteenth century contact and trade with Europeans. The paper concludes that aboriginal Micmac population probably exceeded 35,000.
J

303. Newton, Norman. ON SURVIVALS OF ANCIENT ASTRONOMICAL IDEAS AMONG THE PEOPLES OF THE NORTHWEST COAST. *BC Studies [Canada] 1975 Summer (26): 16-38.* Describes the ancient astronomical and calendar systems of the Northwest Coast Indians in British Columbia. The ten-month year is outlined

in detail. The systems are of long local development yet resemble Chinese and Near Eastern systems. Primary and secondary sources; 90 notes.
W. L. Marr

304. Padden, R. C. ON DIFFUSION AND HISTORICITY. *Am. Hist. R. 1973 78(4): 987-1004.* Reviews Cyrus H. Gordon's *Before Columbus: Links Between the Old World and Ancient America.* (New York: Crown Publishers, 1971), and Carroll L. Riley *et al.,* ed. *Man Across the Sea: Problems of Pre-Columbian Contacts* (Austin: U. of Texas Press, 1971). Diffusion theories of the spread of civilization were brought to a climax by A. L. Kroeber for his *Oikoumenê.* Gordon has extended his *Oikoumenê* to include the Americas, and predicates Old World Bronze Age origins for the cultures of Mesoamerica despite major chronological discrepancies and lack of evidence. In his use of the myth of the Plumed Serpent and other gratuitous assumptions he betrays his lack of understanding of Mesoamerican culture and tradition. *Man Across the Sea* had its origin on a symposium on the subject of pre-Columbian contacts between the hemispheres held by the Society for American Archaeology in May, 1968. The volume is divided into sections on theory, transoceanic contacts, and cultural geography, and should mark "the end of traditional transoceanic diffusionist postulation, especially as epitomized in the former work." 38 notes.
R. V. Ritter

305. Saylor, Stanley G. DHLB-1: EARLY PERIOD OCCUPATION NEAR GLACIAL LAKE AGASSIZ, SOUTHEAST MANITOBA. *Plains Anthropologist 1975 20(70, Part 1): 241-252.* DhLb-1 is a Paleo-Indian site situated just north of the International Boundary in southeastern Manitoba. It was excavated in 1972, and found to be an area of tool manufacturing. It was dated by association with a gravel lens, deposited shortly after the formation of the Campbell strandline, 9,500 to 10,000 years B.P. The site is of significance because it demonstrates early period migration into southeastern Manitoba immediately after Lake Agassiz withdrawal.
J

306. Syms, E. Leigh. HISTORY OF A REFUSE PIT: INTERPRETING PLAINS CAMP ACTIVITY AT A MICROCOSMIC LEVEL. *Plains Anthropologist 1974 19(66, Part I): 306-315.* During the summer of 1970, a storage pit [in southwestern Manitoba] filled with camp debris was excavated by depositional levels at site DgMg-15. The pit had been used repeatedly while slowly being filled with habitation debris. Six hearths were in the pit, several of which had been carefully covered with layers of sterile gravel. The earliest hearth yielded a carbon-14 date of A.D. 1610 XXX 130 (GSC-1546). Evidence from these excavations indicates that important information can be lost by treating storage pits as single, homogeneous units of activity.
J

307. Syms, E. Leigh. CULTURAL ECOLOGY AND ECOLOGICAL DYNAMICS OF THE CERAMIC PERIOD IN SOUTHWESTERN MANITOBA. *Plains Anthropologist 1977 22(76, pt. 2): 1-142.* A new research paradigm—the Co-Influence Sphere Model—is developed and applied to the archaeological record to account for the variability in prehistoric ceramics of Southwestern Manitoba. The Co-Influence Sphere Model emphasizes the co-existence, interaction, and territorial overlapping of groups in the prehistoric and early historic periods. The model requires an evaluation of the seasonally fluctuating resource potential across the Plains, Aspen Parkland, and Boreal Forest; the mobility and multiple biome utilization of historic groups; and the interaction of historic groups through formalized trade networks, conflict, and sharing of similar resources. The earlier emphasis on chronology and mutually exclusive home territories of historic groups is replaced by a more realistic and dynamic model of groups with core, secondary, and tertiary subsistence-settlement areas in which groups interact to varying degrees. For Southwestern Manitoba, the earlier Chronological Model (with one identifiable phase and one historic tribe per period and area) is replaced by a complicated record of four complexes during the Middle Woodland Stage, nine complexes during the Late Woodland Stage, and possibly 15 different ethnic groups in the protohistoric and early historic periods. Furthermore, there is a shift in interrelationships between territorially overlapping occupants from the Boreal Forest and Plains with the advent of the Late Woodland Stage that is accompanied by the development of horticultural villages, the growth and fission of human populations, and symbiotic relationships between horticulturalists and hunters. Use of the dynamic Co-Influence Sphere Model requires a shift away from defining

complexes and seeking causal relationships or processes within a small research region. The environmental limitations, cultural history, and cultural processes of any region, and particularly a region like Southwestern Manitoba (which partly straddles an ecotone) can be determined only by an exhaustive study of fluctuating resources, ethnohistory, archaeological history, and variation in subsistence-settlement patterns beyond the region. In order to apply the Co-Influence Sphere Model to Southwestern Manitoba, local data have been related to developments in the Boreal Forest, Upper Great Lakes, Upper Mississippi, and Northern Plains. Relationships are determined by assessing regions and areas beyond the local research universe, rather than attempting to discover processes on the basis of limited local data.   J

308. Syms, E. Leigh. EARLY MAN IN SOUTHWEST MANITOBA. *Can. Geographical J. 1976 93(2): 64-68.* Discusses artifacts of Indians discovered in southwestern Manitoba dating from approximately 10,000 B.C. to 1600 A.D., emphasizing tools and weapons.

309. Wendland, Wayne M. HOLOCENE MAN IN NORTH AMERICA: THE ECOLOGICAL SETTING AND CLIMATIC BACKGROUND. *Plains Anthropologist 1978 23 (82, pt. 1): 273-287.* Patterns of human occupation and vegetation are delineated on maps of North America for one thousand year intervals through the Holocene. The raw data for this review include radiocarbon-dated pollen cores and archaeological information and tree-ring records. Dynamic changes in the Laurentide Ice limits and major ecotones are observed through the middle Holocene, when both features reach essentially post-glacial stability. Significant changes in the vegetation boundaries continue to the present, but the scale of change is much diminished. Early Holocene occupation apparently expanded from Alaska south to California, then east, parallel to the southern boundary of the grasslands, to the Mississippi River and northeastward to the east coast. The absence of occupation in late-Atlantic time is noted through much of the Great Plains and continued until about 4,000 BP. Within the next millennium, evidence of human occupation virtually covered the United States (except for the northwest) and much of coastal Canada. Environmental conditions and occupation over North America are reviewed within the framework of Holocene climatic episodes.   J

310. Wilson, Michael. FOSSIL BISON AND ARTIFACTS FROM THE MONA LISA SITE, CALGARY, ALBERTA. PART I: STRATIGRAPHY AND ARTIFACTS. *Plains Anthropologist 1974 19(63): 34-45.* "In November, 1968, salvage excavations at the site of an art gallery under construction in urban southwest Calgary, Alberta, Canada, revealed a Paleo-Indian bison kill . . . A bone radiocarbon date of 8080 [plus or minus] 150 years B.P. (G.S.C.-1209) was obtained." Article to be continued.   J

311. Woodward, John. AN EARLY CERAMIC TRADITION ON THE PACIFIC COAST. *Masterkey 1977 51(2): 66-72.* Short discussion of diffusion of pottery throughout the New World, 4500-50 B.C.

Inuit (Eskimo)

312. Adams, Doreen B. and Adams, Samuel T. OPHTHALMOLOGY IN THE CANADIAN NORTH. *Arctic [Canada] 1974 27(2): 91-94.* Discusses various eye diseases and difficulties among Eskimos. Among the most serious are trauma, scarred cornea, glaucoma, and myopia. 3 illus.   J. A. Casada

313. Alekseev, V. P. and Balueva, T. S. MATERIALLY PO KRANIOLOGII NAUKANSKIKH ESKIMOSOV (K DIFFERENTSIATSII ARKTICHESKOI RASY) [Materials on the craniology of the Naukan Eskimos (towards a differentiation of the Arctic race)]. *Sovetskaia etnografiia [USSR] 1976 (1): 84-100.* A study of craniological material found in 1971 tends to confirm the hypothesis of the existence of a western and eastern variant within the Eskimo group.

314. Barry, Mary J. CAPTAIN JOSEPH BERNARD: ARCTIC TRADER. *Alaska J. 1973 3(4):246-251.* Discusses the shipping business of Canadian Trader Joseph Francis Bernard, 1903-29, emphasizing his dealings with Eskimos of the Alaskan and Siberian coasts for furs, skins, ivory, and whalebone.

315. Bloom, Joseph D. and Gelardin, Richard D. ESKIMO SLEEP PARALYSIS. *Arctic [Canada] 1976 29(1): 20-26.* Sleep paralysis, a rare condition associated with narcolepsy and ataplexy, is fairly common among Eskimos; presents traditional native thought on the subject including shamanistic tradition, hysterical mechanisms, and traditional causes and cures.

316. Bouchard, Lorne. THE EASTERN ARCTIC: A FIRST IMPRESSION. *Beaver [Canada] 1974 305(3): 4-9.* Results of a 1969 visit to Frobisher Bay. Comments on geography and the local Eskimos with emphasis on art depicting the Eskimos. 9 illus.   D. Chaput

317. Brody, Hugh. COLONIALISM IN THE ARCTIC: FOUR REMINISCENCES. *Hist. Workshop J. [Great Britain] 1976 1: 245-253.* Reproduces four transcripts of discussions with Eskimos, the oldest 60 years old and the youngest 33, about the effect of the white man's colonization of the Arctic and Eskimo life since 1930. The first concerned the Eskimos' fear of the new arrivals and of the forces of law and order they brought. The second revolved around the move to settlements and described the transfer of Eskimos from their original homes to newly designed settlements provided by the whites. The third related the difficulties that Eskimos had with their new work, the English language, and the school subjects which struck them as odd and remote. The fourth considered the future and the land, and how explorations for oil and gas have taught the Eskimos new skills, but have also created new problems.
                                                                            A. J. Evans

318. Brody, Hugh. ESKIMO POLITICS: THE THREAT FROM THE SOUTH. *New Left R. [Great Britain] 1973 (79): 60-68.* The increasing penetration of remote regions (Alaska and Canada) has contributed to the emergence of "an underdeveloped ethnic minority," separated both culturally and economically from the "colonisers." The Alaska Land Settlement of 1971 is a means of reconciling such diverse interests and is a precedent. 11 notes.   P. J. Beck

319. Caillois, Roger. THE STONE MEN OF THE CANADIAN ARCTIC. *Diogenes [Italy] 1976 (94): 78-93.* Discusses the man-shaped piles of stones, called inkshuks, found on the coasts of the Canadian Arctic, whose purpose is not known even by the Eskimos now inhabiting the area.

320. Coldevin, Gary O. ANIKI AND ISOLATION: TELEVISION IN THE LIVES OF CANADIAN ESKIMOS. *J. of Communication 1977 27(4): 145-153.* Surveys the impact of television on Eskimos on Baffin Island at Frobisher Bay; transition has taken place in Eskimo culture, but the deep-seated social customs remain intact because of television's irrelevance to their lives.

321. Coldevin, Gary O. SOME EFFECTS OF FRONTIER TELEVISION IN A CANADIAN ESKIMO COMMUNITY. *Journalism Q. 1976 53(1): 34-39.* A study of the impact of one year of television service on an Eskimo community in Baffin Island. Most of the Eskimos do not understand English, which was used for the programs. The primary impact was on socioeconomic aspirations, with little effect on knowledge of national unit identification and international affairs. Radio, which is broadcast in the Eskimo language, is perceived as the most important information source. Based on primary sources; 3 tables, 9 notes.
                                                                            K. J. Puffer

322. Damas, David. SOCIAL ANTHROPOLOGY OF THE CENTRAL ESKIMO. *Can. R. of Sociol. and Anthrop. 1975 12(3): 252-266.* Current and recent literature on the anthropology of Central Eskimos deals mainly with family and local social organization, authority structure, alliance mechanisms, and cultural ecology.

323. Douglas, W. O. THE QUANGWAK AFFAIR. *Beaver [Canada] 1976 307(1): 15-21, (2): 45-49.* Part I. Reminiscences of RNWMP sergeant who in 1919 went to Baker Lake District, Northwest Territory, to apprehend an Eskimo, Quangwak, who had murdered two brothers and taken the wife of one. The village was in confusion, and trade had halted. Discusses the apprehension of Quangwak, legal-interpretation problems, and the long journey with Quangwak and his wife to Ottawa. 8 illus., map. Part II. Involves travel from Manitoba to Ottawa to Chesterfield Inlet. At the Inlet, Douglas was joined by a coroner-officer, who

was new to the area and unsympathetic to the prisoner. He insisted on chaining Quangwak. The Eskimo escaped, taking a sled and rifle. His body was found by other Eskimos. Douglas and the coroner argued frequently over the treatment of the prisoner, and Douglas was informed that he would face charges for permitting the Eskimo to escape. Nothing came of the matter, but Douglas left the RCMP to join the Hudson's Bay Company. 5 illus.   D. Chaput

324. French, Alice. MY NAME IS MASAK. *Beaver [Canada] 1976 307(2): 28-31.* Autobiographical account of a young Eskimo girl from Cambridge Bay who in 1937 was taken to a boarding school at Aklavik. Recounts the adjustments to a new language and changing values. 5 illus.
                                                                      D. Chaput

325. Grainge, Jack W. and Royle, John C. HOW ARCTIC COMMU-NITY LIFE HAS CHANGED. *Can. Geographical J. 1975 91(6): 38-45.* Describes changes occurring in the living conditions of Canada's Inuit since the early 1950's.

326. Hinds, Margery. MINA. *Beaver [Canada] 1976 307(3): 20-24.* Mina was an Eskimo woman living on an island in Hudson's Bay. In February 1941, based on celestial changes and reading the Bible, she caused the death of 10 reluctant Eskimos in an effort "to meet Jesus." After a trial at Moose Factory, she was judged mildly insane, but author-ities felt that she would best survive if returned to a familiar environment. She was sent to Port Harrison (now Inoucdjouac, Quebec), where she spent the rest of her days as a household helper and cook. She adjusted well, was proud of her earlier messiah role, was usually in good spirits, and proved to be an effective, reliable worker. Mina worked for the author, a teacher at Port Harrison. 3 illus.   D. Chaput

327. Hippler, Arthur E. SOME OBSERVATIONS ON WITCH-CRAFT: THE CASE OF THE AIVILIK ESKIMOS. *Arctic [Canada] 1973 26(3): 198-207.* Analyzes "continuities and changes in witchcraft behaviour" among the Aivilik of Roes Welcome Sound north of Hudson Bay since the 1953 study of E. S. Carpenter. The changes are minimal and are explained by altered cultural circumstances. Based on field research and printed sources; biblio.   J. A. Casada

328. Marsh, Donald B. THE STONE WINTER HOUSES OF THE SADLERMIUT. *Beaver [Canada] 1976 307(3): 36-39.* Presents remi-niscences of the late Donald B. Marsh, Anglican Bishop of the Arctic, who in 1938 interviewed Jimmy Gibbons, an Eskimo, about the Sadler-miut of Southampton Island near Hudson Bay. The tribe was decimated at the turn of the century, probably by disease. While a few members were still alive, young Jimmy asked them questions about their unusual homes. Examines details of house construction, and discusses furniture and use of bone and other materials. 6 illus.   D. Chaput

329. Mays, Robert G. MASS COMMUNICATIONS AND CANA-DA'S ESKIMOS. *Polar Record [Great Britain] 1973 16(104): 683-690.* Satellite service will reach half of the 21,000 residents of the Canadian Arctic. To ameliorate the effect of southern TV programs on Eskimo society the federal government plans a 5-year program setting up local radio stations and videotaping projects prior to introducing TV to addi-tional communities. Documented from government documents and sec-ondary sources.   L. L. Hubbard

330. O'Connell, Sheldon. TELEVISION AND THE CANADIAN ESKIMO. *J. of Communication 1977 27(4): 140-144.* Examines the impact of television on Eskimos in 1976-77; certain attitudes have changed, but basic Eskimo values remain intact.

331. Oswalt, Wendell H. THE ESKIMO PEOPLE: THE EARLIEST ACCOUNTS. *Beaver [Canada] 1977 308(2): 21-27.* Summarizes the earliest accounts and art work, beginning with reports and drawings from the 1500's. The first important study was by Hans P. Egede, *A Descrip-tion of Greenland* (1745). Accurate information on Eskimo culture was accumulated from east to west. The Polar Eskimos were first detailed in a solid work by Elisha K. Kane, *Arctic Explorations* (1856). Includes an early map and contemporary artistic views.   D. Chaput

332. Russell, Chesley. THE DEVON ISLAND POST. *Beaver [Can-ada] 1978 308(4): 41-47.* In 1934 the author, with the Hudson's Bay

Company, organized a move of 50 Eskimos from Baffin Island to North Devon Island where game was supposedly more abundant. The agree-ment was to stay for at least two years, after which if the Eskimos wished to return home, the Company would arrange the move. Although the hunting was adequate, the weather was fierce, and the Eskimos did not adjust to Devon Island. In 1936 the company decided to move to Arctic Bay, on the north side of Baffin Island, far from where the Eskimos lived. Although the Company did not keep its bargain, Russell feels that the experiments in moving in Arctic lands prepared the way for modern settlements on Cornwallis and Ellesmere Islands. 7 illus., map.
                                                                      D. Chaput

333. Schaefer, Otto. ESKIMO PERSONALITY AND SOCIETY: YESTERDAY AND TODAY. *Arctic [Canada] 1975 28(2): 87-91.* Examines traditional and contemporary Inuit Eskimos, comparing familial respect, closeness, love, and social values, attitudes, and practices, 1974.

334. Schledermann, Peter. THULE CULTURE COMMUNAL HOUSES IN LABRADOR. *Arctic [Canada] 1976 29(1): 27-37.* Studies of excavations near Saglek Bay, Labrador, indicate that construction of large sod-stone and whalebone communal houses of the Thule culture Eskimos was begun in the latter half of the 17th century as a response to economic or social stress; variation in styles was due to areal construction materials.

335. Smith, T. G. MANAGEMENT RESEARCH ON THE ES-KIMO'S RINGED SEAL. *Can. Geographical J. 1973 86(4): 118-125.*

336. Spiess, Arthur and Cox, Steven. DISCOVERY OF THE SKULL OF A GRIZZLY BEAR IN LABRADOR. *Arctic [Canada] 1976 29(4): 194-200.* Discovery of a grizzly bear skull in an excavation of an Eskimo encampment proves the presence of the *Ursus arctos* in the Labrador region and its exploitation by native peoples, 18th-19th centu-ries.

337. Tyrrell, J. W. ESKIMOS OF THE KAZAN. *Beaver [Canada] 1975 305(4): 40-46.* Travel notes of an 1894 journey on the west side of Hudson Bay, compiled by J. W. Tyrrell for his brother, J. B. Tyrrell, who conducted the expedition for the Geological Survey of Canada. The notes, 7 August-18 September, record temperatures, Eskimo personalities, geo-logical features, types of transportation, and diet of both Eskimos and members of the expedition. 8 illus., map.   D. Chaput

338. Usher, Peter J. NORTHERNERS AND THE LAND. *Can. Dimension 1975 11(2): 23-30.* Eskimos want to have a say in the development of their land, notably in oil production, to control both industrial expansion and pollution in 1975.

339. Warner, Iris. HERSCHEL ISLAND. *Alaska J. 1973 3(3): 130-143.* Discusses the history and Eskimo inhabitants of Herschel Island, in Mackenzie Bay on the southern edge of the Arctic Ocean, 1826-1972, emphasizing whaling and polar explorations in that region.

340. White, Gavin. MISSIONARIES AND TRADERS IN BAFFIN ISLAND 1894-1913. *J. of the Can. Church Hist. Soc. 1975 17(1): 2-10.* Describes the problems of the Anglican Church Missionary Society in their work with the Eskimos of Baffin Island. Because whalers and traders constituted the only government there, E. J. Peck and the other mission-aries had to use the traders' ships for transportation and huts for living. Relations between missionaries and traders deteriorated, as the former accused the latter of exploitation and immorality vis-a-vis the Eskimos. The Hudson's Bay Company ultimately took over all trade on the island, and the missionaries seemed to fare better. Based mainly on archival materials of the Church Missionary Society; 26 notes.
                                                              J. A. Kicklighter

Indian

341. Adams, George F. COMMERCIAL FISHING IN NORTH-ERN ONTARIO. *Can. Geographic [Canada] 1978 97(1): 62-69.* Chronicles the fresh water fishing industry on the lakes of northern Ontario among the Chippewa and Cree Indians, 19th century-1978.

342. Ames, Michael. INDIANS OF THE NORTHWEST COAST. *Am. West 1973 10(4): 12-17.* The natural year-round abundance of the river mouths and sea of the Pacific Northwest helped produce an extraordinary complex of rich cultures from northern California to southern Alaska, some of the most advanced hunting-gathering societies ever. The Yurok, Karok, and Hupa of the California-Oregon border country were rich hoarders who took great pride in displaying their wealth. The Chinook occupied the strategic Columbia River Valley and were prosperous middlemen in the commerce between the inland and coastal tribes. The Nootka and Kwakiutl who dominated the coastal areas of British Columbia were famous for their elaborate feasts and protocol. Of indefinite prehistoric origins, these peoples responded differently to intrusive white culture. All are now succumbing to the modern world that exacts a toll of their timeless ancestral cultures. Adapted from a forthcoming volume. 4 illus.   D. L. Smith

343. Andrews, Isabel. INDIAN PROTEST AGAINST STARVA-TION: THE YELLOW CALF INCIDENT OF 1884. *Saskatchewan Hist. [Canada] 1975 28(2): 41-51.* Located on the Crooked Lakes Reserves in the Lower Qu'Appelle Valley, the incident of the title occurred because of a change in farm instructors and a strict enforcement of Department of Indian Affairs' rations policies. The firing of James Setter by Edgar Dewdney for laxity of policy enforcement and Hilton Keith's subsequent rigid enforcement of a new minimum rations policy established by Assistant Indian Commissioner Hayter Reed nearly brought on a revolt by Yellow Calf's Cree Indians. The validity of the Indians' complaints is documented from several contemporary sources. The incident portended the troubles of the following year. 60 notes.
                                                        C. Held

344. Battiste, Marie. CULTURAL TRANSMISSION AND SUR-VIVAL IN CONTEMPORARY MICMAC SOCIETY. *Indian Hist. 1977 10(4): 2-13.* The Micmac Indians of the Canadian Maritime Provinces have been converted to Christianity and otherwise assimilated into white culture for several generations, but they have maintained many cultural traits unique to their tribe. Customs relating to family ties, the rearing of children, funerals, and social control are preserved and in many cases integrated into the outward conformation to Christianity and western civilization. For example, the Catholic Feast of St. Anne has become the focal point of a tribal celebration. Illus., biblio.
                                                        E. D. Johnson

345. Bauer, George W. HOW THE JAMES BAY INDIANS COPE IN THE WHITE MAN'S WORLD. *Can. Geographic [Canada] 1978/79 97(3): 26-31.* Discusses sociological, psychological, and economic acculturation of the Cree Indians living near James Bay in Quebec, 1970's.

346. Berkes, Fikret. JAMES BAY: THE CREE INDIAN COASTAL FISHERY. *Can. Geographical J. 1976/77 93(3): 60-65.*

347. Bishop, Charles A. ARCHIVAL SOURCES AND THE CUL-TURE HISTORY OF THE INDIANS OF THE EASTERN SUBARC-TIC. *Can. R. of Sociol. and Anthrop. 1975 12(3): 244-251.* Reports on archives which have information on the Indians of the eastern Subarctic.

348. Bishop, Charles A. THE HENLEY HOUSE MASSACRES. *Beaver [Canada] 1976 307(2): 36-41.* In 1754, five traders at this Hudson's Bay Company post were killed by the Cree. Usual interpretations stress this as an episode in the English-French rivalry for local furs, which incited the Cree to kill the traders. The author, using Hudson's Bay manuscripts, claims that the English traders at Albany and Henley House either did not understand or chose to ignore Cree attitudes in sexual matters. For example, Joseph Ibister at Fort Albany kept a Cree woman at the post, yet he prohibited the local Cree chiefs from having their women live at the post. The disgruntled Cree chief, Woudbee, led the attack on Henley House. He and his two sons were killed. 6 illus.
                                                        D. Chaput

349. Blanchette, Jean-François. GUNFLINTS FROM CHICOUTIMI INDIAN SITE (QUÉBEC). *Hist. Archaeol. 1975 9: 41-54.* The aim of this study is to introduce new criteria for the identification and dating of 17th century gunflints. The discovery of a new variety of spall gunflint is explained and the archaeological evidence for the existence of both Dutch and French gunflints on North American archaeological sites before 1663 is demonstrated. The sample used here is composed of all the gunflints from the Indian component of the Chicoutimi site in Québec (39 gunflints). Though small in number, it is shown that this sample can give conclusions which may be checked with the data from 17th-18th century sites in southeastern Massachusetts and other places in North America.   J

350. Bleasdale, Ruth. MANITOWANING: AN EXPERIMENT IN INDIAN SETTLEMENT. *Ontario Hist. [Canada] 1974 66(3): 147-157.* Discusses the attempt to settle Indians on Manitoulin Island, Ontario, in the mid-19th century. Considers the attempt from three perspectives: government, missionary activities, and commercial interests. Concludes with two brief sections considering the failure of the scheme and the reasons for that failure. 44 notes.   W. B. Whitham

351. Boyce, Douglas W. A GLIMPSE OF IROQUOIS CULTURE HISTORY THROUGH THE EYES OF JOSEPH BRANT AND JOHN NORTON. *Pro. of the Am. Phil. Soc. 1973 117(4): 286-294.* Results of an 1801 questionnaire given to Joseph Brant and John Norton by a New York City clergyman, Samuel Miller. The two Indian statesmen were extremely knowledgeable about eastern North American Indians, particularly the Six Nations. Unfortunately, Miller's questionnaire to Brant does not exist, only the answers; yet the replies are worthy for their views on social and political organization, religion, life cycle, and traditional history. 26 notes.   C. W. Olson

352. Bradley, Ian L. A BIBLIOGRAPHY OF THE ARTS AND CRAFTS OF NORTHWEST COAST INDIANS. *BC Studies [Canada] 1975 Spring (25): 78-124.* Includes scholarly studies, catalogs of exhibitions, and literature describing and illustrating the Northwest Indians' plastic and graphic art, dance, and music. Headings are provided. Primary and secondary sources; 719 entries.   W. L. Marr

353. Bradley, Ian L. INDIAN MUSIC OF THE PACIFIC NORTHWEST: AN ANNOTATED BIBLIOGRAPHY OF RE-SEARCH. *BC Studies [Canada] 1976 (31): 12-22.* The literature of the achievements in the creative arts of the Indians of the Pacific Northwest is growing. This 40-entry bibliography includes books, periodical articles, government documents, and an unpublished M.A. thesis. The coverage is a composite of the literature on musical instruments, notated songs, texts and translations of lyrics, and appropriate anthropological observations.   D. L. Smith

354. Bradley, Ian L. REVISED BIBLIOGRAPHY OF INDIAN MUSICAL CULTURE IN CANADA. *Indian Hist. 1977 10(4): 28-32.* Provides 90 entries, mostly of periodical articles but including a few books and theses, relating to all phases of Native American music in Canada.
                                                        E. D. Johnson

355. Braroe, Niels Winther and Braroe, Eva Ejerhed. WHO'S IN A NAME: IDENTITY MISAPPREHENSION ON THE NORTHERN PLAINS. *Diogenes [Italy] 1977 (98): 71-92.* Discusses methods of name assignation among the Cree Indians in the Northern Plains of Canada; asserts that retention of unique name-giving is one of the methods used by native peoples to retain an insularity in their culture and to maintain a barrier against the outside Anglo society which allows for preservation of moral values.

356. Brasser, Ted J. THE CREATIVE VISIONS OF A BLACK-FOOT SHAMAN. *Alberta Hist. [Canada] 1975 23(2): 14-16.* Wolf Collar, an Alberta Blackfoot warrior, had several significant dreams in the 1870's, featuring a large bird, Thunder Woman, and her son, Blue Thunder Lodge. Dreams and voices over the years gave Wolf Collar his medicine-man powers. He also became a noted warrior and competent artist. When warfare was declared illegal, Wolf Collar assisted missionary H. W. G. Stocken with a syllabic system in translating the Bible. He died in 1928.   D. Chaput

357. Brasser, T. J.   METIS ARTISANS.   *Beaver [Canada] 1975 306(2): 52-57.* Canadian Plains Indians originally had decorative arts emphasizing geometric patterns, yet by the mid-1800's circular, floral patterns predominated. Examines the origins of such changes, especially the influence of Chippewa-Cree-Métis groups which originated around the Straits of Mackinac and Sault Sainte. Marie, then by the early 1800's settled around Pembina. From there, the Métis hunted, traveled, and explored a wide territory, probably thus spreading the floral-circular styles. 12 illus.   D. Chaput

358. Brown, Bern Will.   THE HARE INDIANS.   *Beaver [Canada] 1974 305(2): 12-17.* Looks at the past and present daily life of the Hare Indians. These people who live along the Arctic Circle and who were once nomadic hunters and trappers, are now literate inhabitants of permanent settlements. They are attempting to use oil exploration on their former hunting grounds to re-negotiate their treaty with the government. 13 illus.   D. Heermans

359. Carroll, Michael P.   REVITALIZATION MOVEMENTS AND SOCIAL STRUCTURE: SOME QUANTITATIVE TESTS.   *Am. Sociol. R. 1975 40(3): 389-401.* After reviewing some of the methodological difficulties which have faced investigators trying to investigate the rise of revitalization movements, the methodological advantages of studying the acceptance of the Ghost Dance (circa 1889) by North American Indians are delineated. These advantages are: (1) a relatively large number of tribes (N=37) were all exposed to what was more or less the same revitalization movement; (2) information on the degree to which each tribe accepted the movement is available from a source contemporary to the event and (3) information relating to some of the social characteristics of these tribes is available from Murdock's *Ethnographic Atlas.* The sample thus provides what is probably a unique opportunity for quantitatively testing several hypotheses relating to the acceptance of revitalization movements. After ascertaining that diffusion alone could not account for acceptance of the Ghost Dance, several other hypotheses, derived from different theoretical frameworks, were tested. Thus, using a "cultural deprivation" argument, it was predicted, and found, that those tribes recently deprived (because they were living in areas in which the buffalo had only recently been exterminated) were far more likely to accept the Ghost Dance than those not recently deprived. The assertion—implicit in Worsley's analysis of Cargo Cults—that acceptance of a revitalization movement would vary inversely with degree of political centralization was *not* supported by the data. Finally, based upon a consideration of the social conditions promoting "integration" in Durkheim's sense of that word, it was predicted, and found, that acceptance varied inversely with the presence of unilineal kin groups and with the presence of a system of inheritance.   J

360. Carter, David J.   THE REV'D. SAMUEL TRIVETT.   *Alberta Hist. R. 1973 21(2): 13-19, (3): 18-27.* Part I. On his first tour of duty, 1878-85, the Reverend Samuel Trivett (1852-1931) was a missionary to the Cree and Blackfoot Indians in Alberta. This pioneer Anglican churchman also made linguistic contributions. Part II. When the Reverend Trivett returned from furlough to the mission field he built a new mission house for the Church Missionary Society. The location and expense of this house became a source of conflict with his bishop and led to his dismissal from the Indian service in 1891. 4 illus., 36 notes.
D. L. Smith

361. Chalmers, John W.   FEDERAL, PROVINCIAL AND TERRITORIAL STRATEGIES FOR CANADIAN NATIVE EDUCATION, 1960-1970.   *J. of Can. Studies [Canada] 1976 11(3): 37-49.* A marked increase in Indian and Métis populations during the 1940's forced the federal government to take control of native school children away from local authorities. In the 1960's, native education became compulsory, universal, and racially integrated; and day schools replaced residential ones. However, the white man's curriculum did not provide for the social integration of native children, and their parents were dissatisfied with their own exclusion from educational decisions. Based on government reports and author's data; 3 tables, 3 notes.   G. E. Panting

362. Chalmers, John W.   KLEE WYCK.   *Alaska J. 1975 5(4): 231-238.* Discusses the life and paintings of Emily Carr, 1888-1972, a Canadian whose nickname, Klee Wyck, was an Indian name meaning Laughing One, and who spent most of her life painting and drawing the Indians of Western Canada.

363. Chalmers, John W.   TEKAHIONWAKE.   *Alberta Hist. R. [Canada] 1974 22(3): 24-25.* Presents a biographical sketch of the poet and Indian princess Pauline Johnson.   S

364. Chalmers, John W.   TREATY NO. SIX.   *Alberta Hist. [Canada] 1977 25(2): 23-27.* The Cree Treaty of 1876 covered much of modern Alberta and most of Saskatchewan. Under the treaty the Crees agreed to surrender all land rights and have reserves set up without Indian title. Other considerations were cash presents, annuities, agricultural implements, medicine chests, and education whenever the Indians desired it. Subsequently, the government frequently changed the ground rules, especially regarding land use, education, hunting and fishing rights. The treaty also conflicts with the Indian Act, which leads to much confusion. Current Cree unrest is related to treaty misunderstandings. Based on the Treaty and on reminiscences of S. B. Steele; 2 illus.   D. Chaput

365. Clifton, James A.   MERCHANT, SOLDIER, BROKER, CHIEF: A CORRECTED OBITUARY OF CAPTAIN BILLY CALDWELL.   *J. of the Illinois State Hist. Soc. 1978 71(3): 185-210.* Challenges the prevailing characterization of Billy Caldwell (1780-1841) as a successful half-Indian trader and Potawatomi chief on the Great Lakes frontier. Applying ethnohistorical methods, the author concludes that Caldwell was an alien in his tribal Mohawk society, in his childhood in Canada, in his early adulthood in the British Indian Department, and especially in his later years in post-revolutionary America. Far from being a power broker, Caldwell was usually an instrument of others; nor did he think of himself as an Indian. Based on Caldwell papers in Canada, Michigan, Wisconsin, Missouri, and Illinois; Illus., 4 maps, 83 notes.
J/S

366. Corum, Charles Ronald.   A TETON TIPI COVER DEPICTION OF THE SACRED PIPE MYTH.   *South Dakota Hist. 1975 5(3): 229-244.* Much of the Sioux Indians' religion, including the sacred pipe myth, was recorded on a buffalo-hide tipi. These paintings were on the inside of the tipi, although an extant model in Berlin's Royal Museum of Ethnology presents them on the outside for display purposes. The Berlin museum came into possession of the original from a French nobleman who had acquired it through a Quebec collection of artifacts captured from the Sioux. It remained in storage until 1900 when an artist-ethnographer with a description of the tipi from a Sioux medicine man discovered it in the museum's storage. Interpretations of the paintings are here presented insofar as they are understood. Some meanings are still unknown, as is the overall theory and plan of the figures. However, it is clear that they represent the theology of the Sioux in many of its aspects. It may have served to aid memorization of songs, traditions, and dances. Based on primary and secondary sources; 5 photos, 23 notes.
A. J. Larson

367. Cumming, Peter A. et al.   THE RIGHTS OF INDIGENOUS PEOPLES: A COMPARATIVE ANALYSIS.   *Am. Soc. of Int. Law Pro. 1974 68: 265-301.* Discusses the roles of international law, the Organization of American States, and the UN in protecting the interests of Indians in North and South America since the 19th century.

368. Day, Gordon M.   HENRY TUFTS AS A SOURCE ON THE EIGHTEENTH CENTURY ABENAKIS.   *Ethnohistory 1974 21(3): 189-197.* The autobiography of Henry Tufts is introduced as a substantial source of information for a little-known group of Western Abenakis from southern Quebec and northern New England, with whom Tufts lived during 1772-75.   J/S

369. Day, Gordon M.   THE WESTERN ABENAKI TRANSFORMER.   *J. of the Folklore Inst. 1976 13(1): 75-89.* World origin myths of the Wabanaki Indian tribes of the eastern Algonquin area have been well documented. A common Transformer, or world-creator figure known as Gluskap, appears in several of these myths. Personal fieldwork, however, reveals the existence among the Western Abnaki Indians of two mythical Transformers, known as Odzihozo and Bedegwadzo, whose characteristics differ. Based on field notes and published material; 55 notes.   J. L. White

370. Dempsey, Hugh A.   THE CENTENNIAL OF TREATY SEVEN: AND WHY INDIANS THINK WHITES ARE KNAVES.   *Can. Geographical J. [Canada] 1977 95(2): 10-19.* Discusses a centennial

celebration among Canadian Indians (Bloods, Blackfoot, Piegans, Sarcees, and Stoneys) of Treaty Seven, the last of the treaties signed between the British crown and the warlike plains Indians of Canada, in which in exchange for a million acres of land, the Indians received guarantee of education, land reserves, and financial aid, much of which they never received.

371. Denton, Trevor. CANADIAN INDIAN MIGRANTS AND IMPRESSION MANAGEMENT OF ETHNIC STIGMA. *Can. R. of Sociol. and Anthrop. 1975 12(1): 65-71.* Canadian Indian migrants feel that the social category 'Indian' is a discrediting one among whites. Accordingly, migrants act to control their image of Indian self during interaction with whites. They either suppress an Indian identification, or else admit to being Indian but take steps to avoid discreditation. This paper focuses on the impression management strategies involved and relates type of strategy to type of friendship network. J

372. Dickson, Lovat. THE DOUBLE IDENTITY: THE GROWTH OF THE GREY OWL MYTH. *Can.: An Hist. Mag. 1974 1(3): 1-8.* The life of Englishman Archie Belaney, who immigrated to Ontario, married an Ojibway Indian and took on the Indian identity of Grey Owl. S

373. Doig, Ivan. THE TRIBE THAT LEARNED THE GOSPEL OF CAPITALISM. *Am. West 1974 11(2): 42-47.* William Duncan (b. 1832) served from 1857 until his death in 1918 as Anglican missionary to the Tsimshean Indians. He established the village of Metlakahtla, in northern British Columbia, as a self-sustaining community of Christian Indians, isolated from the moral taints of the white frontier. Later he moved the settlement to the southern tip of Alaska. Schooled in the reform atmosphere of Victorian England and apprenticed in its industrial revolution, Duncan emphasized education, Christian living, organization, and mechanization in his missionary efforts. He was very influential with his converts and earned enormous respect, giving them both Christianity and capitalism. Metlakahtla also became Duncan's fiefdom and trouble came as he aged and became too dictatorial. His town still practices Duncan's faith and thrives as a fishing port. 4 illus. D. L. Smith

374. Doutre, Joseph. LES SAUVAGES DU CANADA EN 1852, [Indians in Canada in 1852]. *Études Françaises [Canada] 1973 9(3): 265-273.* Describes voyages to Indian tribes at Caughnawaga and Sault St. Louis. Relates the activities and dress of the Indian women. Includes two accounts of witchcraft and attempts to deal with it. Suggests two causes have maintained the Indians in their originality: their language and the conservation of the Indian woman's traditional dress. Extracted from J.-L. Lafontaine, *L'Institut canadien en 1855*, Montréal, Senécal et Daniel, 1855, p. 190-225; illus. G. J. Rossi

375. Duff, Wilson. MUTE RELICS OF HAIDA TRIBE'S GHOST VILLAGES. *Smithsonian 1976 7(6): 84-91.* Discusses the Haida Indians' totem poles on Anthony Island and Queen Charlotte Islands on the coast of British Columbia left from long-since-abandoned early villages, 1774-95.

376. Dunwiddie, Peter W. THE NATURE OF THE RELATIONSHIP BETWEEN THE BLACKFEET INDIANS AND THE MEN OF THE FUR TRADE. *Ann. of Wyoming 1974 46(1): 123-133.* Examines why the Blackfoot Indians gained a notorious reputation among American trappers in the early 19th century. They were generally friendly toward whites until the advent of major changes in the fur trade. By the 1820's white companies increasingly dealt with Free Trappers rather than trading with the Blackfoot for furs. The companies built permanent forts, depleted animal populations, and provided guns to traditional Blackfoot enemies. These factors, rather than British support in Canada, prompted Blackfoot reprisals against Americans. Based on primary and secondary sources; 40 notes. M. L. Tate

377. Duran, Elizabeth C. and Duran, James A., Jr. INDIAN RIGHTS IN THE JAY TREATY. *Indian Historian 1973 6(1): 33-37.* Discusses recent attempts to validate Article III of Jay's Treaty (1794) which granted free border-crossing rights to Canada for North American Indians. S

378. Eisen, George. GAMES AND SPORTING DIVERSIONS OF THE NORTH AMERICAN INDIANS REFLECTED IN AMERICAN HISTORICAL WRITINGS OF THE SIXTEENTH AND SEVENTEENTH CENTURIES. *Can. J. of Hist. of Sport and Physical Educ. [Canada] 1978 9(1): 58-85.*

379. Faries, Richard. AUTOBIOGRAPHY OF ARCHDEACON RICHARD FARIES (DOCUMENTS OF THE CANADIAN CHURCH-5). *J. of the Can. Church Hist. Soc. 1973 15(1): 14-23.* Born and reared in Canada, Faries (1870-1964) devoted his entire career to missionary work with the Indians. He completed this autobiography in 1961 at the request of a church official. He was ordained deacon in 1896 and immediately thereafter began to teach Indian children and to preach to the Indians of the Albany River district, travelling by canoe, dog-team, or foot. He was shortly named missionary to the Swampy Cree Indians and established headquarters at York Factory. His accomplishments included building a new church, converting many Indians to Christianity, and, later, compiling a dictionary of the Cree language. He was named archdeacon of York in 1917 and was ordained priest so that he could perform sacraments. In later years, poor health forced Faries to spend the winter in Toronto, but during the summers he returned to York Factory. 15 notes. J. A. Kicklighter

380. Finnie, Richard. TREATY TIME AT FORT RAE 1939 AND 1974. *Beaver [Canada] 1975 306(1): 24-31.* In 1939 the author made a film of the Thlingchadinne (Dog-rib) Indians' treaty payments at Fort Rae above Great Slave Lake; he was invited to witness the celebrations again in 1974. Emphasizes the contrasts. In 1939 he had to fly in to the isolated settlement. In 1974 he drove in. The Hudson's Bay Company trading post had been replaced by a supermarket; Dogrib chants were replaced by a rock concert. Dogrib population has increased dramatically, and modern education and housing have supplanted the primitive conditions of the 1930's. 12 illus. D. Chaput

381. Fisher, A. D. THE DIALECTIC OF INDIAN LIFE IN CANADA. *Can. Rev. of Sociol. and Anthrop. 1976 13(4): 458-464.* Canadian Indian communities have been studied as communities that are timeless and functionally coherent, but suffering from disorganization or dysfunctional acculturation. What the aggregations of persons who are brought together by fiat have in common, however, is their formal status as Indians and land. In these settlements the white "contact persons" and Indian "ethnics" may strive for separate goals, but their achievements are limited by population growth and the divorce of power from local authority. The so-called pathology of these settlements is better understood as the dialectic between Indian individuals and their white administrators. The characteristic power relations make these settlements "reflex" or dual societies, dual societies, one might add, which cannot experience true development. J

382. Fisher, Robin. ARMS AND MEN ON THE NORTHWEST COAST, 1774-1825. *BC Studies [Canada] 1976 (29): 3-18.* Questions two assumptions about the destructive effect of European firearms introduced into the Indian cultures of the Pacific Northwest: 1) European-technology-produced weapons were superior to traditional Indian weapons, and 2) Indians wanted guns for the same reason Europeans did, to eliminate their enemies more effectively. European guns were not necessarily more efficient killers. It is possible that the status value of guns was more important to the Northwest Indians than anything else. 63 notes. D. L. Smith

383. Fisher, Robin. AN EXERCISE IN FUTILITY: THE JOINT COMMISSION ON INDIAN LAND IN BRITISH COLUMBIA, 1875-1880. *Can. Hist. Assoc. Hist. Papers [Canada] 1975: 79-94.* Europeans did not want to share land equally with the Indians. Settlers tended to reject Indian rights. Therefore, the provincial government of British Columbia was reluctant to implement the recommendations of the Joint Commission on Indian Land. As a result that body did not alter land policies as they applied to Indians. Based on government reports, papers in the Public Archives of Canada and the Provincial Archives of British Columbia, and secondary sources; 86 notes. G. E. Panting

384. Fleming, Roy F. ARTIST PAUL KANE PAINTS INDIAN LIFE AROUND THE GREAT LAKES. *Inland Seas 1977 33(4): 277-281.* In 1845 the noted Canadian painter Paul Kane (1810-71) visited the

Upper Great Lakes in order to paint Indian daily life. The following year he made a second trip. From them came hundreds of paintings and sketches which provide an especially valuable record of mid-19th-century Indians.   K. J. Bauer

385. Frideres, J. S. EDUCATION FOR INDIANS VS. INDIAN EDUCATION IN CANADA. *Indian Hist. 1978 11(1): 29-35.* Canada's Indians' schools—government, missionary, and military—all were designed to make the Indian into a white man. Today, the integrated public schools continue that process, giving Indian children a white man's education. Fortunately more of the tribes are assuming control of their own educational systems and making progress in bilingual and bicultural programs that better meet the needs of the Indian child. 6 notes.
                                                                                             E. D. Johnson

386. Friesen, John W. JOHN MC DOUGALL: THE SPIRIT OF A PIONEER. *Alberta Hist. R. 1974 22(2): 9-17.* Reverend John McDougall (ca. 1842-1917) was a pioneer Wesleyan Methodist missionary teacher to the Indians in the prairie provinces of Canada. He established several schools, was prominent in church and mission affairs, and was a prolific writer. 5 illus., 25 notes.   D. L. Smith

387. Gagné, Jacques. DE CHRISTIAN LEDEN ET DE SES RECHERCHES AU CANADA, DANS L'OPTIQUE DE L'UTILISATION DU PHONOGRAPHE [Christian Leden and his research in Canada, in light of the use of the phonograph]. *Can. Oral Hist. Assoc. J. 1976/77 2: 64-68.* Ethnomusicologist Christian Leden's songs recorded among the Cris Indians in 1911 still exist in the Public Archives of Canada.

388. Gagnon, François-Marc. "ILS SE PEIGNENT LE VISAGE...": RÉACTION EUROPÉENNE À UN USAGE INDIEN AU XVIᵉ ET AU DÉBUT DU XVIIᵉ SIÈCLES ["They paint their faces . . .": European reaction to an Indian custom in the 16th and beginning of the 17th centuries]. *Rev. d'Hist. de l'Amérique Française [Canada] 1976 30(3): 363-381.* Face and body paint indicated an Indian's societal status. Based on observations by early explorers about Indian body painting, most Europeans thought that Indians were intrinsically white and that if the aboriginal culture could be replaced with that of Europe, the Indians would become civilized, and such customs would cease. Secondary works; 51 notes.   L. B. Chan

389. Gallagher, John and Gonick, Cy W. THE OCCUPATION OF ANICINABE PARK. *Can. Dimension 1974 10(5): 21-39.* Background and commentary on the 1974 occupation of Anicinabe Park in Kenora, Ontario, by members of the Ojibwa Warriors Society.   S

390. Gough, Barry M. SEND A GUNBOAT! CHECKING SLAVERY AND CONTROLLING LIQUOR TRAFFIC AMONG COAST INDIANS OF BRITISH COLUMBIA IN THE 1860'S. *Pacific Northwest Q. 1978 69(4): 159-168.* The intertribal trade in Indian slaves and illegal trafficking in liquor created enormous problems for British Columbia officials during the 1860's. To suppress both nefarious activities and thus reduce the friction between tribes, British gunboats patrolled the coastal areas making arrests and serving as diplomats between feuding groups. Though never adequately funded or staffed, this small force successfully reduced the Indian slave trade. Liquor trafficking, however, was not greatly affected since the demand remained high and the laws proved difficult to enforce. Primary and secondary sources; 4 photos, 30 notes.
                                                                                             M. L. Tate

391. Gregg, Richard B. and Hauser, Gerald A. RICHARD NIXON'S APRIL 30, 1970 ADDRESS ON CAMBODIA: THE "CEREMONY" OF CONFRONTATION. *Speech Monographs 1973 40(3): 167-181.* "This essay examines President Nixon's April 30, 1970 address announcing the American incursion into Cambodia. Examining the perceptual patterns of the speech, the authors found that Nixon's remarks led to a climax which justified the war on ritualistic rather than Cold War premises. The last third of the speech was content analyzed. The resulting term clusters were then interpreted for their symbolic significance. The authors found the President's remarks in conformity with the potlatch ceremony of the Kwakiutl Indians. The essay concludes by relating the perceptual patterns and analogical matrix of the potlatch to trends which may be developing on the international scene, and calls for the rhetorical

critic to become aware of ritualistic elements in public communication."
                                                                                             J

392. Grindstaff, Carl F.; Galloway, Wilda; and Nixon, Joanne. RACIAL AND CULTURAL IDENTIFICATION AMONG CANADIAN INDIAN CHILDREN. *Phylon 1973 34(4): 368-377.* Canadian Indian children are unable to make culturally and racially accurate self-identification; based on a study conducted 1972-73.   S

393. Grumet, Robert Steven. CHANGES IN COAST TSIMSHIAN REDISTRIBUTIVE ACTIVITIES IN THE FORT SIMPSON REGION OF BRITISH COLUMBIA, 1788-1862. *Ethnohist. 1975 22(4): 295-318.* Coast Tsimshian potlatch phenomena in the present Port Simpson area of British Columbia are organized in a diachronic perspective. A human ecological stress-response model is utilized which views potlatching as a cultural subsystemic response that acts to redistribute material and personnel in response to stressful changes in the Coast Tsimshian environmental subsystem. Changes in population, amount of furs traded at Port Simpson, eulachon fishing, and the relative amount of direct subsistence activity are measured and correlated with changes in Coast Tsimshian potlatching. It is proposed that changes in the type, intensity, and frequency of Coast Tsimshian potlatches reflect changes in the complete Coast Tsimshian system from the protohistoric contact period to the time of their removal to the mission community of Metlakatla in 1862.
                                                                                             J

394. Guillemin, Jeanne. THE POLITICS OF NATIONAL LIBERATION: A COMPARISON OF UNITED STATES AND CANADIAN INDIAN ADMINISTRATION. *Social Problems 1978 25(3): 319-332.* Historical parallels and differences between Indian-white relations in the United States and Canada have been reflected in the final institutional form and political direction of contemporary Indian administration. Patterns of early colonial settlement, sequences of demographic growth, and the rise of urban industrialization have been important. Today, Indians face the problem of the decentralization of their community administration accompanied by tighter government controls on native land use. Ref.
                                                                                             A. M. Osur

395. Hall, D. J. CLIFFORD SIFTON AND CANADIAN INDIAN ADMINISTRATION, 1896-1905. *Prairie Forum [Canada] 1977 2(2): 127-151.* Preoccupied with western development, Clifford Sifton (Minister of the Interior and Superintendent General of Indian Affairs) placed unsympathetic officials in positions of authority which increased efficiency and centralized administration, but also led to animosity between the Indians and the government due to reduced spending on medical care, education, and agriculture and because of attempts at forced acculturation, 1896-1905.

396. Hall, D. J. THE HALF-BREED CLAIMS COMMISSION. *Alberta Hist. [Canada] 1977 25(2): 1-8.* The government's sorry record in dealing with the land claims of Métis helped cause the 1885 rebellion. What finally inspired government action was the Klondike gold rush. Indian lands had to be crossed. If the government treated with the Indians, the Métis also would demand justice. A series of government commissions in 1898-1900 treated with both the Indians and the Métis of the Prairie Provinces. Much scrip was issued, but the Métis failed to realize most of the value involved and they did not benefit materially from the lands assigned them. The Liberal Party benefited, because in the election of 1900 they gauged correctly and received the bulk of the Métis vote. 4 illus., 33 notes.   D. Chaput

397. Helbig, Alethea K. NANABOZHO OF THE GREAT LAKES INDIANS: AS HE WAS, AS HE IS. *Michigan Academician 1978 11(1): 49-58.* Explores the personality and powers of Nanabozho, a character in the folklore and oral tradition of the Chippewa and Ottawa Indians, 19th-20th centuries.

398. Henderson, John R. MISSIONARY INFLUENCES ON THE HAIDA SETTLEMENT AND SUBSISTENCE PATTERNS, 1876-1920. *Ethnohistory 1974 21(4): 303-316.* In the last quarter of the nineteenth century Anglican and Methodist missionary societies sent ministers to serve among the Haida of the Queen Charlotte Islands, British Columbia. Each missionary society had its own future goals and appraisals of the Haida's condition. Both approaches lead to the reorganization of the Haida's settlement and subsistence patterns.
                                                                                             J

399. Hohn, E. Otto. MAMMAL AND BIRD NAMES IN THE IN-DIAN LANGUAGES OF THE LAKE ATHABASCA AREA. *Arctic [Canada] 1973 26(2): 163-171.* Glossaries of native names for birds and mammals accompanied by a description of the various tribes involved. Comments on tribal linguistics. 2 tables, 6 notes.
J. A. Casada

400. Howard, Helen Addison. A SURVEY OF THE DENSMORE COLLECTION OF AMERICAN INDIAN MUSIC. *J. of the West 1974 13(2): 83-96.* Reviews five unabridged republications of Frances Densmore's ethnological and musicological studies undertaken for the Bureau of American Ethnology, Washington, D.C.: *Teton Sioux Music* (1918), *Yuman and Yaqui Music* (1932), *Nootka and Quileute Music* (1939), *Choctaw Music* (1943), and *Music of Acoma, Cochiti, and Zuni Pueblos* (1957). 50 notes.
D. D. Cameron

401. Hughes, Kenneth. JACKSON BEARDY: THE ART AND THE ARTIST. *Can. Dimension [Canada] 1977 12(6): 20-26.* White culture and the eventual regaining of Ojibwa Indian culture formed the artist Q. P. Jackson Beardy and his painting, 1944-75.

402. Jessett, Thomas E. ANGLICAN INDIANS IN THE PACIFIC NORTHWEST BEFORE THE COMING OF WHITE MISSIONAR-IES. *Hist. Mag. of the Protestant Episcopal Church 1976 45(4): 387-412.* Whereas other denominations sent missionaries to the Pacific Northwest to convert the Indians, the Episcopalians did not because the Indians had already been reached for the Episcopal Church through the earlier efforts of Hudson's Bay Company employees. Anglican success among the Indians was quite significant, for in 1825 Hudson's Bay employees sent two boys, Spokan Garry and Kottenay Pelly, to the mission school at Fort Garry. They returned to their tribes and taught agriculture and catechism to their people. Since the response to the Anglican faith was favorable, five more boys were sent back for similar training. As Americans pushed into the Oregon Country, other denominational missionaries came with them. These missionaries were surprised to find Christianized Indians among the Spokanes, Cayuses and Nez Perces. Squabbles among the missionaries, disagreement with Anglican theology, and general confusion on the part of the Indians over the missionaries' strategy gradually reduced the Anglican numbers. When Spokan Garry died, he had long been forgotten by the Church in which he was raised and was buried by a Presbyterian. Based on primary and secondary sources; 37 notes.
H. M. Parker, Jr.

403. Josephy, Alvin M., Jr. THE SPLENDID INDIANS OF ED-WARD S. CURTIS. *Am. Heritage 1974 25(2): 40-59, 96-97.* Biographical sketch accompanying a selection of Edward S. Curtis' (1868-1952) photographs from *The North American Indian* (New York: Johnson Reprint Corporation, 1970).
S

404. Kehoe, Alice B. DAKOTA INDIAN ETHNICITY IN SAS-KATCHEWAN. *J. of Ethnic Studies 1975 3(2): 37-42.* Fleeing from the advance of American settlers in the late 19th century, various bands of Dakota (Sioux) Indians resettled within the Canadian province of Saskatchewan. From an anthropological perspective considers the status of these Indians with the Canadian government and with the predominant Canadian Indian bands. 2 notes.
T. W. Smith

405. Kehoe, Alice B. and Kehoe, Thomas F. THE IDENTIFICA-TION OF THE FALL OR RAPID INDIANS. *Plains Anthropologist 1974 19(65): 231-232.* An identification of the "Fall" or "Rapid" Indians of southcentral Saskatchewan as Hidatsa is shown to be unlikely; rather, the Fall Indians of the contact period were Algonkian speaking bison hunters identified as Atsina.
J

406. Kehoe, Thomas F. and Kehoe, Alice B. STONES, SOLSTICES AND SUN DANCE STRUCTURES. *Plains Anthropologist 1977 22(76): 85-95.* Eleven boulder configurations in Saskatchewan were examined in 1975 for possible astronomical alignments. Three were found to contain alignments to summer solstice phenomena. Ethnographic interviewing failed to discover any tradition of solstice marking in the historic tribes of the Northwestern Plains, but did suggest that the boulder configurations may have been constructed for the private observations of calendar-keeping shamans. Ethnoarchaelogical mapping of a 1975 Sun Dance camp revealed that the ceremonial structures were aligned to sunrise, but whether this was deliberate, and if deliberate, traditional, could not be determined.
J

407. Kerri, James Nwannukwu. "PUSH" AND "PULL" FAC-TORS: REASONS FOR MIGRATION AS A FACTOR IN AMERIN-DIAN URBAN ADJUSTMENT. *Human Organization 1976 35(2): 215-220.* Discusses reasons for migration of Indians in the United States and Canada, based on research conducted in 1972.

408. Lagassé, Jean. ALGUNOS COMENTARIOS SOBRE LOS FACTORES SOCIALES QUE AFECTAN EL DESARROLLO IN-DÍGENA EN CANADA [Commentaries on the social factors that affect native development in Canada]. *Am. Indígena [Mexico] 1975 35(1): 101-115.* States "that all native communities are undergoing significant changes. Changes have taken 25 to 50 years to occur compared to a five to ten year span in an average white community. It isn't so much that the potential for leadership is better than in former years since that potential has always been there. Rather, the modern systems of communication leave no one untouched. The new information that reaches native communities daily provides a degree of challenge that perhaps wasn't felt in earlier years. While there won't be a return to the past, cultural change being irreversible, the forms that native culture will take in the future are difficult to predict."
J

409. Leacock, Eleanor. WOMEN IN EGALITARIAN SOCIETIES. Bridenthal, Renate and Koonz, Claudia, ed. *Becoming Visible: Women in European History* (Boston: Houghton Mifflin Company, 1977): 11-35. Examines the anthropological basis for the progression throughout history from a systematized cooperativeness to a systematized competitiveness, as expressed through such social inventions as private property, social stratification, political subjugation, and institutionalized warfare with standing armies. In examining the transformation from egalitarian to stratified societies—emphasizing women's position as the analytical criterion—the author reconstructs the earliest social relations based on archaeological data from Europe and anthropological studies of North American Indians. 34 notes, biblio.
J. Brown

410. Leighton, Douglas. THE MANITOULIN INCIDENT OF 1863: AN INDIAN-WHITE CONFRONTATION IN THE PROV-INCE OF CANADA. *Ontario Hist. [Canada] 1977 69(2): 113-124.* Comments on the failure of 19th-century Indian policy as exemplified by the relatively minor violence at Manitoulin. Describes the Indian communities on the island, and their contacts with whites before 1862. Remarks on Indian policy of the provincial government in the early 19th century, the changes before the violence, press reaction, and on subsequent events and the resolution of the affair. Suggests another explanation for the only death in the incident. 38 notes.
W. B. Whitham

411. Leitch, Adelaide. THE SPOTTED HORSE OF NEW FRANCE: STEEDS OF THE MOUNT-UP? *Can. Geographical J. 1973 87(1): 28-31.* Horses from Canada may have assisted Spanish horses in altering the life-style of the Plains Indians.
S

412. Lillard, Charles. A CHINOOK GAZETEER. *Sound Heritage [Canada] 1977 6(3): 18-25.* Discusses and presents examples from Chinook jargon, an argot of fishing, mining, and logging words unique to the Pacific Northwest and British Columbia, 1830's-1976.

413. Lismer, Marjorie. ADOPTION PRACTICES OF THE BLOOD INDIANS OF ALBERTA, CANADA. *Plains Anthropologist 1974 19(63): 25-33.* "Adoption is practiced in many parts of the world, but its mechanics are rarely spelled out in detail. The following paper is an effort to correct this lack for the Blood (Blackfoot) Indians living in Alberta in 1939. The introduction of a money economy and life on a reservation brought about certain modifications, but at the time this investigation was made 'the Indians themselves' said adoption was 'frequent in former times.' There is reason to believe that the motives for adoption and the varying attitudes of those who adopt and of those who are adopted have not changed radically through the years. Many parallels in adoption are apparent, not only in other Blackfoot tribes, but also in such North American Indian groups as the Crow, Omaha, Winnebago and Ojibwa."
J

414. Lister, Rota. CANADA'S INDIANS AND CANADIAN DRAMA. *Am. Rev. of Can. Studies 1974 4(1): 54-74.* Four stages of native acculturation are identified: initial contact, dependence on European goods, treaties and settlement on reservations, and Indian resurgence; these are examined as they are reflected in Canadian drama, 1606-1886, and most recently in both non-Indian and Indian dramatic activities which emphasize the current fourth stage. 27 notes.

415. Lobb, Allan and Wolfe, Art. GLIMPSES INTO A LOST WORLD: A PHOTOGRAPHIC PORTFOLIO OF NORTHWEST INDIAN BASKETS. *Am. West 1978 15(5): 34-45.* A picture essay of representative examples of late 19th- and early 20th-century baskets of historic Indian tribes of the Pacific Northwest photographed in their native settings. Selected from a recently published volume of the authors —Allan Lobb, a collector of Indian baskets, and Art Wolfe, a photographer. 16 photos.   D. L. Smith

416. Loree, Donald James. SOME FACTORS RELATED TO INDIAN ORGANIZATIONAL DEVELOPMENT IN THE NORTHWEST TERRITORIES OF CANADA. *Plural Societies [Netherlands] 1976 7(2): 3-16.* Factors affecting the organizational development of Indians in the Northwest Territories include Indian-white relations, neocolonialism, geographic and social isolation, economic development, and population growth; covers 1940-76.

417. Low, Jean. GEORGE THORNTON EMMONS. *Alaska J. 1977 7(1): 2-11.* George Thornton Emmons (1852-1945) was a pioneer ethnologist of native Alaskans. While assigned to the *USS Adams* after graduation from Annapolis, Emmons was introduced to Alaska. He became friendly with the Tlingit Indians and began collecting artifacts which he shipped to museums all over the world. He prepared an exhibit for the World's Fair in 1891. In 1902, President Theodore Roosevelt asked him to find the old Russian boundary markers in the Chilkat country, and in 1904 he prepared for Roosevelt a report on the needs of the natives. 9 notes, biblio.   E. E. Eminhizer

418. MacDonald, Duncan. NEZ PERCÉS: THE HISTORY OF THEIR TROUBLES AND THE CAMPAIGN OF 1877. *Idaho Yesterdays 1977 21(1): 2-15, 26-30; 1978 21(4): 2-10, 18-28.* Part I. Presents the Indian argument that the hostilities of the Nez Percé War in Idaho were in reaction to many unpunished abuses by white men. First published in the *New North-West* in 1878 after interviews with Nez Percés in Canada. Map, 5 illus., 28 notes. Part II. Traces the movement of the Nez Percés and their leader, Looking Glass, through Idaho and Montana toward the buffalo country in Canada. Presents the Indian point of view. 6 illus., map, 12 notes.   B. J. Paul

419. MacDonald, Graham A. THE ANCIENT FISHERY AT SAULT STE. MARIE. *Can. Geographical J. 1977 94(2): 54-58.* Describes the system of fishing the whitefishery at Sault Ste. Marie and discusses the fishery's importance to Indian life and inter-tribal trade in the Upper Great Lakes Basin during the 17th to early 20th centuries.

420. MacLaren, George. THE ARTS OF THE MICMAC OF NOVA SCOTIA. *Nova Scotia Hist. Q. [Canada] 1974 4(2): 167-177.* Describes the art forms created by the Micmac Indians, Algonquin-speaking people who occupied the northern part of New Brunswick and Prince Edward Island. The achievements of these migratory people included clay and birchbark cooking pots, birchbark canoes, and weapons of stone and bone. Their decorative designs include seven- and eight-pointed stars, double curves, crosses, and diamonds executed in porcupine quills of various colors. Motifs of animals were also used. 3 notes, biblio.
                                                      H. M. Evans

421. Maranda, E. K. B.C. INDIAN MYTH AND EDUCATION: A REVIEW ARTICLE. *BC Studies [Canada] 1975 Spring (25): 125-134.* Review article on Indian mythology prompted by Kenneth B. Harris' *Visitors Who Never Left* (Vancouver: U. of British Columbia Press, 1974) and Marius Barbeau's novel *The Downfall of Temlaham* (1928) (Edmonton: Hurtig, 1973).   W. L. Marr

422. Marshall, Mortimer Villiers. SILAS TERTIUS RAND AND HIS MICMAC DICTIONARY. *Nova Scotia Hist. Q. 1975 5(4): 391-410.* Silas Tertius Rand (1810-89) was a self-taught linguist, Baptist pastor, and missionary to the Micmac Indians of Nova Scotia. He collected Indian legends, translated the Bible into Micmac and Maliseet, compiled a Micmac dictionary, gathered a great amount of linguistic and philological data on the Micmac and Maliseet languages, and lectured extensively on Indian languages, customs, and traditions, including ethnological and anthropological topics. Though he was without formal schooling, his philological accomplishments were widely recognized in university circles. 20 notes, biblio.   R. V. Ritter

423. Martin, Calvin. THE EUROPEAN IMPACT ON THE CULTURE OF A NORTHEASTERN ALGONQUIAN TRIBE: AN ECOLOGICAL INTERPRETATION. *William and Mary Q. 1974 31(1): 3-26.* Seeks to explain the wildlife extermination through the methodology of cultural ecology. The ecosystem and local human population are the basic units of analysis. The Micmacs of eastern Canada engaged extensively in trade with European fishermen. Taboos and ceremonies governed the preparation of animals as food; other hunting and eating habits affected the environment. The Indians were apostatized by disease, European trade, and Christianity. One important change wrought by the European contact was the unrestrained slaughter of certain wildlife. Based on early French and English records; 94 notes.   H. M. Ward

424. Martin, Calvin. THE FOUR LIVES OF A MICMAC COPPER POT. *Ethnohist. 1975 22(2): 111-133.* What to the seventeenth-century French was little more than a mundane article of commerce became, to the Acadian Micmac, an institution with noteworthy economic, ceremonial, spiritual, and demographic connotations. Utilizing portable kettles, Micmac households became less inclined to camp near their immobile wooden cauldrons which now served a diminishing function as the symbolic locus of settlement. The copper kettle thus afforded these people the opportunity to move about at random as they hunted game for the fur trade.   J

425. Martin, Calvin. WILDLIFE DISEASES AS A FACTOR IN THE DEPOPULATION OF THE NORTH AMERICAN INDIAN. *Western Hist. Q. 1976 7(1): 47-62.* Challenges the theory that European-introduced human epidemic diseases were the sole microbial source of the decimation of the American Indian. Epizootic or wildlife epidemics, most of them from rodents, seem to have been significant factors. The continuing demographic debate on the Indian changes the magnitude of the problem. Fur trade historians will have to revise previous estimates as to Indian responsibility in the decline of the beaver population. 40 notes.
                                                       D. L. Smith

426. Maxwell, Joseph A. THE EVOLUTION OF PLAINS INDIAN KIN TERMINOLOGIES: A NONREFLECTIONIST ACCOUNT. *Plains Anthropologist 1978 23(79): 13-29.* The striking similarity in basic terminological pattern among Plains tribes, and the absence of this pattern elsewhere in North America, is not accounted for by existing general theories of the evolution of kin terminologies. The development of this pattern is explained here in terms of a theory which abandons the assumption that terminological patterns are reflections of social structure. It is argued that the basic process in this development was the tactical or metaphoric extension of sibling terms to cross-cousins as a response to the increased importance of solidarity under the conditions of Plains life, and the subsequent incorporation of this extension into the meanings of the sibling terms. This hypothesis not only accounts for the distribution of terminological patterns in the Plains areas, but illuminates the general relationship of kin terminology to social structure.   J

427. McKinney, Wayne R. THE SIOUX LOOKOUT MEDICAL PROGRAM. *Beaver [Canada] 1973 303(4): 52-57.* Discusses available health services in the Sioux Lookout Zone of northwestern Ontario, and traces the history of medical care from the early 1900's, when tuberculosis treatment was emphasized. In 1969 the University of Toronto began a new model program with air service and a series of satellite treatment centers. 7 illus., map.   D. Chaput

428. Ménard, Camil. LA RELIGION DES AMÉRINDIENS DU NORD-EST DANS LA PERSPECTIVE DE L'ÉCOLOGIE CULTURELLE AMÉRICAINE [Northeastern American Indian religion in relation to American cultural ecology]. *Protée [Canada] 1976 5(2): 19-27.* The religion and social organization of Canadian Indians have been responses to the demands of a hostile environment.

429. Moodie, D. W. and Ray, Arthur J. BUFFALO MIGRATIONS IN THE CANADIAN PLAINS. *Plains Anthropologist 1976 21(71): 45-52.* This paper examines the seasonal movements of buffalo in the Canadian Plains during the fur trade period. Using the primary accounts of fur traders and missionaries, it demonstrates that a regular migration into the parkland in winter, and back onto the prairie in spring and summer, was characteristic of buffalo movements in the region. The migration into the parkland in winter was initiated by the need for shelter. The specific temporal and spatial manifestations of this general movement, however, were conditioned from year to year by a variety of factors whose effects were largely predictable to both the aboriginal and non-aboriginal residents of the region. Most important among these factors were winter mild spells, heavy snow, hunting pressures and fires.   J

430. Morgan, Lael. TRADE BEADS: ALASKA'S NATIVE HEIR-LOOMS. *Alaska J. 1973 3(4): 217-225.* Discusses history of trade bead making and collecting in Alaska during 1649-1973, emphasizing its practice among the Tlingit, Haida, and Tsimshian Indians.

431. Myers, Rex C. THE SETTLERS AND THE NEZ PERCE. *Montana 1977 27(4): 20-29.* Nez Perce Indians moved across Montana from late July to early October, 1877, fleeing the US military and seeking sanctuary in Canada. Preceding Indian movements, a wave of panic spread through Montana civilians who remembered plains Indian wars of 1876 and feared a repetition of the Little Big Horn battle. Letters, diaries, and newspapers of the period reveal that with few exceptions, Nez Perce treated Montana civilians well. Before the campaign ended in the Indians' defeat, Montana residents became derisive of federal military efforts and policy, developing a mood of public sympathy for the Nez Perce. Out of this sympathy grew a popular legacy of Nez Perce greatness which, in the succeeding century, grew to almost epic proportion. Based on letters, diaries, newspapers, and Territorial Records in Montana Historical Society collections, and War Department Records in the National Archives; 21 illus., biblio.   R. C. Myers

432. Nock, David. E. F. WILSON: EARLY YEARS AS A MIS-SIONARY IN HURON AND ALGOMA. *J. of the Can. Church Hist. Soc. 1973 15(4): 78-97.* Anglican missionary and educator Edward F. Wilson was sent to the Indians of the diocese of Huron in 1868. He was enthusiastic about converting Indians, intolerant of others' ideas, and thoroughly imbued with Victorian moral precepts. Most of the Indians were already Christians, and his work caused friction with the Methodists. Then he turned to education; but his Industrial School for Ojibway boys was only partly successful, because results did not come fast enough for his patrons and because he did not understand the significance of cultural barriers. By 1885 he had begun to feel that whites should advise Indians only when asked. This change (a result of the Riel Rebellion) revitalized his career. He retired in 1893. 71 notes.
J. A. Kicklighter

433. Ogilvie, William. FIELD NOTES OF A SURVEYOR. *Alberta Hist. R. 1974 22(2): 18-27.* The author surveyed Indian treaty reserves in Alberta. Reprints his description of the country and of the survey, 20 May 1878—6 January 1879, from his manuscript field book. 4 illus., map, 14 notes.   D. L. Smith

434. Oldham, Evelyn. RENAISSANCE OF COAST INDIAN ART. *Can. Geographical J. 1973 87(5): 32-37.*

435. Palmer, Gwen. CAMPERVILLE AND DUCK BAY. *Manitoba Pageant 1973 18(2): 11-17, (3): 6-10.* Part I. The earliest missions at Camperville and Duck Bay on Lake Winnipegosis were predominantly Roman Catholic. Father C. J. Camper encouraged the settlement of Métis and educational work among the Muskegon Indians. Fathers St. Germain and Adelard Chaumont established a residential school for Indians in 1897. The mission experienced its most productive years under Father Joseph Brachet 1912-38. Part II. A Frenchman (Maurice Bretagne), a Jew (Abe Sanoffsky), and a Negro (Bob Jones) played major roles in the development in the 1920's of the Indian settlement of Duck Bay on the west side of Lake Winnipegosis. Describes their work in furthering religion, education, and business in the community. 4 illus.
D. M. Dean

436. Preston, Richard J. A SURVEY OF ETHNOGRAPHIC AP-PROACHES TO THE EASTERN CREE-MONTGNAIS-NASKAPI. *Can. R. of Sociol. and Anthrop. 1975 12(3): 267-277.* Describes the fieldwork, writings, and language facilities of ethnographers who have worked with the Eastern Cree-Montagnais-Naskapi in Labrador 1908-68.

437. Raczka, Paul. INDIAN DANCERS. *Beaver [Canada] 1978 309(1): 24-29.* Summary of the modern Blackfoot Indians' Indian Days ceremonies, with brief background of the significance of the grass dance in local rituals. Recent changes, such as dance contests and cash prizes, are attributed to the influences from Oklahoma which traveled through the northern plains. 10 illus.   D. Chaput

438. Ramsey, Jarold. THE BIBLE IN WESTERN INDIAN MY-THOLOGY. *J. of Am. Folklore 1977 90(358): 442-454.* Examines the impact of Catholic and Protestant evangelism 1830-50, on the mythologies of the Klamath, Clackamas Chinook, and Northern Paiutes in Oregon, the Dieguña in California, the Klickitats and Cowlitz in Washington, and the Thompson, Okanagan, Lillooet, and Flathead tribes in British Columbia. Bible stories were incorporated, adapted, or sometimes reworked into new tales within the mythologies of the Pacific Northwest Indians. Primary and secondary sources; 28 notes.
W. D. Piersen

439. Ray, Arthur J. SMALLPOX: THE EPIDEMIC OF 1837-38. *Beaver [Canada] 1975 306(2): 8-13.* The smallpox epidemic that smashed the Mandans and other Upper Missouri tribes in 1837 soon crossed to the prairies of Canada. The Hudson's Bay officials were better prepared, as they had on hand a vaccine, and several knowledgeable surgeons. Many Indians, Métis, and traders were inoculated, but those who refused or neglected to receive such preventatives died. Examines the geographical flow of the epidemic and the work of officials such as William Todd who controlled the vaccination program. 6 illus.   D. Chaput

440. Robinson, Helen Caister. THAYENDANEGEA—THE STRONG ONE: THE STORY OF JOSEPH BRANT. *Can.: An Hist. Mag. 1974 2(1): 43-56.* As a boy Joseph Brant (1742-1807) was exposed to Indian and European culture. His knowledge of British ways helped him become a respected spokesman for the Iroquois Confederacy. When the confederacy split during the American Revolution, Brant became the leader of the pro-British Indians. In 1784, he brought his defeated supporters to the Grand River, where until his death he was chief spokesman for the Grand River Iroquois before the British Governors of Upper Canada. Based on secondary accounts; 8 illus., 14 notes.
D. B. Smith

441. Romaniuk, A. MODERNIZATION AND FERTILITY: THE CASE OF THE JAMES BAY INDIANS. *Can. R. of Sociol. and Anthrop. 1974 11(4): 344-359.* "The theory that modernization at its initial stage may result in an increase in fertility through the relaxation of restrictive customs governing procreative behaviours of premodern societies has often been postulated, but little empirical evidence has been provided to support it. Data collected on fertility for Indians living in the James Bay area of Canada tend to confirm the validity of this theory. They reveal, for this population, that intervals between successive births tend to become shorter among younger as compared to older generations of mothers, and this is attributed to three factors related to modernization: 1) changes in lactation habits whereby an increasingly larger proportion of mothers either do not breast-feed at all, or do so for shorter periods of time than did the older generations; 2) reduction in the level of pregnancy wastage resulting both from medical progress and from the fact that hardship and pregnancy accidents to which the pregnant mothers were formerly exposed probably have diminished as James Bay Indians have shifted from a nomadic to a sedentary society; and 3) reduction in the incidence of prolonged temporary separation of spouses as the communication between home villages of spouses has improved and as Indian families have given up their nomadic mode of life."   J

442. Ronaghan, Allen. THE IRON CREEK METEORITE. *Alberta Hist. R. 1973 21(3): 10-12.* The odyssey of this 386-pound meteorite, Canada's largest, is ended; it has been returned to Alberta. It was long venerated by Cree and Blackfoot Indians. Illus., 13 notes.
D. L. Smith

443. Ronaghan, Allen. THE PROBLEM OF MASKIPITON. *Alberta Hist. [Canada] 1976 24(2): 14-19.* Maskipiton ("Broken Arm") was a Cree chief prominent in the Prairie Provinces and along the US border in the mid-1800's. It is difficult to identify him in the various missionary, exploration, and military accounts, as he was known by a variety of Cree, French, English, and Sioux names. Some have even suggested there were two Maskipitons. Examination of the sources suggests there was but one Maskipiton, though this is tentative. 2 illus., 42 notes.   D. Chaput

444. Saban, Vera D. MEN WHO CHALLENGED THE BIG-HORN. *Am.West 1974 11(3): 44-47. 62-63.* Beginning as the Wind River in central Wyoming, the Bighorn River empties into the Yellowstone River in Montana. There is archaeological evidence that the area was inhabited eight to ten thousand years ago. The Crow and Sioux occupied it in a transitory way after the arrival of whites. A fur trading expedition of the North West Company of Canada in 1805 is the first recorded visit by whites. A succession of trappers and traders, topographical engineers, gold seekers, hunters, railroad surveyors, photographers, and adventurers braved the waters and gorges until Yellowtail Dam was completed in 1965. 3 illus.   D. L. Smith

445. Schroeter, Gerd. THE BUCKSKIN CURTAIN AS SHIB-BOLETH AND SECURITY-BLANKET. *J. of Ethnic Studies 1977 4(4): 85-94.* Review article prompted by Howard Adams' *Prison of Grass: Canada from the Native Point of View*, J. E. Chamberlin's *The Harrowing of Eden: White Attitudes Toward North American Natives*, Mark Nagler's *Natives Without a Home* and Henry Zentner's *The Indian Identity Crisis*, all published during 1976-77. The first two take a separationist approach to Indian-White relations; the others are integrationist. Focusing on racism in North American society, Adams has "a decidedly conspiratorial tone," draws dramatic parallels with the Third World, and rejects all participation in the dominant society by Indians. Chamberlin sees land control and attitudes toward private property as underlying the "Indian Problem." Zentner's collection of six essays focuses on the reservation system as cause for demoralization and anomie among Indians and calls for some alternative to the pre-Neolithic ethic of the reservations and the Protestant ethic of white society. Nagler refuses to call native peoples an ethnic group and places on them the onus for their inevitable acculturation to urban-bureaucratic-industrial society. 12 notes.
G. J. Bobango

446. Sharrock, Susan R. CREES, CREE-ASSINIBOINES, AND AS-SINIBOINES: INTERETHNIC SOCIAL ORGANIZATION ON THE FAR NORTHERN PLAINS. *Ethnohistory 1974 21(2): 95-122.* Interethnic social organization on the Far Northern Plains has typically been interpreted within the framework of 'tribe.' According to this concept, a tribe—by non-specific definition—is a discretely bounded unit that corresponds in membership composition to ethnic unit, linguistic unit, territorial coresidential unit, cultural unit, and societal unit. In this paper are presented ethnohistorical data on the Cree and Assiniboine which indicate to the contrary that within each of these five unit categories, the sociocultural units were graded one into another; and that the membership of one unit category was not necessarily correlative with the membership of any other. The society was polyethnic—composed of both monoethnic and polyethnic coresidence units. It is suggested that interethnic social organization can be interpreted on the basis of two independently varying criteria—ethnicity and coresidence. Based on these criteria, three forms of interrelationship are shown to have existed between the Cree and Assiniboine ethnic units: Early Alliance, Intermarriage and Polyethnic Coresidence, and Fused Ethnicity.   J

447. Shaw, P. C. I SAW THE LAST BRAVE. *Alberta Hist. [Canada] 1976 24(4): 28-29.* A pioneer reminiscence of a Blood ceremony in 1894 in which young Indian boys were converted into braves. Mentions medicine man, singing, dancing, and other rituals. The author's father was a dentist at Ft. Macleod near the Blood Agency. Illus.
D. Chaput

448. Sismey, Eric D. "SAUNAS" OF THE OKANAGAN INDIANS. *Can. Geographical J. 1973 87(3): 26-27.*

449. Slobodin, Richard. CANADIAN SUBARCTIC ATHAPAS-KANS IN THE LITERATURE TO 1965. *Can. R. of Sociol. and Anthrop. 1975 12(3): 278-289.* Reports on the fieldwork and literature of professional ethnographers of the Northern Athapaskan peoples, 1900-65.

450. Smith, Donald B. MAUNGWUDAUS GOES ABROAD. *Beaver [Canada] 1976 307(2): 4-9.* Tale of a Chippewa ex-seminarian turned theatrical manager who gathered a group of Ontario Chippewas in the 1840's and toured England and the Continent. They were associated with George Catlin for some time, and they gave special performances for royalty in France and England. Based mostly on a pamphlet published by Maungwudaus, known also as George Henry. One of the rare published versions of an American Indian reflecting on the life of man in Europe. 7 illus.   D. Chaput

451. Smith, Donald B. THE TRANSATLANTIC COURTSHIP OF THE REVEREND PETER JONES. *Beaver [Canada] 1977 308(1): 4-13.* Peter Jones, part Ojibwa, became a Methodist preacher in the 1820's and was successful in converting many of the Indians around Lake Ontario. In 1831 he was sent to England to solicit funds for the missions. He made more than 150 appearances, was successful, and met Eliza Field, daughter of a wealthy factory owner near London. She became interested in mission work, and in him. Jones proposed marriage, which she accepted, though her father resisted for some time. After consent was given, her father found out that Jones' father was still alive, and had two wives. Yet, in 1833, in New York, the couple was married. Based on Jones's accounts and recently discovered diaries kept by Eliza Field; 12 illus.
D. Chaput

452. Smith, Donald B. WHO ARE THE MISSISSAUGA? *Ontario Hist. [Canada] 1975 67(4): 211-222.* Discusses the impact and background of some late-17th-century tribal wars, and remarks on the subsequent changes in location and name. Against this background, attempts to identify the origins of the "Mississauga," and outlines the 18th-century history of tribes in the area in dispute between Britain and France during the early part of that century. Comments on 19th-century confusion of names, and concludes by claiming that the Mississauga of earlier days are the Chippewa of today. Based on primary sources; 81 notes.
W. B. Whitham

453. Smyly, John and Smyly, Carolyn. HAIDA TOTEMS: A SAL-VAGE OPERATION. *Beaver [Canada] 1975 305(4): 55-59.* In 1957 the last major totem pole rescue took place on Anthony Island, an isolated island in the Queen Charlotte group. Museum officials, with cooperation of the Canadian Navy, went to the island and removed the poles after receiving permission from the Indians. This presented many problems, as the poles weighed many tons and were often fifty feet high. Some poles were cut into sections, where carvings were either missing or not noticeable. The poles were crated, then shipped to Victoria. After a drying period, some restoration was done. Some of the totem poles are now on exhibit, and others will be shown in the future. 8 illus., map.
D. Chaput

454. Smyly, John and Smyly, Carolyn. KOONA: LIFE AND DEATH OF A HAIDA VILLAGE. *Am. West 1976 13(1): 14-19.* Traces the broad outlines of the history of Koona, a Haida Indian village, on Louise Island of the Queen Charlotte Island group off the coast of British Columbia. Utilizes totem poles and memorial carvings, archaeological evidence, surviving tribal legends, notations of anthropologists, and the few pictures made by pioneer photographers to describe the village. Koona flourished in the 1830's with upwards of 500 inhabitants, 27 houses, and 56 carved monuments. The village was abandoned about 1890. Adapted from a recent book; 6 illus.   D. L. Smith

455. Smyly, John. THE SHUSWAP KEKULI. *Beaver [Canada] 1973 303(4): 49-51.* Details the building of a replica *kekuli* or pit house at Shuswap Lake Park by the Provincial Museum staff members, with Isaac Willard, a Salish Indian, as consultant. The reconstruction was adequate, but Willard feels that the replica has too much of a teepee look, which was later modified by piling earth at the base of the mound. 6 illus.
D. Chaput

456. Song, Sunmin. ANTHROPOLOGY AND MYTH. *Indiana Social Studies Q. 1975/76 28(3): 8-23.* Surveys 20th-century anthropological approaches to myths, drawing on the "Story of Asdiwal, a myth of the Tsimshian Indians of the Northwest Coast."

457. Spindler, George D. and Spindler, Louise S. IDENTITY, MILITANCY, AND CULTURAL CONGRUENCE: THE MENOMINEE AND KAINAI. *Ann. of the Am. Acad. of Pol. and Social Sci. 1978 436: 73-85.* Recent movements of varying degrees of militancy on the part of American Indians can be better understood if we have a grasp of the kinds of adaptations Indians have made to the long-term and continuing confrontation with white culture, white power, and white world views. Native Americans do not constitute a single group. The Menominee are taken as an example of an Indian tribe with a hitherto unaggressive record that has recently engaged in militant activity. The diversity within the Menominee population is described in terms of four major types of long-standing adaptation that were observed as dominant in the 1950s and 1960s and that emerged some time before that. Recent militancy is regarded as a fifth type of adaptive response to the continuing confrontation between Menominee and white culture. Militancy is interpreted, in part, as an assertion of identity. The responses of the Kainai, the Blood Indians of Alberta, Canada, to white culture and power are contrasted briefly at certain critical points to demonstrate the fact of diversity among American Indians in regard to current actions and to reinforce the interpretation that the degree of difference in cultures and world views between Indian cultures and white culture is a significant factor in the kinds of adaptive response to confrontation native American groups have made and will make.   J

458. Stanbury, W. T. RESERVE AND URBAN INDIANS IN BRITISH COLUMBIA: A SOCIAL AND ECONOMIC PROFILE. *BC Studies [Canada] 1975 Summer (26): 39-64.* In 1971, a survey of Indians living off reserves in British Columbia was undertaken. The sample is used to develop socioeconomic characteristics such as age-sex composition, birth rates, dependency ratios, marital status, and housing. Comparisons are made with on reserve Indians. Primary and secondary sources; 63 notes.   W. L. Marr

459. Stone, Thomas. LEGAL MOBILIZATION AND LEGAL PENETRATION: THE DEPARTMENT OF INDIAN AFFAIRS AND THE CANADIAN PARTY AT ST. REGIS, 1876-1918. *Ethnohist. 1975 22(4): 375-408.* Cases of intra-community dispute taken to the Department of Indian Affairs from the Canadian Party of St. Regis Iroquois between 1876-1918 are analyzed for the light they shed on the relationship between the mobilization of external authority and the penetration of indigenous communities by external legal systems. In the St. Regis case, appeals to Indian Affairs in this period appear to have provided a way of softening the potential impact of external legal penetration during a time of crisis and division concerning legitimate authority within the community.   J

460. Strong, Emory. ENIGMA OF THE PHOENIX BUTTON. *Hist. Archaeol. 1975 9: 74-80.* Phoenix buttons which were produced for the uniforms of the army of King Christophe of Haiti became popular trade items for the Northwest Coast Indians around 1830. When found on archaeological sites, they serve as good time markers. Discussed in this paper are the origin, manufacture, and the method by which the buttons entered the Indian trade.   J

461. Thomas, Gregory. FIRE AND THE FUR TRADE: THE SASKATCHEWAN DISTRICT: 1790-1840. *Beaver [Canada] 1977 308(2): 32-39.* Indians caused many of the prairie fires, out of malice, to control direction of buffalo, and to increase the price of the provisions they provided the fur traders. After 1800, rival traders often caused prairie fires to hamper other companies. Although the Hudson's Bay Company had no written guide for fighting fires, each post reacted according to local conditions. They cleared rubbish, kept supplies of water on hand, and kept the grass down on adjacent areas. Impact of fires on the ecology is still uncertain, though it appears that what are now extensive prairies were once more heavily wooded. Based on Hudson's Bay Company files; 5 illus.   D. Chaput

462. Thompson, Arthur N. THE WIFE OF THE MISSIONARY. *J. of the Can. Church Hist. Soc. 1973 15(2): 35-44.* A study of the wives of early Anglican missionaries in the Canadian Red River settlement from 1820 to 1840. Born and reared in England, some complained bitterly about their new deprivations. Yet the wives vigorously supported their husbands' work. They bore many children, managed households, taught Sunday school classes, and taught in the missionary boarding schools and cared for the students who lived with them. Although some of the women were hostile to the Indians, most missionary wives treated Indians with warmth and visited them in their homes. In short, the missionaries' wives deserve much credit for their part in maintaining the influence of education and religion in the Red River area. Based on primary and secondary sources; 50 notes.   J. A. Kicklighter

463. Ticoll, David and Persky, Stan. WELCOME TO OTTAWA! THE NATIVE PEOPLES' CARAVAN. *Can. Dimension 1975 10(6): 14-31.* Describes the September 1974 protest march to Ottawa of the Native Peoples' Caravan, a militant Indian organization.   S

464. Unrau, William E. AN INTERNATIONAL PERSPECTIVE ON AMERICAN INDIAN POLICY: THE SOUTH AUSTRALIAN PROTECTOR AND ABORIGINES PROTECTION SOCIETY. *Pacific Hist. Rev. 1976 45(4): 519-538.* Adequate understanding of the United States' handling of its Amerindian problems can be gained only through a comparison with the very similar Canadian and Australian experiences. To this end one must study the strengths and weaknesses of the British initiated Aborigines Protection Society, founded in 1837 by British humanitarians, notably Thomas Fowell Buxton, Saxe Bannister, and Thomas Hodgkin, and must study the efforts of the Protector of Aborigines in Australia. In all cases, regardless of ideals and resounding rhetoric, the result was exploitation. 30 notes.   R. V. Ritter

465. Upton, L. F. S. COLONISTS AND MICMACS. *J. of Can. Studies 1975 10(3): 44-56.* Discusses colonization and the Christianization of Micmac Indians in Nova Scotia and New Brunswick during 1803-60.

466. Upton, L. F. S. THE EXTERMINATION OF THE BEOTHUCKS OF NEWFOUNDLAND. *Can. Hist. Rev. [Canada] 1977 58(2): 133-153.* The Beothuck population was eliminated during 1500-1848 as a result of European contact and expansion.

467. Upton, L. F. S. INDIAN POLICY IN COLONIAL NOVA SCOTIA 1783-1871. *Acadiensis [Canada] 1975 5(1): 3-31.* By 1783 Nova Scotia's Indians had become dispossessed wanderers attempting, with little success, to maintain a traditional way of life. Provincial authorities responsible for them classified them as indigent poor until 1800. Humanitarian interest led to the establishment of reserves by 1820, but whites encroached on them. The province denied the Indians the right to vote, and their numbers declined until the mid-19th century. By 1871 the federal government of Canada assumed total responsibility for them. 147 notes.   D. F. Chard

468. Upton, L. F. S. INDIANS AND ISLANDERS: THE MICMACS IN COLONIAL PRINCE EDWARD ISLAND. *Acadiensis [Canada] 1976 6(1): 21-42.* The French regime little affected Prince Edward Island's Indians, but English settlement restricted them by 1782. By 1800 the colony established several Indian families on 1,400 acre Lennox Island, but most lived elsewhere. By 1838 there were perhaps only 200 Indian residents. They hunted, sold handicrafts, and begged. The Assembly showed little concern for them. Several individuals during the 1830's-40's sought to improve their lot, but received little support. In the 1850's the Assembly appointed Indian commissioners and began providing relief. 71 notes.   D. F. Chard

469. Upton, L. F. S. THE ORIGINS OF CANADIAN INDIAN POLICY. *J. of Can. Studies 1973 8(4): 51-61.* Discusses the British Colonial Office's assimilationist Indian policy which eventually became Canadian Indian policy, 1760-1830.

470. Warner, John Anson. CONTEMPORARY ALGONKIAN LEGEND PAINTING. *Am. Indian Art Mag. 1978 3(3): 58-69, 76, 78-79.* Discusses legend painting among artists of the Cree and Chippewa Indians in Manitoba and Ontario, 1960's-70's.

471. Webber, Alika. WIGWAMATEW: OLD BIRCH BARK CONTAINERS. *Am. Indian Art Mag. 1978 4(1): 56-61.* Describes birch bark containers; they are still made by the Têtes de Boule Indians of Quebec, who call them wigwamatew; establishes the complex role of the birch tree in the history and legend of Indians of the northeastern states and eastern Canada.

472. Weinberger, Caspar, Jr. EDWARD S. CURTIS PORTRAYS CLASSIC IMAGES OF INDIANS. *Smithsonian 1975 6(1): 82-89.* Summarizes the photographic career of Edward S. Curtis (1868-1952) who made more than 40,000 photographs of the American Indian during 1906-27, financed by J. P. Morgan. These photographs were collected into the 21-volume *North American Indian*, of which 500 sets were planned but only approximately 300 were actually produced at a cost of nearly $l.5 million.   K. A. Harvey

473. Whyte, John D. THE LAVELL CASE AND EQUALITY IN CANADA. *Queen's Q. [Canada] 1974 81(1): 28-41.* Analyzes the controversial 1973 verdict by the Supreme Court of Canada in the Lavell case. The central issues in the case were "the legitimacy of administration of native peoples in Canada" and "the constitutional value of equality" of sexes. Feels the Supreme Court failed to resolve key points at issue and as a result "cast doubt on the Court's adequacy to perform this duty." 8 notes.   J. A. Casada

474. Wilson, J. Donald. "NO BLANKET TO BE WORN IN SCHOOL": THE EDUCATION OF INDIANS IN EARLY NINE-TEENTH-CENTURY ONTARIO. *Social Hist. [Canada] 1974 7(14): 293-305.* Prior to 1830, Indian schools in Ontario were under military authority. Their main aim was to keep Indian loyalty and prevent hostility. After 1830, when responsibility was shifted to civil governors, the civilizing of the Indians became the ideal. Efforts at teaching skilled trades also began. Church schools during the early 19th century sought to convert the Indians and to give them moral instruction, especially in temperance. Reports by those involved in Indian education show only partial acceptance by the Indians. Based on primary and secondary sources; 62 notes.   W. K. Hobson

475. Wilson, J. Donald. A NOTE ON THE SHINGWAUK INDUSTRIAL HOME FOR INDIANS. *J. of the Can. Church Hist. Soc. 1974 16(4): 66-71.* Describes the philosophies and operations of the Shingwauk Industrial Home for boys and the nearby Wawanosh Home for Indian Girls, both in the Sault Ste. Marie area. Shingwauk trained Indian boys primarily to be tradesmen, and Wawanosh instructed its students in how to perform all varieties of domestic duties. Both were based on the beliefs of E. F. Wilson, missionary-educator to the area (1871-93), who thought that Indians must be completely "amalgamated" into white society. Wilson emphasized the teaching of English and tried to keep the students away from their parents. Such paternalism was in part responsible for Indian alienation and frustration vis-à-vis Canadian society. Secondary and printed primary sources; illus., 20 notes.

J. A. Kicklighter

476. Yerbury, J. C. THE POST-CONTACT CHIPEWYAN: TRADE RIVALRIES AND CHANGING TERRITORIAL BOUND-ARIES. *Ethnohistory 1976 23(3): 237-263.* Discusses the history and culture of the Chipewyan Indians, and their hostile relations with the Cree Indians from the 1680's through the 18th century, in the eastern Mackenzie District and the Prairie Provinces.

4. PRE-COLUMBIAN EXPLORATION AND EXPLOITATION

The Norse Venture

477. Anderson, W. R. NORSEMEN IN MEDIEVAL AMERICA: AN APPRAISAL. *Inland Seas 1978 34(3): 190-199, 210.* Summarizes the evidence for Norse voyages to North America, about which "there is the greatest amount of misinformation." Illus. K. J. Bauer

478. Harmon, Julius Frasch, ed. CONCERNING THE CARVINGS ON THE BRAXTON AND YARMOUTH STONES. *West Virginia Hist. 1976 37(2): 133-139.* Using numerical notation, the author translates petroglyphs on the Braxton stone in West Virginia and the Yarmouth stones in Nova Scotia and suggests that the carvings were made by the same Scandinavians who left the Kensington stone in Minnesota in 1362. 3 illus., 3 tables, 3 notes. J. H. Broussard and S

479. Lee, Thomas E. THE NORSE PRESENCE IN ARCTIC UN-GAVA. *Am. Scandinavian R. 1973 61(3): 242-257.* Describes archaeological excavations in 1965 at two sites near Payne Lake in the center of the Ungava Peninsula in Arctic Quebec. The author believes the ruins are of European origin, probably Norse. He explored the Payne River to the coast with an Eskimo guide and the coast of Ungava Bay as far as 300 miles north into Hudson Strait. He saw great stone beacons and longhouse ruins along some 70 miles of the coast. He believes a stone monument on the Payne River represents the Hammer of Thor. Several longhouses on Pamiok Island just north of Payne Bay were excavated. The description of the largest ruin shows that it was of Norse origin. The author believes that the Saga of Arrow Odd was written about these settlements and that Ögmund lived in the great longhouse and ruled the kingdom of Skuggifjördur on the Ungava Peninsula. Map, 9 photos. J. G. Smoot

480. Lindsay, Charles. WAS L'ANSE AUX MEADOWS A NORSE OUTPOST? *Can. Geographical J. 1977 94(1): 36-43.* Discusses archaeological diggings going on in L'Anse aux Meadows, Newfoundland, where it is believed Vikings had a settlement around 1000.

481. Nitkin, Nathaniel. VIKING NEW ENGLAND. *New-England Galaxy 1976 17(4): 40-45.* Traces the settlements of Vikings in Newfoundland around 1000 A.D. and Viking explorations in Maine and Massachusetts. Runestones found in these areas provide archeological evidence of their presence as early as 986 A.D. Other evidence includes Indian use of Icelandic numerals and sails similar to those of the Vikings. 2 illus., map. P. C. Marshall

482. Seifert, Traudl. DE VINLANDKAART [The Vinland map]. *Spiegel Hist. [Netherlands] 1975 10(3): 138-144.* The so-called Vinland map was found in 1957 and seemed to prove that the Vikings had rather extensive knowledge of the East coast of North America during the second half of the 15th century. The author provides an account of the successful efforts made by various scholars to demonstrate that this map was a forgery. Illus., biblio. G. D. Homan

483. Sullivan, Clare D. and Johnson, Paul E. VIKING TRAILS ALONG AMERICA'S EAST COAST. *Scandinavian Rev. 1976 64(1): 4-15.* Reviews the Norse saga about discoveries beyond Iceland and Greenland in North America. Describes various sites. Photos, maps, biblio. J. G. Smoot

484. Wallis, Helen, et al. THE STRANGE CASE OF THE VINLAND MAP. *Geographical J. [Great Britain] 1974 140(2): 183-214.* "This series of papers comprises contributions to the Symposium on the Vinland Map held at the Royal Geographical Society on 4 February 1974. The Symposium considered the circumstances leading to the publication of the Vinland Map in 1965 and the arguments for and against its authenticity. Physical tests had shown that the ink of the Map was not only unlike that of other seemingly comparable medieval documents but contained a pigment not known to have been available before 1917 at the earliest. The Map did not appear to fit into the framework of medieval cartography as conceived in Western Europe; an early twentieth-century source was suggested. Doubt was also cast (for linguistic reasons) on the alleged date of the *Tartar Relation* with which the Map had been bound and was associated. On the other hand it was argued that the internal evidence for a medieval origin for the Map was so overwhelming that some explanation of the physical evidence consistent with authenticity was bound ultimately to be forthcoming. Reference was made to the Map's interest (if genuine) for the history of geographical ideas. A reconstruction of a possible forgery was also attempted. The Map's importance, however, in relation to the Norse discovery of America was shown to have been grossly exaggerated. In this respect the publicity it had attracted had been particularly misleading." J

European Exploration

485. Herold, David. SAMUEL ELIOT MORISON AND THE OCEAN SEA. *Dalhousie R. [Canada] 1974/75 54(4): 741-748.* Compares Morison to Francis Parkman through Morison's use of "imaginative field work" in sailing the same routes as early explorers. Deals with aspects of Morison's *Admiral of the Ocean Sea* (1942), *The Two-Ocean War* (1963), *Vistas of History* (1964), *The European Discovery of America: Northern Voyages* (1971), *By Land and Sea* (1953), and *Maritime History of Massachusetts: 1783-1860* (1921). 29 notes. C. Held

486. Hubbard, Jake T. W. JOHN CABOT'S LANDFALL: CAPE DEGRAT OR CAPE BONAVISTA? SOME OBSERVATIONS. *Am. Neptune 1973 33(3): 174-177.* Analyzes the significance of a recently discovered letter written by John Day to Christopher Columbus (1446?-1506) in the winter of 1497-98 describing John Cabot's (1451?-99) first voyage in 1497. Samuel Eliot Morison in his *The European Discovery of America, the Northern Voyages, A.D. 500-1600* (New York: Oxford U. Press, 1971) claims that the letter supports Cape Dégrat, northern Newfoundland, as the place of his landfall; but when analyzed in the light of practical sailing conditions, the letter points in a different direction. Contends that Cabot's route culminated in a North American landfall somewhere near Cape Bonavista. Cabot then explored nearby Trinity Bay, and landed somewhere close by the isthmus joining the Avalon peninsula to the rest of Newfoundland. From here he cruised northward along the coastline, taking off for home when he had reached a point with the same latitude as Cape Dursey, Ireland (Cape Dégrat). 8 notes.
R. V. Ritter

487. McGhee, Robert and Tuck, James. DID THE MEDIEVAL IRISH VISIT NEWFOUNDLAND? *Can. Geographical J. [Canada] 1977 94(3): 66-73.* The authors have discovered, near the northern tip of Newfoundland, an inscription on the St. Lunaire boulder. The characters resemble not the Roman alphabet or Indian markings but the ogham alphabet used in pre- and early Christian Ireland. Mentions popular interest in this discovery. Recounts the sixth-century voyage of St. Brendan the Navigator, and Norse voyages. Concludes that the inscription is inexplicable but that apparently it was carved hundreds of years ago with European tools by someone familiar with European alphabets. 11 illus.
D. J. Engler

488. Schomp, Gerald. ST. BRENDAN'S FANTASTIC VOYAGE. *Am. Hist. Illus. 1977 12(1): 22-27.* Discusses an expedition in progress, 1976-77, which intends to retrace the hypothetical voyage of St. Brendan the Navigator, an Irish monk who some feel discovered the New World some 900 years before Columbus; discusses that voyage and others from Ireland.

5. NEW FRANCE, 16TH CENTURY-1763

General

489. Angers, François-Albert. LIONEL GROULX, NOTRE LIB-ÉRATEUR [Lionel Groulx, our liberator]. *Action Natl. [Canada] 1978 67(9): 697-709.* Lionel Groulx, the foremost historian of French Canada, may be compared to Gandhi in his devotion to the achievement of national autonomy by nonviolence. Quebec nationalism had been checked by the repercussions of the rebellions of 1837, and Quebecois saw themselves as an ethnic minority in an Anglicized nation. Groulx helped establish the journal *Action Française* in 1917, signalling the renaissance of a national spirit directly antecedent to contemporary separatism, and a departure from the Bourassa tradition which sought protection of minority rights in the context of confederation. Paper presented at a conference in Quebec on 21 January 1978 commemorating the centenary of Groulx's birth. A. W. Novitsky

490. Blain, Jean. ÉCONOMIE ET SOCIÉTÉ EN NOUVELLE-FRANCE: L'HISTORIOGRAPHIE DES ANNÉES 1950-1960—GUY FRÉGAULT ET L'ÉCOLE DE MONTRÉAL [Economy and society in New France: Historiography during 1950-60—Guy Frégault and the school of Montreal]. *Rev. d'Hist. de l'Amérique Française [Canada] 1974 28(2): 163-186.* The study of history in Montreal after 1950 became more scientific thanks to the work of Guy Frégault.

491. Blain, Jean. ÉCONOMIE ET SOCIÉTÉ EN NOUVELLE-FRANCE: L'HISTORIOGRAPHIE AU TOURNANT DES ANNÉES 1960 [Economy and society in New France: historiography at the beginning of the 1960's]. *Rev. d'Hist. de l'Amérique Française [Canada] 1976 30(3): 323-362.* In 1957, Guy Frégault wrote that the period of French colonial rule was not Canada's golden age, but only a normal evolutionary period. A contemporary, Marcel Rioux, also identified the minority status of the French Canadians, Roman Catholicism, and the French language as the basic forces contributing to a romanticization of the French colonial period. Writers such as Frégault and Rioux distinguished between social history and nationalistic history, and along with others of the Montreal school helped to rejuvenate French Canadian historiography. Secondary works; 124 notes. L. B. Chan

492. Chard, Donald F. CANSO, 1710-1721: FOCAL POINT OF NEW ENGLAND-CAPE BRETON RIVALRY. *Nova Scotia Hist. Soc. Collections [Canada] 1977 39: 49-77.* The pivotal geographical location of Canso rendered it vital in the establishment of attitudes of officials in Great Britain, France, and New England. New England's problem was "to ensure the effective control of the area without disrupting trade with Cape Breton, or the entente which developed between France and Britain" after 1710. New England representatives such as Cyprian Southack sought to defend Canso as the gateway to the French Colony and to insure that the delineation of imperial policy insofar as the French in Acadia (Nova Scotia) were concerned took place in Canso and in Boston. In short, the establishment of colonial-imperial policy by New Englanders for their own ends was aided and abetted (in ignorance) by the British officials. Based on the *Calendar of State Papers, Colonial Series; Public Archives of Nova Scotia papers; Colonial Office Papers,* and secondary sources; 107 notes. E. A. Chard

493. Durrell, Harold Clarke and Dearborn, David Curtis. PHILIP[1] DURRELL AND HIS DESCENDANTS. *New England Hist. and Geneal. Register 1978 132(Apr): 115-122, 132 (Oct): 264-277; 1979 133 (Jan): 40-48.* Part I. The 204 page unindexed notebook of Harold Clarke Durrell (1882-1943) is a detailed history of the Durrell family of New Hampshire and Maine. Philip is believed to have come from Guernsey around 1689. Indians attacked his family in 1703 and 1726. Several children were carried off to Canada and his wife was killed in the second attack. Philip's dates are unknown as is the identity of his wife, who bore him eleven children. Part II. Covers descendants of Philip Durrell in the second and third generations. Part III. Covers five descendants in the third generation. Article to be continued. A. E. Huff/S

494. Miron, Gaston. ROBERT-LIONEL SÉGUIN, HISTORIEN DE L'IDENTITÉ ET DE L'APPARTENANCE [Robert-Lionel Seguin, historian of identity and roots]. *Action Natl. [Canada] 1976 65(8): 539-546.* Robert-Lionel Séguin, historian, ethnologist and professor, has devoted his life to the explication of French Canadian identity in over 200 articles and 17 books, including *La civilisation traditionelle de "l'Habitant" aux 17ᵉ et 18ᵉ siècles* (1972) and *L'injure en Nouvelle-France* (1975). He founded and directs the Centre de documentation en civilisation traditionelle at the University of Quebec at Trois-Rivières. Adapted from a speech given 9 February 1975. A. W. Novitsky

495. Monet, Jacques. COMNAUNAUTÉ ET CONTINUITÉ: VERS UN NOUVEAU PASSÉ [Community and continuity: toward a new past]. *Can. Hist. Assoc. Hist. Papers [Canada] 1976: 1-11.* Quebec's approach to the gradual transformation of her *ancien regime* has been incorporated in the original experience of Canada among New World republics based on revolution. Having concentrated on the study of their particular past, French Canadian historians have much to learn from and to contribute to the history of their neighbors. By providing them with a new past, Quebec's historians will have changed their present and future as well. G. E. Panting

496. Monière, Denis. L'UTILITÉ DU CONCEPT DE MODE DE PRODUCTION DES PETITS PRODUCTEURS POUR L'HISTORIOGRAPHIE DE LA NOUVELLE-FRANCE [The utility of the concept of mode of production of the small producers for the historiography of New France]. *Rev. d'Hist. de l'Amérique Française [Canada] 1976 29(4): 483-502.* The concept of "mode of production of the small producers" is applicable to New France, and helps to describe the complexity of the transition process from feudalism to capitalism under colonialism. The theory regarding the destruction of the Canadian colonial bourgeoisie and its replacement by an English bourgeoisie, by itself, cannot explain adequately the formation of Canadian society after 1760. The MPSP concept clarifies the importance of the petty bourgeoisie in the historical development of Quebec's society. Based on secondary works; 28 notes. L. B. Chan

497. Moodie, D. W. GARDENING ON HUDSON BAY: THE FIRST CENTURY. *Beaver [Canada] 1978 309(1): 54-59.* Due to climate and soil, the Hudson's Bay Company never tried to be self-sufficient in garden crops but wished to supplement the local game and the food sent from England. Although there was much experimentation over the years, it never led to large-scale production. However, the vegetables grown locally broke the monotony of Company tables, and helped in controlling scurvy. 4 illus. D. Chaput

498. Oppen, William A. HOW EARLY MAPS PORTRAYED NORTH AMERICA. *Can. Geographical J. 1975 90(2): 30-35.*

499. Pilgrim, Donald G. FRANCE AND NEW FRANCE: TWO PERSPECTIVES ON COLONIAL SECURITY. *Can. Hist. Rev. [Canada] 1974 55(4): 381-407.* A critique of the theses of William J. Eccles in his *Canada under Louis XIV, 1663-1701* (Toronto, 1964) and *Frontenac: The Courtier Governor* (Toronto, 1962) in explanation of France's claimed neglect of New France. Eccles exaggerated the degree of neglect of the Marquis de Seignelay's (1651-90) administration, has given an unbalanced portrait of the secretary of state himself, and his analysis is incomplete, being "based on a conceptual framework which does not take into account the multitude of factors and considerations which determined French foreign policy during the 1680's." His interpretation overemphasizes New France's isolation. 89 notes.

R. V. Ritter

500. Reck, W. Emerson. FOR THE BLESSINGS OF THE YEAR. *Am. Hist. Illus. 1977 12(7): 4-7, 44-46.* The pilgrims were not the first celebrants of Thanksgiving. Martin Frobisher held the first celebration in North America on 27 May 1578 in Newfoundland. English Captain George Popham held the first celebration in the United States on 9 August 1607 near Phippsburg, Maine. Discusses noteworthy Thanksgiv-

ing celebrations held by English Captain John Woodlief at the Berkeley Plantation in Charles City County, Virginia, on 4 December 1619, the famous celebration at Plymouth in 1621, the Second Continental Congress' celebration on 18 December 1777, and George Washington's celebrations on 26 November 1789 and 19 February 1795. Abraham Lincoln established the last Thursday in November as Thanksgiving Day in 1863 after a sustained campaign by Sarah J. Hale, editor of *Ladies' Magazine* (later *Godey's Lady's Book),* 1828-63. Primary and secondary sources; 6 illus.   D. Dodd

501. Reid, John G. THE SCOTS CROWN AND THE RESTITUTION OF PORT ROYAL, 1629-1632. *Acadiensis [Canada] 1977 6(2): 39-63.* Several historians have accused Charles I of stupidity or duplicity in returning Port Royal to France in 1632. Yet Charles sought arguments to justify retention, and asserted Scotland's claim at some length. But the issue threatened to jeopardize peace, as France insisted on restitution. Scotland agreed to withdraw, while maintaining its claims. French reoccupation and Scottish lack of capital then rendered Scotland's claims futile, and dealt a death-blow to Scottish colonization in North America. 95 notes.   D. F. Chard

502. Rich, E. E. THE COLONY OF RUPERT'S LAND. *Beaver [Canada] 1978 309(1): 4-12.* The Hudson's Bay Company charter of 1670 allowed for colonization rights; however, trade was the primary aim of the company. Only a few individuals can be considered settlers: the family of Governor Henry Sergeant and a few servants. The nonexistent "colony" was the result of publicity given by Daniel Defoe. He interviewed the governor after his defeat, capture by the French, and return to English control. Unfortunately, Defoe used Sergeant's confused, garbled account instead of interviewing other survivors. Based on Hudson's Bay Company documents. 6 illus., map.   D. Chaput

503. Rich, E. E. THE PERPETUAL GOVERNOR. *Beaver [Canada] 1974 305(2): 18-22.* Sir Bibye Lake for 31 years (1712-43) was the Governor of the Hudson's Bay Company, and has become known as the "Perpetual Governor." Under Lake, the company was able to offer its first dividend, survive a price drop in furs, and issue new stock to aid its investors during an economic slump. 4 illus.   D. Heermans

504. Stauffer, Anne Tholen. THE FRENCH-AMERICANS AND THE FRENCH-CANADIANS: A SELECT BIBLIOGRAPHY OF MATERIALS IN THE LIBRARY OF THE VERMONT HISTORICAL SOCIETY. *Vermont Hist. 1976 44(2): 110-114.* Includes 30 titles on Quebec, 7 on Samuel de Champlain, 10 on New England, 14 on Vermont, 4 periodicals, 3 maps, and 2 genealogies.
                                                            T. D. S. Bassett

Exploration

505. Goodman, Elizabeth B. HE FOUNDED THE FIRST "NEW ENGLAND." *Am. West 1976 13(1): 4-13.* The 1577-80 navigation of the globe by Sir Francis Drake (1540?-96) took him along the Pacific coast of North America, possibly as far north as British Columbia. In 1579 he spent five weeks in a California harbor somewhere on or near San Francisco Bay for careening and repairing his ship, the *Golden Hinde.* Discusses the evidence and continuing controversy over the precise location of Drake's Nova Albion. 8 illus., map, biblio.   D. L. Smith

506. Gridgeman, N. T. CHAMPLAIN'S ASTROLABE RE-EXAMINED. *Can. Geographical J. 1977 94(1): 24-27.* Examines facts surrounding Samuel de Champlain's 1613 inland exploration of Canada, especially the contested fact of whether he actually employed the Cobden astrolabe (1603) during this time.

507. Smith, Ralph. ST. CROIX ISLAND. *Beaver [Canada] 1978 308(4): 36-40.* St. Croix Island, only a few hundred yards long, is in the St. Croix River, Maine, close to St. Andrews, New Brunswick. In 1604 this island was discovered by Pierre du Gua, Sieur de Monts, and Samuel de Champlain. The site was abandoned in 1605, but while it was in use the Frenchmen erected a fort accommodating 80 men. The US National Park Service has conducted excavations, and considerable pottery and other materials dating from the early 1600's have been located. 7 illus.
                                                            D. Chaput

508. Vigneras, L.-A. THE VOYAGES OF DIOGO AND MANOEL DE BARCELOS TO CANADA IN THE SIXTEENTH CENTURY. *Terrae Incognitae [Netherlands] 1973 5: 61-64.* Reviews the research of Manuel C. Baptista de Lima, on the discovery of Canadian islands by the Pinheiro family of Barcelos, Terceira. The exploration continued for two generations; Diogo and his son Manoel made several voyages to Canada, 1521-68. They claimed for Portugal land scattered on and off shore at Cape Breton, the Gulf of the St. Lawrence, and southern Labrador. European entanglements prevented Portugal from colonizing the area. Based on primary and secondary sources; 14 notes.
                                                            C. B. Fitzgerald

Colonization and Settlement

509. Charbonneau, Hubert. RECONSTITUTION DE LA POPULATION DU CANADA AU 30 JUIN 1663 SUIVANT MARCEL TRUDEL [The reconstitution of the population of Canada on 30 June 1663 according to Marcel Trudel]. *R. d'Hist. de l'Amérique Française [Canada] 1973 27(3): 417-424.* Marcel Trudel's *La population du Canada en 1663* (Montreal: les Editions Fides, 1973) is representative of a new approach to demographic history based on numerous archival manuscripts and printed materials.

510. Dechêne, Louise. LA CROISSANCE DE MONTRÉAL AU XVIIIᵉ SIÈCLE [The growth of Montreal in the 18th century]. *R. d'Hist. de l'Amérique Française [Canada] 1973 27(2): 163-180.* In spite of the proportionately large number of people inhabiting the cities of New France in the 18th century, the population of the cities did not tend to increase during this period at a significantly higher rate than that of the countryside.

511. Hynes, Gisa I. SOME ASPECTS OF THE DEMOGRAPHY OF PORT ROYAL, 1650-1755. *Acadiensis [Canada] 1973 3(1): 3-17.* Emphasizes immigration to Port Royal, Nova Scotia, from France.

512. Kleber, Louis C. BRITAIN AND FRANCE IN NORTH AMERICA. *Hist. Today [Great Britain] 1971 31(12): 819-826.* Discusses the variant natures of British and French colonization in North America and traces developments up to the capitulation of New France to the British in 1760.

513. Klingelhofer, Eric. THREE LOST CERAMIC ARTIFACTS FROM FROBISHER'S COLONY, 1578. *Hist. Archaeol. 1976 10: 131-134.* In 1578 the Elizabethan explorer, Martin Frobisher, attempted to establish a permanent colony in northern Canada. It was an immediate failure, and all 100 colonists returned to England with Frobisher the same year. The site of the colony was discovered in 1862 by the Arctic explorer, Charles Francis Hall, who brought back to the United States a group of artifacts from the site. All the items have since been lost, but an inventory and a drawing from Hall's records have survived. Based on these sources, three ceramic artifacts are discussed, and their possible identifications are suggested.   J

514. Légaré, Jacques; La Rose, André; and Roy, Raymond. RECONSTITUTION OF THE 17TH CENTURY CANADIAN POPULATION: AN OVERVIEW OF A RESEARCH PROGRAM. *Hist. Methods Newsletter 1975 9(1): 1-8.* Using parish registers and the censuses of 1666, 1667, and 1681 as data, the authors outline their methodology, which uses particulary the Henry Code. They believe that their work has merit for both demographers and historians.   D. K. Pickens

515. Moon, Robert. RESTORING 17TH CENTURY LOWER TOWN QUEBEC. *Can. Geographical J. 1975 91(3): 38-45.* Describes the historic restoration of 17th-century buildings in Lower Town Place Royale, Quebec.   S

Indian Relations

516. Conkling, Robert. LEGITIMACY AND CONVERSION IN SOCIAL CHANGE: THE CASE OF FRENCH MISSIONARIES AND THE NORTHEASTERN ALGONKIAN. *Ethnohist. 1974 21(1): 1-24.* Between 1610 and 1750 the Northeastern Algonkian in Maine and the Maritime provinces experienced charismatic political and religious innovations, which were initiated and directed by the French missionaries in the vacuum left by the disintegration of some native social forms. In line with their recognized charismatic authority, the missionaries were able to persuade the Indians to accept new forms of organization and belief and to generate a considerable number of conversions. The legitimacy of the missionaries' domination in Indian affairs, not just their domination per se, played an important role in these changes. The Indians voluntarily accepted the missionaries' introduction of more intensive, external regulation and, through a kind of empiricism analogous to that of science, judged some of their own ideas to be less useful, and therefore inferior, to the new Christian ideas. J

517. Garrad, Charles. THE ATTACK ON EHWAE IN 1640. *Ontario Hist. [Canada] 1973 65(2): 107-111.* The exact sequence of events in the 1640 battle at Ehwae is unclear. Suggests that the attack was a minor raid by a small band of Seneca Indians. 6 notes.
W. B. Whitham

518. Goulding, Stuart D. FRANCIS PARKMAN AND THE JESUITS. *Hist. Today [Great Britain] 1974 24(1): 22-31.* Gives biographical data on historian Francis Parkman (1823-93) and discusses his treatment of 17th-century Jesuit missionaries in *The Conspiracy of Pontiac: Pioneers of New France in the New World* (1865) and *Jesuits* (1867).

519. Jaenen, Cornelius J. AMERINDIAN VIEWS OF FRENCH CULTURE IN THE SEVENTEENTH CENTURY. *Can. Hist. R. [Canada] 1974 55(3): 261-291.* Examines the traditional interpretation that the Amerindians admired French civilization and welcomed policies of Christianization and assimilation. Despite the paucity of Amerindian sources, there is evidence to indicate selective adaptation of some European technology and cultural patterns, outright rejection of much of French culture and belief systems, development of counter-innovative devices and behaviour, and maintenance of native convictions of superiority to European life-style. Based on French travel literature and unpublished archival materials. S

520. Morrison, Kenneth M. NATIVE AMERICAN HISTORY: THE ISSUE OF VALUES (REVIEW ESSAY). *J. of Ethnic Studies 1978 5(4): 80-89.* Analyzes Cornelius Jaenen's *Friend and Foe: Aspects of French-Amerindian Cultural Contact in the Sixteenth and Seventeenth Centuries* (1976), and Bruce Trigger's *The Children of Aataentsic: A History of the Huron People to 1660* (1976). Both add important new dimensions to Indian history by focusing on Native American values and their relation to ordering intercultural relations, but Trigger is far more successful in explaining the experience of particular Indian peoples at specific times. Jaenen focuses on the French and their ideological postures, and thus does not appreciate the ordered nature of tribal life and repeated Indian rejections of French policies. Trigger is a truer ethnohistorian, who reassesses each stage of Huron history in light of its own values and shows that direct contact with the French "did not alter the direction or nature of cultural change." Internal disunity, as much as Iroquoian aggressions, led to the Hurons' collapse. 4 notes.
G. J. Bobango

521. Porter, John D. THE CALVARY AT OKA. *Beaver [Canada] 1975 305(4): 18-21.* The village of Oka, a few miles from Montreal, was founded in the early 1700's to accommodate various Iroquois and Algonkin groups. The Sulpician missionaries had a definite assignment: to introduce Christianity to the Indians and convert as many as possible. During 1740-42 the Calvary was constructed, consisting of three chapels, three crosses, and four small oratories. Christian paintings, based on prominent European works, were placed in each of the buildings and were used as instructional devices. The Calvary remains in good condition, a remarkable historic site. 5 illus., map.
D. Chaput

522. Pritchard, James S. FOR THE GLORY OF GOD: THE QUINTE MISSION, 1668-1680. *Ontario History [Canada] 1973 65(3): 133-148.* Describes the first major Sulpician mission to the Iroquois Indians. Argues that the mission failed due to a complex of reasons including the fitness of the missionaries, dissent within the order, changing conditions among the Indians, and the erection of Fort Frontenac. This last is viewed as less important than it has been seen in the past. 70 notes.
W. B. Whitham

523. Schlesier, Karl H. EPIDEMICS AND INDIAN MIDDLEMEN: RETHINKING *THE WARS OF THE IROQUOIS*, 1609-1653. *Ethnohistory 1976 23(2): 129-146.* In discussions of historians and ethnohistorians, George T. Hunt's book, *The Wars of the Iroquois*, continues to loom prominently. His interpretation of events in northeastern North America during the seventeenth century, which proposed that the Iroquois fought the French colonials and French-dominated tribes for economic reasons, is widely accepted. This paper re-examines the period. It finds, contrary to Hunt and his followers, that the Iroquois did not fight for economic causes, and that the destruction or dispersal of many tribes around the middle of the seventeenth century did not result from the fur trade. A new look at the period reveals a set of forces destructive to tribes from Quebec to Wisconsin, including the Iroquois. Smallpox emerges as the most significant among those forces. This paper suggests that much of the historical and ethnohistorical literature before and after Hunt propounds biases which not only do injustice to the Iroquois, but prevent a deeper understanding of the historical truth. J

Society

524. Belliveau, J. E. THE ACADIAN FRENCH AND THEIR LANGUAGE. *Can. Geographical J. [Canada] 1977 95(2): 46-55.* Discusses the Acadian presence in Canada (especially the Maritime Provinces), 1605-1800, and the enforced migration of many of the group, 1755-67, because of the outbreak of hostilities between Britain and France.

525. Blain, Jean. LA MORALITÉ EN NOUVELLE-FRANCE: LES PHASES DE LA THÈSE ET DE L'ANTITHÈSE [Morality in New France: thesis and antithesis]. *R. d'Hist. de l'Amérique Française [Canada] 1973 27(3): 408-416.* Examines the historiographical problem of conveying an accurate sense of the life of New France in the 17th and 18th centuries and finds a scientific analysis of the society's morals inadequate.

526. Bouchard, Gérard and La Rose, André. LA RÉGLEMENTATION DU CONTENU DES ACTES DE BAPTÊME, MARIAGE, SÉPULTURE, AU QUÉBEC, DES ORIGINES À NOS JOURS [Regulation of the contents of the acts of baptism, marriage, and burial in Quebec from the beginning to our day]. *Rev. d'Hist. de l'Am. Française [Canada] 1976 30(1): 67-77.* From the 16th century to the present, both the Church and the state have been concerned with registering baptisms, marriages, and burials. Church regulation of these practices has always been more detailed than that of the state. Vicars have been recording performances of these acts, and the state has benefited from such assistance. Based on published Church and state documents and secondary works; 6 tables, 37 notes.
L. B. Chan

527. Charbonneau, Hubert. RÉFLEXIONS EN MARGE D'HABITANTS ET MARCHANDS DE MONTRÉAL DE LOUISE DECHÊNE [Marginal reflections about *Inhabitants and Merchants of Montréal*, by Louise Dechêne]. *Rev. d'Hist. de l'Am. Française [Canada] 1976 30(2): 263-269.* Reviews Louise Dechêne's *Habitants et marchands de Montréal au XVIIᵉ siècle* (Paris, 1974) in light of Hubert Charbonneau's *Vie et mort des nos ancêtres* (Montréal, 1975). Discusses migrations, births, deaths, and family structures in Québec, Trois-Rivières, and Montréal between 1660 and 1713. Secondary works; 14 notes.
L. B. Chan

528. D'Allaire, Micheline. LES INVENTAIRES DES BIENS DE DENIS-JOSEPH RUETTE D'AUTEUIL [Inventories of Denis-Joseph Ruette d'Auteuil's property]. *Rev. de l'U. d'Ottawa [Canada] 1977 47(1-2): 36-45.* The inventory of an estate, besides establishing an individual's financial situation, may reveal the vicissitudes of his life and

career. A comparative analysis of an evaluation of Quebec's Denis-Joseph Ruette d'Auteuil's property following his separation from his wife (1661), and an inventory of his estate at his death (1680), shows an important deterioration of his fortune and discloses the difficulties born from his matrimonial separation. Primary and secondary sources; 26 notes.

G. P. Cleyet

529. Krause, Eric R. PRIVATE BUILDINGS IN LOUISBOURG, 1713-1758. *Can.: An Hist. Mag. 1974 1(4): 47-59.* Discusses the family and business buildings in Louisbourg. One of five articles in this issue on the National Historic Park at Louisbourg. S

530. Lachance, André. LA DÉSERTION ET LES SOLDATS DÉSERTEURS AU CANADA DANS LA PREMIÈRE MOITIÉ DU XVIIIᵉ SIÈCLE [Desertion and soldiers who deserted in Canada in the first half of the 18th century]. *Rev. de l'U. d'Ottawa [Canada] 1977 47(1-2): 151-161.* Military desertions were frequent in New France; soldiers deserted most often because of the fear of getting caught after committing a misdemeanor, on account of unfriendly relations with their officers, or because of a decision made while being drunk. They usually chose the summer months for running away, were 20-24 years old, of varied appearance and good size. They were rarely caught because the environment was favorable to hiding and they had help from the country people. The most frequent punishment was the death penalty. Primary and secondary sources; 4 tables, 50 notes. G. P. Cleyet

531. Lachance, André. UNE ÉTUDE DE MENTALITÉ: LE IN-JURES VERBALE AU CANADA AU XVIIIes SIECLE (1712-1748) [A study of mental attitudes: verbal abuse in Canada in the eighteenth century (1712-1748)]. *Rev. D'Hist. De L'Amérique Française [Canada] 1977 31(2): 229-238.* Judicial records reveal a significant number of cases involving slander, defamation, and other verbal indignities in French Canadian society. Neighborhood women, for example, might question each other's morality; an intoxicated card player might accuse another of cheating. The various "insults" of that era provide a unique view of the contemporary social fabric and strongly suggest that French Canadians placed great emphasis on maintaining their honor and their reputations. 26 notes. M. R. Yerburgh

532. McNally, Paul. TABLE GLASS FROM THE WRECK OF THE *MACHAULT*. *Can. Hist. Sites [Canada] 1977 (16): 35-44.* Table glass from the 1760 French wreck of the *Machault* included a large number of French wine glasses, one French tumbler, and eight English wine glasses. The presence of English glass is presumably indicative of English leadership in the glass industry of the third quarter of the 18th century. Despite the critical situation of Montreal in 1760, the wealthiest citizens of that town apparently still had a desire for relatively fine table wares and the power to have them sent from France. Also, the presence of table glass on a relief ship might indicate that France did not think it was in danger of losing New France permanently. J

533. Moogk, Peter N. IN THE DARKNESS OF A BASEMENT: CRAFTSMEN'S ASSOCIATIONS IN EARLY FRENCH CANADA. *Can. Hist. Rev. [Canada] 1976 57(4): 399-439.* Provides an historical explanation for the scarcity of self-constituted, secular associations among the French Canadians in Quebec before the First World War. The failure of the colonists to transplant the corporate traditions of old France to North America is attributed to the Bourbon administration's hostility to private and unsanctioned groups and gatherings and to the colonists' preoccupation with self-employment and family autonomy. The government attitude is evident from the history of three artisans' religious brotherhoods and a shipwright's strike. The colonists' values are shown by the number and nature of partnerships and journeymen's indentures among craftsmen. Based on the administrative, judicial, and notarial records of New France. A

534. Moogk, Peter N. RANK IN NEW FRANCE: RECON-STRUCTING A SOCIETY FROM NOTARIAL DOCUMENTS. *Social Hist. [Canada] 1975 8(15): 34-53.* The social status of occupations in New France closely paralleled the social status of occupations in France but the hierarchy of occupations did not correlate so closely with wealth in New France as it did in France. Requirements of rank led those in high social standing to conspicuous consumption no matter what their relative wealth, whereas those in low social standing could save. The

wealth hierarchy was reconstructed from estate inventories; the social status hierarchy was reconstructed from marriage contracts. Based on documents in Archives Nationales de France, archives judicaires de Montréal, archives de Québec, archives judicaires de Trois-Rivières, and secondary sources; 2 tables, 38 notes. W. K. Hobson

535. Moogk, Peter N. RÉEXAMEN DE L'ÉCOLE DES ARTS ET MÉTIERS DE SAINT-JOACHIM [Another look at the School of Arts and Crafts of St. Joachim]. *R. d'Hist. de l'Amérique Française 1975 29(1): 3-29.* Reexamines historian Auguste-Honoré Gosselin's study of the School of Arts and Crafts of St. Joachim (New France). Gosselin attributed creation of the school to Bishop François de Laval (ca. 1668) and supposed it an extension of the Petit Séminaire of Quebec. The St. Joachim school, an alternative to traditional apprenticeship, lacked the structure and importance of a modern technical school. Translation of article in English based on primary and secondary sources; 68 notes.

C. Collon

536. Morel, André. RÉFLEXIONS SUR LA JUSTICE CRIMI-NELLE CANADIENNE, AU 18ᵉ SIÈCLE [Reflections on Canadian criminal justice, in the 18th century]. *Rev. d'Hist. de l'Amérique Française [Canada] 1975 29(2): 241-253.* The great severity of justice can be an indication of the real values which people strove to protect. Banishment was the punishment invariably retained during the 17th century for all crimes except rape; in the 18th century, it was only enforced against adulterous men. Secondary works, 2 tables, 13 notes. L. B. Chan

537. Morgan, Robert J. and MacLean, Terrence D. SOCIAL STRUCTURE AND LIFE IN LOUISBOURG. *Can.: An Hist. Mag. 1974 1(4): 60-75* Social classes and daily life of the inhabitants of Louisbourg, 1713-50. One of five articles in this issue on the National Historic Park at Louisbourg. S

538. Ouellet, Fernand. PROPRIÉTÉ SEIGNEURIALE ET GROUPES SOCIAUX DANS LA VALLÉE DU SAINT-LAURENT (1663-1840) [Manorial property and social groups in the St. Lawrence Valley, 1663-1840]. *Rev. de l'U. d'Ottawa [Canada] 1977 47(1-2): 183-213.* The manorial system in the St. Lawrence Valley colony was the privilege of the nobility, but the bourgeoisie gradually pervaded the system. In 1760, the English conquest brought a serious decline in the nobility's political power allowing the bourgeoisie to become more autonomous and increase its manorial ownership. The clergy, not experiencing the nobility's vicissitudes, dominated the society during 17th-18th centuries, even after the partial abolition of the manorial system which kept its social meaning in the 19th century. Secondary sources; 40 notes.

G. P. Cleyet

539. Rousseau, François. HÔPITAL ET SOCIÉTÉ EN NOU-VELLE-FRANCE: L'HÔTEL-DIEU DE QUÉBEC À LA FIN DU XVIIᵉ SIÈCLE [Hospital and society in New France: the chief hospital of Quebec at the end of the 17th century]. *Rev. d'Hist. de l'Am. Française [Canada] 1977 31(1): 29-47.* Quebec's first hospitals were established in the 1640's as part of the policy of evangelizing the American Indians. By 1700, however, Indians accounted for less than four percent of total admissions. Most patients were Canadian colonists. Illness records were started in 1689. From such records, it is possible to study the chief hospital in society, and popular perception of it. Based on published documents and secondary works; 4 tables, 4 graphs, 37 notes.

L. B. Chan

540. Roy, Raymond and Charbonneau, Hubert. LE CONTENU DES REGISTRES PAROISSIAUX CANADIENS DU XVIIᵉ SIÈCLE [The contents of Canadian parish registers of the 17th century]. *Rev. d'Hist. de l'Am. Française [Canada] 1976 30(1): 85-97.* From about 1616 to 1700, more than 26,000 acts of baptism, marriage, and burial affecting Europeans were recorded in Quebec's parish registers. Attempts to analyze Canada's 17th-century population from parish registers. Based on parish registers and secondary works; 3 figs., 12 notes.

L. B. Chan

541. Roy, Raymond; Landry, Yves; and Charbonneau, Hubert. QUELQUES COMPORTEMENTS DES CANADIENS AU XVIIᵉ SIÈCLE D'APRÈS LES REGISTRES PAROISSIAUX [Some comportments of 17th-century Canadians according to parish registers]. *Rev.*

d'Hist. de l'Am. Française [Canada] 1977 31(1): 49-73. The Department of Demography of the University of Montreal has attempted to reconstitute the whole population of Quebec during the 17th century based on parish records. Surviving records show more than 31,000 acts of baptism, marriage, and burial. Scholars may certainly attempt to make conclusions about the social and cultural nature of the early colonial population from such statistics. Based on parish records, published documents, and secondary works; 9 tables, 3 figs., 23 notes, appendix.   L. B. Chan

542. Salter, Michael A. L'ORDRE DE BON TEMPS [The Order of Good Times]. *Nova Scotia Hist. Q. [Canada] 1975 5(2): 143-154.* An account of the founding of L'Ordre de Bon Temps, the first social club in the new world, at Port Royal in 1606. The idea of Samuel de Champlain, its purpose was to help while away the dreary evening hours of the bleak Nova Scotian winter, and, more seriously, to save the colonists from the devastation suffered from disease the previous winter. By this means were avoided poor diets, a passive existence, and a failure in esprit de corps that would again bring disaster. The experiment was successful. 38 notes.   R. V. Ritter

543. Salter, Michael A. L'ORDRE DE BON TEMPS: A FUNCTIONAL ANALYSIS. *J. of Sport Hist. 1976 3(2): 111-119.* In 1606 Saumel de Champlain proposed that a social group be established in New France to while away the evening hours of the Nova Scotian winter. It was to be called L'Ordre de Bon Temps, the first social club structured by Caucasians in North America. The club and its activities are described. 44 notes.   M. Kaufman

544. Séguin, Robert-Lionel. LES DIVERTISSEMENTS AU QUÉBEC AUX XVIIᵉ ET XVIIIᵉ SIÈCLES [Amusements in Quebec during the 17th and 18th centuries]. *Rev. Française d'Hist. d'Outre-Mer [France] 1974 61(222): 5-17.* The social and cultural conditions in New France did not favor parties and amusements. War with the Indians was a real danger. The Church did not approve of balls, dancing, or the theater. Despite the attitudes of secular and ecclesiastical authorities, the people of New France knew how to amuse themselves by dancing, laughing, and singing. Based on notarial registries in the Archives nationales du Québec and secondary works; biblio.   L. B. Chan

545. —. [THE SCHOOL OF ARTS AND CRAFTS OF ST. JOACHIM]. *Rev. d'Hist. de l'Amérique Française [Canada] 1976 29(4): 567-576.*
Campeau, Lucien. À PROPOS DE L'ÉCOLE DES ARTS ET MÉTIERS DE SAINT-JOACHIM [With respect to the School of Arts and Crafts of Saint Joachim], *pp. 567-570.* A critical commentary regarding Peter N. Moogk's study of this school of New France.
Moogk, Peter N. RÉPLIQUE AU COMMENTAIRE DU PÈRE CAMPEAU [Reply to the commentary of Father Campeau], *pp. 571-576.* When a researcher as remarkable as Father Lucien Campeau defends the traditional version of the history of the School of Arts and Crafts of Saint Joachim, his comments merit attention. Father Campeau, however, misunderstood several portions of the earlier article.   L. B. Chan

The Church

546. Campeau, Lucien. MGR DE LAVAL ET LE CONSEIL SOUVERAIN 1659-1684 [Monseigneur Laval and the Sovereign Council 1659-84]. *R. d'Hist. de l'Amérique Française [Canada] 1973 27(3): 323-360.* Discusses the relationship between the ecclesiastical and commercial authorities in New France in the late 17th century and how the provincial governors exploited both.

547. Cliche, Marie-Aimée. LA CONFRÉRIE DE LA SAINTE-FAMILLE À QUÉBEC SOUS LE RÉGIME FRANÇAIS, 1663-1760 [The Brotherhood of the Holy Family in Quebec under the French regime, 1663-1760]. *Sessions d'Étude: Soc. Can. d'Hist. de l'Église Catholique [Canada] 1976 43: 79-93.* Describes the formation, recruitment, and nature of the elitist society, the Brotherhood of the Holy Family, founded through collaboration among Bishop François de Laval, Joseph-Marie-Pierre Chaumonot, and followers in Montreal, and its important influence on religious activities in colonial Canadian society.

548. Hamilton, Raphael N. WHO WROTE *PREMIER ÉTABLISSEMENT DE LA FOY DANS LA NOUVELLE FRANCE* [Who wrote *The First Establishment of the Faith in New France*?]. *Can. Hist. Rev. [Canada] 1976 57(3): 265-288.* Examines evidence about the authorship by others than Crestien Le Clercq who is named on the title page. A Parisian savant, Abbe Claude Bernou, and Eusèbe Renaudot, editor of the *Gazette de France*, seem to have edited the work with the purpose of promoting Robert Cavelier de la Salle and the Comte de Frontenac. Based on the 1691 edition, contemporary printed sources, and unpublished documents from the archives in Montreal (Canada), Paris (France), and Seville (Spain).   A

549. Hurtubise, Pierre. NI JANSENIST, NI GALLICAN, NI ULTRAMONTAIN: FRANÇOIS DE LAVAL [Neither Jansenist, nor Gallican, nor Ultramontane: François de Laval]. *R. d'Hist. de l'Amérique Française [Canada] 1974 28(1): 3-26.* Attempts to place the late-17th-century bishop of Quebec, François de Laval, in relationship to the men and ideas of his time, particularly Jansenism and Ultramontanism.

550. Jaenen, Cornelius J. THE PERSISTENCE OF THE PROTESTANT PRESENCE IN NEW FRANCE, 1541-1760. *Pro. of the Ann. Meeting of the Western Soc. for French Hist. 1974 (2): 29-40.* Outlines the varying fortunes of the Huguenots in New France and examines the small Protestant community of 1759. The Catholic Recollet missionaries and the Jesuits successfully campaigned to exclude Protestants from colonial administration and from further settlement in New France by 1627. Protestants continued to trickle in and during 1669-78 Jean Baptiste Colbert's policy of tolerance outweighed the clergy's demand for exclusion of all Huguenots, but Louis XIV's much harsher policy culminated in the Edict of Fontainbleau. Under the Regency and Louis XV, Huguenots reestablished contacts with Canada. In 1759 there were about 1,000 Protestants of whom 471 are identified by name. Their various national origins, their economic and occupational status, and the number of and reasons for abjurations are cited. Protestantism, although not a major factor, continued to be important in the history of New France. Based on Canadian and French archives and other primary sources; 31 notes.   J. D. Falk

551. Lahey, R. J. THE ROLE OF RELIGION IN LORD BALTIMORE'S COLONIAL ENTERPRISE. *Maryland Hist. Mag. 1977 72(4): 492-511.* Analyzes the facts and the standard versions of Lord Baltimore's involvement in Newfoundland. It is "improbable that Calvert's original interest . . . involved religious considerations of any kind." Assesses how long before 1625 Calvert developed Catholic sympathies. Uses previously unexamined Vatican archives to document the roles of English Carmelite priests who saw in Avalon a potential Catholic mission to offset Puritanism, and a means of reaching the Far East via the supposed Northwest Passage. Calvert's actual attempt to allow Catholics and Protestants to coexist in his colony brought potentially damaging political accusations at home. The inhospitality of land and climate, however, determined Calvert's abandonment of Ferryland in 1629. Primary and secondary sources; 97 notes.   G. J. Bobango

552. La Palm, Loretta. THE HÔTEL-DIEU OF QUEBEC: THE FIRST HOSPITAL NORTH OF THE RIO GRANDE UNDER ITS FIRST TWO SUPERIORS. *Study Sessions [Canada] 1974 41: 53-64.* Gives a history of the Hôtel-Dieu, a hospital founded in 1639 by nuns to provide medical care for the Indians. A paper read at the 1974 annual meeting of the Canadian Catholic Historical Association.   S

553. Noppen, Luc. L'ÉVOLUTION DE L'ARCHITECTURE RELIGIEUSE EN NOUVELLE-FRANCE [The evolution of religious architecture in New France]. *Sessions d'Étude: Soc. Can. d'Hist. de l'Église Catholique [Canada] 1976 43: 69-78.* Discusses the principal architectural types characteristic of the period, 1600-1760.

The Government

554. Dickinson, John A. LA JUSTICE SEIGNEURIALE EN NOU-VELLE-FRANCE: LE CAS DE NOTRE-DAME-DES-ANGES [Seigneurial justice in New France: the case of Notre Dame des Anges]. *R. d'Hist. de l'Amérique Française 1974 28(3): 323-346.* In the fief of Notre Dame des Anges (New France), granted to the Jesuits in 1626, feudal justice was practiced and covered serious crimes. Conflicts between feudal law and the Provost Court of Quebec were settled by an ordinance of 2 August 1706 confirming the competence of feudal lords in the administration of justice, including commerce, inheritances, guardianship, and taxes. Based on primary and secondary sources; 4 tables, 111 notes.
C. Collon

555. Dubé, Jean-Claude. LES INTENDANTS DE LA NOUVELLE-FRANCE ET LA RÉPUBLIQUE DES LETTRES [The intendants of New France and the intellectuals]. *R. d'Hist. de l'Amérique Française 1975 29(1): 31-48.* A series of 15 royal intendants were appointed to administer New France during 1663-1760, all with strong intellectual backgrounds. Notarial documents concerning their personal furnishings attest to their sober tastes and their extensive libraries in theology, jurisprudence, art, science, literature, and history. Based on primary and secondary sources; table, 71 notes.
C. Collon

Fish, Furs, and Farming

556. Alwin, John A. THE UNCELEBRATED BOATS OF THE ALBANY. *Beaver [Canada] 1975 305(4): 47-53.* Henley House, southwest of Fort Albany on James Bay, was established as a post when French traders became too active in the early 1740's. Hudson's Bay Company decided to place a small post there, not to create or divert trade, but to prevent French traders from feeling comfortable. Confronted with the problem of providing adequate transportation between Albany and Henley House, the Company had local Indians build larger canoes. These boats became the prototypes for the later, more famous York boats. A continuing problem was use of the canoes: local Indians were adept at handling them, but most Company employees never attained the skill. This may have been intentional, as they shunned posting at Henley House, an interior, isolated way station. 6 illus., map.
D. Chaput

557. Barkham, Selma. THE BASQUES: FILLING A GAP IN OUR HISTORY BETWEEN JACQUES CARTIER AND CHAMPLAIN. *Can. Geographical J. [Canada] 1978 96(1): 8-19.* Some of the earliest Europeans to settle on the coasts of Labrador were Basques, who set up whaling stations in the 16th century.

558. Barkham, Selma and Grenier, Robert. DIVERS FIND SUNKEN BASQUE GALLEON IN LABRADOR. *Can. Geographic [Canada] 1978/79 97(3): 60-63.* Research in Spanish archives confirmed the presence of a Basque whaling ship, the *San Juan*, in Labrador's Red Bay where it sank in 1565.

559. Barkham, Selma. TWO DOCUMENTS WRITTEN IN LABRADOR, 1572 AND 1577. *Can. Hist. Rev. [Canada] 1976 57(2): 235-238.* Discusses the predominance of Basque as a spoken language in 16th-century Labrador. Documents about the Labrador whaling industry tend to be written in Spanish, since French Basques were more concerned with codfishing prior to 1580. A thorough grounding in Spanish palaeography is a basic requirement for further research in Spain. Based on a 1572 bond and a 1577 will found in the notarial archives of the Province of Guipuzcoa which house the earliest known civil documents written in Canada.
A

560. Bosher, J. F. A FISHING COMPANY OF LOUISBOURG, LES SABLES D'OLONNE, AND PARIS: LA SOCIÉTÉ DU BARON D'HUART, 1750-1775. *French Hist. Studies 1975 9(2): 263-277.* Describes the general character and circumstances of a fishing company organized by Baron d'Huart formed to exchange goods for fish at Louisbourg, Cape Breton. It points out the role of the nobility in capitalistic enterprises. Based on archival materials; 37 notes.
H. T. Blethen

561. Bosher, J. F. A QUEBEC MERCHANT'S TRADING CIRCLES IN FRANCE AND CANADA: JEAN-ANDRÉ LAMALETIE BEFORE 1763. *Social Hist. [Canada] 1977 10(19): 24-44.* The trading merchants of 18th-century Quebec depended on a particular network of associates in other ports and cities of the trading region. These trading circles were usually composed of family members and close friends. This study of the trading circle of Jean-André Lamaletie, a merchant in Quebec from 1741 to 1758, reveals the nature of these business relationships. Lamalatie was not one of the merchants arrested by the French government in 1761 for profiteering and fraud (the *affaire du Canada),* although probably he was not completely innocent. Based on documents in the Public Record Office (London), Quebec Archives, and national and department archives in France; 2 tables, 3 charts, 50 notes.
W. K. Hobson

562. Boulle, Pierre H. PATTERNS OF FRENCH COLONIAL TRADE AND THE SEVEN YEARS' WAR. *Social Hist. [Canada] 1974 7(13): 48-86.* Examines the ties between various French ports and different sectors of the colonial trade. Reveals the need to amend the hinterland thesis for the decline of the most prominent 17th-century French ports and the rise of a new group of ports in the 18th century. Bordeaux, Marseilles, and Le Havre gained control of sugar and slaves, the new colonial products. The Seven Years' War accentuated their rise and the decline of St. Malo, La Rochelle, and Bayonne. Based on documents in the Archives Nationales and in departmental archives, and on published documents and secondary sources; 3 tables, 142 notes, appendix.
W. K. Hobson

563. Campeau, Lucien. LE COMMERCE DES CLERCS EN NOUVELLE-FRANCE [Trade by the clergy in New France]. *Rev. de l'U. d'Ottawa [Canada] 1977 47(1-2): 27-35.* In New France, the clergy was forbidden to exercise trade, which was defined as the resale for a profit of merchandise purchased at a smaller price, without any transformation increasing its value beyond the social service rendered. Members of the clergy, who handled a considerable amount of furs which they used only as currency to pay for imports necessary to church administration activities, were often falsely accused of trading in the manner prohibited by the law.
G. P. Cleyet

564. Carcassonne, Marcel. LA JONQUIÈRE ET LES ORIGINES DE TORONTO [La Jonquière and the origins of Toronto]. *R. française d'hist. d'Outre-Mer [France] 1974 61(224): 366-394.* Toronto, a city with a population of more than two million, was originally established in 1750 as a fortified French fur trading station. Pierre-Jacques de Taffanel (1685-1752), the Marquis de La Jonquière, and governor of New France from 1749-52, suggested that the post be established. Based on documents in the Archives nationales de France, and secondary works; 48 notes.
L. B. Chan

565. Charbonneau, Hubert; Desjardins, Bertrand; and Beauchamp, Pierre. LE COMPORTEMENT DEMOGRAPHIQUE DES VOYAGEURS SOUS LE REGIME FRANÇAIS [The demographic behavior of the Voyageurs in the French regime]. *Social Hist. [Canada] 1978 11(21): 120-133.* Scanty sources prevent thorough research on the voyageurs of Canada, but an analysis of the genealogical work of Archange Godbout indicates that some 16.4% of adult males were involved in the fur trade, with higher proportions from western regions. Godbout's *Nos ancetres au xviiᵉ siecle,* a veritable encyclopedia of first Canadians, thereby helps remedy the traditionally neglected demographic history of migrants such as the voyageurs, usually ignored in favor of their sedentary contemporaries. 12 fig., 12 notes.
D. F. Chard

566. Kenyon, Walter. CHARLTON ISLAND. *Beaver [Canada] 1974 305(1): 24-31.* In 1972 and 1973, the author excavated Hudson's Bay Company sites on Charlton Island in James Bay. In the late 1600's, the company used the island as a trade rendezvous but never established a colony. A French force captured and burned the post in 1686. A house, blacksmith shop, and forge were excavated. Finds included a musket lock, balls, flints, tool chest, tobacco pipe, and evidence of other structures. 19 illus., map.
D. Chaput

567. Kupp, Jan. ASPECTS OF NEW-YORK DUTCH TRADE UNDER THE ENGLISH, 1670-1674. *New-York Hist. Soc. Q. 1974 58(2): 139-147.* The English conquest of New Netherland in 1664 did not end

trade between that colony and Holland. War broke out between the Dutch republic and England and France in 1672, but commerce, particularly the Albany fur trade, was not seriously interrupted. Therefore, revision apparently is in order for historians' previous conclusion that the Iroquois were forced to trade with the French in Montreal rather than the Dutch in Albany after 1672. Primary sources; 3 illus., 18 notes.
C. L. Grant

568. Kupp, Jan. AUBERT DE LA CHESNAYE AND THE DUTCH FUR TRADE 1695-98. *Can. Hist. R. 1973 54(3): 337-341.* Deals with Charles Aubert de la Chesnaye (1630-1702) and his connections with the Dutch. Based on unpublished documents of the Notarial Archives of Holland collected by the author: "Dutch Documents Relating to the Early Furtrade and Cod Fisheries of North America, Vols. IX, X, XI," *Public Archives of Canada.* A and S

569. Kupp, Jan and Hart, Simon. THE EARLY CORNELIS MELYN AND THE ILLEGAL FUR TRADE. *Halve Maen 1975 50(3): 7-8, 15.* During the mid-17th century, Cornelis Melyn engaged in illegal fur trading in New England and Nova Scotia. S

570. Kupp, Jan. LE DÉVELOPPEMENT DE L'INTÉRÊT HOLLANDAIS DANS LA PÊCHERIE DE LA MORUE DE TERRE-NEUVE—L'INFLUENCE HOLLANDAISE SUR LES PÊCHERIES DE TERRE-NEUVE AU DIX-SEPTIÈME SIÈCLE [The development of Holland's interest in the cod fisheries of Newfoundland—the influence of Holland on the fisheries of Newfoundland in the 17th century]. *R. d'Hist. de l'Amérique Française [Canada] 1974 27(4): 565-570.* The participation of the Netherlands in the cod fisheries of Newfoundland began in 1589 and remained very active until 1670, when it disappeared almost as quickly as it began.

571. Massicotte, Jean-Paul and Lessard, Claude. LA CHASSE EN NOUVELLE-FRANCE AU XVIIᵉ SIÈCLE [Hunting in New-France in the 17th century]. *Can. J. of Hist. of Sport and Physical Educ. 1974 5(2): 18-30.* In 17th century Canada, the European hunted for pleasure while the Indians were encouraged to hunt for trading which would benefit the mother country. Describes the Indian's skill at hunting various animals, which supplemented grain cultivation and provided a sportive event. Based on contemporary accounts and secondary literature; 42 notes. L. R. Atkins

572. Miquelon, Dale. HAVY AND LEFEBVRE OF QUEBEC: A CASE STUDY OF METROPOLITAN PARTICIPATION IN CANADIAN TRADE, 1730-1760. *Can. Hist. R. 1975 56(1): 1-24.* The business papers of a French trading company, Robert Dugard et Cie of Rouen, housed in the Archives nationales, Paris, and Canadian private papers and notarial archives have been used to reconstruct the day-to-day business of these 18th-century factors, answering some questions regarding Canadian economic history while posing the larger one of the influence of French business society on Canada. A

573. Moore, Christopher. THE MARITIME ECONOMY OF ISLE ROYALE. *Can.: An Hist. Mag. 1974 1(4): 32-46.* The fishing industry flourished on Isle Royale during the early 18th century. One of five articles in this issue on the National Historic Park at Louisbourg. S

574. Ouellet, Fernand. DUALITÉ ÉCONOMIQUE ET CHANGEMENT TECHNOLOGIQUE AU QUÉBEC (1760-1790) [Dual economy and technological change in Quebec, 1760-1790]. *Social Hist. [Canada] 1976 9(18): 256-296.* The rise in wages for fur trappers in New France during 1760-90 is explained by the increasing commercialization of agriculture in the period and by the growing competition among fur trading companies. Fur trapping was seasonal work for about one-third of New France's peasants. After the Seven Years' War, the number of fur traders increased when Englishmen began to compete with the established francophone traders. During the American Revolution the prices of imported goods rose steeply, squeezing out individual francophone traders, stimulating technological changes, and encouraging the growth of the larger enterprises. Based on statistical analysis of data on trading expeditions, investments, prices, wages, and exports in Public Archives of Quebec and Canada; 53 tables, 70 notes, appendix. W. K. Hobson

575. Plamondon, Lilianne. UNE FEMME D'AFFAIRES EN NOUVELLE-FRANCE: MARIE-ANNE BARBEL, VEUVE FORNEL [A business woman in New France: Marie-Anne Barbel, the widow Fornel]. *Rev. D'Hist. De L'Amérique Française [Canada] 1977 31(2): 165-185.* There has been virtually no systematic examination of the role of women in business and financial affairs during the French hegemony in Canada. Individuals such as Marie-Anne Barbel, however, provide a more realistic portrait of women in colonial society and the ways in which they helped shape that society. Barbel (Widow Fornel) inherited her husband's business holdings and under her management those holdings grew, diversified, and prospered. Partially in response to the military intrusions of the English, she liquidated her assets in 1759 and lived in retirement for another 31 years. 54 notes. M. R. Yerburgh

576. Ray, Arthur J. HIGGLING AND HAGGLING AT YE BAY. *Beaver [Canada] 1977 308(1): 39-46.* By the late 17th century the Hudson's Bay Company had established a "standard of trade" intended to prevent competition between company posts. This standard, used in the fur trade, was for decades the official policy, but there were local variations. By the 1730's, when the French began to trade northwest of Lake Superior, the Indians, keenly aware of competitive prices, forced the company to be flexible in its standards. Based on Hudson's Bay Company archives; 7 illus. D. Chaput

577. Van Kirk, Sylvia. THANADELTHUR. *Beaver [Canada] 1974 304(4): 40-45.* Discusses the life of Thanadelthur (known as "Slave Woman"), a Chippewa Indian who served as interpreter in 1715-16 for a journey in Saskatchewan undertaken by a representative of Hudson's Bay Company, and who secured a peace between the Chippewa and Cree Indians for the benefit of the fur trade. S

Continental Penetration

578. Allain, Mathé. L'IMMIGRATION FRANÇAISE EN LOUISIANE, 1718-1721 [French immigration into Louisiana, 1718-1721]. *Revue d'hist. de l'Amérique française [Canada] 1975 28(4): 555-564.* In 1715 there were no more than 215 French inhabitants in Louisiana, including military personnel. The colony was founded as a check on Spanish and English colonialism, and by 1715 was considered a buffer area of Canada. During 1718-21, a concerted attempt was made to populate Louisiana by exiling many undesirables from France. Not until mid-century would there be another attempt to stimulate emigration to Louisiana. Based on primary and secondary sources; 49 notes. L. B. Chan

579. Bourne, Edward Gaylord. THE ROMANCE OF WESTERN HISTORY. *Missouri Hist. R. 1973 68(1): 55-73.* Discusses various aspects of western history, emphasizing the appreciation of French and Spanish influence on trans-Mississippi history and the value of the romantic element in history. Cites the expeditions of Hernando de Soto and Francisco Vásquez de Coronado and the sightings of the Rio Grande and the Grand Canyon as dramatic examples. Discusses the importance of the French quest for the "Western sea," and the designs and explorations of Father Jacques Marquette, La Motte Cadillac, Pierre LeMoyne, Nicholas de la Salle, and Father P. F. X. de Charlevoix. Credits an early prediction of the westward movement to Pierre LeMoyne d'Iberville, founder of Louisiana, and outlines the early history of the Missouri River area. First given as an address to the State Historical Society of Missouri in 1906. Primary and secondary sources; 6 illus., map, 35 notes. N. J. Street

580. Conrad, Glenn R. LES ACADIENS: LA LEGENDE ET LA REALITE [Acadians: Legend and reality]. *Rev. de Louisiane 1977 6(1): 5-17.* Chronicles the movements of the Acadians from France to, and in, the New World, 17th-20th centuries (including the Cajun culture in Louisiana), and discusses their daily life, customs, and religion, and myths about them; mentions Longfellow's *Evangeline.*

581. Higginbotham, Jay. HENRI DE TONTI'S MISSION TO THE CHICKASAW, 1702. *Louisiana Hist. 1978 19(3): 285-296.* The French Commander of Louisiana, Pierre LeMoyne d'Iberville, in 1702 sent Henri de Tonti to Mississippi and Alabama to attempt to arrange peace between

the Chickasaw and Choctaw nations, in an effort to secure their alliance against the advance of the English from the Carolinas. The Italian-born Tonti and his Canadian force travelled throughout the Choctaw country and persuaded their chiefs of the desirability of peace with the Chickasaw. He had more difficulty with the Chickasaw, owing to the English influence already there, but he eventually brought chiefs from both tribes back to Fort St. Louis "to seal an alliance that for several years, at least, would help stem the tide of English advance." Based on archival research in France, Canada, the United States, and Spain; 37 notes.

R. L. Woodward, Jr.

582. Higginbotham, Jay. PREPARATIONS FOR THE VOYAGE OF THE *PELICAN* TO LOUISIANA, 1703-1704. *Alabama Hist. Q. 1975 37(3): 165-175.* In 1703 Pierre Le Moyne d' Iberville suggested that the sending of marriageable girls to Mobile would provide a basis for natural population growth and encourage the Canadians there to become permanent settlers. Such a program was started, and girls of moral quality were secured in Paris. There were many delays in their sailing, and the number finally on the *Pelican* was only one-fourth the number d'Iberville hoped for. 25 notes. E. E. Eminhizer

583. Holli, Melvin G. FRENCH SEIGNIORIALISM AND THE SOCIAL STRUCTURE OF EARLY DETROIT. *Indiana Social Studies Q. 1975 28(2): 63-74.* Discusses the social, political, and cultural influence of French Seigniorialism in the development of Detroit, Michigan, 1701-1837.

584. Lemieux, Donald J. THE MISSISSIPPI VALLEY, NEW FRANCE, AND FRENCH COLONIAL POLICY. *Southern Studies 1978 17(1): 39-56.* France had several purposes in holding the Louisiana Territory, 1683-1762: to prevent a foreign foothold at the mouth of the Mississippi, to realize commercial gains at Spain's expense, to prevent English expansion, and to increase the sale and consumption of French goods. However, Louisiana was a financial liability. This was caused by domestic problems and distractions in France and the nature of the goods produced in the colonies. The loss of the Louisiana Territory to Spain in 1762 was not a significant loss; the sugar production of the Antilles was of much greater value. Primary and secondary sources; 56 notes.

J. Buschen

585. Marcolin, Lorenzo. SCUBA DIVING FOR HISTORY ON THE GREAT LAKES. *Inland Seas 1975 31(1): 7-13, 45.* While part of an amateur scuba diving team in 1961-62 at Sault Ste. Marie, Ontario, the author discovered the remains of the "old French dock," the *Chicora*, a 150-foot vessel, various pipes, plates, and glassware, a wrecked bateau off St. Joseph's Island, Ontario, and a lock and key which probably came from Fort St. Joseph. Illus. K. J. Bauer

586. Meyer, Larry L. THE FARTHEST WITH THE FEWEST. *Am. West 1975 12(4): 4-9, 61-63.* Discusses French explorers in the West during the 18th century: Louis Juchereau de St. Denis and Jean-Baptiste Bénard de la Harpe in Louisiana, Charles Claude du Tisne in the Indian country of Oklahoma, Etienne Veniard de Bourgmont in the Indian lands of the Missouri River, and Pierre Gaultier de Varennes, Sieur de la Verendrye, and sons in the western Canadian-American border fur territory. 2 illus., map. D. L. Smith

587. Santos Hernández, Angel. PRESENCIA MISIONERA EN LA ANTIGUA LUISIANA [Missionary presence in old Louisiana]. *Missionalia Hispanica [Spain] 1975 32(94): 77-101.* Sketches the history of old Louisiana, dealing with its earliest exploration and evangelization connected with the Canadian Indian missions of the Jesuits. The Franciscan Recollects from Paris and the Capuchins were later entrusted with some areas. There were problems of ecclesiastical jurisdiction during the successive French, Spanish, and American periods. In the 20th century the evangelization of several Indian tribes has been the work chiefly of the Jesuits. Based on secondary sources; 29 notes.

J. Correia-Afonso

588. Solano Costa, Fernando. LOS DESCUBRIMIENTOS DEL MISSISSIPI [Discoveries on the Mississippi]. *Estudios del Departamento de Hist. Moderna [Spain] 1975 (4): 7-18.* Discusses European exploration in the Mississippi River Valley by Spain in the 16th century and by France, beginning in the last third of the 17th century. Examines

formation of the Louisiana territory and its boundaries with Canada and Mexico. P. M. (IHE 95071)

589. Wakefield, Theodore D. A VIEW OF THE LAKES IN 1648: A TRIBUTE TO THE *JESUIT RELATIONS*. *Inland Seas 1976 32(3): 184-191, 206-207.* Reprints with introduction the 16 April 1648 covering letter of Father Paul Ragueneau and excerpts from Chapters I and X of his description of the Huron country around the southern end of Georgian Bay. Illus., 17 notes. K. J. Bauer

Decline and Fall

590. Adams, Blaine. THE 'KING'S BASTION BARRACKS' IN LOUISBOURG. *Nova Scotia Hist. Q. 1973 3(4): 303-308.* Discusses the history, 1716-39, of the Château St-Louis, the barracks building in Louisbourg, and the 1969 research in which the author engaged in order to reconstruct the fortress.

591. Bassett, T. D. Seymour, ed. A BALLAD OF ROGERS' RETREAT, 1759. *Vermont Hist. 1978 46(1): 21-23.* Prints 11 of 34 quatrains from the University of Vermont manuscript of a ballad about the retreat of Robert Rogers' Rangers after they destroyed the Saint Francis Indian village in Quebec; describes how Ebenezer Wheeler starved to death, as reported by Lieutenant Nathan Brigham of Southborough, Massachusetts. 6 notes. A

592. Beattie, Judith and Pothier, Bernard. THE BATTLE OF THE RESTIGOUCHE. *Can. Hist. Sites [Canada] 1977 (16): 5-34.* The battle of the Restigouche, 1760, was fought between the remnants of a French relief fleet bound for Montreal and a British squadron. The three French ships, only half the number that had sailed from Bordeaux in the spring, captured six British vessels in the Gulf of St. Lawrence. On learning that the British had already reached the St. Lawrence River, the French fleet sought refuge in Chaleur Bay and the Restigouche River where its numbers were further increased by 25 to 30 Acadian sloops and schooners. A British fleet from the Fortress of Louisbourg made contact with the French on 22 June. By 8 July, the final day of the engagement, the French had lost, in addition to 10 vessels sunk across channels in the river to halt the British advance, 22 or 23 vessels, most of which the French destroyed to prevent the British from taking them. The loss of the French fleet and its supplies contributed to the fall of New France. The battle was the last naval engagement between France and Great Britain for the possession of North America. J

593. Bosher, J. F. FRENCH PROTESTANT FAMILIES IN CANADIAN TRADE 1740-1760. *Social Hist. [Canada] 1974 7(14): 179-201.* Protestant merchants in Quebec increased in number after the end of the War of Austrian Succession in 1748. By the time Quebec fell in 1759 they may have been preponderant in Franco-Canadian trade. Information on the origins, family ties, and business connections of the 16 identifiable Protestant firms indicates they came from and maintained ties with southwestern France (La Rochelle, Bordeaux, and Montauban) and were willing to trade with anyone, but formed companies and married only with other Protestants. Based on secondary sources and on documents in the Archives nationales, Public Record Office, Bibliothèque de l'Arsenal (Paris), Public Archives of Canada, and departmental and town archives in France; 82 notes. W. K. Hobson

594. Brown, Desmond H. FOUNDATIONS OF BRITISH POLICY IN THE ACADIAN EXPULSION: A DISCUSSION OF LAND TENURE AND THE OATH OF ALLEGIANCE. *Dalhousie Rev. [Canada] 1977-78 57(4): 709-725.* Searches for the roots of the idea of personal loyalty to the king. Traces the development of oaths from Normandy through Saxon England and the writings of jurists such as Henry de Bracton (d. 1268), Sir Thomas Littleton in his 1481 treatise, and Edward Coke in his 1628 interpretation of Littleton. Examines the meaning of the oath of allegiance as it was intended at the time of the 1755 expulsion of the Acadians and as expounded by William Blackstone (1755). Trying to understand the meaning of the oath in today's society is difficult, because no writer has sufficiently explained why the right to possess title to land depended upon allegiance to the crown. Quotes from Nova Scotia Lieutenant Governors Thomas Caulfield (1715), Lawrence Armstrong (1726), Paul Mascarene (1736), and Charles Lawrence (1753). 96 notes.

C. H. Held

595. Chard, Donald F. CANSO, 1710-1721: FOCAL POINT OF NEW ENGLAND-CAPE BRETON RIVALRY. *Nova Scotia Hist. Soc. Collections [Canada] 1977 39: 49-78.* French-English rivalry over Canso, Nova Scotia, occurred during 1710-21.

596. Chard, Donald F. THE IMPACT OF FRENCH PRIVATEERING ON NEW ENGLAND, 1689-1713. *Am. Neptune 1975 35(3): 153-165.* During King William's War (1689-97) and Queen Anne's War (1702-13) French privateers inflicted serious losses on New England's fishing and shipping industries. The privateering, which was intensified during the latter war, was not curbed until England provided military support to its American colonists resulting in the British capture of Acadia (Nova Scotia). Published sources; 56 notes. G. H. Curtis

597. Chard, Donald F. LACK OF A CONSENSUS: THE ATTITUDE OF NEW ENGLAND TO ACADIA (1689-1713). *Nova Scotia Hist. Soc. Collections [Canada] 1973 38: 5-25.* Disputes over the Acadia-New England border, France's proven superiority in guerrilla warfare, and general disunity over whether to wage war resulted in a weak attack on Acadia by Sir William Phips in 1691. This conquest lasted one year. The interwar years 1698-1702 witnessed a lack of consensus in providing public funds for defense, yet in 1704 Acadia was again attacked—although even in Massachusetts there was resistance from several groups over the costs of such a maneuver. Based on printed secondary sources and some original documents, such as pamphlets, sermons, and government minute books; 60 notes. E. A. Chard

598. Codignola, Luca. VINCITORI E VINTI NELLA STORIA AMERICANA: IL CONFLITTO ANGLO-FRANCESE [Winners and losers in American history: The Anglo-French conflict]. *Ponte [Italy] 1975 31(10): 1112-1125.* Considers the historiography of the relations of France and Great Britain as reflected in their respective American colonies and suggests that the distance and independence of Italian historians of the period has allowed them to study the century-long conflict in a new light, one that does not corroborate the traditional interpretation that every American expansionist victory was a victory for progress and civilization.

599. Curry, Richard John. ROGERS' BATTLE ON SNOWSHOES. *New-England Galaxy 1974 15(3): 26-32.* Robert Rogers' (1731-95) expedition against the French was courageous, but futile. S

600. Dunnigan, Brian Leigh. VAUBAN IN THE WILDERNESS: THE SIEGE OF FORT NIAGARA, 1759. *Niagara Frontier 1974 21(2): 37-52.* Describes the battle plans and action of the British Army in its takeover of Fort Niagara, 1759, during the French and Indian War.

601. Fairchild, Byron. SIR WILLIAM PEPPERRELL: NEW ENGLAND'S PRE-REVOLUTIONARY HERO. *New England Hist. and Geneal. Register 1976 130(April): 83-106.* Sir William Pepperrell (1696-1759) was a merchant-trader, representative to the General Court of Massachusetts from Kittery (now in Maine), member of the Governor's Council, commander of the colonial forces against the French fortress of Louisbourg, Nova Scotia, interim governor there after the French defeat, and the only American so honored with a royal title (baronet). Although he was a successful merchant, politics and military affairs occupied most of Pepperrell's later life. He knew three royal governors, Jonathan Belcher (1681/2-1757), William Shirley (1694-1771), and Thomas Pownall (1722-1805), and was involved in efforts to replace Shirley. From commander of the Louisbourg expedition, Pepperrell rose to the rank of British lieutenant general. Primary and secondary sources, especially a newly found collection of approximately 400 Pepperrell Family Papers at the New England Historic Genealogical Society, Boston; 21 notes. S. L. Patterson

602. Fortier, John. PATTERNS OF RESEARCH AT LOUISBOURG: THE RECONSTRUCTION ENTERS ITS SECOND DECADE. *Can.: An Hist. Mag. 1974 1(4): 1-15.* Discusses the historical restoration of the Fortress of Louisbourg. One of five articles in this issue on the National Historic Park at Louisbourg. S

603. Fortier, Margaret. THE DEVELOPMENT OF THE FORTIFICATIONS AT LOUISBOURG. *Can.: An Hist. Mag. 1974 1(4): 16-31.* Discusses plans and architectural drawings for the Fortress of Louis-

bourg. One of five articles in this issue on the National Historical Park at Louisbourg. S

604. Godfrey, W. G. JOHN BRADSTREET AT LOUISBOURG: EMERGENCE OR RE-EMERGENCE? *Acadiensis [Canada] 1974 4(1): 100-120.* Traces the early military career of John Bradstreet (1717-74). At Canso during 1739-74, Bradstreet traded with the French at Louisbourg from which he profited but simultaneously hurt his chances for promotion in the British Army. In an effort to recoup his reputation, he promoted and played an important role in the colonial capture of Louisbourg in 1745, using his special knowledge of the fortress to great advantage. Although suspicions still plagued him, this performance ultimately helped Bradstreet's career. Based on published and unpublished private papers, secondary sources, printed government documents, official papers from Public Archives of Canada and Public Archives of Nova Scotia; 99 notes. E. A. Churchill

605. Greer, Allan. MUTINY AT LOUISBOURG, DECEMBER 1744. *Social Hist. [Canada] 1977 10(20): 305-336.* This mutiny is noteworthy because it occurred in wartime (during King George's War) and involved nearly all of the Fortress of Louisbourg soldiers. Provoked by rotten vegetables, and irritated by other injustices, Swiss troops protested and French troops then rebelled. When New Englanders attacked in 1745, French troops performed well, but later many surviving rebels were punished. Misery and hardship are often given as explanations of the rebellion, but the gap in outlook, background, and material interests between the Louisbourg soldiers and their officers also was important. 134 notes. D. F. Chard

606. Griffiths, Naomi. ACADIANS IN EXILE: THE EXPERIENCES OF THE ACADIANS IN THE BRITISH SEAPORTS. *Acadiensis [Canada] 1974 4(1): 67-84.* Caught between the French and English, the Acadians of Nova Scotia remained neutral, developing their own distinctive character by the time of their dispersion in 1755. Those sent to England maintained their separate identity; French officials, emphasizing similarities in language and religion and ignoring cultural differences, saw these Acadians as dislocated loyal French and got them resettled in France in 1763. The Acadians proved unhappy, uncooperative and troublesome and many later emigrated to New Orleans. Based on materials in the British and French Archives, published primary and secondary sources; 86 notes. E. A. Churchill

607. Gwyn, Julian. WAR AND ECONOMIC CHANGE: LOUISBOURG AND THE NEW ENGLAND ECONOMY IN THE 1740'S. *Rev. de l'U. d'Ottawa [Canada] 1977 47(1-2): 114-131.* An economic survey of New England showing the changes brought by King George's War which ended in 1745 by the capture of the fortress of Louisbourg and the restoration of the latter to the French by the British in 1749. In spite of New England's costly war effort, 1745-49 were years of prosperity, but these were followed by a deflation bringing financial insecurity to citizens already embittered by Britain's restoration of Louisbourg to the French. Based on primary and secondary sources; 11 tables, 49 notes. G. P. Cleyet

608. Hamilton, T. M. and Fry, Bruce W. A SURVEY OF LOUISBOURG GUNFLINTS. *Can. Historic Sites 1975 (12): 101-128.* The discovery of a large cache of gunflints in a defence work protecting Louisbourg harbour led to a study of all measurable flints from this site together with gunflints recovered from nine excavated sites within the 18th-century town of Louisbourg. Two distinct types of gunflints could be distinguished, in accordance with a classification generally accepted by historic archaeologists, although the attribution of types to exclusive areas of manufacture implied by this classification is questioned. In addition, gunflints from the cache are regarded as constituting a distinct group within the whole Louisbourg collection on the basis of manufacturing technique and over-all appearance. Documents dealing with the sites from which the gunflints were recovered were studied in an attempt to define context and chronological limits. Documents concerning the purchase and manufacture of gunflints for Louisbourg and for the French army were also studied in order to compare historical evidence on desirable qualities of military gunflints with archaeologically recovered specimens. J

609. Hudson, J. P. THE ORIGINAL RECONNAISSANCE MAP FOR THE BATTLE OF QUEBEC. *British Lib. J. [Great Britain] 1975 1(1): 22-24.* In 1959 the British Library was presented with some Townshend papers originally kept at Rainham in Norfolk. Among these was a map of Quebec prepared by Patrick Mackellar in 1759, prior to the Battle of Quebec. Reproduces the map, and lists several other items in the Townshend archive. Based on the Townshend papers and secondary works; fig. B. Jacobsen

610. Kaiser, Leo M. JOHN LEVERETT AND THE QUEBEC EXPEDITION OF 1711: AN UNPUBLISHED LATIN ORATION. *Harvard Lib. Bull. 1974 22(3): 309-316.* Discusses the background information on, and text of the 1711 Harvard Commencement Day Address, delivered in Latin to an audience including Admiral Sir Hovenden Walker and General John Hill of the Quebec Expedition (1711). Based on primary sources; 105 notes, chiefly in Latin. L. D. Smith

611. Kaulback, Ruth E. A JOURNAL OF THE PROCEEDINGS . . . (SIR WM. PHIPPS' EXPEDITION TO PORT ROYAL APRIL 23-MAY 30, 1690). *Nova Scotia Hist. Q. 1973 3(2): 131-143.* Recounts the destruction of the French fort at Port Royal with excerpts from the journal of Sir William Phipps, leader of the English expedition. All inhabitants of the area were required to swear allegiance to King William and Queen Mary of England. 9 notes. H. M. Evans

612. Kelsey, Harry. THE AMHERST PLAN: A FACTOR IN THE PONTIAC UPRISING. *Ontario History [Canada] 1973 65(3): 149-158.* Notes that Amherst was not adequately staffed, manned, or equipped to garrison the territory of New France when it was surrendered to him in 1760. Argues that the actions he took to cope with this situation and to modify wartime practices with respect to the Iroquois Indians were to some degree sabotaged by his own officers, who did not share his outlook. Thus, his policies were a contributing factor in Pontiac's Rebellion. Some of the events during 1760-64 are analyzed in detail, especially the activities of some of his subordinates in the field and on the frontier. W.B. Whitham

613. Koyen, Kenneth. FRENCH CANADA'S COLONIAL FORT IS BEING BUILT ANEW. *Smithsonian 1973 4(2): 76-83.* Discusses the restoration of the 18th-century French fortress of Louisbourg, Nova Scotia. S

614. Leefe, John. NOVA SCOTIA AND THE ACADIAN PROBLEM 1710-1755. *Nova Scotia Hist. Q. [Canada] 1974 4(4): 327-343.* Discusses the causes and background of the expulsion of the Acadians from Nova Scotia. In 1710 Great Britain conquered Port Royal, the capital of Acadia. Inhabitants living within three miles of the fort were given two years to change their allegiance from French to British. The dispute was not settled until 1755 when 6,000 Acadians were dispersed among the English colonies in the South. 34 notes. H. M. Evans

615. Lindsay, Charles S. LIME PREPARATION AT 18TH-CENTURY LOUISBOURG. *Can. Historic Sites 1975 (12): 5-45.* The equipment and techniques used in the preparation of lime for mortar in 18th-century Louisbourg are studied against the background of contemporary practices in France. Two basic types of French kilns and limeburning techniques are identified, as are two methods of slaking the burnt lime. Parallels for all these structures and techniques are found at Louisbourg. J

616. Lindsay, Charles S. LOUISBOURG GUARDHOUSES. *Can. Historic Sites 1975 (12): 47-100.* Louisbourg guardhouses are studied from two aspects, architectural and functional, by bringing together primary historical and archaeological evidence from Louisbourg, secondary historical evidence from France, and pictorial evidence of surviving French guardhouses. The results have shown that Louisbourg guardhouses were parallel in building techniques and materials with the simpler guardhouses used in lesser positions in France. In layout and function they were consistent with the principles applied to all French guardhouses. The evidence also shows that, consistent with much of the other construction work at Louisbourg, few concessions were made to the climatic differences between France and North America. J

617. MacLeod, Malcolm. LETTER FROM ANOTHER WORLD, 1757. *Nova Scotia Hist. Q. 1973 3(3): 197-213.* Reprints letters of Henry Pringle to his brother Robert, written while he was stationed in Halifax with the British Army fighting the French elements in Canada, 1757; gives detailed accounts of daily life, geography, and battles.

618. Plumstead, A. W. CRÈVECOEUR: A "MAN OF SORROWS" AND THE AMERICAN REVOLUTION. *Massachusetts Rev. 1976 17(2): 286-301.* Michel Guillaume Jean de Crèvecoeur (1735-1813), born in Caen, France, and best known for his *Letters from an American Farmer*, emigrated to Canada in 1755, was wounded on the Plains of Abraham, and left for New York in 1759. Here he became known as J. Hector St. John, married Mehitabel Tippet, became a farmer, and wrote his *Letters*. These extolled the happy valley syndrome. In 1779 Crèvecoeur left for Great Britain, where his *Letters* were published in 1782. He finally moved to France. Not permitted to return to New York during the French Revolution, he spent his final years in France. E. R. Campbell

619. Proudfoot, Dan. HOW LOUISBOURG RESTORED LOOKS TODAY. *Can. Geographical J. 1976 93(1): 28-33.* Discusses the history of Fort Louisbourg on Cape Breton Island, Nova Scotia, 1720-68; continues with exploration of the fort following contemporary preservation efforts.

620. Reid, Ronald F. NEW ENGLAND RHETORIC AND THE FRENCH WAR, 1754-1760: A CASE STUDY IN THE RHETORIC OF WAR. *Communication Monographs 1976 43(4): 259-286.* Examines New England rhetoric in light of the French and Indian War, 1754-60, discussing war rhetoric as a genre whose aims change as war progresses and as one based on ethnocentrism, territoriality, and optimism.

621. Stokesbury, James L. QUEBEC FALLS! *Am. Hist. Illus. 1975 10(6): 4-11, 42-48.* Describes the taking of Quebec from the French by the British under General James Wolfe, 13 September 1759.

622. Wade, Mason. AFTER THE *GRAND DERANGEMENT*: THE ACADIANS' RETURN TO THE GULF OF ST. LAWRENCE AND TO NOVA SCOTIA. *Am. Rev. of Can. Studies 1975 5(1): 42-65.* Despite numerous attempts by the colonial government of Nova Scotia to remove Acadians, some groups remained in the Gulf of St. Lawrence area and eventually returned to Nova Scotia, 1756-95.

6. BRITISH NORTH AMERICA, 1763-1867

General

623. Allen, Robert S. THE BRITISH INDIAN DEPARTMENT AND THE FRONTIER IN NORTH AMERICA, 1755-1830. *Can. Historic Sites 1975 (14): 5-125.* Initially formed in 1755 during the last great war for empire between France and England in North America, the Indian Department became the keystone of British policy for the wilderness interior. With the support of the local tribes and working closely with the British army, the department provided invaluable service during the American Revolution, the struggle for the Ohio valley and the War of 1812, and thus helped to preserve British jurisdiction and political institutions over much of British North America from the continuing threat of usurpation by American republicanism.
J

624. Allen, Robert S. THE CHAIN OF FRIENDSHIP: A SHORT HISTORY OF THE BRITISH INDIAN DEPARTMENT AND THE FRONTIER IN NORTH AMERICA, 1755-1830. *Military Collector and Hist. 1977 29(3): 111-113, 140.* The British Indian Department, 1755-1830, was formed to court and maintain the allegiance of Indians in Canada and the United States during Great Britain's colonization attempts.

625. Angrave, James. JOHN STRACHAN AND SCOTTISH INFLUENCE IN THE CHARTER OF KING'S COLLEGE, YORK, 1827. *J. of Can. Studies [Canada] 1976 11(3): 60-68.* The charter of King's College, York, in Toronto, was modeled on those of Scottish universities known to John Strachan (1776-1867) which gave considerable powers to an academic senate and provided no religious test for students. But, it did provide for an Anglican faculty, President, and Visitor. Besides fear of Anglican domination, resistance in the Upper Canadian legislature was motivated by a reluctance to use prime revenue-bearing lands to support the college. So, despite its Scottish liberal character, the charter was not accepted until 1843. Based on official correspondence and secondary works; 35 notes.
G. E. Panting

626. Baily, Marilyn. FROM CINCINNATI, OHIO TO WILBERFORCE, CANADA: A NOTE ON ANTEBELLUM COLONIZATION. *J. of Negro Hist. 1973 58(4): 427-440.* Recounts the movement of black people out of Cincinnati after the enforcement there of legislation patterned after southern slave codes in 1829. Several families traveled to a site near London, Ontario, which they called Wilberforce. Though ultimately unsuccessful, the black colony served as a symbol of the escape from slavery and thereby contributed to the struggle against that institution. Based on secondary sources; 35 notes.
N. G. Sapper

627. Bergquist, Harold E. THE RUSSIAN UKASE OF SEPTEMBER 16, 1821: THE NONCOLONIZATION PRINCIPLE, AND THE RUSSO-AMERICAN CONVENTION OF 1824. *Can. J. of Hist. [Canada] 1975 10(2): 165-184.* Examines foreign relations between the United States and Russia pertaining to the Northwest Coast area, 1821-25; examines the role of Great Britain, trade relations among the three, and the ukase issued by Tsar Alexander I in 1821.

628. Brown, Jennifer. ULTIMATE RESPECTABILITY: FUR-TRADE CHILDREN IN THE "CIVILIZED WORLD." *Beaver [Canada] 1977 308(3): 4-10; 1978 308(4): 48-55.* Part I. By the 1840's, most clerks and administrators of the Hudson's Bay Company began to send their children away for an education, because the Red River Academy was thought inadequate. Some went to England and Scotland, and others to Montreal and vicinity. The mixed-blood heritage did not seem to be a problem; there were too few of them in Britain to lead to any generalizing, and in the towns around Montreal, Métis were relatively commonplace. Two major problems faced the fathers. Because of the size of their families, they often had to select one or a few for education, leaving the others illiterate and untrained. It was also difficult to "place" their children. Some company officials favored finding a relative in eastern Canada or Britain, while others felt that strangers could provide the best attitude and environment for their children. Based on author's Ph.D.

thesis, U. of Chicago; 7 illus. Part II. A few of the Métis children could not adjust to society in eastern Canada. Ranald McDonald, after a boring apprenticeship in a bank, became a sailor and managed to get to Japan, "the land of his ancestors." He spent a few years there in the 1840's, teaching several people English; they later served as interpreters when Commodore Perry arrived in the 1850's. McDonald eventually settled in British Columbia and Washington, and died in 1894. In the 1830's, a dozen or so Métis children, studying in eastern Canada, became temporarily infatuated with Dickson's call to arms; a Métis and Indian kingdom would be founded in California. This proved abortive, and the remnants of the group adjusted to life in Canada. The bulk of these fur trade children do not appear to have suffered for their mixed racial backgrounds. In eastern Canada they became clerks, teachers, farmers, or businessmen. It is true that family reputation and "gentleman" status were highly regarded, but it is also true that individual achievement was a major determinant in the careers of these children of mixed blood. 10 illus.
D. Chaput

629. Brown, Wallace. WILLIAM COBBETT IN THE MARITIMES. *Dalhousie Rev. [Canada] 1976 56(3): 448-461.* Deals with the English radical-Tory William Cobbett (1763-1835) who spent 1785-91 in the Maritimes, mostly New Brunswick. This self-taught man gained much of his education and formed many of his attitudes toward England, the British army, the upper class, and North America while on duty with the 54th Regiment of Foot in St. John and Fredericton. 39 notes.
C. Held

630. Brynn, Edward. VERMONT AND THE BRITISH EMPORIUM. *Vermont Hist. 1977 45(1): 5-30.* Great Britain was mercantilist in annexing Canada in 1763, but its administrative policies, although well conceived, were ineffective. The Green Mountain Boy policy to create an independent Vermont between the Connecticut, Mohawk, and St. Lawrence Rivers coincided with British policy to restrain American expansion by means of buffer states, but England conceded Vermont to the United States in 1783. However, the British feared New England emigration north of Vermont as an attempt to annex Canada. As Britain moved into its free trade era, the Champlain-Richelieu trade was allowed to increase in spite of Jefferson's embargo, but Britain virtually turned its back on Canadian interests, and the United States would have annexed Canada by 1850, had not the slavery controversy intervened. The military importance of the Champlain corridor repeatedly affected border negotiations and helped create Canadian unity. Map, 137 notes.
T. D. S. Bassett

631. Careless, J. M. S. TWO RIVER EMPIRES: AN HISTORICAL ANALYSIS. *Am. Rev. of Can. Studies 1975 5(2): 28-47.* Offers a comparative survey of themes in the establishment of empire represented by the St. Lawrence River for Canada and the Mississippi River for the USA; examines the establishment of a federal government in either case and draws juxtapositions along political, social, economic, and intellectual lines, 1760's-1860's.

632. Chartrand, René. NOTES ON THE UNIFORMS OF THE BRITISH INDIAN DEPARTMENT. *Military Collector and Hist. 1977 29(3): 115-117.* No official uniform existed for officers of the British Indian Department from its inception in 1755 until 1823, but there appears to have been a "fashion" for officers as exhibited in portraits 1760-1823.

633. Cole, Douglas and Tippett, Maria. PLEASING DIVERSITY AND SUBLIME DESOLATION: THE 18TH CENTURY BRITISH PERCEPTION OF THE NORTHWEST COAST. *Pacific Northwest Q. 1974 65(1): 1-7.* Studies the aesthetics of landscape as viewed through British eyes conditioned by landscape painting of the 17th and early 18th centuries. Captain George Vancouver and Archibald Menzies emphasized the "pleasant fertility and . . . agreeable diversity" of the Northwest coast of Canada. Explores the origins of these aesthetic ideals in natural scenery. 43 notes.
R. V. Ritter

634.   Craig, G. M.   CANADA'S ROLE IN AMERICAN HISTORY. *Can. Geographical J. 1976 92(2): 30-35.* Discusses Canada's influence in the shaping of US history from 1759 to the 20th century, emphasizing the American Revolution and the War of 1812.

635.   Doyle, John E.   CHICOPEE'S IRISH (1830-1875). *Hist. J. of Western Massachusetts 1974 3(1): 13-23.* Nineteenth-century Irish settlers came to the Chicopee mills via Canada and other parts of Massachusetts, and by 1848 Chicopee became a predominantly immigrant company town. Irish mores encouraged nativism among Protestants, but the record of Irish participation in the Civil War led to respectability. Primary and secondary sources; 2 illus., 34 notes.   S. S. Sprague and S

636.   Evans, Howard V.   THE NOOTKA SOUND CONTROVERSY IN ANGLO-FRENCH DIPLOMACY 1790.   *J. of Modern Hist. 1974 46(4): 609-640.* Discusses the historiographical controversy regarding the missions of William Miles and Hugh Elliot to Paris in 1790 in connection with the Nootka Sound Controversy. Argues that prevailing interpretations require correction and that, contrary to some claims, none of the evidence has been suppressed. Based on British Government sources, and on the Miles and Elliot papers; 125 notes.   P. J. Beck

637.   Farrell, David R.   ANCHORS OF EMPIRE: DETROIT, MONTREAL AND THE CONTINENTAL INTERIOR, 1760-1775. *Am. Rev. of Can. Studies 1977 7(1): 33-54.* After the conquest of New France, Great Britain attempted to insure the military defense, political stability, and economic exploitation of the interior by direct imperial control through regional garrison towns. These outposts were subject to strict military and economic regulations which prevented their developing into urban centers. By 1770, changing trade patterns and unrest in the eastern colonies altered British policy, concentrating interest in the Great Lakes. Some garrison towns were abandoned and the fur-trading centers of Detroit and Montreal became the logical anchors for the realigned empire. Primary and secondary sources; map, 37 notes.
G.-A. Patzwald

638.   Fowler, Marian.   PORTRAIT OF ELIZABETH SIMCOE. *Ontario Hist. [Canada] 1977 69(2): 79-100.* Discusses Mrs. Elizabeth Simcoe, wife of the first Lieutenant Governor of Upper Canada. Illustrated with quotations from her diary and letters, and by examples of the watercolors she painted. Comments on some of the influences on her which led to entries in the diary. Discusses major contemporary aesthetic theories as related to Mrs. Simcoe's paintings. Remarks on her life after she and Lieutenant Governor Simcoe left the province in 1796. In general, Mrs. Simcoe was a typical upper-class woman of the late 18th century, influenced in behavior by rationalism and noblesse oblige, who tried to carry these values with her to the frontier. 12 illus., 36 notes.
W. B. Whitham

639.   Galbraith, John S.   THE ENIGMA OF SIR GEORGE SIMPSON. *Beaver [Canada] 1976 306(4): 4-9.* Biographical questions about Sir George (1787-1860), key Hudson's Bay Company official in the early 19th century. The "Little Emperor of the Plains" is not well known today, due to a variety of factors: he stressed privacy, fought no battles, and sought acceptance from his peers, not from the public. His attitude toward privacy most likely stems from his birth, apparently illegitimate. Drawn mostly from the author's biography, published in 1976. 7 illus.
D. Chaput

640.   Grant, John N.   BLACK IMMIGRANTS INTO NOVA SCOTIA, 1776-1815. *J. of Negro Hist. 1973 58(3): 253-270.* Discusses the background of three waves of black immigration to Nova Scotia: black Loyalists came after the American Revolution, Maroons were exiled to Nova Scotia after their surrender in Jamaica in 1796, and former slaves came after the British liberated them in the Chesapeake campaign of the War of 1812. The first two groups soon emigrated from Nova Scotia to Africa, but the former slaves remained and their descendants still live in Nova Scotia. Based on primary sources in the British Colonial Office and on secondary sources; 68 notes.   N. G. Sapper

641.   Grantmyre, Barbara.   MYSTERIOUS HENRY. *Nova Scotia Hist. Q. [Canada] 1977 7(2): 111-124.* The career of Henry Moore Smith (alias Frederick Henry Moore, Henry Moon, Henry Hopkins, William Newman, and Henry Gibney) as a thief and confidence man began in Windsor in 1812 while he was a tailor-peddler. He moved to Saint John to escape the sheriff but was arrested in Pictou in July 1814 for stealing a horse. He was tried in Kingston, New Brunswick, 4 May 1815 and was sentenced to death. While awaiting his fate he occupied his time making puppets from mattress straw and gave shows to everyone willing to pay; by 10 August there were 24 figures in his productions. Popular sentiment forced his pardon and he boarded a ship on 30 August 1815 for Windsor. In 1827 he was arrested and jailed in Baltimore, Maryland. He was reported to be in prison in Toronto in 1835 for burglary. His ultimate fate is unknown. Biblio.   H. M. Evans

642.   Greenough, John Joseph.   THE HALIFAX CITADEL, 1825-60: A NARRATIVE AND STRUCTURAL HISTORY.   *Can. Hist. Sites [Canada] 1977 (17): 5-197.* As a result of the need to defend Halifax as the base of the British Navy in the North Atlantic, the British government decided in 1828 to build a permanent fortress in Halifax. Originally the work was to take six years and to cost 116,000 [pounds]. Because of a number of problems—inadequate design and climate being the worst—the work was not finished until 1857-60 and cost 242,122 [pounds]. This report discusses the history of the building, the background in which it took place, and the structure of the fortress and its individual components.   J

643.   Greer, Allan.   THE SUNDAY SCHOOLS OF UPPER CANADA.   *Ontario Hist. [Canada] 1975 67(3): 169-184.* The role of Sunday schools in Upper Canada in the early 19th century was to inculcate loyalty to the king, obedience to employers, regular and industrious habits, and fear of God.

644.   Guay, Donald.   PROBLEMES DE L'INTÉGRATION DU SPORT DANS LA SOCIETÉ CANNADIENNE 1830-1865: LE CAS DES COURSES DE CHEVAUX   [Problems of sport's integration in Canadian society in 1830-1865: the case of horse races]. *Can. J. of Hist. of Sport and Physical Educ. 1973 4(2): 70-92.* Horse racing, introduced to Canadian society by Englishmen in the second half of the 18th century, was accepted as a sport by Canadians not sooner than the first decades of the 19th century. There was strong moral, ideological, and cultural resistance against horse racing, because it was viewed as an affair of the high bourgeoisie and aristocracy. Canadian nationalism, primarily anti-English, developed later (about 1860) in a nationalism of conciliation. The attitude toward this English-imported sport changed then. Based on secondary sources; 103 notes.   G. E. Pergl

645.   Gundy, H. Pearson.   THE FAMILY COMPACT AT WORK: THE SECOND HEIR AND DEVISEE COMMISSION OF UPPER CANADA, 1805-1841.   *Ontario Hist. [Canada] 1974 66(3): 129-146.* While much attention has been given to the first Heir and Devisee Commission set up to bring order into the very confused land grant situation of the 1790's, little has been paid to the second commission, despite its very extensive records. Examines the operations of this second commission, set up in 1805, between its genesis and 1841. Includes examples of the problems met and the decisions rendered. 34 notes.
W. B. Whitham

646.   Haering, R. R.   TRACKING MACKENZIE'S TRAIL TO THE COAST.   *Can. Geographical J. 1976 93(2): 12-21.* Discusses the course taken by explorer Alexander Mackenzie in his expedition from the Fraser River to the sea in British Columbia in 1793.

647.   Hansen, Dagny B.   JULY FOURTH, 1789: FIRST INDEPENDENCE DAY CELEBRATION ON THE NORTH AMERICAN PACIFIC COAST.   *Am. West 1976 13(4): 32-34.* Describes the celebration by the personnel of the American ship, the *Columbia Rediviva*, under Captain John Kendrick, along the west shore of Vancouver Island during the Spanish-English Nootka Sound controversy. Illus., note.
D. L. Smith

648.   Hare, John.   SUR LES IMPRIMÉS ET LA DIFFUSION DES IDÉES   [Printed matter and the diffusion of ideas]. *Ann. Hist. de la Révolution Française [France] 1973 45(3): 407-421.* Describes the spread of Enlightenment ideas in Canada. Between 1764 and 1810, 11 newspapers were established and hundreds of pamphlets were printed. *La Gazette de Quebec*, the first newspaper, espoused republican ideas and was sympathetic to the French Revolution. Primary and secondary sources; 31 notes.   S. R. Smith

649. Herndon, G. Melvin. A GRANDIOSE SCHEME TO NAVI-GATE AND HARNESS NIAGARA FALLS. *New-York Hist. Soc. Q. 1974 58(1): 6-17.* Although English-born William Tatham's rather lim-ited fame rests largely on his book on tobacco, he had many interests, most of which he pursued in the United States. However, he was living in England when he proposed his most fantastic scheme, an apparatus to permit ships to traverse Niagara Falls. Based on an inclined plane, the device he envisioned would not only open the Great Lakes to trade, but would promote closer relations between Americans and Canadians. Un-fortunately for Tatham, no one took him too seriously, then or later. Still, his sketches and plans showed a great deal of imagination. Based largely on primary sources; 5 illus., 29 notes.   C. L. Grant

650. Holloway, Trevor. DAVID DOUGLAS: BOTANICAL CO-LUMBUS & PLANT HUNTER EXTRAORDINARY. *Am. West 1976 13(2): 46-51, 60-61.* After apprenticeship and experience in horticul-ture and botany, Scotsman David Douglas (1799-1834) spent most of his adult life on collecting expeditions. His 1823 assignment, to the eastern United States and Canada, focused on commercial fruit tree culture. In 1824-27, he covered much of the Pacific Northwest with headquarters at the Hudson's Bay Company post at Fort Vancouver. Most of the hun-dreds of specimens and seeds he collected were new to his English spon-sors. Although it was previously known, he was the first to obtain the seeds and to introduce into cultivation the giant Douglas fir, named in his honor. His final efforts, 1829-34, concentrated on California, the Pacific Northwest, an unsuccessful attempt to go overland to Alaska, and a fatal overland trek across one of the Hawaiian islands. 4 illus., note.   D. L. Smith

651. Hutchinson, Gerald M. JAMES EVANS' LAST YEAR. *J. of the Can. Church Hist. Soc. [Canada] 1977 19(1-2): 42-56.* James Evans served the Methodist Church in Canada with great distinction both as a minister in the Hudson's Bay territory and as a linguist in the creation of a written language for the Cree Indians. Unfortunately, his later years were clouded with controversy. Involved in conflicts with both the Hud-son's Bay Company and Roman Catholic missionaries, Evans was ac-cused of immorality with some young girls and went to England where the matter was considered by the Missionary Society. He died suddenly before a verdict was reached; but the view was that while Evans may have acted improperly, he was not guilty of any immorality. The matter has remained a mystery ever since because, until recently, scholars were not permitted to examine the relevant documents. Now it is possible to con-sider his great accomplishments and explain the great tragedy of his last year. This issue is *J. of the Can. Church Hist. Soc.* 1977 19(1-2) and *Bull. of the United Church of Can.* 1977 26. Primary and secondary sources; 13 notes.   J. A. Kicklighter

652. Jackson, Donald. LEDYARD AND LAPÉROUSE: A CON-TRAST IN NORTHWESTERN EXPLORATION. *Western Histori-cal Q. 1978 9(4): 495-508.* In 1778, English explorer Captain James Cook charted the Pacific Northwest coast as far as Bering Strait. Seven years later, French explorer Jean François Lapérouse (1741-ca. 1788) was sent to explore areas not seen by Cook and to search for the fabled Northwest Passage. American John Ledyard (1751-89), who had accompanied Cook and who wrote the chronicle of Cook's voyage, set out by foot in 1786 to cross Siberia eastward to North America and explore its interior. Lapérouse collected much scientific and geographic information before shipwreck ended the expedition. Ledyard was arrested by Russian police in Siberia, but that did not end his dreaming and planning. Studies the impact of Lapérouse and Ledyard upon Thomas Jefferson. Suggests Le-dyard's influence is reflected in the Lewis and Clark expedition. 41 notes.   D. L. Smith

653. Johnson, Arthur L. THE TRANSPORTATION REVOLU-TION ON LAKE ONTARIO, 1817-1867: KINGSTON AND OG-DENSBURG. *Ontario Hist. [Canada] 1975 67(4): 199-209.* Discusses the growth of steamboating on Lake Ontario, suggests some of the causes, and indicates the impact of the changing transportation patterns on the two towns named. These were seen as comparable, and in both cases towns which did not develop as their citizens had hoped, largely due to shifts in the inland transportation patterns feeding the lake steamers. Some examples of cargoes are given, as are some generalized descriptions of selected vessels to indicate changes over the years. Based on primary sources; 43 notes.   W. B. Whitham

654. Jones, Howard. ANGLOPHOBIA AND THE AROOSTOOK WAR. *New England Q. 1975 48(4): 519-539.* The Maine-Canada boundary dispute of 1837-39 arose from vague passages in the existing treaty. Each side claimed the disputed territory, tempers flared, and troops were sent, but no shooting occurred. President Martin Van Buren sent Winfield Scott to work out a compromise. A neutral area was created and the controversy gradually died down. Great Britain and the United States should have used this time to work out a permanent settlement, but nothing was done. War was avoided simply because neither side wanted it. 30 notes.   V. L. Human

655. Kaplanoff, Mark D., ed. NOOTKA SOUND IN 1789: JOSEPH INGRAHAM'S ACCOUNT. *Pacific Northwest Q. 1974 65(4): 157-163.* Examines the history of European contact with Nootka Sound on the west coast of Vancouver Island. The Spanish first arrived in 1774, followed by James Cook in 1778. Others followed as a result of Cook's discovery of the profit to be had in the fur trade. Among these was the American ship, *Columbia*, with Joseph Ingraham as first mate. At the request of Don Esteban Josè Martinez, commander of the Spanish ship *Princesa*, Ingraham wrote an account in 1789 of what he had learned of the area and its inhabitants after having wintered on the island. Published here for the first time, it describes the flora and fauna of the area and the people, their amusements, customs, and religion. 24 notes.   R. V. Ritter

656. Katz, Michael B. ORIGINS OF THE INSTITUTIONAL STATE. *Marxist Perspectives 1978 1(4): 6-22.* Institutions from 1750 to 1860 in North America developed from volunteer-oriented to publicly financed formal bureaucracies which delineated sharp boundaries in so-cial organization and became specialized, demeaning, and all-encompass-ing during social change and industrial capitalism.

657. Kushner, Howard I. THE RUSSIAN-AMERICAN DIPLO-MATIC CONTEST FOR THE PACIFIC BASIN AND THE MONROE DOCTRINE. *J. of the West 1976 15(2): 65-80.* Discusses the events leading up to President James Monroe's message to Congress in December, 1823, which became the Monroe Doctrine. Proposes that the policies laid out in the Monroe Doctrine were aimed at Russia rather than at Great Britain, but even more directly at domestic foes. The 1821 ukase, issued by Tsar Alexander I, closed the entire Northwest Coast of America. This challenge was answered directly and in no uncertain terms by diplomatic messages. A contingent in Congress called for direct action. The Monroe Doctrine was the answer to this demand. Also involved were the Presidential aspirations of Henry Clay and John Quincy Adams.   R. Alvis

658. Lambert, James H. THE REVEREND SAMUEL SIMPSON WOOD, BA, MA: A FORGOTTEN NOTABLE AND THE EARLY ANGLICAN CHURCH IN CANADA. *J. of the Can. Church Hist. Soc. 1974 16(1): 2-22.* Describes the career of Samuel Wood (1795-1868), an English-born clergyman in the Anglican diocese of Quebec. Educated at the conservative Richmond Grammar School and Cambridge, Wood began his work in Quebec as a missionary. In 1822 he became the first rector of Drummondsville. In 1829 he went to Three Rivers, and re-mained some 30 years. His chief efforts were devoted to ending the British government's discrimination against Canadian Anglican clergy and to establishing church-related schools and seminaries. His later years were spent as rural dean of Upper Durham, where he was primarily involved in missionary work. Though neither powerful nor spectacular, Wood's career represented many important trends in the evolution of Canadian Anglicanism. Based largely on primary sources; 132 notes.   J. A. Kicklighter

659. Landon, Richard. IMPULSIVE FRONTIER HACKS. *Can. Lib. J. 1974 31(4): 362-364.* Reviews *William Henry Bartlett (1809-1854): Artist, Author & Traveller* (University of Toronto Press, 1973) by Alexander M. Ross and *Braves and Buffalo: Plains Indian Life in 1837 —Watercolours of Alfred J. Miller* by Michael Bell (University of Toronto Press). Bartlett was a Canadian, and Miller an American artist.   S

660. Landry, Yves. ÉTUDE CRITIQUE DU RECENSEMENT DU CANADA DE 1765 [Critical study of the census of Canada of 1765]. *R. d'hist. de l'Amérique française [Canada] 1975 29(3): 323-351.* The

census of 1765, ordered by the imperial government, was taken with the help of the Catholic clergy. A total population of 76,675 persons was reported. The census was not taken in all parishes, and approximately 10% of the population were not counted. A total figure of 80,000 is more realistic. Criticism of statistical sources is an essential prerequisite in determining historical reality. Based on documents in the Public Record Office (London), Archives Publiques du Canada, Archives Nationales du Québec, and secondary works; 5 tables, 47 notes.   L. B. Chan

661. Lass, William E. HOW THE FORTY-NINTH PARALLEL BECAME THE INTERNATIONAL BOUNDARY. *Minnesota Hist. 1975 44(6): 209-219.* In spite of an ignorance of geography, lack of British concern over the fate of the Canadian lands, and the existence of a myth that the boundary had been set by commissioners named under Article X of the Treaty of Utrecht, the US-Canadian border was partly established in 1818 on a due course from the northwest corner of the Lake of the Woods to the 49th parallel and thence to the continental divide. Based on primary and secondary sources.   N. Lederer

662. Lates, Richard. THE LINE WHICH SEPARATES VERMONTERS FROM CANADIANS: A SHORT HISTORY OF VERMONT'S NORTHERN BORDER WITH QUEBEC. *Vermont Hist. 1976 44(2): 71-77.* The French claimed the Champlain Valley until defeated in 1761. The British Proclamation of 1763 named Lat. 45 degrees as Quebec's southern boundary and the Treaty of 1783 confirmed it. John Collins of Quebec and Thomas Valentine of New York surveyed and marked this line in 1771-72, and west from Lake Champlain (by Collins and Sauthier) in 1773-74. It was not agreed upon until the Webster-Ashburton Treaty of 1842, including Fort Montgomery ("Fort Blunder") near Rouses Point, from .25 to 1.1 miles north of 45 degrees. The gore between Halls Stream and the Connecticut River, awarded to Vermont in a US Supreme Court decision settling its New Hampshire boundary in 1933, is almost completely surrounded by New Hampshire. 2 maps, 20 notes.   T. D. S. Bassett

663. Leechman, Douglas. "COMODITYES BESIDES FURRES." *Beaver [Canada] 1974 304(4): 46-52.* Describes attempts of the Hudson's Bay Company to find saleable products in the New World.   S

664. Lemieux, Lucien. LA PREMIÈRE CAISSE ECCLÉSIASTIQUE DU CLERGÉ CANADIEN [The first ecclesiastical fund of the Canadian clergy]. *Sessions d'Étude: Soc. Can. d'Hist. de L'Église Catholique [Canada] 1977 44: 5-22.* Discusses the establishment and administration of a fund for ill and aged priests of the Canadian Catholic Church during the 1790's, as well as further financial aid during the 1830's.

665. Maclean, Hugh D. AN IRISH APOSTLE AND ARCHDEACON IN CANADA. *J. of the Can. Church Hist. Soc. 1973 15(3): 50-67.* Irish-born William McMurray (1810-94) was an important Canadian Anglican clergyman. Brought to Toronto when he was one, McMurray became a theology student at age 18. In 1832, he became the missionary to the Ojibway Indians in the Sault Ste. Marie area. He was ordained deacon in 1833 and priest in 1839. His work with the Indians was successful, but he resigned after the provincial governor stopped all projects involved in "civilizing" the Indians. He served as assistant curate and rector of Ancaster and Dundas, and in 1857 became rector of Niagara. He received two honorary doctorates as a result of extensive fund-raising in the United States and of lobbying for the church at the Parliament in Quebec City. He rounded out his career as a fund-raiser in Great Britain as rural dean of Lincoln and Welland, and as archdeacon of the new diocese of Niagara 1876-94. 58 notes.   J. A. Kicklighter

666. Mansvelt, A. CAPTAIN GEORGE VANCOUVER: BRITS ZEEVAARDER VAN NEDERLANDSE AFKOMST [Captain George Vancouver: British navigator of Dutch extraction]. *Spiegel Hist. [Netherlands] 1977 12(2): 98-104.* The ancestors of the British navigator George Vancouver (1757-98) came from the Dutch community of Coevorden. In the Netherlands, the family name was spelled Van Coeverden. George's great grandfather settled in England in the 17th century and the family name was anglicized to Vancouver. George joined the British navy in 1772 and sailed with Captain James Cook (1728-79) in the Pacific in 1778. In 1791 Vancouver was charged with the task of charting the American continent between the 30th and 60th meridian. He was very successful in this undertaking and returned in 1795. He named the island

of Vancouver after himself. In 1886 the city of Vancouver, British Columbia, was named after him. Illus., biblio.   G. D. Homan

667. Martin, Ged. THE APPOINTMENT OF SIR FRANCIS BOND HEAD AS LIEUTENANT-GOVERNOR OF UPPER CANADA IN 1835. *J. of Imperial and Commonwealth Hist. [Great Britain] 1975 3(2): 280-291.* Reassesses the appointment of Sir Francis Bond Head to the Lieutenant-Governorship of Upper Canada; he may have been sent to Canada in 1835 because of a mistake in identity.

668. Martin, Ged. BRITISH OFFICIALS AND THEIR ATTITUDES TO THE NEGRO COMMUNITY IN CANADA, 1833-1861. *Ontario Hist. [Canada] 1974 66(2): 79-88.* Discusses the Negro in Canada in a broader perspective than that of fugitive slaves. Points to differences in the position of the Negro in different provinces and observes some variations in the attitudes of these communities toward the United States. Notes that these attitudes were basically hostile, and further that the British tried to divert fugitives to the West Indies. Similar efforts made to divert resident Negroes were also resisted. There was no official policy toward Negroes in Canada other than to see and basically treat them as legally free citizens or residents of the provinces. 28 notes.   W. B. Whitham

669. Martin, Ged. THE SIMCOES AND THEIR FRIENDS. *Ontario Hist. [Canada] 1977 69(2): 101-112.* Discusses, through extensive quotations from letters, the friendship between the Simcoe's and Burge's families. Shows the relationships with the Heads, from which family came the last Lieutenant Governor of Upper Canada before the Durham Report disrupted the original pattern. Speculates on Simcoe's influence on Bond-Head, as they knew each other, albeit for a short time. 32 notes.   W. B. Whitham

670. Mathews, Robin. SUSANNA MOODIE, PINK TORYISM, AND NINETEENTH CENTURY IDEAS OF CANADIAN IDENTITY. *J. of Can. Studies 1975 10(3): 3-15.* Discusses the social stratification theory of Canadian writer Susanna Moodie (*Roughing It in the Bush*, *Life in the Clearings*), 1832-53, including her conception of Canada's national self-image.

671. McNairn, Norman A. MISSION TO CANADA. *Methodist Hist. 1975 13(4): 46-60.* An account of the efforts of the Methodist Episcopal Church to expand Methodism into the Provinces of Upper and Lower Canada during 1788-1812. 30 notes.   H. L. Calkin

672. Millar, W. P. J. GEORGE P. M. BALL: A RURAL BUSINESSMAN IN UPPER CANADA. *Ontario Hist. [Canada] 1974 66(2): 65-78.* Analyzes an unusually complete set of recently found mid-19th century business records. The records are significant because they throw light on the activities of a small businessman in a time of marked economic change and depression. Outlines the events of Ball's life and relates them to events in the province. Discusses the economic aspects of his activities in response to the problems he faced in the depression of the late 1840's. 42 notes.   W. B. Whitham

673. Millar, W. P. J. THE REMARKABLE REV. THADDEUS OSGOOD: A STUDY IN THE EVANGELICAL SPIRIT IN THE CANADAS. *Social Hist. [Canada] 1977 10(19): 59-76.* Traces career of nondenominational traveling preacher Thaddeus Osgood (1775-1852) in Canada after 1807. He attempted to stimulate a vast spiritual awakening. He believed such an awakening could not be left to faith alone, but must be assisted by such means as day and Sunday schools, education of Indians, temperance movements, sabbatarianism, organization of tract societies, and an attack on urban poverty and vice. By the 1820's he met strong resistance from the sources of denominationalism. By 1835 he had narrowed his activities to the moral improvement of the urban poor, especially children. Based on documents in Public Archives of Canada, Public Record Office, on newspapers, and on other primary sources; 105 notes.   W. K. Hobson

674. Neidecker, John F. ROBERT E. LEE VISITS THE GREAT LAKES COUNTRY. *Inland Seas 1974 30(2): 125-127.* During an Army boundary survey in 1835 for Ohio and Michigan, Lieutenant Robert E. Lee apparently was involved in an incident in Canada in which a Canadian lighthouse keeper was killed. Neither the location nor the details of the incident are known.   K. J. Bauer

675. Norris, John. THE STRAIT OF ANIAN AND BRITISH NORTHWEST AMERICA: COOK'S THIRD VOYAGE IN PERSPECTIVE. *BC Studies [Canada] 1977-78 (36): 3-22.* Captain James Cook put into Nootka, British Columbia, for a brief stay in 1778 on his third voyage, before making a perfunctory exploration of the coast to the north and a detailed examination of the Alaska coast. His instructions were to search for the "strait of Anián" which supposedly separated Asia from North America and was a key to a Northwest Passage across North America. Analyzes the significance of Cook's voyage for British sovereignty and settlement of British Columbia and the reasons for his search north of the 65th parallel. 7 maps, 15 notes.   D. L. Smith

676. Olsen, Ruth A. RAPE: AN "UN-VICTORIAN" ASPECT OF LIFE IN UPPER CANADA. *Ontario Hist. [Canada] 1976 68(2): 75-79.* Points out that rape was probably widespread in the early to mid-19th century but reliable statistics are not available. Suggests reasons for this. Charges brought in court were often reduced since there are considerably more convictions for "assault with intent to ravish" than for rape. Suggests that, since the penalty for the latter was death, juries were unwilling to convict for rape no matter what the evidence. The sole exception was when a child was involved. 18 notes.   W. B. Whitham

677. Phinney, William R. THE NEW YORK CONFERENCE AND CANADIAN METHODISM. *J. of the Can. Church Hist. Soc. [Canada] 1977 19(1-2): 27-41.* Summarizes the Canadian missionary activities of five Methodist missionaries who were affiliated with the New York Conference of the United Methodist Church: Darius Dunham, James Coleman, Nathan Bangs, Peter Vannest, and Samuel Coate. They all went to Canada as volunteers because of their strong personal convictions and, perhaps, their senses of adventure. They enjoyed considerable success in their efforts to bring about the growth of Methodism in Canada, showing how important the New York Conference was to that development. Primary and secondary sources, 30 notes. This issue is *J. of the Can. Church Hist. Soc.* 1977 19(1-2) and *Bull. of the United Church of Can.* 1977 26.   J. A. Kicklighter

678. Pirenne, J.-H. LA COMPAGNIE RUSSO-AMÉRICAINE ET LA POLITIQUE MONDIALE D'ALEXANDRE I^e [The Russian-American Company and Alexander I's world policy]. *Bull. des Séances de l'Acad. Royale des Sci. d'Outre-Mer [Belgium] 1976 (3): 316-342.* Examines the origins, development, and decline of the Russian-American Company, a Russian mixed-economy company founded in 1799 to promote the expansion of Siberian merchants' commerce along the American Northwest coast. It momentarily affected Russian maritime ascendancy in the Northern Pacific at the apogee of Alexander I's international influence. The company's rise and decline were due to changes in his foreign policy. 46 notes, biblio.   R. O. Khan

679. Purdy, J. D. JOHN STRACHAN AND THE DIOCESAN THEOLOGICAL INSTITUTE AT COBOURG, 1842-1852. *Ontario Hist. [Canada] 1973 65(2): 113-123.* John Strachan had pondered the problems of his church before internal disputes (tractarians v. evangelicals) and external attacks (political reform and rival denominations) brought a crisis in the 1840's. Strachan was concerned with obtaining clergy trained to handle frontier conditions. Discusses the resolution of that problem in light of the disputes in the Church of England. Primary and secondary sources; 51 notes.   W. B. Whitham

680. Reibel, Daniel B. THE BRITISH NAVY ON THE UPPER GREAT LAKES, 1760-1789. *Niagara Frontier 1973 20(3): 66-75.* Discusses the Great Lakes as an area necessary to naval strength in North America, emphasizing the French ignorance of this fact and the British concentration on the area as one for shipbuilding and naval strength. 2 reproductions, 25 notes.

681. Ross, W. Gillies. WHALING IN HUDSON BAY. *Beaver [Canada] 1973 303(4): 4-11, 304(1): 40-47, (2): 52-59.* Part I. Examines the Hudson's Bay Company's first whaling period, 1765-1772, which was unsuccessful. Most efforts were near Marble Island north of Churchill. In this period the company, wishing to supplement its food supply, only killed five small whales. They did not stay long enough for each search, had inadequate provisions as well as poor leadership, and erroneously limited their search to Marble Island, while the whales were usually farther north. 8 illus., map, chart. Part II. 1866-67. Part III. The voyages of the *Perseverance* and the whaling industry of the Hudson's Bay Company, 1892-97.   S

682. Ruggles, R. I. GOVERNOR SAMUEL WEGG, INTELLECTUAL LAYMAN OF THE ROYAL SOCIETY, 1753-1802. *Notes and Records of the Royal Soc. of London [Great Britain] 1978 32(2): 181-199.* As deputy governor and governor of the Hudson's Bay Company, 1774-99, and treasurer of the Royal Society, 1768-1802, Samuel Wegg (1723-1802) facilitated communication and cooperation between the two organizations and was instrumental in reversing the Company's policy of extreme secrecy and hoarding of information of interest to the scientific community. Plate, 2 fig., 33 notes.   T. L. Underwood

683. Ruggles, Richard I. GOVERNOR SAMUEL WEGG: 'THE WINDS OF CHANGE.' *Beaver [Canada] 1976 307(2): 10-20.* In 1748, Samuel Wegg inherited some of his father's stock in the Hudson's Bay Company. He accumulated more shares, was elected to the Committee of the Co. in 1760, eventually became governor, and died in 1802. Wegg had a typical gentry upbringing. He became a barrister and joined the right clubs. It was the club affiliations that had an impact on the Company. Wegg for years attended and participated in activities of the Royal Society, the Thursday Club, and the Society of Antiquaries. He was an intimate of naturalists, cartographers, and explorers; and these interests, coupled with his position with the Company, led to many changes in Hudson's Bay Co. policy and knowledge of geography. 7 illus., 2 maps.   D. Chaput

684. Ruggles, Richard I. HOSPITAL BOYS OF THE BAY. *Beaver [Canada] 1977 308(2): 4-11.* Summarizes education in Great Britain of orphan and indigent children, their selection for certain charity schools, methods and tools of education, and changing curriculum. Emphasizes the Grey Coat Hospital, Westminster, and the Blue Coat School (Christ's Hospital), London. The Hudson's Bay Company encouraged enlistment of many of these boys in the late 1700's, feeling that their training in mathematics and reading would be useful on the northern frontier. Dozens entered the Company service, but other than David Thompson, none became notable explorers, cartographers, or administrators. 7 illus.   D. Chaput

685. Schelbert, Leo. PIERRE-FRÉDÉRIC DROZ: THE 'AMERICAN': THE STORY OF AN ITINERANT WATCHMAKER. *Swiss Am. Hist. Soc. Newsletter 1977 13(1): 11-20.* Pierre-Frédéric Droz, a Swiss watchmaker, journeyed through Europe and British North America, 1768-70.

686. Smith, Donald. THE MISSISSAUGA AND DAVID RAMSAY. *Beaver [Canada] 1975 305(4): 4-8.* David Ramsay, born in Scotland, settled north of Lake Ontario in the 1760's and engaged in the fur trade while also acting as a messenger. He was involved in numerous escapades with the local Mississauga Indians, a branch of the Chippewas. Over a period of years Ramsay killed at least a dozen Indians, usually over liquor, illegal trading, or misunderstandings. The Superintendent of Indian Affairs, Sir William Johnson, realized that not only was Ramsay guilty, but that the authorities would not punish him. Ramsay, who despised the Indians, took to their way of life, yet continued in his attitudes. After the American Revolution, incoming Loyalist settlers became familiar with the Ramsay legend and passed the tales into local folklore. The Mississauga also remembered Ramsay, naming him the man most responsible for their move north, away from their traditional homeland. 3 illus., map.   D. Chaput

687. Smith, Shirlee A. JAMES SUTHERLAND, INLAND TRADER, 1751-1797. *Beaver [Canada] 1975 306(3): 18-23.* Sutherland was a moderately successful trader for the Hudson's Bay Company. He worked at posts from Lake of the Woods to Albany, was effective working with the Indians, and got along well with rival traders such as Cameron, who traded in his vicinity. Sutherland, described as a "worthy officer" of the Company, was one of the middle-level traders whose careers are not generally known. Based on manuscripts in the Hudson's Bay Co. Archives; 5 illus., 2 maps.   D. Chaput

688. Socwell, Clarence P. PETER SKENE OGDEN: FUR TRADER EXTRAORDINAIRE: TRAPPING, EXPLORATION, AND ADVENTURE ON THE CANADIAN AND AMERICAN FRONTIERS.

Am. West 1973 10(3): 42-47, 61. The 17-year-old Montreal-born Ogden (1794-1854) signed on as a clerk with the North West Company. His ability and daring as a fur trapper, Indian fighter, and explorer advanced him in the company and in the Hudson's Bay Company. He supervised trapping expeditions in unmapped regions from the American Southwest to Alaska and from the western Great Lakes to the Pacific. His 1824-30 expeditions worked over the formidable Snake River Country and parts of the Great Basin where his name now graces several geographic features. In 1835 Ogden was commissioned chief factor, the highest rank in the company. His last venture was a failure: negotiations with President Millard Fillmore for compensation for the property which his company had lost to the Americans. 4 illus.   D. L. Smith

689. Sweet, Jessie M. ROBERT JAMESON AND THE EXPLORERS: THE SEARCH FOR THE NORTH-WEST PASSAGE. *Ann. of Sci. [Great Britain] 1974 31(1): 21-47.* Part I. Discusses the life and work of Robert Jameson (1774-1854) with particular reference to the search for the Northwest Passage and to his influence on others' explorations while he was professor of natural history at the University of Edinburgh, 1804-54. Article to be continued.

690. Verney, Douglas V. and Verney, Diana M. A CANADIAN POLITICAL COMMUNITY: A CASE FOR TRIPARTITE CONFEDERALISM. *J. of Commonwealth and Comparative Pol. [Great Britain] 1974 12(1): 1-19.* Examines the problems of a permanent francophone minority in Canada, the possible separatist, confederate, majoritarian, and bicultural solutions, and their origins in Canada's political history. Traces the workings of confederalism and federalism in Canada, the historic definition of Canada itself between 1763 and 1867, its significance for the future of the Canadian parliamentary process, and the argument for a new political system of Tripartite Confederalism. An appendix details five perspectives on the Canadian political system. 10 notes.   C. Anstey

691. Webb, Paul. THE NAVAL ASPECTS OF THE NOOTKA SOUND CRISIS. *Mariner's Mirror [Great Britain] 1975 61(2): 133-154.* Discusses the politics, diplomacy, and trade behind the question of territorial rights in Nootka Sound (Vancouver, British Columbia) between Great Britain and Spain, 1790.

692. Williams, Glyndwr. ANDREW GRAHAM AND THOMAS HUTCHINS: COLLABORATION AND PLAGIARISM IN 18TH CENTURY NATURAL HISTORY. *Beaver [Canada] 1978 308(4): 4-14.* Andrew Graham served more than 30 years in various Hudson's Bay Company posts, became a trained observer, and accumulated much information on people, plants, and the natural history of the region. Hutchins came to the area in 1772 as a surgeon and also became a natural history enthusiast. Within a few years, many natural history works were published in England and Europe, often crediting the two men, but mostly praising the work of Thomas Hutchins. However, it appears that Hutchins gleaned most of his information from data gathered by Graham. Hutchins died in 1790, Graham in 1815. The mystery is heightened by the fact that Graham had nothing but praise for Hutchins, though he must have been aware that the other man was earning a wide reputation based on pilfered materials. Based on Hudson's Bay Company materials; 8 illus., map.   D. Chaput

693. Wise, S. F. LIBERAL CONSENSUS OR IDEOLOGICAL BATTLEGROUND: SOME REFLECTIONS ON THE HARTZ THESIS. *Can. Hist. Assoc. Hist. Papers 1974: 1-14.* Discusses recent trends in Canadian historiography, emphasizing Louis Hartz' conception of the 1760-1800 period.

694. Wonders, William C. THE TOAST AT THE PUNCH BOWL. *Alberta Hist. [Canada] 1974 22(4): 26-30.* 19th-century fur-traders crossing the Continental Divide paused at the Committee's Punch Bowl, a lake at the summit of Athabasca Pass, for a ritual toast with a glass of rum.   S

695. Woodcock, George. CAPTAIN COOK AT NOOTKA, 1778: THE POLITICAL AFTERMATH. *Hist. Today [Great Britain] 1978 28(2): 97-104.* Original explorations in the area of Nootka Sound on Vancouver Island by British Captain James Cook were primarily to prove existence or nonexistence of the Northwest Passage and secondarily to

claim land; his presence there in 1778 touched off a competition for control of the area between Great Britain and Spain until 1794.

Accommodation to the French

696. Angers, François-Albert. LE DOSSIER DE L'ACTE DE QUEBEC [The Quebec Act file]. *Action Natl. [Canada] 1974 64(1): 871-922.* Comments on the Quebec Act, 1774, which marked the official founding of Quebec, with documents by three great Canadian historians, Thomas Chapais, François Xavier Garneau, and Lionel Groulx.

697. Dessaules, Louis-Antoine. PREMIÈRE "LECTURE" SUR L'ANNEXION [First "reading" on annexation]. *Études Françaises [Canada] 1973 9(3): 205-236.* Far from being the freest people on earth as claimed by Great Britain, 19th-century inhabitants of Lower Canada were subjected to the oppressive political policies of the British colonial administration. To free themselves of this oppression, they ought to seek unification with the United States of America. Extracted from *Six lectures aur l'annexion du Canada auz États-Unis*, Montreal, Gendron, 1851, p. 42-54.   G. J. Rossi

698. Fahmy-Eid, Nadia. ULTRAMONTANISME, IDÉOLOGIE ET CLASSES SOCIALES [Ultramontanism, ideology and social classes]. *R. d'Hist. de l'Amérique Française 1975 29(1): 49-68.* During the 19th century, the French middle class of Lower Canada united with the ultramontane clergy against the economic power being wielded by the English middle class of Upper Canada. The clergy of Lower Canada aimed at a state governed by the Church and effectively influenced education and government until Lower Canada became a modern capitalist state. Based on primary and secondary sources; 25 notes.
                                                              C. Collon

699. Greenwood, E. Murray. ANALYSE DE L'EXPOSÉ DE N.-E. DIONNE SUR LE DISCOURS DE PIERRE BÉDARD AU SUJET DE LA LANGUE OFFICIELLE, 1793 [Analysis of N.-E. Dionne's account about Pierre Bédard's discourse on the subject of the official language, 1793]. *Rev. d'Hist. de l'Am. Française [Canada] 1976 30(2): 259-262.* In his analysis of the linguistic conflict of 1792-93 in the Legislative Assembly of Lower Canada, Mason Wade cites a discourse of Pierre-Stanislas Bédard. The *Gazette de Québec* did not publish it, nor do historians F.-X. Garneau and Thomas Chapais refer to it. Wade cites Narcisse-Eutrope Dionne, *Pierre Bédard et ses fils* (Québec, 1909). Dionne's views were probably based on Hugh Gray's francophobic public commentary published in the newspaper *Le Canadien* on 30 December 1809. Based on letters in the Public Archives of Canada and secondary works; 10 notes.   L. B. Chan

700. Hare, John E. LA FORMATION DE LA TERMINOLOGIE PARLEMENTAIRE ET ÉLECTORALE AU QUÉBEC, 1792-1810 [The formation of parliamentary and electoral terminology in Quebec: 1792-1810]. *Rev. de l'Université d'Ottawa [Canada] 1976 46(4): 460-475.* As a result of the Constitutional Act of 1791, Quebec, then known as Lower Canada, was given its own Parliament to be elected by the voters of the province. Parliamentary institutions were strange to the French-speaking Québécois, because France lacked parliamentary bodies when Canada was ruled by the French. Some of the terminology used in the electoral process and the new Quebec Parliament were pure French, but much was borrowed, either in the form of calques or of direct loaning, from English electoral and parliamentary terminology. Many of these borrowings have persisted. Canadian French electoral and parliamentary vocabulary is quite different from that of the mother country, whose history has been a good deal less stable and tranquil than that of Quebec. 56 notes, biblio.   J. C. Billigmeier

701. Hare, John. L'ASSEMBLÉE LÉGISLATIVE DU BAS-CANADA, 1792-1814: DÉPUTATION ET POLARISATION POLITIQUE [The legislature of Lower Canada, 1792-1814: the deputies and political polarization]. *R. d'Hist. de l'Amérique Française [Canada] 1973 27(3): 361-396.* Analyzes the membership of the legislative assembly of Lower Canada in the late 17th and early 18th century, and assesses its conduct and voting patterns.

702. Igartua, José. A CHANGE IN CLIMATE: THE CONQUEST AND THE *MARCHANDS* OF MONTREAL. *Can. Hist. Assoc. Hist. Papers 1974: 115-134.* Discusses the change from French to British commercial ascendancy among the middle classes of Montreal, Quebec, 1750-92, emphasizing the fur trade.

703. Igartua, José E. THE MERCHANTS OF MONTREAL AT THE CONQUEST: SOCIO-ECONOMIC PROFILE. *Social Hist. [Canada] 1975 8(16): 275-293.* Of the 200 merchants and traders who can be identified in Montreal 1750-75, 92 form a core group of those in business for an extended period of time. Examinations of the core group reveals that they were not wealthy, their social mobility was restricted, and a distinct hierarchy existed among them. Importers and wholesale merchants formed the highest group; they married within their group or one notch below. Fifty-five fur trade outfitters formed the second category. They also tended to marry within their group, but had few social or business connections with the colony's governing elite. The third category, "shopkeepers," was not a socially cohesive group. The fourth category consisted of assorted traders, artisans, and one moneylender. Based on published primary sources and documents in the Public Archives of Canada and the National Archives of Quebec. 82 notes, 2 appendixes.
W. K. Hobson

704. LaBrèque, Marie-Paule. LES ÉGLISES DANS LES CANTONS DE L'EST, 1800-1860 [The churches in the Eastern Townships, 1800-1860]. *Sessions d'Étude: Soc. Can. d'Hist. de l'Eglise Catholique 1974 41: 87-103.* A history of the establishment of churches in the Eastern Townships of Quebec, including the great material obstacles and the psychological and moral difficulties faced in French settlement. Analyzes the problem of maintaining French education and religion in the isolated colony after the establishment of other settlers (American, Scotch, Irish). Studies the decline of colonization and validity of French rule on Anglo-Saxon land. Describes the establishment of Catholicism and the propagation of the faith under various bishops. Regional and diocesan archives and secondary sources; 49 notes.
S. Sevilla

705. Laforce, Ernest. IMMIGRATION ET IMMIGRANTS [Immigration and immigrants]. *Action Natl. [Canada] 1978 67(7): 547-558.* The first immigrants to Canada arrived after the cession of New France to England, and immediately attempted anglicization of the country. Immigration has continued as an instrument of repression against French Canadian society. To counter the possible French majority in the province of Manitoba, John A. MacDonald actively recruited immigrants from Europe, Asia, and Africa who would become part of a dominant British culture, ensuring its preponderance in western Canada. After the election of 1896, with the appointment of Clifford Sifton as minister of immigration, the rate of new arrivals passed 500,000 per year. Thus, despite a strong birthrate, French Canadians remained a perpetual minority.
A. W. Novitsky

706. Lamonde, Yvan. CLASSES SOCIALES, CLASSES SCOLAIRES: UNE POLÉMIQUE SUR L'ÉDUCATION EN 1819-1820 [Social classes, scholarly classes: A controversy on education in 1819-1820]. *Sessions d'Étude: Soc. Can. d'Hist. de l'Eglise Catholique 1974 41: 43-60.* A history of the educational controversy raised by French-Canadian priest Abbot de Calonne on the importance of doctrinal vigilance by counter-revolutionary clergy in Canada against liberal "Lancastrian" schools modeled after British secular teaching. Studies de Calonne's letters to the *Trois-Rivieres Gazette* against public schools. Debate centers on the control of schools, the extent of modernization, and protection of the existing social order. Failure of the liberal primary schools was due to clerical efforts. Based on a previous study by Fernand Ouellet, *Éléments d'Histoire Sociale du Bas-Canada* (Cahiers du Quebec, 1972). 49 notes.
S. Sevilla

707. Tishkov, V. A. K ISTORII VOZNIKNOVENIIA FRANKO-KANADSKOGO NATSIONAL'NOGO VOPROSA [On the history of the origin of the French Canadian national problem]. *Voprosy Istorii [USSR] 1974 (1): 76-90.* Drawing on archive materials and historical documents, the author traces the origin of the national question among French Canadians in connection with the British conquest of Canada. The article contains a critical analysis of the various trends existing in the bourgeois historiography of Canada, which give widely differing interpretations to this question. The author draws the conclusion that the origin of the national question in Canada should be directly attributed to the policy pursued by Britain and her colonial top crust in relation to the indigenous French-speaking population. He makes a point of stressing that from the very outset the national question in Canada was distinguished by its class character, for it concerned relations between the privileged English minority and the ruthlessly exploited and disfranchised mass of colonists of French extraction.
J

708. Tousignant, Pierre. LA PREMIÈRE CAMPAGNE ÉLECTORALE DES CANADIENS EN 1792 [The first Canadian electoral campaign in 1792]. *Hist. sociale—Social Hist. [Canada] 1975 8(15): 120-148.* In the first electoral campaign in Canada, in 1792, the francophone majority elected a disproportionately anglophone Legislative Assembly. Although corruption may have played some role, an analysis of the available returns of the propaganda disseminated prior to the election suggests that the anglophone candidates' appeal to colonial unity and loyalty had a stronger attraction than the francophone candidates' appeal to ethnic loyalty, especially among the French-speaking upper and middle classes. Based on newspapers and documents in Canadian Public Archives, Quebec Seminary Archives, and National Library of Quebec; 77 notes, appendix.
W. K. Hobson

709. Tousignant, Pierre. LE CONSERVATISME DE LA PETITE NOBLESSE SEIGNEURIALE [The conservatism of the petit seigneurial nobility]. *Ann. Hist. de la Révolution Française [France] 1973 45(3): 322-343.* Under French rule in Canada, a class of small landowning gentry developed. British policy cultivated the support of this class and during both the American and French Revolutions, they remained loyal to Great Britain in the hope of maintaining and consolidating their status. The article was originally presented in 1969 at the University of Montreal and includes a transcript of part of a discussion that followed. Primary and secondary sources; 42 notes.
S. R. Smith

710. Tousignant, Pierre. PROBLÉMATIQUE POUR UNE NOUVELLE APPROCHE DE LA CONSTITUTION DE 1791 [Thoughts toward a new approach concerning the Constitution of 1791]. *R. d'Hist. de l'Amérique Française [Canada] 1973 27(2): 181-234.* Attempts to place in a new perspective the establishment of a parliamentary government in Lower Canada which takes into account the ambitions of the Scottish-English middle class, the sociopolitical concepts of British leaders, and the peculiar problems raised by the "Old Colonial System."

711. Wallot, Jean-Pierre. THE LOWER CANADIAN CLERGY AND THE REIGN OF TERROR (1810). *Study Sessions: Can. Catholic Hist. Assoc. 1973 40: 53-60.* Studies the Catholic clergy's reactions and conduct during the crisis of 1810, in which Governor Sir James Craig implemented repressive measures to fend off the threat of democracy and French Canadian nationalism.
S

712. Wallot, Jean-Pierre. RÉVOLUTION ET RÉFORMISME DANS LE BAS-CANADA (1773-1815) [Revolution and reformism in Lower Canada (1773-1815)]. *Ann. Hist. de la Révolution Française [France] 1973 45(3): 344-406.* During the American Revolution, most French-speaking Canadians adopted an attitude of neutrality, despite American propaganda. Several reasons for this are suggested. However, Canadians were generally familiar with the trends of Enlightenment thought and many hailed the beginning of the French Revolution as the dawn of a new era. Despite the zeal of some revolutionaries and several local uprisings against the established government, reformers saw greater hope in expanding their influence within a British-style parliamentary system. Local issues and anticlericalism played major roles. Primary and secondary sources; 213 notes.
S. R. Smith

The American Revolution

713. Bird, Lilah Smith. THE TRAGIC SHIPWRECK OF THE BRIGANTINE *ST. LAWRENCE*. *Nova Scotia Hist. Q. [Canada] 1978 8(2): 165-170.* The brigantine *St. Lawrence*, enroute from Quebec to New York carrying British Army dispatches, ran into a severe storm and on 5 December 1780 was wrecked two miles off Port Hood Island. Some of the crew were able to launch a boat and struggle ashore. The dispatches were delivered to Sir Henry Clinton nine months later in New York.
H. M. Evans

714. Bowler, R. Arthur. SIR GUY CARLETON AND THE CAMPAIGN OF 1776 IN CANADA. *Can. Hist. R. 1974 55(2): 131-140.* A re-examination of the British army's campaign of 1776 in Canada to retake the Province of Quebec from American forces and carry the war to the Revolutionary colonies. Based primarily on army administration material in the Public Record Office, London. The failures of the campaign, traditionally blamed on excessive caution and poor military judgement on the part of General Sir Guy Carleton, are found to have been due to logistical problems, for the most part the result of an inefficient and inadequate army logistical organization.
A

715. Brown, Wallace. THE AMERICAN COLONIES AND THE WEST INDIES. *Am. Hist. Illus. 1974 9(2):12-23.* Considers the interrelationships between Britain's North American colonies and the British West Indies. The islands produced abundant sugar, which for a time made them more important than the mainland colonies. The colonials needed sugar and molasses for rum manufacture and traded wood and food products in return. Slaves were used extensively in the islands. The American Revolution caused many loyalists to move to the West Indies and re-directed island trade patterns to Canada. The old order was never fully reestablished. 12 photos, map.
V. L. Human

716. Dull, Jonathan R. FRANCE AND THE AMERICAN REVOLUTION: QUESTIONING THE MYTHS. *Pro. of the Ann. Meeting of the Western Soc. for French Hist. 1973 1: 110-118.* Attempts to dispel six prevalent myths concerning France and the American Revolution. France intervened because of dispassionate calculation, not because of Anglophobia or a desire to avenge the loss of Canada. French participation reflected the desperate French diplomatic position on the European continent. The war was a tragic failure for France: American independence failed to weaken Great Britain. The Battle of Saratoga provided only the occasion for French participation, a policy which had already been decided. The Spanish navy was vital to the maintenance of the military initiative by the allies. France was desperate for peace but did not attempt to betray the United States. The French government was overwhelmed by debt maintenance, but war led to the financial crisis "which provided the immediate occasion for the release of those forces which shattered the French political and social order." Based on French diplomatic and naval correspondence.
L. S. Frey

717. Hare, John E. LE COMPORTEMENT DE LA PAYSANNERIE RURALE ET URBAINE DE LA RÉGION DE QUÉBEC PENDANT L'OCCUPATION AMÉRICAINE, 1775-1776 [The behavior of the rural and urban peasantry of the Quebec region during the American occupation]. *Rev. de l'U. d'Ottawa [Canada] 1977 47(1-2): 145-150.* During the American occupation of the province of Quebec (1775-76), a minority of the rural, peasant militiamen responded favorably to Governor Guy Carleton's appeal to resistance; however, the majority of them remained neutral with sometimes a friendly attitude toward Americans and a small group of activists rebelled against the governor's orders. In the city of Quebec, an equal lack of enthusiasm to resistance was shown by the urban peasantry. The expulsion of the American army from the province proved for the rebels a humiliating defeat which ensured the clergy and the gentry a favorable position toward the British government. Primary and secondary sources; 2 tables, 15 notes.
G. P. Cleyet

718. Kershaw, Gordon E. JOHN WENTWORTH VS. KENNEBECK PROPRIETORS: THE FORMATION OF ROYAL MAST POLICY 1769-1778. *Am. Neptune 1973 33(2): 95-119.* Reviews legal actions between John Wentworth, Surveyor-General of New England, and the Kennebeck Purchase Company, involving a pine forest. In his official position, Wentworth was protector of such trees for the king, for they were used for ships' masts. The Company argued that it owned the forest and could dispose of the trees at will. Lengthy and complicated legal proceedings vindicated the company's claims and altered royal mast policy. By then the War of Independence was underway, Wentworth had fled to Canada, and the Company was unable to profit from its victory. 86 notes.
V. L. Human

719. Ketchum, Richard M. MEN OF THE REVOLUTION XVI—DANIEL MORGAN. *Am. Heritage 1976 27(2): 34-35, 97.* Leadership of a group of unrestrained riflemen from the frontier fell to Daniel Morgan (ca. 1735-1802), who had never had much use for authority. During the American Revolution he saw action on several fronts—in Cambridge in 1775, and in Quebec with Benedict Arnold, where he was captured. Held until late 1776, Morgan rejoined George Washington's army in April 1777 and was sent off to New York. Morgan's most celebrated battle came in early 1781 at Cowpens, where his small force inflicted heavy casualties on the British. After Cowpens, sciatica forced him out of action. In his later years he operated a gristmill, speculated in western lands, and, in 1797, won a seat in the House of Representatives. Illus.
J. F. Paul

720. McLeod, Carol. PRIVATEERS AND PETTICOATS. *Nova Scotia Hist. Q. [Canada] 1978 8(3): 205-214.* The fishing village of Lockport, on the southern coast of Nova Scotia, was settled by Americans from New England searching for new homes and good fishing. Their loyalties were to their former home rather than the British Crown or their new government. During the American Revolution the community profited from trade goods supplied by American privateers. By 1779 sympathy had changed and the privateers began to raid the settlements on the coast. One raid was discouraged by the women of Lockport who draped red petticoats on trees to stimulate British soldiers. The privateers withdrew. Biblio.
H. M. Evans

721. Mintz, Max M. HORATIO GATES, GEORGE WASHINGTON'S RIVAL. *Hist. Today [Great Britain] 1976 26(7): 419-428.* Discusses the military strategy of Continental Army General Horatio Gates in the battle of Saratoga, and George Washington's and Congress' opposition to his plans for the invasion of Canada, 1777-80.

722. Nelson, Paul David. GUY CARLETON VERSUS BENEDICT ARNOLD: THE CAMPAIGN OF 1776 IN CANADA AND LAKE CHAMPLAIN. *New York Hist. 1976 57(3): 339-366.* The numerically superior British forces failed to crush American invaders in Canada and in upper New York State in 1776 because of Sir Guy Carleton's excessive caution as a military commander, leniency toward Americans, and vacillation between civil policy and efficient military operations. Historians have exaggerated the effectiveness of Benedict Arnold's flotilla on Lake Champlain in preventing a British attack on American-held Fort Ticonderoga during the autumn of 1776. 3 illus., 45 notes.
R. N. Lokken

723. Nicholson, N. L. THE U.S. NORTHWEST ANGLE: EAST OF MANITOBA. *Can. Geographical J. [Canada] 1978 96(1): 54-59.* Describes a piece of territory cut off from the United States in the Lake of the Woods, Canada, and its part in the border settlement of the Treaty of Paris (1783) and subsequent treaties.

724. Nihart, Brooke. OUR PRE-COLONIAL EXPERIENCE. *Marine Corps Gazette 1976 60(7): 29-34.* Discusses early prototypes of the US Marines in naval expeditions and amphibious operations in the Nova Scotia region, 1654-1798, including their role in the American Revolution.

725. Rawlyk, G. A. CANADA AND THE AMERICAN REVOLUTION: 200 YEARS OF REALIZING THAT REJECTION WAS REALLY ACCEPTANCE. *Queen's Q. [Canada] 1976 83(3): 377-387.* Surveys the changing attitudes toward the United States by the Canadians, especially those in eastern Canada. Beginning with strong antiAmerican feelings in the Revolutionary period, traces the way in which this was increasingly offset and finally overcome through the overwhelming presence of American mass culture. This has been furthered by the impetus and influence of several dynamic American leaders. Both cultural and economic factors have drawn the two nations together, however there is

growing undercurrent of nationalism as well as other differences. 28 notes.
R. V. Ritter

726. Siegenthaler, David. NOVA SCOTIA, 1784: A LETTER OF JACOB BAILEY. *J. of the Can. Church Hist. Soc. [Canada] 1977 19(3-4): 131-137.* A letter of an Anglican clergyman in Nova Scotia to another, his close friend, in Massachusetts. Though the letter does not reveal any important information that could not have been acquired from other sources, it has both value and interest because of its unconscious, intimate approach to contemporary events. The Rev. Jacob Bailey (1731-1808) thus remarks on the American Revolution which had forced his removal from Maine to Canada, the severe financial limitations of his current position in Nova Scotia, and the wide diversity of Christian sects in the area. In the letter one can sense some of the difficulties a North American clergyman faced in the later 18th century. Based on secondary sources and an unprinted primary source; 17 notes.
J.A. Kicklighter

727. Skaggs, David Curtis. LORD SHELBURNE'S GIFT: THE OLD NORTHWEST. *Military Rev. 1976 56(9): 56-57.* Discusses British Prime Minister Sir William Petty, Second Earl of Shelburne's diplomatic concessions of the Old Northwest region to the Americans in exchange for the strategic Great Lakes region for British Loyalists at the Peace of Paris (1783) following the American Revolution.

728. Skinner, Andrew S. ADAM SMITH AND THE AMERICAN REVOLUTION. *Presidential Studies Q. 1977 7(2-3): 75-87.* Great Britain had three choices for pacifying the American colonies: 1) creating a union by granting representation in Parliament, 2) military coercion, and 3) emancipation with the return of Canada to France and Florida to Spain to ensure an American alliance with England. Adam Smith favored taxation of the colonies to help meet British fiscal needs, American representation in Parliament, and free trade within the empire. Union was the best solution for solving the differences within the empire, but Britain lost the opportunity through delay, and was destined to face humiliation and disgrace for losing the colonies. Smith foresaw a close relationship between Britain and America because of the common heritage. Based on the *Wealth of Nations* and other primary and secondary sources; 30 notes.
R. D. Hurt

729. Spindel, Donna J. ANCHORS OF EMPIRE: SAVANNAH, HALIFAX, AND THE ATLANTIC FRONTIER. *Am. Rev. of Can. Studies 1976 6(2): 88-103.* A comparison of pre-Revolutionary Nova Scotia and Georgia reveals reasons for their different loyalties. Georgia's economic prosperity fostered political independence while Nova Scotia's heavy financial dependence on Great Britain promoted loyalty. While both colonies attracted immigrants from other colonies, those who emigrated to Nova Scotia did so too early to bring the revolutionary ideas that later immigrants carried to Georgia. An influx of British immigrants to Nova Scotia during 1770-75 further strengthened her ties to Britain. The numerous military personnel in Halifax tended to deter revolutionary activity such as the resistance to the Stamp Act which occurred in Savannah where the military was virtually absent. Primary and secondary sources; 51 notes.
G. A. Patzwald

730. Squires, J. Duane. A SUMMARY OF EVENTS OF 1777 WHICH LED TO GENERAL STARK'S MARCH TO AND VICTORY AT BENNINGTON. *Hist. New Hampshire 1977 32(4): 165-170.* In June 1777 the British Major General John Burgoyne launched a two-pronged attack on New York from Canada along the Lake Champlain-Hudson River route. To replenish dwindling supplies, Burgoyne sent 600 men to Bennington, Vermont, in early August. John Stark of New Hampshire led a force of 2,000 New Englanders which routed the first British unit and then a detachment of 600 reinforcements, in encounters which the British historian, George Otto Trevelyan, called the turning point of the Saratoga campaign, and of the war.
D. F. Chard

731. Stewart, Catharine McArthur. QUEBEC CITY IN THE 1770'S. *Hist. Today [Great Britain] 1973 23(2): 116-121.* "Life in Quebec was considerably changed by the arrival of merchants from Britain and by the effects of the American Revolution."

732. Stewart, Gordon. CHARISMA AND INTEGRATION: AN 18TH CENTURY NORTH AMERICAN CASE. *Comparative Stud-*

ies in Soc. and Hist. 1974 16(2): 138-149. Considers "the case of Henry Alline, a popular religious leader in Nova Scotia during the years of the American Revolutionary War."
S

733. Taylor, George Rogers. NANTUCKET OIL MERCHANTS AND THE AMERICAN REVOLUTION. *Massachusetts Rev. 1977 18(3): 581-606.* The Nantucket Island whale oil merchants were disturbed at the coming of the American Revolution. They were predominantly Quakers and thus were pacifists. The causes of the Revolution did not trouble these merchants. They saw only ruin in separation. These merchants, therefore, set out to found whaling colonies in other places. These new settlements included Dartmouth, Nova Scotia, Milford Haven, Wales, Dunkirk, France, and Hudson, New York. The merchants could register their ships under three flags and pursue their business as neutrals. Even their crews and other workers were pacifists. Primary and secondary sources; 44 notes.
E. R. Campbell

734. Upton, L. F. S. DOUBLE JEOPARDY: CANADIANS IN THE AMERICAN REVOLUTION. *Can. Rev. of Am. Studies [Canada] 1977 8(2): 180-183.* As recounted by Allan Seymour Everest in *Moses Hazen and the Canadian Refugees in the American Revolution* (Syracuse: Syracuse U. Pr., 1976), Moses Hazen (1733-1803) enlisted 250 Canadians for service in the so-called Second Canadian Regiment in 1776. The regiment ultimately contained both American and Canadian recruits. Quarrels between the Americans and Canadians and Hazen's poor leadership made the regiment ineffective. Congress provided rewards for service that were unsatisfactory to Hazen and the Canadian recruits after the American Revolution.
H. T. Lovin

735. Whiteley, W. H. NEWFOUNDLAND, QUEBEC, AND THE ADMINISTRATION OF THE COAST OF LABRADOR, 1774-1783. *Acadiensis [Canada] 1976 6(1): 92-112.* Merchants in Quebec and England argued over the Labrador fisheries from the conquest in 1763 until the implementation of the Quebec Act in 1775, when Labrador reverted to Quebec. British fishermen retained the right to fish cod where there were no Canadian posts. During the American Revolution, Quebec lacked the means to administer Labrador. The Newfoundland governors assumed primary responsibility for the coast and regularly sent warships there, although American privateers inflicted considerable damage to the fishery. 77 notes.
D. F. Chard

736. Wilson, Bruce. THE STRUGGLE FOR WEALTH AND POWER AT FORT NIAGARA, 1775-1783. *Ontario Hist. [Canada] 1976 68(3): 137-154.* Discusses the reasons for a particular merchant and his associates emerging as politically and economically powerful in the Niagara Peninsula before 1812. Notes that the pattern emerged during the American Revolution, and had existed embryonically before 1776. Personal rivalries, more or less systematized corruption, and patronage were relevant factors. Most important was a good reputation with the military command which overtly despised merchants and their practices, usually for good cause. Thus, the conviction of one early merchant and his associates for activities beyond the tolerance of the command structure is seen as the key factor in the rise of the ultimately successful man. 8 illus., 98 notes.
W. B. Whitham

737. Zurlo, John A. BLACK ODYSSEY. *Crisis 1977 84(8): 409-410.* The rhetoric of liberty during the American Revolution, together with offers of freedom from British commanders, caused a continuous flow of black slaves escaping from their masters to take shelter under the British. More than 3,000 fugitive slaves sailed under British protection to Nova Scotia during the summer of 1783. Racial segregation and food shortages there stimulated another move—to West Africa. These transplanted black Americans laid the groundwork for what would later become Liberia.
A. G. Belles

Loyalist Influx

738. Brown, Wallace. 'VICTORIOUS IN DEFEAT': THE AMERICAN LOYALISTS IN CANADA. *Hist. Today [Great Britain] 1977 27(2): 92-100.* Discusses the settlement of British Loyalists in Nova Scotia, New Brunswick, Prince Edward Island and Quebec near the end of the American Revolution, 1782-90's.

739. Carroll, Kenneth L. IRISH AND BRITISH QUAKERS AND THEIR AMERICAN RELIEF FUNDS, 1778-1797. *Pennsylvania Mag. of Hist. and Biog. 1978 102(4): 437-457.* Philadelphia mainly utilized Irish funds which also relieved New England and southern Quakers. London funds aided Nova Scotian Quaker loyalists and later were utilized by Philadelphia Friends. Based on manuscripts, Friends' House Library, London; Friends' Historical Library, Dublin; Philadelphia Meeting for Sufferings; printed sources and secondary works; 108 notes.
T. H. Wendel

740. Crowson, E. T. JOHN SAUNDERS: AN EXILED VIRGINIA LOYALIST AND A FOUNDER OF NEW BRUNSWICK. *Virginia Cavalcade 1977 27(2): 52-57.* John Saunders, a determined loyalist forced to flee his native Virginia in 1782, helped found New Brunswick and lived in that British colony, 1784-1834.

741. Duffy, Dennis. UPPER CANADIAN LOYALISM: WHAT THE TEXTBOOKS TELL. *J. of Can. Studies [Canada] 1977 12(2): 17-26.* Discusses the mythology of Loyalism in Upper Canada, as depicted in history textbooks. Describes the changing attitudes toward the Loyalist heritage, and discusses different viewpoints. Suggests the need in Canada's national mythology for the civilized character of Loyalism. Based on primary and secondary school history textbooks approved by the educational authorities of Ontario; 36 notes.
J. B. Reed

742. Fellows, Jo-Ann. THE "BRITISH CONNECTION" IN THE JALNA NOVELS OF MAZO DE LA ROCHE: THE LOYALIST MYTH REVISITED. *Dalhousie Rev. [Canada] 1976 56(2): 283-290.* The idea that the "Loyalists" or "Tories" of the American Revolution were monolithic in their ideologies is a myth which did not survive the First World War except in fantasy, patriotic speeches, bad poetry, and the Jalna novels. Through analysis of several novels in the series the author declares that "Jalna is the Loyalist Myth." However, the "Loyalist tradition is only one of many in the pantheon of Canadian national ethics or myths." 29 notes.
C. Held

743. Gross, Leonard, ed. "PREPARING FOR '76": A CANADIAN-MENNONITE PERSPECTIVE. *Mennonite Hist. Bull. 1974 35(2): 2-4.* Though "many Canadian and 'American' Mennonites share a common Pennsylvania heritage, "some evidence suggests that from the American Revolution through the War of 1812 many Mennonites left Pennsylvania for Canada because of their allegiance to the British Crown. Prints excerpts from the introduction and text of Ezra E. Eby's *A Biographical History of Waterloo Township . . .* (Berlin, Ontario, 1895).
S

744. Lambert, Robert S. A LOYALIST ODYSSEY: JAMES AND MARY CARY IN EXILE, 1783-1804. *South Carolina Hist. Mag. 1978 79(3): 167-181.* Forced to leave the United States in 1781 because of his commitment to the British cause, James Cary spent the remainder of his life in Jamaica, Great Britain and Nova Scotia seeking compensation for losses suffered because of this loyalty.

745. MacKinnon, Neil. THE ENLIGHTENMENT AND TORYISM: A LOYALIST PLAN FOR EDUCATION IN BRITISH NORTH AMERICA. *Dalhousie Rev. [Canada] 1975 55(2): 307-314.* Outlines the growth of governmental responsibility for education in Nova Scotia, noting the optimistic concept of education and its potential in the age of Enlightenment. Financial inducements were necessary to encourage the most able students into the teaching profession. Based on "A Plan of Liberal Education for the Youth of Nova Scotia and the Sister Province in North America" in *Nova Scotia Magazine* (1789) and probably authored by Professor William Cochran of the then newly founded King's College.
C. Held

746. MacNutt, W. S. THE LOYALISTS: A SYMPATHETIC VIEW. *Acadiensis [Canada] 1976 6(1): 3-20.* Throughout the American Revolution, many Loyalists suffered severe persecution. Eventually, those who had too openly sided with the British crown left for Nova Scotia and Canada. Struggling against shortages, resentful of their fate, and critical of British aid, some Loyalists returned home while those who remained clung to marginal settlements for decades. For 30 years they were the principal English-speaking element in British North America, and they assured the language's continuance. 50 notes.
D. F. Chard

747. Moir, John S. ROBERT MCDOWALL AND THE DUTCH REFORMED CHURCH MISSION TO CANADA, 1790-1819. *Halve Maen 1978 53(2): 3-4, 14-15.* Robert James McDowall, a minister in the Reformed Dutch Church from New York, during 1790-1819, was a missionary to Loyalists exiled in present-day Ontario during the American Revolution.

748. Morgan, Robert J. THE LOYALISTS OF CAPE BRETON. *Dalhousie R. [Canada] 1975 55(1): 5-22.* The loyalists of Cape Breton, though relatively unknown because of later Scottish migration, played an important role in the history of the area from their arrival in 1784 until its annexation to Nova Scotia in 1820. Some of the important early settlers mentioned are Abraham Cuyler, Jonathan Jones, David Smith, Jacob Sparling, David Mathews, and Neil Robertson. The Cape Breton loyalists were generally either officials, farmers, or soldiers from northern New England. Includes a seven page list of Cape Breton loyalists. 46 notes.
C. Held

749. Osborne, Brian S. THE CEMETERIES OF THE MIDLAND DISTRICT OF UPPER CANADA: A NOTE ON MORTALITY IN A FRONTIER SOCIETY. *Pioneer Am. 1974 6(1): 46-55.* Illustrates demographic information that can be taken from gravestones. The Midland District of Upper Canada (fronting onto the Bay of Quinte at the eastern end of Lake Ontario) was selected for study because little is known of the birth rate, death rate, life expectancy, etc., of the Americans who left the former colonies following the War of Independence to settle in this region. Since this was a pioneer society which predated the major advancements in science and technology, the analysis bore out the hypotheses that the hardships associated with this life accounted for the high infant and female mortality and peak years of mortality associated with outbreaks of epidemics. Primary and secondary sources; 3 photos, map, 4 tables, 2 figs., 20 notes.
C. R. Gunter, Jr.

750. Punch, Terrence M. and Marble, Allan E. JOHN HOWE GENEALOGY. *Nova Scotia Hist. Q. [Canada] 1976 6(3): 317-328.* Given the genealogy of John Howe, a Loyalist in Nova Scotia and King's printer in Halifax, in the 18th and 19th centuries.

751. Thomas, C. E. THE WORK OF THE S.P.G. IN NOVA SCOTIA, SECOND HALF-CENTURY. *Nova Scotia Hist Soc. Collections [Canada] 1973 38: 63-90.* The Loyalists' arrival opened a new chapter in the history of the Society for the Propagation of the Gospel in Foreign Parts as 18 of the 31 Church of England clergymen who came as Loyalists remained in the Maritime Provinces. In 1787, Charles Inglis became the first Anglican bishop of Nova Scotia; in 1788, King's College, Windsor was founded; and thereafter new missionary stations were established. All increased the S.P.G.'s work so that hardships were ever present, notably after 1833 when the British government drastically reduced its support to overseas missionaries. A new missionary society from England, The Colonial Church Society, arose; then in 1864, the Nova Scotian Diocesan Synod.
E. A. Chard

752. Williams, Linda K. EAST FLORIDA AS A LOYALIST HAVEN. *Florida Hist. Q. 1976 54(4): 465-478.* When the American Revolution broke out, George III ordered Patrick Tonyn, Governor of East Florida from 1774-84, to invite all loyalists in the colonies to seek refuge in St. Augustine. As the influx of refugees grew, the government made various provisions for them. When the colony was returned to Spain in 1783, loyalist refugees were evacuated to the Bahamas, Jamaica, England, Nova Scotia, and other British territories. Based mainly on the records of the Colonial Office and British Headquarters-Public Record Office and secondary sources; 4 portraits, 90 notes.
P. A. Beaber

The War of 1812

753. Allen, Robert S. A HISTORY OF FORT GEORGE, UPPER CANADA. *Can. Hist. Sites 1974 (11): 61-93.* "Fort George was built between 1796 and 1799 and subsequently served as British military headquarters in Upper Canada. During the War of 1812 the post was engaged in several artillery duels with Fort Niagara across the river on the American side, and was the site of a fierce battle and two sieges. Although by 1815 Fort George was in a state of decay and disrepair, British troops continued to garrison the fort until the 1830s, when the star-shaped fort at Mississauga Point became the major military installation of His Majesty's forces in the Niagara area. The work of reconstruction was begun in 1937 by the Niagara Parks Commission and completed in 1940. Fort George was transferred to the Department of Indian Affairs and Northern Development in 1969 and declared a national historic park." J

754. Brown, Stephen W. CONGRESSMAN JOHN GEORGE JACKSON AND REPUBLICAN NATIONALISM, 1813-1817. *West Virginia Hist. 1977 38(2): 93-125.* John George Jackson served in Congress from northwestern Virginia, during 1813-17, as a firm supporter of the War of 1812 and Madison's administration. He saw impressment as the war's chief cause, denied that Republicans wanted to conquer Canada, and blasted domestic antiwar sentiment. He supported federal internal improvements and a new national Bank but criticized New England commercial interests. Primary and secondary sources; 91 notes.
J. H. Broussard

755. Chartrand, René. UNIFORMS OF THE CANADIAN VOLTIGUERS AND THE GLENGARRY LIGHT INFANTRY, 1812-1816. *Military Collector and Historian 1974 26(1): 14-18.*

756. Hickey, Donald R., ed. A DISSENTING VOICE: MATTHEW LYON ON THE CONQUEST OF CANADA. *Register of the Kentucky Hist. Soc. 1978 76(1): 45-52.* Reprints a letter from Matthew Lyon to James Monroe in 1811. Lyon, a Congressman first from Vermont and later from Kentucky, and formerly a strong supporter of Jefferson and the Republicans, takes issue with the drift toward war in 1811 and urges against any attempt to conquer Canada. Letter taken from the James Monroe papers, Library of Congress; 18 notes.
J. F. Paul

757. Hickey, Donald R. NEW ENGLAND'S DEFENSE PROBLEM AND THE GENESIS OF THE HARTFORD CONVENTION. *New England Q. 1977 50(4): 587-604.* Concludes that historians have been wrong to reject Federalists' claims that the Hartford Convention was called to meet a growing defense problem in 1814. In 1812, the governors of Massachusetts, Connecticut, and Rhode Island refused to meet federal requisitions for militiamen because they did not want to lose control of them or to help prosecute what they considered an unjust war. Governors did call out militia units to protect their coasts in 1813 and 1814 and worked out agreements with federal officers to allow militiamen to serve under state rather than regular army officers. Officials in Washington refused to pay and supply the troops under these conditions. Wartime depression precluded state tax increases to support the troops, national forces were invading Canada, and British raids along the coast became more common. The only solution was to tap federal revenue sources in the region and this led directly to the Hartford Convention. Based on correspondence, newspaper articles and secondary sources; 52 notes.
J. C. Bradford

758. Keller, Alan. THE BATTLE OF LAKE CHAMPLAIN. *Am. Hist. Illus. 1978 12(9): 4-9, 47-48.* In September 1814, US Brigadier General Alexander Macomb had a land force of less than 5,000 against British General Sir George Prevost's invading army of 14,000. Also, US Lieutenant Thomas Macdonough's hastily constructed fleet was smaller than Captain George Downie's squadron. Macdonough won the lake battle and Prevost retreated, leaving a half million dollars' worth of supplies. It was the last effort of an enemy to invade the United States from Canada. Winston Churchill in his *History of the English Speaking People* called it "the most decisive engagement of the war." Primary and secondary sources; 9 illus., map.
D. Dodd

759. Leefe, John. THE ATLANTIC PRIVATEERS. *Nova Scotia Hist. Q. [Canada] 1978 8(1): 1-17; (2): 109-124.* Part I. Privateering vessels from Newfoundland and New Brunswick provided a means of defense for coastal towns, helped the empire, and often reaped profits from their ventures. The schooner *Liverpool Packet* was the most successful of the Canadian privateers. Her prizes exceeded a quarter of a million dollars during 1812-14. The vessels *Lucy* and *Resolution* were much less successful. Part II. Recounts the exploits of the brig *Rover,* the sloop *Lucy,* the *Liverpool Packet,* the *Herald,* the *Charles Mary Wentworth,* and their captains during 1800-15. Privateering was sometimes profitable, but not often.
H. M. Evans

760. Lohnes, Barry J. BRITISH NAVAL PROBLEMS AT HALIFAX DURING THE WAR OF 1812. *Mariner's Mirror [Great Britain] 1973 59(3): 317-333.* Analyzes the problems at the British naval base and argues that the major difficulty was incompetent administration. Unseaworthy ships and insufficiently trained seamen to form the cores of the various crews were other problems. These and other problems were a result of preoccupation with the European theaters of war and long predated the War of 1812. The 1797 mutiny on HMS *Lotus* in Halifax was indicative that the problems were already serious. 99 notes.
W. B. Whitham

761. Muller, H. Nicholas, III. A "TRAITOROUS AND DIABOLICAL TRAFFIC": THE COMMERCE OF THE CHAMPLAIN-RICHELIEU CORRIDOR DURING THE WAR OF 1812. *Vermont Hist. 1976 44(2): 78-96.* While Canadian officials restricted export of war materials and encouraged other trade, Americans smuggled tobacco, naval stores, timber, and local produce into Canada. C. P. Van Ness, Collector of Customs, devised legal tricks to circumvent the law against trading with the enemy; a privateer avoided customs by capturing prizes and selling them in the United States. Macdonough stopped much timber, but two-thirds of the British army was fed on American beef at triple prewar prices. The Catlin firm in Burlington made large profits with Manzuco under the Spanish flag. This trade was less harmful to the United States than total embargo. 90 notes.
T. D. S. Bassett

762. Snow, Richard F. THE BATTLE OF LAKE ERIE. *Am. Heritage 1976 27(2): 14-21, 88-90.* In 1812 Great Lakes merchant captain Daniel Dobbins convinced President James Madison to build a fleet of warships at Presque Isle (Erie) on Lake Erie. Oliver Hazard Perry was given command of the operation early in 1813. The British were forced to challenge Perry's fleet in September 1813. Perry won a decisive victory. 8 illus.
B. J. Paul

763. Suthren, Victor J. H. THE BATTLE OF CHÂTEAUGUAY. *Can. Hist. Sites 1974 11: 95-150.* "On 26 October 1813, on the banks of the Châteauguay River some 30 miles south of Montreal, an engagement was fought between the lead elements of an invading American army and a smaller Canadian force under British command. The result of this engagement was the withdrawal of the American army from Canada and the subsequent retirement of another American army descending the St. Lawrence. This ended the most serious invasion threat of the War of 1812 that Canada would be called upon to face, and demonstrated the ability of Canadians to effectively participate in the defence of their country."
J

764. Tanner, Dwight. YOUNG TEAZER: THE MAKING OF A MYTH. *Nova Scotia Hist. Q. [Canada] 1976 6(4): 405-412.* Discusses the mythology surrounding the *Young Teazer,* an American privateer destroyed in Mahone Bay, Nova Scotia, during the War of 1812 and since reported as a ghost ship haunting the local waters.

765. Wallace, Lee A., Jr. THE PETERSBURG VOLUNTEERS, 1812-1813. *Virginia Mag. of Hist. and Biog. 1974 82(4): 458-485.* In the fall of 1812, approximately 100 men from Petersburg volunteered for an infantry company to serve in Ohio. Under the command of Gen. William Henry Harrison, the Petersburg volunteers helped defend Fort Meigs and prevented a British invasion from Canada. Based on primary and secondary sources; 115 notes.
R. F. Oaks

766. Whitfield, Carol. THE BATTLE OF QUEENSTON HEIGHTS. *Can. Hist. Sites 1974 11: 9-59.* "The village of Queenston, Upper Canada, was the scene of the second major American invasion of British territory in the War of 1812. Early on 13 October 1812, the Americans, under Stephen and Solomon Van Rensselaer, crossed the

Niagara River and gained a foothold, despite the efforts of the small British force stationed there. Major General Isaac Brock and his provincial aide-de-camp, Lieutenant Colonel John Macdonell, were killed in unsuccessful attempts to dislodge the invaders. Late in the day a large group of reinforcements under Major General Roger Hale Sheaffe defeated the Americans, taking more than nine hundred prisoners. The British losses, although slight, were significant because Brock, the president and commanding officer of Upper Canada, was killed." J

767. Wood, G. N. THE DEFENCE OF CANADA 1812-14. *Army Q. and Defence J. [Great Britain] 1975 105(3): 336-342.* Discusses Great Britain's defense of Canada from US attacks during the War of 1812.

Settlement and Economic Growth

768. Armstrong, Frederick H. JOHN ARMOUR OF DUNNVILLE: FROM CANAL SUPERVISOR TO VILLAGE PATRIARCH. *Inland Seas 1973 29(2): 83-90.* Armour (1791-1881) came to Canada in 1828 from Scotland. He was a school teacher before becoming clerk (1829) to William H. Merritt, the promotor and manager of the Welland Canal. Armour settled in Dunnville, Ontario, becoming postmaster and one of the leading citizens. Reprints three letters written 1830-34 from Armour to his family in Scotland. 8 notes. K. J. Bauer

769. Baehre, Rainer. ORIGINS OF THE PENITENTIARY SYSTEM IN UPPER CANADA. *Ontario Hist. [Canada] 1977 69(3): 185-207.* The first penitentiary in Upper Canada opened in 1835. The penitentiary was a reform of the early justice system, conceived as a place to induce penitence (hence its name) for crimes. The motives for this reform, and the approach taken by reformers are analyzed. Notes that a legislator examined penitentiaries, which led to a legislative committee visiting the United Kingdom and the United States before defining practices to be followed in the Canadian institution. Those practices and subsequent modifications are described. An 1849 report on the institution is quoted. 101 notes. W. B. Whitham

770. Bilson, Geoffrey. THE FIRST EPIDEMIC OF ASIATIC CHOLERA IN LOWER CANADA, 1832. *Medical Hist. [Great Britain] 1977 21(4): 411-433.* In 1832, Lower Canada faced an epidemic of cholera. Canadian doctors learned of British and French treatments, and debated whether cholera was contagious. French doctors were more likely to see a link between emigrant ships and the disease, while English doctors were more inclined to think that climatic conditions created the disease. Doctors exposed their patients to a variety of treatments, leaning heavily on calomel, opium, and bleeding. Doctors faced some hostility, but no violence. There were some accusations, however, that cholera had been introduced to kill off the French Canadians. Quarantine was tried, but it did not prevent the spread of the disease. When disease struck, people fled the cities. Cholera contributed to the tensions of a year marked by ethnic and political divisions. 118 notes. M. Kaufman

771. Brown, Jennifer. "A COLONY OF VERY USEFUL HANDS." *Beaver [Canada] 1977 307(4): 39-45.* Examines the growth of mixed-blood population around Hudson Bay and the Hudson's Bay Company's attitudes toward employment and education. As the population grew, some efforts toward schooling were attempted. Some of the boys were apprenticed to positions formerly reserved for young English boys. Company policy was to take advantage of this talented reservoir, educate them to some degree, and move them into appropriate positions. By the 1820's educational efforts were largely abandoned. By then schooling was concentrated at Lord Selkirk's Red River settlement. 6 illus. D. Chaput

772. Bulkley, P. B. HORACE FABYAN, FOUNDER OF THE WHITE MOUNTAIN GRAND HOTEL. *Hist. New Hampshire 1975 30(2): 53-77.* Horace Fabyan (1807-81) accumulated capital in the Portland provisions trade, and then became a hotel keeper. In 1837 he entered the White Mountain hotel trade, and prospered in the 1840's as Portland extended its economic influence over the area with the construction of the Grand Trunk Railway's Montreal-Portland line. In the 1850's Fabyan suffered reverses from a fire and legal disputes. By 1861 he had left New

Hampshire and settled in Bradford, Vermont, where he died. Deified as "the pioneer good landlord," Fabyan also symbolized the commercialization of the hotel trade. 4 illus, 72 notes, 3 appendixes. D. F. Chard

773. Burns, R. J. GOD'S CHOSEN PEOPLE: THE ORIGINS OF TORONTO SOCIETY, 1793-1818. *Can. Hist. Assoc. Hist. Papers 1973: 213-228.* Lieutenant-governor John Graves Simcoe (1752-1806) and the original officials of Upper Canada regarded themselves as people with a mission. They were to perpetuate and spread a type of society which provided an alternative to the American Revolution. By 1818, having established themselves and their families in Toronto, the official elite awaited a leader who could carry their ideas throughout Upper Canada. Anglican Archdeacon John Strachan (1778-1867) arrived at that point and took up the task. Based on primary and secondary sources; 59 notes. G. E. Panting

774. Cameron, J. M. CANADA'S UNKNOWN COLONY: JOHN GALT AND HIBERNIA. *Ontario Hist. [Canada] 1973 65(2): 81-85.* Discusses John Galt's little-known attempt to promote settlement in Lower Canada after leaving the Canada Company. These settlements were rejected by the Imperial Government and failed when private support was not forthcoming. 13 notes. W. B. Whitham

775. Cameron, Wendy. THE PETWORTH EMIGRATION COMMITTEE: LORD EGREMONT'S ASSISTED EMIGRATIONS FROM SUSSEX TO UPPER CANADA, 1832-37. *Ontario History [Canada] 1973 65(4): 231-246.* Describes the activities of the Petworth Emigration Committee and the emigrations from Petworth to Upper Canada during 1832-37. Notes that there were six emigrant groups sent at annual intervals, but major attention is paid to the first. Its progress from Sussex to York, Upper Canada, is described, and the problems it encountered are outlined. 68 notes. W. B. Whitham

776. Chaput, Donald. THE "MISSES NOLIN" OF RED RIVER. *Beaver [Canada] 1975 306(3): 14-17.* Discusses the story of two daughters of Jean-Baptiste Nolin, and the origin of the first school for girls in western Canada, St. Boniface, in 1829. Also includes data on the role of the Métis Nolin family in the Red River country, as well as the Earl of Selkirk's plans for utilizing key merchants such as Nolin, who had previously lived in the United States. Based on church records and Lord Selkirk's Papers; 4 illus. A

777. Clarke, John. ASPECTS OF LAND ACQUISITION IN ESSEX COUNTY, ONTARIO, 1790-1900. *Social Hist. [Canada] 1978 11(21): 98-119.* Essex County includes the most westerly of the four earliest Ontario settlement centers. Analysis of land patent data in relation to accessibility and the physical environment reveals that before 1815 land speculators acquired large tracts of land. Afterwards, the Canada Company replaced individual speculators. By 1865 most lands had been acquired. The most accessible, best drained areas along Lake Erie had an initial development advantage, but the back townships were acquired more rapidly, for political reasons. 11 fig., 46 notes. D. F. Chard

778. Clarke, John. LAND AND LAW IN ESSEX COUNTY: MALDEN TOWNSHIP AND THE ABSTRACT INDEX TO DEEDS. *Social Hist. [Canada] 1978 11(22): 475-493.* Ontario's Abstract Index to Deeds, as yet little used, has tremendous potential for historians and geographers. It was begun in 1865 to cover deeds since the 18th century, and originally was deposited in district and county registry offices. It is also available on microfilm, at the Public Archives of Ontario, or from the Genealogical Society of Latter Day Saints. Explains some of the legal devices, or instruments, used in transactions (such as deed, patent, bargain and sale, mortgage, grant, quit claim, and power of attorney). 10 illus., 2 tables, 11 notes. D. F. Chard

779. Fingard, Judith. THE WINTER'S TALE: THE SEASONAL CONTOURS OF PRE-INDUSTRIAL POVERTY IN BRITISH NORTH AMERICA, 1815-1860. *Can. Hist. Assoc. Hist. Papers 1974 65-94.* Discusses poverty and unemployment in British Canada during winter months of 1815-60.

780. Gidney, R. D. ELEMENTARY EDUCATION IN UPPER CANADA: A REASSESSMENT. *Ontario Hist. [Canada] 1973 65(3):*

169-185. Remarks that all political parties agreed that provincial education was inadequate during the early 19th century. Points out that there were others who disagreed, arguing that for all its admitted flaws, it was as good as could reasonably be expected under the existing circumstances. Analyzes the situation and argues that the second group was closer to the truth. Some significant efforts were made to upgrade the existing level of education. The major problems faced by educators were a widely dispersed population, costs, the rapidly rising population, and in the rural areas, the great distances to be travelled by some children. 81 notes.
W. B. Whitham

781. Gillis, Robert Peter. GREAT BRITAIN'S WOODYARD: A CRITICAL APPRAISAL. *J. of Forest Hist. 1974 18(4): 110-112, 125-127.* Reviews Arthur Lower's *Great Britain's Woodyard: British America and the Timber Trade, 1763-1867* (Montreal, 1973). Based on Lower's doctoral dissertation concerning the pine timber trade between Great Britain and Canada; 6 notes.
L. F. Johnson

782. Golladay, V. Dennis. THE UNITED STATES AND BRITISH NORTH AMERICAN FISHERIES, 1815-1818. *Am. Neptune 1973 33(4): 246-257.* A study of the diplomatic struggle between the United States and Great Britain over American rights to fish off the coast of British America and the Newfoundland banks. The American case was handled largely by James Monroe, Secretary of State (and President, 1817-25), and John Quincy Adams, one of the Ghent commissioners (1814) and shortly to be minister to Britain. Both nations compromised their positions, with the United States the largest beneficiary. Knowing that Britain was anxious for settlement, the United States had a main tactic of delay. 49 notes.
R. V. Ritter

783. Gough, Barry M. CANADA'S "ADVENTURE TO CHINA" BETWEEN 1784 AND 1821. *Can. Geographical J. 1976/77 93(3): 28-37.* Discusses trade with China carried on by Canada's North West Company 1784-1821 until its merger with the Hudson's Bay Company.

784. Gough, Barry M. JAMES COOK AND THE ORIGINS OF THE MARITIME FUR TRADE. *Am. Neptune 1978 38(3): 217-224.* Captain James Cook's last voyage opened a new branch of commerce quite by accident. Beginning in March 1778 in Nootka Sound, Cook's crews traded for curios and souvenirs along the northwest coast of North America, resulting in their acquisition of sea-otter pelts. Upon their arrival in Macao, China (November 1779), Cook's officers and crews discovered that the pelts were highly prized by the Chinese. Thus began the development of a profitable maritime fur trade along the rim of the Pacific basin. Based on published journals; 8 notes.
G. H. Curtis

785. Gough, Barry M. THE NORTH WEST COMPANY'S "ADVENTURE TO CHINA." *Oregon Hist. Q. 1975 76(4): 309-332.* Early in the European development of Canada, the economic promise of the Pacific and the China market drew explorers west. A focal point of the North West Company's interest in the China market and the Pacific was Astoria, "where furs were collected for export and where suppliers and trade items for the vast interior were received." In 1814 the *Isaac Todd* began taking all the furs from the Columbia River Basin to Canton and returning to England with tea on account for the East India Company. High costs were offset by the good prices received for the furs. Illus., map, 66 notes.
E. P. Stickney

786. Gross, Leonard, ed. EARLY NINETEENTH-CENTURY PENNSYLVANIA-ONTARIO LETTERS. *Mennonite Hist. Bull. 1975 36(3): 4-7.* Excerpts letters and diary entries of Jacob Brubacher and his brother Henry; the writings reveal their closeness despite the physical distance of the Mennonites in Pennsylvania and Ontario, and describe daily life and economic and social history, 1817-46.

787. Heisler, John P. THE CANALS OF CANADA. *Can. Historic Sites 1973 (8): 1-183.* "Canals have played an important part in the economic and social development of Canada. Undertaken but never completed during the French regime, they were begun soon after 1760 and reached the peak of their development and use during the mid-19th century. The financing and construction of canals to improve navigation on the St. Lawrence and the Great Lakes; the Rideau Canal constituting a waterway between the Ottaway and the St. Lawrence, and the canals communicating with the American waterway system of New York state

are discussed in detail. Several waterways were proposed and some actually constructed in the Maritimes and in the West. Part of this deep waterway system culminated in the St. Lawrence Seaway, a successful venture in international cooperation."
J

788. Jarvis, Eric. MILITARY LAND GRANTING IN UPPER CANADA FOLLOWING THE WAR OF 1812. *Ontario Hist. [Canada] 1975 67(3): 121-134.* Discusses the two phases of the military land granting policy in Upper Canada, 1816-17 and 1819-20, in order to analyze the dissimilarities between them and to formulate conclusions as to settlement patterns and the relative success or failure of each.

789. Le Goff, T. J. A. THE AGRICULTURAL CRISIS IN LOWER CANADA, 1802-12: A REVIEW OF A CONTROVERSY. *Can. Hist. R. 1974 55(1): 1-31.* Assesses the methods used and the issues at stake in the controversy between Fernand Ouellet and J.-P. Wallot and Gilles Paquet over the existence and impact of an agricultural crisis in the Lower Canadian economy in the 1800's. Shows from published material that price rises in the 1800's were not only caused by worldwide inflation but had mostly a local cause: a population whose growth outstripped food supply. Local farmers appear to have been unable to profit from higher prices. Stresses the need for a new approach to the transformation of the Lower Canadian economy in the 1800's, based on detailed social analysis of well-defined groups. 7 tables, 3 graphs, 64 notes.
A

790. McCalla, Douglas. THE CANADIAN GRAIN TRADE IN THE 1840'S: THE BUCHANANS' CASE. *Can. Hist. Assoc. Hist. Papers 1974: 95-114.* Discusses Peter and Isaac Buchanan's profitable grain trade in Canada during the commercial crisis of the 1840's.

791. McIlwraith, Thomas F. FREIGHT CAPACITY AND UTILIZATION OF THE ERIE AND GREAT LAKES CANALS BEFORE 1850. *J. of Econ. Hist. 1976 36(4): 852-877.* This paper deals with the relationship between tonnage capacity and utilization of the Erie, Welland and St. Lawrence River canals before 1850. Estimates are presented for the capacities of the canals, as built and modified. Comparison with the actual tonnage carried eastward for selected years shows that the British canals were grossly and increasingly underutilized, while the Erie's utilization was closely correlated with its capability, particularly through its eastern half. Reasons for this situation are given and it is argued that had British funds been redirected away from canal enlargement and applied to the construction of vessels and harbor facilities, the British might have entered upon a prosperous carrying trade within North America in the second quarter of the 19th century.
J

792. McKenzie, Ann. ANIMAL HUSBANDRY IN THE 1840'S AS REFLECTED IN THE AGRICULTURAL JOURNALS OF CANADA WEST. *Ontario Hist. [Canada] 1974 66(2): 114-128.* Comments on the character of the livestock available in the province in the early 19th century and discusses the efforts of a small group to upgrade the stock. Discusses the role of the press and analyzes the major species of stock kept, showing the problems and the means taken to improve its quality. Summarizes the content of typical articles in contemporary agricultural journals. 3 illus., 16 notes.
W. B. Whitham

793. Norton, William. THE PROCESS OF RURAL LAND OCCUPATION IN UPPER CANADA. *Scottish Geographical Mag. [Great Britain] 1975 91(3): 145-152.* Discusses factors in the process of rural land occupation in Upper Canada 1782-1851, emphasizing the establishing of townships by settlers and land speculation.

794. Norton, William. THE PROCESS OF RURAL LAND OCCUPATION IN UPPER CANADA. *Scottish Geographical Mag. [Great Britain] 1975 91(3): 145-152.* The location decisions of settlers to Upper Canada, 1782-1851, are related to several factors. Initial settlement cores resulted from the previous pattern of French occupation and the need to strengthen the border with the United States. The availability of surveyed land influenced location decisions throughout the period. Of less significance were the land-granting procedure and the various official policies which prompted land speculation and resulted in areas of reserved land.
J

795. Paquet, Gilles and Wallot, Jean-Pierre. GROUPES SOCIAUX ET POUVOIR: LE CAS CANADIEN AU TOURNANT DU XIXe

SIÈCLE [Social groups and power: the case of Canada at the turn of the 19th century]. *Rev. d'Hist. de l'Amérique Française [Canada] 1974 27(4): 509-564.* Shows how Canada participated in its own way in the great social and political changes that occurred in Europe and America around the turn of the 19th century by contributing both men and ideas to the efforts to modernize and liberalize society.

796. Paquet, Gilles and Wallot, Jean-Pierre. LES INVENTAIRES APRÈS DÉCÈS À MONTRÉAL AU TOURNANT DU XIXᵉ SIÈCLE: PRÉLIMINAIRES À UNE ANALYSE [Inventories after death in Montreal at the turn of the 19th century: preliminaries to an analysis]. *Rev. d'Hist. de l'Am. Française [Canada] 1976 30(2): 163-221.* At the turn of the 19th century, Lower Canada's role in the trans-Atlantic commercial economy was transformed by external and internal forces. Presents research regarding wealth distribution, social stratification, and behavioral adjustment. Based on notarial documents and secondary works; 3 tables, 96 notes, 2 appendixes.   L. B. Chan

797. Parr, G. J. THE WELCOME AND THE WAKE: ATTITUDES IN CANADA WEST TOWARD THE IRISH FAMINE IMMIGRATION. *Ontario Hist. [Canada] 1974 66(2): 101-113.* The initial reaction to Irish immigration into the Canadas in the late 1840's was sympathetic in Canada West and the concept of immigration allied to settlement was favorably received. But the scale of the problem was not realized at first, so that when available funds were exhausted a backlash developed, especially when the problem of disease became public knowledge. Yet even in this situation there was marked public sympathy, although the situation forced the reappraisal of some basic concepts. Canadian anger was directed less at the immigrants than at the landlords and others in Ireland who were seen as exploiting the famine. Concludes that the incident produced a marked shift in the attitude toward immigration in the province. 76 notes.   W. B. Whitham

798. Phillips, Paul. LAND TENURE AND ECONOMIC DEVELOPMENT: A COMPARISON OF UPPER AND LOWER CANADA. *J. of Can. Studies 1974 9(2): 35-45.* The seigneurial system of New France and Lower Canada did not provide a potential investment frontier because there was a limited total income unequally distributed with secondary economic institutions concentrated in Montreal and Quebec. By contrast, in Upper Canada the method of land tenure led to high labor productivity among widely distributed small independent landholders. Secondary sources; 2 tables, 40 notes.   G. E. Panting

799. Raudzens, George K. THE MILITARY IMPACT ON CANADIAN CANALS, 1815-25. *Can. Hist. R. 1973 54(3): 273-286.* Discusses the sustained effort of high military officers in Canada (Drummond, Sherbrooke, Richmond, Dalhousie) to divert imperial funds allocated for civilian communications improvements into the Ottawa-Rideau military canal project. The soldiers succeeded at the expense of Canadians seeking aid for more commercially viable canals on the St. Lawrence. Based on unpublished government documents at the Public Record Office, London, the Scottish Record Office, Edinburgh, and the Public Archives of Canada, Ottawa.   A

800. Rigby, G. Reginald and Legget, Robert F. RIDDLE OF THE TREADWELL TRENCHES. *Can. Geographical J. 1974 88(3): 38-42.* Several boulders were mysteriously moved out of the Ottawa River in order to aid river travel.   S

801. Rubin, Julius. NOTES ON THE COMPARATIVE STUDY OF THE AGRICULTURE OF WORLD REGIONS. *Peasant Studies Newsletter 1973 2(4): 1-4.* Reports on three studies of agricultural growth: 18th-century frontiers in China and North America, central Russia in the 19th century, and the South of the United States in the 19th century, with reference to Ester Boserup's model.   S

802. Russell, Hilary. THE CHINESE VOYAGES OF ANGUS BETHUNE. *Beaver [Canada] 1977 307(4): 22-31.* In 1813 and 1815, Angus Bethune, a partner for the North West Company, led two trading expeditions to Canton. He carried mostly furs, and in return received Oriental foods, tea, and fireworks. Bethune touched at the Hawaiian Islands, the California coast, and Alaska. The Company was not pleased with the ventures. Expenses were too high, repairs costly, quarreling was common, and there was much bribery and red tape in China. The author

details some of the contacts with officials in Hawaii, California, and China. 10 illus., map.   D. Chaput

803. Schechter, Rebecca. CANADIAN PIONEER COOKERY: A STRUCTURAL ANALYSIS. *J. of Can. Studies [Canada] 1977 12(4): 3-11.* Discusses foodstuffs available to Canadian pioneers, and the development of methods for food preparation, particularly as these reflect the structure of society on the Canadian frontier from 1750 to 1850. It was necessary at first to produce at home many ingredients, e.g. yeast, which could be bought by even the poorer Britons. This made for more variety in the finished product, as did the gradual introduction of newer cooking methods, which supplemented without replacing the kettle and spit. Discusses the "ubiquitous" pie. The meat and berries for filling pies, available only to the upper classes in Britain, could be had by all in Canada, the pie thus symbolizing an "upward levelling" of society, while the crust concealed the more meager variety of foodstuffs available in rural areas. Based on instructional materials used by pioneers and on secondary sources; 4 charts, 32 notes.   L. W. Van Wyk

804. Spray, W. A. THE SETTLEMENT OF THE BLACK REFUGEES IN NEW BRUNSWICK, 1815-1836. *Acadiensis [Canada] 1977 6(2): 64-79.* In 1815, 371 black fugitives from the United States arrived in New Brunswick. In 1816 they applied for land, receiving temporary licenses of occupation to 50 acres each rather than the minimum 100-acre lots granted free to white settlers. The Assembly apparently rejected requests to assist blacks, but aided Scottish settlers. Grants of land to whites in the black settlement began in 1822, occasioning disorders lasting until 1826. The Assembly settled the land questions in 1836, although other problems persisted. 85 notes.   D. F. Chard

805. Sunter, Ronald. THE SCOTTISH BACKGROUND TO THE IMMIGRATION OF BISHOP ALEXANDER MACDONNELL AND THE GLENGARRY HIGHLANDERS. *Study Sessions: Can. Catholic Hist. Assoc. 1973 40: 11-20.* The British Navy attempted to impress Catholics emigrating to Canada where Bishop Alexander Macdonnell and the Glengarry Highlanders settled and figured prominently in the history of Ontario. Covers the period 1770's-1814.

806. —. [THE AGRICULTURAL CRISIS IN LOWER CANADA]. *Can. Hist. R. 1975 56(2): 133-168.*
Paquet, Gilles and Wallot, Jean-Pierre. THE AGRICULTURAL CRISIS IN LOWER CANADA, 1802-12: MISE AU POINT. A RESPONSE TO T. J. A. LE GOFF, *pp. 133-161.* Assesses Le Goff's contribution to the debate over the thesis of a crisis in Lower Canadian agriculture starting circa 1802 and giving rise to the "first French-Canadian nationalism" (F. Ouellet). The authors assert that Le Goff's statistical exercises are based on insufficient and biased data and that his demography oriented interpretation, although valuable in some European contexts, does not take into account the extension of colonization in a North American setting. Finally, they stress that the struggles of the 1800's are simply another round in the more-and-more insistent struggle for global power (political, economic, social).
Le Goff, T. J. A. A REPLY, *pp. 162-168.* Maintains that Paquet and Wallot fail to refute his criticisms of their work. Their analytical model of foreign demand for Lower Canadian produce is meaningless in a preindustrial economy; their description of domestic demand is based only on impressions; their discussion of supply shows ignorance of the limitations on good accessible and available land in the colony. There was a "structural" crisis after the turn of the century. Expresses a general lack of interest in Paquet and Wallot's global models of socio-economico-political transformations drawn from systems analysis, etc., but suggests that those models may be undercut by the flimsiness of the evidence presented by Paquet and Wallot on the state of the agricultural economy and of people in the countryside.   A

807. —. [LAND INHERITANCE IN 19TH-CENTURY ONTARIO]. *J. of Econ. Hist. 1976 36(1): 126-146.*
Gagan, David P. THE INDIVISIBILITY OF LAND: A MICROANALYSIS OF THE SYSTEM OF INHERITANCE IN NINETEENTH-CENTURY ONTARIO, *pp. 126-141.* Although they had recourse to both the perfectly partible and the perfectly impartible systems of inheritance, nineteenth-century Ontario farmers

commonly employed a unique English-Canadian variation on the perfectly impartible pattern. They devised their estates upon one, or occasionally two of their children, binding them to pay out of their inheritance or other resources the provisions for remaining survivors made in the will. The purpose of this system was to allow land rich and money poor agrarians to pass on their principal asset intact, and it reflects their belief that favorable man/land ratios were the essence of security and prosperity. At the same time, the system made the principal heir the instrument of the deceased parent's desire to treat all of his surviving dependents more or less equally in terms of the value of their inheritances. The system guaranteed that those who inherited land would acquire sufficient land to pursue time tested agricultural methods, but it promoted severe demographic and social dislocations.

McInnis, Marvin. DISCUSSION, *pp. 142-146.* J

The Rebellions of 1837

808. Beck, J. M. "A FOOL FOR A CLIENT": THE TRIAL OF JOSEPH HOWE. *Acadiensis [Canada] 1974 3(2): 27-44.* Discusses the 1835 libel trial of Joseph Howe, editor of the *Novascotian,* for publicizing the corruption in the local Halifax government. Truth was not yet considered a defense, so conviction seemed inevitable. Howe defended himself, however, and because he was a lawyer, could present otherwise unallowable evidence. He thereby convinced the jury to acquit him despite the law. Several local officials then resigned, but the system was unimproved. Realizing his new popularity and determined to bring change, Howe entered Nova Scotia politics. Based on archives, newspapers, and primary and secondary sources; 103 notes. E. A. Churchill

809. Craig, G. M. TWO CONTRASTING UPPER CANADIAN FIGURES: JOHN ROLPH AND JOHN STRACHAN. *Tr. of the Royal Soc. of Can. 1974 12: 237-248.* Compares and contrasts the careers of John Rolph and John Strachan. Rolph left few records whereas Strachan left many. Both men were born in Britain and were better educated than the average Canadian. Although both men were Anglicans, Rolph opposed the idea of an established church and Strachan strongly supported it and the land endowment allowed the church in Canada. Strachan became the bishop of Toronto; Rolph had a career in law and medicine. In politics Strachan was a tory and Rolph a rebel who had to flee to the United States after the rebellion of 1837. Only Rolph held elective office, but Strachan held more power. Each man was an eloquent speechmaker, had taught, and was influential in the development of the University of Toronto. Although students may prefer Rolph's reform ideas and his opposition to an established church and the family compact to Strachan's fight for the benefit of a minority denomination, encouragement of the family compact, and francophobia, the latter did provide good leadership to his church and, despite his faults, emerges as the bigger man. J. D. Neville

810. Duffy, John and Muller, H. Nicholas, III. THE GREAT WOLF HUNT: THE POPULAR RESPONSE IN VERMONT TO THE *PATRIOTE* UPRISING OF 1837. *J. of Am. Studies [Great Britain] 1974 8(2): 153-169.* Chronicles the failure of the *patriote* in Vermont to assist Canadian rebels in their 1837-38 rebellion against British rule of Canada. Governor Silas Jennison and other Vermont authorities condemned the *patriote.* President Martin van Buren (1782-1862) intervened and used force to curb *patriote* activities along the Vermont-Canada border. Based on American and British archival materials; 49 notes. H. T. Lovin

811. Hardy, René. LA RÉBELLION DE 1837-38 ET L'ESSOR DU PROTESTANTISME CANADIEN-FRANÇAIS [The rebellion of 1837-38 and the scope of French-Canadian Protestantism]. *Rev. d'Hist. de l'Amérique Française [Canada] 1975 29(2): 163-189.* English and Swiss Protestant evangelists considered the rebellion of 1837-38 in Lower Canada as a good opportunity to destroy the influence of the Catholic clergy. The English residents of Montreal thought that the conversion of the French-Canadians to Protestantism would guarantee cohesion between the two ethnic groups. Colonial administrators, however, considered the Catholic clergy indispensable to the maintenance of law and order. Based on documents in the Archives de la paroisse Notre-Dame

de Québec, Archives de la Chancellerie de l'Archevêché de Montréal, Archives de l'Université du Québec à Trois-Rivières, and secondary works; 106 notes. L. B. Chan

812. Johnson, J. K. THE U.C. CLUB AND THE UPPER CANADIAN ELITE, 1837-1840. *Ontario Hist. [Canada] 1977 69(3): 151-168.* Mentions some of the historiographic problems that once existed around the early years of the Upper Canada Club. Discusses its origins and early years. Comments on the characteristics and interests of some early members. The picture of the club as excluding businessmen is not valid. In appendixes, lists the names of the politically significant in Toronto 1837-40, public offices held by members, some business directorships and interests, and the memberships of the management committees of the club in those years. There is considerable overlapping of the lists. Mainly secondary sources; 50 notes. W. B. Whitham

813. Kesteman, Jean-Pierre. LES PREMIERS JOURNAUX DU DISTRICT DE SAINT-FRANÇOIS (1823-1845) [The first newspapers in the district of Saint Francis (1823-1845)]. *Rev. D'Hist. De L'Amérique Française [Canada] 1977 31(2): 239-253.* An overview of the principal newspapers published in a single distrcit of Lower Canada's (Quebec's) Eastern Townships. Though many of these pioneering ventures, e.g., the *British Colonist* and the *Farmer's Advocate* were initiated by Americans, they clearly reflected the social, political, and economic polarization that developed before the French Canadians' Rebellion of 1837. 82 notes. M. R. Yerburgh

814. Martin, Ged. THE CANADIAN REBELLION LOSSES BILL OF 1849 IN BRITISH POLITICS. *J. of Imperial and Commonwealth Hist. [Great Britain] 1977 6(1): 3-22.* Examines the Canadian Rebellion Losses Bill of 1849, which was to compensate for losses resulting from the rebellions of 1837-38 in Lower Canada, from the standpoint of its impact on British politics. William Ewart Gladstone and Lord Henry Peter Brougham were the key figures in attempting to have the bill vetoed, and in so doing they brought into question the whole definition of responsible government and imperial authority. In the end parliament did not intervene in Canadian affairs and thus gave responsible government a chance to mature as a constitutional concept. 71 notes. J. A. Casada

815. Muller, H. N., III and Duffy, John J. JEDIDIAH [sic] BURCHARD AND VERMONT'S 'NEW MEASURE' REVIVALS: SOCIAL ADJUSTMENT AND THE QUEST FOR UNITY. *Vermont Hist. 1978 46(1): 5-20.* Jedediah Burchard, a traveling actor and circus performer, brought the anxious seat and protracted meetings, techniques used by C. G. Finney in New York and Ohio, to a dozen Vermont villages during 1835-36. His sensationalism and vernacular speech polarized Protestants. A symptom of social unrest, the short-lived Burchard revival was replaced by other excitements, beginning with sympathy for the Canadian Rebellion of 1837-38. 7 illus., 43 notes. T. D. S. Bassett

816. Muller, H. Nicholas, III. TROUBLE ON THE BORDER, 1838: A NEGLECTED INCIDENT FROM VERMONT'S NEGLECTED HISTORY. *Vermont Hist. 1976 44(2): 97-102.* "During the . . . winter of 1837-1838, . . . nearly the entire population of northern Vermont showed "frenzied excitement" over the Canadian Rebellion of 1837. The 1 March letter of N. R. Woods of Potton, north of Troy, Vermont, in the Eastern Townships of Lower Canada, in the Vermont Historical Society, here edited with introduction, described a raid of some 60 *patriotes* which seized arms. By November the excitement died down. 16 notes. T. D. S. Bassett

817. Read, Colin. THE DUNCOMBE RISING, ITS AFTERMATH, ANTI-AMERICANISM, AND SECTARIANISM. *Social Hist. [Canada] 1976 9(17): 47-69.* The Duncombe Rising of 1837 was a haphazard and disorganized revolt in Upper Canada, resulting from political discord. Rebels came from isolated agrarian townships populated largely by people born in North America. Although religion was not important in the revolt, most churches suffered setbacks in the aftermath of the rebellion because accusations were made against their members. Many church-going settlers fled the area. The smaller sects and the American sects suffered the most. Based on papers in public and church archives, on church periodicals, and on published primary sources; 3 maps, 88 notes. W. K. Hobson

818. Read, Colin. THE SHORT HILLS RAID OF JUNE, 1838, AND ITS AFTERMATH. *Ontario Hist. [Canada] 1976 68(2): 93-115.* Discusses the events of the Short Hills raid, a minor incident following the rebellion of 1837. Comments on the organization of the raid and some of the persons involved. Suggests the participants' motives. The trials subsequent to the capture of the raiders also are remarked upon. Posttrial appeals and the international atmosphere of the time are mentioned. 111 notes, 3 appendixes.   W. B. Whitham

819. Rudé, George. IDEOLOGY AND POPULAR PROTEST. *Hist. Reflections [Canada] 1976 3(2): 69-77.* The American and French Revolutions of the 18th century and the Lower Canada Rebellions of 1837-38 show that revolutions and rebellions involve a distinctive popular element. In the American Revolution the common people shared the dominant ideology which the revolutionary elites transmitted. The French Revolution also suggest the impact of the ideology of the revolutionary middle class and liberal aristocracy on the common people. The common people of France added something of their own to the notions of the French bourgeoisie. The Canadian rebellions show a popular ideology distinguishable from that of the leadership.   P. Travis

820. Senior, Elinor. THE PROVINCIAL CAVALRY IN LOWER CANADA, 1837-50. *Can. Hist. Rev. [Canada] 1976 57(1): 1-24.* Examines the colonial cavalry's role assisting British regulars during the insurrections of 1837-38, its use as frontier guards in the post-rebellion period, and its aid to civil power in Montreal during the turbulent 1840's. Although its disbandment in 1850 was owing partly to alleged annexationist sympathies among its officer corps, no evidence of such sympathies was found. Based on documents in the military "C" series, the memoirs of Sydney Bellingham and Thomas Wily, in the Public Archives in Ottawa, and the McCord Papers in the McCord Museum, Montreal.   A

821. Senior, H. OGLE GOWAN, ORANGEISM, AND THE IMMIGRANT QUESTION 1830-1833. *Ontario Hist. [Canada] 1974 66(4): 193-210.* Discusses the effect of Irish immigration and Irish influence on the political life of Upper Canada in the early 19th century, with an emphasis on the continuing contest between reformers and the governing circles, popularly known as the "Family Compact."

822. Trépanier, Pierre. RUMILLY ET SON PAPINEAU [Rumilly and his Papineau]. *Action Natl. [Canada] 1978 67(9): 727-736.* For 50 years, Robert Rumilly has published several volumes per year on Quebec history, including his monumental *Histoire de la province de Québec*. He has recently published his second biography of Louis-Joseph Papineau, *Papineau et son temps* (Montreal, 1977, 2 vols.). There are some modifications from Rumilly's earlier *Papineau* (Paris, 1934), but the author's ideological position remains the same. The rebellions of 1837-38 were ideological, a local manifestation of the struggle which agitated the West since the French Revolution of 1789 and subsequent counterrevolution. Ethnic, cultural, and economic conflicts were secondary. For Trepanier, Rumilly's interpretation is somewhat narrow and simplistic. 40 notes.
A. W. Novitsky

823. Walton, Bruce. THE 1836 ELECTION IN LENNOX AND ADDINGTON. *Ontario Hist. [Canada] 1975 67(3): 153-168.* Examines the switch in allegiance which occurred in the 1836 election in Lennox and Addington, suggests possible reasons for the results, and offers some conclusions as to the nature of Tory electoral politics in the mid-1830's.

Responsible Government and Self-Government

824. Banks, Margaret A. UPPER AND LOWER CANADA OR CANADA WEST AND EAST, 1841-67? *Can. Hist. R. 1973 54(4): 475-482.* Seeks to determine the official names of the constituent parts of the Province of Canada. There was no uniform official terminology until April 1849, but from then until the end of the union, Upper Canada and Lower Canada were the names authorized for use in the statutes and generally employed in official documents. It would therefore be preferable for historians to use these names instead of calling the constituent parts

of the province Canada West and East, as many of them do. Based on statutes, journals of the Legislative Assembly, and other contemporary sources.   A

825. Beer, D. B. SIR ALLEN MCNAB AND THE RUSSELL-SYDENHAM REGIME. *Ontario Hist. [Canada] 1974 66(1): 37-.* Examines the political career of Sir Allan McNab, 1839-42. McNab's adherence to the beliefs of the Family Compact, the dominant political faction in upper Canada prior to the 1840's, caused a shift in his popularity during the following period of rapid constitutional and political reform. 64 notes.   W. B. Whitham and S

826. Colthart, J. M. EDWARD ELLICE AND THE DECISION FOR SELF-GOVERNMENT, 1839. *Can. Hist. Assoc. Hist. Papers [Canada] 1975: 113-133.* Edward Ellice (1781-1863) was influential in shaping British imperial policy during 1838-40. His objective was to preserve the Whig government, 1835-41, and not to protect his income from North America. Ellice was consulted about the missions to British North America of Lord Gosford (1776-1849) and Lord Durham (1792-1840). He helped shape Durham's recommendations and advised Charles Poulett Thomson (1799-1841). Throughout, Ellice emphasized the need to retain Canada as an imperial outpost. Based on Hansard, various collections of the Public Archives of Canada, the Public Records Office, and secondary sources; 77 notes.   G. E. Panting

827. Gibson, James A. POLITICAL PRISONERS, TRANSPORTATION FOR LIFE, AND RESPONSIBLE GOVERNMENT IN CANADA. *Ontario Hist. [Canada] 1975 67(4): 185-198.* Argues that the Colonial Office conceded "responsible government" to the Canadas during 1838-45, less as a result of the Earl of Durham's report on the two provinces, than as an effort to divert attention from penal transportation from the Canadas as punishment for the 1837-38 uprisings. Analyzes events in Upper Canada only, and sees a trend in public opinion initially forcing the substitution of transportation for execution, and then against transportation. In passing, comments on the treatment of transportees in Australia. Based on primary sources; 33 notes.   W. B. Whitham

828. Inness, Lorna. JOSEPH HOWE: JOURNALIST. *Nova Scotia Hist. Q. 1973 3(3): 159-170.* Discusses Joseph Howe's career in journalism, especially for the Halifax newspaper, the *Novascotian*, ca. 1824-38.

829. Newbound, I. D. C. LORD DURHAM, THE WHIGS AND CANADA, 1838: THE BACKGROUND OF DURHAM'S RETURN. *Albion 1976 8(4): 351-374.* Lord Durham's (1792-1840) personal and petty attacks on his fellow ministers and his vainglorous and pompous conduct made him very unpopular in his own party. When he exceeded his authority in Canada, end-of-session fatigue and the need to get Irish legislation through a Tory-dominated House of Lords made impractical a Whig defense of Durham against censure. Thus, although he was coauthor of the first Reform Act and the author of the Durham Report, he was considered an outcast by his own government and failed to earn the respect usually accorded a public figure of his significance. 118 notes.
T. L. Underwood

830. Nourry, Louis. L'IDÉE DE FÉDÉRATION CHEZ ÉTIENNE PARENT 1831-1852 [The idea of federation in Étienne Parent's thinking 1831-52]. *R. d'Hist. de l'Amérique Française [Canada] 1973 26(4): 533-557.* French Canadian politician Étienne Parent defended the idea of an almost independent Canada, with more or less protectorate status in the British Empire, in his newspaper *Le Canadien*. Parent felt such status would enable Canada to win its independence gradually from England, rather than be absorbed by the United States. Based on primary and secondary sources; 102 notes.   C. Collon

831. Patterson, Graeme. AN ENDURING CANADIAN MYTH: RESPONSIBLE GOVERNMENT AND THE FAMILY COMPACT. *J. of Can. Studies [Canada] 1977 12(2): 3-16.* Traces the meaning and significance of the terms "family compact" and "responsible government" in 19th-century Canada. Describes the political attitudes and connotations of each term, giving examples from newspapers, books, and speeches of political and literary figures. Shows how neither term was commonly defined, and analyzes the mythology surrounding each term and its changing relationship to current politics. 65 notes.
J. B. Reed

CAMROSE LUTHERAN COLLEGE
LIBRARY

832. Patterson, Graeme H. WHIGGERY, NATIONALITY, AND THE UPPER CANADIAN REFORM TRADITION. *Can. Hist. R. 1975 56(1): 25-43.* An historiographical critique and reinterpretation of Upper Canadian political and intellectual history. Treating 19th-century colonial political theory, the structure of parties of opposition, and misconceptions involving the concept of "responsible government," this article, by implication, relates also to the study of the political history of the other British North American colonies for the period prior to 1848.

A

833. Senior, Elinor. THE BRITISH GARRISON IN MONTREAL IN THE 1840'S. *J. of the Soc. for Army Hist. Res. 1974 52 (210): 111-127.* From its capitulation (1760) until 1870, "Montreal was a British garrison town" and was "never without a regiment of the line, a battery of Royal Artillery and some Royal Engineers." For those 110 years it rivalled "Quebec as the major British military station" in Canada. For much of the 1840's, in fact, "when the city was also the political capital of the united province of Canada, Montreal resembled a European metropolis, having the seat of government and military headquarters located in the most important commercial city of the country," and "it is difficult to touch any aspect of Montreal history without encountering the influence or, at least, the presence of the military." Probably the most important duty of the British garrison was aiding the civil authorities in times of disturbance—"and the forties in Montreal proved exceptionally disturbing"—and particularly during the annual municipal elections, the provincial elections in 1844 and 1848, and the troubles during the summer of 1849 "as the house of assembly debated the Rebellion Losses Bill." 110 notes.

A. N. Garland

Mid-Century Developments

834. Anders, Leslie. "FARTHEST NORTH": THE HISTORIAN AND THE BATTLE OF ATHENS. *Missouri Historical R. 1975 69(2): 147-168.* The battle of Athens, Missouri, on 5 August 1861 was a northern victory wedged between disasters at Bull Run on 21 July and Wilson's Creek on 10 August. Pointing to the St. Albans, Vermont, raid and John Morgan's raid in Ohio, the author rejects an old belief that Athens was the "farthest north" penetration of Confederate forces. He also rejects a belief that troops from Iowa were largely responsible for the victory and concludes that the Union Guards of Scotland and Clark counties under David Moore almost unaided routed the secession forces of half a dozen counties under Martin E. Green. Based on primary and secondary sources; 8 illus., map, 30 notes.

W. F. Zornow

835. Anderson, Stuart. BRITISH THREATS AND THE SETTLEMENT OF THE OREGON BOUNDARY DISPUTE. *Pacific Northwest Q. 1975 66(4): 153-160.* Examines one aspect of the historiographical debate about the United States' acquisition of Oregon from Great Britain. Disputes Julius Pratt's interpretation that President James K. Polk withdrew his demand for 54° 40' and accepted the 49th parallel because of British threats of military action against the United States. On the contrary, Polk had sought compromise on the 49th parallel from the beginning and used skillful diplomacy to insure it. Yet, despite Frederick Merk's assertion that British military threats played no role, Polk's timing on a final settlement plan was affected by the consideration of possible war. The correct interpretation therefore lies somewhere between the extremes of Pratt and Merk. Based on primary sources; 39 notes.

M. L. Tate

836. Barthe, Joseph-Guillaume. LE CANADA RECONQUIS PAR LA FRANCE [Canada reconquered by France]. *Études Françaises [Canada] 1973 9(3): 257-263.* Increased intellectual and commercial ties between France and French Canada would allow the democratic institutions already established in the New World to continue to flourish, based on an expansion of French immigration to Canada and the continuance of Anglo-French cooperation. Extracted from *Le Canada reconquis par la France*, Paris, Ledoyen, 1855, p. 291-302; illus.

G. J. Rossi

837. Baskerville, Peter. DONALD BETHUNE'S STEAMBOAT BUSINESS: A STUDY OF UPPER CANADIAN COMMERCIAL AND FINANCIAL PRACTICE. *Ontario Hist. [Canada] 1975 67(3): 135-149.* Discusses the financial fortunes of the mid-19th-century Canadian steamboat proprietor, Donald Bethune, for the purpose of illuminating the changing and increasingly reckless commercial and financial environment in which he operated.

838. Brumgardt, John R. PRESIDENTIAL DUEL AT MIDSUMMER: THE "PEACE" MISSIONS TO CANADA AND RICHMOND, 1864. *Lincoln Herald 1975 77(2): 96-102.* To silence critics and to capitalize on supposed discontent in the North, Jefferson Davis in 1864 sent Jacob Thompson and Clement C. Clay as emissaries to Canada. They were to give the appearance of a South willing to negotiate for peace. Abraham Lincoln, at the insistence of Horace Greely, offered to meet with any emissary authorized to discuss reunion and emancipation. The emissaries were unable to meet Lincoln's conditions, but some Northern leaders believed Lincoln had deliberately stifled the Southern initiative. Southern leaders had hoped for just such results thinking they would weaken Lincoln's chances for reelection in 1864. Lincoln countered the southern initiative by sending James F. Jacquess and James R. Gilmore on an unofficial mission to Richmond to propose reunion, emancipation, amnesty, and compensation to slaveholders owning less than 50 slaves. Davis said the South would accept only independence. Gilmore and Jacquess returned north and published an account of their discussions with Davis. With the South's true intentions made clear Lincoln had little trouble winning reelection. Based on primary sources; illus., 33 notes.

B. J. LaBue

839. Carroll, Daniel B. AMERICA IN 1861: A FRENCH VIEW. *J. of the Illinois State Hist. Soc. 1974 67(2): 132-153.* An extensive North American trip in 1861 was undertaken by French Prince Jerome Napoleon Bonaparte, son of Napoleon's brother Jerome. Bonaparte's diary, Lieutenant Colonel Camille Ferri Pisanis and Maurice Sand's published accounts, and French ambassador Henri Mercier's foreign affairs reports provide a descriptive French view of America as seen by this bourgeois party. The French party visited Northern, Southern, and Canadian military, industrial, and political leaders. Based on the four travelers' accounts and manuscripts in the Archives du Ministere des Affaires etrangeres, Paris; 35 notes.

A. C. Aimone

840. Cottrell, Philip L. THE ROLE OF THE INTERNATIONAL FINANCIAL SOCIETY IN THE BUYING-OUT OF THE HUDSON'S BAY COMPANY, 1863. *Rev. Int. d'Hist. de la Banque [Italy] 1975 10: 192-200.* Discusses recently discovered papers of the International Financial Society (IFS), one of several investment banks established in London in the early 1860's, which shed new light on its role in buying the Hudson's Bay Company. Several interests in both Canada and Great Britain wished to push railroad building into Rupert's Land, the area controlled by the Hudson's Bay Company, but they needed the investment of a major financial institution. This they received from the IFS, several of the members of which had interests in Canadian railroad promotion. The IFS papers do not sustain earlier interpretations that the IFS was founded solely to purchase the Hudson's Bay Company and profit from its recapitalization. Based on the board minutes of the IFS and secondary sources; 49 notes.

D. McGinnis

841. Cousins, Leone B. LETTERS OF NORMAN WADE. *Nova Scotia Hist. Q. [Canada] 1974 4(2): 117-146.* In 1859 Norman Wade (1837-62) left his home and family in Granville Ferry to become a sailor on the brig *Cyrene*. The letters he wrote to family members from May 1859 to September 1862 give some flavor of his life aboard ship, his rise to Captain of the forecastle, and the dangers of blockade running during the American Civil War. He died aboard ship at age 25 and was buried on the coast of Florida.

H. M. Evans

842. Cousins, Leone Banks. A NOVA SCOTIAN IN THE UNION NAVY: THE LETTERS OF NORMAN WADE. *Canada 1975 2(3): 58-73.* An introductory note outlines the life of Wade (1837-62). Provides 12 letters, 7 photos, 37 notes, biblio.

W. W. Elison

843. Cunningham, O. Edward. "IN VIOLATION OF THE LAWS OF WAR": THE EXECUTION OF ROBERT COBB KENNEDY. *Louisiana Hist. 1977 18(2): 189-202.* Born in Georgia and raised in Claiborn Parish, Louisiana, Robert C. Kennedy attended West Point for two years before settling down to farming. When the Civil War began he was commissioned a Captain in the First Louisiana Infantry. Wounded at Shiloh, Kennedy was later transferred to General Joe Wheeler's cav-

alry. He was captured in the Chattanooga campaign, but escaped from Johnson's Island Prison in Ohio a year later. Recruited as a saboteur, Kennedy participated in an abortive attempt to burn New York City after the 1864 election. He escaped to Canada, but was later captured in Michigan while attempting to cross to Confederate lines. Tried in New York City for espionage, he was the last Confederate executed before the end of hostilities. Primary sources; 18 notes.   A

844. Dessaules, Louis-Antoine. CONTRE LES DÉTRACTEURS DE L'INSTITUT CANADIEN [Against the detractors of the Canadian Institute]. *Études Françaises [Canada] 1973 9(3): 197-204.* Ostensibly addressed to Canadian ecclesiastics, refutes the legitimacy of the *Index* in determining the suitability of a book for inclusion in a library. Extracted from *Le Pays*, March 11, 1862.   G. J. Rossi

845. Dodds, Ronald. U.S. BALLOON LOST OVER CANADA—IN 1859! *Can. Geographical J. 1974 88(3): 22-27.* Describes the experiences of two American balloonists, John LaMountain and John A. Haddock— the first to fly over Canada, who were forced to land in the Quebec wilderness and hike back to civilization.   S

846. Edwards, Malcolm. "THE WAR OF COMPLEXIONAL DISTINCTION": BLACKS IN GOLD RUSH CALIFORNIA AND BRITISH COLUMBIA. *California Hist. Q. 1977 56(1): 34-45.* Describes how blacks in the California gold rush, disillusioned at discriminatory laws passed by the state legislature and at court decisions upholding unfair actions against them, migrated to British Columbia in the late 1850's. The state of California attempted several times to exclude free blacks from admission to California; blacks could not testify in civil and criminal actions involving whites, were excluded from jury service, and lived under other legal restrictions. Such cases as the Archy Lee case, in which the state supreme court bent the law in order to restore Lee to slave status, indicated the views of white Californians on blacks. In 1858 blacks began to migrate to British Columbia because of an indirect invitation from its Governor, James Douglas. As many as 800 blacks may have headed north. Unfortunately, although British Columbia did not codify discrimination into law, whites there displayed overt prejudice. They refused to attend integrated church services and denied blacks public accommodations. In 1864 a black militia, organized for protection of the colony against Indians, was refused permission to take part in public ceremonies. Finding their welcome little better than in California, most blacks returned to the United States after the Civil War and the enactment of new constitutional amendments. Primary and secondary sources; photos, 37 notes.   A. Hoffman

847. Francis, Daniel. WHALING ON THE EASTMAIN. *Beaver [Canada] 1977 308(1): 15-19.* In 1852, Governor George Simpson predicted that whaling in the rivers on the east coast of Hudson Bay would become more meaningful to the Hudson's Bay Company than the beaver trade. After a series of poor starts, the business improved under James Anderson and reached its peak during 1854-60. The whaling was a stationary operation in which the whales were caught in nets and then killed. However, the weather frequently interfered, it was difficult to provision the area, and, for reasons unknown, the whales avoided the rivers whenever the men and nets were ready. The project was abandoned in 1870. Based on Hudson's Bay Co. archives; 7 illus.   D. Chaput

848. Gagan, David P. ENUMERATOR'S INSTRUCTIONS FOR THE CENSUS OF CANADA, 1852 AND 1861. *Social Hist. [Canada] 1974 7(14): 355-365.* Reprints the 1852 and 1861 Canadian census enumerator's instructions. Comments on special problems for using the census that the instructions and the returns themselves reveal. Both censuses were poorly planned and poorly executed. The 1852 instructions are from private papers in the University of Western Ontario Library, and the 1861 instructions are from the *Hamilton Weekly Spectator*; 5 notes.
                                                                      W. K. Hobson

849. Gagan, David. GEOGRAPHICAL AND SOCIAL MOBILITY IN NINETEENTH-CENTURY ONTARIO: A MICROSTUDY. *Can. R. of Soc. and Anthrop. 1976 13(2): 152-164.* Mobility studies are central to the analysis of historical populations. The rate and direction, both vertical and horizontal, of the movement of individuals and families are indices of the nature and pace of demographic and social structural change in past time. This microstudy focuses on geographical mobility in a mid-nineteenth-century rural Canadian community and seeks to explain it in terms of levels of vocational opportunity. Automated record linkage across three census returns is the method used to distinguish between permanent and transient households. Vocational mobility, that is, movement into, out of, and through the ranks of various occupational groups, is employed as the measure of economic opportunity in the community. The evidence suggests that levels of migration were as high in this rural community as they were in contemporary urban societies as individuals moved into and out of the community seeking to improve their economic status. But it is also shown that vocational mobility was a function of displacement or replacement and not of an expanding demand for goods and services. Thus the limited opportunities for vertical mobility were predicated on persistence; however, emigration was the usual response in the face of limited opportunities. Within this context nineteenth-century rural communities were able to assimilate, however temporarily, large numbers of transient employables.   J

850. Gagan, David. LAND, POPULATION, AND SOCIAL CHANGE: THE 'CRITICAL YEARS' IN RURAL CANADA WEST. *Can. Hist. Rev. [Canada] 1978 59(3): 293-318.* Competition for land among a rural community's families in the 1850's to increase productivity and provide landed inheritances for children created a land shortage, wildly fluctuating land prices and increased rural indebtedness during a period of general economic and agricultural instability. The land and economic crises resulted in the adoption of a more restrictive system of inheritance, later ages of marriage and lower marital fertility. But because these adjustments were essentially unpalatable an alternative prospect— emigration to a new farming frontier—proved more attractive; hence agrarian support for the creation of the new Canadian nation in 1867 and its territorial objectives—westward expansion. A microanalysis which employs manuscript census returns, aggregate census data, probate and real property records, record linkage, family reconstitution and quantitative analysis.   A

851. Gaster, Patricia, ed. HOGAN OUREN IN NEBRASKA AND COLORADO, 1861-1866. *Nebraska Hist. 1977 58(2): 219-249.* Hogan Ouren left Norway for Canada in 1853. After working briefly on railroad construction in Quebec he crossed the border into the United States. During the 1860's he sometimes freighted across the Nebraska plains to Colorado. Reminiscences of these early years mention Indian affairs, mining, freighting, cattle driving, and military operations.
                                                                      R. Lowitt

852. Graff, Harvey J. WHAT THE 1861 CENSUS CAN TELL US ABOUT LITERACY: A REPLY. *Social Hist. [Canada] 1975 8(16): 337-349.* Replies to criticism by H. J. Mays and H. F. Manzl that the census is an unsatisfactory source for the systematic study of literacy in Canada in comparison to signatory documents. Contemporary literacy research in several countries has established a high level of accuracy in census self-reports. Proof that admission of illiteracy on census forms was not random can be found in the fact that literacy rates were quite similar in four cities of Upper Canada, and that the rates varied by age, sex, ethnicity, occupation, and wealth in a predictable manner. Although signatures are a direct indication of the ability to read and perhaps of some ability to write, nonsigners cannot immediately be classed as nonreaders. Using signatory documents alone poses a serious problem of unrepresentativeness in terms of sex, wealth, and probably ethnicity and occupation. 20 notes.   W. K. Hobson

853. Greenberg, Dolores. YANKEE FINANCIERS AND THE ESTABLISHMENT OF TRANS-ATLANTIC PARTNERSHIPS: A RE-EXAMINATION. *Business Hist. [Great Britain] 1974 16(1): 17-35.* Traces the role of non-Jewish Americans in the establishment of American private banking houses abroad, mainly London and Paris, in the 1860's. Focuses on the key role of Levi Parsons Morton who was successively a country storekeeper, importer and jobber, and international banker connected with the Morgans, the Drexels, George Peabody, and Sir John Rose, a Canadian. Based on primary sources.
                                                                      B. L. Crapster

854. Greening, W. E. CANADA'S FIRST INTERNATIONAL RAILWAY. *Can. Geographical J. 1974 89(6): 24-27.*

855. Griezic, Foster. JOHN HILLYARD CAMERON AND THE QUESTION OF CONSERVATIVE LEADERSHIP IN CANADA WEST 1854-1856. *Ontario Hist. [Canada] 1974 66(4): 223-240.* Discusses the actions of the prominent Conservative John Hillyard Cameron toward the establishment of a Conservative-centered coalition and a change of leadership in 1856.

856. Harris, Donald A. REPORT OF THE 1972 ARCHAEOLOGICAL EXCAVATIONS OF THE MARKET SHOAL TOWER, KINGSTON, ONTARIO. *Can. Historic Sites 1976 15: 171-223.* Archaeological excavations were conducted on the Market Shoal Martello tower during the month of February, 1972. These excavations uncovered the ground floor of the tower and exposed the No. 1 ordnance store, No. 2 ordnance store, the powder magazine, the barracks store and the commissariat. Most of the structural material remaining in these rooms was flooring. Sections of the second level were also excavated including one window, the roof of the powder magazine, the boiler and the vault above the No. 2 ordnance store. A latrine was excavated on the gun platform and a small quantity of mid-19th-century artifacts was collected from the site.   J

857. Headon, Christopher F. DEVELOPMENTS IN CANADIAN ANGLICAN WORSHIP IN EASTERN AND CENTRAL CANADA 1840-1868. *J. of the Can. Church Hist. Soc. 1975 17(2): 26-38.* Many Canadian Anglican clergy with Tractarian backgrounds wanted to increase ritual and introduce a variety of innovations in the Canadian Church. These included the increased use of the surplice, more frequent celebration of the Holy Communion, and development of plainsong for congregational singing. The vast number of low churchmen viewed these changes as very dangerous, seeing an obvious drift toward Roman Catholicism. The attitudes of both high and low churchmen toward the innovations cannot be understood without reference to the great changes affecting 19th-century Canada. Secondary and printed primary sources; 51 notes.   J. A. Kicklighter

858. Hite, Roger W. VOICE OF A FUGITIVE: HENRY BIBB AND THE ANTE-BELLUM BLACK SEPARATISM. *J. of Black Studies 1974 4(3): 269-284.* Black leader Henry Bibb promoted the movement to encourage blacks to settle in Canada during the Antebellum period. 8 notes, biblio.   K. Butcher

859. Holmgren, E. J. THOMAS BLAKISTON, EXPLORER. *Alberta Hist. [Canada] 1976 24(1): 15-22.* Thomas Blakiston, an army officer, was assigned in 1857 to assist in the Palliser-British North American Exploring Expedition. Blakiston's role was to record magnetic observations and at the same time to explore unknown regions. Blakiston disagreed with John Palliser and the rest of the party, mainly wanting more military discipline. Blakiston led a major search party through the Kootenay Pass and the valley of the Flathead River; he then resigned and refused to cooperate further with Palliser. Blakiston later explored the upper Yangtze in China, and then lived in Japan for 20 years, becoming a leading merchant and an authority on birds. In 1885 he married and settled in New Mexico, spending most of his time on ornithology. He died in 1891 while visiting in San Diego. 4 illus., 17 notes.   D. Chaput

860. Houston, C. Stuart. A BIRD-WATCHER'S OUTING IN 1858. *Saskatchewan Hist. [Canada] 1976 29(1): 14-25.* Describes contributions to the natural history of the Saskatchewan River during the past two centuries. The published observations of such men as Samuel Hearne, John Richardson, Robert Hood, and Thomas Drummond were profitably added to by the notes and specimens of Captain Thomas Wright Blakiston who was sent on a separate mission at the time of the Palliser expedition of 1857-59. Blakiston did notable ornithological work in many parts of the world. The bulk of this article is a transcript of a series of letters he wrote while on the Saskatchewan expedition. Map, 17 notes.
C. Held

861. Hussey, John A. FORT VANCOUVER: FUR TRADE CAPITAL OF THE PACIFIC NORTHWEST. *Am. West 1977 14(5): 12-19, 68-71.* Fort Vancouver was established in 1825 as headquarters of the Hudson's Bay Company in the Oregon country. Under Chief Factor John McLoughlin (1784-1857), it dominated the economic and political life of the area. The balance of power began to shift away from McLoughlin's jurisdiction in the 1840's with the coming of large-scale American immigration and merchants south of the Columbia River. After the Oregon Treaty of 1846, Fort Vancouver became a subsidiary depot and administrative center to Fort Victoria on Vancouver Island. The last HBC officials left in 1860. 8 illus., note, biblio.   D. L. Smith

862. Hussey, John A. "UNPRETENDING" BUT NOT "INDECENT": LIVING QUARTERS AT THE MID-19TH CENTURY HBC POSTS. *Beaver [Canada] 1975 305(4): 12-17.* Legend has replaced reality when historians discuss living conditions in most of the posts of the Hudson's Bay Company. Life at the posts was spartan, in many cases crude. A few posts did have decent furniture and other measures of the comfortable life, but in most cases the items of refinement were the personal possessions of the employees, not part of company policy. 7 illus.
D. Chaput

863. Huyda, R. EXPLORATION PHOTOGRAPHER: HUMPHREY LLOYD HIME AND THE ASSINIBOINE AND SASKATCHEWAN EXPLORING EXPEDITION OF 1858. *Tr. of the Hist. and Sci. Soc. of Manitoba [Canada] 1973-74 (30): 45-59.* Discusses Humphrey Lloyd Hime (1833-1903) and his pioneer work as a photographer, focusing on the 1858 Canadian expedition led by Henry Youle Hind to the region to the west of Lake Winnipeg and Red River, and between the Saskatchewan and Assiniboine rivers as far west as "South Branch House." Packed with collodion wet-plate process photographic apparatus, Hime joined the expedition to the Red River following the old Northwest Co. Pigeon River canoe route. The 50 remaining photographs, including scenes of Fort Frances, Iroquois voyageurs, Little Souris Valley, Fort Ellice, Fort Pelly, and the Red River Settlement, are an enduring monument to early photography in the Western Interior.
S. R. Quéripel

864. Kendall, John C. THE NEW YORK CITY PRESS AND ANTI-CANADIANISM: A NEW PERSPECTIVE ON THE CIVIL WAR YEARS. *Journalism Q. 1975 52(3): 522-530.* Canadian opinion during the US Civil War has been debated. The proposition that Canada was pro-Northern is partly based on studies of the Toronto *Globe*. The proposition that Canada was pro-Confederate is partly based on believed Canadian reaction to anti-Canadian editorials in the New York City press. However, except for the *Herald*, the New York press was annexationist, but not aggressive. This was surely not enough to turn Canada against the Union. Based on primary and secondary sources; 30 notes.
K. J. Puffer

865. Knight, David. 'BOOSTERISM' AND LOCATIONAL ANALYSIS: OR ONE MAN'S SWAN IS ANOTHER MAN'S GOOSE. *Urban Hist. Rev. [Canada] 1973 3: 10-16.* Discusses the role of boosterism, the exaggerated proclamation of one place over another, in the location of Ottawa as the national capital, 1857-59; offers a brief history of the development of Bytown (as Ottawa was previously known), 1822-59.

866. Langdon, Steven. THE EMERGENCE OF THE CANADIAN WORKING CLASS MOVEMENT, 1845-75. *J. of Can. Studies 1973 8(2): 3-13, (3): 8-26.*

867. Liebler, William F. JOHN BULL'S AMERICAN LEGION: BRITAIN'S ILL-STARRED RECRUITING ATTEMPT IN THE UNITED STATES DURING THE CRIMEAN WAR. *Pennsylvania Mag. of Hist. and Biog. 1975 99(3): 309-335.* Describes Great Britain's efforts to recruit American soldiers for military service in the Crimean War. A Nova Scotian, Joseph Howe, was put in charge of the enlistment in clear violation of the Neutrality Act (1818). James Buchanan, US minister in London, protested to the British government which decided that the American enlistment issue wasn't worth a quarrel with the United States. Palmerston's new government, however, kept diplomatic relations unsatisfactory by dismissing the British minister in Washington, John F. Crampton. Anglophobia was intensified in the press, and war might have taken place but for the fact that England's commercial and industrial interests were too closely linked with the United States. 82 notes.   C. W. Olson

868. Lindsey, David. "ST. ALBANS HAS BEEN SURPRISED." *Am. Hist. Illus. 1976 10(9): 14-22.* On 19 October 1864, Lt. Bennett H. Young and some 20 CSA cavalrymen raided St. Albans, Vermont, about

15 miles south of Philipsburg, Canada. The raiders took $170,000 from the town's three banks and killed one citizen who fired upon them. Young and seven subordinates were captured in Canada, but George N. Sanders, the CSA agent who planned the raid, employed an able Canadian attorney, J. G. K. Houghton, who convinced the judge the raid was an authorized CSA operation and not a felony which would permit extradition via the Webster-Ashburton Treaty. After the war Young was a lawyer, railroad president, and Confederate Veterans Association President. Primary and secondary sources; 9 illus., map.   D. B. Dodd

869. Lischke-McNab, Ute and McNab, David. PETITION FROM THE BACKWOODS. *Beaver [Canada] 1977 308(1): 52-57.* Katherine Parr Traill, an English settler who lived near Peterborough, wrote several popular emigrant guides, especially *The Backwoods of Canada* (1836). In 1854, she petitioned Queen Victoria for a "reward" for her literary services to the Empire. Various administrative and colonial officials considered the petition and even brought it to the Queen's attention. No land was granted Traill, however, mostly due to Colonial Office lethargy and a shifting colonial policy for Canada. In succeeding years, the author wrote other emigrant travel works. In the 1860's she received a small cash grant from British Prime Minister Lord Palmerston, but for her fern collecting and research, and not her literary efforts. 5 illus.
                                                                   D. Chaput

870. Maier, C. R., ed. A LETTER FROM NEW WESTMINSTER. *Beaver [Canada] 1976 307(2): 42-44.* Reprints an 1864 letter by Arthur N. Birch, colonial secretary in New Westminster, British Columbia, to his brother, John, in London. Comments on local government, sports, climate, population, and the local militia. Especially resents the numerous "decayed Gentlemen" that were flooding the colony. 3 illus.
                                                                   D. Chaput

871. McDonald, R. H. NOVA SCOTIA AND THE RECIPROCITY NEGOTIATIONS, 1846-1854: A RE-INTERPRETATION. *Nova Scotia Hist. Q. [Canada] 1977 7(3): 205-234.* Details Nova Scotian public opinion toward the reciprocity treaty with the United States by examining newspaper reports, legislative arguments, and economic conditions. Concludes that most inhabitants were aware of the advantages of free trade regulations but were unhappy when Great Britain reached an agreement with the United States without their consent or approval. Primary and secondary sources; 114 notes.   H. M. Evans

872. McDonald, R. H. SECOND CHESAPEAKE AFFAIR: 1863-1864. *Dalhousie R. [Canada] 1974/75 54(4): 674-684.* As the American Civil War began most Nova Scotians favored the North, but this later changed because of the Republican Party's reluctance to abolish slavery and the war's impact on the Nova Scotian economy. Two Confederates, John C. Braine and Vernon Locke, had obtained a letter of marque from the Confederate Secretary of State with the object of capturing the Union steamer *Chesapeake*, selling her cargo and converting her into a Confederate privateer. The capture took place on 7 December 1863, resulting in a series of exciting chases and narrow escapes across the Bay of Fundy, followed by union recapture at Sambro on the Atlantic coast. International complications followed when the ship was towed to Halifax by the three Northern warships. Following an exciting escape by John Wade, a Confederate privateer, international complications threatened British and Northern relations. A Canadian court, however, ruled in favor of returning the *Chesapeake* to her former owners and this eased the situation. 54 notes.   C. Held

873. Millman, T. R. DOCUMENTS OF THE CANADIAN CHURCH—7. *J. of the Can. Church Hist. Soc. 1973 15(3): 71.* Reprints excerpts from the Letters of Patent of 18 July 1850 which created the diocese of Montreal and appointed its first bishop; and from an act of the Parliament of United Canada, 9 June 1852. Sent in response to the June 1973 publication in the *Journal* of a special legal instrument granting the prelate of Quebec the title of lord bishop, these documents demonstrate that the title of lord bishop was given to the bishops of both Montreal and Quebec.   J. A. Kicklighter

874. Millman, Thomas R. A SKETCH OF THE LIFE OF FRANCIS FULFORD. *J. of the Can. Church Hist. Soc. 1975 17(4): 82-93.* Francis Fulford was bishop of Montreal, 1850-68. A native of England, Fulford was aristocratic, well-educated, and experienced as a minister at home.

As a bishop in Canada, Fulford made important contributions, especially in establishing diocesan synods, ecclesiastical provinces, and provincial synods in the Canadian Anglican Church. He was also responsible for ecclesiastical legislation which led to the self-governance of the church in Canada and for the construction of a new cathedral after the old one burned down. A man of great faith, Fulford strove for peace within the church and at all times acted in a spirit of moderation. Based on printed primary sources; 30 notes.   J. A. Kicklighter

875. Mitchell, Betty L. REALITIES NOT SHADOWS: FRANKLIN BENJAMIN SANBORN, THE EARLY YEARS. *Civil War Hist. 1974 20(2): 101-117.* An account of the involvement of Massachusetts abolitionist Franklin Benjamin Sanborn in John Brown's raid on Harpers Ferry. "More of a storybook revolutionary than a day-to-day political activist," Sanborn fled to Canada after the raid, returned, was seized by agents for a United States Senate investigating committee, but was liberated by friends. Like Brown, Sanborn thirsted for a war that would end slavery, but when war came, he "stepped back into the shadows, and did not serve." Based on the Sanborn Papers.   E. C. Murdock

876. Neidhardt, W. S. THE FENIAN TRIALS IN THE PROVINCE OF CANADA, 1866-7: A CASE STUDY OF LAW AND POLITICS IN ACTION. *Ontario Hist. [Canada] 1974 66(1): 23-.* Discusses the trial of prisoners taken during the Fenian raids in the 1860's. Also discusses American reaction to the trials and international ramifications. Proves that the eventual commutation of the sentences was highly unwelcome to Fenian leaders in the United States. Primary and secondary sources; 85 notes.   W. B. Whitham and S

877. Nicholls, Robert V. V. THE CONSTRUCTION OF AN OPERABLE REPLICA OF AN EARLY 19TH CENTURY STEAM LOCOMOTIVE: A CASE HISTORY OF CANADIAN-JAPANESE-SCOTTISH COOPERATION. *XIVth International Congress of the History of Science, Proceedings No. 3* (Tokyo and Kyoto: Science Council of Japan, 1975): 177-180. Discusses the replication of a Scottish-built 1849 steam locomotive, the *John Molson,* constructed in Japan and housed in the Canadian Railway Museum at Montreal, 1969.

878. Ostenstad, W. L. A LUCRATIVE CONTRACT: THE HBC AND THE PACIFIC ICE TRADE. *Beaver [Canada] 1977 308(3): 36-40.* The California Gold Rush led to a demand for northern ice. The Hudson's Bay Company, which had been leasing part of the coastal waters from the Russian-American Company, filled the ice needs at San Francisco for a few years. The profit was impressive: they received much more for the sale of the ice than it cost to lease the Russian lands. A new lease in 1859 ended the HBC's exclusive trade rights in the coastal waters. Based on Company archives; 5 illus.   D. Chaput

879. Portes, Jacques. LA REPRISE DES RELATIONS ENTRE LA FRANCE ET LE CANADA APRÈS 1850 [The revival of relations between France and Canada after 1850]. *Rev. Française d'Hist. d'Outre-Mer [France] 1975 62(3): 447-461.* Before 1850 France and Canada were linked only by a few private contacts. In 1855 a French warship, the *Capricieuse,* visited Quebec City. A French consulate was established there in 1858, and trade between the two countries started to grow. However, the French had no Canadian policy, and wished to avoid arousing British suspicions. Therefore the volume of trade was kept at a low level. Such ties as existed were mainly cultural and sentimental. Based on documents in the Archives nationales, the Archives du Ministère des Affaires étrangères, and secondary works; 40 notes.   L. B. Chan

880. Prentice, Alison. THE FEMINIZATION OF TEACHING IN BRITISH NORTH AMERICA AND CANADA 1845-1875. *Social Hist. [Canada] 1975 8(15): 5-20.* Entry of women into Canadian public school teaching was facilitated in the second half of the 19th century when school administrators wanted to divide schools into grade levels and promote the pay and status of the male teaching profession. Women were brought in at lower grade levels and at lower pay and status while the pay and status of men at higher levels was increased. Women were attracted to teaching because even low salaries provided an avenue for respectable independence not otherwise available. They may also have been attracted by the ideology that women were especially suited to early childhood education. Based on documents in the Public Archives of Nova Scotia and

Ontario, published school reports, and secondary sources; 4 tables, 40 notes.   W. K. Hobson

881. Preston, Adrian. GENERAL SIR WILLIAM FENWICK WILLIAMS, THE AMERICAN CIVIL WAR AND THE DEFENSE OF CANADA, 1859-65: OBSERVATIONS OF HIS MILITARY CORRESPONDENCE TO THE DUKE OF CAMBRIDGE, COMMANDER-IN-CHIEF AT THE HORSE GUARDS. *Dalhousie Rev. [Canada] 1976-77 56(4): 605-629.* Narrates the activities of William Fenwick Williams, the senior British officer in North America, from his posting there in 1859 to his appointment as Lieutenant Governor of Nova Scotia in 1865 and his eventual reassignment out of Canada in late 1867. The bulk of the material concerns military matters and contemporary military figures such as Henry Ponsonby and Sir John Michel. Based on William's correspondence of about 300 letters with the Duke of Cambridge; 52 notes.   C. Held

882. Rankin, Ernest H., Sr. THE 'INLAND SEAS' OF 1862. *Inland Seas 1978 34(1): 26-31, 43.* Describes *The Great Lakes, or 'Inland Seas' of America* compiled by John Disturnell and published by Charles Scribner in 1862. A traveler's handbook, it describes the Great Lakes and their ports, resorts, and steamer services. Illus.   K. J. Bauer

883. Reinders, Robert C. THE JOHN ANDERSON CASE, 1860-1: A STUDY IN ANGLO-CANADIAN IMPERIAL RELATIONS. *Can. Hist. Rev. [Canada] 1975 56(4): 393-415.* Reexamines the John Anderson case. Reveals the close connections between British and Canadian anti-slavery societies, relations among the United States, Canada, and Great Britain, and the contentious character of Canadian politics in the early 1860's. Particularly important were the case's legal aspects and the implications of the various court decisions for Anglo-Canadian relations. 76 notes.   R. V. Ritter

884. Robb, Andrew. EDWARD WATKIN AND THE PACIFIC TELEGRAPH: 1861-1865. *Ontario History [Canada] 1973 65(4): 189-209.* Summarizes Edward Watkin's background and outlook, discussing the immediate cause of his arrival in Canada in 1861. Analyzes the political and diplomatic maneuverings involved in the proposed development of a Pacific railroad and the problems of existing railroads in Canada. When the Pacific railroad plan proved to be impossible, Watkin's emphasis shifted to the telegraph, and his subsequent efforts to attain this, especially in the face of political opposition, are discussed in detail. The ultimate failure of his schemes is explained. 119 notes.
                                                          W. B. Whitham

885. Schweninger, Loren. A FUGITIVE NEGRO IN THE PROMISED LAND: JAMES RAPIER IN CANADA, 1856-1864. *Ontario Hist. [Canada] 1975 67(2): 91-104.* Examines the life of James Thomas Rapier while he was a refugee in Canada and finds it representative of the experience of many Negroes who, seeking freedom in a foreign land, found their lives profoundly changed.

886. Schweninger, Loren. JOHN H. RAPIER, SR.: A SLAVE AND FREEDMAN IN THE ANTE-BELLUM SOUTH. *Civil War Hist. 1974 20(1): 23-34.* As a free Negro and relatively prosperous barber in Florence, Alabama, before the Civil War, Rapier raised two families, educated his numerous children, acquired extensive real estate holdings in Alabama, Minnesota, and Canada West, and was respected by both white and black communities. Based largely on the Rapier Papers at Howard University.   E. C. Murdock

887. Stouffer, Allen P. CANADIAN-AMERICAN RELATIONS IN THE SHADOW OF THE CIVIL WAR. *Dalhousie Rev. [Canada] 1977 57(2): 332-346.* That Canadian-American affairs spiralled downward during the Civil War is clear, but that this downward spiral lasted after 1866 is disputed. Presents evidence that the St. Albans Raid was the nadir and that marked improvement was made until the unfortunate Fenian raid of 1866. Considerable evidence from American, British, and Canadian sources is marshalled to support this thesis. 31 notes.
                                                          C. H. Held

888. Turner, Wesley. "80 STOUT AND HEALTHY LOOKING GIRLS." *Canada 1975 3(2): 36-49.* Discusses the immigration of approximately 80 penniless Irish girls and women sent to Canada from Irish workhouses by British Poor Law Commissioners in 1865, the demoralization and victimization of some of them, their eventual employment as domestic servants, and official investigation in Ireland and Canada.
                                                          S

889. Wade, Norman. "WE ARE ON THE BLOCKADING AGAIN." *Civil War Times Illus. 1977 15(10): 28-36.* Norman Wade left his home in 1859 for a seafaring career. He was a native of Nova Scotia. Five months after the Civil War broke out he was in Boston and joined the Union Navy. Wade was on blockade duty near Hampton Roads from the time of his enlistment until his death a year later. Reproduces six of his letters to his family and a letter to his sister from his best friend telling of his death.   R. Alvis

Confederation

890. Baker, William M. SQUELCHING THE DISLOYAL, FENIAN-SYMPATHIZING BROOD: T. W. ANGLIN AND CONFEDERATION IN NEW BRUNSWICK, 1865-6. *Can. Hist. R. 1974 55(2): 141-158.* Examines the nature of the "loyalty" issue which was a major contributor to the victory of the pro-Confederation forces in New Brunswick in 1866. Concludes that the loyalty issue involved an anti-Catholic campaign which utilized the Fenian scare and directed itself against the prominent anti-Confederate and lay leader of New Brunswick Catholics, Timothy W. Anglin.   S

891. Baker, W. M. TURNING THE SPIT: TIMOTHY ANGLIN AND THE ROASTING OF D'ARCY MCGEE. *Can. Hist. Assoc. Hist. Papers 1974: 135-155.* Discusses debates between Irish Catholic leaders Timothy Warren Anglin and Thomas D'Arcy McGee in Canada, 1863-68, on the character of Irish Canadians, and on McGee's proposed British North American Union, support for Confederation, and attacks on the Fenians.

892. Fergusson, C. B. HOWE AND CONFEDERATION. *Nova Scotia Hist. Q. [Canada] 1974 4(3): 223-244.* Joseph Howe, editor, writer, and Lieutenant Governor of Nova Scotia, was outspoken concerning confederation of the Canadian Colonies. Examines the opinions expressed by Howe during 1832-69.   H. M. Evans

893. Forsey, Eugene. IN DEFENCE OF MACDONALD'S CONSTITUTION. *Tr. of the Hist. and Sci. Soc. of Manitoba [Canada] 1972/73 Series 3(29): 41-47.* Examines the Constitution of 1867 from the standpoint of John A. Macdonald's contribution to the document. The Constitution was essentially "Macdonald's Constitution," and "one of the most successful" in the world. Based on printed sources; 28 notes.
                                                          J. A. Casada

894. Knox, Bruce A. THE BRITISH GOVERNMENT, SIR EDMUND HEAD, AND BRITISH NORTH AMERICAN CONFEDERATION, 1858. *J. of Imperial and Commonwealth Hist. [Great Britain] 1976 4(2): 206-217.* Reprints letters written in 1858 between Sir Edmund Walker Head, an advocate of confederation of Great Britain's North American colonies, and Lord Stanley of Preston (later 15th Earl of Derby) which reveal their attitudes toward the British Empire and the possibility of Canadian confederation.

895. McDonald, R. H. HASTINGS DOYLE AND THE ANTI-CONFEDERATES. *Nova Scotia Hist. Q. [Canada] 1976 6(4): 413-430.* Hastings Doyle, Lieutenant-Governor of Nova Scotia at the time of Confederation, found himself between two hostile camps—his confederationist superiors in the federal government, and anticonfederationist local government—yet he successfully fought a repeal movement within the province setting the government on a course of confederation, 1867-68.

896. Papineau, Louis-Joseph. UN TESTAMENT POLITIQUE [A political testament]. *Études Françaises [Canada] 1973 9(3): 237-255.* Praises Aristotle's political thought as the best explication of the science of government. Unlike Montesquieu, who allowed his social position to affect his writings, Aristotle searched for the truth. Describes the outrages of the English victory in the battle of Quebec and rejects the justice of the 1867 Act of Confederation. Calls for liberty of political, religious, and

scientific thought. Text of *Discours de l'Honorable Louis-Joseph Papineau devant l'Institut canadien, à l'occasion du 23 anniversaire de la fondation de l'Institut canadien, le 17 décembre 1867*, Montréal, Imprimerie du journal *Le Pays*, 1868, 20p.   G. J. Rossi

897. Swaison, Donald. SIR HENRY SMITH AND THE POLITICS OF UNION. *Ontario Hist. [Canada] 1974 66(3): 161-179.* Notes that in pre-Confederation politics local interests and individual men were sometimes of importance on the national level. Discusses Henry Smith, who had his power base in Kingston. Outlines Smith's life and career, and analyzes the main stages. Details some of the changing political alliances associated with the immediate pre-Confederation years. Makes an effort to show Smith's significance as a representative MPP. 117 notes.
                                                    W. B. Whitham

898. Trépanier, Lise and Trépanier, Pierre. NATIONALISME ET PARTISANERIE: LOUIS ARCHAMBEAULT (1815-1890) [Nationalism and partisanism: Louis Archambeault (1815-1890)]. *Action Natl. [Canada] 1975 64(8): 649-655.* Studies the views of Louis Archambeault on the Confederation and Canadian unity, as seen during his long career of public official and spokesman for Canadian politics, stressing his evolution from the Conservative to the Liberal Party.

7. EMERGENT NATIONALISM, 1867-1914

General

899. Acheson, T. W. CHANGING SOCIAL ORIGINS OF THE CANADIAN INDUSTRIAL ELITE, 1880-1910. *Business Hist. R. 1973 47(2): 189-216.* Two groups of Canada's manufacturing elites are compared and contrasted, 1880-85 and 1905-10. The latter group tended to be organization men rather than owner-entrepreneurs, and social mobility seems to have decreased for them. Overall, differences between the two groups outweighed any continuity. Based primarily on standard biographical sources; 18 tables, 50 notes. C. J. Pusateri

900. Avery, Donald and Neary, Peter. LAURIER, BORDEN AND A WHITE BRITISH COLUMBIA. *J. of Can. Studies [Canada] 1977 12(4): 24-34.* Studies Oriental immigration to British Columbia from its beginnings in the 1850's until 1914, and Dominion policy toward it under the Laurier (1896-1911; Liberal) and Borden (1911-20; Conservative) governments. The Canadian Pacific Railroad was active in recruiting, transporting, and employing unskilled Asian workers. Chinese immigration virtually ended in 1903 with the imposition of a prohibitively high entry tax, whereupon Japanese and East Indian immigration increased. Japanese immigrants were granted freedom from interference by the 1894 Anglo-Japanese treaty, but the Japanese government agreed to restrict emigration. Still, a riot in Vancouver (1907) underlined continuing hostility (based largely but not solely on economics) to *all* Asian immigration. Mentions the intervention of Theodore Roosevelt in this matter (1908). 66 notes. L. W. Van Wyk

901. Bacchi, Carol. LIBERATION DEFERRED: THE IDEAS OF THE ENGLISH-CANADIAN SUFFRAGISTS, 1877-1918. *Social Hist. [Canada] 1977 10(20): 433-434.* The Canadian suffrage movement, initially committed to sexual equality, was infiltrated by social reformers in the 1880's. Mainly middle class traditionalists, the reformers wanted to preserve and strengthen the old order and their own positions. They regarded the family as the fundamental social unit and believed woman suffrage would give mothers a political voice and strengthen the family by doubling its representation. Feminists reactivated the movement in 1906 after an 11-year lull, but feminist concerns declined. D. F. Chard

902. Bacchi, Carol. RACE REGENERATION AND SOCIAL PURITY: A STUDY OF THE SOCIAL ATTITUDES OF CANADA'S ENGLISH-SPEAKING SUFFRAGISTS. *Social Hist. [Canada] 1978 11(22): 460-474.* Most suffragists believed that woman's most valuable roles were as wife and mother. Rather than demand sexual freedom, they "upheld the Victorian idea that women stood above sex." These attitudes derived from the suffragists' origins in the Anglo-Saxon, Protestant middle class. Suffragists subscribed to the goal of a strong healthy race, but through environmental improvements rather than eugenics. Opposition to drinking and prostitution stemmed from the threat they represented to Protestant middle-class values. Primary and secondary sources; 76 notes. D. F. Chard

903. Barrea, Jean. THE COUNTER-CORE ROLE OF MIDDLE POWERS IN PROCESSES OF EXTERNAL POLITICAL INTEGRATION. *World Politics 1973 25(2): 274-287.* In political integration, the middle power is the natural rival of the leading state of its region. Tests the counter-core area hypothesis by examining the political integration of the Canadian, Australian, and South African superstates, and adds the German political integration movement as a non-English-speaking example. In the Canadian situation, Nova Scotia resisted the process of federation and provided the first prime ministers of the Dominion. In Australia, New South Wales and Queensland were the countercore areas which repeatedly adopted a hostile attitude toward the movement for political integration. Among the South African colonies, Cape Colony was the region's middle power, far less dynamic economically than the Transvaal, but it did not display any lasting hostility to the unification movement. The Prussian-directed movement for integration was persistently resisted by Bavaria, the intermediate power. 18 notes. E. P. Stickney

904. Beckow, S. M. FROM THE WATCH-TOWERS OF PATRIOTISM: THEORIES OF LITERARY GROWTH IN ENGLISH CANADA 1864-1914. *J. of Can. Studies 1974 9(3): 3-15.* Literary philosophers concluded that Canada enjoyed the conditions prerequisite to the development of a distinctive national literature. They were convinced that they lived in both the best period of world history and the best country. Their theories must have elicited a patriotic response from English Canadian readers. Based on periodicals and secondary works; 122 notes. G. E. Panting

905. Best, Gary Dean. JACOB H. SCHIFF'S GALVESTON MOVEMENT: AN EXPERIMENT IN IMMIGRANT DEFLECTION, 1907-1914. *Am. Jewish Arch. 1978 30(1): 43-79.* Although the career of Jacob H. Schiff is usually associated with the world of high finance, Professor Best has carefully documented Schiff's involvement with a plan to send hundreds of thousands of immigrant Jews into the interior regions of the United States and Canada and away from the congested cities of America's east coast. The city of Galveston, Texas, would serve as the departure point for many of these Jews. The Galveston Plan, as it came to be known, necessitated complex political and financial maneuverings on the parts of Schiff, the American immigration authorities, and the English Territorialist, Israel Zangwill. J

906. Bicha, Karel D. SPRING SHOOTING: AN ISSUE IN THE MISSISSIPPI FLYWAY, 1887-1913. *J. of Sport Hist. 1978 5(2): 65-74.* During the late 19th century, there was a major controversy over the "spring shooting" of game animals, resident species, and migratory wildfowl, and especially the latter. During the 1880's, game populations in the upper midwest rapidly declined, while game harvests increased considerably. The most common explanation was the prevalence of shooting waterfowl during the spring migration to nesting grounds in the northern Great Plains and Canada. States in the Mississippi Flyway, the leading migratory route, permitted hunting of waterfowl in seasons extending into April or May. Naturalists like "Frank Forester" (William Henry Herbert) and George Bird Grinnell criticized the "spring shooting," but legislatures were not receptive to demands for hunting reforms. Before 1915, the states paid little attention to the demand for reform, but they often passed laws that were not enforced. Wisconsin, Michigan, and Minnesota, however, established game warden systems, as early as 1887. Spring shooting finally disappeared due to the intrusion of the federal government, and declining game populations. 39 notes. M. Kaufman

907. Boissonnault, Charles-Marie. GOUVERNEMENTS SANS MAJORITÉ ABSOLUE [Governments without absolute majority]. *Tr. of the Royal Soc. of Can. 1973 11: 147-157.* Describes internal battles for power in the Canadian Assembly and the Chamber of Deputies, involving constitutional conflict stemming from abuse of power by elected representatives, which retarded the creation of a real parliamentary regime, 1858-1900.

908. Burchell, Howard B. OSLER: IN QUEST OF THE GNOSTIC GRAIL IN MORBID ANATOMY. *J. of the Hist. of Medicine & Allied Sci. 1975 30(3): 235-249.* Sir William Osler (1849-1919) "had early been imbued with a spiritual quest for medical insights through morbid anatomy, and had clearly dedicated himself to this role at the time of his graduation." Osler's preoccupation with pathology is shown from his own medical problems, and from his dreams. 72 notes. M. Kaufman

909. Bush, Edward F. THOMAS COLTRIN KEEFER. *Ontario Hist. [Canada] 1974 66(4): 211-222.* Recounts the life of the Canadian railroad promoter Thomas Coltrin Keefer (b. 1821), emphasizing his accomplishments as a professional engineer.

910. Consentino, Frank. A HISTORY OF THE CONCEPT OF PROFESSIONALISM IN CANADIAN SPORT. *Can. J. of Hist. of Sport and Physical Educ. 1975 6(2): 75-81.* Discusses social factors in the development of professional sports in Canada during 1835-1909.

911. Cook, Ramsay. THE PROFESSOR AND THE PROPHET OF UNREST. *Tr. of the Royal Soc. of Can. 1975 13: 227-250.* In the 19th century, when Canada was considered an intellectual wasteland, Canadian writers were concerned with religious and philosophical duties. Goldwin Smith "never lost sight of the relationship between religious uncertainty and social unrest." Smith supported the ideas of liberal capitalists, much the same as Adam Smith's ideas. Among his critics were W. D. LeSueur and T. Phillips Thompson. Henry George had some influence on the latter. 101 notes.   J. D. Neville

912. Cook, Terry. GEORGE R. PARKIN AND THE CONCEPT OF BRITANNIC IDEALISM. *J. of Can. Studies 1975 10(3): 15-31.* Discusses the role of Sir George R. Parkin's concept of Britannic idealism in the development of Canadian imperialism and nationalism from 1871 to 1922.

913. De Villiers-Westfall, William E. THE DOMINION OF THE LORD: AN INTRODUCTION TO THE CULTURAL HISTORY OF PROTESTANT ONTARIO IN THE VICTORIAN PERIOD. *Queen's Q. [Canada] 1976 83(1): 47-70.* Attempts to delineate the interacting forces of religion and culture in Ontario during the Victorian era. Particular emphasis is placed on the Gothic revival and its relationship "to the general structure of social forces that defined the character of Victorian Canada." Suggests that the leading secular themes of the period's social history were articulated by Lord Durham in his *Report.* Through their religious convictions, Protestants in Ontario (and elsewhere in Canada) became convinced that theirs was a land of boundless possibilities. Based on printed sources; 49 notes.   J. A. Casada

914. Eadie, James A. THE NAPANEE MECHANICS' INSTITUTES. *Ontario Hist. [Canada] 1976 68(4): 209-221.* Discusses the origins of the Mechanics' Institute movement and comments on its expansion to Canada, concentrating on the Napanee Mechanics' Institute. Ironically, it began as a private subscription library, and was transformed into a public library. The main reason for the failure of the Institute movement, and, thus, of the Napanee one, is that the movement was primarily seen as a middle-class movement intended to "improve the morals of the lower classes." Covers the period 1850-1900. 61 notes.
                                                           W. B. Whitham

915. Eagle, John A. RAILWAYS AND CANADIAN DEVELOPMENT. *Acadiensis [Canada] 1978 7(2): 159-164.* Studies on Canadian railways, such as P. Berton's works (1970 and 1971), and J. L. McDougall's *Canadian Pacific* (1968), have praised the Canadian Pacific unabashedly. Robert Chodos' *The CPR: A Century of Corporate Welfare* (1977) rebuts Berton, but is less objective and balanced than Kaye Lamb's *History of the Canadian Pacific Railway* (1977). In part, Lamb analyses the railway's impact on British Columbia generally, and on Vancouver's rise to metropolitan status particularly. T. D. Regehr's *The Canadian Northern Railway: Pioneer Road of the Northern Prairies 1895-1918* rejects the metropolitan approach, but admits that the railway was identified with Toronto interests. 3 notes.   D. F. Chard

916. Fingard, Judith. MASTERS AND FRIENDS, CRIMPS AND ABSTAINERS: AGENTS OF CONTROL IN 19TH CENTURY SAILORTOWN. *Acadiensis [Canada] 1978 8(1): 22-46.* During 1850's-90's three agencies competed for control of sailors in eastern Canadian ports. Boardinghouse keepers exploited them, but enhanced their wage rates. Despised by civic elites, the keepers were tolerated as agents of control. The government shipping office, intending to reduce desertion and control wage rates, lacked the means to do either. Social reformers promoted temperance and sailors' homes, but failed because of their paternalism. By the 1880's the need for control declined as working conditions improved. 87 notes.   D. F. Chard

917. Fox, M. F. BIRD'S-EYE VIEWS OF CANADIAN CITIES: A REVIEW. *Urban Hist. Rev. [Canada] 1977 (1): 38-45.* Reviews the exhibition of bird's-eye maps of Canadian cities (ca. 1865-1905) at the Public Archives of Canada from July to November 1976, and discusses their potential and limitations for the historical researcher. The detail and design of the maps suggest some uses that could be made of them by the researcher. 3 illus.   C. A. Watson

918. Gerson, Carole. CANADA'S RESPONSE TO THOMAS HARDY: A LOOK AT NINETEENTH-CENTURY LITERARY ATTITUDES. *Dalhousie R. [Canada] 1975 55(2): 252-262.* Explores the conservatism of the late 19th-century Canadian literary scene through the reaction of authors and literary critics to the works of Thomas Hardy. Cites the following Canadian journals: *Canadian Magazine, Rose-Belford's, Week, Monthly Review,* and the *Dominion Illustrated Monthly.* While Hardy was not unknown in Canada, his impact was not great. 41 notes.   C. Held

919. Gough, Barry M. CANADA AND THE NORTH PACIFIC, 1871-1914: PROBLEMS OF A LION'S CUB IN AN OPEN DEN. *South Atlantic Q. 1977 76(3): 348-365.* Although the North Pacific had provided commercial and strategic opportunity for Canada during 1871-1914, the Canadians failed to establish a national presence in the area. Great Britain also neglected the strategic value despite the first-rate port of Vancouver, the naval drydocks at Esquimalt, the trans-Pacific cable station, and the Canadian Pacific Railroad terminus. As the *Pax Britannica* withdrew from the North Pacific in the late 19th century, the rise of foreign naval powers and influence grew beyond Canada's control. Neither Britain nor Canada could prevent American advances in Hawaii, the Yukon, Alaska, and the Bering Sea. Ultimately, Canada's interest remained in the east coast and Canadian leaders allowed American and Japanese protection of British Columbia by World War I. Based on primary and secondary sources; 32 notes.
                                                    W. L. Olbrich/G. Fox

920. Green, Janet. THE FEDERAL GOVERNMENT AND MIGRATORY BIRDS: THE BEGINNING OF A PROTECTIVE POLICY. *Can. Hist. Assoc. Hist. Papers [Canada] 1976: 207-227.* The International Migratory Bird Treaty (1916) resulted from the dedication of civil servants. It was a landmark in Canadian wildlife conservation because the federal government assumed responsibility for a presumptively provincial resource. The Canadian movement ran parallel to one in the United States and the authority of the central government was upheld by the courts in both countries. Based on the records of American and Canadian Department, conservation organization, and secondary sources; 62 notes.   G. E. Panting

921. Guest, Henry James. THE OLD MAN'S SON: SIR HUGH JOHN MACDONALD. *Tr. of the Hist. and Sci. Soc. of Manitoba [Canada] 1972/73 Series 3(29): 49-67.* As the son of one of Canada's most famous political figures, Sir Hugh John Macdonald always labored in his father's shadow, but he nonetheless carved for himself a successful career in law and politics. A true gentleman in an era marked by its lack of politeness and cordiality in politics, the younger Macdonald (1850-1929) was in some ways "almost a puppet in the hands of the Conservative party leaders." However, he had distinctly expressed views on Anglo-Saxon superiority and in regard to his belief that Canada's future lay in close imperial ties with Britain. Based on manuscript sources (notably the Macdonald Papers), and printed materials; 102 notes.
                                                           J. A. Casada

922. Hall, D. J. "THE SPIRIT OF CONFEDERATION": RALPH HEINTZMAN, PROFESSOR CREIGHTON, AND THE BICULTURAL COMPACT THEORY. *J. of Canadian Studies 1974 9(4): 24-42.* Discusses the government of Canada from the 1850's to the 1890's, political problems between the French Canadian minority and English Canadians, and the work of Ralph Heintzman and D. G. Creighton on this subject.   S

923. Headon, Christopher. WOMEN AND ORGANIZED RELIGION IN MID AND LATE NINETEENTH CENTURY CANADA. *J. of the Can. Church Hist. Soc. [Canada] 1978 20(1-2): 3-18.* Within the Christian denominations of Canada, women in the mid- and late-19th century had an alternative to their traditional role. Some served as preaching evangelists, while others joined religious orders to help the poor. The most important of all activities in which Canadian churchwomen were involved was missionary work, both foreign and domestic, in which they acted to alleviate poverty, teach the young, and eliminate as much as possible the most crude and overt forms of female subordination. Yet, there were many limitations in this advance. Women's organizations in the church were usually considered subordinate and dependent on those dominated by men; and most churchwomen con-

ducted themselves and their activities in accordance with traditional notions of female subservience. Primary and secondary sources; 51 notes.
J. A. Kicklighter

924.　Hughes, Ken.　POET LAUREATE OF LABOUR.　*Can. Dimension [Canada] 1976 11(4): 33-40.* Describes the life of the radical Alexander McLachlan, who was born in Scotland in 1818 and died in Ontario, Canada, in 1896; discusses his poetry on the working class and social reform.

925.　Jarvis, Eric.　THE GEORGIAN BAY SHIP CANAL: A STUDY OF THE SECOND CANADIAN CANAL AGE: 1850-1915. *Ontario Hist. [Canada] 1977 69(2): 125-147.* Remarks that the railroad did not terminate interest in canals. Comments on several projects designed to connect Georgian Bay with the St. Lawrence system, and discusses the origins and vicissitudes of some of these projects. One of the more ambitious projects was to link Goergian Bay with Montreal. Others were more practicable, although equally ambitious. Causes of the failures of the schemes are suggested: one common one being lack of government financial backing, or substantial landgrants although the railroads got both. 89 notes.　　W. B. Whitham

926.　Livermore, John Daniel.　THE PERSONAL AGONIES OF EDWARD BLAKE.　*Can. Hist. R. 1975 56(1): 45-58.* Analyzes Edward Blake's (1833-1912) psychological problems and the implications of his nervous ailments on his political career in Canada. Emphasizes the close link, hitherto largely ignored, between Blake's seemingly erratic career and his emotional problems. Based on contemporary memoirs and personal papers, some currently in private hands.　　A

927.　MacLeod, David.　A LIVE VACCINE: THE YMCA AND MALE ADOLESCENCE IN THE UNITED STATES AND CANADA 1870-1920.　*Social Hist. [Canada] 1978 11(21): 5-25.* In the 1850's and 1860's the Young Men's Christian Association (YMCA) engaged in evangelism for all ages, but as job opportunities for teenagers shrank and formal schooling increased, officials devoted more attention to middle-class adolescent boys, who needed protection from corruption, could pay fees, and would be receptive to Christianity. Around 1900, G. Stanley Hall's studies of adolescent psychology further stimulated boy's work. Workers emphasized objective, masculine religious expression, and dealt with sexuality through distraction and sublimation. During 1910-20 Taylor Statten instigated standardized programs. 87 notes.
D. F. Chard

928.　McCalla, Douglas.　TOM NAYLOR'S *A HISTORY OF CANADIAN BUSINESS, 1867-1914:* A COMMENT.　*Can. Hist. Assoc. Hist. Papers [Canada] 1976: 249-253.* Maintains that the banks would not provide the capital necessary to create a class of national industrial entrepreneurs during 1867-1914. Some industry did develop in Canada and the banks did provide commercial capital that was needed for equipment. 22 notes.　　G. E. Panting

929.　McLaren, Angus.　BIRTH CONTROL AND ABORTION IN CANADA, 1870-1920.　*Can. Hist. Rev. [Canada] 1978 59(3): 319-340.* Based on religious, medical, legal and journalistic reports of the birth control debate. Shows why and how traditional contraceptive methods were employed by Canadian couples and, if these failed, how abortion was employed as a second line of defense against unwanted pregnancies. Reveals the importance of women's desires to control their physical functions, the view taken of women's health by the medical profession, and the differences in male and female attitudes toward sexuality.　　A

930.　Metcalfe, Alan.　SOME BACKGROUND INFLUENCES ON NINETEENTH CENTURY CANADIAN SPORT AND PHYSICAL EDUCATION.　*Can. J. of Hist. of Sport and Physical Educ. 1974 5(1): 62-73.* Focuses on ideas that influenced middle class attitudes toward sports and recreation.　　S

931.　Miller, J. R.　D'ALTON MCCARTHY, EQUAL RIGHTS, AND THE ORIGINS OF THE MANITOBA SCHOOL QUESTION. *Can. Hist. R. 1973 54(4): 369-392.* Examines the historiography of the origins of provincial legislation in Manitoba to eliminate Catholic denominational education in 1890. Offers a revised view of the role of Conservative Member of Parliament D'Alton McCarthy and the Equal Rights

Association in this process. There was little connection between McCarthy and the schools legislation. The 1890 Acts were the result of the social transformation of Manitoba, 1870-90. Based on newspaper, pamphlet, and manuscript sources in the Public Archives of Canada, the Public Archives of Manitoba, and the Archiepiscopal Archives of St. Boniface.　　A

932.　Millman, T. R.　THE DOMESTIC AND FOREIGN MISSIONARY SOCIETY OF THE CHURCH OF ENGLAND IN CANADA, 1883-1902.　*J. of the Can. Church Hist. Soc. [Canada] 1977 19(3-4): 166-176.* Describes the major events in the history of the short-lived Domestic and Foreign Missionary Society of the Canadian Anglican Church. First established in 1883, the Society was replaced in 1902 by the Missionary Society of the Church of England in Canada. During its existence it assisted both domestic and foreign missionary efforts. In Canada itself it supported the missionary diocese of Algoma as well as the diocese of the West and Northwest, thus continuing the efforts of earlier groups. The Society was also responsible for the initiation of the Canadian Church's first foreign mission. Although there had been Canadian Anglican missionaries in Japan in earlier years, it was only with the support of the Society that the Church undertook its first major mission there. Based on secondary, printed and unprinted primary sources; 19 notes.
J. A. Kicklighter

933.　Naylor, R. T.　TRENDS IN THE BUSINESS HISTORY OF CANADA, 1867-1914.　*Can. Hist. Assoc. Hist. Papers [Canada] 1976: 255-267.* Historians have tended to divorce the politics and the business interests of Canadian leaders. *A History of Canadian Business, 1867-1914,* 2 vols. (Toronto, 1975), was written to reverse this trend. Its methodology is deliberately antiquantitative. There are two interrelated themes in Canadian business history which date back to 1663. A close relationship with big business led the federal government to foster economic concentration while foreign capital was used to finance infrastructure and heavy industry.　　G. E. Panting

934.　Parker, George.　THE CANADIAN COPYRIGHT QUESTION IN THE 1890'S.　*J. of Can. Studies [Canada] 1976 11(2): 43-55.* The Canadian book trade was not primarily concerned with producing and distributing books of Canadian authorship. Its objective was to sell illegal editions of foreign works. The Copyright Act (Canada, 1900) provided for the existing agency system and subsidiary companies with which Canadian authors could identify. Copyright was accepted by the Canadian government as a protection for the creator. Based on statutes, Copyright Commission (Great Britain) Report, Laurier Papers, MacDonald Papers, and secondary sources; table, 61 notes.
G. E. Panting

935.　Parker, W. J. Lewis.　TO 'THE RIVER,' AN OFFSHORE SCHOONER TRADE.　*Am. Neptune 1975 35(1): 5-19.* From the 1860's until World War I a tremendous number of offshore voyages were successfully accomplished by schooners of 300 tons or more. Describes the long-range voyages taken by schooners from North American Atlantic ports to the River Plate and its tributaries. Based on manuscripts and secondary sources; 8 photos, 59 notes.　　G. H. Curtis

936.　Paterson, D. G.　THE NORTH PACIFIC SEAL HUNT, 1886-1910: RIGHTS AND REGULATIONS.　*Explorations in Econ. Hist. 1977 14(2): 97-119.* Using mathematical modelling techniques, shows that Canadian offshore and US onshore hunting combined to threaten the seals with extinction. Based on manuscripts in the Public Archives of Victoria, British Columbia, published documents, and secondary accounts; 7 tables, 16 notes, 2 appendixes, 32 ref.　　P. J. Coleman

937.　Rapprich, William F.　THE *NORTH WEST* AND *NORTH LAND.*　*Inland Seas 1973 29(1): 3-15, 29-30.* The *North West* (1894-1921) and *North Land* (1895-1941) were the two most famous and luxurious 19th-century Great Lakes passenger steamers. Built by the Globe Iron Works in Cleveland, they sailed in the Buffalo-Duluth service of the Northern Steamship Company. The *North West* burned in 1911 but its hulk was not scrapped for 10 years. The *North Land* was converted to a Canadian freighter *(Maplecourt)* in 1919-20. In 1940 it sailed for England as part of a convoy but was sunk by German aircraft off the Hebrides on 6 February 1941. Illus.　　K. J. Bauer

938. Redmond, Gerald.   APART FROM THE TRUST FUND: SOME OTHER CONTRIBUTIONS OF LORD STRATHCONA TO CANADIAN RECREATION AND SPORT.   *Can. J. of Hist. of Sport and Physical Educ. 1973 4(2): 59-69.* A wealthy philanthropist, Lord Strathcona (1820-1914) made large contributions to Canadian sport. He set up the oft-noted $500,000 trust fund for national physical and military training. Strathcona contributed an approximately equal amount to numerous sports, athletic clubs, and particularly Young Men's Christian Associations. Greater research into Strathcona's philanthropy is needed. Based on primary sources, including the Strathcona papers; 39 notes.
R. A. Smith

939. Russell, Loris S.   "CARBIDE" WILLSON.   *Canada 1975 3(1): 20-33.* Discusses the life and career of inventor Thomas Leopold "Carbide" Willson in Canada, 1860-1915, emphasizing his work in electrochemistry and the manufacture of calcium carbide.

940. Rutherford, Paul F. W.   THE PEOPLE'S PRESS: THE EMERGENCE OF THE NEW JOURNALISM.   *Can. Hist. R. 1975 56(2): 169-191.* Analyzes a group of cheap daily newspapers, founded in the late 19th century and designed to appeal to the whole of the urban public. Examines their particular style of journalism and their opportunistic radicalism. Suggests they were the pioneers of the mass circulation dailies in Canada, comparable to Pulitzer's *World* and Harmsworth's *Mail*. Suggests also they were a vehicle for the democratization of Victorian Canada. Concludes that, although their impact on journalism was significant, they were unable to survive as an independent force and soon were absorbed into the existing network of party newspapers.
A

941. Schlabach, Theron F.   THE HUMBLE BECOME "AGGRESSIVE WORKERS": MENNONITES ORGANIZE FOR MISSION, 1880-1910.   *Mennonite Q. Rev. 1978 52(2): 113-126.* For a time the traditionally humble Mennonites became much more aggressive in the United States and Canada, having missions, Sunday Schools, revivalism, etc. Conflicts arose at once; it was not easy to reconcile the old doctrine of defenselessness with the new aggressiveness. The extent of aggressiveness may be questioned: perhaps it was more apparent than real. Many of the institutional changes seem to have been intended to support the much older and traditional Mennonite value system. 47 notes.
V. L. Human

942. Smith, Allan.   THE MYTH OF THE SELF-MADE MAN IN ENGLISH CANADA, 1850-1914.   *Can. Hist. Rev. [Canada] 1978 59(2): 189-219.* Examines how the myth of the self-made man influenced Canadian social thought, in spite of Canada's strong attachment to the values of the rights of the community over those of the individual.

943. Wolff, Julius F., Jr.   CANADIAN SHIPWRECKS ON LAKE SUPERIOR.   *Inland Seas 1978 34(1): 32-42, (2): 113-120, (3): 200-206, 208.* Part I. Very little Canadian shipping traversed Lake Superior before 1870. Only two wrecks are recorded before then. During 1872-90 approximately 15 Canadian vessels were lost on the lake. Part II. Only four Canadian vessels sank in Lake Superior during the 1890's, but over the next 10 years approximately 15 others went down. Six of those sank during 1906 alone. Part III. During 1908-19 there was a bad shipping season, and the "Great Storm of 1913," but the most catastrophic event occurred in the fall of 1918 when two Canadian-built French minesweepers disappeared in a storm east of Isle Royale. Illus. Article to be continued.
K. J. Bauer

944. —.   A DISAGREEMENT: CANADIAN BUSINESS 1867-1914.   *Social Hist. [Canada] 1977 10(19): 152-163.*
Naylor, R. Thomas.   THE HISTORY OF CANADIAN BUSINESS: A REPLY,   *pp. 152-159.* Point-by-point response to Michael Bliss' 1976 review of Naylor's *The History of Canadian Business* in this journal. The main issue is ideological. Naylor's analysis presupposes venality and corruption as the norm among a set of individuals whom Bliss was fondly typed as "captains of industry" and "the men who were building the nation." 5 notes.
Bliss, Michael.   THE HISTORY OF CANADIAN BUSINESS: REVIEWER'S RESPONSE,   *pp. 160-163.* Point-by-point response to Naylor's responses. Bliss's presupposition is that "business ethics were and are probably about the same as academic ethics."
W. K. Hobson

Western Expansion

945. Arnold, A. J.   JEWISH PIONEER SETTLEMENTS.   *Beaver [Canada] 1975 306(2): 20-26.* A series of settlements of Russian Jews was started in the 1880's at the instigation of Sir Alexander Galt. Three bad crop years led to dissatisfaction; some of the Jews went to Manitoba, others began "peddling." Mentions other contemporary Jewish settlements, occupations, travel problems, family life, and relations with neighboring communities. Provides details on the family of Alter Kaplun of Wapella, who settled there in 1891 and whose descendants are still on the farm. 12 illus., map.
D. Chaput

946. Benoit, Virgil.   GENTILLY: A FRENCH-CANADIAN COMMUNITY IN THE MINNESOTA RED RIVER VALLEY.   *Minnesota Hist. 1975 44(8): 278-289.* Gentilly and its environs in northwestern Minnesota was heavily settled during the 1870's-80's by French Canadians emigrating from Quebec. The French Catholic community has been held together by its religion, conservative family life, and the rural environment. Extensive ties with Canadian relatives still exist. Gentilly achieved a modicum of prosperity through the efforts to establish a cheese factory by the powerful Catholic priest Elie Theillon. Father Theillon was the spiritual and secular leader of Gentilly's French Canadians during 1888-1935. The Catholic Church has been a major factor in preserving the conservative social and economic world view of Gentilly's residents. Based on French and English language primary sources.
N. Lederer

947. Berry, Virginia.   WASHINGTON FRANK LYNN: ARTIST AND JOURNALIST.   *Beaver [Canada] 1978 308(4): 24-31.* Washington Frank Lynn, an Englishman trained as an artist, came to the New World in the 1860's as a correspondent for the Toronto *Globe*. He covered the Civil War in the United States. He became interested in Canadian settlement, and after a few years in England returned to Canada and the United States to study the lives of the immigrants. During 1871-72, he traveled via Minnesota to the Red River country, making copious notes on the inhabitants and painting many scenes, including "The Dakota Boat," "Pembina," and "Flat-Boats on the Red River." 5 illus.
D. Chaput

948. Bingaman, Sandra Estlin.   THE TRIALS OF POUNDMAKER AND BIG BEAR, 1885.   *Saskatchewan Hist. [Canada] 1975 28(3): 81-94.* Details the trials of Poundmaker and Big Bear, both Métis who participated in the North-West Rebellion of 1885. 52 notes.

949. Brooks, W. H.   THE PRIMITIVE METHODISTS IN THE NORTH-WEST.   *Saskatchewan Hist. [Canada] 1976 29(1): 26-37.* The branch of evangelical Methodists known as Primitive Methodists since their origin in early 19th-century England, founded an agricultural colony near Grenfell, Saskatchewan, in 1882. Mentions early leaders such as Hugh Bourne, William Clowes, and Lorenzo Dow, as well as a very active leader of the colony, the Reverend William Bee. Presents excerpts from Reverend Bee's letters. Photos, 65 notes.
C. Held

950. Brooks, William H.   THE UNIQUENESS OF WESTERN CANADIAN METHODISM 1840-1925.   *J. of the Can. Church Hist. Soc. [Canada] 1977 19(1-2): 57-74.* Methodism in western Canada was never truly established as it had been in eastern Canada and the United States. The Ontario missionaries who hoped to find in the west a frontier in which to gain success were bound to be disappointed, because both metropolitanism and railroads began to take hold there quite early. Moreover, the extreme mobility of the settlers and the harsh physical environment made the establishment of western Methodism even more difficult. All these problems meant that the church was not established with any definite character. Some of its members clung to traditional ideas; others turned to social utility. The result was that the institutionalized western Methodist church was devoid of vitality and fell apart. Primary and secondary sources; 35 notes.
J. A. Kicklighter

951. Brown, D. H.   THE MEANING OF TREASON IN 1885.   *Saskatchewan Hist. [Canada] 1975 28(2): 65-73.* In 1885 Louis Riel, then a naturalized US citizen living in Saskatchewan, was charged with treason against the British crown. Examines whether the charge was legitimate, and the evolving nature of treason in British law from 1352 to 1885. Also

examines whether Riel could renounce his British citizenship by taking US citizenship. 69 notes.

C. Held

952. Codignola, Luca. LOUIS RIEL E LE RIVOLTE DELL'OVEST CANADESE (1870-1885) [Louis Riel and the West Canadian revolts (1870-1885)]. *Riv. Storica Italiana [Italy] 1976 88(1): 127-142.* In 1869 the Hudson's Bay Company gave up its possessions to the government in Ottawa. This action provoked revolts in North Western Canada and in particular Red River. These revolts were the culmination of important themes in American history; the colonization of Western Canada and the Western United States, agrarian protest movements in the West, the history of the Indians, the history of relations between Canada and the United States, and the conflict between the French and English in North America. Louis Riel (1844-1885) was the leader of the major part of these revolts. On 15 May 1885, Riel was arrested by Canadian authorities and the entire movement was suppressed. Refusing to allow his lawyers to plead insanity, he was condemned to death and was hung in Regina on 16 November 1885. Primary and secondary sources; 85 notes.

M. T. Wilson

953. Comfort, D. J. WILLIAM MC MURRAY: THE NAME BEHIND THE FORT. *Alberta Hist. [Canada] 1975 23(4): 1-5.* Fort McMurray, at the fork of the Athabasca and Clearwater Rivers, was named for William McMurray, a Hudson's Bay Company factor there in 1870. The site was chosen by McMurray because it could serve the Indians of the region and act as a guard station for the Peace, Athabasca, and Mackinzie districts. His obscurity is a result of Henry John Moberly's biography, *When Fur Was King*, one of the few public writings about Fort McMurray's past, in which Moberly emphasizes his own role in the establishment of the trading post. 2 photos, 3 notes.

D. Chaput and S

954. Criddle, Percy. THE CRIDDLES OF AWEME. *Beaver [Canada] 1978 308(4): 15-19.* In 1882, Percy Criddle of London migrated to Canada and settled at Aweme, southeast of Brandon, Manitoba. With him were his wife Alice, friend Elise Vane, and nine children. Criddle kept a diary for over 35 years, excerpts of which appear here. He discusses various homestead situations, including digging a well, cutting logs, hosting guests, and earning a living from the land. He was particularly impressed with that great Canadian predator, the field mouse, an "all-devouring monster." 6 illus.

D. Chaput

955. Day, John P. EDMONTON CIVIC POLITICS 1891-1914. *Urban Hist. Rev. [Canada] 1978 (3): 42-68.* The coming of the Canadian Pacific Railway in 1891 stimulated the typical prairie town prewar boom in Edmonton. Describes the wide variety of political groupings which contended for political power in the prewar boom period. Primary sources; 3 tables, 3 fig., 57 notes.

C. A. Watson

956. Dempsey, Hugh A. DOROTHY AND THE BACHELORS. *Alberta Hist. [Canada] 1976 24(1): 12-14.* Although males greatly outnumbered females on the frontier, such a ratio did not necessarily lead to quick marriages for females. In 1895 "Dorothy" wrote to the Calgary *Herald* complaining that the men of the city resisted marriage for a strange variety of bad reasons. She challenged them, and in a series of exchanges in the *Herald*, was challenged by the bachelors. A promising courtship between "Dorothy" and a correspondent named "P. Kaboo" never materialized, as a few crimes and scandals shifted the readers' interest away from the question. Illus., 9 notes.

D. Chaput

957. Dempsey, Hugh A. THE REDCOAT DETACHMENT AT WRITING-ON-STONE. *Montana, the Mag. of Western Hist. 1974 24(4): 2-15.* In 1887, the North West Mounted Police established a patrol post at Writing-On-Stone, in rimrocks along the Milk River, five miles north of the Montana border. A small force stationed there attempted to suppress Indian raids and horse thievery, while supervising traffic crossing the international boundary. Later, a chief duty was repelling Montana cattle straying north to the river. The post closed in 1918. Illus., 16 notes.

S. R. Davison

958. DenOtter, A. A. COAL TOWN IN WHEAT COUNTRY: LETHBRIDGE, ALBERTA, 1885-1905. *Urban Hist. Rev. [Canada] 1976 76(1): 3-5.* Lethbridge's development as the first industrial city of western Canada resulted principally from the collieries and railways es-

tablished during 1882-90 by Sir Alexander T. Galt (1817-93). The town grew like other prairie cities, with a youthful and energetic population, but was unique in that the transient mine workers produced an unruly society and the Galt family dominated its early life. Lists sources for the study of Lethbridge. Based on the author's dissertation; note.

C. A. Watson

959. Den Otter, A. A. LETTERS FROM ELLIOTT GALT: TRAVELLING THE PRAIRIES, 1879-80. *Alberta Hist. [Canada] 1978 26(3): 21-33.* Prints five letters Elliott Galt wrote to his parents in 1879-80. Galt, grandson of John Galt and son of Alexander T. Galt, a father of Confederation, at age 29 became secretary to Edgar Dewdney, Indian commissioner of the North-West Territories. Elliott accompanied him on several trips, negotiating with western tribes. His letters (now in the Public Archives of Canada) stressed the hardships of travel in the west and the plight of the Indians. 6 illus., map.

D. Chaput

960. Den Otter, A. A. SIR ALEXANDER TILLOCH GALT, THE CANADIAN GOVERNMENT AND ALBERTA'S COAL. *Can. Hist. Assoc. Hist. Papers 1973: 21-42.* Discusses contributions of sophisticated entrepreneurs such as Sir Alexander Tilloch Galt (1817-93) to the settlement of the Canadian prairies. During the 1880's and 90's the economic climate was unfavorable for major business ventures in the North West. As a result, Galt needed and received generous concessions from the Canadian government to support his coal mining enterprise at Lethbridge. Based on papers in the Public Archives of Canada, House of Commons Debates, government reports, and newspapers; 80 notes.

G. E. Panting

961. Doerksen, A. D. "Tony". THE BRANDON WHEAT KINGS —1887 VINTAGES. *Manitoba Pageant [Canada] 1976 22(1): 11-17.* Immigrants from eastern Canada and England began farming in the Brandon district of Manitoba during 1879-80. Wheat was the principal crop. By 1887, even with single-furrow plows and hand-broadcast seeding, the area produced 1,920,000 bushels. In 1881 General Rosser of the Canadian Pacific Railway selected the site of Brandon for a major divisional point. The Great North West Central and the Northern Pacific and Manitoba Railways both connected with Brandon making it become the commercial center of the Northwest. 2 illus.

B. J. Lo Bue

962. Dreisziger, N. F. THE CANADIAN-AMERICAN IRRIGATION FRONTIER REVISITED: THE INTERNATIONAL ORIGINS OF IRRIGATION IN SOUTHERN ALBERTA, 1885-1909. *Can. Hist. Assoc. Hist. Papers [Canada] 1975: 211-229.* Focuses on the St. Mary and Milks River Basins that straddle the Canadian-United States border and have similar climates. Mormons began irrigating land in Southern Alberta. Public opinion and the competition of the national governments stimulated the development. After 1909, the Boundary Waters Treaty made possible a cooperative and realistic assessment of the irrigation needs of the area. Based on papers in the Public Archives of Canada, House of Commons Sessional Papers, Records of the International Joint Commission, government reports of Canada and the United States, secondary sources; 70 notes.

G. E. Panting

963. Driedger, Leo. NATIVE REBELLION AND MENNONITE INVASION: AN EXAMINATION OF TWO CANADIAN RIVER VALLEYS. *Mennonite Q. R. 1972 46(3): 290-300.* Discusses how Mennonites have reaped settlement benefits from government eviction of Métis and Indian groups, specifically in the Red River Valley of Manitoba and the Saskatchewan River Valley (1869-95).

S

964. Dunlop, Allan C. LETTER FROM A SOLDIER TOURIST. *Alberta Hist. 1975 23(3): 24-30.* William Johnston Tupper, grandson of Sir Charles Tupper and son of the premier of Nova Scotia, went west in 1885 with the Halifax Prov. Battalion. From Medicine Hat, he and other soldiers were given permission to visit the Rocky Mountains. This July letter to his mother details the trip, emphasizing tourist spots, conditions of travel, people met in the provinces, and a visit with some Sioux Indians. 2 illus., 23 notes.

D. Chaput.

965. Dunlop, Allan C. WILLIE GOES TO WAR. *Nova Scotia Hist. Q. [Canada] 1975 5(1): 1-20.* Discusses the initial publication of two letters by William Johnston Tupper, youngest son of Sir Charles Tupper and Lady Frances Amelia Tupper, containing his impressions and reac-

tions to the formation and dispatching of the Halifax Provisional Battalion to the North West Rebellion of 1885. "The excitement of military adventure, tempered by the realization of the delicate 'political' position in which he found himself, brings to his correspondence a careful, circumspect and accurate portrayal of events. As such they represent one of the few surviving contemporary Nova Scotian descriptions of this crisis in our nation's development. With the exception of a brief introductory setting for the letters and a number of explanatory notes, the letters tell the story." 17 notes, biblio.   R. V. Ritter

966. Ens, Adolph and Penner, Rita. QUEBEC PASSENGER LISTS OF THE RUSSIAN MENNONITE IMMIGRATION, 1874-1880. *Mennonite Q. R. 1974 48(4): 527-531.*

967. Essar, D. A LETTER FROM AN EARLY SASKATCHEWAN SETTLER. *Saskatchewan Hist. [Canada] 1976 29(2): 65-72.* Reprints a letter from Septimus Alfred Clark, of "Ardencroft, Township 19-Range 19, N. Regina, Assiniboia, Canada" to his sister, Lady Mary Radcliffe of Liverpool, written in 1884. It describes the journey from Great Britain the previous year and the hardships of Western Canadian life for a man trained to be an architect in England. He ultimately became a successful hardware merchant in Saskatoon and died there in 1909. 11 notes.   C. Held

968. Evans, Simon M. STOCKING THE CANADIAN RANGE. *Alberta Hist. [Canada] 1978 26(3): 1-8.* In the late 19th century, the cattle on the Canadian prairie range were mostly from Montana. In turn, the Montana ranches acted as clearing areas for cattle from the prairie states and from Oregon. Eastern Canadians and British financiers dominated the early ranching; yet, this ranching frontier was a blend of British, Canadian, and American open-range traditions. The type and quantity of cattle in the Prairie Provinces varied greatly, depending on whether the food supply was in the foothills or on the short-grass prairie. Based primarily on cattle literature and Canadian government reports; 3 illus., map.   D. Chaput

969. Ewanchuk, Michael. LORD DUFFERIN TRAIL AT GIMLI. *Manitoba Pageant [Canada] 1975 20(2): 5-9.* Examines Dufferin's 1877 trip to Gimli, Manitoba; attempts to ferret out the route taken and the farms in the Icelandic community which Dufferin visited.

970. Flanagan, Thomas. LOUIS "DAVID" RIEL: PROPHET, PRIEST-KING, INFALLIBLE PONTIFF. *J. of Can. Studies 1974 9(3): 15-25.* Louis Riel's letters, written after his entry into a mental hospital, reveal a traditional Christian eschatological faith with the overtones of a Joachimite dispensation. The letters are well organized rather than demented ravings. During the 1885 Rebellion, Riel tried to put his messianic religious convictions into practice. Based on Public Archives of Canada, and of Manitoba, Archives of the Archdiocese of Montreal and the Seminary of Quebec, periodicals, monographs; 54 notes.
                                                              G. E. Panting

971. Flanagan, Thomas. THE MISSION OF LOUIS RIEL. *Alberta Hist. [Canada] 1975 23(1): 1-12.* Examines visionary Louis Riel's conception of the North-West Rebellion as a messianic religious movement.   S

972. Flanagan, Thomas. POLITICAL THEORY OF THE RED RIVER RESISTANCE: THE DECLARATION OF DECEMBER 8, 1869. *Can. J. of Pol. Sci. [Canada] 1978 11(1): 153-164.* The document, written by a missionary and inspired by the Metis [people of French-Canadian and Amerindian descent] led by Louis Riel, is presented in English and French. 16 notes.   R. V. Kubicek

973. Flanagan, Thomas. THE RIEL "LUNACY COMMISSION": THE REPORT OF DR. VALADE. *Rev. de l'U. d'Ottawa [Canada] 1976 46(1): 108-127.* Discusses the report of Dr. François-Xavier Valade on the insanity of Louis Riel, who was hanged for high treason at Regina, Saskatchewan, 1885. Dr. Valade's appointment and subsequent report were "meaningless political sop." The government misinterpreted and later forged a telegram by Valade, in an attempt to disguise Valade's original opinion that Riel could not "distinguish between right and wrong on political and religious questions." Includes the published text of the report. Primary and secondary sources; 59 notes.   M. L. Frey

974. Flanagan, Thomas E. LOUIS RIEL'S RELIGIOUS BELIEFS: A LETTER TO BISHOP TACHÉ. *Saskatchewan Hist. [Canada] 1974 27(1): 15-28.* Louis Riel (1844-85) claimed to be a religious prophet in addition to being a separatist leader. Argues that Riel's religious leadership was "an essential part of the attempt to recover the integrity of the Métis way of life," and that his religious theories were not as fantastic or nonsensical as missionaries and his defense attorneys pointed out. Too much information is gathered from hostile sources. His letter to Bishop Alexandre Taché tends to ameliorate this condition despite Bishop Taché's opinion that Riel was hopelessly insane. 2 portraits, 16 notes.
                                                                 C. Held

975. Gaskin, Fred. RETRACING TYRRELL'S TRIP INTO THE BARREN LANDS. *Can. Geographical J. 1976/77 93(3): 46-53.* Retraces a canoe trip taken by Joseph Burr Tyrrell in 1893 in order to explore Rupert's Land, acquired from the Hudson's Bay Company in 1869.

976. Gilman, Carolyn. PERCEPTIONS OF THE PRAIRIE: CULTURAL CONTRASTS ON THE RED RIVER TRAILS. *Minnesota Hist. 1978 46(3): 112-122.* The French and Métis hunters, farmers, trappers, and fishermen living around present-day Winnipeg saw the Red River trails as a means to transport goods to St. Paul and in this manner obtain those few commodities necessary for their comfort or survival in their near-subsistence economy. As St. Paul developed American traders visualized the Red River trails from a south to north vantage point instead of the north to south perception of the Métis. They saw the trails as a means of generating commerce with the growing settlements in Manitoba. The Métis visualized the prairie as a sea, employing French nautical terms to describe natural phenomena. They were highly conscious of the dangers of the trails, especially in regard to the menace of storms, drought, and prairie fires. Later Americans on the scene began to comment on the beauty of the environment along the trail and especially its potential as a site for agricultural progress and the building of towns and cities. While the Métis favored Red River trails that would provide the most rapid form of transportation with available provisions, the Americans saw the trails as linkages between settlements.   N. Lederer

977. Gizycki, Horst von. ALTERNATIVE LEBENSFORMEN [Alternative life-styles]. *Frankfurter Hefte [West Germany] 1975 30(10): 45-54.* In his search for alternative life-styles, the author visited the Hutterites of Canada and South Dakota, a religious, communalistic group formed in central Europe centuries ago, which fled persecution by Habsburgs and Tsars, coming to the new world during 1874-79.

978. Goldring, Philip. THE CYPRESS HILLS MASSACRE—A CENTURY'S RETROSPECT. *Saskatchewan Hist. 1973 26(3): 81 103.* In June 1873 a small party of whites killed an undetermined number of Assiniboin Indians and destroyed 40 lodges in the Cypress Hills Massacre in southwestern Saskatchewan. Although there is a wealth of published information on the subject, relatively few of the facts are above dispute. Discusses the types of evidence available, the reasons an accurate account probably will never be reconstructed, and the real significance of the massacre. 3 illus., 63 notes.   D. L. Smith

979. Gough, Barry. THE CHARACTER OF THE BRITISH COLUMBIA FRONTIER. *BC Studies [Canada] 1976-77 (32): 28-40.* The British Columbia frontier, 1846-71, is defined as "the zone of influence of imperial administration" issuing from London and the colonial capitals of Victoria and New Westminster. The frontier process consists of the Europeans' methods to occupy land, manage a resource base, develop an Indian policy, establish sites for exploitation of the land mass and the sea coast, and extend their jurisdiction. Environmental determinants and British and American influences helped mold the character of the British Columbia frontier and its uniqueness in relation to adjacent American states, to other Canadian provinces, and to certain Commonwealth countries. 34 notes.   D. L. Smith

980. Greenberg, Dolores. A STUDY OF CAPITAL ALLIANCES: THE ST. PAUL & PACIFIC. *Can. Hist. R. 1976 57(1): 25-39.* Views the St. Paul & Pacific [Railroad] as opening a route to foreign capital for the Canadian Pacific supplied by United States and English financial intermediaries. Reveals the negotiations of [George] Stephen with Morton, Bliss & Company of New York, their termination by Stephen, and

the subsequent direct investment and policymaking role of this firm in the [Canadian Pacific Railroad]. The bankers' letterbooks revise the premise that Stephen and associates were responsible for financing CP construction and point to a New York-London-Canadian financial nexus.

981. Gross, Leonard, ed. and Bender, Elizabeth, trans. THE COMING OF THE RUSSIAN MENNONITES TO AMERICA: ANALYSIS OF JOHANN EPP, MENNONITE MINISTER IN RUSSIA 1875. *Mennonite Q. R. 1974 48(4): 460-475.* Introduces and reprints Johann Epp's letter of 1875 arguing against Mennonites' emigration from Russia to North America.

982. Guitard, Michelle. LA ROLANDERIE. *Saskatchewan Hist. [Canada] 1977 30(3): 110-114.* Examines an estate near Whitewood in Eastern Assiniboia, its founder, Rudolf Meyer, and his successor owner, Count Yves de Roffignac, who came to Saskatchewan with Meyer in 1886. The economic ventures of a series of French owners were disasters; however, the culture and social manners these French aristocrats provided were talked about in the district for several decades. 30 notes.
C. Held

983. Holmgren, Eric J. WILLIAM NEWTON AND THE ANGLICAN CHURCH. *Alberta Hist. [Canada] 1975 23(2): 17-25.* William Newton founded the Church of England in Edmonton in 1875 and remained there until 1900. Born, educated, and married in England, his Edmonton years were neither pleasant nor successful. He seemed to be mostly interested in Indians and Métis, possibly because so many whites were Methodist or Roman Catholic, and he antagonized many with his undiplomatic bearing. His book, *Twenty Years on the Saskatchewan*, appeared in 1897. 3 illus., 30 notes.
D. Chaput

984. Horrall, Stan W. A POLICEMAN'S LOT IS NOT A HAPPY ONE: THE MOUNTED POLICE AND PROHIBITION IN THE NORTH-WEST TERRITORIES, 1874-91. *Tr. of the Hist. and Sci. Soc. of Manitoba [Canada] 1973-74 (30): 5-16.* Discusses the formation of the romantic and heroic myth of the Royal Canadian Mounted Police, based on their success in creating law and order on the western frontier and the reversal of their reputation after 1880 (attributed almost entirely to the enforcement of the territorial liquor laws). The stringent liquor law of 1875 primarily was intended to "protect the Indian population from the nefarious activities of the whiskey traders," but as emigration increased, white settlers were determined not to have their drinking habits dictated. The rigorous but ambiguous enforcement of the prohibition laws threatened the survival of the mounted police until about 1900, when provincial police assumed this responsibility. Based on documents in the Public Archives of Canada and secondary works; 58 notes.
S. R. Quéripel

985. Humphrys, Ruth. DR. RUDOLF MEYER AND THE FRENCH NOBILITY OF ASSINIBOIA. *Beaver [Canada] 1978 309(1): 17-23.* Rudolf Meyer, a German fluent in French, came to Pipestone Creek, Saskatchewan, in 1885, with backing from French capitalists. He started an agricultural settlement with modest success. Soon around a dozen members of the French nobility and their families arrived. They continued with their aristocratic airs, dancing, dressing well, riding, and hunting. They even created the Whitewood town band, which included a marquis, a count, and a viscount. They tried a variety of farming and business ventures, but their inexperience and lack of direction led to constant failures. The colony disappeared after a few years. The only moderate success was Viscount de Langle, who operated a store in Whitewood. 7 illus., map.
D. Chaput

986. Humphrys, Ruth. [THE SHINY HOUSE]. THE SHINY HOUSE... AND THE MAN WHO BUILT IT. *Beaver [Canada] 1977 307(4): 49-55.* James Humphrys, retired British naval architect, moved to Assiniboia in 1888 for his health. There he acquired land for a farm. Within a few months he erected a large, comfortable home for his family of eight children and his wife, who remained in England until the home was completed. The Humphrys home was at Cannington Manor in southeastern Saskatchewan. Humphrys adjusted well, helped initiate medical and educational services, and looked forward to life in a progressive community. 8 illus.

EARLY DAYS IN THE SHINY HOUSE. *Beaver [Canada] 1977 308(1): 20-28.* Concludes the story of the family of James Humphrys. Discusses education, church life, entertainment, and other social affairs. 17 illus.
D. Chaput

987. Kerstan, Reinhold J. THE HUTTERITES: A RADICAL CHRISTIAN ALTERNATIVE. *Fides et Hist. 1973 5(1/2): 62-67.* The Hutterite sect was founded in 1528 in Moravia. They have maintained an agricultural communal form of society and culture. Caught often in the European wars at grave threat to their existence, they migrated to Canada and the United States in the 1870's. They are highly innovative and invariably successful farmers, but cling tenaciously to their original cultural and social patterns. Based on secondary sources; 6 notes.
R. Butchart

988. Klippenstein, Lawrence. AELTESTER DAVID STOESZ AND THE BERGTHAL STORY: SOME DIARY NOTES. *Mennonite Life 1976 31(1): 14-18.* Chronicles the years 1872-76 in the life of David Stoesz, a bishop of the Bergthaler Mennonites, during his immigration from the Ukraine to Manitoba. Article to be continued.

989. Klippenstein, Lawrence. DIARY OF A MENNONITE DELEGATION (1873). *Manitoba Pageant 1973 18(2): 18-23.* A delegation of 12 Russian Mennonites visited Manitoba during the summer of 1873. They travelled by steamboat from Moorhead, Minnesota, to Fort Garry and then visited the East Reserve and the Assiniboine River district from Winnipeg West. Records brief observations of their survey. The favorable findings of the delegation were instrumental in sending thousands of Mennonite families to North America. Illus., 4 notes.
D. M. Dean

990. Klippenstein, Lawrence. MANITOBA METIS AND MENNONITE IMMIGRANTS: FIRST CONTACTS. *Mennonite Q. R. 1974 48(4): 476-488.* Discusses the first experiences of Russian Mennonites who immigrated to Manitoba in 1873, especially their relationship to the Chippewa Indians and the Métis, natives of mixed blood.
S

991. Klippenstein, Lawrence. MANITOBA SETTLEMENT AND THE MENNONITE WEST RESERVE. *Manitoba Pageant 1975 21(1): 13-24.* Seven thousand Russian Mennonites entered Manitoba 1870-80. The peak year was 1875. Many of the Mennonites arriving that year settled on the plains west of the Red River, an area not dissimilar to what they had just left in Russia. Based on secondary works; 7 notes.
B. J. LaBue

992. Klippenstein, Lawrence. MOVING TO MANITOBA: JACOB Y. SHANTZ, ONTARIO BUSINESSMAN, PROMOTED SETTLEMENT ON THE PRAIRIE. *Mennonite Life 1974 29(3): 51-53.* Discusses efforts of Jacob Y. Shantz to encourage friends of his remaining in the Ukraine to come to Manitoba, 1870's; includes excerpts from Shantz' letters.

993. Klippenstein, Lawrence. A VISIT TO MANITOBA IN 1873: THE RUSSIAN MENNONITE DELEGATION. *Canada 1975 3(1): 48-61.* Discusses a visit by Russian Mennonites to Manitoba for the purpose of investigating settlement possibilities in 1873, emphasizing the role of Mennonite Reverend John F. Funk.

994. Krahn, Cornelius. A CENTENNIAL CHRONOLOGY. *Mennonite Life 1973 28(1): 3-9, (2): 40-45.* Part I. Describes Mennonite immigration from Russia to the American prairies, noting the underlying causes of the migration and the chronology of the key events in the movement. 9 illus., biblio. Part II. Chronology of events among Mennonite immigrants in Manitoba, Canada, 1871-74.
J. A. Casada/G. A. Hewlett

995. Lalonde, André N. THE NORTH-WEST REBELLION AND ITS EFFECTS ON SETTLERS AND SETTLEMENT IN THE CANADIAN WEST. *Saskatchewan Hist. [Canada] 1974 27(3): 95-102.* The positive effects of a completed railroad and cash for their crops to support the troops brought in by the rebellion were more than offset in the minds of the settlers by the violence occasioned by Riel's men. While actual casualties were light the widespread rumors of violence, often erroneous, effected a serious reduction in immigration for the remaining years of the 1880's. 38 notes.
C. Held

996. Legebokoff, Peter P. PORTRAIT OF DOUKHOBORS: IN-TRODUCTION. *Sound Heritage [Canada] 1977 6(4): 12-21.* Offers a history, 1652-1908, of the Christian Community of Universal Brotherhood, also known as Dukhobors; recounts early oppression in Russia and immigration to Nova Scotia in 1899, Saskatchewan in 1905, and British Columbia in 1908.

997. Letourneau, Rodger. THE GRAND RAPIDS TRAMWAY: A CENTENNIAL HISTORY. *Beaver [Canada] 1977 308(2): 47-54.* The tramway, built in 1877, provided a route which avoided the rapids of the Saskatchewan River near Grand Rapids. Horse and mule power pulled six four-wheeled cars over three and one-half miles of narrow gauge track. For the next 20 years the tramway was a success, particularly in supplying troops during the 1885 Rebellion. Rail developments in the 1890's, and the decline of the fur trade at Grand Rapids in 1909, led to the closing of the tramway. 6 illus., map.   D. Chaput

998. Lowes, Ellen McFadden. PAGES FROM A PIONEER DIARY: THE DIARY OF ELLEN MC FADDEN LOWES 1882-1886. *Manitoba Pageant [Canada] 1976 22(1): 21-25.* The diary covers the move to Elliott Settlement, and the first year there of the diarist and her future husband, Johnnie Lowes. Article to be continued.
B. J. Lo Bue

999. MacKay, Daniel S. C. THE RED RIVER EXPEDITION, 1870. *Military Collector and Hist. 1977 29(3): 101-110.* Describes the gear, arms, and composition of the expeditionary force of Sir James Lindsay into western Canada, which was intended to seize land from insurgent Métis who refused to acknowledge the sale of their lands by the Hudson's Bay Company.

1000. McCook, James. HORSES. *Beaver [Canada] 1974 304(4): 18-23.* Discusses the use and treatment of horses during the pioneer days of Alberta in the 1870's and 1880's.   S

1001. McCormick, P. L. THE DOUKHOBORS IN 1904. *Saskatchewan Hist. [Canada] 1978 31(1): 12-19.* The year 1904 was pivotal in the early history of the Doukhobors in Canada. The earliest groups came from three different backgrounds and had varying commitments to communal life. They also lacked leadership. The arrival of Peter Verigin in the Yorkton colonies in December 1902 solved the leadership problem and brought a vigorous move to reimpose communalism. A major objective in this, self-sufficiency, was nearly achieved in 1904. The same year, however, saw the arrival of the railway in the area of some of the settlements and the isolation the group had sought was gone forever. Photo, map, 35 notes.   C. Held

1002. McCracken, Jane. YORKTON DURING THE TERRITORIAL PERIOD, 1882-1905. *Saskatchewan Hist. [Canada] 1975 28(3): 95-110.* Discusses the importance of Canadian national policy in the settlement and economic growth of Yorkton, Saskatchewan, and specifically the effects of colonization companies and the extension of the Manitoba and North Western Railways lines. Map, 3 photos, 25 notes.

1003. McLean, W. J. TRAGIC EVENTS AT FROG LAKE AND FORT PITT DURING THE NORTHWEST REBELLION. *Manitoba Pageant 1972 18(1): 22-24, 1973 18(2): 4-8, (3): 11-16.* Continued from a previous article. Part III. Diary account by the author, Chief Factor of the Hudson Bay Company, of his captivity by the Plains Cree during the Riel Rebellion in 1885. The Plains Cree failed to induce the Wood Cree to join the fight against government troops at the Battle of Frenchman's Butte. In this encounter the cannonfire caused the Indians to flee. Part IV. Held captive, McLean and his family had to accompany the Cree on an arduous flight after the battle. He urged his captors to free him so that he could negotiate a peace settlement. Part V. McLean successfully urged his captors to free all their white prisoners so that he could negotiate a peace settlement. Details the return journey of 140 miles to Fort Pitt.   D. M. Dean

1004. McLeod, Evelyn Slater. OUR SOD HOUSE. *Beaver [Canada] 1977 308(2): 12-15.* Wesley Williams came from North Dakota in 1909 to settle west of Stettler, Alberta. Explains methods and materials used in construction of a sod house. Provides a photo of the completed sod house, plus floor plan, cut-away view, and sod slabbing diagrams. 5 illus.   D. Chaput

1005. McLeod, Finlay J. C. RECOLLECTIONS OF VIRDEN 1882. *Manitoba Pageant [Canada] 1976 22(1): 6-10.* Presbyterian Finlay J. C. McLeod was minister for the construction crews of the Canadian Pacific Railway during the winter of 1881-82 when they were passing through the Virden area. His recollections include mention of the earliest settlers and the religious life in the area.   B. J. Lo Bue

1006. Meyer, Larry L. THE COMPLEAT AND UNLIKELY PLAINSMAN. *Westways 1974 66(10): 24-29, 68.* Jerry Potts served the North West Mounted Police as scout, guide, and Indian interpreter.
S

1007. Morgan, E. C. THE NORTH-WEST MOUNTED POLICE: INTERNAL PROBLEMS AND PUBLIC CRITICISM, 1874-1883. *Saskatchewan Hist. 1973 26(2): 41-62.* The discipline and high morale of the Royal North West Mounted Police in the first decade were imperiled by internal problems aggravated by the isolation of the frontier and by inadequate awareness of higher authorities of the needs of the force. The resultant resignations, desertions, and improper conduct in relations with the local populations generated spirited debates in the press and parliament. Acclaim exceeded criticism. 5 illus., 121 notes.
D. L. Smith

1008. Morton, Desmond. CAVALRY OR POLICE: KEEPING THE PEACE ON TWO ADJACENT FRONTIERS, 1870-1900. *J. of Can. Studies [Canada] 1977 12(2): 27-37.* Compares the activities and peace-keeping roles of the US Army and the Royal Canadian Mounted Police, finding more differences than similarities. Focuses on the background and history of the establishment of the Mounted Police in 1873. The Canadian government felt that the tax burden of law enforcement would only increase as settlement advanced, which gave the Mounted Police a more mediatory role than that of the US Army. Discusses common conditions on both sides of the border, and the declining living conditions of the Indians as settlement advanced in the 19th century. 73 notes.   J. B. Reed

1009. Morton, W. L. TWO YOUNG MEN, 1869: CHARLES MAIR AND LOUIS RIEL. *Tr. of the Hist. and Sci. Soc. of Manitoba [Canada] 1973-74 (30): 33-43.* Discusses political tension between the nationalist group Canada First and the Red River Rebellion, 1869-70. Poet Charles Mair, seen as a representative of Canada First, "the forerunner of Canadian Manifest Destiny," believed the future of the new nation was to be assumed by annexing the Northwest. Canada's future martyr, poet Louis Riel, defended the rights of the Métis and Indian groups occupying the area. The 1879 decision of Sir John MacDonald would create the province of Manitoba on the basis of Riel's Bill of Rights, but for now Riel was forced into exile while Mair returned to the Northwest and continued his literary career. Primary and secondary works; 9 notes.
S. R. Quéripel

1010. Naftel, William. THE COCHRANE RANCH. *Can. Hist. Sites [Canada] 1977 (16): 74-153.* The Cochrane ranch at Big Hill (now Cochrane, Alberta) and its successor and corporate cousin, the British American ranch, telescoped into a few years the various pioneer stages of large-scale Canadian ranching. Beginning in 1881 as the favoured child of a government that saw it as a means of profitably occupying a vacant area, the Cochrane ranch fell victim within two years to over-confidence, hard winters and mismanagement, and its cattle operations were moved to a more equable climate south of Fort MacLeod. The Big Hill site was transferred to the British American Ranche Company for sheep raising yet by 1888 this ranch was the victim of management and market problems and the rush of settlement to the West. The Cochrane ranch became successful on its southern range, but after the death of its founder was sold in 1905. Cochrane's efforts had brought other ranches into the empty land and demonstrated to settlers that the Red River Valley was not the only attractive area of the Northwest.   J

1011. Nicholson, L. H. NORTH-WEST MOUNTED POLICE 1873-1885: "HIGHLIGHTS OF THE FIRST YEARS." *Can. Geographical J. 1973 86(5): 142-154.*

1012. Norrie, K. H. THE RATE OF SETTLEMENT OF THE CANADIAN PRAIRIES, 1870-1911. *J. of Econ. Hist. 1975 35(2): 410-427.* Continental patterns of agricultural expansion delayed settlement of the Canadian prairies from the Homestead Act (Canadian) of 1872 until the late 1890's. The riskiness of dry-farming and the availability of humid lands in the United States until the late 1880's discouraged use of Canadian lands until grain prices turned upward after 1895. The lack of railway branch lines was a symptom, not a cause, of delayed expansion. Based on secondary sources and published statistics; table, 34 notes.

J. W. Williams

1013. Painchaud, Robert. LES ORIGINES DES PEUPLEMENTS DE LANGUE FRANÇAISE DANS L'OUEST CANADIEN, 1870-1920 MYTHES ET RÉALITÉS [The origins of the French-speaking people in the Canadian West, 1870-1920: Myths and realities]. *Tr. of the Royal Soc. of Can. 1975 13: 109-121.* Discusses the origins of French-speaking people in Western Canada, with emphasis on Manitoba, and describes the efforts, especially by ecclesiastical leaders, to get them to settle there. In Manitoba they settled largely in a contiguous area; hence, they were concentrated and retained their identity. They came from three major areas—Quebec, the United States, and French-speaking Europe (i.e., France, Belgium, and Switzerland). Many of them were farmers; however, some of them worked in the coal mines. 30 notes.

J. D. Neville

1014. Pannekoek, Frits. THE REV. GRIFFITHS OWEN CORBETT AND THE RED RIVER CIVIL WAR OF 1869-70. *Can. Hist. Rev. [Canada] 1976 57(2): 133-149.* Examines the period 1863-69 in Red River. Argues that Red River was a civil war between the English- and French-speaking half-breeds. Based primarily on unpublished documents in the Hudson's Bay Company Archives and the Church Missionary Society Archives, London.

A

1015. Pearson, William. RECOLLECTIONS AND REMINISCENCES: COLONIZATION WORK IN LAST MOUNTAIN VALLEY. *Saskatchewan Hist. [Canada] 1978 31(3): 111-113.* An excerpt from William Pearson's *Memoirs* written in 1928 primarily to preserve his experiences for his family. This passage describes how his company, Wm. Pearson Co., Ltd., organized extensive excursions during 1903-13 to bring settlers to Saskatchewan and to sell company lands.

C. H. Held

1016. Pennefather, John P. A SURGEON WITH THE ALBERTA FIELD FORCE. *Alberta Hist. [Canada] 1978 26(4): 1-14.* Reminiscences of Pennefather, a British surgeon who moved to Manitoba in the early 1880's. During the Second Riel Rebellion in 1885, he served as surgeon of the Winnipeg Light Infantry. Discusses some of the fighting, means of transportation and communication, and general dealing with and treatment of the Métis and Indians. Material extracted here is from a rare pamphlet published in 1892. 5 illus.

D. Chaput

1017. Rees, Ronald. ECCENTRIC SETTLEMENTS IN THE CANADIAN WEST, 1882-1900. *Hist. Today [Great Britain] 1977 27(9): 607-614.* Discusses the settlement of Cannington, Saskatchewan, which, unlike most frontier towns, was settled by a group of British who enjoyed the hunt, tennis, cricket, horseracing, and rugby, 1882-1900.

1018. Richtik, James M. THE POLICY FRAMEWORK FOR SETTLING THE CANADIAN WEST, 1870-1880. *Agric. Hist. 1975 49(4): 613-628.* To compete with the free land for homesteading available on the American frontier, Canada implemented government policy decisions designed to make settlement on the Prairie Provinces more desirable than settlement further to the south. More generous to the railroad, the Canadian government withheld land for large groups of immigrants and revised the grid system of settlement to make land in Canada more attractive than land in the United States. Based on primary and secondary sources; 48 notes.

R. T. Fulton

1019. Ridge, Alan D.   C. C. MCCAUL, PIONEER LAWYER. *Alberta Hist. R. 1973 21(1): 21-25.* Charles Coursolles McCaul (1858-1928) achieved fame as a criminal lawyer, consultant counsel, and fluent writer in pioneer western Canada. 2 illus., 34 notes.   D. L. Smith

1020. Ronaghan, Allen. THREE SCOUTS AND THE CART TRAIN. *Alberta Hist. [Canada] 1977 25(1): 12-14.* In 1875 several Cree chiefs stopped the installation of a telegraph line near Vermilion, Alberta. Richard Fuller, the contractor, was told that no further work could be

done until a treaty with the government had determined all rights. Hudson's Bay Company officials were asked to mediate, and they confirmed the Cree position. A treaty was signed the following year. Illus., 12 notes.

D. Chaput

1021. Rowand, Evelyn. THE REBELLION AT LAC LA BICHE. *Alberta Hist. R. 1973 21(3): 1-9.* The Northwest Rebellion, 1885, was felt in northeastern Alberta. Presents two versions of what happened, one by Peter Erasmus, a mixed-blood participant, and one by Bishop Faraud whose episcopal seat was in Lac la Biche when the events occurred. 4 illus., 3 notes.   D. L. Smith

1022. Schwieder, Dorothy A. FRONTIER BRETHREN. *Montana 1978 28(1): 2-15.* Hutterites found in the American West land and isolation, which persecution as European Anabaptists had denied them during the 16th-19th centuries. Communal colonies were first established during 1874-77 near Yankton, South Dakota, spreading during the next century to North Dakota, Montana, Washington, Alberta, Saskatchewan, and Manitoba. Training and education in each colony perpetuated traditions, strengthened communal goals, and reinforced male/female roles in adult life. Colonies are led by an elected minister and a council of 5 to 7 men. When the population reaches 130, a colony seeks to establish a new unit. Intercolonial marriages and religious traditions strengthen group ties. Hutterites were not a product of the American frontier, nor were they shaped by it. Thus Frederick Jackson Turner's frontier thesis and the Great Plains hypothesis of Walter Prescott Webb do not apply to the Hutterite colonies' experiences. Accompanying photographs by Kyrn Taconis are central to the article. Based on secondary sources and author's M.A. thesis; 12 illus., map, biblio.   R. C. Myers

1023. Selwood, John and Baril, Evelyn. LAND POLICIES OF THE HUDSON'S BAY COMPANY AT UPPER FORT GARRY: 1869-1879. *Prairie Forum [Canada] 1977 2(2): 101-119.* Though precise plans were drafted for the layout of Hudson's Bay Company lands surrounding Upper Fort Garry (now Selkirk, Manitoba), tradition, environmental factors, and politics caused much compromise in the original city planning, 1869-79.

1024. Shantz, Jacob Y. NARRATIVE OF JOURNEY TO MANITOBA. *Manitoba Pageant 1973 18(3): 2-6.* In 1873 Jacob Y. Shantz, at the request of the Canadian government, travelled with Bernard Warkentin of South Russia to see what the Manitoba prairies offered Russian Mennonites who wished to migrate. Shantz described the villages and the burgeoning town of Winnipeg. He visited farms owned by recent immigrants and recorded crop prices. His account was translated into several languages and distributed to prospective settlers.

D. M. Dean

1025. Silverman, Elaine. IN THEIR OWN WORDS: MOTHERS AND DAUGHTERS ON THE ALBERTA FRONTIER. *Frontiers 1977 2(2): 37-44.* Interviews from a wide-ranging project involving 130 female pioneers reveal daughters' attitudes toward their mothers; part of a special issue on women's oral history.

1026. Stanley, George F. INDIAN RAID AT LAC LA BICHE. *Alberta Hist. 1976 24(3): 25-27.* During the North-West Rebellion, this Hudson's Bay post was under control of trader Patrick Pruden. The post was plundered in April. Pruden's memorial includes details of the takeover by Beaver Indians. They came to the post and insisted on removing items for "safe-keeping" as they feared Big Bear's tribe had theft in mind. Pruden, faced with the armed Beaver Lake men, agreed. Most of the furs and supplies and some oxen were taken, and the post was gutted, thanks to the "safe-keeping" of the friendly Indians. Illus., 3 notes.

D. Chaput

1027. Steward, Donald M. LEESON & SCOTT. *Alberta Hist. [Canada] 1976 24(4): 12-17.* George Leeson and James Scott were Scotch Canadians who entered the freight business in western Canada in the early 1880's. They transported beef, had several regular stage runs, and acted as special couriers for mail and provisions during the Rebellion of 1885. Discusses firm personnel, commodities, stage robberies, and a special coinage-token system that began in the early 1900's. 3 illus., biblio.

D. Chaput

1028. Tegelberg, Laurie. CATHERINE SUTHERLAND OF POINT DOUGLAS—WOMAN OF HEAD AND HEART. *Manitoba Pageant 1975 21(1): 19-24.* Catherine McPherson Sutherland endured many hardships as a pioneer wife and mother along the Red River.
B. J. LaBue

1029. Threinen, Norman J. EARLY LUTHERANISM IN WESTERN CANADA. *Concordia Hist. Inst. Q. 1974 47(3): 110-117.* Discusses the role (ca. 1870) of William Wagner, a German immigrant, in establishing Township Berlin, in Manitoba, and his relation to the Lutheran Church, Missouri Synod.
S

1030. Turner, C. Frank. JAMES WALSH: FRONTIERSMAN. *Can.: An Hist. Mag. 1974 2(1): 29-42.* Due to his previous military training, James Walsh (1840-1905) was appointed a superintendent of the new North West Mounted Police in 1873. Walsh led the initial trek west to the Red River. When Sitting Bull and the Sioux came north after the Battle of the Little Big Horn in 1876, Walsh successfully pacified them. After retirement Walsh became the first commissioner of the Yukon in 1897. Based on MS. material in the Public Archives of Manitoba, and on published primary and secondary sources; 6 illus., 9 notes.
D. B. Smith

1031. Williams, W. H. A TERRIBLE TRIP TO EDMONTON. *Alberta Hist. [Canada] 1974 22(4): 1-13.* A newspaper reporter made a stormy trip north from Calgary in 1881 to assess Edmonton's agricultural potential.
S

1032. Wonders, William C. SCANDINAVIAN HOMESTEADERS. *Alberta Hist. 1976 24(3): 1-4.* Scandinavian settlement in the Prairie Provinces and British Columbia was secondary to the initial thrust, homesteading in the United States. However, after completion of the Calgary & Edmonton Railroad in 1891, and the immigrant quotas in the United States in the 1920's, Scandinavian population in central Canada increased markedly. Examines reasons for settlements, homesteading policies, and percentages of population. Unanswered questions are many and must be asked now, as assimilation is so rapid that there is seldom any second Scandinavian generation. 2 illus., 6 notes.
D. Chaput

1033. Woodcock, George. THE SPIRIT WRESTLERS: DOUKHOBORS IN RUSSIA AND CANADA. *Hist. Today [Great Britain] 1977 27(3): 152-158; (4): 249-255.* Part I. Outlines the history of the Dukhobor sect in Russia 1654-1890's and their emigration to Canada in 1898-99 because of religious persecution. Part II. Describes the Dukhobors as a militant religious sect led by Peter Nerigin, and their emigration from tsarist Russia to Canada, 1898-1902.

1034. Woywitka, Anne B. HOMESTEADER'S WOMAN. *Alberta Hist. [Canada] 1976 24(2): 20-24.* Dominka Roshko, born in 1893 in the Ukraine, came to Manitoba with her family in 1900. In 1912 she married Monoly Zahara, and they went to homestead in the Peace River country. Examines frontier living, such as clearing the land, farming, lack of medical facilities, and education. 2 illus.
D. Chaput

1035. —. THE DOUKHOBORS. *Sound Heritage [Canada] 1977 6(4): 23-77.* Fourteen members of the Christian Community of Universal Brotherhood, also known as Dukhobors, reminisce about immigration, the early days in Russia, and daily life in British Columbia, 1880's-1976.

1036. —. MENNONITE BEGINNINGS AT ROSTHERN. *Mennonite Life 1976 31(4): 4-15.* Presents an anonymous personal account, perhaps by Peter Klassen, of the first years of the Russian Mennonite settlement in Rosthern, Saskatchewan. In early spring 1892, 27 families staked out homesteads and began planting crops, building homes, and establishing a community. A split between Old Colony Mennonites and liberal Mennonites prevented the establishment of a church until Elder Peter Regier united factions in 1894. Despite frequent prairie fires, a food shortage during the harsh winter of 1892-93, and an 1895 shoot-out with rebellious Cree chief Almighty Voice, morale remained high. Settlers continued to arrive, crop yield was good, and the area prospered. Based on material in the archives of the Conference of Mennonites in Canada; 5 photos, map.
B. Burnett

1037. —. THE RATE OF SETTLEMENT OF THE CANADIAN PRAIRIES, 1870-1911. *J. of Econ. Hist. 1978 38(2): 471-475.*
Grant, K. Gary. A COMMENT, *pp. 471-473.* Examines the use of the long-run equilibrium model of the number of homesteads in Kenneth H. Norrie's previous article. Norrie's mistaken use of new homestead entries to estimate the model is not consistent with his interpretation that agricultural expansion of the wheat-producing Canadian frontier did not occur until 1) the unoccupied subhumid land disappeared, 2) dry-farming techniques increased in use, and 3) the price of wheat increased, 1896-1911. Table, 6 notes.
Norrie, Kenneth H. A REPLY, *pp. 474-475.* The standard logged adjustment model does not seem appropriate for explaining the delayed reaction of settlement in the semiarid Prairie Provinces. Only a small number of homesteaders were initially attracted; their success contributed to further migration. Note.
C. W. Olson

The Conservative Years, 1867-1896

1038. Allen, Richard. SALEM BLAND: THE YOUNG PREACHER. *J. of the Can. Church Hist. Soc. [Canada] 1977 19(1-2): 75-93.* After World War I, Salem Bland became recognized as a leader in the social gospel and liberal theology movements. The formative period for Bland was his early years as a Methodist minister in Canada. Though successful as a preacher, he held some suspect views and disliked the numerous theological controversies going on around him. Using his various talents, Bland sought to show that there was no important difference between science and religion and that Christian perfection meant not freedom from mistakes, but the constant desire to do what was right. Seeking at all times to combine the good from his own culture and fundamental Christian ideas, Bland rejected the evangelistic approach of both the Methodists and the Salvation Army because he felt that they could not help combine the old and the new. Primary and secondary sources; 69 notes. This issue is *J. of the Can. Church Hist. Soc.* 1977 19(1-2) and *Bull. of the United Church of Can.* 1977 26.
J. A. Kicklighter

1039. Baker, W. M. T. W. ANGLIN: SPEAKER OF THE HOUSE OF COMMONS, 1874-1878. *Queen's Q. [Canada] 1973 80(2): 256-266.* Timothy Warren Anglin was Canada's second Speaker of the House of Commons. Anglin was avowedly partisan but such conduct was acceptable politically at the time. The paucity of studies of Speakers and of the key constitutional issues of the period makes Anglin's years in office particularly important. His Speakership is illustrative of the immaturity of Canadian politics and constitutional development in the early years of Confederation, and offers insight into the lack of delineation between personal and public interests. The difficulties of his career were resolved, in typical Canadian fashion, "by compromise if necessary, evolution if permissible, and procrastination if possible." Based on the author's unpublished Ph.D. dissertation; 5 notes.
J. A. Casada

1040. Bella, Leslie. JOHN A. MACDONALD'S REALISM SAVED BANFF. *Can. Geographic [Canada] 1978 97(2): 20-27.* Seeing a possibility for profit through tourism as well as exploitation of natural resources, Canada's Prime Minister John A. Macdonald fought for and gained the first national park at Banff, Alberta in 1885.

1041. Birrell, A. J. D.I.K. RINE AND THE GOSPEL TEMPERANCE MOVEMENT IN CANADA. *Can. Hist. Rev. [Canada] 1977 58(1): 23-42.* Examines the rise, message, success, and sudden downfall of D.I.K. Rine and the Gospel Temperance Movement, in Canada during 1877-82. This moral suasionist movement, begun in New England by Francis Murphy, combined religious revivalism with the temperance message in attempting to reclaim alcoholics and hard drinkers. In Canada, led by Rine, a reformed alcoholic and an ex-convict, it met with enormous success, although unlike other contemporary movements it refused to campaign for legislated prohibition. Rine's arrest for indecent assault marked the end of the movement in Canada.
A

1042. Consentino, Frank. NED HANLAN—CANADA'S PREMIER OARSMAN A CASE STUDY IN 19TH CENTURY PROFESSIONALISM. *Ontario Hist. [Canada] 1974 66(4): 241-250.* Examines the influence of the Canadian oarsman Edward "Ned" Hanlan in helping professional athletes in general gain public acceptance in the 1870's and 1880's.

1043. Cosentino, Frank. NED HANLAN—CANADA'S PREMIER OARSMAN: A CASE STUDY IN 19TH CENTURY PROFESSIONALISM. *Can. J. of Hist. of Sport and Physical Educ. 1974 5(2): 5-17.* Canada's rowing hero of the 1870's and 1880's, Ned Hanlan, defeated 300 straight scullers who raced against him including the celebrated American rower, Charles Courtney. The Hanlan-Courtney series of matches indicates a high pitch of nationalism reached in both countries. Based on 30 primary and secondary notes.					R. A. Smith

1044. Graff, Harvey J. "PAUPERISM, MISERY, AND VICE": ILLITERACY AND CRIMINALITY IN THE NINETEENTH CENTURY. *J. of Social Hist. 1977 11(2): 245-268.* A study of the Middlesex County, Ontario, gaol registers of 1867-68 indicates that the popular concept that crime is committed by the uneducated is in error. Instead, such crimes as property offenses and prostitution were committed by some of the most literate members of society. Judging from this study, it was really "social inequality" that was the "prime determinant of criminality . . . Stratification by ethnic or sexual factors influenced the hierarchy of class, status, and wealth; in similar fashion, they turned the wheels of justice. Rather than illiteracy or ignorance leading directly to lives of crime, ethnicity, class, and sex lay behind and strongly mediated the relationships most commonly drawn." 6 tables, 62 notes.					L. E. Ziewacz

1045. Gundy, H. Pearson. FLOURISHES AND CADENCES: LETTERS OF BLISS CARMAN AND LOUISE IMOGEN GUINEY. *Dalhousie R. [Canada] 1975 55(2): 205-226.* Contains background information on the Canadian poet William Bliss Carman's early years, especially in Boston, and mentions a number of acquaintances in his circle including Josiah Royce, Charles Eliot Norton, Bernard Berenson and Louise Imogen Guiney. Special attention is paid to his relationship with Guiney and includes 22 letters in whole or in part in the text. The correspondence began in 1887 and continued into 1898.					C. Held

1046. Hancock, Harold B. MARY ANN SHADD: NEGRO EDITOR, EDUCATOR, AND LAWYER. *Delaware Hist. 1973 15(3): 187-194.* Mary Ann Shadd (d. 1893) was the daughter of Abraham D. Shadd, a Delaware Negro abolitionist prominent in the Negro convention movement. She was nursed on Quaker teachings and antislavery witness. The family moved to Ontario, Canada, in 1851, but the Shadd family maintained contacts with Wilmington (Delaware) and West Chester (Pennsylvania) friends. Mary Ann Shadd first earned her antislavery reputation by investigating the possibilities of Negro settlement in Canada to escape the baneful effects of the invigorated Fugitive Slave Act of 1850. In a pamphlet in 1852 she called attention to opportunities for Negroes in Canada, and lectured widely on the subject. Her most significant contribution was her leading role as editor, 1854-59, in the publication of the weekly *Provincial Freeman,* the first antislavery newspaper in Ontario. From its inception in 1854 the *Freeman* attacked the mismanagement of experimental Negro communities, opposed segregation, and assaulted slavery in the United States. She lectured in the United States in 1855. She also taught school, initially through the American Missionary Association, participated in women's rights reform, and published articles encouraging Negroes to patronize Negro businesses. Based on newspapers and unpublished letters; 27 notes.					R. M. Miller

1047. Harvey, Fernand. UNE ENQUÊTE OUVRIÈRE AU XIXᵉ SIÈCLE: LA COMMISSION DU TRAVAIL, 1886-1889 [A working inquiry in the 19th century: the Labour Commission, 1886-89]. *Rev. d'Hist. de l'Am. Française [Canada] 1976 30(1): 35-53.* During the latter part of December 1886, the federal government established the Royal Commission of Inquiry into the Relations between Capital and Labour. The commission investigated the poor working and living conditions of laborers in Ontario, Quebec, New Brunswick, and Nova Scotia. In February 1889, the commissioners issued reports and made recommendations. Even though federal legislation did not immediately result from the inquiry, the public nevertheless was informed about the capitalist system's abuses. Based on letters in the Public Archives of Canada (Bowell and Macdonald Papers), published government documents, newspapers, and secondary works; 2 tables, 34 notes.					L. B. Chan

1048. Hirthe, Walter M. WHERE IS THE *TWO FRIENDS?* *Inland Seas 1975 31(3): 186-191, 214.* Although most maritime histories and wreck charts of the area indicate that the Canadian bark *Two Friends* was sunk in North Bay, Wisconsin, on 16 October 1880, she was salvaged and rebuilt in Milwaukee in 1881 as the schooner *Pewaukee.* Based on local newspapers; illus., 16 notes.					K. J. Bauer

1049. Joyner, Christopher C. THE HEGIRA OF SITTING BULL TO CANADA: *DIPLOMATIC REALPOLITIK,* 1876-1881. *J. of the West 1974 13(2): 6-18.* An account of the hegira of Sitting Bull to Canada following the Custer Massacre of 25 June 1876. The northward movement of the Sioux Indians into Canada "precipitated an international crisis over the American-Canadian boundary. In 1877, President Hayes appointed a commission to deal with the problem, and on 19 July 1881, "Sitting Bull surrendered at Fort Buford. . . . Whoever was responsible, officials in both countries welcomed this action by the old medicine man." 64 notes.					D. D. Cameron

1050. Kealey, Gregory S. ARTISANS RESPOND TO INDUSTRIALISM: SHOEMAKERS, SHOE FACTORIES AND THE KNIGHTS OF ST. CRISPIN IN TORONTO. *Can. Hist. Assoc. Hist. Papers 1973: 137-157.* Traces the part played by the Knights of St. Crispin in the organization of boat and shoe factory workers. The Crispins, beginning as a craft society, adapted to the industrialization of their trade in Toronto during the early 1870's. They were regarded as leading working class intellectuals and their spirit and tactics were carried into the Knights of Labor. Based on primary and secondary sources; 3 tables, 75 notes.					G. E. Panting

1051. Koerper, Phillip E. CABLE IMBROGLIO IN THE PACIFIC: GREAT BRITAIN, THE UNITED STATES AND HAWAII. *Hawaiian J. of Hist. 1975 9: 114-120.* During the Colonial Conference at Ottawa, in 1894, a resolution was passed calling for a study and survey relating to construction of a communications cable from Vancouver, Canada, to Australia and New Zealand. Deals with the attempt by the British to use one of the smaller Hawaiian islands as a cable relay point.					R. Alvis

1052. Lai, Chuen-Yan David. HOME COUNTY AND CLAN ORIGINS OF OVERSEAS CHINESE IN CANADA IN THE EARLY 1880'S. *BC Studies [Canada] 1975 (27): 3-29.* The composition and spatial distribution of home county and clan origins of the Chinese in British Columbia in the early 1880's is studied. The effects of county and clan affiliation on the organization of voluntary associations and the monopoly of certain occupations and trades in Chinese communities is examined. Primary and secondary sources; 11 tables, 7 figs., 24 notes.					W. L. Marr

1053. Larivière-Derome, Céline. UN PROFESSEUR D'ART AU CANADA AU XIXᵉ SIÈCLE: L'ABBÉ JOSEPH CHABERT [An art teacher in 19th-century Canada: Abbé Joseph Chabert]. *R. d'Hist. de l'Amérique Française 1974 28(3): 347-366.* Describes the history of the National Institute for Arts and Crafts of Montreal founded in 1870 and directed by the French Abbé Joseph Chabert. Courses in engraving, sculpture, architecture, drafting, and various scientific subjects were offered to the working classes. The school declined following the Abbé's involvement in a scandal, later changed location several times, and finally disappeared after his death in 1894. Based on primary and secondary sources; 126 notes.					C. Collon

1054. Lawrence, Robert G. EUGENE A. MCDOWELL AND HIS CONTRIBUTIONS TO THE CANADIAN THEATRE 1875-1890. *Dalhousie Rev. [Canada] 1978 58(2): 249-259.* McDowell (1845-93) was a US actor, theater manager, and impressario with the courage to tour Canada extensively during important years of Canadian cultural development. Using newspaper commentary from 1875 to 1890, the author covers many productions in the small towns of Ontario, Manitoba, and the Maritime Provinces as well as the usual stopping places of Toronto, Montreal, and Ottawa. One of the favorite productions was W. H. Fuller's political satire, *H.M.S. Parliament.* The only identifiable Canadian actors in the troupe were John H. Gilmour, Albert Tavernier, and Joe Banks. 31 notes.					C. Held

1055. Lozynsky, Artem. WALT WHITMAN IN CANADA. *Am. Book Collector 1973 23(6): 21-23.* The devotion of Dr. Richard Maurice Bucke (1837-1902) to Walt Whitman exceeded that of even the most enthusiastic collector. His deification of the poet in a speech in London, Ontario, 27 February 1880, aroused resentment. Reprints an interview with Whitman in the *London Free Press,* 5 June 1880, which reveals his admiration for Sir Walter Scott and his dislike for "Bret Harte and that class of humourists" who would turn Homeric poetry into burlesque. Illus.   D. A. Yanchisin

1056. Marble, Allan E. and Punch, Terrence M. SIR J. S. D. THOMPSON: A PRIME MINISTER'S FAMILY CONNECTIONS. *Nova Scotia Hist. Q. [Canada] 1977 7(4): 377-388.* Outlines the genealogy of John S. D. Thompson (1844-94), a native of Halifax and Prime Minister of Canada 1892-94. The listings trace the family from 1796 in Waterford, Ireland, to 1903 and include both female and male lines. Primary and secondary sources.   H. M. Evans

1057. Miller, J. R. 'AS A POLITICIAN HE IS A GREAT ENIGMA': THE SOCIAL AND POLITICAL IDEAS OF D'ALTON MC-CARTHY. *Can. Hist. Rev. [Canada] 1977 58(4): 399-422.* Based on McCarthy's (1836-98) speeches (in Hansard and newspaper accounts), as well as political manuscript collections and unpublished dissertations. Analyzes the views of the Conservative Member of Parliament for North Simcoe [Ontario] in an effort to explain the evolution of his political career and the development of his thought. An understanding of McCarthy's career requires an appreciation of his concern for social reform in an age of industrialization and urbanization, as well as his better-known theories on language and imperial relations.   A

1058. Miller, J. R. THE JESUITS' ESTATES ACT CRISIS: "AN INCIDENT IN A CONSPIRACY OF SEVERAL YEARS' STANDING." *J. of Can. Studies 1974 9(3): 36-50.* Rejects Orange bigotry and general Protestant opposition as a satisfactory explanation for the furor over the Jesuits' Estates Act. Slow economic growth brought pre-Confederation conflicts to the surface of politics, and the Jesuit Estates agitation was in the mainstream of English Canadian life. Based on personal papers, House of Commons debates, newspapers, periodicals, theses, secondary works; 71 notes.   G. E. Panting

1059. Miller, James R. "THIS SAVING REMNANT": MACDONALD AND THE CATHOLIC VOTE IN THE 1891 ELECTION. *Study Sessions [Canada] 1974 41: 33-52.* Discusses the issues involved in the 1891 election in Canada and shows how conservative John Macdonald retained the Catholic vote. A paper read at the 1974 annual meeting of the Canadian Catholic Historical Association.   S

1060. Morrison, Rodney J. THE CANADIAN-AMERICAN RECIPROCAL TRADE AGREEMENT OF 1874: A PENNSYLVANIAN'S VIEW. *Pennsylvania Mag. of Hist. and Biog. 1978 102(4): 457-468.* Widely influential Henry C. Carey, fearing England, rejected English free-trade political economy in the name of nationalism and protectionism. He therefore opposed the Treaty of Washington (1871) and the Canadian- and British-proposed Reciprocity Treaty (1874) which the US Senate rejected in February 1875. 33 notes.
                                                        T. H. Wendel

1061. O'Brien, Kevin H. F. "THE HOUSE BEAUTIFUL": A RECONSTRUCTION OF OSCAR WILDE'S AMERICAN LECTURE. *Victorian Studies 1974 17(4): 395-418.* Reconstructs the text of the lecture, "The House Beautiful," delivered by Oscar Wilde (1854-1900) during his 10-month tour of Canada and the United States in 1882. Based on contemporary sources; 25 notes.   C. B. Fitzgerald

1062. Powell, William E. EUROPEAN SETTLEMENT IN THE CHEROKEE-CRAWFORD COAL FIELD OF SOUTHEASTERN KANSAS. *Kansas Hist. Q. 1975 41(2): 150-165.* Underground coal mining started in southeastern Kansas during the 1870's reached a peak during 1890-1920. Adverse conditions in Europe, coupled with economic opportunity and lax immigration laws, drew large numbers of immigrants from Europe and Canada to Kansas coal fields, where they settled in existing towns or company mining camps. When the mines declined after 1920 many immigrants moved to northern industrial cities. Based on primary and secondary sources; 3 photos, 2 tables, fig., 51 notes.
                                                        W. F. Zornow

1063. Roberts, Barbara. "THEY DROVE HIM TO DRINK" . . . DONALD CREIGHTON'S MACDONALD AND HIS WIVES. *Canada 1975 3(2): 50-64.* Discusses historian Donald Creighton's biographic portrayal of the personal and family life of Prime Minister John A. Macdonald in Canada, 1843-91, emphasizing Macdonald's relations with women.

1064. Ross, Brian R. RALPH CECIL HORNER: A METHODIST SECTARIAN DEPOSED, 1887-95. *Methodist Hist. 1977 16(1): 21-32.* Ralph Cecil Horner (1854-1921) was ordained a minister in the Methodist Church in 1887 and was suspended seven years later for evangelistic activities. In 1900 he created a separate denominational group, the Holiness Movement Church, in Canada. 24 notes.   H. L. Calkin

1065. Ross, Brian R. RALPH CECIL HORNER: A METHODIST SECTARIAN DEPOSED. *J. of the Can. Church Hist. Soc. [Canada] 1977 19(1-2): 94-103.* Finding salvation through an evangelical experience in 1872, Ralph C. Horner dedicated himself to winning souls through evangelism and was ordained a minister in the Montreal Conference of the Methodist Church of Canada in 1887. Horner was very successful as an evangelist but found considerable problems with the authorities of the church. They found his methods excessive and discovered that he would not follow their orders. Though told to accept an assignment as a regular minister, Horner refused to do so. The Conference leaders tried to work out an arrangement with him but to no avail. In 1894 Horner was deposed from the ministry of the Methodist Church. Ultimately, in 1900, he organized his own successful Holiness Movement Church in Canada. His strong belief in freedom and his self-confidence in the rightness of his mission made him unable to accept direction from others. Primary sources; 24 notes. This issue is *J. of the Can. Church Hist. Soc.* 1977 19(1-2) and *Bull. of the United Church of Can.* 1977 26.
                                                        J. A. Kicklighter

1066. Spector, David. THE 1883 LOCOMOTIVE ENGINEERS' STRIKE IN THE CANADIAN NORTH WEST. *Manitoba Pageant [Canada] 1976 22(1): 1-4.* To avert bankruptcy and to encourage investors with its skillfull business techniques the Canadian Pacific Railway (CPR) reduced engineers' wages six dollars per month and had them sign statements agreeing to the cut. In 1883 the engineers received $3.50-$3.75 per day. They petitioned William Van Horne, the General Manager of CPR, and asked for $4.00 per day. The petition was rejected and the engineers and firemen went out on strike. James Slavin, Acting President of the Brotherhood of Locomotive Engineers, coordinated the strike from Winnipeg. Scabs imported from Chicago broke the strike and after eight days the union agreed to company terms. Primary and secondary sources; illus., 24 notes.   B. J. Lo Bue

1067. Spigelman, Martin S. "DES PAROLES EN L'AIR": QUEBEC, MINORITY RIGHTS AND THE NEW BRUNSWICK SCHOOLS QUESTION. *Dalhousie Rev. [Canada] 1978 58(2): 329-345.* The New Brunswick Schools question vexed Canada during most of the 1870's. The Common Schools Act (1871) ordered taxation of all, including Catholics, for public schools, but withdrew long-standing grants to Catholic schools. That Quebec gave vocal support to the Acadians was to be expected; but that little real support was forthcoming greatly disappointed the French-speaking New Brunswickers. Catholic newspapers and politicians gave vocal support to the Acadians and Irish Catholics in New Brunswick but always stopped short of changing their political allegiance to the governing Conservative Party. Names such as Georges Cartier, Hector Langevin, and John A. Macdonald appear frequently, as do references to the newspapers *La Minerve, L'Opinion Publique,* and *Le Nouveau Monde.* Quebec's first concern was not a Catholic minority in another province but its own security. 70 notes.
                                                        C. Held

1068. Sylvain, Philippe. LES CHEVALIERS DU TRAVAIL ET LE CARDINAL TASCHEREAU [The Knights of Labor and Cardinal Taschereau]. *Industrial Relations [Canada] 1973 28(3): 550-564.* The Noble and Holy Order of the Knights of Labor, formed in 1869, was one of many secret societies born of militant, discouraged workers. Elzéar Alexandre Taschereau (1820-98), Archbishop of Quebec, was among those who feared an association with Freemasonry in the rapid spread of the secret Knights of Labor. He was instrumental in having the Knights condemned by the Catholic Church in 1884. James Gibbons (1834-1918),

Archbishop of Baltimore, however, as a warm supporter of the Knights journeyed to Rome and succeeded in having the ruling overturned. His efforts helped prepare the way for the encyclical *Rerum Novarum* (1891), the charter of Catholic social thought. Based on published Church documents and secondary works; 46 notes.   L. R. Atkins

1069. Sylvain, Philippe. LES CHEVALIERS DU TRAVAIL ET LE CARDINAL ELZÉAR-ALEXANDRE TASCHEREAU [The Knights of Labor and Cardinal Elzéar-Alexandre Taschereau]. *Tr. of the Royal Soc. of Can. 1973 11: 31-42.* Records the history of Cardinal Taschereau's condemnation and later pardon of the Noble and Holy Order of the Knights of Labor for secretiveness, 1884-94, suggesting that this secret society, founded in Philadelphia in 1869, had some influence on the history of French Canadian labor unions.

1070. Tallman, Ronald. PETER MITCHELL AND THE GENESIS OF A NATIONAL FISHERIES POLICY. *Acadiensis [Canada] 1975 4(2): 66-78.* After the United States abrogated its Reciprocity Treaty with Canada in 1866, American fishermen continued to fish along the coasts of the Maritime provinces even though they had lost the legal right to. Peter Mitchell, head of Canada's Ministry of Marine and Fisheries, first tried to make the New Englanders buy licenses. Failing that, in 1870 he began forcibly excluding them from the coast, which brought some American concessions and bolstered Canadian confidence and self-respect. Primary and secondary materials and government sources; 67 notes.   E. A. Churchill

1071. Tallman, Ronald D. RECIPROCITY, 1874: THE FAILURE OF LIBERAL DIPLOMACY. *Ontario Hist. [Canada] 1973 65(2): 87-105.* Discusses efforts to negotiate a new reciprocity treaty in 1874. Attributes the failure partly to Ottawa's diplomacy. Because a majority of Congress was either not in favor or was uninterested, there was no significant American lobby for a treaty. Identifies some interest groups and gives much attention to the efforts of George Brown to negotiate the treaty. Primary sources; 127 notes.   W. B. Whitham

1072. Tepperman, Lorne. ETHNIC VARIATIONS IN MARRIAGE AND FERTILITY: CANADA, 1871. *Can. R. of Sociol. and Anthrop. 1974 11(4): 324-343.* "The Canadian census of 1871 provided data for the estimation of ethnic variations in marriage and fertility. These variations largely account for the observed provincial variations in mean age at marriage, marital fertility, and birth rate, in 1871. Ethnic identity exercised an extremely strong influence on nuptiality and fertility, both directly and indirectly through the impact of ethnic custom on land distribution. Customs of inheritance and land partibility affected land inequality and mean size of landholdings, which in turn increased or decreased the feasibility of high levels of nuptiality and fertility. However, nuptiality was less influenced by land distribution than was fertility, implying that ethnic customs of nuptiality continued to predominate in the direct determination of marriage levels. It is concluded that regional and provincial variations in nuptiality and fertility can be satisfactorily accounted for by variations in ethnic composition and, perhaps secondarily, by historical patterns of land settlement. Ethnic reproductive practices were part of the cultural heritage brought to Canada by its immigrants, and they continued largely unaffected by the changed environment. Their continuity signified and maintained ethnic distinctiveness in Canadian society, but may also have had implications for the development of the Canadian 'vertical mosaic.'"   J

1073. Toner, Peter M. THE UNSTRUNG HARP: CANADA'S IRISH. *Acadiensis [Canada] 1978 7(2): 156-159.* Two recent works illuminate the Irish experience in 19th-century Canada. W. S. Neidhardt's *Fenianism in North America* (1975) is the first work on the Fenians in the Canadian context, but fails to explain the phenomenon of Fenianism or the reaction of Canadian Irish. W. M. Baker's *Timothy Warren Anglin* (1977) emphasizes Anglin's search for power through respectability, and his inability to decide who to represent: Irish, Catholics, or Liberals. As a result, when he lost his seat in 1882, his political career was virtually over.   D. F. Chard

1074. Tusseau, Jean-Pierre. LA FIN "ÉDIFIANTE" D'ARTHUR BUIES [The "edifying" end of Arthur Buies]. *Études Françaises [Canada] 1973 9(1): 45-54.* Discusses the return of French Canadian pamphleteer Arthur Buies to the Catholic Church. Based on works of Buies, newspapers, and works of Gagnon; illus., 31 notes.   C. Bates

1075. Waite, P. B. ANNIE AND THE BISHOP: JOHN S. D. THOMPSON GOES TO OTTAWA, 1885. *Dalhousie Rev. [Canada] 1977-78 57(4): 605-618.* Presents the background for John S. D. Thompson's move out of the Supreme Court of Nova Scotia and into the larger world of Canadian politics centering in Ottawa, 1867-94. Details his motives, and especially the motives and influence of his wife, Annie Affleck, through excerpts from their correspondence, which was considerable because of their close emotional ties. Examines the role of the Bishop of Antigonish, John Cameron, and the reluctance of Sir Alexander Campbell in giving up the Ministry of Justice. 40 notes.
                     C. H. Held

1076. Weaver, Bill. THE TWAIN-CABLE LECTURES IN KENTUCKY, 1884-1885. *Register of the Kentucky Hist. Soc. 1974 72(2): 134-142.* Mark Twain's and George Washington Cable's lecture tour between 5 November 1884 and 28 February 1885 encompassed 85 cities in 16 states and Canada. Stops in Louisville and Paris, Kentucky, were well-received. Based on newspapers and secondary sources; 40 notes.
                     J. F. Paul

1077. —. THE SHAFSKY BROTHERS OF FORT BRAGG: A MENDOCINO COUNTY VIGNETTE. *Western States Jewish Hist. Q. 1976 9(1): 49-54.* The Shafsky family, Russian emigrants, came to the United States by way of Canada. Starting as pack peddlers in the lumber camps of northern California, two of the brothers, Abraham Harry and Samuel, opened a general merchandise store in Fort Bragg. The business prospered and is still operated by a son and grandson of Abraham Harry Shafsky. Based on interviews, family records, and published works; 3 photos, 13 notes.   B. S. Porter

The Laurier Years, 1896-1911

1078. Armstrong, Christopher. HORNY HANDS ACROSS THE BORDER. *Can. R. of Am. Studies 1976 7(1): 93-94.* Review article prompted by Robert H. Babcock's *Gompers in Canada: A Study of American Continentalism before the First World War* (Toronto: U. of Toronto Pr., 1974) follows the events and analyzes the forces which enabled Samuel Gompers (1850-1924) and the American Federation of Labor to dominate the organized labor movement in Canada.
                     H. T. Lovin

1079. Avery, Donald. CONTINENTAL EUROPEAN IMMIGRANT WORKERS IN CANADA 1896-1919: FROM 'STALWART PEASANTS' TO RADICAL PROLETARIAT. *Can. R. of Sociol. and Anthrop. 1975 12(1): 53-64.* This paper challenges the traditional interpretation of European immigration to Canada between 1896 and 1919 and the Canadian experience of these immigrants in this period. The author rejects the view that most of the European immigrants settled on the land; instead, he concludes that large numbers became unskilled industrial workers. The author also emphasizes the serious class and ethnic tension which developed between the 'foreign' worker and the Anglo-Canadian business community, especially during the First World War and the 'Red Scare' of 1919. Indeed, in response to the apparent radicalism of many immigrant workers the Immigration Act was dramatically altered in the spring of 1919. Immigrants who advocated Bolshevist ideas were not only excluded from the country, but were also subject to rapid deportation. Ethnic, cultural, and ideological acceptability became temporarily a more important factor than economic utility in determining Canadian immigration policy.   J

1080. Bercuson, D. J. ORGANIZED LABOUR AND THE IMPERIAL MUNITIONS BOARD. *Relations Industrielles/Industrial Relations [Canada] 1973 28(3): 602-616.* "Examines the fight for fair wage clauses in Canadian munitions production at the beginning of this century."   J

1081. Bliss, Michael. ANOTHER ANTI-TRUST TRADITION: CANADIAN ANTI-COMBINES POLICY, 1889-1910. *Business Hist. R. 1973 47(2): 177-188.* While Canada may have preceded the United States in the passage of the first anti-monopoly statute, this solution was not followed up in later years. Canadian politicians came to defend the large corporations on the grounds of efficiency, concentrating instead on the tariff issue. Based primarily on public and documentary sources; 37 notes.   C. J. Pusateri

1082. Bradley, James G. WHEN SMOKE BLOTTED OUT THE SUN. *Am. West 1974 11(5): 4-9.* On 20-21 August 1910, the largest forest fire in North American history consumed three million acres of timber, some 100 lives, and four towns. The smoke blacked out the sun for five days over northern United States and southern Canada. The devastated area was a semicircle 160 miles long and 50 miles wide, stretching to the Canadian border in northern Idaho and Montana. The Great Idaho Fire of 1910 was met by the first organized resistance ever given to a forest fire. It stimulated fire protection legislation and policies that gave foundation to present day fire control. 3 illus.
D. L. Smith

1083. Brannigan, Colm J. THE LUKE DILLON CASE AND THE WELLAND CANAL EXPLOSION OF 1900: NON-EVENTS IN THE HISTORY OF THE NIAGARA FRONTIER REGION. *Niagara Frontier 1977 24(2): 36-44.* Luke Dillon (1848-1929), a member of the Clan-na-Gael, an Irish Republican group, was convicted "on very flimsy evidence" in the bombing of the Welland Canal, at Thorold, Ontario, in 1900; he was sentenced to life imprisonment in Kingston Penitentiary, and Irish American and Canadian groups did not obtain his release until 1914.

1084. Clements, Kendrick A. MANIFEST DESTINY AND CANADIAN RECIPROCITY IN 1911. *Pacific Hist. R. 1973 42(1): 32-52.* Describes the reactions in Canada and the United States to the proposed trade reciprocity agreement of 1911. Although American imperialism was by then on the wane, the conservative party in Canada was able to use the threat of annexation to successfully defeat the passage of the agreement. American debate on the issue gave support to Canadian fears by tactless and blundering statements, deliberately misleading statements by protectionists, and widespread faith in the idea of ultimate union with its tacit implications of the inequality of the two countries. 65 notes.
E. C. Hyslop

1085. Clifford, N. K. THE ORIGINS OF THE CHURCH UNION CONTROVERSY. *J. of the Can. Church Hist. Soc. 1976 18(2-3): 34-52.* The key figure of William Patrick in the Presbyterian Church Union controversy has heretofore been neglected. Writers on church union have not emphasized his role, because Patrick was not a Canadian. A Scottish liberal, Patrick rose quickly to a position of leadership in the Presbyterian Church and in 1902 daringly proposed organic union to the Methodist General Conference. This naturally engendered great controversy in the Presbyterian ranks, but Patrick never faltered, believing union was divinely ordained. As the first liberal in a place of authority in the Presbyterian Church and as a newcomer to Canada, Patrick was in a good position to further the cause of union, yet his ignorance of the special conditions of the Canadian situation and his inability to develop many social ties helped to frustrate efforts at union and caused great polarization within the Canadian Presbyterian Church. Based on printed and unprinted primary sources; 45 notes.   J. A. Kicklighter

1086. Cook, George L. ALFRED FITZPATRICK AND THE FOUNDATION OF FRONTIER COLLEGE (1899-1922). *Canada 1976 3(4): 15-39.* To combat the brutal conditions in Canadian railroad, mining, and lumber camps, and to help assimilate immigrant laborers into Canadian society, Alfred Fitzpatrick (1862-1932) established the Frontier College. In its final development the laborer-teachers of the Frontier College faculty traveled and worked side-by-side with the camp laborers during the day and taught them evenings or Sundays. 12 photos, 43 notes, biblio.   W. W. Elison

1087. Dosey, Herbert W. THE INTERNATIONAL SHIP MASTERS ASSOCIATION. *Inland Seas 1977 33(4): 272-276.* In 1886 a group of Great Lakes ship captains in Buffalo, New York, formed a life insurance association called The Excelsior Marine Benevolent Association. Seven years later the organization, now grown to nine lodges and 900 members, changed its name to The Ship Masters Association. In 1897 it recognized its many Canadian members by changing its name again, to The International Ship Masters Association of the Great Lakes. It continues active as a benevolent and fraternal organization of 11 lodges.
K. J. Bauer

1088. Dreisziger, N. F. THE CAMPAIGN TO SAVE NIAGARA FALLS AND THE SETTLEMENT OF UNITED STATES-CANADIAN DIFFERENCES, 1906-1911. *New York Hist. 1974 55(4): 437-458.* The environmentalist concern about the preservation of Niagara Falls stimulated improvement in United States-Canadian relations. Power plants and tourist-oriented retailers threaten to spoil the natural beauty of Niagara Falls. New York Senator Thomas C. Platt called for the establishment of the International Waterway Commission in 1905. Sir Wilfred Laurier, Canadian Prime Minister and Governor General Albert Henry Grey of Canada combined to negotiate first with the State of New York and then the United States in preserving Niagara Falls in the Boundary Waters Treaty of January, 1909. Primary sources; 3 illus., 8 photos, 43 notes.   A. C. Aimone

1089. Emery, George N. THE ORIGINS OF CANADIAN METHODIST INVOLVEMENT IN THE SOCIAL GOSPEL MOVEMENT 1890-1914. *J. of the Can. Church Hist. Soc. [Canada] 1977 19(1-2): 104-119.* The massive, rapid transformation of Canada in the early 20th century through urbanization, immigration, and industrialization brought about the growth of Methodism and other Christian denominations of the social gospel movement. There were a number of reasons. First was the decline of the evangelical tradition with the growing affluence of Methodists and the development of the higher criticism. Moreover, the strong belief in individual perfectionism evolved into concern about society as a whole. In their nationalism, pietism, optimism about the future of man, and desire to avoid theological controversy, many Methodists saw in the social gospel movement an opportunity to express their concern about the growing problems caused by the modern changes. All these factors helped bring Canadian Methodists into the forefront of the social gospel movement in Canada. Primary and secondary sources; table, 38 notes. This issue is *J. of the Can. Church Hist. Soc.* 1977 19(1-2) and *Bull. of the United Church of Can.* 1977 26.
J. A. Kicklighter

1090. Feaver, George. THE WEBBS IN CANADA: FABIAN PILGRIMS ON THE CANADIAN FRONTIER. *Can. Hist. Rev. [Canada] 1977 58(3): 263-276.* Surveys the thought of Sidney James Webb (1859-1947) and Beatrice Webb (1858-1943) on Canada and Canadians, as revealed by their 1911 diary of a six-week trip across Canada, and by an article written as they were leaving Canada and published in *The Crusade* (September 1911), entitled "Destitution in Canada." They found Canada, a sprawling dominion, in the midst of transition and social change, with "the failings of the capitalist way of life of the parent European stock . . . already evidencing themselves in its youthful North American progeny." 14 notes.   R. V. Ritter

1091. Fulford, Frederick M. J. RECOLLECTIONS OF A MONUMENT SETTER. *Beaver [Canada] 1976 306(4): 10-16.* As a teenager the author worked on the US-Canadian boundary setting team in 1908-12. The earlier line, set in 1875, had deteriorated. Fulford's crew used metal markers, rock-metal cairns, and other permanent materials. Discusses construction and supply problems, as well as contacts with immigrants and farmers along the boundary. 9 illus., map.   D. Chaput

1092. Gooch, John. GREAT BRITAIN AND THE DEFENCE OF CANADA, 1896-1914. *J. of Imperial and Commonwealth Hist. [Great Britain] 1975 3(3): 369-385.* Great Britain's Committee of Imperial Defence, the War Office, and the civil service disagreed on a defense policy for Canada, and generally avoided the issue, 1896-1914.

1093. Isaacson, John A. AMERICAN-SWEDISH HISTORY OF MANY, ILLUSTRATED BY EXPERIENCE. *Swedish Pioneer Hist. Q. 1975 26(4): 247-259.* Autobiography of John A. Isaacson (1892-1974), who emigrated from Sweden to Canada in 1911. He worked at laboring jobs, he tried investing in real estate, attended Minnesota College in Minneapolis (at the end of his second year he was offered a bank position), volunteered for World War I and became a US citizen, studied banking, and went to Chicago in 1927. 2 illus.   K. J. Puffer

1094. Jeffreys-Jones, Rhodri. THE MONTREAL SPY RING OF 1898 AND THE ORIGINS OF "DOMESTIC" SURVEILLANCE IN THE UNITED STATES. *Can. R. of Am. Studies [Canada] 1974 5(2): 119-134.* Chronicles responses by the William McKinley administration to potentially serious espionage by a Spanish "spy ring" at Montreal

during the Spanish-American War. Lyman Gage (1836-1927) directed the wartime American counterintelligence work. In these operations, John Wilkie (1860-1934) was "America's master spy." Wilkie's agents, using questionable methods, dealt with the menace posed by the Spanish "spy ring." Based on Canadian and American archival sources; 54 notes.
H. T. Lovin

1095. Jessop, David. THE COLONIAL STOCK ACT OF 1900: A SYMPTOM OF THE NEW IMPERIALISM? *J. of Imperial and Commonwealth Hist. [Great Britain] 1976 4(2): 154-163.* Passage of the Colonial Stock Act (1900), which allowed British trustees to invest in colonial stock, was the result of pressure from Sir Wilfrid Laurier's government in Canada, which exploited Great Britain's imperialist leanings to improve its trade position.

1096. Lewis, Frank. THE CANADIAN WHEAT BOOM AND PER CAPITA INCOME: NEW ESTIMATES. *J. of Pol. Econ. 1975 83(6): 1249-1257.* Reexamines a 1966 study of the impact of prairie wheat expansion on per capita income growth in Canada (1901-11), coming to very different conclusions.

1097. Matheson, Gwen. NELLIE MCCLUNG. *Can. Dimension 1975 10(8): 42-48.* Provides a biographical sketch of early 20th century feminist Nellie McClung and reviews her book *In Times Like These*, first published in 1915 and recently edited by Veronica Strong-Boag (Toronto: U. of Toronto Pr., 1972).
S

1098. Miller, Carman. ENGLISH CANADIAN OPPOSITION TO THE SOUTH AFRICAN WAR AS SEEN THROUGH THE PRESS. *Can. Hist. R. 1974 55(4): 422-438.* Examines the English Canadian opposition to Canadian participation in the Boer War, 1899-1902, attempting to suggest the intellectual and social pattern of dissent. English Canadian opposition, though neither large nor widespread, found its strongest support among farmers, radical labour, Protestant clergy and anglophobic Canadians notably of Irish and German descent who defended their cause with a mélange of arguments from isolationism to Socialism and Christian pacifism. Based primarily on English language Canadian newspaper sources.
A

1099. Miller, Carman. A PRELIMINARY ANALYSIS OF THE SOCIO-ECONOMIC COMPOSITION OF CANADA'S SOUTH AFRICAN WAR CONTINGENTS. *Social Hist. [Canada] 1975 8(16): 219-237.* Presents a statistical analysis of socioeconomic characteristics of 5,825 of the 7,368 Canadian volunteers for British military service in the South African War, 1899-1902, and reveals they were disproportionately urban, white collar, and British-born. Patriotism probably best explains their motivation, especially since when British fortunes in the war improved an adventure-seeking, more representative, group volunteered: blue collar, Canadian-born, and younger. The analysis of the data is preliminary. It has been cross-tabulated only by regiment for each of the socioeconomic characteristics. The data is retrievable and more complex analyses could be done. Based on attestation papers, North West Mounted Police records, published census, and contemporary newspapers and periodicals; 10 tables, 43 notes.
W. K. Hobson

1100. Nelles, H. V. and Armstrong, Christopher. PRIVATE PROPERTY IN PERIL: ONTARIO BUSINESSMEN AND THE FEDERAL SYSTEM, 1898-1911. *Business Hist. R. 1973 47(2): 158-176.* Economic policy in Canada at the beginning of the 20th century was a struggle between two rival groups within the business community: large scale financiers operating on a national level, and small local businessmen and manufacturers. Unlike the American experience, the local forces were able to use provincial powers successfully to gain the upper hand. Based on documentary materials, private papers, and secondary sources; 27 notes.
C. J. Pusateri

1101. Ramirez, Bruno C. U. S. RESPONSES TO THE CANADIAN INDUSTRIAL DISPUTES INVESTIGATION ACT. *Industrial Relations [Canada] 1974 29(3): 541-557.* The author analyses the impact that the Canadian Industrial Disputes Investigation Act (1907) had in the U.S. His article also tries to show the extent to which the question of arbitration tended to transcend the narrow boundaries of industrial relations practice and acquire a wider political significance.
J

1102. Richard, Bruce. THE NORTH ATLANTIC TRIANGLE AND CHANGES IN THE WHEAT TRADE BEFORE THE GREAT WAR. *Dalhousie Rev. [Canada] 1975 55(2): 263-271.* Canada challenged US dominance of the wheat trade after the turn of the century because of changing economic and social conditions in the United States, booming expansion of Canadian wheat areas geared specifically for the export market, and Great Britain's role as a primary dealer in grain favored Canada. Government interest and support of an orderly development of wheat lands, quality control of exports, and support for transportation facilities played a major role in the Canadian challenge to the United States. The theme of empire self-sufficiency for food also helped the Canadians. 53 notes.
C. Held

1103. Roberts, Wayne. ARTISANS, ARISTOCRATS AND HANDYMEN: POLITICS AND UNIONISM AMONG TORONTO SKILLED BUILDING TRADES WORKERS, 1896-1914. *Labour [Canada] 1976 1: 92-121.* During the pre-World War I building boom, contracting and subcontracting methods, including use of immigrant and unskilled workers, caused marked but diverse alterations to the building trades' artisanal character and engendered varied political responses. Using Toronto carpenters, woodworkers, plumbers, ironworkers, stone and granite cutters, and bricklayers' unions to "sample this diversity," concludes that the greater the retention of artisanal character, the lesser the degree of politicization; the greater the retention of craft consciousness, the lesser the degree of class consciousness. Primary and secondary sources; 154 notes.
W. A. Kearns

1104. Sawula, Lorne W. NOTES ON THE STRATHCONA TRUST. *Can. J. of Hist. of Sport and Physical Educ. 1974 5(1): 56-61.* Sir F. W. Borden, not Lord Strathcona (as noted by most physical education historians), was the major force in the formation and function of the Strathcona Trust fund which provides for physical and military drill instruction in Canadian schools. Borden, the Minister of Militia and Defense for Canada in the early 1900's, proposed the idea to Strathcona, who provided the half-million dollar trust around 1910. The trust still exists and provides about $20,000 annually. Primary sources.
R. A. Smith

1105. Sherrin, P. M. SPANISH SPIES IN VICTORIA, 1898. *BC Studies [Canada] 1977-78 (36): 23-33.* The outbreak of the Spanish-American War in 1898 evoked a British proclamation of neutrality and nonintervention for the Empire. Spanish espionage efforts were mounted in Canada against the United States. One such operation was based in Victoria, British Columbia. American agents closely monitored the situation in Victoria but Canadian, provincial, and Victoria officials gave it little attention. The Spanish agents gathered information about West Coast merchant shipping and military preparations, and fostered fears of Spanish naval raids on the American West Coast and privateer attacks on Yukon gold shipments. The goal was to divert American attention and efforts from the Caribbean theater of operations. Americans were somewhat disquieted by Spanish intelligence gathering and spurious threats, but the activities of the Spanish agents had no discernible effect on the short war. 42 notes.
D. L. Smith

1106. Shields, R. A. THE CANADIAN TARIFF AND THE FRANCO-CANADIAN TREATY NEGOTIATIONS OF 1901-1909: A STUDY IN IMPERIAL RELATIONS. *Dalhousie Rev. [Canada] 1977 57(2): 300-321.* Examines the Canadian demand for more autonomy in foreign relations where they involved Canada's trade and territory, with particular reference to Laurier's administration. The period following the Alaska boundary decision was crucial to the Canadians because of their bitterness over Great Britain's role in that disappointment. William Fielding and Louis Philippe Brodeur were given authority to act for Canada in the negotiations for the tariff arrangement with France in 1907; this marked a clear gain for Canada. Comments on the less-than-harmonious relationship between Fielding and Brodeur. 60 notes.
C. H. Held

1107. Shields, R. A. IMPERIAL POLICY AND CANADIAN-AMERICAN RECIPROCITY, 1909-11. *J. of Imperial and Commonwealth Hist. [Great Britain] 1977 5(2): 151-171.* International trade agreements between the United States and Canada, 1909-11, without British diplomats, proved to be an initial step toward national sovereignty for Canada.

1108. Sugimoto, Howard H. THE VANCOUVER RIOT AND ITS INTERNATIONAL SIGNIFICANCE. *Pacific Northwest Q. 1973 64(4): 163-174*. The Vancouver branch of the Asiatic Exclusion League put on a parade and public meeting on 7 September 1907 to convince officials of the seriousness of anti-Japanese sentiment in British Columbia during a time of depression and high job competition. A riot broke out involving heavy property loss to much of the Japanese community. Despite recriminations from all involved, the occasion became a landmark in Canadian diplomatic history because Britain allowed Canada to enter into direct discussions with foreign powers on questions of Asiatic immigration. Japanese claims were settled and ultimately the and the situation resulted in a spirit of cooperation between the United States and Canada abrogation of the Anglo-Japanese Treaty of Alliance (1902) in 1922. 65 notes.   R. V. Ritter

1109. Thomas, Clara. CANADIAN SOCIAL MYTHOLOGIES IN SARA JEANETTE DUNCAN'S *THE IMPERIALIST*. *J. of Can. Studies [Canada] 1977 12(2): 38-49*. Discusses the novel *The Imperialist* (1904) by Sara Jeanette Duncan. After living outside of Canada for 13 years, she decided to write a novel with the political motif of imperialism, set in a typical town in southern Ontario. Duncan wrote the novel after requesting materials from John Willison, editor of the *Globe* in Toronto, which included all of Sir W. Laurier's speeches and *Globe* editorials dealing with imperial federation. 12 notes.   J. B. Reed

1110. Travis, Paul D. GORE, BRISTOW AND TAFT: REFLECTIONS ON CANADIAN RECIPROCITY, 1911. *Chronicles of Oklahoma 1975 53(2): 212-224*. Attempts by Canada and the United States to negotiate reciprocal trade agreements in 1911 produced considerable reaction from the agricultural Midwest. Favoring the measure was Democratic Senator Thomas Gore of Oklahoma who faced stiff opposition from Republican Senator Joseph Bristow of Kansas. Debate went beyond the tariff issue into the structure of party politics as Bristow led Insurgent Republicans in opposition to President Taft who promoted the compromise agreement. In the election of 1912 Kansas and other Republican strongholds dumped Taft and supported the successful Democratic candidate Woodrow Wilson. Based on primary and secondary sources; 68 notes.   M. L. Tate

1111. Tuck, J. H. UNION AUTHORITY, CORPORATE OBSTINACY, AND THE GRAND TRUNK STRIKE OF 1910. *Can. Hist. Assoc. Hist. Papers [Canada] 1976: 175-192*. The relationship between railroad workers and management in Canada worsened by 1896. In 1910, approximately 3,500 workers participated in a two-week strike against the Grand Trunk Railway. The president of the Grand Trunk Railway resisted implementation of the strike settlement in full. While the Federal Labour Minister acted as a mediator in the strike, his government refused a Royal Commission of inquiry into the company's actions. Despite the strength of the international brotherhoods, concerted union action was prevented because two unions and international representatives were involved in the situation. Based on King, Laurier and Labour Department Papers, union proceedings, and secondary sources; 90 notes.
                                                        G. E. Panting

1112. Vipond, M. BLESSED ARE THE PEACEMAKERS: THE LABOUR QUESTION IN CANADIAN SOCIAL GOSPEL FICTION. *J. of Can. Studies 1975 10(3): 32-43*. Discusses the ideological evolution of social gospel Christianity in Canada in the 1890's as a reaction to increasing industrialization, including the issue of Christian responsibility toward labor.

1113. Whitney, Harriet. SIR GEORGE C. GIBBONS, CANADIAN DIPLOMAT, AND CANADIAN-AMERICAN BOUNDARY WATER RESOURCES, 1905-1910. *Am. Rev. of Can. Studies 1973 3(1): 65-75*. Discusses the role of Canadian diplomat Sir George Christie Gibbons in maritime law disputes between the United States and Canada, 1905-10, involving the water resources of the Great Lakes and Niagara Falls.

1114. Whitney, Harriet E. SIR GEORGE GIBBONS, CANADIAN DIPLOMAT, AND THE BOUNDARY WATERS TREATY. *Inland Seas 1973 29(2): 99-109*. Gibbons, Chairman of the International Waterways Commission after 1905, was instrumental in negotiating the Boundary Waters Treaty of 1909. Although the American Secretary of State, Elihu Root, wished only a treaty to preserve Niagara Falls, Gibbons through patient negotiation secured equal rights for Canada in the Great Lakes and international rivers. Based on official documents and personal papers; 77 notes.   K. J. Bauer

8. ACHIEVEMENT OF NATIONHOOD, 1914-1945

General

1115.   Beck, Jeanne M.   HENRY SOMERVILLE AND SOCIAL RE-FORM: HIS CONTRIBUTION TO CANADIAN CATHOLIC SO-CIAL THOUGHT.   *Study Sessions: Can. Catholic Hist. Assoc. 1975 42: 91-108.* Henry Somerville, editor of the *Catholic Register* 1933-53, provided an impetus for his generation through his contributions to the development of Catholic social thought and action in Canada by combining the influences of Edwardian England and his own Canadian immigrant experiences since his arrival in 1915.

1116.   Brown, Lorne.   PEACE AND HARMONY: BREAKING DOWN MYTHS OF CANADIAN LABOR HISTORY.   *Can. Dimension 1973 9(5): 11-14.* Summarizes labor history in Canada over the last 50 years. Concentrates on violent incidents to depict inevitable violence in strikes. Includes a long interview with one of the leaders of the 1919 Winnipeg General Strike. Defends the more radical strike leaders and denigrates employers, nonstrikers, moderates, and the public. Summarizes a federal committee's report. 25 photos.   W. B. Whitham

1117.   Cain, Louis P.   UNFOULING THE PUBLIC'S NEST: CHICAGO'S SANITARY DIVERSION OF LAKE MICHIGAN WA-TER.   *Technology and Culture 1974 15(4): 594-613.* In the 1890's the Sanitary District of Chicago began to flush the city's sewage into the Mississippi drainage area with water diverted from the Great Lakes. This incurred "legal resistance over the next 40 years from the War Department, other Great Lakes states, and Canada." By 1930, faced with a court decree limiting the amount of water it could divert from Lake Michigan, the Sanitary District had shifted to sewage disposal by the activated sludge method. Illus., 45 notes.   C. O. Smith

1118.   Cole, Douglas.   PAUL RAND'S WEST.   *Beaver [Canada] 1976 307(1): 22.* German-born artist Paul Rand was active in the 1930's and 1940's. A professional commercial artist, he also painted in private. He did many landscapes, but he is most remembered for strong laboring and farming scenes, the most famous being "Coal Diggers" and "Picking the Zucca." No Rand works are in public collections. 4 illus.
   D. Chaput

1119.   Duffy, Dennis.   ART-HISTORY: CHARLES WILLIAM JEF-FREYS AS CANADA'S CURATOR.   *J. of Can. Studies [Canada] 1976 11(4): 3-18.* Charles William Jeffreys (1869-1951), a popular illustrator in Canada, 1920's-50, illustrated children's books, the popular press, and historical texts for public schools.

1120.   Hillmer, Norman.   PROFILE OF O. D. SKELTON.   *Int. Perspectives [Canada] 1973 (September-October): 46-49.* O. D. Skelton, Under-Secretary of State for External Affairs, 1925-41, influenced Canadian foreign relations and national security and was responsible for establishing the modern External Affairs Department.

1121.   Hinz, Evelyn J.   D. H. LAWRENCE AND "SOMETHING CALLED 'CANADA.' "   *Dalhousie R. [Canada] 1974 54(2): 240-250.* When seeking a place of freedom, the liberated characters in *Lady Chatterley's Lover* (1927) turn to Canada. Lawrence had never visited Canada, yet he used Canada as a refuge for his characters in an earlier novel, *The White Peacock* (1911). Canada also receives negative treatment since those of his characters who go there show a loss of identity and sense of security which traditionalist Great Britain offers. Lawrence's interest and knowledge of Canada came originally through acquaintances in Saskatchewan. The subject appears again in *John Thomas and Lady Jane* (1972). 11 notes.   C. Held

1122.   Hurford, Grace Gibberd.   MISSIONARY SERVICE IN CHINA.   *J. of the Can. Church Hist. Soc. [Canada] 1977 19(3-4): 177-181.* A personal recollection by a Canadian missionary-educator in China. During her years of service she was a nurse, English instructor, and Christian teacher. Her work offered many rewarding experiences, but from 1937 on she and her fellow workers had to contend with the problems caused by the Japanese invasion. She was injured only once by Japanese bombs, but the danger was omnipresent. Consequently, her work in China was disrupted by the necessity to move on several occasions and by the orders of the Chinese government to close all schools. Her service in China ended with the conclusion of World War II.
   J. A. Kicklighter

1123.   Jones, Kevin G.   DEVELOPMENTS IN AMATEURISM AND PROFESSIONALISM IN EARLY 20TH CENTURY CANA-DIAN SPORT.   *J. of Sport Hist. 1975 2(1): 29-40.* During 1900-20, interest in amateur sports helped inspire an increase in Canadian professional teams, including hockey, baseball, lacrosse, and later football. The development of amateur associations in Canada is described, and developments within several of the assocations are emphasized. 64 notes.
   M. Kaufman

1124.   Kasurak, Peter.   AMERICAN FOREIGN POLICY OFFI-CIALS AND CANADA, 1927-1941: A LOOK THROUGH BUREAU-CRATIC GLASSES.   *Int. J. [Canada] 1977 32(3): 544-558.* Examines the background and views of State Department and Commerce Department officials in the US legation at Ottawa. Based on the author's recently completed Ph.D. thesis; 11 notes.   R. V. Kubicek

1125.   Kresl, Peter Karl.   BEFORE THE DELUGE: CANADIANS ON FOREIGN OWNERSHIP, 1920-1955.   *Am. Rev. of Can. Studies 1976 6(1): 86-125.* Discusses the growth, extent, and impact of US investment and ownership in Canadian industries and resources during 1920-55.

1126.   Kresl, Peter.   THE "NEW NATIONALISM" AND ECO-NOMIC RATIONALITY.   *Am. Rev. of Can. Studies 1974 4(1): 2-19.* Examines the conflict between Canadian nationalism and economic rationality, pre-World War I-1960's; discusses three political viewpoints, Continentalist, Liberal-Nationalist, and Radical-Nationalist, and suggests that power in private sector institutions may hold a key to resolution of the conflict. 28 notes.

1127.   Lappage, Ronald S.   SPORT AS AN EXPRESSION OF WESTERN AND MARITIME DISCONTENT IN CANADA BE-TWEEN THE WARS.   *Can. J. of Hist. of Sport and Physical Educ. [Canada] 1977 8(1): 50-71.* Examines the reform movement in sports in the Prairie and Atlantic Provinces as a rebellion against the domination of Quebec and Ontario; discusses social acceptance of hostility and aggression in sports, 1920-40.

1128.   Lavigne, Marie et al.   LA FÉDÉRATION NATIONALE SAINT-JEAN-BAPTISTE ET LES REVENDICATIONS FÉMI-NISTES AU DÉBUT DU XXᵉ SIÈCLE [The Saint John the Baptist National Federation and feminist demands at the start of the 20th century].   *R. d'hist. de l'Amérique française [Canada] 1975 29(3): 353-373.* Surveys the history of the Fédération Nationale Saint-Jean-Baptiste from 1907-33, and discusses the role of its founder, Marie Gérin-Lajoie (1867-1945). In order to develop in French-Canadian society, the Fédération, a feminist group, had to make alliances with the Catholic clergy and compromises with the prevailing ideology. While calling for increased political rights for women, it supported the integrity of the family and the traditional female familial role. The organization did not succeed in synthesizing these paradoxical interests, and its influence declined after 1933. Based on documents in the Archives de la Fédération Nationale Saint-Jean-Baptiste (Montréal), Archives de la Communauté des Soeurs de Notre-Dame-du-Bon Conseil (Montréal), and secondary sources; 31 notes.   L. B. Chan

1129.   MacPherson, G. R. I.   THE CO-OPERATIVE UNION OF CANADA AND POLITICS, 1909-31.   *Can. Hist. R. 1973 54(2): 152-175.* Examines why the leaders of the Co-operative Union became suspicious of political action for both themselves and cooperative institutions. The disenchantment grew out of the Rochdale emphasis on political neutrality, the union leaders' experience with local politics, the Progressive movement, and the Liberal and Communist parties. Based on the collected papers and publications of the Co-operative Union of Canada and the papers of the Communist Party of Canada.   J

1130. Morrow, Dan. THE STRATHCONA TRUST IN ONTARIO, 1919-1939. *Can. J. of Hist. of Sport and Physical Educ. [Canada] 1977 8(1): 72-90.* Despite its paramilitary nature the Strathcona Trust was largely responsible for the progress in physical education curricula in Canadian public schools, 1919-39.

1131. Murray, David. GARRISONING THE CARIBBEAN: A CHAPTER IN CANADIAN MILITARY HISTORY. *Revista/Review Interamericana [Puerto Rico] 1977 7(1): 73-86.* During both World Wars, Canada's soldiers have provided garrison duty for Great Britain in the Caribbean, freeing English troops to serve in Europe. 56 notes.   J. A. Lewis

1132. Neatby, H. Blair. MACKENZIE KING AND FRENCH CANADA. *J. of Can. Studies [Canada] 1976 11(1): 3-13.* William Lyon Mackenzie King (1874-1950), as Liberal Party leader, understood that French Canada was a society with a collective identity. He developed an organizational structure for ascertaining the political situation within that society. His closest and most trusted colleague was always a French Canadian, first Ernest Lapointe and then Louis St. Laurent. This arrangement goes far to explain the dominance of the Federal Liberal Party in Quebec during King's years as its leader. Based on King Papers and secondary sources; 22 notes.   G. E. Panting

1133. Nicholson, G. W. L. ARCHER FORTESCUE DUGUID, 1887-1976. *Can. Hist. Assoc. Hist Papers [Canada] 1976: 268-271.* Obituary of Archer Fortescue Duguid, director of the Historical Section of the Canadian General Staff, 1921-45, and official historian of the Canadian Expeditionary Force, 1945-47. He was a founder of the Heraldry Society of Canada and planned the mural decoration for the Memorial Chamber in the Peace Tower at Ottawa. Colonel Duguid was noted for his work on regimental battle honors and battlefield memorials.   G. E. Panting

1134. Oden, Jack P. CHARLES HOLMES HERTY AND THE BIRTH OF THE SOUTHERN NEWSPRINT PAPER INDUSTRY, 1927-1940. *J. of Forest Hist. 1977 21(2): 76-89.* Early sources of newsprint for American newspapers were forests of northeastern United States and Canada. Paper mills in those regions could produce enough newsprint for both countries. Pine trees of southeastern United States were considered unsuitable for newsprint because they were presumed to have a high resin content. Charles Holmes Herty (d. 1938) was a prominent Georgia chemist who discovered that the presumption about the unsuitability of pines for newsprint was erroneous. He organized and ran a research laboratory that worked out a process for making newsprint from pines. Primary and secondary sources; 11 photos, 64 notes.   F. N. Egerton

1135. Parks, M. G. THE LETTERS OF FREDERICK PHILIP GROVE. *Dalhousie Rev. [Canada] 1976 56(3): 574-579.* Review article prompted by *The Letters of Frederick Philip Grove* (Toronto: U. of Toronto Pr., 1976). This is the only edition of all the known letters written by Grove during his years in Canada, 1912-48. Desmond Pacey, the editor, died before this work was published. For years Pacey had decried the lack of "genuine scholarly research" concerning Canadian authors and it is fitting that this volume should be a "first." The unfounded condescension directed toward editors of scholarly materials prevents a large body of such materials in Canadian literature.   C. Held

1136. Patterson, R. S. and Wilson, Leroy R. THE INFLUENCE OF THE DANISH FOLK HIGH SCHOOL IN CANADA. *Paedagogica Historica [Belgium] 1974 14(1): 64-79.* In the three decades following World War I, the Danish folk school concept had a significant impact on the growth of adult education in Canada, beginning in the western part of the nation and proceeding eastward.   J. M. McCarthy

1137. Ross, Brian. JAMES EUSTACE PURDIE: THE STORY OF PENTECOSTAL THEOLOGICAL EDUCATION. *J. of the Can. Church Hist. Soc. 1975 17(4): 94-103.* Describes the foundations of theo-

logical education in the Pentecostal Assemblies of Canada (PAOC). Evangelical, fundamentalist, charismatic, and sectarian, PAOC rather feared theology with its connotations of incessant, cold argument. Yet Pentecostals wanted individuals knowledgeable in biblical subjects to preach and teach. Such a task fell to an evangelical ex-Anglican, James Eustace Purdie, selected to head the Pentecostal Bible School, established in Winnipeg in 1925. Although beginning with a faculty of three and student body of 33, the school under Purdie's direction was very successful. In 1930 the school was moved to Toronto near the church's headquarters, but financial exigencies forced its return to Winnipeg in 1932. There Purdie maintained his leadership of the school for the next 18 years, training individuals of all backgrounds in a biblical, fundamentalist, premillennial, practical atmosphere. Based on primary and secondary sources; 19 notes.   J. A. Kicklighter

1138. Russell, Hilary. ALL THAT GLITTERS: A MEMORIAL TO OTTAWA'S CAPITOL THEATRE AND ITS PREDECESSORS. *Can. Historic Sites 1975 (13): 5-125.* This paper is one result of the 1970 destruction of Ottawa's Capitol Theatre, a movie palace built in 1920. Movie palaces were those gigantic, extravagantly embellished theatres built between about 1914 and 1932 in which vaudeville and motion picture entertainment was presented. One movie palace, the Capitol in Ottawa, is examined in terms of its construction, decoration, equipment and ownership. The investigation includes a general discussion of the movie palace phenomenon and the major developments in the evolution of motion picture exhibition that contributed to the building of movie palaces. Certain American prototypes are considered, as many Canadian palaces were built by American-controlled theatre circuits, designed by American architects, and exhibited American movies.   J

1139. Salaff, Stephen. THE DIARY AND THE CENOTAPH: RACIAL AND ATOMIC FEVER. *Can. Dimension [Canada] 1978 13(3): 8-11.* Discusses excerpts from the diary of former Canadian Prime Minister William Lyon MacKenzie King dealing with Canada's participation in the atomic bomb enterprise of the 1940's, and the racist (specifically, anti-Japanese) policies carried out during his 1921-48 administration.

1140. Smith, Donald B. THE BELANEYS OF BRANDON HILLS: GREY OWL'S CANADIAN COUSINS. *Beaver [Canada] 1975 306(3): 46-50.* Biography of Grey Owl, born Archibald Stansfeld Belaney in England. He moved to Canada in 1906 and concocted a new identity, claiming he was Scotch and Apache. Until his death in 1938 he was a well-known spokesman for various conservation movements. Discusses the family connections of Grey Owl in England and in Canada, his successful attempt at covering his identity tracks, his success as an early environmentalist. 6 illus.   D. Chaput

1141. Torrelli, Maurice. CHARLES MAURRAS ET LE NATIONALISME CANADIEN FRANÇAIS [Charles Maurras and French Canadian nationalism]. *Action Natl. [Canada] 1977 67(2): 102-113.* Despite the lack of any direct connection between the two, there are many similarities in the thought of French royalist nationalist Charles Maurras and French Canadian nationalist Lionel Groulx. Both founded journals entitled *L'Action française.* Both emphasized the French national heritage, favoring a corporative rather than an individualistic view of society. Both emphasized the concept of a nation as a natural society founded on blood, history, faith, and culture, repudiating the liberal contract theory. Both questioned the value of democratic forms of government, and asserted that only history could provide the basis for the discovery and verification of natural laws of society which individualism neglected. Covers 1910-40. Primary and secondary sources; 39 notes.   A. W. Novitsky

1142. Trofimenkoff, Susan Mann. HENRI BOURASSA AND "THE WOMAN QUESTION." *J. of Can. Studies 1975 10(4): 3-11.* Discusses the opposition of writer Henry Bourassa to feminism, woman suffrage and divorce in Canada, 1913-25.

1143. Vanger, Max. MEMOIRS OF A RUSSIAN IMMIGRANT. *Am. Jewish Hist. Q. 1973 63(1): 57-88.* The author, a retired businessman, recounts his experiences since his arrival in Canada before World War I. He worked as a shoemaker, junk peddler, cloth cutter, fish merchant, cattle buyer, lumber dealer, shoe store operator, millinery and sweater manufacturer, and finally garage operator and owner in New York City.   F. Rosenthal

1144. West, J. Thomas. PHYSICAL FITNESS, SPORT, AND THE FEDERAL GOVERNMENT 1909 TO 1954. *Can. J. of Hist. of Sport and Physical Educ. 1973 4(2): 26-42.* The Canadian government has cautiously assisted physical fitness and sport, leaving most problems to the private sector. Federal programs for physical fitness have generally encouraged amateur sport, and cost-sharing arrangements have been worked out with the provinces. Mentions the Strathcona trust fund (1909), the Provincial Recreation Movement Programs of the 1930's, and the National Physical Fitness Act of 1943. Federal interest was strong when military preparedness or international prestige were concerned. Based on primary sources; 60 notes. R. A. Smith

1145. Wittlingern, Carlton O. THE ADVANCE OF WESLEYAN HOLINESS AMONG THE BRETHREN IN CHRIST SINCE 1910. *Mennonite Q. Rev. 1976 50(1): 21-36.* In 1910 the Brethren in Christ, located mainly in Canada and the North Central States, adopted in their general conference a statement embodying the Wesleyan perfectionism. Charles Baker, Bishop of Nottawa District, Ontario, objected to the view that the sanctified no longer had inner desire to sin. No one challenged his view until 1916. In that year, the perfectionists gained control of the *Visitor* and controversy followed. By 1930 the perfectionists were seeking change in the 1910 statement to say "second work of grace." Following this there developed holiness camp meetings. 75 notes. E. E. Eminhizer

1146. Wrong, Hume. THE CANADA-UNITED STATES RELA-TIONSHIP 1927/1951. *Int. J. [Canada] 1976 31(3): 529-545.* Contains lengthy statements on relations between the two countries. Editorial comment by John W. Holmes (U. of Toronto). Wrong (1894-1954), a former senior Canadian diplomat, was ambassador to the United States, 1946-53. 6 notes. R. V. Kubicek

1147. —. [PRIME MINISTERIAL CHARACTER: ASSESSING POLITICAL LEADERSHIP].
Courtney, John C. PRIME MINISTERIAL CHARACTER: AN EX-AMINATION OF MACKENZIE KING'S POLITICAL LEAD-ERSHIP. *Can. J. of Pol. Sci. 1976 9(1): 77-100.* Examines the Canadian prime minister's abilities through the model of presidential character developed by James David Barber in *The Presidential Character: Predicting Performance in the White House* (Englewood Cliffs, 1972). 84 notes.
Esberey, J. E. PRIME MINISTERIAL CHARACTER: AN ALTER-NATIVE VIEW. *Can. J. of Pol. Sci. 1976 9(1): 101-106.* 27 notes.
Courtney, John C. "AN ALTERNATIVE VIEW" OF MACKENZIE KING: A REJOINDER. *Can. J. of Pol. Sci. 1976 9(2): 308-309.* 2 notes. R. V. Kubicek

1148. —. [THIRD PARTIES IN CANADA]. *Can. J. of Pol. Sci. 1973 6(3): 399-460.*
White, Graham. ONE-PARTY DOMINANCE AND THIRD PAR-TIES: THE PINARD THEORY RECONSIDERED, pp. 399-421. Tests Maurice Pinard's theories about the rise of third parties, as expressed by Pinard in a previous article (see abstract 5:1226) and in his *The Rise of a Third Party: A Study in Crisis Politics* (Englewood Cliffs, N.J.: Prentice-Hall, 1971). Examines the United Farmers of Ontario, The United Farmers of Alberta, and the Social Credit Party of Alberta. 4 tables, 88 notes.
Blais, André. THIRD PARTIES IN CANADIAN PROVINCIAL POLITICS, pp. 422-438. Examines Pinard's hypothesis that one-party dominance is a necessary but not sufficient condition for the rise of third parties. 4 tables, 38 notes.
Pinard, Maurice. THIRD PARTIES IN CANADA REVISITED: A REJOINDER AND ELABORATION OF THE THEORY OF ONE-PARTY DOMINANCE, pp. 439-460. Offers a more general theory, of which one-party dominance is said to be a subclass. 2 tables, 56 notes. R. V. Kubicek

World War I

1149. Bercuson, David J. WESTERN LABOUR RADICALISM AND THE ONE BIG UNION: MYTHS AND REALITIES. *J. of Can. Studies 1974 9(2): 3-11.* Western labor radicals adopted socialist political action and industrial unionism. The One Big Union (O.B.U.) was not an industrial union and its leaders tried to discourage labor parliamentary activity. It was a tangential movement rather than a child of western labor radicalism. Based on Public Archives of Canada and of Manitoba, departmental reports, union proceedings, newspapers, secondary works; 51 notes. G. E. Panting

1150. Boudreau, Joseph A. INTERNING CANADA'S "ENEMY ALIENS," 1914-1919. *Can.: An Hist. Mag. 1974 2(1): 15-28.* At the outbreak of World War I, roughly 200,000 "Austrians," mainly of Uk-rainian descent, resided in Canada. Until the government released or paroled them, they constituted the majority of enemy aliens interned. The main camps were at Amherst, Nova Scotia; old Fort Henry at Kingston, Ontario; Kapuskasing, Ontario; and Vernon, British Columbia. Administration of the internment camps was unimaginative and bureaucratic. Based on primary materials in the Public Archives of Canada; 8 illus., 24 notes. D. B. Smith

1151. Buckley, Suzann. ATTEMPTS AT IMPERIAL ECONOMIC CO-OPERATION, 1912-1918: SIR ROBERT BORDEN'S ROLE. *Can. Hist. R. 1974 55(3): 292-306.* Examines Sir Robert Borden's lack of cooperation (1912-18) with schemes for Empire economic unity, especially his avoidance of the issues of British tariff preferences and of imperial self-sufficiency in raw materials. Based on British Colonial Office and Cabinet documents, and on Canadian and British private papers. A

1152. Buckley, Suzann C. SIR GEORGE FOSTER'S "IMPERIAL JUNKET": THE FAILURE TO PROMOTE IMPERIAL ECO-NOMIC ORGANIZATION, 1912-1917. *Am. Rev. of Can. Studies 1973 3(2): 14-29.* Discusses Canadian Imperial Conference member Sir George Foster's unsuccessful attempt to persuade the British government to abandon its free trade policy in favor of extending tariff preferences to nations of the British Empire, during 1912-17.

1153. Dodds, Ronald. LONG BRANCH: CANADA'S FIRST FLY-ING SCHOOL. *Can. Geographical J. 1974 88(4): 22-29.*

1154. Eagle, John A. SIR ROBERT BORDEN, UNION GOVERN-MENT AND RAILWAY NATIONALIZATION. *J. of Can. Studies 1975 10(4): 59-66.* Discusses Prime Minister Robert Borden's program of nationalization of railroads in Canada, 1915-19.

1155. Ellis, Frank H. CANADA'S FIRST MILITARY AERO-PLANE. *Beaver [Canada] 1974 305(2): 48-53.* In 1914, Captain Ernest L. Janney, the first Provincial Commander of the Canadian Aviation Corps, was allotted $5,000 to purchase the Corps' first airplane, a second-hand Burgess-Dunne Seaplane. After an adventurous and delayed delivery flight from Marblehead, Massachusetts, to Quebec City, the plane was shipped to England, where it was retired and finally sold for scrap. 7 illus., map. D. Heermans

1156. Hyatt, A. M. J. SIR ARTHUR CURRIE. *Canada 1975 2(3): 4-15.* General Currie's (1875-1933) brilliant military career in World War I became controversial when the former Minister of Militia and Defence, Sir Sam Hughes (1853-1921) accused Currie of needlessly sacrificing Canadian lives. Actually, Currie constantly worked to reduce casualties and to increase the fighting efficiency of his various commands, but his unpopular image was strengthened by his formal demeanor. 7 photos, 26 notes, biblio. W. W. Elison

1157. Larsen, Lawrence H. THE REACTION TO A SCHOLARLY PAPER. *North Dakota Q. 1976 44(4): 67-71.* Author discusses the unprecedented and unexpected reaction to a paper which he presented in 1975 before the Northern Great Plains History Conference in which he examined the 1919 plan put forth by the US Army to defend the United States from unspecified invaders who might be coming from Canada through North Dakota.

1158. Larsen, Lawrence H. THE UNITED STATES ARMY'S 1919 CONTINGENCY PLAN TO DEFEND NORTH DAKOTA AGAINST AN UNSPECIFIED INVADER FROM CANADA. *North Dakota Hist. 1976 43(4): 22-27.* In 1919 the Army Corps of Engineers, under the direction of Colonel Clarence O. Sherrill, developed plans to protect the US boundary with Canada from invasion between Northgate, in western North Dakota, and the approaches to Glacier National Park some 500 miles away in Montana. Despite no possibility of an invasion from Canada, Sherrill ordered his subordinates to construct contingency plans, evidently in an effort to enhance the scope and influence of his command. The resultant plans were based on sketchy, sometimes inaccurate, and even absurd explorations of the terrain involved. Some of the information was obtained through Canadian official sources. The plans were completed and filed in Washington. They came to light only recently. Based on files in the Kansas City Archives and Records Center.   N. Lederer

1159. Morton, Desmond. POLLING THE SOLDIER VOTE: THE OVERSEAS CAMPAIGN IN THE CANADIAN GENERAL ELECTION OF 1917. *J. of Can. Studies 1975 10(4): 39-58.* Discusses the voting preferences of Canadian soldiers in France and Great Britain during World War I, emphasizing political campaign issues of the 1917 general election.

1160. Morton, Desmond. THE SHORT, UNHAPPY LIFE OF THE 41ST BATTALION CEF. *Queen's Q. [Canada] 1974 81(1): 70-80.* The 41st Canadian Expeditionary Force was the second French Canadian battalion to be sent overseas during the First World War and its story lends poignant insight into divisive forces at work in Canadian society prior to the war's outbreak. The Battalion's experiences symbolized the failure of Canada's military forces to attract competent French Canadians in the pre-war era and exemplifies a recurrent military problem in Canada. Based on printed and manuscript sources. 27 notes.
J. A. Casada

1161. Morton, Desmond. SIR WILLIAM OTTER AND INTERNMENT OPERATIONS IN CANADA DURING THE FIRST WORLD WAR. *Can. Hist. R. 1974 55(1): 32-58.* During World War I, more than 8,500 German, Austrian, and Turkish subjects were interned in Canada. Examines the work of the director of internment operations amidst the cross-pressures of official reluctance to act and a rising hysteria of anti-alien feeling. Based on records of the Canadian Departments of Justice and of Militia & Defence, and on the newly available papers of General Sir William Otter; 100 notes.   A

1162. Samardžić, Dragana. ZASTAVE DOBROVOLJACA IZ SEVERNE AMERIKE 1917-1918 GOD [Flags of the volunteers from North America, 1917-1918]. *Vesnik Vojnog Muzeja-Beograd [Yugoslavia] 1974 (19-20): 101-120.* The military museum in Belgrade contains World War I flags carried by volunteer fighters consisting of Yugoslav emigrants in the United States and Canada. The flags can be divided into three groups: 1) military flags carried by combatants from North America, 2) flags of different societies (mainly *Sokols*) which organized the recruiting and expeditions of the volunteers, and 3) American flags which were carried beside the flags belonging to the volunteers and various societies. Describes all the flags and insignias carried and worn by Yugoslav volunteers. 14 photos, 35 notes.   A. C. Niven

1163. Smith, Donald B. THE 1919 ROYAL VISIT. *Alberta Hist. [Canada] 1977 25(2): 9-14.* In late summer of 1919, Edward, Prince of Wales, made a three-month tour of Canada. From New Brunswick to British Columbia he was enthusiastically received. His tour was such a success because of Canada's tremendous sacrifice during World War I. His popularity was at its peak, however; from 1919 on, Canada became increasingly independent in her relations with the British Empire. 4 illus., 13 notes.   D. Chaput

1164. Thompson, John H. PERMANENTLY WASTEFUL BUT IMMEDIATELY PROFITABLE: PRAIRIE AGRICULTURE AND THE GREAT WAR. *Can. Hist. Assoc. Hist. Papers [Canada] 1976: 193-206.* During World War I, the Dominion Department of Agriculture encouraged Canadian farmers to grow cereals but also to abandon good techniques. Tariffs and transportation policies did not help to prevent rising agricultural production costs. Rather than retire debts, farmers

expanded their holdings, though they did not diversify production. Therefore, the war resulted in greater concentration upon cereal growing with declining efficiency. Based on Borden, Crerar and Dunning Papers, provincial and private archives; secondary sources, 65 notes.
G. E. Panting

1165. Wong, George G. CLASS STRUGGLE AND THE WINNIPEG GENERAL STRIKE. *Bull. of the Soc. for the Study of Labour Hist. 1975 (30): 80-85.* Reviews David Jay Beruson's *Confrontation at Winnipeg: Labour Industrial Relations and the General Strike* (Montreal: McGill-Queens U. Press, 1974) and the social structure of industrial relations. 3 notes.   L. L. Athey

The Twenties

1166. Barratt, Glynn. JOSEPH-FIDÈLE BERNARD: *ON THE BERING SEA FRONTIER* (1921-1922). *Polar Record [Great Britain] 1977 18(115): 341-349.* During a period of struggle in Chukotka, USSR, 1921-22, when the Soviet government was attempting to cut off relations between the Chukchi natives of the area and Canadian and American traders following the Russian Revolution, Joseph-Fidèle Bernard, a Canadian trader in guns, maintained trade relations and left a diary of his other activities.

1167. Bercuson, David Jay. THE ONE BIG UNION IN WASHINGTON. *Pacific Northwest Q. 1978 69(3): 127-134.* Traces the development of the One Big Union movement in the Pacific Northwest (particularly in Washington) whereby laborers in Canada and the United States would join hands in a common effort. While leftist groups such as the Industrial Workers of the World branded the movement as nonrevolutionary, leaders of the mainstream American Federation of Labor attempted to undercut its influence during 1919. The AFL's secretary Frank Morrison worked behind the scenes in the state of Washington and successfully discredited the movement which never established strong grass roots support. Primary sources; 2 photos, 26 notes.
M. L. Tate

1168. Chevrier, Bernard. LA POLITIQUE ISOLATIONNISTE DU CANADA DE 1919 A 1921 [The isolationist policy of Canada from 1919 to 1921]. *Rev. de l'U. d'Ottawa [Canada] 1976 46(2): 234-241.* After World War I, Canadians wished to assert their diplomatic independence and avoid entanglements abroad. Highlights Canadian opposition to Article X of the Versailles Treaty and the renewal of the Anglo-Japanese Pact as well as the effects of Canada's diplomatic maneuvers. Primary and secondary sources; note, biblio.   M. L. Frey

1169. Crone, Ray H. THE UNKNOWN AIR FORCE. *Saskatchewan Hist. [Canada] 1977 30(1): 1-17.* An air training school for Chinese pilots and aeronautical engineers was operated in Saskatoon from May 1919 until mid-1922. The King Wah Aviation field, known to Saskatonians as "the Chinese airfield" was founded to aid the armies of Dr. Sun Yat-Sen's Nationalists. The first instructor, Douglas Fraser, of the Royal Air Force, taught a class of six starting in July 1919. Fraser was the brother-in-law of a Mr. Lee, an ardent member of the Chinese Nationalist League. Lee's friend, Stanley Bring Mah, was also active in the founding of the air school. Fraser's successor as instructor was Lt. Harry Lobb, a partner in Stan McClelland's aviation business. The first graduate of this school was Y. M. Lim On. 6 photos, 49 notes.   C. Held

1170. Davis, Ann. THE WEMBLEY CONTROVERSY IN CANADIAN ART. *Can. Hist. R. 1973 54(1): 48-74.* The Wembley controversy occurred when Canada was invited to participate in the 1923 British Empire Exhibition at Wembley in London, England. Conservative painters had traditionally gravitated to the Royal Canadian Academy, and modernist artists to the National Gallery of Canada. As members of the two principal artistic institutions, they competed for representation at Wembley. Examines the history of both institutions to show that the conflict was as much an "institutional power-play" as a "division of taste" and style. Based on unpublished documents in the National Gallery of Canada, the Archives of the Province of Ontario, and the Public Archives of Canada, and on private papers.   A. R. Shipton

1171. Dyck, Peter J. THE DIARY OF ANNA BAERG. *Mennonite Life 1973 28(4): 121-125.* Anna Baerg and other Russian Mennonites emigrated to Canada after the Russian Revolution; excerpts from her diary, 1917-23, detail Russian life, the Revolution, and the trip to Canada.

1172. Ellis, Frank H. FLYING DUTCHMAN OF THE SKIES. *Can. Geographical J. 1973 87(6): 22-27.* The place of two Junker mono-planes in Canadian aviation history in the 1920's.   S

1173. Epp, Frank H. 1923: THE BEGINNINGS OF THE GREAT MIGRATION. *Mennonite Life 1973 28(4): 101-103.* Economic depression and cholera in the Ukraine inspired a group of Russian Mennonites to begin immigration to Canada, a country ripe for settlement.

1174. Esberey, J. E. PERSONALITY AND POLITICS: A NEW LOOK AT THE KING-BYNG DISPUTE. *Can. J. of Pol. Sci. 1973 6(1): 37-55.* A psychoanalytic study attempts to account for the clash between Canadian prime minister William Lyon Mackenzie King (1874-1950) and the governor general, Lord Byng (1862-1935), in 1926 over the latter's constitutional role in accepting or rejecting the advice of ministers of the crown. Based on primary sources; 56 notes.

R. V. Kubicek

1175. Frank, David. THE CAPE BRETON COAL INDUSTRY AND THE RISE AND FALL OF THE BRITISH EMPIRE STEEL CORPORATION. *Acadiensis: J. of the Hist. of the Atlantic Region [Canada] 1977 7(1): 3-34.* Factors such as the concentration and centralization of capital in Central Canada deepened Canadian regional disparities in the early 20th century. The results are seen clearly in industrial Cape Breton, which produced about half of Canada's coal by 1914. The Canadian national economic structure favored Cape Breton as a supplier of raw materials and labor. A viable regional economy could not develop, as the rise and fall of the British Empire Steel Corporation in the 1920's demonstrates. 99 notes.   D. F. Chard

1176. Fraser, Nancy W. THE DEVELOPMENT OF REALISM IN CANADIAN LITERATURE DURING THE 1920'S. *Dalhousie Rev. [Canada] 1977 57(2): 287-299.* Discusses realism, Canadian authors and early critics such as Thomas Marquis, Pelham Edgar, Archibald MacMechan, J. D. Logan, Donald French, Lionel Stevenson, and George Bugnet. Three 1920's novels which brought a new approach to realism receive special attention: *Grain* (Robert Stead), *Wild Geese* (Martha Ostenso), and *Settlers of the Marsh* (Frederick Philop Grove). 19 notes.

C. H. Held

1177. George, Benjamin. THE FRENCH-CANADIAN CONNECTION: WILLA CATHER AS A CANADIAN WRITER. *Western Am. Literature 1976 11(3): 249-261.* Although Willa Cather has appeared to be a distinctively American writer, she also held a close affinity with Canadian ideals and attitudes. The development of these ideals and attitudes is shown more clearly in her work after World War I, and reached its peak in her novel *Shadows on the Rock* (1931).

M. Genung

1178. Godler, Zlata. DOCTORS AND THE NEW IMMIGRANTS. *Can. Ethnic Studies [Canada] 1977 9(1): 6-17.* Expands upon H. E. MacDermot's thesis that the Canadian medical profession was politically active both before and after the Department of Health's establishment in 1919. This is especially noticeable in immigrant legislation. Revealing in their journals that their opinions were based more often on racial fears than on scientific fact, Canada's physicians helped inhibit the infusion of Southern and Eastern Europeans. Such prejudice and its legislation peaked in the 1920's when the United States imposed an immigration quota system.   K. S. McDorman

1179. Hatch, F. J. SHIP-TO-SHORE AIRMAIL SERVICES IN THE 1920'S. *Can. Geographic [Canada] 1978 97(1): 56-61.* Ship-to-shore air mail services between Montreal and Rimouski, New Brunswick were inaugurated to provide speedy delivery of the mail in the 1920's-30's, as well as to gain firm command of North Atlantic air routes.

1180. Hillmer, Norman. A BRITISH HIGH COMMISSIONER FOR CANADA, 1927-28. *J. of Imperial and Commonwealth Hist. [Great Britain] 1973 1(3): 339-356.* Discusses the changing relationship of Britain with the dominions in the 1920's and the manner in which the need for "establishing an institutional framework of Empire so that information and ideas could be exchanged day by day at the highest level" was met in Canada through the appointment of a high commissioner. Both the negotiations of the British cabinet and the sentiments of Canadian leaders on the matter are analyzed. The creation of the post was one means of slowing the disintegration of the Empire. Based on manuscript and printed sources; 55 notes.   J. A. Casada

1181. Lauder, Brian. TWO RADICALS: RICHARD MAURICE BUCKE AND LAWREN HARRIS. *Dalhousie Rev. [Canada] 1976 56(2): 307-318.* Examines the influence of a book by English-born Canadian doctor Richard Bucke, *Cosmic Consciousness*, on the artist, writer, and mystic Lawren Harris. Bucke, who was also Walt Whitman's literary executor, had a powerful influence on the theosophical movement during the 1920's and the book remains in print. The influence of Bucke on Harris is indirect, but a comparison of passages from Bucke with Harris' theories of art shows the strong relationship. 45 notes.   C. Held

1182. Levitt, Joseph. HENRI BOURASSA AND THE PROGRESSIVE "ALLIANCE" OF 1926. *J. of Canadian Studies 1974 9(4): 17-23.*

1183. Luodesmeri, Varpu. AMERIKANSUOMALAISTEN TYÖVÄENJÄRJESTÖJEN SUHTAUTUMINEN SUOMESTA VUODEN 1918 SODAN JÄLKEEN TULLEISIIN SIIRTOLAISIIN: "HILJAN SUOMESTA TULLEITTEN TUTKIJAKOMITEAT" [The attitudes of the Finnish American workers' movement toward immigrants coming from Finland after the 1918 war: the "Committees of examination of recent arrivals from Finland"]. *Turun Hist. Arkisto [Finland] 1974 29: 63-113.* Describes radical labor organizations of Finnish immigrants in the United States and Canada. Recent immigrants were screened to determine their roles in the 1918 Finnish civil war before that person was allowed to join the local organization. At least 68 local committees were established, ceasing in the United States after 1924, but continuing longer in Canada. Based on newspapers, manuscripts and interviews collected at Turku University, Finland; map, 195 notes, English summary.   R. G. Selleck

1184. McCorkell, Edmund J. CHESTERTON IN CANADA. *Chesterton R. 1975/76 2(1): 39-54.* Reports on the two lectures given by the British intellectual Gilbert Keith Chesterton in Canada, 1921 and 1930.

1185. Moore, Donald S. PRESBYTERIAN NON-CONCURRENCE AND THE UNITED CHURCH OF CANADA. *Bull. of the United Church of Can. 1975 (24): 28-39.* Examines the two major factors "motivating Presbyterian non-concurrence in the Canadian church union of 1925. . . . One was distaste for the social gospel movement, and the other dislike of the centralized, semi-episcopal structure of the United Church." This paper offers no new interpretations but "is an attempt to detail these attitudes." Based on newspapers; 41 notes.

B. D. Tennyson

1186. Piédalue, Gilles. LES GROUPES FINANCIERS ET LA GUERRE DU PAPIER AU CANADA, 1920-1930 [Financial groups and the paper war in Canada, 1920-30]. *Rev. d'Hist. de l'Am. Française [Canada] 1976 30(2): 223-258.* During the 1920's, the upper bourgeoisie was headed by those associated with the Bank of Montréal, the Canadian Bank of Commerce, and the Royal Bank. The Royal Bank hastened consolidation in the newsprint industry. The International Power and Paper Company, tied to American interests, opposed the formation of a Canadian newsprint monopoly. Price cutting occurred. The Royal Bank suffered defeat because of Canadian dependence on the American market and International's greater diversification of investment and production. Based on documents in company archives, published government documents, and secondary works; 6 tables, 2 figs., 54 notes, appendix.

L. B. Chan

1187. Russell, Francis. BUBBLE, BUBBLE—NO TOIL, NO TROUBLE. *Am. Heritage 1973 24(2): 74-80, 86.* In late 1919, Italian-born Charles Ponzi (1882-1949) opened his Securities and Exchange Company in Boston, Massachusetts. He promised, and paid, 50 percent and higher interest rates for investments. His secret was to take advantage of varying currency exchange rates in different parts of the world. The Boston *Post* finally discovered that Ponzi was an ex-convict, Charles Bianchi, who had been involved in a similar scheme in Canada. His collapse in 1920 brought tangled legal situations, failure of several banks, and revelation of other criminal activities. It did not end his colorful career in other activities. 8 illus.   D. L. Smith

1188. Scott, Bruce. 'A PLACE IN THE SUN': THE INDUSTRIAL COUNCIL AT MASSEY-HARRIS, 1919-1929. *Labour [Canada] 1976 1: 158-192.* Analysis of the industrial council at the Massey-Harris Toronto plant suggests that such organizations had greater importance than historians have acknowledged. Intended as an alternative to unions and a means to increased productivity, the council was essentially a management public relations tool. It operated, after 1922, with "smooth formality." The balance of power favored management, but worker representatives developed organizational and leadership skills. Despite general employee indifference to the council, workers made gains in control of work conditions, especially relating to safety. The council helped "achieve a decade of relative labour peace." Primary and secondary sources; 137 notes.   W. A. Kearns

1189. Strong-Boag, Veronica. CANADIAN FEMINISM IN THE 1920'S: THE CASE OF NELLIE L. MC CLUNG. *J. of Can. Studies [Canada] 1977 12(4): 58-68.* Nellie L. McClung managed to be simultaneously "Canada's foremost woman warrior" and a conscientious mother. A popular novelist, she was a leading proponent of woman suffrage (achieved in 1918) and prohibition, for social reform laws, and (as an active Methodist) for the ordination of women. In 1921 she was elected to the Alberta legislature as a Liberal despite a landslide for the United Farmers of Alberta. As a legislator she was overshadowed by Irene Parlby, who was a UFA member and a cabinet minister. McClung narrowly failed to win reelection, partly because of her continued support for prohibition. The collapse in the 1920's of the moral earnestness of the war years undermined the reform movement generally, and McClung's career in particular. Based on the McClung Papers and secondary sources; 45 notes.   L. W. Van Wyk

1190. Struthers, James. PRELUDE TO DEPRESSION: THE FEDERAL GOVERNMENT AND UNEMPLOYMENT, 1918-29. *Can. Hist. Rev. [Canada] 1977 58(3): 277-293.* Studies Canada's economic slump in the post-World War I years and the federal government's handling of the unemployment problem. "Back-to-the-Land," and "Work or Maintenance," were the dominant emphases in Canadian social policy. The federal government considered the problem more provincial than federal, and lost its opportunity to anticipate the social and economic problems which more liberal reformers foresaw in this policy. Experience in federal leadership in labor exchanges, unemployment relief, and unemployment insurance during 1918-21 was thereby lost. 51 notes.
R. V. Ritter

1191. Threinen, Norman J. THE STUERMER UNION MOVEMENT IN CANADA. *Concordia Hist. Inst. Q. 1973 46(4): 148-157.* An early (1922) attempt at unity among Lutheran synods in Western Canada.   S

1192. Traves, Thomas D. THE BOARD OF COMMERCE AND THE CANADIAN SUGAR REFINING INDUSTRY: A SPECULATION ON THE ROLE OF THE STATE IN CANADA. *Can. Hist. R. 1974 55(2): 159-175.* Examines the relationship between the Board of Commerce of Canada, a selective price control agency which was established as a response to the social unrest which followed World War I, and the Canadian sugar refining industry. It is found that the board was designed and served as a device to allay social unrest and that its relationship with the industry served the industry's needs, 1919-20. Based on the papers of the board and of the principal political figures of the period; 2 charts, 69 notes.   A

1193. Vipond, Mary. CANADIAN NATIONALISM AND THE PLIGHT OF CANADIAN MAGAZINES IN THE 1920'S. *Can. Hist. Rev. [Canada] 1977 58(1): 43-63.* An examination of the campaign of Canadian magazine publishers for a tariff against American magazines in the 1920's, showing how self-interested both the publishers and their opponents were, and how their definitions of what it meant to be "Canadian" differed. Based on unpublished transcripts of hearings before the Advisory Board on Tariff and Taxation and Minute Books of the publishers' organizations.   A

1194. Vipond, Mary. CANADIAN NATIONAL CONSCIOUSNESS AND THE FORMATION OF THE UNITED CHURCH OF CANADA. *Bull. of the United Church of Can. 1975 24: 4-27.* Examines "the extent to which a feeling of national consciousness and a sense of national responsibility motivated the unionists in the post World War I period." The movement for church union was directly related to the heavy European immigration and the need to evangelize and 'Canadianize' the west." Concludes that the United Church was intended "to accomplish a double mission for a nation whose unity was threatened by ethnic and geographic divisions. . . . The unity of the three Protestant churches was a religious goal, but it was also a national one." Based on United Church archival material, newspapers, and secondary sources; illus., 82 notes.   B. D. Tennyson

1195. Vipond, Mary. THE IMAGE OF WOMEN IN CANADIAN MASS CIRCULATION MAGAZINES IN THE 1920'S. *Modernist Studies [Canada] 1974-75 1(3): 5-13.* The assumptions made in Canadian periodicals about women's occupations reflect an ambivalent and contradictory image of their sex roles.

The Great Depression

1196. Betcherman, Lita-Rose. THE EARLY HISTORY OF CANADA'S ANTI-DISCRIMINATION LAW. *Patterns of Prejudice [Great Britain] 1973 7(6): 19-23.* Discusses the passing of anti-discrimination legislation in Canada in the 1930's as a reaction against the anti-Semitism of Nazism.

1197. Comeau, Robert. LA CANADIAN SEAMEN'S UNION (1936-1949): UN CHAPITRE DE L'HISTOIRE DU MOUVEMENT OUVRIER CANADIEN [The Canadian Seamen's Union, 1936-49: a chapter in the history of the Canadian labor movement]. *Rev. d'Hist. de l'Amérique Française [Canada] 1976 29(4): 503-538.* During the depression period of the 1930's and the decade of the 1940's, the Canadian Seamen's Union contributed to the growth of Canadian syndicalism. Its activities illustrated the inherent polarization among militant workers who wanted to improve working conditions in the face of collusion among the shipowners, the federal government, and the corrupt directors of an international union. Discusses the important role of the militant Communists. Based on journals, newspapers, and published monographs; 73 notes.   L. B. Chan

1198. Granatstein, J. L. and Bothwell, Robert. 'A SELF-EVIDENT NATIONAL DUTY': CANADIAN FOREIGN POLICY, 1935-1939. *J. of Imperial and Commonwealth Hist. [Great Britain] 1975 3(2): 212-233.* Canada's foreign policy under Prime Minister William Lyon Mackenzie King provided strong moral (if not political) support for Great Britain and attempted to conciliate American and British interests during 1935-39.

1199. Hillmer, Norman. DEFENCE AND IDEOLOGY: THE ANGLO-CANADIAN MILITARY "ALLIANCE" IN THE 1930S. *Int. J. [Canada] 1978 33(3): 588-612.* While Canada expressed concern for the welfare of Britain in a threatening world, it gave almost nothing in the way of material assistance and no commitments for the future. Primary material; 78 notes.   R. V. Kubicek

1200. Horn, Michael. LEONARD MARSH AND THE COMING OF A WELFARE STATE IN CANADA: A REVIEW ARTICLE. *Social Hist. [Canada] 1976 9(17): 197-204.* Reprints Leonard Marsh's *Report on Social Security for Canada* (1943) and discusses his career. He pioneered social welfare research in Canada during the 1930's, and in the 1940's he became one of the main designers of the slowly developing Canadian welfare state. Marsh was strongly influenced by Fabianism and was active in the League for Social Reconstruction which stood for a reformist and constitutionalist socialism committed to thorough-going changes in the distribution of income, wealth, and power. Secondary sources; 27 notes.   W. K. Hobson

1201. Horn, Michiel. THE GREAT DEPRESSION: PAST AND PRESENT. *J. of Can. Studies [Canada] 1976 11(1): 41-50.* The middle classes during the 1930's were people who had either no experience with economic hardship or believed that they had left it behind. A repetition of the Great Depression still is regarded as the worst thing that could happen, and we are not yet certain that it is safely behind us. R. B. Bennett Papers, Avison Papers in the Public Archives of Canada, and secondary works; 24 notes.   G. E. Panting

1202. Kidd, Bruce. CANADIAN OPPOSITION TO THE 1936 OLYMPICS IN GERMANY. *Can. J. of Hist. of Sport and Physical Educ. [Canada] 1978 9(2): 20-40.* Canadian Communists and others campaigned against the holding of the Olympic Games in Berlin and persuaded some Canadian athletes to sail to Spain for the proposed People's Olympic Games, which were cancelled when the Spanish Civil War started.

1203. Kottman, Richard N. HERBERT HOOVER AND THE SMOOT-HAWLEY TARIFF: CANADA, A CASE STUDY. *J. of Am. Hist. 1975 62(3): 609-635.* Analyzes the role of President Herbert C. Hoover and the Smoot-Hawley Tariff of 1930 in the deterioration of Canadian-American relations. Hoover's insensitivity to nationalist feeling and agricultural interests in Canada, reflected in his signing of the Smoot-Hawley Tariff, led to tariff retaliation, prolonged neglect of the St. Lawrence seaway project, and the Liberal electoral defeat in Canada in 1930. Recent scholarship which attempts to rehabilitate Hoover's image faces a contradiction in Hoover's handling of Canadian-American relations, 1929-33. Based on Hoover's writings, documents in the public archives of Canada, records of the Department of State, newspapers, journals, and secondary works; 117 notes.   J. B. Street

1204. Kottman, Richard N. HERBERT HOOVER AND THE ST. LAWRENCE SEAWAY TREATY OF 1932. *New York Hist. 1975 56(3): 314-346.* Describes President Herbert Hoover's negotiations with Canada of the St. Lawrence Seaway Treaty of 1932. Negotiations were politically complicated by New York state's and Chicago's interests in several aspects of the proposed seaway. Based on recently opened manuscripts in the United States, Canada, and Great Britain; 5 illus., 61 notes.   R. N. Lokken

1205. Kottman, Richard N. THE HOOVER-BENNETT MEETING OF 1931: MISMANAGED SUMMITRY. *Ann. of Iowa 1974 42(3): 205-221.* Examines the 1931 Washington summit conference between Herbert Hoover and Canadian Prime Minister R. B. Bennett against a background of several areas of dispute, including tariff protection, prohibition, restriction of laborers from Canada into the United States, and joint development of the St. Lawrence River. The January 1931 visit of Bennett did nothing to settle national differences, and activities of the press raised false hopes. 41 notes.   C. W. Olson

1206. McAndrew, William J. "WEIGHING A WILD-CAT ON THE KITCHEN SCALES": CANADIANS EVALUATE THE NEW DEAL. *Am. Rev. of Can. Studies 1974 4(2): 23-45.* Anti-Americanism, a strong theme in Canadian attitudes toward the United States, shows through in their interpretation of the New Deal, which takes one of two attitudes; disillusionment over Roosevelt's initial rejection of the internationalist option in lieu of stimulating domestic economy, and argument over whether the New Deal actually represented continuity or discontinuity in the overall sweep of American policy, 1930's.

1207. Petryshyn, J. R. B. BENNETT AND THE COMMUNISTS: 1930-1935. *J. of Can. Studies 1974 9(4): 43-54.* Discusses the campaign of Richard Bedford Bennett and the Conservative Party against the Communist Party of Canada.   S

1208. Read, Colin and Forster, Donald. "OPERA BOUFFE": MACKENZIE KING, MITCH HEPBURN, THE APPOINTMENT OF THE LIEUTENANT GOVERNOR AND THE CLOSING OF GOVERNMENT HOUSE, TORONTO, 1937. *Ontario Hist. [Canada] 1977 69(4): 239-256.* The controversy between the federal and provincial governments in 1937 originated in personal frictions and disagreements between the federal Prime Minister (William Lyon Mackenzie King) and the provincial Premier (Mitchell F. Hepburn). These spilled over into a squabble over patronage, discontent over differing interpretations of "liberalism," and depression economics. Analyzes how the position and role of the Lieutenant Governor was dragged into the affair after it became clear that Lieutenant Governor Herbert Bruce was resigning and the two

principals could not agree on his successor. Outlines the resolution of the affair. Mainly primary sources; 75 notes.   W. B. Whitham

1209. Seager, Allen. THE PASS STRIKE OF 1932. *Alberta Hist. [Canada] 1977 25(1): 1-11.* The depression in the coal district by the British Columbia-Alberta border started in the early 1920's, with a decline in the price of coal. The worldwide depression led to confrontations between management and labor. In 1932, violence erupted in several mining communities, and the Mounties were called in. Management tried unsuccessfully to separate the Eastern European workers from the Canadians. An unusual aspect of the strike was the participation of women and children in parades and other demonstrations. By the mid-1930's the workers had the upper hand, and in 1936 they joined the United Mine Workers of America. 5 illus., 53 notes.   D. Chaput

1210. Snow, Duart. THE HOLMES FOUNDRY STRIKE OF MARCH, 1937: "WE'LL GIVE THEIR JOBS TO WHITE MEN!" *Ontario Hist. [Canada] 1977 69(1): 3-31.* The Holmes strike grew out of the Depression and was one of the few sitdown strikes in Canadian labor history. Presents the origins of the strike, its course, and its resolution. There were significant anti-immigrant, antilabor sentiments as well as simple antiunionism. 3 illus., 90 notes.   W. B. Whitham

1211. Soward, F. H. FORTY YEARS ON: THE CAHAN BLUNDER RE-EXAMINED. *BC Studies [Canada] 1976-77 (32): 126-138.* Japan's invasion of Manchuria raised the question of whether the League of Nations Covenant had been violated. If so, sanctions should be applied against Japan. The Canadian position, like many others, was not to define it as a violation but to handle the problem in some other fashion. Charles H. Cahan, Secretary of State, was Canada's delegate to a 1932 international conference to discuss the matter. Cahan's address to the conference, considered very pro-Japanese, did not follow his instructions and caused Canada embarrassment. 22 notes.   D. L. Smith

1212. Stokes, Lawrence D. CANADA AND AN ACADEMIC REFUGEE FROM NAZI GERMANY: THE CASE OF GERHARD HERZBERG. *Can. Hist. Rev. [Canada] 1976 57(2): 150-170.* Examines Gerhard Herzberg's experience in coming to Canada in 1935 as a visiting Carnegie Fellow and in later obtaining landed immigrant status. Refugees, including displaced scholars, had great difficulty entering Canada before 1945 because of high unemployment, antiforeign sentiment, narrow university hiring practices, and restrictive immigration policies. Only those refugees were successful whose cases were energetically presented to the government, as was Herzberg's by University of Saskatchewan president Walter Murray.   A

1213. Thompson, Lee Briscoe. POETIC PRISM: THE *CANADIAN FORUM* IN THE GREAT DEPRESSION. *Am. Rev. of Can. Studies 1976 6(1): 56-85.* Examines the poetic output of the *Canadian Forum* during the Great Depression of the 1930's and assesses the condition of literary consciousness and its growth in relation to social stress.

1214. Unsigned. THE HUNGRY THIRTIES IN WESTERN CANADA: A VISUAL RECORD. *Can.: An Hist. Mag. 1974 1(3): 17-24.* Photo essay of western Canada during the Great Depression.   S

1215. Unsigned. THE STORY OF THE R-100. *Can. Geographical J. 1973 86(1): 24-35.* The dirigible R-100's historic round trip between England and Canada July-August 1930.   S

1216. Wagner, Jonathan. THE *DEUTSCHER BUND CANADA* 1934-39. *Can. Hist. Rev. [Canada] 1977 58(2): 176-200.* The *Deutscher Bund Canada* was a radical movement which conducted a propaganda campaign to convert German Canadians to Nazism.

1217. Webb, Jonathan. ADVICE TO A GOVERNOR-GENERAL 1935. *Dalhousie Rev. [Canada] 1975-76 55(4): 631-642.* A copy of Sir Alan Lascelles' memorandum of 27 May 1935, entitled "Apochrypha," to the recently appointed governor-general of Canada, John Buchan (1875-1940). Published with the permission of the Douglas Library Archives, Queen's University, where it is included with the Buchan Papers. 5 notes.   C. Held

1218. Wilbur, J. R. H. CANADIAN-AMERICAN TRADE WAR DURING THE GREAT DEPRESSION. *Int. Perspectives [Canada] 1975 Mar.-Apr.: 16-20*. Discusses the effects which the depression, 1929-33, had on Canadian-US relations, including Canada's integration into the American trade and economic sphere, and the tendency toward consolidation between two major political factions (one led by MacKenzie King, the other by R. B. Bennett), eventually agreeing that tariff barriers were no longer feasible and economic integration with the United States was a necessity.

World War II

1219. Barry, P. S. THE PROLIFIC PIPELINE: FINDING OIL FOR CANOL. *Dalhousie Rev. [Canada] 1977 57(2): 205-223*. Canol, coined from "Canada" and "oil," was conceived by the US War Department in the spring of 1942 as a 600-mile pipeline from Norman Wells on the Mackenzie River to Whitehorse, Yukon. Its "hydra-headed monster" nature was commented on by Colonel S. W. Dzuiban, an American historian, and Canada's Major General W. W. Foster attempted to control it in 1943. Before the project ended in 1945 it included roadbuilding, river freighting, airfields, wildcat oil drilling, and other minor projects unrelated to the original authorization. During World War II there were several full-blown investigations of Canol by the United States and Canadian Governments. The wildcatting by Imperial Oil is noted. 44 notes.
C. H. Held

1220. Campbell, John P. THE SKIES OVER DIEPPE, AUGUST 19, 1942. *Canada 1975 3(1): 3-19*. Discusses the Royal Canadian Air Force's participation in the air battle of Dieppe during World War II in 1942, emphasizing the military strategy of British Air Vice-Marshal Trafford Leigh-Mallory.

1221. Douglas, W. and Greenhous, Brereton. L'HISTORIOGRAPHIE CANADIENNE ET LA SECONDE GUERRE MONDIALE [Canadian historiography and the Second World War]. *Rev. d'Hist. de la Deuxième Guerre Mondiale [France] 1976 26(104): 67-87*. Analyzes historical writing concerning Canada during World War II, referring to approximately 50 works. 28 notes.
G. H. Davis

1222. Fry, Garry L. "BOISE BEE": THE DUANE BEESON STORY. *Am. Aviation Hist. Soc. J. 1978 23(4): 242-259*. Duane Beeson (1921-47) of Boise, Idaho, joined the Royal Canadian Air Force in June 1941 and in 1942 was transferred with his outfit to the US Army Air Force; in P-47's and P-51's he scored 24 victories, was shot down by antiaircraft fire, and spent 1944-April 1945 as a POW in Germany.

1223. Granatstein, J. L. GETTING ON WITH THE AMERICANS: CHANGING CANADIAN PERCEPTIONS OF THE UNITED STATES, 1939-1945. *Can. R. of Am. Studies 1974 5(1): 3-17*. Geographic, economic, and security considerations produced growing Canadian-American cooperation during World War II. Policies of William Lyon Mackenzie King (1874-1950), designed to effect closer ties to the United States, speeded the achievement of that end. Based on the King and Franklin Roosevelt Papers and other archival sources; 44 notes.
H. T. Lovin

1224. Granatstein, J. L. and Cuff, Robert D. THE HYDE PARK DECLARATION 1941: ORIGINS AND SIGNIFICANCE. *Can. Hist. R. 1974 55(1): 59-80*. Examines the intricacies of Canadian-American war finance, 1939-41, as part of a broader Anglo-American-Canadian nexus. Concludes that the Hyde Park Declaration was a result of Canadian negotiating success—and American benevolence. Based on Canadian, British and American governmental and private collections.
A

1225. Granatstein, J. L. INDÉPENDANCE ET DÉPENDANCE: LA POLITIQUE ÉTRANGÈRE DU CANADA PENDANT LA SECONDE GUERRE MONDIALE [Independence and dependence in Canadian foreign policy during the Second World War]. *Rev. d'Hist. de la Deuxième Guerre Mondiale [France] 1976 26(104): 49-66*. Despite independence in foreign affairs since 1929, Canada was a minor world power before World War II. Canada acknowledged limited responsibility in the war. Economic problems included dislocation of foreign exchange, high

costs of a British-Canadian air training program, suspicion of British financial negligence, and a major dislocation which threatened when the United States offered the United Kingdom armaments which Canada insisted on being paid for. Canada wrote off a donation of $1,000,000,000 as a comradely act toward Great Britain, but received little gratitude for it. Canada struggled to be included in Allied decisionmaking, especially in mixed commissions. Canadian-US relations emerged from the war in a positive condition, partly because Canada feared the Soviet Union. 23 citations from Canadian and British archives.
G. H. Davis

1226. Granatstein, J. L. LE QUÉBEC ET LE PLÉBISCITE DE 1942 SUR LA CONSCRIPTION [Quebec and the Plebiscite of 1942 regarding conscription]. *R. d'Hist de l'Amérique Française [Canada] 1973 27(1): 43-62*. Quebec voted against conscription on 27 April 1942, while English-speaking provinces voted in favor of it. The LPDC (Ligue pour la Défense du Canada) actively worked against conscription. Premier William Lyon Mackenzie King, who had initiated the plebiscite, respected Quebec's decision until 1944, when limited conscription was decided upon. 62 notes.
C. Collon

1227. Granatstein, J. L. SETTLING THE ACCOUNTS: ANGLO-CANADIAN WAR FINANCE, 1943-1945. *Queen's Q. [Canada] 1976 83(2): 234-249*. Examines the nature of Canada's financial contribution in World War II, especially its impact on relations with Great Britain. The period saw the triumph of Keynesian economics as well as something of a reversal of Canada's traditional financial role vis-à-vis Britain, but Canada's generosity was justified. Table, 46 notes.
J. A. Casada

1228. Gravel, J. Yves. LE CANADA FRANÇAIS ET LA GUERRE 1939-1945 [French Canada and the war, 1939-45]. *Rev. d'Hist. de la Deuxième Guerre Mondiale [France] 1976 26(104): 31-47*. World War II accentuated the differences between the English and French Canadians. In general, the French opposed conscription and participation in overseas warfare. As a compromise, only volunteers went overseas but conscription was instituted for home defense. Anglo Canadians tended to volunteer and readily supported the Commonwealth, but French Canadians tended to wait for conscription. Officers' schools and entrance exams were conducted in English only. French-speaking officers came from a different class (bilinguals or teachers) than the English-speaking officers. Before 1941 the air force ignored French Canadians, but after that some classes were taught in English and French, and courses in mechanics were offered in French. One of 85 squadrons was French Canadian. The navy modeled itself after the British fleet and gave no chance to French-speaking volunteers. 107 notes.
G. H. Davis

1229. Greenhous, B. and Douglas, W. A. B. CANADA AND THE SECOND WORLD WAR: THE STATE OF CLIO'S ART. *Military Affairs 1978 42(1): 24-28*. Reviews the state of the historiography of Canada's participation in World War II. Works document Canada's emergence from a colonial status to true independence. Others show the growth of social reforms, strengthening of the economy, and the role of the military services—the main weakness is in the realm of military aviation. Interest is increasing but more so on the social, political, and economic impact rather than military developments. 10 notes.
A. M. Osur

1230. Greenhous, Brereton. CANADA AND THE SECOND WORLD WAR: A HISTORIOGRAPHICAL PERSPECTIVE. La seconda guerra mondiale nella prospettiva storica a trent'anni dall'epilogo (Como: Casa Editrice Pietro Cairoli, 1977): 411-417. The extent of Canadian historiographical consideration of World War II is severely limited, despite several excellent works. Canadian preoccupation with federal-provincial relationships and the sociopolitical clash of two cultures pervades World War II historiography. 5 notes.
M. T. Wilson

1231. Hatch, F. J. ALLIES IN THE ALEUTIANS. *Aerospace Hist. 1974 21(2): 70-78*. Discusses the Aleutian campaign during World War II, "the only instance in the conflict in which Canadian squadrons served under American command."
S

1232. Hunter, T. Murray. COAST DEFENCE IN BRITISH COLUMBIA, 1939-1941: ATTITUDES AND REALITIES. *BC Studies [Canada] 1975/76 (28): 3-28*. Traces the history of Canada's west-coast defenses since 1862 and examines the attitudes and realities governing military preparations 1939 to December 1941, specifically the coast defense artillery. Based on primary and secondary sources; map, 3 tables, 70 notes. W. L. Marr

1233. Iwaasa, David B. THE JAPANESE IN SOUTHERN ALBERTA, 1941-45. *Alberta Hist. [Canada] 1976 24(3): 5-19.* At the outbreak of World War II, many Japanese from British Columbia were removed to southern Alberta, which already had Japanese communities at Raymond and Hardieville. At first limited to working in sugar beet fields, the newly arrived Japanese had severe housing, school, and water problems. In the following years some of the Japanese were permitted to work in canning factories, sawmills, and other businesses. There was constant controversy in the press about the role and freedom of the local Japanese. Farm production increased markedly, and after the war few of the Japanese took advantage of the repatriation plan. The Japanese in Alberta today are well assimilated, but little of Japanese heritage remains. Based on newspaper accounts and government documents; 6 illus., 76 notes. D. Chaput

1234. LePan, Douglas. PORTRAIT OF NORMAN ROBERTSON. *Int. Perspectives [Canada] 1978 (July-Aug.): 3-8.* Norman Alexander Robertson (1904-68) was Under Secretary of State for External Affairs, Canadian High Commissioner in the United Kingdom, and Ambassador to the United States. Superbly intelligent, highly literate, and possessing a wide-ranging expertise, he served Canada well, particularly in the formation of foreign economic policies. Although generally considered a poor administrator, he was a master of all aspects of Canada's economy, and considered a knowledge of economics part of the equipment of the complete diplomat. He enjoyed his greatest influence when he served under Mackenzie King in 1941-46. E. S. Palais

1235. Martens, Hildegard M. ACCOMMODATION AND WITHDRAWAL: THE RESPONSE OF MENNONITES IN CANADA TO WORLD WAR II. *Social Hist. [Canada] 1974 7(14): 306-327.* Canadian Mennonite response to World War II was primarily in the direction of assimilation. There was no united Mennonite policy. Church leaders divided over whether to try and protect baptized members only or to include adherents. They also divided over whether to accept alternative service. The Conference of Historic Peace Churches was formed to negotiate agreements with the Government on matters affecting pacifists. Some individual Mennonites chose jail when unable to satisfy a Mobilization Board of their conscientious objection. Many others, especially recent immigrants, volunteered for active duty. Based on secondary sources and the Conrad Grebel Archives; 79 notes. W. K. Hobson

1236. Massicotte, Guy. LES ÉDITORIALISTES CANADIENS-FRANÇAIS ET LES ORIGINES DE LA SECONDE GUERRE MONDIALE [French Canadian editorialists and the origins of World War II]. *Recherches Sociographiques [Canada] 1976 17(2): 139-165.* Juxtaposes the opinions of eight contemporary historians concerning the origins of World War II with the perceptions of French Canadian editorialists writing in five newspapers during 1938-39. The editorialists perceived the movement of international politics in the same light as the contemporary historians. 91 notes. A. E. LeBlanc

1237. McEvoy, Fred. CANADIAN-IRISH RELATIONS DURING THE SECOND WORLD WAR. *J. of Imperial and Commonwealth Hist. [Great Britain] 1977 5(2): 206-226.* Despite Ireland's choice to remain neutral during World War II, Canada, alone among the British Commonwealth, retained open and friendly relations with Ireland and often arbitrated when other Commonwealth countries attempted to harry Ireland from the group.

1238. Munton, Don and Page, Don. PLANNING IN THE EAST BLOCK: THE POST-HOSTILITIES PROBLEMS COMMITTEES IN CANADA 1943-5. *Int. J. [Canada] 1977 32(4): 687-726.* An account of the creation, successes, and demise of formal foreign policy planning mechanism within the Canadian government. Primary sources; 62 notes. R. V. Kubicek

1239. Murray, D. R. CANADA'S FIRST DIPLOMATIC MISSIONS IN LATIN AMERICA. *J. of Inter-Am. Studies and World Affairs 1974 16(2): 131-152.* In 1939 Canada declared war on the Axis powers and became the only Western Hemisphere state directly involved in the war. Canada had few diplomatic missions in Latin America and was not a member of the Pan-American Union. The first legations were established in Brazil, Argentina, and Chile. In 1941, the United States blocked Canadian membership in the PAU, and Canadian interest in the inter-American system has remained low. Based on Canadian government documents, private papers, and secondary sources; biblio. J. R. Thomas

1240. Pierson, Ruth. WOMEN'S EMANCIPATION AND THE RECRUITMENT OF WOMEN INTO THE CANADIAN LABOUR FORCE IN WORLD WAR II. *Can. Hist. Assoc. Hist. Papers [Canada] 1976: 141-173.* The federal and provincial bureaucrats of Canada regarded women as temporary replacements for men in the operation of a war economy. The extent of women's employability was categorized according to their positions in the family system. Because they were required to work in wartime, their needs as working women were handled in the context of the war effort. After World War II they were expected to return to the home or to traditional women's occupations. Based on Public Archives of Canada, Series RG 27 and 35, Orders-in-Council, secondary sources; 176 notes. G. E. Panting

1241. Rothwell, David R. UNITED CHURCH PACIFISM OCTOBER 1939. *Bull. of the United Church of Can. 1973 (22): 36-55.* Examines the reasons for the issuance of "A Witness Against War," a manifesto signed by 68 United Church of Canada ministers in October 1939 proclaiming opposition to Canadian participation in World War II. The central figure was Reverend R. Edis Fairbairn, who hoped to force the church to recognize the moral dilemma posed by the war and to advertise his conscientious commitment. The manifesto called for no action but sought merely "to bring into fellowship . . . all the Christian pacifists in the United Church." The church moderator suggested that "it is a very serious thing for a minister to split his congregation through controversy," but counselled "tolerance and acceptance of the conscientious rights of others." Concludes that "the pure form of idealism that underlay both the effort to Christianize the social order and to reform international affairs by pacific means was largely a victim of the Second World War." Based on newspapers, interviews and secondary sources; 90 notes. B. D. Tennyson

1242. Roy, Patricia E. THE SOLDIERS CANADA DIDN'T WANT: HER CHINESE AND JAPANESE CITIZENS. *Can. Hist. Rev. [Canada] 1978 59(3): 341-358.* Draws on the records of many federal government departments and politicians as well as British Columbia sources. Argues that the Mackenzie King government was reluctant to enlist Chinese and Japanese Canadians in the armed forces during World War II partly for considerations of military morale but especially because of its sympathies with British Columbia's fears that military service would give Asian Canadians a strong claim to the franchise. Only late in the war, and under special circumstances, were Chinese and Japanese recruited. A

1243. Roy, Reginald H. THE DEFENCE OF PRINCE RUPERT: AN EYEWITNESS ACCOUNT. *BC Studies [Canada] 1976 (31): 60-77.* Lieutenant R. Thistle was the Area Intelligence Officer for the Prince Rupert Defences when the Japanese attacked Pearl Harbor in 1941. His diary, from which several entries and excerpts from December 1941 to June 1942 are included here, gives a valuable eye-witness account of developments in the northern British Columbia Pacific coastal area. The last entry, 21 June 1942, tells of the first and only enemy shells which fell on British Columbia. 32 notes. D. L. Smith

1244. Stacey, C. P. POLITIQUE ET OPERATIONS MILITAIRES (1939-1945) [Canadian politics and military operations, 1939-45]. *Rev. d'Hist. de la Deuxième Guerre Mondiale [France] 1976 26(104): 1-30.* The Canadian Army was very small before revival after 1936 under Prime Minister William Lyon W. L. Mackenzie King. Immediately after Great Britain entered World War II, Canada joined as a loyal member of the Commonwealth. The first task was to train and supply almost 30,000 airmen to support Britain. French Canadians opposed conscription and many politicians called for "limited engagement." Canada took an active part in the direction and operations of the European but not the Pacific war, although Canadians did defend Hong Kong in 1941. Canadians were involved in the operation at Dieppe in August 1942. Other operations summarized here include the Italian and northwest European campaigns, and aerial and naval activity. One of four articles in a special edition on Canada during World War II. 29 notes.   G. H. Davis

1245. Tanaka, June K.   FRUIT OF DIASPORA: THE JAPANESE EXPERIENCE IN CANADA.   *Japan Interpreter [Japan] 1978 12(1): 110-117.* Anti-Japanese prejudice and discrimination led to early anti-Japanese immigration restrictions in British Columbia, and culminated in the forced relocation of all Japanese from the Province after Pearl Harbor. Relocation proved beneficial for many Japanese Canadians. Stresses the lack of racial prejudice in eastern Canada.   F. W. Iklé

1246. Wagner, Jonathan F.   THE DEUTSCHER BUND CANADA IN SASKATCHEWAN.   *Saskatchewan Hist. [Canada] 1978 31(2): 41-50.* The Deutscher Bund Canada, founded in Waterloo, Ontario, during January 1934, was closely linked to the pan-German movement sponsored by Hitler's Germany. Its move into western Canada began in the summer of 1934 with a tour by Karl Gerhard, the first national leader. Explains organizational terms such as *Gau, Gebeit, Bezirke, Ortsgrupper,* and *Stutzpunkt.* The number of members was relatively small, representing less than one percent of Saskatchewan's German population. The attempts to propagandize the Nazi ideology through German cultural programs and the speeches of Bernhard Bott, Horst Jerosch, and Henrich Seelheim were overt, and probably telling, until the summer of 1938. At

that time the mood all over Canada began to change toward fear of Hitler's Germany. By late 1939 the movement had notably failed. Photo, map, 55 notes.   C. H. Held

1247. Ward, W. Peter.   BRITISH COLUMBIA AND THE JAPANESE EVACUATION.   *Can. Hist. Rev. [Canada] 1976 57(3): 289-309.* Explores fluctuations in popular feeling against Japanese in British Columbia during 1937-42. Particularly examines the outburst of sentiment after the bombing of Pearl Harbor and reveals the great impact which public opinion had on the federal government's decision to evacuate Japanese from the coastal region of the province. This decision was a response to popular and political pressures stimulated by the widespread, irrational westcoast belief that Japanese residents threatened the military security of the region. Based on newspaper reports, published public documents, and unpublished documents in major archival collections, notably the Mackenzie King and Ian Mackenzie papers in the Public Archives of Canada and records of the Canadian departments of External Affairs and National Defence.   A

1248. Woodman, Lyman L.   THE TRANS-CANADIAN, ALASKA, AND WESTERN RAILWAYS.   *Alaska J. 1974 4(4): 194-202.* Discusses 1942-43 plans made by the US War Department to build railways from British Columbia to Alaska in order to provide supplies to the USSR during World War II.

9. THE CONTEMPORARY SCENE, SINCE 1945

General

1249. Aleksandrov, Iu. PARLAMENT KANADY: ORGANIZAT-SIONNAIA STRUKTURA [Canada's Parliament: Organizational structure]. *Sovetskoe Gosudarstvo i Pravo [USSR] 1976 (3): 106-109.* Reviews differences between the British and Canadian parliamentary systems and discusses changes in structure and procedure introduced by the British North America Act (1867) and subsequent constitutional amendments through 1962. The first really important changes were made by Canadian Prime Minister Pierre Elliott Trudeau, head of the Liberal Party, since his election in 1968. 9 notes.   N. Frenkley

1250. Couve de Murville, Maurice. PEARSON ET LA FRANCE [Pearson and France]. *Internat. J. [Canada] 1973/74 29(1): 24-32.* Comments on the wish of former Canadian prime minister Lester B. Pearson, to strengthen French-Canadian relations, and his world view as it contrasted with that of General de Gaulle.   R. V. Kubicek

1251. Elford, Jean. THE ST. CLAIR RIVER: CENTER SPAN OF THE SEAWAY. *Can. Geographical J. 1973 86(1): 18-23.*

1252. Farb, Judith and Farb, Nathan. THEY CAN'T GO HOME AGAIN. *Present Tense 1973 1(1): 59-61.* Jewish deserters and exiles in Canada.   S

1253. Leach, Richard H. CANADA IN PERSPECTIVE. *Current Hist. 1974 66(392): 145-149.* Examines problems facing the various regions, relations between Canada and the United States, and Canadian politics and economics.   S

1254. Nappi, Carmine. DES MÉTHODES QUANTITATIVES AP-PLIQUÉES AU SECTEUR DES EXPORTATIONS QUÉBÉCOISES, 1969 [Quantitative methods and the Quebec export sector, 1969]. *Actualité Écon. [Canada] 1974 50(4): 491-511.* "This paper explores the relationship between the structural models and different trade indices which can be used to quantify Quebec and other Canadian regions export sector. An attempt is made to measure the degrees of specialization of exports for 50 goods, the interprovincial and international export intensity indices for the five Canadian regions, and the export performance indices for the provinces under study. The conclusion highlights the importance of the east-west Canadian trade, specially for the internal provinces. Finally, the Quebec commercial characteristics in relation with those of other Canadian provinces (and the need to take them into account when formulating a federal trade policy) are outlined and stressed."   J

1255. Page, Don. A VISUAL DIMENSION TO ORAL HISTORY. *Can. Oral Hist. Assoc. J. [Canada] 1976/77 2: 20-23.* Explores the possibilities of recording oral history through videotaping, using as a case study the program initiated by the Historical Division of the External Affairs Department of Canada in 1971.

1256. Raynauld, André. CANADA'S INDUSTRIAL POLICY. *Atlantic Community Q. 1974 12(3): 358-370.* "Canada, too, is joining the 'post-industrial' world. The Chairman of the Economic Council of Canada examines the implications of this and other factors in discussing future industrial policy."   J

1257. Rogers, A. Robert. CANADIAN LITERATURE IN AMERICAN LIBRARIES. *Lib. Q. 1973 43(1): 1-26.* "Acquisition of Canadian literature by American libraries was investigated in three ways. Questionnaires were sent to selected large libraries in 1961 and 1971, Canadian literature titles for 1956-60 and 1965-69 were checked against the *National Union Catalog,* and published literature describing major collections was examined. The Library of Congress greatly surpasses all other United States libraries in the acquisition of new titles and in the rate of increase of current acquisitions in recent years. Several other libraries tend to acquire works by established Canadian authors on a retrospective basis, but very few purchase more than 10 percent of Canada's current literary output."   J

1258. Rossetto, Luigi. A FINAL LOOK AT THE 1971 WHITE PAPER ON DEFENCE. *Queen's Q. [Canada] 1977 84(1): 61-74.* Examines the role of Canada's armed forces. The *White Paper on Defence —Defence in the 70s* offered no solutions but only a basis for further debate. Its premises are no longer valid. Canada has a difficult choice of dependence on the United States, the heavy costs of an independent military policy, or the questionable reliance on a Swiss-type neutrality. 32 notes.   J. A. Casada

1259. Rotstein, Abraham. CANADA: THE NEW NATIONALISM. *Foreign Affairs 1976 55(1): 97-118.* A new phase of Canadian nationalism exists, albeit in a still frail way. In the economy a majority of manufacturing, of corporations, of resources, of capital, and of the trade unions is controlled by foreigners (mainly Americans). Culturally Canada is even more completely dominated by foreigners whose book sales, for example, total, 83 percent of all sales in Canada. American presence so completely permeates Canadian life that after a time it is hardly noticed, but occasionally the numbness is broken by strange events. Such an episode was unveiled in a government report which related testimony from American sociologists (they dominate Canadian universities) who stated "that they would not hire Canadians" for fear that their departments would then be overwhelmed by Canadians. But, Canada is awakening and beginning to explore ways of establishing a new national identity. Reactions in the United States are those of nonunderstanding coupled with obstructionism. Ultimately the question of power is the one needing to be resolved, and Canada's "new" nationalism is an attempt to assert final control. 2 notes.   R. Riles

1260. Rowe, Ian. PUMORI: CANADA'S FIRST HIMALAYAN CONQUEST. *Can. Geographical J. [Canada] 1978 96(2): 42-49.* Chronicles the first Canadian assault on a Himalayan peak, Pumori (23,442 feet) in 1977, sponsored by the Alpine Club of Canada and supported through a grant by the Royal Canadian Geographical Society.

1261. Schwartz, Mildred A. CITIZENSHIP IN CANADA AND THE UNITED STATES. *Tr. of the Royal Soc. of Can. [Canada] 1976 14: 83-96.* Defines citizenship and compares attitudes in Canada and the United States concerning that status. Notes the efforts in Canada to pass a Citizenship Act and a Bill of Rights, and discusses the British tradition in Canada and the effect of the Citizenship Act on British subjects. Compares treatment of Japanese in the United States and Canada during World War II. 8 notes, biblio.   J. D. Neville

1262. Scovil, G. C. Coster. MSCC [MISSIONARY SOCIETY OF THE CANADIAN CHURCH] AND MY CHINA EXPERIENCE. *J. of the Can. Church Hist. Soc. [Canada] 1977 19(3-4): 182-185.* The recollections of a Canadian missionary to China. Inspired to his task by a Chinese bishop and earlier Canadian missionaries to China, he entered that country after considerable training in its language, history and culture by the Missionary Society of the Canadian Church. He remained there some 15 months and was very impressed by the ecumenical spirit that characterized the missionaries of other Christian faiths whom he encountered. He was also pleased by the careful supervision provided by the MSCC. With the recommendation of the Chinese church leaders and the MSCC, however, it was determined that he and his fellow missionaries should leave China because of the growing possibility of a Communist takeover in the years after World War II.   J. A. Kicklighter

1263. Sealock, Richard B. and Powell, Margaret S. PLACE-NAME LITERATURE, UNITED STATES AND CANADA 1971-1974. *Names 1974 22(4): 150-164.*

1264. Stursberg, Peter. BANQUET SPEECH TO THE 1976 CANADIAN ORAL HISTORY CONFERENCE. *Can. Oral Hist. Assoc. J. [Canada] 1976/77 2: 6-10.* Author reminisces about his work in oral history during 1957-75, especially for his books on Prime Minister John Diefenbaker.

1265. Taylor, Hugh A. ORAL HISTORY AND ARCHIVES: KEYNOTE SPEECH TO THE 1976 CANADIAN ORAL HISTORY CONFERENCE. *Can. Oral Hist. Assoc. J. [Canada] 1976/77 2: 1-5.* Discusses the facilities and materials available through the Public Archives of Canada and evaluates their value for oral historians.

1266. Teeple, Gary. FREE TRADE AND GOVERNMENT AID. *Queen's Q. [Canada] 1973 80(2): 274-277.* Reviews Philip Mathias' *Forced Growth: Five Studies of Government Involvement in the Development of Canada* (Toronto: James, Lewis, and Samuel, 1971), and *Canada in a Wider Economic Community* (Toronto: U. of Toronto Press, 1972). Both have serious limitations. Mathias does not go beyond "a vision of competitive capitalism" while the second "vacuous" study "amounts to a modern-day call for annexation to the USA."
J. A. Casada

1267. Treddenick, J. M. QUEBEC and CANADA: SOME ECONOMIC ASPECTS OF INDEPENDENCE. *J. of Can. Studies 1973 8(4): 16-31.* Discusses Quebec's desire for economic independence, the political influence of the Parti Québécois, and United States influence in political and social affairs in Canada and Quebec.

1268. Warner, Malcolm and Peccei, Riccardo. TOWARDS "PARTICIPATIVE" MULTINATIONALS. *Industrial Relations [Canada] 1977 32(2): 172-181.* If the labour movement is strong, this may not only simultaneously make for more effective participation at the national plant levels but also via pressure on the State, to very much limit the role of the multi-national corporations.
J

1269. Warnock, John. IMPERIALISM AND THE CANADIAN LEFT. *Can. Dimension 1976 11(4): 15-25.* Reviews Steve Moore and Debi Wells' work, *Imperialism and the National Question in Canada* (Toronto, 1975), concerning the views of the Left in Canada on Canadian nationalism and imperialism.

The Domestic Scene

General

1270. Dixon, Marlene. WOMEN'S LIBERATION: OPENING CHAPTER TWO. *Can. Dimension 1975 10(8): 56-69.* The problems before the women's movement in North America are that since the 1960's it has come to be dominated by a middle-class leadership and has become "a politically and ideologically co opted reformist movement."
S

1271. Aird, Paul L. PLEA FOR A NATIONAL ENVIRONMENT PLAN. *Can. Geographical J. 1973 87(4): 24-29.*

1272. Amody, Francis J. COLD COUNTRY BANSHEES (THE MC DONNELL F2H-3) IN ROYAL CANADIAN NAVY SERVICE. *Am. Aviation Hist. Soc. J. 1978 23(3): 226-229.* Provides photos, description, design drawings, and a list of the McDonnell Aircraft Corporation F2H-3 aircraft with the Royal Canadian Navy, 1956-63.

1273. Baldwin, John R. THE EVOLUTION OF TRANSPORTATION POLICY IN CANADA. *Can. Public Administration [Canada] 1977 20(4): 600-631.* Examines how government regulation of transportation controls economic development and population distribution, 1945-77.

1274. Biswas, Asit K. and Biswas, Margaret R. ENERGY, ENVIRONMENT AND WORLD DEVELOPMENT. *Can. Geographical J. 1975 91(6): 4-13.* Discusses relations between energy and environment in light of current energy shortages in both developed and developing nations, and urges that Canada adopt a rational energy-environment policy.

1275. Brack, D. M. LIVING WITH SNOW. *Can. Geographical J. 1973 86(4): 106-117.* Man's many ways to overcome the obstacle of snow.
S

1276. Butler, Richard W. HOW TO CONTROL 1,000,000 SNOWMOBILES? *Can. Geographical J. 1974 88(3): 4-13.*

1277. Byers, R. B. THE CANADIAN MILITARY. *Current Hist. 1977 72(426): 173-175, 181-183.* Examines Canada's military operations and weapons systems, 1970-76, questioning equipment purchases in light of swift political and technological change.

1278. Byers, R. B. THE CANADIAN MILITARY AND THE USE OF FORCE: END OF AN ERA? *Int. J. [Canada] 1975 30(2): 284-298.* Discusses attitudes toward force in the military strategy and defense policy of Canada in the 1970's.

1279. Chapman, J. H. THE ROYAL SOCIETY OF CANADA: WHAT IS IT? *Tr. of the Royal Soc. of Can. 1973 11: 263-274.* Describes the present role of the Royal Society of Canada, incorporated in 1883, in encouraging scholarly research, publishing, advising and aiding government, carrying on an active international exchange, etc., and explores possibilities for development of increased activities.

1280. Cody, Howard. THE ONTARIO RESPONSE TO QUEBEC'S SEPARATIST CHALLENGE. *Am. Rev. of Can. Studies 1978 8(1): 43-55.* Since the election of Quebec's separatist government, Ontario Premier William Davis has employed overtures of friendship, economic arguments, and a new concern for Franco-Ontarians in his attempt to convince the Quebec people of the advantages of continued confederation. Further, Davis has proposed creation of a Federal-Provincial Secretariat to resolve inter-provincial conflicts. Ontario's opposition parties, both opposed to separation, "have been jockeying against the Premier and each other for the position of Ontario's champion of a united Canada." Primary and secondary sources including interviews with unidentified persons; 57 notes.
G.-A. Patzwald

1281. Conacher, J. B. GRADUATE STUDIES IN HISTORY IN CANADA: THE GROWTH OF DOCTORAL PROGRAMMES. *Can. Hist. Assoc. Hist. Papers [Canada] 1975: 1-15.* Surveys various reports and discussions on graduate studies in history. While Canada, like the United States, is producing too many graduate students, the right specialists are not being produced at the right time. Agrees with a report of the Canadian Historical Association that graduate schools should accept only outstanding applicants in research fields where there is some demand for people. Based on reports of the Ontario government, universities, the Canadian Historical Association and the Canada Council, and secondary sources; 38 notes.
G. E. Panting

1282. Cook, George I. THE FRONTIER COLLEGE HISTORY PROJECT. *Can. Oral Hist. Assoc. J. [Canada] 1975/76 1: 25-29.* Discusses the technical aspects of the Frontier College history project, including financing, organization, method of data collection, and use of the Public Archives of Canada, 1974-75.

1283. Cotton, Charles A.; Crook, Rodney K. and Pinch, Frank C. CANADA'S PROFESSIONAL MILITARY: THE LIMITS OF CIVILIANIZATION. *Armed Forces and Soc. 1978 4(3): 365-390.* Since World War II Canada has relied on voluntary recruitment for its military forces, thus it can serve as a model for other all volunteer armies emerging currently in many advanced industrial democratic nations. During 1966-76 Canada's military forces became "civilianized" as many traditional military functions and practices converged towards civilian norms. Recruiting stressed analytical and learning skills over physical and manual aptitudes. Poor reenlistment rates, however, caused personnel managers to construct three functional traces: combat arms, sea operations, and administration and technical support. Based on institutional research, primary interviews, secondary literature, statistical data; 29 notes.
J. P. Harahan

1284. Crane, David. CANADA'S ENERGY POLICIES IN A GLOBAL CONTEXT. *Int. Perspectives [Canada] 1973 (July-August): 32-37.* Canada must assess its present energy needs and power resources to assure sufficient supplies in the future.

1285. Critchley, W. Harriet. DOES DOCTRINE PRECEDE WEAPONRY? *Int. J. [Canada] 1978 33(3): 524-556.* Discusses defense policy and weapons with special reference to the re-equipment of the

Canadian Armed Forces with new tanks, aircraft, and ships. Table, 14 notes.   R. V. Kubicek

1286. Currie, Donald. CANADA'S ENERGY RESOURCES. *Communist Viewpoint [Canada] 1973 5(2): 37-46.*

1287. DuPasquier, Thierry. RAPPORTS ENTRE LES PROTESTANTS FRANCAIS ET L'AMÉRIQUE DU NORD [Connections between French Protestants and North America]. *Bull. de la Soc. de l'Hist. Protestantisme Français [France] 1976 122(3): 191-199.* Lists principal Huguenot settlements in North America, American Revolution leaders of French Protestant descent, some Protestant members of the French expeditionary force in America, Americans involved in the whaling industry in France in 1786-91 and 1817-30, and some contemporary French Huguenot societies in the United States and Canada. Summarized in English. Based on monographs; 16 notes.   O. T. Driggs

1288. Dwivedi, P. P. THE CANADIAN GOVERNMENT RESPONSE TO ENVIRONMENTAL CONCERN. *Internat. J. [Canada] 1972/73 28(1): 134-152.* In the mid-1960's "growing public concern about environmental problems impelled the Canadian government to respond by undertaking certain legislative, administrative, and international actions." Reviews the history of the formation of the Department of Environment in 1970, and examines its organization and function.
S

1289. Falkner, Ann. THE CANADIAN INVENTORY OF HISTORIC BUILDING. *Can. Geographical J. 1973 86(2): 44-53.* How architectural elements and building techniques are inventoried.   S

1290. Farr, Robin. A REALISTIC APPROACH TO PUBLISHING AND NATIONALISM. *Scholarly Publishing 1973 4(4): 387-396.* Discusses the report by the Royal Commission on Book Publishing, *Canadian Publishers and Canadian Publishing* (Toronto, 1973). The recommendations in the publication are discussed in the context of their application beyond Canada and their implications for government involvement in publishing.   J. A. Casada

1291. Gellner, John. STRATEGIC ANALYSIS IN CANADA. *Int. J. [Canada] 1978 33(3): 493-505.* The Canadian military effort is still hampered by ineffectual strategic analysis and a lack of an independent defense policy. 10 notes.   R. V. Kubicek

1292. Genest, Jean. LA BAIE JAMES [James Bay]. *Action Natl. [Canada] 1973 62(10): 761-784.* Discusses the development of the James Bay area for the production of electricity, its costs, its problems, and its environmental impact, within the context of the world energy crisis.

1293. Glazier, Kenneth M. THE SURGE OF NATIONALISM IN CANADA TODAY. *Current Hist. 1974 66(392): 150-154.*

1294. Gonick, Cy. A LONG LOOK AT THE CCF/NDP. *Can. Dimension 1975 11(1): 24-34.* Discusses the failures of the Co-operative Commonwealth Federation and the National Democratic Party to represent labor in Canada from 1933-75, and suggests socialism as a solution.
S

1295. Gonick, Cy. ON THE ROAD TO TRIPARTISM. *Can. Dimension [Canada] 1977 12(1): 3-6.* Examines the attitudes of the current federal government, the Canadian Labour Congress, and the business community in Canada on the subject of Tripartism, 1977.

1296. Goodwin, Clive E. POLLUTION. *Can. Labour 1973 18(4-6): 21-24.*

1297. Haddrell, Glenn. PENSION FUNDS FOR CO-OP HOUSING? *Can. Labour 1973 18(7-9): 19-20, 41.*

1298. Hand, Wayland D. MEASURING AND PLUGGING: THE MAGICAL CONTAINMENT AND TRANSFER OF DISEASE. *Bull. of the Hist. of Medicine 1974 48(2): 221-233.* Treats 20th-century folk medicine in the United States and Canada. Read at the 46th annual meeting of the American Association for the History of Medicine, Cincinnati, Ohio, 4 May 1973.   S

1299. Hannigan, John A. THE NEWSPAPER OMBUDSMAN AND CONSUMER COMPLAINTS: AN EMPIRICAL ASSESSMENT. *Law and Soc. Rev. 1977 11(4): 679-699.* The results of a survey of approximately 300 clients of a Canadian newspaper ombudsman. The data show that the newspaper ombudsman is more successful as a facilitator in a consumer-business dispute than as a mediator. Also, this service tends to benefit middle classes as opposed to higher or lower classes.
H. R. Mahood

1300. Hartland-Rowe, Richard. CONTROLLING WATER POLLUTION: WHAT IS NEEDED? *Can. Geographical J. 1975 91(5): 34-41.* Discusses the problem of water pollution in Canada during the 1960's and 70's.

1301. Heap, James L. WARRANTING INTERPRETATIONS: A DEMONSTRATION. *Can. Rev. of Sociol. and Anthrop. [Canada] 1978 15(1): 41-49.* The problem of warranting interpretations of social action is discussed in terms of the controversy over *aktuelles Verstehen.* Borrowing from ordinary language philosophy, a method of warranting is proposed. The method is demonstrated by explicating the grammar of the concept of justification and showing how the conditions were satisfied in Trudeau's War Measures Act speech for interpreting three of his (speech) acts as justification.   J

1302. Hennessey, R. A. INDUSTRIAL ARCHAEOLOGY IN EDUCATION. *Hist. Teacher 1975 9(1): 29-55.* Discusses the status of industrial archaeology, its place in the study of history, and opportunities for study in this field in Great Britain, Canada, and the United States. Offers specific suggestions for placing the study of industrial archaeology in historical context. The article includes a listing of "Useful Addresses in the United States and Canada." 2 illus.   P. W. Kennedy

1303. Hodgins, Bruce W. and Smith, Denis. CANADA AND QUÉBEC: FACING THE REALITY. *J. of Can. Studies [Canada] 1977 12(3): 124-126.* English-speaking Canada and Quebec-French Canada are really separate nations, though the Anglophones are not as aware of their identity as are the French. Whether the result of the current confrontation is sovereignty for Quebec or some new type of confederation, English-speaking Canadians should become more aware and confident of their own purpose and will to survive as a distinct entity.
J. C. Billigmeier

1304. Horowitz, Irving Louis. THE HEMISPHERIC CONNECTION. *Queen's Q. [Canada] 1973 80(3): 327-359.* Critiques "the entrepreneurial thesis of development with special emphasis on the Canadian case." Takes issue with Seymour Martin Lipset on basic questions of American political sociology. After examining the Canadian identity and social values, supplemented by statistical data, the author concludes that in broad areas of sociological significance such as murder, divorce, religion, and education, it is difficult "to bifurcate and bipolarize general data on the United States and Canada." Canada is characterized by its own special set of international connections and a unique form of advanced capitalism, and these complexities necessitate rejection of Lipset's thesis. 9 tables, biblio.   J. A. Casada

1305. Howes, Helen C. THE WORLD'S LARGEST RAILWAY MUSEUM. *Can. Geographical J. [Canada] 1977 94(3): 42-47.* The Canadian Railway Museum in St. Constant, near Montreal, Quebec, was created by the Canadian Railroad Historical Association. Discusses the Museum's history since the 1940's and the locomotives and railroad cars in its collection. Map, 12 photos.   D. J. Engler

1306. Hutchison, Bruce. CANADA'S TIME OF TROUBLES. *Foreign Affairs 1977 56(1): 175-189.* Though the 1976 provincial victory of René Lévesque and his Parti Quebecois added new momentum to the cause of French Canadian separatism, an independent Quebec is by no means inevitable. After years of indecision and hesitation, the federal government clearly has committed itself to a bicultural and bilingual Canada.   M. R. Yerburgh

1307. Jensen, Robert. THE UPSIDE OF UNDERGROUNDS. *Horizon 1978 21(2): 72-77.* Discusses design evolution in subways, 1940's-70's, in the United States, Mexico, Canada, and Europe.

1308. Kirschbaum, J. M. SLOVAKS HELP SET PACE IN CAN-ADA. *Jednota Ann. Furdek 1977 16: 109-114.* Discusses Slovak Canadians and their contribution to public life, politics, sports, and fine arts in Canada, 1950-77.

1309. Laponce, J. A. OF GODS, DEVILS, MONSTERS, AND ONE-EYED VARIABLES. *Can. J. of Pol. Sci. 1974 7(2): 199-209.* Urges his fellow political scientists to ask fewer questions and seek, through a more comprehensive multifactor approach, to answer them more adequately. 30 notes.   R. V. Kubicek

1310. Larsen, H. K. SWEDISH PLANNING: A LESSON FOR CANADA. *Queen's Q. [Canada] 1975 82(1): 98-106.* A survey of the socioeconomic development of Sweden suggesting how it is applicable to Canada. Suggests that Sweden's experiences indicate that Canada should have longer-range budgets, comprehensive industrial and resource usage strategy, and a more formal communication and consultation network.   J. A. Casada

1311. Lochead, Richard. THREE APPROACHES TO ORAL HISTORY: THE JOURNALISTIC, THE ACADEMIC, AND THE ARCHIVAL. *Can. Oral Hist. Assoc. J. [Canada] 1975/76 1: 5-12.* Examines three aspects of oral history in Canada, 1960-75.

1312. MacDonald, H. A. CANADIAN COMMAND AND STAFF COLLEGE. *Marine Corps Gazette 1975 59(8): 40-43.* Discusses the role of the Canadian Armed Forces Command and Staff College in training officers for the Canadian military (1966-74).   S

1313. Main, John. PUBLICATION AND COPYRIGHT OF ORAL HISTORY MATERIALS: THE OISE EXPERIENCE. *Can. Oral Hist. Assoc. J. [Canada] 1975/76 1: 37-41.* Through the experience of the Oral Institute for Studies in Education, presents findings concerning copyright laws and publication possibilities for those working in oral history, 1960's-75.

1314. Manor, F. S. WILL CANADA BREAK UP? *Encounter [Great Britain] 1977 49(2): 68-76.* Discusses current political and economic trends in Canada: a resurgence of nationalism, a foreign trade deficit, rising inflation, cultural isolation, declining labor production, and a rising taxation percentage which is squelching the spirit of free enterprise.

1315. McCracken, Jane. THE ROLE OF ORAL HISTORY IN MUSEUMS. *Can. Oral Hist. Assoc. J. [Canada] 1975/76 1: 34-36.* Examines oral history as a method by which museums, as public institutions, can better educate the public, 1970's; discusses the use to which specific museums in Canada might put this information.

1316. Miller, Robert F. WRITING ABOUT COMMUNISM. *Australian J. of Pol. and Hist. [Australia] 1975 21(3): 167-171.* A review of four books: *The Communist Party in Canada: A History* by Ivan Avakumovic (Toronto, 1975); *The Politics of Modernization in Eastern Europe: Testing the Soviet Model* ed. by Charles Gati (New York and London, 1974); *Bureaucracy and Revolution in Eastern Europe* by Chris Harman (London, 1974); and *Organizacija i Funkcije Javne Uprave: Osnovne Uporedne i Istorijske Karakteristike* [The organization and function of public administration: basic comparative and historical characteristics] by Aleksandar Stojanović (Belgrade, 1972). The author compares the books, each of which respectively illustrates four different analytical perspectives viz., that of the traditional political and historical scholar; that of the current Western (mainly American) scholar striving for scientific objectivity in the comparative analysis of communist systems; that of the Western New Left critiques of existing socialist systems; and finally, the sympathetic but critical analyses of insiders (mainly Yugoslavs) who seek basically nonrevolutionary change to enhance the humanistic and popular elements of their societies. Secondary sources; 4 notes.   R. G. Neville

1317. Norris, Darrell A. SOME COMMENTS CONCERNING A MEETING OF ONTARIO HISTORICAL GEOGRAPHERS. *Urban Hist. Rev. [Canada] 1976 76(1): 14-20.* Reports on the papers of the urban historical geography of Ontario and the prehistoric and historical geography of the native peoples of Canada, presented at a meeting at McMaster University, 20 March 1976. Summarizes the papers and calls for more interdisciplinary study and cooperation between urban historians and historical geographers.   C. A. Watson

1318. O'Farrell, John K. A. THE CANADIAN CATHOLIC HISTORICAL ASSOCIATION'S FORTIETH ANNIVERSARY: A RETROSPECTIVE VIEW. *Study Sessions: Can. Catholic Hist. Assoc. 1973 40: 61-68.* Discusses the Canadian Catholic Historical Association.   S

1319. Ogmundson, Rick. PARTY CLASS IMAGES AND THE CLASS VOTE IN CANADA. *Am. Sociol. R. 1975 40(4): 506-512.* Canada stands out sharply as a country in which the relationship of social class to electoral politics appears to be almost non-existent. The class vote in Canada is re-examined using a new measure which takes into account voter perceptions of the class positions of the political parties. The results indicate that voter interest in class issues is greater than previously thought. This, in turn, suggests that the main source of the anomaly associated with the Canadian case resides, not with the Canadians themselves, but with the nature of the electoral options presented to them. This finding suggests that one cannot assume that the politics of a democracy faithfully reflect the salient concerns of its citizens. The results also suggest that conventional measures of voting behavior, which normally fail to take into account the variable nature of electoral options, provide a poor indicator of the nature of mass sentiment.   J

1320. Oliver, Peter. ORAL HISTORY: ONE HISTORIAN'S VIEW. *Can. Oral Hist. Assoc. J. [Canada] 1975/76 1: 13-19.* Affirms the importance of oral history as a tool for the historian to assess daily life and popular thought during the modern age.

1321. Ossenberg, Richard J. UNITY IN SPITE OF OURSELVES. *Queen's Q. [Canada] 1974 81(3): 431-436.* Examines separatism in Quebec and alienation in Canada's hinterlands, suggesting that, somewhat paradoxically, conflict forces are a factor making for national unity. Biblio.   J. A. Casada

1322. Ostry, Bernard. DISCOURS ADRESSÉ AU COLLOQUE SUR L'HISTOIRE ORALE, 1976 [Address to the Oral History Conference, 1976]. *Can. Oral Hist. Assoc. J. [Canada] 1976/77 2: 11-19.* Discusses the origin and growth in popularity of oral history, emphasizing the need to be granted credence by academic history circles, 1975-76.

1323. Ostry, Bernard. SPEECH DELIVERED TO THE 1976 ORAL HISTORY COLLOQUIUM. *Can. Oral Hist. Assoc. J. [Canada] 1978 3(1): 1-9.* Provides examples of the use of oral history by academic, amateur, and museum researchers in Canada, 1930's-70's.

1324. Paquin, Michel and Migué, Jean-Luc. EFFICACITE ECONOMIQUE ET LUTTE CONTRE LA POLLUTION DE L'EAU [Economic efficiency and the struggle against water pollution]. *Actualité Econ. [Canada] 1973 49(2): 163-174.* There is no way for all individuals in a society to state their preferences for water usage. What is pollution for one use is not necessarily pollution for another. Starting from an idealized situation of only two persons with different uses for a single water source, the author builds up to more complex situations. He summarizes and evaluates current policies, primarily those of Quebec. Much of the earlier study of the problem and solutions proposed were premised on an ideal world which has produced more or less dubious results. A "least evil" theory and approach would be more applicable to the current situation. Graph, 5 notes.   W. B. Whitham

1325. Parry, Geraint. ELITES AND INFLUENCES. *Government and Opposition [Great Britain] 1975 10(2): 240-243.* Reviews Robert Presthus's *Elites in the Policy Process* (London: Cambridge U. Pr., 1974) and Bridget Pym's *Pressure Groups and the Permissive Society* (Newton Abbot: David and Charles, 1974), which study pressure groups in Great Britain, Canada, and the United States.

1326. Philips, R. A. J. HERITAGE CANADA—AND WHAT IT MEANS. *Can. Geographical J. 1973 87(5): 4-11.* Heritage Canada preserves historic buildings and sites.   S

1327. Polyani, J. C. A NATION'S SCIENCE AND TECHNOLOGY. *Bull. of the Atomic Scientists 1976 32(3): 8-12.* Discusses the relationship between national self-image, intellectual traditions and attitudes toward the development of science and technology in Canada in the 1970's.

1328. Reford, Robert W. PROBLEMS OF NUCLEAR PROLIFERATION. *Behind the Headlines [Canada] 1975 34(1): 1-22.* Canada has furthered knowledge of peacetime uses of atomic energy but declined to develop its own nuclear arms stockpile.

1329. Richmond, Anthony H. and Verma, Ravi P. THE ECONOMIC ADAPTATION OF IMMIGRANTS: A NEW THEORETICAL PERSPECTIVE. *Int. Migration Rev. 1978 12(1): 3-38.* Compares classical "functionalist" migration theories with neo-Marxian models, and finds both inadequate to explain international trends in migration and the Canadian experience of immigration since World War II. Advances an alternative "global systems model" of international and internal migration which takes into account the movements within and between industrial and postindustrial societies, as well as movements from less developed to more developed areas. The most mobile sections of the population will continue to be those with higher education, professional and technical skills, or managerial experience. C. Moody

1330. Rubinoff, Lionel. NATIONALISM AND CELEBRATION: REFLECTIONS ON THE SOURCES OF CANADIAN IDENTITY. *Queen's Q. [Canada] 1975 82(1): 1-13.* Examines nationalism in a Canadian context from the viewpoint that it is intimately connected with economic and political interests. Because nationalism is already becoming an outdated concept, argues that the diversity of the Canadian cultural traditions which has led to the development of a Canadian consciousness should be a cause for celebration. 13 notes. J. A. Casada

1331. Stewart, William. MAOISM IN CANADA. *Communist Viewpoint [Canada] 1973 5(2): 9-13.*

1332. Sullivan, Richard F. LES ASPECTS ÉCONOMIQUES DE LA PROTECTION DE LA SOCIÉTÉ [Economic perspectives of problems in social defense]. *Actualité Écon. [Canada] 1974 50(4): 512-519.* "In this paper, the author describes some views that economists have of the problems of criminology together with the means accessible to them by which they attempt to answer certain interesting questions. Sketches of the economic arguments which are challenging a dominant view of the theory of criminal law and challenging as well the concept of 'rehabilitation' are presented. The author proposes to review, briefly, the arguments for a systems approach and to outline new 'industry' approaches to criminology problems. Finally, he tries to demonstrate why many traditional criminology studies are obsolete, and he indicates in passing the reason why the displacing of crime in time is a social benefit." J

1333. Trezise, Philip H. THE ENERGY CHALLENGE. *Pro. of the Acad. of Pol. Sci. 1976 32(2): 113-123.* Existing or predictable energy reserves are still considerable and new technology will no doubt develop before reserves are depleted. The energy challenge, insofar as Canada and the United States are concerned, consists of regulating energy use so that it maximizes benefits. Neither has acted efficiently, up to this point, but existing agencies and policies hold hope for improvement. A single energy policy and resource coordination is officially out of the question, but something similar may result from purely nationalistic motives. Note. V. L. Human

1334. Webber, L. R. SOLID WASTES. *Can. Geographical J. 1973 86(6): 192-201.* Canadians must become aware of the problems of pollution while technology still has solutions. S

1335. Wilgat, T. PROBLEMES GEOGRAPHIQUES DE L'EXPLOITATION DES RESSOURCES EN [Some geographical problems concerning the exploitation of our water resources]. *R. de l'U. d'Ottawa [Canada] 1973 43(3): 373-389.* In spite of the plenitude of water, planning its use, and the judicious use of hydroelectric power, are indispensable. M. L. Frey

1336. Wilkinson, Ron. LABELLING THE LAND: CANADA NEEDS 2,000,000 MORE PLACE NAMES. *Can. Geographical J. 1973 87(1): 12-19.*

1337. —. CANADA AND QUEBEC NATIONALISM. *Can. Dimension 1975 10(7): 32-37.*
Piotte, Jean-Marc. A QUESTION OF STRATEGY, pp. 32-34.
Resnick, Philip. STRATEGY AND ITS DISCONTENTS, pp. 35-37.

1338. —. [HUMANIST DEMOCRACY, MARXISM, AND C. B. MACPHERSON]. *Can. J. of Pol. Sci. 1976 9(3): 377-430.*
Minogue, K. R. HUMANIST DEMOCRACY: THE POLITICAL THOUGHT OF C. B. MACPHERSON, pp. 377-394. Discusses the mixture of individualism and communal sentiment in the work of Canadian political theorist C. B. MacPherson. 37 notes.
Svacek, Victor. THE ELUSIVE MARXISM OF C. B. MACPHERSON, pp. 395-422. The work of political theorist C. B. MacPherson includes all the necessary minima of a Marxist position except its revolutionary prescriptions. 133 notes.
MacPherson, C. B. HUMANIST DEMOCRACY AND ELUSIVE MARXISM: A RESPONSE TO MINOGUE AND SVACEK, pp. 423-430. Responds to the two critiques (one liberal and one Marxist). 13 notes. R. V. Kubicek

Society and Culture

1339. Abu-Laban, Sharon and Abu-Laban, Baha. WOMEN AND THE AGED AS MINORITY GROUPS: A CRITIQUE. *Can. Rev. of Sociol. and Anthrop. [Canada] 1977 14(1): 103-116.* Critically examines contrasting arguments [among North American sociologists] over the extension of the minority group concept to two subgroups outside the traditional minority perspective: women and the aged. The participants in these debates have tended to utilize an essentially similar definition of minority group which encompasses both social structural and social psychological elements. But they have disagreed on the relative importance of these elements and on the evaluations and interpretations of relevant empirical evidence. The debates reveal that the minority group concept, though ideologically attractive, is still ambiguously defined, poorly operationalized, and insensitive to changes in a group's position over time. Recent attempts at redefining it and broadening its referents have not succeeded in clarifying the conceptual and methodological issues underlying the current debates. Suggestions are made toward this clarification. J

1340. Adamson, Christopher R.; Findlay, Peter C.; Oliver, Michael K.; and Solberg, Janet. THE UNPUBLISHED RESEARCH OF THE ROYAL COMMISSION ON BILINGUALISM AND BICULTURALISM. *Can. J. of Pol. Sci. 1974 7(4): 709-720.* Provides a reference to more than 100 unpublished reports deposited in mimeographic form in the Public Archives of Canada, Ottawa. 2 notes, appendix. R. V. Kubicek

1341. Andrews, Margaret W. REVIEW ARTICLE: ATTITUDES IN CANADIAN WOMEN'S HISTORY 1945-1975. *J. of Can. Studies [Canada] 1977 12(4): 69-78.* A consistently polemic intent characterizes recent literature on Canadian women's history. From 1945 to 1970, English-language authors emphasized the compatibility of a life inside and outside the home, and sought to recall women to the activism of earlier years through the example of those whose lives they described. French-language writers praised the traditional roles of mother and nun, especially as they helped to preserve French Canadian culture. In the 70's, trends in the two literatures tended to converge. Canadian writing on women tended to be less devoted to great individuals, and to be influenced by the ideas and rhetoric of a revitalized but much-changed women's movement. Based on the texts reviewed and secondary sources; 55 notes. L. W. Van Wyk

1342. Arès, Richard. LES MINORITÉS FRANCO-CANADIENNES: ÉTUDE STATISTIQUE [French-Canadian minorities: A statistical study]. *Action Natl. [Canada] 1976 66(1): 34-47.* Census returns of 1971 indicate that outside the province of Quebec, francophones tend to become strongly anglicized. Ethnic French tend to consider English as their maternal language and to speak English within the family. The trend is most pronounced in the western provinces. It is also strong in Ontario and appears in the Maritime provinces where only New Brunswick maintains a strong French influence. 5 tables. A. W. Novitsky

1343. Askey, Donald E.; Gage, Gene G.; and Rovinsky, Robert T. NORDIC AREA STUDIES IN NORTH AMERICA: A SURVEY AND DIRECTORY OF THE HUMAN AND MATERIAL RESOURCES. *Scandinavian Studies 1975 47(2): 109-256.* In separate subsections the authors define their methodology in compiling the data and defend the validity of their results. The first area covered in this survey is the Humanities. Enrollment in the Nordic languages apparently is down but enrollment in non-language courses such as culture, history, and social sciences has risen. There is a slight increase in enrollment in Scandinavian studies majors at all levels. The second area covered is Social Studies. Enrollment in Scandinavian social studies increased by nearly 50% during 1970-73. Includes a directory of scholars and a section on Nordic Library resources in North America. 20 tables, 20 notes.
O. W. Ohrvall

1344. Audet, Louis-Philippe. BILAN DE LA CONTRIBUTION DE LA SECTION DES LETTRES ET DES SCIENCES HUMAINES AUX ÉTUDES CANADIENNES, 1952-72 [Perspective on the contribution of the Letters and Social Sciences Section on Canadian studies, 1952-72]. *Tr. of the Royal Soc. of Can. 1973 11: 131-146.* Offers a comprehensive inventory of studies presented to the Letters and Social Sciences Section of the Royal Society of Canada, 1952-72; the studies are an important contribution to the knowledge of French civilization in Canada.

1345. Baldus, Bernd and Tribe, Verna. THE DEVELOPMENT OF PERCEPTIONS AND EVALUATIONS OF SOCIAL INEQUALITY AMONG PUBLIC SCHOOL CHILDREN. *Can. Rev. of Sociol. and Anthrop. [Canada] 1978 15(1): 50-60.* One hundred and eight children in Toronto-area public schools participated in a study designed to find out when and how children employ concepts of social inequality to identify and order their environment. The findings indicate that by the time they are 11 years old, most of the children have not only developed an ability to recognize inequality, but also use evaluative prejudgments which link specific expectations concerning moral and performance behaviour with social class. The findings are discussed in the context of the legitimation of social inequality in contemporary capitalist societies.
J

1346. Bate, Peter. LEARNING HISTORICAL THINKING DOES MAKE A DIFFERENCE. *Teaching Hist. 1975 4(13): 9-12.* Tests of Canadian high school students showed that lessons developed by Edwin Fenton to teach historical thinking resulted in higher scores in critical thinking abilities.
S. D. Smith

1347. Beckman, Margaret. LIBRARY NETWORKS IN THE '70'S: UNIVERSITY LIBRARIES. *Can. Lib. J. 1974 31(3): 197-198, 200.* Discusses the need for and possible benefits of a university library network in Canada.
S

1348. Beveridge, James. CULTURE AND THE MEDIA IN CANADA. *Am. Rev. of Can. Studies 1973 3(1): 135-145.* Discusses television and films in Canada during the 1960's and 70's, highlighting audience acceptance, sources, finance, and distribution.

1349. Bird, Florence. THE GREAT DECADE FOR CANADIAN WOMEN. *Current Hist. 1977 72(426): 170-172, 179-180.* Examines the status of women in Canada, 1966-76; despite progress, women do not yet have equal status or opportunity.

1350. Bohne, Harald. THE CRISIS OF SCHOLARLY PUBLISHING. *J. of Can. Studies 1975 10(2): 9-15.* Discusses difficulties encountered in scholarly publishing in Canada during 1974, including high publishing costs and relatively low circulation.

1351. Bourgeon, C. Y. LES ARCHIVES DE PROGRAMMES A RADIO-CANADA, C'EST QUOI? [Program Archives of Radio Canada: What's That?]. *Can. Oral Hist. Assoc. J. [Canada] 1975/76 1: 42-47.* Examines the Radio Canada Archives, an archive established in Montreal in 1959 to preserve radio and some television broadcasts.

1352. Bourne, L. S. THE CENTRE FOR URBAN AND COMMUNITY STUDIES. *Urban Hist. Rev. [Canada] 1978 78(2): 100-104.* Describes the research themes and the objectives of the Centre for Urban and Community Studies, University of Toronto and suggests ways in

which urban historians can utilize it. Urban history and urban studies can both benefit by such interdisciplinary links.
C. A. Watson

1353. Bourne, L. S. SOME MYTHS OF CANADIAN URBANIZATION: REFLECTIONS ON THE 1976 CENSUS AND BEYOND. *Urbanism Past and Present 1977-78 (5): 1-11.* Examines misconceptions derived from empirical research depending on statistics and images from past periods: emerging trends are overlooked until they are obvious. This dependence results in analyzing problems and processes of the past rather than those of the present or future. Future projections result in errors of interpretation. Critiques current thinking based on 1976 Canadian Census, including preoccupations of urban growth fixation, metropolitan concentration and growth, regional depopulation, high urban migration, peripheral growth of the industrial and financial heartland, stability of urban growth, and institutional reorganization. Concludes with policy implications and plea for future-oriented and politically-sensitive research. 5 tables, 7 notes.
B. P. Anderson

1354. Boutet, Odina. LA GRENOUILLE BICULTURELLE ET LE BOEUF UNICULTUREL [The bicultural frog and the unicultural bull]. *Action Natl. [Canada] 1977 67(1): 61-73.* Canadian federalism and biculturalism are opportunities for English Canadians to retain their identity while assimilating and destroying the identity of French Canadians. Quebec's weakness has been caused not only by the strength of English culture in North America but also by the absence of a French culture even within the province. French Canadian educational institutions and news media have been especially negligent in preserving French culture. While presenting a facade of seeking unity to the outside world, internally English Canadians have exercised a policy of intimidation and deprived French Canadians of perspective and a sense of accomplishment.
A. W. Novitsky

1355. Boyd, Monica. FAMILY SIZE IDEALS OF CANADIANS: A METHODOLOGICAL NOTE. *Can. R. of Sociol. and Anthrop. 1974 11(4): 360-370.* "Using data from Canadian Gallup Poll questions on the number of children considered ideal, this paper suggests that the frequently cited 1960 figure of 4.2 children is erroneously inflated. The discussion compares responses in 1960 to responses of an earlier 1957 poll. Comparisons are also made between American and Canadian responses to recent questions on ideal family size."
J

1356. Breton, Raymond; Burnet, Jean; Hartmann, Norbert; Isajiw, Wsevolod; and Lennards, J. RESEARCH ISSUES ON CANADIAN CULTURES AND ETHNIC GROUPS. AN ANALYSIS OF A CONFERENCE. *Can. Rev. of Sociol. and Anthrop. 1975 12(1): 81-94.* Synopsis of discussions on Canadian ethnic groups at the National Conference on Canadian Culture and Ethnic Groups in Canada, October 1973, including ethnicity and stratification, prestige, social class, pluralism, ethnic boundaries, immigration, and generational differences.

1357. Brusegard, David A. *SOCIAL INDICATORS '76 AND PERSPECTIVE CANADA II:* ELIXERS OF REASON OR OF SLEEP? *Ann. of the Am. Acad. of Pol. and Social Sci. 1978 (435): 268-276.* Both *Social Indicators, 1976* and its Canadian counterpart, *Perspective Canada II,* are produced by government organizations with the intent to develop social indicators and provide a social report on the condition and progress of their respective nations. Having examined both publications, the author suggests that neither goal has been accomplished or properly dealt with. It is argued that to accomplish either objective in a satisfactory manner, both *Social Indicators, 1976* and *Perspective Canada II* must change their organization, commentary, authorship, and intended audience. Among other things, such publications must seek authors outside of government and actively draw them to the attention of education and public audiences.
J

1358. Buchignani, Norm. A REVIEW OF THE HISTORICAL AND SOCIOLOGICAL LITERATURE ON EAST INDIANS IN CANADA. *Can. Ethnic Studies [Canada] 1977 9(1): 86-108.* Provides additions to the bibliographic studies of East Indian immigration into Canada. The introductory essay compares major sources. The 286 listings were published before 1970. Most are readily available through library sources, though doctoral dissertations are more difficult to obtain. The listings include sociological, historical, bibliographical, educational, and quantitative references. Primary sources include folk historical commentary from the immigrants and government documents from England, the United States, and Canada.   K. S. McDorman

1359. Budakowska, Elżbieta. STRUKTURA DEMOGRAFICZNA POLONII KANADYJSKIEJ [Demographic structure of the Poles in Canada]. *Kultura i Społeczeństwo [Poland] 1976 20(1): 107-116.* The largest center of the Canadian Polonia is still Toronto, followed by Winnipeg, Montreal, Edmonton, Hamilton, Vancouver, Calgary, and Ottawa. The Canadian Polonia, hindered by foreign heritage and low income, shows a considerable rise in its professional structure since World War II. The educated or partly educated pre- and postwar Polish emigration greatly influenced this because it increased the number of intellectuals and scholars. The number of Polish students at Canadian universities also has risen considerably.   M. Swiecicka-Ziemianek

1360. Cameron, David. DOWN AND OUT OF THE IVORY TOWER. *J. of Can. Studies [Canada] 1976 11(4): 1-2, 69-72.* Discusses the relationship between social responsibility and academic responsibility in the university in Canada, concluding that more specific knowledge is necessary concerning university autonomy and public accountability, especially in the area of Canadian studies, 1970's.

1361. Campbell, H. C. METROPOLITAN PUBLIC LIBRARY SYSTEMS IN CANADA. *Pakistan Lib. Bull. [Pakistan] 1973 6(1-2): 1-28.* Regional quality of public library service necessitated by metropolitan growth was achievable only by consolidation. This has been hampered by municipalities clinging to control over their libraries. Secondary sources; 8 tables, 23 notes.   V. Samaraweera

1362. Careless, J. M. S. URBAN DEVELOPMENT IN CANADA. *Urban Hist. Rev. [Canada] 1974 74(1): 9-13.* Examines the effect of Canadian urbanization on the hinterland and rural areas surrounding urban centers, during 1955-75.

1363. Carpentier, Rene, et al. LA FONCTIONNALITÉ DE LA FORMATION ACADÉMIQUE DU SOCIOLOGUE [The functionality of the academic formation of sociologists]. *Recherches sociographiques [Canada] 1974 15(2/3): 313-334.* In addition to a sound preparation in the fundamentals of sociology, the universities should provide their students with practical experience so as to prepare them for the realities of the work world. Based on a masters level seminar in which several practicing sociologists were interviewed.   A. E. LeBlanc

1364. Castonguay, Charles and Marion, Jacques. L'ANGLICISATION DU CANADA [The Anglicization of Canada]. *Action Natl. [Canada] 1974 63(8/9): 733-749.* A study comparing language usage in Canada, 1961-71, indicates a trend toward the assimilation of French-speaking Canadians to English, even in Quebec.

1365. Clark, S. D. THE ATTACK ON THE AUTHORITY STRUCTURE OF THE CANADIAN SOCIETY. *Tr. of the Royal Soc. of Can. [Canada] 1976 14: 3-15.* Discusses the effect of the protest movements of the 1960's on Canadian society. In Canada the middle class was more narrowly based than in the United States; hence, there was less opportunity for individual advancement. Dissatisfied Canadians, both working class and middle class, sought opportunities to the south. After World War II there were more economic opportunities in Canada with the resulting population shift from rural to urban; but, in the 1960's, more young people entered the work force than there were positions. At the same time, dissatisfied Americans emigrated to Canada where they became leaders in opposition to the old order. Although in the United States the protest movement was more violent, in Canada it had a more lasting effect because many Canadian officials had little experience in running newly created educational and governmental agencies and more readily yielded to pressure. 2 notes.   J. D. Neville

1366. Clark, S. D. CANADIAN URBAN DEVELOPMENT. *Urban Hist. Rev. [Canada] 1974 74(1): 14-19.* Urbanization in Canada during 1955-75 followed the pattern in northern Ontario and Quebec; rural persons moved into cities to find employment and gave cities a rural, conservative attitude rather than a metropolitan one.

1367. Clark, S. D. THE POST SECOND WORLD WAR CANADIAN SOCIETY. *Can. R. of Sociol. and Anthrop. 1975 12(1): 25-32.* The primary concern of this paper is with what has happened to Canadian society since the Second World War. In seeking to understand the changes that have been taking place in this society, however, the author argues that it is necessary to go back and examine the way in which Canadian society developed over the years before the Second World War. One can speak of an 'old order' of Canadian society, not simply of an old order of the society of French Canada, and what has happened since the war, in English-speaking as well as French-speaking Canada, can be described as a 'quiet revolution.'   J

1368. Clarkson, Stephen. THE AMBIGUITIES OF ANALYSIS: THE PROBLEM OF KNOWING OURSELVES. *J. of Can. Studies [Canada] 1976 11(4): 50-54.* The T. H. B. Symons report, *To Know Ourselves: The Report of the Commission on Canadian Studies* (Ottawa: Assoc. of U. and Coll. of Can., 1975) deals with higher education in Canada and the need for advanced Canadian studies.

1369. Clement, Wallace. INEQUALITY OF ACCESS: CHARACTERISTICS OF THE CANADIAN CORPORATE ELITE. *Can. R. of Sociol. and Anthrop. 1975 12(1): 33-52.* Modelled after John Porter's 1951 corporate elite study, this paper updates an analysis of the social characteristics of this elite to 1972. By comparing means of mobility into the elite and class of origin for the two periods it finds that access to dominant corporations has become increasingly confined to members of the upper class. Mobility from working class origins has declined. Compradorization, the elite reflection of foreign penetration of Canada's economy, has provided more mobility for middle class Canadians than has the indigenous elite. There remains a powerful core of indigenous Canadian capitalists firmly rooted in the upper class. The private world of powerful people is examined as a means of elite interaction and selection. It is shown that traditional social forces tend to become more exclusive while new social forces bring new social types to power.   J

1370. Corry, J. A. THE ROLE OF THE UNIVERSITY AND THE SCHOLAR IN CONTEMPORARY SOCIETY. *Tr. of the Royal Soc. of Can. [Canada] 1973 11: 255-260.* Discusses relevance in Canada's colleges and universities and stresses the need for the university to maintain touch with the society it serves.

1371. Crampton, Esmé. PREPARATION FOR AN ORAL BIOGRAPHY OF GWENETH LLOYD, TEACHER OF DANCE. *Can. Oral Hist. Assoc. J. [Canada] 1976/77 2: 49-53.* The author discusses preparation for an oral biography of Gweneth Lloyd, and use of newspaper clippings and oral interviews with Lloyd, 1969-75.

1372. Crowley, Ronald W. TOWARDS FREE POST-SECONDARY EDUCATION? *J. of Can. Studies 1973 8(3): 43-57.* Presents a case for providing tuition-free higher education opportunities in Canada.

1373. Cuneo, Carl J. and Curtis, James E. SOCIAL ASCRIPTION IN THE EDUCATIONAL AND OCCUPATIONAL STATUS ATTAINMENT OF URBAN CANADIANS. *Can. R. of Sociol. and Anthrop. 1975 12(1): 6-24.* This paper reports on a replication and extension of the Blau-Duncan model of the process of social stratification—an extension to urban Canadian samples and additional independent variables. We focus on the nature and extent of social ascription—the effect of family background, language, and gender on the educational and occupational status attainment of respondents. The analysis is comparative for four subsamples of urban Canadians: francophone men and women and anglophone men and women. The findings show that social ascription is strong in this country in that family background has rather strong and different effects on occupational attainment, through its influence on respondent's education, among women and men and among francophones and anglophones. Some parallel findings from a comparable subgroup of Blau and Duncan's American respondents are also briefly reported on. Among our Canadian findings are the following: mother's education has, of all family background variables, the strongest effect on respondent's education among French males; family size has a greater negative impact on education among anglophones than among francophones; respondent's education has greater effects on occupation among francophones than among anglophones, and among men than among women. Interpretations of these patterns are given and a set of considerations requiring future investigations are presented. In particular, argues that previous American and Canadian data on social mobility have often shown strong ascriptive effects in stratification in contrast to the achievement interpretation which has been placed on them.   J

1374. Curtis, James E. and Lambert, Ronald D. STATUS DISSATIS-FACTION AND OUT-GROUP REJECTION: CROSS-CULTURAL COMPARISONS WITHIN CANADA. *Can. R. of Sociol. and Anthrop. 1975 12(2): 178-192.* An analysis of data on negative affect towards selected religious, racial, and ethnic out-groups is reported. This is guided by an hypothesis from the literature concerning the effect of status dissatisfaction on attitudes towards minority out-groups. The analysis is for working subsamples of English-speaking Catholics and Protestants and French-speaking Catholics, all native born. The independent variable, status dissatisfaction, is measured by four alternative procedures. Education and occupational status are control variables, employed in analyses within each of the three linguistic-religious groups. There are some slight, but statistically significant, direct relationships between status dissatisfaction and negative affect toward Jews and Blacks in evaluations by French Catholics. However, these findings do not obtain for the other two linguistic-religious subgroups. Interpretations and implications of the findings are discussed.   J

1375. de Valk, Alphonse A. M. THE ABORTION ISSUE IN CON-TEMPORARY CANADIAN HISTORY: THE UNFINISHED DE-BATE. *Study Sessions [Canada] 1974 41: 81-100.* Presents Canadian press and public opinion surrounding the abortion issue. A paper read at the 1974 annual meeting of the Canadian Catholic Historical Association.   S

1376. Dobell, Peter and d'Aquino, Susan. THE SPECIAL JOINT COMMITTEE ON IMMIGRATION POLICY 1975: AN EXERCISE IN PARTICIPATORY DEMOCRACY. *Behind the Headlines [Canada] 1976 34(6): 1-24.* Evaluates the steps taken by Martin O'Connell, chairman, and the special committee to discover public opinion about the "green paper," or suggested changes in the immigration law.
                                  S. G. Yntema

1377. Donahue, Jim. A CANADIAN APPRECIATION OF AMERICAN FOLK MUSIC. *Can. Dimension 1976 11(6): 60-61.* A Canadian musician discusses why he admires American folk music, particularly as an expression of American political protest, culture, and values, and as a vehicle for social change.

1378. Dove, Jack. CANADA AND U.S.A., 1972. *Lib. R. [Great Britain] 1973/74 24(4): 159-161.* Recounts a five-week tour in 1972 of libraries in North America. Describes each library and mentions holdings (almost totally audiovisual) and services of each institution. Covers four libraries in Canada and others in the northeastern United States and Chicago.   T. H. Bauhs

1379. Driedger, Leo. CANADIAN MENNONITE URBANISM: ETHNIC VILLAGERS OR METROPOLITAN REMNANT? *Mennonite Q. R. 1975 49(3): 226-241.* Presents a study of the effect of urbanization on traditional Mennonite beliefs and practices in an attempt to determine the amount of erosion, if any, on urban Mennonites in contrast to those in rural areas. Urban Mennonites are lost to other groups in lesser numbers. Institutions (colleges, etc.) are shifting to urbanized areas successfully. The study shows that Canadian Mennonites have suffered less than their American counterparts in urbanization. 3 charts, 19 notes.   E. E. Eminhizer

1380. Driedger, Leo. IN SEARCH OF CULTURAL IDENTITY FACTORS: A COMPARISON OF ETHNIC STUDENTS. *Can. R. of Sociol. and Anthrop. 1975 12(2): 150-162.* Factor analysis of Likert-type items administered to undergraduate students suggests that modes of ethnic identification can be described in terms of six factors: religion, endogamy, language use, ethnic organizations, parochial education, and choice of ingroup friends. A comparison of the factor profiles of seven ethnic groups revealed considerable variations. For example, the Jewish students identified strongly with endogamy and ingroup choice of friends but ranked low on the importance of religion and the use of their ethnic language. The French students' identification with their language and religion was high. Both the French and the Jewish students valued parochial education. Scandinavian and Polish ethnic ingroup identification was the lowest of all seven groups compared. The modes of identification

tended to vary with the historically important experiences of ethnic groups. Therefore the measures of the modes exhibited a multifactor structure.   J

1381. Driedger, Leo and Zehr, Dan. THE MENNONITE STATE-CHURCH TRAUMA: ITS EFFECTS ON ATTITUDES OF CANA-DIAN STUDENTS AND LEADERS. *Mennonite Q. R. 1974 48(4): 515-526.* Discusses some of the social causes for the Canadian Mennonites' perception of social issues, and gives a 1970 statistical analysis of the views of differing Mennonite Conference leaders and university students.   S

1382. England, Claire. COMMENTS ON OBSCENITY: A RE-VIEW OF RECENT LAW REFORM COMMISSIONS. *Can. Lib. J. 1973 30(5): 415-419.*

1383. Falcone, David J. and Mishler, William. LEGISLATIVE DETERMINANTS OF PROVINCIAL HEALTH POLICY IN CAN-ADA: A DIACHRONIC ANALYSIS. *J. of Pol. 1977 39(2): 345-367.* Provincial health policy in Canada results from the interaction of the socioeconomic environment with aspects of the political system such as the degree of constituency and legislative party competition, the partisan composition of provincial legislatures, and the level of legislative institutionalization and professionalism. Data from the 10 provinces, at five year intervals during 1945-65, span the period when provincial health care programs experienced their greatest growth. Supports the Hybrid Environmental Model of policy formation and suggests that the legislative system has a significant, independent effect. Based on primary and secondary sources; 6 tables, 24 notes.   A. W. Novitsky

1384. Farine, Avigdor. LA RESPONSIBILITE COMPTABLE EN MATIERE D'EDUCATION [Accountability in educational content]. *Actualité Econ. [Canada] 1973 49(1): 134-140.* "Accountable responsibility" in education is a new administrative concept which since 1970 has been discussed in numerous publications. This concept can contribute toward the effective utilization of resources and can create an innovative atmosphere for teaching. Previous administrative concepts were based on a private-enterprise model in which efficiency was the supreme goal.
                                  S

1385. Fathi, Asghar. DIFFUSION OF A "HAPPY" NEWS EVENT. *Journalism Q. 1973 50(2): 271-277.* Examines the news diffusion in Calgary of Prime Minister Pierre Trudeau's marriage (1971).
                                  S

1386. Fink, Howard. THE CBC RADIO DRAMA PROJECT AND ITS BACKGROUND. *Can. Oral Hist. Assoc. J. [Canada] 1976/77 2: 54-63.* Examines the Canadian Broadcasting Corporation's radio drama presentations and its influence on drama in Canada, 1940's-50's; also discusses the author's current research on the history of Canada's radio drama.

1387. Fireman, Janet R. REFLECTIONS ON TEACHING WOM-EN'S HISTORY: FIRST DOWN AND GOAL TO GO! *J. of the West 1973 12(2): 197-211.* "The subject of women has generally been neglected by historians." There has been little historical literature about women except from the feminist viewpoint. "Though incomplete and naive, the work of the feminist writers is important today as a catalog of the women's rights movement." Notes various libraries and research centers on women's history. Today more than 1000 women's studies courses are taught in Canada and the United States. 26 notes.
                                  E. P. Stickney

1388. Freeman, Milton M. R. ANTHROPOLOGISTS AND SO-CIAL INVOLVEMENT IN CANADA. *Human Organization 1974 33(4): 391-393.* Examines the opportunities for anthropologists to assist in social reforms.   S

1389. Friedler, Egon et al. JEWS WITHOUT MONEY TODAY. *Present Tense 1975 2(2): 62-67.* Discusses Jews currently living in poverty in Uruguay, Canada, France, and Great Britain.

1390. Fulford, Robert. GENERAL PERSPECTIVES ON THE CA-NADIAN CULTURE. *Am. Rev. of Can. Studies 1973 3(1): 115-121.*

Discusses the growth in Canadian fine arts and the present tendency among the artists to pay more attention to cultural trends in Canada than to depend on US artistic influences.

1391. Genest, Jean. LA JEUNESSE ET SES MILLE MAÎTRES [Youth and its thousand teachers]. *Action Natl. [Canada] 1975 65(4): 298-315.* Since the 1920's, the traditional role of teachers has been replaced by the mass media which undermines values and creates new ways of conceiving ideas by stressing emotions over the scientific approach.

1392. Grabowski, Yvonne. SOME FEATURES OF POLISH AND OTHER SLAVIC LANGUAGES IN CANADA. *Polish Rev. 1977 22(2): 62-72.* Many of the changes in Polish, as spoken in Canada, are the results of extralinguistic factors shared with other tongues. Among these are the size and length of residence of a given language group, its level of education and social class, and its time of arrival. The changes in Polish are stabilized by the second generation, but its use tends to disappear entirely by the third generation. Primary and secondary sources; 20 notes. E. M. McLendon

1393. Groffier, Ethel. PRINCIPAUX PROBLÈMES DE L'ADOP-TION AU CANADA, EN FRANCE ET EN BELGIQUE [Main adoption problems in Canada, France, and Belgium]. *Rev. Int. de Droit Comparé [France] 1974 26(2): 263-294.* The adoption laws of Quebec and the common law provinces of Canada, France, and Belgium, attempt to deal with the problems arising from the effort to equalize the status of the adopted child to the legitimate child. These laws, which in their present form date from the post-World War I period, set forth the conditions under which adoption can take place, regulate the granting and revocation of consent to adoption, and determine the various effects of adoption in regard to the changes in the rights and obligations of the various parties involved. Based on published works, statutes, and judicial decisions; 145 notes. J. S. Gassner

1394. Hawkins, Freda. CANADIAN IMMIGRATION: A NEW LAW AND A NEW APPROACH TO MANAGEMENT. *Int. Migration Rev. 1977 11(1): 77-94.* The 1976 Immigration Bill before the House of Commons would institute an integrated method of management of employment problems and immigration policy.

1395. Hawkins, Freda. CANADIAN IMMIGRATION: PRESENT POLICIES, FUTURE OPTIONS. *Round Table [Great Britain] 1977 (265): 50-64.* Traces Canada's immigration policy since 1945. Discusses the 1962 immigration regulations, the Department of Manpower and Immigration, and the problems of settlement and assimilation. Because the fertility rate is below the replacement level, the Canadian government has adopted the Australian idea of planned population growth through immigration. C. Anstey

1396. Haycock, Ken. COMMUNITY INVOLVEMENT IN SCHOOL LIBRARIES: A PUBLIC RELATIONS APPROACH. *Can. Lib. J. 1973 30(2): 110-115.*

1397. Hayes, Saul. CANADIAN JEWISH CULTURE: SOME OB-SERVATIONS. *Queen's Q. [Canada] 1977 84(1): 80-88.* Canadian Jews have been affected by the broader culture and are heterogeneous, but their "all important propulsion is an *élan vital* of folk, group, [and] people." J. A. Casada

1398. Hedley, R. Alan and Warburton, T. Rennie. THE ROLE OF NATIONAL COURSES IN THE TEACHING AND DEVELOP-MENT OF SOCIOLOGY: THE CANADIAN CASE. *Sociol. R. [Great Britain] 1973 21(2): 299-320.* Using 1971 data from university departments across Canada, empirically examines the increase in courses focusing on Canadian social structure. Based on primary and secondary sources; 3 tables, 36 notes. M. L. Lifka

1399. Henripin, Jacques. L'AVENIR DES FRANCOPHONES AU CANADA [The future of French-speaking people in Canada]. *Tr. of the Royal Soc. of Can. 1975 13: 133-139.* Discusses French-speaking Canadians, noting that they have retained their percentage of the population because of their much higher birthrate. Each year the percentage of Canadians whose primary language is French declines as they emigrate or assimilate. Assimilation is greater in areas far from Quebec, areas in

which the French-speaking population is very small. Discusses Robert Maheu's predictions concerning French-speaking Canadians. Also, even in Quebec the percentage of the population which is French-speaking is declining gradually. 2 notes. J. D. Neville

1400. Hill, Charles C. ORAL HISTORY AND THE HISTORY OF CANADIAN ART. *Can. Oral Hist. Assoc. J. [Canada] 1976-77 2: 31-35.* The author discusses his oral history tape recordings in preparation for an exhibit for the National Gallery of Canada, *Canadian Painting in the Thirties;* discusses possible mutual benefits for oral history and art history.

1401. Hobbs, R. Gerald. THE NATURE AND EXERCISE OF AU-THORITY IN THE UNITED CHURCH OF CANADA. *Bull. of the United Church of Can. 1973 (22): 21-35.* Attempts to determine "the reality of the latitudinarian church" which lies behind the "image of institutionalized ecclesiastical anarchy" projected by the United Church of Canada. Concludes that the church is committed to the authority of the Scriptures and of tradition as enshrined in the Basis of Union, and that the church courts possess the necessary authority to exercise discipline. The results of a survey of 24 ministers, "indicate a tentative shift in the direction of a more effective self-discipline administered in a spirit of grace, whether through forms already in existence or as a result of a move closer to the Anglican communion." Based on a questionnaire and records of church conferences; 63 notes. B. D. Tennyson

1402. Howell, Maxwell L. and Mutimer, Brian T. TOWARD COM-PARATIVE PHYSICAL EDUCATION AND SPORT. *Can. J. of Hist. of Sport and Physical Educ. 1974 5(1): 31-37.* Comparative study of physical education and sport should be in context of the total framework of man; thus the need for borrowing extensively from a variety of disciplines. The desire to know, the possibility of bettering relations and the exchange of different views and ideas justify comparative studies. To facilitate them, working relations should be developed with experts in other disciplines, and some expertise in the subject matter and methodology of the social sciences is vital. 10 notes. R. A. Smith

1403. Hughes, Kenneth. ASESSIPPI EVERYWHERE! *Can. Dimension [Canada] 1978 13(3): 26-37.* Analyzes the work of contemporary Canadian artist Don Proch, in relation to his roots in Ukrainian cultural tradition.

1404. Hull, W. H. N. THE 1971 SURVEY OF THE PROFESSION. *Can. J. of Pol. Sci. 1973 6(1): 89-120.* A 64% return of 1000 questionnaires provides a profile of the nationality, education, research, publication, and funding of political scientists in Canada. 29 tables, 3 notes, appendix. R. V. Kubicek

1405. Hunt, Peter. A CHESTERTONIAN CRITIQUE OF CANA-DIAN SOCIETY TODAY. *Chesterton Rev. [Canada] 1976/77 3(1): 43-84.*

1406. Hurley, Jefferson. "THE NATIONAL FILM BOARD OF CANADA IS FRIGHTENED OF ITS OWN IMAGES." *Communist Viewpoint [Canada] 1973 5(3): 36-42.* The National Film Board's attempts to censor French-language documentaries from Quebec. S

1407. Isajiw, Wsevolod W. DEFINITIONS OF ETHNICITY. *Ethnicity 1974 1(2): 111-124.* Based on an analysis of 27 definitions of ethnicity, a list of features ranked by frequency was compiled. A definition applicable specifically to North America was sought. Concluded by defining ethnicity as referring to an involuntary group of people (one is born into such a group), sharing a common culture, ancestry, peoplehood, *Gemeinschaft*-type relations, and immigrant background. They identify themselves and/or are identified by others as belonging to that group. They possess either a majority or minority status. Biblio.

E. Barkan

1408. Isajiw, Wsevolod W. OLGA IN WONDERLAND: ETH-NICITY IN TECHNOLOGICAL SOCIETY. *Can. Ethnic Studies [Canada] 1977 9(1): 77-85.* Not the marketplace but technological culture most affects immigrant assimilation. Componential, materialistic technology creates a yearning for the maintenance of holistic, natural ethnicity. Impersonal technological culture "heightens the need for identity and

creates the search for identity." The revival of ethnic identities in modern society promises a real pluralism which accepts and affirms all human differences. Discusses Canada and the United States.
K. S. McDorman

1409. Jones, Frank E. CURRENT SOCIOLOGICAL RESEARCH IN CANADA: VIEWS OF A JOURNAL EDITOR. *J. of the Hist. of the Behavioral Sci. 1977 13(2): 160-172*. Sociology in Canada, 1960's-70's, has focused on studies of social problems in an empirical and a theoretical context; discusses ethnic studies and immigrant adjustment.

1410. Jones, H. R. CANADA REVIEWS IMMIGRATION POLICY. *Geography [Great Britain] 1978 63(3): 217-219*. The passage of a new Immigration Act by Canada's Parliament in 1977 marks the culmination of a long debate over immigration. Until recently few industrial nations besides Canada had an expansionist immigration law, yet that policy seems destined to change. From the 1950's to the present Canada has changed from a quota system giving preference to certain nationalities to a system giving preference to immigrants with qualification of education, experience, and skill. But throughout these decades, the constant in her policy towards immigration has been the state of unemployment among Canadians: there is an inverse relationship between unemployment and immigration. This is not likely to change. Canada's immigration policies are apt to become increasingly restrictive, and she is probably going to step up efforts to counsel immigrants abroad, hoping that they will settle outside the main urban centers of Toronto, Montreal, and Vancouver. Table, fig.
J. W. Leedom

1411. Jones, Richard R. L'IDÉOLOGIE DE L'ACTION CATHOLIQUE, 1917-1939 [The ideology of the *Action Catholique*, 1917-39]. *R. d'Hist. de l'Amérique Française [Canada] 1973 27(1): 63-78*. The French Canadian newspaper *L'Action Catholique* steadily defended Catholic ideology 1917-39, criticizing the Bolshevik Revolution of 1917 and the Socialist and Communist organizations of Canada. It did not support Nazism but attacked the Jews and their immigration to Canada (1936-39), for they appeared as natural enemies of the Catholic Church. It supported private enterprise and all the traditional moral principles of the Catholic Church, notably the Sabbath. Based on the *Action Catholique* and secondary sources; 27 notes.
C. Collon

1412. Kapiszewski, Andrzej. PROBLEMS IN CANADIAN MULTICULTURALISM AND THE POLISH-CANADIAN COMMUNITY. *Polish Western Affairs [Poland] 1976 17(1-2): 145-151*. The Canadian Commission on Bilingualism and Biculturalism Affairs reported that Polish Canadians actively participate in Canadian cultural life. Polish schools are the third most numerous among ethnic groups. Poles received substantial subsidies to develop cultural enterprises. In November 1972, Dr. Stanley Haidasz, a Polish Canadian, was appointed Minister of State responsible for multiculturalism.
M. Swiecicka-Ziemianek

1413. Kelly, John J. ALTERNATIVE ESTIMATES OF THE VOLUME OF EMIGRATION FROM CANADA, 1961-1971. *Can. Rev. of Sociol. and Anthrop. [Canada] 1977 14(1): 57-67*. The contribution of immigration to Canada's population growth has received considerable analytical attention. However, much less is known about the impact which emigration has had on the nation's population growth, particularly since actual data are not available on the number of persons emigrating from Canada. This paper presents three different emigration estimates for Canada for the 1961-71 intercensal period derived from different estimation procedures, endeavours to determine which estimate is the most reliable one, and demonstrates the importance of considering emigration in the continuing reformulation of Canada's immigration policies. J

1414. Kerwin, Larkin. PROVINCIALISME INTELLECTUEL AU CANADA [Intellectual provincialism in Canada]. *Tr. of the Royal Soc. of Can. [Canada] 1977 15: 3-7*. Presidential address to the Royal Society based on a similar speech by Monseigneur Camille Roy in 1929. Notes that societies are rarely monolithic and homogeneous; instead most of them are pluralist. Some have accepted ideas from several cultures from which they have then created their own culture such as Italian, English, Dutch, French, and Spanish. Canada, of course benefits from two of these cultures. Cautions against the division of countries into many small regions and notes that Quebec is not the only Canadian area with this

tendency. Also notes the role of the Royal Society of Canada in bringing together the two cultures in Canada.
J. D. Neville

1415. Kiker, B. F. and Traynham, Earle C., Jr. A COMMENT ON "RESEARCH ON INTERNAL MIGRATION IN THE UNITED STATES: A SURVEY." *J. of Econ. Lit. 1976 14(3): 885-888*. Prompted by Michael J. Greenwood's earlier article, discusses reasons for return migration in the internal migration of the United States and Canada in the 1960's and 70's, emphasizing wages, cost of living, and employment factors.

1416. Kirschbaum, J. M. JESUITS FIND A HOME IN CANADA. *Jednota Ann. Furdek 1977 16: 107-109*. Jesuits from Czechoslovakia came to Canada in 1950 following the dissolution of religious communities under Communism.

1417. Kleindienst, Richard G. et al. REHABILITATING OUR CONTINENTAL NEIGHBORHOOD: THE PROBLEM OF DRUGS. *Am. Soc. of Int. Law Pro. 1974 68: 169-189*. Primarily discusses international cooperation in North America to end drug abuse, 1960's-74.

1418. Klement, Susan. FEMINISM AND PROFESSIONALISM IN LIBRARIANSHIP: AN INTERVIEW WITH SHERRILL CHEDA. *Can. Lib. J. 1974 31(6): 520-528*. Sherrill Cheda, campus librarian at Seneca College, Willowdale, Ontario, discusses the current feminist movement, unions, community involvement of librarians, and the Canadian Library Association Committee on the Status of Women. S

1419. Kraszewski, Piotr. POLSKA GRUPA ETNICZNA W KANADZIE [The Polish ethnic group in Canada]. *Przegląd Zachodni [Poland] 1975 31(5-6): 129-159*. Discusses the periodization and the social and professional structure of immigration to Canada during 1900-65, with special reference to the Polish immigrant group—its geographical distribution and its social mobility, in relation to other ethnic groups.

1420. Labovitz, Sanford. SOME EVIDENCE OF CANADIAN ETHNIC, RACIAL, AND SEXUAL ANTAGONISM. *Can. R. of Sociol. and Anthrop. 1974 11(3): 247-254*. "Two studies designed to tap the nature of ethnic, racial, and sexual antagonism in mid-western Canada were carried out in 1972 and 1973. A definite pattern of such antagonism was discovered by using the evaluation of name types that represented selected ethnic groups. Respondents differentially evaluated the names of Edward Blake (English-Canadian male), Edith Blake (English-Canadian female), Joseph Walking Bear (Canadian Indian male), and Marcel Fournier (French-Canadian male). The rank ordering of names on an evaluational scale ranging from highly favourable to highly unfavourable was: (1) Edward Blake, (2) Edith Blake, (3) Joseph Walking Bear, (4) Marcel Fournier. The Indian and the French names were ranked well below the two names representing English Canadians." J

1421. Lacroix, Robert and Proulx, M. UNE EVALUATION PARTIELLE DES PERTES OU DES GAINS DES PROVINCES RESULTANT DE LA MOBILITE DES ETUDIANTS ET DIPLOMES UNIVERSITAIRES [A partial evaluation of the losses or gains to the provinces from the mobility of students and graduates of universities]. *Actualité Econ. [Canada] 1973 49(3): 379-395*. During recent negotiations over federal aid to postsecondary education, certain provinces have shown marked interest in the question of interprovincial mobility of students and graduates. The authors 1) attempt to estimate the extent of this interprovincial mobility, and its relationship to educational grants, 2) provide a mathematical model of the real costs of this mobility, and 3) attempt to evaluate net financial gains and losses. Future negotiations and discussion of the problem must take this mobility into account, because it results in injustices to some provinces. Offers proposals for further investigation. 6 tables, 41 notes.
W. B. Whitham

1422. Lambert, Ronald D. and Curtis, James. NATIONALITY AND PROFESSIONAL ACTIVITY CORRELATES AMONG SOCIAL SCIENTISTS: DATA BEARING ON CONVENTIONAL WISDOMS. *Can. R. of Sociol. and Anthrop. 1973 10(1): 62-80*. "Analysis of data from a recent CSAA survey of sociologists and anthropologists is offered to provide perspective on propositions raised in current debates on the nature of Americanization of academe in [Canada]. Similarities and differences between American and English-Canadian sociologists are explored for a range of professional background and professional activity characteristics. Nationality is operationalized in terms of birthplace, citizenship, and places of BA and highest degrees. Comparisons are also made for 'pure' Canadians and 'pure' Americans defined in terms of three and four criteria of nationality and for Canadian- and American-born sociologists controlling for highest degree." J

1423. Landes, Ronald G. PRE-ADULT ORIENTATIONS TO MULTIPLE SYSTEMS OF GOVERNMENT: A COMPARATIVE STUDY OF ENGLISH-CANADIAN AND AMERICAN SCHOOL-CHILDREN IN TWO CITIES. *Publius 1977 7(1): 27-39.* The analysis is derived from a questionnaire administered in 1972 to pupils in grades 4-8 in Belleville, Ontario, and Watertown, New York. Children of both nations are aware of the federal nature of their respective political structures. Canadians view the provincial government as most important in their lives, while American youngsters downgrade state and local governments, placing greater faith in the federal government. The political structure of a system thus influences children's perception of the polity. 4 tables, 16 notes. A. Clive

1424. Landy, Sarah. THE CULTURAL MOSAIC: SOME PSYCHOLOGICAL IMPLICATIONS. *Can. Lib. J. [Canada] 1976 33(3): 245-247.* Urges more psychological analyses of relations between immigrants and receiving societies. Aspects of the relations include alienation, ambiguity, loss of status, and residential alienation; at the same time, attachment and amalgamation with the new society occur. In societies demanding too early or too thorough assimilation, migrants exhibit psychological regression, behavioral breakdown, and psychopathological difficulties. Multiculturalism attempts to allow the individual to integrate at his own pace, to retain his uniqueness, and to appreciate his own and other cultures. Implications are drawn for libraries serving multicultural groups. 11 notes. L. F. Johnson

1425. Lawson, Robert F. ON THE IDEOLOGICAL CONDITIONS OF CANADIAN INDEPENDENCE. *British J. of Educ. Studies [Great Britain] 1975 23(1): 24-48.* Examines international professional migration in Canada during economic progression and developing political autonomy; highlights education and its impact on feelings for independence among Canadians, 1945-75.

1426. Légaré, Jacques. DEMOGRAPHIC HIGHLIGHTS ON FERTILITY DECLINE IN CANADIAN MARRIAGE COHORTS. *Can. R. of Sociol. and Anthrop. 1974 11(4): 287-307.* "The purpose of this study is to examine the family-formation behaviour of marriage cohorts in Canada, using data from the 1961 census. Some comparisons are made with similar data from the 1960 United States census. Since the mean age of women at first marriage was fairly constant for the cohorts involved, fertility trends are then independent of the average nuptiality behaviour. Levels and trends in average family size are different for each country. In Canada, the average family size has gone down to 2.9 children per family for couples married between 1945 and 1950, while in the United States, the level has been rather constant—around 2.5 children per family—for couples married between 1920 and 1950. When age at marriage is taken into account, the comparisons of average family size and of the proportion of childless marriages in Canada and the United States become more interesting. The analysis for Canada of the distribution of families by size and of the parity progression ratios indicates the part played in the past by age at marriage: the younger the bride the larger the family. These differences are much less important for the latest cohorts, however. Unfortunately, childspacing could be estimated in only a crude way, and it appears that in Canada birth intervals are rather long. Finally, for Canadian couples married after 1950, recent trends in birth statistics suggest that the average family size will not remain at the level of 2.9 children per family but rather will decline to a level equivalent to that attained in the United States." J

1427. Légaré, Jacques. LES GROUPES ETHNIQUES ET LINGUISTIQUES AU CANADA [Ethnic and linguistic groups in Canada]. *Can. R. of Sociol. and Anthrop. 1973 10(1): 81-84.* Report on three recent studies of bilingualism and biculturalism in Canada by authors of differing origins. Apart from the original contribution of each, all agree that outside of Quebec and an encircling zone, French has little chance of survival as an everyday language in Canada. 3 notes. L. R. Atkins

1428. Leman, Christopher. PATTERNS OF POLICY DEVELOPMENT: SOCIAL SECURITY IN THE UNITED STATES AND CANADA. *Public Policy 1977 25(2): 261-291.* Presents a comparative analysis of the development of social security systems in the United States and Canada. Utilizing brief histories of the evolution of social security in both nations and tracing modifications of the original systems to the present, offers explanations of how and why the two systems differ. Canada's social security systems grew out of a political process which has forced accommodation because of the nature of provincial-federal relationships. Canada has thus developed a social security system financed by contributions and out of the federal treasury. In the United States, the program has been financed entirely out of contributions. This has led to speculation about the long-range viability of the US social security system. The varying responses of both countries to political crises are studied as part of the contexts within which social security programs emerged. Primary and secondary sources; 5 notes, biblio. J. M. Herrick

1429. Lovell, Emily Khalled. A SURVEY OF THE ARAB-MUSLIMS IN THE UNITED STATES AND CANADA. *Muslim World 1973 63(2): 139-154.* Analyzes Arab Muslims in North America, based on a 1970 questionnaire sent to Islamic centers, mosques, and individuals. The mosques, usually in major cities, were not large but often served social and educational, as well as religious, needs. Arab nationalism stimulated American Muslims to organize and build more mosques. The third generation had become somewhat assimilated, but generally the Muslims, while reconciled to their Christian environment, had maintained their ethnic identity. Based on a questionnaire and secondary sources; 38 notes. P. S. J. Mattar

1430. Mackie, Marlene. ON CONGENIAL TRUTHS: A PERSPECTIVE ON WOMEN'S STUDIES. *Can. Rev. of Sociol. and Anthrop. [Canada] 1977 14(1): 117-128.* Critiques research in women's studies from the perspective of the sociology of knowledge. Argues that as a result of dual commitment to feminist social movement sympathies and research activities, the temptation is there to mistake our ideological preferences and pronouncements for social 'reality.' However, value neutrality on the part of individuals is neither possible nor desirable. Instead, 'triangulation' of ideologies, or conflict of perspectives, is advocated. J

1431. MacPherson, Kay. THE SEEDS OF THE 70'S. *Can. Dimension 1975 10(8): 39-42.* Surveys the Canadian Women's Liberation Movement's progress during the last 20 years. S

1432. Maghami, Farhat Ghaem. POLITICAL KNOWLEDGE AMONG YOUTH: SOME NOTES ON PUBLIC OPINION FORMATION. *Can. J. of Pol. Sci. 1974 7(2): 334-340.* Devised a political knowledge scale to test a sampling of Canadian college and university students. Relates findings to socio-economic background, religion, sex, and education. 5 tables, 8 notes, 2 appendices. R. V. Kubicek

1433. Marsden, Lorna R. IS CANADA BECOMING OVERPOPULATED? *Can. Geographical J. 1974 89(5): 40-47.*

1434. Marshall, John U. CITY SIZE, ECONOMIC DIVERSITY, AND FUNCTIONAL TYPE: THE CANADIAN CASE. *Econ. Geography 1975 51(1): 37-49.*

1435. Masse, Jacqueline C. ATTRACTION INTERPERSONNELLE DANS UN GROUPE MUTLI-ETHNIQUE [Interpersonal attraction among a multiethnic group]. *Can. R. of Sociol. and Anthrop. 1973 10(2): 160-170.* "This research studies interpersonal attraction among a multi-ethnic group composed of 324 students, men and women, who lived in a university residence. A correlational and multiple regression analysis shows the relationship between different levels of attraction in pairs of individuals (these pairs being the unit of analysis), and degrees of homogeneity in these pairs with regard to nationality, length of residence, and proximity of residence. The results confirm balance theory: in both groups of women and groups of men interpersonal attraction is linked with similarity and reciprocity of choice. Relationships between men and women depend on different types of similarity." J

1436. Matejko, Alexander. MULTICULTURALISM: THE POLISH-CANADIAN CASE. *Polish Rev. 1976 21(3): 177-194.* Discusses the presence of Polish immigrants in Canada, their incorporation into the predominantly Anglo culture, 1945-75, and their efforts to be both Poles and Canadians ethnically.

1437. McClure, J. Derrick. THE SEMANTICS OF A SOCIAL PROBLEM. R. de l'U. d'Ottawa [Canada] 1973 43(1): 152-159. Proposes scrutiny of attitudes toward the language used in discussing race relations. What term is used in discussing Negroes does not matter because nothing "will alter the history or present-day predicament of the Negroes."   M. L. Frey

1438. McRoberts, Kenneth. BILL 22 AND LANGUAGE POLICY IN CANADA. Queen's Q. [Canada] 1976 83(3): 464-477. Surveys the struggles for language equality throughout all the Canadian provinces and the federal government's support of such programs. Bill 22 seems a reversal of the language equality policy for the Province of Quebec because it calls for the primacy of French over English within Quebec. For some it does not go far enough, for others it violates the general equality of language ideal. An analysis of the bill indicates some weaknesses, especially at operational levels. Bill 22 may point the way to a more appropriate language regime for Quebec and for Canada as a whole. 23 notes.   R. V. Ritter

1439. Migué, Jean-Luc. LE PRIX DE LA SANTÉ ET LE PRIX DES RÉFORMES DES SERVICES DE SANTÉ [The price of health and the price of health care service reforms]. J. of Can. Studies 1973 8(3): 26-32. Discusses the enactment of guaranteed national public health care plans and reforms in the administration of that health care by the Canadian legislature in 1972.

1440. Milcs, Edward J. ANDREW HILL CLARK. Am. Rev. of Can. Studies 1975 5(2): 2-3. Serves as an introduction to an article appearing in the same issue written by Andrew Hill Clark, as well as an obituary briefly examining Clark's academic and literary career, 1911-75.

1441. Moreau, Jean-Paul. VINGT-QUATRE HEURES AVEC MARCEL OUIMET [Twenty-four hours with Marcel Ouimet]. Can. Oral Hist. Assoc. J. [Canada] 1978 3(1): 10-21. Discusses Marcel Ouimet's career with Radio Canada, 1939-75.

1442. Myers, C. R. AN ORAL HISTORY OF PSYCHOLOGY IN CANADA. Can. Oral Hist. Assoc. J. [Canada] 1975/76 1: 30-33. Discusses the Canadian Psychological Associations's oral history project, 1970-75.

1443. Negrete, J. C. CULTURAL INFLUENCES ON SOCIAL PERFORMANCE OF ALCOHOLICS: A COMPARATIVE STUDY. Q. J. of Studies on Alcohol 1973 34 (3, pt. A): 905-916. "The records of 3 groups of men alcoholics, patients in a residential treatment center in Montreal, were studied: 34 English-speaking Protestants (EP), 28 English-speaking Catholics (EC) and 29 French Catholics (FC). Their mean ages were about 49 years, over half of each group had less than 11 years of education, over 60% were unskilled workers. The mean age at onset of regular drinking was 20 years in the EP, 17 in the EC and 16 in the FC. The proportion of patients reporting symptoms of alcoholism was similar in each group (over 90% reported morning drinking and tremors; over 30% a history of delirium tremens and hallucinosis); however, 74 and 86% of the EP and EC, but only 45% of the FC, reported frequent blackouts. Personality disorders were diagnosed in 41, 25 and 17% of the EP, EC and FC; neuroses in 18, 36 and 48%, respectively. On admission, 31% of the EP were single, 12% married or widowed, 68% separated or divorced; among the EC the respective percentages were 25, 25 and 50, and among the FC, 38, 31 and 31. Over 60% of each group were unemployed at admission; but 56, 27 and 22% of the EP, EC and FC became unemployed before age 35. A history of police arrests was reported by 74, 57 and 38% of the EP, EC and FC. It seems that the social manifestations of alcoholism are influenced by cultural attitudes toward drinking and alcoholism and toward role expectations. Definitions of alcoholism in English-speaking cultures emphasize the sociopathic characteristics of alcoholism; French-speaking cultures put more emphasis on the physical consequences of excessive drinking. The Catholic alcoholics of the present study tended to adopt an 'incapacitated' role while the Protestants adopted a 'sociopathic' role."   J

1444. Nossal, Frederick. POPULATION PLANNING: THE PUZZLES A CROWDED PLANET MUST SOLVE. Internat. Perspectives [Canada] 1973: 40-46. Analyzes demographic trends of recent years and the effects on population growth of industrial and agricultural revolutions, various family planning projects, and the commitment of various nations, such as India, the United States, and Canada, to population control.   L. S. Frey

1445. Novogrodsky, Myra. SCHOOLS. Can. Dimension 1974 10(3): 50-54. Canadian public schools today continue to reinforce the existing class structure.   S

1446. Ostry, Sylvia. EDUCATION AND THE "NEW HOME ECONOMICS." Queen's Q. [Canada] 1975 82(4): 495-498. Assessing the value of the expansion of higher education in the developed countries in the 1960's, the "new home economics" views education as an investment in human capital, both in the labor market and in society. Present youth unemployment, scarcity of "choice" jobs, and underemployment of the elite suggest a declining labor market return on investment in education. However, increased social returns from education are enjoyed by college graduates who are healthier, better informed citizens and more efficient consumers. Note.   T. Simmerman

1447. Paltiel, Freda L. INTERNATIONAL PERSPECTIVE ON EQUAL OPPORTUNITY. Can. Labour 1975 20(2): 19-22. Presents the efforts of national (including US and Canadian) and international organizations against sex discrimination since the 1960's.

1448. Parai, Louis. CANADA'S IMMIGRATION POLICY. Int. Migration Rev. 1975 9(4): 449-477. Discusses economic and employment factors of Canada's immigration policy from 1962-74.

1449. Paučo, Joseph. CULTURAL REVIVAL OF AMERICAN AND CANADIAN SLOVAKS. Slovakia 1973 23(46): 72-81. During the past decade there has been a revival of interest by Slovak Americans and Slovak Canadians in their cultural heritage, strengthened by Slovaks who migrated after the Second World War. This revival has resulted in an increase in books, pamphlets, periodicals, and newspapers that are devoted to the history and culture of Slovakia. Slovak organizations are placing increasing emphasis on Slovak achievements in art, music, and literature.   J. Williams

1450. Paulston, Rolland G. and LeRoy, Gregory. STRATEGIES FOR NONFORMAL EDUCATION. Teachers Coll. Record 1975 76(4): 569-596. Discusses types of nonformal education (NFE) and their role in achieving more equitable income distribution and greater personal growth. NFE, that is "organized systematic educational activity outside . . . the formal school system," seems more capable than does formal education of achieving such goals. Most scholars, particularly Frederick H. Harbison and Philip H. Coombs, see NFE's goals as primarily imposed upon target groups from outside and aimed at national economic development. However, successful but rarely studied programs developed by various economic and ethnic groups and aimed at greater self-realization have been initiated in Scandinavia, Canada, and the United States. These programs offer hope of expanding the scope of NFE. Based on primary and secondary sources; diagram, 59 notes.   E. C. Bailey

1451. Pike, Robert. LEGAL ACCESS AND THE INCIDENCE OF DIVORCE IN CANADA: A SOCIOHISTORICAL ANALYSIS. Can. R. of Sociol. and Anthrop. 1975 12(2): 115-133. Long-term trends in divorce rates in Canada are examined within the framework of Canadian divorce law and of changes in social attitudes and family structure. It is suggested, in particular, that an essential concept in an analysis of the changing incidence of divorce is that of 'legal access,' by which is meant the impact on divorce rates of the nature of the legal grounds for divorce, as well as the impact of the provision, or lack of provision, of divorce court facilities. More specifically, Canadian divorce rates prior to the divorce law reforms of 1968 are shown to have provided a very poor indication of the actual rate of marriage breakdown owing to the stringent nature of the legal grounds of divorce and the lack of divorce court facilities in some provinces. Furthermore, the existence of major legal barriers to divorce fostered patterns of institutionalized evasion amongst those seeking divorces including migratory divorces and fraudulent divorce actions. However, the continued existence of large, and long-term, variations in divorce rates between the Canadian provinces highlights the need for further analysis of a wide variety of social, cultural, and demographic variables which appear to be associated with the differential regional incidence of divorce in this country.   J

1452. Plato, W. R. THE UNITED CHURCH OF CANADA AND EUCHARISTIC WORSHIP. *Bull. of the United Church of Can. 1973 (22): 16-20.* Initial results of a questionnaire sent to 1,000 United Church ministers in 1972 in an attempt to ascertain trends in United Church of Canada eucharistic worship. This is part of a larger study which will seek also to establish possible differences in practice according to geographical location and denominational background. Concludes that over the past 20 years there has been an obvious trend toward more frequent celebration of the Lord's Supper, and that there has been a renewal of interest and personal concern for worship on the part of many ministers.
B. D. Tennyson

1453. Pool, D. I. and Bracher, M. D. ASPECTS OF FAMILY FORMATION IN CANADA. *Can. R. of Sociol. and Anthrop. 1974 11(4): 308-323.* "Fertility is declining in Canada. We attempt to account for this change and to suggest policy implications. We review recent Canadian studies fitting them into an adaptation of the Davis-Blake framework. This permits the formulation of hypotheses at two levels implicit in the framework: 1) social structural (independent variables); 2) proximate ("intermediate" variables). Hypotheses were tested against available data, but a problem remained: does the decline result from deferring or averting of births?"
J

1454. Pringle, Jim. FORCED RETIREMENT: A DEATH SENTENCE. *Can. Dimension [Canada] 1977 12(7): 33-35.* Discusses positive and negative aspects of forced retirement in Canada during the 1970's.

1455. Quarter, Jack. SHIFTING IDEOLOGIES AMONG YOUTH IN CANADA. *Youth & Soc. 1974 5(4): 448-474.* Industrialization has modified the attitudes of Canadian youths toward the work ethic since the 1950's.
S

1456. Raeithel, Get. DER ANATOMISCHE SHICKSALGLAUBE UND DIE AMERIKANISCHE FRAU [Belief in anatomical fate and the American woman]. *Frankfurter Hefte [West Germany] 1976 31(1): 25-34.* Discusses the current status of women in the United States (with a single reference to contemporary Canada), tracing that status through its historical development from colonial times. Emphasizes such topics as the lack of women's rights under the English common law, the slow development of female suffrage, the double standard for sexual behavior, and the Kinsey Report. Also discusses changes in sexual mores (especially those instituted by utopian religious experiments), black-white sexual relations, and the changing familial configurations of recent decades. The conclusion is that American women today are, through hard struggles, defining their new and different roles in American life. 20 notes.
J. L. Colwell

1457. Raitz, Karl B. ETHNIC MAPS OF NORTH AMERICA. *Geographical Rev. 1978 68(3): 335-350.* Reviews the methods of mapping American cultural or ethnic groups that indicate major trends in ethnic research. Because ethnicity has a number of forms, the most difficult methodological problems in the United States and Canada are to define ethnicity and to find reliable data sources. The most innovative techniques have been developed by those who make medium and large-scale maps based on several types of information. The most useful maps sometimes require accuracy in a distance as short as a street width, and they involve a considerable amount of fieldwork. Based on maps and on secondary sources; 59 notes.
W. R. Hively

1458. Rakhmanny, Roman. THE CANADIAN OPTION FOR 1975 AND BEYOND: UNITY THROUGH DIVERSITY. *Ukrainian Q. 1974 30(2): 151-165.* Discusses the role of minorities in Canada, particularly French Canadians and Ukrainians.
S

1459. Redekop, John H. AUTHORS AND PUBLISHERS: AN ANALYSIS OF TEXTBOOK SELECTION IN CANADIAN DEPARTMENTS OF POLITICAL SCIENCE AND SOCIOLOGY. *Can. J. of Pol. Sci. 1976 9(1): 107-120.* Academics in these departments,

whatever their region, citizenship, or type of university, have a strong proclivity to select US textbooks. 12 tables, 10 notes.
R. V. Kubicek

1460. Reed, Walt. JOHN CLYMER: HISTORIAN WITH A PAINTBRUSH. *Am. West 1976 13(6): 18-29.* After several years as a commercial illustrator in the East, artist John Clymer decided to paint historical events of the West. He systematically explored the American and Canadian West and studied its history. His paintings are widely exhibited and have earned several awards. Adapted from a recent book; 6 illus.
D. L. Smith

1461. Reynolds, Arthur. WRITING A LOCAL CHURCH HISTORY. *J. of the Canadian Church Hist. Soc. 1976 18(3): 2-5.* The most important matter in writing local church history is to gather and use the most accurate information. Thus a history must take into account the different impressions events may make on various observers. Also, a history should not be merely a compilation of names and dates, but should tell a story of the interaction of the human and the divine. Finally, the writer of a local church history must always relate it to the universal church and to the larger community of which it is a part.
J. A. Kicklighter

1462. Rich, Harvey. THE VERTICAL MOSAIC REVISITED: TOWARD A MACROSOCIOLOGY OF CANADA. *J. of Can. Studies [Canada] 1976 11(1): 14-31.* John Porter's *The Vertical Mosaic: An Analysis of Class and Power in Canada* (U. of Toronto Pr., 1965) presented a caricature of Canadian society. Refutes Porter's assertions concerning equality of opportunity and upward mobility. Lacking a coherent theoretical framework Porter reached a series of incompatible conclusions. Radicals accepted the conclusions because Canadian society as presented seemed to have a high potential for radicalism. Secondary works; 4 tables, 52 notes.
G. E. Panting

1463. Richert, Jean Pierre. CANADIAN NATIONAL IDENTITY: AN EMPIRICAL STUDY. *Am. Rev. of Can. Studies 1974 4(1): 89-98.* Examines differences in Canadian children and American children as they experience feelings of nationalism; further, discusses the tendency of Canadian anglophone children to identify with Canada, while Francophone children identify with Quebec; examines tendency for nationalistic feelings to weaken with age, 1971-72.

1464. Richert, Jean Pierre. THE IMPACT OF ETHNICITY ON THE PERCEPTION OF HEROES AND HISTORICAL SYMBOLS. *Can. R. of Sociol. and Anthrop. 1974 11(2): 156-163.* "The object of this paper is to verify empirically a hypothesis suggested by the Royal Commission on Bilingualism and Biculturalism. The Commission suggests that there are two Canadian historical traditions, one Anglophone, the other Francophone, and that they are mutually exclusive. The data were derived from a survey of 960 English- and French-Canadian elementary pupils, essays written by children, and in-depth interviews and observations. The findings generally confirmed the hypothesis and showed, first of all, that children overwhelmingly identified with historical symbols of their own culture, and that their ethnocentric perception of historical figures increased with age. Second, the data showed that Francophone and Anglophone children identified with different eras of Canadian history. The former identified primarily with the pre-1760 era, while the latter identified mostly with the post-1760 era. It was concluded from these data that there are few *reconciliation* symbols in Canadian history which was, therefore, viewed as a divisive rather than a binding force."
J

1465. Richmond, Anthony H. LANGUAGE, ETHNICITY, AND THE PROBLEM OF IDENTITY IN A CANADIAN METROPOLIS. *Ethnicity 1974 1(2): 175-206.* Discusses a central Canadian problem, cultural diversity and national identity, and determines types of self-identification among a Toronto sample from 1970. The analysis focuses on competing identifications, the influence of age at time of arrival and length of residence in Canada, the effects of status and mobility, attitudes toward Canadian society, and the relationship of language to identification. Age, language, mobility, and length of residence are critical factors. 20 tables, biblio.
E. Barkan

1466. Richmond, Anthony H. and Rao, G. Lakshmana. RECENT DEVELOPMENTS IN IMMIGRATION TO CANADA AND AUSTRALIA: A COMPARATIVE ANALYSIS. *Int. J. of Comparative Sociol. [Canada] 1976 17(3-4): 183-205.* Analyzes immigration to Canada and Australia during 1967-75. Considers the numbers involved, racial and national discrimination, educational and occupational selection, opposition to immigration, and government sponsored studies. Government immigration policy is debated in the political arena and forms an accommodation of conflicting interests and ideologies. The most influential opposition to immigration in Australia and Canada now comes from those concerned with the environmental consequences of population growth. Counteracting them are those who support moderate growth. Even in the face of high unemployment, immigration has continued. In both countries fertility has declined, and continued immigration is seen as a means of avoiding future population decline and ameliorating the consequences of an otherwise aging population. Primary and secondary sources; 5 tables, 7 notes, biblio.   R. G. Neville

1467. Rowat, Donald C. THE DECLINE OF FREE RESEARCH IN THE SOCIAL SCIENCES. *Can. J. of Pol. Sci. 1976 9(4): 537-547.* Finds alarming a shift in the federal government's budget for social science research, a shift from scholar-initiated research to government-commissioned research. Presidential address to the annual meeting of the Canadian Political Science Association at Laval University, 1 June 1976. 24 notes.   R. V. Kubicek

1468. Sawula, Lorne W. WHY 1970, WHY NOT BEFORE? *Can. J. of Hist. of Sport and Physical Educ. 1973 4(2): 43-58.* Postwar government involvement in sport can be attributed to the need for physical fitness and the desire to improve Canada's prestige in international sporting events. In 1970 the Minister of Health and Welfare announced that sport "has an equal right to government attention as . . . the arts." Government involvement has become a way of life in Canada and has softened the opposition to government control of sport. Sport tied to nationalistic aspirations and international prestige has come of age. Based on primary works; 55 notes.   R. A. Smith

1469. Schlesinger, Benjamin. THE SINGLE WOMAN IN SECOND MARRIAGES. *Social Sci. 1974 49(2): 104-109.* "The topic of remarriage has been neglected in the field of family sociology in North America. With more and more persons deciding to marry again, we need to examine the adjustment problems in these unions. The few available studies have focused on the person who marries for the second time. This paper examines some of the selected findings of a Canadian study which included 28 single women, who married men who had been married previously. Their feelings, attitudes, and problems in this type of union give us direction for further research in this important and growing area of family life."   J

1470. Schreiber, E. M. CULTURAL CLEAVAGES BETWEEN OCCUPATIONAL CATEGORIES: THE CASE OF CANADA. *Social Forces 1976 55(1): 16-29.* The applicability of the neo-Marxian and middle majority models to cultural cleavages between occupational categories was investigated with 1965-71 Canadian Gallup poll data. While the summary cultural scores showed modest differences by occupation, the largest cleavage separated professionals from nonprofessionals. For the 18 individual topics, marked differences appeared between nonmanual and manual (neo-Marxian cleavage) for economic topics and between professionals and nonprofessionals for "compassionate" topics, but there were essentially no differences for the remaining topics. The mostly small effects of occupation on cultural scores suggest that the typically low level of class voting in Canadian federal elections is attributable less to the lack of class-differentiated choice provided by the two major parties than to the Canadian electorate's non-class opinions on most topical issues.   J

1471. Sheehan, Bernard S. FEDERAL FUNDS AND UNIVERSITY RESEARCH. *Can. J. of Pol. Sci. 1973 6(1): 121-130.* The current financial contribution of the Canadian government to university research can only be estimated; and estimates range widely. 8 tables, 19 notes.   R. V. Kubicek

1472. Sirois, Antoine. LITTÉRATURE ET NATIONALISME [Literature and nationalism]. *J. of Can. Studies [Canada] 1976 11(4):*

54-56. Discusses the T. H. B. Symons report (1975) on Canadian higher education, as it relates to Quebec; the report does not adequately deal with national educational needs or with the needs of those who are not strictly English Canadian.

1473. Smiley, Donald. MUST CANADIAN POLITICAL SCIENCE BE A MINIATURE REPLICA? *J. of Can. Studies 1974 9(1): 31-42.* American political scientists are numerous, highly specialized, and insular in outlook. Canadian political scientists, who can call upon a native tradition of political and social inquiry, do not have to be "miniature replica" of this community. This native approach is historical, eclectic and individualistic. Based on periodicals and secondary works; 54 notes.   G. E. Panting

1474. Smith, Dorothy E. AN ANALYSIS OF IDEOLOGICAL STRUCTURES AND HOW WOMEN ARE EXCLUDED: CONSIDERATIONS FOR ACADEMIC WOMEN. *Can. Rev. of Soc. and Anthrop. 1975 12(4): 353-369.* A distinctive feature of this form of society is the significance of ideology in the processes of ordering its social relations. Women have historically and in the present been excluded from the production of the forms of thought, images, and symbols in which their experience and social relations are expressed and ordered. Marx and Engels' original account of ideology is used to focus on the control of ideological production by a ruling class, and on how ideas and images are thus imposed on others whose perspectives, interests and experience are not represented. Those who occupy the positions from which ideologies are produced and controlled are almost exclusively men. It is therefore their perspectives and interests which are represented. A series of historical instances of repression illustrate how women's exclusion has been an active and sometimes brutal process. For contemporary Canada, data on the position of women in the educational system describe institutionalized practices which exclude women from positions of influence and control in ideological structures. Further, studies are cited showing a general pattern which constitutes what men say as authoritative and depreciates what women say. The metaphor of a 'circle' is used to describe the control of ideological development through restricting participation to properly authorized persons. Women as a social category are not among them. This is observable at the level of face-to-face interaction. Studies describe distinctive patterns of interpersonal talk which restrict women's part in the development of topics. The consequence of these exclusions is that the established knowledges and modes of thinking constitute women as objects. The perspective of men has become in the academic context institutionalized as the 'field' or 'discipline.' This is true of sociology as of other intellectual enterprises. The conclusion proposes that a major critique and rethinking of academic disciplines is needed. In sociology this means constructing a sociology *for* rather than *of* women and from the position of women in society.   J

1475. Spates, James L. COUNTERCULTURE AND DOMINANT CULTURE VALUES: A CROSS-NATIONAL ANALYSIS OF THE UNDERGROUND PRESS AND DOMINANT CULTURE MAGAZINES. *Am. Sociol. Rev. 1976 41(5): 868-883.* A content analysis of values in dominant culture magazines in the United States, Canada and Great Britain during 1957-59, 1967-69 and 1970-72 indicated a priority on instrumentalism and little shifting in overall value preference over time. This appears to be contrary to predictions made by counterculture observers that Western society was changing rapidly toward a countercultural ideology. A similar analysis of the underground press in the same countries during 1967-69 and 1970-72 revealed a marked shift from expressive priorities during the earlier period to political priorities during the later period. These findings and their implications are discussed.   J

1476. Stager, David A. A. FEDERAL GOVERNMENT GRANTS TO CANADIAN UNIVERSITIES, 1951-66. *Can. Hist. Rev. [Canada] 1973 54(3): 287-297.* Origins of federal government grants to Canadian universities are traced by reference primarily to published and unpublished papers of the National Conference of Canadian Universities. Close relationships among NCCU officers, the Massey Commission, and the federal cabinet, combined with an appeal to the national interest served by universities and their impending financial crisis, enabled the universities to gain federal support at a critical time. Had there been consultation with provincial governments, Quebec's rejection of the grants might have been avoided.   A

1477. Stone, Leroy O. WHAT WE KNOW ABOUT MIGRATION WITHIN CANADA—A SELECTIVE REVIEW AND AGENDA FOR FUTURE RESEARCH. *Internat. Migration R. 1974 8(2): 267-281.* Reviews several papers on internal migration in Canada 1964-74, identifying major questions for migration research and summarizing partial answers.

1478. Sussman, Leonard R. NORTH AMERICA: IN TRANSITION. *Freedom At Issue 1973 (17): 11-14.* The status of human rights, freedoms, and race relations in North America.   S

1479. Tate, Eugene D. and Surlin, Stuart H. AGREEMENT WITH OPINIONATED TV CHARACTERS ACROSS CULTURES. *Journalism Q. 1976 53(2): 199-203.* Uses survey research techniques to show that Canadian adults find less humor and realism in the television show *All in the Family* than US adults. Both American and Canadian adults exhibiting high levels of dogmatism agree significantly more with the views of Archie Bunker. Concludes that people in a foreign culture identify more with an opinionated TV character when they possess the same social and psychological characteristics. The results are based on surveys of 276 adults each in Athens, Georgia, and in Saskatoon, Saskatchewan. 2 tables, 14 notes.   E. Gibson

1480. Unsigned. THE PRESS AND THE POOR. *Can. Labour 1973 18(10-12): 33-40.* Extracts from the National Council of Welfare's August 1973 report on Canada's newspaper coverage of poverty.   S

1481. Van Dyke, Vernon. HUMAN RIGHTS WITHOUT DISTINCTION AS TO LANGUAGE. *Int. Studies Q. 1976 20(1): 3-38.* Examines policies throughout the world relating to language differentiation and discrimination in international organizations, government and politics, and education since the 1960's, concentrating on the United States and Canada.

1482. Wakil, S. Parvez. CAMPUS MATE SELECTION PREFERENCES: A CROSS NATIONAL COMPARISON. *Social Forces 1973 51(4): 471-476.* Very little research has been done in Canada on mate selection preferences. This survey of such preferences allows comparisons with some earlier studies conducted in the United States. Findings indicate that there may not be much difference in these preferences between U.S. and Canadian university students. They also indicate that sex status explains more about such preferences than rural-urban background.

1483. Ward, E. Neville and Cranmer, Valerie. CANADA HAS LAND "CRISES" FROM SEA TO SEA. *Can. Geographical J. 1974 89(6): 34-41.*

1484. Warkentyne, H. J. CONTEMPORARY CANADIAN ENGLISH: A REPORT OF THE SURVEY OF CANADIAN ENGLISH. *Am. Speech 1971 46(3-4): 193-199.* In 1972 the Survey of Canadian English was sponsored by the Canadian Council of Teachers of English with the support of the Canadian Linguistic Association and funding by the Canada Council. This first national survey of Canadian English compared the language of youth with that of their parents, showing that youth are tending toward American English usage. The survey also indicated that Canada could be divided into three main dialect areas: Newfoundland, Eastern Canada, and Western Canada, with Newfoundland most distinct in its speech habits. Based on mailed questionnaire; 5 notes.
P. A. Beaber

1485. Watts, Ronald L. FREEDOM WITH RESPONSIBILITY: UNIVERSITIES, GOVERNMENTS AND THE PUBLIC. *Queen's Q. [Canada] 1975 82(1): 14-21.* Discusses the role of universities in regard to how they function as opposed to what the world at large expects of them. Analyzes problems concerning the objectives of universities. Concludes, "It is time for us in the universities to speak out and to warn society that its declining support is now seriously threatening our ability to provide the kind of higher education which it needs."
J. A. Casada

1486. Weinfeld, Morton. A NOTE ON COMPARING CANADIAN AND AMERICAN JEWRY. *J. of Ethnic Studies 1977 5(1): 95-103.* Evaluates the two factors usually cited to account for the greater commu-

nal identification of Canadian Jews compared with their American brethren: 1) that the Canadian community is one generation younger or closer to Europe and 2) that the Canadian mosaic is more accepting and supportive of ethnic diversity than is the conformity of the American melting pot ethos. Sees the major empirical differences between the two groups as somewhat misleading because of variations in statistical criteria between the United States and Canada. Still, Canadian Jews rate of intermarriage is much lower, day school enrollment far exceeds that in the United States, retention of Yiddish is stronger in Canada, and religious affiliation of Canadian synagogues leans more to Orthodoxy than does that of American Jews. Canada's new national preoccupation with fostering national sentiment, its official multiculturalism, and its government expenditures to promote ethnic maintenance, which are four times those of the United States explain the greater sense of Jewish identity in Canada. Primary and secondary sources; 3 tables, 13 notes.
G. J. Bobango

1487. Whitaker, Reg and Panitch, Leo. THE NEW WAFFLE: FROM MATHEWS TO MARX. *Can. Dimension 1974 10(1): 51-56.* Reviews *The Political Economy of Dependency,* (Toronto: McClelland and Stewart, 1973), a collection of Socialist critiques on Canadian society.
S

1488. Wilson, Marion C. LIBRARY DOCUMENTATION CENTRE, NATIONAL LIBRARY OF CANADA. *Can. Lib. J. 1973 30(2): 116-118.*

1489. Wilson, V. Seymour. THE RELATIONSHIP BETWEEN SCIENTIFIC MANAGEMENT AND PERSONNEL POLICY IN NORTH AMERICAN ADMINISTRATIVE SYSTEMS. *Public Administration [Great Britain] 1973 51(2): 193-205.* Analyzes those aspects of the philosophy of scientific management which deal with human resources within organizations, and the relationship between the philosophy and the system of personnel administration introduced into Canadian and American bureaucracy in the early 20th century. The philosophy of scientific management is "so deeply ingrained in North American society that it is difficult to envisage any substantial changes in these tenets taking place." 51 notes.   L. Brown

1490. Woods, John. REPATRIATING THE CANADIAN UNIVERSITY. *J. of Can. Studies [Canada] 1976 11(4): 56-68.* Analyzes the T. H. B. Symons report (1975) on higher education in Canada, examines the evolution of the university system in Canada, and calls for a strict policy on foreign students and government support of graduate programs and faculty research.

1491. Wright, Donald K. AN ANALYSIS OF THE LEVEL OF PROFESSIONALISM AMONG CANADIAN JOURNALISTS. *Gazette [Netherlands] 1974 20(3): 133-144.* Results of a 1973 survey in Ontario, British Columbia, Saskatchewan, Alberta, and Manitoba, indicate journalists are dissatisfied with the lack of both opportunities for improvement within the field and availability of adequate professional and academic training outside on-the-job-training.

1492. Wukasch, Peter. BALTIC IMMIGRANTS IN CANADA, 1947-1955. *Concordia Hist. Inst. Q. 1977 50(1): 4-22.* Fleeing Russian expansion, a number of people from Estonia, Latvia, and Lithuania entered Canada during 1947-55. To assist these immigrants the Lutheran Church responded with a multifaceted program led by Rev. Ernest Hahn and Rev. Donald Ortner of St. John's Lutheran Church in Toronto. The church involved itself in social, economic, cultural, and political efforts to safeguard the interests of the displaced Baltic people. Primary sources; 28 notes.   W. T. Walker

1493. Ziegler, Suzanne. THE FAMILY UNIT AND INTERNATIONAL MIGRATION: THE PERCEPTIONS OF ITALIAN IMMIGRANT CHILDREN. *Int. Migration Rev. 1977 11(3): 326-333.* Examines through a series of interviews with children of Italian immigrants the postwar migratory process to Canada, the centrality of the 20th-century family, and the importance of intergenerational ties and commitments; family ties have survived migration and even been fortified because of it.

1494. Zielinska, Marie F. MULTICULTURALISM: THE IDEA BEHIND THE POLICY. *Can. Lib. J. [Canada] 1976 33(3): 223-225.* A selection of quotations providing definitions of multiculturalism and insights into Canadian multiculturalism policy. 10 notes.
L. F. Johnson

1495. —. MORE REFLECTIONS ON THE SYMONS REPORT AND CANADIAN STUDIES. *J. of Can. Studies [Canada] 1977 12(4): 95-107.*
Blishen, Bernard. THE SEARCH FOR IDENTITY, *pp. 95-99.* Discusses T. H. B. Symons's *To Know Ourselves: The Report of the Commission on Canadian Studies* of the Association of Universities and Colleges of Canada. The report fails to reprimand Canadian university planners for underestimating future enrollments and thus creating the need to hire many American professors. It understates the amount of specifically Canada-oriented work being done in sociology. 4 ref.
Applebaum, Louis. A REASONABLE BALANCE: THE ARTS AND CANADIAN STUDIES, *pp. 100-102.* Stresses the need for Canadian universities to give more attention to "the arts and to Canadianism within the arts."
Bumsted, J. M. THE MOUSE THAT MUST ROAR: SOME THOUGHTS ON CANADIAN STUDIES PROGRAMMES TODAY, *pp. 102-107.* Advocates the creation of separate departments of Canadian studies.
L. W. Van Wyk

Economic Matters

1496. Adams, George W. COLLECTIVE BARGAINING BY SALARIED PROFESSIONALS. *Industrial Relations [Canada] 1977 32(2): 184-199.* Examines whether the traditional approach to collective bargaining fits the needs of the salaried professionals or if special treatment is necessary.
J

1497. Aggarwal, Arjun P. ADJUDICATION OF GRIEVANCES IN PUBLIC SERVICE OF CANADA. *Relations Industrielles/Industrial Relations [Canada] 1973 28(3): 497-549.* "Employer-employee relations in the Federal Public Service of Canada entered a new era with the proclamation on March 13, 1967, of three Acts—*The Public Service Staff Relations Act; The Public Service Employment Act;* and an *Act to Amend the Financial Administration Act.* The employees have been guaranteed the right to organize, the right to bargain, the right to strike and the right to get grievances adjudicated by an independent tribunal. The statutory right to grieve and get the grievances adjudicated have provided to the federal public employees a sense of justice and 'fairplay'. The adjudication system has made the private sector of industrial jurisprudence applicable to the federal public services with a remarkable success. This article deals with the function and operation of the statutory Grievance Process and Adjudication."
J

1498. Alexander, David. CANADIAN HIGHER EDUCATION: A REVIEW OF THE GRAHAM ROYAL COMMISSION. *Dalhousie R. [Canada] 1975 55(3): 491-504.* John Graham's report assumes that universities should be different from high schools and should not be vocationally oriented as other post-secondary institutions. Those who can profit from a true university are students who are both able and interested in undertaking higher intellectual study. He believes standards have fallen under pressure to satisfy society's misplaced emphasis on "credentials." The system of increasing compulsory education should be reversed. Universities offer higher education to a minority and if it is a worthwhile investment they should be expected to pay for it. Discussion of arguments counter to Graham's comprises two-thirds of the article. 27 notes.
C. Held

1499. Allard, Jean-Louis. LES FRANCO-ONTARIENS ET L'EDUCATION POSTSECONDAIRE [French Ontarians and postsecondary education]. *R. de l'U. d'Ottawa [Canada] 1973 43(4): 518-531.* Analyzes education problems, especially in postsecondary schools, and the progress in making Canada, especially Ontario, bilingual and bicultural. Based on secondary sources; 5 notes.
M. L. Frey

1500. Anderson, John C. and Kochan, Thomas A. COLLECTIVE BARGAINING IN THE PUBLIC SERVICE OF CANADA. *Industrial Relations [Canada] 1977 32(2): 234-248.* Examines the existing system of collective bargaining in the Public Service of Canada and the legislative suggestions of the Parliamentary Committee on Employer-Employee Relations in the Public Service in light of the results of two major empirical investigations of collective bargaining in the federal public service of Canada.
J

1501. Anton, F. R. THE PRICES AND INCOMES COMMISSION IN RETROSPECT. *Relations Industrielles/Industrial Relations [Canada] 1973 28(3): 457-475.* "Reviews the Canadian Prices and Incomes Commission's findings and comments on some of the conclusions drawn."
J

1502. Armstrong, Hugh and Armstrong, Pat. THE SEGREGATED PARTICIPATION OF WOMEN IN THE CANADIAN LABOUR FORCE, 1941-71. *Can. Rev. of Soc. and Anthrop. 1975 12(4): 370-384.* Using primarily census data, we examine the jobs held by Canadian women. Despite changing attitudes to women's work and despite the substantial growth in the labour force participation of women, occupational segregation stays virtually unchanged between 1941 and 1971. Most working women remain concentrated in a few jobs, jobs which are dominated by female workers. Economic need has been chiefly responsible for their joining the labour force, and a link can be established between increasing female participation and growing economic disparity by analysing shifts over the years in income distribution and in the number of income recipients per family. Finally, both the low pay for women workers and the growing disparity between high and low individual income recipients have been camouflaged by the tremendous growth in the number of married women in the labour force.
J

1503. Baba, Vishwanath and Jamal, Muhammad. COMPANY SATISFACTION, COMPANY COMMITMENT AND WORK INVOLVEMENT: AN EMPIRICAL EXAMINATION OF BLUE COLLAR. *Industrial Relations [Canada] 1976 31(3): 434-447.* This study investigates the relationships among company satisfaction, company commitment and work involvement for a sample of blue-collar workers drawn from packaging, power distribution and manufacturing industries in Canada. Guttman scaling, factor analysis and correlational analysis are the statistical techniques employed to analyze the data. The results confirm the hypothesized positive relationship among the three attitudes.
J

1504. Bauer, Charles. "LOFTY" MAC MILLAN—ORGANIZER. *Can. Labour 1973 18(3): 6-9, 23.* Career (1935-) of John F. "Lofty" MacMillan (b. 1918).
S

1505. Bauer, Charles. OLD PEOPLE DO NOT DIE, THEY ONLY FADE AWAY. *Can. Labour 1973 18(2): 6-9.* Senior citizens need improved social security and pension programs.
S

1506. Beauregard, Ludger. LA GEOGRAPHIE DU FER AU CANADA: UNE MUTATION EN COURS [The geography of iron ore in Canada: a mutation in process]. *Cahiers de Géographie de Québec [Canada] 1973 17(40): 85-106.* In the last decade, Canada has become one of the leading producers and shippers of iron ore. Because of the huge reserves of the Quebec-Labrador region and the utilization of modern technology and equipment, Canada is in a favorable position to capture world markets, but difficulty arises from foreign control of Canadian reserves. Map, 3 photos, 2 tables, 14 notes, biblio.
A. E. LeBlanc

1507. Beeching, W. C. FARMERS IN THE ANTI-MONOPOLY STRUGGLE. *Communist Viewpoint [Canada] 1973 5(2): 19-27.*

1508. Beigie, Carl E. THE OPTIMUM USE OF CANADIAN RESOURCES. *Pro. of the Acad. of Pol. Sci. 1976 32(2): 164-175.* Reviews new and pending Canadian policies designed to optimize the use of natural resources. Many Canadians do not believe the nation is benefiting from its resources to the degree that it should. Canada will be charging firms a higher price to operate. New emphasis is being placed on exporting finished products rather than raw materials. Stabilization of markets will also be pursued more vigorously. Other than the decision to phase out oil exports, the new decisions will provoke little ire in the United States. Table, 2 notes.
V. L. Human

1509. Bellerose, Pierre-Paul. LE REVENU ANNUEL GARANTI: NOUVELLE FORME DE SÉCURITÉ DU REVENU [Guaranteed annual income: a new form of income security]. *Actualité Écon. [Canada] 1974 50(4): 520-532.* "This paper discusses guaranteed annual income (GAI) as a mean of income redistribution and an alternative to current income security programs, with an emphasis on some basic facts commonly overlooked in recent debates. In the first part, GAI is shown to be, conceptually and technically, a logical evolution rather than a revolution considering the current income security program. In the second part, we show that the cost of income security programs must essentially be related to the amount of 'net transfers.' As a consequence, GAI programs will be costlier than the present system, because they require greater net transfers. In the third part, given a distribution of families by level of income, we show that the rate of decrease of poverty through any GAI program depends on the relative values of both the arbitrarily chosen poverty threshold and on the selected breaking point of 'zero net transfer.' Finally, rules are established pertaining to the effect of various GAI programs on poverty." J

1510. Belzile, Bertrand and Larouche, Viateur. MOTIVATION AU TRAVAIL DES PARENTS DE FAMILLES À FAIBLE REVENU: MODÈLE CONCEPTUEL [Motivation to work of parents of low-income families: Conceptual framework]. *Industrial Relations [Canada] 1974 29(4): 643-670.* "The authors attempt to discover the factors that motivate parents of low-income families to find jobs (to work), or not to find them (to not work)." Presents a motivation model relying on a literary magazine and interviews with key informants. In addition, "the authors formulate a hypothesis on the relation between motivation and the rate of participation in manpower."

1511. Bentley, C. Fred. AGRICULTURAL CHANGES AND RE-SOURCE ENDOWMENTS. *Tr. of the Royal Soc. of Can. [Canada] 1977 15: 29-47.* Discusses changes in Canadian agriculture. Good farm land even in a country as large as Canada is limited and it is in the rich farming areas that urban growth is greatest. In the Atlantic Provinces, Quebec, and Ontario, much farm land has been abandoned; thus, less land is available for farming. Changes in climate could reduce it even more. Energy shortages could reduce productivity. Fertility of soil has already declined; thus, with increased population and changed work habits and food requirements Canada could become no longer self-sufficient in food production. 3 tables, 6 fig., biblio. J. D. Neville

1512. Berlin, Simon; Jones, Paul; and Torge, Janet. DECLINE OF A UNION. *Can. Dimension [Canada] 1977 12(7): 40-46.* Discusses the International Ladies' Garment Workers' Union, 1937-77, and assesses present union activity in Montreal.

1513. Bernard, Jean-Thomas. L'INTÉGRATION VERTICALE DANS L'INDUSTRIE MINIÈRE [Vertical integration in the mining industry]. *Actualité Écon. [Canada] 1977 53(4): 648-665.* Vertical integration occurs when a transaction between two consecutive stages of production is carried through an internal organisation rather than the market. For most mineral products that are found in Canada, we can observe a fairly high degree of vertical integration from exploration up to refining. The purpose of this paper is to review the various approaches that have been used to study vertical integration in economic analysis and to evaluate their applicability to the Canadian mining sector. Thus far economists have approched vertical integration from three different standpoints: first, the efficiency of interval organisation relative to the market in dealing with uncertainty under certain circumstances; second, the capacity to extend market power through vertical integration, and third, vertical integration can arise as an adjustment to some institutional constraints resulting mostly from government interventions. Although the efficiency and the monopolistic arguments have contributed to vertical integration in the Canadian mining sector, government intervention in the form of special tax rules has also played a major role. J

1514. Bjarnason, Emil. THE TECHNOLOGICAL REVOLUTION AND THE LABOR MOVEMENT. *World Marxist R. [Canada] 1975 18(1): 114-123.* Discusses trade unions in Canada during the 1970's.

1515. Bone, Ronald. THE OPEIU IN CANADA. *Can. Labour 1973 18(3): 16-19.* The Office and Professional Employees International Union. S

1516. Boyd, Monica. OCCUPATIONS OF FEMALE IMMIGRANTS AND NORTH AMERICAN IMMIGRATION STATISTICS. *Internat. Migration R. 1976 10(1): 73-80.* Discusses labor force potential and occupations of women immigrants to the United States and Canada, 1964-71.

1517. Breton, Albert. TRENDS IN THE CANADIAN ECONOMY. *Current Hist. 1974 66(392): 165-166, 184.*

1518. Brown, Malcolm C. ECONOMIC DIMENSIONS OF THE UNEMPLOYMENT PROBLEM. *J. of Canadian Studies 1974 9(4): 55-61.*

1519. Bruce, C. J. and Marshall, J. H. JOB SEARCH AND FRICTIONAL UNEMPLOYMENT: SOME EMPIRICAL EVIDENCE. *Industrial Relations [Canada] 1976 31(3): 402-416.* The purpose of this paper is to report on some recent empirical research undertaken in order to provide additional information concerning the frictionally unemployed. J

1520. Carrothers, A. W. R. WHO WANTS COLLECTIVE BARGAINING ANY WAY? *Industrial Relations [Canada] 1975 30(3): 319-330.* Collective bargaining in Canada is undergoing strains today, as it has in different circumstances, which are challenging the process and are causing responsible people to question whether it can be improved or should be replaced. J

1521. Castonguay, Claude. LE PROGRAMME CANADIEN DE LUTTE À L'INFLATION [The Canadian anti-inflation program]. *Industrial Relations [Canada] 1976 31(4): 522-536.* The Canadian wage and price control program modifies programs of remuneration and collective agreements, but a climate of mutual respect must be reestablished between labor and management. S

1522. Chant, John F. and Acheson, Keith. MYTHOLOGY AND CENTRAL BANKING. *Kyklos [Switzerland] 1973 26(2): 362-379.* Many recent contributions to the theory of bureaucracy have viewed the bureau as choosing its discretionary options from a given opportunity set. Less frequently have writers recognized that the bureau may be concerned with the maintenance and generation over time of an opportunity set which allows the bureau scope for discretionary action. The flow of information to the public initiated by any bureau is one means for enhancing its range of choice. In this paper a general hypothesis concerning the nature and emphasis of material released by the bureau is outlined and tested with respect to the behaviour of the Canadian central bank. Specifically the theory of bureaucracy predicts that the central bank would attempt to reduce expectations regarding its performance and to rationalize its past activities as appropriate. By countering attempts to specify the desired "output" of the central bank and by denying the efficacy of monetary policy in certain situations the Bank maintains its scope for discretion. In general it is found that the views of economic relationships adopted and expounded by the Bank are consistent with the hypothesis put forward in this paper. J

1523. Cheda, Sherrill. WOMEN AND MANAGEMENT: A SELECTIVE BIBLIOGRAPHY 1970-73. *Can. Lib. J. 1974 31(1): 18-19, 22, 24, 26-27.* Lists eight books, three essays, 26 articles and two bibliographies that deal with the subject. S

1524. Chung, Joseph H. SPECULATION FONCIERE ET BANQUE DE SOL URBAIN [Speculative funding and an urban land bank]. *Actualité Écon. [Canada] 1973 49(1): 39-57.* Urban land costs are increasingly a major factor in housing costs. Examines the rate of increase of such costs in recent years for Canada, and forecasts the rate of increase up to 1981. Specific causes include speculation and realtors. A land bank will be a necessary component of any effective solution. 7 tables, 12 notes, appendix. W. B. Whitham

1525. Clark, John. CYRIL STRONG: A DREAM IN REVERSE. *Can. Labour [Canada] 1977 22(3): 32-35.* Discusses Cyril Strong, a labor organizer and instrumental member of the American Federation of Labor and the Canadian Labour Congress, 1949-77.

1526. Clark, John. THE FIRST MINISTERS AND THE UNEM-PLOYED: TWO SOLITUDES. *Can. Labour [Canada] 1978 23(1): 11-14.* Discusses inadequacies in Canada's unemployment policy, 1978.

1527. Clark, John. "NICKLE JOE" LEAVES BIG SHOES. *Can. Labour [Canada] 1978 23(3): 29-33.* Reviews the accomplishments of Joe Morris, past president of the Canadian Labour Congress, and includes an interview with him.

1528. Cousineau, Jean-Michel and Green, Chris. STRUCTURAL UNEMPLOYMENT IN CANADA: 1971-1974: DID IT WORSEN? *Industrial Relations [Canada] 1978 33(2): 175-191.* The paper examines the question whether "structural" unemployment in Canada worsened during the period 1971-1974. Structural unemployment is here defined as a mismatch between the location and skill of job seekers and the location and skill requirements of available jobs (vacancies).   J

1529. D'Aoust, Claude. L'EFFET DE LA GRÈVE SUR LE CON-TRACT INDIVIDUEL DE TRAVAIL: L'AFFAIRE MCGAVIN TOASTMASTER [The effect of strikes in individual work contracts: The McGavin Toastmaster affair]. *Industrial Relations [Canada] 1977 32(3): 456-460.* Canada's Supreme Court upheld the right to strike in situations of individual work contracts; assesses the impact of this deci-sion on collective bargaining and salary negotiations based on the case of *McGavin Toastmaster Limited* v. *Ainscough et al.* (Canada, 1975).

1530. Daub, Mervin. A COMPARISON OF THE ACCURACY OF AMERICAN AND CANADIAN SHORT-TERM PREDICTIONS OF GROSS NATIONAL PRODUCT. *J. of Business 1974 47(2): 173-185.* Comparison with the accuracy of other nations' aggregate economic forecasts is one way to assess one's own national predictions, but method-ological problems discourage comparisons with the United States. Partly due to relative sizes of Gross National Product, American forecasters did significantly (.05 level) better than Canadians on absolute measures. Ex-trapolative adjustments, however, gave the Canadians higher relative predictive efficiency. Conclusions based solely on absolute accuracy can mislead, if the economies are dissimilar. Based on statistics and secondary sources; 2 tables, 19 notes.   J. W. Williams

1531. Davis, Douglas F. LOGGING, LUMBERING, AND FOR-ESTRY MUSEUMS. *J. of Forest Hist. 1974 17(4): 28-31.* This review of selected logging, lumber, and forestry museums in the United States and Canada is the beginning of an effort by the Forest History Society to create an informal association of logging museums to exchange infor-mation and promote increased visitor use of such museums. 6 photos.   D. R. Verardo

1532. Deaton, Rich. FISCAL SQUEEZE. *Can. Dimension 1973 9(4): 36-42, 49.* Since 1950 Canadian government expenditures, especially on the provincial and municipal levels, have outstripped incoming reve-nues. On the federal and provincial levels the corporate share of income tax revenues has declined while the individual taxpayer's share has in-creased. "Because of . . . this fiscal crisis, there will be a massive effort to hold down the wages of workers in the public sector." As the crisis grows, public employees will be forced to take action and political alliances between public workers and the users of social public services will inevita-bly result.   S

1533. Della Valle, P. A. and Meyer, B. CHANGES IN RELATIVE FEMALE-MALE UNEMPLOYMENT: A CANADIAN-UNITED STATES COMPARISON. *Industrial Relations [Canada] 1976 31(3): 417-433.* This paper seeks to examine the impact of the level of cyclical economic activity and of the relative female-male participation rates on the structure of the relative unemployment rates of women and men.   J

1534. Dion, Gérard. L'ORIGINE DE LA FORMULE RAND [The origin of the Rand formula]. *Industrial Relations [Canada] 1975 30(4): 747-761.* Studies the origin of the Rand formula in industrial unionism. Retraces the background behind the famous decision by Judge Ivan C. Rand after the Ford Motor Company of Canada strike of Septem-ber 1945 in Windsor, Ontario. The strike concerned 9,500 workers of the United Automobile Workers (Canadian Region) and extended to include workers from the Chrysler Corporation factories as well. The Rand deci-

sion, passed 29 January, guaranteed union security, outlined solid princi-ples for cooperation between companies and employees, gave unions the right to collect dues, assured unions the freedom to join or not join, and included a "strike vote" provision giving all workers equal vote. Stresses the impact of this decision on all Canadian labor relations, and says similar decisions today have been deprived of certain essential elements. Primary and secondary sources; 18 notes.   S. Sevilla

1535. Dodge, William. WAGES AND FOOD COSTS. *Can. Labour 1973 18(7-9): 4-6.*

1536. Doern, G. Bruce. THE POLITICAL ECONOMY OF REGU-LATING OCCUPATIONAL HEALTH: THE HAM AND BEAUDRY REPORTS. *Can. Public Administration [Canada] 1977 20(1): 1-35.* Examines the results and recommendations of the Ham Royal Commission on the Health and Safety of Workers in Mines in Ontario and the Beaudry Report on the Quebec asbestos industry, 1972-74.

1537. Dudley, Leonard. SUR L'OPTIMALITE DE LA ZONE MONETAIRE CANADIENNE [On the desirability of a Canadian monetary zone]. *Actualité Econ. [Canada] 1973 49(1): 7-19.* Canada has a dual economy composed of the "western prosperous zone" and the "eastern, somewhat less-favored zone." Western Canada has a 20% higher per capita revenue than eastern Canada. Discusses the reasons for the disparity and suggests that a modification of tariff barriers and a dual monetary system would correct the problem. Table, 2 graphs, 14 notes.   W. B. Whitham and S

1538. Edwards, Claude A. L'AVENIR DU SYNDICALISM DANS LA FONCTION PUBLIQUE FÉDÉRALE DU CANADA [The fu-ture of federal public service unionism in Canada]. *Industrial Relations [Canada] 1974 29(4): 804-824.* Comments on the current state of collec-tive bargaining in the Canadian federal public service. Stresses that present method of giving salary raises has considerably increased differ-ences in salaries, especially of small revenue civil servants, and that this will create great tension in future negotiations. Also discusses institution-alized consultation, planned negotiation, and the role that the Public Service Commission of Canada will be called upon to play.

1539. Elford, Jean. WHAT LAKE TANKERS MEAN TO CEN-TRAL CANADA. *Can. Geographical J. 1974 88(5): 24-31.* Describes the Great Lakes tankers which carry oil and petroleum products on the St. Lawrence Seaway.   S

1540. Farid, Z. and Kuyek, Joan. WHO SPEAKS FOR WORKING-CLASS WOMEN? *Can. Dimension 1975 10(8): 80-82.* The Women's Liberation Movement in Canada, dominated by middle-class women, ought to turn its attention to working-class women and such goals as equal access to jobs and promotions, state-supported day nurseries, and equality before the law.   S

1541. Ferguson, Norman. A CRITIQUE OF THE ECONOMIC COUNCIL OF CANADA. *Communist Viewpoint [Canada] 1973 5(3): 27-29.*

1542. Finkelman, Jacob. REPORT ON EMPLOYER-EMPLOYEE RELATIONS IN THE PUBLIC SERVICE OF CANADA. *Industrial Relations [Canada] 1974 29(4): 786-803.* In this article, the author ex-plains the rationale behind the Finkelman report which contains many proposals for legislative change in the Public Service Staff Relations Act. Some of the key recommendations are discussed but substantial consider-ation is also given to the constraints the committee had to deal with.   J

1543. Finn, Ed. BEYOND THE STRIKE STATISTICS. *Industrial Relations [Canada] 1973 28(4): 826-841.* "Before examining many of the myths surrounding the strike phenomenon, the author of this paper feels that the accuracy of the strike figures themselves should be questioned."   J

1544. Gelber, Sylva. WOMEN AND WORK: THE LEGISLATIVE BASE. *Can. Labour 1975 20(2): 7-10.* Presents Canada's labor laws as they pertain to women since 1951.   S

1545. Globerman, Steven. MARKET STRUCTURE AND R & D IN CANADIAN MANUFACTURING INDUSTRIES. *Q. R. of Econ. and Business 1973 13(2): 59-68*. "Least-squares multiple regression analysis was employed to determine the empirical relationship between different market structure characteristics and the overall research intensity of an industry. Using a sample of 15 Canadian manufacturing industries, it was determined that the relationship is industry specific. For technologically progressive industries, increased foreign ownership and decreased concentration contributes to increased research intensity. The relationship is reversed for technologically unprogressive industries. The findings help to explain why previous industry studies relating research intensities to concentration have given inconclusive results." J

1546. Glorieux, Guy. LA STAGFLATION ET LA CONJONCTURE ÉCONOMIQUE AU CANADA EN 1974 [Stagflation and statistical economic projections in Canada in 1974]. *Actualité Écon. [Canada] 1975 51(2): 367-374*. Canada, like other industrial nations, has suffered a conjunction of inflation and recession in recent years, and for many of the same reasons.

1547. Goldenberg, Shirley B. DISPUTE SETTLEMENT IN THE PUBLIC SECTOR: THE CANADIAN SCENE. *Relations Industrielles/Industrial Relations [Canada] 1973 28(2): 267-294*. "A brief overview of the current provisions for impasse resolution at all levels of public employment is followed by a more detailed discussion of policy and practice in jurisdictions that grant the right to strike to the employees of senior levels of government. Finally, the author tries to identify some of the problems that complicate the settlement of disputes in the public sector and considers the challenge and the prospects of resolving these problems in the light of the Canadian experience." J

1548. Gonick, Cy. [INFLATION IN CANADA]. INVESTMENT BOOM . . . AND BUST. *Can. Dimension 1974 10(3): 10-12, 63-64*. Continued from a previous article. Deals with the effects of inflation on income distribution and investment. INFLATION AND THE COMING CRISIS. *Can. Dimension 1974 10(4): 45-48*. Deals with the economic crisis of inflation. THE CURRENT CRISIS MARKS THE END OF THE KEYNESIAN ERA. *Can. Dimension 1974 10(5): 4-9*. Inflation in the 1970's disproves John Maynard Keynes' economic theory.

1549. Gonick, Cy. LABOUR'S NEW MANIFESTO: CLC CONVENTION NOTES. *Can. Dimension 1976 11(5): 23-32*. Discusses the Labour Manifesto (1976) of the Canadian Labour Council's convention in Quebec City, emphasizing issues in economics, politics, and collective bargaining.

1550. Gonick, Cy. UNEMPLOYMENT: THE MYTHS AND REALITIES. *Can. Dimension [Canada] 1978 12(8): 24-31*. Answers common assumptions about unemployment in the 1970's; discusses its causes, extent, and possible solutions in Canada.

1551. Goodman, Eileen. COOPRIX SUPERMARKETS EXPAND. *Can. Labour 1973 18(7-9): 13-15*.

1552. Hameed, Syed M. A. EMPLOYMENT IMPACT OF FRINGE BENEFITS IN CANADIAN MANUFACTURING SECTOR: 1957-1965. *Relations Industrielles/Industrial Relations [Canada] 1973 28(2): 380-396*. "Analyzes the growing costs of various fringe benefits in Canada and their impact on expanding employment. The empirical evidence is in support of fringe barrier hypothesis but not until labour turnover costs are added to fringe costs. It emphasizes that Canadian data on fringe benefits and overtime are extremely inadequate; therefore, at the present time, no conclusive study is possible without collecting data on overtime, describing the causes of assigning it internally in a factory. This study attempted to fill in this gap by suggesting that external factors such as skill shortages and capacity output are not significant determinants of overtime." J

1553. Hamilton, Richard and Pinard, Maurice. POVERTY IN CANADA: ILLUSION AND REALITY. *Can. Rev. of Sociol. and Anthrop. [Canada] 1977 14(2): 247-252*. Based on taxation statistics, in 1946 the richest 10% of earners received about 20 times as much income as the poorest 10%. In 1971, they received 45 times as much. The actual experi-

ence is far different. The only valid data would be for family units, not individual taxpayers. More individuals are employed part-time or short-term and more are reporting than previously. "There has been . . . a significant increase in the welfare effort and that contribution has come disproportionately to the benefit of the poorest families." 2 tables, 5 notes, ref.   E. P. Stickney

1554. Jain, Harish C. and Hines, Robert J. CURRENT OBJECTIVES OF CANADIAN FEDERAL MANPOWER PROGRAMS. *Industrial Relations [Canada] 1973 28(1): 125-148*. "In this paper some of the factors leading to renewed interest in Manpower in the 1960's are enumerated; the present course of Federal Manpower Programs is examined and the objectives of these programs are evaluated. It is suggested that the emphasis of the Federal Manpower Programs on economic growth and stabilization of the economy is misguided; that the Department of Manpower and Immigration has failed to foresee shifts in labour market composition; and that in the face of counter-productive fiscal policy, manpower programs and objectives as originally conceived do not have the capability to resurrect a sick economy." J

1555. Jenness, R. A. TAUX DE ROULEMENT ET PERMANENCE DE L'EMPLOI DANS L'INDUSTRIE CANADIENNE [Turnover and worker tenure in Canadian industry]. *Actualité Écon. [Canada] 1974 50(2): 152-176*. "This study poses the question: 'How long will the average new employee likely stay with his employer?' This question has considerable relevance to the study of labour market activity, and to the obverse question: 'How likely will a person, once employed, be unemployed again?' This paper explores the relevance of the tenure question on a number of fronts, and then develops a simple model for estimating the expected tenure of workers joining specific industries in Canada. Although the findings are based on somewhat dated statistics and lack a vector related to age, sex and other personal characteristics, they nonetheless confirm within reasonable degrees of confidence that the average new employee will remain with his employer a remarkably short time—less than two years in most industries and only a few months in some others. They suggest that employers are wise to defer costly training, pension and other non-wage expenditures until their new employees have built up some attachment to the firm. By the same token they affirm the usefulness of public income support programs to tide those who are laid off or quit through the transition to their next job, and for public retraining and mobility facilities to make the investments in human skills and allocation that employers will not." J

1556. Johnson, John H. THE GREENING OF THE BLACK CONSUMER MARKET. *Crisis 1976 83(3): 92-95*. At one time, most American goods and services were marketed without the black consumer in mind. But the blacks' is one of the largest secondary markets in the world, exceeding those of Canada, Australia, or the Netherlands. And it is a general market, not a special one. Only recently has business and industry recognized the spending power resting in the black community.   A. G. Belles

1557. Kehoe, Mary. AUTOMATION ALIENATION. *Can. Labour 1973 18(1): 15-17*.

1558. Kehoe, Mary. CLC CONFERENCE ON EQUAL OPPORTUNITY. *Can. Labour [Canada] 1978 23(1): 30-33*. Discusses the proceedings of the Canadian Labour Conference on Equal Opportunity and Treatment for Women Workers, 1978, which found that though laws exist to provide equal employment opportunities for women, it does not exist in the Canadian labor market.

1559. Kliman, M. L. CONTROLLING INFLATION IN CANADA. *Current Hist. 1977 72(426): 166-169*. Examines federal anti-inflation measures 1970-76 and investigates action appropriate for "post-controls" policymaking in Canada.

1560. Kravtsov, A. K. GOSUDARSTVENNYE KORPORATSII KANADY [Canada's state corporations]. *Sovetskoe Gosudarstvo i Pravo [USSR] 1978 (3): 101-105*. Reviews the make-up, classification, and functions of Canada's crown corporations (federal, provincial, and jointly held). The Financial Administration Act (1951) and subsequent legislation protect state-owned corporations from losses inflicted by private organizations in the chaotic conditions of capitalist market economy. 18 notes.   N. Frenkley

1561. Kuzminov, I. THE 1969-1971 ECONOMIC CRISIS: ITS CHARACTER AND CONSEQUENCES. *Int. Affairs [USSR] 1973 (9): 38-43.* Sees economic crisis and industrial and manufacturing slowdown in the United States, Great Britain, Canada, Italy, France, and West Germany, 1969-71.

1562. Kwavnick, David. THE PURSUIT OF ORGANIZATIONAL OBJECTIVES: THE CASE OF THE NON-EXISTENT CONTRADICTORY VERSION. *Can. J. of Pol. Sci. 1975 8(2): 307-311.* A rejoinder to an article by Raymond Hudon, which was a critique of a previous article by Kwavnick. The articles are concerned with the organizational ambitions of the leadership of the Confederation of National Trade Unions (CNTU), also known as the Confédération des Syndicats Nationaux (CSN).
R. V. Kubicek

1563. LaBerge, Roy. NATIONAL DAY OF PROTEST. *Can. Labour [Canada] 1976 21(4): 14-17.* Discusses workers' strike and political protest against the federal government in Canada in October, 1976 for the purpose of eradicating wage controls. Considers the role of the Canadian Labour Congress and its President Joe Morris.

1564. Lanphier, C. M. and Morris, R. N. STRUCTURAL ASPECTS OF DIFFERENCES IN INCOME BETWEEN ANGLOPHONES AND FRANCOPHONES. *Can. R. of Sociol. and Anthrop. 1974 11(1): 53-66.* "This paper compares the data on French-British income differences presented by Raynauld et al. with more recent survey data. It mentions several methodological criticisms of Raynauld's analysis. Comparisons between data gathered in 1961 and 1968 indicate a levelling of the income differences during that period. Although the nation-wide ration of francophone to anglophone incomes is now closer to unity, the income disparity has increased for persons in lower-skilled occupations. These and other findings invite various interpretations of 'discrimination' as a variable related to income."
J

1565. Lasserre, Jean-Claude. LE COMPLEXE PORTUAIRE DE LA COTE-NORD ET SON ROLE DANS LA NAVIGATION SUR LE SAINT-LAURENT [The port complex of the north shore and its role in navigation on the Saint Lawrence River]. *Cahiers de Géographie de Québec [Canada] 1973 17(40): 155-169.* The north shore of the St. Lawrence River benefits from a relatively new system of ports that in terms of tonnage have risen to the top in Quebec and Canada. Specializing in bulk cargo, they serve as one of the two large termini for internal navigation of the St. Lawrence-Great Lakes system. A comparison with the ports at the head of the lakes is mandatory. Photo, 8 figs., 9 notes, biblio.
A. E. LeBlanc

1566. Laudadio, Leonard and Percy, Michael. SOME EVIDENCE OF THE IMPACT OF NON-WAGE LABOUR COST ON OVERTIME WORK AND EMPLOYMENT. *Relations Industrielles/Industrial Relations [Canada] 1973 28(2): 397-402.* "Total labour costs can be considered to be a function of the hourly wage, a quasi-fixed component (mainly fringe benefits and training cost) and overtime rate. The theoretical model employed in this paper suggests that an increase in the ratio of quasi-fixed cost to overtime rate leads to an increase in the amount of scheduled overtime work instead of employment. The model, tested with Canadian data, yields statistically significant results."
J

1567. Layton, Jack. NATIONALISM AND THE CANADIAN BOURGEOISIE: CONTRADICTIONS OF DEPENDENCE. *Can. Rev. of Studies in Nationalism [Canada] 1976 3(2): 146-171.* Examines nationalistic thought within the Canadian economic elite and business communities, concluding that the "nationalism of the middle" offers little possibilities for the establishment of a strong independent Canadian economy and only symbolic pacification of the left or ineffectual pursuits of self-interest among certain components of the bourgeoisie, 1968-76.

1568. Lazar, Fred and Donner, Arthur. THE DIMENSION OF CANADIAN YOUTH UNEMPLOYMENT: A THEORETICAL EXPLANATION. *Relations Industrielles/Industrial Relations [Canada] 1973 28(2): 295-324.* "This paper looks beneath the national unemployment numbers to examine in detail the dimension of Canada's youth unemployment problem. After an outline of the empirical dimensions of youth unemployment in Canada, a theoretical framework is set out to explain the particular characteristics of youth unemployment. Finally, some policy recommendations are presented."
J

1569. LeGoff, Jean-Pierre. IMPACT DES INCITATIONS À L'INVESTISSEMENT DU GOUVERNEMENT FÉDÉRAL CANADIEN DANS LE SECTEUR MANUFACTURIER, DE 1965 À 1974 [Impact of Canadian federal government investment incentives in the manufacturing sector, 1965 to 1974]. *Actualité Écon. [Canada] 1977 53(3): 370-389.* The Canadian federal government called upon substantial fiscal incentives between 1965 and 1974 to increase the flow of capital expenditures in the manufacturing sector, in order to reduce regional disparities, to alleviate an excessive unemployment rate and to insure a higher growth rate. The objective of our research is to evaluate the effectiveness of these incentives in inducing larger investment expenditures. We use econometric investment functions based on neoclassical and "hybrid" models of firm behavior, applied to Canadian yearly manufacturing time series from 1946 to 1974. The neoclassical and hybrid models agree that the incentives have a substantial impact during the years 65-69; and a marginal impact during the 69-74 years. The neoclassical model explains the marginal impact of incentives in the 69-74 period by a displacement through time of investment projects; there is an acceleration-deceleration effect attributed to the incentives. Investment expenditures of the 69-74 period are submitted to an upward pressure because of the 69-74 incentives, and to a downward pressure because of a deceleration effect associated with the 65-69 incentives. We conclude that the incentives are effective in the short run in stimulating investment expenditures (the mean lag of their impact is approximately eighteen months) but that an acceleration-deceleration effect shows up after three years.
J

1570. Lerette, Jack L. THE NATIONAL PENSIONERS AND SENIOR CITIZENS' FEDERATION. *Can. Labour 1973 18(2): 2-5.* Covers the period 1954-73.
S

1571. Lindberg, Leon N. ENERGY POLICY AND THE POLITICS OF ECONOMIC DEVELOPMENT. *Comparative Pol. Studies 1977 10(3): 355-382.* Analyzes energy policies of Great Britain, Canada, France, Hungary, India, Sweden, and the United States from 1945 to 1976, with special attention to the post-1973 response and to a comparison of pluralist and elite explanations for the emergence and persistence of this pattern, and addresses the prospects for adaptation and change in energy policies and policymaking systems.

1572. Lipsey, Richard G. LE CONTRÔLE DES PRIX ET DES REVENUS AU CANADA [Prices and incomes controls in Canada]. *Actualité Écon. [Canada] 1976 52(3): 271-310.* This paper is a summary of the Legal Factum submitted by the Canadian Labor Congress to the Supreme Court of Canada. It intends to demonstrate the irrelevance of the Anti-Inflationnary Act of October 1975. Three main questions are dealt with. First, was there an economic crisis in October 1975? Analysing various sets of data, the paper concludes that, by no stretch of imagination, could October 1975 be called an economic crisis. Second, was there a policy crisis in the sense that traditional methods had been tried and failed? It establishes here that no serious attempt had been made to contain inflation by traditional fiscal and monetary tools by October 1975. Third, what results can be expected from income policies? This part gives a summary of the voluminous evidence for the U.K. and the U.S., and concludes that the evidence of other incomes policies is that their efforts on slowing the rate of inflation are small and often transitory.
J

1573. Lizee, Ruth Rose. INFLATION, IMPÔTS SUR LE REVENU ET REVENU RÉEL DISPONIBLE [Inflation, income taxes and real disposable income]. *Actualité Écon. [Canada] 1974 50(4): 533-548.* "The purpose of this text is to examine how federal and Quebec provincial income tax policies have affected real disposable income of taxpayers in the context of the rapid inflation of the last five years. It finds that the net effect of federal fiscal reform since 1970 has been to make the tax structure more progressive. Low-income taxpayers have benefitted from lower tax rates in real terms but real tax rates have risen for those with incomes above approximately $14,000. On the provincial level, on the other hand, there has been virtually no change in the tax structure except for an increase in the threshold level below which no tax is paid. All, except the very poorest taxpayers (single persons earning less than $2,578 in 1970 or $3,200 in 1974 and married couples with two children earning less than $5,200 in 1970 or $6,300 in 1974), have paid higher taxes in real terms every year from 1970 to 1974. This is true even when provincial family allowances (which the province considers as a tax credit and as a substitute for personal exemptions for children under 16) are deducted from provincial income tax. The net result of federal and provincial tax policies, family allowance payments and deductions for various social security programs is as follows: real disposable income increased for single persons earning less than $4,000 in 1970 ($5,000 in 1974) and for two-children families earning less than $8,000 ($10,000 in 1974); it stayed about the same for single persons earning between $4,000 and $6,000 ($5,000 to $7,500 in 1974) and families earning $8,000 to $10,000 ($10,-000 to $12,500 in 1974) in 1970; it fell for those with higher levels of income."   J

1574. Magnuson, Bruce. LABOR UNITY AGAINST DOMINATION OF STATE-MONOPOLY POWER. *Communist Viewpoint [Canada] 1973 5(1): 19-25.*

1575. Magnuson, Bruce. TRADE UNIONS AND INDEPENDENCE OF CANADA. *World Marxist R. [Canada] 1975 18(12): 77-86.* The Communist Party of Canada has encouraged a recent move by the Canadian Labour Congress to adopt a more militant and reform-oriented position.

1576. Maki, Dennis R. UNEMPLOYMENT INSURANCE, UNEMPLOYMENT DURATION AND EXCESS SUPPLY OF LABOUR. *Industrial Relations [Canada] 1976 31(3): 368-378.* This paper examines the effect of the unemployment insurance scheme on the duration of unemployment spells in Canada in the period 1953-73.   J

1577. Marmor, Theodore R. RETHINKING NATIONAL HEALTH INSURANCE. *Public Interest 1977 (46): 73-95.* Plans to deal with medical care problems in the United States include the American Medical Association Medicredit, the Kennedy-Corman Bill, the major-risk-insurance proposal of Martin Feldstein, the Long-Ribicoff bill, and the Ford administration's Comprehensive Health Insurance Plan. The Canadian experience with government health insurance is relevant to the United States. The United States needs a plan that provides protection against disastrous medical costs, encourages preventive care, is an incentive to efficient medical practice, and has a reasonable price. Proposes an introductory comprehensive health insurance program for all preschool children and pregnant women, combined with universal catastrophic protection. If desired, the child insurance program would be expanded for the first five years, with the possibility of extending it to the rest of the population at that time. 3 tables, 9 references.
                                                                  S. Harrow

1578. Mastromatteo, Ernest. INDUSTRIAL DISEASES. *Can. Labour 1973 18(4-6): 17-20, 34.*

1579. McCaffrey, Gordon. COASTING TRADE POLICY—PROFITS OR JOBS. *Can. Labour 1973 18(10-12): 29-32.*

1580. McDonald, Charles. UAW RETIRED MEMBERS' PROGRAMME. *Can. Labour 1973 18(2): 10-11.* The United Automobile Workers (Canadian Region).   S

1581. McIvor, R. Craig. POSTWAR TRENDS IN THE FINANCING OF CANADIAN ECONOMIC ACTIVITY. *Tr. of the Royal Soc. of Can. 1973 11: 199-228.* Summarizes the functioning of financial institutions in serving the ever-changing economic objectives of Canadian society, with an assessment of the capital market's success in meeting these financial requirements, 1947-72.

1582. Mehmet, Ozay. ECONOMIC RETURNS ON UNDERGRADUATE FIELDS OF STUDY IN CANADIAN UNIVERSITIES, 1961-1972. *Industrial Relations [Canada] 1977 32(1): 321-337.* This paper provides comparable estimates of private rates of return on a set of 21 undergraduate courses of study at Canadian Universities in 1961, 1969, and 1972, and then attempts to explain observed shifts in the college labour market using a simple multiple regression model.   J

1583. Moore, Larry F. and Daly, William G. OCCUPATIONAL CHARACTERISTICS OF LEADING CANADIAN EXECUTIVES. *Industrial Relations [Canada] 1973 28(1): 110-123.* "The purpose of this study is to investigate the geographic origins, the social and educational

backgrounds and the occupational and career patterns of top executives in Canadian Companies."   J

1584. Morris, Joe. LABOUR'S ROLE IN REHABILITATION. *Can. Labour 1973 18(4-6): 5-6, 24.*

1585. Moy, Joyanna and Sorrentino, Constance. AN ANALYSIS OF UNEMPLOYMENT IN NINE INDUSTRIAL COUNTRIES. *Monthly Labor Rev. 1977 100(4): 12-24.* Analyzes unemployment rates during 1974-76 in relation to age, sex, population, national development, and labor market factors in countries including Canada and the United States.

1586. Nousiainen, Seppo. THE COST OF FRINGE BENEFITS. *Can. Labour 1973 18(7-9): 21-23.*

1587. Onibokun, Adepoju G. EVALUATING CONSUMERS' SATISFACTION WITH HOUSING: AN APPLICATION OF A SYSTEMS APPROACH. *J. of the Am. Inst. of Planners 1974 40(3): 189-200.* "This study develops a research method of assessing people's satisfaction with housing. Instead of the old approaches which consider in fragmented ways the characteristics of the dwelling, or the neighborhood, or the social environment, the author proposes a systems approach in which various interdependent factors are studied in relation to one another. Using the techniques developed, the relative satisfaction of tenants in public housing projects in certain areas of Canada is identified, analyzed, and discussed."   J

1588. Passaris, Constantine. THE COST-BENEFIT IMPACT OF IMMIGRANTS ON ECONOMY. *Internat. Perspectives [Canada] 1975 (5): 9-13.* Discusses the effect of immigration on the economics of Canada in the 1970's, emphasizing employment and wages.

1589. Pearson, Norman. PRESERVING CANADIAN FARMLAND. *Queen's Q. [Canada] 1974 81(4): 598-604.* Discusses the importance of Canada's vast farmlands in a global perspective, based on how they relate to ongoing population problems. Enumerates areas where greater research into productivity possibilities is needed. The goal is "prosperous farmers in a productive landscape." It is essential that good farmland be preserved.   J. A. Casada

1590. Peitchinis, Stephen G. THE INFLUENCE OF PUBLIC OPINION IN LABOR-MANAGEMENT RELATIONS AND DISPUTE SETTLEMENT. *Industrial Relations [Canada] 1977 32(2): 268-273.* Assesses the influence of Canadian public opinion on labor disputes and settlement, 1940's-70's.

1591. Poon, L. C. L. RAILWAY EXTERNALITIES AND RESIDENTIAL PROPERTY PRICES. *Land Econ. 1978 54(2): 218-227.* Constructs a multiple-linear regression model using data from four sample tracts in London, Ontario, in 1972, to identify the effect of railroads on housing prices. At distances to 900 feet from the railway, the railroad depresses the sale value of a house. This is an indication of the economic effect of railroad pollution and should be considered by planners. Map, 2 tables, 16 notes, 19 ref.   E. S. Johnson

1592. Porter, Glenn. RECENT TRENDS IN CANADIAN BUSINESS AND ECONOMIC HISTORY. *Business Hist. R. 1973 47(2): 141-157.* Reviews recent historical writing in Canadian business and economic history. Notes that the economic interpretation of Canada's history, referred to as the Laurentian thesis, has begun to lose its force of late. However, the need for other instructive generalizations supported by sound evidence continues. Secondary sources; 66 notes.
                                                                  C. J. Pusateri

1593. Pritchett, Craig H. TECHNOLOGY AND THE LONGSHOREMEN. *Can. Labour 1973 18(1): 6-8, 17.*

1594. Rainville, Jean-Marie and Guerin, Gilles. FACTEURS EXPLICATIFS DE LA SATISFACTION DANS LE TRAVAIL [Explicative factors of work satisfaction]. *Can. Rev. of Sociol. and Anthrop. [Canada] 1978 15(1): 16-30.* The efforts some researchers have made since the early sixties to "prove" that intrinsic factors are more important than extrinsic ones in explaining the satisfaction of individuals in their work, borrow a conceptual framework of doubtful value. In this article, it is contended that attempts to use this hypothesis to explain workers' motivation overlook the fact that blue collar work, even if it is enriched, cannot gain any intrinsic value. Taking this into account, intrinsic factors can have only limited value in explaining job satisfaction. This study tested the working hypothesis just suggested. Data were collected from a group of blue workers in a Montreal area (N-269). Results were obtained through the use of discriminant analysis which supported the working hypothesis.   J

1595. Rand, Ivan C. DÉCISION TOUCHANT LA SÉCURITÉ SYNDICALE DANS LE CONFLIT FORD 1946 [Decision concerning union security in the Ford conflict, 1946]. *Industrial Relations [Canada] 1975 30(4): 761-771.* Presents the text of the famous Judge Rand decision, 29 January 1946, in the arbitration between the Ford Motor Company of Canada Limited and the International United Automobile Workers (Canadian Region). Develops a general philosophy of labor relations in a democratic industrial society, and considers individual rights and social duty. Lays out principles for management and labor, asserting that labor unions are natural and necessary organizations, and that collective negotiation is an accepted and desirable social institution. Some points include: mandatory payment of union dues through employer salary deduction, worker freedom to participate in activities, equal vote of all members in strike decision, and simple majority in strike decision. This decision sets new principles where none were yet established, and reinforces the security of unionism.   S. Sevilla

1596. Raynauld, André. INFLATION ET FISCALITÉ [Inflation and fiscal policy]. *Industrial Relations [Canada] 1975 30(3): 299-315.* We live in a period of growing inflation. In this context the analysis of postwar politics exposes the necessity to have recourse to new instruments of analysis.

1597. Reschenthaler, G. B. REGULATORY FAILURE AND COMPETITION. *Can. Public Administration [Canada] 1976 19(3): 466-486.* Examines policymaking and regulation of industry in Canada, to detect failure of regulatory actions, to determine techniques for measuring the cost of regulatory failure, and to identify sectors of the economy which would profit better from competition than from direct regulation.

1598. Richards, John. FEAR AND LOATHING AT CALGARY'S CONVENTION CENTRE. *Can. Dimension 1975 10(6): 45-51.* A report on a conference held in Calgary, where the topic to be discussed was "How should the Revenues from Canada's Resources be Shared?"   S

1599. Rinehart, James W. CONTRADICTIONS OF WORK-RELATED ATTITUDES AND BEHAVIOUR: AN INTERPRETATION. *Can. Rev. of Sociol. and Anthrop. [Canada] 1978 15(1): 1-15.* Attitude studies show that manual workers are satisfied with or indifferent to their jobs, but observations of workers' actions indicate a dissatisfaction with and resistance to work. A conceptual framework is developed to interpret this discrepancy. Workers evaluate jobs in terms of the limited alternatives open to them; hence, "satisfied" responses are minimal and qualified. This reduces the magnitude of the attitude-behaviour disparity but does not explain it. The remaining discrepancy stems from the conjuncture of workers' subordinate position at the workplace and their adherence to dominant values which justify capitalist authority and production. The necessity to accumulate capital obliges employers to cheapen labour and divest workers of their control over the work process. Workers, in their attempt to work with the greatest possible degree of security, ease, and autonomy, are compelled to resist the debasement of the labour process. Such resistance occurs despite and in contradiction to workers' own beliefs and values.   J

1600. Robinson, Kenneth R. CARGO HOOKS AND COMPUTERS: THE ILWU AND AUTOMATION. *Can. Labour 1973 18(1): 2-5.*

1601. Robinson, Kenneth R. LONGSHOREMEN AND SAFETY. *Can. Labour 1973 18(1): 9-11, 17.*

1602. Robinson, Kenneth R. A SILVERY BONANZA FROM THE SEA—FOR WHOM? *Can. Labour 1973 18(2): 14-15, 24.* Canada's commercial fishermen are not profiting from record catches.   S

1603. Rose, Joseph B. ACCREDITATION AND THE CONSTRUCTION INDUSTRY: FIVE APPROACHES TO COUNTERVAILING EMPLOYER POWER. *Relations Industrielles/Industrial Relations [Canada] 1973 28(3): 565-582.* "In this paper, the author aims at describing the various legislative approaches to accreditation which have been adopted and at evaluating the strengths and weaknesses of different efforts to reduce employer fragmentation and redress the imbalance of power within the industry."   J

1604. Rose, Joseph B. CONSTRUCTION LABOUR RELATIONS ASSOCIATIONS IN CANADA. *Industrial Relations [Canada] 1977 32(1):: 35-47.* This paper examines the relatively recent movement by employers in the construction industry toward province-wide associations specializing in labour relations. Beginning with the formation of the Construction Labour Relations Association of British Columbia (CLRA) it reviews the influences of contractor cooperation, union opposition and labour laws on the ability of these organizations to bring unity to contractor ranks and alleviate what has been described as the imbalance of power in construction labour relations. There is also an examination of the organizational characteristics of these CLRA-type organizations which reveals how they have been able to maintain control of members and reduce fragmentation.   J

1605. Rousseau, Henri-Paul. UNE NOTE SUR LA RÉALISATION DES INTENTIONS D'INVESTISSEMENT DES PROVINCES ET DES MUNICIPALITÉS 1950-1973 [A note on the realization of provincial and municipal investment intentions, 1950-73]. *Actualité Écon. [Canada] 1976 52(1): 111-121.* Except for the years 1968 and 1969, *Statistique Canada*'s annual predictions of public and private investments have been accurate within a fraction of one percent. Provinces have underestimated their expected income, resulting in larger-than-anticipated surpluses. Municipalities usually have budgetary deficits. A regression analysis supports the theory that interest rates influence provincial capital expenditures; in the case of municipalities, the question remains open. The realization of investment intentions is influenced by monetary policy through fluctuations in interest rates, which are generally counter-cyclical. Based on government statistics and secondary sources; 3 tables, 10 notes.   W. R. Hively

1606. Ruggeri, Giuseppe C. HIDDEN UNEMPLOYMENT BY AGE AND SEX IN CANADA: 1957-1970. *Industrial Relations [Canada] 1975 30(2): 181-196.* This study presents yearly estimates of hidden unemployment and job requirements for full employment in Canada by age and sex for the period 1957 to 1970. The method employed in deriving these estimates involved the calculation of the potential labour force, total and by specific age-sex groups, and the formulation of a relationship relating group employment to total employment.   J

1607. Russell, Peter H. THE *ANTI-INFLATION* CASE: THE ANATOMY OF A CONSTITUTIONAL DECISION. *Can. Public Administration [Canada] 1977 20(4): 632-665.* The Canadian Supreme Court's upholding of the Anti-Inflation Act gave wage-price controls and the peacetime use of emergency powers constitutional mandate, 1976.

1608. Schaafsma, Joseph. CAPITAL-LABOR SUBSTITUTION AND THE EMPLOYMENT FUNCTION IN MANUFACTURING: A MODEL APPLIED TO 1949-72 CANADIAN DATA. *Q. Rev. of Econ. and Business 1977 17(3): 33-42.* In this paper an employment function for the manufacturing sector is derived in which desired employment is a function of output and relative factor prices, and in which actual employment adjusts with a lag to desired employment. The parameters of the employment function are estimated using annual Canadian data for the period 1949-72. The empirical results indicate the existence of constant returns to scale in the long run and an elasticity of substitution substantially less than unity. Actual employment adjusts to desired employment within two years with 72 percent of the adjustment occurring in the first year.   J

1609. Scherer, F. M. THE DETERMINANTS OF INDUSTRIAL PLANT SIZES IN SIX NATIONS. *Rev. of Econ. and Statistics 1973 55(2): 135-145.* Covers Europe and North America, 1963-67.

1610. Seymour, Edward E. THE TILCO STRIKE. *Can. Labour 1973 18 (10-12): 18-28, 43.* Example of how trade unions can protect employees of small firms through strikes and the courts.   S

1611. Steed, Guy P. F. CENTRALITY AND LOCATIONAL CHANGE: PRINTING, PUBLISHING, AND CLOTHING IN MONTREAL AND TORONTO. *Econ. Geography 1976 52(3): 193-205.* Examines locational clustering of publishing and clothing industries in metropolitan areas, centering on Montreal and Toronto, 1949-67.

1612. Swidinsky, Robert. UNEMPLOYMENT AND LABOUR FORCE PARTICIPATION: THE CANADIAN EXPERIENCE. *Industrial Relations [Canada] 1973 28(1): 56-74.* "In an analysis of the short-run sensitivity of the Canadian labour force time series regression results appear inconclusive whereas cross-section regression results suggest a strong negative response to unemployment. Generally, the findings from the cross-section are comparable neither qualitatively nor quantitatively with those from the time series."					J

1613. Tandon, B. B. and Tandon, K. K. WAGE DIFFERENTIALS BETWEEN NATIVE AND FOREIGN BORN CANADIANS. *Industrial Relations [Canada] 1977 32(2): 202-214.* Estimates the extent of male-female wage differential in a local labor market among the native born and foreign born Canadians.					J

1614. Thompson, Mark J. and Moore, Larry F. MANAGERIAL ATTITUDES TOWARD INDUSTRIAL RELATIONS: PUBLIC AND PRIVATE SECTORS. *Industrial Relations [Canada] 1976 31(3): 359-367.* The authors analyse possible differences in managerial attitudes toward unionism and collective bargaining in the public and private sectors in Canada. Distinct patterns of attitudes emerge showing more favorable views in the public sector.					J

1615. Thompson, Mark and Moore, Larry F. MANAGERIAL ATTITUDES TOWARD INDUSTRIAL RELATIONS: A US-CANADIAN COMPARISON. *Industrial Relations [Canada] 1975 30(3): 331-340.* This paper analyses possible differences in managerial attitudes toward unionism and collective bargaining in Canada and the United States. Divergent patterns of attitudes emerge that are consistent with other observable differences between Canadian and US industrial relations.					J

1616. Unsigned. CLC INCOMES POLICY. *Can. Labour 1975 20(2): 28-30.* Discusses the 1975 efforts by the Executive Committee of the Canadian Labour Congress and the ministers of finance, labour and manpower, and immigration to combat inflation in Canada.					S

1617. Unsigned. CUPE PROGRAMME FOR WOMEN'S YEAR. *Can. Labour 1975 20(2): 16-18.* Notes the efforts of the Canadian Union of Public Employees to fight sex discrimination in 1975.					S

1618. Unsigned. IAM RETIREES' PLANS AND PROJECTS. *Can. Labour 1973 18(2): 12-13, 24.* The International Association of Machinists and Aerospace Workers.					S

1619. Unsigned. UNEMPLOYMENT INSURANCE. *Can. Labour 1975 20(1): 28-31.* Gives text of statement approved in December 1974 by the Canadian Labour Congress Executive Council.					S

1620. Vanderberg, Richard D. RAILWAY UNIONS AND TECHNOLOGICAL CHANGE. *Can. Labour 1973 18(1): 12-14, 17.*

1621. Veeman, Terrence S. and Veeman, Michele M. CANADIAN AGRICULTURE TODAY. *Current Hist. 1977 72(426): 162-165.* Marked by relatively little government intervention, agriculture in Canada is plagued by low income production and promises to remain so.

1622. Waldie, Ken. PRODUCTIVITY AND COMPETITIVENESS IN CANADIAN MANUFACTURING. *Can. Labour [Canada] 1977 22(4): 8-11.* There is no decline in competitiveness and productivity among Canadian corporations; wage increases have not stifled competition.

1623. Wallace, Iain. RAILWAYS IN THE SERVICE OF CANADIAN MINING. *Can. Geographical J. [Canada] 1978 96(1): 66-71.* Meeting the new transportation demands of the Canadian mining industry, especially the railroads, is important to all of Canada for economic reasons.

1624. Walsh, William D. THE CANADIAN EXPERIMENT WITH VOLUNTARY INCOMES RESTRAINT, DEGREE OF LABOUR ORGANIZATION AND CYCLICAL SENSITIVITY OF EMPLOYMENT. *Industrial Relations [Canada] 1975 30(3): 390-406.* This paper provides a measure of the industrial distribution of the employment impact of monetary and fiscal policies and suggests that organized labour could have expected to have realized very little differential employment benefits from the Commission's package of proposals—prices and incomes restraint in combination with less monetary and fiscal restraint than would otherwise be possible.					J

1625. Weiermair, Klaus. THE ECONOMIC EFFECTS OF LANGUAGE TRAINING TO IMMIGRANTS: A CASE STUDY. *Internat. Migration R. 1976 10(2): 205-219.* Discusses the role of English language training in the employment and economic assimilation of immigrants in Toronto, Ontario, 1968-70.

1626. Wertheim, Edward G. WORKER PARTICIPATION AND INDUSTRIAL RELATIONS: THE TREND TOWARD DECENTRALIZATION. *Industrial Relations [Canada] 1976 31(1): 98-110.* Examines worker participation and industrial relations, concluding that in the United States and Canada where much decentralization has already taken place, worker control is not so badly needed, unlike Europe, where employee input appears as a complement to traditional worker-management relations, 1960's-70's.

1627. Whitehouse, John R. W. HERITAGE OF LABOUR EDUCATION IN CANADA. *Can. Labour 1973 18(4-6): 26-29.*

1628. Williams, C. Brian. COLLECTIVE BARGAINING IN THE PUBLIC SECTOR: A RE-EXAMINATION. *Industrial Relations [Canada] 1973 28(1): 17-31.* "This paper calls for a new direction in the study of public sector collective bargaining away from the 'issue' and 'problem' approach in favor of a re-examination, in the light of our experience over the past decade, of the physiology of the technique itself with particular reference to the appropriateness of current public sector collective bargaining structures."					J

1629. —. [A DOLLAR STANDARD]. *Actualité Écon. [Canada] 1973 49(3): 323-348.*
Leroy, Vély. UN ÉTALON-DOLLAR: PASSÉ ET FUTUR [A dollar standard: past and future], pp. 323-341. Adherence to a dollar standard was reasonable in the past, but contemporary developments necessitate a reconsideration. The term "standard" has been abused; many economists deny that a worldwide standard has ever existed. Neither gold nor the dollar will serve to reestablish stable conditions for international exchange. 2 tables, graph, 39 notes, biblio.
Drakos, Georges E. and Eastman, H. C. COMMENTAIRES SUR L'EXPOSÉ DE MONSIEUR V. LEROY [Comments on V. Leroy's article], pp. 342-348. Drakos (pp. 342-346) essentially agrees with Leroy's paper, but questions certain interpretations of data. Eastman (pp. 346-348) also accepts Leroy's basic argument, but questions certain details and interpretations.
					W. B. Whitham and S

1630. —. THE IMPACT OF WAGE CONTROLS ON COLLECTIVE BARGAINING. *Can. Labour 1976 21(1): 9-13.* Explains the impact of the Anti-Inflation Board and its regulations on collective bargaining and on labor unions since free collective bargaining was suspended in Canada in October, 1975.

Government and Politics

1631. Albinski, Henry S. CURRENTS IN CANADIAN POLITICS. *Current Hist. 1977 72(426): 158-161, 178.* Discusses political parties in Canada, 1975-77, emphasizing the continuing rift between French-speaking and English-speaking Canadians and the threatened separatism of Quebec.

1632. Andrew, Caroline; Blais, André; and Des Rosiers, Rachel. LES ÉCHEVINS ET LA FORMULATION DES POLITIQUES:

NOTE MÉTHODOLOGIQUE [Councillors and the formulation of politics: a methodological note]. *Can. Public Administration [Canada] 1977 20(2): 231-242*. Examines the role of local government councillors in formulating Canadian public policy, 1968-75.

1633. Baar, Carl. PATTERNS AND STRATEGIES OF COURT ADMINISTRATION IN CANADA AND THE UNITED STATES. *Can. Public Administration [Canada] 1977 20(2): 242-274*. Canadian courts are administered primarily by the executive branch and US courts are administered primarily by the judicial branch because of basic differences in constitutional principles.

1634. Babe, Robert E. REGULATION OF PRIVATE TELEVISION BROADCASTING BY THE CANADIAN RADIO-TELEVISION COMMISSION: A CRITIQUE OF ENDS AND MEANS. *Can. Public Administration [Canada] 1976 19(4): 552-586*. The Canadian Radio-Television Commission has protected private broadcasters' revenue to promote indigenous broadcasting, but has been lax in regulating their programming, 1968-75.

1635. Baldwin, Bob. TAXATION POLICY. *Can. Labour [Canada] 1977 22(4): 20-24*. The taxation policy of the Canadian federal government is aimed at a reduction of unemployment through individual and corporate incentive plans which encourage savings and investments; however, $1.5 billion in revenue is used to implement the policy, which creates a wealth distribution favoring the upper classes and capital, not the middle and lower classes and labor.

1636. Balls, Herbert R. DECISION-MAKING: THE ROLE OF THE DEPUTY MINISTER. *Can. Public Administration [Canada] 1976 19(3): 417-431*. Theoretical policymaking and practical policy administration and execution are intermingled; though official committees and outside advisors contribute to decisionmaking, government decisions are made by ministers in Canada's federal government system.

1637. Blake, Donald E. CONSTITUENCY CONTEXTS AND CANADIAN ELECTIONS: AN EXPLORATORY STUDY. *Can. J. of Pol. Sci. [Canada] 1978 11(2): 279-305*. Examines riding-to-riding variability in party support produced by different distributions of individuals and different environments using a form of variance decomposition. Data from 261 ridings on voting for the Liberal Party in the 1968 election. 10 tables, 36 notes, appendix.   R. V. Kubicek

1638. Blake, Donald E. "THE LAND IS STRONG(?)": AN INTERPRETATION OF THE 1972 CANADIAN ELECTION. *Australian J. of Pol. and Hist. 1973 19(1): 48-62*. Analyzes the 1972 Canadian election in which the Liberal Government's House of Commons majority was reduced to two. Disagrees with simple explanations which posit an English-Canadian backlash, or smug paternalism on the part of Premier Pierre Elliott Trudeau. Suggests that Liberal support was simply returning to earlier levels after the 1968 Trudeau honeymoon, and that a general dissatisfaction by electors with the Liberal Government's record of 1968-72 was the chief factor. By-products of the policies of bilingualism, the new Department of Regional Expansion, and tax changes affected the Liberal role adversely, while foreign policy successes did not have much electoral appeal.   W. D. McIntyre

1639. Brown-John, C. Lloyd. MEMBERSHIP IN CANADIAN REGULATORY AGENCIES. *Can. Public Administration [Canada] 1977 20(3): 513-533*. Results from a 1974 questionnaire on the ability, self-perception, and political predilection of employees of federal and provincial regulatory agencies in Canada indicate that, though of a high quality, they are neither as judicial nor as politically neutral as they think.

1640. Brown-John, C. Lloyd. PARTY POLITICS AND THE CANADIAN FEDERAL PUBLIC SERVICE. *Public Administration [Great Britain] 1974 52(4): 79-93*. Discusses legal issues in the rights of federal public employees to participate actively in party politics in Canada 1967-70's, emphasizing the implications of the 1967 Public Service Employment Act.

1641. Burke, Mike; Clarke, Harold D.; and LeDuc, Lawrence. FEDERAL AND PROVINCIAL POLITICAL PARTICIPATION IN CANADA: SOME METHODOLOGICAL AND SUBSTANTIVE CONSIDERATIONS. *Can. Rev. of Sociol. and Anthrop. [Canada] 1978 15(1): 61-75*. Employing the 1974 national election study data, the authors develop scales measuring participation rates in Canadian federal and provincial politics. Analyses using these scales reveal that, although there is discernable interprovincial variance in participation in federal, and especially, provincial politics, at the individual level, there are strong positive correlations between federal and provincial participation rates in all provinces. Further, it appears that Canadians are somewhat more active politically than earlier studies have indicated. Regarding correlates of participation, the data suggest that conventional sociodemographic and attitudinal variables do not provide adequate explanations of participation in either federal or provincial politics. Additional analyses indicate the possible significance of regional differences in Canadian political culture for understanding variations in participation rates.   J

1642. Cairns, Alan C. THE GOVERNMENTS AND SOCIETIES OF CANADIAN FEDERALISM. *Can. J. of Pol. Sci. [Canada] 1977 10(4): 695-725*. Presidential address to the Canadian Political Science Association meeting of June 1977. Argues that studies of Canadian politics have underestimated the ability of governments to manufacture conditions necessary to their growth and survival. 81 notes.
                    R. V. Kubicek

1643. Campbell, Colin and Reese, Thomas. THE ENERGY CRISIS AND TAX POLICY IN CANADA AND THE UNITED STATES: FEDERAL-PROVINCIAL DIPLOMACY V. CONGRESSIONAL LAWMAKING. *Social Sci. J. 1977 14(1): 17-32*. Compares the respective roles of government and tax policy in dealing with the energy crisis in Canada and the United States, 1973-75; Canada responded to the crisis in the form of federal-provincial diplomacy, while the US federal government and Congress acted unilaterally.

1644. Campbell, Colin. THE INSTITUTIONAL ORIENTATIONS OF CANADIAN SENATORS: SOME IMPLICATIONS FOR THE THEORY OF LIBERAL DEMOCRACY IN NORTH AMERICA. *Am. Rev. of Can. Studies 1973 3(1): 76-87*. Examines the attitudes of senators in the Senate of Canada toward that legislative body and the impact of special interest groups and constituencies as they relate to senatorial roles; relates findings to broad liberal democratic theory, 1970's.

1645. Campbell, Colin. "THE PROTESTANT ETHIC," "RATIONALITY" AND CANADA'S POLITICAL ELITE: ETHNIC AND RELIGIOUS INFLUENCE ON SENATORS. *Soc. Sci. J. 1976 12(3): 159-173*. Analyzes the religious and ethnic values held by Canadian senators in a 1971 study.

1646. Chandler, William M. CANADIAN SOCIALISM AND POLICY IMPACT: CONTAGION FROM THE LEFT? *Can. J. of Pol. Sci. [Canada] 1977 10(4): 755-780*. Socialist parties in opposition have significantly affected public policy in Canada, but the evidence indicates that it is simplistic to assume that government initiative is entirely conditioned by them. 4 tables, 61 notes.   R. V. Kubicek

1647. Clarke, Harold D.; Price, Richard G.; and Krause, Robert. CONSTITUENCY SERVICE AMONG CANADIAN PROVINCIAL LEGISLATORS: BASIC FINDINGS AND A TEST OF THREE HYPOTHESES. *Can. J. of Pol. Sci. 1975 8(4): 520-542*. Data from a mail survey of members of provincial legislatures from the political parties in all 10 provinces show most of them spend substantial amounts of time on constituency service tasks. 9 tables, 44 notes.   R. V. Kubicek

1648. Courtney, John C. RECOGNITION OF CANADIAN POLITICAL PARTIES IN PARLIAMENT AND IN LAW. *Can. J. of Pol. Sci. [Canada] 1978 11(1): 33-60*. Parliamentarians have chosen to ignore one of the essentials of Canadian politics by continuing to claim that parties are not to be acknowledged formally. This claim has widened the gap between theory and practice. 4 tables, 53 notes.
                    R. V. Kubicek

1649. Cunningham, Robert B. and Winham, Gilbert R. COMPARATIVE URBAN VOTING BEHAVIOR: CANADA AND THE UNITED STATES. *Am. Rev. of Can. Studies 1973 3(2): 76-100*. Compares the roles of social classes, ethnicity, religion, and political party identification in the voting behavior of urban residents of Canada and the United States in elections 1952-68.

1650. Curtis, James E. and Lambert, Ronald D. VOTING, ELECTION INTEREST, AND AGE: NATIONAL FINDINGS FOR ENGLISH AND FRENCH CANADIANS. *Can. J. of Pol. Sci. 1976 9(2): 293-307.* Analysis from a sample survey conducted in 1968 shows that, contrary to prevailing notions, there is no drop-off in political interest with age and perhaps even some modest increases. 3 tables, 18 notes.
R. V. Kubicek

1651. Dion, Léon. POLITIQUE ET SCIENCE POLITIQUE [The political use of political science]. *Can. J. of Pol. Sci. 1975 8(3): 367-380.* Questions whether political scientists, as part of a very strong and formidable science establishment, should be beyond the scrutiny of elected representatives.
R. V. Kubicek

1652. Dyck, Rand. THE CANADA ASSISTANCE PLAN: THE ULTIMATE IN COOPERATIVE FEDERALISM. *Can. Public Administration [Canada] 1976 19(4): 587-602.* The Canada Assistance Plan (1966) succeeded because of deference to professional norms, provincial initiation of cooperative activities, and the federal government's positive attitude toward the provincial governments.

1653. Elkins, David J. THE MEASUREMENT OF PARTY COMPETITION. *Am. Pol. Sci. Rev. 1974 68(2): 682-700.* Most measures of party competition were designed for the United States or other two-party systems. The measure proposed here is intended for multi-party as well as two-party systems. It is a formalization of the notion of uncertainty: election outcomes are competitive to the degree we are uncertain who will win. By ascertaining through survey research the degree of party loyalty over time, one can calculate the chances of alternative outcomes in hypothetical replications of any given election. Since the chance that a losing party might have won is one measure of the importance of that party, this approach to party competition also provides a precise indicator of the number of parties in the system (i.e., whether it is two-party, three-party, etc.). The method is applied here to data on Canadian federal elections in 1965 and 1968.
J

1654. Elkins, David J. THE PERCEIVED STRUCTURE OF THE CANADIAN PARTY SYSTEMS. *Can. J. of Pol. Sci. 1974 7(3): 502-524.* Analysis based on spatial models of competitive behavior to examine evidence from the 1965 and 1968 federal election studies. Suggests that besides the left-right continuum, another dimension structures parties in Canada, namely a center-periphery axis. 5 tables, 3 figs., 43 notes.
R. V. Kubicek

1655. Elkins, David J. and Blake, Donald E. VOTING RESEARCH IN CANADA: PROBLEMS AND PROSPECTS. *Can. J. of Pol. Sci. 1975 8(2): 313-325.* Isolates areas in which previous work has concentrated and points out gaps in which future studies on voting behavior should operate. 75 notes.
R. V. Kubicek

1656. Fletcher, Frederick J. THE PRIME MINISTER, THE PRESS AND THE PUBLIC: THE CASE OF THE ANTI-INFLATION PROGRAM. *Queen's Q. [Canada] 1976 83(1): 75-84.* Examines Prime Minister Pierre Trudeau's promotion of his anti-inflation program through public speeches and media interviews. Argues "that the anti-inflation program is in essence a public relations program." This approach has raised questions regarding the Prime Minister's credibility and whether he should act as an educator or as an outright propagandist for his programs. 17 notes.
J. A. Casada

1657. Forcese, Dennis and de Vries, John. OCCUPATION AND ELECTORAL SUCCESS IN CANADA: THE 1974 FEDERAL ELECTION. *Can. Rev. of Sociol. and Anthrop. [Canada] 1977 14(3): 331-340.* Occupational data were examined for all candidates for Parliament in 1974. For all parties, high status occupations were over-represented, relative to labour force statistics, especially in the Liberal and Progressive Conservative parties. Only in the Social Credit party did we find a numerical majority of lower status candidates. In examining electoral success, it was found that regardless of political affiliation, a high status candidate had almost twice as high a probability of election as a low status candidate. The data illustrate a two-step phenomenon, wherein the pool of all

candidates contains a larger proportion of higher status persons than the total adult Canadian population, while the elected members contain yet a larger proportion of high status persons.
J

1658. Fraser, John D. INTELLECTUALS AND THE PARTY. *Communist Viewpoint [Canada] 1973 5(3): 30-35.*

1659. Garant, Patrice; Kenniff, Patrick; Lemieux, Denis; and Carrier, Denis. LA CÔNTROLE POLITIQUE DES ORGANISMES AUTONOMES À FONCTIONS REGULATRICES ET QUASI-JUDICIAIRES [Political control of autonomous regulatory and quasijudicial bodies]. *Can. Public Administration [Canada] 1977 20(3): 444-468.* Examines control by the Canadian Parliament over autonomous regulatory and quasijudicial bodies and the implications of such regulation for administrative tribunals and other autonomous bodies having regulatory and quasijudicial functions, 1970's.

1660. Gardner, C. James. ORGANIZATION AND METHODS DEVELOPMENT IN THE GOVERNING OF CANADA. *Public Administration [Great Britain] 1976 54(3): 283-318.* Discusses the operations of the Organization and Methods Development activities of the Canadian Civil Service Commission, 1946-76, and to illustrate the difficulties encountered in trying to institute innovation and change from within.

1661. Goldman, Ralph M. MEMOIRS: CASE MATERIALS FOR STUDYING POLITICAL BEHAVIOR? *Polity 1975 7(4): 542-552.* A review essay prompted by ten books concerned with the political experiences and careers of world leaders, including Lester Pearson and Lyndon Johnson. These works all make interesting source material for the study of the political psychology of major twentieth-century political leaders. 5 notes.
V. L. Human

1662. Grayson, J. Paul. SOCIAL POSITION AND INTEREST RECOGNITION: THE VOTER IN BROADVIEW, OR ARE VOTERS FOOLS? *Can. J. of Pol. Sci. 1973 6(1): 131-139.* Members of particular social groupings do not necessarily support a political party because of perceived interest. Based on a random survey conducted in a federal riding of Toronto; 9 tables, 16 notes, appendix.
R. V. Kubicek

1663. Hagan, John. CRIMINAL JUSTICE IN RURAL AND URBAN COMMUNITIES: A STUDY OF THE BUREAUCRATIZATION OF JUSTICE. *Social Forces 1977 55(3): 597-612.* This paper inquires into the effects of urbanization and bureaucratization on one type of institutionalized decision-making: judicial sentencing. Theoretical and empirical links between urbanization, bureaucratization, and sentencing are reviewed. Then, two data sets from a Canadian province (Alberta) are analyzed: (1) 507 questionnaires based on pre-sentence reports completed in all provincial probation departments, and (2) 974 offenders admitted to the five major provincial prisons. The analysis is built on comparisons of sentencing patterns for North American Indians and whites in urban and rural communities. The results reveal that probation officers in rural jurisdictions, as contrasted with those in urban communities, sentence Indians severely, without the justification of correlated legal variables. In addition, Indians are more likely to be sent to jail in default of fine payments in rural, than in urban communities. The implications of these findings for an understanding of the bureaucratization of criminal justice are discussed.
J

1664. Hagan, John and Leon, Jeffrey. PHILOSOPHY AND SOCIOLOGY OF CRIME CONTROL: CANADIAN-AMERICAN COMPARISONS. *Sociol. Inquiry [Canada] 1977 47(3-4): 181-208.* Outlines differences in crime control strategy in Canada and the United States, 1950's-76, examining the influence of national values, historical conditions, and economic constraints; different strategies may reach the same ends.

1665. Hamel, J. M. AN ELECTION EXPENSES ACT FOR CANADA. *Natl. Civic R. 1974 63(11): 565-568.* "The Canadian Election Expenses Act [1973], passed last January, represents long-awaited reform in a field where there has never been any comprehensive legislation. Significant sources of contributions for candidates and political parties must be disclosed, and limits are placed on election expenses that may be incurred by either."
J

1666. Headey, B. W. THE ROLE SKILLS OF CABINET MINIS-
TERS: A CROSS-NATIONAL REVIEW. *Pol. Studies [Great Britain]*
1974 22(1): 66-85. Examines the political recruitment of cabinet officers
to determine their role skills in Canada, Australia, Great Britain, the
Netherlands, and the United States, 1940's-60's.

1667. Hodgetts, J. E. BUREAUCRATIC INITIATIVE, CITIZEN
INVOLVEMENT, AND THE QUEST FOR ADMININSTRATIVE
ACCOUNTABILITY. *Tr. of the Royal Soc. of Can. 1974 12: 227-236.*
Discusses the growth of bureaucracy as the state has aggrandized, contrary to the Marxist belief that as administration replaced politics the
state would wither away. In Great Britain, the United States, and Canada
there is the fixation of freeing administration from politics, an idea that
has resulted in an efficient rational administration but has not solved the
problem of accountability. Today bureaucracies have great powers, some
of which are quasi-judicial without provision for review. The ombudsman
is insufficient as a remedy. Bureaucracies need individuals who have a
sense of responsibility and are sensitive to the interests they serve. They
must develop their own code of professional ethics and encourage citizen
participation in decisions.   J. D. Neville

1668. Horowitz, Gad. [CONSERVATISM, LIBERALISM, AND
SOCIALISM IN CANADA].
CONSERVATISM, LIBERALISM, AND SOCIALISM IN CAN-
ADA. *Can. J. of Econ. and Pol. Sci. [Canada] 1966 32(2): 143-
171.* Relates socialism to conservatism and liberalism. Discusses
why socialism is a significant political force in Canada but not in
the United States. Based on the thesis of Louis Hartz. 87 notes.
NOTES ON 'CONSERVATISM, LIBERALISM AND SOCIALISM
IN CANADA.' *Can. J. of Pol. Sci. [Canada] 1978 11(2): 383-399.*
Replies to criticism of the above article. 50 notes.
                                                            R. V. Kubicek

1669. Hyson, Stewart. THE ROLE OF THE BACKBENCHER: AN
ANALYSIS OF PRIVATE MEMBERS' BILLS IN THE CANADIAN
HOUSE OF COMMONS. *Parliamentary Affairs [Great Britain] 1974
27(3): 262-272.* An analytical study of private members' bills not only
from the perspective of the initiation of legislation but also in relation to
their expressive function (affording an opportunity for backbenchers to
express their views on issues). Studies the significance of private members'
bills in the House of Commons, covering three parliaments: 24th (1958-
62), 26th (1963-65), and the 28th (1968-72). Concludes their role as a
means of introducing policy is of little significance. 6 tables, 18 notes.
                                                            R. V. Ritter

1670. Irvine, William P. EXPLAINING THE RELIGIOUS BASIS
OF THE CANADIAN PARTISAN IDENTITY: SUCCESS ON THE
THIRD TRY. *Can. J. of Pol. Sci. 1974 7(3): 560-563.* Uses a political
socialization model and data from the 1965 national survey to discount
religion as a source of electoral cleavage in Canada. 2 tables, 5 notes.
                                                            R. V. Kubicek

1671. Jenson, Jane. PARTY LOYALTY IN CANADA: THE
QUESTION OF PARTY IDENTIFICATION. *Can. J. of Pol. Sci.
1975 8(4): 543-553.* Asserts that Canadians do alter their party ties more
frequently and more easily than do voters elsewhere. Written in rebuttal
to a previous article by P. M. Sniderman, et al., "Party Loyalty and
Electoral Volatility: A Study of the Canadian Party System" (see abstract
12A:219). 6 tables, 23 notes.   R. V. Kubicek

1672. Jenson, Jane. PARTY STRATEGY AND PARTY IDEN-
TIFICATION: SOME PATTERNS OF PARTISAN ALLEGIANCE.
Can. J. of Pol. Sci. 1976 9(1): 27-48. Adapts, through redefinition, the
concept of party identification and uses it to analyze the Progressive
Conservative Party under the leadership of John Diefenbaker. Shows and
accounts for instability and loss of membership in the party, the consequence of Diefenbaker's reorientation of it. Covers the period 1956-67. 10
tables, 29 notes.   R. V. Kubicek

1673. Johansen, Peter W. TELEVISING PARLIAMENT: WHAT
THE COMMONS REPORT LEFT OUT. *J. of Can. Studies 1973 8(4):
39-51.* Discusses the effects of televising Canada's Parliament, and television's compatibility with the institution of Parliament and the influence
(good or ill) which television might have on the popular understanding
of Parliamentary process.

1674. Johnson, John M. REVIEW ARTICLE: POLICE POLITICS.
Queen's Q. [Canada] 1975 82(4): 606-609. Police patrollers, dispatchers,
and executives wield vast discretionary powers that enable them to interpret legislation through their selective enforcement of the plethora of
laws. Myths obscuring this fact and deterring public scrutiny of police
have been "that policing a community is a completely objective and
value-free function" and that legislation is "fully enforced against all
transgressors at all times." One of the first studies of police decisionmaking in Canada is Brian A. Grosman's *Police Command: Decisions and
Discretion* (Toronto: Macmillan, 1975), which focuses on police executives, their bureaucracies, and organizational difficulties that hinder reform.   T. Simmerman

1675. Johnson, Leo; Brown, Lorne; Cameron, Donald; and Gonick, Cy.
WHAT SHAPE CANADA IS IN: THOUGHTS ON THE ELECTION
RESULTS. *Can. Dimension 1973 9(2/3): 6-10, 64.* Comments on the
1972 Canadian elections. The future of the New Democratic Party (NDP)
is dubious in view of election defeats and internal division. The Liberal
Party is also weakened by its identification with a single province. The
ability of the Conservative Party to win a federal election in the near
future is questionable and is one of several reasons for the minority
government which resulted from the elections.   W. B. Whitham

1676. Kashtan, William. THE FEDERAL ELECTION AND THE
ROAD AHEAD. *Communist Viewpoint [Canada] 1973 5(1): 5-18.*

1677. Kashtan, William. WHAT THE CANADIAN BAROMETER
INDICATES. *World Marxist R. 1973 16(4): 50-60.* The Communist
Party's political policies and election tactics, 1972-73.   S

1678. Kernaghan, Kenneth. CHANGING CONCEPTS OF POWER
AND RESPONSIBILITY IN THE CANADIAN PUBLIC SERVICE.
Can. Public Administration [Canada] 1978 21(3): 389-406. Discusses the
evolution of the concepts of administrative power and responsibility of
Canadian federal public servants since the 1940's and examines efforts to
reconcile the two through accountability and the values of neutrality,
responsiveness, and efficiency.

1679. Kernaghan, Kenneth. POLITICS, POLICY AND PUBLIC
SERVANTS: POLITICAL NEUTRALITY REVISITED. *Can. Public
Administration [Canada] 1976 19(3): 432-456.* Examines the traditional
and modern models of political neutrality among public employees in
Canada in six areas: politics and administration, patronage, political activity, public comment, anonymity and ministerial responsibility, and
permanency in office; concludes that public servants are politically involved in Canada by necessity of policy development and by choice of
political partisanship.

1680. Kirby, M. J. L.; Kroeker, H. V.; and Teschke, W. R. THE
IMPACT OF PUBLIC POLICY-MAKING STRUCTURES AND
PROCESSES IN CANADA. *Can. Public Administration [Canada]
1978 21(3): 407-417.* Discusses the implications for Canadian public
servants of the change from a personalized style of policy development
in the 1950's to a more collectivist approach which relies on structures
and processes to ensure the expressions of relevant interests in the 1960's
and 70's.

1681. Kornberg, Allan; Smith, Joel; Clarke, Mary-Jane; and Clarke,
Harold D. PARTICIPATION IN LOCAL PARTY ORGANIZA-
TIONS IN THE UNITED STATES AND CANADA. *Am. J. of Pol.
Sci. 1973 17(1): 23-47.* This analysis of variations in the level of participation in party organization affairs, measured by aspects of the time allocated to party work, entailed interviews with 1,252 men and women who
hold the highest offices in the several party organizations of Seattle,
Minneapolis, Vancouver, and Winnipeg. A political participation index
was constructed, and each party official was assigned a participation
score. These scores together with 29 independent variables were employed
in a series of regression analyses to ascertain the correlates of high participation. The single best predictor of differences in the level of participation
is found to be national origins, United States party officials devoting
substantially more time to party affairs than their Canadian counterparts.
The research serves two useful purposes: First, the several analyses suggest that good predictors of mass political behavior do not provide equally
good explanations of behavior in elite political organizations, especially

behavior that takes place in a relatively amorphous organization such as a political party. Second, it is felt that behavior within such elite political organizations can be best explained by attitudinal variables that measure matters such as institutional commitment and reactions to activity within the institutions.   J

1682. Koulack, Esther. "IT COULD HAVE BEEN ANY ONE OF US." *Can. Dimension 1976 11(6): 23-27.* Examines political repression in the US and Canada, 1940's-50's, resulting from the espionage case of Julius and Ethel Rosenberg.

1683. Laponce, J. A. and Uhler, R. S. MEASURING ELECTORAL CLEAVAGES IN A MULTIPARTY SYSTEM: THE CANADIAN CASE. *Comparative Pol. Studies 1974 7(1): 3-25.* Taking Canada and its four-party system as an example, measures party cleavages by means of an extension of the logit model suggested by Theil (1969), then translates these cleavages into measures of electoral homogeneity by use of the entropy concept derived from Shannon's (1948) information theory.   S

1684. Laskin, Bora. THE JUDGE AS LEGISLATOR AND ADMINISTRATOR. *Tr. of the Royal Soc. of Can. 1973 11: 183-198.* Analyzes the role of the judge and the process of judicial review as a core part of administrative law, with examples.

1685. Lederman, W. R. CONTINUING CONSTITUTIONAL DILEMMAS: THE SUPREME COURT AND THE FEDERAL ANTI-INFLATION ACT OF 1975. *Queen's Q. [Canada] 1977 84(1): 90-98.* Examines the legal implications of the Anti-Inflation Act (1975) passed by the Canadian Parliament. One basic question raised by the Act was whether Parliament possessed "the legislative power to enact such total measures, whatever their economic merit." Studies this question and the Canadian Supreme Court's seven-to-two decision supporting its constitutionality. 12 notes.   J. A. Casada

1686. LeDuc, Lawrence. POLITICAL BEHAVIOUR AND THE ISSUE OF MAJORITY GOVERNMENT IN TWO FEDERAL ELECTIONS. *Can. J. of Pol. Sci. [Canada] 1977 10(2): 311-339.* Discusses public concern for majority government and potential deviations in voting behavior which appear to have declined in 1974. 13 tables, 4 figs., 25 notes, appendix.   R. V. Kubicek

1687. LeDuc, Lawrence, Jr. MEASURING THE SENSE OF POLITICAL EFFICACY IN CANADA: PROBLEMS OF MEASUREMENT EQUIVALENCE. *Comparative Pol. Studies 1976 8(4): 490-500.* Discusses methods of measuring public opinion about political issues in Canada in the 1970's.

1688. Lemieux, Vincent. ESQUISSE D'UNE THÉORIE ORGANISATIONNELLE DES PARTIS [Outline of an organizational theory of parties]. *Can. J. of Pol. Sci. [Canada] 1977 10(4): 841-856.* Explores a theory which assumes that certain component groups within political parties choose quite different objectives and strategies. 5 diagrams, 12 notes.   R. V. Kubicek

1689. Loney, Martin. BANKROLLING THE REVOLUTION. *Can. Dimension [Canada] 1977 12(2): 2-5.* Government financing of radical organizations via social services and citizen projects is divisive and destructive to the political development and social protest of militant activists.

1690. Lovink, J. A. A. IS CANADIAN POLITICS TOO COMPETITIVE? *Can. J. of Pol. Sci. 1973 6(3): 341-379.* Offers two new hypotheses to explain variations in electoral competition and provides an approach to measuring it. The author applies these hypotheses to Canadian federal constituencies in which he finds competition extraordinarily high. 15 tables, fig., 64 notes.   R. V. Kubicek

1691. Lundqvist, Lennart J. DO POLITICAL STRUCTURES MATTER IN ENVIRONMENTAL POLITICS? THE CASE OF AIR POLLUTION CONTROL IN CANADA, SWEDEN, AND THE UNITED STATES. *Am. Behavioral Scientist 1974 17(5): 731-750.*

1692. Luxton, Meg. HOUSEWORK. *Can. Dimension [Canada] 1977 12(7): 35-38.* Examines the connection between housework and wage work and assesses the political potential of Canadian housewives during the 1970's.

1693. Maxwell, James A. FEDERAL GRANTS IN CANADA, AUSTRALIA, AND THE UNITED STATES. *Publius 1974 4(2): 63-75.* Compares how the federal governments in Canada, Australia, and the US gave revenue to their provincial or state governments, 1787-1974.

1694. McInnes, Simon. IMPROVING LEGISLATIVE SURVEILLANCE OF PROVINCIAL PUBLIC EXPENDITURES: THE PERFORMANCE OF THE PUBLIC ACCOUNTS COMMITTEES AND AUDITORS GENERAL. *Can. Public Administration [Canada] 1977 20(1): 36-86.* Assesses the effect of Public Accounts committees and Auditors General in provincial government on controlling public spending, 1970-75.

1695. McKinsey, Lauren S. DIMENSIONS OF NATIONAL POLITICAL INTEGRATION AND DISINTEGRATION, THE CASE OF QUEBEC SEPARATISM, 1960-75. *Comparative Pol. Studies 1976 9(3): 335-360.* Discusses Canadian government attempts to maintain centralization and political stability to counteract separatist movements in Quebec 1960-75.

1696. Meisel, John. POLITICAL CULTURE AND THE POLITICS OF CULTURE. *Can. J. of Pol. Sci. 1974 7(4): 601-615.* The 1974 presidential address to the Canadian Political Science Association urges members to study various leisure activities and their interaction with politics. Such activities include recreation, sports, the arts, and environmental concerns. Fig., 34 notes.   R. V. Kubicek

1697. Migué, Jean-Luc. ENCADREMENT JURIDIQUE DES INSTITUTIONS FINANCIERES: EVOLUTION ET SIGNIFICATION [Judicial grouping of financial institutions: evolution and significance]. *Actualité Econ. [Canada] 1973 49(1): 58-67.* During the last 10 years, regulation of financial institutions has liberalized. The powers of controllers and government oversight have concurrently become more direct. Analyzes the significance of this development, including nonfinancial factors. Chart, 3 notes.   W. B. Whitham

1698. Morley, Terence. THE CONSTITUTIONAL IMPLICATIONS OF PRICE CONTROL LEGISLATION. *Queen's Q. [Canada] 1973 80(4): 596-600.* Any government attempt to regulate Canada's rampant rise in prices would encounter severe constitutional difficulties. Suggests possible circumventions of such problems.   J. A. Casada

1699. Morrison, Ian. TINKERING WITH ADULT TRAINING POLICIES. *Can. Labour [Canada] 1977 22(4): 17-19, 24.* Examines the debate in the Canadian government over allocation of funds for adult education and manpower training programs, 1967-77.

1700. Murray, Donald. THE RALLIEMENT DES CREDITISTES IN PARLIAMENT, 1970-1971. *J. of Can. Studies 1973 8(2): 13-31.* Chronicles the origins of the Ralliement des Creditistes during the 1930's-70 and their participation in Canada's Parliamentary politics, 1970-71.

1701. Paltiel, Khayyam Z. PARTY AND CANDIDATE EXPENDITURES IN THE CANADIAN GENERAL ELECTION OF 1972. *Can. J. of Pol. Sci. 1974 7(2): 341-352.* Notes a sharp increase over previous elections in spending on the broadcasting as opposed to printed media, and the employment of sophisticated computerized direct mail techniques and surveys. 5 tables, 8 notes, 2 appendices.   R. V. Kubicek

1702. Pammett, Jon H.; LeDuc, Lawrence; Jenson, Jane; and Clarke, Harold D. THE PERCEPTION AND IMPACT OF ISSUES IN THE 1974 FEDERAL ELECTION. *Can. J. of Pol. Sci. 1976 10(1): 93-126.* Focuses on three issues—inflation, leadership, and majority government. Stresses the diversity of concerns influencing voter behavior. 11 tables, 2 figs., 35 notes, appendix.   R. V. Kubicek

1703. Pearson, Geoffrey. THE LINKS BETWEEN ACADEMIC AND POLICYMAKER. *Int. Perspectives [Canada] 1973 (November-*

December): 43-46. Examines the narrowing gap between political scientists and government officials and diplomats during the 1970's; assesses attempts to reconcile the two camps in Canada.

1704. Presthus, Robert. INTEREST GROUP LOBBYING: CANADA AND THE UNITED STATES. *Ann. of the Am. Acad. of Pol. and Soc. Sci. 1974 413: 44-57.* Political theory usually assumes that interest groups play an essential role in democratic polities, providing an instrument through which the individual may participate to some extent in the making of public policy. Such groups synthesize, express and provide technical and ideological support for collective social demands which provide critical inputs into the political subsystem. Despite these contributions, interest groups are often regarded as both normatively and operationally marginal. Using cross-national survey data on interest group lobbying, the present study shows that group activities are common in two political systems. Regardless of variations in political culture and political structure and despite variations in group legitimacy and the intensity of lobbying, groups play a critical linkage role, bringing into concert the private and public sectors of North American society. J

1705. Regenstreif, Peter. CANADIAN PARTIES AND POLITICS. *Current Hist. 1974 66(392): 173-176, 184.* Canadian political parties, 1958 to the present. S

1706. Rich, Harvey. THE CANADIAN CASE FOR A REPRESENTATIVE BUREAUCRACY. *Pol. Sci. [New Zealand] 1975 27(1-2): 97-110.* Discusses representative bureaucracies as they relate to the Canadian Public Service; considers the anglophone and francophone communities as well as the corresponding binational character of the Canadian national government, 1944-75.

1707. Robertson, Gordon. CANADIAN DEVELOPMENTS IN DECENTRALIZING DECISIONMAKING. *Am. Soc. of Int. Law Pro. 1974: 68 192-197.* Discusses the decentralization of government decisionmaking in Canada, especially in the 1970's.

1708. Rutan, Gerard F. WATERGATE NORTH: HOW THE MOUNTIES GET THEIR MEN. *Civil Liberties Rev. 1978 5(2): 17-26.* Describes the systematic abuse of civil rights by the Royal Canadian Mounted Police, including illegal wiretapping, theft, coercion, break-in, kidnapping, and arson, said by the government to have been carried out in the interests of Canada's security.

1709. Sankoff, David and Mellos, Koula. LA RÉGIONALISATION ÉLECTORALE ET L'AMPLIFICATION DES PROPORTIONS [Electoral regionalization and the swing ratio]. *Can. J. of Pol. Sci. 1973 6(3): 380-398.* The authors examine models of electoral systems concerned with probing the disproportion between votes obtained and seats won through empirical studies of elections in Quebec, Ontario, and the Canadian federal systems. One of the authors' models provides an index of electoral regionalization and accounts for the small deviation between seats and votes in Quebec. 2 tables, 9 graphs, 27 notes.
R. V. Kubicek

1710. Sayeed, Khalid B. THE ROLE OF SOCIAL SCIENTISTS IN SHAPING PUBLIC POLICY. *Queen's Q. [Canada] 1973 80(4): 567-578.* Examines the avenues through which social scientists can contribute to the formulation of public policy. The thoughts of social scientists must be tinctured by a degree of pragmatic realism, but nonetheless theirs is potentially a crucial role. 20 notes.
J. A. Casada

1711. Sharman, G. C. THE POLICE AND THE IMPLEMENTATION OF PUBLIC LAW. *Can. Public Administration [Canada] 1977 20(2): 291-304.* The lack of precise federal and provincial police jurisdictions has caused problems in framing legislative policy, invoking legislative norms, and administering public law in different regions, 1970's.

1712. Sigelman, Lee and Vanderbok, William G. LEGISLATORS, BUREAUCRATS, AND CANADIAN DEMOCRACY: THE LONG AND THE SHORT OF IT. *Can. J. of Pol. Sci. [Canada] 1977 10(3): 615-623.* Assesses the cross-national validity of the thesis, offered by Norton Long for the US experience, that the decline of legislative power and the expansion of bureaucratic power are democratizing forces. 2 tables, 28 notes.
R. V. Kubicek

1713. Smiley, Donald V. THE DOMINANCE OF WITHINPUTS?: CANADIAN POLITICS. *Polity 1973 6(2): 276-281.* A review article of John Meisel's *Working Papers on Canadian Politics* (Montreal: McGill-Queen's U. Press, 1972) and Richard Simeon's *Federal-Provincial Diplomacy; The Making of Recent Policy in Canada* (Toronto: U. of Toronto Press, 1972). The longest of Meisel's papers are interim reports on the study of the 1968 federal general elections, while others deal with linguistic groups and with relations between the English and the French in Canada. Examines intensively three sets of federal-provincial interactions in the middle and late 1960's. Speculates that "there are relatively weak linkages between political decision makers and their environment." Further investigation is necessary. 10 notes.
E. P. Stickney

1714. Sniderman, Paul M.; Forbes, H. D.; and Melzer, Ian. PARTY LOYALTY AND ELECTORAL VOLATILITY: A STUDY OF THE CANADIAN PARTY SYSTEM. *Can. J. of Pol. Sci. 1974 7(2): 268-288.* Describe a study based mostly on the 1965 and 1968 election surveys of John Meisel and his colleagues. Contrary to notions generally accepted by political scientists, identification with a party is the rule not the exception, and the vote is marked by continuity, not volatility. 8 tables, 55 notes.
R. V. Kubicek

1715. Solerlund, Walter C. and Wagenberg, Ronald H. A CONTENT ANALYSIS OF EDITORIAL COVERAGE OF THE 1972 ELECTION CAMPAIGNS IN CANADA AND THE UNITED STATES. *Western Pol. Q. 1975 28(1): 85-107.* While the American and Canadian federal systems are similar in some respects, a content analysis of editorials written in selected newspapers in the two countries reveals important differences in attitudes toward them. The bicultural society of Canada was reflected in much greater Canadian concern with the stability of their union. The central position of the American presidency was emphasized by the much larger number of references to Richard Nixon and George McGovern in American papers than mention of Pierre Trudeau and Robert Stanfield in Canadian papers. Unexpectedly, there was little difference between the coverage given the parties in each country despite the Canadian parliamentary system of government. Documentation comes from newspapers; 10 tables, 40 notes.
G. B. McKinney

1716. Srebnik, Henry. THE LIBERAL PARTY: CANADA'S PROTECTION RACKET. *Can. Dimension [Canada] 1978 13(1): 22-27.* Concludes that the popularity of Canada's Liberal Party, which has maintained national rule for 43 years, is due to its basic unifying nature, and that though many French Canadians vote in the Liberal Party nationally and in the Parti Québécois locally and provincially, such votes allow them to protect their collective interests vis-à-vis English Canada.

1717. Steele, G. G. F. "NEEDED—A SENSE OF PROPORTION!": NOTES ON THE HISTORY OF EXPENDITURE CONTROL. *Can. Public Administration [Canada] 1977 20(3): 433-443.* Examines implementation of recommendations of the Glassco Commission on control over public finance, 1960's-70's, and the possible impact of the proposed office of Financial Comptroller on government expenditure.

1718. Subbarao, A. V. THE IMPACT OF THE TWO DISPUTE RESOLUTION PROCESSES IN NEGOTIATIONS. *Industrial Relations [Canada] 1977 32(2): 216-233.* Answers the questions as to why the federal public servants alter their options from the arbitration process to the conciliation process.
J

1719. Swankey, Ben. COMMUNISTS AND THE NDP. *Communist Viewpoint [Canada] 1973 5(3): 15-26.* Discusses the New Democratic Party in Canada, 1961-73.
S

1720. Teeple, Gary. LIMITS TO NATIONALISM. *Can. Dimension [Canada] 1977 12(6): 27-36.* Examines the presence of nationalism in Canadian national politics, 1957-75; discusses several political movements spawned by it and the possibility of social change because of nationalistic feelings.

1721. Truman, Tom. A SCALE FOR MEASURING A TORY STREAK IN CANADA AND THE UNITED STATES. *Can. J. of Pol. Sci. 1977 10(3): 597-614.* Reports on an attitude scale to be used in measuring conservatism in English-speaking countries. 8 tables, 20 notes.
R. V. Kubicek

1722.   Wagenberg, Ronald H. and Soderlund, Walter C.   THE INFLU-ENCE OF CHAIN-OWNERSHIP ON EDITORIAL COMMENT IN CANADA.   *Journalism Q. 1975 52(1): 93-98.* Examines newspaper editorial coverage of the 1972 Canadian federal election campaign to determine the effects of chain ownership. Editorial coverage was found to be influenced more by local or regional interests and the interests of the editorialist than by type of ownership. There was no apparent relationship between chain ownership and partisanship except that Free Press newspapers did not give editorial support for the New Democratic Party. Based on primary sources; 7 tables, 5 notes.   K. J. Puffer

1723.   Warnock, John.   PEARSON PASSES.   *Can. Dimension 1973 9(4): 5-7.* Discusses the career of Lester Bowles Pearson (1897-1972), civil servant, government official, and former Canadian prime minister. During the Pearson era no attempt was made to deal with any of the fundamental problems facing Canada.   S

1724.   Welch, Susan.   DIMENSIONS OF POLITICAL PARTICIPA-TION IN A CANADIAN SAMPLE.   *Can. J. of Pol. Sci. 1975 8(4): 553-559.* Sample shows that Canadian political participation is similar to that found in some recent studies in other national settings. 4 tables, 14 notes.   R. V. Kubicek

1725.   Williams, Roger and Bates, David.   TECHNICAL DECI-SIONS AND PUBLIC ACCOUNTABILITY.   *Can. Public Administration [Canada] 1976 19(4): 603-632.* Discusses the need for public accountability in the federal government and the problems in implementing technical advice, 1950's-70's.

1726.   Wilson, John.   THE CANADIAN POLITICAL CULTURES: TOWARDS A REDEFINITION OF THE NATURE OF THE CANA-DIAN POLITICAL SYSTEM.   *Can. J. of Pol. Sci. 1974 7(3): 438-483.* Suggests Canadian politics should be understood not in terms of a two-fragment society, but on the basis of several distinctive cultures. Develops this argument by determining differences in political development, particularly with reference to party systems, among the provinces viewed as largely independent units. 10 tables, 12 figs., 60 notes.   R. V. Kubicek

1727.   Zipp, John F.   LEFT-RIGHT DIMENSIONS OF CANA-DIAN FEDERAL PARTY IDENTIFICATION: A DISCRIMINANT ANALYSIS.   *Can. J. of Pol. Sci. [Canada] 1978 11(2): 251-277.* Data drawn from Vancouver and Winnipeg subjected to multiple discriminant analysis stresses importance of major-minor party dichotomy and weakness of standard left-right categorizations. 5 tables, 3 fig., 51 notes.   R. V. Kubicek

1728.   —.   [EXPENDITURE AND POLITICAL SUCCESS].   *J. of Law & Econ. 1975 18(3): 745-780.*
Palda, Kristian S.   THE EFFECT OF EXPENDITURE ON POLITI-CAL SUCCESS, *pp. 745-771.* Explores the relationship between campaign expenditures and political success, concluding that the concepts are too vague to be successfully compared at present; proposes models that might evaluate the effects of expenditures on ballots cast, and presents models used to explore the influence of electoral outlays on voting in Manitoba and Quebec.
Madansky, Albert.   COMMENT, *pp. 773-774.*
Cole, Roland J.   COMMENT, *pp. 775-777.*
Palda, Kristian S.   REPLY, *pp. 779-780.*   G. A. Hewlett

1729.   —.   [REVIEW OF TEXTBOOKS ON CANADIAN GOV-ERNMENT].   *Can. J. of Pol. Sci. 1974 7(1): 101-134.*
Cairns, Alan C.   ALTERNATIVE STYLES IN THE STUDY OF CA-NADIAN POLITICS, pp. 101-128.   A review article generally about textbooks on Canadian government and specifically about two recent works: James R. Mallory, *The Structure of Canadian Government* (Toronto: St. Martin Press, 1971) and R. J. Van Loon and Michael S. Whittington, *The Canadian Political System: Environment, Structure and Process* (Toronto: McGraw, 1971); and the previous standard work by R. MacGregor Dawson, *The Government of Canada* (Toronto, 1947; 5th revised edition: U. of Toronto Press, 1970).
Ward, Norman.   ALTERNATIVE STYLES: A COMMENT, pp. 128-129.   The reviser of Dawson's text finds the review article "admirable."

Mallory, J. R.   STYLE AND FASHION: A NOTE ON ALTERNA-TIVE STYLES IN CANADIAN POLITICAL SCIENCE, pp. 129-132.   Responds to the review's "thorough dissection" of his book.
Van Loon, Richard J. and Whittington, Michael S.   ALTERNATIVE STYLES IN THE STUDY OF CANADIAN POLITICS: A BRIEF REJOINDER, pp. 132-134.   Reflections on the "constructive," "critical" and "careful" review of their book.   R. V. Kubicek

1730.   —.   [UTILITY OF PARTY IDENTIFICATION].   *Can. J. of Pol. Sci. [Canada] 1978 11(2): 419-446.*
Elkins, David J.   PARTY IDENTIFICATION: A CONCEPTUAL ANALYSIS,   *pp. 419-435.* Probes the concept of party identification on voting decisions with reference to Canada and the United States. 41 notes.
Jenson, Jane.   COMMENT: THE FILLING OF WINE BOTTLES IS NOT EASY.   *pp. 437-446.* Criticizes the limitation of Elkins's approach. 27 notes, table.   R. V. Kubicek

1731.   —.   YOU AND ME AND THE RCMP.   *Can. Dimension [Canada] 1978 13(3): 3-8.* Interviews Ian Adams, author of *S: Portrait of a Spy: RCMP Intelligence—the Inside Story,* about the abusive practices of the security services of the Royal Canadian Mounted Police.

International Posture

1732.   (Kika) et al. SHOULD PEOPLE STAY HOME? REGULA-TION OF FREE MOVEMENT AND RIGHT OF ESTABLISHMENT BETWEEN THE U.S., CANADA, AND MEXICO.   *Am. Soc. of Int. Law Pro. 1974 68: 38-58.* Discusses the public policies regulating immigration among the US, Canada, and Mexico from 1910 to 1974.

1733.   Ali, Mehrunnisa.   A SURVEY OF PAKISTAN'S FOREIGN RELATIONS—1973: PAKISTAN-CANADA RELATIONS.   *Pakistan Horizon [Pakistan] 1974 27(1): 77-79.* Pakistan has close relations with Canada; substantial amounts of economic grant aid, as well as commodity assistance, indicate Canada's goodwill for Pakistan. 4 notes.   H. M. Evans

1734.   Andrew, A. J.   PROBING THE RAISON D'ÊTRE OF A CA-NADIAN DIPLOMAT ABROAD.   *Internat. Perspectives [Canada] 1974 (2): 54-56.*

1735.   April, Serge.   EXAMINING THE RIGHT OF ASYLUM: THE CHOICES AND THE LIMITATIONS.   *Internat. Perspectives [Canada] 1974 (3): 44-47.* Discusses this right particularly in Canada and Latin America.

1736.   Armstrong, Gregory.   AID POLICIES AS A REFLECTION OF CANADIAN DOMESTIC CONCERNS.   *Int. Perspectives [Canada] 1975 Mar.-Apr.: 44-48.* Examines Canada's foreign aid policy, 1950-69, from the initiation of the Colombo Plan until the creation of the Canadian International Development Agency.

1737.   Balthazar, Louis.   LE STYLE CANADIEN ET LA POLI-TIQUE ÉTRANGÈRE   [Canadian style and foreign policy].   *Pol. Étran-gère [France] 1973 38(2): 131-148.* Outlines a few traits of Canadian national style to show how it determines and affects foreign policy, defining style as the British Canadian historical perspective, and speculating on the curious lack of French Canadian interest or influence, 1973.

1738.   Barros, James.   PEARSON OR LIE: THE POLITICS OF THE SECRETARY-GENERAL'S SELECTION, 1946.   *Can. J. of Pol. Sci. [Canada] 1977 10(1): 65-92.* Examines the motives and methods of the United States, Great Britain, and the USSR in the selection of the UN's first secretary-general. Based on primary sources; 74 notes.   R. V. Kubicek

1739.   Beesley, J. Alan.   GUERRE, PAIX ET DROIT DANS UN MONDE DIVISÉ   [War, peace and law in a divided world].   *Études Internationales [Canada] 1974 5(1): 45-71.* The Judicial Counsel to the

Canadian Foreign Office reviews the nature of conflict since World War II and notes a high correlation between developing nations and violence. Comments on the present structure of international society which features nation states, miltinational enterprises, and a supranational organization. Examines the relationship of international law to sanction and force and notes Canada's role in implementing UN policies. International law is replacing force as the vehicle to resolve conflicts. Primary and secondary sources; 102 notes.   J. F. Harrington

1740. Behuncik, Edward V. FORTIETH ANNIVERSARY CANADIAN SLOVAK LEAGUE. *Slovakia 1973 23(46): 48-52.* Speech by Edward J. Behuncik, President of the Slovak League of America, on the 40th anniversary of the founding of the Canadian Slovak League (5 August 1972). Calls upon all Slavs to support the Slovak World Congress organized in New York in 1970.   J. Williams

1741. Bergeron, Gérard. FOREIGN POLICY: 1950-1975 (OR SHOULD THAT BE 1945-1970?) *Internat. Perspectives [Canada] 1975 (6): 57-61.* Discusses Canada's foreign policy toward the United States, Europe, Japan and Third World nations from 1950-75, including its participation in the UN and NATO.

1742. Berry, Glyn R. IMMIGRATION IN CANADA—WEST INDIES RELATIONS: AN UNWELCOME RETRENCHMENT. *Revista/Review Interamericana [Puerto Rico] 1977 7(1): 87-98.* Many West Indians view Canada's recent restrictive immigration policy as a classical example of racism. In addition, the decision to allow only trained and educated immigrants into Canada has contributed to the Caribbean brain drain. 2 tables, 50 notes.   J. A. Lewis

1743. Black, J. B. and Blanchette, A. E. INFLUENCE OF THE MASS MEDIA ON THE CONDUCT OF FOREIGN POLICY. *Internat. Perspectives [Canada] 1974 (4): 42-45.* Brief discussion of the media in the 19th and 20th centuries.

1744. Blanchette, Arthur. [HISTOIRE ORALE ET POLITIQUE ÉTRANGÈRE] [Oral History and Foreign Policy]. *Can. Oral Hist. Assoc. J. [Canada] 1975/76 1: 20-24.* Discusses a program initiated by the Minister of External Affairs in Canada in documentation and research in foreign policy through oral history of such affairs, 1970-75.

1745. Boardman, Robert. CANADA AND COMMUNITY: ONE YEAR AFTER. *World Today [Great Britain] 1977 33(10): 395-404.* The Framework Agreement for Commercial and Economic Co-operation, was signed by Canada and the European Economic Community, 1976, to promote trade and investment links in Europe to raw material and semimanufactured goods in Canada.

1746. Bothwell, Robert and English, John. CANADIAN TRADE POLICY IN THE AGE OF AMERICAN DOMINANCE AND BRITISH DECLINE, 1943-1947. *Can. Rev. of Am. Studies [Canada] 1977 8(1): 52-65.* Traces the development of Canadian tariff, monetary, and other fundamental economic policies between 1943 and 1947. Canada alternately followed policies designed to preserve its preferential trading position in the British Empire, bilateral trade policies characterized by special agreements between Canada and its "trading partners," and finally multilateral trade policies that the United States favored and Canada accepted as a means of curing its post-World War II economic ills. Canada made its postwar economic choices largely out of fear of returning to the poverty experienced during the 1930's. Based on Canadian archival sources and secondary works; 52 notes.   H. T. Lovin

1747. Brazeau, J. A. R. SPECIAL PROBLEM OF REFUGEES RECEIVES SPECIAL ATTENTION. *Internat. Perspectives [Canada] 1975 (5): 13-17.* Discusses Canada's immigration policy toward refugees fleeing from international political crises during the 1950's-70's, emphasizing emigration from developing nations.

1748. Brecher, Irving. THE CONTINUING CHALLENGE OF INTERNATIONAL DEVELOPMENT: A CANADIAN PERSPECTIVE. *Queen's Q. [Canada] 1975 82(3): 323-343.* The problems of the developing nations—overpopulation, poverty, unequal income, rural underdevelopment—are formidable and have been compounded by the food and energy crises of 1972 and 1973. During the 1960's-70's the developed

nations' foreign aid efforts became more sophisticated, aiming for social justice as well as economic growth. Canadian aid must continue to grow in quality and quantity through research on types of effective assistance, improved policy planning and coordination of government agencies, easing of trade restrictions, and mobilization of public opinion to support the war on world poverty. 4 notes.   T. Simmerman

1749. Brown, LaVerne. JAMES H. ROBINSON'S UNFINISHED TASK. *Crisis 1973 80(5): 159-161.* Discusses Operation Crossroads Africa, the organization established in 1958 by James H. Robinson which enabled US and Canadian students to work and learn in Africa.

1750. Buick, Glen. CONSULS LEND A HELPING HAND TO INNOCENTS ABROAD—AND OTHERS. *Int. Perspectives [Canada] 1977 (July-August): 23-27.* Canada's Bureau of Consular Services, a division of the Department of External Affairs, serves a growing number of Canadians who live or travel abroad. The Bureau issues passports and provides medical, financial, or legal services to those in trouble. The most serious problems concern Canadians in foreign prisons and those holding dual nationality who are trapped in countries which do not recognize their Canadian citizenship. Consular personnel are trained to administer the regulations with compassion and common sense.
                              E. S. Palais

1751. Byers, R. B. and Leyton-Brown, David. CANADIAN ÉLITE IMAGES OF THE INTERNATIONAL SYSTEM. *Int. J. [Canada] 1977 32(3): 608-639.* Variations among images held by elite groups including government officials, parliamentarians, and academics were found to be limited. Based on 343 interviews completed during 1975-76; 8 tables, 45 notes.   R. V. Kubicek

1752. Byers, R. B. DEFENCE AND FOREIGN POLICY IN THE 1970'S: THE DEMISE OF THE TRUDEAU DOCTRINE. *Int. J. [Canada] 1978 33(2): 312-338.* Reviews circumstances preventing the realization of the protection-of-Canada role and prompting the renewal of emphasis on NATO (North Atlantic Treaty Organization) and peacekeeping. 28 notes.   R. V. Kubicek

1753. Cadieux, Marcel. FRAMEWORK AGREEMENT IS THE KEY TO CLOSER RELATIONS. *Int. Perspectives [Canada] 1976 (6): 3-7.* Discusses Canada's 1976 "contractual link" with the European Economic Community to strengthen economic relations.

1754. Calkin, G. A. THE DEVELOPMENT OF RELATIONS BETWEEN CANADA AND MEXICO. *Internat. Perspectives [Canada] 1973 (3): 55-58.* Discusses the evolution and importance of Canada's relation with Mexico since 1944.   L. S. Frey

1755. Carson, John. NATO'S 25TH ANNIVERSARY: ALLIANCES FUTURE POLITICAL ROLE STILL KEYED TO DEFENCE FUNCTION. *Internat. Perspectives [Canada] 1974 (2): 58-62.* Comments on NATO's military and political strategy since 1969.

1756. Caves, Richard E. CAUSES OF DIRECT INVESTMENT: FOREIGN FIRMS' SHARES IN CANADIAN AND UNITED KINGDOM MANUFACTURING INDUSTRIES. *R. of Econ. and Statistics 1974 56(3): 279-293.*

1757. Caves, Richard. THE MULTINATIONAL FIRM IN THE NORTH AMERICAN ECONOMY. *Am. Rev. of Can. Studies 1973 3(1): 107-114.* Presents statistical research on the effects of multinational corporations in Canada, concluding that foreign subsidiaries make some contribution by reducing monopolies in secondary manufacturing, 1970's.

1758. Chevrier, Lionel. THE PRACTICAL DIPLOMACY OF LESTER PEARSON. *Internat. J. [Canada] 1973-74 29(1): 122-135.* An appreciation by a former colleague of the skillful diplomacy of the late Canadian prime minister, Lester B. Pearson, including negotiations with the United States on the Saint Lawrence Seaway project.
                              R. V. Kubicek

1759. Copithorne, M. D. THE SETTLEMENT OF INTERNATIONAL CLAIMS BETWEEN CANADA AND CHINA: A STATUS REPORT. *Pacific Affairs [Canada] 1975 48(2): 230-237.* Examines the negotiations leading to the settlement of international claims between Canada and the People's Republic of China. The question of repayment for the 1946 Canadian loan for the building of the Ming Sung Yangtse ships was acknowledged by the Chinese for years, but in the absence of formal diplomatic relations there was no way to pursue the claims. After the Stockholm 1969-70 recognition negotiations, the matter was resolved by the payment of a lump sum in Canadian dollars and a transfer of ship's registration to the Chinese. The compensation to the Canadians for their confiscated embassy property in Nanking was finally secured, but the financial settlement was not satisfactory to the Canadians. The 1946 inter-governmental loan has not been recognized by the government of the People's Republic of China, and they refuse to assume any of these obligations. The Chinese are prepared to negotiate seriously for settlements of private Canadian claims which are few in number and relatively small in value. Secondary sources; 11 notes.   S. H. Frank

1760. Cordier, Andrew W. and Russell, Ruth B.   PATTERN FOR A SPECIAL WAR DAMAGE FUND.   *Internat. Perspectives [Canada] 1973 (1): 21.* Advocates the adoption of international assistance in Vietnam and a war damage repair agency to operate in Indochina.
L. S. Frey

1761. Coull, J. R.   SECOND BRITISH-CANADIAN SYMPOSIUM IN HISTORICAL GEOGRAPHY.   *Scottish Geographical Mag. [Great Britain] 1977 93(3): 186-187.* Describes the first part of the second British-Canadian Symposium held 6-9 May 1977 at Anstruther; lists paper topics and speakers.

1762. Craig, A. W.   BRITAIN, CANADA AND EUROPE FACE RESURGENT REGIONALISM.   *Int. Perspectives [Canada] 1977 (July-August): 37-42.* Examines the phenomenon variously described as regionalism, separatism, home-rule, devolution, subnationalism, or minority nationalism in Great Britain and Canada. Such movements may be the result of excessive centralization (e.g., Scotland, Wales) or weakness of national identity (e.g., Quebec), but neglect of perceived regional needs is a common factor. Governments must respond to such regional pressures. Federal systems, such as Canada's, appear better equipped to make the required adjustments. Secondary sources; photo, 6 notes.
E. S. Palais

1763. Crispo, John.   MULTINATIONAL CORPORATION, INTERNATIONAL UNIONS AND INDUSTRIAL RELATIONS: THE CANADIAN CASE.   *Industrial Relations [Canada] 1974 29(4): 673-684.* This paper highlights several generalizations about the conduct in Canada of both multi-national corporations and international unions. Their impact on Canadian collective bargaining is examined and sets the stage for a discussion of selected issues and problems growing out of their presence.   J

1764. Critchley, W. Harriet.   CANADA'S MARITIME FORCES AND THE LAW OF THE SEA.   *Int. Perspectives [Canada] 1978 (Mar.-Apr.): 3-8.* Among participants in the UN Conference on the Law of the Sea (UNCLOS), coastal states favor a restrictive attitude toward international use of the sea, while global-maritime powers are interested in the maximum possible freedom. Although Canada shares both sets of interests, her position at UNCLOS successfully strikes a balance between the two. Canada also has no problem in balancing the military and civil-regulatory tasks of her armed forces operating in the Atlantic and Pacific Oceans, but a new policy is needed for the Arctic, where maritime security needs far outstrip capabilities. 3 photos.   E. S. Palais

1765. Cutler, Maurice.   FOREIGN DEMAND FOR OUR LAND AND RESOURCES.   *Can. Geographical J. 1975 90(4): 4-19.* Looks at Canada's growing concern in recent decades over foreign domination of its natural resources and its industrial and financial life.   S

1766. Cutler, Maurice.   HOW FOREIGN OWNERS SHAPE OUR CITIES.   *Can. Geographical J. 1975 90(6): 34-48.* Discusses foreign use and Canadian control of Canada's land and resources.   S

1767. Dack, W. L.   CANADA'S STEEL INDUSTRY EXPANDS IN A BIG WAY.   *Can. Geographical J. 1975 91(4): 32-41.* Discusses Canada's expanding steel industry including projections for foreign trade through 1980.   S

1768. Dayal, Rajeshwar.   THE POWER OF WISDOM.   *Internat. J. [Canada] 1973/74 29(1): 110-121.* Considers the efforts of Lester B. Pearson (1897-1972), former Canadian prime minister, to support local self-determination and promote international understanding. Reviews his diplomacy at the UN during the Korean War. Note.
R. V. Kubicek

1769. De Goumois, Michel.   LE CANADA ET LA FRANCOPHONIE   [Canada and "Francophonie"].   *Études Internationales [Canada] 1974 5(2): 355-366.* Discusses Canada's bilateral relations with France, Belgium, and the French-speaking African states as well as Ottawa's involvement with multinational francophone institutions, especially the Agency for Cultural and Technical Cooperation, the Conference of Education Ministers (1960), the Conference of Ministers for Youth and Sports (1969), and various private French-speaking associations.
J. F. Harrington

1770. Delvoie, L. A.   GROWTH IN ECONOMIC RELATIONS OF CANADA AND THE ARAB WORLD.   *Int. Perspectives [Canada] 1976 (6): 29-33.* Examines the increase in Canada's bilateral economic assistance programs and trade with Arab States in the 1960's and 70's; considers the magnitude of the flow of Arab oil capital into Canada.

1771. Dickerman, C. Robert.   TRANSGOVERNMENTAL CHALLENGE AND RESPONSE IN SCANDINAVIA AND NORTH AMERICA.   *Int. Organization 1976 30(2): 213-240.* Eighty interviews with bureaucratic and political actors in five national capitals illustrate the Keohane/Nye theoretical argument concerning the importance of transnational and, specifically, transgovernmental factors in world politics. Focusing upon the development and application of integrative techniques between countries which have no formal supranational integrative institutions, the paper reports on the practice of transgovernmental politics within the dyad of Canada and the United States, and the triad of Denmark, Norway, and Sweden. Dealing both with middle-level bureaucratic practitioners concerned with horizontal coordination of policy and administration between countries, and with bureaucratic and political actors responsible for the cohesiveness of national policies, the paper explores situations in which the demands of external and domestic harmonization are inconsistent, and sometimes mutually contradictory. The problem of maintaining "dual coherence" in domestic and external policy and administration is identified, and procedures for attempting such coordination are discussed. Of importance are modifications within the traditional institutions of inter-state communication: foreign offices and embassies. Recommendations are made on the basis of the intra-North American and intra-Scandinavian experiences. It is suggested that considerable insight into managing policy and administrative areas which are neither purely domestic nor purely external may be gained by the study of bureaucratic experience only infrequently considered by students or governmental managers. Insights which may be gained from such study, it is argued, may be of great relevance in dealing with the challenge which transgovernmental horizontal harmonization now poses for national administrations.   J

1772. Diebold, William, Jr.   CANADA IN THE WORLD ECONOMY OVER TEN YEARS.   *Int. J. [Canada] 1978 33(2): 432-437.* Pragmatic economic nationalism has dominated the economic foreign policy of the Trudeau government. Note.   R. V. Kubicek

1773. Dmitriev, S.   GOSUDARSTVENNO-MONOPOLISTICHESKII KAPITALIZM KANADY   [The state-monopolistic capitalism of Canada].   *Mirovaia Ekonomika i Mezhdunarodnye Otnosheniia [USSR] 1975 (8): 45-55.* Studies the unique role in Canada's economy of foreign capital, its influence on governmental economic policy, and the economic ties between Canada and the United States.

1774. Dobell, W. M.   A 'SOW'S EAR' IN VIETNAM.   *Internat. J. [Canada] 1974 29(3): 356-392.* Discusses Canada's participation in the International Commission for Supervision and Control (ICSC) in Vietnam with reference to Canada's general attitude toward participation in peacekeeping operations. 10 notes.   R. V. Kubicek

1775. Dobell, W. M.   UNITED NATIONS: SEA LAW, PEACEKEEPING, AND SOUTHERN AFRICA.   *Int. J. [Canada] 1978 33(2): 415-424.* A critique of aspects of Canada's policy towards the UN with particular reference to the Trudeau administration's 1970 *Foreign Policy for Canadians*. 26 notes.   R. V. Kubicek

1776. Donneur, André P. ADVOCATING SCIENTIFIC APPROACH FOR DIPLOMATS AND ACADEMICS. *Internat. Perspectives [Canada] 1974 (1): 47-49.* Comments on the discipline of international relations and its application to Canada's foreign policy.
                                                                    S

1777. Donneur, André P. CANADA'S IMAGE IN EUROPE STILL NEEDS IMPROVEMENT. *Int. Perspectives [Canada] 1977 Mar.-Apr.: 16-21.* Discusses Canada's "Third Option" policy, an attempt to assert economic independence from the United States by strengthening trade and economic ties with western Europe.

1778. Douglas, W. A. B. WHY DOES CANADA HAVE ARMED FORCES? *Int. J. [Canada] 1975 30(2): 259-283.* Discusses the need for armies and defense in Canada as a means of asserting self-determination in international relations in the 1970's, including political factors.

1779. Dow, Alexander. INTERNATIONAL MINERALS POLICY SHOULD BE ADOPTED BY CANADA. *Int. Perspectives [Canada] 1977 (Nov.-Dec.): 19-25.* As a major producer of minerals, particularly nickel, zinc, lead and copper, Canada shares certain economic interests with the mineral-producing developing nations. Canada's mines are largely foreign-controlled and undertaxed because of the threat to locate elsewhere. Cooperation with the developing nations should include the harmonization of policies concerning the collection of resource rents and the taxation of monopoly profits. Canada should also assist the efforts of producer associations such as the Inter-Governmental Council of Copper-Exporting Countries (CIPEC) to devise workable commodity price stabilization programs. Photo.   E. S. Palais

1780. Eayrs, James. DEFINING A NEW PLACE FOR CANADA IN THE HIERARCHY OF WORLD POWER. *Int. Perspectives [Canada] 1975 (3): 15-24.* Discusses Canada's role in world affairs as a "foremost power" in the context of what power is; describes recent changes in the international system, and the decline of the United States.

1781. Eckhardt, Konstantine and Korey-Krzeczowski, George. PROPOSAL FOR ACTION: NEW ROLE FOR THE CANADIAN ECONOMY IN THE AGE OF WORLD FOOD CRISIS. *Polish Rev. 1976 21(1-2): 129-144.* The world is in the midst of a food crisis, one that can only grow worse as population increases. Canada is in an excellent position to help meet this emergency. By drawing on its largely untapped natural and demographic resources, Canada can produce more food at little more cost. Primary sources; 6 tables, 5 notes.
                                                               E. M. McLendon

1782. English, H. Edward. FOREIGN INVESTMENT IN MANUFACTURING. *Pro. of the Acad. of Pol. Sci. 1976 32(2): 88-99.* Analyzes the effects of foreign investments, primarily US, in Canadian manufacturing. The question is whether Canada gets as much as it gives. The present arrangement is hardly an example of harsh exploitation, but improvements could be made. More federal regulation is required. A policy of encouraging quality and durability, and using taxation to discourage their opposites, would result in products bearing a distinctively Canadian stamp and better able to compete in world markets. 5 notes.
                                                                    V. L. Human

1783. Evans, Brian. THE CHINA-CANADA STUDENT EXCHANGE: THE FIRST TWENTY. *Pacific Affairs [Canada] 1976 49(1): 93-101.* Describes the experience of 20 exchange students from Canada in China from 1973-75. These students were recruited in Canada at the request of the Education and Science Groups under the State Council and took up residence in Peking in November 1973. Unfortunately, the Peking Language Institute was caught up in the unrest caused by the Criticize Confucius, Criticize Lin Piao Campaign. The students adapted to the Spartan living conditions but did not conform to the administrative policies of the Language Institute. In 1974 tension between the students and the authorities ebbed with the coming of Spring and the easing of the Anti-Confucius Campaign. During the second year the Canadian students who remained in China were quite restricted in their fields of study. Subsequent negotiations regarding the Canadian students

in China gave the Chinese authorities greater control over student stipends and discipline. The author was Sinologist-in-Residence in the Canadian Embassy in Peking where he studied the materials for this article.
                                                                    S. H. Frank

1784. Fauriol, Georges A. CANADIAN RELATIONS WITH HAITI: AN OVERVIEW. *Revista/Review Interamericana [Puerto Rico] 1977 7(1): 109-117.* Canada's diplomatic and economic ties with Haiti traditionally have been minimal. In recent years, however, contact between the two nations has increased because of their common French background. 28 notes.   J. A. Lewis

1785. Finkle, Peter Z. R. CANADIAN FOREIGN POLICY FOR MARINE FISHERIES: AN ALTERNATE PERSPECTIVE. *J. of Can. Studies 1975 10(1): 10-24.* Generally, Canadian foreign policy is shaped by a desire to further international cooperation. As a result, marine fisheries policy is based upon the acceptance of existing international agreements, even though these have failed to prevent the depletion of fish stocks off Canadian shores. The alternative practical policy is to assert the right of a coastal fishing state and take control of the offshore fishery. The foreign fishing nations involved could then obtain an uninterrupted supply of fish by trading with Canada. Based on United Nations documents, Canadian documents, and secondary sources; 36 notes.
                                                                    G. E. Panting

1786. Finkle, Peter Z. R. REALITIES OF ENVIRONMENTAL MANAGEMENT: THE CASE OF MARINE FISHERIES. *Queen's Q. [Canada] 1974 81(2): 240-46.* Studies the disruption of society inherent in regulations designed to protect the environment while ignoring other factors. Marine fisheries offer a useful example, in an international context, of tempering ecological sanctity to meet the realities of existing situations. We should strive for flexible, sensible solutions that all concerned parties find acceptable. Note.   J. A. Casada

1787. Fleurot, Jean. AMBITIONS ET LIMITES DE LA POLITIQUE EXTÉRIEURE DU CANADA [Ambitions and limitations of Canada's foreign policy]. *Défense Natl. [France] 1974 30(7): 85-93.* Describes the principal historical elements of Canada's foreign policy and traces its evolution in the recent past when Pierre Trudeau became Prime Minister, 1968-74.

1788. Franck, Thomas M. INTERNATIONAL LAW IN CANADIAN PRACTICE: THE STATE OF THE ART AND THE ART OF THE STATE. *Int. J. [Canada] 1975-76 31(1): 180-214.* Uses a review of *Canadian Perspectives on International Law and Organization*, edited by R. St. J. Macdonald et al. (Toronto, 1974), to set out what should be the duties and functions of international lawyers. 3 notes.
                                                                    R. V. Kubicek

1789. Freifeld, Sidney A. THE PRESS OFFICER AND EXTERNAL AFFAIRS. *Int. J. [Canada] 1976 31(2): 255-269.* Recommends improvements in the role and function of the press officers in Canada's Department of External Affairs. 11 notes.   R. V. Kubicek

1790. Garner, Joseph John. CANADIAN DIPLOMACY: THE MEMOIRS OF TWO PUBLIC SERVANTS. *Round Table [Great Britain] 1974 (253): 85-94.* Review article on *Mike: The Memoirs of the Right Honourable Lester B. Pearson, Vol. I* (Ontario: U. of Toronto Press, 1972) and Arnold D. P. Heeney's *The Things That Are Caesar's* (Ontario: U. of Toronto Press, 1972). Considers the parallel careers of Pearson and Heeney in the context of Canada's historical relationship with Britain and her geographical connection with the United States. Discusses how these relationships may develop in the future.
                                                                    R. G. Neville

1791. Garner, Joseph John. MIKE: AN ENGLISHMAN'S VIEW. *Internat. J. [Canada] 1973/74 29(1): 33-45.* An appreciation of Lester B. Pearson, stressing his tolerant internationalism, by a retired senior British civil servant who knew the late Canadian prime minister from 1936 on.
                                                                    R. V. Kubicek

1792. Garnier, Gérard. LES INVESTISSEMENTS DIRECTS DU CANADA A L'ETRANGER [Direct Canadian foreign investments]. *Actualité Econ. [Canada] 1973 49(2): 211-.* Canada is, among other things, a major capital-exporting nation, and its external investments are highly concentrated by industrial group and geographical location. Based on secondary sources; 3 tables, 22 notes.   W. B. Whitham

1793. Gérin-Lajoie, Paul. TOWARDS A NEW GLOBAL ORDER: REFLECTIONS ON 25 YEARS OF DEVELOPMENT CO-OPERATION. *Int. Perspectives [Canada] 1975 (6): 38-42.* Discusses Canada's foreign policy and economic assistance programs to developing nations in the 1970's, including the roles of technology and industrialization.

1794. Goldblatt, Murray. CANADA AND EUROPEAN SECURITY. *Internat. Perspectives [Canada] 1973 (1): 35-38.* In Canada's view the proposed European Security Conference would attempt to resolve the underlying causes of division and tension in Europe. The Helsinki talks should prepare the ground before the conference is convened, which also will focus on economic, cultural and scientific questions.
                L. S. Frey

1795. Goldblatt, Murray. CANADA'S ROLE IN VIETNAM. *Internat. Perspectives [Canada] 1973: 47-51.* Examines Canadian commitment to "participate with Poland, Hungary, and Indonesia in the new four-power international supervisory organization" in Vietnam.
                L. S. Frey

1796. Gordon, J. King. SPECIFIC POLICIES MUST REFLECT A RETURN OF GLOBAL PERSPECTIVE. *Int. Perspectives [Canada] 1976 (5): 3-6.* Canada needs to adopt humanitarian attitudes toward poverty in developing nations in light of its election to the UN Security Council in the 1970's.

1797. Gotlieb, Allan and Dalfen, Charles. NATIONAL JURISDICTION AND INTERNATIONAL RESPONSIBILITY: NEW CANADIAN APPROACHES TO INTERNATIONAL LAW. *Am. J. of Internat. Law 1973 67(2): 229-258.* Discuss Canada's interpretation of international law regarding outer space and the oceans.   S

1798. Graham, John W. RECENT GROWTH OF INTEREST IN CANADIAN STUDIES ABROAD. *Int. Perspectives [Canada] 1976 (5): 38-42.* Discusses the role of academic exchange programs in Canada's Five-Year Cultural Plan in the 1970's; examines government funding and the distribution of Canadian journals and periodicals to other nations.

1799. Green, L. C. FOCUS ON INTERNATIONAL LAW. *Internat. Perspectives [Canada] 1974 (5): 52-55.* Reviews the *Canadian Perspectives on International Law and Organization*, edited by R. St. J. MacDonald, Gerald L. Morris and Douglas M. Johnston (Toronto: University of Toronto Press, 1974).   S

1800. Grenier, Raymond. LA "CRISE GLOBALE" ET LA COOPÉRATION CANADIENNE AU DÉVELOPPEMENT DE L'AFRIQUE FRANCOPHONE ["Global crisis" and Canadian cooperation in development of French-speaking Africa]. *Études Internationales [Canada] 1974 5(2): 367-375.* Examines Canada's financial commitment to cooperation with French-speaking African states since 1968, and notes attempts to regionalize programs rather than maintain numerous bilateral endeavors. 4 charts.   J. F. Harrington

1801. Grenon, Jean-Yves. CANADA'S DEVELOPING RELATIONS WITH THE EUROPE OF "EIGHTEEN." *Int. Perspectives [Canada] 1976 (2): 37-42.* Discusses Canada's attempt to establish foreign relations with the nations of the Council of Europe, chiefly in matters of international law from 1965-70's; stresses Canada's similarity to European political systems.

1802. Guy, James John. CANADA AND LATIN AMERICA. *World Today [Great Britain] 1976 32(10): 376-386.* Since 1968 Canadian Prime Minister Pierre Elliott Trudeau has implemented a new international trade policy toward Latin America in an attempt to foster good mercantile and foreign relations with Latin countries and to maintain independence in relations previously dominated by the United States.

1803. Guy, James. THE GROWING RELATIONSHIP OF CANADA AND THE AMERICAS. *Int. Perspectives [Canada] 1977 (Jul.-Aug.): 3-6.* Canada has had economic ties with Latin America since 1865,

but no established policy goals existed until Prime Minister Pierre Elliott Trudeau's foreign policy review in 1968-70. The resulting reassessment of Canada's international role included expanded relations with Latin America. The new policy, marked by the establishment of a Bureau of Western Hemisphere Affairs in the Department of External Affairs, is characterized by increased participation in inter-American organizations (e.g., permanent observer status—but not membership—in the Organization of American States and the Andean Community), inauguration of a bilateral assistance program, and increased frequency of ministerial trade missions. Photo.   E. S. Palais

1804. Guy, James John. TRUDEAU'S FOREIGN POLICY AND LATIN AMERICA. *Rev. Interamericana [Puerto Rico] 1977 7(1): 99-108.* Canadian interest in Latin America was slight until the election of Pierre Elliott Trudeau in 1968. Trudeau viewed Canada as primarily a North American nation with a unique mission to perform in the Western Hemisphere. Therefore since 1968, Canada has cultivated close ties with selected Latin American countries. 25 notes.   J. A. Lewis

1805. Hajjar, Sami G.; Bowman, James S.; and Brzezinski, Steven J. THE LITERATURE OF POLITICAL SCIENCE: PROFESSIONAL JOURNALS IN FOUR NATIONS. *Int. Social Sci. J. [France] 1977 29(2): 327-332.* Assesses professional political science journals in the United States, Great Britain, Canada and India to determine scope and methodology in international political science during the 1970's.

1806. Hamilton, Edward K. THOUGHTS ON THE CHAIRMAN. *Internat. J. [Canada] 1973/74 29(1): 136-142.* An appreciation of Lester B. Pearson, late prime minister of Canada, in his work as chairman of the Commission on International Development by the former executive secretary of the commission. 4 notes.   R. V. Kubicek

1807. Harbron, John D. CANADA RECOGNIZES CHINA: THE TRUDEAU ROUND OF 1968-1973. *Behind the Headlines [Canada] 1974 33(5): 1-22.* Although diplomatic recognition of China was popular in Canada, some warn of the overidentification of Canadian values with those of a communist system. Determined to recognize China before his election, Pierre Trudeau pushed it through without any comment on Peking's claim to Taiwan. Sino-Canadian relations have been very good.   R. D. Frederick

1808. Harbron, John. GROWING PRESSURES ON CANADA TO SEEK HEMISPHERIC IDENTITY. *Internat. Perspectives [Canada] 1974 (3): 31-35.* Discusses relations between Canada and Latin America in the 1970's.

1809. Hawkins, Freda. CANADA'S GREEN PAPER ON IMMIGRATION POLICY. *Internat. Migration R. 1975 9(2): 237-249.* Discusses Canada's current Green Paper on immigration policy, focusing on its implications for future immigration and development policies.

1810. Hawkins, Freda. CANADIAN IMMIGRATION POLICY AND MANAGEMENT. *Internat. Migration R. 1974 8(2): 141-153.* Discusses present immigration policy and management in Canada, including major features of the Canadian immigration situation since the end of World War II.

1811. Hawkins, Freda. DEMOGRAPHIC STUDIES NEEDED TO SUPPLEMENT GREEN PAPER. *Internat. Perspectives [Canada] 1975 (5): 3-9.* Discusses the need for demographic research in Canada's immigration policy in the 1970's, emphasizing the implications for federal and local government.

1812. Hawkins, Freda. PUBLIC AFFAIRS: DIFFICULT DECISIONS IN IMMIGRATION POLICY. *Queen's Q. [Canada] 1975 82(4): 589-599.* In 1975 the Canadian Liberal government published a Green Paper on Immigration Policy to elicit the attitudes of citizens on immigration, to amend 1967 and 1972 immigration acts, and to develop long-term national goals. Since 1967 international pressure has resulted in increased rates of immigration, yet by 1975 internal pressure from overcrowded metropolitan areas and labor shortages has shown a need to limit these rates. Immigration policies should be nondiscriminatory, respect family immigration, freely admit refugees, ensure the survival of the French language and culture, improve services for arriving immigrants, and (most importantly) tie immigration to national labor and economic, urban, and social goals.   T. Simmerman

1813. Heald, Henry F. SCANNING THE BROAD IMPLICA-TIONS OF SHARP'S TRIP TO SOVIET UNION. *Internat. Perspectives [Canada] 1974 (1): 16-20.* Discusses the diplomacy of Canadian External Affairs Minister Mitchell Sharp in November 1973.

1814. Heeney, Stephen. COMMON GOAL OF EXPANSION UNITES CANADA AND JAPAN. *Internat. Perspectives [Canada] 1975 (1): 15-20.* Canada must achieve a less vulnerable economic base and must broaden its spectrum of markets. In spite of the economic imbalance between Canada and Japan, their economic goals open possibility for closer relations.   L. S. Frey

1815. Held, Robert. CANADIAN FOREIGN POLICY: AN OUT-SIDER'S VIEW. *Int. J. [Canada] 1978 33(2): 448-456.* An assessment of Canadian foreign policy under the Trudeau administration from the point of view of a West German journalist. Note.
                                                     R. V. Kubicek

1816. Helleiner, G. K. INTERNATIONAL DEVELOPMENT EIGHT YEARS ON. *Int. J. [Canada] 1978 33(2): 395-401.* A critique of Canada's assistance programs for the Third World with particular reference to the Trudeau administration's 1970 position paper on the subject, *International Development.* 5 notes.   R. V. Kubicek

1817. Hervouet, Gérard. SINO-CANADIAN RELATIONS: RES-IGNATION AND OPTIMISM. *Int. Perspectives [Canada] 1977 (Nov.-Dec.): 25-28.* After Canada established diplomatic relations with China in 1970, the two countries negotiated a contract for the largest wheat transaction ever made and Canada became China's main wheat supplier. However, the volume of trade decreased during 1975-76 and Canadian diplomats have learned that they must be prepared to accept a more gradual development of foreign relations with China, and that Canadians must court the Chinese. There is cause for optimism in the October 1977 visit of the Chinese Minister of Foreign Affairs and the significant increase in scientific, technological, cultural, and sports ex-changes. Photo.   E. S. Palais

1818. Hockin, Thomas. AFTER THE OTTAWA DECLARATION THE STRUCTURAL PROBLEMS REMAIN. *Internat. Perspectives [Canada] 1974 (5): 36-39.* Assesses the results of the Declaration of Atlantic Principles of NATO of June 1974.

1819. House, J. D. THE SOCIAL ORGANIZATION OF MULTI-NATIONAL CORPORATIONS: CANADIAN SUBSIDIARIES IN THE OIL INDUSTRY. *Can. Rev. of Sociol. and Anthrop. [Canada] 1977 14(1): 1-14.* Based on a study of Canadian oil subsidiaries, this paper attempts to contribute to an economic sociology of multinational corpora-tions by examining four organizational principles basic to their economic success: internalized financing, transnational technology, local mobiliza-tion of manpower, and the collectivization of entrepreneurship. Direct foreign investment in the industry is then examined in this context. Al-though formerly beneficial as a financial starting mechanism, and of continuing benefit for technological access, foreign ownership now per-petuates cooptation of Canadian entrepreneurship and expropriation of economic surplus. The industry could be Canadianized with surprisingly little economic dislocation.   J

1820. Humphreys, David. CANADA'S LINK WITH EUROPE STILL NOT WIDELY UNDERSTOOD. *Int. Perspectives [Canada] 1976 (2): 32-36.* Discusses the lack of press coverage of political and foreign policy factors in Canada's desire to establish economic relations with the European Common Market in 1974-75.

1821. Ignatieff, George. BOOK REVIEW: PEARSON IN THE POSTWAR DECADE: HELPING KEEP THE COLD WAR COLD. *Internat. Perspectives [Canada] 1974 (1): 50-53.* Reviews the memoirs of a former Canadian Secretary of State for External Affairs, *Mike: The Memoirs of the Right Honourable Lester B. Pearson, Volume II (1948-1957)* (University of Toronto Press, 1973), edited by John A. Munro and Alex I. Inglis.   S

1822. Ignatieff, George. SITTING ON THE HOT SEAT OF THE UN SECURITY COUNCIL. *Int. Perspectives [Canada] 1976 (5): 7-11.* Discusses potentially explosive political decisions Canada will be forced to make in issues involving the Middle East and egalitarianism in develop-ing nations while serving on the UN Security Council in 1976.

1823. Inglis, Alex I. PEACEKEEPING AND PEACEMAKING SHOULD BE REVIEWED TOGETHER. *Internat. Perspectives [Can-ada] 1975 (1): 31-34.* "In an interdependent world, the sovereignty of Canada, the defense of North America and peace in the Atlantic may depend very much on the avoidance" of conflict or at least its contain-ment. The Canadian forces are made more efficient by their participation in the UN peacekeeping operations. Canada must estimate the effect of its decisions on the world community and its influence on other powers.
                                                     L. S. Frey

1824. Inglis, Alex I. PROLOGUE: THE CHANGING WORLD OF 1950-75. *Int. Perspectives [Canada] 1975 (6): 3-7.* Discusses political, economic, and military developments in foreign relations from 1950 to 1975, emphasizing Canada, the United States, the USSR, China, and the developing nations.

1825. Jacomy-Millette, Anne-Marie. CANADA'S VOTING PAT-TERN AT 30TH GENERAL ASSEMBLY. *Int. Perspectives [Canada] 1976 (5): 21-26.* Analyzes Canada's voting on issues involving disarma-ment and alleged racism in Israel, and decolonization in developing na-tions at the 30th UN General Assembly in 1975; considers Canada's UN decisions as an extension of its foreign policy.

1826. Johnson, Barbara and Langdon, Frank. TWO HUNDRED MILE ZONES: THE POLITICS OF NORTH PACIFIC FISHERIES. *Pacific Affairs [Canada] 1976 49(1): 5-27.* Analyzes the history of mari-time diplomacy leading to the Third Law of the Sea Conference. Exam-ines the political interplay among Canada, the United States, the Soviet Union, and Japan regarding 200-mile zones and fisheries issues. All of these nations became major economic powers and major trading nations in the 20th century and sought to maintain an unimpeded flow of ocean-borne commerce. These North Pacific states have the longest coastline in the world. Canada and Japan were primarily concerned with maintaining their coastal integrity and fishing opportunities and the United States and the Soviet Union were preoccupied with maintaining the rights of their warships to insure national security. Based on secondary sources; map, 13 notes, biblio.   S. H. Frank

1827. Joxe, Alain. SÉCURITÉ DE L'EUROPE OCCIDENTALE ET DU CANADA DANS LE SYSTÈME ATLANTIQUE: RÉTRO-SPECTIVE ET PERSPECTIVE [Western European and Canadian se-curity in the Atlantic system: retrospect and perspectives]. *Pol. Étrangère [France] 1973 38(2): 201-212.* Views Canada and Europe as pawns in the US strategic system since World War II, in the US economic plan, in the military domain, and in political leadership.

1828. Kavic, Lorne. CANADA AND THE COMMONWEALTH: SENTIMENT, SYMBOLISM, AND SELF-INTEREST. *Round Table [Great Britain] 1975 (257): 37-49.* Outlines changing Canadian attitudes toward the British Commonwealth since 1947. Although positive support for continued membership has been declining since the mid-1950's as links with Britain have been superseded by bilateral relations with indi-vidual members, ties with Australia, the Commonwealth Caribbean, Africa, and India have multiplied. Commonwealth trade relations con-tinue to be important to the Canadian economy. Based on newspapers; 19 notes.   C. Anstey

1829. Keenleyside, T. A. CANADA AND THE PACIFIC: PERILS OF A POLICY PAPER. *J. of Can. Studies 1973 8(2): 31-49.* Discusses Canadian foreign policy in the Pacific region dealing specifically with economic growth, social justice, quality of life, and peace and security, 1969-73.

1830. Keenleyside, T. A. CANADA AND THE PACIFIC: POLI-CIES FOR ECONOMIC GROWTH. *Pacific Affairs [Canada] 1973 46(1): 5-28.* Questions the Canadian government's effectiveness in imple-menting Pacific trade policies set forth in its major foreign policy study of 1970. The dramatic rise in trade 1965-70 probably caused the govern-

ment to overestimate Canadian trade prospects in the Pacific. Although the government has given increased attention to this area, new trade restrictions and a relative decline in investment developed in the 1970's. Canada will need to follow the Japanese pattern of government-industry cooperation in order to compete successfully. A policy of economic growth for Canada may be incompatible with the interests of developing countries in the Pacific. Based on government documents; 87 notes.
S. H. Frank

1831. Kempthorne, Marlene. AMNESTY INTERNATIONAL. *Can. Labour 1975 20(2): 31-34.* Reports on the work of Amnesty International, "founded in 1961 in London, England, by Peter Benenson, a lawyer, who was appalled at the prison conditions under which political prisoners were held." Mentions Canadian chapters.

1832. Kennedy, John F. ON *DIPLOMACY IN THE NUCLEAR AGE. Internat. J. [Canada] 1973/74 29(1): 67-70.* Republishes a review which appeared in the *Saturday Review* (August 1, 1959) of lectures given by late Canadian prime minister, Lester B. Pearson, and published as *Diplomacy in the Nuclear Age* (Harvard University Press, 1959).   S

1833. Keyfitz, Nathan. CONTINENTAL POPULATION AND RESOURCES. *Am. Rev. of Can. Studies 1973 3(1): 146-163.* Proposes a strategy for the use, both domestic and foreign, of Canadian natural resources, taking into account use, 1950's-70's, and concluding that export of natural resources can bring about continental security as well as economic prosperity; covers timber, metals, water, fossil fuel, and raw materials.

1834. Khripunov, I. CANADA AND LATIN AMERICA. *Int. Affairs [USSR] 1976 (9): 110-114.* To diminish US political and economic influence in the Western Hemisphere, Canada and several Latin American countries have opened diplomatic relations during 1970-76.

1835. Kinsman, Jeremy. PURSUING THE REALISTIC GOAL OF CLOSER CANADA EEC LINKS. *Internat. Perspectives [Canada] 1973 (1): 22-27.* Closer economic ties with an enlarged European Economic Community will diversify Canada's external economic relations. This diversification will reduce the vulnerability of the Canadian economy.
L. S. Frey

1836. Kirton, John J. FOREIGN POLICY DECISION-MAKING IN THE TRUDEAU GOVERNMENT: PROMISE AND PERFORMANCE. *Int. J. [Canada] 1978 33(2): 287-311.* Notes considerable imperfections in decisionmaking although there is some indication of new initiatives following the victory of the Parti Québécois in 1976. 11 notes.
R. V. Kubicek

1837. Kojima, Kiyoshi. TAIHEIYŌ CHIIKI NO KEIZAI TŌGŌ [Economic integration in the Asian-Pacific region]. *Hitotsubashi ronsō [Japan] 1975 74(4): 1-21.* Advocates organizing a Pacific Free Trade Area to develop the economy and trade of the Pacific area, with the United States, Canada, Japan, Australia, and New Zealand as the leading countries. Compares PAFTA with other existing economic organizations, and considers its role and prospects in the modern international economy. Notes.
T. Kamika

1838. Kyba, Patrick. ENVIRONMENTAL CO-OPERATION TO MEET POLITICAL OBJECTIVES. *Int. Perspectives [Canada] 1977 (July-August): 11-14.* Of the 60 international environmental organizations to which Canada belongs, NATO's Committee on the Challenges of Modern Society (CCMS) is unique in that Canada's motives for membership are political, not environmental. The value of CCMS-sponsored pilot projects is generally recognized, but the committee suffers from many weaknesses and will never be a high-priority environmental organization. Canada remains a member because it pleases the United States and presents an additional platform for explanation of Canada's environmental views.
E. S. Palais

1839. Langley, James. CANADA'S DIALOGUE WITH THE EEC: PROBLEMS OF MAKING IT EFFECTIVE. *Internat. Perspectives [Canada] 1974 (1): 28-31.*

1840. Laux, Jeanne Kirk. CSCE: SYMBOL OF THE SEARCH FOR EAST-WEST CO-OPERATION. *Internat. Perspectives [Canada] 1974 (5): 23-26.* Evaluates the work of the Conference on Security and Cooperation in Europe, 1973-74, and international relations among Europe, Canada, and the United States.

1841. Laxer, James. IMPERIAL OIL CALLS THE TUNE. *Can. Dimension [Canada] 1976 11(8): 27-33.* Discusses the Imperial Oil Company, a multinational oil corporation in Canada; because of major distrust of the aims of the oil company (and its head, Jack A. Armstrong), proposes public ownership of Imperial Oil in order to establish priorities in energy development.

1842. Leach, Richard H. CANADA AND THE COMMONWEALTH—ASSUMING A LEADERSHIP. *Internat. Perspectives [Canada] 1973 (3): 24-29.* "Canada has moved from automatic and ritualist support of the Commonwealth to active leadership in it." The Trudeau government in particular has played a prominent role in British Commonwealth activities.
L. S. Frey

1843. LeBlanc, Lawrence J. ECONOMIC, SOCIAL AND CULTURAL RIGHTS AND THE INTERAMERICAN SYSTEM. *J. of Interam. Studies and World Affairs 1977 19(1): 61-82.* Concern for human rights is a relatively new (post-World War II) concern in foreign relations. The principal inter-American human rights documents—the American Declaration of the Rights and Duties of Man and the American Convention on Human Rights—reflect the trend toward more successful responses to civil and political rights than social, economic, and cultural rights. This is probably because the former only require noninterference by the states, while the latter require active assistance and involvement of the state in society. Ref.
T. D. Schoonover

1844. Legault, Albert. NUCLEAR POLICY SHOULD BE MORE OPEN AND LESS AMBIGUOUS. *Internat. Perspectives [Canada] 1976 (1): 8-13.* Discusses the need for less government secrecy about Canada's supplying nuclear technology to India and other nations, 1968-70's, emphasizing the implications of the Treaty on the Non-Proliferation of Nuclear Weapons (1968).

1845. Léger, Jean-Marc. BUILDING THE FRENCH-SPEAKING COMMUNITY: AN EXCITING VENTURE IN THE ART OF CO-OPERATION. *Int. Perspectives [Canada] 1975 (6): 50-57.* Discusses attempts to form cooperative bonds between French-speaking nations in international relations, 1950's-70's, including France, regions of Africa, and Quebec, Canada.

1846. Lemelin, Claude. OBJECTIVES VIEWED AS TOO VAGUE IN OTTAWA'S APPROACH TO EUROPE. *Internat. Perspectives [Canada] 1974 (1): 32-36.*

1847. Lentner, Howard H. FOREIGN POLICY DECISION MAKING: THE CASE OF CANADA AND NUCLEAR WEAPONS. *World Pol. 1976 29(1): 29-66.* Foreign policy decision making is the result of a complex political process in which the political values and style of the chief executive play a large part. The case of Canada's decision, in 1963, to acquire nuclear weapons illustrates that external events and pressures generated by Canada's international obligations were processed through complex political interactions. The Government of Prime Minister Diefenbaker was unable to take the nuclear weapons decision because of two splits in the Cabinet, only one of which was pertinent to nuclear weapons policy. The decision was taken by Leader of the Opposition Pearson alone and in conformity with his personal values, because of his political style which commanded deference. The approach used combines historical detail with political analysis.
J

1848. Levy, David. MAKING A MARK IN MOSCOW... *Internat. Perspectives [Canada] 1974 (1): 20-22.* Discusses the 1973 diplomatic mission of Canadian External Affairs Minister Mitchell Sharp to Moscow.

1849. Levy, Gary. CANADIAN PARTICIPATION IN PARLIAMENTARY ASSOCIATIONS. *Can. J. of Pol. Sci. 1974 7(2): 352-357.* Reviews procedures used to select Canadian parliamentarians who attend meetings of six such informal organizations designed to promote international understanding through personal contact. 27 notes.
R. V. Kubicek

1850. Leyton-Brown, David. CANADA, FRANCE AND BRITAIN AS HOSTS TO MULTINATIONALS. *Int. Perspectives [Canada] 1975 (5): 39-43.* Discusses political and economic aspects of multinational corporations in Canada, France, and Great Britain in the 1960's and 70's, emphasizing labor relations, export controls, and antitrust policy.

1851. Litvak, Isaiah A. and Maule, Christopher J. CANADIAN INVESTMENT ABROAD: IN SEARCH OF A POLICY. *Int. J. [Canada] 1975-76 31(1): 159-179.* Illustrates, through examples of corporate activity in Guyana, Peru, Spain, and Malaysia, problems associated with Canadian direct investment abroad and what government response should be. 3 tables, 24 notes.   R. V. Kubicek

1852. Litvak, Isaiah and Maule, Christopher J. NATIONALISATION IN THE CARIBBEAN BAUXITE INDUSTRY. *Internat. Affairs [Great Britain] 1975 51(1): 43-59.* Examines the role of the Canadian government in the light of the Guyanan government's nationalization of a bauxite subsidiary of Alcan Aluminium, Ltd. in 1971. Suggests implications for Canadian foreign policy and Canadian-based multinational corporations. Primary and secondary sources; 30 notes.   P. J. Beck

1853. Litvak, I. A. and McMillan, C. H. A NEW UNITED STATES POLICY ON EAST-WEST TRADE: SOME IMPLICATIONS FOR CANADA. *Internat. J. [Canada] 1973 28(2): 297-314.* Improved relations between the United States and the USSR and between the United States and Communist China will produce a freer climate for trade. Because this trade will be more competitive than that which Canadian business firms have enjoyed, they will have to be far better informed and more imaginative and aggressive in their commercial dealings with the East. 11 notes, appendix.   R. V. Kubicek

1854. Lotz, Jim. 200-MILE LIMIT REVIVES ATLANTIC FISHERIES. *Can. Geographic [Canada] 1978 97(2): 34-39.* Formerly monopolized by large foreign fleets, Canada's rich Atlantic fishing grounds began reenergizing Canada's fishing industry when the government declared a 200-mile limit on off-shore fishing, 1977.

1855. Lyon, Peyton V. THE KEY QUESTION FOR PEARSON: WHAT KIND OF WORLD DO WE WANT? *Internat. Perspectives [Canada] 1974 (2): 73-75.* Reviews the memoirs of one of Canada's Secretaries of State for External Affairs, *Mike: The Memoirs of the Right Honourable Lester B. Pearson, Volume II (1948-1957)* (University of Toronto Press, 1973), edited by John A. Munro and Alex I. Inglis.   S

1856. MacEachen, Allan J. EPILOGUE—THE CHALLENGE OF CONTINUITY: DIRECTIONS FOR FOREIGN POLICY. *Internat. Perspectives [Canada] 1975 (6): 62-66.* Discusses economic, political and military aspects of Canada's overall foreign policy from the 1950's-70's.

1857. MacLaren, Alasdair. CANADA NEEDS TO RECONCILE FOREIGN AND DEFENSE POLICIES. *Int. Perspectives [Canada] 1977 Mar.-Apr.: 22-25.* Following the onset of the "Third Option" program in which independence from the United States was asserted, Canada's defense policy has been out of kilter with its foreign policy exhibiting a preference for nationalism rather than internationalism.

1858. Mahant, E. E. CANADA AND THE EUROPEAN COMMUNITY: THE NEW POLICY. *Int. Affairs [Great Britain] 1976 52(4): 551-564.* Examines the course of Canadian policy toward the European Economic Community, especially the factors resulting in the adoption of a "new policy" in the 1970's, as seen in the conclusion of the Framework Agreement in July 1976. Primary and secondary sources; 35 notes.   P. J. Beck

1859. Malmgren, Harald B. THE EVOLVING TRADING SYSTEM. *Pro. of the Acad. of Pol. Sci. 1976 32(2): 124-136.* Analyzes Canadian and American trade patterns, both bilateral and global. Both see the need to change the existing system, but differ markedly on how to do so because their objectives are different. The United States is concerned with the whole world trade system. Canada is concerned with its own trade, much of which is with the United States. But Canada is the more reliant of the two on world trade. Each nation has made wrong moves, though for different reasons, and when the economic chickens come home to roost, Canada will be the major loser. Note.   V. L. Human

1860. Manning, Bayless et al. ENTENTE CORDIALE? DIVERGENCE AND ACCOMMODATION: APPROACHES TO MULTILATERAL ISSUES. *Am. Soc. of Int. Law Pro. 1974 68: 204-225.* Examines the similarities among US, Canadian, and Mexican positions on foreign policy issues 1945-74, and discusses attempts by each nation to reach diplomatic understandings when their policies diverged.

1861. Manor, F. S. BY ABANDONING PEACE-KEEPING NATO COULD BE REINFORCED. *Int. Perspectives [Canada] 1977 (July-Aug.): 28-32.* Canada has been an enthusiastic supporter of a UN police force since 1956, when Prime Minister Lester B. Pearson sent troops to Suez. Because of the high cost of maintaining such forces and the failure of subsequent peace-keeping missions, Canada should withdraw its forces from Cyprus and reassign them to NATO. Other reasons cited are the morale-destroying nature of such assignments, the low prestige of the UN service, the lack of cooperation from Communist members, and the relative impotence of lightly armed forces.   E. S. Palais

1862. Marshall, C. J. NEGOTIATING NATO DECLARATION: THE DIFFICULT ROAD TO CONSENSUS. *Internat. Perspectives [Canada] 1974 (5): 32-36.* Studies the Declaration of Atlantic Principles signed by the members of NATO in June 1974 in Ottawa, Canada.

1863. Marshall, C. J. OF ARMIES AND POLITICS: CANADA'S FORCES TAKE STOCK IN DEFENSE STRUCTURE REVIEW. *Internat. Perspectives [Canada] 1976 (1): 26-30.* Discusses government reviews of economic aspects of Canada's defense policy, military strategy, and role in NATO from 1973-76.

1864. Matthews, Robert O. CANADA'S RELATIONS WITH AFRICA. *Int. J. [Canada] 1975 30(3): 536-568.* Examines the ambivalence in Canada's foreign aid and trade relations with Africa, 1970-75; 4 tables, 27 notes.   R. V. Kubicek

1865. Maybee, J. R. THE PROBLEMS IN PROVIDING AID TO CANADIANS IN TROUBLE ABROAD. *Internat. Perspectives [Canada] 1974 (3): 39-44.* Discusses the diplomacy of Canada's External Affairs Department in handling travelers' problems.   S

1866. Meekison, J. Peter. PROVINCIAL ACTIVITY ADDS NEW DIMENSION TO FEDERALISM. *Int. Perspectives [Canada] 1977 Mar.-Apr.: 8-11.* Assesses the foreign policy role of Canada's provincial governments in the 1970's.

1867. Mégélas, Roger. A NEW KIND OF DIALOGUE BETWEEN CANADA AND CUBA. *Int. Perspectives [Canada] 1976 (4): 19-21.* Discusses the role of the creation of new economic markets for Canadian products in improved foreign relations and trade between Canada and Cuba in 1975-76.

1868. Meredith, Brian. THE POLITICS OF THOSE MULTINATIONAL ENTITIES. *Int. Perspectives [Canada] 1975 (5): 43-47.* Discusses the political influence of multinational corporations in foreign relations, the UN, and Canada in the 1970's.

1869. M'Gonigle, R. Michael and Zacher, Mark W. INTERNATIONAL PROBLEM OF MARINE POLLUTION. *Int. Perspectives [Canada] 1978 (Mar.-Apr.): 8-12.* Because of a growing environmental concern, Canada has become one of the most active participants in international efforts to control marine pollution. Pollution caused by ships and land-based sources is the subject of deliberations of such bodies as the United Nations Conference on the Law of the Sea (UNCLOS) and the Intergovernmental Maritime Consultative Organization (IMCO). Because marine pollution is a small part of the global environmental crisis, Canada and other nations must not only ratify conventions in this area but should also change their domestic laws to conform to such agreements. Photo.   E. S. Palais

1870. Moynagh, Michael. THE NEGOTIATION OF THE COMMONWEALTH SUGAR AGREEMENT, 1949-1951. *J. of Commonwealth and Comparative Pol. [Great Britain] 1977 15(2): 170-190.* Examines the background to the signing of the Commonwealth Sugar Agreement, the attitudes of Canada, New Zealand, and Great Britain, the arguments for and against the continuation of Britain's wartime system of bulk purchase, and the establishment of a permanent consumer subsidy. Analyzes the negotiations, the economic implications of the various proposals, the divergent positions of colonies and Dominions, and the economic aims of each. Britain wanted an agreement to promote economic development in the colonies and to alleviate its dollar shortage; it did not want an extension of bulk purchase unaltered, nor did it desire to include the Dominions. Based on the Minutes of the CSA Conference, and correspondence between H. R. F. Watson and the Head Office (Correspondance Dept. CSR Ltd. Sydney). 9 tables with details of Commonwealth production and export of raw sugar, proposed export quotas between Britain and Australia, Colonial Office proposals for allocating colonial quotas, and guaranteed price markets for Commonwealth producers. 101 notes.　　　　　　　　　　　　　　C. Anstey

1871.　Munro, Gordon R.　EXTENDED FISHERIES JURISDICTION AND INTERNATIONAL CO-OPERATION.　*Int. Perspectives [Canada] 1978 (Mar.-Apr.): 12-18.* Over-exploitation of commercial fisheries has resulted in strong pressure on the Canadian government to exclude foreign fishing fleets. The establishment in 1977 of an exclusive fishing zone extending 200 miles off Canada's coast was a significant step in that process. Nevertheless, Canada has implemented this policy in a spirit of international cooperation: she permits ships from other nations to fish in Canadian waters under special arrangements and participates in the United Nations Conference on the Law of the Sea (UNCLOS). Canada also intends to support the proposed Northwest Atlantic Fisheries Consultative Organization (NAFCO). 2 photos.
　　　　　　　　　　　　　　　　　　E. S. Palais

1872.　Munton, Don and Poel, Dale H.　ELECTORAL ACCOUNTABILITY AND CANADIAN FOREIGN POLICY: THE CASE OF FOREIGN INVESTMENT.　*Int. J. [Canada] 1977-78 33(1): 217-247.* Analysis of 1974 election survey data shows that the influence of the foreign investment issue did not provide much support for the argument that voters hold governments accountable for their foreign policies. 3 tables, 75 notes.　　　　　　　　　　R. V. Kubicek

1873.　Murray, Geoffrey.　GLIMPSES OF SUEZ 1956.　*Internat. J. [Canada] 1973/74 29(1): 46-66.* Reviews Canada's contribution to the UN when coping with the Suez crisis (1956), particularly the efforts of Lester B. Pearson, Canadian prime minister.　R. V. Kubicek

1874.　Murray, J. Alex and Gerace, Mary C.　MULTINATIONAL BUSINESS AND CANADIAN GOVERNMENT AFFAIRS. *Queen's Q. [Canada] 1973 80(2): 222-232.* Discusses an attempted meeting in April 1972 between the Canadian government and international corporations with Canadian interests. In light of strong nationalism and other issues relating directly to multinational businesses, communication between the two is important; but the talks proposed by the American firm, Business International, fell through. This failure revealed "the lack of an organizational structure within the . . . government to deal with foreign investment problems, American business' frequent insensitivity to Canadian problems, and the growing concern of the public over foreign control and takeover." Analyzes the events which caused the proposal to fail and advocates the formal establishment of communication channels. 4 notes.　　　　　　　　　　　　　J. A. Casada

1875.　Murray, J. Alex and LeDuc, Lawrence.　PUBLIC OPINION AND FOREIGN POLICY OPTIONS IN CANADA.　*Public Opinion Q. 1976-77 40(4): 488-496.* This article examines the role of public opinion in Canada's attempt to lessen its dependence on the United States and seek closer ties with European and Asian countries. Employing national survey data collected over a three-year period, the authors argue that widespread public support for new directions in foreign policy has not developed in Canada in spite of the climate of increasing nationalism and the shift in government policy. Attitudes toward the problem of foreign investment, domestic economic issues, trade agreements, and Canadian participation in international peacekeeping forces are also reported.
　　　　　　　　　　　　　　　　　　　　　J

1876.　Noble, John J.　CANADA'S CONTINUING SEARCH FOR ACCEPTABLE NUCLEAR SAFEGUARDS.　*Int. Perspectives [Canada] 1978 (July-Aug.): 42-48.* As a supplier of both nuclear fuel and reactor technology, Canada has developed stringent safeguards in support of nuclear nonproliferation. Her injunction on the use of Canadian ura-

nium for military purposes was intended to offset weaknesses in provisions of the International Atomic Energy Agency and the Treaty on the Non-Proliferation of Nuclear Weapons. Canada's experience with this policy indicates that unilateral safeguards are insufficient and that international consensus among suppliers and recipients of nuclear materials and technology is required.　　　　　　　　　E. S. Palais

1877.　Nossal, Kim Richard.　CHUNGKING PRISM: COGNITIVE PROCESS AND INTELLIGENCE FAILURE.　*Int. J. [Canada] 1977 32(3): 559-576.* Examines the perceptions of the government of China held by Canada's first ambassador to China, Victor Wentworth Odlum. Covers 1943-46. Primary sources; 52 notes.　R. V. Kubicek

1878.　Ogelsby, J. C. M.　LATIN AMERICA.　*Int. J. [Canada] 1978 33(2): 401-407.* A critique of Canada's Latin American policies with particular reference to the Trudeau administration's 1970 position paper on the subject, *Latin America.* 19 notes.

1879.　Oglesby, Jack.　CONTINUING U.S. INFLUENCE ON CANADA-CUBA RELATIONS.　*Int. Perspectives [Canada] 1975 (5): 34-38.* Emphasizes politics, trade, and sugar prices, 1960's-70's.

1880.　Okuma, Tadayuki.　PASSIVE JAPAN: ACTIVE CANADA. *Int. J. [Canada] 1978 33(2): 443-448.* An assessment of Canadian foreign policy under the Trudeau administration from the point of view of Japan. 4 notes.　　　　　　　　　　　　　R. V. Kubicek

1881.　O'Neill, Robert.　CONSTRAINT WITH HONOUR.　*Internat. J. [Canada] 1974 29(3): 350-355.* Reviews Denis Stairs' *The Diplomacy of Constraint: Canada, the Korean War, and the United States* (Toronto: University of Toronto Press, 1973).　R. V. Kubicek

1882.　Orr, Dale.　THE INDUSTRIAL COMPOSITION OF U.S. EXPORTS AND SUBSIDIARY SALES TO THE CANADIAN MARKET: A COMMENT.　*Am. Econ. Rev. 1975 65(1): 230-235.* In questioning the conclusions of an earlier paper by Thomas Horst, Orr believes that Horst's findings are weakened at the three-digit level analysis of his model. Tariffs, nevertheless, help determine whether US firms penetrate the Canadian markets by imports or production in Canada. In his reply Horst maintains that both common sense and published research indicate the complexity of the issue and that his paper was an oversimplification.　　　　　　　　　　　　　D. K. Pickens

1883.　Ørvik, Nils.　SEMI-NEUTRALITY AND CANADA'S SECURITY.　*Internat. J. [Canada] 1974 29(2): 186-215.* NATO members' selective participation in NATO only when NATO's objectives coincide with national interests is a kind of semi-neutrality and is occurring more and more frequently. Canada, in these circumstances, should define its role to ensure an effective contribution to Atlantic security. 32 notes.
　　　　　　　　　　　　　　　　　　R. V. Kubicek;

1884.　Page, Donald M.　CANADA AS THE EXPONENT OF NORTH AMERICAN IDEALISM.　*Am. Rev. of Can. Studies 1973 3(2): 30-46.* Canada set a tone of idealism for peace in international relations which has influenced the United States, 1904-32; includes Canada's advocacy of international arbitration, conciliation, and disarmament, and its policy toward the League of Nations.

1885.　Page, Don.　CANADIAN IMAGES OF THE COLD WAR 1946-7.　*Int. J. [Canada] 1977 32(3): 577-604.* It is misleading to ascribe Canadian support for a Western alliance merely to a supposed hostile image of a Communist threat posed by the Soviet Union. Based on secret documents by Canadian diplomats recently made available for study; 47 notes.　　　　　　　　　　　　　R. V. Kubicek

1886.　Painchaud, Paul.　FÉDÉRALISME ET THÉORIES DE POLITIQUE ÉTRANGÈRE [Federalism and theories of foreign policy]. *Études Internationales [Canada] 1974 5(1): 25-44.* Examines the theories of foreign policy as a facet of international relations. Questions whether federalism is a legitimate vehicle to discuss foreign policy. Notes the problem in federalism which permits the coexistence of individual state relations and national foreign policy. Examines the types of international activity a federal state may embrace; uses Canada as a model. Secondary sources; chart, 51 notes.　　　　　　　J. F. Harrington

1887. Passaris, Constantine. "INPUT" OF FOREIGN POLICY TO IMMIGRATION EQUATION. *Int. Perspectives [Canada] 1976 (6): 23-28.* Examines population and skilled labor concerns in Canada's immigration policy and its relationship to foreign policy and refugees, from the 1950's-70's.

1888. Peacock, Don. SELLING CANDU TO BRITAIN: A VENTURE IN PUBLIC DIPLOMACY. *Int. Perspectives [Canada] 1976 (1): 3-8.* Discusses Canada's use of public relations techniques in attempting to convince Great Britain to maintain Canadian nuclear power technology in 1973-74.

1889. Pearson, G. A. H. ORDER OUT OF CHAOS? SOME REFLECTIONS ON FOREIGN-POLICY PLANNING IN CANADA. *Int. J. [Canada] 1977 32(4): 756-768.* Discusses the founding and work of the Policy Analysis Group of Canada's Department of External Affairs.   S

1890. Pentland, C. C. L'ÉVOLUTION DE LA POLITIQUE ÉTRANGÈRE DE LA COMMUNAUTÉ EUROPÉENE: LE CONTEXTE TRANSATLANTIQUE [The development of the European Community's foreign policy: the transatlantic context]. *Études Int. [Canada] 1978 9(1): 106-125.* Discusses the nature of the European Economic Community's foreign policy. Analyzes EEC relations with the United States, and to a lesser degree with Canada, through two models: externalization, which utilizes a stimulus-reaction approach, and extension, which emphasizes traditional transatlantic relations. Secondary sources; 16 notes.   J. F. Harrington, Jr.

1891. Pentland, Charles. LINKAGE POLITICS: CANADA'S CONTRACT AND THE DEVELOPMENT OF THE EUROPEAN COMMUNITY'S EXTERNAL RELATIONS. *Int. J. [Canada] 1977 32(2): 207-231.* Examines the shaping of the Framework Agreement for Commercial and Economic Cooperation signed by Canada and the European Economic Community on 6 July 1975. Notes the difficulty a state such as Canada has to get the EEC to develop a foreign policy toward it. 45 notes.   R. V. Kubicek

1892. Pick, Alfred. PROTOCOL SIGNED AT SAN JOSE PROVIDES REFORM OF RIO TREATY. *Int. Perspectives [Canada] 1975 (5): 25-30.* Discusses Canada's role in attempts to reform the administrative structure of the Organization of American States, emphasizing issues in territorial and international law in the 1945 Rio Treaty and the 1975 San José resolution.

1893. Pilisi, Paul. BOTH EUROPE AND CANADA CAN BENEFIT FROM THE LINK. *Int. Perspectives [Canada] 1976 (6): 8-11.* Discusses Canada's 1976 "contractual link" with the European Economic Community to strengthen economic relations.

1894. Plumptre, T. DIPLOMACY: OBSOLETE OR ESSENTIAL. *Queen's Q. [Canada] 1973 80(4): 503-520.* Analyzes foreign affairs and the present and future functions of diplomats. Assesses contemporary diplomacy and evaluates the currently fashionable attacks on that profession. Diplomats fill a vital and important role in government. 8 notes.   J. A. Casada

1895. Povolotskii, V. INOSTRANNYI KAPITAL VO VNESHNEI TORGOVLE KANADY [Foreign capital in the foreign trade of Canada]. *Mirovaia Ekonomika i Mezhdunarodnye Otnosheniia [USSR] 1976 (11): 64-74.* Statistical analysis of the role of multinational corporations in Canada's foreign trade, with discussion of attempts made since 1973 to control foreign investment.

1896. Preeg, Ernest H. ECONOMIC BLOCS AND US FOREIGN POLICY. *Internat. Organization 1974 28(2): 233-246.* Points out that the most far-reaching configuration of economic blocs "would be the evolution of regional groupings within and around the three industrialized concentrations of economic power in North America, Europe, and Japan . . . Each of the three has a highly self-contained industrial structure, and a well-developed trade which is concentrated internally within the region and is extended to a number of neighboring countries . . . A well-functioning, cooperative, international economic system will depend on the policies of the advanced industrialized countries for some time to come." Within this grouping, there appears to be emerging a three-tiered policy framework: 1) multilateral or non-discriminatory policies; 2) harmonized policies among the industrialized countries as a group; and 3) tripolar policies, where there are three distinct policy approaches to meet the special needs and circumstances of Western Europe, North America, and Japan. Note.   D. D. Cameron

1897. Regenstreif, Peter. CANADA'S FOREIGN POLICY. *Current Hist. 1977 72(426): 150-153, 180-181.* Chronicles Canada's foreign policy 1945-76, including post-1970 diplomacy and attempts to build relations with world powers other than the United States.

1898. Rigin, Y. CANADA IN THE MODERN WORLD. *Int. Affairs [USSR] 1973 (2): 57-62.* Examines how US foreign investment in Canada has led to military-political alliances between the two nations and considers the development of foreign relations between Canada and the USSR since 1970.

1899. Ritchie, Charles. WHAT ARE DIPLOMATS MADE OF? *Int. J. [Canada] 1974-75 30(1): 15-23.* Discusses recent Canadian writings about the role of diplomacy, questioning the relevance of traditional methods and channels of diplomacy and negotiations.

1900. Ritchie, Ronald S. ASSESSING THE ENERGY ISSUES FROM A CANADIAN PERSPECTIVE. *Internat. Perspectives [Canada] 1974 (2): 13-18.*

1901. Romanow, Walter Ivan. A DEVELOPING CANADIAN IDENTITY: A CONSEQUENCE OF A DEFENSIVE REGULATORY POSTURE FOR BROADCASTING. *Gazette [Netherlands] 1976 22(1): 26-37.* Though considered censorship by some, the regulations governing Canadian content enacted by the Board of Broadcast Governors in 1959 (which stipulated that 55% of all broadcasting in both public and private television stations had to be of Canadian origin), have proven effective, leading to the recognition that Canada lacks institutions offering adequate programs to study mass media, and point to a certain concentration in media ownership.

1902. Ruddick, Valley. CAN THE UN AGREE UPON UNDERSEA RIGHTS? *Can. Geographical J. 1975 90(3): 12-21.* Discusses Canada's position at the UN Conference on the Law of the Sea held in 1974 to discuss undersea rights, marine pollution, and protection of the world's marine environment.   S

1903. Safarin, A. E. FOREIGN INVESTMENT IN PRIMARY INDUSTRIES. *Pro. of the Acad. of Pol. Sci. 1976 32(2): 75-87.* Canadian concern about foreign influence in the national economy is increasing. Most of this influence is from the United States. Canada did not have the money or technical skills to develop its natural resources, so foreign investments were necessary. This has changed. The national government wants to use its resources and economic power as bargaining instruments. The problem is complicated by economic competition between the provinces. Harsh nationalization policies are unlikely, but international firms will find it more difficult to establish themselves in Canada.
                                                               V. L. Human

1904. Sanger, Clyde. THE INTERNATIONAL DEVELOPMENT RESEARCH CENTRE: CANADA'S HELP TO THE WORLD'S RURAL POOR. *Can. Geographical J. 1974 88(5): 14-21.* Describes the Centre's projects in developing nations.   S

1905. Saul, John S. CANADA AND SOUTHERN AFRICA. *Can. Dimension [Canada] 1977 12(1): 46-51.* Despite condemnation by many Canadian political groups since the 1960's, trade with South Africa and Rhodesia continues.

1906. Sauter, John V. SPECIALIZATION AND TRADE: CASE STUDY: THE NORTH AMERICAN BICYCLE MARKET: MEXICO, CANADA, AND THE UNITED STATES. *Inter-Am. Econ. Affairs 1977 30(4): 3-15.* Compares bicycle production costs and methods of North American countries and finds that increased US and Canadian productivity has been used to offset lower Mexican labor costs. Originally presented to the North American Economic Studies Association during the annual meeting of the Southern Economic Association, November 1976. Primary and secondary sources; 4 tables, 14 notes.
                                                               D. A. Franz

1907. Saywell, William. PIERRE AND THE PACIFIC: A POST-MORTEM. *Int. J. [Canada] 1978 33(2): 408-414.* A critique of the Trudeau administration's policies toward Asia, particularly China and Japan.   R. V. Kubicek

1908. Seastone, D. A. THE POTENTIAL IMPACT OF CANADA ON NORTH AMERICAN ENERGY SUPPLIES. *Am. Rev. of Can. Studies 1973 3(1): 26-38.* Offers statistics for Canadian fuel and energy consumption and production during the 1960's and 70's with projections concerning Canada's impact on world energy policy and supply.

1909. Sewell, James P. CANADA AND THE FUNCTIONAL AGENCIES: THE NIEO'S CHALLENGE, TRUDEAU'S RESPONSE. *Int. J. [Canada] 1978 33(2): 339-356.* Reviews Canada's commitments and options concerning the specialized agencies of the UN, especially with reference to the establishment of NIEO (a New International Economic Order). 21 notes.   R. V. Kubicek

1910. Sherfield, Lord. ON THE DIPLOMATIC TRAIL WITH LBP: SOME EPISODES 1930-1972. *Internat. J. [Canada] 1973/74 29(1): 71-89.* Short accounts of several international meetings including the League of Nations on economic sanctions, the Quebec conference (1943) and Hyde Park meeting (1944) on nuclear energy, and the United Nations and the formation of the FAO and UNRRA (1943-1944) in which the author and Lester B. Pearson, the late Canadian prime minister, were involved. 10 notes.   R. V. Kubicek

1911. Siemens, L. B. SUCCESS OF CANADA-THAI UNIVERSITY AID. *Can. Geographical J. 1974 88(3): 14-21.* Describes experiences in 1965-67 and in 1973 with the Canadian International Development Agency and the Thai government's contract for University of Manitoba professors to assist in developing a new university, Khon Kaen, in the northeastern part of the country; 20 photos.   S

1912. Small, A. Douglas. THE DEVELOPING DIALOGUE BETWEEN CANADA AND ASEAN. *Int. Perspectives [Canada] 1978 (Mar.-Apr.): 28-31.* The purpose of the Association of Southeast Asian Nations (ASEAN), founded in 1967, is to achieve closer political, economic, social and cultural cooperation among countries of the region. Because ASEAN recognizes the need for constructive relations between industrialized and developing nations, the organization has established formal communications ("dialogues") with Australia, New Zealand, Japan, the United States, and Canada. Canada, which has a long history of involvement in the region, held two such dialogues in 1977, in which agreements were reached to expand trade, development assistance and industrial cooperation. 2 photos.   E. S. Palais

1913. Smart, Ian. ALASTAIR BUCHAN AS STRATEGIST. *Int. J. [Canada] 1976 31(4): 631-647.* Evaluates the work and insight of the late Alastair Buchan (1918-75), an expert on the Atlantic region and former director of the [International] Institute of Strategic Studies. 24 notes.   R. V. Kubicek

1914. Smith, Arnold. COMMONWEALTH: CAN IT COMBAT THE WORLD'S DIVISIVE TRENDS? *Internat. Perspectives [Canada] 1973 (3): 18-24.* Analyzes the evolution of the British Commonwealth in the post-war years and stresses the Canadian role in this development.   L. S. Frey

1915. Smith, Norman. PEARSON, PEOPLE, AND PRESS. *Internat. J. [Canada] 1973/74 29(1): 5-23.* Recollections in praise of the diplomacy and rapport with journalists of Lester B. Pearson, late prime minister of Canada, by a retired journalist who knew him well from 1936 on.   R. V. Kubicek

1916. Soames, Christopher; Creery, Tim; and Sharp, Mitchell. CANADA AND THE EUROPEAN COMMUNITY. *Behind the Headlines [Canada] 1974 32(6): 1-39.* Soames envisions an expanded and energetic worldwide community tackling and mastering all types of economic problems. Creery of the *Montreal Gazette* sees Canada expanding its relations and interests in Europe. Sharp declares that Canada will not substitute a unified Europe for the United States, and will seek a policy of economic and political diversification.   R. D. Frederick

1917. Soderlund, Walter C. and Wagenberg, Ronald H. THE EDITOR AND EXTERNAL AFFAIRS: THE 1972 AND 1974 ELECTION CAMPAIGNS. *Int. J. [Canada] 1976 31(2): 244-254.* Content analysis of election editorials from a sample of 16 newspapers notes lack of treatment of foreign affairs generally and of Canada's external relations specifically. 3 tables, 9 notes.

1918. Stairs, Denis. PRESENT IN MODERATION: LESTER PEARSON AND THE CRAFT OF DIPLOMACY. *Internat. J. [Canada] 1973/74 29(1): 143-153.* A review article of the second volume of *Mike: The Memoirs of the Right Honourable Lester B. Pearson,* edited by John A. Munro and Alex I. Inglis (Ontario, U. of Toronto, 1973).   S

1919. Stairs, Denis. THE PRESS AND FOREIGN POLICY IN CANADA. *Int. J. [Canada] 1976 31(2): 223-243.* On the basis of interviews with Ottawa journalists and foreign service officers, examines the coverage Canadian newspapers give to international affairs and the foreign policy of their country. 31 notes.   R. V. Kubicek

1920. Starnes, John. QUEBEC, CANADA, AND THE ALLIANCE. *Survival [Great Britain] 1977 19(5): 212-215.* Speculates about the effects of successful Quebec separatism on its relations with Canada and in the Western Alliance.

1921. Stethem, Nicholas. CANADA'S CRISIS: THE DANGERS. *Foreign Policy 1977-78 (29): 56-64.* The independence of Quebec would disrupt the strong and united North America which has been so vital in the East-West balance of power. Strategically important, Quebec lies athwart the major bombing route from the Soviet Union to the most populous and industrialized areas of Canada and the United States. The loss of that province would cripple the NORAD system of continental defense. There are domestic dangers involved as well, for the question already may have gone far enough to make inevitable some form of internal violence, whether from separatists, the federal government, or antiseparatist minorities within Quebec. Note.   T. L. Powers

1922. Stevens, Geoffrey. MR. TRUDEAU WOOS EUROPE: CANADA'S ATTEMPTS TO LESSEN DEPENDENCE ON THE UNITED STATES. *Round Table [Great Britain] 1975 (260): 401-409.* Explores Canada's attempts to form a closer relationship with Europe, focusing on Prime Minister Pierre Elliott Trudeau's efforts to establish a "contractual link" with the European Economic Community. Traces US-Canadian relations. Since Confederation, Canada had to resist the "continental pull" of the United States. Canada cannot afford to adopt a European policy antithetical to American interests. The Canada-EEC agreement will be vague, designed to satisfy the architects of the "third option" and placate the United States.   C. Anstey

1923. Story, Donald C. REFLECTING ON THE 'CONCEPTUAL FRAMEWORK.' *Int. J. [Canada] 1978 33(2): 379-387.* A critique of Canadian foreign policy with particular reference to the Trudeau administration's 1970 policy papers, *Foreign Policy for Canadians.* 21 notes.   R. V. Kubicek

1924. Sussman, Leonard R. L'IMPATTO DEI "NEWS MEDIA" SULLA POLITICA ESTERA [The impact of the news media on foreign policy]. *Affari Esteri [Italy] 1977 9(36): 565-576.* Evaluates the differing impact of the mass media on foreign policy in totalitarian and democratic governments (including North American) during the last two decades.

1925. Swanson, Roger Frank. DETERRENCE, DETENTE, AND CANADA. *Pro. of the Acad. of Pol. Sci. 1976 32(2): 100-112.* The Cold War caused a meeting of minds between Canada and the United States on military matters. The USSR must be contained and readiness to fight was unquestioned. The present era of detente has weakened these bonds, though not fatally. Canada is now pursuing a more independent policy, emphasizing detente more and deterrence less than is the case in the United States. This attitude has caused some concern in American councils, but Canada has pursued its own interests in ways which seem calculated to maximize benefits and minimize dangers. 16 notes.   V. L. Human

1926. Tatz, Colin M. FOUR KINDS OF DOMINION. (COMPARATIVE RACE POLITICS IN AUSTRALIA, CANADA, NEW ZEALAND AND SOUTH AFRICA). *Patterns of Prejudice [Great Britain] 1973 7(2): 1-8.* Governments respond to nonwhites with policies of assimilation, integration, or segregation. These policies are all ethnocentric, based on the assumption of white superiority; hence they are racist. Politicians should accept and respond to self-perceived nonwhite realities. Based on primary and secondary sources; 7 notes.

M. W. Szewczyk

1927. Tejchmann, Miroslav. OTÁZKA PŘIJETÍ BULHARSKA, MAĎARSKA A RUMUNSKA DO OSN V LETECH 1947-1955 [The question of Bulgarian, Hungarian, and Rumanian admission to the UN, 1947-55]. *Slovanský Přehled [Czechoslovakia] 1976 62(5): 337-344.* Surveys the difficulties of Bulgaria, Hungary, and Rumania in gaining admission to the UN. The United States exploited the UN in its antisocialist stand, while the USSR used the UN for international understanding and cooperation. Over nearly 10 years these three countries were denied admission five times, allegedly for the violation of human rights. John Foster Dulles was the most persistent opponent of admission, but his ploys led to a dead end when even his allies, Canada and Great Britain, supported admission. The new presence in the UN strengthened the Soviet camp against the imperialist camp. 20 notes.   B. Kimmel

1928. Thakur, Ramesh C. CHANGE AND CONTINUITY IN CANADIAN FOREIGN POLICY. *India Q.: J. of Int. Affairs [India] 1977 33(4): 401-418.* Analyzes Canadian foreign policy during 1947-77. Examines the relations of Canada with the United States and India in particular. Also studies conflicts with the Soviet Union, the emergence of the new nations of Asia and Africa, and issues of trade and sovereignty in the Western Hemisphere. Traces the changing Canadian interests in collective security and unilateralism. Secondary sources; 48 notes.

S. H. Frank

1929. Thapar, Romesh. CANADA'S TRANSITION. *Int. J. [Canada] 1978 33(2): 437-443.* An assessment of Canadian foreign policy under the Trudeau administration from the point of view of the developing nations.   R. V. Kubicek

1930. Thordarson, Bruce. POSTURE AND POLICY: LEADERSHIP IN CANADA'S EXTERNAL AFFAIRS. *Int. J. [Canada] 1976 31(4): 666-691.* Compares the styles and priorities of four prime ministers in the making of Canadian foreign policy. The leaders are Louis St. Laurent, John Diefenbaker, Lester Pearson, and Pierre Trudeau. 19 notes.   R. V. Kubicek

1931. Toh, Swee-Hin. CANADA'S BRAIN GAIN FROM THIRD WORLD BRAIN DRAIN, 1962-1974. *Studies in Comparative Int. Development 1977 12(3): 25-45.* The brain drain (gain), especially from the Third World, is a major politico-economic issue in international relations. Unlike other research this study focuses on one nation's gains during a short period (1962-74). The influx of brain power results from a revised immigration policy. Replacement cost savings, social returns, and national income input analyses indicate that Canada's financial gains are substantial. This repays a goodly portion of Canada's foreign aid dollars. There is little likelihood that the immigration policy will change; hence the Third World brain drain will continue. Primary and secondary sources; 9 tables, 3 notes, 61 ref.   S. A. Farmerie

1932. Tovell, Freeman M. THE CANADIAN EXPERIENCE IN CULTURAL RELATIONS. *Int. Perspectives [Canada] 1976 (5): 32-38.* Discusses Canada's academic and cultural exchange programs as an aspect of its diplomacy and foreign policy from 1963-70's.

1933. Travis, Ralph. POLICING OUR ENLARGED COASTAL FISHING ZONES. *Can. Geographic [Canada] 1978 97(2): 46-51.* Canada's 1977 extension of fishing boundaries to a 200-mile limit in 1977 necessitated strict enforcement of boundaries to assure compliance among foreign fishing fleets.

1934. Turcotte, Claude. THE TRUDEAU VISIT TO CHINA: SHOWING CANADA NO CARBON COPY OF U.S., A KEY GOAL IN PEKING. *Internat. Perspectives [Canada] 1974 (1): 7-12.*

1935. Turrittin, Jane Sawyer. NETWORKS AND MOBILITY: THE CASE OF WEST INDIAN DOMESTICS FROM MONTSERRAT. *Can. Rev. of Soc. and Anthrop. 1976 13(3): 305-320.* Case studies of fifteen women from Montserrat were made in order to show how a group of migrants create and use their social networks to promote their geographic and occupational mobility. The pattern of West Indian migration to Canada is shown to be related to the availability of domestic work as an occupation open to West Indian women. The role of white Canadians sponsoring women to work as domestics is described and the chain migration initiated by women who came to 'do domestic' illustrated. Friendships created in Canada and contacts with West Indians made at points central to the networks of several women enabled them to leave domestic work, obtain blue-collar jobs, and enter the school system. For unskilled women, entrance into white-collar jobs was contingent on receiving more education in Canada, and the ways women solicited Manpower's financial aid to go to school are described. Finally, the ways in which two women who now work as keypunch operators mobilized their networks to promote their geographic and occupational mobility are contrasted to show how a woman's island social status influenced but cannot predict her economic integration.   J

1936. Unsigned. FOREIGN OWNERSHIP. *Can. Labour 1973 18(7-9): 24-26, 43.*

1937. Unsigned. ILGWU WOMEN'S YEAR SEMINAR. *Can. Labour 1975 20(2): 26-27, 36.* Reviews the International Ladies' Garment Workers' Union's efforts on behalf of the International Women's Year at their 1975 Montreal seminar.   S

1938. Unsigned. WEIGHING A NEW PEACEKEEPING ROLE. *Internat. Perspectives [Canada] 1973 (1): 16-17.* The costs and conditions of Canada's participation in a supervisory commission in Vietnam are surveyed.   L. S. Frey

1939. Valaskakis, Kimon. LA CEE A-T-ELLE POLITIQUE COHÉRENTE VIS-À-VIS DU CANADA? [Is the EEC's policy toward Canada coherent?]. *Études Int. [Canada] 1978 9(1): 126-136.* Discusses general arguments in favor of a European Economic Community-Canada rapprochement. Examines the numerous obstacles confronting this entente, and analyzes the effect that transformations in the international production system will have on the external policies of the EEC. Secondary sources; chart, 6 notes.   J. F. Harrington, Jr.

1940. VonRiekhoff, Harald. THE IMPACT OF PRIME MINISTER TRUDEAU ON FOREIGN POLICY. *Int. J. [Canada] 1978 33(2): 267-286.* Evaluates the prime minister's foreign policy in terms of criteria which he himself set, and stresses his contribution to the underlying rationales upon which policy is based. 19 notes.   R. V. Kubicek

1941. Wagner, J. Richard and O'Neill, Daniel J. THE GOUZENKO AFFAIR AND THE CIVILITY SYNDROME. *Am. Rev. of Can. Studies 1978 8(1): 31-42.* The theory that Canadian political culture has provided a more humane and decent tradition than the American can be tested by comparing the two countries' responses to the same situation, employing a norm called the "civility syndrome" which examines: moderation in style and policy; conformity to law; and respect for the rights of others. Using as an example the American attempt to pressure Canada into permitting a US congressional committee to interview Soviet defector Igor Gouzenko in 1953, Canadian political culture appears superior to American in terms of the "civility syndrome." Primary and secondary sources; 28 notes.   G.-A. Patzwald

1942. Waisglass, Harry J. LABOUR AND MANAGEMENT ADJUSTMENTS TO A CHANGING INTERNATIONAL ECONOMIC ENVIRONMENT. *Industrial Relations [Canada] 1974 29(3): 579-589.* In this paper the author delivers some thoughts on the international setting in which Canada is striving to achieve its social and economic goals.   J

1943. Ward, Norman, ed. A PRINCE ALBERTAN IN PEIPING: THE LETTERS OF T.C. DAVIS. *Int. J. [Canada] 1974-75 30(1): 24-33.* Discusses and presents the letters of Canadian diplomat Thomas Clayton Davis during his stay in China, 1946-49.

1944. Weir, John. CANADA-U.S.S.R. RELATIONS. *Communist Viewpoint [Canada] 1973 5(6): 43-46.* To the working class of Canada, the 56th anniversary of the USSR has special significance.   S

1945. Winberg, Alan R. RAW MATERIAL PRODUCER ASSOCIATIONS AND CANADIAN POLICY. *Behind the Headlines [Canada] 1976 34(4): 1-28.* Discusses qualifications for membership in blocs of developing nations to control part of the world economy. The Organization of Petroleum-Exporting Countries is an example of a bloc that succeeded. Cooperation is essential in related groups, such as CIPEC, Conseil Intergouvernemental des Pays Exportateurs de Cuivre, Intergovernmental Council of Copper Exporting Countries, and International Bauxite Association. Discusses Canada's position as stated in April 1974 by Mitchell Sharp, Secretary of State for External Affairs. Opposition leader Robert Stanfield asked for and received clarification on this point a year later. The US position influences Canada. Thomas Enders, Assistant Secretary of State for Economic Affairs, stated that America had the goal of the demise of OPEC. But Henry A. Kissinger, Secretary of State, declared that the United States had changed policies and would support agreements on commodities. Differentiates between short-run good and long-run good and points out the complexities of the problem.   S. G. Yntema

1946. Wright, Gerald. EUROPE: POLICY PLANNING ON A SEE-SAW. *Int. J. [Canada] 1978 33(2): 387-395.* A critique of Canada's policy toward Europe with particular reference to the Trudeau administration's 1970 policy paper, *Foreign Policy for Canadians.* 10 notes.   R. V. Kubicek

1947. Yuzyk, Paul. THE NEW CANADIAN CONSTITUTION AND THE RIGHTS OF ETHNIC GROUPS. *Ukrainian Q. 1978 34(1): 61-66.* Reviews the report of the Special Joint Committee of the Canadian Senate and House of Commons to review the Canadian constitution, particularly in regard to language rights. The Committee recommended that French and English be recognized as the two official languages of Canada but that other languages be given official recognition at the provincial level when appropriate.   K. N. T. Crowther

1948. —. THE ATLANTIC DECLARATION OF OTTAWA. *Internat. Perspectives [Canada] 1974 (4): 46-48.* Presents the text of this declaration of the aims of NATO, June 1974.

1949. —. CANADA AND AUSTRALIA: A POSITIVE AND EVOLVING RELATIONSHIP. *Australian Foreign Affairs Record 1975 46(12): 681-683.* Australia and Canada have been regarded traditionally as "sister countries" as a result of their shared Anglo-Saxon heritage, joint participation in two world wars, membership of the Commonwealth, and a common English-language culture. This traditional relationship has established a genuine goodwill between the inhabitants of the two countries, facilitating the exchange of information and people at all levels. However, it is a limited basis for the conduct of modern business, and, of course, has little relevance to the twenty-eight per cent of the Canadian population who are French-speakers.   J

1950. —. [CANADA EXTENDS ITS TRIAL PERIOD IN VIETNAM]. *Internat. Perspectives [Canada] 1973 (3): 14-17.*
—. VIETNAM: A FURTHER TRIAL PERIOD, *pp. 14-16.* External Affairs Minister Mitchell Sharp emphasizes that unless there is some "substantial improvement" in the Vietnam situation or "distinct progress . . . toward a political settlement" in two months, Canada will withdraw from the International Commission of Control and Supervision in Vietnam.
Gauvin, Michel. AN AMBASSADOR'S VIEW OF THE ICCS LIMITS, *pp. 16-17.* Excerpts from a speech delivered in Saigon 9 April 1973 by Ambassador Michel Gauvin, who believes that the ICCS is not performing the tasks assigned to it.   L. S. Frey

1951. —. FINANCIAL SUPPORT OF OPPRESSION. *Can. Labour [Canada] 1977 22(1): 12-14, 25.* The Task Force on the Churches and Corporate Responsibility depicts and protests against the policies and activities of the Royal Bank of Canada with its loans to the governments of South Africa and Chile.

1952. —. [FRANCO-CANADIAN RELATIONS]. *Internat. Perspectives [Canada] 1975 (1): 3-11.*
Halstead, John G. H. RESTORING RELATIONS WITH FRANCE AND OPENING NEW DOORS TO EUROPE, *pp. 3-6.* Trudeau's visit to Europe promoted "new levels of mutual understanding and awareness on both sides of the Atlantic" and emphasized Canada's concern with the problems of security and detente.
Painchaud, Paul. THE NEW TRIANGLE: CANADA-FRANCE-QUEBEC, *pp. 6-11.* The renewed entente between Paris and Ottawa will affect Franco-Quebec relations. De Gaulle's visit in 1967 initiated a rapid growth in Franco-Quebec relations. Quebec must now "adopt a strategy and soundly-based doctrine on the international level."   L. S. Frey

1953. —. [INTELLECTUAL RECIPROCITY AND CULTURAL IMPERIALISM: ART TREASURES—MEDIA—DATA TRANSFER]. *Am. Soc. of Int. Law Pro. 1974 68: 117-137.*
Bernal, Ignacio. PROTECTION OF NATIONAL TREASURES, *pp. 117-121.*
Castel, J.-G. POLISH ART TREASURES IN CANADA—1940-1960: A CASE HISTORY, *pp. 121-127.*
Gotlieb, Allan E. THE TRANSNATIONAL FLOW OF INFORMATION: A CANADIAN PERSPECTIVE, *pp. 127-134.*
Flemming, Brian. COMMENTS BY BRIAN FLEMMING, *p. 134.*
Nafziger, James A. R. COMMENTS BY JAMES A. R. NAFZIGER, *pp. 135-136.*
O'Connell, Robert J. COMMENTS BY ROBERT J. O'CONNELL, *p. 136.*
Olsson, Harry R., Jr. COMMENTS BY HARRY R. OLSSON, JR., *pp. 136-137.*
Rogers, William D. COMMENTS BY WILLIAM D. ROGERS, *p. 137.*
An evaluation of international cultural relations in North America, 1940-74, including the protection of art treasures, Canada's return of art treasures to Poland, and Canadian efforts to regulate the mass media in order to lessen US influence on Canadian culture.

1954. —. A NORTH AMERICAN MARKET? U.S.-MEXICAN-CANADIAN PERSPECTIVES ON TERMS OF TRADE AND RATIONALIZATION OF PRODUCTION; ANTIDUMPING AND COUNTERVAILING DUTIES. *Am. Soc. of Int. Law Pro. 1974 68: 92-117.*
Goldman, Robert K. REMARKS BY THE CHAIRMAN, *pp. 92-93.*
Metzger, Stanley D. U.S.-CANADIAN-MEXICAN TRADE RELATIONS, *pp. 93-100.*
Feltham, Ivan R. CANADIAN PERSPECTIVES ON TERMS OF TRADE, RATIONALIZATION OF PRODUCTION, ANTIDUMPING AND COUNTERVAILING DUTIES, *pp. 100-107.*
Del Villar, Samuel I. U.S.-MEXICAN ECONOMIC RELATIONS, *pp. 107-110.*
Aquilina, Gerald G. COMMENTS BY RICHARD W. EDWARDS, JR., *pp. 110-111.*
Aquilina, Gerald G. COMMENTS BY DAVID POLLOCK, *pp. 112-113.*
Aquilina, Gerald G. DISCUSSION, *pp. 113-117.*
Discusses tariff and nontariff barriers of trade among the US, Canada, and Mexico, 1946-74, and analyzes the prospects for trade liberalization.

1955. —. [OPERATING IN MORE THAN ONE JURISDICTION: THE CAPTAIN'S PARADISE? (A) BUSINESS; (B) LABOR]. *Am. Soc. of Int. Law Pro. 1974 68: 250-265.*
Moorhead, Thomas B. REMARKS BY THE CHAIRMAN, *pp. 250-251.*
Vagts, Detlev. OPERATING IN MORE THAN ONE JURISDICTION—BUSINESS, *pp. 251-254.*
Johnson, Keith. A TRADE UNION POINT OF VIEW, *pp. 254-258.*
Wionczek, Miguel S. THE LATIN AMERICAN VIEW ON TRANSNATIONALS, *pp. 258-260.*

Schwartz, Louis B. COMMENTS, *pp. 261-262.*
Jager, Elizabeth. COMMENTS, *pp. 262-263.*
Olive, David Allen. DISCUSSION, *pp. 263-265.*
Considers the international legal problems in North America created by the divergent regulation of multinational corporations and international labor unions in the United States, Canada, and Mexico since 1937.

Canadian-American Relations

1956. Armstrong, Willis C. THE AMERICAN PERSPECTIVE. *Pro. of the Acad. of Pol. Sci. 1976 32(2): 1-13.* Analyzes the American view of Canada. Americans know little of Canada, and are indifferent. Even government officials are scarcely knowledgeable. The business community is less ignorant, but its relations with Canadian counterparts are abstruse and poorly understood by the general public. Government waits until Canada acts, then quietly reacts. French nationalism has produced some change. Americans are no longer as eager to regard Canadians as friendly brothers. Canada is increasingly perceived as a doubtfully friendly foreign power, but fundamental attitude changes are unlikely.
V. L. Human

1957. Arroyo, Gilberto. EL SISTEMA DE INSCRIPCIÓN ELECTORAL DE PUERTO RICO: ADAPTACIÓN DEL SISTEMA CANADIENSE DE ENUMERACIÓN DE ELECTORES [The Puerto Rican voter registration system: An adaptation of the Canadian form of listing voters]. *Revista/Review Interamericana [Puerto Rico] 1977 7(1): 21-29.* In order to combat political apathy, Puerto Rico enacted in 1974 the Canadian form of voter registration, in which state employees go door-to-door to enroll voters. Although the results have been mildly disappointing, more Puerto Ricans than ever before have the right to cast their ballot on election day. Based on primary and secondary sources; table, 23 notes.
J. A. Lewis

1958. Austin, Jack et al. POWER TO THE PEOPLE: U.S.-CANADIAN ENERGY POLICY. *Am. Soc. of Int. Law Pro. 1974 68: 76-92.* Discusses US-Canadian commercial relations concerning energy from the 1950's to 1974.

1959. Balthazar, Louis. A NEW ATMOSPHERE PERVADES CANADIAN-AMERICAN RELATIONS. *Int. Perspectives [Canada] 1977 (Sept.-Oct.): 25-29.* In 1975, Canadian adoption of nationalist policies such as restricting foreign investment caused a state of tension between Canada and the United States. By 1977, relations again were excellent. The most significant factor in this transformation is the threat of an independent Quebec, which is viewed by both the United States and English Canada as a disastrous venture. Other reasons cited are the fragility of Canadian nationalism, growing mutual understanding due to the acceptance by Americans of Canadian policies and the ending of the Vietnam War, and a recognition that the poor performance of the economy make US investment in Canada desirable. Genuine problems remain, and Americans no longer feel that Canada is just an extension of their own country, but there is no possibility of real conflict.
E. S. Palais

1960. Barnds, William J. NIXON'S AMERICA AFTER VIETNAM. *Worldview 1973 16(4): 5-10.* Analyzes the United States' "basically competitive relationship with the Soviet Union and China," "basically cooperative relationship with other advanced industrial nations —chiefly Western Europe, Japan, and Canada," and a "relationship with the poor nations designed to help them develop economically and to mitigate local and regional violence . . . and thus reduce the dangers of outside involvement."
M. L. Frey

1961. Barr, Lorna. NAWAPA: A CONTINENTAL WATER DEVELOPMENT SCHEME FOR NORTH AMERICA? *Geography [Great Britain] 1975 60(2): 111-119.* "The past decade has witnessed an important change in the approach to water management in North America. While technological horizons have continued to expand and have made it possible to develop truly enormous river development schemes and to undertake interregional transfers on a mammoth scale, the traditional technological approach to water management has been subjected to increasing criticism. With the escalating costs of development and the increasing doubts raised concerning the environmental impacts of major

schemes, the possibilities of achieving more efficient use of existing supplies are receiving greater attention. The reluctance of Canada to draw up agreements for water transfer to the United States may well have some major long-term benefits for the latter. Perhaps the most important of these is the need to reconsider the merits of transfer schemes versus the other alternatives."
J

1962. Bergsten, C. Fred. COMING INVESTMENT WARS? *Foreign Affairs 1974 53(1): 135-152.* Examines the multinational corporation, with special reference to US-Canadian policies, in the setting of the collapse of the post-World War II economic order (evidenced by the globalization of inflation, international monetary instability, growing use of export controls, the search for oil and other natural resources, and the dire needs of the poor countries of the "Fourth World"). Stresses the need for new international economic cooperation in order to prevent the series of retaliatory and counter-retaliatory measures adopted in home and host countries over the emotion-charged issue of multinational corporations. 9 notes.
C. W. Olson

1963. Bonenfant, Jean-Charles. LES INFLUENCES ÉTATS-UNIENNES SUR LA CONCEPTION CANADIENNE DES DROITS DE L'HOMME [The US influence on the Canadian conception of human rights]. *Tr. of the Royal Soc. of Can. 1973 11: 85-96.* Notes the great influence in Canada of the American development of the civil liberties concept since 1930, and the judicial legislation following on civil rights, showing that much Canadian federal and provincial law imitated or directly copied its US counterpart.

1964. Brecher, Irving. THE MYTH AND REALITY OF CANADA-U.S. RELATIONS. *Internat. Perspectives [Canada] 1975 (6): 29-37.* Discusses economic, business and trade aspects of foreign relations between Canada and the United States from the 1950's-70's.

1965. Chossudovsky, Michel and Sellekaerts, Willy. A COMPARISON OF OPTIMAL AND ACTUAL POLICIES FOR HIGH EMPLOYMENT AND PRICE STABILITY UNDER EXTERNAL INFLATIONARY CONDITIONS: THE CANADIAN EXPERIENCE. *Southern Econ. J. 1974 41(2): 206-214.* Considers the social and economic impact of US inflation during 1954-72 in a comparison of actual and optimal economic policies designed to promote high employment and price stability in Canada.
S

1966. Cleaver, Harry. HOW THE U.S. RULING CLASS VIEWS CANADA. *Can. Dimension 1974 10(2): 26-30, 54.* Discusses views of US business and government, expressed in publications of the Council on Foreign Relations, towards the Canadian crisis brought on by Nixon's economic policy.
S

1967. Cohen, Maxwell. CANADA AND THE UNITED STATES—POSSIBILITIES FOR THE FUTURE. *Columbia J. of Transnatl. Law 1973 12(2): 196-212.*

1968. Conant, Melvin A. "A PERSPECTIVE ON DEFENCE: THE CANADA-UNITED STATES COMPACT." *Behind the Headlines [Canada] 1974 33(4): 1-36.* Meaningful consultation, "at heart an expression of will," is crucial to continued US-Canadian defense accommodation. Canada will observe her own priorities and thus guard her sovereignty as she contributes to Western defense.
R. D. Frederick

1969. Cullen, Dallas; Jobson, J. D.; and Schneck, Rodney. TOWARDS THE DEVELOPMENT OF A CANADIAN-AMERICAN SCALE: A RESEARCH NOTE. *Can. J. of Pol. Sci. [Canada] 1978 11(2): 409-418.* Provides data for the measurement of anti-Americanism. 4 tables, 6 notes.
R. V. Kubicek

1970. Cuneo, Carl J. EDUCATION, LANGUAGE, AND MULTIDIMENSIONAL CONTINENTALISM. *Can. J. of Pol. Sci. 1974 7(3): 536-550.* Uses data from opinion polls conducted in Canada during 1956-71 to test hypotheses about the willingness of Canadians to support annexation by the United States. 2 tables, 20 notes.
R. V. Kubicek

1971. Cutler, Maurice. THE SALE OF CANADA'S RESOURCES. *Can. Geographical J. 1975 91(1/2): 14-25.* Expresses concern over American foreign investment in Canada's natural resources since the 1960's.   S

1972. Dion, Gérard. L'INFLUENCE ÉTATSUNIENNE SUR LE SYNDICALISME CANADIEN [US influence on Canadian unionism]. *Tr. of the Royal Soc. of Can. 1973 11: 119-130.* Studies the history and current effect of US influence on the organization, structure, activity, and ideology of Canadian unionism, ca. 1970-73, with future possibilities for "Canadization" of the existing unions.

1973. Dirlik, Andre and Sawyer, Tom. TOWARDS A NEW FOREIGN POLICY—STRATEGY FOR INTERDEPENDENCE: A COMMON MARKET WITH THE U.S. *Int. Perspectives [Canada] 1976 (2): 46-49.* Examines the dimensions of Canada's North American Air Defense treaty with the United States and its impact on trade and degrees of economic interdependence between the two nations in the 1970's; stresses the role of US foreign investments in Canada.

1974. Dobell, Peter C. THE INFLUENCE OF THE UNITED STATES CONGRESS ON CANADIAN-AMERICAN RELATIONS. *Internat. Organization 1974 28(4): 903-929.* Discusses the impact of the US Congress on US-Canadian foreign relations (1950's-73).

1975. Dobell, P. C. A MATTER OF BALANCE. *Internat. J. [Canada] 1973 28(2): 315-324.* Reviews two recent memoirs by Canadian statesmen involved in American-Canadian diplomatic relations: *Mike: The Memoirs of the Right Honourable Lester B. Pearson. I: 1897-1948* (Toronto: Quadrangle Books, Inc., 1972), and Arnold D. P. Heeney's *The Things That Are Caesar's: Memoirs of A Canadian Public Servant* (Toronto: U. of Toronto Press, 1972). 7 notes.   R. V. Kubicek

1976. Doucet, Paul. ENGLISH CANADIAN NATIONALISM: A QUEBEC VIEW. *Queen's Q. [Canada] 1975 82(2): 259-262.* Analyzes developing nationalism among the English-origin people of Canada. Persons of French origin went through the same process 25 years ago. Oil has provided the economic impetus. It will no longer be exported to the United States unless all other markets fail. Americans will soon be forbidden to purchase certain properties in Canada. The old ideal of a single continent with single aims is dead. The most important remaining task is to create an English Canadian culture, the burden of which will fall on the universities.   V. L. Human

1977. Dunn, Robert M., Jr. CANADA AND ITS ECONOMIC DISCONTENTS. *Foreign Affairs 1973 52(1): 119-140.* In 1973 relations between Canada and the United States are strained, especially because of US investments in Canada and Canada's emerging effort to change its basic economic structure. Both elements stem from Canada's desire to become more independent of the United States. The Canadian and US governments should acknowledge each other's legitimate interests and work toward long-range solutions. 11 notes.   R. Riles

1978. Dunn, Robert, Jr. CANADIAN ECONOMIC ISSUES AND THEIR RELATION TO THE UNITED STATES: A VIEW FROM THE SOUTH. *Am. Rev. of Can. Studies 1973 3(1): 101-106.* Examines Canadian-US relations in terms of economic ties; examines the issue of foreign ownership in Canada and suggests a Canadian industrial strategy designed to increase domestic use of natural resources, increase imports, and stabilize the national economy to ease regional tensions within the overall nationalistic Canadian movement, 1970's.

1979. Dunton, Davidson. THE RESPONSE TO CULTURAL PENETRATION. *Pro. of the Acad. of Pol. Sci. 1976 32(2): 63-74.* Analyzes US cultural influence in Canada, which is pervasive. Most Canadians are within easy reach of American cultural attractions. Original cultural productions are costly, and Canada has but a small population to support the cost, whereas distribution of cultural productions is rather inexpensive. American television and radio, newspapers and magazines, are everywhere. Many American professors staff the universities. Canadian talent has difficulty becoming known. There is no movement to a closed society, but the government should increase support for Canadian efforts.   V. L. Human

1980. English, H. Edward. THE ROLE OF CANADA-U.S. RELATIONS IN THE PURSUIT OF CANADA'S NATIONAL OBJECTIVES. *Am. Rev. of Can. Studies 1976 6(1): 32-55.* Reviews the features of Canadian-US relations, particularly economic ones, and discusses their relation to the stated goals of the Canadian government, 1950-74.

1981. Farrell, R. Barry. CANADA AND THE UNITED STATES. *Atlantic Community Q. 1976 14(1): 69-75.* A new, timely survey of U.S.-Canadian affairs. Reprinted (with permission) from the Review of International Affairs, Belgrade, Yugoslavia.   J

1982. Feldman, Mark B. et al. REHABILITATING OUR CONTINENTAL NEIGHBORHOOD: RIVERS, LAKES, FISHERIES, AND POLLUTION ZONES. *Am. Soc. of Int. Law Pro. 1974 68: 138-156.* Primarily discusses the international regulation of the water quality in North American rivers, lakes, and coastal areas, from 1960's-74.

1983. Filion, Gérard. L'INFLUENCE DES FIRMES AMÉRICAINES SUR L'ÉCONOMIE CANADIENNE ET PARTICULIÈREMENT CELLE DU QUÉBEC [The influence of American firms on the Canadian economy, and especially that of Quebec]. *Tr. of the Royal Soc. of Can. 1973 11: 65-74.* Studies the question of vast American involvement in the French Canadian economy, 1960-73, with investment concentrated away from services to the primary and secondary sectors by Canadian governmental regulation, which is aimed at encouraging rapid development, leading to economic dependence and psychological detriment.

1984. Fowler, R. M. SCANNING THE "TROUBLED WATERS" OF CANADIAN-AMERICAN RELATIONS. *Internat. Perspectives [Canada] 1973 (3): 35-39.* The United States and Canada must "recapture a sense of mutual regard and understanding" in order to solve their mutual economic problems. In particular, "oil and gas policy should not loom so large as a cause of friction" between the two countries.
                                                            L. S. Frey

1985. Fox, Annette Baker and Hero, Alfred O., Jr. CANADA AND THE UNITED STATES: THEIR BINDING FRONTIER. *Internat. Organization 1974 28(4): 999-1014.* Concluding discussion of articles in a special issue on US-Canadian interdependence and foreign relations (1900-74).

1986. Fox, Annette Baker. CANADIAN-AMERICAN COOPERATION IN FOREIGN POLICY AND DEFENSE. *Am. Rev. of Can. Studies 1973 3(1): 173-182.* Discusses foreign policy and defense cooperation between the United States and Canada under the aegis of NATO and the North American Air Defense Command, 1950's-70's; includes areas where the two nations' policies have differed, such as arms control.

1987. Freeman, Susan. CANADA'S CHANGING POSTURE TOWARD MULTINATIONAL CORPORATIONS: AN ATTEMPT TO HARMONIZE NATIONALISM WITH CONTINUED ECONOMIC GROWTH. *New York U. J. of Internat. Law and Pol. 1974 7(2): 271-315.* Analyzes Canada's special relationship with the United States and her recent attempts to "foster a sense of nationhood in the face of cultural divisiveness, great economic disparities among the provinces and pervasive American corporate power and American cultural influences on their society. Discusses Canada's recent economic concerns and policies, concluding that "Canadian compromises with nationalism and ambivalence toward American investment endure" and that Canada's first concern is with a high standard of living, not with foreign investment. Primary and secondary sources; 252 notes.   M. L. Frey

1988. Gellner, John. IN DEFENDING THE CONTINENT THERE CAN BE NO "THIRD OPTION." *Int. Perspectives [Canada] 1976 (Special Issue): 27-30.* Discusses the influence of US security requirements on Canada's defense policy and military strategy from the 1930's-70's; examines the evolution of the joint defense principle between the two nations and the current role of the North American Air Defense Command (NORAD).

1989. Gillespie, Alastair. CANADA-UNITED STATES TRADE: TOWARDS A BALANCED UNDERSTANDING. *Am. Rev. of Can.*

Studies 1973 3(1): 11-19. Examines Canadian-American relations in international trade; Canada desires a strong internationally competitive manufacturing sector, national sharing of economic wealth, and greater domestic control of the Canadian economy.

1990. Gilpin, Robert. INTEGRATION AND DISINTEGRATION ON THE NORTH AMERICAN CONTINENT. *Internat. Organization 1974 28(4): 851-874.* Discusses how economic forces affected Canadian national unity and US-Canadian interdependence ca. 1910-73.

1991. Gray, Colin S. STILL ON THE TEAM: NORAD IN 1973. *Queen's Q. [Canada] 1973 80(3): 398-404.* In an earlier article, the author maintained that Canada should seriously consider its role in the North American Air Defense Command (NORAD) before agreeing to renewal in 1973. The agreement has been extended for two years, until 1975, despite the fact that Canadian participation in NORAD cannot be justified by strategic considerations. Any justification of such participation lies in foreign policy considerations. Canadian decisionmaking on even this matter reflects timidity, failure to consider logical alternatives, and some short-sightedness.   J. A. Casada

1992. Greenwood, Ted. CANADIAN-AMERICAN TRADE IN ENERGY RESOURCES. *Internat. Organization 1974 28(4): 689-710.* Discusses how economic and political interests in the United States and Canada affected bilateral trade in power resources (1950's-73).

1993. Hero, Alfred, Jr. QUELQUES REACTIONS AMERICAINES AU REGIME DU PARTI QUÉBÉCOIS DEPUIS LE 15 NOVEMBRE 1976 [American reactions to the Parti Québécois government since 15 November 1976]. *Études Int. [Canada] 1977 8(2): 356-373.* Few Americans ever have been interested in Canada. Those presently interested are the influential; they are concerned by the 15 November 1976 Quebec vote. That much of their information on Canada comes from English Canadians colors their perceptions of the economic, cultural, and collective security ramifications in Ottawa and Washington of an independent Quebec. Examines the future of Canadian-US relations, noting that Quebec's separatism could make the Maritime Provinces US satellites. Secondary sources; 6 notes.   J. F. Harrington, Jr.

1994. Hollick, Ann L. CANADIAN-AMERICAN RELATIONS: LAW OF THE SEA. *Internat. Organization 1974 28(4): 755-780.* Discusses US-Canadian negotiations during 1958-73 regulating use of the oceans.

1995. Holmes, John W. IMPACT OF DOMESTIC POLITICAL FACTORS ON CANADIAN-AMERICAN RELATIONS: CANADA. *Internat. Organization 1974 28(4): 611-635.* Discusses how US-Canadian relations have been affected in the 1970's by changes in economic conditions and politics in Canada.

1996. Holsti, Kal J. and Levy, Thomas Allen. BILATERAL INSTITUTIONS AND TRANSGOVERNMENTAL RELATIONS BETWEEN CANADA AND THE UNITED STATES. *Internat. Organization 1974 28(4): 875-901.* Discusses the formal international organizations and informal contacts between government bureaucracies developed by the United States and Canada during 1909-74 to control their mutual relations.

1997. Inglis, Alex I. A NEW APPROACH TO THE DISCUSSION OF CANADIAN AMERICAN RELATIONS. *Int. Perspectives [Canada] 1975 Mar.-Apr.: 3-11.* Extensive quotation from US and Canadian diplomats and politicians are used to elaborate the current state of Canadian US relations, 1972-75.

1998. Juneau, Pierre. QUELQUES PROBLÈMES DE VOISINAGE ET D'INFLUENCE, HIER, AUJOURD'HUI ET DEMAIN [A few problems of proximity and influence, yesterday, today, and tomorrow]. *Tr. of the Royal Soc. of Can. 1973 11: 97-108.* Studies the detrimental effect on the Canadian economy of the overabundance and availability of US products in Canada, the problem of competition with efficient US transportation and communication media, and the cultural identity crisis that Canadians face today.

1999. Kattan, Naim. L'INFLUENCE AMÉRICAINE SUR LE ROMAN CANADIEN [American influence on the Canadian novel]. *Tr. of the Royal Soc. of Can. 1973 11: 81-84.* Describes the relatively recent influence of the United States on Canadian fiction and the novel, maintaining that the strongest influence is found especially in the radio and television media (ca. 1960-72).

2000. Katz, Brian. THE POTENTIAL IMPACT OF CANADA'S ENVIRONMENTAL PROTECTION EFFORTS ON CANADIAN-U.S. RELATIONS. *Am. Rev. of Can. Studies 1973 3(1): 39-55.* Discusses environmental policy affecting both the USA and Canada, including shipping, air and water pollution, preservation of wildlife, and land use and conservation which because of their stricter adherence in Canada might cause rifts in Canadian-US relations, 1960's-70's.

2001. Keenleyside, Terence A.; LeDuc, Lawrence; and Murray, J. Alex. PUBLIC OPINION AND CANADA: UNITED STATES ECONOMIC RELATIONS. *Behind the Headlines [Canada] 1976 35(4): 1-26.* Discusses public opinion polls concerning US-Canadian economic relations. The public has become more wary of dependence on the United States and legislation has followed suit. Specific proposals were initiated by Robert Winters, Mitchell Sharp, Allan MacEachen, and Prime Minister Trudeau. Most Canadians favor trade relations with the United States as opposed to Europe or Asia.   S. G. Yntema

2002. Keohane, Robert O. and Nye, Joseph S., Jr. INTRODUCTION: THE COMPLEX POLITICS OF CANADIAN-AMERICAN INTERDEPENDENCE. *Internat. Organization 1974 28(4): 595-607.* Introduction by the editors of *International Organization* to a special issue on Canadian-American relations in the 1960's and 1970's.

2003. Kierans, Eric. UTILIZING CANADIAN NATURAL RESOURCES. *Am. Rev. of Can. Studies 1973 3(1): 96-100.* Offers a short background, 1950's-70's, for the exchange of natural resources between Canada and the USA, maintaining that Canadian needs and economic demands have not been met; concludes that Canada should, given the increasing scarcity of natural resources and the growing role of multinational corporations, begin exploration for and development of domestic sources for natural resources.

2004. Kronenberg, Vernon. DEVELOPMENT OF THE CANADIAN ARMED FORCES: IMPLICATIONS FOR THE UNITED STATES. *Am. Rev. of Can. Studies 1973 3(1): 183-191.* Discusses the implications of changes in Canada's defense and military structure for the United States 1963-70's; concludes that a unitary form of defense organization such as Canada has attempted to achieve would be impractical for the United States because of the larger size of the US armed forces.

2005. Latouche, Daniel. QUEBEC AND THE NORTH AMERICAN SUBSYSTEM: ONE POSSIBLE SCENARIO. *Internat. Organization 1974 28(4): 931-960.* Examines, in a special issue on US-Canadian foreign relations, the history of Quebec (1950's-73) to determine if the province could become independent and what the impact of independence would be on Quebec's relations with the US and the rest of Canada.

2006. Laxer, Jim. BETWEEN FRIENDS: THE TRIALS OF CANADIAN PRIME MINISTERS IN CANADIAN-AMERICAN RELATIONS. *Can. Dimension 1976 11(6): 12-15.* Relates economic policy in Canada to foreign relations with the US during the 1960's-70's, particularly under Pierre Elliott Trudeau.

2007. Lea, Sperry and Volpe, John. CONFLICT OVER INDUSTRIAL INCENTIVE POLICIES. *Pro. of the Acad. of Pol. Sci. 1976 32(2): 137-148.* The United States and Canada have in recent years instituted a number of industrial incentive policies which each views as hidden tariffs designed to promote national industries. These policies have resulted in conflict and retaliation. Balance of payments may be disrupted in consequence, but this can backfire on the instituting nation because the two economies are closely interrelated. Trade structure, resource allocation, and tax patterns are more seriously disrupted. For these reasons, Canada and the United States should act to prevent such abrasive policies in the future. Table, 12 notes.   V. L. Human

2008. Leach, Richard H. CANADA AND THE UNITED STATES: A SPECIAL RELATIONSHIP. *Current Hist. 1977 72(426): 145-149, 180.* Discusses international trade, economic, and diplomatic relations between Canada and the United States, 1945-76, emphasizing Canada's concern over US Bureau of Reclamation affairs, the Great Lakes Water Quality Agreement (1972), and oil tankers carrying Alaskan oil to the United States.

2009. Lebel, Maurice. INFLUENCES AMÉRICAINES SUR LES UNIVERSITÉS CANADIENNES [American influence on the Canadian universities]. *Tr. of the Royal Soc. of Can. 1973 11: 43-64.* Views the multiple influence of US education on teaching in Canada, which includes strong similarities in administration, student attitude, teaching method, and personnel; notes the international appeal of Canadian education and emphasizes the negative results of the US influence.

2010. Le Duc, Lawrence and Murray, J. Alex. PUBLIC ATTITUDES TOWARDS FOREIGN POLICY ISSUES. *Int. Perspectives [Canada] 1976 (3): 38-40.* Assesses the influence of Canadian public opinion in shaping foreign policy toward US foreign investments in Canada from 1973-75.

2011. LeMarquand, David and Scott, Anthony D. CANADA-UNITED STATES ENVIRONMENTAL RELATIONS. *Pro. of the Acad. of Pol. Sci. 1976 32(2): 149-163.* Sharing a lengthy border, it is inevitable that beneficial projects to either the United States or Canada may sometimes be harmful to the other. A number of environmentally-oriented trouble spots now exist. No common policy settles these irritations. They are fought out on a case-by-case basis at great cost in terms of time and money. Canada is more often the victim than the perpetrator. No moves are afoot to collectively prevent or solve these problems, so the future may mirror the past, though the likelihood of serious disruption of Canadian-American friendship is slim.   V. L. Human

2012. Levy, Thomas and Munton, Don. FEDERAL-PROVINCIAL DIMENSIONS OF STATE-PROVINCIAL RELATIONS. *Int. Perspectives [Canada] 1976 (2): 23-27.* Discusses the effect of Canadian economic development on the range of US federal government involvement into arrangements and relations between American states and Canadian provinces from the 1950's-70's.

2013. Levy, Thomas A. THE INTERNATIONAL ECONOMIC INTERESTS AND ACTIVITIES OF THE ATLANTIC PROVINCES. *Am. Rev. of Can. Studies 1975 5(1): 98-113.* Examines the political economy of Canada's Atlantic Provinces with special attention paid to provincial government dealings in international affairs: free trade, foreign investment, external representation, and energy policy, all important parts of Canadian-American relations, 1960's-70's.

2014. Leyton-Brown, David. THE MULTINATIONAL ENTERPRISE AND CONFLICT IN CANADIAN-AMERICAN RELATIONS. *Internat. Organization 1974 28(4): 733-754.* Analyzes conflicts in Canada between the Canadian federal government and US multinational corporations (1945-71).

2015. Litvak, Isaiah A. and Maule, Christopher J. CANADIAN-UNITED STATES CORPORATE INTERFACE AND TRANSNATIONAL RELATIONS. *Internat. Organization 1974 28(4): 711-731.* Discusses the impact of US multinational corporations and their Canadian subsidiaries on US-Canadian foreign relations during the 1960's-70's.

2016. Litvak, Isaiah A. and Maule, Christopher J. INTEREST-GROUP TACTICS AND THE POLITICS OF FOREIGN INVESTMENT: THE TIME-READER'S DIGEST CASE STUDY. *Can. J. of Pol. Sci. 1974 7(4): 616-629.* Criticizes the preferred status under Canada's income tax act given to Canadian editions of two US journals. 52 notes.   R. V. Kubicek

2017. LoGalbo, John R. THE TIME AND READER'S DIGEST BILL: C-58 AND CANADIAN CULTURAL NATIONALISM. *New York U. J. of Int. Law and Pol. 1976 9(2): 237-275.* Traces the development of Canadian protectionism to stem the tide of US publication in Canada previous to Bill C-58. Time Canada adjusted its advertis-ing rate base to less than half of its pre-1976 rate. "The net effect has been to make Time magazine's operations in Canada more profitable." The Bill C-58 on the contrary has resulted in the effective Canadianization of Reader's Digest. "A more satisfactory solution could have been achieved through the Canadianization, rather than the expulsion, of Time Canada . . . Ensuring Canadian ownership and editorial control, as was done with the Reader's Digest, would have been a more effective solution." Analyzes the Davey Report and Bill C-58 in detail. Creating high quality consumer magazines is the "only solution to Canada's goal of cultural nationalism." 201 notes.   E. P. Stickney

2018. Logan, Roderick M. SALMON PROBLEMS IN THE PACIFIC NORTHWEST. *Social Sci. J. 1977 14(1): 39-45.* Discusses US and Canadian violations of fishing rights treaties in Salmon interceptions in the Vancouver Island and Strait of Juan de Fuca areas in the 1970's; recommends assigning regulatory authority to the International Pacific Salmon Fisheries Commission.

2019. Lyon, Peyton. THE CANADIAN PERSPECTIVE. *Pro. of the Acad. of Pol. Sci. 1976 32(2): 14-26.* Analyzes Canadian views of the United States. Public rhetoric is more nationalistic than the people actually are. Canada is pulling away from the United States because no military threat is perceived, and the people are not necessarily in agreement with even this limited foray into independence. Certainly Canadians want more control over their economy—or do they? The future may hold more of the same. Canada will move away from the United States in fair weather and will move closer in foul weather. 13 notes.   V. L. Human

2020. Lyon, Peyton V. and Leyton-Brown, David. IMAGE AND POLICY PREFERENCE: CANADIAN ELITE VIEWS ON RELATIONS WITH THE UNITED STATES. *Int. J. [Canada] 1977 32(3): 640-671.* Notes the underlying blend of fear and trust, abhorrence and admiration, rejection and emulation that has characterized political attitudes among Canadian bureaucrats toward the United States. Based on interviews with 179 senior government officials; 2 tables, 40 notes, 2 appendices.   R. V. Kubicek

2021. Manor, F. S. CANADA'S CRISIS: THE CAUSES. *Foreign Policy 1977-78 (29): 43-55.* The Canadian crisis is due less to political nationalism in Quebec than to economic nationalism among English-speaking Canadians which has taken the form of a socialistic assault on the American-dominated business system. The resulting flight of foreign capital has wrecked the economy, encouraging Quebec's separatism. An independent Quebec would be economically weak and politically leftist, and therefore susceptible to Soviet penetration. This would pose a threat to the entire continent. The Alaska gas pipeline project will pump $10 billion (US) into Canada and should, by restabilizing the economy, make separatism less attractive.   T. L. Powers

2022. Milsten, Donald E. THE LAW OF THE SEA: IMPLICATIONS FOR NORTH AMERICAN NEIGHBORS. *Am. Rev. of Can. Studies 1973 3(2): 2-13.* Discusses the implications of recent UN resolutions in maritime law for the United States and Canada in the 1970's; includes issues involving fishing rights, free shipping transit, and environmental concerns.

2023. Mount, Graeme S. CANADA AND THE 1971-72 CULEBRA CONTROVERSY. *Revista/Review Interamericana Rev. [Puerto Rico] 1975 5(3): 378-390.* The Royal Canadian Navy played a secondary, albeit briefly significant, role in the controversy over whether the island of Culebra should be used for target practice by the United States and allied navies. The Canadians decided to use the Culebran target range in 1971 and became the object of heated protests on the island and in Puerto Rico. As a result of these protests, the Canadians stopped using the range. Based on primary and secondary sources; 62 notes.   J. A. Lewis

2024. Munro, John A. and Inglis, Alex I. THE ATOMIC CONFERENCE 1945 AND THE PEARSON MEMOIRS. *Internat. J. [Canada] 1973/74 29(1): 90-109.* The authors, who have been appointed to edit the remaining volumes of *Mike: The Memoirs of the Right Honourable Lester B. Pearson* (Ontario: U. of Toronto Press, 2 vols., 1972-73), quote here long passages from two documents of 1945 about Canadian-United States discussions on nuclear arms in order to make a point about the late prime minister's character.   R. V. Kubicek

2025. Munton, Don. BEHIND ALL THE RHETORIC THE HARD REALITIES REMAIN. *Int. Perspectives [Canada] 1978 (July-Aug.): 23-27.* Although differences between the United States and Canada have been muted in recent years by threats to Canadian unity and by economic stagnation, the sources of Canadian-American conflict remain. The "hard realities" include disputes over fishing zones, potential oil spills, and the inequities of the 1965 Auto Pact. Moreover, a Delphi exercise, employed to analyze the opinions of Canadian experts in foreign relations, predicted that the two governments would have more conflicts during the next decade. E. S. Palais

2026. Murphy, Cornelius J., Jr. THE FUTURE OF NORTH AMERICA. *Queen's Q. [Canada] 1975 82(3): 426-433.* Economic ties and geographical proximity bind Canada and the United States and both nations would benefit from closer economic and political integration than from the present autonomous decision-making based on self-centered sovereign discretion. Superficial differences in attitudes and policies in the 1970's on economic growth versus environmental protection, cultural diversity, form of government and foreign policy belie fundamental compatability in these areas which provides a basis for cooperation and a "creative partnership" leading to "shared abundance." 3 notes. T. Simmerman

2027. Murray, J. Alex and Helmers, Henrik O. MARKET STRUCTURE AND TRADE LIBERALIZATION—A CASE STUDY. *J. of World Trade Law [Switzerland] 1973 7(1): 117-125.* "Examines the structure of the market for auto replacements in North America. It is characterized by a highly concentrated pattern of ownership, running across the U.S.-Canadian frontier. The authors conclude that regional integration along the lines of the U.S.-Canadian Automotive Agreement would be appropriate for this sector." J

2028. Nuechterlein, Donald E. AN AMERICAN LOOKS AT CANADA. *Int. Perspectives [Canada] 1978 (July-Aug.): 31-35.* Americans no longer take Canada for granted, particularly since 1972, when Prime Minister Pierre Elliott Trudeau adopted the Third Option as a basis for economic and foreign policy decisions. A more serious concern to US citizens is the threat to Canadian unity from René Lévesque's Parti Québécois. The United States could accept an independent Quebec if the separation were peaceful. However, if there were danger of an external threat, the United States might take forceful measures to prevent foreign interference. Photo. E. S. Palais

2029. Nye, Joseph S., Jr. TRANSNATIONAL RELATIONS AND INTERSTATE CONFLICTS: AN EMPIRICAL ANALYSIS. *Internat. Organization 1974 28(4): 961-996.* Analyzes disputes between the governments of the US and Canada (1920's-70's) in order to determine if informal relations between US and Canadian societies have grown.

2030. Orr, Dale. THE DETERMINANTS OF ENTRY: A STUDY OF THE CANADIAN MANUFACTURING INDUSTRIES. *R. of Econ. and Statistics 1974 56(1): 58-66.* Examines economic factors affecting the expansion of US industries into Canada. S

2031. Ostman, Ronald E. CBC'S "THE WORLD AT SIX" LOOKS AT THE U.S.: CONTENT ANALYSIS AS AN AID TO UNDERSTANDING THE MEDIA. *Am. Rev. of Can. Studies 1977 7(2): 33-50.* A content analysis of CBC radio news coverage showed items about Canada to dominate, being more numerous, more prominent, longer, and more complex. Items about the US, many rewritten from US wire service reports, ranked second. These tended toward sensationalism and often conveyed an impression of the US as either favorable or unfavorable. The analysis confirmed previous observations of journalists and scholars, many of whom see a need for improved US-Canadian news flow. Based mainly on analysis of "The World at Six," 5-20 June 1975 and views of participants in a Syracuse, New York conference, September, 1976; 45 notes. G. A. Patzwald

2032. Page, Donald M. AN ENERGY CRISIS IN REVERSE: CANADA AS NET OIL IMPORTER. *Internat. Perspectives [Canada] 1974 (2): 18-21.* Discusses the first oil shortage during the winter of 1947-48 in Canada and the United States. S

2033. Page, Don. SELLING THE CANADIAN IMAGE IN THE UNITED STATES: THE CONSULATES. *Social Sci. J. 1977 14(1): 59-69.* Discusses Canadian consulates' interest in promoting the image of Canada in the United States in order to maintain friendly foreign relations and economic cooperation between the two nations, 1941-70's.

2034. Parenteau, Roland. L'INFLUENCE ÉTATS-UNIENNE DANS LES ÉCOLES D'ADMINISTRATION AU CANADA ET PLUS PARTICULIÈREMENT AU QUÉBEC [US influence on management schools in Canada and especially in Quebec]. *Tr. of the Royal Soc. of Can. 1973 11: 109-118.* Outlines the catastrophic proportions of Americanization in Canadian business education, stressing the influence of US-educated professors, US textbooks, and US ideological inspiration on business schools in Quebec, where the language barrier protects to some extent, but cultural alienation is still strongly felt.

2035. Peterson, Hans J. THE CABIN CREEK COAL PROJECT: AN ENVIRONMENTAL PROBLEM AND RECOMMENDATIONS. *Social Sci. J. 1977 14(1): 33-38.* Discusses Montana residents' environmental complaints regarding coal explorations along Cabin Creek, in southeastern British Columbia, 1973-75; considers possible violations of the Boundary Waters Treaty (1909) between the United States and Canada.

2036. Pratt, Larry. SYNCRUDE: THE CANADIAN STATE AS AGENT OF FOREIGN CORPORATIONS. *Can. Dimension 1975 10(7): 28-31.* Describes plans for the American petroleum industry to develop the Athabasca tar sands. S

2037. Preston, Richard A. THE NEW NATIONALISM VIEWED FROM ACROSS THE BORDER: CHAUVINISM OR SURVIVAL? A BACKGROUND STUDY. *Am. Rev. of Can. Studies 1975 5(2): 48-65.* Examines the present rift between Canada and the United States, attempting to extend analysis beyond current growth in Canadian nationalism; examines roots of the issue and concludes that periods of stress have existed before and that proper cooperation between the two nations will lead to mutual understanding and economic, political, and social cooperation.

2038. Preston, Richard A. TOWARD A DEFENSE POLICY AND MILITARY DOCTRINE FOR CANADA. *Armed Forces and Soc. 1977 4(1): 127-141.* Analyzes contemporary Canadian defense policy in this review article prompted by four historical studies and three policy essays. The historians, James Eayers, John McLin, and Dennis Stairs, trace the origins and evolution of Canada's post-World War II defensive alignment with the United States. The political strategists, Colin Gray, John Warnock, and John Sloan Dickey, provide insights into the consequences of recent history, specifically the emerging nationalism in Canada and the continuing satellite status of that nation to the United States. J. P. Harahan

2039. Reuber, Grant L. CANADIAN INDEPENDENCE IN AN ASYMMETRICAL WORLD COMMUNITY: A NATIONAL RIDDLE. *Internat. J. [Canada] 1974 29(4): 535-556.* Argues Canada's international interdependence is primarily characterized by its bilateral, asymmetrical, interdependence with the United States. R. V. Kubicek and S

2040. Riddell, John and Fidler, Dick. THE TORONTO CONVENTION: A STEP FORWARD FOR CANADIAN TROTSKYISM. *Int. Socialist Rev. 1973 34(7): 10-13.* Discusses and presents Trotskyists' resolutions at the 1973 meeting of the Canadian League for Socialist Action regarding Canada's relationship to US imperialism and class struggle in Quebec.

2041. Rigin, Y. CANADA AND THE US OIL BUSINESS. *Int. Affairs [USSR] 1975 (6): 91-97.* Discusses economic competition between the United States and Canada for control of the oil industry, 1973-75, including controversy surrounding the Alaska pipeline.

2042. Robinson, Gertrude Joch and Sparkes, Vernone M. INTERNATIONAL NEWS IN THE CANADIAN AND AMERICAN PRESS: A COMPARATIVE NEWS FLOW STUDY. *Gazette [Netherlands] 1976 22(4): 203-218.* Assesses international news flow in US and

Canadian newspapers, discussing factors affecting the presence of foreign news: newsworthiness, trade, and population. Also investigates the flow of news between Canada and the United States, 1974-76.

2043. Rowley, Kent. MY FIGHT FOR AN INDEPENDENT UNION MOVEMENT. *Can. Dimension 1973 9(4): 30-35.* The influence and control of U.S. labor unions over the Canadian labor front subvert the true interests of Canadian workers. Foreign control removes some types of decisionmaking from local labor leaders, eroding Canada's capacity for autonomous growth. Canadian unions should form one powerful center, and Canadian members of American unions should declare their independence.   S

2044. Roy, Jean-Louis. THE FRENCH FACT IN NORTH AMERICA: QUEBEC-UNITED STATES RELATIONS. *Int. J. [Canada] 1976 31(3): 470-487.* Accounts for and describes Quebec government initiatives to establish a presence in the US. 9 notes.
                                                       R. V. Kubicek

2045. Rutan, Gerard F. DOCTRINAL FOLLY IN THE NAME OF CANADIANISM: DOCTRINES OF THE 'NEW' NATIONALISM IN CANADA. *Am. Rev. of Can. Studies 1974 4(1): 37-53.* Examines Canada's 'New' Nationalism, a movement since the mid-1960's, as a doctrinal movement composed of three interrelated parts: Anti-Americanism, anti-Continentalism, and suspicion and distrust for corporate capitalist economy and lifestyle. 26 notes.

2046. Rutan, Gerard F. STRESSES AND FRACTURES IN CANADIAN-AMERICAN RELATIONS: THE EMERGENCE OF A NEW ENVIRONMENT. *Orbis 1974 18(2): 582-593.* Analyzes foreign relations between Canada and the United States since 1967.   S

2047. Rutan, Gerard F. THE UGLY CANADIAN: CANADIAN PURCHASE AND OWNERSHIP OF LAND IN WHATCOM COUNTY, WASHINGTON. *Social Sci. J. 1977 14(1): 5-15.* Discusses problems in jurisdictional law in Canadians' foreign investments in and land ownership of areas of Whatcom County, Washington, in the 1970's; examines economic, political, and ecological relations between Washington state and British Columbia.

2048. Schramm, Carl J. UNITED STATES STRATEGIES FOR WORLD HUNGER. *Behind the Headlines [Canada] 1976 35(1): 1-20.* Outlines US foreign aid in foodstuffs. Explains how the international market system functions. The unpredictability of demand makes a "food-for-concessions" policy ill-fated. Other nations who have a grain surplus, such as Canada, can undermine US policy and cause internal or external friction. If US policy followed supply and demand, the increasing indebtedness of other countries would bring visibility to the United States and instability to importing nations. William and Paul Paddock's *Famine-1975! America's Decision: Who will Survive* (Boston: Little, Brown, 1976) provides an answer to the starvation problem of developing nations, who are divided into countries who cannot survive, are walking wounded, or can be saved. The United States can not be responsible for the decisions of other nations.   S. G. Yntema

2049. Scott, Anthony. FISHERIES, POLLUTION, AND CANADIAN-AMERICAN TRANSNATIONAL RELATIONS. *Internat. Organization 1974 28(4): 827-848.* Discusses Canada's environmental protection movements and US-Canadian environmental protection efforts (1900-72).

2050. Sigler, John H. and Goresky, Dennis. PUBLIC OPINION ON UNITED STATES-CANADIAN RELATIONS. *Internat. Organization 1974 28(4): 637-668.* Analyzes Canadian and American public opinion (1950's-73) on US-Canadian relations in a special issue on foreign relations between the two nations.

2051. Silverman, Bernie I. and Battram, Shelley. CANADIANS' AND AMERICANS' NATIONAL IMPRESSIONS. *Sociol. and Social Res. 1975 59(2): 163-170.* "Canadian and American students evaluated the concepts Canada, Canadians, America, and Americans. Canadian students rated the concept Canadians more positively than American students rated the concept Americans, while American students rated the concepts Canada and Canadians more positively than

Canadians rated the concepts America and Americans. The pattern of these evaluations was discussed in terms of Canadians' concern over American control of Canadian institutions and Canadians' perception of Americans' opinion of Canada."   J

2052. Slimman, Donald J. THE PARTING OF THE WAVES: CANADA-UNITED STATES DIFFERENCES ON THE LAW OF THE SEA. *Behind the Headlines [Canada] 1975 33(6): 1-21.* The United States and Canada agree on matters of conservation, pollution, and mineral exploitation at sea, but the United States considers the mobility of its naval and air forces throughout the world most important. Should freedom of navigation be guaranteed, the United States would ease its position on naval issues. Canada, however, hopes to extend its control seaward.   R. D. Frederick

2053. Smedresman, Peter S. INTERNATIONAL JOINT COMMISSION (UNITED STATES-CANADA) AND THE INTERNATIONAL BOUNDARY AND WATER COMMISSION (UNITED STATES-MEXICO): POTENTIAL FOR ENVIRONMENTAL CONTROL ALONG THE BOUNDARIES. *New York U. J. of Internat. Law and Pol. 1973 6(3): 499-532.* Compares two bilateral commissions devoted to boundary-related problems, particularly with regard to the commission's potential for environmental control. Primary and secondary sources; 145 notes.   M. L. Frey

2054. Smith, Burton M. THE UNITED STATES IN RECENT CANADIAN NATIONALISM. *World Affairs 1978 140(3): 195-205.* Reviewing Canadian attitudes toward the United States from the 19th century to the 1970's, finds that Canadian nationalism more frequently has been anti-American than pro-Canadian. Canadian nationalism has grown more vocal in recent years (especially since the 1960's, when many Canadians were appalled by the assassinations, civil disorders, urban deterioration, and environmental disasters in the United States), but Canada has not been able to present a viable alternative to American culture.

2055. Sparkes, Vernone M. THE FLOW OF NEWS BETWEEN CANADA AND THE UNITED STATES. *Journalism Q. 1978 55(2): 260-268.* Compared to the percentage of US foreign trade that is conducted with Canada, the level of coverage of Canadian news by the United States press is low, but it is commensurate with the relative size of Canada's population and gross national product. Canadian newspapers focus on social, economic and political news from the United States, while the US press emphasizes human interest stories from Canada. For most of their foreign news, Canadian newspapers remain greatly dependent on US news services. Based on an analysis of selected 1975 editions of 10 Canadian and 29 US newspapers; 27 notes.
                                                       R. P. Sindermann, Jr.

2056. Sparkes, Vernone. TV ACROSS THE CANADIAN BORDER: DOES IT MATTER? *J. of Communication 1977 27(4): 40-47.* Surveys preferences among Canadians and Americans living along the Canadian-American border for television programs broadcast from either country into the other's television receiving range; concludes that American television is more widely received by Canadians than the reverse and there is little attitudinal change associated with watching foreign television programs.

2057. Stedman, Charles. CANADA-U.S. AUTOMOTIVE AGREEMENT: THE SECTORAL APPROACH. *J. of World Trade Law [Switzerland] 1974 8(2): 176-185.* The sectoral approach to multilateral trade negotiations has been proposed by Canada as a negotiating strategy for the current trade talks. This article reviews the experience of one such arrangement with a view to applying the formula to other product groups.   J

2058. Stevenson, Garth. THE THIRD OPTION. *Int. J. [Canada] 1978 33(2): 424-431.* A critique of the Trudeau administration's policies toward the United States. The third option is defined as reducing Canada's vulnerability to American actions. 9 notes.   R. V. Kubicek

2059. Stieb, Ernst W. I REMEMBER WHEN . . . A PERSONAL SILVER ANNIVERSARY OF MY ASSOCIATION WITH AIHP, ALONG WITH VARIOUS AND SUNDRY REMINISCENCES, NOT NECESSARILY RELATED, BUT INCLUDING SOME

THOUGHTS ON AMERICAN/CANADIAN PHARMACO-HISTORICAL RELATIONS. *Pharmacy in Hist. 1977 19(4): 127-143.* The author highlights his association with the American Institute of the History of Pharmacy (founded 1941) and with its prominent leaders, notably Directors George Urdang, Glenn Sonnedecker, and John Parascandola. Close Canadian-American pharmaco-historical relations were enhanced by the election of the first non-U.S. "American," Canadian Ernst W. Stieb, to the presidency of AIHP during 1977-79. Stieb, presently Assistant Dean and Professor of the History of Pharmacy at the University of Toronto, and Director of the Canadian Academy of the History of Pharmacy, recognizes his immediate ties with CAHP (founded 1955) and its leading personality G. R. Paterson. Inaugural message of AIHP President Stieb (1977-1979), May 1977.   S. C. Morrison

2060. Stranges, John B. DUALISM AND DEPENDENCE: THE MULTINATIONAL CORPORATION IN CANADA. *Peace and Change 1976 4(1): 40-49.* Examines US multinational corporations' heavy foreign investment in Canada's industry and manufacturing, bringing about an unwanted economic dependence on the United States in the 1970's; considers the threat to Canada's national sovereignty.

2061. Suthren, Victor J. H. THE NORTH AMERICAN PARTNERSHIP: ITS PAST, ITS PITFALLS, AND ITS PROMISE. *New York Hist. 1977 58(1): 69-81.* The fundamental differences between Canadians and Americans result from different historical experiences and physical environments. In many respects, however, Canadians and Americans are more like each other than peoples of neighboring countries in Europe and Asia. Canada and the United States are essentially brother nations. Despite some lack of understanding between Canadians and Americans, future world developments will force them into a mutual dependence. The article was a speech delivered at the College Conference on New York History in Plattsburgh, New York, April 1976. 3 illus.
                                                    R. N. Lokken

2062. Swanson, Roger Frank. AN ANALYTIC ASSESSMENT OF THE UNITED STATES-CANADIAN DEFENSE ISSUE AREA. *Internat. Organization 1974 28(4): 781-802.* Discusses US-Canadian defense policies and interdependence from World War II to the 1970's in a special issue on foreign relations between the US and Canada.

2063. Swanson, Roger F. CANADA AND THE UNITED STATES: THE RANGE OF DIRECT RELATIONS BETWEEN STATES AND PROVINCES. *Int. Perspectives [Canada] 1976 (2): 18-23.* Discusses the US State Department's research into types of arrangements between American states and Canadian provinces in the 1970's; findings indicated that most arrangements involved licensing procedures at borders and occasional issues in constitutional law.

2064. Swanson, Roger Frank. THE FORD INTERLUDE AND THE U.S.-CANADIAN RELATIONSHIP. *Am. Rev. of Can. Studies 1978 8(1): 3-17.* During his presidency, Gerald R. Ford met with Canadian Prime Minister Pierre Elliott Trudeau five times. Their first meeting (Washington, 1974) did much to relieve strained US-Canadian relations as each leader agreed to notify the other of proposed policy changes affecting their respective countries. They also discussed energy, security, trade, and environmental matters. Subsequent meetings at Brussels and Helsinki (1975) and Washington and Puerto Rico (1976) featured discussions of NATO, NORAD, energy, world affairs, and US-Canadian issues. Overall, "the Ford interlude normalized a highly unstable period in the US-Canadian relationship." Based on confidential interviews; 16 notes.
                                                    G.-A. Patzwald

2065. Swanson, Roger Frank. THE UNITED STATES CANADIANA CONSTELLATION, II: CANADA. *Internat. J. [Canada] 1973 28(2): 325-367.* Continued from a previous article. Studies the intra and interorganizational structure of the decisional interaction of Canada and the United States, particularly the organization and function of the U.S. diplomatic and consular presence in Canada. 2 tables, 42 notes.
                                                    R. V. Kubicek

2066. Trezise, Philip H. INTERDEPENDENCE AND ITS PROBLEMS. *Internat. J. [Canada] 1974 29(4): 523-534.* With regard to Canadian-US relations, author suggests subordinating some illusions of independence to ensure both political viability and economic interdependence.
                                                    R. V. Kubicek

2067. Trooboff, Peter D. et al. SHOULD INVESTMENT CAPITAL STAY HOME? A CANADIAN-U.S. DIALOGUE. *Am. Soc. of Int. Law Pro. 1974 68: 16-38.* Discusses the economic policies of the United States, Quebec, and the remainder of Canada concerning American capital investment in Canada in the early 1970's.

2068. Vaughan, Frederick. THE AMERICANIZATION OF CANADIAN LAW? THE CASE OF CHIEF JUSTICE BORA LASKIN. *Round Table [Great Britain] 1974 (256): 445-450.* Examines the controversial appointment of Bora Laskin to the office of chief justice in December 1973. The appointment has been criticized as a slap at western Canada. Chief Justice Bora Laskin has been accused of Americanizing Canadian law, especially in criminal procedure. Cites his judgment in *Hogan* v. *The Queen* (Canada, 1972).
                                                    C. Anstey

2069. Wagner, J. Richard. BORDER PROBLEMS OF THE UNITED STATES AND CANADA: ISSUES OF THE SEVENTIES. *Social Sci. J. 1977 14(1): 1-3.* Discusses economic, ecological, and diplomatic aspects of transborder friction between the United States and Canada, 1970's.

2070. Wagner, J. Richard. CONGRESS AND CANADIAN-AMERICAN RELATIONS: THE NORMAN CASE. *Rocky Mountain Social Sci. J. 1973 10(3): 85-92.* Congress' role in the investigation of a Communist espionage case involving E. Herbert Norman, a Canadian diplomat.   S

2071. Wagner, J. Richard. CONGRESS AND UNITED STATES-CANADA WATER PROBLEMS: SENATOR NEUBERGER AND THE COLUMBIA RIVER TREATY. *Rocky Mountain Social Sci. J. 1974 11(3): 51-60.* Oregon Senator Richard Neuberger's participation (1955-61) in the negotiations between the United States and Canada on the Columbia River Treaty (1955) is an example of how a congressman can influence foreign policy.   S

2072. Wallace, Iain. CONTAINERIZATION AT CANADIAN PORTS. *Ann. of the Assoc. of Am. Geographers 1975 65(3): 433-448.* "The volume of Canadian container cargo reflects competition between Canadian and US ports and their hinterland transport systems, the role of labor problems in influencing carriers' choice of port, and the nature of export commodities."   S

2073. Warnock, John W. INTERNATIONAL RELATIONS AS A CANADIAN ACADEMIC DISCIPLINE. *J. of Can. Studies 1973 8(1): 46-57.* Discusses the influence which American methodology has had in the teaching of International Relations in Canadian colleges and universities.

2074. Weiss, J. M. IMAGES DES ETATS-UNIS DANS LE ROMAN QUEBECOIS MODERNE [Images of the United States in contemporary Quebec novels]. *Am. Rev. of Can. Studies 1975 5(2): 82-103.* Examines images of the United States in Quebec novels, especially those of Ringuet, Roger Lemelin, and Anne Hébert; discusses themes expressed through the use of US imagery in much French Canadian literature, 1960's-70's.

2075. White, Arthur. THE NIAGARA GRAB AND THE PRECEDENT OF FEDERAL REGULATION OF NIAGARA FALLS. *Niagara Frontier 1975 22(4): 78-87.* Chronicles negotiations between Canada and the United States 1895-1906 concerning Niagara Falls as an electric power source; highlights environmental attitudes as well as power needs and federal regulation extant in the 1960's-70's.

2076. Whynot, G. Keith. SOME BUSINESS ASPECTS OF TANKER TRANSPORTATION IN THE GREAT LAKES AND ST. LAWRENCE RIVER AREA. *Inland Seas 1974 30(4): 268, 277-286.* Sketches the development of tank vessels on the Great Lakes with special attention to developments in the oil industry which have influenced the size and character of the inland tanker trade. Particularly important is the use of pipelines which have reduced the demand for tankers in areas of dense population. Photo.   K. J. Bauer

2077. Willoughby, William R. THE ROOSEVELT CAMPOBELLO INTERNATIONAL PARK COMMISSION. *Dalhousie R. [Canada]*

1974 54(2): 289-297. Roosevelt Campobello International Park in New Brunswick is a significant milestone in the evolution of Canadian-American friendship in that it is truly an international park. Earlier parks at Waterton-Glacier (Alberta-Montana) and International Peace Garden (Manitoba-North Dakota) are operated by the two countries as separate entities. The land for the park was given by Dr. Armand Hammer who had bought it from the Roosevelt family. Both countries had thought of the site as a park at one time or another, but both had rejected it. The problem was one of Canadian land with US historical interest. A joint commission plus Hammer's offer as a gift was the ideal solution, with the costs of development equally shared. 18 notes.   C. Held

2078. Wilson, W. A.   A CANADIAN APPRAISAL OF THE STATE OF THE UNION: GRAVE PROBLEMS NEED NEW SOLUTIONS. *Int. Perspectives [Canada] 1976 (Special Issue): 31-35.* Assesses social, political, military, foreign policy, and economic conditions in the United States and their implications for Canada in the 1970's; emphasizes race relations and the aftereffects of the Vietnam War.

2079. Wonnacott, R. J.   THE POLITICAL ECONOMY OF LIBERALIZED TRADE. *Internat. J. [Canada] 1974 29(4): 577-590.* Argues that political problems associated with free trade with the United States would not be as forbidding for Canada as often supposed. 28 notes.
R. V. Kubicek

2080. Wright, Gerald and Molot, Maureen Appel.   CAPITAL MOVEMENTS AND GOVERNMENT CONTROL. *Internat. Organization 1974 28(4): 671-688.* Discusses Canadian political and economic responses during the 1960's and early 1970's to US capital flow restrictions in a special issue on foreign relations between the US and Canada.

2081. Young, Christopher.   END OF AN ERA OR A CONSTANT IN POLITICAL VOCABULARY? *Int. Perspectives [Canada] 1975 Mar.-Apr.: 12-15.* Examines changing Canadian-US relations, 1948-75, including the nature of Canadian nationalism, desire for economic independence, and basic differences in cultural values.

2082. —.   CANADA AND THE CRISIS OF WORLD IMPERIALISM. *Int. Socialist Rev. 1973 34(7): 14-35.* Discusses Canada's political and economic vulnerability to US imperialism and foreign investment in the 1960's and 70's; considers the relation of social class to Canadian nationalism.

2083. —.   CANADA-U.S. RELATIONS: OPTIONS FOR THE FUTURE. *Behind the Headlines [Canada] 1973 32 (1): 1-10, (2): 1-14.*
Diebold, William, Jr.; Fleming, Louis B.; Gullion, Edmund; and Trezise, Philip H.   AMERICAN REACTION, (1): 1-10. Prompted by Mitchell Sharp's recent "green paper" on Canadian-U.S. relations. Diebold (pp. 1-3) expects the citizenry to pull the United States and Canada closer, although Canada can reverse the process at a cost. Fleming (pp. 4-5) stresses similarities and calls for good leadership to preserve sovereignty. Gullion (pp. 6-8) believes that Canada overlooks its effects on the United States. Trezise (pp. 8-11) sees economic integration as inevitable and multilateral development as Canada's only option.
Rolland, Solange Chaput; Howard, Peter; Lyon, Peyton V.; St. John, Peter; and Smith, Norman.   CANADIAN REACTION (2): 1-14. Rolland (pp. 1-4) maintains that only Canadians can decide the question of national distinctiveness (at the possible cost of American generosity) and that Canadian independence (including the French-speaking parts) is good for both countries. Howard (pp. 4-7) suggests the impossibility of maintenance of current ties and that cultural and political factors outweigh economic factors, however important to Canada. Lyon (pp. 7-9) favors economic integration but an international bias to enhance Canadian autonomy and to increase cultural self-awareness. St. John (pp. 9-12) views Sharp's paper as an expression of hopeful intent rather than as a serious blueprint. Smith (pp. 12-14) believes that Canadian leaders must dissuade Canadians from exaggerated concern over American "infiltration."
R. D. Frederick

2084. —.   SELECTED BIBLIOGRAPHY OF LITERATURE ON CANADIAN AMERICAN RELATIONS. *Internat. Organization 1974 28(4): 1015-1023.* Concludes a special issue on US-Canadian foreign

relations and interdependence (1900-74) with a list of relevant books and articles.

Constitutional Crisis

2085. Angers, François-Albert.   LE QUÉBEC: ÉCONOMIQUEMENT ACCULÉ À L'INDÉPENDANCE   [Quebec: economically forced to independence].
LE QUÉBEC EST ACCULÉ À L'INDÉPENDANCE   [Quebec is forced toward independence]. *Action Natl. [Canada] 1973 63(1): 7-22.* Gives the history of Canadian federalism since 1867 as an appeal for the independence of Quebec.
LA THÈSE FÉDÉRALISTE   [The federalist thesis]. *Action Natl. [Canada] 1973 63(3): 188-205.* The political liberation of Quebec must precede its economic expansion and raise its standard of living.
LES DÉMENTIS DE L'EXPÉRIENCE VÉCUE À LA THÈSE FÉDÉRALISTE   [The denials of life under federalism]. *Action Natl. [Canada] 1973 63(4): 268-277.* Present worldwide economic conditions have cast doubt on the liberal theory of international economic relations and, by analogy, on the validity of the federalist thesis in Canada.
LE FÉDÉRALISME CANADIEN: UNE THÉORIE NON SEULEMENT PAR LES FAITS, MAIS THÉORIQUEMENT RETARDATAIRE   [Canadian federalism: both actually and theoretically regressive]. *Action Natl. [Canada] 1974 63(7): 523-538.* The preconceptions of politicians and theoreticians toward political centralization prevent them from adapting their federalist economic theory to new scientific knowledge.

2086. Beaudoin, Gerald.   LES ASPECTS CONSTITUTIONNELS DE REFERENDUM   [The constitutional aspects of a referendum]. *Études Int. [Canada] 1977 8(2): 197-207.* Discusses the legal basis for and the political ramifications of a referendum in connection with Quebec's aspirations for independence. Secondary sources; 20 notes, biblio.
J. F. Harrington, Jr.

2087. Bergeron, Gerard.   PROJECT D'UN NOUVEAU COMMONWEALTH CANADIEN   [Proposal for a new Canadian commonwealth]. *Études Int. [Canada] 1977 8(2): 240-253.* Rejoices in the 15 November 1976 vote and wants to insure that Quebec's victory is lasting. Suggests as an alternative to Ottawa's federalism and Quebec's separatism, a "Commonwealth *Canadien"* which reflects the bilingual and distinctive nature of the British and French parts of Canada. Discusses the political design of the proposed Commonwealth, emphasizing its two-state construction: one would be federative and English-speaking and the other would be unitary and French-speaking.
J. F. Harrington, Jr.

2088. Brossard, Jacques.   LE DROIT DE PEUPLE QUÉBECOIS A L'AUTODETERMINATION ET A L'INDEPENDANCE   [The right of the people of Quebec to self-determination and independence]. *Études Int. [Canada] 1977 8(2): 151-171.* Examines the constitutional aspect of Quebec's legal right to self-determination and to secede from Ottawa's control. Considers the establishment of a French-Canadian state from the viewpoint of international law and UN precedents. Concludes that the Quebec people have the legal right to determine their own form of government and that their wishes can be discerned easily through a referendum. Primary and secondary sources; 26 notes.
J. F. Harrington, Jr.

2089. Dobkin, Donald S.   CIVIL LIBERTIES AND THE CANADIAN BILL OF RIGHTS. *Policy Studies J. 1975 4(2): 167-171.* Criticizes the antiquarian proclivities of the Canadian Supreme Court's interpretation of the Canadian Bill of Rights which took effect in 1960.

2090. Guindon, Hubert.   LA MODERNISATION DU QUÉBEC ET LA LÉGITIMITÉ DE L'ÉTAT CANADIEN   [The modernization of Quebec and the legitimacy of the Canadian state]. *Recherches Sociographiques [Canada] 1977 18(3): 337-366.* The foundation of the present Canadian crisis flows from the modernization of the political economy of Quebec. The rise of a new middle class, supported by the expanding role of the Quebec provincial government, created a new series of expectations. With time the question of language was to surface as a political issue and the federal government established its language policy to cope with the new expectations. This has proven inadequate and a renegotiation of the Canadian federal structure is now a necessity. Based on studies on the Royal Commission on Bilingualism and Biculturalism and secondary sources; table, 58 notes. A. E. LeBlanc

2091. Hodgetts, J. E. INTERGOVERNMENTAL RELATIONS IN CANADA. *Ann. of the Am. Acad. of Pol. and Social Sci. 1974 416: 170-180.* "Intergovernmental relations in Canada have tended to be viewed in light of the paper distribution of powers contained in the British North America Act, and, as a result, debate and research have focused on judicial interpretation and amendment as means of adapting intergovernmental relations. The tremendous augmentation of governmental functions (and spending) at all levels has necessitated the creation of extra-constitutional mechanisms for providing the flexibility required to meet the contemporary trend toward the merging and blending of jurisdictions that had been thought to exist in relatively watertight compartments. What is unique about the processes termed executive federalism is the way in which adjustment of regional and local relations tends to move to the top for resolution in a species of diplomatic conferences. While the new procedures have injected a realistic flexibility into the system, a high price is exacted in terms of Canada's capacity to arrive at an overall set of national policies." J

2092. Holmes, Jean. A NOTE ON SOME ASPECTS OF CONTEMPORARY CANADIAN AND AUSTRALIAN FEDERALISM. *J. of Commonwealth and Comparative Pol. [Great Britain] 1974 12(3): 313-322.* Examines the constitutional crises in Canada and Australia resulting from a breakdown in the relations between the state and federal governments and compares the constitutional conferences prompted in Canada by Quebec and in Australia by Victoria. Discusses the importance of bargaining in a federal system, the freedom of action of political leaders as compared with their counterparts in unitary systems, and the problems inherent in financial policymaking and the allocation of revenue. Based on extracts from newspapers; 112 notes. C. Anstey

2093. Koehler, Wallace C., Jr. THE IMPACT OF CANADIAN ENERGY POLICY ON CHANGING FEDERAL-PROVINCIAL RELATIONS: COMPETITION AND CONFLICT BETWEEN ALBERTA AND OTTAWA. *Am. Rev. of Can. Studies 1977 7(1): 1-32.* As a result of the energy crisis of the 1970's, Canadian federal energy policy has shifted from laissez-faire to an attempt to exercise direct control over marketing of energy products. Designed to assure adequate supplies to meet domestic needs and to maintain reasonable prices, the program favors consumer provinces over the producer provinces which have been committed to profiting from sales to the United States. Since provinces traditionally have controlled development of their natural resources, the success of the Trudeau government's attempts to extend federal authority into the economic sphere appears to require a redefinition of Canadian federalism. Primary and secondary sources; table, 45 notes. G. A. Patzwald

2094. Kwavnick, David. QUEBEC AND THE TWO NATIONS THEORY: A RE-EXAMINATION. *Queen's Q. [Canada] 1974 81(3): 357-376.* A critical rejoinder to Hugh Thorburn's article "Needed: A New Look at the Two-Nations Theory." Suggests that English Canadian reactions to separatism in the 1960's had irrational bases, particularly those that centered on the "More Power to Quebec" theory, and that Quebec was a nation in a "sociological" sense. 15 notes. J. A. Casada

2095. Kwavnick, David. QUÉBECOIS NATIONALISM AND CANADA'S NATIONAL INTEREST. *J. of Can. Studies [Canada] 1977 12(3): 53-68.* Quebec nationalism, whether separatist or "moderate," has been damaging to Canada's national interest. In fact, the "moderates" are worse, for they want to remain in Canada, while making other Canadians repay them for this magnanimity by giving them all sorts of special privileges. Canada's national interest lies in minimizing Quebec nationalism in Canada at the least possible cost to Canada. This might be done by allowing only hard-core, French-speaking nationalist districts along the St. Lawrence to secede. Outside of this "Republic of Lévésquiana," the rest of Quebec would continue as a Canadian province. 5 notes. J. C. Billigmeier

2096. Lalande, Gilles. THE FEDERAL EXPERIENCE. *Am. Rev. of Can. Studies 1973 3(1): 90-95.* Examines various writings of Canadian scholars pertaining to the success or failure of the Canadian federal system, concluding that in order for the system to continue regional economic disparities must be reduced and closer ties established between national and provincial governments, 1960's-70's.

2097. Lamontagne, Maurice. FEDERALISME OU ASSOCIATION D'ETATS INDEPENDANTS [Federalism or an association of independent states]. *Études Int. [Canada] 1977 8(2): 208-230.* A Canadian Senator reviews the arguments supporting Quebec's independence and examines alternatives to such separation, including an association of independent states, and federalism (his own preference). J. F. Harrington, Jr.

2098. Latouche, Daniel. IT TAKES TWO TO . . . DIVORCE AND REMARRY. *J. of Can. Studies [Canada] 1977 12(3): 24-32.* Canadians, both Anglophone and Francophone, should calm down and realize that neither independence for Quebec nor continued federalism would be the end of the world. Independence is not inevitable, and it isn't the only alternative to federalism. Québécois and English Canadians need to sit down together and calmly and rationally discuss *all* alternatives, including *indépendance-association,* federalism, and new approaches. 5 notes. J. C. Billigmeier

2099. Latouche, Daniel. LES PROGRAMMES ÉLECTORAUX LORS DE L'ÉLECTION PROVINCIALE DE 1973: UNE DESCRIPTION QUANTITATIVE [The electoral programs during the provincial elections of 1973: a quantitative description]. *Can. Rev. of Studies in Nationalism [Canada] 1974 1(2): 263-275.* Analyzes Quebec's four major parties: the secessionist Parti Québécois, the Liberals, Crédit Social, and Union Nationale, and their positions on social, economic, environmental, and constitutional questions, including the issue of Quebec's ties to Canada. The Parti Québécois, despite its secessionist views, stressed social issues more in its campaign literature, relegated Quebec's independence to third place, and appealed to voters as a general party of the Left. The Union Nationale discussed its main issue, Québec's relationship to the federal government, more than did any other party. 2 fig., 9 tables, 6 notes. J. C. Billigmeier

2100. LeDuc, Lawrence. CANADIAN ATTITUDES TOWARD QUEBEC INDEPENDENCE. *Public Opinion Q. 1977 41(3): 347-355.* The coming to power of the Parti Quebecois in Quebec has focused much attention on the climate of opinion in Quebec and the rest of Canada, particularly with the prospect of a future referendum on independence. Using data from a national election study and from recent public opinion polls in Quebec, this article examines the strength and stability of support for independence in Quebec and of electoral support for the Parti Quebecois which led to its victory. The data suggest that support for the Parti Quebecois is neither a transient phenomenon nor unrelated to support for independence, which has remained relatively constant over a number of years. Finding that support for both independence and the Parti Quebecois is highest among younger, better educated respondents, and that it relates to fundamental attitudes toward the country, the article hypothesizes that the struggle for independence in Quebec is likely to be a protracted one whose outcome is as yet uncertain. J

2101. Levine, Marc V. INSTITUTION DESIGN AND THE SEPARATIST IMPULSE: QUEBEC AND THE ANTEBELLUM AMERICAN SOUTH. *Ann. of the Am. Acad. of Pol. and Social Sci. 1977 433: 60-72.* Regional autonomy and separatist movements severely test the conflict management capacities of a nation's political system. Following Calhoun, a series of institutional arrangements and political practices which depart from majority rule decision making have been identified in the literature as contributing to the peaceful management of subcultural cleavages. Such arrangements provide minority subcultures with institutionalized means of self-protection and guarantees against stable unrepresentation and official cultural stigmatization. But, as Schattsneider pointed out, conflicts are best regulated before they start and institutional arrangements such as those above must be made before regional cleavages become too politicized. At a certain stage of conflict, peaceable partition may be the only solution. In Canada and the antebellum U.S., failure to set up "formal modes of sectional self-protection" led to conflict regulation failure and the emergence of separatist movements in Quebec and the

South. Without mechanisms of the type noted above and in the context of mass politics, the machinery of national political parties and intersubcultural elite accommodation which had held regional cleavages in check simply proved inadequate.   J

2102. Levitt, Joseph. THE FEDERAL N.D.P. AND QUÉBEC. *J. of Can. Studies [Canada] 1977 12(3): 118-123.* Canada's social democratic New Democratic Party (NDP) favors a strong federal government. The Parti Québécois (PQ) is also social democratic, but wants Quebec to be independent. The NDP, with its social democratic program, may be able to win Quebecois from support of the PQ to a renewed, reformed federalism. If Quebec does secede, the NDP may be crucial in ensuring that secession is peaceful.   J. C. Billigmeier

2103. Lithwick, N. H. and Winer, Stanley L. FALTERING FEDERALISM AND FRENCH CANADIANS. *J. of Can. Studies [Canada] 1977 12(3): 44-52.* The current debate over Quebec's relationship to Canada consists of two separable but closely interwoven themes: one concerns the meaning of and role for French Canada, and the second involves the nature of Canadian federalism. Quebec's independence would be disastrous economically; moreover, it would be a catastrophe for the many French Canadians who live outside Quebec. The solution lies in severely limiting the powers and taxation of the federal government. This done, Québécois (and British Columbians, Ontarians, etc.), as individuals and as a provincial collectivity, would have more power and more money to run their own lives and enliven their own culture. 14 notes.   J. C. Billigmeier

2104. Mallory, J. R. AMENDING THE CONSTITUTION BY STEALTH. *Queen's Q. [Canada] 1975 82(3): 394-401.* Canada's Representation Act of 1974 attempted to solve the historical constitutional conflict between proportional representation by population favored by English-speaking Canadians in the larger provinces, and equitable representation of minorities, espoused by French Canadians in Quebec and in the smaller provinces. Although the reapportionment act amended the constitution by altering the legislated formula for representation in the House of Commons, this fact was not openly debated, probably to facilitate a practical political compromise. 6 notes.   T. Simmerman

2105. Mallory, J. R. CONFEDERATION: THE AMBIGUOUS BARGAIN. *J. of Can. Studies [Canada] 1977 12(3): 18-23.* Confederation, as an alternative to federalism and to the division of Canada into two independent States, one Anglophone, the other (Quebec) Francophone, has many disadvantages. Rather, the solution to the present impasse between the governments of Canada and Quebec lies in a renewal and revitalization of federalism, a federalism that will pay more attention to the needs of Quebec and Francophone Canadians generally. 6 notes.   J. C. Billigmeier

2106. Mallory, J. R. RESPONSIVE AND RESPONSIBLE GOVERNMENT. *Tr. of the Royal Soc. of Can. 1974 12: 207-225.* Discusses the evolution of the Canadian government and questions the parliamentary system. In Canada the combination of a strong executive and weak legislature had led to the development of presidential politics without the restraints found in the United States. Although cabinet governments are flexible and made up of members who are more or less equal, they cannot act quickly, yet they can thrash out problems in secret. Since the Canadian Cabinet is too large, there have been attempts to reduce its size. An important part of the Government Reorganization Act of 1971 was the Ministers and Ministries Act which created two new classes of ministers called ministers of state. One such minister, that of Science and Technology, according to the Lamontagne report does not have sufficient authority to do the job effectively. A significant development has been the growth of committees, especially of the Committee of Priorities and Planning as a new inner core of the Cabinet. The next step in the evolution of the government may be to group functions under a single minister. Also discusses the increasingly important role of civil servants in governments. Since nearly all business in the House of Commons is that of the government, the question period has great value. The emergence of the speaker as an impartial presiding officer is significant, but the most important change in procedure concerns financial business because the opposition can no longer withhold supply in order to force the government to give in or dissolve parliament. 20 notes.   J. D. Neville

2107. McRoberts, Kenneth. ENGLISH CANADA AND THE QUEBEC REFERENDUM: THE STAKES AND THE DANGERS. *J. of Can. Studies [Canada] 1977 12(3): 108-113.* The accession to power of the Parti Québécois (with its program of separation from Canada) has created a tremendous potential for destructive conflict between English and French Canada. Whatever happens—whether Quebec becomes independent or not—we must prevent the growth of a climate of hostility that will haunt this part of North America for decades to come. This is the real stake in the debate over Quebec independence.

J. C. Billigmeier

2108. Miller, D. R. A SHAPELY VALUE ANALYSIS OF THE PROPOSED CANADIAN CONSTITUTIONAL AMENDMENT SCHEME. *Can. J. of Pol. Sci. 1973 6(1): 140-143.* A mathematical analysis to determine the voting power which would be assigned to each province under the Canadian constitutional scheme of 1971. 2 tables, 7 notes.   R. V. Kubicek

2109. Orban, Edmond. CANADA-QUÉBEC: POUR UN PROCESSUS ACCÉLÉRÉ DE CRÉATIVITÉ [Canada-Quebec: For an accelerated process of creativity]. *J. of Can. Studies [Canada] 1977 12(3): 39-43.* Calls for creative thinking to deal with the problems between Quebec and the Canadian federal government. The eventual solution may be federalism, independence, or a confederation, but Canada needs what Henri Bergson called *l'évolution créatrice.* 14 notes.

J. C. Billigmeier

2110. Penner, Norman. QUEBEC EXPLODES A BOMBSHELL: RENÉ LEVESQUE AND THE CHALLENGE OF SEPARATISM. *Round Table [Great Britain] 1977 (266): 153-160.* Examines the growth of the Parti Québécois, focusing on its separatism and René Levesque's success in the November 1976 election. Discusses the position of Prime Minister Pierre Elliott Trudeau and the options open to separatists and federalists.   C. Anstey

2111. Rempel, Henry David. THE PRACTICE AND THEORY OF THE FRAGILE STATE: TRUDEAU'S CONCEPTION OF AUTHORITY. *J. of Can. Studies 1975 10(4): 24-39.* Discusses the conception of government of Canadian Prime Minister Pierre Elliott Trudeau during the 1950's-70's.

2112. Smiley, Donald. AS THE OPTIONS NARROW: NOTES ON POST-NOVEMBER 15 CANADA. *J. of Can. Studies [Canada] 1977 12(3): 3-7.* The elections of 15 November 1976, in which the Parti Québécois (PQ), led by René Lévesque, captured a majority in the provincial Parliament of Quebec with a program based on independence from Canada, have irreversibly altered the situation in Canada. Either the federal system has to be reformed—and explained to the people more clearly—or Quebec will leave Canada. Intensified resistance to the PQ independence policy could result in either a retreat from independence by the relatively moderate Lévesque leadership, or replacement of that leadership by extremists. A purely English Canada would be born in an atmosphere of rejection and failure. 6 notes.   J. C. Billigmeier

2113. Smiley, Donald V. FEDERAL-PROVINCIAL CONFLICT IN CANADA. *Publius 1974 4(3): 7-24.* World War II saw the establishment of a reasonably strong central government, but the provinces moved to reclaim lost ground during the late 1950's because of the failure of so many national programs. The battle wages warm at present. Judicial review of the constitution, partisan politics, territorial pluralism within the central government, and executive federalism represent forces and forums within which the issues are both fought out and settled. The central government retains control of many critical functions, but lacks the institutional structure to effectively pursue them. 35 notes.

V. L. Human

2114. Stein, Michael. QUÉBEC AND CANADA: THE CHANGING EQUILIBRIUM BETWEEN "FEDERAL SOCIETY" AND "FEDERAL POLITICAL SYSTEM." *J. of Can. Studies [Canada] 1977 12(3): 113-117.* In 1968, just before Pierre Elliott Trudeau became Prime Minister and René Lévésque formed the Parti Québécois, the author argued that Canada is a "federal society" supported and shaped by a "federal political system." Since then, both "society" and "system" have changed radically, and there has arisen a severe disjunction between them. Reform of the federal system is needed to create a bilingual or plurilingual "federal society" as in Belgium and Switzerland. Much reform will be informal—personnel changes in the government and judicial institutions to give French Canadians equal representation. 3 notes.

J. C. Billigmeier

2115. Thorburn, Hugh. NEEDED: A NEW LOOK AT THE TWO-NATION THEORY. *Queen's Q. [Canada] 1973 80(2): 268-273.* The disaffection of French Canada has introduced a malaise into Canadian politics, with increasing sentiment in Quebec for a permanent separation. Too much Americanization and too rapid a depletion of economic resources pose economic problems for the country. Canada must solve these problems to have a successful future by tackling existing constitutional arrangements which cause frustrations and animosities.

J. A. Casada

2116. Tremblay, Marc-Adélard. LE 15 NOVEMBRE ET SES LENDEMAINS: LES DÉFIS DE LA SOUVERAINETÉ POLITIQUE [The 15th of November and after: The challenges of political sovereignty]. *J. of Can. Studies [Canada] 1977 12(3): 100-105.* The people of Quebec certainly have a right to self-determination or even independence, but they will realize that the road to political sovereignty is strewn with obstacles. The government of the Parti Québécois seems to underestimate the problems associated with accession to sovereignty. The PQ should concentrate on political reform and on building a strong economic infrastructure for Quebec. If it succeeds—and if other necessary conditions are present—then independence will be a viable option, which it is not at present. 2 notes.

J. C. Billigmeier

2117. Trent, John. TERRAIN D'ENTENTE ET TERRITOIRES CONTESTES: LES POSITIONS FEDERALES ET PROVINCIALES A L'EGARD DE L'AVENIR CONSTITUTIONNEL DU CANADA [Common ground and disputed territory: Federal and provincial positions concerning Canada's constitutional future]. *Études Int. [Canada] 1977 8(2): 172-197.* Discusses arguments and constitutional debates concerning federalism and provincialism in Canada and relates these issues to Quebec's quest for independence. Graphically contrasts the theories and positions of Trudeau and Levesque and illustrates in tabular form the proposals for constitutional reform from 1968-77. Primary and secondary sources; 2 tables, 25 notes.

J. F. Harrington, Jr.

2118. Trent, John F. REFORM OF THE CANADIAN FEDERAL SYSTEM: A NOTE. *Pol. Sci. Rev. [India] 1978 17(1-2): 62-90.* Outlines the rationale for reform of the Canadian federal system. Although Canada's federalism began in 1848 when Ontario and Quebec were joined, the two cultural communities never fully accommodated to one another. The

French-speaking Quebec area continued to fear a loss of identity and power to the English-speaking majority. Even after the reforms of the Victorian era and subsequent judicial and legislative adjustments, the problems of official languages, human rights, taxing powers, and structural mechanisms persisted. Evaluates the major elements of the constitutional reforms proposed from 1968 to 1977. Secondary sources; 6 notes.

S. H. Frank

2119. Trépanier, Pierre. L'OPINION PUBLIQUE ANGLO-QUÉBÉCOISE ET L'AUTONOMIE PROVINCIALE (1945-1946) [Anglo-Quebec public opinion and provincial autonomy (1945-46)]. *Action Natl. [Canada] 1977 67(1): 34-55.* The depression and World War II prompted the Canadian federal government to formulate social welfare proposals. At a federal-provincial conference during August 1945-May 1946, the William Lyon Mackenzie King government proposed to assume taxation powers previously reserved to the provinces in exchange for fixed, per capita, welfare grants. Ontario and Quebec opposed the plan, citing an infringement on provincial sovereignty. Two conservative Anglo-Canadian newspapers in Quebec, the Montreal *Daily Star* and the *Gazette,* deplored the failure of the conference. The *Star* supported new fiscal arrangements increasing federal responsibility and power and blamed the provincial autonomists for the lack of results. The *Gazette,* less favorable to social security and more influenced by economic liberalism, de-emphasized the controversy over autonomy and blamed the federal government for the deadlock. Based on newspapers and secondary sources; 52 notes.

A. W. Novitsky

2120. Young, R. A. NATIONAL IDENTIFICATION IN ENGLISH CANADA: IMPLICATIONS FOR QUEBEC INDEPENDENCE. *J. of Can. Studies [Canada] 1977 12(3): 69-84.* English-speakers among Canadians may be divided into four groups, according to their attitudes on the possibility of Quebec's separation from Canada and other issues: Dogmatists, Locals, Cosmopolitans, and Individualists. Dogmatists oppose separation, being strong Canadian nationalists, but they might accept it if a corridor to the Maritime Provinces were left within Canada. Locals, being oriented toward local and provincial entities, would let the Québécois go if they wished, while considering it a mistake. Cosmopolitans will tolerate secession if economic and communications links are maintained unimpaired. Individualists, wrapped up in themselves, seem to care little about any public issues. 21 notes.

J. C. Billigmeier

2121. Yuzyk, Paul. THE NEW CANADIAN CONSTITUTION AND THE RIGHTS OF ETHNIC GROUPS. *Ukrainian R. [Great Britain] 1973 20(1): 85-94.* Discusses the need for a new Constitution for Canada and the importance of insuring the rights of non-English, non-French ethnic groups (1972).

S

10. CANADA: REGIONS

General

2122. Alwin, John A. THE HISTORIC WINNIPEG RIVER. *Can. Geographical J. 1976 92(1): 44-51.* Presents a history of the Winnipeg River of Ontario and Manitoba from the 1730's to the 1960's.

2123. Appavoo, Patricia J., ed. ALTERNATIVES CANADA: A CONFERENCE REPORT. *Behind the Headlines [Canada] 1978 36(3): 1-28.* Synopsizes the proceedings of a student-organized and -run conference on future alternatives for Canada in the arts, language, culture, and in terms of regionalism and its effects on Canada's political future.

2124. Burry, Shierlaw. EDMONTON TO THE KLONDIKE. *Alberta Hist. R. 1973 21(2): 20-25.* Thomas Burry joined the gold rush to the Klondike in 1897. His party traveled the 2,400-mile "back-door" route by way of Edmonton and the Athabasca, Slave, and Mackenzie Rivers, and across to the Yukon River system. 2 illus.
D. L. Smith

2125. Forbes, Ernest R. NEVER THE TWAIN DID MEET: PRAIRIE-MARITIME RELATIONS, 1910-27. *Can. Hist. Rev. [Canada] 1978 59(1): 18-37.* Based on the correspondence of the politicians and journalists of Canada's three Prairie and three Maritime provinces, the essay explores sources of conflict and failures in cooperation between the two regions in matters of common interest involving freight rates, subsidies and tariffs. Emphasized are the roles of leadership, ideology and the metropolis' playing off one portion of the hinterland against the other. Rejecting the stereotype of Maritime conservatism, the essay attributes the collapse of farmers' protest movement in the Maritimes to "Prairie imperialism."
A

2126. Forward, Charles N. PARALLELISM OF HALIFAX AND VICTORIA. *Can. Geographical J. 1975 90(3): 34-43.* Highlights some similarities between provincial capitals Halifax and Victoria (1749-1971).
S

2127. Frank, J. A. and Kelly, Michael. ETUDE PRÉLIMINAIRE SUR LA VIOLENCE COLLECTIVE EN ONTARIO ET AU QUÉBEC, 1963-1973 [A preliminary study on collective violence in Ontario and Quebec, 1963-73]. *Can. J. of Pol. Sci. [Canada] 1977 10(1): 145-157.* Uses newspaper sources which show there were 125 cases of collective violence in Ontario and 121 in Quebec during 1963-73. Correlates the violence with social and economic trends. 8 tables, 1 fig., 14 notes.
R. V. Kubicek

2128. Frideres, James S. OFFSPRING OF JEWISH INTERMARRIAGE: A NOTE. *Jewish Social Studies 1973 35(2): 149-156.* In sociological investigation of a Jewish community in the Canadian Midwest, the author found that the incidence of intermarriage could be correlated with the size of the Jewish community, the previous pattern of intermarriage, and the availability of Jewish education. Based on primary and secondary sources; 21 notes.
P. E. Schoenberg

2129. Gainer, Walter D. WESTERN DISENCHANTMENT AND THE CANADIAN FEDERATION. *Pro. of the Acad. of Pol. Sci. 1976 32(2): 40-52.* Reviews Canadian regional differences and their underlying causes during 1965-75. With the exception of Quebec, differences are diffuse and well-distributed. All of Canada objects to the concentration of industry in central Canada, and rumblings of discontent can usually be traced to this cause. Freight rates, taxes, royalties, and other economic policies emanating from Ontario are immediately suspect by the western provinces. These grumblings are not based on factual government discrimination and generally are not even justified, though they stubbornly refuse to disappear. 7 notes.
V. L. Human

2130. Gill, Don and Cooke, Alan D. CONTROVERSIES OVER HYDROELECTRIC DEVELOPMENTS IN SUB-ARCTIC CANADA.

Polar Record [Great Britain] 1974 17(107): 109-127. Discusses hydroelectric projects in sub-Arctic Canada (1971-74), including the Aishihik Lake, Peace River, Churchill River, and James Bay projects.

2131. Howell, William Maher. "MY TWELVE-YEAR WAIT." *Inland Seas 1978 34(3): 176-181, 209.* Describes the author's recollections of a trip as a 12-year-old in 1928 from Erie, Pennsylvania, to Quebec on steamers and interurban trolleys. Photo.
K. J. Bauer

2132. Isbister, John. AGRICULTURE, BALANCED GROWTH, AND SOCIAL CHANGE IN CENTRAL CANADA SINCE 1850: AN INTERPRETATION. *Econ. Development and Cultural Change 1977 25(4): 673-697.* Analyzes differences in the agricultural development in the Quebec and Ontario provinces of Canada between 1850 and 1970 and "shows how Quebec's industrial sector was able to develop at a relatively rapid rate without the support of a dynamic agricultural sector." "The differences in the rural cultures of the two provinces have been largely responsible for the differences in urban social stratification and political mores." Based on published materials; 5 tables, 51 notes, appendix.
J. W. Thacker, Jr.

2133. Johannson, P. R. A STUDY IN REGIONAL STRATEGY: THE ALASKA-BRITISH COLUMBIA-YUKON CONFERENCES. *B.C. Studies [Canada] 1975/76 (28): 29-52.* Reviews the historical background of the three 1960-64 meetings about economic development. Provides an overview of the issues discussed, the results, and the participants. Based on secondary sources; table, 51 notes.
W. L. Marr

2134. Lavender, David. FIRST CROSSING: ALEXANDER MACKENZIE'S QUEST FOR THE PACIFIC. *Am. West 1977 14(5): 4-11, 67-68.* Alexander Mackenzie (1763-1820), in the service of the North West Company, searched for a viable fur-trade route across Canada to the Pacific. Based on Lake Athabasca, in 1789 he traveled to Great Slave Lake, discovered the Mackenzie River, and followed it to the Arctic Ocean. During 1792-93, from the same base, he followed the Peace River over the Rocky Mountains, the Parsnip, Fraser, and Bella Coola rivers to the Pacific. He had made the first crossing of the continent north of Mexico. 3 illus., map.
D. L. Smith

2135. Levy, Thomas Allen. DEVELOPING REGIONALISM IN THE MARITIMES AND WESTERN CANADA. *Current Hist. 1974 66(392): 167-172, 183.*

2136. MacPherson, Ian. APPROPRIATE FORMS OF ENTERPRISE: THE PRAIRIE AND MARITIME CO-OPERATIVE MOVEMENTS, 1900-1955. *Acadiensis [Canada] 1978 8(1): 77-96.* Maritime and Prairie cooperative movements had closer exchanges than any other Canadian regional cooperative movements. Before 1919 exchanges were largely personal and informal. In the 1920's closer ties emerged but not strong institutions. In the 1930's the cooperative press and credit unions helped strengthen ties. Then, in the 1940's, the Co-operative Union of Canada, kept alive since 1909 mainly because of support from Cape Breton and Saskatchewan, was restructured and became the focal point of Maritime-Prairie links during 1945-55. 48 notes.
D. F. Chard

2137. Marple, David. THE UTILITY OF QUANTITATIVE SOURCES IN THE STUDY OF TRANSPORTATION AND THE GROWTH OF ONTARIO AND QUEBEC URBAN HIERARCHY, 1861-1901: AN EXAMPLE. *Urban Hist. Rev. [Canada] 1973 (2): 2-7.*

2138. Nelles, H. V. PUBLIC OWNERSHIP OF ELECTRICAL UTILITIES IN MANITOBA AND ONTARIO, 1905-30. *Can. Hist. Rev. [Canada] 1976 57(4): 461-484.* Two Canadian provinces embarked upon experiments with public ownership of electrical utilities at the same time. In Ontario the public power movement achieved near-monopoly status within two decades; in Manitoba private utilities continued to dominate the industry. Based on primary sources from municipal, provincial, and national archives.
A

2139. Parenteau, Roland. L'INFLUENCE DE L'ESPACE SUR LA VIE CANADIENNE [The influence of space on Canadian life]. *Tr. of the Royal Soc. of Can. [Canada] 1976 14: 123-125.* Canada's large size and small population has greatly influenced Canadian life. It has encouraged the development of regional peculiarities which probably needed no extra incentives since Canada's multitude of ethnic groups had already given the provinces a plethora of peculiarities. Although Canada has cut its umbilical cord with Great Britian, British influence is still great in Canada. Many postwar actions of the Canadian government reflected policies of the British government. American influence has increased largely because of geographical influences. Although Canada is a horizontal country, East-West, its lines of communication are vertical, North-South. New York and Boston are as close to Montreal as is Toronto, and closer than Winnipeg, Vancouver, or Halifax.   J. D. Neville

2140. Patterson, F. H. SIR CHARLES HIBBERT TUPPER. *Nova Scotia Hist. Soc. Collections [Canada] 1977 39: 121-154.* Deals with certain incidents in the political life of Charles Hibbert Tupper (1855-1927) both as a federal member for Pictou County, during 1882-1904, then as a member of the federal cabinet during 1888-96. To understand the political climate of Pictou County in the 1880's, one must know about the various branches of the Presbyterian Church represented by the early settlers. Being the son of Sir Charles Tupper, coupled with his proven ability as a debater and an extremely hard worker, Tupper was assured success in politics. His friendship with Sir John Thompson brought him to the fore of the Conservative Party within a short period of time and in 1894 he became Minister of Justice and had to deal with the contentious "Manitoba School Question." By 1898, Tupper had moved to British Columbia for personal, financial, and medical reasons and there he created a sensation by charging maladministration against Clifton Sifton, the Minister of the Interior. By the age of 45 his public career had ended, but for the next 27 years his influence in party circles, both in Nova Scotia and in British Columbia, was considerable. 10 notes.
                                                                         E. A. Chard

2141. Polèse, Mario. LE SECTEUR TERTIAIRE ET LE DÉVELOPPEMENT ÉCONOMIQUE RÉGIONAL. VERS UN MODÈLE OPÉRATIONNEL DES ACTIVITÉS MOTRICES [The role of service activities in regional economic growth: towards an operational model]. *Actualité Écon. [Canada] 1974 50(4): 475-490.* "Tertiary activity is rapidly growing in all industrialized nations: it already accounts for almost two third of Canada's (and Québec's) total production and employment. It thus becomes increasingly reasonable to think that many service activities are becoming autonomous agents of economic growth rather than simply being induced (non-basic) activities as is generally postulated in classical regional development models. This paper discusses in what manner certain services might be involved in the growth process, and particularly how we might identify and measure them. The framework of the paper is regional rather than national growth since it is felt that it is on the regional level that the growth impact of the service sector is most easily discernible. We propose a largely conceptual model of the regional growth impact of service activities. The model leans heavily on certain theories prevalent in regional economics, especially export-base theory and central place theory. The main problem, we observe, as in all impact models, is not measuring short-run impacts but rather that of measuring long-run dynamic impacts."   J

2142. Scott, Beverly. COMPILING A REGIONAL BIBLIOGRAPHY. *Can. Lib. J. [Canada] 1978 35(2): 103-105, 107, 109.* Proposes a national system to compile local bibliographies based on the method devised by the Algonquin College Resource Centre for the Ottawa area. Suggests improvements in bibliographic control through policies such as including the holdings of libraries of municipal governments and community groups. Describes search strategies by the Centre staff and its publication procedures. Canadian readers need a national regional bibliography published serially. 11 notes.   D. J. Mycue

2143. Simeon, Richard and Elkins, David J. REGIONAL POLITICAL CULTURES IN CANADA. *Can. J. of Pol. Sci. 1974 7(3): 397-437.* Explores marked differences in Canada's political cultures on the basis of three sets of attitudes towards efficacy, trust, and involvement. Data drawn from 1965 and 1968 national post-election surveys. 17 tables, 54 notes.   R. V. Kubicek

2144. Simeon, Richard. REGIONALISM AND CANADIAN POLITICAL INSTITUTIONS. *Queen's Q. [Canada] 1975 82(4): 499-511.* "The regionalized character of Canadian politics . . . is not only a function of the territorial character of our underlying ethnic, economic and cultural diversity, but also, perhaps more important, a result of the operation of three major institutional characteristics of Canadian Government: the federal system, the electoral system and British-style cabinet." These political institutions reinforce the territorial dimensions of politics and minimize nonregional, national cleavages. 6 notes.   T. Simmerman

2145. Soroka, Lewis. LES DIFFÉRENCES INTER-PROVINCIALES DANS LES CYCLES DE L'EMPLOI MANUFACTURIER, 1949-1970 [Interprovincial differences in the cycles of manufacturing employment, 1949-70]. *Actualité Écon. [Canada] 1978 54(1): 92-103.* Canada's provinces show considerable differences in how they respond to cycles in manufacturing employment. Nova Scotia, Ontario, Newfoundland, and Alberta have been relatively unstable. The unstable provinces have been less able to profit from federal revenue sharing than have the stable provinces. Exports and imports seem to play a large role in the transmission of these cycles to regional economies, and the key to a better comprehension of provincial cycles lies in the exports from the provinces on an interregional and international level. 3 tables, 20 notes, biblio., appendix.   J. C. Billigmeier

2146. Stegner, Wallace. LETTER FROM CANADA. *Am. West 1974 11(1): 28-30.* Finds that the current search for Canadian national identity is similar to past preoccupations with regionalism south of the border, particularly in the American West. The parallels are striking and numerous. The common effort to define Canadian identity is fraught, however, with the basic contradictions posed by regionalism and ethnicity —the intractable French Canada-English Canada division, and the ethnic "vertical mosaic" instead of the melting pot.   D. L. Smith

2147. Stevenson, Garth. FOREIGN DIRECT INVESTMENT AND THE PROVINCES: A STUDY OF ELITE ATTITUDES. *Can. J. of Pol. Sci. 1974 7(4): 630-647.* Uses information derived from questionnaires given members of the 10 Canadian provincial legislatures to gauge attitudes toward foreign investment and programs for economic nationalism. 9 tables, 21 notes.   R. V. Kubicek

2148. Vaillancourt, François. LE COMMERCE INTERPROVINCIAL QUÉBEC-ONTARIO: UN ESSAI D'ANALYSE PAR LA THÉORIE DU COMMERCE INTERNATIONAL [Quebec Ontario interprovincial commerce. An attempt at analysis through the theory of international commerce]. *Actualité Écon. [Canada] 1974 50(2): 259-269.* This study aims at explaining commerce between Quebec and Ontario by the generally used Hecksher-Ohlin theory of international exchange. Concludes that this theory is not valid. If data were available, it would be interesting to follow the suggestions of Dales, Faucher, and Lamontagne. Based on governmental data and secondary sources; 5 tables, 26 notes.   L. R. Atkins

2149. —. [CANADIANS, IMMIGRANTS, AND OCCUPATIONAL STATUS]. *Can. Rev. of Sociol. and Anthrop. 1973 10(4): 366-372.*
Warburton, T. Rennie. CANADIANS, IMMIGRANTS, AND OCCUPATIONAL STATUS: A COMMENT, *pp. 366-370.* Criticizes article by Bernard Blishen on the regional class distribution of Canadian-born and immigrant males in the labor force, claiming he omitted a vast array of potential cultural influences, restricting occupational levels to those entered on coming to Canada. The author offers a proposition which incorporates some of the factors Blishen omits including important social structural variables. Biblio.
Blishen, Bernard R. CANADIANS, IMMIGRANTS, AND OCCUPATIONAL STATUS: A REJOINDER, *pp. 370-372.* States that the point of his previous article is that the level of education has an important influence on the class distribution of immigrants. Biblio.   E. P. Stickney

2150. —. L'ÉCONOMIE ET LES DISPARITÉS RÉGIONALES [The economy and regional disparities]. *Action Natl. [Canada] 1978 67(8): 607-623.* Despite favorable rhetoric, Canada remains far from genuine biculturalism. The English sector is strongly influenced and supported by the United States. The maintenance of French culture in North America requires a stronger Quebec economy, and the leveling of regional economic disparity in which Quebec suffers in comparison with Ontario. This is a necessary, but not sufficient condition to render French Canada viable. The cooperative movement can make a major contribution to Quebec's economic development. Since 1951, Montreal has increased its dominance over Quebec, while falling farther behind Toronto on the national scale. Quebec must modernize her paper industry and agriculture, develop asbestos and aluminum mills, restructure weak industries, and consolidate and expand metal fabrication. Primary and secondary sources; 7 tables, 13 notes.   A. W. Novitsky

The Atlantic Provinces

General

2151. Alexander, David. ECONOMIC GROWTH IN THE AT-LANTIC REGION, 1880 TO 1940. *Acadiensis [Canada] 1978 8(1): 47-76.* The Maritime Provinces and Newfoundland have traditionally been treated as two regions, but certain similarities exist and suggest the utility of a systematic, comparative, quantitative assessment as a means of understanding Newfoundland's economic history. During 1880-1910 Newfoundland and the Maritimes grew at the same rate (2.2%), which was 50% less than the growth rate in Canada (3.8%). During 1910-39 Newfoundland's aggregate growth of output matched Canada's, while the Maritimes lagged behind. But in the key sector—fishing—Newfoundland failed to achieve reasonable growth. 69 notes.   D. F. Chard

2152. Allen, James P. FRANCO-AMERICANS IN MAINE: A GEOGRAPHICAL PERSPECTIVE. *Acadiensis [Canada] 1974 4(1): 32-66.* Depicts geographical and social characteristics of Maine's Franco-Americans, many of whom immigrated to the state during the later 19th and early 20th centuries. Major immigration included southward expansion of rural settlements along the upper St. John River and the migration of Canadians to textile and later pulp and paper manufacturing centers. Generally settling together and maintaining their language and Catholic faith, the Franco-Americans retained their ethnic identity surprisingly well, although there has been slippage in the last two decades due to changing conditions. Based on private and official census reports, published government materials, newspapers, and secondary sources; 3 maps, 7 tables, 85 notes.   E. A. Churchill

2153. Beck, J. Murray. THE MARITIMES: A REGION OR THREE PROVINCES. *Tr. of the Royal Soc. of Can. [Canada] 1977 15: 301-313.* Notes that outsiders and statisticians are more likely to refer to a Maritime Region than are the inhabitants of the three provinces. The people, except for the French, come from the same national origin and have the same economic problems, but continue to think of themselves in terms of provincial rather than regional loyalty. Thus, by abstract and impersonal criteria, the three provinces form a region; however, using personal characteristics one sees that regionalism is poorly developed.
J. D. Neville

2154. Brookes, Alan A. OUT-MIGRATION FROM THE MARI-TIME PROVINCES, 1860-1900: SOME PRELIMINARY CONSID-ERATIONS. *Acadiensis [Canada] 1976 5(2): 26-56.* Emigration from the Maritime Provinces during 1860-1900 was largely because of persistent depressions and economic dislocation. By the 1880's the exodus had spread into rural areas not previously affected, and to industrializing urban centers. Beginning with young, single people, the movement later embraced older, more stable elements and whole families. Most went to New England, especially Boston, where they "assumed a wide range of better jobs." Transportation and communication links and commercial orientation favored Boston. 78 notes.   D. F. Chard

2155. Byrne, Cyril. THE MARITIME VISITS OF JOSEPH-OCTAVE PLESSIS, BISHOP OF QUEBEC. *Nova Scotia Hist. Soc. Collections [Canada] 1977 39: 23-48.* The diary of the Bishop of Quebec, Joseph-Octave Plessis, provided considerable detail of the visits which he undertook in 1812 and 1815 to his diocese in Prince Edward Island, Cape Breton, and mainland Nova Scotia, as well as New Brunswick. Several

outstanding characteristics of Plessis's attitude are noted: his implicit and explicit acceptance of the British dominance; his adverse judgment of the Acadians; his observation of the "most perfect harmony [which] existed" between the Scotch and Acadian Catholics on Prince Edward Island; his consciousness of his episcopal office and the dignity which it deserved together with the respectfulness due the performance of the sacred offices of the Church. Interesting details of daily life of the whites and Indians are delineated, as are frequent references to the geography and topography of the Maritime Provinces.   E. A. Chard

2156. Cormier, Clement. LA SOCIÉTÉ ACADIENNE D'AU-JOURD'HUI [Acadian society today]. *Tr. of the Royal Soc. of Can. 1975 13: 73-90.* Discusses the survival of the Acadian population in Canada from its first colonization in 1604 until today. Emphasizes a demographic study of French-speaking Canadians showing a decline in the percentage of the population outside of Quebec which has French as its first or only language. Centers on the Maritime Provinces which have had little immigration which is neither British nor French in origin. More people of French origin are bilingual than are those of English origin, but in North America there are only six million French-speaking people and 250 million English-speaking ones. Utilizes the work of the Laurendeau-Dunton Commission and suggests that the French-speaking population holds its own in areas where there is some population density, especially in the areas with close proximity to Quebec. Cites aids to survival of French culture. 12 tables, 12 notes.   J. D. Neville

2157. Fingard, Judith. THE RELIEF OF THE UNEMPLOYED POOR IN SAINT JOHN, HALIFAX AND ST. JOHN'S, 1815-1860. *Acadiensis [Canada] 1975 5(1): 32-53.* Overseas immigration, economic recession, and other factors forced urban poverty to the forefront of public attention in the major centers of eastern British North America after the Napoleonic Wars. Responses were influenced by "interest in economy, order, and the wider welfare of the town. . . ." Heavy outdoor labor, such as stonebreaking, and indoor factory work were seen as solutions. Generally, however, organizations dispensed charity rather than campaigning for economic reform, and capitalists exploited patterns of unemployment. 101 notes.   D. F. Chard

2158. Forbes, E. R. T. THE ORIGINS OF THE MARITIME RIGHTS MOVEMENT. *Acadiensis [Canada] 1975 5(1): 54-66.* During 1900-19 a broadly based regional protest movement developed in the Atlantic Provinces. It climaxed in the 1920's with the Maritime Rights Movement which promoted the regionally oriented Intercolonial Railway against the national government system, and promoted the ports of Halifax and St. John as entrepots for Canada's winter trade. The clergy, labour, farm, and professional organizations espoused progressive reforms through the movement which provided an uncommon amount of regional unity. 60 notes.   D. F. Chard

2159. Francis, Daniel. THE DEVELOPMENT OF THE LUNATIC ASYLUM IN THE MARITIME PROVINCES. *Acadiensis [Canada] 1977 6(2): 23-38.* Considers treatment of the insane in Nova Scotia and New Brunswick in the 18th and 19th centuries. In Nova Scotia the insane were first housed in a workhouse, but the law-abiding and reasonably responsible insane were left alone. Both provinces opened asylums in the 1840's and 1850's. Moral treatment (compassion and lenience within a controlled environment) was the principal therapeutic technique. Crowding and inadequate attention, however, led to the asylums becoming filthy jails rather than hospitals. 65 notes.   D. F. Chard

2160. Karr, Clarence G. THE ATLANTIC PROVINCES AND THE DEVELOPMENT OF THE CANADIAN HISTORIOGRAPH-ICAL TRADITION. *Dalhousie Rev. [Canada] 1977 57(1): 90-106.* Following the collapse of the Canada First movement, the consciousness of nationhood languished until the late 19th century. It revived in central Canada, and central Canadian ideas of what was Canadian history became dominant. There is a need to develop areas of Canadian history that are not centralist in tone; special reference is made of a maritime point of view. Because many of the dominant personalities in Canadian historiography are passing from the scene and because this group was largely centralist in its approach, now is the time to push for a wider concept of the Canadian historical theme. 52 notes.   C. Held

2161. Kealey, Gregory; McKay, Ian; and Reilly, Nolan. CANADA'S "EASTERN QUESTION": A READER'S GUIDE TO REGIONAL UNDERDEVELOPMENT. *Can. Dimension [Canada] 1978 13(2): 37-39.* Annotated bibliography of books and periodicals on economic development, political movements, and social classes in the Atlantic Provinces, 1920's-70's.

2162. Kennedy, Albert J. "THE PROVINCIALS," WITH AN INTRODUCTION BY ALAN A. BROOKES. *Acadiensis [Canada] 1975 4(2): 85-101.* During the mid-1910's at Boston's South End settlement house, social worker Albert J. Kennedy wrote a description of Canadians who had fled to Boston from the Atlantic Provinces because of economic conditions. Titled "The Provincials," the description is opinionated and dated but still offers numerous insights. The provincials were largely unskilled or semi-skilled, fairly religious, and generally had high morals. Although the first generation was clannish and uninterested in politics or unions, the second generation soon became Americanized. Based on published secondary materials, United States and Canadian census reports; 9 notes. E. A. Churchill

2163. Leefe, John. THE BOUNTY HUNTER. *Nova Scotia Hist. Q. 1973 3(4): 333-340.* Described the events of 1755 which brought Sylvanus Cobb, owner and captain of the sloop *York*, into government service, and the bounties which he collected by the seizure of ships engaged in illegal trade on the Bay of Fundy.

2164. Lomas, A. A. THE COUNCIL OF MARITIME PREMIERS: REPORT AND EVALUATION AFTER 5 YEARS. *Can. Public Administration [Canada] 1977 20(1): 188-200.* Evaluates the effectiveness of the Council of Maritime Premiers, 1971-76, centering on the original seven tasks and the impact of the council members.

2165. MacPherson, Ian. PATTERNS IN THE MARITIME COOPERATIVE MOVEMENT 1900-1945. *Acadiensis [Canada] 1975 5(1): 67-83.* Despite initial adversity for cooperatives in the Maritime Provinces, several new ones opened in Nova Scotia's coal mining towns in the early 1900's. Most failed. The British-Canadian one prospered but was reluctant to lead the movement. Toward the end of World War I more cooperatives opened, but they withered in the 1920's depression. In the 1930's, the Antigonish Movement inspired the establishment of 29 stores. Difficulties such as differences between rural and urban elements prevented the cooperatives from uniting, although by 1939 there were some 250 cooperatives, and in 1945 some 36,000 members. 51 notes. D. F. Chard

2166. Muise, D. A. THE DUN AND BRADSTREET COLLECTION: A REPORT. *Urban Hist. Rev. [Canada] 1975 (3): 23-26.* Discusses records of the New York City credit agency Dun and Bradstreet that pertain to Canadian Atlantic provinces 1842-1968 and which are currently located at the Harvard Graduate School of Business' Baker Library.

2167. Neill, Robin F., Jr. NATIONAL POLICY AND REGIONAL DEVELOPMENT: A FOOTNOTE TO THE DEUTSCH REPORT ON MARITIME UNION. *J. of Can. Studies 1974 9(2): 12-20.* The metropolitan centers of the Maritime Provinces sought free trade within confederation and then accepted the federal policy of industrial protection in order to promote Nova Scotian coal and iron, commodities not found in Central Canada. The Maritime Union Movement has now generated a demand for self-generating growth. This fits the new national policy in which the federal government has ceased to be the initiator of economic growth. Based on governmental reports, periodicals and secondary works; 30 notes. G. E. Panting

2168. Penner, Peter. MENNONITES IN THE ATLANTIC PROVINCES. *Mennonite Life 1976 31(4): 16-20.* Mennonites did not settle in the Canadian Atlantic Provinces until after World War II. Three motivations brought Mennonites to the area after 1954: a desire to withdraw from crowded metropolitan life, an orientation toward social and evangelical service in underdeveloped areas, and the availability of jobs in teaching, engineering, research, and medicine. 5 photos, map, 7 notes. B. Burnett

2169. Pluta, Leonard A. and Kontak, Walter J. THE SOCIAL ECONOMICS OF THE ANTIGONISH MOVEMENT. *R. of Social Econ. 1976 34(1): 63-70.* Analyzes the Antigonish movement of economic self-help through formation of cooperatives in the Canadian Maritime Provinces (1920's-40's), focusing on the philosophical underpinnings of the movement and on the institutions which were formed to further this philosophy.

2170. Smith, James F. CROSSING THE CATASTROPHE. *Nova Scotia Hist. Q., 1973 3(4): 309-322.* Attempts the reconstruction from newspaper and firsthand accounts of the events leading up to the sinking of the *Fairy Queen*, a passenger steamer which went down in 1853 on a trip between Charlottetown and Pictou, Nova Scotia.

2171. Theriault, Leon. CHEMINEMENT INVERSE DES ACADIANS ET DES ANGLOPHONES DES MARITIMES [Inverse progress among Acadians and the English-speaking population of the Maritimes]. *Tr. of the Royal Soc. of Can. [Canada] 1977 15: 145-168.* Discusses the change in status of French-speaking people in the Maritime Provinces from the defeat of France in 1763 to the present. For the first century, especially after the influx of American Loyalists, the English-speaking population dominated the area. Gradually, the Acadians developed an identity and began to play a more active role. The Catholic Church expanded until it was able to establish dioceses in the area. Conflict between French parishoners and an Irish hierarchy was a problem. Henry Wadsworth Longfellow's poem "Evangeline" and Napoleon Bourassa's novel *Jacques et Marie* helped create an Acadian identity. Colleges such as Saint Anne's founded in 1890 and Sacred Heart founded in 1899 also helped. By the 1970's the Acadians had become an important force in the area, the economy of which had declined. In New Brunswick they have achieved a bilingual province. 55 notes, biblio. J. D. Neville

2172. Veltmeyer, Henry. "PEOPLE ARE OUR BIGGEST PRODUCT": ATLANTIC CANADA AND THE INDUSTRIAL RESERVE ARMY. *Can. Dimension [Canada] 1978 13(2): 33-37.* Analyzes growth in capital concomitant with differentiation of social classes and rising unemployment in the Atlantic Provinces, 1972-77.

2173. Wilson, Alan. MARITIME BUSINESS HISTORY: A RECONNAISSANCE OF RECORDS, SOURCES AND PROSPECTS. *Business Hist. R. 1973 47(2): 260-276.* Argues that the business history of Canada's Maritime Provinces—Nova Scotia, New Brunswick, and Prince Edward Island—offers rich opportunities for the researcher as well as some substantial handicaps. Surveys the available primary source materials and the areas where gaps exist. 22 notes. C. J. Pusateri

2174. Young, Murray. W. STEWART MACNUTT, 1908-1976. *Can. Hist. Assoc. Hist. Papers [Canada] 1976: 271-273.* Obituary of a Professor Emeritus of the University of New Brunswick and Chairman of the International Programme for Loyalist Studies. He received awards for local history from the American and Canadian Historical Associations and was noted as an interpreter of the Atlantic Provinces. G. E. Panting

Newfoundland

2175. Alexander, David. THE COLLAPSE OF THE SALT FISH TRADE AND NEWFOUNDLAND'S INTEGRATION INTO THE NORTH AMERICAN ECONOMY. *Can. Hist. Assoc. Hist. Papers [Canada] 1976: 229-248.* As parts of an Atlantic economy, Newfoundland and Canada faced dependence upon foreign trade and after 1945, sterling nonconvertibility. From 1934 to the founding of the Newfoundland Association of Fish Exporters Limited, in 1949, the coordination of Newfoundland's salt fish exports increased. Faced with declining salt fish markets, Canada rejected NAFEL's experience and encouraged a shift to inadequate American fresh and frozen fish markets dominated by corporate foods conglomerates. Based on DBS figures, Newfoundland Documents, NAFEL Papers, secondary sources; 5 tables, 83 notes. G. E. Panting

2176.   Alexander, David.   A DESCRIPTION OF INDEXING PRO-
CEDURES FOR THE "AGREEMENT ON ACCOUNT OF CREW."
Archives [Great Britain] 1973 11(50): 86-93. In 1971 the Maritime His-
tory Group of the Memorial University of Newfoundland took possession
at St. John's of shipping documents (1863-1913) of the Agreements on
Account of Crew (crew lists), and some Official Logs formerly in the
Public Record Office, London.   B. L. Crapster

2177.   Alexander, David.   DEVELOPMENT AND DEPENDENCE
IN NEWFOUNDLAND, 1880-1970.   *Acadiensis [Canada] 1974 4(1):
3-31.* Traces Newfoundland's economic conditions to a failure of internal
entrepreneurship and an overdependence on outside economic leadership
and capital. Believes a major mistake was not to modernize the fishing
industry, incorporating new advances. Nineteenth century attempts to
encourage commercial agriculture and secondary industry failed, while
the country's railroads, mines, and pulp and paper companies were owned
and operated by outside concerns. Overall, Newfoundland's economy
suffered greatly. Suggests that the country should concentrate on fishing
and other export industries dominatable by domestic factors and avoid
outside capital or entrepreneurs for economic development. Primary and
secondary sources, published government documents; 5 tables, 73 notes.
E. A. Churchill

2178.   Alexander, David.   NEWFOUNDLAND'S TRADITIONAL
ECONOMY AND DEVELOPMENT TO 1934.   *Acadiensis [Canada]
1976 5(2): 56-78.* Settlement of Newfoundland flowed largely from shifts
in fishing techniques in the late 16th century, and grew rapidly in the late
18th century as French and New England fisheries declined. Late-19th-
century attempts to diversify and attract foreign investments changed
Newfoundland from a domestically-owned one-product economy to a
substantially foreign-owned three-product economy. During 1884-1911
almost 30 percent of the labor force abandoned fishing. During 1929-30
fish, forest, and mineral products dominated exports, but unemployment
still caused considerable emigration. 54 notes.   D. F. Chard

2179.   Alexander, David.   THE POLITICAL ECONOMY OF FISH-
ING IN NEWFOUNDLAND.   *J. of Can. Studies [Canada] 1976 11(1):
32-40.* In 19th-century Newfoundland the codfishery provided incomes
for fishermen similar to those of workers elsewhere. By the 1950's Newfoundland fish was being priced out of European fish markets. Newfoundland needs a strong, socially and economically efficient, domestically
owned and managed fishing industry. But the Canadian government pays
little attention to Canadian self-interest and confuses corporate size and
technical expertise with economic and social efficiency. Based on government reports and secondary sources; 16 notes.   G. E. Panting

2180.   Baker, Melvin.   THE POLITICS OF MUNICIPAL REFORM
IN ST. JOHN'S, NEWFOUNDLAND, 1888-1892.   *Urban Hist. Rev.
[Canada] 1976 76(2): 12-29.* Describes the reform movement in St. John's
during 1888-92. Because the Newfoundland government was slow to
respond to municipal needs and was burdened by an archaic, unwieldy
administration, a reform movement for responsible city government began in the 1880's. Immersed in partisan party politics and opposed by the
local business and professional elite, the movement compromised with the
Municipal Act (1888). Because the colonial government retained its influence in city government, reform efforts remained frustrated until 1902.
Based on secondary sources, newspapers, and legislative debates; 58
notes.   C. A. Watson

2181.   Bayliss, Robert A.   THE TRAVELS OF JOSEPH BEETE
JUKES, F.R.S.   *Notes and Records of the Royal Soc. of London [Great
Britain] 1978 32(2): 201-212.* Joseph Beete Jukes (1811-69) was a geological surveyor in Newfoundland, Australia, Java, and New Guinea. Having
joined the Geological Survey in 1846, he became local director in Ireland
and lectured at the Royal College of Science in Dublin. Based on his own
two-volume account of his adventures in Newfoundland and a collection
of his letters; plate, 78 notes.   T. L. Underwood

2182.   Coakley, Thomas M.   GEORGE CALVERT AND NEW-
FOUNDLAND: "THE SAD FACE OF WINTER."   *Maryland Hist.
Mag. 1976 71(1): 1-18.* "No other man of state of his generation threw
himself so energetically into the colonial enterprise" as did George Calvert, but the 20,000-30,000 pounds cost him by his Newfoundland venture
is hard to account for. Traces the evolution of Calvert's Avalon charter

of 1623, comparing it to the later Maryland charter, both with the strong
"Bishop of Durham's clause." Calvert's efforts to recover losses due to
French naval incursions, and major problems in the plantation due to
weather and disease are surveyed against the background of Calvert's own
role as secretary of state and the promotion of the Spanish Match. Growing trouble over his suspected Catholicism forced him out of office,
whereupon he took a more active role in Avalon's fortunes. The problems
of the colony seemed insuperable, and largely motivated his seeking another grant in the region of Virginia. Gold and glory were not forthcoming from Newfoundland, and it is erroneous to explain Calvert's
motivation as specifically due to a long religious or intellectual quest.
"His cruel apprenticeship" as a colonizer yet left him wiser and un-
daunted. Primary sources; 65 notes.   G. J. Bobango

2183.   Cohen, Anthony P.   THE DEFINITION OF PUBLIC IDEN-
TITY: MANAGING MARGINALITY IN OUTPORT NEWFOUND-
LAND FOLLOWING CONFEDERATION.   *Sociol. R. [Great
Britain] 1975 23(1): 93-119.* Discusses the perception of self-image in
Newfoundland since the Canadian Confederation, 1949-75, emphasizing
life-styles, religious sects, and socioeconomic stratification.

2184.   Gluek, Alvin C., Jr.   PROGRAMMED DIPLOMACY: THE
SETTLEMENT OF THE NORTH ATLANTIC FISHERIES QUES-
TION, 1907-12.   *Acadiensis [Canada] 1976 6(1): 43-70.* During 1905-06,
Newfoundland revoked US fishing privileges in order to force US ratifica-
tion of the reciprocal Hay-Bond Treaty. To avoid quarrels with a bluster-
ing United States, Great Britain imposed a temporary settlement on
Newfoundland. Not until 1909 did both sides agree on procedure and
practice for arbitration. The Hague Tribunal made an award in 1910. A
1912 Treaty confirmed and implemented it. The British won many points
and the Americans maintained their fishing liberties. 97 notes.
D. F. Chard

2185.   Greene, John P.   PROVINCIAL ARCHIVES OF NEW-
FOUNDLAND.   *Acadiensis [Canada] 1973 3(1): 72-77.* Discusses the
history of provincial government archives in Newfoundland during 1825-
1973.

2186.   Jelks, Edward B.   ARCHAEOLOGICAL EXPLORATIONS
AT SIGNAL HILL, NEWFOUNDLAND, 1965-1966.   *Can. Historic
Sites 1973 (7): 10-126.* "Archaeological investigations were carried out
during 1965 and 1966 at three areas in Signal Hill National Historic Park,
St. John's, Newfoundland, to determine what remained of the military
installations that formerly occupied the hill. These areas included the
Queen's Battery, Lady's Lookout and the area where a new interpretation
Centre was to be constructed. Significant finds were made primarily in
the first two areas. Structural remains found were typical of buildings of
the first half of the 19th century, although these structures had had to be
accommodated to the topography of the hill. Artifacts included clay
pipes, buttons, bottle and ceramic fragments, and military insignia and
accoutrements. The structural and artifact data are presented descrip-
tively as a sample of British colonial materials dating from 1800 to 1860."
J

2187.   Jones, Frederick.   BISHOPS IN POLITICS: ROMAN CATH-
OLIC V. PROTESTANT IN NEWFOUNDLAND 1860-2.   *Can. Hist.
R. 1974 55(4): 408-421.* Adds to what has already been written about the
ousting of the Liberal government in Newfoundland in 1861 by detailing
the several newspaper interventions of the Anglican Bishop, Edward
Feild. Describes how these interventions so upset the Roman Catholic
Bishop, John Thomas Mullock, an influential reformer, that he lost his
growing misgivings about the Liberals and worked for their victory with
such imprudence that he facilitated their downfall. Based mainly on
Colonial Office correspondence, Society for the Propagation of the Gospel letters and records, and Newfoundland newspapers.   A

2188.   Jones, Frederick.   THE EARLY OPPOSITION TO BISHOP
FEILD OF NEWFOUNDLAND.   *J. of the Can. Church Hist. Soc.
1974 16(2): 30-41.* Newfoundland was torn between two rival groups
when Edward Feild became Anglican bishop there in 1844. The liberals
included most of the fishermen, Roman Catholic in religion and Irish in
nationality, while the conservatives were Anglican, of English background and included a majority of the merchants. The Protestant Dissent-
ers, Methodists and Presbyterians, were ambivalent in their attitude

towards the two groups. Feild's appointment was unfortunate, since the new bishop was High Church and ritualistic while most Anglicans in Newfoundland were Low Church and evangelical. Thus a new source for dispute arose. Feild fought the evangelicals on many issues, and his relations with Roman Catholics and Methodists were not good, either. The conflict between Feild and his Anglican flock typifies the division in the Church of England as a whole. Primary sources; 74 notes.

J. A. Kicklighter

2189. Jones, Frederick. JOHN BULL'S OTHER IRELAND—NINETEENTH-CENTURY NEWFOUNDLAND. *Dalhousie Rev. [Canada] 1975 55(2): 227-235.* Compares the role of sectarian religion in the politics of 19th-century Newfoundland with that of Ireland, evaluating the reasons for the dissimilar outcome. From early predictions of disaster for Protestants if responsible government should come, to being considered a model at a later date, the fate of Newfoundland is followed through the careers of three important leaders of the day, Roman Catholic bishop John Thomas Mullock, politician Philip Little, and Anglican bishop Edward Feild. 21 notes.   C. Held

2190. Jones, Frederick. THE MAKING OF A COLONIAL BISHOP: FIELD OF NEWFOUNDLAND. *J. of the Can. Church Hist. Soc. 1973 15(1): 2-13.* Studies the career of Edward Feild, second bishop of Newfoundland (1844-76), before his accession to the episcopate. Feild was born in Worcester, England, in 1801 and was ordained to the priesthood in 1826. As curate-in-charge of Kidlington and rector of English Bicknor, Gloucestershire, Feild dealt with the many difficult problems of his parishes, demonstrating great concern for miseries resulting from industrialization. Believing that education would help alleviate some of the problems, Feild built day schools for his churches. He became widely known as an authority on education and was an Inspector of Schools for the church. In 1844 he reluctantly accepted appointment as a colonial bishop. Based on primary and secondary sources; 79 notes.

J. A. Kicklighter

2191. Kewley, Arthur E. THE FIRST FIFTY YEARS OF METHODISM IN NEWFOUNDLAND 1765-1815: WAS IT AUTHENTIC WESLEYANISM? *J. of the Can. Church Hist. Soc. [Canada] 1977 19(1-2): 6-26.* Examines the origins of Methodism in Newfoundland to discover whether the United Church represents the only continuous tradition of pure Methodism in Canada. Finds Methodism in Newfoundland to be totally unique and unconnected, except in name, to any Wesleyan group. Its founder, an Anglican free-lance missionary named Lawrence Coughlin, had practically no connection with English Wesleyans during his stay in Newfoundland and demonstrated little adherence to Wesley's doctrines or to Methodist discipline. The Methodist movement there seemed to fall apart after he left but gradually revived through solid organization, revived missionary concern and skill, and positive popular response. Primary and secondary sources, 43 notes. This issue is *J. of the Can. Church Hist. Soc.* 1977 19(1-2) and *Bull. of the United Church of Can.* 1977 26.   J. A. Kicklighter

2192. Martin, Ged. CONVICT TRANSPORTATION TO NEWFOUNDLAND IN 1789. *Acadiensis [Canada] 1975 5(1): 84-99.* In 1789 authorities in Ireland transported 114 convicts to Newfoundland. Authorities there seized and returned 80. The affair threatened to upset Anglo-Irish relations, because the British government had ceased transporting convicts to America after 1783. The authorities in Ireland actually had not violated this policy because Newfoundland technically was not a colony then. The affair confirmed inadequacies of the system and ended convict transportation to British North America. 90 notes.

D. F. Chard

2193. Martin, Ged. ROYAL IMPRESSIONS OF NEWFOUNDLAND IN 1786. *Canada 1976 3(4): 54-60.* Describes Prince William's (1765-1837) visit as captain of H.M.S. *Pegasus* to Newfoundland. While there, the Prince put down a riot, observed the progress of the fishing industry, and noted the bleak weather. 3 photos, 3 notes.

W. W. Elison

2194. Matthews, Keith. THE CLASS OF '32: ST. JOHN'S REFORMERS ON THE EVE OF REPRESENTATIVE GOVERNMENT. *Acadiensis [Canada] 1977 6(2): 80-94.* The contest for representative government was largely an internal struggle against indif-

ference and apathy. In 1820 there was no active opposition from British politicians. In 1830 only a few Poole merchants, individual Newfoundlanders, and some officials opposed representative government. By 1832 there was virtually no active opposition. Reformers overcame apathy by blaming problems on external forces. Sincere, but unrepresentative of the general population, and mistaken in their analysis of the colony's problems, they faced bitter factionalism with Newfoundland's first elections. 55 notes.   D. F. Chard

2195. Matthews, Ralph. PERSPECTIVES ON RECENT NEWFOUNDLAND POLITICS. *J. of Can. Studies 1974 9(2): 20-35.* Confederation, religion, patronage, and government mismanagement are the important factors in Newfoundland politics. Patronage and mismanagement existed because a commercial elite dominated society unopposed. During 1949-71, a countervailing force to the Liberal party administration appeared, allowing the Progressive Conservative party by 1972 to carry every major commercial and industrial center in the province. The Liberals were left with the outlying Protestant districts. Based on government reports, newspapers, periodicals, secondary works; 4 tables, 58 notes.   G. E. Panting

2196. McCurdy, Earle. THE CRISIS IN THE NEWFOUNDLAND FISHERY. *Can. Dimension [Canada] 1978 13(2): 24-27.* Newfoundland's fishing industry could be revitalized through refurbishment and expansion of facilities and involvement of the provincial government.

2197. McCurdy, Earle. THE FISHERMEN'S UNION IN NEWFOUNDLAND. *Can. Dimension [Canada] 1978 13(2): 28-29.* Despite few material gains, Newfoundland's young labor organization, the Newfoundland Fishermen, Food, and Allied Workers, has instilled pride in the workers of the fishing industry, 1970-77.

2198. Mifflen, Jessie B. NEWFOUNDLAND REGIONAL LIBRARY SYSTEM: DISTRIBUTION OF BOOKS IN SPARSELY POPULATED AREAS. *Can. Lib. J. 1968 25(2): 92-96.*

2199. Neary, Peter F. "TRADITIONAL" AND "MODERN" ELEMENTS IN THE SOCIAL AND ECONOMIC HISTORY OF BELL ISLAND AND CONCEPTION BAY. *Can. Hist. Assoc. Hist. Papers 1973: 105-136.* In Conception Bay a traditional peasant culture revealed a balance between man and nature. However, by 1900 one economic mainstay, the seal fishery, was gone and another, the Labrador cod fishery, was declining. Outside capital established iron mining on Bell Island in the Bay; however, a modern urban and industrial work force emerged slowly from the local population. The history of Bell Island has been like that of other Canadian communities based upon primary resource extraction. Based on primary and secondary sources; 2 maps, 10 tables, 96 notes.   G. E. Panting

2200. O'Flaherty, Patrick. LOOKING BACKWARDS: THE MILIEU OF THE OLD NEWFOUNDLAND OUTPORTS. *J. of Can. Studies 1975 10(1): 3-9.* Refutes the idea that the Confederation destroyed the culture of the outports. Outport life was a burdensome round of labor with people living on the edge of poverty. When Newfoundlanders voted for union with Canada in 1948, they were looking for a secure and decent mode of life. Based on personal observation and experience; 2 notes.

G. E. Panting

2201. Pocius, Gerald L. "THE FIRST DAY THAT I THOUGHT OF IT SINCE I GOT WED": ROLE EXPECTATIONS AND SINGER STATUS IN A NEWFOUNDLAND OUTPOST. *Western Folklore 1976 35(2): 109-122.* Explores the importance of social status and male-female roles among recognized singers in Calvert, Newfoundland, an outport village. The author believes social recognition and sex roles often lead to neglect of some "areas of the singing tradition." Based on primary and secondary sources; 17 notes.   S. L. Myres

2202. Scott, John R. PRACTICAL JOKES OF THE NEWFOUNDLAND SEAL FISHERY. *Southern Folklore Q. 1974 38(4): 275-283.* Practical jokes provided means by which sealers could exist as a harmonious group during periods of isolation (16c-1914).   S

2203. Whiteley, William H. JAMES COOK AND BRITISH POLICY IN THE NEWFOUNDLAND FISHERIES, 1763-7. *Can. Hist.*

R. 1973 54(3): 245-272. Examines the Newfoundland surveys of James Cook against the background of efforts to expand the British fisheries in the region in the 1760's. While developing his skills as a nautical surveyor, Cook aided his government in diplomatic struggles with the French, and provided fisheries information which revealed the economic potential of previously unexploited areas. His contributions help to explain his selection to command the Pacific expedition in 1768. Based chiefly on unpublished documents and charts in the Public Archives of Canada, Ottawa, the Public Record Office, London, and the Hydrographic Department of the Ministry of Defence, Taunton, Somerset.　　A

Prince Edward Island

2204. Cowan, G. K. COLLECTIVE BARGAINING IN THE PUBLIC SECTOR: PRINCE EDWARD ISLAND. *Industrial Relations [Canada] 1974 29(1): 200-208.* The author reports on Prince Edward Island's attempt to solve some of the key issues of public sector bargaining through its recent collective bargaining regulations for teachers and the public service.　　J

2205. Cutler, Maurice. SHALL CANADA'S LAND GO TO THE RICHEST BIDDERS? *Can. Geographical J. 1975 91(1/2): 26-41.* Much of Canada's natural resources are controlled by foreign investments, but Prince Edward Island has taken legal steps to control the situation.　　S

2206. McNally, Paul. TABLE GLASS EXCAVATED AT FORT AMHERST, PRINCE EDWARD ISLAND. *Can. Historic Sites 1974 (9): 111-116.* The table glass from Fort Amherst is limited to 16 objects but provides a good representation of English glass in the third quarter of the 18th century. Objects include twist and facet-cut stemware, a cut-glass cruet, a monteith, a stopper finial, firing glasses and tumbler fragments. The dates established for the glass coincide with the 1758 to 1771 period of known occupation of the fort. The glass is more expensive than is typical of military sites excavated in Canada. The small quantity and relative fineness of the glass appear to indicate selective use and availability of table glass in the limited period during which Fort Amherst was occupied.　　J

2207. Robertson, Ian Ross. THE BIBLE QUESTION IN PRINCE EDWARD ISLAND FROM 1856 TO 1860. *Acadiensis [Canada] 1976 5(2): 3-25.* In 1856 the head of Prince Edward Island's teachers' college suggested daily Bible lessons. The Board of Education rejected the suggestion, but evangelical Protestants launched a campaign for public school Bible-reading. Supported by most Tories, the campaign became the colony's most important political issue until 1860. Sectarian animosity replaced class and ideological divisions as the moving force in Island politics and resulted in an all-Protestant government in a nearly half-Catholic colony. 99 notes.　　D. F. Chard

2208. Robertson, Ian Ross. PARTY POLITICS AND RELIGIOUS CONTROVERSIALISM IN PRINCE EDWARD ISLAND FROM 1860 TO 1863. *Acadiensis [Canada] 1978 7(2): 29-59.* Sectarian bitterness erupted in Prince Edward Island over a debate over Board of Education membership and the Prince of Wales College Act (1860), seen as a Protestant effort to gain state funds for their college. Feuding escalated from 1861, with attempts to incorporate the Grand Orange Lodge, and because of measures threatening Acadian schools. In 1863 bickering declined. Although verbal, not physical, the battles further divided Islanders and diverted attention from land reform. 132 notes.　　D. F. Chard

2209. Weale, David. THE TIME IS COME! MILLENARIANISM IN COLONIAL PRINCE EDWARD ISLAND. *Acadiensis: J. of the Hist. of the Atlantic Region [Canada] 1977 7(1): 35-48.* Hardships led many early 19th-century settlers in Prince Edward Island to despair of their future. Many turned to the millenarian preaching of the Reverend Donald McDonald for consolation. McDonald experienced a conversion in 1828, and led a revival in 1829. At his death in 1867 he had about 5,000 followers, most of them immigrants from the Highlands of Scotland. Millenarianism may have restored their sense of a meaningful future and provided them with an identity. 46 notes.　　D. F. Chard

Nova Scotia

2210. Alexander, David and Panting, Gerry. THE MERCANTILE FLEET AND ITS OWNERS: YARMOUTH, NOVA SCOTIA, 1840-1889. *Acadiensis [Canada] 1978 7(2): 3-28.* Yarmouth lacked a significant hinterland, but had the resources and tradition to compete in international shipping. Yarmouth had 5,500 tons of registered shipping in 1840; but 179,400 tons in 1879, or more than one-quarter of the Maritimes' tonnage. Schooners comprised 62% of the registered tonnage in the 1840's and 40% in the 1870's. About 2,200 individuals invested in ships during 1840-89. Some 5% of investors, dominated by a 12-man elite, owned 66% of the tonnage. The elite invested extensively in nonshipping ventures in the 1860's and 1870's, but by the 1890's ceased to reinvest in shipping. 51 notes.　　D. F. Chard

2211. Armstrong, Christopher and Nelles, H. V. GETTING YOUR WAY IN NOVA SCOTIA: "TWEAKING" HALIFAX, 1907-1917. *Acadiensis [Canada] 1976 5(2): 105-131.* During 1909-17 Montreal-dominated interests incorporated a company in Nova Scotia to develop and distribute hydroelectric power. The syndicate then obtained control of the Halifax street railway. A new charter exempting the company from the jurisdiction of the Public Utilities Commission enabled the syndicate to issue watered stock. The syndicate then effected a merger and recapitalization, ensuring itself of large profits. It retained high electricity rates and tram fares, and neglected to develop promised hydroelectric power. 104 notes.　　D. F. Chard

2212. Auwarter, Ruth. A GENEALOGICAL FILE. *Nova Scotia Hist. Q. [Canada] 1976 6(2): 167-172.* Author discusses her experience in compiling a genealogy for the family of Waitsill Lewis of Yarmouth, Nova Scotia, giving tips on finding sources and methodology, 1976.

2213. Bains, Yashdip Singh. THE AMERICAN COMPANY OF COMEDIANS IN HALIFAX IN 1768. *Dalhousie Rev. [Canada] 1976 56(2): 240-246.* The first visiting professional company to appear anywhere in what is now Canada performed in Halifax on 26 August 1768. Puritan Nova Scotians opposed the production of plays through a spokesman known as Anti-Thespis. A supporter known as Theatricus countered the criticism in the same journal, the *Nova-Scotia Gazette*. The troupe was gathered by an actor and his wife known only as Mr. and Mrs. Mills from North Carolina and contained such persons as Henry Giffard, Mrs. Giffard, and a man and wife known only as Mr. and Mrs. Platt, who appeared in David Douglass' troupe in Philadelphia in 1766. The last production of the troupe in Halifax was 28 October 1768. 5 notes.　　C. Held

2214. Bains, Yashdip Singh. THE ARTICULATE AUDIENCE AND THE FORTUNES OF THE THEATRE IN HALIFAX IN 1816-1819. *Dalhousie Rev. [Canada] 1977-78 57(4): 726-736.* Halifax critics valued the theater, but their dilemma was, should they condemn Halifax drama if it was poor, or continually aspire to London? Examines the question through the writings of pseudonymous critics. The dilemma is never clearly solved. 30 notes.　　C. H. Held

2215. Baird, Frank, Jr., ed. A MISSIONARY EDUCATOR: DR. THOS. MCCULLOCH. *Dalhousie R. [Canada] 1972/73 52(4): 611-617.* Discusses Thomas McCulloch's early life, his work as a Presbyterian minister, and efforts in establishing Nova Scotia's Pictou Academy, ending with his acceptance of the presidency of Dalhousie College. 4 notes.　　R. V. Ritter

2216. Banks, Herbert Robertson. CAPE SABLE ISLAND FERRIES. *Nova Scotia Hist. Q. [Canada] 1975 5(3): 265-276.* An account of the ferry services operating between 1850 and 1949, when a causeway was built to connect Cape Sable Island to the mainland. The service was begun by local residents at opposite ends of the passage, but operated under government subsidy after 1847. It was converted to steam about 1875. The company was organized as the Barrington and Cape Island Steam Ferry Company. Increased automobile traffic in the 1920's demanded enlarged facilities, and finally the causeway supplanted it to handle the increased trucking demands.　　R. V. Ritter

2217. Bates, George T. THE GREAT EXODUS OF 1749. *Nova Scotia Hist. Soc. Collections [Canada] 1973 38: 27-62.* The names of Robert Kirshaw and John Hudson do not appear in the ships' rolls, among the original grantees of land, on the 1752 census rolls, or among the first members of Saint Paul's Church; the situation is similar to for approximately 56% of the total number of families who in 1749 came to Halifax with Honorable Edward Cornwallis, and who constitute 43% of the entire number on the ships' Mess Lists. Cites several examples to show the extent of incomplete records kept of births, marriages, and deaths, as well as of the arrival of new settlers in the vicinity of Halifax. Seventeen pages of appendices provide a composite list of "the Cornwallis Settlers Who Didn't."   E. A. Chard

2218. Bauckman, Frank A. JOHN BAPTIST BACHMAN OF LUNENBURG TOWNSHIP, NOVA SCOTIA. *Nova Scotia Hist. Q. [Canada] 1975 5(3): 297-306.* A genealogy of John Baptist Bachman (1720-94), who arrived in Halifax in 1752 among a company of German immigrants. Mentions his descendants down to 1952.
                                                                R. V. Ritter

2219. Bilson, Geoffrey. DR. ADAMSON'S CHOLERA CURE. *Nova Scotia Hist. Q. 1973 3(4): 323-332.* Discusses the ineffective cholera cures devised by John Adamson, a doctor (though of dubious medical training) in Halifax, and the conclusion of his career in 1834 due to poor medical practices.

2220. Birchall, Stella. PHYSICIAN AND SURGEON, AGED TWENTY TWO. *Nova Scotia Hist. Q. [Canada] 1975 5(3): 242-246.* Reviews extracts from the letters of Ebenezer Annan (1820-47), a young physician from Edinburgh who had come to Halifax as a result of a dispute with his father. The letters are to his wife, Susan, who was still in Edinburgh awaiting the birth of their first child. Describes life in Halifax at that time.   R. V. Ritter

2221. Bird, Lilah Smith. MY ISLAND HOME. *Nova Scotia Hist. Q. 1975 5(4): 323-336.* Contains nostalgic recollections of early years on Port Hood Island off the coast of Cape Breton. Describes the simple, and, in some ways, primitive manner of life during the first part of the 20th century. The first English settlers, David Smith and family (the author's ancestor), came from New England in 1786.   R. V. Ritter

2222. Black, Mary Ellouise. CAPE BRETON'S EARLY ROADS. *Nova Scotia Hist. Q. [Canada] 1975 5(3): 277-296.* The first roads on Cape Breton were animal trails used also by the Indians, and then further developed by the first settlers. When Judge John George Marshall received his judicial appointment in 1823 he was also instructed to inspect and report on the condition of all existing roads. Reprints the judge's own account of his travels to meet court responsibilities, and an official road and bridge report made for Sir James Kempt, Lieutenant Governor of Nova Scotia at the close of 1826.   R. V. Ritter

2223. Black, Mary E. JOHN GEORGE'S HURRICANE. *Nova Scotia Hist. Q. [Canada] 1978 8(2): 153-158.* Excerpts from a diary of Judge John George Marshall, of Guysborough County, relate his personal experiences of a severe hurricane in 1811. The storm levelled a church, overturned a ship in the harbor, and blew down many trees. He travelled on foot eight days to reach his home, a distance of 100 miles.
                                                                H. M. Evans

2224. Blakeley, Phyllis Ruth. "AND HAVING A LOVE FOR PEOPLE." *Nova Scotia Hist. Q. [Canada] 1975 5(2): 167-176.* A tribute to and biographical memoir of Elizabeth O. M. P. Doane (1715-98) of Barrington, Nova Scotia, grandmother of John Howard Payne, writer of "Home, Sweet Home." She was better educated than most women of her day, had acquired some medical skills, and had married three times. She and her third husband, Edmund Doane, moved to Nova Scotia from Cape Cod where she practiced medicine and was long remembered in her new home.   R. V. Ritter

2225. Blakeley, Phyllis R. W. J. ANCIENT: HERO OF SHIPWRECK *ATLANTIC.* *Nova Scotia Hist. Q. 1973 3(3): 215-224.* Describes the accolades given to William J. Ancient for his part in the rescue of people (including the first mate J. W. Firth) from the shipwreck of the *Atlantic* near Terence Bay, Nova Scotia, 1873.

2226. Bliss, Edwin T. ALBION MINES, PICTOU COUNTY, NOVA SCOTIA. *Nova Scotia Hist. Soc. Collections [Canada] 1977 39: 5-22.* Discusses coal mining in Pictou County, 1767-1881.

2227. Bliss, Edwin T. ALBION MINES, PICTOU COUNTY, NOVA SCOTIA. *Nova Scotia Hist. Soc. Collections [Canada] 1977 39: 5-22.* Chronicles Pictou County and the Albion Mines during 1798-1881. Details are provided with respect to the efforts of the firm of Rundell, Bridge and Rundell and its successor in 1825, "The General Mining Association of London" especially in Albion Mines (later Stellarton). Discusses geologist Robert Bakewell, and Joseph Howe's interest in coal mining. Captures the romance of mining via the development of railways in this region.   E. A. Chard

2228. Brannan, Beverly W. and Thompson, Patricia T. ALEXANDER GRAHAM BELL: A PHOTOGRAPHIC ALBUM. *Q. J. of the Lib. of Congress 1977 34(2): 72-96.* Photographs from the Gilbert J. Grosvenor Collection, recently donated to the Library by the National Geographic Society, present professional and personal facets of the life of Alexander Graham Bell. In 1870 he moved with his parents from Scotland to Canada, and then to Boston. There he was absorbed by his work with the deaf. He developed a respiratory device which was the forerunner of the iron lung. His wife helped finance his work with tetrahedral kites and the Aerial Experiment Association. He continued his work with the deaf, and helped Helen Keller's father locate Annie Sullivan, "who became Helen's miracle worker." Illus., 12 notes.
                                                                E. P. Stickney

2229. Buggey, Susan. HALIFAX WATERFRONT BUILDINGS: AN HISTORICAL REPORT. *Can. Historic Sites 1974 (9): 119-168.* The study attempts to explain and document the historical role and associations of a complex of 19th-century Halifax waterfront buildings. It undertakes as well to distinguish their architectural features and structural alterations.   J

2230. Byers, G. THE NORTH SHORE LANGILLES OF NOVA SCOTIA. *Nova Scotia Hist. Q. [Canada] 1977 7(3): 267-289.* Traces the history and descendants of the Langille family through David Langille (1718-1804), who left France with his son, a half-brother, and two cousins to escape persecution. They arrived in Halifax in 1752. Primary and secondary sources; biblio.   H. M. Evans

2231. Cameron, James M. DISASTERS IN THE PICTOU COLLIERIES. *Nova Scotia Hist. Soc. Collections [Canada] 1973 38: 127-173.* Admitting the impossibility of tabulating the number of men injured in the collieries, some of whom died prematurely as a result, and all of whom were adversely affected for a short or long period of time, the author notes 48 major fires (and countless minor outbreaks) in the Pictou coal fields between 1832 and 1957. These, together with explosions, resulted in many deaths. Details the Drummond Explosion, Foord Pit Flood and Explosion, Vale Explosion, Marsh Mine Dynamite Explosion, English Slope Explosion, Drummond Boiler Explosion, the Allan Shaft Explosions (1924 and 1935), and MacGregor Explosion (1925).
                                                                E. A. Chard

2232. Cameron, James M. THE PICTOU BANK. *Nova Scotia Hist. Q. [Canada] 1976 6(2): 119-144.* The Pictou Bank, 1872-85, served the citizens of Pictou, Nova Scotia, until it went bankrupt and was taken over by the Bank of Nova Scotia.

2233. Campbell, Bertha J. EARLY HISTORY OF ST. ANDREW'S WESLEY UNITED CHURCH OF CANADA: SPRINGHILL, NOVA SCOTIA. *Nova Scotia Hist. Q. [Canada] 1976 6(2): 173-192.* Discusses St. Andrew's Presbyterian Church and the Wesley Methodist Church in Springhill, Nova Scotia, 1800-1976; originally separate congregations, the two amalgamated in 1964.

2234. Campbell, Bertha J. EARLY HISTORY OF PRESBYTERIANS OF SPRINGHILL, NOVA SCOTIA. *Nova Scotia Hist. Q. [Canada] 1977 7(1): 1-30.* Traces the history of the Presbyterian Church and its clergy in Springhill, Nova Scotia, from 1874, when the first elders were elected, until 1925, when the congregation joined the United Church of Canada. Primary sources; 48 notes.   H. M. Evans

2235. Campbell, Lyall. SHIPWRECKS AND THE COLONIZA-
TION OF SABLE ISLAND. *Canada 1975 2(3): 16-29.* The history of
Sable Island is the history of shipwreck in the North Atlantic. A rescue
station established there in 1801 continued to aid survivors until the
technology of the 20th century began to prevent shipwrecks. Now Sable
Island's image as a graveyard is changing because several resident genera-
tions have regarded it as their home. 5 photos, map, 11 notes, biblio.
W. W. Elison

2236. Campbell, Lyall. SIR JOHN WENTWORTH AND THE SA-
BLE ISLAND HUMANE ESTABLISHMENT. *Nova Scotia Hist. Q.
[Canada] 1976 6(3): 292-310.* Discusses Sir John Wentworth's role in the
establishment in 1801 of the lifesaving service on Sable Island off Nova
Scotia to aid endangered ships.

2237. Campbell, P. MacKenzie. CO-OP DEVELOPMENT IN
CAPE BRETON. *Can. Labour 1973 18(7-9): 7-9, 42.*

2238. Cockburn, Robert. NOVA SCOTIA IS MY *DWELEN PLAS:*
THE LIFE AND WORK OF THOMAS RADDALL. *Acadiensis
[Canada] 1978 7(2): 135-141.* Thomas Raddall (born at Hythe, England,
in 1903) came to Nova Scotia in 1913. Too poor to attend university, he
became a wireless operator, then a bookkeeper with a lumber company.
His autobiography, *In My Time: A Memoir,* reveals the context of his
development as Canada's foremost historical novelist. It is noteworthy for
its candor and lucid prose, although the latter part is less interesting,
concentrating on his uneasy relations with publishers, other writers, and
academics. 2 notes.   D. F. Chard

2239. Collins, Lewis W. LOYAL SUBJECTS, ABLE ARTISTS
AND HONEST MEN. *Nova Scotia Hist. Q. 1973 3(3): 225-244.*
Presents a commentary on the growth of the profession of architecture
in Halifax, 1749-1973.

2240. Cousins, Leone B. THE FELLOWS FAMILY OF GRAN-
VILLE, NOVA SCOTIA. *Nova Scotia Hist. Q. [Canada] 1978 8(1):
81-91.* Traces the genealogy of William Fellows, or Fellowes (1609-?)
who came to Massachusetts from Hertfordshire, England, in 1635. His
great-grandson Israel Fellows (1740-1815) emigrated to Nova Scotia in
1768 and reared a family of 11 children. Among his descendants were
members of the clergy, a ship-builder, chemist, legislators, and a US naval
officer. Includes nine generations. Primary and secondary sources; 25
notes.   H. M. Evans

2241. Cousins, Leone B. WOMAN OF THE YEAR: 1842. *Nova
Scotia Hist. Q. [Canada] 1976 6(4): 349-374.* Eliza Ruggles Raymond of
Nova Scotia married a minister who was a missionary to escaped slaves
and who eventually had a mission on Sherbro Island; she aided slaves on
slaving vessels, accompanied her husband to Africa, and defended
wrongly accused slaves against imprisonment, 1839-50.

2242. Crathorne, Ethel. THE MORRIS FAMILY: SURVEYORS-
GENERAL. *Nova Scotia Hist. Q. [Canada] 1976 6(2): 207-216.*
Genealogy of the Morris family of Great Britain, Nova Scotia, and Mas-
sachusetts in the 18th and 19th centuries.

2243. Creighton, Edith. A HALIFAX TRAGEDY. *Nova Scotia
Hist. Q. 1973 3(3): 191-196.* Reconstructs the events of an 1816 Halifax
murder in which John Westmacott was killed by two thieves, Michael
M'Grath and Charles Devit, both of whom were brought to trial, found
guilty, and publicly executed.

2244. Currie, Justice L. D. THE EMIGRANTS OF ST. ANN'S.
Nova Scotia Hist. Soc. Collections [Canada] 1973 38: 113-126. Against
the background of chaos produced by the abolition of the ancient land-
holding system of the clans, the dynamic and courageous Norman Mac-
Leod (1780-1866) vowed he would be college-educated. After attending
Aberdeen University where he acquired an M.A. and a gold medal in
philosophy, as a lay preacher he traveled to Middle River, Nova Scotia,
with about 400 Scottish settlers. In 1820, after intending to travel to Ohio,
MacLeod and supporters were shipwrecked at St. Ann's Bay, Cape
Breton, where one year later they built the first Presbyterian Church in
Cape Breton. The Nova Scotia government soon appointed MacLeod
schoolmaster, Justice of the Peace, and postmaster. In the fall of 1851,

MacLeod led 140 people from St. Ann's to Adelaide, South Australia;
then to Waipu, New Zealand. Favorable comments later caused more
than 1,000 people to follow MacLeod's example.   E. A. Chard

2245. Curry, Starr. EARLY EFFORTS TO IMPROVE SERVICES
FOR THE MENTALLY RETARDED IN NOVA SCOTIA. *Nova
Scotia Hist. Q. 1975 5(4): 381-390.* Inquires into steps in the early 20th
century for improving facilities and care for the "feebleminded." Several
agencies were involved before the formation of the Royal Commission
Concerning Mentally Deficient Persons in Nova Scotia, in 1926. Among
them were the Halifax Local Council of Women, the Provincial Council
of Women, and the Victorian Order of Nurses. The Imperial Order of the
Daughters of the Empire established a home and improved services. The
Report of the Royal Commission recommended the establishment of a
training facility, educational improvements, legal guardianship, and interest in the female feebleminded. 25 notes.   R. V. Ritter

2246. Cuthbertson, Brian C. THOMAS BEAMISH AKINS: BRIT-
ISH NORTH AMERICA'S PIONEER ARCHIVIST. *Acadiensis: J. of
the Hist. of the Atlantic Region [Canada] 1977 7(1): 86-102.* Thomas
Beamish Akins (1809-91), Commissioner of Public Records for Nova
Scotia (1857-91), was largely responsible for the proper preservation of
early Nova Scotian public records. Previous efforts only organized small
parts of the public records. Akins's *Selections from the Public Documents
of the Province of Nova Scotia* (1869) occasioned considerable controversy because its incomplete nature appeared deliberately selective concerning the Acadian expulsion, but Akins took pains to publish all
relevant documents as they came to light. 74 notes.   D. F. Chard

2247. Dunlop, Allan C. PHARMACIST AND ENTREPRENEUR
PICTOU'S J. D. B. FRASER. *Nova Scotia Hist. Q. [Canada] 1974 4(1):
1-21.* James Daniel Bain Fraser (1807-69), pioneer pharmacist of Pictou,
Nova Scotia, served the community as Justice of the Peace, dentist,
Commissioner of Streets, and inventor. He is best remembered, however,
for the first use of chloroform in childbirth. Based on documents in the
Public Archives of Nova Scotia (W721) and secondary sources; 69 notes.
H. M. Evans

2248. Dunlop, Allan C. THE PICTOU LITERATURE AND
SCIENTIFIC SOCIETY. *Nova Scotia Hist. Q. 1973 3(2): 99-116.*
Traces the 20-year history of the Pictou Literature and Scientific Society
formed in 1834 by 23 men at Pictou Academy. Lecture subjects included
hydrodynamics, oxygen properties, mineralogy, physiology, languages,
chemistry, and bridge construction. Politics and religion were banned as
topics for discussion. Based on letters and primary sources; 58 notes,
biblio., 2 appendices.   H. M. Evans

2249. Easton, Alan. BEYOND THE LIMIT. *Nova Scotia Hist. Q.
1977 7(2): 135-160.* Discusses Nova Scotia Captain Gabriel Pentz, the
schooner *Hazel E. Herman,* and their involvement in a rum-running
episode off Florida and Alabama.   H. M. Evans

2250. Eaton, E. L. ADDITIONAL KINGS COUNTY SHIP
BUILDING RECORDS. *Nova Scotia Hist. Q. [Canada] 1978 8(3):
243-247.* Ebenezer Cox (1828-1915) designed and built 30 sailing vessels
in Kingsport. Lists the names and tonnage of many of these ships.
H. M. Evans

2251. Eaton, E. L. THE FORGOTTEN CHRISTIANS OF CORN-
WALLIS TOWNSHIP. *Nova Scotia Hist. Q. 1977 7(1): 41-53.* Sketches
the history of the Christian Church (Disciples of Christ) in Cornwallis
Township. In 1812, Thomas Campbell established the denomination in
Ontario. In 1901, J. A. L. Romig brought the sect to Cornwallis. In 1910,
the last minister was recorded.   H. M. Evans

2252. Eaton, Ernest Lowden. WHO WAS JACOB WALTON?
Nova Scotia Hist. Q. 1975 5(4): 367-380. Inquires into the identity of the
two Jacob Waltons whose epitaphs appear on gravestones in the public
cemetery in the Township of Cornwallis, the first a merchant who died
in 1811, and the second his son, a physician, who died in 1840. They and
two other Jacob Waltons are identified and the findings summarized in
"The Waltons of Canard Genealogy."   R. V. Ritter

2253. Evans, G. R.   THE ANNAPOLIS ROAD: ITS WEAKEST LINK.   *Nova Scotia Hist. Soc. Collections [Canada] 1973 38: 91-112.* Notwithstanding earlier interest and schemes, it was not until 1816 that John Harris surveyed and recommended the best route for the Halifax-to-Annapolis road. Lieutenant-Governor Dalhousie surpported the construction of this inland link. For 13 years such support continued, although on such a reduced scale that by the 1830's it was evident that the government was, by default, reaching the conclusion that the road was too ambitious for the means of road construction then available. Based in part on documents on file in the Public Archives of Nova Scotia; 20 notes.   E. A. Chard

2254. Fergusson, Charles Bruce.   THE FLORAL EMBLEM OF NOVA SCOTIA.   *Nova Scotia Hist. Q. [Canada] 1974 4(1): 49-61.* Recounts the efforts of Nova Scotia citizenry to win acceptance for the Trailing Arbutus (Epigaea repens, Linn), commonly known as the Mayflower, the Provincial Flower of Nova Scotia.   H. M. Evans

2255. Fergusson, C. Bruce.   HALIFAX HAS A WINNER: HISTORIC PROPERTIES.   *Can. Geographic [Canada] 1978 97(2): 34-39.* Halifax Historic Properties, a group of seven historic buildings, dating 1825-1905, were renovated and restored, providing an authentic representation of wharf and waterfront life for tourists.

2256. Fergusson, Charles Bruce.   WILLIAM SABATIER—PUBLIC SPIRITED CITIZEN OR MEDDLING BUSYBODY.   *Nova Scotia Hist. Q. [Canada] 1975 5(3): 203-230.* William Sabatier (1753-1826), an Englishman of French extraction, came to North America as a young man and in 1780 went from New York to Halifax, where he spent most of his life. He was deeply involved in successful business ventures, but also found time to interest himself and be involved in public affairs and local politics to the point that he was called a "busy-body" by Lord Dalhousie.   R. V. Ritter

2257. Ficken, Robert E. and Sherrard, William R.   THE PORT BLAKELY MILL COMPANY, 1888-1903.   *J. of Forest Hist. 1977 21(4): 202-217.* Port Blakely, on the tip of Bainbridge Island across Puget Sound from Seattle, was the site of the largest sawmill in the world in the 1890's. Sailing vessels carried its wood to South America, Hawaii, Japan, Australia, and China. Nova Scotian William Renton (1818-91) had founded the mill in 1864 and rebuilt it when it burned in 1888. The company was sold in 1903 for about $3 million to John W. Eddy and David E. Skinner. Based on records of the PBM Company and on secondary sources; 11 illus., 52 notes.   F. N. Egerton

2258. Fingard, Judith.   ENGLISH HUMANITARIANISM AND THE COLONIAL MIND: WALTER BROMLEY IN NOVA SCOTIA, 1813-25.   *Can. Hist. R. 1973 54(2): 123-151.* "Examines the career of Walter Bromley as a social activist in Nova Scotia and as an agent of Christian imperialism in both the Maritimes and South Australia, concentrating particularly on the response in Nova Scotia to his self-help projects for relieving the urban poor and ameliorating the condition of the Micmacs. The degree of success enjoyed by Bromley's schemes depended almost entirely on his tireless energy and dedication rather than on the support of the local population which was channelled through voluntary associations. Concludes that the colonial response to Bromley's pioneering efforts at social improvement was characterized by a parasitic reliance on the benevolence and financial assistance of the mother country."   J

2259. Fingard, Judith.   HOW THE "FOREIGN" PROTESTANTS CAME TO NOVA SCOTIA, 1749-1752.   *Can. Geographical J. [Canada] 1976/77 93(3): 54-59.* Discusses German immigrants who settled in Nova Scotia, 1749-52.

2260. Fowlie, W. D.   NOVA SCOTIA, A LEADER IN WORLD-WIDE COMMUNICATIONS.   *Nova Scotia Hist. Soc. Collections [Canada] 1977 39: 79-88.* In 1847, F. N. Gisborne won for Nova Scotia the title "A Leader in World Communication" when he had partially constructed a telegraph line to connect Quebec City and Halifax. Prior to that, under the direction of Edward, Duke of Kent, semaphore stations had been constructed and a pony express established to convey "news packets" to Boston and New York from ships arriving in Halifax. After the establishment of telegraph lines, the Nova Scotia Electric Company

was formed under Gisborne's management in 1851. Then followed the Trans-Atlantic Cable project under the direction of Cyrus Field. After many years of experimentation, the first Trans-Atlantic Wireless Station was built in 1902 at Glace Bay, amid many difficulties. Sir Sandford Fleming campaigned for a wireless connection between Canada, Australia, and New Zealand. Sir Alexander Graham Bell's efforts are discussed as well as the 1964 Mill Village, Nova Scotia communication link.   E. A. Chard

2261. Fowlie, W. D.   NOVA SCOTIA, A LEADER IN WORLD-WIDE COMMUNICATIONS.   *Nova Scotia Hist. Soc. Collections [Canada] 1977 39: 79-88.* Examines communication in Nova Scotia since prehistory.

2262. Gouett, Paul M.   THE HALIFAX ORPHAN HOUSE, 1752-87.   *Nova Scotia Hist. Q. [Canada] 1976 6(3): 281-291.* Discusses the Orphan House in Halifax, Nova Scotia, and its function as provider of food, shelter, and education for poor and orphaned children during 1752-87.

2263. Grant, Dorothy Metie.   THE TRAGEDY OF CATHERINE THOMPSON.   *Nova Scotia Hist. Q. [Canada] 1976 6(1): 49-55.* Recounts the story of Catherine Thompson, wife of George Thompson (an English ensign), and the strange circumstances of her death in Dartmouth, Nova Scotia in 1846.   H. M. Evans

2264. Grant, Francis W.   GEORGE WOODLAND: MASTER BUILDER.   *Nova Scotia Hist. Q. 1977 7(1): 55-67.* George Woodland (1867-1969) was born in Nova Scotia but he moved to Boston, Massachusetts when he was 19 years old, built his first house at the age of 22, and became a US citizen in 1896. He is remembered for the fine houses he built and for his wood carvings of birds and animals.   H. M. Evans

2265. Grant, John N.   A SHIPBUILDING DOCUMENT FROM SHERBROOKE VILLAGE.   *Nova Scotia Hist. Q. [Canada] 1976 6(2): 159-166.* Reprints the text of a contract between Alexander N. McDonald, shipbuilder, and Peter Sutherland, purchaser, to build a ship, 1873-74 in Sherbrooke, Nova Scotia.

2266. Grant, John N.   TRAVEL AND TRAVELERS ON THE EASTERN SHORE.   *Nova Scotia Hist. Q. [Canada] 1976 6(1): 17-32.* Rocky terrain, scarcity of funds, and scattered population made it difficult to maintain roads on Nova Scotia's eastern Shore from Dartmouth to Cape Canso. The discovery of gold in 1862 resulted in regular road improvements and mail service. Primary and secondary sources; 48 notes.   H. M. Evans

2267. Grant, Laurier C.   THE MATTHEW WELSH ESTATE.   *Nova Scotia Hist. Q. 1974 4(4): 393-405.* Matthew Welsh, a 19th-century Nova Scotian blacksmith, left instructions in his 1818 will for the proceeds from the sale of his estate to be invested and used for free education for the children of the town of Guysborough.   H. M. Evans

2268. Grant, Laurier C.   PRIVATE ENTERPRISE IN GUYSBOROUGH, NOVA SCOTIA.   *Nova Scotia Hist. Q. [Canada] 1976 6(4): 391-404.* Discusses six businessmen who pooled money to start an electrical generating plant to bring electrification to Guysborough, Nova Scotia, in 1927.

2269. Grantmyre, Barbara.   … AND DEATH THE JOURNEY'S END: DRYDEN.   *Nova Scotia Hist. Q. [Canada] 1976 6(1): 33-47.* Extracts from a journal of A. Stanley MacKenzie of a canoe trip from Dartmouth to Windsor, 29 August-10 September 1885. Stanley MacKenzie was accompanied by his brother George, Frederick L. Harvey, Robert Cutler, and Sandy Morrison. One of the canoes capsized, and Frederick Harvey was drowned. Biblio.   H. M. Evans

2270. Grantmyre, Barbara.   THE CANAL THAT BISECTED NOVA SCOTIA.   *Can. Geographical J. 1974 88(1): 20-27.*

2271. Grantmyre, Barbara.   TWO PERIPATETIC GENTLEMEN.   *Nova Scotia Hist. Q. [Canada] 1976 6(4): 375-390.* Discusses Nova Scotia residents Titus Smith and Valentine Gill, who surveyed much of Nova Scotia during 1800-15, and estimated its natural resources.

2272. Graves, Ross. THE WEATHERHEAD FAMILY OF UPPER RAWDON. *Nova Scotia Hist. Q. [Canada] 1975 5(2): 177-188.* Presents a genealogy of the James Weatherhead (ca. 1802-67) family from the late 1820's when he came to Hants County as a weaver from southern Scotland; carries the line down to 1946.   R. V. Ritter

2273. Hamilton-Edwards, Gerald. EDWARD, DUKE OF KENT, AND THE LYONS FAMILY IN NOVA SCOTIA. *J. of the Soc. for Army Hist. Res. [Great Britain] 1978 56(225): 39-47.* Despite a reputation for brutal discipline among his military underlings, Prince Edward was kind to the wives and families, as evidenced by his careful watch over the widow and orphaned children of Captain Charles Lyons, former Town Major of Halifax, Nova Scotia, 1812-63.

2274. Harris, Jane E. GLASSWARE EXCAVATED AT BEAUBASSIN, NOVA SCOTIA. *Can. Historic Sites 1975 (13): 127-142.* Approximately 200 glass objects, mostly bottles for wine, snuff or medicine, were recovered from the Acadian townsite of Beaubassin, Nova Scotia. The settlement was occupied by the French from the 1670s to about 1750, and by the British from the 1750s to the early 1800s. The French occupation is represented by fragments of bottles, tumblers, and stemware bowls; the British period by bottles, a small amount of plain stemware and a decanter stopper.   J

2275. Hartlen, John. WHEN WAVERLEY WISHED FOR GOLD. *Nova Scotia Hist. Q. [Canada] 1977 7(4): 331-350.* The earliest discovery of gold in Nova Scotia was recorded in May 1860 at Tangier. By the end of 1861 gold had been found in nine other locations, one of which was Waverley. Six gold mining companies were working at the site in 1866, and the town's population had increased from a few families to 1,000. By 1939 only eight men were involved in the work. The total gold production from Waverley during 1862-1976 was 73,353 ounces, or 6.4% of the Province's gold. More than one-half of Waverley's gold was extracted by 1868. Primary and secondary sources; 78 notes.   H. M. Evans

2276. Harvey, Robert Paton. JOHN HARVIE (1730-1822) OF NEWPORT, NOVA SCOTIA: THREE GENERATIONS OF DESCENDANTS. *Nova Scotia Hist. Q. [Canada] 1976 6(4): 431-442.* Genealogy of the John Harvie family (Hervie, Herve, Harvey) which originated in Great Britain and settled and flourished in Nova Scotia, 1730-1945.

2277. Harvey, Robert Paton. THE TEACHER'S REWARD: ALEXANDER FORRESTER AT TRURO. *Nova Scotia Hist. Q. 1975 5(1): 47-68.* A study of the career and innovative ideas of Alexander Forrester (d. 1869), the first principal of the Truro Normal School and the second Superintendent of Education in Nova Scotia. His attempts at improving teacher preparation and at selling the idea of a general property tax for the support of free education for all were strongly opposed and for a time frustrated by petty political feuding. Never during his lifetime was he properly recognized for his work and beliefs. 41 notes.
                                                        R. V. Ritter

2278. Harvey, Robert Paton. WHEN VICTOR HUGO'S DAUGHTER WAS A HALIGONIAN. *Nova Scotia Hist. Q. [Canada] 1977 7(3): 243-256.* Recounts the story of Adèle Hugo, daughter of Victor Hugo, the circumstances of her residence in Nova Scotia (1863-66), and her later history. Primary and secondary sources; biblio.
                                                        H. M. Evans

2279. Hatchard, Keith A. THE HISTORY OF THE APPLE INDUSTRY OF NOVA SCOTIA. *Nova Scotia Hist. Q. [Canada] 1977 7(3): 235-241; (4): 367-375; 1978 8(1): 39-49, (3): 195-204.* Continued from a previous article (see abstract 15A3:6739). Part III. Presents a brief history of the Starr family of Connecticut (Dr. Comfort Starr) and Nova Scotia (Samuel Starr) and their contributions to the early history of Nova Scotia. Biblio. Part IV. Ahira Calkin (1752-1828) farmed in Cornwallis and introduced the Calkin Pippin apple to the Nova Scotia apple industry. The Calkin family contributed a great deal to the early history of both Canada and the United States: John Burgess Calkin (b. 1829), educator and author in Canada; Dr. Marshal Calkins (1828-1922), pioneer in gynecology in Massachusetts; Charles Walbridge Calkins (1842-1918), lawyer and scholar in Michigan; and Benjamin Howes Calkin (1819-93), businessman in Canada, are the most prominent. The American descen-

dants added an 's' to the family name, while the Canadian branch retained the singular. 12 notes. Part V. Charles Inglis (1734-1816), first Anglican Bishop of Nova Scotia, retired to the Annapolis Valley and through experiments produced the Bishop Pippin apple during 1796-1808. Discusses the lives of his daughters, Margaret and Ann, and his son, John. 9 notes. Part VI. In 1872 Robert Grant Halliburton (1831-1901) urged the fruit growers of Nova Scotia to form an association to control and supervise the apple industry and to widen the market to include England. 6 notes. Article to be continued.   H. M. Evans

2280. Hatchard, Keith A. THE NOVA SCOTIA APPLE INDUSTRY. *Nova Scotia Hist. Q. 1977 7(1): 31-39, (2): 125-133.* Part I. Traces the history of the apple industry in Nova Scotia from 1851 to the present time. Uses statistics of crop yields. 4 tables, 8 notes, biblio. Part II. Outlines the family history of Charles Ramage Prescott (1772-1859) and his efforts to improve the apple industry in Nova Scotia. Primary and secondary sources; 11 notes, biblio.   H. M. Evans

2281. Hautecoeur, Jean-Paul. NATIONALISME ET DEVELOPPEMENT EN ACADIE [Nationalism and development in Acadia]. *Recherches sociographiques [Canada] 1976 17(2): 167-188.* The traditional nationalism fostered by the Acadian elites and reinforced by the principal national institutions setup over the years came into contact with a neonational movement in the 1960's. Constructed to establish new social structures to bring about development, the neonational ideology conflicted with the small bourgeoisie class of the dominant elites. Based on writings of Acadian leaders and contemporary political theorists; 44 notes.
                                                        A. E. LeBlanc

2282. Hayes, F. Ronald. TWO PRESIDENTS, TWO CULTURES, AND TWO WARS: A PORTRAIT OF DALHOUSIE AS A MICROCOSM OF TWENTIETH-CENTURY CANADA. *Dalhousie R. [Canada] 1974 54(3): 405-417.* Compares the direction taken by Dalhousie University through two presidents' administrations: A. Stanley Mackenzie (1911-31) and Carleton Stanley (1931-45). 9 notes.   C. Held

2283. Huber, Paul B. TEMPORAL ASPECTS OF THE REGULATION OF GASOLINE MARKETING IN NOVA SCOTIA. *Dalhousie Rev. [Canada] 1976-77 56(4): 645-662.* Examines the activities of the Nova Scotia Board of Commissioners of Public Utilities during the 1960's-74, based on powers given to it by the Gasoline Licensing Act (1934) as amended up to 1974. The interpretation of the act by the Board is so broad that "it may well be *ultra vires*." 2 tables, 24 notes.
                                                        C. Held

2284. Hutten, Joanna. END OF THE WHITE PLAGUE. *Nova Scotia Hist. Q. [Canada] 1978 8(3): 215-223.* A sanatorium was established at Kentville in 1904 by the provincial government to care for tuberculosis patients. It began with one nurse, space for 18 patients and depended on irregular visits from town doctors for medical supervision. The sanatorium was renamed Miller Hospital, for Dr. A. F. Miller its first full-time medical doctor, and now has five staff physicians, 114 bed capacity, and a competent nursing staff. The present emphasis is treatment for all respiratory diseases, not just tuberculosis.
                                                        H. M. Evans

2285. Inglis, R. E. LOCHABER: A TYPICAL RURAL COMMUNITY. *Nova Scotia Hist. Soc. Collections [Canada] 1977 39: 89-106.* Discusses the Lochaber region through a portion of the descriptive poem "Acadie" by Joseph Howe. This geographical region is used as a prototype of "what has happened in many rural districts of eastern Nova Scotia since [the] arrival of the first white settlers." Immigration may have commenced as early as 1795 so that by 1830, the pattern of settlement was almost complete. The next 20 years witnessed many important changes such as the replacement of log cabins with frame houses, central heating, and the development of small orchards. During 1850-80, the Lochaber region "reached the zenith of its progress," yet by 1880 in retrospect, a downward trend was noted as the youth began to move to the Boston States, and later to Western Canada, creating a lack of interest in the land. Discusses Lochaber churches, schools, industries, and professionals. 16 notes.   E. A. Chard

2286. Inglis, R. E. SKETCHES OF TWO CHIEF JUSTICES OF NOVA SCOTIA. *Nova Scotia Hist. Soc. Collections [Canada] 1977 39:*

107-120. Starting in 1887, Charles James Townshend (1844-1924) served on the Supreme Court of Nova Scotia, for 28 years, including the last eight as Chief Justice. His decisions were characterized "by lucidity and reasoning." He devoted considerable time to his research and his writings, some of which were read before the Nova Scotia Historical Society and preserved in their collections. Robert Edward Harris's (1860-1931) chief interest, corporation law, brought him involvement with several businesses, including the Nova Scotia Steel & Coal Company, the presidency of which he assumed in 1904, and The Eastern Trust Company. His later friendship with Sir Robert Borden is reputed to have brought him a seat on the Supreme Court of Nova Scotia in 1915. In 1918 he became Chief Justice. E. A. Chard

2287. Johnson, Arthur L. THE BOSTON-HALIFAX STEAMSHIP LINES. *Am. Neptune 1977 37(4): 231-238.* Presents a history of the steamship lines (Cunard, the Yarmouth Steam Navigation Company, the Boston & Colonial Steamship Company) which operated between Boston, Massachusetts, and Halifax, Nova Scotia, 1840's-1917. Based on newspapers and monographs; 25 notes. G. H. Curtis

2288. Johnson, Arthur L. FROM *EASTERN STATE* TO *EVANGELINE*: A HISTORY OF THE BOSTON-YARMOUTH, NOVA SCOTIA, STEAMSHIP SERVICES. *Am. Neptune 1974 34(3): 174-187.* Account of steamship transportation between two North American ports through four phases of development (1855-1955). Competition with the automobile and rising operating costs led to its decline. Based on primary and secondary sources; 48 notes. G. H. Curtis

2289. Keane, Patrick. ADULT EDUCATION IN NOVA SCOTIA. *Nova Scotia Hist. Q. [Canada] 1975 5(2): 155-166.* A study of the pioneer steps by which the colonial legislature aided the education of adults. Between 1819 and 1824 the first step was taken, with an appropriation to the Central Board of Agriculture for this purpose. The Board established an agricultural library, published instructional pamphlets, and organized new societies. The movement spread to other areas: industry and commerce, and a Mechanics' Library Association. Governmental financial aid was sought and mechanics' institutes were organized. The efforts were more on the part of key individuals rather than any widespread governmental interest, yet government did make some response. 40 notes. R. V. Ritter

2290. Keane, Patrick. JOSEPH HOWE AND ADULT EDUCATION. *Acadiensis [Canada] 1973 3(1): 35-49.* Discusses the influence of publisher and educator Joseph Howe in establishing adult education in Nova Scotia, 1827-66.

2291. Keane, Patrick. A STUDY IN EARLY PROBLEMS AND POLICIES IN ADULT EDUCATION: THE HALIFAX MECHANICS' INSTITUTE. *Social Hist. [Canada] 1975 8(16): 255-274.* The Halifax Mechanics' Institute, founded in 1831, reflected the hopes of its middle-class sponsors of molding the urban working class in its own image. The Institute failed to attract large numbers of mechanics, and soon became a center of occasional middle-class entertainment and recreation. It failed in its original purpose because its sponsors never came to grips with the needs and aspirations of Halifax workingmen. Based on documents in Public Archives of Nova Scotia, newspapers, and secondary sources. 98 notes. W. K. Hobson

2292. Kernaghan, Lois Kathleen. "MJKL"—A VICTORIAN CONTRADICTION. *Nova Scotia Hist. Q. [Canada] 1975 5(3): 231-241.* Contains a biographical study of the career of Mary Jane Katzman Lawson (1828-90), the first Nova Scotian woman to achieve lasting literary recognition. She is remembered primarily for her social history, *History of the Township of Dartmouth, Preston and Lawrencetown.* She also edited a successful though short-lived periodical, and was an able businesswoman in a circle dominated by male initiative. R. V. Ritter

2293. Landry, Dollard. LA NATURE ET LES CAUSES DES DISPARITES SOCIO-ECONOMIQUES SUR LE TERRITOIRE ACADIEN [The nature and the causes of socioeconomic disparities in the Acadian territory]. *Tr. of the Royal Soc. of Can. [Canada] 1977 15: 169-195.* Discusses the economy of Acadia noting the difficulties in making such a study. Explains economic circumstances of the area, i.e. a largely rural, undeveloped area with a stagnant economy. Emigration has been great. Notes the different types of employment in the area and discusses the distribution of English-speaking and French-speaking elements of the population. Makes several hypotheses concerning degrees of urbanization, population, employment, women, and ethnicity. 25 tables. J. D. Neville

2294. Leefe, John, ed. SYDNEY MORTON'S DIARY. *Acadiensis [Canada] 1974 4(1): 121-129.* Details the diary of Sydney Morton (1868-1955) on a trip from Liverpool, Nova Scotia, to Halifax and back again in 1874. As he was just six his mother wrote the entries for him, but the diary is the story of his experiences. The diary provides numerous glimpses of Halifax society in 1874 as seen through a child's eyes and includes many insights into childhood at that time. E. A. Churchill

2295. Lemay, J. A. Leo. THE AMERICAN ORIGINS OF "YANKEE DOODLE." *William and Mary Q. 1976 33(3): 435-464.* Refutes traditional stories on the origins of the song and offers evidence that it is an American folk song, dating back to before the 1740's. Comments on first printed broadsides of the song, ca 1775, compares Yankee Doodle with other patriotic songs, and shows how it was used in the theater. Also provides textual comparisons and criticism of various versions with an emphasis in analyzing the "Cape Breton" stanzas and the "Corn stalk" motif of the various versions, which underline its folk origins. Based on early newspapers, broadsides, and comparison of the versions; 91 notes, appendix. H. M. Ward

2296. Little, C. H. HALIFAX CONTAINER PORT. *Can. Geographical J. 1973 86(4): 126-133.*

2297. Lotz, Jim. THE HISTORICAL AND SOCIAL SETTING OF THE ANTIGONISH MOVEMENT. *Nova Scotia Hist. Q. [Canada] 1975 5(2): 99-116.* Studies the Antigonish Movement as a significant Canadian contribution to the theory and practice of social change. It combined educational, economic, and cooperative merchandising elements to solve serious problems developing in rural areas of eastern Nova Scotia. Traces its history from its inception in the 1920's in response to various social trends (urbanization, industrialization, and rural depopulation) as part of the social action movement of the Catholic Church, and as an alternative to the left-wing and right-wing ideologies of the period. "The Movement has acted as a model and a stimulus for grassroots organization elsewhere in Canada and throughout the world." 14 notes. R. V. Ritter

2298. Macgillivray, Don. MILITARY AID TO THE CIVIL POWER: THE CAPE BRETON EXPERIENCE IN THE 1920'S. *Acadiensis [Canada] 1974 3(2): 45-64.* Historians have long felt that the use of the militia in Canada to quell disturbances has reduced violence and has been socially beneficial. The author analyzed three labor disputes on Cape Breton in the 1920's which involved the use of militia. At least twice their presence probably increased the amount of violence. Furthermore, sure of military support, industry was non-conciliatory, forcing workers to accept substandard conditions and ultimately making them more class-conscious, radical, and violence-prone. Based on archives, private papers, published government material, newspapers, and secondary sources; 119 notes. E. A. Churchill

2299. MacKenzie, A. A. THE PICTOU CATTLE DISEASE. *Acadiensis [Canada] 1975 4(2): 79-84.* Between the mid-19th century, when it was accidently brought from Great Britain, and the early 20th, when it was generally eradicated, the ragwort weed (or "Stinking Willie") poisoned and killed over 6,000 cattle in Nova Scotia. Only after a variety of ineffectual actions had been taken was the true nature of the weed understood, and programs were then developed to bring it under control. Based on *Journals of the Nova Scotia House of Assembly, Canadian Sessional Papers*, other government documents, newspapers, and published secondary materials; 25 notes. E. A. Churchill

2300. MacLaren, George. EARLY AUTOMOBILES IN NOVA SCOTIA. *Nova Scotia Hist. Q. [Canada] 1974 4(1): 37-48.* Recounts the history of the first appearance of automobiles in Nova Scotia in 1899 and the legislation passed to regulate their use. Lists vehicles manufactured in Canada 1906-13. 4 notes, appendix. H. M. Evans

2301. MacLaren, George. NOVA SCOTIA'S FIRST SCULPTOR. *Nova Scotia Hist. Q. 1973 3(2): 117-120.* Provides a brief biographical sketch of John A. Wilson (1877-1954), Nova Scotia's first sculptor. He studied at the Cowes Art School of the Boston Museum of Fine Arts. In 1902 The Royal Canadian Academy of Arts accepted one of his works for exhibit in Montreal and in 1905 he was commissioned by the state of Pennsylvania to make a monument to the men who served in the American Civil War; "Pennsylvania Volunteers" was erected in front of Independence Hall, Philadelphia. In 1917 he was appointed Instructor in the Harvard Modelling School of Architecture. His sculpture is displayed throughout the United States.   H. M. Evans

2302. MacLaren, George. PASSENGER LIST OF THE SHIP "HECTOR." *Nova Scotia Hist. Q. 1973 3(2): 121-129.* Recalls the hardships endured by the immigrants who sailed from Scotland to Pictou Harbor in 1773. They arrived in September, too late in the year to erect shelters or plant crops, and barely managed to survive the first cold winter. A passenger list is appended. (Quoted from an article by Alexander Mackenzie, "First Highland Emigrant to Nova Scotia," *Celtic Magazine*, Jan. 1883, pp. 141-144.)   H. M. Evans

2303. Major, Marjorie. THE GREAT PONTACK INN. *Nova Scotia Hist. Q. 1973 3(3): 171-190.* Presents a history of the Great Pontack Inn, one of the waterfront inns in Halifax, 1754-1837.

2304. Major, Marjorie. MELVILLE ISLAND. *Nova Scotia Hist. Q. [Canada] 1974 4(3): 253-272.* Reviews the history of Melville Island near Halifax. These four acres have been used as an Indian encampment, a naval prison, and currently as a modern yacht club. Biblio.   H. M. Evans

2305. Marble, Allan E. THE BURNS FAMILY OF WILMOT TOWNSHIP: SCOTCH-IRISH FOLK IN ANNAPOLIS COUNTY. *Nova Scotia Hist. Q. [Canada] 1978 8(2): 171-180.* Traces the genealogy of the Burns family through four generations; Francis Burns (d. 1789) came to Wilmot Township with his brother William (1733-1818) from the North of Ireland in 1764. Primary and secondary sources.   H. M. Evans

2306. Marble, Allan Everett. JAMES MC CABE GENEALOGY. *Nova Scotia Hist. Q. 1975 5(4): 411-422.* The genealogy of James McCabe, native of Belfast who emigrated to Philadelphia about 1743, and came to Pictou on 10 June 1767. Descendants are traced to 1917. Lists sources.   R. V. Ritter

2307. Marble, A. E. SOME NOTABLE ACHIEVEMENTS OF NATIVE NOVA SCOTIANS. *Nova Scotia Hist. Q. 1973 3(4): 259-279.* Synopsizes achievements of Nova Scotians in the 19th and 20th centuries in politics and government, judiciary, business, industry, military, religion, education, art, literature, music, athletics, drama, and science.

2308. Marshall, J. Furber. A BANKS FAMILY OF NOVA SCOTIA. *Nova Scotia Hist. Q. 1977 7(2): 175-188.* Traces the genealogy of Moses Banks (1739-1833) and Joshua Banks (1749-1843), of Granville, Nova Scotia. Primary sources; biblio.   H. M. Evans

2309. Marshall, Mortimer Villiers. MY THREE GRANDFATHERS. *Nova Scotia Hist. Q. 1974 4(4): 373-381.* Presents biographical sketches of three Nova Scotia pioneers: Captain Samuel Marshall, Trooper Charles E. Villiers (who fought in the Crimean War), and Reverend William Mortimer Knollin, a Free Baptist Minister.   H. M. Evans

2310. Marshall, M. V. YARMOUTH AND ARGYLE, 1814-1851. *Nova Scotia Hist. Q. 1973 3(4): 281-301.* Reprints excerpts from the Grand Jurors' Book from the district of Yarmouth and Argyle which served as the minutes of the semiannual meetings of local government for the area.

2311. Marshall, Vera G. GREAT GRANDMOTHER ISABEL: A STORY OF THE TURN OF THE CENTURY. *Nova Scotia Hist. Q. [Canada] 1976 6(1): 57-66.* Reminiscences of "Grannie Belle" and early daily life in Nova Scotia.   H. M. Evans

2312. McDonald, R. H. NOVA SCOTIA NEWSPAPERS VIEW THE UNITED STATES 1827-1840. *Nova Scotia Hist. Q. [Canada] 1976 6(1): 1-16.* Examines editorial policies of the *Colonial Patriot* and the *Yarmouth Herald* of Pictou and Yarmouth and contrasts them with the newspapers of Halifax during 1827-40. The Halifax press was more critical of US policies in foreign relations and domestic affairs. 61 notes.   H. M. Evans

2313. McLaughlin, K. M. W. S. FIELDING AND THE LIBERAL PARTY IN NOVA SCOTIA, 1891-1896. *Acadiensis [Canada] 1974 3(2): 65-79.* The Liberal Party of Nova Scotia fared badly in national elections during the 1880's and early 1890's. The national party advocated policies that would discontinue the national coal subsidy and, for all practical purposes, eliminate Catholic schools in Manitoba, policies disliked by provincial coal miners and Catholics respectively. William Stevens Fielding influenced a more moderate coal policy and defused the school issue. Thus in 1896 the provincial Liberals improved their showing in the national election. Primary and secondary sources; 60 notes.   E. A. Churchill

2314. McLeod, Carol. BALTIMORE: SHIP OF DOOM. *Nova Scotia Hist. Q. [Canada] 1978 8(2): 125-133.* An account of the mystery of the brigantine *Baltimore* which was found in the harbor of Chebogue, Nova Scotia, on 5 December 1735. Attempts to explain the deserted, blood-spattered ship's appearance in the harbor were inconclusive. The convict passengers might have been murdered by the Indians; the testimony of the one survivor, Susannah Buckler, was not to be trusted. Secondary sources; 6 notes.   H. M. Evans

2315. McNairn, Norman A. MISSION TO NOVA SCOTIA. *Methodist Hist. 1974 12(2): 3-18.* Freeborn Garrettson and James Cromwell became the first foreign missionaries of the Methodist Episcopal Church when they went to Nova Scotia in 1785. From 1785 to 1800, 13 American missionaries went there. In 1799, however, William Black decided there was no hope of further help from the United States and turned to England. 36 notes.   H. L. Calkin

2316. Miller, Carman. FAMILY, BUSINESS AND POLITICS IN KING'S COUNTY, N.S.: THE CASE OF F. W. BORDEN, 1874-1896. *Acadiensis [Canada] 1978 7(2): 60-75.* First elected to Parliament in 1874, Frederick W. Borden survived 37 years with only one defeat, despite an initial narrow victory and lack of high-level Liberal Party support. He achieved wealth by exploiting the existing economic system based on family alliances. Borden invested first in small lots and coastal shipping, then in lumbering, farming, and wholesaling. Borden's political hold was shaky initially with his support coming from stagnating coastal areas. After 1882 he supported growing Kentville and the County's railway interests. 62 notes.   D. F. Chard

2317. Mills, Eric L. H.M.S. *CHALLENGER*, HALIFAX, AND THE REVEREND DR. HONEYMAN. *Dalhousie R. [Canada] 1973 53(3): 529-545.* Describes the discoveries made on the expedition of HMS *Challenger*, a floating oceanographic laboratory which docked in Halifax and was visited by the geologist David Honeyman (1817-89).   S

2318. Moss, Robert. CRICKET IN NOVA SCOTIA DURING THE NINETEENTH CENTURY. *Can. J. of Hist. of Sport and Physical Educ. [Canada] 1978 9(2): 58-75.*

2319. Mount, Graeme S. THE CANADIAN PRESBYTERIAN MISSION TO TRINIDAD, 1868-1912. *Revista/Review Interamericana [Puerto Rico] 1977 7(1): 30-45.* Presbyterian missionaries from Nova Scotia began to work with the East Indian population of Trinidad in 1868. Their most effective tool of conversion was their parochial school system, which was the first to educate East Indians on the island. 4 photos, 2 tables, 78 notes.   J. A. Lewis

2320. Newton, David. WHAT IS HAPPENING IN CAPE BRETON. *Can. Geographical J. 1973 87(5): 24-31.* The Canso Causeway created an ice-free, deep-water harbor which has aided economic development.   S

2321. Patterson, F. H. SIR CHARLES HIBBERT TUPPER. *Nova Scotia Hist. Soc. Collections [Canada] 1977 39: 121-154.* Examines the political career of Charles H. Tupper during 1882-1904 as a Federal member for Pictou County, Nova Scotia, and as a member of the Federal Cabinet, 1888-1896.

2322. Perry, Ruth B. THE WRECK OF THE COBEQUID. *Nova Scotia Hist. Q. [Canada] 1974 4(1): 31-36.* The *Cobequid*, a passenger steamer, ran into freezing temperatures and stormy weather returning to Halifax from the West Indies in January 1914. Although distress signals were heard early in the morning, the storm delayed rescue operations until late in the afternoon. Three ships were involved in saving the passengers and the crew. H. M. Evans

2323. Powell, R. B. THE CROSSING OF BEAR RIVER. *Nova Scotia Hist. Q. [Canada] 1976 6(2): 145-158.* Discusses a bridge built over the Bear River, Nova Scotia, in order to connect two adjoining counties, Annapolis and Digby, 1853-66.

2324. Powell, R. Baden. NEW FRANCE DIGBY COUNTY. *Nova Scotia Hist. Q. [Canada] 1974 4(1): 63-74.* Traces the history of Emile Charles Adolph Stehelin (1837-1918), Nova Scotia pioneer lumberman, and the impact he and his family made on the early history of Digby County. H. M. Evans

2325. Powell, Robert Baden. YARMOUTH STEAM PACKETS 1839-1889. *Nova Scotia Hist. Q. 1975 5(1): 31-46.* Investigates the history of steamboats out of Yarmouth to the rest of Nova Scotia and New England. The promotion of a steamship company began with a meeting to that end in December 1839. The first steamboat entering the port was (in 1842) that of James Whitney, the steamboat promoter of Saint John, New Brunswick; his project was strongly supported by the community, holding as it did the prospect of faster communication. The pioneer efforts were followed by the organization of the Yarmouth Steam Navigation Company in 1856. Narrates developments through 1889. R. V. Ritter

2326. Pullen, Hugh Francis. THE LOSS OF THE H.M.S. TRIBUNE OFF HERRING COVE, 23 NOVEMBER 1797. *Nova Scotia Hist. Q. 1975 5(4): 353-366.* A detailed description of the last military action of H.M.S. *Tribune* when taken from the French in 1796 and commissioned into the Royal Navy, followed by a description of its grounding off Halifax Harbor on Thrumcap Shoal in November 1797, and subsequent loss off Herring Cove on 23 November. Divers in recent years have located the wreck. 13 refs. R. V. Ritter

2327. Punch, Terrence M. HALIFAX TOWN: THE CENSUS OF 1838. *Nova Scotia Hist. Q. [Canada] 1976 6(3): 233-258.* Reprints the results of an 1838 census taken of Halifax, Nova Scotia.

2328. Punch, Terrence M. MAPLE SUGAR AND CABBAGES: THE "PHILOSOPHY" OF THE "DUTCH VILLAGE PHILOSOPHER." *Nova Scotia Hist. Q. [Canada] 1978 8(1): 19-38.* Titus Smith (1769-1850) is remembered as a conservationist, land surveyor, gardener, road overseer, and writer. He was a practical man who believed in God as a Wise Providence. In 1801 he accepted an assignment to survey and report on the timber, soil conditions, plants, lakes, rivers, and game resources of the "unfrequented parts" of Nova Scotia. Excerpts from his journal indicate that he fulfilled the obligation and show that he believed that man must not destroy his environment. Secondary sources; 48 notes. H. M. Evans

2329. Punch, Terrence Michael. TOBIN GENEALOGY. *Nova Scotia Hist. Q. [Canada] 1975 5(1): 71-82.* Contains a genealogy of Thomas Tobin (d. 1783), merchant tailor, who established his home in Halifax about 1759. He came from Newfoundland and, earlier, Ireland. Mentions his descendants down to 1936. R. V. Ritter

2330. Punch, Terrence M. THE WESTS OF HALIFAX AND LUNENBURG. *Nova Scotia Hist. Q. [Canada] 1976 6(1): 69-84.* Traces the history and genealogy of the family of Johann Wendel Wuest, or Wiest (1724-1811). Born in Hesse-Darmstadt, a small German state, he emigrated to Halifax in 1751 and was one of the founders of Lunenburg. The family name was changed to West in the second generation. Primary sources; 9 notes. H. M. Evans

2331. Raymond, Ann. DANIEL RAYMOND OF YARMOUTH: A PRE-LOYALIST SETTLER IN WESTERN NOVA SCOTIA. *Nova Scotia Hist. Q. [Canada] 1978 8(3): 249-259.* Traces the genealogy of Daniel Raymond (1744-90's) who settled in Chebogue in 1772, through his third son, Jonathan Raymond (1780-1869). Jonathan settled in Beaver River, Digby County, and fathered nine sons and five daughters. Appendix. Part II. Traces the genealogy of the Raymond Family through Daniel (1744-99) and his 11 children (eight sons and three daughters). Based on vital statistics and probate and church records; 16 notes, appendix. H. M. Evans

2332. Richardson, Evelyn M. THE HALIFAX EXPLOSION: 1917. *Nova Scotia Hist. Q. [Canada] 1977 7(4): 305-330.* Presents an eyewitness account of the explosion of the *Mont Blanc*, a French munitions ship, in the Halifax harbor. The French vessel collided with the *Imo*, a Norwegian relief ship, on 6 December 1917 at 9:05 A.M. and caught fire. The disaster killed 2,000 people, maimed or blinded 6,000 and left 6,000 homeless. There was also extensive property damage. H. M. Evans

2333. Richardson, Evelyn M. THY KINGDOM COME. *Nova Scotia Hist. Q. [Canada] 1975 5(3): 247-264.* A sailing vessel named the *Kingdom Come, Ark of the Holy Ghost and Us Society* ran aground on Big Mud Island approximately 20 miles from Yarmouth in August 1910. Recounts some of the stories of the strange cult and their leader, the Reverend Frank Sanford, who owned the ship—the self-proclaimed incarnation of the prophet Elijah. The cult had as headquarters a communal community near Bangor, Maine. Various legal actions were brought against the leader, and many stories were spread about. The ship, after repair, was ultimatley wrecked off the west coast of Africa, its crew taken off by the companion yacht *Coronet*, also owned by Sanford. Sanford was ultimately imprisoned for manslaughter. He died in 1948. R. V. Ritter

2334. Ricker, Helen S. GLENWOOD, YARMOUTH COUNTY: 1895-1909. *Nova Scotia Hist. Q. [Canada] 1977 7(3): 257-265.* Reminisces about early Glenwood, including names of early residents. Winter boots were handmade, mail was delivered only twice a week, and the school was a one-room building accommodating only 30 pupils. Biblio. H. M. Evans

2335. Rutherford, Paul. A PORTRAIT OF ALIENATION IN VICTORIAN CANADA: THE *PRIVATE MEMORANDA* OF P. S. HAMILTON. *J. of Can. Studies [Canada] 1977 12(4): 12-23.* Studies the memoirs of Pierce Stevens Hamilton (1826-93), lawyer, editor (1853-61) of the Halifax (Nova Scotia) *Acadian Recorder,* stock speculator, government administrator, and at one time Commissioner of Mines for Nova Scotia. His death, in obscure poverty, was declared a suicide. Hamilton felt his failures were due largely to his strict code of honor and the amorality of his contemporaries, who seemed interested only in "getting on in the world." Concludes by placing Hamilton's sometimes self-serving reflections in the context of a short analysis of the moral and social climate of Victorian Canada. Presents a picture of an aristocrat adrift in an entrepreneurial society. Based on Hamilton's *Private Memoranda* and on secondary sources; 48 notes. L. W. Van Wyk

2336. Sancton, Andrew. THE APPLICATION OF THE "SENATORIAL FLOOR" RULES TO THE LATEST REDISTRIBUTION OF THE HOUSE OF COMMONS: THE PECULIAR CASE OF NOVA SCOTIA. *Can. J. of Pol. Sci. 1975 6(1): 56-64.* Certain rules from the British North America Act for allocation of House of Commons seats among the provinces may have been interpreted in an unwarranted manner regarding Nova Scotia. Table, 14 notes. R. V. Kubicek

2337. Scotland, James. EDUCATION IN OLD AND NEW SCOTLAND. *Nova Scotia Hist. Q. 1974 4(4): 355-371.* Reviews the early history of formal education in Nova Scotia from its beginnings with Thomas McCullouch's Pictou Grammar School (established in 1811). H. M. Evans

2338. Secouman, R. James. UNDERDEVELOPMENT AND THE STRUCTURAL ORIGINS OF ANTIGONISH MOVEMENT CO-OPERATIVES IN EASTERN NOVA SCOTIA. *Acadiensis: J. of the Hist. of the Atlantic Region [Canada] 1977 7(1): 66-85.* In the 1920's and

1930's many farmers, fishermen, and coal miners joined cooperatives in eastern Nova Scotia. The Antigonish Movement's successes generally have been attributed to local distress and dynamic leadership. Social structure factors may explain the area's receptivity to the cooperative movement. The Antigonish Movement was most successful in underdeveloped areas where it could provide links across class boundaries. The incomplete nature of proletarianization, which lessened class differences, may have facilitated such links. 57 notes.   D. F. Chard

2339. Sharman, V. THOMAS MCCULLOCH'S STEPSURE: THE RELENTLESS PRESBYTERIAN. *Dalhousie R. [Canada] 1972/73 52(4): 618-625.* A critical study of the *Letters of Mephibosheth Stepsure*, a series of 16 letters written by Thomas McCulloch, Secessionist Presbyterian minister, educator, and first principal of Pictou Academy, Nova Scotia. The letters were originally sent to the *Acadian Recorder* in 1821-22, and later published in book form (Halifax, 1862). Half are satiric sketches of those who fail to live productive lives, yet Stepsure, the ideal Presbyterian settler, emerges as an "unsocial, self-centered, and priggish materialist . . . The *Letters* deserve a place in Canadian literature because of the image of the relentless puritan that is so important in our writing." 6 notes.   R. V. Ritter

2340. Sherwood, Roland H. LANDING OF THE *HECTOR*. *Nova Scotia Hist. Q. 1973 3(2): 87-97.* In 1773 the brig *Hector* brought 200 Scottish immigrants from Loch Broom to Pictou Harbor. The passengers experienced smallpox, dysentery, food shortages, and a dwindling water supply on the 11-week voyage.   H. M. Evans

2341. Sherwood, Roland H. THE LAWS OF PICTOU. *Nova Scotia Hist. Q. [Canada] 1977 7(2): 101-109.* The early laws of Pictou were severe and inconsistent. The first Court House was built in 1813; before that private homes and sometimes taverns were used. Recounts details of early trials and punishments.   H. M. Evans

2342. Sherwood, Roland Harold. PICTOU ISLAND. *Nova Scotia Hist. Q. [Canada] 1975 5(2): 131-142.* Includes an account of life on Pictou Island, and describes the character of the islanders. Also contains an account of the rum-running incident of 1930 when the runner dumped his cargo to escape revenue agents.   R. V. Ritter

2343. Sherwood, Roland Harold. PICTOU'S PIONEER MINISTER. *Nova Scotia Hist. Q. 1975 5(4): 337-352.* Describes the primitive way of life and the hardships patiently accepted for the sake of his calling by the Reverend James MacGregor, sent to the "Township of Pictou" in 1786 as a missionary by the Presbyterian Church of Scotland. Records the main events in his 44-year ministry in this parish, until his death on 3 March 1830.   R. V. Ritter

2344. Sherwood, Roland H. THEY BUILT A FORTUNE. *Nova Scotia Hist. Q. [Canada] 1976 6(2): 109-118.* Discusses the Crerar brothers of Pictou, Nova Scotia, who built a family fortune around their shipping and shipbuilding operations, 1840's-50's.

2345. Silver, Marietta. WAS THERE NEVER A GARDEN? *Nova Scotia Hist. Q. [Canada] 1974 4(2): 147-154.* Points out some early flower gardens in Nova Scotia (1850-1900) and lists unusual plants from colonial gardens in the province.   H. M. Evans

2346. Sinclair, D. M. REV. DUNCAN BLACK BLAIR, D.D. (1815-1893): PIONEER PREACHER IN PICTOU COUNTY, GAELIC SCHOLAR AND POET. *Nova Scotia Hist. Soc. Collections [Canada] 1977 39: 155-168.* Duncan Black Blair's poem "Eas Niagara" is regarded as one of the "two most celebrated Gaelic poems composed on Canadian soil." His Gaelic *Diary* provides not only interesting information on society but also on the youthful author's education, including 1834-38, when he was enrolled at the University of Edinburgh. In 1846 he came to Nova Scotia as a Free Church [Presbyterian] missionary, remained slightly more than one year, only to return in 1848 to accept the call of the congregation at Barney's River-Blue Mountain where he remained until his death in 1893. Regarded as "the best Gaelic scholar in America, in his time" Blair wrote *Rudiments of Gaelic Grammar,* "a most complete Gaelic dictionary," as well as some poetry, examples of which are provided in this article.   E. A. Chard

2347. Sinclair, D. M. THE STRATHBEG READING SOCIETY, 1866-1869. *Nova Scotia Hist. Q. [Canada] 1974 4(3): 273-276.* The literary venture called the Strathbeg Reading Society held its first meeting 30 October 1866 with 20 members. Its purpose was "the advancement of its members in religious, literary, and scientific knowledge by means of a library and lectures." Two and one-half years later the library was sold to the YMCA.   H. M. Evans

2348. Smith, James. ANDREW MC KIM, REFORMER. *Nova Scotia Hist. Q. [Canada] 1978 8(3): 225-242.* Andrew McKim (1779-1840), farmer, shoemaker, and Baptist lay preacher, began his political career as a campaigner for Thomas Roach, county M. P. P. At the age of 56 he ran for a seat in the House of Assembly; the final vote was disputed for two years. He entered a final plea and was awarded a seat in the legislature in February 1838. He served until 1840 when the legislature was dissolved. He entered again but died before the voting was completed. 26 notes.   H. M. Evans

2349. Smith, James Francis. CUMBERLAND COUNTY HATCHET MURDER. *Nova Scotia Hist. Q. [Canada] 1975 5(2): 117-130.* An account of the axe murder of farmer John Clem in June 1838 in the Pugwash-River Philip area of Nova Scotia. A transient farm laborer, Maurice Doyle, was charged, tried, and hung. 12 notes.
                R. V. Ritter

2350. Smith, James F. "OFFICIALS AND WALKING GENTLEMEN." *Nova Scotia Hist. Q. [Canada] 1974 4(2): 89-116.* Reviews the early history of New Glasgow from its incorporation in 1875 to 1926 by examining people, projects, and issues important in the town's election campaigns.   H. M. Evans

2351. Steinberg, Charles. THE ECONOMICS OF BARGAINING RIGHTS IN THE FISHERIES OF NOVA SCOTIA AND ATLANTIC CANADA. *Industrial Relations [Canada] 1975 30(2): 200-214.* This paper contends that the legal precedents which have until so recently discouraged positive Canadian legislation, and which could still invalidate fresh legislative efforts, are based on an outdated view of the economic relations of fishermen and fish buyers. The following briefly examines the economic underpinnings of the Canadian fishermen's right to bargain, with special reference to Nova Scotia and Atlantic Canada.   J

2352. Stephens, David E. BOOMTOWN OF IRON AND STEEL. *Nova Scotia Hist. Q. [Canada] 1974 4(1): 23-30.* Traces the history of the iron and steel industry in the town of Londonderry, on the Bay of Fundy, from 1844 (when iron ore was discovered) through 1898 (when the plant ceased operations).   H. M. Evans

2353. Stephens, David E. THE CHIGNECTO SHIP RAILWAY. *Nova Scotia Hist Q. [Canada] 1978 8(2): 135-145.* An account of the building of a ship railway across the isthmus between Nova Scotia and the rest of Canada. Work on the project progressed rapidly during 1888-91, but financial difficulties prevented its completion within the seven year period required by the original charter. The Canadian government refused to extend the charter and the line was never completed. Henry George Clepper Ketchum (1839-96) was the engineer for the project. Primary and secondary sources; 9 notes.   H. M. Evans

2354. Stewart, Gordon. SOCIO-ECONOMIC FACTORS IN THE GREAT AWAKENING: THE CASE OF YARMOUTH, NOVA SCOTIA. *Acadiensis [Canada] 1973 3(1): 18-34.* Discusses social and economic tensions of colonial society in Yarmouth, Nova Scotia, during the Great Awakening of the 1760's and 70's.

2355. Stewart, Nellie R. MUSQUODOBOIT REMEMBERS FONDLY ILLUSTRIOUS NEIGHBOUR, J. HOWE. *Nova Scotia Hist. Q. [Canada] 1974 4(3): 245-251.* Describes Joseph Howe's rapport with the people of Upper Musquodoboit, where he lived, 1845-47.
                H. M. Evans

2356. Sutherland, David. HALIFAX, 1815-1914: "COLONY TO COLONY." *Urban Hist. Rev. [Canada] 1975 75(1): 7-11.* Discusses colonial affairs and economic and urban growth in Halifax, Nova Scotia, 1815-1914; one of eight articles in this issue on the Canadian city in the 19th century.

2357. Tallman, Richard S. WHERE STORIES ARE TOLD: A NOVA SCOTIA STORYTELLER'S MILIEU. *Am. Rev. of Can. Studies 1975 5(1): 17-41.* Examines social, psychological, biographical, and historical influences which affect folklore in the form of oral tradition in Nova Scotia, 20th century.

2358. Tennyson, B. D. CAPE BRETON IN 1867. *Nova Scotia Hist. Q. [Canada] 1976 6(2): 193-206.* Reprints the text of an article written in 1867 by John Bournot describing his impressions of Cape Breton, Nova Scotia.

2359. Thomas, C. E. REV. WILLIAM TUTTY, M.A.: FIRST MISSIONARY TO THE ENGLISH IN NOVA SCOTIA. *Nova Scotia Hist. Soc. Collections [Canada] 1977 39: 169-186.* Born in Hertfordshire, England (ca. 1715), William Tutty was one of two missionaries appointed by the Society for the Propagation of the Gospel in Foreign Parts (S.P.G.) to sail with Edward Cornwallis in 1749 to what would soon become Halifax. By September 1750, he succeeded in having St. Paul's Church constructed and preached the first service. Tutty then established records of vital statistics for the infant colony. He obtained the appointment of the Reverend Jean Baptiste Moreau as his assistant with the title of "Missionary to the French in Nova Scotia" and ministered to the colony for a little over three years. His letters and reports to the S.P.G. during this interval provided invaluable data with respect to the beginnings of the colony at Halifax. E. A. Chard

2360. Tolson, Elsie Churchill. FIRST TWO YEARS OF THE BEDFORD FIRE DEPARTMENT. *Nova Scotia Hist. Q. [Canada] 1976 6(3): 311-316.* Discusses the organization, funding, and establishment of the Fire Department in Bedford, Nova Scotia, 1921-22.

2361. Ullman, Stephen H. NATIONALISM AND REGIONALISM IN THE POLITICAL SOCIALIZATION OF CAPE BRETON WHITES AND INDIANS. *Am. Rev. of Can. Studies 1975 5(1): 66-97.* Examines methods of political socialization among the extremely regionally loyal Cape Bretoners, both Indians and whites, 1860's-1970's.

2362. Vincent, Thomas B. JONATHAN BELCHER: CHARGE TO THE GRAND JURY, MICHAELMAS TERM, 1754. *Acadiensis: J. of the Hist. of the Atlantic Region [Canada] 1977 7(1): 103-109.* Jonathan Belcher, first Chief Justice of Nova Scotia, swore in the first Grand Jury on 18 October 1754. The three cases pending decision involved one charge of breaking and theft, another of robbery, and one of the murder of two British sailors who had been searching for contraband. These cases, and the Lunenburg riots in January 1754, no doubt influenced the tone and substance of Belcher's first charge, as Belcher attempted to impress the Jury with the need for peace and order. 6 notes. D. F. Chard

2363. Wallace, Mrs. Ernest. THE HISTORY OF THE MUNICIPALITY OF EAST HANTS. *Nova Scotia Hist. Q. [Canada] 1978 8(1): 51-79.* Outlines the early history (1861-1923) of East Hants, Nova Scotia. Examines the records of the officers, councillors, and wardens of the town in relation to actions on the development of roads and bridges, establishment of a Board of Health, a system of education, fisheries industry, the effects of a railway, election procedures, and farm legislation. Lists names of justices, commissioners and wardens. Primary and secondary sources; 7 notes. H. M. Evans

2364. White, Stephen A. THE ARICHAT FRENCHMEN IN GLOUCESTER: PROBLEMS OF IDENTIFICATION AND IDENTITY. *New England Hist. and Genealogical Register 1977 131(April): 83-99.* Describes the settlement of the Acadians of the Arichat region of Nova Scotia in Gloucester, Massachusetts, in the late 19th century. Gloucester had always been dominated by the fishing industry, and the winter fishery of Georges Banks was just started when the Acadians, already skilled fishermen, began to arrive. Determining how many Acadians arrived and when is difficult, for a strong desire to "become American," as well as cultural and religious prejudice, caused the Frenchmen to change their names (LeBlanc to White, Fogeron to Smith) and to work diligently to banish any trace of a French accent. The high mortality on the seas encouraged intermarriage. In addition, the absence of French priests made interaction with other non-French—and later non-Catholic—groups almost inevitable, eventually contributing to the breakdown of a sense of community. Based on oral interviews and on primary and secondary sources; 3 charts, 80 notes. S. L. Patterson

2365. White, Stephen A. THE LAVACHE FAMILY OF ARICHAT, CAPE BRETON. *Nova Scotia Hist. Q. 1977 7(1): 69-85.* Gives a genealogy of the LaVache family beginning in 1774. Traces the name changes from LaVache, Lavache, to Lavash. Primary and secondary sources; 9 notes. H. M. Evans

2366. Williams, Rick. NOVA SCOTIA: "FISH AT MY PRICE OR DON'T FISH." *Can. Dimension [Canada] 1978 13(2): 29-33.* Examines the maritime fishing industry in Nova Scotia and attempts by fishermen to form the Maritime Fishermen's Union, 1977.

2367. Wright, A. Jeffrey. THE HAPLESS POLITICIAN: E. H. ARMSTRONG OF NOVA SCOTIA. *Nova Scotia Hist. Q. [Canada] 1976 6(3): 259-280.* Discusses E. H. Armstrong's reluctant assumption of the office of Premier of Nova Scotia, 1923-24, after the retirement of G. H. Murray; examines the lack of support from the Liberal Party and Armstrong's unachieved hope for appointment to the Supreme Court.

2368. Wright, Jeffrey. THE HALIFAX RIOT OF APRIL, 1863. *Nova Scotia Hist. Q. [Canada] 1974 4(3): 299-310.* Recounts the circumstances leading to the difficulties, later referred to as the "riot," between the military and the civilian population of Halifax. The uprising lasted from 14-23 April 1863. 35 notes, biblio. H. M.Evans

2369. Young, Alexander. "THE BOSTON TARBABY." *Nova Scotia Hist. Q. [Canada] 1974 4(3): 277-298.* Sam Langford (1886-1956) fought in all weight classes from featherweight to heavyweight. Born in Nova Scotia, he left the Province and became famous as the "Boston Tarbaby." Explores his influence on racial equality and boxing. 101 notes, biblio. H. M. Evans

2370. —. NOVASCOTIANA: IN-PRINT TITLES AS OF MAY, 1974. *Nova Scotia Hist. Q. [Canada] 1974 4(2): 179-205.* Provides a subject list of more than 200 titles. Topics include Agriculture, Children's Stories, Cookery, Description and Travel, History, Politics, Science, and the Sea. H. M. Evans

2371. —. NOVASCOTIANA, 1976. *Nova Scotia Hist. Q. 1977 7(2): 161-174.* A subject listing of 108 1976 publications in 22 categories, compiled by the Nova Scotia Legislative Library. H. M. Evans

New Brunswick

2372. Argaez, C. THE ECONOMIC IMPACT OF THE SHIPBUILDING AND SHIPPING INDUSTRIES ON NINETEENTH CENTURY NEW BRUNSWICK. *Tr. of the Royal Soc. of Can. [Canada] 1977 15: 315-323.* Discusses the growth of shipbuilding as New Brunswick's major secondary industry throughout much of the 19th century. When the American Revolution cut off its source of pine masts, the British navy turned to New Brunswick. Eventually entrepreneurs took advantage of cheap timber and cheap labor to create a shipbuilding industry there. It remained important until superseded by steam and steel ships and then almost ceased. 18 notes, biblio. J. D. Neville

2373. Baker, William M. AN IRISH-CANADIAN JOURNALIST-POLITICIAN AND CATHOLICISM: TIMOTHY ANGLIN OF THE SAINT JOHN FREEMAN. *Study Sessions: Can. Catholic Hist. Assoc. [Canada] 1977 44: 5-24.* Timothy Warren Anglin during 1849-83 supported Catholicism while acting as editor of the *Freeman,* a newspaper in Saint John, New Brunswick.

2374. Barclay, C. N. BENEDICT ARNOLD: TURN-COAT AND INTERNATIONAL ADVENTURER. *Army Q. and Defence J. [Great Britain] 1975 105(2): 208-213.* Emphasizes the activities of Benedict Arnold and his wife Peggy Arnold in Great Britain, the West Indies, and New Brunswick, 1781-1801.

2375. Barkley, Murray. THE LOYALIST TRADITION IN NEW BRUNSWICK: THE GROWTH AND EVOLUTION OF AN HISTORICAL MYTH, 1825-1914. *Acadiensis [Canada] 1975 4(2): 3-45.* Examines the New Brunswick loyalist tradition from 1825 to 1914, including the loyalists' elitist origins, their loyalty to England, their suffering and self-sacrifice, and a recurring anti-Americanism, which usually emerged during periods of crisis and weakness in New Brunswick. The loyalist tradition has been seriously undercut by 20th-century historical scholarship. Primary and secondary sources; 133 notes.

E. A. Churchill

2376. Barton, K. J. THE WESTERN EUROPEAN COARSE EARTHENWARES FROM THE WRECK OF THE *MACHAULT*. *Can. Hist. Sites [Canada] 1977 (16): 45-71.* The bulk of the coarse earthenware ceramics recovered from the *Machault*, a French ship sunk in the Restigouche River in 1760, comprises three types: Type 1, green-glazed white-fabric ware; Type 2, slip-decorated red-fabric ware, and Type 3, undecorated, unglazed and partly glazed red-fabric ware. The remainder are miscellaneous decorated and undecorated coarse earthenwares. The coarse earthenwares originated in Western Europe: a source in southwestern France is postulated for Type 1 and in the south of France or southwestern France for Types 2 and 3. The evidence suggests that Types 1, 2 and 3 were part of the cargo of the *Machault* and that the miscellaneous coarse earthenwares were ship's goods.

J

2377. Brookes, Alan A. "DOING THE BEST I CAN": THE TAKING OF THE 1861 NEW BRUNSWICK CENSUS. *Social Hist. [Canada] 1976 9(17): 70-91.* The 1861 New Brunswick census contained numerous inconsistencies and inaccuracies because of political propaganda motives, patronage, informality, enumerator incompetency, and respondent distrust. Despite these problems, the census provides the most comprehensive information available on social and economic conditions in mid-19th century New Brunswick. Based on letters from census enumerators in the Provincial Archives of New Brunswick and on published primary sources; 80 notes, appendix.

W. K. Hobson

2378. Bumsted, J. M., ed. THE AUTOBIOGRAPHY OF JOSEPH CRANDALL. *Acadiensis [Canada] 1973 3(1): 79-96.* Discusses the autobiography and memoirs of Reverend Joseph Crandall, patriarch of the Baptist Church in New Brunswick, 1795-1810.

2379. Carter, Joseph Cleveland. XENOPHON CLEVELAND: A NINETEENTH-CENTURY ARTIST AND HIS STENCILS. *Old-Time New England 1973 63(4): 108-112.* The artist's grandson traces the life and artistic work of Xenophon Cleveland (1839-1899), a native of Sussex, New Brunswick, who lived at one time or another in Moncton, New Brunswick, and in several locations in Massachusetts. 2 illus., 7 notes.

R. N. Lokken

2380. Chapman, James K. HENRY HARVEY STUART (1873-1952): NEW BRUNSWICK REFORMER. *Acadiensis [Canada] 1976 5(2): 79-104.* In his generation Henry Harvey Stuart was the most prominent and widespread voice of dissent in New Brunswick. A single theme dominated his multifarious activities: the regeneration of society through education and social reform. Stuart grew up in poverty. He began teaching in the 1890's, when his Christianity led him to socialism and the social gospel. He organized the province's first socialist party in 1902, promoted unions, edited a union newspaper, and played a role in municipal and provincial politics. 97 notes.

D. F. Chard

2381. Cogswell, Dale. WILLIAM HARLEY'S REPORT ON THE ACADIANS. *Acadiensis [Canada] 1978 7(2): 103-106.* William Harley, a Deputy-Surveyor of Lands in New Brunswick, submitted a detailed report to the Surveyor-General in 1829, describing the Acadians of northeastern New Brunswick. In his report, reproduced here, Harley states that the area was densely populated, despite poor land. The Acadians survived by hunting wildfowl in spring, then fishing for herring and cod. They practised little agriculture, and spent their winters "in a state of inactivity," except when at dancing frolics, which could last for days. Note.

D. F. Chard

2382. Cogswell, Frederick. LITERARY TRADITIONS IN NEW BRUNSWICK. *Tr. of the Royal Soc. of Can. [Canada] 1977 15: 287-299.* Discusses five literary movements in New Brunswick noting outside influences—the ballad and folktale tradition popular among lumberjacks and later captured by the country and western music of Nashville, Tennessee; the 18th-century British literary tradition brought by the Loyalists; British romanticism; cosmopolitan modernism; and post-modern eclecticism. Notes the roles of Charles G. D. Roberts, Bliss Carman,

Alfred Bailey, *The Fiddlehead* poetry magazine and the Fiddlehead movement, the Bliss Carman Poetry Society, and others.

J. D. Neville

2383. Day, Douglas. FUNDY NATIONAL PARK: SMALL BUT IMPRESSIVE. *Can. Geographical J. [Canada] 1977 94(3): 28-35.* Discusses an area of New Brunswick (now Fundy National Park) since the 1870's, chronicling its settlement, lumber industry, and eventual inclusion in the national park system.

2384. d'Entremont, Harley and Robardet, Patrick. MORE REFORM IN NEW BRUNSWICK: RURAL MUNICIPALITIES. *Can. Public Administration [Canada] 1977 20(3): 469-480.* Elimination of rural county government in 1967 has dissatisfied rural residents (who claim they have no government) and incorporated areas (who claim rural residents are undertaxed). In 1975 the new Task Force on Non-Incorporated Areas in New Brunswick recommended the creation of rural municipalities.

2385. Finn, Jean-Guy. LA SITUATION SOCIO-POLITIQUE DES ACADIENS: AUJOURD' HUI ET DEMAIN [The socio-political situation of the Acadians: today and tomorrow]. *Tr. of the Royal Soc. of Can. [Canada] 1977 15: 197-205.* Discusses the role of the French-speaking population of New Brunswick, noting that, although they have increased at a rate higher than the English-speaking population, emigration has reduced their number. They make up about 40% of the population. They are also rural; thus, their influence is less than the urbanized English-speaking population. Gradual assimilation also reduces their number. Moncton is the center of French-speaking culture in the Maritimes. 12 notes.

J. D. Neville

2386. Geoffrey, Bilson. THE CHOLERA EPIDEMIC IN SAINT JOHN, N.B., 1854. *Acadiensis [Canada] 1974 4(1): 85-99.* When St. John experienced an outbreak of cholera in 1854, efforts to counter the epidemic or eradicate its causes were half-hearted and ineffectual. Uncertain what caused the disease, townspeople were unsure how to combat it, while local politicians avoided such potentially unpopular solutions as quarantining infested neighborhoods or introducing expensive cleanup programs. Realizing by fall that the disease was probably contagious, the city bought and overhauled the polluted water system, which eased political pressure. Based on provincial archives of New Brunswick, printed government documents, private papers, newspapers, printed secondary sources; 95 notes.

E. A. Churchill

2387. Harris, Jane E. GLASSWARE EXCAVATED AT FORT GASPEREAU, NEW BRUNSWICK. *Can. Historic Sites 1974 10: 74-95.* "Most of the glassware excavated at Fort Gaspereau, New Brunswick (1751-56) consists of bottles and a small number of tumblers. French glass of the mid-18th century is represented by three distinct bottle types and a number of non-lead glass tumblers. English glass of the same period is also present with examples of only two bottle types. No tableglass could be identified as being of English manufacture. A variety of bottles and a few tumblers, many of probable North American manufacture, indicate the limited use of the site from the mid-19th century to at least the first half of the 20th century."

J

2388. Hatfield, Michael. H. H. PITTS AND RACE AND RELIGION IN NEW BRUNSWICK POLITICS. *Acadiensis [Canada] 1975 4(2): 46-65.* In 1871 New Brunswick adopted a free nonsectarian school system, avoiding an Acadian rebellion only by allowing "a sectarian bias within the non-sectarian system." The dispute resurfaced in 1890 when the Catholic-dominated Bathurst board of trustees began reinstituting strong sectarian policies in their local schools. Herman H. Pitts, a newspaper editor and radical Protestant reformer, cited Bathurst excesses in prodding the province's Protestant majority to institute a "British cultural hegemony." His militant approach failed as the people refused to rekindle the sectarian conflict. Primary and secondary sources; 3 tables, 80 notes.

E. A. Churchill

2389. Headon, Christopher. AN UNPUBLISHED CORRESPONDENCE BETWEEN JOHN MEDLEY AND E. B. PUSEY. *J. of the Can. Church Hist. Soc. 1974 16(4): 72-74.* Selections from letters written by John Medley (1804-92), an Englishman who became first Anglican bishop of Fredericton, New Brunswick, to Edward Bouverie Pusey (1800-

82), one of the most prominent leaders of the Oxford Movement. Written during 1840-44 when Medley was in England, the letters were found among Pusey's correspondence at Pusey House, Oxford.

J. A. Kicklighter

2390. Johnson, Arthur L. THE INTERNATIONAL LINE: A HISTORY OF THE BOSTON-SAINT JOHN STEAMSHIP SERVICE. *Am. Neptune 1973 33(2): 79-94.* A history of the coastal trade between Boston and New Brunswick. The vessels used on the line were constructed solely to carry light cargo and passengers. The company prospered until World War I, surviving the temporary disruption of the Civil War and powerful railroad competition. It could not, however, successfully compete with the automobile, and World War II brought the International or the Eastern Steamship Company, as it had become, to a close. Efforts to revive the service after the war were unsuccessful. 8 photos, 50 notes.

V. L. Human

2391. Kalisch, Philip A. TRACADIE UND PENIKESE LEPROSARIA: A COMPARATIVE ANALYSIS OF SOCIETAL RESPONSE TO LEPROSY IN NEW BRUNSWICK, 1844-1880, AND MASSACHUSETTS, 1904-1921. *Bull. of the Hist. of Medicine 1973 47(5): 480-512.* "The incarceration of the 'lepers' " in New Brunswick and Massachusetts in different eras illustrates the traditional stigma associated with the disease. Presented at the 45th annual meeting of the American Association for the History of Medicine at Montreal, Canada, 4 May 1972.

S

2392. Kennedy, Estella. IMMIGRANTS, CHOLERA, AND THE SAINT JOHN SISTERS OF CHARITY, 1854-1864. *Study Sessions: Can. Catholic Hist. Assoc. [Canada] 1977 44: 25-44.* Following a cholera epidemic in 1854, the Sisters of Charity of the Immaculate Conception, was founded in Saint John, New Brunswick, to care for orphaned children, but expanded to include education of youth and care for the elderly during 1854-64.

2393. Kothari, Vinay. A CROSS-CULTURAL STUDY OF WORKER ATTITUDES IN A BICULTURAL ECONOMIC ENVIRONMENT. *Industrial Relations [Canada] 1973 28(1): 150-163.* "This research study examines the attitudes of French and English workers of New Brunswick, and it attempts to show similarities and differences in the attitudes of the two cultural groups. Specifically, the worker's attitudes towards his coworkers, economic benefits, administrative practices, physical conditions, and the work itself are examined and analyzed. Overall, the study points out that there are no significant differences between the attitudes of French and those of English. But the differences are likely to increase in the years to come because of social trends."

J

2394. Magee, Eleanor E. RALPH PACKARD BELL LIBRARY, MOUNT ALLISON UNIVERSITY. *Can. Lib. J. 1973 30(3): 210-212.*

2395. McGahan, Elizabeth. THE PORT OF SAINT JOHN, NEW BRUNSWICK, 1867-1911: EXPLORATION OF AN ECOLOGICAL COMPLEX. *Urban Hist. Rev. [Canada] 1976 (3): 3-13.* Using Saint John, New Brunswick, as a model, examines how one urban community was integrated, through its transport mode, into a larger ecosystem of cities. The stimulus for the integration was the impact of the Industrial Revolution on its provincial-based prosperity. Saint John sought to expand its economic horizons in the 1880's by seeking a railroad connection with central Canada. The integration into a national transportation system caused organizational and spatial changes within the city. Secondary sources, 4 maps, table, 18 notes.

C. A. Watson

2396. Morrison, Monica. WEDDING NIGHT PRANKS IN WESTERN NEW BRUNSWICK. *Southern Folklore Q. 1974 38(4): 285-297.*

2397. Phillips, Doris. NOVA SCOTIA'S AID FOR THE SUFFERERS OF THE GREAT SAINT JOHN FIRE (JUNE 20TH, 1877). *Nova Scotia Hist. Q. [Canada] 1977 7(4): 351-366.* Saint John, New Brunswick, was virtually demolished by a fire which started in bales of hay in a warehouse. The 20 June 1877 fire was the 16th recorded fire in the city and the worst in its history. It burned out of control for nine hours despite efforts to contain it. The conflagration reduced two-fifths of the city to ashes and left 20,000 homeless. Food, tents, clothing, and donations of money came from all over Canada, the United States, and Great Britain; but the disaster relief from other cities in Nova Scotia was particularly appreciated by Saint John's residents. 2 notes, biblio.

H. M. Evans

2398. Potvin, Claude. THE ALBERT-WESTMORLAND-KENT REGIONAL LIBRARY. *Can. Lib. J. 1973 30(3): 213-216.* History of the Moncton, New Brunswick, library system since 1911.

S

2399. Rees, Ronald. CHANGING ST. JOHN: THE OLD AND THE NEW. *Can. Geographical J. 1975 90(5): 12-17.* Largely rebuilt after the 1877 fire, St. John, New Brunswick, comprises a variety of mid-Victorian architecture, now endangered by unprecedented industrial expansion.

S

2400. Roberts, David. SOCIAL STRUCTURE IN A COMMERCIAL CITY: SAINT JOHN, 1871. *Urban Hist. Rev. [Canada] 1974 74(2): 15-18.* Using the Dominion Census of 1871, effects a methodology for interpreting information provided and applies it to analysis of the social organization in Saint John, New Brunswick.

2401. Rosenberg, Neil V. GOODTIME CHARLIE AND THE BRICKLIN: A SATIRICAL SONG IN CONTEXT. *Can. Oral Hist. Assoc. J. [Canada] 1978 3(1): 27-46.* A song by "Goodtime" Charlie Russell of New Brunswick satirized the production of the Bricklin, a Canadian-designed sports car intended for American markets; examines the place of satire, folk, and popular culture in local politics and in New Brunswick oral tradition, 1970's.

2402. Spigelman, Martin S. RACE ET RELIGION: LES ACADIENS ET LA HIÉRARCHIE CATHOLIQUE IRLANDAISE DU NOUVEAU-BRUNSWICK [Race and religion: the Acadians and the Irish Catholic hierarchy of New Brunswick]. *R. d'Hist. de l'Amérique Française 1975 29(1): 69-85.* In 1900, increasing population and economic power led the French-speaking Acadians of New Brunswick to vie for high clerical positions in the Irish dominated Catholic Church. The conflict centered on racial and linguistic issues. The Irish feared the Acadians might reach a compromise with the English Protestant population of New Brunswick and sabotaged attempts to teach the French language and to publish French language newspapers. Based on primary and secondary sources; 62 notes.

C. Collon

2403. Spray, William A. THE 1842 ELECTION IN NORTHUMBERLAND COUNTY. *Acadiensis [Canada] 1978 8(1): 97-100.* The defeated candidate in the 1842 Northumberland County, New Brunswick, election, John Ambrose Street, called for a scrutiny of the votes cast for the winner. The sheriff refused, but forwarded a report, reproduced here, to the Provincial Secretary. He reported irregularities at some polls, with intimidation of Street's supporters. On one occasion in Chatham a mob destroyed doors and windows. The sheriff characterized the proceedings on one day of the seven-day poll as "lawless and riotous."

D. F. Chard

2404. Stanley, George F. G. JOHN CLARENCE WEBSTER: THE LAIRD OF SHEDIAC. *Acadiensis [Canada] 1973 3(1): 51-71.* Discusses the life and works of Canadian educator and writer John Clarence Webster, 1882-1950, emphasizing his stay at Mount Allison University in Sackville, New Brunswick.

2405. Tennyson, Brian D. SCHOOLDAYS, SCHOOLDAYS . . . COCAGNE ACADEMY IN THE 1840'S BY GEORGE MCCALL THEAL. *Acadiensis [Canada] 1976 5(2): 132-137.* Presents Canadian-born George McCall Theal's (1837-1919) recollections of the Cocagne Academy, which he attended in the 1840's. He indicates that the Academy, believed representative of Canadian schools, encouraged fear and truancy rather than an enthusiastic thirst for knowledge. Revisiting New Brunswick from South Africa in 1894, Theal found the Academy's replacement "an improvement so great that the young people of the present day can hardly realize it." 3 notes.

D. F. Chard

2406. Trueman, Stuart. IN THE HEART OF NEW BRUNSWICK: FREDERICTON AND THE NASHWAAK MIRAMICHI TRAIL. *Can. Geographical J. 1973 87(6): 12-21.*

2407. Trueman, Stuart. TOURING NEW BRUNSWICK EAST AND NORTH. *Can. Geographical J. 1974 88(3): 28-37.* Map, 21 photos.   S

2408. Upton, L. F. S. INDIAN AFFAIRS IN COLONIAL NEW BRUNSWICK. *Acadiensis [Canada] 1974 3(2): 3-26.* The first Indian program in New Brunswick, developed by Lieutenant Governor Sir William Colebrook and Moses H. Perley in the 1840's, attempted to settle the natives as farmers on individual lots, eliminating annual relief payments. The remaining lands would be leased, creating funds for social uplift projects; white squatters would be kicked off. The assembly, instead, tried to sell the excess lands and create a relief fund. Their plan failed, resulting in the sale of nearly 20% of Indian lands. Based on archives and primary sources; 106 notes.   E. A. Churchill

2409. Vincent, Thomas B., ed. CREON: A SATIRE ON NEW BRUNSWICK POLITICS IN 1802. *Acadiensis [Canada] 1974 3(2): 80-98.* "Creon," a political poem, relates the New Brunswick Assembly's effort to assert itself in 1802 by electing its own clerk, Samuel Denny Street. Street served, but Lieutenant Governor Thomas Carleton had the clerk's salary paid to his choice, Dugald Cambell. The Poem, probably by Street, portrays the Governor's forces as despotic and Street's group as defending English traditions. "Creon" provides good insights into intellectual and cultural history of the period. Government publications and secondary sources; 2 notes.   E. A. Churchill

2410. Wallace, C. M. SAINT JOHN BOOSTERS AND THE RAILROADS IN THE MID-NINETEENTH CENTURY. *Acadiensis [Canada] 1976 6(1): 71-91.* In 1851 Saint John had 31,174 people, its population grew 2.5 percent annually, and it was the third largest city in British North America. It saw itself as a great trading center. Eight selected residents illustrate this. They were either Presbyterian or Low Church Anglican, were successful businessmen, entrepreneurs, or lawyers, and promoted railways for New Brunswick. They gave Saint John vitality, but by the end of the 1870's its population was declining because the railways failed to make it a metropolis. 87 notes.
                                                          D. F. Chard

2411. Wallace, C. M. SAINT JOHN, NEW BRUNSWICK (1800-1900). *Urban Hist. Rev. [Canada] 1975 75(1): 12-21.* Examines economic growth, urbanization, manufacturing, population, religious composition, social organization, and environment in Saint John; one of eight articles in this issue on the Canadian city in the 19th century.

2412. Wyn, Graeme. ADMINISTRATION IN ADVERSITY: THE DEPUTY SURVEYORS AND CONTROL OF THE NEW BRUNSWICK CROWN FOREST BEFORE 1844. *Acadiensis: J. of the Hist. of the Atlantic Region [Canada] 1977 7(1): 49-65.* For two decades before 1844, 12 to 20 men were responsible for the field work required to control the exploitation of New Brunswick's crown forests. Deputy surveyors enjoyed a reasonably secure financial basis from 1822, but they still were frustrated by the many opportunities lumberers had for evasions. Trespass was difficult to prove. The short, hectic nature of the spring drive complicated checking. Some deputy surveyors were careless and inefficient, but most were diligent and surprisingly effective. 61 notes.
                                                          D. F. Chard

2413. Wyn, Graeme. NEW BRUNSWICK PARISH BOUNDARIES IN THE PRE-1861 CENSUS YEARS. *Acadiensis [Canada] 1977 6(2): 95-105.* Quantitative data on early New Brunswick are scarce. Much pre-confederation material is fragmentary and difficult to use, but records of the evolution of parish boundaries are useful in studying spatial patterns. The number of parishes increased from 34 in 1784, to 80 in 1834, and 100 in 1851. Statistics from each census reflect parish boundary patterns. Indicates sources of information on boundary changes. Includes maps of boundaries in 1824, 1834, 1840, and 1851. 4 illus., 10 notes.
                                                          D. F. Chard

Quebec

General

2414. Allen, Patrick. LES JEUX OLYMPIQUES: ICEBERGS OU RAMPES DE LANCEMENTS? [The Olympic Games: Icebergs or launching pads?]. *Action Natl. [Canada] 1976 65(5): 271-323.* Pierre de Coubertin proposed the reestablishment of the Olympic Games at a conference at the Sorbonne on 25 November 1892. The first games in the modern series took place four years later at Athens, and they have been held every four years since, except in 1916, 1940, and 1944 during major wars. Canadians have participated since 1900, but the 1976 games at Montreal were the first to be held in Canada. The entire province of Quebec prepared for the games and allied activities and there has been a resurgence of amateur athletic participation throughout the province. The spirit of cooperation in the preparations may be a manifestation of Quebec nationalism. 8 tables.   A. W. Novitsky

2415. Archibald, Clinton and Paltiel, Khayyam Z. DU PASSAGE DES CORPS INTERMÉDIARES AUX GROUPES DE PRESSION: LA TRANSFORMATION D'UNE IDÉE ILLUSTRÉE PAR LE MOUVEMENT COOPÉRATIF DESJARDINS [From common interest groups to pressure groups: The transformation of a concept as seen in the Desjardins cooperative movement]. *Recherches Sociographiques [Canada] 1977 18(1): 59-91.* The notion of common interest groups has deep roots in Catholic Quebec and it is one of the foundation stones of the Desjardins cooperative movement. The notion, however, has undergone profound change in the past few decades as the Quebec government has sought to increase its role in all facets of the province's life. Common interest groups have overtly accepted the mantle of a pressure group to achieve their respective ends. Table, 2 graphs, 96 notes.
                                                          A. E. Le Blanc

2416. Audet, Louis-Philippe. HISTOIRE DE LA COMMISSION PARENT [History of the Parent Commission]. *Tr. of the Royal Soc. of Can. 1974 12: 127-137.* Discusses the royal commission of enquiry in Quebec in 1961—its creation, mission, and recommendations. During 1944-59, Maurice-L. Duplessis of the National Union headed the government of Quebec and attempted to regain powers granted to the federal government during World War II. In 1960, the Liberals headed by Jean Lesage took over. Their secretary of education, Paul Gerin-Lajoie, suggested a royal commission to study the school system. Members were Alphonse-Marie Parent, president; Gérard Filon, vice-president; Paul Larocque; David Munroe; Sister Maire-Laurent de Rome; Jeanne Lapoint; John McIlhone; and Guy Rocher. Staff members were Louis Philippe Audet, Michel Giroux, C. W. Dawson, Guy Houle, and Rémi Levigne. They studied programs in other provinces, the United States, and several European countries. They recommended that a Minister of Education coordinate educational programs and called for the creation of an advisory council of education. They published the report in five volumes. Reactions to the report were varied but the commission dealt realistically with problems in education in the 20th century. Biblio.
                                                          J. D. Neville

2417. Bélanger, Gérard. LA SYNDICALISATION DES PROFESSEURS D'UNIVERSITÉ [Unionism of university professors]. *Industrial Relations [Canada] 1974 29(4): 857-864.* Perspectives on the great effect of growing unionism on the development of higher education in Quebec since 1972, especially its effect on the growth of resources, on the structure of tenure and promotion, and on university management and faculty-student tension.

2418. Bélanger, Gérard. QUESTIONS DE BASE A TOUTE RÉFORME DU FINANCEMENT MUNICIPAL [Basic questions of municipal financial reform]. *Can. Public Administration [Canada] 1977 20(2): 370-379.* Examines financial support given to Quebec's local governments by the provincial government; discusses the degree of autonomy granted to municipalities, 1960-73.

2419. Bélanger, Marcel. LA RAPPORT BÉLANGER: DIX ANS APRÈS [The Bélanger Report: Ten years after]. *Can. Public Administration [Canada] 1976 19(3): 457-465.* Examines the effects of recommendations of the Commission of Inquiry on Taxation in Quebec (1966); discusses differences in provincial, municipal, and school taxation and problems solved by the Commission report.

2420. Benjamin, Jacques. CONSÉQUENCES DE L'ÉLECTION DU 15 NOVEMBRE 1976 AU QUÉBEC: DE NOUVELLES FLAMBÉES DE VIOLENCE? [The consequences of the elections of 15 November 1976 in Quebec: Some new flare-ups of violence?]. *J. of Can. Studies [Canada] 1977 12(3): 85-92.* During 1960-68, under the Union Nationale, Quebec was a consensual society, moving to modernize its traditional institutions; this was the so-called Révolution Tranquille (Quiet Revolution). During 1969-76, it was a conflictual society, in which forces desiring change, some violent (the FLQ), some nonviolent (labor unions, the PQ) opposed the ruling Liberals and each other. With the election of the Parti Québécois, Quebec has become more of a consensus society again; opposition to the PQ comes from the federal government and marginal groups (English-speakers, corporations). The PQ government does not stress its independence plank, but rather social reform; it is this that is winning it support from the Québécois. 43 notes.

J. C. Billigmeier

2421. Betcherman, Lita-Rose. CANADA'S HUMAN RIGHTS AFTER THE QUEBEC ELECTIONS. *Patterns of Prejudice [Great Britain] 1977 11(3): 23-27.* The 1 April 1977 promulgation of the French Language Charter by the Parti Quebecois government of René Levesque disturbs the province's 116,000 Jews, who sense anti-Semitism is implied in the law, in a climate of extreme French-Canadian nationalism.

2422. Blais, André; DesRosiers, Rachel; and Renaud, François. L'EFFET EN AMONT DE LA CARTE ÉLECTORALE: LE CAS DE LA RÉGION DE QUÉBEC À L'ÉLECTION FÉDÉRALE DE 1968 [The effect of redistributing municipalities: the case of Quebec in the federal election of 1968]. *Can. J. of Pol. Sci. 1974 7(4): 648-671.* The impact of redistribution on voter response was found to vary according to the regional or national strength of the parties contesting the election. 6 tables, 3 graphs, 45 notes.

R. V. Kubicek

2423. Bourgault, Jacques. L'ATTITUDE DES MASS MEDIA VIS-À-VIS DU GOUVERNEMENT QUÉBECOIS [The attitude of the mass media toward the Quebec government]. *Études Int. [Canada] 1977 8(2): 320-336.* Analyzes the attitudes of the Montreal press toward René Levesque's government. Examines the coverage of *La Presse, Le Devoir, Montreal-Matin, Dimanche-Matin,* and one English-language paper, the *Montreal Star,* on eight political events during 16 November 1976-1 April 1977. The topics included the result of the elections, the new Council of Ministers, the first two sessions of the legislature, the Prime Minister's trip to New York and his automobile accident, the budget, and the French White Book. Primary sources; 11 notes.

J. F. Harrington, Jr.

2424. Boutet, Odina. LA CULTURE ET L'INDÉPENDANCE DU QUÉBEC [Culture and the independence of Quebec]. *Action Natl. [Canada] 1974 63(10): 838-849.* The goals of the Parti Québécois are to develop French culture, promote the idea of a viable Quebec currency, and secure the independence of Quebec.

2425. Caya, Marcel. APERÇU SUR LES ÉLECTIONS PROVINCIALES DU QUÉBEC DE 1867 À 1886 [Survey on the provincial elections in Quebec from 1867 to 1886]. *Rev. d'Hist. de l'Amérique Française [Canada] 1975 29(2): 191-208.* A statistical interpretation using hierarchical analysis. The Conservatives dominated the political scene by carrying four of six elections. Honoré Mercier's victory in 1886 (usually cited as the beginning of Liberal success in Quebec) resulted more from the debates on the hanging of Louis Riel than from an increase in voting. Actually, electoral participation was greatest in 1878. Based on unpublished theses and on secondary works; 9 tables, 14 notes.

L. B. Chan

2426. Cestre, Gilbert. QUÉBEC: ÉVOLUTION DES LIMITES MUNICIPALES DEPUIS 1831-1832 [The city of Québec: development of its municipal limits since 1831-32]. *Cahiers de Géographie de Québec [Canada] 1976 20(51): 561-567.* Studies and interprets the evolution of the administrative limits of the city of Québec, 1831-1972.

2427. Charbonneau, Michel. LA COMMISSION DES VALEURS MOBILIÈRES DU QUÉBEC [The Quebec Securities Commission]. *Can. Public Administration [Canada] 1977 20(1): 87-139.* Examines the structure, statutory responsibilities, and operation of Quebec's Securities Commission, 1970's.

2428. Contandriopoulos, A. P.; Lance, J. M.; and Meunier, C. UN REGROUPEMENT DES COMTÉS DE LA PROVINCE DE QUÉBEC EN RÉGIONS HOMOGÈNES [A regrouping of the counties of the province of Quebec into homogeneous regions]. *Actualité Écon. [Canada] 1974 50(4): 572-586.* The purpose of this study, partly financed by the national government, is to present both a method of identifying the regions of Quebec and to propose a classification of its counties into homogeneous regions for use in the administration of medical services and in planning socioeconomic development. Proposes eight regional groupings. 3 tables, 5 notes, biblio.

J. C. Billigmeier

2429. Dion, Léon and deSeve, Micheline. QUEBEC: INTEREST GROUPS AND THE SEARCH FOR AN ALTERNATIVE POLITICAL SYSTEM. *Ann. of the Am. Acad. of Pol. and Soc. Sci. 1974 413: 124-144.* Nearly 15 years ago Quebec entered an active period of sociopolitical unrest. A people who had undergone considerable changes in their objective conditions of living without a corresponding change in their social consciousness suddenly found themselves forced, by their political leaders, to realize the extent of their maladjustment to a predominantly urban and highly industrialized society and pressured to readjust their position. The *Union Nationale* Party was thrown into temporary disarray by the sudden deaths of Maurice Duplessis—uncontested master of the province—on August 30, 1959 and of his successor, Paul Sauvé, scarcely four months after he came to power. The Liberal Party under Jean Lesage was thus able to win the provincial election in June 1960. This event precipitated what has been labelled the quiet revolution. The Lesage program manifested a new desire to modernize the mechanisms of the state and to seize the initiative in policies of economic and social development. This set off a reform movement which, we can safely say, went beyond the ambitions of its initiators. The process of rationalizing the administrative mechanisms of a modern bureaucratic state created a wave of cultural shock which was felt at all levels of the society. Such changes could not occur without putting great pressures on the population or without having unexpected consequences, the most important being the rebirth of the Quebec nationalist ideology as a political movement and the formation of various kinds of popular movements.   J

2430. Doyle-Frenière, Murielle. LES ARCHIVES DE LA VILLE DE QUÉBEC [The archives of the city of Quebec]. *Urban Hist. Rev. [Canada] 1977 (1): 33-37.* Describes the historical background and contents of the Quebec city archives and lists general information on the facilities available and their use by researchers.   C. A. Watson

2431. Faucher, Albert. LA REVOLUTION TRANQUILLISANTE [The tranquilizing revolution]. *Can. J. of Pol. Sci. 1973 6(1): 3-21.* Explores the economic and social history of the United States 1920-40 in order to establish a perspective through which to probe the quiet revolution in Quebec. Contrary to some claims, this was not a period of revolutionary change because capitalism was not fundamentally altered. 24 notes.   R. V. Kubicek

2432. Fredette, Jean-Guy. LES PERSPECTIVES DE L'ÉNERGIE AU QUÉBEC [Perspectives of energy in Quebec]. *Actualité Écon. [Canada] 1974 50(2): 272-292.* Outlines the present energy situation in Quebec. Analyzes reserves and capacities of production for electricity, oil, gas, coal, and uranium, and projects consumption and price. Despite uncertainties, the future seems to belong largely to conventional forms of energy, major substitutions not being produced before the next century. Based on data from an incomplete study undertaken by the Ministry of Natural Resources; 2 graphs.   L. R. Atkins

2433. Gay, Daniel. LA PRESSE D'EXPRESSION FRANÇAISE DU QUÉBEC ET L'AMÉRIQUE LATINE INVENTAIRE D'EDITORIAUX ET DE PARA-EDITORIAUX, 1959-1973 [The French press of Quebec on Latin America: An inventory of editorials, 1959-73]. *Études Int. [Canada] 1976 7(3): 359-392.* This subject-author inventory of signed and unsigned editorials appearing daily in *l'Action Catholique* and *Le Soleil* of Quebec, and *le Devoir* and *La Presse* of Montreal, 1959-73, facilitates the study of Canadian-Latin American and Quebec-Latin American relations. Secondary sources; 3 notes.

J. F. Harrington, Jr.

2434. Gérin-Lajoie, Henri. LES ARCHIVES MUNICIPALES DE LA VILLE DE MONTRÉAL [Municipal archives in the city of Montreal]. *Urban Hist. Rev. [Canada] 1974 74(2): 2-4.* Chronicles the Montreal city archives, 1913-74; mentions library facilities, collections, and research possibilities.

2435. Gow, James Iain. LA GESTION DU PERSONNEL DANS LES MINISTÈRES DU GOUVERNEMENT DU QUÉBEC [Personnel management in the departments of the government of Quebec]. *Industrial Relations [Canada] 1974 29(3): 560-578.* Claims that personnel management in government departments receives less attention than do the activities of central management and control agencies, 1972-74.

2436. Gow, James Iain. L'HISTOIRE DE L'ADMINISTRATION PUBLIQUE QUÉBÉCOISE [The history of Quebec's public administration]. *Recherches Sociographiques [Canada] 1975 16(3): 385-411.* Studies the role of the Quebec provincial government in the historical development of the province's public administration and highlights various centralizing tendencies. The role and activities of provincial civil servants in this process receive considerable attention. Based on secondary sources; chart, 74 notes.

A. E. LeBlanc

2437. Halliday, Hugh A. THE LONELY MAGDALEN ISLANDS. *Can. Geographical J. 1973 86(1): 2-13.*

2438. Harrington, Lyn and Harrington, Richard. COVERED BRIDGES IN ABITIBI COUNTY OF *NOUVEAU QUÉBEC. Can. Geographical J. 1976/77 93(3): 66-69.* Chronicles covered bridges 1820-1950's.

2439. Hudon, Raymond. POUR UNE ANALYSE POLITIQUE DU PATRONAGE [Toward a political analysis of patronage]. *Can. J. of Pol. Sci. 1974 7(3): 484-501.* Uses an analytical model inspired by cybernetics to explain the practice of patronage by political parties in Quebec during 1944-72. 2 figs., 46 notes.

R. V. Kubicek

2440. Leeke, James. LA PLUS ÇA CHANGE: PATRONAGE IN QUEBEC. *Can. Dimension 1975 11(1): 6-12.* Discusses political patronage of the Liberal Party under Prime Minister Robert Bourassa since 1970.

S

2441. Linteau, Paul-André. MONTREAL, 1850-1914. *Urban Hist. Rev. [Canada] 1975 75(1): 31-35.* Discusses urbanization in Montreal, Quebec, 1850-1914, examining physical and economic growth, living conditions, and the beginning of administrative positions in municipal government; one of eight articles in this issue on the Canadian city in the 19th century.

2442. Linteau, Paul-André. QUELQUES RÉFLEXIONS AUTOUR DE LA BOURGEOISIE QUÉBÉCOISE, 1850-1914 [Some reflections about the Quebec bourgeoisie, 1850-1914]. *Rev. d'Hist. de l'Am. Française [Canada] 1976 30(1): 55-66.* Examines the Quebec bourgeoisie at three levels: upper, middle, and lower. The upper bourgeoisie was primarily English-speaking, and directed the banks, insurance companies, trusts, railroads, steamship lines, and other major business enterprises of a national or international nature headquartered in Montreal. The middle bourgeoisie included a greater number of French Canadians, and concentrated on regional business and finance. The lower bourgeoisie served in clerical and managerial capacities at the municipal or parish levels. Based on unpublished theses and secondary works; 8 notes.

L. B. Chan

2443. Lord, Gary T., ed. JOURNAL OF ALONZO JACKMAN'S EXCURSION TO QUEBEC, 1838. *Vermont Hist. 1978 46(4): 244-259.* A recent graduate of Norwich University in Northfield, Vermont, and thereafter an instructor in mathematics and science, Jackman patterned his trip by stage, steamboat, and on foot, according to the excursions conducted by Alden Partridge, founder and president of the school. Fortification, and battles at Ticonderoga, Crown Point, Plattsburgh, Isle aux Noix, Mount Royal, and Quebec, were at the center of Jackman's broad interests, which included mills, cathedrals, farming, and the homes of his college friends, but not so much the Canadian rebellions. 34 notes.

T. D. S. Bassett

2444. MacLeod, Alex. THE REFORM OF THE STANDING COMMITTEES OF THE QUEBEC NATIONAL ASSEMBLY: A PRELIMINARY ASSESSMENT. *Can. J. of Pol. Sci. 1975 8(1): 22-39.* The standing committees of the Quebec National Assembly have contributed to government effectiveness by increasing the participation of deputies in the affairs of the assembly. Table, 25 notes.

R. V. Kubicek

2445. Massam, Bryan H. FORMS OF LOCAL GOVERNMENT IN THE MONTREAL AREA, 1911-71: A DISCRIMINANT APPROACH. *Can. J. of Pol. Sci. 1973 6(2): 243-253.* Probes, with the aid of a linear discriminant function (LDF), the variables (socioeconomic and size attributes) which account for municipalities opting for city-manager or mayor-council forms of government. The calculations are made at 10-year intervals coinciding with census years. Based on census data from Statistics Canada; 3 tables, 16 notes.

R. V. Kubicek

2446. Migner, Robert Maurice. LE BOSSISME POLITIQUE À MONTRÉAL: CAMILLIEN HOUDE REMPLACE MÉDERIC MARTIN (1923-1929) [Bossism politics in Montreal: Camillien Houde replaces Méderic Martin (1923-1929)]. *Urban Hist. Rev. [Canada] 1974 74(1): 2-8.* Examines bossism in Montreal politics; rivalry between Méderic Martin and Camillien Houde led to Houde's replacement of Martin as local government "boss" in 1928.

2447. Ryerson, Stanley B. SOCIAL CREDIT IN QUEBEC. *Queen's Q. [Canada] 1974 81(2): 278-283.* Reviews Maurice Pinard's *The Rise of a Third Party: A Study in Crisis Politics* (New York: Prentice-Hall, 1971) and Michael B. Stein's *The Dynamics of Right-wing Protest: A Political Analysis of Social Credit in Quebec* (Toronto: University of Toronto Press, 1973), which discuss the works in comparison with others dealing with the rise of the *Créditiste* movement in French Canada. Both works are accorded qualified praise with the reservation that much work remains to be done in the field.

J. A. Casada

2448. Saguin, André-Louis. TERRITORIALITÉ, ESPACE MENTAL ET TOPOPHILIE AU SAGUENAY [Territorialism, mental space and topophilia in Saguenay]. *Protée [Canada] 1975 4(1): 53-66.* Studies collective and individual behaviorism regarding spatial perception in Saguenay County 1969-74, and the emergence of strong territorialism of a topographical, circulatory, urban, and landscape nature, which opens new promising avenues toward establishment of a political geography in the area.

2449. Savard, Pierre. UN QUART DE SIÈCLE D'HISTORIOGRAPHIE QUÉBÉCOISE, 1947-1972 [A quarter century of Quebec historiography, 1947-72]. *Recherches sociographiques [Canada] 1974 15(1): 77-96.* With the establishment of historical institutes at Laval University and at the University of Montreal in 1947, the quantitative and qualitative development of historical writing in French-speaking Quebec entered into a quarter century period of impressive production. Until this point historical writing glorified the past and sought to defend French Canada's traditional way of life. This gave way in the late 1940's to a varied methodological and ideological exploration of the reality of French Quebec.

A. E. LeBlanc

2450. Schenck, Ernest. EUGÈNE LAPIERRE, MUSICIEN ET NATIONALISTE [Eugène Lapierre, musician and nationalist]. *Action Natl. [Canada] 1974 64(2): 154-169.* The late Eugène Lapierre, a musician and a fervent nationalist, was president of the Historical Society of Montreal (Société historique de Montréal).

2451. Simard, Jean-Jacques. LA LONGUE MARCHE DES TECHNOCRATES [The long march of the technocrats]. *Recherches Sociographiques [Canada] 1977 18(1): 93-132.* The Quiet Revolution has resulted in the ascendency of an enormous civil service in Quebec that is directed by a middle class technocracy allied with business interests to insure control of the State. Table, 76 notes.

A. E. Le Blanc

2452. Trépanier, Pierre. LE 2 MARS 1878 [March 2, 1878]. *Action Natl. [Canada] 1977 66(5): 372-390.* On 2 March 1878 Lieutenant Governor Luc Letellier de Saint-Just, a Liberal, dismissed the Conservative Prime Minister Boucherville of Quebec and called upon Liberal Henri-Gustave Joly to form a new government. The dismissal was precipitated by the provincial government's railroad and fiscal policies, but the major issues of the following election campaign were the validity of the dismissal as well as religious and ethnic conflicts. Election results demonstrated the continuing rise of the Liberal Party in Quebec, supported by Anglo-Protestants. The replacement of Letellier by Théodore Robitaille as Lieutenant-Governor in July, however, may be seen as a victory of Canadian federalism over Quebec autonomy. Chart, 50 notes.

A. W. Novitsky

2453. Trépanier, Pierre. NOTRE PREMIER XIXᵉ SIÈCLE (1790-1890) [Our first 19th century (1790-1890)]. *Action Natl. [Canada] 1978 67(9): 745-751.* Quebec has produced a prodigious number of historians since the time of Perrault, Viger, Bibaud, and Garneau. Since the 1950's, Fernand Ouellet and his colleagues have reoriented Quebec historiography on the model of the French *Annales* school, with great reliance on statistical methods, integration of sociology, psychology, and politics, and an emphasis on economics. Recent studies of 19th-century Quebec history in this tradition include: Ouellet, *Le Bas-Canada, 1791-1840, Changements structuraux et crise* (Ottawa, 1976), Richard Chabot, *Le Curé de campagne et la contestation locale au Québec* (Montreal, 1975), and Jean-Louis Roy, *Édouard-Raymond Fabre, libraire et patriote canadien (1799-1854)* (Montreal, 1974). 10 notes.

A. W. Novitsky

2454. Waterston, Elizabeth. HOWELLS AND THE CITY OF QUEBEC. *Can. Rev. of Am. Studies [Canada] 1978 9(2): 155-167.* Travel accounts, a flourishing literary genre of the 1800's, often covered Quebec. But accounts by Americans differed from the writings of others, because American men-of-letters mostly were impressed by Quebec's rich imperial heritage and monuments of past wars, its Catholic cultural milieu, and its quaint preindustrial setting. In *Their Wedding Journey* (1871) and *A Chance Acquaintance* (1872), William Dean Howells (1837-1920) pictured Quebec as charming for the same reasons as did other Americans. However, Howells preferred the "rawer countryside" surrounding that "antique city." Based on Howells's writings; 4 photos, 9 notes.

H. T. Lovin

Society and Culture

2455. Allaire, Georges. INFLUENCE DU MILIEU ÉTUDIANT QUÉBÉCOIS SUR L'ACTION DE L'ÉGLISE CATHOLIQUE [The influence of Quebec student culture on the action of the Catholic Church]. *Action Natl. [Canada] 1978 67(9): 737-744.* In the 1970's, Quebec university students dramatically have abandoned the practice of Catholicism, and many have adopted agnosticism as well. Students generally are indifferent to the Church, and strongly support total freedom of religion, opposing indoctrination in schools. In response, Catholic college chaplains have developed a mission of evangelization, attempting to form Christian campus communities capable of attracting more sophisticated student participation. Biblio.

A. W. Novitsky

2456. Andrew, Caroline; Blais, André; and Des Rosiers, Rachel. LE LOGEMENT PUBLIC À HULL [Public housing in Hull]. *Can. J. of Pol. Sci. 1975 8(3): 403-430.* The authors try to explain through the use of several indices why the municipal government began the housing program enthusiastically in 1968, but later allowed its commitment to dwindle. 5 tables, 2 figs., 82 notes.

R. V. Kubicek

2457. Angers, François-Albert. ESDRAS MINVILLE ET L'ÉCOLE DES HAUTES ÉTUDES COMMERCIALES [Esdras Minville and the School of Higher Commercial Studies]. *Action Natl. [Canada] 1976 65(9-10): 643-676.* Esdras Minville was the first Canadian to direct the École des Hautes Études Commerciales. He was appointed in 1938 and succeeded the Belgians A.-J. Bray, who served during 1910-16, and Henry Laureys, who served during 1916-38. Minville stressed faculty research, academic freedom, and rigorous standards for admission and degrees.

A. W. Novitsky

2458. Angers, François-Albert. LA SITUATION LINGUISTIQUE AU QUÉBEC APRÈS LA LOI 22 [The language situation in Quebec after Law 22].
LA SITUATION DE DROIT DU FRANÇAISE [The de jure situation of French]. *Action Natl. [Canada] 1974 64(3): 207-228.*

APRÈS L'ÉTAT DE DROIT, L'ÉTAT DE FAIT [After the de jure situation, the de facto situation]. *Action Natl. [Canada] 1974 64(4): 287-301.*
Law 22, the Official Language Act (Quebec, 1974), "establishes" French as the official language in Quebec but still favors the English-speaking because of intrinsic differences between written law and common law. Law 22 does *not* make French the only official language of Quebec.

2459. Angers, François-Albert. LE SENS D'UNE VIE [The sense of a life]. *Action Natl. [Canada] 1976 65(9-10): 800-803.* Reprints the funeral oration for Esdras Minville presented at the church of Saint-Pascal Baylon, 12 December 1975. Minville was, above all else, a Christian. His life was devoted exclusively to the common good of the French Canadian people and was based on the Christian virtues of faith, hope, and charity.

A. W. Novitsky

2460. Angers, François Albert. MOUVEMENT QUÉBEC FRANÇAIS: À PROPOS DU BILL 22 [French Quebec Movement: On the Bill 22]. *Action Natl. [Canada] 1974 64(1): 923-946.* A declaration of outrage by the President of the French Quebec Movement concerning the Official Language Act (1974), passed by the Canadian government, and affirming the use of English in French-speaking Quebec.

2461. Arès, Richard. LANGUES MATERNELLES ET LANGUES D'USAGES AU QUÉBEC [Mother tongue and idiom in Quebec]. *Action Natl. [Canada] 1973 63(3): 228-234.* Discusses the extent to which mother tongues are commonly used by various social classes in Quebec and forecasts the possibility of complete anglicization.

2462. Arès, Richard. LES MINORITÉS FRANCO-CANADIENNES: ÉTUDE STATISTIQUE [The French Canadian minority: a statistical study]. *Tr. of the Royal Soc. of Can. 1975 13: 123-132.* Presents a statistical study of the French-speaking minority in Canada, first defining what a French Canadian is and making a distinction between French Canadian and French Quebecois. Shows trends 1871-1971 and notes that although most French Canadians continue to live in Quebec, a greater percentage of them now live in other sections of the country. In each of the other four areas—the Maritimes, Ontario, and the Western Provinces—French Canadians continue to be a small and declining percentage of the population. Also, whereas in Quebec French is their first language, in the other areas, English increasingly is their first language and an increasing number know no French. The Maritimes, because of the large French population in New Brunswick, have a larger percentage of French-speaking people than other non-Quebec areas, but except for that one province the Maritimes have a small percentage, too. 5 tables.

J. D. Neville

2463. Arès, Richard. QUI FERA L'AVENIR DES MINORITIES FRANCOPHONES AU CANADA? [Who will be responsible for the future of French-speaking minorities in Canada?]. *Action Natl. [Canada] 1973 62(5): 349-377.* The French "fact" has influenced Canadian history. This influence, however, is not such that it can assure the normal development of French language minorities throughout Canada. Quebec, with 84 percent of Canada's French-speaking population, is able to assure its own destiny but it is not necessarily able or willing to do the same for French minority groups. The future of these minorities is a collective responsibility.

A. E. LeBlanc

2464. Barrett, F. A. THIS CHANGING WORLD: THE RELATIVE DECLINE OF THE FRENCH LANGUAGE IN CANADA: A PRELIMINARY REPORT. *Geography [Great Britain] 1975 60(Part 2): 125-129.* The number of French-speaking people in Canada, notably in Montreal, has been declining during the past decade, partly because of decreasing birth rates in the French population.

2465. Beaupré, Viateur. LA LOI 22 LE FRANGLAIS OU LA SCHIZOPHRÉNIE [Law 22, "Frenglish" or schizophrenia]. *Action Natl. [Canada] 1974 64(3): 229-238.* Law 22 (the Official Language Act, 1974) institutionalized "Frenglish" (franglais) while theoretically making French the official language of Quebec.

2466. Bélanger, Noël. MGR. COURCHESNE ET L'ACTION CATHOLIQUE [Monsignor Courchesne and Action Catholique]. *Sessions d'Étude: Soc. Can. d'Hist. de l'Église Catholique [Canada] 1976 43:*

49-67. Studies Monsignor Georges Courchesne's work in the Rimouski diocese, 1940-67, with an outline of major dates in the organization of Action Catholique and his rupture with the Church in 1942.

2467. Bergevin, André. NOTES BIOGRAPHIQUES ET RÉPERTOIRE BIBLIOGRAPHIQUE DES OEUVRES D'ESDRAS MINVILLE [Biographic notes and bibliography of the works of Esdras Minville]. *Action Natl. [Canada] 1976 65(9-10): 762-783.* Lists Esdras Minville's academic career, activities, awards, books, pamphlets, articles for *L'Action Française, L'Action Canadienne-Française, L'Action Nationale, L'Actualité Économique,* and other publications.
A. W. Novitsky

2468. Billette, André. LES INÉGALITÉS SOCIALES DE MORTALITÉ AU QUÉBEC [Social inequalities of death in Quebec]. *Recherches Sociographiques [Canada] 1977 18(3): 415-430.* Analyzes a sampling of deceased Quebecois, ages 25-64, which shows that those of the lower class die younger due to greater incidence of accident, bronchitis, pneumonia, liver ailments, and stomach cancer. Government statistical documents; 7 tables, 25 notes, appendix.
A. E. LeBlanc

2469. Blow, David J. THE ESTABLISHMENT AND EROSION OF FRENCH-CANADIAN CULTURE IN WINOOSKI, VERMONT, 1867-1900. *Vermont Hist. 1975 43(1): 59-74.* In 1867, French-speaking natives of Quebec and their children comprised 49% of the 1,745 people in Winooski village, Vermont, a woolen mill town with a machine shop and 10 other small industries. Bishop Louis de Goësbriand appointed a young Canadian priest, Jean Fréderic Audet, in 1868. Supported by three lay councillors in a "fabrique" organized in 1873, he enlarged a parochial school, built the church of St. Francis Xavier, 1870-84 (see table of its financial history), and presided over a francophone enclave with mutual aid societies and basically Democratic Party politics. The second generation gradually identified with anglophone Vermont rather than with Quebec. 41 notes.
T. D. S. Bassett

2470. Bonenfant, Joseph. GASTON MIRON ET L'IDENTITE POLITIQUE DU QUEBEC [Gaston Miron and Quebec's political identity]. *Am. Rev. of Can. Studies 1974 4(2): 46-54.* Examines the poetry of Gaston Miron, a Quebecois poet whose belief in linguistic, cultural, and political sovereignty for Quebec has come to be represented in his work, identifying him as the national poet of Quebec, 1969-74.

2471. Bouchard, Gérard. FAMILY STRUCTURE AND GEOGRAPHIC MOBILITY AT LATERRIÈRE, 1851-1935. *J. of Family Hist. 1977 2(4): 350-369.* Using both family reconstitution and census records, examines demographic trends in Laterrière, Quebec. There was a high degree of population turnover and net migration was the key determinant of the rate of population change. Examines the influence of the community's hybrid system of farming and lumbering on its general economic development. Map, 8 tables, 4 graphs, 26 notes, biblio.
T. W. Smith

2472. Bouchard, Gérard. INTRODUCTION À L'ÉTUDE DE LA SOCIÉTÉ SAGUENAYENNE AUX XIXᵉ ET XXᵉ SIÈCLES [Introduction to the study of Saguenayan society in the 19th and 20th centuries]. *Rev. d'Hist. de l'Am. Française [Canada] 1977 31(1): 3-27.* Relates developments in agriculture and industry to the mobility of various classes of Saguenayan society since the late 19th century. Secondary works; map, graph, 43 notes.
L. B. Chan

2473. Bouchard, Gérard. L'HISTOIRE DE LA POPULATION ET L'ÉTUDE DE LA MOBILITÉ SOCIALE AU SAGUENAY, XIXᵉ-XXᵉ SIÈCLES [History of the population and a study of social mobility in Saguenay, 19th-20th centuries]. *Recherches Sociographiques [Canada] 1976 17(3): 353-372.* Studies more than 125,000 birth, marriage, and death records of the Saguenay region. The underemployment and the socioprofessional instability recorded almost from the beginning are characteristics of a sick society and economic base. 2 tables, 3 charts, diagram, 22 notes.
A. E. LeBlanc

2474. Bouchard, Gérard. L'HISTOIRE DÉMOGRAPHIQUE ET LE PROBLÈME DES MIGRATIONS: L'EXEMPLE DE LATERRIÈRE [Historical demography and the problem of geographical mobility: the example of Laterrière]. *Social Hist. [Canada] 1975 8(15):*

21-33. Family reconstitution studies at the parish level for the 19th century are seriously hampered by the high rate of geographical mobility. Prior to the 19th century, the parish was a more natural unit; for later periods the historical demographer should focus on larger units. These problems were discovered in the study of the village of Laterrière in Québec during 1855-70. Less than 10 per cent of the families were sedentary enough to permit a complete family reconstitution study. Based on parish records and secondary sources; 3 tables, graph, 15 notes.
W. K. Hobson

2475. Bouchard, Gérard. SUR L'ÉGLISE CATHOLIQUE ET L'INDUSTRIALISATION AU QUÉBEC: LA RÉLIGION DES EUDISTES ET LES OUVRIERS DU BASSIN DE CHICOUTIMI, 1903-1930 [The Catholic Church and the industrialization of Quebec: religion as practiced by the Eudists and the workers of the Chicoutimi Basin, 1903-30]. *Protée [Canada] 1976 5(2): 31-43.* A tacit alliance between the Church and the working class helped shape religious practices in a working-class parish.

2476. Brunet, Michel. LA MINORITÉ ANGLOPHONE DU QUÉBEC: DE LA CONQUÊTE À L'ADOPTION DU BILL 22 [The English-speaking minority of Quebec: from the conquest to the passing of Bill 22]. *Action Natl. [Canada] 1975 64(6): 452-466.* Reviews the struggle of French-speaking Canadians, first in Lower Canada and then in Quebec, against the English-speaking population, now a minority, and the consequences of Bill 22 (the Official Language Act, 1974) for the French-speaking community.

2477. Cabatoff, Kenneth. RADIO-QUÉBEC: A CASE STUDY OF INSTITUTION-BUILDING. *Can. J. of Pol. Sci. [Canada] 1978 11(1): 125-138.* This educational television service evolved into an institution with impact its founders had not anticipated. Fig., 30 notes.
R. V. Kubicek

2478. Cabatoff, Kenneth. RADIO-QUÉBEC: UNE INSTITUTION PUBLIQUE À LA RECHERCHE D'UNE MISSION [Radio-Québec: A public institution looking for a mission]. *Can. Public Administration [Canada] 1976 19(4): 542-551.* Radio-Québec, an educational television service, 1969-76, is seeking public access to the airwaves and self-regulation status from the federal government.

2479. Caldwell, Gary and Czarnocki, B. Dan. UN RATTRAPAGE RATÉ: LE CHANGEMENT SOCIAL DANS LE QUÉBEC D'APRÈS-GUERRE, 1950-1974: UNE COMPARAISON QUÉBEC-ONTARIO [Failure to recover: social change in Quebec after World War II, 1950-1974: a comparison of Quebec/Ontario]. *Recherches Sociographiques [Canada] 1977 18(1): 9-58.* Compares 96 socioeconomic variables for Ontario and Quebec. From this analysis, it appears that a major structural change has taken place in Quebec since World War II. Quebec's modernization during this period was at the expense of its industrial development, which may mean future compromising social advances. 3 tables, 71 notes.
A. E. Le Blanc

2480. Castonguay, Charles. POUR UNE POLITIQUE DES DISTRICTS BILINGUES AU QUEBEC [Toward a policy for bilingual districts in Quebec]. *J. of Can. Studies [Canada] 1976 11(3): 50-59.* The role of bilingual districts is intended to be largely symbolic. Federal census data from 1971 reveal that everywhere in Canada, including Quebec, the French language is losing ground to English. Therefore, at present, there is no point in establishing bilingual districts in order to protect the English language in Quebec. Such action should be postponed until the census data reveal that, in certain areas of Quebec, English has lost its power to attract users. Based on census data and language reports; 4 tables, ref.
G. E. Panting.

2481. Claval, Paul. ARCHITECTURE SOCIALE, CULTURE ET GÉOGRAPHIE AU QUÉBEC: UN ESSAI D'INTERPRÉTATION HISTORIQUE [Social structure, culture and geography in Quebec: an essay of historical interpretaiton]. *Ann. de Géographie [France] 1974 458: 394-419.* "How can be explained Quebec's persistent originality within North America? Its isolation, its peripheric situation are often cited but are not sufficient reasons. The analysis of the spatial organization systems and of the types of social relations that create them allows to go further in the explanation and to take into account the historic and cultural data.

It seems the difficulty French Canadians experience when trying to create modern bureaucracies explains at the same time their resistance to the Anglo-Saxon world and their dominated position. The fragile equilibrium which had built itself little by little is jeopardized by the ever larger opening of Quebec's economy and society. Will the sense of an original historic mission be sufficient to incite the readjustments without which the province's individuality is endangered? That is the question the last part tries to answer."   J

2482. Côté, André. LE MONASTÈRE DE MISTASSINI: SA SUP-PRESSION OU SA FORMATION EN PRIEURÉ, 1900-1903 [The monastery of Mistassini: its suppression or formation in the priory, 1900-03]. *Sessions D'Étude: Soc. Can. d'Hist. de l'Eglise Catholique 1973 40: 92-111.* Examines the religious controversy between Cistercian authorities and the Archbishop of Quebec, Monseigneur Bégin (and his successor Msgr. Labrecque) over the establishment of a monastery for Trappists.   S

2483. Cotnam, Jacques. AMERICANS VIEWED THROUGH THE EYES OF THE FRENCH-CANADIANS. *J. of Popular Culture 1977 10(4): 784-796.* Examines French Canadians' attitudes toward Americans, during 1837-1973.

2484. DeBonville, Jean. LA LIBERTÉ DE PRESSE À LA FIN DU XIXᵉ SIÈCLE: LE CAS DE *CANADA-REVUE* [Freedom of the press at the end of the 19th century: the case of *Canada-Revue*]. *Rev. d'Hist. de l'Amérique Française [Canada] 1978 31(4): 501-523.* The short life of the journal *Canada-Revue* (1890-94) clearly illustrates the capacity of the Catholic Church in French Canada to limit the freedom of the press. When the editors of *Canada-Revue* used their accusation of immoral activities against one cleric to declare that clerical reform was needed, the Archbishop of Montreal declared a total boycott against the journal. *Canada-Revue* eventually won damages in court, but never was able to reverse its financial losses. 63 notes.   M. R. Yerburgh

2485. Deffontaines, Pierre. ULTIMES VICTOIRES SUR L'HIVER AU CANADA FRANÇAIS [Ultimate victories over winter in French Canada]. *Rev. de l'U. d'Ottawa [Canada] 1977 47(1-2): 61-64.* The extremely severe climate of French Canada has impelled settlers to find ways of struggling against its inconveniences and dangers. Beginning with gradually perfecting the structures of houses and improving the heating systems, today, central heating allows the discontinuance of the former work of preparing logs for the winter and a conversion of many wooden areas into pastures or farming zones, thus bringing the Canadians' struggle against winter into complete victory. Note.   G. P. Cleyet

2486. De Koninck, Rodolphe und Langevin, Jean. LA PERENNITE DES PEUPLEMENTS INSULAIRES LAURENTIENS: LE CAS DE L'ILE SAINT-IGNACE ET DE L'ILE DUPAS [Settlement permanency on the islands of the St. Lawrence River: the case of St. Ignace and Dupas Islands]. *Cahiers de Géographie de Québec [Canada] 1974 18(44): 317-336.*

2487. Delude-Clift, Camille and Champoux, Edouard. LE CONFLIT DES GÉNÉRATIONS [The generations conflict]. *Recherches Sociographiques [Canada] 1973 14(2): 157-201.* An analysis of the perceptions of adults and adolescents with respect to family, religion, and education shows that the socioeconomic milieu of the individual determines attitudes concerning social integration, whereas age is an important factor in the quest for identity. Intergenerational tension is largely due to this emergence of a private self among members of the younger generation. Based on 196 interviews conducted in Québec City.
                                                             A. E. LeBlanc

2488. Desmeules, Jean. STATISTIQUES DE LA POPULATION DE QUEBEC SUR LA BASE DES BASSINS VERSANTS HYDRO-GRAPHIQUES [Population statistics of Quebec based on hydrographic regions]. *Cahiers de Géographie de Québec [Canada] 1974 18(44): 367-370.*

2489. Dion, Léon. ANTI-POLITICS AND MARGINALS. *Government and Opposition [Great Britain] 1974 9(1): 28-41.* Discusses the political stability of liberal democracy and the Canadian government's tolerance of dissent in Quebec in the 1960's-70's.

2490. Dion, Marc and DeKoninck, Rodolphe. L'ÉTAT ET L'AMÉNAGEMENT: ORLÉANS, UNE ÎLE À VENDRE [The state and planning powers: Orléans, island for sale]. *Cahiers de Géographie de Québec [Canada] 1976 20(49): 39-67.* Although the rural St. Lawrence River island of Orléans near Quebec was classified a historical district and a community heritage in 1969, it is becoming urbanized to serve the capital's interests.

2491. Dominique, Richard. L'ETHNOHISTOIRE DE LA MOYENNE-CÔTE-NORD [The ethnohistory of the middle North Shore of the St. Lawrence estuary]. *Recherches Sociographiques [Canada] 1976 17(2): 189-220.* The testimony of numerous inhabitants of the middle North Shore of the St. Lawrence estuary is used to provide a retrospective. Concepts such as economy, work, politics, family, education, religion, and leisure show a way of life that has been radically transformed since the turn of the century. Map, 3 tables.
                                                             A. E. LeBlanc

2492. Doucette, Laurel. FAMILY STUDIES AS AN APPROACH TO ORAL HISTORY. *Can. Oral Hist. Assoc. J. [Canada] 1976/77 2: 24-31.* Excerpts a tape-recorded collection from research on the James Kealey family in Hull, Quebec, whose history lends itself to both folklore and oral history, 1974-75.

2493. Drolet, Jean Claude. UNE MOUVEMENT DE SPIRITUA-LITÉ SACERDOTALE AU QUEBEC AU XXᵉ SIÈCLE (1931-1950): LE LACOUTURISME [A movement of priestly spirituality in Quebec in the 20th century (1931-50): Lacouturism]. *Sessions D'Étude: Soc. Can. d'Hist. de l'Eglise Catholique 1973 40: 55-91.* Researches the spiritual movement provoked by Jesuit priest Onésime Lacouture during 1931-39 as it emerged in Quebec.   S

2494. Dumais, Alfred and St.-Arnaud, Pierre. LE DÉVELOPPE-MENT DE LA SOCIOLOGIE DE LA SANTÉ AU QUÉBEC [The development of sociology of health in Québec]. *Recherches Sociographiques [Canada] 1975 16(1): 9-20.* Interest in the sociological impact of health and health services in Québec dates from the end of the 19th century. However, it is with the scientific and technological advances of the post-1950 period, and under the influence of US social scientists, that the field has come into its own. The strides taken during the past 20 years are unknown by the general public, and sociologists should attempt to change this lack of awareness.   A. E. LeBlanc

2495. Dumais, François. JOCELYNE LORTIE: UNE ARTISTE PEINTRE [Jocelyne Lortie: Painter]. *Action Natl. [Canada] 1978 67(8): 644-653.* Lortie, born in 1939 at La Tuque, Quebec, is a foremost contemporary interpreter of the Laurentian landscape: forests, mountains and rivers. Influenced by Sisley and the impressionists, she especially admires the simplicity and space of Corot and the luminous technique of Rembrandt.   A. W. Novitsky

2496. Falaise, Noël. BIOGRAPHIE ET BIBLIOGRAPHIE DE BE-NOÎT BROUILLETTE [Biography and bibliography of Benoit Brouillette]. *Cahiers de géographie de Québec [Canada] 1973 17(40): 5-34.* Benoit Brouillette, first Quebec geographer of international repute, was a professor at Montreal's École des Hautes Études Commerciales, 1931-69. He was responsible for establishing the Montreal Geographical Society and was a member of the Commission of Geography in Education. Biblio.   A. E. LeBlanc

2497. Falardeau, Jean-Charles. ANTÉCÉDENTS, DÉBUTS ET CROISSANCE DE LA SOCIOLOGIE AU QUÉBEC [Antecedents, beginnings and growth of sociology in Quebec]. *Recherches Sociographiques [Canada] 1974 15(2/3): 135-165.* Until the late 1930's sociology in French-speaking Quebec was dominated by theological and doctrinal preoccupations. This was followed by a period of broader and more scientific activity. It was not until the late 1940's, under the impact of American influences, that sociology came into its own. In close relationship to the rapid modernization of Quebec, sociology was to know a rapid maturation and diversification.   A. E. LeBlanc

2498. Foggin, Peter M. L'ACCESSIBILITÉ À L'ENSEIGNEMENT COLLÉGIAL: UNE ANALYSE GÉOGRAPHIQUE DE LA FRÉ-QUENTATION DES CEGEP DU SAGUENAY [The accessibility of the college education: A geographical analysis of the attendance of Saguenay's CEGEP's]. *Protée [Canada] 1975 4(1): 20-37.* Researches the nature of student populations in six secondary schools (CEGEP) in Saguenay, including the origin of the students, their attendance and behavior, and the phenomenon of democratization in college education, with some comparison of American high schools and the colleges of Ile de Montréal.

2499.   Fournier, Marcel.   LA SOCIOLOGIE QUÉBÉCOISE CONTEMPORAINE   [Contemporary Quebec sociology]. *Recherches sociographiques [Canada] 1974 15(2/3): 167-199.* The 1960's and 1970's were characterized by a rapid development in sociology departments at French-language universities in Quebec. This expansion was dictated by the demand of government, unions, and other organizations for university graduates to fill numerous posts. The result was not necessarily good for the profession even though it was to serve immediate needs within the province.   A. E. LeBlanc

2500.   Frigon, F. J.   CATHOLICISM AND CRISIS: L'ECOLE SOCIALE POPULAIRE AND THE DEPRESSION IN QUEBEC, 1930-1940.   *R. de l'U. d'Ottawa 1975 45(1): 54-70.* Analyzes the Roman Catholic Church's reaction to the depression and stresses the importance of the École Sociale Populaire "in promoting a profound reexamination of the church's relationship to the other institutions of French Canada and in encouraging the growth of new ones such as labor unions." Based on primary and secondary sources; 62 notes.   M. L. Frey

2501.   Gagnon, Serge.   L'HISTOIRE DES IDÉOLOGIES QUÉBECOISES: QUINZE ANS DE REÁLISATIONS   [The history of ideas in Quebec: Fifteen years of development]. *Social Hist. [Canada] 1976 9(17): 17-20.* Before the 1950's the study of the history of ideas in Quebec utilized categories drawn from European intellectual history and traced the influence of European ideas in Quebec. Since then there has been increasing emphasis on the social and class context of ideas in Quebec, but many works have suffered from an inadequate analysis of social structure. Secondary sources; 8 notes.   W. K. Hobson

2502.   Galarneau, Claude.   L'ENSEIGNEMENT DES SCIENCES AU QUÉBEC ET JÉRÔME DEMERS (1765-1835)   [Teaching sciences in Quebec and Jérôme Demers, 1765-1835]. *Rev. de l'U. d'Ottawa [Canada] 1977 47(1-2): 84-94.* Discusses scientific education in Quebec, especially at the Quebec seminary, mentioning professors' names, subject matter, and methods. Stresses that, in the 18th century, philosophy and sciences were not separate disciplines, but united under the name of sciences-philosophy, including mathematics, physics, chemistry and philosophy. Analyzes the career of Jerôme Demers, one of the most brilliant men of the time, as a professor of sciences-philosophy at the Quebec seminary during 1800-35. Primary and secondary sources; 52 notes.
                                                          G. P. Cleyet

2503.   Garon-Audy, Muriel and Vandycke, Robert.   LA CHARTE DU FRANÇAIS ET LES DROITS DES MINORITÉS   [The Charter of the French language and the rights of minorities]. *J. of Can. Studies [Canada] 1977 12(4): 85-94.* Argues in favor of *Projet no.* 1 (or 101), also called the *Charte du Français,* regulations proposed by the new provincial government for strengthening the French language in Quebec. The rhetoric of "free competition" in language, employed by the new law's opponents (e.g. Canadian Prime Minister Trudeau), is interested and inapplicable to the Canadian situation. Discusses parts of the proposed legislation which limit the right to an English-language education, arguing that they are not, in international law, discriminatory. Compares *Projet no.* 1 with its "timid" predecessor, Law 22, passed by the former Liberal government of Quebec. Based on government documents, publications of international bodies, newspaper articles, and secondary sources; 14 notes.   L. W. Van Wyk

2504.   Gaulin, André.   LE RAPPORT GENDRON   [The Gendron Report]. *Action Natl. [Canada] 1973 62(9): 716-721.* Criticizes the report of the Gendron commission, its recognition of Quebec as a bilingual area, and its recommendation of bilingual instruction in the schools.

2505.   Gauvin, Lise.   LES REVUES LITTÉRAIRES QUÉBÉCOISES DE L'UNIVERSITÉ À LA CONTRE-CULTURE   [Quebec literary magazines from the university to the counterculture]. *Études Françaises [Canada] 1975 11(2): 161-183.* Describes various contemporary Quebec literary magazines and their histories within an intellectual context. Primary and secondary sources; 15 notes.   G. J. Rossi

2506.   Genest, Jean-Guy.   LES POINNIERS DE L'ENSEIGNEMENT UNIVERSITAIRE AU SAGUENAY (1948-1969)   [Pioneers of university instruction in Saguenay (1948-1969)]. *Protée [Canada] 1977 6(1): 15-128.* Chronicles the beginnings of university education, with L'Ecole de Génie (1949) and L'Ecole de Commerce (1950) in Saguenay-Lac-Saint-Jean, Quebec and discusses the development of educational programs and administrative policy during 1948-69.

2507.   Greer, Allan.   THE PATTERN OF LITERACY IN QUEBEC, 1745-1899.   *Social Hist. [Canada] 1978 11(22): 293-335.* Parish registers, petitions, censuses, and the Buller Commission's report of 1838 suggest that before the mid-19th century French-Canadian literacy was extremely low in rural areas, but relatively high in Montreal and Quebec. In the first half of the 19th century English Canadians and their children were much more literate than French Canadians. Literacy rates among French Canadians were low before the Conquest and remained low until the 1840's and 1850's. Progress thereafter was impressive, particularly among women and in the Montreal area. 17 illus., 66 notes.   D. F. Chard

2508.   Grenier, Manon; Roy, Maurice; and Bouchard, Louis.   L'EVOLUTION DE LA POPULATION DES ENFANTS AU CENTRE DE LA VILLE DE QUEBEC ET EN BANLIEU, 1951-1971   [The evolution of the population of children in downtown Quebec City and the suburbs, 1951-1971]. *Cahiers de Géographie de Québec 1974 18(45): 541-552.*

2509.   Guitard, Michelle.   POUR UNE HISTOIRE DE L'INSTITUT CANADIEN DE MONTRÉAL   [On behalf of a history of the Canadian Institute of Montreal]. *R. d'Hist. de l'Amérique Française [Canada] 1973 27(3): 403-407.* Expresses the desire to collect the names of members of the Canadian Institute of Montreal, 1845-73, as a basis for a social history of the institute.

2510.   Gutwirth, Jacques.   HASSIDIM ET JUDAÏCITÉ À MONTRÉAL   [Hasidism and Judaicity in Montreal]. *Recherches Sociographiques 1973 14(3): 291-325.* The Hasidic groupings that established themselves in Montreal during 1941-52 have, through their sociocultural and religious presence, had a direct and salutary impact on the Jewish community of the city. This has become possible through common reference points of Judaism where institutional collaboration takes place. In turn, Montreal's Jewish faction has permitted the Hasidic groupings to implant themselves. Based on field research and secondary sources; 87 notes.   A. E. LeBlanc

2511.   Hamel, Jacques and Thériault, Yvon.   LA FONCTION TRIBUNITIENNE ET LA DÉPUTATION CRÉDITISTE À L'ASSEMBLÉE NATIONALE DU QUÉBEC: 1970-73   [The tribunicial function and the créditiste group in the Quebec National Assembly, 1970-73]. *Can. J. of Pol. Sci. 1975 8(1): 3-21.* Tribunicial function is defined as the defence of the interests of disadvantaged social classes. Shows how the Creditiste (Social Credit) party in Quebec has fulfilled this function. 2 tables, 36 notes.   R. V. Kubicek

2512.   Hare, John.   LA POPULATION DE LA VILLE DE QUÉBEC, 1795-1805.   [The population of the city of Queébec, 1795-1805]. *Social Hist. [Canada] 1974 7(13): 23-47.* Parish censuses of 1795 and 1805 reveal a strong pattern of religious group residential segregation and high rates of geographic mobility. The special occupational and ethnic character of each of the city's four districts is also apparent. Ethnic differences strongly influenced patterns of social stratification in 1795. Based on published census schedules; 9 maps, 17 tables, 3 graphs, 31 notes.
                                                          W. K. Hobson

2513.   Harvey, Fernand.   PRÉLIMINAIRES À UNE SOCIOLOGIE HISTORIQUE DES MALADIES MENTALES AU QUÉBEC   [A preliminary to a historical sociology of mental diseases in Québec]. *Recherches Sociographiques [Canada] 1975 16(1): 113-117.* An analysis of research materials available for the writing of sociological history of mental disease in Québec suggests three areas that merit attention: study of institutions, study of the development of psychiatry as a science and

as a practice, and study of the sociological composition of mental disease.
                                                                A. E. LeBlanc

2514. Jacob, Paul. CROIX DE CHEMIN ET DÉVOTIONS POPULAIRES DANS LA BEAUCE [Roadside crosses and popular devotions in La Beauce]. *Sessions d'Étude: Soc. Can. d'Hist. de l'Église Catholique [Canada] 1976 43: 15-34.* Studies 17 roadside shrines in La Beauce County as a key to popular devotion, religious practice, and social customs of the area.

2515. Jarrell, R. A. THE RISE AND DECLINE OF SCIENCE AT QUEBEC, 1824-1844. *Social Hist. [Canada] 1977 10(19): 77-91.* The marked interest during the first half of the period declined after 1836 because of a split in the social elite between the English and French. Also, elite interests shifted to politics from the mid-1830's on. The French elite, especially, came to find literature, history, journalism, and the arts more important than science in their fight for cultural survival. Based on published primary and secondary sources; 2 tables, 41 notes.
                                                                W. K. Hobson

2516. Johnstone, John W. C. SOCIAL CHANGE AND PARENT-YOUTH CONFLICT: THE PROBLEM OF GENERATIONS IN ENGLISH AND FRENCH CANADA. *Youth and Soc. 1975 7(1): 3-26.* The high degree of tension between Quebec French Canadian youth and their parents is based primarily on the decline of the Roman Catholic Church as a dominant force and significant changes in the educational system. Conflicts are strongest over dating and religion, and are strong also over politics and occupational plans. There is much less tension in English Canadian families. Based on a 1965 sample of Canadian youth (ages 13-20), and on primary and secondary sources, 5 tables, 8 notes, biblio.
                                                                J. H. Sweetland

2517. Kardonne, Rick. MONTREAL, QUEBEC. *Present Tense 1975 2(2): 50-55.* Discusses the social and religious life of the Jews of Montreal, Quebec during the 1970's and the problems presented by the emigration of Jews from Morocco in the 1960's.

2518. Katz, Elliott. THE GOLDEN ERA OF LAURENTIAN SKIING. *Can. Geographic [Canada] 1978/79 97(3): 12-19.* Chronicles skiing in Quebec's Laurentian Mountains, 1900's-70's.

2519. Kennedy, Frederick James. HERMAN MELVILLE'S LECTURE IN MONTREAL. *New England Q. 1977 50(1): 125-137.* Examines Herman Melville's (1819-91) first appearance (1857) as a lecturer before a non-New England audience. Reprints newspaper accounts and reviews of his "Statues in Rome" address. 22 notes.
                                                                J. C. Bradford

2520. Kesteman, Jean-Pierre. LES TRAVAILLEURS À LA CONSTRUCTION DU CHEMIN DE FER DANS LA RÉGION DE SHERBROOKE (1851-1853) [The railway construction workers in the Sherbrooke region (1851-53)]. *Rev. d'Hist. de l'Amérique Française [Canada] 1978 31(4): 525-545.* Construction of the railroad connecting Montreal with Portland, Maine, attracted many migrant laborers. The census reports issued for the Sherbrooke region of Quebec in 1851 and 1852 enable the historian to more clearly understand the lives, conditions, and activities of this traditionally "invisible" group. Most of the workers were young Irishmen who, with their wives and children, lived in overcrowded railway camps. Local newspaper accounts reveal their most sensational activities, e.g., drinking, brawling, and resisting arrest, but the census materials represent a richer, more systematic vein of information. 8 tables, 45 notes.
                                                                M. R. Yerburgh

2521. Kidd, Bruce. CANADIAN ATHLETES VS. MAYOR DRAPEAU. *Can. Dimension 1973 9(4): 8-10.* Attacks Mayor Jean Drapeau of Montreal for trying to use the 1976 Olympic games in Montreal for political ends. Argues that athletic benefits will ensue eventually. The 1976 Olympics should combine the sports competition with events for other art forms such as music, painting, and dance. The Olympics should be demilitarized and denationalized.   W. B. Whitham and S

2522. LaFrance, Marc and Ruddell, Thiery. ELEMENTS DE L'URBANISATION DE LA VILLE DE QUEBEC: 1790-1840 [Elements of urbanization in the city of Quebec: 1790-1840]. *Urban Hist. Rev. [Can-*

ada] 1975 75(1): 22-30. Discusses urbanization in Quebec, Quebec, 1790-1840, examining the rapid physical expansion and the military, administrative, and commercial functions in the city; one of eight articles in this issue on the Canadian city in the 19th century.

2523. Lambert, James H. "LE HAUT ENSEIGNEMENT DE LA RELIGION": MGR BOURGET AND THE FOUNDING OF LAVAL UNIVERSITY. *R. de l'U. d'Ottawa [Canada] 1975 45(3): 278-294.* Concentrates "solely on the role of Mgr. Ignace Bourget, second bishop of Montreal," in founding Laval University. "The founding of Laval must be seen in the context of a Catholic ultramontane reaction to a liberal and secularist outburst during and following the French Revolution." Bourget saw the university as the principal instrument for "wresting the elite from the clutches of liberalism." Based on primary and secondary sources; 72 notes.
                                                                M. L. Frey

2524. Lamonde, Yvan. INVENTAIRE DES ÉTUDES ET DES SOURCES POUR L'ÉTUDE DES ASSOCIATIONS "LITTÉRAIRES" QUÉBÉCOISES FRANCOPHONES AU 19ᵉ SIÈCLE (1840-1900) [Inventory of monographs and sources for the study of Quebec French-language "literary" associations in the 19th century (1840-1900)]. *Recherches Sociographiques [Canada] 1975 16(2): 261-275.* The inventory includes an introductory bibliography of studies involving various forms of voluntary associations in Quebec, the United States, and Europe. This is followed by an inventory of sources, both manuscript and secondary, on French language literary associations that existed in Quebec during 1840-1900.
                                                                A. E. LeBlanc

2525. Lamonde, Yvan. LE MEMBERSHIP D'UNE ASSOCIATION DU 19ᵉ SIÈCLE. LE CAS DE L'INSTITUT CANADIEN DE LONGUEUIL (1857-1860) [The membership of a 19th century association. The case of the Canadian Institute of Longueuil, 1857-1860]. *Recherches Sociographiques [Canada] 1975 16(2): 219-240.* In the Canadian Institute of Longueuil the membership came from a variety of occupations, although the leadership was assumed by a merchant-commercial group rather than by individuals coming from the liberal profession. This rendered the Longueuil institute more practically-oriented than other such associations. The study utilizes occupational classification techniques for analytical purposes.
                                                                A. E. LeBlanc

2526. Lamonde, Yvan. LES ASSOCIATIONS AU BAS-CANADA: DE NOUVEAUX MARCHÉS AUX IDÉES (1840-1867) [Literary associations of Lower Canada: New markets of ideas (1840-1867)]. *Social Hist. [Canada] 1975 8(16): 361-369.* The literary association movement in Lower Canada was promoted by lawyers and journalists, members of the liberal bourgeoisie. They saw the movement as a solution to the problems faced by the younger generation of a society in transition from a subsistence to a market economy. They considered education via literary associations as a solution to the distinctions of class, wealth, race, and religion, and as a solution to the political isolation of young French Canadians. They believed old institutions were no longer capable of performing such functions. The promotional literature for the associations was permeated with applications of free-market idiom to the discussion of education. Based on literary association promotional periodicals. Graph, 51 notes.
                                                                W. K. Hobson

2527. Lamontagne, Maurice. LA FACULTÉ DES SCIENCES SOCIALES DE LAVAL: PRELUDE DE LA RÉVOLUTION TRANQUILLE [The faculty of social sciences at Laval: Prelude to the quiet revolution] *Social Hist. [Canada] 1977 10(19): 146-151.* The history of Quebec has been marked by an opposition between the sources and orientation of economic growth (external), on the one hand, and the tenor of the dominant ideology of the traditional elites on the other hand. Ideology has opposed the trends of economic growth and proposed impossible alternatives. The Faculty of Social Sciences of Laval University, founded by R.-P. Lévesque, has sought to develop a more realistic and positive approach to the problems of contemporary Quebec society. As a result, a new educated elite is emerging and is inspiring a new dynamic in the popular movements.   W. K. Hobson

2528. Lapointe, Pierre-Louis. LA NOUVELLE EUROPÉENNE ET LA PRESSE QUÉBÉCOISE D'EXPRESSION FRANÇAISE (1866-1871) [European news and the French-language press of Quebec (1866-1871)]. *R. d'hist. de l'Amérique française [Canada] 1975 28(4): 517-537.*

CANADA: REGIONS

During the Austro-Prussian and Franco-Prussian Wars, the French-language newspapers of Quebec covered events in Europe mainly by reproducing published French-language articles from European and American sources. After completion of the trans-Atlantic cable, some of Quebec's French-language newspapers subscribed to the Associated Press dispatch system, and received news from Europe in English on a two-days delayed basis via New York. Most French newspapers in Quebec lacked the funds to subscribe, and had to be content with reproducing articles. Based on newspapers and secondary works; 5 tables, 84 notes.   L. B. Chan

2529. Lavallée, Jean-Guy. L'ÉGLISE DE SHERBROOKE ET LES TRAPPISTES (1880-1948) [The Sherbrooke Church and the Trappists]. *Sessions d'Étude: Société Can. d'Histoire de l'Église Catholique [Canada] 1974 41: 9-24*. A history of relations between the Sherbrooke Church and the Trappist Order. Touches on the great anticlerical and secular crises in France in the 19th and 20th centuries, the internal structure and formation of the Order, and broader problems such as the emigration of French-Canadians to the United States, their repatriation in Quebec, and the colonization of less developed regions of the province. The Trappists failed in their attempt to establish a permanent order in Quebec. Based on Archives of the Sherbrooke Arch-diocese; 41 notes.
                                                                S. Sevilla

2530. Lefebvre, Jean-Jacques. LA FAMILLE PAGE, DE LAPRAIRIE, 1763-1967 [The Page Family of Laprairie, 1763-1967]. *Tr. of the Royal Soc. of Can. [Canada] 1976 14: 209-220*. Notes that earlier genealogical studies were of families of men knighted by the British monarch and suggests the other French Canadians have been ignored. Studies the genealogy of the family of Page, from Laprairie, beginning with Jean Page who was born in 1730 and probably came to Canada as a soldier during the Seven Years War. He married Madeleine Circe. Traces the family up to the present. 11 notes.   J. D. Neville

2531. Lejeunesse, Marcel. LES CABINETS DE LECTURE À PARIS ET À MONTRÉAL AU 19ᵉ SIÈCLE [Reading rooms in Paris and Montreal in the 19th century]. *Recherches Sociographiques [Canada] 1975 16(2): 241-247*. The reading room was one of the major sociocultural forces at work in Paris during the first half of the 19th century, but its popularity only began in Montreal in the late 1850's. Its development in Montreal was closely related to the interests of the Roman Catholic Church.   A. E. LeBlanc

2532. LeMoignan, Michel. LA VISION AUDACIEUSE DE MGR. F.-X. ROSS, PREMIER ÉVÊQUE DE GASPÉ [The audacious vision of Monsignor F.-X. Ross, first bishop of Gaspé]. *Sessions d'Étude: Soc. Can. d'Hist. de l'Église Catholique [Canada] 1976 43: 35-47*. A biography of Bishop-founder François Xavier Ross (1869-1945), emphasizing his contributions to the educational system, medical facilities, and socioeconomic organization of Gaspé and its environs, 1923-45, and stressing the importance of his writings to the historian.

2533. Létourneau, Firmin. ESDRAS MINVILLE. *Action Natl. [Canada] 1976 65(9-10): 621-625*. Esdras Minville wrote his first article for *Action Française* (Canada) in 1922. Later he became a director of the Ligue d'Action Français. In 1928, with Gerard Parizeau, Fortunat Fortier, François Vézina, and others, he founded *Actualité Économique,* the official publication of the École des Hautes Études Commerciales in Montreal.   A. W. Novitsky

2534. Little, J. I. THE PARISH AND FRENCH CANADIAN MIGRANTS TO COMPTON, QUEBEC, 1851-1891. *Social Hist. [Canada] 1978 11(21): 134-143*. The Catholic Church in Quebec clearly wanted a society of small independent landowners because of fear that landless laborers would eventually abandon French and Catholicism. In Compton County rural communities were the most stable and homogeneous, reinforcing this bias, but the parish was still an effective institution in towns and where French Canadian farmers were a minority. Studies of a colonization parish, a mixed rural parish, and an industrial parish confirm this. 30 notes.   D. F. Chard

2535. Louder, Dean R.; Bisson, Michel; and La Rochelle, Pierre. ANALYSE CENTROGRAPHIQUE DE LA POPULATION DE QUEBEC DE 1951 A 1971 [Centrographic analysis of Quebec population, 1951-1971]. *Cahiers de Géographie de Québec 1974 18(45): 421-444*.

2536. Lunardini, Rosemary. "TUQUE BLEUE." *Beaver [Canada] 1976 307(3): 40-45*. Relates the history of the Montreal Snowshoe Club. Officially founded in Montreal in 1843, the club met weekly in the winters to tramp cross-country and to have annual races. Club members competed against Indian guests who usually won. The club grew, but by the turn of the century social activities and charitable works threatened to replace the snowshoe aspects, as few members kept up an interest in the rigorous sport. Today there are many snowshoe clubs in Quebec, totaling more than 5,000 members. They socialize and practice the sport, as well as emphasize the historic role of snowshoeing in discovery and exploration. Based on materials in the Public Archives of Canada; 5 illus.
                                                                D. Chaput

2537. Menard, Johanne. L'INSTITUT DES ARTISANS DU COMTÉ DE DRUMMOND, 1856-1890 [The Drummond County Mechanics Institute, 1856-1890]. *Recherches Sociographiques [Canada] 1975 16(2): 207-218*. Established in 1856, the Drummond County Mechanics Institute was largely composed of farmers and by 1861, French-Canadian Roman Catholics were in the majority. Until 1880 the institute was a vital part of the community; however, the changing composition of its membership brought an end to this dynamism.
                                                                A. E. LeBlanc

2538. Metcalfe, Alan. THE EVOLUTION OF ORGANIZED PHYSICAL RECREATION IN MONTREAL, 1840-1895. *Social Hist. [Canada] 1978 11(21): 144-166*. Before 1840, organized physical recreation in Montreal was elitist. In the 1840's public concern at the lack of recreational facilities developed, but throughout the 19th century most facilities remained private. In the 1870's and 1880's the number of baseball, lacrosse, and hockey clubs grew significantly, and new sports, such as golf, swimming, and biking, emerged. Public concern about parks grew in the 1870's, but not until the 1890's did mass sports, still largely Anglophone, develop. Commercial spectator sports increased gradually after 1870. 56 notes.   D. F. Chard

2539. Morin, Rosaire. L'AVENIR DU QUÉBEC, C'EST LE PRÉSENT [Quebec's future is the present]. *Action Natl. [Canada] 1973 62(6): 451-457*. The crisis management in vogue in Quebec must go, and the government must set priorities. The fundamental priority is to integrate the two million Quebecers who live within the poverty level. Full employment and a realistic system of social reconstruction must be initiated.   A. E. LeBlanc

2540. Nguyen, Hung. ASPECT REGIONAL DE LA CONSOMMATION ET DE LA PRODUCTION DES SERVICES DE SANTE AU QUEBEC [Regional aspects of the consumption and supply of health services in Quebec]. *Actualité Écon. [Canada] 1974 50(2): 125-151*. "In this study we are trying to measure the influence of health services supply (or better, the availability of health services) on the consumption. We first examine the regional disparity of available services and the impact of this difference on the production and (the) consumption of services. Then we do a projection of resources based on a standardized consumption. At the regional level, we find: 1) a disparity of resources in numbers and structure; 2) the consumption increases with the availability of services; 3) the production decreases with the availability of services."   J

2541. O'Gallagher, Marianna. CARE OF THE ORPHAN AND THE AGED BY THE IRISH COMMUNITY OF QUEBEC CITY, 1847 AND YEARS FOLLOWING. *Study Sessions: Can. Catholic Hist. Assoc. [Canada] 1976 43: 39-56*. Indicates the history and development of St. Bridget's Home in Quebec, and the work of Father Patrick McMahon, Irish immigrants, and the Catholic Church to provide for the needy, 1847-1972.

2542. Paré, Marius. LE ROLE DES ÉVÊQUES DE CHICOUTIMI DANS L'OEUVRE DU SÉMINAIRE [The role of the bishops of Chicoutimi in the work of the seminary]. *Sessions D'Étude: Soc. Can. d'Hist. de l'Eglise Catholique 1973 40: 113-124*. Gives a history of the bishops of the Séminaire de Chicoutimi in Quebec from its foundation in 1873 to the present.   S

2543. Porter, John R. L'HÔPITAL-GÉNÉRAL DE QUÉBEC ET LE SOIN DES ALIÉNÉS (1717-1845) [Quebec's General Hospital and the care of the insane (1717-1845)]. *Sessions d'Étude: Soc. Can. d'Hist.*

de l'Église Catholique [Canada] 1977 44: 23-56. Discusses establishing the General Hospital in Quebec during 1692-1717 by the Augustinians and assesses methods of treating the insane, their acceptance within the local community, and the role of the Catholic Church during 1717-1845. Biblio.

2544. Porter, John R. UN PROJET DE MUSÉE NATIONAL À QUÉBEC À L'ÉPOQUE DU PEINTRE JOSEPH LÉGARÉ (1833-1853) [A proposed National Museum in Quebec during the era of painter Joseph Légaré, 1833-1853]. *Rev. d'Hist. de l'Am. Française [Canada] 1977 31(1): 75-82.* The painter Joseph Légaré (1795-1855) was one of the first promoters of a national museum in Quebec. He suggested such a project in 1833, but the public was indifferent. The National Gallery was not established until 1880, in Ottawa instead of Quebec. In 1874, Laval University purchased the old collection of Légaré's paintings. When the provincial Museum of Quebec opened in 1933, the university's collections were not integrated with it. Based on periodicals and secondary works; 23 notes.   L. B. Chan

2545. Pouyez, Christian and Bergeron, Michel. L'ÉTUDE DES MIGRATIONS AU SAGUENAY (1842-1931): PROBLÈMES DE MÉTHODE [The study of migrations to the Saguenay (1842-1931): methodological problems]. *Social Hist. [Canada] 1978 11(21): 26-61.* This study, part of a social history project on the population of Quebec's Saguenay district, relies on four main sources: federal censuses (available for only 1852, 1861, and 1871), parish censuses and annual reports, and civil registers (misleading where parishes and municipalities were subdivided, thereby suggesting moves where none occurred). Methods devised to identify such problems justify the research, and show that the problem of the equivalence of territories needs resolution to put the study of migrations on a solid methodological basis. 3 tables, 62 notes.
                                                                    D. F. Chard

2546. Raymondis, L. M. LA CONCEPTION COMMUNAUTAIRE DU DROIT ET LA PSYCHIATRIE COMMUNAUTAIRE [The concept of community law and community psychiatry]. *Recherches Sociographiques [Canada] 1973 14(1): 9-39.* Sets forth approaches to psychiatric care legislation in North America and France and their influence on recently drafted legislation in Quebec.   A. E. LeBlanc

2547. Renaud, François and von Schoenberg, Brigitte. L'IMPLANTATION DES CONSEILS RÉGIONAUX DE LA SANTÉ ET DES SERVICES SOCIAUX: ANALYSE D'UN PROCESSUS POLITIQUE [The establishment of regional councils of health and social services: Analysis of a political process]. *Can. J. of Pol. Sci. 1974 7(1): 52-69.* Interested, well established health and social service institutions are found to establish dominant roles in these councils (formed in 1971 by the Quebec government) which had been designed to provide effective representation for the population at large. 17 notes.   R. V. Kubicek

2548. Richert, Jean Pierre. POLITICAL PARTICIPATION AND POLITICAL EMANCIPATION: THE IMPACT OF CULTURAL MEMBERSHIP. *Western Pol. Q. 1974 27(1): 104-116.* Examines and tests a hypothesis using Quebec as an example that suggests how two cultural groups differ in the formation of political attitudes.   S

2549. Richert, Jean Pierre. POLITICAL SOCIALIZATION IN QUEBEC: YOUNG PEOPLE'S ATTITUDES TOWARD GOVERNMENT. *Can. J. of Pol. Sci. 1973 6(2): 303-313.* English- and French-Canadian children differed in their perception of the character and purpose of government but held similar views about its performance. Based on data gathered from a survey of elementary school children; 8 tables, 42 notes.   R. V. Kubicek

2550. Robert, Jean-Claude. LES NOTABLES DE MONTRÉAL AU XIXᵉ SIÈCLE [Montreal's "worthies" in the 19th century]. *Social Hist. [Canada] 1975 8(15): 54-76.* In 1892 J. Douglas Bothwick (1832-1912) published the *History and Biographical Gazetteer of Montreal to the Year 1892.* It includes usable biographical sketches of 491 Montreal notables. "Intellectuals" and professionals are overrepresented and businessmen are underrepresented, but it is otherwise a good source on the social composition of the 19th century Montreal elite. Almost 50 per cent of the notables were born outside Lower Canada, in Great Britain for the most part. The elite was proportionately more English-speaking than the

population. Occupations showed ethnic specialization. British-born tended to be in business; Canadian-born tended to be doctors or lawyers. Francophones formed the majority of the political class. Anglophones formed the majority of the business class. 4 tables, 28 notes.
                                                                    W. K. Hobson

2551. Rocher, Guy. L'INFLUENCE DE LA SOCIOLOGIE AMÈRICAINE SUR LA SOCIOLOGIE QUÉBECOISE [The influence of American sociology on Quebec sociology]. *Tr. of the Royal Soc. of Can. 1973 11: 75-79.* Compares American and French influence on the field of sociology in Quebec, blaming these two elements for the indetermination, weakness, and lack of creativity in Quebec sociology, and for its failure to develop its own potential.

2552. Rodin, Alvin E. OSLER'S AUTOPSIES: THEIR NATURE AND UTILIZATION. *Medical Hist. [Great Britain] 1973 17(1): 37-48.* From 1876 to 1884, Sir William Osler (1849-1919) performed 786 autopsies while he was pathologist at Montreal General Hospital and a teacher at McGill Medical College. Then, while professor of medicine at the University of Pennsylvania, he performed an additional 162 autopsies. Osler utilized the material gathered in his extensive experience in the morgue; he prepared museum specimens for the McGill Medical College, wrote a medical text (*The Principles and Practice of Medicine,* 1892), and used the specimens in preparing papers for publication and presentations before medical societies. 47 notes.   M. Kaufman

2553. Rogel, Jean-Pierre. LA PRESSE QUEBECOISE ET L'INFORMATION SUR LA POLITIQUE INTERNATIONALE [Quebec's Press and Information on International Politics]. *Études Int. [Canada] 1974 5(4): 693-711.* Analyzes foreign news coverage in three major Quebec daily newspapers, *La Presse, Le Soleil,* and *Le Devoir.* Discusses the sources for foreign news, notably the impact of the US press, international news agencies, and journalists. Examines the treatment afforded foreign developments, including editorials. Covers 1962-74. Primary and secondary sources; 3 tables, 25 notes, biblio.
                                                                    J. F. Harrington, Jr.

2554. Roy, Jean-Yves. MÉDECINE: CRISE ET DÉFI [Medicine: crisis and challenge]. *Recherches Sociographiques [Canada] 1975 16(1): 43-67.* Medicine in Quebec is facing a crisis as classical medical thinking comes under fire from all quarters. The individualistic notion of sickness has to be replaced by a collective notion of health in order to reestablish the destroyed equilibrium. In this manner, medicine will recover its respected position in society and will be ready to confront the future.
                                                                    A. E. LeBlanc

2555. Rudin, Ronald. REGIONAL COMPLEXITY AND POLITICAL BEHAVIOUR IN A QUEBEC COUNTY, 1867-1886. *Social Hist. [Canada] 1976 9(17): 92-110.* Examines voting patterns on the parish level within the strongly Liberal county of Saint-Hyacinthe in Quebec, 1867-86, not previously revealed in earlier county studies. The city's Liberal tradition developed largely because of the political stance of local church leaders. Saint-Denis parish's anti-Liberal tradition can be traced to that parish's subordinate position within the Saint-Hyacinthe regional economy. Based on sessional papers of Canada and Quebec and other published primary sources; 48 notes, appendix.
                                                                    W. K. Hobson

2556. Ryan, Claude. ANDRÉ LAURENDEAU. *J. of Can. Studies 1973 8(3): 3-7.* Discusses the thought of André Laurendeau, a French Canadian from Quebec who urged his fellow French Canadians to gain knowledge and understanding of English Canadians.

2557. Savard, Pierre. SUR LES NOMS DE PAROISSES AU QUÉBEC, DES ORIGINES À 1925 [On parish names in Quebec, from the beginning until 1925]. *Sessions d'Étude: Soc. Can. d'Hist. de l'Eglise Catholique 1974 41: 105-113.* Studies the religious orientation of town and parish names in Quebec, and evaluates the evolution of religious feeling during 1600-1925. Discusses the question of the origin of church names, stressing chronology as a key to recurring themes particular to Quebec: Irish names accompanying emigration, and Jesuit and Franciscan cycles. Catalogues names by number and subject. Based on departmental archives and secondary sources; 9 notes.   S. Sevilla

2558. Séguin, Normand. COLONISATION ET IMPLANTATION RÉLIGIEUSE AU LAC SAINT-JEAN, DANS LA SECONDE MOI-TIÉ DU XIXᵉ SIÈCLE [Settlement and the establishment of religion around Lake Saint John, in the second half of the 19th century]. *Protée [Canada] 1976 5(2): 55-59.* The Catholic Church was eminently success-ful in establishing its influence in the region of Lake St. John, Quebec, beginning with the settlement of Hébertville in 1840.

2559. Sheriff, Peta. PREFERENCES, VALEURS ET DIFFEREN-TIATION INTRAPROFESSIONNELLE SELON L'ORIGINE ETH-NIQUE [Preferences, values, and intraoccupational distribution according to ethnic origin]. *Can. R. of Sociol. and Anthrop. 1974 11(2): 125-137.* "For some time, sociologists have been concerned with the unequal distribution of members of different ethnic groups on the Cana-dian occupational scale. Using a sample of French- and English-speaking engineers of the city of Montreal, the author tests the hypothesis that their occupational values influence their distribution within the profession. The results of the study suggest that the *values* of the two ethnic groups are similar; however, their occupational *preferences,* which reflect social con-straints, are more closely linked to their professional situation. In empha-sizing the importance of the distinction between values and preferences, the author suggests that a structural approach to intraoccupational distri-bution would be more fruitful."   J

2560. Silver, A. I. SOME QUEBEC ATTITUDES IN AN AGE OF IMPERIALISM AND IDEOLOGICAL CONFLICT. *Can. Hist. Rev. [Canada] 1976 57(4): 440-460.* Uses French-Quebec newspapers, pam-phlets, and other printed material to examine late 19th- and early 20th-century attitudes toward world affairs. Finds considerable sympathy for the "civilising mission" in colonial imperialism and for the Catholic, conservative camp in a perceived division of the world on ideological grounds. These sympathies and perceptions seem to have influenced atti-tudes toward French Canada's place in Canada and in the British Empire.   A

2561. Simard, Jean. CULTES LITURGIQUES ET DÉVOTIONS POPULAIRES DANS LES COMTÉS DE PORTNEUF ET DU LAC-SAINT-JEAN [Liturgical cults and popular devotions in the counties of Portneuf and Lac-Saint-Jean]. *Sessions d'Études: Soc. Can. d'Hist. de l'Église Catholique [Canada] 1976 43: 5-14.* Presents the results of re-search and surveys on the close relation between liturgical cults and popular devotions in Quebec, comparing them to similar developments in France.

2562. Simard, Jean Paul and Riverin, Bérard. ORIGINE GÉOGRA-PHIQUE ET SOCIAL DES ETUDIANTS DU PETIT-SÉMINAIRE DE CHICOUTIMI ET LEUR ORIENTATION SOCIO-PROFES-SIONNELLE: 1873-1930 [Geographic and social origins of the students of the Petit-Séminaire de Chicoutimi and their socioprofessional orienta-tion: 1873-1930]. *Sessions D'Étude: Soc. Can. d'Hist. de l'Eglise Cath-olique 1973 40: 33-54.*

2563. Simard, Ovide-D. SÉMINAIRE DE CHICOUTIMI, 1873-1973: COUP D'OEIL SUR LE SIÈCLE ECOULÉ [Séminaire de Chicoutimi, 1873-1973: a glance at the past century]. *Sessions D'Étude: Soc. Can. d'Hist. de l'Eglise Catholique 1973: 40: 125-130.* The oldest living Superior of the Chicoutimi seminary reflects on its hundred-year existence.   S

2564. Simard, Sylvain. LES FRANÇAIS ET LE CANADA, 1850-1914: IDENTITÉ ET PERCEPTION [The French and Canada, 1850-1914: identity and perception]. *Rev. d'Hist. de l'Amérique Française [Canada] 1975 29(2): 209-239.* More than 700 books and brochures about Canada were published in late 19th-century France. Their authors were chiefly interested in Quebec for ethnic and linguistic reasons. They at-tributed the survival and development of the French in Canada to the leadership of the French-speaking Roman Catholic clergy. Secondary works; 10 tables, 26 notes.   L. B. Chan

2565. Smith, Elsie B. WILLIAM J. ANDERSON: SHOREHAM'S NEGRO LEGISLATOR IN THE VERMONT HOUSE OF REPRE-SENTATIVES. *Vermont Hist. 1976 44(4): 203-213.* Elected almost unanimously to the House of Representatives as a Republican in 1944 and 1946, William J. Anderson met a favorable press but was excluded from

lodging at Montpelier's two major hotels. He killed a civil rights bill as unnecessary and worked through Senator Warren R. Austin to increase the percentage of black army officers. Trained at the Mount Herman School, Anderson managed its laundry during 1900-20, and saved enough to return to Shoreham where he planted an apple orchard. The orchard expanded profitably and reached a peak of 40,000 bushels in 1943, but declined because of Anderson's inability to change methods, and from mismanagement during his increased absences. Anderson's mother was French Canadian and Indian, and he was bilingual. He belonged to the otherwise white Whitehall Masonic lodge and earned a reputation for his excellent rhetoric and sonorous voice. Primary sources.
                                    T. D. S. Bassett

2566. Sorrell, Richard S. FRANCO-AMERICANS IN NEW EN-GLAND. *J. of Ethnic Studies 1977 5(1): 90-94.* Reiterates the distinc-tion between French and French Canadian as ethnic backgrounds, two out of three Franco-Americans will be French Canadian in ancestry and nearly three-fourths are found in New England, mainly in New Hamp-shire. Majority of the article is a bibliographic essay on Franco-Ameri-cans, including unpublished dissertations and manuscripts. Focuses on the *survivance* idea, the realization of slow acculturation.
                                    G. J. Bobango

2567. Sylvain, Philippe. UN FRÈRE MÉCONNU D'ANTOINE GÉRIN-LAJOIE: ELZÉAR GÉRIN [Elzéar Gérin, Antoine Gérin-Lajoie's brother not rightly recognized]. *Rev. de l'U. d'Ottawa [Canada] 1977 47(1-2): 214-225.* Because of adverse circumstances and a premature death, Elzéar Gérin 1843-87 was not as well-known as his brother, jour-nalist, poet, novelist, and historian, Antoine Gérin-Lajoie. A talented, alert, and witty journalist with a combative spirit, Elzéar contributed to various important French Canadian newspapers and had many faithful readers; he was involved in political dissensions, once between the Vatican and the French government because of his publication of a confidential document. He founded his own newspaper and was elected a deputy of Quebec. Primary and secondary sources; 41 notes.   G. P. Cleyet

2568. Thomson, Dale C. QUEBEC AND THE BICULTURAL DI-MENSION. *Pro. of the Acad. of Pol. Sci. 1976 32(2): 27-39.* Analyzes the present position and possible future of French Quebec in Canada. The present provincial government is committed to the Canadian federation, supporting separatist sentiment just enough to remain in power. Separa-tion is unlikely. French Canadians are primarily concerned with making English Canada endure what they have endured, at least in Quebec, and in wringing financial and other concessions from the federal government. Declining birthrates augur ill for the future, though this trend will proba-bly reverse.   V. L. Human

2569. Tremblay, Marc-Adélard. LES QUÉBÉCOIS À LA RECHER-CHE DE LEUR IDENTITÉ CULTURELLE [Quebecers in search of their cultural identity]. *Action Natl. [Canada] 1973 62(6): 439-450.* French-speaking Quebecers suffer from cultural alienation brought about by rapid change in their historical roots and by the adoption of the North American material value system. Unless redressed, this process of aliena-tion will lead to complete assimilation of the French-language group.
                                    A. E. LeBlanc

2570. Trépanier, Pierre. SIMÉON LE SAGE (1835-1909): UN NO-TABLE D'AUTREFOIS DANS L'INTIMITÉ [Simeon Le Sage (1835-1909): The personal life of a notable of the past]. *Action Natl. [Canada] 1978 67(6): 469-496.* Biographical sketch and study of the social mobility of a Quebec lawyer and public official in the late 19th century. His father was an unlettered craftsman, but Simeon Le Sage completed classical studies, became a lawyer, and married into a landed family. Although defeated twice in legislative elections (1862 and 1867) he was appointed deputy director of the Department of Agriculture and Public Works by Quebec premier P.-J.-O. Chauveau. A staunch conservative and French Canadian nationalist, he was a patron of the arts and letters, especially French Canadian history. Primary and secondary sources; 150 notes.
                                    A. W. Novitsky

2571. Trudel, Marcel. LES DÉBUTS DE L'INSTITUT D'HIS-TOIRE À L'UNIVERSITÉ LAVAL [The beginnings of the Institute of History at Laval University]. *R. d'Hist. de l'Amérique Française [Can-ada] 1973 27(3): 397-402.* Discusses the founding of the Institute of

History at Laval University in 1947 which effectively established the study of history as an academic discipline.

2572. Trudel, Pierre. LA PROTECTION DES ANGLO-QUÉBÉCOIS ET LA PRESSE CONSERVATRICE (1864-1867) [The protection of the Anglo-Quebecans and the Conservative Press (1864-1867)]. *R. de L'U. d'Ottawa [Canada] 1974 44(2): 137-157.* Analyzes the economic and political power of the "Anglo-Québécois" and their desire, as a minority, to retain their rights. The conservative press argued for the majority of the Franco-Québécois by stressing the importance of the French language, the Catholic religion, and the basic institutions of lower Canada. Based on primary and secondary sources; 133 notes.   M. L. Frey

2573. Tunis, B. R. MEDICAL LICENSING IN LOWER CANADA: THE DISPUTE OVER CANADA'S FIRST MEDICAL DEGREE. *Can. Hist. R. 1974 55(4): 489-504.* A legal controversy, over the right of medical graduates of a Canadian university to practice medicine without further examination by medical licensing authorities, was settled in 1834 in favor of McGill University. Gives some insight into conflict within the medical profession in Lower Canada, both over control of the medical boards and on the larger political scene. Based on unpublished documents of the Court of King's Bench, Archives de la Cour Supérieure de Montréal, 1833-34, and on contemporary newspaper accounts of the meetings of the Montreal Medical Board.   A

2574. Vaillancourt, Pauline. STOP THE PRESS! EN GRÈVE. *Can. Dimension [Canada] 1978 13(1): 37-41.* Discusses the strike by journalists and support staff of three major newspapers in Quebec to protest the stranglehold which major industry has on the Quebec press and for better job conditions and benefits, 1977-78.

2575. Veltman, Calvin J. DEMOGRAPHIC COMPONENTS OF THE FRANCISATION OF RURAL QUEBEC: THE CASE OF RAWDON. *Am. Rev. of Can. Studies 1976 6(2): 22-41.* Explores francisation of the village of Rawdon about 40 miles from Montreal. The population was divided into groups based on ethnic and religious characteristics and each was studied in terms of 19th- and 20th-century patterns of marriage, family size, and migration. The study concludes that the Irish emigrated and were replaced by French Canadians whose higher marriage rate and tendency to have larger families produced a predominance of francophones. The relatively stable Anglican population became the most significant part of the anglophone community. 5 tables, 11 notes, biblio.
G. A. Patzwald

2576. Veltman, Calvin J. ETHNIC ASSIMILATION IN QUEBEC: A STATISTICAL ANALYSIS. *Am. Rev. of Can. Studies 1975 5(2): 104-129.* Examines linguistic transfers in 1971 census reports to determine whether the use of the French language in Quebec is really in danger of extinction; there is some linguistic transfer, but the French-speaking community is presently growing.

2577. Veltman, Calvin J. THE EVOLUTION OF ETHNO-LINGUISTIC FRONTIERS IN THE UNITED STATES AND CANADA. *Social Sci. J. 1977 14(1): 47-58.* Examines the political and ethnic implications of linguistic nationalism in the Official Language Act (1974) in Quebec restricting the use of the English language in favor of French; the United States and Canada should provide government services in minority languages in any region where the minority language population is sufficiently numerous.

2578. Vigod, B. L. IDEOLOGY AND INSTITUTIONS IN QUEBEC: THE PUBLIC CHARITIES CONTROVERSY, 1921-1926. *Social Hist. [Canada] 1978 11(21): 167-182.* In late 1920 a brief but severe recession strained the resources of Quebec's charitable institutions. The Public Charities Act (1921) provided relief but also demanded greater accountability. The Church objected to what it saw as anticlerical state interference. The patronage-ridden regime of Premier Alexandre Taschereau, with his personal reputation for impatience and intolerance, was another cause for concern. There was also uncertainty about the most appropriate concept of social welfare. The Act provided relief, but no systematic reform occurred. 72 notes.   D. F. Chard

2579. Voisine, Nive. L'ÉPISCOPAT QUÉBÉCOIS AU MOMENT DE LA FORMATION DU DIOCÈSE DE SHERBROOKE, 1874 [The Quebec episcopate at the time of the formation of the diocese of Sherbrooke, 1874]. *Sessions d'Étude Soc. Can. d'Hist. de l'Eglise Catholique 1974 41: 25-41.* A biographical sketch of six bishops of the Sherbrooke Diocese studying conflicts dividing the episcopate, such as opposition to modern thought, to liberalism, and to changes in education. A reunion (1872) to celebrate the bicentennial of the Quebec seat became a confrontation between the two rival clans of bishops, the "idealists": Taschereau, La Rocque, and Langevin; and the "realists": Bourget, and Laflèche. Based on correspondence and publications in Diocese Archives; 43 notes.   S. Sevilla

2580. Voisine, Nive. UN DIOCÈSE DIVISÉ CONTRE LUI-MÊME, TROIS-RIVIÈRES (1852-1885) [A diocese divided against itself: Trois-Rivières, 1852-85]. *Rev. de l'U. d'Ottawa [Canada] 1977 47(1-2): 226-236.* The Trois-Rivières diocese which extended north and south of the St. Lawrence River was divided in 1885, the southern part becoming the Nicolet diocese. It ended a 15 year feud inside the diocese between the north and the south among the clergy of opposite philosophies, added to financial difficulties, and the threat of the transfer of the Nicolet seminary. Primary and secondary sources; 51 notes.   G. P. Cleyet

2581. Wawrzysko, Aleksandra. A BIBLIOGRAPHIC GUIDE TO FRENCH-CANADIAN LITERATURE. *Can. Lib. J. [Canada] 1978 35(2): 115-117, 119-121, 123-131, 133.* Covers not only French Canadian literature but also other disciplines that study the French in Canada. Focuses on reference works in the humanities and fine arts. Emphasizes writings since the late 19th century but contains some from the early 17th century. Encompasses catalogs, translations (from French into English and vice versa), biobibliographies, dictionaries of quotations, encyclopedias, indexes and abstracts, dissertations, literary history, drama, fiction, poetry, and literary periodicals. Annotates 108 works and 41 journals.
D. J. Mycue

2582. Whiteley, Albert S. COMMUNICATIONS ON THE LOWER NORTH SHORE. *Can. Geographical J. [Canada] 1977 95(1): 42-47.* The development of intertown communication on Quebec's lower north shore, along the St. Lawrence Seaway, 16th-20th centuries, includes land, sea, air, and (only since the 1950's) telephone communication.

2583. Woolfson, Peter. THE HERITAGE AND CULTURE OF THE FRENCH-VERMONTER: RESEARCH NEEDS IN THE SOCIAL SCIENCES. *Vermont Hist. 1976 44(2): 103-109.* Reviews the limited historiography on an ethnic minority comprising nearly 10 percent of the population, and urges more study. 20 refs.
T. D. S. Bassett

2584. —. ACCROISSEMENT ET STRUCTURE DE LA POPULATION À QUÉBEC AU DÉBUT DU XIXᵉ SIÈCLE [Growth and structure of the Quebec population at the beginning of the 19th century]. *Social Hist. [Canada] 1976 9(17): 187-196.*
Paillé, Michel P. ACCROISSEMENT ET STRUCTURE DE LA POPULATION À QUÉBEC AU DÉBUT DU XIXᵉ SIÈCLE (À PROPOS D'UN ARTICLE DE JOHN HARE) [Growth and structure of the Quebec population at the beginning of the 19th century (with respect to an article by John Hare)], *pp. 187-193.* Reviews John Hare's article on the population of the city of Quebec during 1795-1805. Corrects several compilation errors, defines several concepts, and illustrates methodology for studying population growth and age structure. 3 tables, 33 notes.
Hare, John E. À PROPOS DES COMMENTAIRES DE MICHEL PAILLÉ [Response to Michel Paillé], *pp. 193-196.* Michel Paillé's reexamination is flawed because he relies on the published census' summary tables, which do not correspond to the census' details when examined street by street and house by house. Studying the age structure cannot be as exact as Paillé believes because it must be based on census data using the age of communicants. During 1703-1840, the age for communion was not precise; it was allowed to vary between 10 and 14 years old. 3 tables.
W. K. Hobson

Economic Matters

2585. Allaire, Yvan and Toulouse, Jean-Marie. PROFIL PSY-CHOLOGIQUE DES ETUDIANTS CANADIENS-FRANÇAIS AU M.B.A. [Psychological profile of French Canadian M.B.A. students: consequences for a selection policy]. *Industrial Relations [Canada] 1973 28(3): 476-496.* The results of a study of the *psychological profile* of French Canadian students enrolled in programs for the degree of Master in Business Administration. The aim of the study is to compare the profile of these students to the profiles of the entrepreneur and the manager suggested by past studies of those two types of economic agent. As a whole, the students have a profile closer to that of the manager than to that of the entrepreneur; a sizable proportion of students, however, shows a profile matching neither manager nor entrepreneur. This information could be used by a M.B.A. program in the formulation of its selection policy for candidates. Based on secondary works; 7 tables, 2 diagrams, 2 notes, biblio.   L. R. Atkins

2586. Angers, François-Albert. LA PENSÉE ÉCONOMIQUE D'ES-DRAS MINVILLE [The economic thought of Esdras Minville]. *Action Natl. [Canada] 1976 65(9-10): 727-761.* Esdras Minville opposed liberal capitalism, but was not an agrarian. He sought a balanced industrializa-tion for Quebec. He saw in *Rerum Novarum* and *Quadragesimo Anno* support for his corporatism and personalism. His nationalism was based on respect for French Canadian culture. 7 notes.
                        A. W. Novitsky

2587. Angle, John. MAINLAND CONTROL OF MANUFAC-TURING AND REWARD FOR BILINGUALISM IN PUERTO RICO. *Am. Sociol. R. 1976 41(2): 289-307.* The literature on language group relations in the economy of Quebec Province suggests that more French Canadians are bilingual than English Canadians because many businesses use English and are owned or operated by English Canadians. Bilingual French Canadians are rewarded, on the average, by placement into better occupations. The hypothesis is made that a similar reward exists for bilingualism in English in the Spanish mother tongue labor force in Puerto Rico. The 1970 Census of Population in Puerto Rico provides data for a test of this hypothesis in which the reward is demonstrated. It is also hypothesized that it is mainland American ownership of businesses which accounts for this reward. This hypothesis is tested on the labor force in manufacturing. It is not confirmed.   J

2588. Babcock, Robert. SAMUEL GOMPERS AND THE FRENCH-CANADIAN WORKER, 1900-1914. *Am. Rev. of Can. Studies 1973 3(2): 47-66.* Discusses Samuel Gompers and the American Federation of Labor's policy toward trade unions and the organization of the working class in Quebec 1900-14.

2589. Bauer, Charles. RECOLLECTIONS OF PHILIPPE VAIL-LANCOURT. *Can. Labour 1977 22(2): 39-43.* Philippe Vaillancourt discusses his role in the labor movement in Quebec during 1936-76.

2590. Bauer, Charles and Laplante, Pierre. TRICOFIL—WHERE WORKERS ARE MANAGERS. *Can. Labour 1975 20(3): 2-6.* Textile workers in St. Jérôme, Quebec, organized a collective, the *Société popu-laire Tricofil*, in 1974 to reopen and operate their factory which had closed.

2591. Bauer, Julien. ATTITUDE DES SYNDICATS [The political position of unions]. *Études Int. [Canada] 1977 8(2): 307-319.* Examines the relationship of workers' movements and unions with the Parti Québé-cois before and after the 15 November 1976 elections. Explains differences in attitude among the labor organizations. Primary and secondary sources; 30 notes.   J. F. Harrington, Jr.

2592. Bauer, Julien. PATRONS ET PATRONAT AU QUÉBEC [Employers and their associations in Quebec]. *Can. J. of Pol. Sci. [Can-ada] 1976 9(3): 473-491.* Explores disunity and cleavages within employ-ers' groups in the province. Table, chart, 40 notes.
                        R. V. Kubicek

2593. Beaudry, Richard. LES DETERMINANTS DES MIGRA-TIONS AU QUEBEC [Determinants of internal migration in Quebec].

Actualité Écon. [Canada] 1973 49(1): 113-127. Develops a mathematical model for geographic mobility within Quebec. The traditional concept sees the mobility of laborers only as a factor of production within a broad theory of resource allocation. This concept is flawed because free mobility of workers is often checked by family and social ties. The mathematical model used, which tried to account for these obstacles, was formulated by Ira S. Lowry. Analyzes its application to Quebec. 3 tables, 29 notes, biblio.   W. B. Whitham

2594. Bernard, Jean-Paul; Linteau, Paul-André; and Robert, Jean-Claude. LA STRUCTURE PROFESSIONNELLE DE MONTRÉAL EN 1825 [The professional structure of Montreal in 1825]. *Rev. d'Hist. de l'Amérique Française [Canada] 1976 30(3): 383-415.* In 1825, Mon-treal was a mercantile city uninfluenced by the industrial revolution. Petty bourgeois merchants and artisans competed for the business of a small commercial economy. Based on published government statistics and on secondary works; 4 tables, 28 notes, appendix.
                        L. B. Chan

2595. Bernier, Bernard. THE PENETRATION OF CAPITALISM IN QUEBEC AGRICULTURE. *Can. Rev. of Sociol. and Anthrop. [Canada] 1976 13(4): 422-434.* The transformation of Quebec agriculture under the impact of capitalism has not resulted in the use of wage labour in agriculture, i.e. has not followed the "classic" English case analysed by Marx. Rather, smallholding agriculture has been established and main-tained in Quebec, despite an accelerated rate of dispossession of peasants. This type of agricultural development, resulting in a real crisis in the 1970's, has its cause in the preference of monopoly capital (whether industrial, commercial, or financial) in an indirect exploitation of peas-ants effected through the market.   J

2596. Bernier, Jacques. LA CONSTRUCTION DOMICILIAIRE À QUÉBEC 1810-1820 [House construction in Quebec 1810-20]. *Rev. d'Hist. de l'Amérique Française [Canada] 1978 31(4): 547-561.* Examines domestic building contracts in Quebec during a period of sustained popu-lation growth. Details the geographical and architectural development of the city. Contracts, for example, reveal type, size, and location of house, name of builder, mode of payment, etc. These documents provide little information on the daily life of the construction worker, but are a valuable source of information in their own right. 12 notes.
                        M. R. Yerburgh

2597. Besner, Jacques and Bertrand, Louis-Claude. LA COOPÉR-ATIVE FÉDÉRÉE DE QUÉBEC [The federated cooperative in Que-bec]. *Action Natl. [Canada] 1973 62(9): 746-756.* Discusses the diverse activities of the Coopérative Fédérée de Québec, a federation of farming cooperatives, focusing on the extent of its enterprise, its ideology, present problems, and future directions.

2598. Besner, Jacques and Bertrand, Louis-Claude. LES CAISSES POPULAIRES DESJARDINS [The Desjardins' credit unions]. *Action Natl. [Canada] 1973 62(6): 458-471.* The international extension of credit unions more than attests to the value of this cooperative venture. From their inception in Quebec via the "Caisses Populaires Desjardins," credit unions have adapted to changing needs and thus have assured their legitimacy.   A. E. LeBlanc

2599. Bessette, Luc. DÉTERMINATION DES SALARIES DANS LA FONCTION PUBLIQUE FÉDÉRALE AMÉRICAINE: AP-PLICABILITÉ AU QUÉBEC [Salary determination in the US Federal Service: Applicability to Quebec]. *Industrial Relations [Canada] 1977 32(2): 161-171.* Examines characteristics of the salary structure and de-termination in the Civil Service, compares them to similar ones in Quebec, and assesses the possibility of applying the US situation to Quebec, 1970's.

2600. Bilodeau, Therese. THE FRENCH IN HOLYOKE (1850-1900). *Hist. J. of Western Massachusetts 1974 3(1): 1-12.* Nicholas Proulx, one of the first French Canadians to migrate to Holyoke, re-cruited workers in Quebec. Management found them obedient, non-union workers whose life revolved around the Catholic Church. Primary and secondary sources; 3 illus., chart, 58 notes.   S. S. Sprague

2601. Blais, André. POLITIQUE AGRICOLE ET RÉSULTATS ÉLECTORAUX EN MILIEU AU QUÉBEC [Agricultural policy and election results in rural Quebec]. *Can. J. of Pol. Sci. [Canada] 1978 11(2): 333-381.* Provincial government policy is effective in such results if highly visible and implemented a short time before an election. 13 tables, 75 notes.   R. V. Kubicek

2602. Boivin, Jean. LA NEGOCIATION COLLECTIVE DANS LE SECTEUR PUBLIC QUEBECOIS: UNE EVALUATION DES TROIS PREMIERES RONDES (1964-1972) [Collective bargaining in the public sector of the Province of Quebec: an evaluation of the first three rounds (1964-1972)]. *Industrial Relations [Canada] 1973 27(4): 679-717.* Analyzes Quebec's experience in collective bargaining for public employees (excepting municipalities and universities) from the period immediately preceding the adoption of the New *Labor Code* (September 1964) until the last negotiations (ending 15 October 1972). Describes the legal framework before and after adoption of the *Labor Code*, and analyzes the three rounds of negotiations 1964-72. Concludes by characterizing the major issues involved: 1) the political nature of the conflict, 2) the strategy used by the parties, and 3) the impact on the institution of collective bargaining. Based on newspaper references and secondary sources; 12 notes.
L. R. Atkins

2603. Boucher, Michel. UNE ANALYSE ÉCONOMIQUE DES LOTERIES QUÉBÉCOISES [An economic analysis of the Quebec lotteries]. *Actualité Écon. [Canada] 1974 50(1): 63-78.* Analyzes the success of the provincial lotteries, which have contributed some $95 million to the general funds of the province in the first three years of operation. 3 tables, 21 notes.   W. B. Whitham

2604. Brooks, Stanley; Gilmour, James M.; and Murricane, Kenneth. THE SPATIAL LINKAGES OF MANUFACTURING IN MONTREAL AND ITS SURROUNDINGS. *Cahiers de Géographie de Québec [Canada] 1973 17(40): 107-122.* Material linkages of manufacturing in Montreal, correlated to size and location of enterprises within the industrial complex, seem to show that overall linkage is weak and that the strength of linkage varies inversely with the size of establishments studied. There does not seem to be a diminution of linkage from the center to the edge of the industrial complex, although the opposite occurs in the case of purchase linkages. Further investigation is needed. 10 tables, 2 figs., biblio.   A. E. LeBlanc

2605. Brouillette, Normand. LES FACTEURS DU DECLIN INDUSTRIEL DE SHAWINIGAN, PROVINCE DE QUEBEC [The factors underlying the industrial decline of Shawinigan, Province of Quebec]. *Cahiers de Géographie de Québec [Canada] 1973 17(40): 123-133.* After a period of phenomenal industrial growth, Shawinigan has declined since the early 1960's. Explains the decline in terms of the dynamics of industrial location. Shawinigan is no longer situated favorably to foster technological progress; as such, its industrial development is suffering. 2 figs., 14 notes, biblio.   A. E. LeBlanc

2606. Burgess, Joanne. L'INDUSTRIE DE LA CHAUSSURE À MONTRÉAL 1840-1870: LE PASSAGE DE L'ARTISANAT À LA FABRIQUE [The shoe industry in Montreal 1840-1870: The transformation from craft to factory]. *Rev. D'Hist. De L'Amérique Française [Canada] 1977 31(2): 187-210.* The production of shoes formed a central element in the economic life of 19th-century Montreal. During three decades, it evolved from a traditional craft into a highly organized industry. The division of labor, the introduction of machinery, and the advent of the factory system slowly displaced the traditional modes of production, despite strikes and disruptions. The transition from the artisan's shop to the factory was harsh, however it operated progressively over a relatively long period of time. 71 notes.   M. R. Yerburgh

2607. Carvalho, Joseph, III and Everett, Robert. STATISTICAL ANALYSIS OF SPRINGFIELD'S FRENCH CANADIANS (1870). *Hist. J. of Western Massachusetts 1974 3(1): 59-63.* Ninety-six percent of all Canadians in Ward 8, in Springfield, Massachusetts, worked in cotton mills. A majority were under the age of 21 and less than one-eighth of those over 21 were US citizens. They were a church centered group. Primary and secondary sources; 4 tables, 17 notes.
S. S. Sprague

2608. Cermakian, Jean. L'INFRASTRUCTURE ET LE TRAFIC DU PORT DE TROIS-RIVIERES [The infrastructure and traffic of the port of Three Rivers]. *Cahiers de Géographie de Québec [Canada] 1973 17(40): 171-191.* Three-Rivers has always benefited in times of economic prosperity despite its midway location between the ports of Quebec City and Montreal. When the economic situation of the St. Maurice valley manufacturing plants and forest operation deteriorated, however, there was a direct impact on the port. The opening of the St. Lawrence Seaway in 1959 strengthened the transshipment side of the port, but in recent years better-equipped ports in eastern Quebec and on the Pacific coast have cut into this development. The detailed traffic analysis for 1961-70 can be used as a model for most other Canadian ports. 3 tables, 6 figs., 7 notes, biblio.   A. E. LeBlanc

2609. Chouinard, Denys. ALFRED CHARPENTIER FACE AU GOUVERNEMENT DU QUÉBEC, 1935-1946 [Alfred Charpentier in relation to the Quebec government, 1935-1946]. *Rev. D'Hist. De L'Amérique Française [Canada] 1977 31 (2): 211-227.* Though the Confederation of Catholic Workers of Canada (CTCC) has been the subject of intense scrutiny, its ideological/philosophical moorings can be appreciated fully only by examining the relationship between its leadership and the Quebec government. President of the C.T.C.C. during 1935-46, Alfred Charpentier imbued the movement with a fresh sense of mission and morality, but his concepts of corporatism and worker-employer entente never caught on. His moderate stance vis-à-vis the provincial government alienated the more radical elements in the movement. 44 notes.
M. R. Yerburgh

2610. Chung, Joseph H. LA NATURE DU DÉCLIN ÉCONOMIQUE DE LA RÉGION DE MONTRÉAL [The nature of the economic decline in the Montreal area]. *Actualité Econ. [Canada] 1974 50(3): 326-338.* Montreal's economic decline, not a new phenomenon, is caused by the competition of newer markets in the west and by the incapacity to adapt its older industrial structure to contemporary demands.   S

2611. Comeau, Robert. L'HISTOIRE OUVRIÈRE AU QUÉBEC: QUELQUES NOUVELLES AVENUES [The working class history of Quebec: some new avenues]. *R. d'hist. de l'Amérique française [Canada] 1975 28(4): 579-583.* Recent histories of Quebec's working class emphasize the exploitation of workers. New approaches are needed in retracing and interpreting the evolution of political consciousness among members of that class. Geographic precision, specific job descriptions, accurate wage and salary scales, and full knowledge about living conditions are necessary. A good history of Quebec's working class should be integrated with the general social and economic history of Quebec. Based on secondary works; 7 notes.   L. B. Chan

2612. Côté, André and McComber, Marie. SOURCES DE L'HISTOIRE DU SAGUENAY-LAC-SAINT-JEAN: INVENTAIRE DU FONDS DUBUC [Historical resources of Saguenay-Lac-Saint-Jean: inventory of the Dubuc Estate]. *Protée [Canada] 1975 4(1): 129-153.* Gives an inventory of the Dubuc family papers of three generations, 1892-ca. 1963, dealing with some 50 pulp and paper companies founded and directed by J.-E. Alfred Dubuc of Chicoutimi and by his son Antoine Dubuc, with personal correspondence of his wife and family.

2613. Durand, Guy. LE TISSU URBAIN QUÉBÉCOIS, 1941-1961: ÉVOLUTION DES STRUCTURES URBAINES DE L'INDUSTRIE ET DES OCCUPATIONS [The Quebec urban fabric, 1941-61: Evolution of the urban structures of industry and the work force]. *Recherches Sociographiques [Canada] 1977 18(1): 133-157.* Industrialization was crucial in the urban development of Quebec until the beginning of the 1950's. From this point on, the industrialization process lagged behind the urbanization of the province. From an occupational perspective, this resulted in the dominance of occupations related to the tertiary sector which took over as the driving force behind urban development. 16 tables, 14 notes.   A. E. Le Blanc

2614. Dussault, Gilles. LES MÉDECINS DU QUÉBEC (1940-1970) [Doctors in Québec (1940-1970)]. *Recherches Sociographiques [Canada] 1975 16(1): 69-84.* During the past 30 years a movement toward greater specialization and unionization of the medical profession has been growing in Québec, along with a questioning of doctors' professional status. These trends will undoubtedly lead to significant change and medical reforms.   A. E. LeBlanc

2615. Dussault, Gilles. L'ÉVOLUTION DU PROFESSION-NALISME AU QUÉBEC [The evolution of professionalism in Quebec]. *Industrial Relations [Canada] 1978 33(3): 428-469.* After having examined the sociological literature on the definition of the idea of "profession," the author studies the evolution of professionalism in Quebec, applying himself particularly to the criteria which determine the granting of the legal title of professional corporation.   J

2616. Faucher, Albert. EXPLICATION SOCIO-ÉCONOMIQUE DES MIGRATIONS DANS L'HISTOIRE DU QUÉBEC [Socioeconomic explication of migrations in the history of Quebec]. *Tr. of the Royal Soc. of Can. 1975 13: 91-107.* Discusses the causes of emigration in Quebec in the 19th and 20th centuries, noting several explanations. One was by contemporaries such as the Chicoyne Committee which noted the depopulation of rural areas caused by the industrial revolution. Most emigrants sought both a job and a better life as they left the agricultural areas of Quebec where there were fewer chances for economic advancement, especially as its two primary employers, agriculture and forestry, went into a decline. French Canadians moved both to other areas of Canada and to the United States, leaving an area which had a high birth rate and an economy that could not absorb new people. Thus, Quebec had to industrialize in order to find a solution to its decline in population, which had affected the entire province rather than just the rural areas. By contrast, areas such as Ontario with diversified economies grew rapidly in population during the same period. 76 notes.
                                                        J. D. Neville

2617. Faucher, Albert. LA NOTION DE LUXE CHEZ LES CANADIENS FRANÇAIS DU DIX-NEUVIÈME SIÈCLE [The concept of luxury among French Canadians in the 19th century]. *Tr. of the Royal Soc. of Can. 1973 11: 175-180.* The outlook on luxury in Quebec 1849-1900 was derived in large part from moralistic literature of the time, such as the writings of David Hume; clarifies the economic reality, and studies the social consequences, of the luxury concept.

2618. Faucher, Albert. PSUEUDO-MARXISME ET RÉVOLUTION AU QUÉBEC: RÉFLEXIONS SUR LA PROPAGANDE DE LÉANDRE BERGERON [Pseudo-Marxism and revolution in Quebec: Reflections on Léandre Bergeron's propaganda]. *Action Natl. [Canada] 1975 64(6): 487-508.* Sees in Léandre Bergeron's *Petit Manuel d'Histoire du Québec* (Editions Québecoises, 1970) an oversimplified Marxist interpretation of Quebec history.

2619. Gagnon, Gabriel. POPULISME ET PROGRÈS: LES CRÉDITISTES QUÉBÉCOIS [Populism and progress: The Quebec creditistes]. *Recherches sociographiques [Canada] 1976 17(1): 23-34.* Discusses recent interpretations of the rise of Social Credit in the Province of Quebec. Suggests that the Social Credit movement cannot be easily identified as belonging either to the right or the left. It was made up of small farmers and industrial workers affected by the expansion phase of monopolistic capitalist production, and their protests necessarily were expressed differently. 22 notes.   A. E. LeBlanc

2620. Garon, Jean. ALLOCUTION CHEZ PROVIGO [Allocution at Provigo]. *Action Natl. [Canada] 1977 67(1): 56-60.* Since 1902 Provigo has modernized the Quebec food industry by uniting independent grocers under a common trademark and uniform price structure. It now has sales of $572 million, with 2092 affiliated stores and 3021 employees. The Quebec government has established a policy of encouraging the purchase of Quebec food products, expanding worldwide agriculture markets, and rebuilding local control of the province's food industry. Speech of the Quebec Minister of Agriculture at the opening of the Provi-Viande Center, Laval, Quebec, 6 May 1977.   A. W. Novitsky

2621. Gaudette, Gabriel. LA CULTURE POLITIQUE DE LA C.S.D. [The political culture of the D.U.C.]. *Recherches sociographiques [Canada] 1976 17(1): 35-67.* Born of a schism in the Confederation of National Trade Unions, the Democratic Union Central (DUC) returned to a union tradition that was much more conservative. Seeking security for its members rather than fighting for social change, it tried to remain close to its members rather than create a highly efficient and distant organization. The DUC made its greatest inroad among workers belonging to the traditional mining and manufacturing sectors of the province of Quebec. 9 tables, 72 notes.   A. E. LeBlanc

2622. Genest, Jean. J'AI VU FIRE LAKE [I have seen Fire Lake]. *Action Natl. [Canada] 1976 66(2): 81-117.* Fire Lake, a new iron mining community located near Gagnon and Fermont, Quebec, was developed by SIDBEC, a Quebec-controlled consortium. The region of New Quebec north of the 52nd parallel is rich in natural resources, especially hydroelectric power, iron, and uranium. A judgment of the London Privy Council in 1927 ceded Labrador to Newfoundland, and multinational corporations based in the United States and Ontario have provided most of the development capital. Historically, raw materials have been shipped out of the province for transformation into finished products. The consortium's project will help open the Great North and increase employment opportunities throughout the province. 4 notes, biblio.
                                                        A. W. Novitsky

2623. Genest, Jean. LA COMMISSION DES ACCIDENTS DU TRAVAIL [The Commission on Industrial Accidents]. *Action Natl. [Canada] 1978 67(9): 710-726.* In 1890, a Quebec royal commission on labor relations noted the hazards of industry. The Turgeon Commission found similar conditions in 1936-38. Quebec's Catholic bishops issued pastoral letters on the subject in 1941 and 1950. Strikes and public demonstrations in 1948, 1949, and 1972 kept the issue before the public. A Commission on Industrial Accidents was established by legislation in 1931, victims of criminal acts were indemnified in 1971, and protection was extended to victims of asbestosis and silicosis in 1975. In 1976, some 282,684 cases had been brought before the commission under the three laws. Table.   A. W. Novitsky

2624. Gonick, Cy W. WILDCATS, PRICES AND PROFITS. *Can. Dimension 1974 10(2): 5-8, 52-53.* Lists causes of present inflation and shows that the strikes in Quebec in 1974 are a result of worker anger at this inflation and corporations' profits.   S

2625. Gourd, Benoît-Beaudry. APERÇU CRITIQUE DES PRINCIPAUX OUVRAGES POUVANT SERVIR À L'HISTOIRE DU DEVELOPPEMENT MINIER DE L'ABITIBI-TÉMISCAMINGUE (1910-1950) [Critical survey of the principal works relating to the history of mining development in Abitibi-Témiscamingue, 1910-50]. *Rev. d'Hist. de l'Am. Française [Canada] 1976 30(1): 99-107.* The Abitibi-Témiscamingue region was developed much later than the rest of Quebec. Most historical studies have dealt with its agricultural development. Mining activity, however, was a major factor in populating the region. Presents critical summaries of basic works: Raoul Blanchard, *L'Ouest du Canada français* (Montréal: Beauchemin, 1954), Pierre Bays, *Les marges de l'oekoumène dans l'Est du Canada* (Québec: Presses de l'Université Laval, 1964), Marcien Villemure, *Les villes de la Faille de Cadillac* (Rouyn: Conseil économique régional du Nord-Ouest québécois, 1971), E. S. Moore, *American Influence in Canadian Mining* (Toronto: U. of Toronto Pr., 1941), Leslie Roberts, *Noranda* (Toronto: Clarke and Irwin, 1952), Émile Benoist, *L'Abitibi, pays de l'or* (Montréal: Éditions du Zodiaque, 1938), and Evelyn Dumas, *Dans le sommeil de nos os* (Montréal: Leméac, 1971). 14 notes.   L. B. Chan

2626. Halliday, Hugh A. PUSHING THE ROAD TO HAVRE-ST. PIERRE—AND WHAT THEN? *Can. Geographical J. 1973 87(6): 28-35.*

2627. Harvey, Fernand. TECHNOLOGIE ET ORGANISATION DU TRAVAIL À LA FIN DU XIXᵉ SIÈCLE: LE CAS DU QUÉBEC [Technology and the organization of labour at the end of the XIXth century: the Quebec experience]. *Recherches Sociographiques [Canada] 1977 18(3): 397-414.* Analyzing technological and organizational change in the tobacco, shoe, cotton, coopers, and foundry trades at the end of the 19th century reveals the emergence of traits specific to the industrialization of Quebec: the economic structure, monied interests divided amongst linguistic lines, and backwardness of labor law. Royal Commission of Enquiry on Capital and Labour and secondary sources; chart, 52 notes.
                                                        A. E. LeBlanc

2628. Harvey, Jacquelin. HAVRE-SAINT-PIERRE: LE PLUS ANCIEN DES PORTS MINIERS QUEBECOIS [Saint Pierre Harbor: Quebec's oldest mining port]. *Cahiers de Géographie de Québec 1974 18(44): 357-365.*

2629. Harvey, Pierre. LES IDÉES ÉCONOMIQUES D'ESDRAS MINVILLE DES DÉBUTS À LA MATURITE (1923-1936) [The economic ideas of Esdras Minville from the beginning to maturity (1923-36)]. *Action Natl. [Canada] 1976 65(9-10): 626-642.* Esdras Minville's primary concern was the economic development of Quebec and the institution of a corporative order to replace liberal capitalism. He believed that forestry would play a major role in the province, and was one of the first authors to note the domination of Quebec by American multinational corporations. 23 notes.   A. W. Novitsky

2630. Heap, Margaret. LE GRÈVE DES CHARRETIERS À MONTRÉAL, 1864 [The teamsters' strike in Montreal, 1864]. *Rev. d'Hist. de l'Amérique Française [Canada] 1977 31(3): 371-395.* In September 1864, the Montreal teamsters launched a spectacular, highly organized strike; the commercial life of the city was completely paralyzed. The teamsters demanded a cessation of certain monopolistic practices employed by the Grand Trunk Railway Company—practices which seriously jeopardized their livelihood. Despite the solidarity of the teamsters, the courts would not consider their demands. The rising tide of industrial capitalism continued to erode the status of the working classes. 76 notes.   M. R. Yerburgh

2631. Hébert, Gérard. LA LOI 9 ET LES RELATIONS DU TRAVAIL DANS L'INDUSTRIE DE LA CONSTRUCTION AU QUÉBEC [Bill 9 and labor relations in the Quebec construction industry]. *Industrial Relations [Canada] 1973 28(4): 697-719.* "Bill 9 has brought substantial amendments to the *Construction Industry Labour Relations Act* (Bill 290). It was adopted by the Quebec Legislature and sanctioned 1 June 1973."   J

2632. Hébert, Gérard. LES RELATIONS DU TRAVAIL DANS LA FONCTION PUBLIQUE AU QUÉBEC [Public service labor relations in Quebec]. *Industrial Relations [Canada] 1974 29(4): 750-775.* "The author summarizes the latest developments occurring in the Quebec public sector since the 1972 general strike. After arriving at a brief retrospect of the incidents encountered in this negotiation, he describes major directions, which show as much the point of view of the negotiating structures as that of the regulatory mechanisms of conflict, with a view to the next round of negotiations."

2633. Houde, Pierre et al. LA PROPRIÉTÉ FONCIÈRE AU SAGUENAY, 1840-1975: ORIENTATION DE LA RECHERCHE [Land ownership in Saguenay, 1840-1975: Research directions]. *Protée [Canada] 1975 4(1): 67-86.* Defines types, problems, and present basic techniques of research in regional land ownership in Saguenay, including exploitation of local historical resources and the construction of spatial graphs and geographical matrices.

2634. House, J. Douglas. ENTREPRENEURIAL CAREER PATTERNS OF RESIDENTIAL REAL ESTATE AGENTS IN MONTREAL. *Can. R. of Sociol. and Anthrop. 1974 11(2): 110-124.* "Real estate agents are best understood as a type of modern entrepreneur. A model of their entrepreneurial behaviour is developed here which includes an explanation of strategies producing short- and long-term success. Given this model, five career patterns are distinguished: abortives, marginals, regulars, upwardly mobiles, and perennial high producers. Finally, these patterns are *explained* in terms of three determinants: sales success through implementing productive entrepreneurial strategies; mobility opportunities or structurally imposed barriers to mobility, which in turn depend upon ascribed ethnicity and sex status; and individual decisions at crucial career phases."   J

2635. Jouandet-Bernadet, Roland. UNE EXPERIENCE DE COMPTABILITE REGIONALE ET SES ENSEIGNEMENTS [An experience with regional accounting and its lessons]. *Actualité Econ. [Canada] 1973 49(1): 19-38.* The financial accounts of the province of Quebec, 1951-66, show that the Montreal region has experienced much economic growth since 1951 whereas the rest of Quebec has had a mediocre growth rate. These two trends apparently will continue, although the estimates will have to be updated with 1971 census figures. 8 tables, 7 graphs, 10 notes.   S

2636. Laperrière, Guy. L'ÉGLISE ET L'ARGENT: LES QUÊTES COMMANDÉES DANS LE DIOCÈSE DE SHERBROOKE, 1893-

1926 [The church and money: the collections ordered in the diocese of Sherbrooke, 1893-1926]. *Sessions d'Etude Soc. Can. d'Hist. de l'Eglise Catholique 1974 41: 61-86.* Studies the financial sources of the Church in the Quebec diocese of Sherbrooke, based on the collections ordered during the episcopate of Bishop Paul LaRocque. Seeks an explanation for changes in church income and in financial administration. Draws conclusions on the development of the population and agricultural production during this time, as well as on the mentality and the religiousness of the ministers and congregation. Based on diocesan archives and secondary sources; 4 tables, 11 graphs, 55 notes.   S. Sevilla

2637. Larocque, Paul. APERÇU DE LA CONDITION OUVRIÈRE À QUÉBEC, 1896-1914 [A look at the condition of workers in Quebec, 1896-1914]. *Labour [Canada] 1976 1: 122-138.* Examines workers' lives in Quebec City's Lower Town when industries were diversifying, growing, and becoming mechanized. In crowded neighborhoods near the factories and commercial areas, workers lived in or close to misery and were plagued by poor working conditions and pay, disease, unemployment, fires, and monotony. In frustration, many turned to alcohol. Despite efforts by charitable organizations such as the St. Vincent de Paul Society and some feeble action by government, neither the law nor the social system provided much to alleviate conditions which produced a fundamental alienation of the working class. Primary and secondary sources; 93 notes.   W. A. Kearns

2638. Larocque, Paul. LES PÊCHEURS GASPÉSIENS ET LA MOUVEMENT COOPÉRATIF (1939-1948) [Gaspé fishermen and the cooperative movement (1939-1948)]. *Social Hist. [Canada] 1975 8(16): 294-313.* Gaspé Peninsula (Québec) fishermen, who suffered economic hardship in the 1930's, united during World War II in more than 30 local producers' cooperatives, which federated into the Pêcheurs-Unis. Promotion by the government and clergy were important factors in the cooperatives' founding and success, as was the wartime economic boom. The rapid growth of the cooperatives created an unstable structure, which partially collapsed when the boom ended. Based on documents in Pêcheurs-Unis du Québec Archives (Montreal) and published primary sources; 126 notes.   W. K. Hobson

2639. Larouche, Fernand. L'IMMIGRANT DANS UNE VILLE MINIÈRE: UNE ÉTUDE DE L'INTERACTION [The immigrant in a mining city: A study of interaction]. *Recherches Sociographiques [Canada] 1973 14(2): 203-228.* Three descriptive portraits of workers in a northern Quebec mining community. The immigrant worker prefers to assimilate himself into the English-speaking milieu rather than the French-speaking, because the former appears to offer greater consistency and stability. Secondary sources augmented with on-site field work.   A. E. LeBlanc

2640. Latouche, Daniel. LA VRAI NATURE DE ... LA RÉVOLUTION TRANQUILLE [The true nature of the quiet revolution]. *Can. J. of Pol. Sci. 1974 7(3): 525-536.* Uses statistical techniques associated with functional studies of government and economics to test Marxist theory as to the significance of Quebec's quiet revolution. 6 tables, 26 notes.   R. V. Kubicek

2641. Lee-Whiting, Brenda. LOGGING ON THE SCHYAN 1938-39. *Beaver [Canada] 1978 309(1): 48-53.* Vernon Price went to the Schyan River area in Quebec during 1938-39 to work as a logger. While there he collected dozens of photographic views taken by a commercial photographer. Presents some of these photographs and information from an interview with Price. Details work crews, housing for men and animals, tools, and diet. 9 photos, map.   D. Chaput

2642. Linteau, Paul-André. LA SOCIETE MONTREALAISE AU 19E SIECLE: BILAN DES TRAVAUX [Montreal society in the 19th century: balance of workers]. *Urban Hist. Rev. [Canada] 1973 (3): 17-19.* Explores the work of the Research Group on Montreal Society of the 19th century which set about, in 1971, to write a social history of Montreal during the era when commercial capitalism was changing into industrial capitalism.

2643. Malo, Marie-Claire and Dionne, Georges. ANALYSE PROSPECTIVE DU MOUVEMENT COOPÉRATIF AU QUÉBEC [A prospective analysis of the cooperative movement in Quebec]. *Action*

Natl. [Canada] 1973 62(10): 785-793. Theorizes about the prospects of the cooperative movement in Quebec, based on an analysis of the causes that presently restrict its growth, including public opinion and the attitudes of various business interests.

2644. Martin, Fernand. EFFETS DE LA CRISE DE L'ENERGIE SUR LA CROISSANCE ECONOMIQUE DE MONTREAL ET DU QUEBEC [Effects of the energy crisis on the economic growth of Montreal and Quebec]. *Actualité Econ. [Canada] 1974 50(3): 351-361.*

2645. Miller, J. R. HONORÉ MERCIER, LA MINORITÉ PROTESTANTE DU QUÉBEC ET LA LOI RELATIVE AU RÈGLEMENT DE LA QUESTION DES BIENS DES JÉSUITES [Honoré Mercier, the Protestant minority of Quebec, and the law governing the question of the properties belonging to the Jesuits]. *Rev. d'Hist. de l'Amérique Française [Canada] 1974 27(4): 483-508.* Recounts the attempt of Honoré Mercier, First Minister of Quebec, to resolve the problems occasioned by legislation governing the disposition of lands once granted to the Jesuits, following his rise to power in 1886.

2646. Minville, Esdras. LA VOCATION ÉCONOMIQUE DE LA PROVINCE DE QUÉBEC [The economic vocation of the province of Quebec]. *Action Natl. [Canada] 1976 65(9-10): 784-799.* Quebec's natural resources are appropriate for industrialization, so the province cannot remain agrarian. However, the wise use of forests will guarantee success for Quebec agriculture. A commission of scholars should set forth Quebec's position on Canadian federalism. Includes a letter from Minville to Maurice Duplessis, Premier of Quebec, 15 November 1945.
A. W. Novitsky

2647. Mireault, Réal. LES NOUVEAUX DÉFIS DE L'OFFICE DE LA CONSTRUCTION DU QUÉBEC [The new challenges of the construction office of Quebec]. *Industrial Relations [Canada] 1976 31(4): 553-564.* The Office de la construction du Québec does not intervene in the industrial relations systems of the Québec construction industry, but only administers specific aspects of that industry by intervening not only on the supply side of the labor market, but also on the demand for labor.
S

2648. Morin, Fernand. DIVERGENCE OU CONVERGENCE DU MOUVEMENT SYNDICAL ET DU MOUVEMENT COOPÉRATIF DES CAISSES DESJARDINS [Divergence or convergence of the syndicalist movement and the cooperative movement in the Desjardins credit union]. *Industrial Relations [Canada] 1977 32(2): 262-268.* Assesses similarities and differences in the syndicalist movement and the cooperative movement in Quebec in the case of labor relations; discusses the case of a particular union local, Desjardins, 1972-77.

2649. O'Connor, D'Arcy. THE MONTREAL CITIZENS' MOVEMENT. *Working Papers for a New Soc. 1976 4(1): 22-29.* Discusses the conflict between the Montreal Citizens' Movement since 1974 and Jean Drapeau, Mayor of Montreal since 1957, showing the political and economic effects of the MCM.

2650. Parizeau, Gérard. LE CAPITALISME TRIOMPHANT DANS LE QUÉBEC DE 1870 À 1900 [Triumphant capitalism in Quebec from 1870 to 1900]. *Tr. of the Royal Soc. of Can. 1973 11: 159-174.* The individual entrepreneur enjoyed free rein from federal and provincial governments, and this was a period of great expansion for enterprise.

2651. Parson, Helen E. THE RISE AND FALL OF FARMING IN A MARGINAL AREA: THE GATINEAU VALLEY, QUÉBEC. *Cahiers de Géographie de Québec [Canada] 1975 19(48): 573-582.* Studies the evolution of shield farming using the Gatineau Valley in western Quebec as an example.

2652. Poulin, Antonio. LE CONSEIL DE DÉVELOPPEMENT DE LA CHAUDIÈRE [The council for the development of the Chaudière]. *Action Natl. [Canada] 1974 63(10): 821-829.* Describes the efforts in 1973 of the local Council of the Beauce locality of Saint-Georges Est to reduce pollution in the Chaudière River and to promote tourism and industry in the surrounding region.

2653. Power, Geoffrey. HISTORY OF THE HUDSON'S BAY COMPANY SALMON FISHERIES IN THE UNGAVA BAY REGION. *Polar Record [Great Britain] 1976 18(113): 151-161.* Details the establishment of the three Hudson's Bay Company salmon fisheries in the Ungava Bay region of Canada, 1830's through 1939, including statistics about the operation of the fisheries and on the catches at each fishery.

2654. Racine, Jean-Bernard. LE DISPOSITIF BANCAIRE A LA PERIPHERIE DE LA METROPOLE MONTREALAISE [Location of banks on the periphery of metropolitan Montreal]. *Cahiers de Géographie de Québec [Canada] 1973 17(40): 210-216.* A study of banking in suburban Montreal shows that the establishment of bank branches seems to favor the crystallization of the area. When branches do not emerge, on the other hand, it suggests that the area is considered a risk. The existence of bank branches is not a function of demographic demand nor of distance from the city center. List of references.
A. E. LeBlanc

2655. Rouillard, Jacques. LE QUÉBEC ET LE CONGRÈS DE BERLIN, 1902 [Quebec and the Berlin Congress, 1902]. *Labour [Canada] 1976 1: 69-91.* At the 1902 Trades and Labour Congress of Canada in Berlin (now Kitchener), Ontario, constitutional changes caused the expulsion of all unions having concurrent jurisdiction with an international union. This victory of internationalism over the Knights of Labor, still strong in Quebec, and Canadian national unions was due in part to the "imperialist" drive of Samuel Gompers' American Federation of Labor but was also a direct result of union conflicts in Quebec, especially in Montreal, dating from 1892. Of 23 expelled organizations, 17 were from Quebec. The split in the Canadian labor movement saw the formation of a rival National Trades and Labour Congress, largely dominated by Quebec unions. Primary and secondary sources; 105 notes.
W. A. Kearns

2656. Saint-Germain, Maurice. DÉPENDANCE ÉCONOMIQUE ET FREINS AU DÉVELOPPEMENT: LE CAS DU QUÉBEC [Economic dependence and curbs on development: the Quebec case]. *Recherche Sociale [France] 1974 49: 93-98.* The present economic structure of Quebec suffers from double domination by English Canada and the United States, and from the juxtaposition of two unequal economic sectors having different dynamics and objectives. This dependence and dualism, which are manifested at various levels of the economy and society, are the major obstacles to the development of Quebec.
J. D. Falk

2657. Séguin, N. HERBERTVILLE AU LAC SAINT-JEAN, 1850-1900: UN EXEMPLE QUEBECOIS DE COLONISATION AU XIXᵉ SIECLE [Herbertville in the Lake St. John Region, 1850-1900: An example of 19th-century Quebec colonization]. *Can. Hist. Assoc. Hist. Papers 1973: 251-268.* Herbertville was a traditional market center for the sawmill industry founded in a remote area. It was dominated by the parish priest and a group of families who provided local functionaries: the merchants and moneylenders who throve on the indebtedness of subsistence farmers. The railway, in 1893, tightened the commercial and financial connections with larger centers, while after 1896 a paper mill marked a shift to intensified industrialization and an urban work force. Based on provincial archives, church archives, and secondary sources; 36 notes.
G. E. Panting

2658. Séguin, Normand. L'ÉCONOMIE AGRO-FORESTIÈRE: GENÈSE DU DÉVELOPPEMENT AU SAGUENAY AU XIXᵉ SIÈCLE [The agricultural-forestry economy: genesis of development in Saguenay in the 19th century]. *Rev. d'Hist. de l'Amérique Française [Canada] 1976 29(4): 559-565.* Discusses the principal characteristics of the economy and the process of settlement of Saguenay in the 19th century. Concentrates on the production of timber for export and subsistence agriculture. Saguenay was a hinterland of Quebec and Montreal. Economic control over the region was in the hands of interests located in the two cities. Instead of establishing a new frontier society, the settlers of Saguenay merely reproduced the type of rural society to be found elsewhere in 19th-century Quebec. A summary of a part of the author's *La conquête du sol au XIXᵉ siècle* (The conquest of the soil in the 19th century), in press.
L. B. Chan

2659. Silvia, Philip T., Jr. THE POSITION OF "NEW" IMMIGRANTS IN THE FALL RIVER TEXTILE INDUSTRY. *Internat.*

Migration Rev. 1976 10(2): 221-232. Discusses the reception of Portuguese and Polish immigrants by French Canadians in textile industries and trade unions in Fall River, Massachusetts, 1890-1905.

2660. Slack, B. AN EXPLANATION OF PORT ACTIVITY ON THE SOUTH SHORE OF THE LOWER ST. LAWRENCE RIVER. *Cahiers de Géographie de Québec [Canada] 1973 17(40): 135-154.* Problems in measuring relationships of factors proposed by earlier researchers to port activity cause unsatisfactory measurement of port development on the south shore of the lower St. Lawrence River. Geographers should examine more closely the relationships between hinterland and port size to gain an accurate assessment of what is taking place. A multiple regression analysis, using this area as a model, accounts for over 90% of size variation in the port system. 3 figs., 7 tables, 18 notes, biblio.
                                                                    A. E. LeBlanc

2661. Smith, William. MARKET-FARM LINKAGES AND LAND USE CHANGE: A QUEBEC CASE STUDY. *Cahiers de Géographie de Québec [Canada] 1974 18(44): 297-315.* Discusses the "functional and spatial relationship between individual farm units and their markets."
                                                                    S

2662. Stammers, M. K. THE MONTREAL OCEAN STEAMSHIP COMPANY'S MUTUAL BENEFIT SOCIETY. *Maritime Hist. [Great Britain] 1977 5(1): 68-73.* Discusses the history and administration of the Montreal Steamship Company's friendly society, established in Liverpool in 1863 to benefit seamen, shipping staff, and their relatives in the event of injury or death.

2663. Stevenson, A ARCTIC FUR TRADE RIVALRY. *Beaver [Canada] 1975 306(2): 46-51.* Presents a first-hand account of the 1930's, when a Hudson's Bay employee, was sent to the Quebec Arctic to compete with Jean Berthe, an independent trader. Berthe had spent 20 years in the Arctic as an employee for Revillon Freres of Paris. After the firm was acquired by the Hudson's Bay Company, Berthe went independent. In the winter of 1938-39, Stevenson placed his post seven miles from Berthe's on the Ungava Bay. Both tried to outdo the other with presents and promises to the Eskimos, but the fur harvest that winter was slight. The traders maintained friendly relations with each other, even visiting from time to time. 9 illus., map.
                                                                    D. Chaput

2664. Thompson, Agnes L. NEW ENGLAND MILL GIRLS. *New-England Galaxy 1974 16(2): 43-49.* Describes life in the woolen and cotton mills of Lowell, Massachusetts, in the 1840's and 1850's. Farm girls gained economic independence by working for a few years before marriage, but were closely supervised in the mill, boarding house, and community, and had to cope with long hours, low wages, and limited social and educational opportunities. By 1857 competition forced their replacement by a permanent industrial working class of Irish and French Canadians. 6 illus.
                                                                    P. C. Marshall

2665. Tremblay, Rodrigue. LES QUÉBÉCOIS ET LEUR ÉCONOMIE [The people of Quebec and their economy]. *Action Natl. [Canada] 1975 64(10): 801-809.* Examines the causes for lack of participation by French Canadians in Quebec industry and proposes solutions to the problem.

2666. Tulchinsky, Gerald. UNE ENTREPRISE MARITIME CANADIENNE-FRANÇAISE—LA COMPAGNIE DU RICHELIEU 1845-1854 [A French Canadian maritime enterprise—the Richelieu Company 1845-54]. *R. d'Hist. de l'Amérique Française [Canada] 1973 26(4): 559-582.* The French Canadian Richelieu shipping company created in 1845 successfully competed against the English Canadian companies, in the region of Montreal and notably along the Richelieu River. First involved with freight, it later offered a passenger service. Most of the shareholders of this company were French Canadians and sound businessmen. Based on primary and secondary sources; 91 notes.
                                                                    C. Collon

2667. Vézina, Jean-P.; Masson, Claude; Lamonde, Pierre; and Boisvert, Michel. UNE POLITIQUE ÉCONOMIQUE QUÉBÉCOISE [An economic policy for Quebec]. *Actualité Écon. [Canada] 1974 50(4): 549-571.* Comments by four economists on *Une politique économique québécoise,* a document of the Ministry of Industry and Commerce of Quebec. 3 tables, 23 notes.
                                                                    J. C. Billigmeier

2668. —. ANALYSIS OF FACTORS CAPABLE OF AFFECTING LABOUR SUPPLY: THE CASE OF PARENTS OF LOW-INCOME FAMILIES. *Industrial Relations [Canada] 1975 30(2): 162-165.* The present article presents in part a progress report of a research which tries to estimate the impact of public programs of economic security in Quebec on the work effort of parents of low-income families. Our interest in such a research comes from the recent but increasing effort of our society to fight poverty, and more particularly from the passing of the Social Aid Act by the Quebec Government in 1969. The question of incentive to work takes a particular importance, since, according to this Act, benefits to families are calculated as the difference between income and needs, whatever the labor force participation of their members.
                                                                    J

2669. —. LES RÉPERTOIRES DES INDUSTRIES FRANCO-PHONES [Lists of francophone industries]. *Action Natl. [Canada] 1978 67(8): 624-643.* The Conseil d'expansion économique studies the food, furniture, wood-working, leather, metal fabrication, printing, machine, transportation, electrical, paper, chemical, textile, clothing, and other industries in Quebec 1961-71, updated to 1975, in terms of numbers of establishments and employees, value of salaries and products, and percentage of Canadian production. Corporate headquarters and major manufacturing centers outside of Quebec are noted for the leading companies in each industry, and preferential purchase of the products of Quebec manufacturers is urged. Primary and secondary sources; 14 tables, note.
                                                                    A. W. Novitsky

2670. —. THE MOUNTING CLASS STRUGGLE IN QUEBEC. *Int. Socialist Rev. 1973 34(7): 36-62.* Discusses socialists' potential for exploiting the politicization of the working class and class struggle in Quebec, and for establishing an independent socialist state in the 1970's.

Separatism and Nationalism

2671. Albinski, Henry S. QUEBEC AND CANADIAN UNITY. *Current Hist. 1974 66(392): 155-160.* Discusses Quebec's position within Canada and the problems of unifying Quebec with the nine other Canadian provinces.
                                                                    S

2672. Alessandri, Giuseppe. UN'ALTERNATIVA PER IL QUEBEC [An alternative for Quebec]. *Affari Esteri [Italy] 1973 5(20): 150-161.* The alternative for Quebec in contemporary Canada is to maintain its social and cultural identity within the Canadian confederation.
                                                                    A. R. Stoesen

2673. Angers, François-Albert. LA LANGUE FRANÇAISE AU QUÉBEC (1774-1974) [The French language in Quebec: 1774-1974]. *Action Natl. [Canada] 1974 63(8/9): 618-628.* The Act of Quebec (1774), reestablishing French laws and language, has been the justification for a sovereign Quebec for 200 years and is the basis for the possible establishment of French as the official language.

2674. Angers, François-Albert. LES ORIGINES DE L'INDÉPENDANTISME CONTEMPORAIN AU QUÉBEC: L'ALLIANCE LAURENTIENNE DE RAYMOND BARBEAU [The origins of contemporary independence in Quebec: the Alliance Laurentienne of Raymond Barbeau]. *Action Natl. [Canada] 1975 65(3): 234-244.* Reproduces Pierre Guillemette's "Raymond Barbeau, l'alliance Laurentienne et le début du Souverainisme Quebécois" *Le Jour* (14 August 1975), dealing with the Alliance Laurentienne, a Quebec movement for independence.

2675. Angers, François-Albert. UN DOCUMENT À MÉDITER SUR LE PLAN NATIONAL FRANÇAIS OU QUÉBÉCOIS: COMPARAISON ENTRE LA POLOGNE ET LE QUÉBEC [Meditations on a document on the French or Quebec national plan: A comparison between Poland and Quebec]. *Action Natl. [Canada] 1973 63(4): 324-344.* Evaluates Quebec's future as a nation capable of resisting foreign influences and of maintaining its national identity, based on Marcel Mermoz's "Pologne Vivante sous les Contraintes," *La France Catholique* (18 May 1973), here reproduced.

2676. Arès, Richard. LE COMMISSAIRE ROYAL [The royal commissary]. *Action Natl. [Canada] 1976 65(9-10): 689-705.* Richard Arès served with Esdras Minville on the Tremblay Commission (Commission royale d'enquête sur les problèmes constitutionnels) during 1953-56. Minville stressed that Quebec's primary concern must be security for the French tradition in a bicultural Canada. 5 notes.
A. W. Novitsky

2677. Aubéry, Pierre. NATIONALISME ET LUTTE DES CLASSES AU QUEBEC [Nationalism and class struggle in Quebec]. *Am. Rev. of Can. Studies 1975 5(2): 130-145.* Intellectuals in Quebec are trying to help the proletariat French-speaking community bring about social, political, and economic equality for all Quebecois, 1960's-70's.

2678. Balthazar, Louis. LE NATIONALISME AU QUÉBEC [Nationalism in Quebec]. *Études Int. [Canada] 1977 8(2): 266-281.* Quebec's nationalism has been present for more than two hundred years through tradition, religion, and language. Emphasizes the more recent manifestations of this nationalism, particularly in the 1960's. Primary and secondary sources; 19 notes.
J. F. Harrington, Jr.

2679. Blanchard, Guy. LA POSITION DE FAIBLESSE DU "FRENCH POWER" [The weak position of "French power"]. *Action Natl. [Canada] 1973 62(10): 810-815.* The sense of French inferiority to the English and superior English economic power are at the base of the separatist movement in Quebec.

2680. Chapdelaine, Jean. ESQUISSE D'UNE POLITIQUE EXTERIEURE D'UN QUEBEC SOUVERAIN: GENESE ET PROSPECTIVE [Outline of a sovereign Quebec's foreign policy: Origins and prospects]. *Études Int. [Canada] 1977 8(2): 342-355.* Discusses the possibility of Quebec adopting an independent foreign policy. Examines the influence Paris and Ottawa would have as models for Quebec and considers the ramifications of an independent Quebec in relation to the United States and NATO and other international bodies.
J. F. Harrington, Jr.

2681. Chouinard, Jean-Yves. L'AUTODÉTERMINATION ET LES LAURENTIENS [Self-determination and the Laurentians]. *Action Natl. [Canada] 1977 66(6): 410-422.* Since 1957 the Alliance Laurentienne has provided intellectual support for Quebec separatism with the publication of a reprint of Wilfred Morin's *L'Indépendance du Québec*, first published in 1938 as *Nos Droits a l'indépendance politique*; 20 issues of the *Revue Laurentie*; and three books written by the Director of the Alliance, Raymond Barbeau. The Alliance asserts that Quebec has moral, legal, and constitutional rights to autonomy, and is particularly critical of Pierre Elliott Trudeau, André Laurendeau, and other proponents of a reformed federalism. 6 notes.
A. W. Novitsky

2682. Cuneo, Carl J. and Curtis, James E. QUEBEC SEPARATISM: AN ANALYSIS OF DETERMINANTS WITHIN SOCIAL-CLASS LEVELS. *Can. R. of Sociol. and Anthrop. 1974 11(1): 1-29.* "This paper reports a secondary analysis of 1968 survey data on the extent and correlates of separatist opinion among French-speaking adults in Quebec. The analysis focuses on determinants of separatism within new middle-class occupational levels, but some comparative data are provided for the lower classes and farmers as well. A model of separatist support is constructed based on an interpretation of the previous literature and, controlling for occupational level, the effects of seven independent and intervening variables are explored in path analyses. The model of separatist support fits the new middle class best and explains 40 percent of the variance in the dependent variable for professionals and semi-professionals and 43 percent for managers, officials, and proprietors. The effect of the independent variables on separatist support varied by occupational level. For example, French-Canadian ethnic consciousness, distrust of the federal government and personal dissatisfaction had their strongest independent effects within the new middle class, while economic insecurity and left politico-economic orientation generally had their strongest effects on separatist support among unskilled workers and farmers." J

2683. Dobell, Peter C. QUÉBEC SEPARATISM: DOMESTIC AND INTERNATIONAL IMPLICATIONS. *World Today [Great Britain] 1977 33(4): 149-159.* Examines separatism among French Canadians in Quebec, 1974-76.

2684. Durocher, René. L'HISTOIRE PARTISANE: MAURICE DUPLESSIS ET SON TEMPS VUS PAR ROBERT RUMILLY ET CONRAD BLACK [Partisan history: Maurice Duplessis and his times as seen by Robert Rumilly and Conrad Black]. *Rev. d'Hist. de l'Amérique Française [Canada] 1977 31(3): 407-426.* A comparison of Conrad Black's *Duplessis* (Toronto: McClelland and Stewart, 1976) and Robert Rumilly's *Maurice Duplessis et Son Temps* (Montreal: Fides, 1973). Duplessis was the controversial Prime Minister of Quebec during 1936-39 and 1944-59. These two massive studies are the first to incorporate materials from the Duplessis archives. Though Black's treatment is somewhat more critical than Rumilly's, neither presents a clear or convincing portrait of their fascinating subject.
M. R. Yerburgh

2685. Filion, Jacques. DE GAULLE, LA FRANCE ET LE QUEBEC [de Gaulle, France and Quebec]. *Rev. de l'U. d'Ottawa [Canada] 1975 45(3): 295-319.* Analyzes Charles de Gaulle's views of French Canadians and their political milieu. All Frenchmen, according to de Gaulle, represent a particular interest in the world. Primary and secondary sources; 66 notes.
M. L. Frey

2686. Fontaine, André. LA FRANCE ET LE QUEBEC [France and Quebec]. *Études Int. [Canada] 1977 8(2): 393-402.* Discusses foreign relations between France and Canada from the 18th century to 1967. Reflects on the effect of deGaulle's 1967 Montreal address calling for a free Quebec and notes the new relationship between Pierre Elliott Trudeau and Valery Giscard d'Estaing. Secondary sources; 3 notes.
J. F. Harrington, Jr.

2687. Frenette, Jean-Vianney. LA RECHERCHE D'UN CADRE REGIONAL AU QUEBEC MERIDIONAL: QUELQUES ETAPES, DE 1932 A 1966 [The search for a regional framework for Southern Quebec Province: some steps from 1932 to 1966]. *Cahiers de Géographie de Québec 1973 17(40): 69-84.* Regional divisions in Quebec evolved in much the same context as those in North America and Europe. Quebec's regions changed from agricultural areas to statistical and administrative units 1932-66. The impact of provincial and federal government geographers and bureaucrats was great. 8 maps, 25 notes, biblio.
A. E. LeBlanc

2688. Gagnon, Marcel-Aimé. ESDRAS MINVILLE ET L'ACTION NATIONALE [Esdras Minville and *Action Nationale*]. *Action Natl. [Canada] 1976 65(9-10): 677-688.* In 1933, under the direction of Esdras Minville, the Ligue d'Action Nationale established *L'Action Nationale*, successor to *L'Action Française* and *L'Action Canadienne-Française*, as an organ of thought and action to serve the religious and national traditions of the French element in America. Its major inspiration was the papal encyclical *Rerum Novarum*, and its philosophy was corporatist.
A. W. Novitsky

2689. Glazier, Kenneth M. SEPARATISM AND QUEBEC. *Current Hist. 1977 72(426): 154-157, 178-179.* Examines economic issues in Quebec separatism, the breakdown of minorities in the province, and the militant French-speaking population.

2690. Gonick, Cy. THE NEW PATRIOTS. *Can. Dimension [Canada] 1977 12(2): 32-36.* Traces the historical development of nationalism in Quebec and analyzes the relations among nationalism, the Parti Quebecois, the business community, and the working class in the 1970's.

2691. Hallett, Mary E. THE QUEBEC TERCENTENNIAL: LORD GREY'S IMPERIAL BIRTHDAY PARTY. *Can. Hist. R. 1973 54(3): 341-352.* Governor General Lord Grey (Albert Henry George Grey, 4th Earl Grey), tried to foster imperial feeling in Canada and in particular to win French Canadians to the imperial cause by using the occasion of Quebec City's tercentennial for a display of imperial pageantry and power. The long-term results were probably negligible. This episode in relations between Canadians of English and French descent (1904-06) had an amusing imperial involvement. Based on the Grey and Laurier papers in the Public Archives of Canada, newspapers and periodicals. A

2692. Hamel, Jacques. LE MOUVEMENT NATIONAL DES QUÉBÉCOIS À LA RECHERCHE DE LA MODERNITÉ [The Quebecers national movement and the search for modernity]. *Recherches Sociographiques [Canada] 1973 14(3): 341-361.* The Movement has directed its attention to the emergence of a political objective, the State of Québec. Since the movement is an outgrowth of the St. John the Baptist Society of a preceeding era, this has led to significant problems. The latter, concerned with the French-Canadian family and the Church, created a distinct mode of thinking and action. The former has found it necessary to turn to other sources for inspiration and elite support. Based on interviews and official pronouncements of both groups; 44 notes.

A. E. LeBlanc

2693. Hamilton, Richard and Pinard, Maurice. THE BASES OF PARTI QUÉBÉCOIS SUPPORT IN RECENT QUEBEC ELECTIONS. *Can. J. of Pol. Sci. 1976 9(1): 3-26.* Based on a cross-sectional sample of eligible voters in the 1973 election. Excludes for methodological reasons anglophone population and distinguishes between Montreal and the rest of the province. Voters who in terms of socioeconomic status should be most attracted the the PQ give the party either the same or less support than do the more privileged. 9 tables, 30 notes.

R. V. Kubicek

2694. Hare, John. LE DÉVELOPPEMENT D'UNE PENSÉE CONSTITUTIONNELLE AU QUEBEC, 1791-1814 [The development of constitutional thought in Quebec, 1791-1814]. *R. de l'U. d'Ottawa 1975 45(1): 5-25.* Analyzes the development of constitutional thought in Quebec and stresses the influence of the constitution of Great Britain and writers such as Montesquieu, Blackstone, and Jean-Louis Delolme. Based on primary and secondary sources; 66 notes. M. L. Frey

2695. Hudon, Raymond. THE 1976 QUEBEC ELECTION. *Queen's Q. [Canada] 1977 84(1): 18-30.* Analyzes the 1976 provincial election in Quebec in terms of both French and English Canada. Details causes of the election, the nature of the campaign, and recent developments. Clearly the election marks a new era in Quebec politics, but the question of the long-term impact of the victorious Parti Québécois remains. 15 notes. J. A. Casada

2696. Kopkind, Andrew. QUEBEC: A DECLARATION OF INDEPENDENCE BUT NO REVOLUTION. *Working Papers for a New Soc. 1978 6(5): 32-40.* Discusses the aims of the Parti Québécois which seeks cultural and lingual hegemony for French-speaking citizens, placing political and economic ends in a secondary position, 1973-78.

2697. Lemieux, Pierre. WHAT'S HAPPENING IN QUEBEC. *Reason 1978 10(3): 24-27, 36.* Examines political attitudes of the Parti Québécois, 1976-78, toward French language, separatism, statism, socialism, and anti-capitalism.

2698. Lemieux, Vincent. QUEL ETAT DU QUEBEC? [What type of state for Quebec?]. *Études Int. [Canada] 1977 8(2): 254-265.* Discusses the social, cultural, political and economic implications of statehood for Quebec. Mentions three political functions a state can assure: It can maintain order, it can be a benefactor to citizens, and it can provide organizational structures. Secondary sources; 5 notes.

J. F. Harrington, Jr.

2699. Lévesque, Delmas. UN QUÉBEC EN REDÉFINITION [Quebec in redefinition]. *Action Natl. [Canada] 1977 67(1): 16-33.* At the turn of the 20th century, English Canadians saw Quebec as a backward, priest-ridden province dominated by the Catholic Church. Quebec was transformed only by industrialization imported from New England and Ontario, which absorbed the excess farm population. In 200 years, the hegemony of the Catholic Church was challenged only during the 1830's. Catholicism thwarted modernization, but also protected Quebec from the American cultural imperialism which conquered English Canada. In an independent Quebec, the state would be expected to assume the role formerly held by the Church. The text is a lecture prepared for students of L'École Internationale de Bordeaux at the École des Hautes Études Commerciales, Montreal, August, 1972. 5 notes.

A. W. Novitsky

2700. Lévesque, Georges-Henri. PRÉLUDE À LA RÉVOLUTION TRANQUILLE AU QUÉBEC: NOTES NOUVELLES SUR D'ANCIENS INSTRUMENTS [Prelude to the quiet revolution in Quebec: New notes on old instruments]. *Social Hist. [Canada] 1977 10(19): 134-146.* Personal comments on the historial background to the "quiet revolution"

in Quebec. From its founding in 1903 until the 1930's the A.C.J.C. was the only movement of young French Canadians. Its focus was on both Catholicism and nationalism. The dual emphasis was not compatible with the needs of the 1930's, and purely nationalist and purely Catholic youth movements were formed. The author adopted the nationalist position, and a major controversy developed over an article he planned to publish outlining these views in the *Revue Dominicaine* in 1935. 10 notes.

W. K. Hobson

2701. Lévesque, René. FOR AN INDEPENDENT QUEBEC. *Foreign Affairs 1976 54(4): 734-744.* Briefly discusses the historical position of the French of Quebec from the beginning of English domination in 1763 to the present. The Québécois remained outside the national development carried on by the Anglo-Saxons and assimilated immigrant groups, but their prolific numbers ensured them a continued presence on the land and the use of their own language. After World War II, nationalism took hold; by the 1960's it had become the Quiet Revolution. The author, president of the Parti Québécois, argues for sovereignty with a new kind of healthy association with Canada. C. W. Olson

2702. Loh, Wallace D. NATIONALIST ATTITUDES IN QUEBEC AND BELGIUM. *J. of Conflict Resolution 1975 19(2): 217-249.* Nationalist attitudes were studied in relation to ethnicity and social class in Quebec and Belgium, two bilingual multiethnic societies, during the 1970's.

2703. MacLeod, Alex. NATIONALISM AND SOCIAL CLASS: THE UNRESOLVED DILEMMA OF THE QUEBEC LEFT. *J. of Can. Studies 1973 8(4): 3-15.*

2704. Orban, Edmond. FIN D'UN NATIONALISME: LE CAS RECENT DES FRANCO-AMÉRICAINS DE LA NOUVELLE-ANGLETERRE [End of a nationalism: The recent case of the New England Franco-Americans]. *Can. Rev. of Studies in Nationalism [Canada] 1976 4(1): 91-99.* Studies the nationalism of the Franco-Americans, a group of unassimilated French Canadians in New England, who were distinguished by the use of the French language and the practice of a rural and conservative Catholic faith distinct from the Irish one. After 1940, such nationalism gradually deteriorated and has disappeared today, because of Franco-Americans' exogamous marriages, their mobility due to economic causes, their mixed parishes where priests officiate in English, and a general decrease in their resistance to anglicization. Based on primary and secondary sources; 2 tables, graph, 13 notes.

G. P. Cleyet

2705. Pageau, René. L'IDÉOLOGIE POLITIQUE DE GUSTAVE LAMARCHE [The political ideology of Gustave Lamarche]. *Action Natl. [Canada] 1975 64(9): 758-777.* Surveys the political philosophy of Catholic Father Gustave Lamarche, an active supporter of the independence of Quebec.

2706. Painchaud, Paul. LE ROLE INTERNATIONAL DU QUEBEC: POSSIBILITES ET CONTRAINTES [Quebec's international role: Possibilities and constraints]. *Études Int. [Canada] 1977 8(2): 374-392.* Notes the problems of dealing with a state that has not yet determined its form of independence. Nonetheless, two criteria are useful in anticipating foreign policy: first, states are influenced by their commercial, scientific, technical, and cultural environment, and second, they are influenced by ideology. Quebec must determine its affiliation with NATO and NORAD as well as its cultural alliances with such areas as Francophonia, the African states, and Latin America. Concludes by examining the methods available to implement an independent foreign policy. Primary and secondary sources; 21 notes.

J. F. Harrington, Jr.

2707. Pinard, Maurice and Hamilton, Richard. THE INDEPENDENCE ISSUE AND THE POLARIZATION OF THE ELECTORATE: THE 1973 QUEBEC ELECTION. *Can. J. of Pol. Sci. [Canada] 1977 10(2): 215-259.* Uses data acquired by a telephone poll conducted shortly after the 1973 Quebec election to examine the forces which led to the rapid polarization of the electorate between the Liberals and the Parti Québécois. Findings anticipated the results of the 1976 election. 10 tables, 71 notes. R. V. Kubicek

2708. Portes, Jacques. LE PROBLÈME DES IDÉOLOGIES DU CANADA FRANÇAIS À LA FIN DU XIXᵉ SIÈCLE ET AU DÉBUT DU XXᵉ SIÈCLE [The problem of the ideologies of French Canada at the end of the 19th century and at the beginning of the 20th century]. *Rev. d'Hist. Écon. et Sociale [France] 1975 53(4): 574-577.* Review article prompted by J. P. Bernard's *Les idéologies au Canada français, 1900-1929* (Quebec, 1974), A.-J. Bélanger's *L'apolitisme des idéologies québécoises, le Grand Tournant de 1934-36* (Quebec, n.d.), and G. Laloux-Jain's *Les manuels d'Histoire du Canada, au Québec et en Ontario (de 1867 à 1914)* (Quebec, 1973). The ideological response of French Canadians to British hegemony was ambiguous and did not lead to serious demands for separatism. The books under review give no clue about how French Canadian nationalism survived in spite of this ambiguity and how it could subsequently influence policy and economic development. 4 notes.
U. Wengenroth

2709. Roy, Jean-Louis. DYNAMIQUE DU NATIONALISME QUÉBÉCOIS (1945-1970) [The dynamics of Quebecois nationalism (1945-70)]. *Can. Rev. of Studies in Nationalism [Canada] 1973 1(1): 1-13.* Quebec nationalism obtained its postwar dynamism from complex social, economic, and political forces. The cultural isolation of French Canadian Catholic life has broken down, forcing a redefinition of Quebec's identity in a secular, nationalist sense. The centralizing tendencies of Canadian federal bureaucrats and planners have provoked strong reactions from inside Quebec. 36 notes.
J. C. Billigmeier

2710. Sabourin, Louis. LA RECHERCHE D'UN STATUT ENDOGENE QUÉBÉCOIS: TROIS STADES DE CONNAISSANCE MUTUELLE [Quebec's search for an endogenous statute: Three stages of mutual understanding]. *Études Int. [Canada] 1977 8(2): 231-239.* Analyzes the perceptions, fears, and understandings that affect Quebec-Ottawa relations as a result of that French-speaking province's demand for independence. Primary and secondary sources; 17 notes.
J. F. Harrington, Jr.

2711. Sabourin, Louis. QUEBEC'S INTERNATIONAL ACTIVITY RESTS ON IDEA OF COMPETENCE. *Int. Perspectives [Canada] 1977 Mar.-Apr.: 3-7.* Discusses attempts of Quebec to initiate foreign relations as a separate entity within Canada; examines the ascension of the Parti Québécois in politics and the aims of the French speaking populace, 1960-76.

2712. Sigler, John. STABILITE, CHANGEMENT SOCIAL ET SEPARATISME DANS LES SOCIETES DEVELOPPEES: LE CAS QUEBECOIS [Stability, social change and separatism in developed societies: The case of Quebec]. *Études Int. [Canada] 1977 8(2): 282-291.* Examines the political and sociological implications of Quebec's separatism. Gives considerable attention to the work of the Norwegian sociologist Johan Galtung and shows the average salary of male workers in Quebec in 1961 according to their ethnic origin. Primary and secondary sources; chart, 6 notes.
J. F. Harrington, Jr.

2713. Singer, Howard L. INTERNAL CONFLICTS WITHIN THE PARTI QUEBECOIS. *Dalhousie Rev. [Canada] 1977 57(1): 5-17.* The Parti Quebecois has had two major sources of cleavage since its founding in 1968. The first was an ideological one between radical and moderate members, and the second was an institutional one between the executive council and the parliamentary wing. René Lévesque represents the moderate group and has thus far defeated radical attempts by Pierre Bourgault and André Larocque to gain supremacy. The several crises of the party during 1969-73 are explained. Following the 29 October 1973 election and the pequiste position of official opposition in the National Assembly, the move to tone down the separatist issue caused several more party quarrels including a renewed questioning of Lévesque's party leadership. The position of holding a referendum on independence should the party form a government was a reassuring one for the moderates in the party. If the referendum on independence votes to remain in confederation, the conflict within the party will severely escalate. 36 notes.
C. Held

2714. Stein, Michael. LE ROLE DES QUÉBECOIS NON FRANCOPHONES DANS LE DEBAT ACTUEL ENTRE LE QUÉBEC ET LE CANADA [The role of non-Francophone Quebecers in the current Canadian debate]. *Études Int. [Canada] 1977 8(2): 292-306.* More than one million non-French-speaking people live in Quebec province. Dis-

cusses the historic self-perception of these people, and the impact of Bill 22 which made French the official language in Quebec and the landmark vote of 15 November 1976. Examines the role these people can play in Quebec's future. Secondary sources; 31 notes.
J. F. Harrington, Jr.

2715. Tremblay, Marc-Adélard. ESPACES GÉOGRAPHIQUES ET DISTANCE CULTURELLE: ESSAI DE DEFINITION DU FONDEMENT DES MENTALITÉS REGIONALES AU QUEBEC [Geographical space and cultural distance: essay on the definition of the cause of regionalism in Quebec]. *Tr. of the Royal Soc. of Can. [Canada] 1976 14: 131-147.* Questions the influence of space on the Canadian and Quebecois mentalities. Canada is made up of many diverse ethnic groups each settled in its own region. The railroad changed Canadians' view of space and brought more cultural interaction. Canada is multicultural with four main geographical regions: the west coast, the Prairies, the central region, and the Atlantic region. Notes Alfred Kroeber's studies concerning ethnic groups. The spaces are too vast and culture too heterogeneous to make valid studies in all cases. Studies the effect of space on French Canadians and discusses the impact of urbanization on areas such as Quebec. 4 notes, biblio.
J. D. Neville

2716. Tremblay, Marc-Adélard. EXISTE-T-IL DES CULTURES REGIONALES AU QUEBEC [Do regional cultures exist in Quebec?]. *Tr. of the Royal Soc. of Can. [Canada] 1977 15: 137-144.* Notes that Quebec has a regional culture made up of subregions. Makes use of the disciplines of geography, economics, political science, sociology and anthropology. Suggests that the French language draws together about eight distinct regions. Notes the criteria for identifying regional cultures. Concludes that with limitations there are distinct regional cultures within Quebec.
J. D. Neville

2717. Trépanier, Pierre. SIMÉON LE SAGE (1835-1909): L'IDÉOLOGIE D'UN HAUT FONCTIONNAIRE NATIONALISTE [Simeon LeSage (1835-1909): the ideology of a nationalist government official]. *Action Natl. [Canada] 1978 67(8): 654-684.* The nationalism of Le Sage was essentially defensive. It reflected a faith in the providential mission of French Canada to maintain the traditions and faith of *ancien régime* France. Quebec civilization was to be based on agriculture fortified by religion. While a loyal member of the Conservative party, Le Sage had reservations about confederation and especially the Anglo-Protestant policies of John A. MacDonald. The Riel Rebellion posed a conflict between his conservatism and his nationalism. While he supported clemency for Louis Riel, Le Sage opposed the transformation of his execution into martyrdom. While accepting the dogma of papal infallibility, Le Sage rejected ultramontanism. He supported church control of education and condemned anticlericalism. Based on primary sources, especially the Simeon Le Sage collection of the Archives nationale du Québec, and secondary sources; 149 notes.
A. W. Novitsky

2718. Vaugeois, Denis. LA COOPÉRATION DU QUÉBEC AVEC L'EXTÉRIEUR [Quebec and Cooperation with the Outside World]. *Études Internationales [Canada] 1974 5(2): 376-387.* Reviews Quebec's relations with Belgium, the French-speaking African states, and France. Primary and secondary sources; chart, 7 notes.
J. F. Harrington

2719. Walsh, Sam. FOR RECOGNITION OF THE FRENCH-CANADIAN NATION. *World Marxist R. [Canada] 1974 17(10): 126-133.* Oppression of French Canadians can be ended by making Quebec a separate nation in a confederated republic.
S

2720. Walsh, Sam. 4TH CONVENTION OF THE PARTI QUÉBÉCOIS. *Communist Viewpoint [Canada] 1973 5(3): 8-14.*

2721. Weinfeld, Morton. LA QUESTION JUIVE AU QUÉBEC [The Jewish question in Quebec]. *Midstream 1977 23(8): 20-29.* With the victory of René Levesque's Parti Québécois in the Quebec provincial elections in 1976, many Quebec Jews (most of whom are English-speaking) began to fear that the separatist philosophy of the P.Q. would lead to disenfranchisement for non-French residents of Quebec (even those able to speak French).

2722. Weiss, Jonathan M. *LES PLOUFFE* ET L'AMERICANISME AU QUÉBEC [*Les Plouffe* and Americanism in Quebec]. *Can. Rev. of Studies in Nationalism [Canada] 1976 3(2): 226-230.* Discusses Roger Lemelin's 1948 novel *Les Plouffe* and the author's attitude toward the Americanism in Quebec nationalism, 1938-45.

2723. Wisse, Ruth R. and Cotler, Irwin. QUEBEC'S JEWS: CAUGHT IN THE MIDDLE. *Commentary 1977 64(3): 55-59.* With the rise of Quebec's separatist movement and the 1976 *Quebecois* victory, the prevailing French-English tension, formerly a stimulant to Jewish cohesiveness, began to cause uncertainty in the Jewish community. Sympathetic toward French Canadian aspirations, yet fearful of negative repercussions, Jews in Montreal face a crisis of conscience. Should they strive to adapt to the new political situation in order to preserve and nuture their many achievements? Or should they accept their latest difficulty as evidence corroborating the Zionist judgment that the Diaspora will never treat Jews altogether kindly?						D. W. Johnson

Ontario

2724. Adam, Judith. TORONTO GETS INTO THE "ACTE." *Can. Labour 1973 18(3): 3-5, 24.* Labor unions work to organize white-collar employees.						S

2725. Anderson, Michael. FAMILY AND CLASS IN NINE-TEENTH-CENTURY CITIES. *J. of Family Hist. 1977 2(2): 139-149.* Reviews the first book-length product of the Canadian Social History Project at the University of Toronto, Michael B. Katz's *The People of Hamilton, Canada West: Family and Class in a Mid-Nineteenth-Century City.* Analyzes each of Katz's main themes: the distribution of wealth and power, social and geographic mobility, and the structure and role of the family. 10 notes, biblio.						T. W. Smith

2726. Armstrong, Frederick H. CAPT. HUGH RICHARDSON: FIRST HARBOR MASTER OF TORONTO. *Inland Seas 1975 31(1): 34-40, 42, 49-50.* Hugh Richardson (1784-1870) emigrated to York (Toronto), Upper Canada, in 1821. He became a shipowner and maintained aids to navigation around Toronto at his own expense until the city and provincial governments assumed responsibility. In 1850 he was appointed Harbor Master of Toronto and actively directed the improvement of the harbor, notably the reconstruction of Queen's Wharf. Based on materials in the Public Archives of Ontario and newspapers; 22 notes.						K. J. Bauer

2727. Armstrong, Frederick H. and Phelps, Edward C. H. IN ALMOST PERPETUAL CIRCLES: URBAN PRESERVATION AND THE MUNICIPAL ADVISORY COMMITTEE IN LONDON, ONTARIO. *Urban Hist. Rev. [Canada] 1977 (2): 10-19.* The authors, members of the committee concerned with the urban architectural heritage of London, Ontario, describe the antecedents of a coalition of groups and individuals in the early 1970's to preserve London's architecture. Over protests, the Mutual Advisory Committee pressured the city administration to recognize preservation when dealing with city planning and development. Using their experiences as an example, they urged preservation groups to: 1) list buildings deserving of preservation, 2) have the municipality obtain the legal power to designate buildings and areas, and 3) have the city appoint an official committee.						C. A. Watson

2728. Baldwin, Doug. PRIMARY SOURCE MATERIALS FOR THE HISTORY OF NORTHERN ONTARIO MINING TOWNS: THE CASE OF COBALT, ONTARIO. *Urban Hist. Rev. [Canada] 1978 (3): 80-85.* Details the types of sources available for historical research in Cobalt, Ontario, a northern mining town. Urges investigation in similar towns before the early records are destroyed by fire, rot, or neglect. 2 illus., 3 notes.						C. A. Watson

2729. Ball, Rosemary R. "A PERFECT FARMER'S WIFE"—WOMEN IN 19TH CENTURY RURAL ONTARIO. *Canada 1975 3(2): 2-21.* Discusses the social status of women, emphasizing attitudes toward education, marriage, and child care.

2730. Ballard, Robert M. POLLUTION IN LAKE ERIE 1872-1965. *Special Lib. 1975 66(8): 378-382.* Reviews the literature and some of the primary sources covering the development of pollution in Lake Erie from 1872-1965.						S

2731. Banks, Margaret A. GEORGE WARBURTON SPRAGGE, 1893-1976. *Ontario Hist. [Canada] 1976 68(2): 116-118.* Outlines the life of George Warburton Spragge and comments on some of the papers he published, especially those in *Ontario History.* Remarks on his career in the public service and his services to the Ontario Historical Society.						W. B. Whitham

2732. Bannister, Geoffrey. POPULATION CHANGE IN SOUTHERN ONTARIO. *Ann. of the Assoc. of Am. Geographers 1975 65(2): 177-188.* Uses autocovariance procedures to study the temporal and spatial patterns of population change in an urban system.						S

2733. Bannister, Geoffrey. SPACE-TIME COMPONENTS OF URBAN POPULATION CHANGE. *Econ. Geography 1976 52(3): 228-240.* Uses activity levels and spatial structure of urban systems to identify associations between population change and urban hierarchies in southern Ontario, 1941-71.

2734. Barker, G., Penney, J., and Seccombe, W. THE DEVELOPERS. *Can. Dimension 1973 9(2/3): 19-50.* Discusses urbanization and housing in Toronto (although the data could be applied elsewhere). Comments on demographic shifts, industrial concentration, and the role of government in financing development. Certain development corporations maintain inflated prices, evade taxes, and exploit labor. Some neighborhoods intended for development have fought back. Based on a forthcoming book; 11 photos, 7 graphs, 3 charts, 2 tables.						W. B. Whitham

2735. Battistelli, Fabrizio. L'AUTONOMIA CULTURALE COME STRUMENTO DI ASSIMILAZIONE: I MASS MEDIA ITALIANI NELLA COMMUNITÀ IMMIGRATA DI TORONTO, [Cultural autonomy as means of assimilation: Italian mass media in the Toronto immigrant community]. *Rassegna Italiana di Sociologia [Italy] 1975 16(3): 449-465.* A study of Italian mass media in Toronto during the 1970's shows that the media, by carrying the message of Anglo-Canadian capitalism to immigrants, tends to assimilate and thus eradicate the minority community.

2736. Bawtinhimer, R. E. THE DEVELOPMENT OF AN ONTARIO TORY: YOUNG GEORGE DREW. *Ontario Hist. [Canada] 1977 69(1): 55-75.* Presents the major influences in George Drew's early career and analyzes his development into a leading Tory. Outlines his Loyalist family background. He served in the army in World War I before being invalided home. His early postwar career was devoted to the family law practice, until he entered local politics. Analyzes his attitudes and campaigns, along with his election in 1925 as mayor of Guelph. 72 notes.						W. B. Whitham

2737. Begnal, Calista. THE SISTERS OF THE CONGREGATION OF NOTRE DAME, NINETEENTH-CENTURY KINGSTON. *Study Sessions: Can. Catholic Hist. Assoc. 1973 40: 27-34.* Examines the efforts of religious women during 1841-48, important years in the history of religious education.						S

2738. Bendickson, Jamie. RECREATIONAL CANOEING IN ONTARIO BEFORE THE FIRST WORLD WAR. *Can. J. of Hist. of Sport and Physical Educ. [Canada] 1978 9(2): 41-57.* Covers 1888-1914.

2739. Bergey, Lorna L. MENNONITE CHANGE: THE LIFE HISTORY OF THE BLENHEIM MENNONITE CHURCH, 1839-1974. *Mennonite Life 1977 32(4): 23-27.* Pennsylvania Germans settled Waterloo and Oxford Counties in southwest Ontario 1830-50, forming a prosperous agricultural community. In 1839 they organized the Blenheim Mennonite Church. Jacob Hallman was pastor. Membership in the church averaged 50 people for 135 years until it merged with the Biehn congregation to form the Nith Valley Mennonite Church in 1975. Reasons for its lack of growth are its location on the fringe of the Waterloo County settlement, the appeal of the livelier Methodist Church, a schism which led to the formation of the Missionary Church, and population changes in the area.						B. Burnett

2740. Beszedits, S. TORNTO'S 19TH CENTURY ARCHITECTS. *Can. Geographic [Canada] 1978/79 97(3): 52-59.* Discusses architects John G. Howard, Henry B. Lane, William Thomas, F. W. Cumberland, and W. G. Storm.

2741. Bird, Michael. ONTARIO FRAKTUR ART: A DECORA-TIVE TRADITION IN THREE GERMANIC SETTLEMENTS. *Ontario Hist. [Canada] 1976 68(4): 247-272.* Fraktur art is "the embellishment of a written or printed text . . . to produce a pleasing and often personalised work of art within a religio-ethnic tradition." This tradition is associated with Pennsylvania Germans. Points out minor variations and analyzes the background in Europe and Pennsylvania. Details the arrival and development of this art form in Ontario. Discusses specific artists and analyzes characteristic applications. 36 illus., notes.
W. B. Whitham

2742. Brown, Ronald. DEPOT HARBOUR, BUSY LAKES PORT: 1900-1928. *Can. Geographical J. [Canada] 1977-78 95(3): 56-61.* Ontario's Depot Harbour on Georgian Bay in Lake Huron was an important outlet for the lumber industry, 1900-28; examines shipping, harbor layout, and extant buildings.

2743. Brozowski, R.; Romsa, G.; and Lall, A. SOME FACTORS INFLUENCING POPULATION CHANGE IN RURAL ONTARIO. *Scottish Geographical Mag. [Great Britain] 1973 89(2): 131-137.* The hypothesis of the study is that external influences play a more dominant role than internal factors in influencing village population growth. Furthermore, the importance of any given index associated with village population growth may oscillate through given time periods. Factors selected are size of place, occupational grouping, urban influence and regional location. Their association with the population changes of Ontario villages are examined for three time periods, 1941-1951, 1951-1961, 1961-1966. The analysis indicates that external factors, regional location, and urban influences are most important.
J

2744. Burley, Kevin. OCCUPATIONAL STRUCTURE AND ETHNICITY IN LONDON, ONTARIO, 1871. *Social Hist. [Canada] 1978 11(22): 390-410.* London grew rapidly in the three decades before 1871. Its population of 15,826 made it the fourth largest town in Ontario. The foreign-born, particularly those from Great Britain, dominated London's work force. London's percentage of foreign-born (54%) was well below the national average, but typical of western Ontario towns. The Canadian-born were more active in the city's commercial sector and in some professions. Occupations apparently differed widely between ethnic groups, but the distribution by socioeconomic class was remarkably alike for all ethnic groups. Based on the 1871 census and on other primary and secondary sources; 9 tables, 45 notes.
D. F. Chard

2745. Carter, Donald D. LEGAL REGULATION OF COLLECTIVE BARGAINING IN THE ONTARIO PUBLIC SECTOR. *Industrial Relations [Canada] 1974 29(4): 776-785.* In this paper, the author describes the major features of the legal structure for collective bargaining in the Ontario public sector. The emphasis is mostly placed upon the *Crown Employees Collective Bargaining Act* which applies to a substantial portion of the Ontario public sector labor force. The basic issues dealt with include: disputes settlement, scope of bargaining, determination of bargaining units, representation elections and political activities.
J

2746. Charron, Marguerite. MARIE D'AQUIN ET LE NOUVEAU DÉPART DE L'INSTITUT JEANNE D'ARC (1914-1919) [Marie d'Aquin and the new start of the Joan of Arc Institute (1914-19)]. *Sessions d'Étude: Soc. Can. d'Hist. de l'Église Catholique [Canada] 1977 44: 63-80.* The Joan of Arc Institute was established during 1903-14 by Ottawa Catholic nuns for young employment-seeking women who needed security or lodgings. Examines the growth of the Institute during 1914-19 under the leadership of Marie Thomas d'Aquin and the eventual establishment of the Congregation of Sisters of the Institute of Joan of Arc in 1919.
G. A. Hewlett

2747. Choquette, Robert. L'EGLISE D'OTTAWA SOUS MGR GUIGUES, 1848-1874 [The church of Ottawa under Monseigneur Guigues, 1848-74]. *Session d'Étude: Soc. Can. d'Hist. de l'Église Catholique [Canada] 1977 44: 57-62.* The Ottawa diocese was administered by

Joseph-Eugène Guigues during 1848-74, where he actively pursued French Canadian colonization in Ontario, church funding, and spiritual and social programs.

2748. Clarke, Harold D.; Price, Richard G.; Stewart, Marianne C.; and Krause, Robert. MOTIVATIONAL PATTERNS AND DIFFERENTIAL PARTICIPATION IN A CANADIAN PARTY: THE ONTARIO LIBERALS. *Am. J. of Pol. Sci. 1978 22(1): 130-151.* Little is known about the motivations and activity patterns of party workers in Western democracies other than the United States. Equally important, linkages between different motives for initiating and sustaining party work and levels of activity within party organizations are virtually unexplored, and hence, the analytic utility of motivational variables remains problematic. To help fill these lacunae in the scholarly literature, this paper focuses on the motivational patterns and activity levels of members of one Canadian party—the Ontario Liberals. In accordance with expectations, the data reveal considerable motivational diversity as well as substantial motivational "reorientation and change" over time. Regression analyses indicate that "partisanship" and "friendship for candidate" motives have statistically significant independent effects on intraparty participation rates. Additionally, the regression analyses suggest that variables repeatedly found to correlate with political participation in studies of mass publics may have little power to explain *differential* participation within party organizations.
J

2749. Clarke, Harold D.; Kornberg, Allan; and Lee, James. ONTARIO STUDENT PARTY ACTIVISTS: A NOTE ON DIFFERENTIAL PARTICIPATION IN A VOLUNTARY ORGANIZATION. *Can. R. of Sociol. and Anthrop. 1975 12(2): 213-227.* Although there have been a number of studies of political participation among mass publics, there have been virtually no efforts made to study differential participation among those conventionally designated as political activists. This research note focuses on differential participation within university political party clubs, using data derived from questionnaires sent to a sample of political club activists in the several Ontario universities in the spring of 1970. Multiple classification analysis is used to assess the impact of several variables on differential participation. A major finding is that some variables, useful for explaining who joins a voluntary organization such as a political club, are unable to explain level of participation in the club's activities.
J

2750. Corbett, Beatrice. SUSAN MOULTON FRASER MC MASTER. *Inland Seas 1975 31(3): 192-200.* Born in Rhode Island in 1819, Susan Moulton married James Fraser, a Bay City, Michigan, lumberman and Indian agent, in 1851. After Fraser's death in 1866 she built a Baptist church in his memory in Bay City. She married the Toronto banker Senator William McMaster in 1871 and continued to be an active Baptist. She convinced her husband to establish McMaster Hall as a theological college. Based on family information.
K. J. Bauer

2751. Cross, L. Doreen. LOCATING SELECTED OCCUPATIONS: OTTAWA, 1870. *Urban Hist. Rev. [Canada] 1974 74(2): 5-14.* The city directory and a historical atlas provide the basis for an examination of the occupational structure in Ottawa, Ontario, 1870; focuses on professional and skilled labor.

2752. Dahms, Frederic A. HOW ONTARIO'S GUELPH DISTRICT DEVELOPED. *Can. Geographical J. [Canada] 1977 94(1): 48-55.* Discusses the urban development which waxed and waned, 1824-1971.

2753. Dahms, Frederic A. SOME QUANTITATIVE APPROACHES TO THE STUDY OF CENTRAL PLACES IN THE GUELPH AREA, 1851-1970. *Urban Hist. Rev. [Canada] 1975 (2): 9-30.* Explores methodology available to urban geographers and urban historians, in the Guelph Central Place System of 1970.

2754. Davey, Ian E. TRENDS IN FEMALE SCHOOL ATTENDANCE IN MID-NINETEENTH CENTURY ONTARIO. *Social Hist. [Canada] 1975 8(16): 238-254.* Although there was a steady increase in female attendance at schools in Ontario in the 1850's-60's, it was more spectacular in cities than in rural areas. The increase seems directly attributable to the greater availability of public schools. Despite these trends, the long-standing class and sex biases in school attendance persisted. Girls were more likely than their brothers to be withdrawn from school in times of economic hardship. Middle-class girls were far more likely to attend school than were children of the working class. Based on superintendents' annual reports, Hamilton school records, and the Hamilton manuscript census. 10 tables, 20 notes.   W. K. Hobson

2755. Davis, William E. and McKiernan, F. Mark. THE MIGHTY MISSISSIPPI: TWO 19TH CENTURY ACCOUNTS. *Louisiana Hist. 1977 18(3): 338-348.* George Forman's 1883 manuscript, "Biographical Sketch of the Life and Ancestry of Geo. Forman of Stratford-Ontario-Canada," includes a description of his boating and logging on the Mississippi River from Wisconsin to New Orleans in 1849-51. That portion of the 402-page typescript is published here, along with four illustrations of shipping scenes on the Mississippi from Henry Lewis's *Das Illustrite Mississippithal* [The Mississippi Illustrated] (Dusseldorf, 1854).
R. L. Woodward, Jr.

2756. Decarie, M. G. PAVED WITH GOOD INTENTIONS: THE PROHIBITIONISTS' ROAD TO RACISM IN ONTARIO. *Ontario Hist. [Canada] 1974 66(1): 15-.* Examines the prohibition movement in the late 19th century in Ontario and its effect on other aspects of reform. Traces the logic of prohibition (as distinct from temperance) from stereotyping users of alcohol to racism. 20 notes.
W. B. Whitham and S

2757. Denton, Frank T. and George, Peter J. SOCIO-ECONOMIC CHARACTERISTICS OF FAMILIES IN WENTWORTH COUNTY, 1871: SOME FURTHER RESULTS. *Social Hist. [Canada] 1974 7(13): 103-110.* Study of 429 urban and 671 rural families in Wentworth County, Ontario in 1871 reveals that most occupational, religious, birthplace, and ethnic origin variables were not significantly related to number of children; only the wife's birthplace was. The observed urban-rural difference in family size was not due to the differences in socio-economic characteristics of rural and urban families. School attendance was significantly related to father's occupation, parental birthplace, and to basic urban-rural differences, but not to religion or ethnic origin. Based on manuscript census; 2 tables, 6 notes.   W. K. Hobson

2758. Dewees, Donald N. TRAVEL COSTS, TRANSIT, AND CONTROL OF URBAN MOTORING. *Public Policy 1976 24(1): 59-79.* Studies the effects of mass transit systems on private urban motoring in North America. Reduction of motoring has not been achieved and will not be achieved. Mass transit is more expensive than private motoring. A review of mass transit experience in Toronto, Canada, reveals that time is the factor that keeps people in their automobiles. Property values and population density increase near rapid transit stops. Riders return to their cars as soon as mass transit reduces surface travel; thus congestion redevelops. Private motoring can be reduced only by penalizing motorists by means of taxes on gasoline, miles driven, or freeway access. 2 tables, 15 notes.   V. L. Human

2759. Doucet, Michael J. DISCRIMINANT ANALYSIS AND THE DELINEATION OF HOUSEHOLD STRUCTURE: TOWARD A SOLUTION TO THE BOARDER/RELATIVE PROBLEM ON THE 1871 CANADIAN CENSUS. *Hist. Methods Newsletter 1977 10(4): 149-157.* Using knowledge about Hamilton's boarders and relatives during 1851-71 it is possible to distinguish between the two groups in 1871. Many of the boarders were female Catholics of Irish birth. "In the final analysis, most of the associations seem to be inherently logical." 5 tables, 12 notes.   D. K. Pickens

2760. Doucet, Michael J. MASS TRANSIT AND THE FAILURE OF PRIVATE OWNERSHIP: THE CASE OF TORONTO IN THE EARLY TWENTIETH CENTURY. *Urban Hist. Rev. [Canada] 1978 (3): 3-33.* Discusses the trials and tribulations of Torontonians and the street railway system during its most important period of development. The first franchise to a private company expired in 1891 at which time Toronto, not yet ready for public ownership, gave the next 30 year franchise to the private Toronto Railway Company. The subsequent clash of interests—the TRC efforts to make profits and the city administration and civic groups' efforts to get the TRC to provide better service—led to the municipal takeover of the street railway system in 1921 as a public utility. Primary and secondary sources; 3 tables, 3 fig., 70 notes.
C. A. Watson

2761. Elford, Jean. THE ICELANDERS—THEIR ONTARIO YEAR. *Beaver [Canada] 1974 304(4): 53-57.* Describes the 1872 arrival and first year of life in Ontario, Canada for 352 immigrants from Iceland.
S

2762. Ellis, Walter E. GILBOA TO ICHABOD: SOCIAL AND RELIGIOUS FACTORS IN THE FUNDAMENTALIST-MODERNIST SCHISMS AMONG CANADIAN BAPTISTS, 1895-1934. *Foundations 1977 20(2): 109-126.* Examines the socioeconomic makeup of the Jarvis Street Baptist Church in Toronto, and the change that occurred during the Fundamentalist-Modernist controversy. As the Fundamentalists gained control, the professional and entrepreneur class left to form churches in new upper-class areas. Contrasts the Jarvis Street Church with the Central Baptist Church and compares it to the Conventional churches and Union churches. The Fundamentalist Union churches attracted the working class (91 percent), while the Conventional churches attracted the professional class. This increased the social stratification of the church. 23 notes.   E. E. Eminhizer

2763. Emery, George N. ADAM OLIVER, INGERSOLL AND THUNDER BAY DISTRICT, 1850-82. *Ontario Hist. [Canada] 1976 68(1): 25-43.* Discusses the entrepreneurial activities of Adam Oliver, who began his career in Ingersoll in the 1850's and expanded his activities to Thunder Bay in the 1870's. Talks about Oliver's life, some of the political aspects of his activities, and the development of Ontario. Oliver's involvement with fraternal orders, his participation in provincial politics, and the legislative investigations into some of his operations are mentioned. Oliver alleged that the investigations were the result of partisan politics. This allegation is examined in the context of the political practices of the day. The allegations, while not proven, do not seem to have been groundless. 93 notes.   W. B. Whitham

2764. Fetherling, Doug. TORONTO'S CULTURAL FERMENT, 1978-STYLE. *Can. Geographical J. [Canada] 1978 96(2): 28-35.* Discusses Toronto's cultural events and municipal encouragement of the arts programs, including, art galleries, opera, theater, public art fairs, ballet, civic orchestra, and municipal educational television, 1978.

2765. Flynn, Louis J. THE HISTORY OF SAINT MARY'S CATHEDRAL OF THE IMMACULATE CONCEPTION, KINGSTON, ONTARIO, 1843-1973. *Study Sessions: Can. Catholic Hist. Assoc. 1973 40: 35-40.*

2766. Fowler, Marian E. PORTRAIT OF SUSAN SIBBALD: WRITER AND PIONEER. *Ontario Hist. [Canada] 1974 66(1): 50-.* Describes the life of Susan Sibbald, based on her *Memoirs* (1926) and other sources. Photo, 62 notes.   W. B. Whitham and S

2767. Fretz, J. Winfield. THE PLAIN AND NOT-SO-PLAIN MENNONITES IN WATERLOO COUNTY, ONTARIO. *Mennonite Q. Rev. 1977 51(4): 377-385.* The Mennonite community in Waterloo County, Ontario, is unique for its mixture of liberal and conservative elements and diversity of ethnic origin. Describes 12 grades of social action ranging from ultraconservative to ultraliberal. However, all factions work together surprisingly well as a result of a governing committee that is loose and resilient. In fact, the groups are not very different beneath the surface, except in their methods. This fact makes accommodation possible. The various groups cooperate if movement by an individual or a family from one group to another is desired. 4 tables.
V. L. Human

2768. Frideres, J.; Goldenberg, S.; and Reeves, W. THE ECONOMIC ADAPTATION OF WEST INDIANS IN TORONTO. *Can. Rev. of Sociol. and Anthrop. [Canada] 1978 15(1): 93-96.* A review and critique of an article by S. Ramcharan, "The Economic Adaptation of West Indians in Toronto, Canada" (see abstract 15A:414). It falls short in both structure and content, much being doubtful, ambiguous, or in error. This applies to its interpretation of economic adaptation, the analysis of racial background and racial discrimination, the sampling procedures, and the choice of data analysis techniques, and their interpretation.
R. V. Ritter

2769. Gaffield, Chad and Levine, David. DEPENDENCY AND ADOLESCENCE ON THE CANADIAN FRONTIER: ORILLIA,

ONTARIO IN THE MID-NINETEENTH CENTURY. *Hist. of Educ. Q. 1978 18(1): 35-47.* Using Orillia, Ontario, argues that social changes in a 19th-century community, particularly employment opportunities, affected aspects of adolescence and dependency. For example, age at time of marriage was lowered as job opportunities increased. Makes some comparison with urban studies on Hamilton. Primary and secondary sources; 4 tables, 11 notes.   L. C. Smith

2770. Gagan, David and Mays, Herbert. HISTORICAL DEMOGRAPHY AND CANADIAN SOCIAL HISTORY: FAMILIES AND LAND IN PEEL COUNTY, ONTARIO. *Can. Hist. R. 1973 54(1): 27-45.* The authors discuss population studies and quantitative methodology as an approach to Canadian social history. Describe the Peel County History Project and examine its findings on transiency among one township's population. The rate and persistence of transiency among all social and economic groups 1840-80 seems to contradict previous assumptions about the stability of rural society in Upper Canada and suggests the need for more quantitative, microanalytical studies of Canadian populations and social structures.   A. R. Shipton

2771. Gagan, David. THE PROSE OF LIFE: LITERARY REFLECTIONS OF THE FAMILY, INDIVIDUAL RESPONSES AND SOCIAL STRUCTURE IN NINETEENTH CENTURY CANADA. *J. of Social Hist. 1976 9(3): 367-381.* Travel and immigration records offer clues to the quest for a one-class society in early Ontario. The unity of the family, children, servants, relatives, land, labor, and emotional outlook are explored.   M. Hough

2772. Gervais, Gaetan. LORENZO CADIEUX, S.J., 1903-1976. *Ontario Hist. [Canada] 1977 69(4): 214-218.* Father Cadieux was born in Granby, Quebec, educated in Montreal and Edmonton, and closely associated with the study of northern Ontario. Outlines his career as a teacher, and mentions organizations he was associated with. Gives examples of his work, and lists some titles of his publications. The obituary is in English and French.   W. B. Whitham

2773. Geschwender, James A.; Rinehart, James W.; and George, P. M. SOCIALIZATION, ALIENATION, AND STUDENT ACTIVISM. *Youth & Soc. 1974 5(3): 303-325.* Uses data from a sample of students at the University of Western Ontario in 1970 to test hypotheses which predict that certain characteristics of youths are associated with student activism.   S

2774. Gillis, Robert Peter. THE OTTAWA LUMBER BARONS AND THE CONSERVATION MOVEMENT, 1880-1914. *J. of Can. Studies 1974 9(1): 14-30.* Rejects the Robber Baron interpretation of the 19th-century lumber industry entrepreneurs. Like the proponents of Theodore Roosevelt's New Nationalism, the Ontario lumber barons wanted to cooperate with the state in carrying out the planned use of resources, but were thwarted by the upholders of exploitative liberal capitalism. Based on Laurier Papers, industrial reports, company papers and proceedings, and secondary works; 79 notes.   G. E. Panting

2775. Griezic, F. J. K. "POWER TO THE PEOPLE": THE BEGINNING OF AGRARIAN REVOLT IN ONTARIO: THE MANITOULIN BY-ELECTION, OCTOBER 24, 1918. *Ontario Hist. [Canada] 1977 69(1): 33-54.* Discusses the Manitoulin election against the background of pre-World War I farm problems in a thinly settled area. An incident in 1915-16 was interpreted by many farmers as political corruption, and in this period began a significant swing against the provincial government by farmers. Illus., 84 notes.   W. B. Whitham

2776. Gruneir, Robert. THE HEBREW MISSION IN TORONTO. *Can. Ethnic Studies [Canada] 1977 9(1): 18-28.* Focuses primarily on the Presbyterian Church and the Protestant-supported Jewish mission founded in 1912. Examines efforts to convert immigrant Jews to Protestantism. Though presented as an aid to social assimilation, conversion (even the hybrid Hebrew-Protestant variety which allowed maintenance of ethnic identity), failed to attract large numbers of Jews. The movement faded after World War I.   K. S. McDorman

2777. Gunderson, Morley. TIME PATTERN OF MALE-FEMALE WAGE DIFFERENTIALS: ONTARIO 1946-1971. *Industrial Relations [Canada] 1976 31(1): 57-68.* Examines whether male-female wage differentials have narrowed over time, whether such differentials narrow or widen at the peak of a business cycle, and whether the stricter enforcement of equal pay legislation in recent years has influenced these differentials.   J

2778. Hall, Frederick A. MUSICAL LIFE IN WINDSOR: 1875-1901. *U. of Windsor R. [Canada] 1974 9(2): 76-92.* Traces the development of live musical performances in Windsor, Ontario. Early local efforts were concentrated in town churches and featured religious, classical, and popular pieces. Notes the establishment in the city of music education schools and programs and describes important music clubs and societies. A brief history is provided of the 1874-1901 Windsor Opera House. Emphasizes the difficulties of establishing a viable and independent Windsor musical tradition in close proximity to similar American activities in much-larger Detroit. In spite of this competition, Windsor succeeded in inaugurating and maintaining an active musical life. 25 notes.   H. S. Shields

2779. Halliday, Hugh A. HISTORIC QUEENSTON. *Can. Geographical J. 1973 86(3): 96-104.*

2780. Hamilton, Douglas F. REHABILITATION SERVICES OF THE ONTARIO WCB. *Can. Labour 1973 18(4-6): 10-14.*

2781. Harding, Jim. MERCURY POISONING. *Can. Dimension 1976 11(7): 14-23.* Discusses industrial pollution and mercury poisoning in northwestern Ontario in the 1970's, alleging cover-up attempts by the Ontario regional government.

2782. Harney, Robert F. BOARDING AND BELONGING. *Urban Hist. Rev. [Canada] 1978 78(2): 8-37.* A recent study of immigrants has focused on the relationship between ethnic colonies and their acculturation or lack of it. There is now a need to make comparative studies of the migration of immigrants, their sojourning, and finally their settling patterns. The boardinghouse as an institution in the acculturation process of sojourners is described with an emphasis on the Italian boardinghouse in Toronto. Interviews, published government reports, and secondary sources; illus., 59 notes.   C. A. Watson

2783. Harney, Robert F. CHIAROSCURO: ITALIANS IN TORONTO 1885-1915. *Italian Americana 1975 1(2): 143-167.* Discusses the settlement of Italian immigrants who lived and found employment in Toronto before World War II.   S

2784. Harney, Robert F. and Troper, Harold. INTRODUCTION [TO AN ISSUE ON IMMIGRANTS IN THE CITY]. *Can. Ethnic Studies [Canada] 1977 9(1): 1-5.* Seeking to offer broader perspectives than the Anglo-Celtic political historian's approach to urban studies, this issue analyzes 19th- and 20th-century Toronto through its immigrant communities. The eight contributors, using a variety of nontraditional sources (demotic and oral), examine tensions along ethnic boundaries. They conclude that immigrants who encountered overt hostility to their urban settlement reluctantly identified themselves, personally and economically, by their Canadian "caretakers' " stereotypes. This ethnocultural research provides a new and "more honest" dimension in urban history.   K. S. McDorman

2785. Harney, R. F. THE NEW CANADIANS AND THEIR LIFE IN TORONTO. *Can. Geographical J. [Canada] 1978 96(2): 20-27.* Discusses the influx of immigrants from Spain, Portugal, Hungary, Germany, Greece, Yugoslavia, Korea, France, and the United Kingdom, 1950's-70's and their acculturation in Toronto.

2786. Harney, Robert F. A NOTE ON SOURCES IN URBAN AND IMMIGRANT HISTORY: (INCLUDING EXCERPTS FROM PRIMARY MATERIALS ON MACEDONIANS IN TORONTO). *Can. Ethnic Studies [Canada] 1977 9(1): 60-76.* Of the three major sources on immigrants in Toronto (municipal statistics, "caretakers' " records, and immigrant literature), the last has been the most ignored and offers the greatest enrichment to urban history. Provides four types of immigrant sources: a description of the Canadian Baptist mission for Macedonians, the actual records of a Macedonian church, a community historian's depiction of the founding of a Macedonian church in Toronto, and an interview with Gina Petroff, a Macedonian immigrant. Interviews with living immigrants will better document the ethnic community's experience.   K. S. McDorman

2787. Harvey, Edward B. and Charner, Ivan. SOCIAL MOBILITY AND OCCUPATIONAL ATTAINMENTS OF UNIVERSITY GRADUATES. *Can. R. of Sociol. and Anthrop. 1975 12(2): 134-149.* This paper presents an analysis of the changing rates of social mobility and the changes in occupational attainment patterns of 2137 Ontario males who received BA or BSC degrees in 1960, 1964, and 1968. Although some findings are mixed, there is general support for hypotheses that a declining proportion of recent university graduates are likely to be upwardly mobile and that this decline will be more pronounced for graduates from middle level socioeconomic backgrounds than for those from lower socioeconomic backgrounds. Hypotheses relating the effect of socioeconomic background, year of graduation, major field of study, and postgraduate training on occupational attainment are also tested.   J

2788. Haycock, R. THE 1917 FEDERAL ELECTION IN VICTORIA-HALIBURTON: A CASE STUDY. *Ontario Hist. [Canada] 1975 67(2): 105-118.* Through an examination of the 1917 election campaign in the riding of Victoria and Haliburton Counties, one gains a useful illustration of the way the national campaign was fought in the pivotal province of Ontario as a whole, in which the Unionists won a large majority.

2789. Helleiner, F. M. SANDY INLET: PEACE IN A POPULAR WILDERNESS. *Can. Geographical J. [Canada] 1977 94(2): 59-61.* Describes the settlement at Lake Temagami's Sandy Inlet from 1895, when Father Charles Paradis (1848-1926) lived there, to the site's current use as Camp Wanapitei.

2790. Hill, Daniel G. RACISM IN ONTARIO. *Can. Labour 1977 22(2): 24-26, 36.* Examines methods sought by Ontario officials and human rights agencies to deal with racism toward ethnic groups, minorities, and native peoples during 1973-77.

2791. Horn, Michiel. KEEPING CANADA "CANADIAN": ANTI-COMMUNISM AND CANADIANISM IN TORONTO, 1928-29. *Canada 1975 3(1): 34-47.* Discusses the role of immigration and national self-image in anti-Communist movements and anti-Semitism in Toronto, Ontario, in 1928-29, emphasizing freedom of speech issues.

2792. Hovinen, Elizabeth. QUAKERS OF YONGE STREET. *Can. Geographical J. 1976 92(1): 52-57.* Discusses the members of the Society of Friends who lived in southern Ontario in the 19th century.

2793. Humphreys, Barbara A. THE ARCHITECTURAL HERITAGE OF THE RIDEAU CORRIDOR. *Can. Historic Sites 1974 10: 12-71.* "In 1969, an architectural survey was made [by the National Historic Sites Service of the National and Historic Parks Branch for the Canada-Ontario-Rideau-Trent-Severn (CORTS) Study Committee] of all pre-1880 buildings in the Rideau Corridor, an area extending from Ottawa to Kingston (though not including these two cities) along the Rideau Canal. Of the 1,800 buildings recorded, 1,677 were considered to be within the relevant time period. This report describes, analyzes and illustrates a representative collection of these structures as well as some of their architectural details."   J

2794. Humphreys, Barbara A. ARCHITECTURE OF THE RIDEAU CANAL REGION. *Can. Geographical J. 1975 90(6): 20-29.*

2795. Huot, John. FIGHT-BACK AGAINST RACISM. *Can. Dimension [Canada] 1978 12(8): 2-5.* Discusses recent efforts by South Asians of Toronto to organize against social and political injustice and racist violence.

2796. Jacek, Henry; McDonough, John; Shimizu, Ronald; and Smith, Patrick. SOCIAL ARTICULATION AND AGGREGATION IN POLITICAL PARTY ORGANIZATIONS IN A LARGE CANADIAN CITY. *Can. J. of Pol. Sci. 1975 8(2): 274-298.* Examines how three political parties in Hamilton, Ontario, relate to that city's socioeconomic groups. 18 tables, 23 notes.   R. V. Kubicek

2797. James, R. Scott. THE CITY OF TORONTO ARCHIVES. *Urban Hist. Rev. [Canada] 1973 (3): 2-9.* Assesses the accessibility, archival holdings, future plans, and history of the City Archives of Toronto, Ontario, 1959-73.

2798. Jarvis, Eric. MUNICIPAL COMPENSATION CASES: TORONTO IN THE 1860'S. *Urban Hist. Rev. [Canada] 1976 (3): 14-22.* Toronto seems to stand out as an exception to the generally accepted belief that 19th-century government lacked social responsibility. The Toronto City Council compensated private citizens for injuries received from faulty sidewalks and streets while municipal employees were compensated for long-time service, injuries sustained on the job, and layoffs. Compensation was partly voluntary and partly demanded by provincial statute. Based on Toronto City Council Minutes; 20 notes.   C. A. Watson

2799. Johnson, J. K. THE BUSINESSMAN AS HERO: THE CASE OF WILLIAM WARREN STREET. *Ontario Hist. [Canada] 1973 65(3): 125-132.* Discusses William Warren Street's background and the reasons for his embezzlement of substantial funds from the bank of which he was an officer, and his town, of which he was treasurer. Argues that he became involved in land speculation, and that the depression of 1857 led to the discovery of his defalcations and to his flight to the United States, where he remained for the rest of his life. 46 notes.   W. B. Whitham

2800. Kalter, Bella Briansky. A JEWISH COMMUNITY THAT WAS: ANSONVILLE, ONTARIO, CANADA. *Am. Jewish Arch. 1978 30(2): 107-125.* "Oh, it was lovely, lonely, lighted with snow in the wintertime. . . ." So begins the author's poignant memoir of Jewish life in the harsh climate of Canada's northern Ontario province. There are glimpses in her recollection of an existence which many North American Jews have forgotten or never experienced: a sense of community, traditional in nature, which put its emphasis upon sharing and caring; a life of hardship modified by the celebration of simple joys; a sense of continuity, uninterrupted by the geographic rootlessness of our time.   J

2801. Katz, Michael. THE ENTREPRENEURIAL CLASS IN A CANADIAN CITY. *J. of Social Hist. 1975 8(2): 1-29.* Although an entrepreneurial elite ruled Hamilton, Ontario, in the mid-19th century, the individual members of the elite often varied—"the identity of its members swirled with the vicissitudes of commerce, the whims of creditors, the logic of character and the vagaries of chance." 2 tables, 42 notes.   L. Ziewacz

2802. Katz, Michael B. THE ORIGINS OF PUBLIC EDUCATION: A REASSESSMENT. *Hist. of Educ. Q. 1976 16(4): 381-408.* Assesses the expectations for and outcomes of public schools as tools for socialization in Hamilton, Ontario, during 19th-century industrialization.

2803. Kealey, Gregory S. 'THE HONEST WORKINGMAN' AND WORKERS' CONTROL: THE EXPERIENCE OF TORONTO SKILLED WORKERS, 1860-1892. *Labour [Canada] 1976 1: 32-68.* Local coopers', iron moulders', and printers' unions in Toronto exemplified variants of "shop floor control." Adaptation to increasing industrialization and to pressures from management and government gave craftsmen greater production control than generally realized. Struggles to maintain that control brought varied results. Mechanization defeated the coopers. Organizational strength, solidarity with unskilled coworkers, and the failure of technological developments sufficient to replace their skills brought general success to the moulders. The printers "met the machine and triumphed" by increasing the degree of control. Political activity and workers' cooperatives were two effects of the unions' efforts. Primary and secondary sources; 162 notes.   W. A. Kearns

2804. Kilbourn, William. THE NEW TORONTO: A GREAT MODERN CITY. *Can. Geographical J. [Canada] 1978 96(2): 10-19.* Discusses city planning which has aided in the controlled growth and beautification of Toronto, Ontario; examines shopping facilities, business districts, architectural standards, historic renovation, and transportation systems, 1970's.

2805. Killan, Gerald. THE GOOD, THE BAD, AND AN OCCASIONAL TOUCH OF THE UGLY: THE ONTARIO HISTORICAL

SOCIETY *PAPERS AND RECORDS*. *Ontario Hist. [Canada] 1975 67(2): 57-67.* Recounts the inception in 1899 and subsequent history of the Ontario Historical Society's publication, *Papers and Records*, until its name was changed to *Ontario History* in 1947.

2806. Kirley, Kevin. A SEMINARY RECTOR IN ENGLISH CANADA DURING AND AFTER THE SECOND VATICAN COUNCIL. *Study Sessions: Can. Catholic Hist. Assoc. [Canada] 1976 43: 57-74.* Surveys the state of the Catholic Church in Toronto before and after Pope John XXIII convoked Vatican Council II in Rome, records some of the rapid and profound transformation in Canada during the Council, 1962-65, and examines the Council's influence on St. Basil's Seminary 1964-67.

2807. Kutcher, Stan. J. W. BENGOUGH AND THE MILLENNIUM IN HOGTOWN: A STUDY OF MOTIVATION IN URBAN REFORM. *Urban Hist. Rev. [Canada] 1976 76(2): 30-49.* The career of John Wilson Bengough (1851-1923), cartoonist and author, illustrates the idealism of certain aspects of the urban reform movement. Religiously motivated, he believed in worshiping God by serving mankind. Concerned with the social conditions of Toronto, he used his weekly satirical magazine, *Grip*, to promote morality in city government. He became involved in politics by serving as an alderman for three years. Frustrated by the necessity of political compromise, he retired from office in 1909, preferring the freedom of an outside critic. Based on the Bengough Papers, secondary sources, and newspapers; 76 notes.   C. A. Watson

2808. LaFave, Laurence F.; Haddad, Jay; and Marshall, Nancy. HUMOR JUDGEMENTS AS A FUNCTION OF IDENTIFICATION CLASSES. *Sociol. and Social Res. 1974 58(2): 184-194.* "The present experiment tests a modified version of Hobbes' superiority theory of humor in relation to identification classes—i.e., a *vicarious superiority* theory of humor. 'Joke content' concerns the sit-in which occurred in the Theology Department at the University of Windsor in February, 1969. Samples were University of Windsor students, 25 pro-occupiers and 25 opposed. Consistent with prediction each group found that permutation of jokes funnier in which its positive identification class was victorious and its negative the butt rather than the opposite permutation. Reasons for preferring the identification classes construct to that of reference group are discussed."   J

2809. Lambert, Ronald D. CANADIAN NATIONALISM IN ONTARIO: A REVIEW OF TWO ONTARIO GOVERNMENT INQUIRIES. *Can. Rev. of Sociol. and Anthrop. [Canada] 1977 14(3): 347-352.* Review article prompted by the publications of the Ontario Royal Commission on Book Publishing and the Select Committee on Economic and Cultural Nationalism of the Legislative Assembly of the Province of Ontario. The Royal Commission concluded that publication of books of a specifically Canadian character depends upon the continued existence of major Canadian-owned publishing houses alongside the American-owned subsidiaries. The Select Committee enumerated disadvantages to Canadians arising from the prominence of American-owned subsidiaries in the Canadian economy generally. The American economic and cultural presence in Canada is a "persistent background concern" for Canadians, yet there is wide disagreement on the extent to which Canada's internal policies should reflect nationalist priorities. 4 notes.
          L. W. Van Wyk

2810. Landon, Fred. BY CANOE TO LAKE SUPERIOR IN 1838. *Inland Seas 1973 29(1): 33-36, 45-46.* Wesleyan Methodist missionary James Evans (1801-46) traveled from Port Sarnia, Ontario, to his new post at Michipicoten River, Ontario. Mentions his comments on his station.   K. J. Bauer

2811. LeDuc, Lawrence, Jr. and White, Walter L. THE ROLE OF OPPOSITION IN A ONE-PARTY DOMINANT SYSTEM: THE CASE OF ONTARIO. *Can. J. of Pol. Sci. 1974 7(1): 86-100.* Notes the prevalence historically of one-party dominance in Canadian provincial politics. Through questionnaires and interviews of members of the Ontario legislature shows that a particular pattern of opposition behavior is partly the result of this historical pattern. 14 tables, 23 notes.
          R. V. Kubicek

2812. Lee-Whiting, Brenda. THE CRAIGMONT CORUNDUM BOOM, 1900-13. *Can. Geographical J. 1975 90(4): 22-29.* Describes the mining of corundum from 1900 to 1913 in Craigmont, Ontario—the world's leading producer of corundum.   S

2813. Lee-Whiting, Brenda. ENERGY CRISIS OF 1905 RUINED OSCEOLA. *Can. Geographical J. 1976 93(2): 32-37.* Describes how a water power and dam malfunction ruined farms in Osceola, Canada, from 1902-05.

2814. Li, Peter S. THE STRATIFICATION OF ETHNIC IMMIGRANTS: THE CASE OF TORONTO. *Can. Rev. of Sociol. and Anthrop. [Canada] 1978 15(1): 31-40.* Recent developments in the study of ethnic stratification have placed a greater emphasis on differential opportunities by way of explanation, as opposed to the more traditional interpretation of motivational variations. Building on the basic stratification model of Blau and Duncan, this research seeks to evaluate the theory of differential opportunities with regard to occupational status differences among eight European immigrant groups in Toronto. It is found that a wide range of gross status differences exist among the various immigrant groups, and that inequality persists despite adjusting for intergroup differences in social origin, education, and prior achieved occupational status. To the extent that immigrants with similar qualifications are received differently in the occupational structure on the basis of ethnic origin, this study gives support to the theory of differential opportunities.   J

2815. Lochhead, Douglas. JOHN ROSS ROBERTSON, UNCOMMON PUBLISHER FOR THE COMMON READER: HIS FIRST YEARS AS A TORONTO BOOK PUBLISHER. *J. of Can. Studies [Canada] 1976 11(2): 19-26.* Comments on John Ross Robertson, publisher of the Toronto *Telegram,* as a pirate-publisher. He reprinted American titles, without consideration of copyright. He published selections deemed appropriate for the common reader. Discusses the problems involved in this kind of research. Covers 1877-90. 3 notes.
          G. E. Panting

2816. Lowe, Mick. INCO'S NICKELMANIA. *Can. Dimension [Canada] 1977 12(7): 2-8.* Discusses labor-management conflicts at Inco, Ltd., over layoffs in Sudbury, Ontario, nickel mines, 1977.

2817. Lucas, Richard. THE CONFLICT OVER PUBLIC POWER IN HAMILTON, ONTARIO, 1906-1914. *Ontario Hist. [Canada] 1976 68(4): 236-246.* Analyzes the attitudes in Hamilton to public power in the years between the formation of Ontario Hydro and the coming of Ontario Hydro power to the city. Hamilton's private power company provided cheap power to industrial users, but not to private consumers. Analyzes divisions within the Hamilton public, the influence of the power company, various pressure groups, the "blocs" on city council, etc. 41 notes.
          W. B. Whitham

2818. Lutman, John H. CONDUCTING URBAN HERITAGE SURVEYS: A CASE STUDY OF LONDON, ONTARIO. *Urban Hist. Rev. [Canada] 1977 (1): 46-54.* The Heritage Act (Ontario, 1975) empowered provincial municipalities to set up a Local Architectural Conservation Advisory Committee to recommend to its city council the designation of buildings having architectural or historical value. The author describes the organization and procedures used by the city of London in surveying that city under the terms of the Heritage Act, in the hopes of providing a model for other cities doing the same.
          C. A. Watson

2819. MacCallum, Elizabeth. CATHERINE PARR TRAILL: A NINETEENTH-CENTURY ONTARIO NATURALIST. *Beaver [Canada] 1975 306(2): 39-45.* Catherine Parr Traill married in England and emigrated to Canada with several family members in the 1830's. Until her death in 1899, she lived mostly near Peterborough. After the death of her husband she devoted most of her time to collecting botanical types and publishing. Her most notable works are *Studies of Plant Life in Canada* (1885) and *Pearls and Pebbles*. Includes family history as well as aspects of botanical research. 12 illus., map.   D. Chaput

2820. MacGillivray, Royce. NOVELISTS AND THE GLENGARRY PIONEERS. *Ontario Hist. [Canada] 1973 65(2): 61-.* Discusses eight novels about Glengarry County, Ontario. Only five writers used the early pioneers in Glengarry as subject matter in a total of eight novels. Of these, four dealt with the south of the county before 1815-16, and the rest with the north of the county in the 1860's. 9 notes.
          W. B. Whitham

2821. Marsden, Lorna; Harvey, Edward; and Charner, Ivan. FEMALE GRADUATES: THEIR OCCUPATIONAL MOBILITY AND ATTAINMENTS. *Can. Rev. of Soc. and Anthrop. 1975 12(4): 385-405.* The social mobility and occupational attainment of 1905 female arts and science graduates in Ontario are studied in comparison to those of 2137 male colleagues. The findings show that over-all fewer females experience upward occupational mobility than males. The labour market changes in the mid-sixties, which had such a positive impact on male mobility followed by a downturn at the end of the decade, affected females in a similar fashion, but for them the degree of both upward and downward impact is less dramatic. The explanation offered is in terms of occupational sex segregation. In terms of occupational attainment, the findings indicate that females reach greatest attainment when the opportunity exists for them to succeed in visible ways such as high academic performance and graduating in science. For women from a low socioeconomic background high academic performance and attending graduate school are even more important. The authors conclude that fewer tracks and a harder race emerge as the essential properties of female mobility and occupational attainment patterns. J

2822. Mays, H. J. and Manzl, H. F. LITERACY AND SOCIAL STRUCTURE IN NINETEENTH-CENTURY ONTARIO: AN EXERCISE IN HISTORICAL METHODOLOGY. *Social Hist. [Canada] 1974 7(14): 331-345.* The manuscript census has very serious limitations for students of literacy in 19th-century Canada, particularly in rural areas. Linkage of mortgage and probate records with the 1861 census in Peel County, Ontario, revealed a very significant underenumeration of illiterates by the census-takers. Inconsistencies in the census forms filled out by urban residents in three wards in Hamilton cast doubt on their accuracy as an indicator of literacy. Based on the manuscript census in the Public Archives of Canada, and mortgage and probate records in the Public Archives of Ontario; 5 tables, 33 notes. W. K. Hobson

2823. McCalla, Douglas. THE DECLINE OF HAMILTON AS A WHOLESALE CENTER. *Ontario History [Canada] 1973 65(4): 247-254.* Briefly discusses basic aspects of mid-19th century business practices, and analyzes shifts of business activity in Hamilton, Ontario, during 1840-70. Drawn from the records of Hamilton's largest wholesale house. Map, 2 tables, 16 notes, appendix. W. B. Whitham

2824. McIlwraith, Thomas F. ONTARIO'S BEAUTIFUL CREDIT RIVER VALLEY. *Can. Geographical J. [Canada] 1977 94(3): 10-19.* Discusses economic development and population growth since the 1820's.

2825. McLean, Anne. SNUFFING OUT SNUFF: FEMINISTS REACT. *Can. Dimension [Canada] 1978 12(8): 20-23.* Reviews feminist responses since 1975 to the government crackdown on prostitution-related offenses and the increase of rape in Toronto.

2826. Meakin, Alexander C. FOUR LONG AND ONE SHORT: A HISTORY OF THE GREAT LAKES TOWING COMPANY. *Inland Seas 1974 30(4): 231-241, 269.* Organized in 1899, the Great Lakes Towing Company quickly acquired most of the salvage and towing concerns on the Lakes. Illus. Article to be continued. K. J. Bauer

2827. Miller, J. R. "EQUAL RIGHTS FOR ALL": THE E.R.A. AND THE ONTARIO ELECTION OF 1890. *Ontario Hist. [Canada] 1973 65(4): 211-230.* Discusses one manifestation of Ontario reaction to Quebec legislation that seemed to breach the principle of separation of church and state. Shows that some of the motivation for the violence of this reaction to a sister-province's internal business came from unresolved Ontario problems which touched the same principle. Particular attention is paid to the "Anti-Jesuit Convention," and the Equal Rights Association which emerged from the convention. Examines the activities of the ERA in relation to provincial politics, especially the 1890 election. Concludes that the ERA had less influence than had been expected. 2 photos, 96 notes. W. B. Whitham

2828. Mitchell, Elaine Allen. FREDERICK HOUSE MASSACRE. *Beaver [Canada] 1973 303(4): 30-33.* In the winter of 1812-13, three traders and at least nine Indians were killed at Frederick House, the Hudson's Bay Company post in Ontario. Evidence pointed to an Abitibi Indian named Capascoos, but he was never apprehended and his motives in the crime were unclear. He had apparently been at the post all winter, waylaying all who came to trade. The post, never very productive, was not reopened. Illus., map. D. Chaput

2829. Morrison, K. L. THE BUSINESSMAN VOTER IN THUNDER BAY: THE CATALYST TO THE FEDERAL-PROVINCIAL VOTING SPLIT? *Can. J. of Pol. Sci. 1973 6(2): 219-229.* Businessmen support the Liberals federally and the Conservatives provincially. They see an advantage in federal power being checked by provincial opposition. This behavior among influential businessmen may account for the general public's similar voting habit. Based on results of elections in 1968 and 1971 and on answers to a questionnaire; 3 tables, 20 notes. R. V. Kubicek

2830. Morrison, W. R. "THEIR PROPER SPHERE": FEMINISM, THE FAMILY, AND CHILD CENTERED SOCIAL REFORM IN ONTARIO, 1875-1900. *Ontario Hist. [Canada] 1976 68(1): 45-64; (2): 65-74.* Part I. Argues that 19th-century feminists saw family instability resulting from social changes as something women should try to correct. Mentions variations of viewpoints among feminist groups and the attitudes of antifeminists. Both outlooks saw the home as central to women's lives but with varying degrees of emphasis. Also discusses the relationships between the women's movement and other social reform movements, especially the temperance movement. 88 notes. Part II. Discusses the National Council of Women, which originated as a means of coordinating the activities of several organizations. Looks at the activities of a selection of individual women (e.g., Mrs. Hoodless in education) and organizations (e.g., the Victorian Order of Nurses) which were seen as part of the women's movement specifically, and reformism in general. A final section attempts to set the movement in perspective. Photo, 35 notes. W. B. Whitham

2831. Neatby, Hilda. QUEEN'S COLLEGE AND THE SCOTTISH FACT. *Queen's Q. [Canada] 1973 80(1): 1-11.* Discusses the educational and religious controversies behind the founding of Queen's College in 1842. William Morris was the key figure in leading the struggle for Scottish Presbyterians' rights in Canada against the Anglican establishment. His inability to win acceptable concessions for Presbyterian participation on King's College Council led to the decision to found a separate university and thus provided the first chapter in the history of Queen's University. An adaptation of a portion of the author's forthcoming history of Queen's University. J. A. Casada

2832. Newark, Michael J. TORNADOES IN ONTARIO BEFORE 1900. *Ontario Hist. [Canada] 1977 69(4): 257-276.* Tornadoes do occur in Canada more frequently than is commonly recognized. Details some examples. In an appendix, lists, by date, Ontario tornadoes between 1 July 1792 and 7 September 1899. In each case, states location and damage, with any other available and relevant information. Mainly secondary sources; 16 notes. W. B. Whitham

2833. O'Driscoll, Dennis. DIVERGENT IMAGES OF AMERICAN AND BRITISH EDUCATION IN THE ONTARIO CATHOLIC PRESS 1851-1948. *Study Sessions: Can. Catholic Hist. Assoc. [Canada] 1976 43: 5-22.* Examines Canadian attitudes on American and British education through the images presented by the editors of a series of Catholic newspapers published in Ontario 1851-1948.

2834. Osmond, Oliver R. THE CHURCHMANSHIP OF JOHN STRACHAN. *J. of the Can. Church Hist. Soc. 1974 16(3): 46-59.* Describes the ecclesiological views of the first bishop of Toronto, John Strachan. Famed as a founder of educational institutions, Strachan was equally devoted to the defense of the Anglican position in Canada. Though born a Presbyterian, Strachan was never fully committed to its beliefs and first received communion at an Anglican church in Kingston. Greatly influenced by the High Church bishop of New York, J. H. Hobart, Strachan insisted that the Anglican Church was a branch of the universal church. He added to this view the idea that the church was independent of both Pope and king. Accusing the Roman Catholic Church of corruption, he emphasized in his own ministry the ancient practices of the church. Fundamentally a High Churchman, Strachan was broadminded and devoted to unity within his diocese. Based on primary and secondary sources; 56 notes. J. A. Kicklighter

2835. Papageorgiou, George J. and Brummell, A. C. CRUDE IN-FERENCES ON SPATIAL CONSUMER BEHAVIOR. *Ann. of the Assoc. of Am. Geographers 1975 65(1): 1-12.* Explores the current use of urban shopping centers as indicators of population center density in Ontario.   S

2836. Patterson, Nancy-Lou. ANNA WEBER HAT DAS GE-MACHT: ANNA WEBER (1814-1888)—A *FRAKTUR* PAINTER OF WATERLOO COUNTY, ONTARIO. *Mennonite Life 1975 30(4): 15-19.*

2837. Patterson, Nancy-Lou. THE IRON CROSS AND THE TREE OF LIFE: GERMAN-ALSATIAN GRAVEMARKERS IN THE WA-TERLOO REGION AND BRUCE COUNTY ROMAN CATHOLIC CEMETERIES. *Ontario Hist. [Canada] 1976 68(1): 1-16.* Gravemark-ers throw light on social values and beliefs. In the Roman Catholic districts of Ontario settled by German Alsatians iron working was an art and iron gravemarkers are characteristic examples of this skill. Discusses the distribution and location of iron gravemarkers in these areas and analyzes the basic characteristics and variations in the design of markers and associated appendages. 8 illus., 55 notes.   W. B. Whitham

2838. Paupst, Kathy. A NOTE ON ANTI-CHINESE SENTIMENT IN TORONTO. *Can. Ethnic Studies [Canada] 1977 9(1): 54-59.* Anti-Chinese prejudice is usually associated with British Columbia, but Toronto, which lacked a large Chinese community, also feared and hated the "yellow peril." Before World War I journals such as *Jack Canuck* repeatedly hammered out racial hatred and stereotyped Orientals as de-ceitful, seductive, and morally degraded.   K. S. McDorman

2839. Pennefather, R. S. THE ORANGE ORDER AND THE UNITED FARMERS OF ONTARIO, 1919-1923. *Ontario Hist. [Can-ada] 1977 69(3): 169-184.* Discusses the attitudes of the Orange Order, and the United Farmers of Ontario toward the Ontario election of 1920. Issues were the "Keep Ontario British" campaign, and "Regulation 17", as well as the role of Orangemen in the legislature. Mentions the Orange attitude to the Federal Conservative party and their policies. Concludes that in the 1924 election, which saw the United Farmers (who had won in 1920) badly defeated, Orangeism and the Orange Order had some influence, but the extent is debatable. 73 notes.   W. B. Whitham

2840. Petroff, Lillian. MACEDONIANS: FROM VILLAGE TO CITY. *Can. Ethnic Studies [Canada] 1977 9(1): 29-41.* Because they believed that Slavic peoples were inferior immigrants, Canadian Protes-tants, educators, and health officials urged major programs of Canadiza-tion upon the Macedonian community in Toronto's East End. Though aided by elementary language education and nursing services, most of Toronto's first-generation Macedonian population refused to adopt Prot-estantism or surrender their unique traditions. By World War I second-generation Macedonian Canadians had begun to accept their adopted country's culture. Despite some assimilation a distinct ethnic community remains.   K. S. McDorman

2841. Petroff, Lillian. MACEDONIANS IN TORONTO: FROM ENCAMPMENT TO SETTLEMENT. *Urban Hist. Rev. [Canada] 1978 78(2): 58-73.* Before 1914 most Macedonians in Toronto felt they were migrants expecting to return home after earning sufficient money. Conditions in Europe after 1918 led them to decide to settle permanently in Canada. The men, who normally lived in boardinghouses, then tended to marry and set up their own homes, often in slums. Bad conditions were knowingly tolerated in order to live cheaply to save to improve living conditions later. Owning a private home, however, was not quite as important a goal for Macedonians as it was for other immigrant groups: they apparently preferred to invest in commercial enterprises. Interviews, official reports, and secondary sources; 2 illus., map, 50 notes.
C. A. Watson

2842. Phelan, Josephine. A DUEL ON THE ISLAND. *Ontario Hist. [Canada] 1977 69(4): 235-238.* Describes and analyzes the back-ground to and causes of a duel in 1812 between John McDonnell, acting Attorney-General for Upper Canada, and William Warren Baldwin, a local lawyer and doctor. Both men deliberately fired wide. Mainly pri-mary sources; 6 notes.   W. B. Whitham

2843. Phelan, Josephine. THE TAR AND FEATHER CASE, GORE ASSIZES, AUGUST 1827. *Ontario Hist. [Canada] 1976 68(1): 17-23.* In 1826, George Rolph, brother of John Rolph, the prominent reformer, was assaulted and tarred and feathered, allegedly as a punish-ment for adultery. The case came to trial in 1827. Among the defendants were politically prominent opponents of John Rolph. The damages awarded were inadequate in the eyes of the plaintiff, and he appealed. The appeal became entangled in provincial as well as local politics. Outlines the legal controversy, the press reactions, and the court hearings. 26 notes, biblio.   W. B. Whitham

2844. Piva, Michael J. WORKERS AND TORIES: THE COL-LAPSE OF THE CONSERVATIVE PARTY IN URBAN ONTARIO, 1908-1919. *Urban Hist. Rev. [Canada] 1976 (3): 23-39.* Examines the Canadian election of 1919 with regard to the major losses by Conservative Party candidates in southern Ontario urban areas as compared with the prewar elections of 1908, 1911, and 1914. The analysis shows that class was more important in determining voting patterns than either ethnicity or religion and that the class patterns of voting in 1919 represent a culmination of prewar social and political trends rather than an aberra-tion in working class voting behavior. Based on papers in the Public Archives of Canada and on secondary sources; 2 tables, 20 notes.
C. A. Watson

2845. Polyzoi, Eleoussa. THE GREEK COMMUNAL SCHOOL AND CULTURAL SURVIVAL IN PRE-WAR TORONTO. *Urban Hist. Rev. [Canada] 1978 78(2): 74-94.* Communal language schools, often ignored by historians, were established to maintain an immigrant group's cultural heritage. Toronto had a growing Greek population in the early decades of this century concerned that their children retain their ethnic and religious heritage. After one Greek school was founded and failed in the early 1920's, a permanent After-Four school was established in 1926. It grew in numbers and received strong parental and community support. The school was successful in helping Greek immigrants become an ethnic group although some former students remembered resentment at extra hours spent in school. Interviews, census reports, and secondary sources; 5 illus., diagram, 53 notes.   C. A. Watson

2846. Pomfret, Richard. THE MECHANIZATION OF REAPING IN NINETEENTH-CENTURY ONTARIO: A CASE STUDY OF THE PACE AND CAUSES OF THE DIFFUSION OF EMBODIED TECHNICAL CHANGE. *J. of Econ. Hist. 1976 36(2): 399-415.* This paper aims to provide an economic explanation of the pace and causes of the diffusion of the mechanical reaper in Ontario, 1850-1870. The analysis is based on Paul David's diffusion model, extended by the introduction of the size distribution of farms. The model is able to capture the reaper's S-shaped diffusion path. The major explanatory variable is improvements in reaper design, followed in importance by increased scale of operations and changes in factor prices. A third finding is that the effect of change in one of the three explanatory variables depends on the level of the other variables.   J

2847. Price, Brian J. THE ARCHIVES OF THE ARCHDIOCESE OF KINGSTON. *Study Sessions: Can. Catholic Hist. Assoc. 1973 40: 21-26.* Describes material in Kingston archives, including information on bishops of the Archdiocese of Kingston, beginning with Alexander Mac-donell (1760?-1840).   S

2848. Pugh, Donald E. ONTARIO'S GREAT CLAY BELT HOAX. *Can. Geographical J. 1975 90(1): 19-24.* Attributes the rapid and badly planned settlement of northern Ontario's Great Clay Belt between 1900 and 1931 to distorted and exaggerated colonization literature.   S

2849. Ramcharan, Subhas. THE ECONOMIC ADAPTATION OF WEST INDIANS IN TORONTO, CANADA. *Can. Rev. of Soc. and Anthrop. 1976 13(3): 295-304.* This study analyses the economic adapta-tion of West Indian immigrants in Metropolitan Toronto. Two hundred and ninety heads of household were interviewed during the summer of 1972. The experiences of migrants in the economic system differed consid-erably, with the major explanatory variables appearing to be occupational status and length of residence in Canada. Highly educated, white-collar workers were less likely to be have suffered initial status dislocation and more likely to report a fulfillment of their aspirations and a high satisfac-tion with their new society than blue collar workers. Skin colour gradations within the West Indian group did not prove to be a variable causing differing experiences in the economic system, although comparisons between West Indians and white immigrant groups with similar educational levels and length of residence, suggest that the incidence of discrimination in employment is higher for West Indians.   J

2850. Reaburn, Ronald and Reaburn, Pauline. LIME KILNS—REMAINS OF PIONEER TECHNOLOGY. *Can. Geographical J. 1973 86(1): 14-17.*

2851. Rhodes, J. NEW LIFE FOR A TIRED SYSTEM—THE PRISON LIBRARY. *Can. Lib. J. 1973 30(3): 246-249.* At Collins Bay Penitentiary in Kingston, Ontario, an expanded library helped in resocialization of inmates.   S

2852. Roberts, Terry. THE INFLUENCE OF THE BRITISH UPPER CLASS ON THE DEVELOPMENT OF THE VALUE CLAIM FOR SPORT IN THE PUBLIC EDUCATION SYSTEM OF UPPER CANADA FROM 1830 TO 1875. *Can. J. of Hist. of Sport and Physical Educ. 1973 4(1): 27-47.* The British upper-class elite, educated in public schools, had the means necessary to inculcate the idea that team sports build Christian character into the educational system of Upper Canada. There is little evidence of this belief 1830-75, although its existence at that time has been suggested by several writers. Similarly there is no strong evidence of the transmission of this value claim by normal schools, the Council of Public Instruction, or teachers. Sport was probably little used for educational purposes until after 1875. Based on primary and secondary sources, principally the *Journal of Education for Upper Canada;* 48 notes.   R. A. Smith

2853. Romney, Paul. THE ORDEAL OF WILLIAM HIGGINS. *Ontario Hist. [Canada] 1975 67(2): 69-89.* Discusses the removal and imprisonment in 1834 of William Higgins, Toronto's first High Bailiff, whose downfall illustrates the often sordid nature of Upper Canadian politics at that time.

2854. Romney, Paul. WILLIAM LYON MACKENZIE AS MAYOR OF TORONTO. *Can. Hist. R. 1975 56(4) 416-436.* Reviews data relating to Mackenzie's mayoralty. Criticizes Frederick H. Armstrong's disparaging account of it in *Canadian Historical Review* 1967 48 [see abstract 5:1288], and his conclusions as to Mackenzie's personality and historical importance. Mackenzie was not the arbitrary, corrupt and incompetent executive depicted by Armstrong. Rather, he was an honest, hard-working and reasonably effective mayor. Based on municipal records and contemporary newspapers.   A

2855. Rubin, Don. THEATRE HISTORY AND ORAL HISTORY. *Can. Oral Hist. Assoc. J. [Canada] 1976/77 2: 46-48.* Discusses oral history techniques for theater history; details the Ontario Historical Studies Series Oral History Project, 1973-75.

2856. Sainsbury, George V. RE-ROUTING THE HISTORIC WELLAND CANAL. *Can. Geographical J. 1974 89(3): 36-43.* Describes the relocation of the Welland Canal lying between Port Robinson and Ramsey's Bend, Ontario.   S

2857. St. John, Edward S. THE IMAGE OF THE FRENCH CANADIAN IN GLENGARRY LITERATURE. *Ontario Hist. [Canada] 1973 65(2): 69-80.* The image of French Canadians in Glengarry County novels usually is basically negative. Details the major exception. Primary and secondary sources; 52 notes.   W. B. Whitham

2858. Scollard, Robert J. REVEREND WILLIAM RICHARD HARRIS, 1846-1923. *Study Sessions [Canada] 1974 41: 65-80.* Gives a biography of William Richard Harris, priest of the Archdiocese of Toronto. A paper read at the 1974 annual meeting of the Canadian Catholic Historical Association.   S

2859. Scollie, F. Brent. EVERY SCRAP OF PAPER: ACCESS TO ONTARIO'S MUNICIPAL RECORDS. *Can. Lib. J. 1974 31(1): 8-10, 11-16.* Gives guidelines for making Ontario's public records more accessible to historians, librarians, and city planners.   S

2860. Sheffield, Edward F. *THE LEARNING SOCIETY:* AN OVERSTATEMENT. *Queen's Q. [Canada] 1973 80(3): 434-449.* A review article of *The Learning Society* (Toronto: Ministry of Government Services, 1972), a report by the Commission on Post-Secondary Education in Ontario. Reviews the situation which led to the creation of the commission in 1967, outlines the commission's tasks, and describes and evaluates the essence of its report. The author concludes that the commission's work was only partially successful. 11 notes.   J. A. Casada

2861. Sibert, C. Thomas. ARCHITECTURAL ACCURACY AND THE ARTISTS. *Inland Seas 1974 30(2): 95-109, 115.* Identifies and discusses accurate portraits of ships on the Great Lakes painted by Charles W. Norton (1848-1901), Vincent D. Nickerson (1844-99), Howard F. Sprague (1871-99), and Seth A. Whipple (1855-1901). All four produced careful and accurate likenesses of their subjects. Based on newspapers, directories, and local histories; illus., 25 notes.
                                                                    K. J. Bauer

2862. Smith, Michael D. THE LEGITIMATION OF VIOLENCE: HOCKEY PLAYERS' PERCEPTIONS OF THEIR REFERENCE GROUPS' SANCTIONS FOR ASSAULT. *Can. R. of Sociol. and Anthrop. 1975 12(1): 72-80.* Interviews with Toronto high school hockey players yielded data pertaining to players' perceptions of their normative reference groups' sanctions for assault. Results indicated that although players viewed each reference group's sanctions as somewhat distinctive, there was approval of a variety of assaultive behaviors. Factor analysis revealed that the sanctions of 1) father, 2) mother, 3) nonplaying peers, and 4) teammates and coach formed independent conceptual dimensions. In light of the concept of legitimation, much of the violence in sport, as in other social spheres, is not aberrant, but rather is socially acquired normative conduct.   J

2863. Spencer, Stephen. THE GOOD QUEEN OF HOGS: TORONTO, 1850-1914. *Urban Hist. Rev. [Canada] 1975 75(1): 38-42.* Discusses the economic and governmental growth of Toronto, Ontario, concentrating on Toronto's image as a center of manufacturing, culture, and "righteousness"; one of eight articles in this issue on the Canadian city in the 19th century.

2864. Stamp, Robert M. EMPIRE DAY IN THE SCHOOLS OF ONTARIO: THE TRAINING OF YOUNG IMPERIALISTS. *J. of Can. Studies 1973 8(3): 32-42.* Discusses Empire Day celebrations, 1890-1930's, as an expression of nationalism as well as British imperialism.

2865. Stamp, Robert M. SCHOOLS ON WHEELS: THE RAILWAY CAR SCHOOLS OF NORTHERN ONTARIO. *Can.: An Hist. Mag. 1974 1(3): 34-42.*

2866. Stevens, Neil. THE SOLUTION? WIPE OUT THE TOWN, NOT THE POLLUTION. *Can. Dimension 1974 10(5): 10-12.* In the Falconbridge-Sudbury area (Happy Valley) of Ontario, people are being relocated with government aid to escape pollution.   S

2867. Stieb, Ernst W. PHARMACEUTICAL EDUCATION IN ONTARIO: I. PRELUDE AND BEGINNINGS (THE SHUTTLEWORTH ERA). *Pharmacy in Hist. 1974 16(2): 64-71.* Discusses the development of pharmaceutical education in Ontario, Canada, 1868-92, emphasizing the contributions of Edward Buckingham Shuttleworth.

2868. Stiff, John. SILVER ISLET: CURSED BONANZA. *Can. Geographical J. 1973 87(2): 14-19.* A silver mining operation in the late 19th century.   S

2869. Struthers, J. R. ALICE MUNRO AND THE AMERICAN SOUTH. *Can. R. of Am. Studies 1975 6(2): 196-204.* Analyzes the works of Alice Munro, a Canadian writer of fiction. She was most influenced by early 20th century literary and historical suppositions about the nature and character of white society in the American South. She believed that many of the values, biases, and cultural peculiarities of the American South flourished in the rural sections of Ontario. Based on Munro's writings and secondary sources; 42 notes.   H. T. Lovin

2870. Sturino, Franc. A CASE STUDY OF A SOUTH ITALIAN FAMILY IN TORONTO, 1935-60. *Urban Hist. Rev. [Canada] 1978 78(2): 38-57.* City directories are used to trace the occupational and residential history of one immigrant family. Part of a larger research project, the history of this one family seems typical. The family was upwardly mobile in residence, moving from a working-class to a middle-class district, and in occupation, the sons moving from factory to white collar jobs. Many of the upward moves were a result of aid given because of kinship ties. Interviews, city directories, and secondary sources; illus., 2 tables, fig., 18 notes.   C. A. Watson

2871. Tandon, B. B. EARNING DIFFERENTIALS AMONG NATIVE BORN AND FOREIGN BORN RESIDENTS OF TORONTO. *Int. Migration Rev. 1978 12(3): 406-410.* Immigrants entering the Canadian labor market start with lower earnings than native born residents, but their earnings equalize within a period of five years.

2872. Taylor, John. OTTAWA: THE CITY AS CONGLOMERATE. *Urban Hist. Rev. [Canada] 1975 75(1): 36-37.* The physical, economic, and political growth of Ottawa, Ontario, during the 19th century resembled that of a geological conglomerate more than that of a biological organism; one of eight articles in this issue on the Canadian city in the 19th century.

2873. Thoman, Richard S. A CHECKLIST FOR CALIFORNIA. *Cry California 1974 9(4): 13-17.* Argues the need for comprehensive regional planning in California, and presents Ontario, Canada's *Design for Development* (1966) as a key example.   S

2874. Thure, Karen. MARTHA HARPER PIONEERED IN THE HAIR BUSINESS. *Smithsonian 1976 7(6): 94-100.* Discusses the beauty shop run by Martha Matilda Harper in Oakville, Ontario, 1857-93 and the school of hair care which bloomed around her, gaining immediate popularity and extending to the present.

2875. Tomasi, Lydio F. THE ITALIAN COMMUNITY IN TORONTO: A DEMOGRAPHIC PROFILE. *Int. Migration Rev. 1977 11(4): 486-513.* Examines Italian immigration during 1946-72; Italian Canadians are a cohesive, socially active group in Toronto.

2876. Trimble, Paul E. INCONCEIVABLE COMMERCE. *Inland Seas 1974 30(3): 168-177.* Winter use of the Great Lakes to move bulk cargo was unthinkable 20 years ago. Improvement of navigation and port facilities, changes in cargo, better weather forecasting, and improvements in icebreaking make a longer navigation season feasible.   K. J. Bauer

2877. Troper, Harold. IMAGES OF THE "FOREIGNER" IN TORONTO, 1900-1930: A REPORT. *Urban Hist. Rev. [Canada] 1975 (2): 1-8.* Describes a 1974 archival project to assemble photographs of early immigrants in Ontario, 1900-30.

2878. Turner, C. Frank. CUSTER AND THE CANADIAN CONNECTIONS. *Beaver [Canada] 1976 307(1): 4-11.* Gives a biographical sketch of Lt. (Bvt. Lt.-Col.) Willie Cooke, Custer's adjutant at the Battle of the Little Big Horn. Cooke, son of socially prominent parents of Hamilton, Ontario, had served with Union forces in the Civil War. He became a close friend to the George A. Custer family, and in 1869 induced the general to visit with his family in Hamilton. Also discusses the 16 Canadians with the Custer expedition. Analyzes the impact of Sitting Bull and the Sioux band that fled to Saskatchewan after the Little Big Horn. 11 illus.   D. Chaput

2879. Turner, Wesley B. MISS RYE'S CHILDREN *Ontario Hist. [Canada] 1976 68(3): 169-203.* Discusses the attitudes of the press toward the immigration of more or less officially sponsored British pauper children into Ontario, following the publication in Great Britain of a highly critical report on such immigration. This began in 1869 with the work of a Miss Rye; discusses her life and activities. In general, the Ontario press favored ths movement. 89 notes.   W. B. Whitham

2880. Wadley, W. THE DIOCESE OF ALGOMA—1873-1973. *J. of the Can. Church Hist. Soc. 1973 15(3): 68-70.* The diocese of Algoma is observing its 100th anniversary as a missionary diocese separated from the diocese of Toronto. Unlike similar dioceses, Algoma was not self-sustaining. It depended for financial support on missionary organizations such as the English Church's Society for the Propagation of the Gospel in Foreign Parts, and on the collective dioceses of the Ecclesiastical Province of Canada. The diocese, covering 70,000 square miles but with only 100,000 communicants, posed a tremendous challenge for the eight original clergy. Summarizes the careers of Algoma's six bishops: Frederick Dawson Fauquier (1873-1881), Edward Sullivan (1882-1896). George Thorneloe (1897-1926), Rocksborough Remington Smith (1927-1939), George Frederick Kingston (1940-1943) and William Lockridge Wright (1944-). In 1955 the diocese became self-supporting.
                          J. A. Kicklighter

2881. Walker, Gerald. HOW HOLLAND MARSH COMMUNITY DEVELOPED. *Can. Geographical J. 1976 93(1): 42-49.* Discusses the settlement of Holland Marsh by foreign ethnic groups, 1930's-76, which remains one of the true rural settlements in southern Ontario.

2882. Warwick, Peter. PIONEER SHIPBUILDER OF THE GREAT LAKES. *Can. Geographical J. [Canada] 1978 96(3): 26-29.* Discusses the career in shipbuilding, 1835-80, of Louis Shickluna, whose yards at St. Catharines, Ontario, produced some 130 ships.

2883. Weaver, John C. FROM LAND ASSEMBLY TO SOCIAL MATURITY: THE SUBURBAN LIFE OF WESTDALE (HAMILTON), ONTARIO, 1911-1951. *Social Hist. [Canada] 1978 11(22): 411-440.* Studies Westdale (begun in 1911) as a Canadian measure of 20th-century urban trends. It started as a 100-acre residential development, then expanded to 800 acres. Like many suburbs, new transportation links made it possible. World War I and postwar problems prevented half of its approximately 1,700 lots from being developed until 1931. Westdale by design was overwhelmingly Protestant at first, although restrictive covenants did not prohibit native-born Catholics or Jews. By 1951 racial aspects of restrictive covenants were eliminated, and the area had become more diversified. 3 illus., 11 tables, 60 notes.   D. F. Chard

2884. Weaver, John C. THE MEANING OF MUNICIPAL REFORM: TORONTO, 1895. *Ontario Hist. [Canada] 1974 66(2): 89-100.* Analyzes in detail the background to and shift from the municipal government of Toronto "by Council to that by Council and an Executive branch." The shift occurred during a depression, following exposure of serious corruption and graft in the Council. Additional exposure of financially powerful businesses and other pressure groups influencing city government to their own advantage also aided the reform movement. The final influence came from a major public health scare, stimulating sufficient public pressure to push reforms through. Briefly comments on the character and biographic data of some of the major figures involved. The role of the press is also analyzed. 67 notes.   W. B. Whitham

2885. Weaver, John C. ORDER AND EFFICIENCY: SAMUEL MORLEY WICKETT AND THE URBAN PROGRESSIVE MOVEMENT IN TORONTO, 1900-1915. *Ontario Hist. [Canada] 1977 69(4): 218-234.* Wickett represented the strand of urban progressivism which pressed for professionalization of urban government through the city management approach. His father had been an alderman in Toronto, on a reform ticket, in the late 19th century. Wickett's studies at University of Toronto, and postgraduate work in Vienna and then several German centers, exposed him to other influences. He returned to teach political economy at the University of Toronto for years, with time out for the family business. Details his life and services to the city government, both before and after his election as alderman in 1913. Examines his economic ideas and sets them in a broader context than local politics and interests. He died in 1915 of a heart attack, some of his work unfinished. Mainly primary sources; 92 notes.   W. B. Whitham

2886. Welch, Edwin. THE CITY OF OTTAWA ARCHIVES. *Urban Hist. Rev. [Canada] 1976 76(1): 10-13.* The author, Ottawa city archivist, describes the status of the records of Canada's capital city. Archives have not been well maintained nor have records been available for study. Other organizations such as the Public Archives of Canada, the Provincial Archives of Ontario, and local societies hold various records concerned with Ottawa history. A professional archivist was first appointed in 1975 and a start has been made on organizing and cataloging the records. Because of the conditions of some records and lack of study space, visits are by appointment only.   C. A. Watson

2887. Weller, G. R. HINTERLAND POLITICS: THE CASE OF NORTHWESTERN ONTARIO. *Can. J. of Pol. Sci. [Canada] 1977 10(4): 727-754.* Subprovincial regions of Canada have been little analyzed. This article argues that the region, so dependent upon outside forces, features politics characterized by frustration and parochialism. Map, fig., 47 notes.   R. V. Kubicek

2888. Williamson, Eileen. BUSH WIFE. *Beaver [Canada] 1975 306(3): 40-45.* In 1932, the author and her family flew to Casummit Lake in northern Ontario where the family had discovered gold. Discusses the weather, living conditions, food, and camp personnel, which consisted mostly of Swedes and Irishmen. Improvements were made at the mine in 1932, and the company, bought out by Jason Gold Mines, continued in operation until 1952. 5 illus., map.   D. Chaput

2889. Winn, Conrad and McMenemy, John. POLITICAL ALIGNMENT IN A POLARIZED CITY: ELECTORAL CLEAVAGES IN KITCHENER, ONTARIO. *Can. J. of Pol. Sci. 1973 6(2): 230-242.* Examines characteristics and sources of support for or rejection of redevelopment of Kitchener's downtown core through an analysis of municipal and provincial elections during 1967-71. Finds that the electorate was polarized on a left-right axis for which there was ample historical precedent. 4 tables, 33 notes, appendix.   R. V. Kubicek

2890. Winn, Conrad and Twiss, James. THE SPATIAL ANALYSIS OF POLITICAL CLEAVAGES AND THE CASE OF THE ONTARIO LEGISLATURE. *Can. J. of Pol. Sci. [Canada] 1977 10(2): 287-310.* Evaluates alternative spatial models used in the study of the party systems of Canada and Ontario, 1957-74. "A factor analysis of the attitudes of Ontario legislators yielded cultural, left right, Babbittry, ethnocentrism, and collectivism in descending order of importance." 2 figs., 5 tables, 51 notes.   R. V. Kubicek

2891. Wollock, Jeffrey. DID STINSON JARVIS HYPNOTIZE "KIT OF THE MAIL?" *Ontario Hist. [Canada] 1975 67(4): 241-245.* Suggests a relationship between Kathleen Watkins ("Kit of the Mail"), the newspaperwoman, and Stinson Jarvis, the novelist. Argues that this relationship grew from a mutual interest, typical of the time and place, in psychic phenomena and especially hypnotic ones. From this, speculates on the extent and nature of the link between them. Based on primary sources; 20 notes.   W. B. Whitham

2892. Zerker, Sally. THE DEVELOPMENT OF COLLECTIVE BARGAINING IN THE TORONTO PRINTING INDUSTRY IN THE NINETEENTH CENTURY. *Industrial Relations [Canada] 1975 30(1): 83-97.* Analysts of collective bargaining have tended to stress predominant functional characteristics, in general classed as marketing, governmental, and managerial theories. Less emphasis has been placed on the importance of power relationships between organizations. A careful review of the development of collective bargaining in the Toronto printing industry in the 19th century suggests that the latter is the most significant factor in the historical process.   J

2893. Zerker, Sally. GEORGE BROWN AND THE PRINTERS UNION. *J. of Can. Studies 1975 10(1): 42-48.* George Brown (1818-80), publisher of the Toronto *Globe*, fought the typographical union consistently from 1843-72. He paid union wages not because of liberal commitment, but only when the relative power of the union forced him to do so. He also formed an association that interfered with each employer's freedom to make a contract with the workers. Based on records of the Toronto Typographical Union, newspapers, and secondary sources; table, 53 notes.   G. E. Panting

2894. —. A PARISH BORN IN THE GREAT DEPRESSION. *Jednota Ann. Furdek 1977 16: 101-106.* Catholic Slovak Canadians founded Saints Cyril and Methodius Parish in Toronto, Ontario, in 1934; a church was completed in 1941.

2895. —. A SHORT HISTORY OF THE SLOVAK CATHOLICS OF THE BYZANTINE PARISH OF THE ASSUMPTION OF THE B.V.M. *Jednota Ann. Furdek 1977 16: 207-209.* This Uniate parish in Hamilton, Ontario, was founded in 1952, and in 1963 the Shrine of Our Lady of Klococov was dedicated there; Father Francis J. Fuga has been pastor since 1954.

The Western Provinces

General

2896. Baer, Hans A. THE EFFECT OF TECHNOLOGICAL INNOVATION ON HUTTERITE CULTURE. *Plains Anthropologist 1976 21(73, pt. 1): 187-198.* The Hutterites of North America are often envied by their rural neighbors as being efficient and productive agriculturalists who combine twentieth century technology with a life style reminiscent of an earlier age. A closer examination of Hutterite culture reveals that a tension exists between these two elements.   J

2897. Baudoux, Maurice. LES FRANCO-CANADIENS DE L'OUEST: CONSTITUTIFS D'UNE SOCIÉTÉ FRANCOPHONE CANADIENNE [The French Canadians in the West: Elements of a French-speaking Canadian society]. *Tr. of the Royal Soc. of Can. 1975 13: 141-149.* "The West" consists of both the coast and the prairies, the latter being the object of this article. Several generations of French Canadians have now lived in this area. Gradually they are declining in number as younger generations assimilate into English-speaking Canada. Schools and universities are predominantly English-speaking, as are radio and television. In intercultural marriages the children frequently speak only English. The French Canadians in the prairies are separated from Quebec both geographically and psychologically, the result being more assimilation.   J. D. Neville

2898. Becker, A. THE GERMANS IN WESTERN CANADA. *Study Sessions: Can. Catholic Hist. Assoc. 1975 42: 29-49.* A history of the oldest and largest German settlements of western Canada, ca. 1891-1931, using modern census figures on population and ethnic division, which appear inaccurate due to inadequate wording of questions and coverups by German descendants during the racially tense atmosphere of World War I.

2899. Bercuson, David Jay. LABOUR RADICALISM AND THE WESTERN INDUSTRIAL FRONTIER: 1897-1919. *Can. Hist. Rev. [Canada] 1977 58(2): 154-175.* The frontier has been called the great leveller, but the industrial frontier in Canada was the main stimulus in the development of class consciousness and radical working-class attitudes in the Canadian west.

2900. Bercuson, David J. RECENT DEVELOPMENTS IN PRAIRIE HISTORIOGRAPHY. *Acadiensis [Canada] 1974 4(1): 138-148.* Details the revision of Canadian prairie provinces' historiography. New interpretations include the following: 1) there was little difference between Social Credit in Alberta and the Cooperative Commonwealth Federation in Saskatchewan; 2) the French role in western settlement was neither very aggressive, nor antagonistic; 3) the Northwest Mounted Police did little for the Indians; and 4) mistreatment of western Indians resulted from the actions of local officials as well as from national policies. Notes that radical unionism and urbanization in the West are finally being seriously studied. Secondary sources; 19 notes.   E. A. Churchill

2901. Bicha, Karel D. PRAIRIE RADICALS: A COMMON PIETISM. *J. of Church and State 1976 18(1): 79-94.* The "Prairie Radicals" were the activists in the plains area of the United States and Canada following the end of the populist movement. There men had no real common ideological ties. Some were leftist, some rightist, some poor, some wealthy. Argues that pietism was the common tie. There was a prominence of ministerial personnel among the radicals. Their values were pietistic. Most were Baptist, Methodist, Disciples of Christ or Pietistic Lutheran. The influence of their religious origins is analyzed in detail, showing the close similarities of each case. 59 notes.

E. E. Eminhizer

2902. Breen, D. H. THE CANADIAN PRAIRIE WEST AND THE "HARMONIOUS" SETTLEMENT INTERPRETATION. *Agric. Hist. 1973 47(1): 63-75.* Conflict between ranchers and farmers on the southwestern Canadian prairie during the 1880's and 1890's was similar to that between their American counterparts, although armed violence did not occur. Canadian scholars have overlooked these conflicts, assuming that the Canadian prairie was a homogeneous region and failing to note subregional variation. Discusses the land policy of the Canadian government and the role played by big ranching companies. Based on Canadian archives and newspapers; 40 notes. D. E. Brewster

2903. Casterline, Gail Farr, comp. SOURCES AND LITERATURE FOR WESTERN AMERICAN HISTORY: A LIST OF DISSERTATIONS. *Western Hist. Q. 1974 5(3): 319-334.* List of dissertations selected from *Dissertation Abstracts,* volumes 33 and 34, covering the 1973 calendar year. Includes author, title, institution, date, and an occasional annotation. Classified under 19 headings for the American and Canadian West. D. L. Smith

2904. Chalmers, John W. DAVID J. GOGGIN, PROTOTYPE PEDAGOGUE. *Saskatchewan Hist. [Canada] 1974 27(2): 66-72.* The early educational pattern in Manitoba and the Northwest Territories was based on that of Quebec. By 1890, a change toward the Ontario model brought a great need for teachers, curricula revision, training for teaching, inspection of teaching, and testing of learning. The man hired to do all these things was David James Goggin. Portrait, 8 notes. C. Held

2905. Chapman, Terry L. DRUG USE IN WESTERN CANADA. *Alberta Hist. [Canada] 1976 24(4): 18-27.* Analyzes the extent of use and addiction to drugs in western Canada in the late 19th century. Especially widespread were opium and morphine, usually granted without prescription for use in teething powders, asthma, fatigue, etc. Racial issues became confused, as Chinese were said to be opium addicts, yet thousands of Canadians were using opium as an additive to sherry, and were holding cocaine parties. Only in 1919 was nonmedicinal use of drugs prohibited in Canada. Based on newspaper accounts, advertisements, and government documents. 6 illus., 94 notes. D. Chaput

2906. Chapman, Terry L. EARLY EUGENICS MOVEMENT IN WESTERN CANADA. *Alberta Hist. [Canada] 1977 25(4): 9-17.* Following the impact of heavy immigration from southern and eastern Europe in the early 1900's, Canadian officials and the press began to examine the possibility of eugenics. Traces immigration history, as well as forces for control. James S. Woodsworth, prominent mission official of Winnipeg, pushed for popular acceptance of eugenics policies. Convinced that recent immigrants had more than a reasonable share of vices, the Alberta legislature in 1928 passed an Act of Sexual Sterilization, the first such law in western Canada. 61 notes. D. Chaput

2907. Choquette, Robert. PROBLÈMES DES MOEURS ET DE DISCIPLINE ECCLÉSTIASTIQUE: LES CATHOLIQUES DES PRAIRIES CANADIENNES DE 1900 À 1930 [Problem of morality and ecclesiastical discipline: Catholics of the Canadian prairies from 1900 to 1930]. *Social Hist. [Canada] 1975 8(15): 102-119.* During 1900-30 the Catholic minority (20 per cent of the population) in the Canadian prairies was split between francophone and anglophone, with the latter in the majority. Francophone clerics were more intransigent than anglophones in enforcing their authority, interpreting doctrine, and in relations with the Protestant majority on such matters as dancing, clerical dress, public schools, and mixed marriages. Adélard Langevin, archbishop of Saint-Boniface, Manitoba (1895-1915), and Monsignor Legal de Saint-Albert of Edmonton provide examples of especially intransigent francophone clerics. John Thomas McNally (1871-1952), archbishop of Calgary, 1913-1924, provides an example of a more liberal anglophone cleric. Based on Edmonton and Saint Boniface archbishopric archives and Calgary diocese archives; table, 55 notes. W. K. Hobson

2908. Clark, Peter. LEADERSHIP SUCCESSION AMONG THE HUTTERITES. *Can. Rev. of Sociol. and Anthrop. [Canada] 1977 14(3): 294-302.* Forty-two Hutterite colonies were examined in order to determine the degree to which succession to leadership positions departs from a model of complete equality of opportunity. Variation in political mobility patterns within colonies is explained by utilizing a 'demography of opportunity' hypothesis. This hypothesis posits that the degree of inequality of opportunity exhibited by a colony varies directly with the degree to which population growth (growth in the supply of potential position holders) exceeds organizational expansion (expansion in the supply of positions). J

2909. Cooke, Edgar D. PETER POND: FORGOTTEN DEVELOPER OF THE NORTH WEST. *Alberta Hist. R. 1974 22(1): 18-27.*

Biographical sketch of Peter Pond (b. 1740), North West Company fur trader, and explorer and cartographer of the Canadian West. 2 illus., 3 maps, biblio. D. L. Smith

2910. Dorge, Lionel. THE METIS AND CANADIEN COUNCILLORS OF ASSINIBOIA: PART III. *Beaver [Canada] 1974 305(3): 51-58.* Continued from a previous article. Emphasizes the 1860's as a prelude to the Riel Rebellion. The Council of Assiniboia, faced with problems of famine, peace-keeping, road building, and Sioux presence, was unable to keep pace with political changes. A key factor in their failures was the composition of the Council. Métis and Canadiens were included, but in inadequate numbers, and the men chosen were often too closely allied to the Hudson's Bay Co. The tendency to rank all "French speaking" members as a unit was fallacious, as the Metis did not always agree with Canadien policies or plans. The Council could not govern, but the Metis and Canadien members learned some of the intricacies of governing, and they were later active in municipal and provincial affairs in Manitoba. 7 illus., map. D. Chaput

2911. Dorge, Lionel. THE METIS AND THE CANADIEN COUNCILLORS OF ASSINIBOIA. *Beaver [Canada] 1974 305(1): 12-19, (2): 39-45.* Part I traces type of legislation and policies favored by the French-Métis representatives governing Assiniboia in the Northwest Territories. Part II discusses the growing influences of the French-speaking Métis population of the Red River settlement. 9 illus. D. Heermans

2912. Erideres, James S. ATTITUDE AND BEHAVIOUR: PREJUDICE IN WESTERN CANADA. *Patterns of Prejudice [Great Britain] 1973 7(1): 17-22.* Summarizes research on Canadian anti-Semitism to the early 1960's and explores continued anti-Semitism, and its causes and its study. Active anti-Semitism continues in Canada; a large percentage of Canadians have strong anti-Semitic attitudes. Based on secondary sources and a study of 315 randomly selected households in an urban location; 2 tables, 36 notes. G. O. Gagnon

2913. Fee, Art. STEAM TRACTORS: MONSTERS THAT CHANGED THE WEST. *Am. West 1973 10(3): 24-31.* The heyday of steam tractors on the Great Plains of Canada and the United States was 1890-1925. The larger models weighed as much as 30 tons and could pull more than 20 plows. Steam tractors were used all over Canada and the United States. They were also intimately involved in other enterprises such as Death Valley ore, northwest lumber, freighting on the Canadian tundra, Caribou gold operations, and road construction. Case, Reeves, Garr Scott, Rumely, Avery, and Best are all familiar names to today's steam tractor enthusiasts. 13 illus. D. L. Smith

2914. Fidler, Vera. CYPRESS HILLS: PLATEAU OF THE PRAIRIE. *Can. Geographical J. 1973 87(3): 28-35.*

2915. Frideres, J. S. and Goldenberg, Sheldon. HYPHENATED CANADIANS: COMPARATIVE ANALYSIS OF ETHNIC, REGIONAL AND NATIONAL IDENTIFICATION OF WESTERN CANADIAN UNIVERSITY STUDENTS. *J. of Ethnic Studies 1977 5(2): 91-100.* Notes the problematic nature of the concept of identity and its systematic relationship to other structural and contextual features. Relates this to the upsurge of interest in ethnic identity in Canada in recent years and the official policy of multiculturalism. Urges social scientists to pay greater attention to these phenomena. Reports the results of a questionnaire survey of 213 native born and naturalized Canadian students as to their levels of ethnic, regional, and national identity consciousness. Results display high national identification, slightly lower regional identity, and very low ethnic identity. Possible social and psychological factors such as age, sex, father's occupation, residential mobility seem to have no significant bearing on the intensity or salience patterns of the three dimensions of identity. Some sense of unified Canadian history is therefore emerging, although in the West it must compete with a high regional identity; or, perhaps, ethnic oriented youths do not attend universities. Primary sources; 2 tables, fig., 3 notes.

G. J. Bobango

2916. Friesen, Gerald. THE WESTERN CANADIAN IDENTITY. *Can. Hist. Assoc. Hist. Papers 1973: 13-19.* Regional consciousness has been used to present the role of the West in Canada's experience. Regionalism, defined as midway between the provincial and the national viewpoints, had an impact upon the Trades and Labour Council of Canada, the Methodist Church, and the two-party system. Based on periodicals and newspapers; 8 notes. G. E. Panting

2917. Friesen, Gerald. 'YOURS IN REVOLT': REGIONALISM, SOCIALISM AND THE WESTERN CANADIAN LABOUR MOVEMENT. *Labour [Canada] 1976 1: 139-157.* Two decades of worker militancy in western Canada culminated in 1919 with secessions from the American Federation of Labor and the Trades and Labour Congress of Canada, the establishment of One Big Union, and strikes from Winnipeg westward. Responsible for the formation of the regional labor organization, leaders of the Socialist Party of Canada saw in the strength of western consciousness the means to labor reform and possible revolution. Committed to constitutional means until the "day of revolution," they did not intend the strikes to inaugurate an overthrow of the government. Primary and secondary sources; 58 notes. W. A. Kearns

2918. Friesen, Victor Carl. THE RURAL PRAIRIE NOVEL AND THE GREAT DEPRESSION. *Prairie Forum [Canada] 1977 2(1): 83-96.* Agrarian fiction described rural life during the Depression in the Prairie Provinces; identifies three literary themes: treatment of political and socioeconomic background, the West as a "garden," and the psychological impact of the Depression.

2919. Gartner, Gerry J. A REVIEW OF COOPERATION AMONG THE WESTERN PROVINCES. *Can. Public Administration [Canada] 1977 20(1): 174-187.* Discusses cooperation in western Canada, 1960's-70's, in economic development.

2920. Gibbins, Roger and Ponting, J. Rick. CONTEMPORARY PRAIRIE PERCEPTIONS OF CANADA'S NATIVE PEOPLES. *Prairie Forum [Canada] 1977 2(1): 57-82.* Examines the attitudes of non-Indians in the Prairie Provinces toward Indians in Canada; differences among the provinces are based primarily on education and age and do not mitigate the support given to Indians in their changing social roles.

2921. Gibbins, Roger. MODELS OF NATIONALISM: A CASE STUDY OF POLITICAL IDEOLOGIES IN THE CANADIAN WEST. *Can. J. of Pol. Sci. [Canada] 1977 10(2): 341-373.* Uses an ethnocentric and historical model to examine nationalism. Discerns strong apolitical and politicized regional orientations. Based on personal interviews conducted in Calgary, Alberta; 11 tables, 47 notes, 2 appendixes. R. V. Kubicek

2922. Glover, R. THE MAN WHO DID NOT GO TO CALIFORNIA. *Can. Hist. Assoc. Hist. Papers [Canada] 1975: 95-112.* Joseph Burke, under-gardener to the thirteenth Earl of Derby, was sent by the Earl and the Director of the Royal Botanic Gardens at Kew to collect specimens in the Hudson's Bay Company territory. Tells of Burke's difficulties and successes, and concludes that he is a valuable informant on the mid-19th century Canadian West. Covers the period 1843-45. Primary and secondary sources; 61 notes. G. E. Panting

2923. Good, W. S. and Beckman, M. D. A PRAIRIE DISTRIBUTION SYSTEM IN TRANSITION: THE CASE OF FARM MACHINERY PARTS IN MANITOBA. *Prairie Forum [Canada] 1977 2(1): 43-56.* Examines the distribution of farm machinery parts from manufacturer to distributor, 1974; the business center is in Regina rather than Winnipeg, there is a notable decline in local dealerships, and there is a change in the way parts are transported.

2924. Hart, Edward J. THE EMPEROR'S ICE-AXE. *Alberta Hist. R. [Canada] 1974 22(3): 1-7.* Relates the adventures of a Japanese climbing party in the Canadian Rockies. S

2925. Henson, Tom M. KU KLUX KLAN IN WESTERN CANADA. *Alberta Hist. [Canada] 1977 25(4): 1-8.* The Ku Klux Klan began in British Columbia in 1921, then moved into Alberta and Saskatchewan. Primarily anti-French at first, the Klan soon advocated immigration restriction, especially of Orientals and Eastern Europeans. The Klan also became antiunion, as most of the recent immigrants were union affiliated. The Klan was influential in several local elections, but overall lasting impact of the organization in western Canada was slight. By the early 1930's, the Klan was practically dead, due to local scandals (embez-

zlement) and to effective opposition from the Communist and working-class parties. 49 notes. D. Chaput

2926. Holdsworth, Deryck and Mills, Edward. PIONEER PREFAB BANKS ON THE PRAIRIES. *Can. Geographical J. [Canada] 1978 96(2): 66-69.* Discusses the buildings of the Canadian Bank of Commerce, 1904-22, which were prefabricated by a Vancouver, British Columbia firm, the British Columbia Mills, Timber, and Trading Company, and shipped to small towns on the Canadian prairies, creating a uniform architecture.

2927. Horn, Michiel, ed. FRANK UNDERHILL'S EARLY DRAFTS OF THE REGINA MANIFESTO 1933. *Can. Hist. R. 1973 54(4): 393-418.* Three edited documents, drafts of what in July 1933 became the manifesto and program of the Cooperative Commonwealth Federation. The final version of the Regina Manifesto is also reproduced. No drafts were believed extant until the editor found these misfiled in Professor Frank Underhill's private papers in 1972. An introduction traces the history of the drafting of the Regina Manifesto (1933). Textual comparisons show close similarities between it and the earlier drafts, and the manifesto of the League for Social Reconstruction, a social democratic group founded by intellectuals in Toronto and Montreal in 1931-32. Underhill shared the responsibility of drafting the CCF manifesto with other members of the LSR. A

2928. Houston, C. Stuart. BIRDS BY HOOD. *Beaver [Canada] 1974 305(1): 4-11.* Robert Hood, with the Franklin Expedition of 1819-21, kept a diary and painted watercolors of birds in western Canada. These were recently discovered in Ireland and are in print for the first time. The emphasis is on winter birds and waterfowl in the vicinity of the Saskatchewan River. Summarizes the expedition and comments on Hood's field techniques. 13 illus. D. Chaput

2929. Huel, Raymond. THE FRENCH LANGUAGE PRESS IN WESTERN CANADA: *LE PATRIOTE DE L'OUEST,* 1910-41. *Rev. de l'Universite d'Ottawa [Canada] 1976 46(4): 476-499.* The newspaper *Le Patriote de l'Ouest* was founded in Saskatchewan in 1910 with the encouragement of the Roman Catholic bishop and clergy, who regarded the maintenance of the French language and of the Catholic faith as inseparable. *Le Patriote* was located at first in remote Duck Lake, and after 1913 in Regina. The newspaper faced constant financial difficulties. It had to be subsidized constantly by Catholic clergymen, and had a difficult time capturing the imagination of French-speakers in Saskatchewan. In 1933, the Oblates of Mary Immaculate of the Province of Alberta-Saskatchewan took over the newspaper and its publishing company to save it from the Depression. In 1941, *Le Patriote* was merged with *La Liberté* of Winnipeg in the hope that the new, merged journal would survive and help preserve the French language in the West. 142 notes. J. C. Billigmeier

2930. Huel, Raymond. THE IRISH-FRENCH CONFLICT IN CATHOLIC EPISCOPAL NOMINATIONS: THE WESTERN SEES AND THE STRUGGLE FOR DOMINATION WITHIN THE CHURCH. *Study Sessions: Can. Catholic Hist. Assoc. 1975 42: 51-69.* Describes the bitter competition and internal rivalry between the French-speaking minority and the aggressive Irish Catholics in western Canada for ascendancy in the hierarchy of the Church, showing how the problem went beyond episcopal nomination to concern the nature of Catholicism in Canadian society today (1900-75).

2931. Hunter, R. H. FIVE R'S ON THE PRAIRIES. *Saskatchewan Hist. [Canada] 1978 31(1): 34-36, 31(2): 69-73.* In two parts. The author reminisces about his life as a teacher in western Canada during 1923-67. Born in New Brunswick, Mr. Hunter was educated at Regina Normal School where he was employed as a professor following an extensive career as a teacher and administrator in a number of Saskatchewan cities and towns. C. H. Held

2932. Inman, Ivan D. THE RANCHERS' ROUND-UP. *Alberta Hist. 1975 23(3): 1-6.* Examines a series of round-ups from 1911 to the last one in 1919. Discusses personnel, entertainment, Wild West plays, alcohol and saloons, and returning soldiers in the last round-up. The 1919 affair was elaborate, with visiting dignitaries, contests, dramatic presentations, gambling, and Indian shows. Round-ups were successful because

they represented a combination of ranchers, cowboys, and farmers. 3 illus.
D. Chaput

2933.   Klymasz, Robert B.   FROM IMMIGRATION TO ETHNIC FOLKLORE: A CANADIAN VIEW OF PROCESS AND TRANSITION.   *J. of the Folklore Inst. 1973 10(3): 131-139.* Examines dissolution as well as acquisition techniques of immigrant folklore in terms of Ukrainian folklore in Western Canada; maintains that study of such change must be evaluated and a new framework for observation formulated.

2934.   Klymasz, Robert B. and Porter, James.   TRADITIONAL UKRAINIAN BALLADRY IN CANADA.   *Western Folklore 1974 33(2): 89-132.* Discusses the function, content, poetics, structure, and style of traditional Ukrainian balladry still popular among Ukrainian immigrants in the prairie provinces of Canada. Includes the music, text, and translations of 11 ballads. Based on primary and secondary sources and oral interviews; 18 notes, 7 music examples (in addition to the ballads), appendix.
S. L. Myres

2935.   Koester, C. B.   THE AGITATION FOR PARLIAMENTARY REPRESENTATION OF THE NORTH-WEST TERRITORIES, 1870-1887.   *Saskatchewan Hist. 1973 26(1): 11-23.* When Manitoba was created in 1870 and granted federal representation, public agitation began for similar representation for the Northwest Territories. Neither the Conservatives nor the Liberals embodied this in their platforms. It was not included in designs for Confederation. Only after the Northwest Rebellion (1885), the last of a sequence of events, was representation granted in 1887. 60 notes.
D. L. Smith

2936.   Lalonde, André N.   ARCHBISHOP O. E. MATHIEU AND FRANCOPHONE IMMIGRATION TO THE ARCHDIOCESE OF REGINA.   *Study Sessions: Can. Catholic Hist. Assoc. [Canada] 1977 44: 45-60.* Olivier-Elzéar Mathieu, Archbishop of the Regina Archdiocese during 1911-31, promoted the immigration of Catholic French Canadians, French, and Americans to Canada's Prairie Provinces, especially Manitoba and Saskatchewan.

2937.   Lehr, John C.   THE UKRAINIAN PRESENCE ON THE PRAIRIES.   *Can. Geographic [Canada] 1978 97(2): 28-33.* Chronicles the immigration and settlement of Ukrainians in Canada's Prairie Provinces, 1910-31.

2938.   MacPherson, Ian, ed.   GEORGE CHIPMAN, EDUCATOR.   *Alberta Hist. [Canada] 1978 26(4): 31-40.* George Chipman, born in Nova Scotia, went to the Prairie Provinces in 1903 as a teacher. He worked only a few years, then during 1909-31 was editor of the *Grain Growers' Guide.* Reprinted here are several articles Chipman wrote while a prairie teacher, in which he discusses the students, curriculum, and other educational conditions and concepts. Based on manuscripts in Queen's University Archives; 3 illus.
D. Chaput

2939.   Martin, Ged.   BRITISH ATTITUDES TO PRAIRIE SETTLEMENT.   *Alberta Hist. R. 1974 22(1): 1-11.* From the late 1840's to the late 1860's the British public held vague but grand ideas about the destiny of the Canadian western prairies: they would be settled from Canada on the east and Vancouver Island on the west; an easily built transcontinental railway would link the eastern and western British colonies; and British North America would become a transcontinental union. 4 illus., 43 notes.
D. L. Smith

2940.   McCormack, A. Ross.   THE INDUSTRIAL WORKERS OF THE WORLD IN WESTERN CANADA: 1905-1914.   *Can. Hist. Assoc. Hist. Papers [Canada] 1975: 167-190.* Assesses the contribution of the Industrial Workers of the World (IWW) to the radical tradition. In a continental and regional setting the IWW organized unskilled, itinerant, ethnically heterogeneous, and nonpolitical workers outside the classic labor movement. This situation led to friction with the American Federation of Labor, the Trades and Labour Congress of Canada, and the Socialist Party of Canada. Although it sought immediate improvements for workers, the IWW stood for sabotage and the general strike as weapons to defeat capitalism. Based on Frontier College Papers in the Public Archives of Canada, Public Records in the Public Archives of British Columbia, union proceedings, and secondary sources; 119 notes.
G. E. Panting

2941.   Mills, G. E. and Holdsworth, D. W.   THE B. C. MILLS PREFABRICATED SYSTEM: THE EMERGENCE OF READYMADE BUILDINGS IN WESTERN CANADA.   *Can. Historic Sites 1975 (14): 127-169.* Between 1904 and 1910 the Vancouver-based British Columbia Mills, Timber and Trading Company marketed a patented system of prefabricated sectional buildings in western Canada. Initially this system was devised as a means of supplying small inexpensive huts to incoming settlers in newly opened agricultural regions. Such structures were prefabricated, prepainted, packaged and shipped by rail to local distributors in towns and villages throughout western Canada. With a set of accompanying instructions, the purchaser could erect his dwelling in a minimum amount of time with little assistance or equipment. This sectional system was subsequently adapted to a variety of larger permanent homes and ultimately to institutional and commercial structures such as schools, churches and banks. It was with a series of classical banks manufactured for the Canadian Bank of Commerce that the system achieved its greatest success as an enduring western Canadian landmark.
J

2942.   Moodie, D. W. and Kaye, Barry.   TAMING AND DOMESTICATING THE NATIVE ANIMALS OF RUPERT'S LAND.   *Beaver [Canada] 1976 307(3): 10-19.* From the beginning of fur trade days, supplies of meat were limited. Many experiments were carried out, unsuccessfully, to provide needed protein on the frontier. Domesticating fox, caribou, bear, geese, beaver, buffalo, and various songbirds was tried. Some adjusted well to being pets, but the meat question was unsolved. At the beginning of the Red River colony in the 1820's, it seemed that buffalo would become good work animals, as well as provide meat, but experiments failed. Introduction of Missouri cattle in 1822 ended these various experiments. After that time, domesticated native animals were curiosities only. 11 illus.
D. Chaput

2943.   Norrie, Kenneth.   DRY FARMING AND THE ECONOMICS OF RISK BEARING: THE CANADIAN PRAIRIES, 1870-1930.   *Agric. Hist. 1977 51(1): 134-148.* After 1896 the semiarid lands of North America were settled using dry farming techniques. Canadian farmers responded to the uncertain nature of dry farming by using summer fallow rather than the risky but more productive use of substitute crops or the planting of wheat every year. Similarly tenants in the driest areas preferred the safety of sharecropping to the hazards of cash rental, and showed an interest in crop insurance. Because farmers were averse to risk, grain production was less than it might have been. Table, 34 notes.
D. E. Bowers

2944.   Olling, R. D.   AN ATTEMPT AT PARLIAMENTARY REFORM.   *Alberta Hist. [Canada] 1978 26(3): 9-12.* The farmers' political parties, which blossomed in the Prairie Provinces in the 1920's, deviated from traditional party policies and loyalties; in particular they resented cabinet-dominated government. In Alberta, two contrary forces were at work in the 1920's: the new farmers' group and the tradition-oriented legislators. For some years the United Farmers' group held some control, but this dissipated in the 1930's, leading to the formation of the Social Credit Party.
D. Chaput

2945.   Parker, Keith A.   ARTHUR EVANS: WESTERN RADICAL.   *Alberta Hist. 1978 26(2): 21-29.* Arthur Evans, born in Toronto in 1889, spent years in Kansas City, Colorado, and Seattle before settling in western Canada. By the mid-1930's, he was a well-known Communist labor organizer who had spent time in prison for illegally using union funds; instead of forwarding the funds, he spent the money on food for needy families. In 1935 he was one of the organizers of the Trek from western Canada to Ottawa, where he exchanged bitter words with Prime Minister Bennett. After a riot in Regina in July, 1935, Evans was temporarily jailed on charges of being a Communist and a member of the Workers Unity League. Following his release he made a speaking tour across Canada. Evans was a shipwright and shop steward in British Columbia at the time of his death in 1944. Based on government hearings and newspaper accounts. 6 illus., 26 notes.
D. Chaput

2946.   Peake, F. A.   THE ACHIEVEMENTS AND FRUSTRATIONS OF JAMES HUNTER.   *J. of the Can. Church Hist. Soc. [Canada] 1977 19(3-4): 138-165.* Describes the missionary work of the Anglican priest James Hunter, an Englishman, in what is now western Canada, during 1844-64. Hunter maintained good relations with the Hudson's Bay Company which had power in the area and made significant contributions to the missionary effort. First, he translated the *Book of Common Prayer* and other religious works into the Cree Indian language. Second, he worked hard to expand Anglican missionary efforts throughout the area known as Rupert's Land, despite some opposition from the Company. His attempts in this area were rewarded by success, but in 1864 Hunter decided to return to England permanently. Ostensibly he did so for the education of his children, but he also may have been frustrated in his desire to occupy a position of leadership within the Church. Upon his return to England, his opportunities in this area were greatly improved. Based on printed and unprinted primary sources; 59 notes, 2 appendixes.   J. A. Kicklighter

2947. Poelzer, Irene A.   THE CATHOLIC NORMAL SCHOOL IS-SUE IN THE NORTHWEST TERRITORIES, 1884-1900. *Study Sessions: Can. Catholic Hist. Assoc. 1975 42: 5-28.* The real reason behind the loss of the Catholic Church's right to separate normal schools was not its inability to meet legitimate requirements, but political opportunism and growing intolerance in the North-West during 1884-1900.

2948. Provencher, John N.   MEMOIR OR ACCOUNT. *Beaver [Canada] 1973 303(4): 16-23.* The author, priest and then bishop of the Red River Settlement from 1818-53, summarizes the activities of Lord Selkirk, founder of the colony, early education attempts, and his own missionary work among the Métis and Chippewa Indians there and in Quebec, and gives an account of his relations with the Hudson's Bay Company. Based on a memoir recently discovered in archives of Propaganda of the Faith in Rome. 8 illus.   D. Chaput

2949. Ray, Arthur J.   DIFFUSION OF DISEASES IN THE WESTERN INTERIOR OF CANADA, 1830-50. *Geographical R. 1976 66(2): 139-157.* The records of the Hudson's Bay Company are examined and the patterns of diffusion of a series of epidemics that occurred in the Western Interior of Canada between 1830 and 1850 are outlined. The patterns of diffusion clearly show that fur company supply brigades were the primary carriers of disease. The extent to which a given epidemic spread was largely determined by the contagiousness of the disease and the timing of transmission. Diseases that broke out during the summer generally spread more widely than did those that erupted in winter because of the spatial clustering of Indian populations during the summer and the movement of supply brigades between districts at that time of the year.   J

2950. Richtik, James and Hutch, Danny.   WHEN JEWISH SET-TLERS FARMED IN MANITOBA'S INTERLAKE AREA. *Can. Geographical J. [Canada] 1977 95(1): 32-35.* In an effort to escape persecution in tsarist Russia, Jews migrated to Canada in 1884, settling primarily in the interlake districts of Manitoba; in the 1920's they set up agricultural communities in Saskatchewan and Alberta.

2951. Schoonover, Cortlandt.   FRANK SCHOONOVER'S FRONTIER: ILLUSTRATOR-ARTIST OF THE CANADIAN AND AMERICAN WEST. *Am. West 1977 14(2): 38-47.* Frank Schoonover (1877-1972), popular illustrator-painter, painted more than 4,000 pictures. Most of them were commissioned drawings for books and periodicals. He made extensive excursions to the Canadian West and North and to the American West to study and sketch his subjects. His works are characterized by vitality and drama, and his models were invariably forceful. 10 illus.   D. L. Smith

2952. Spry, Irene M.   A VISIT TO RED RIVER AND THE SASKATCHEWAN, 1861, BY DR. JOHN RAE, FRGS. *Geographical J. [Great Britain] 1974 140(1): 1-17.* "In 1861 Dr. John Rae, the Arctic explorer, made a journey with two young big game hunters, Henry (later Viscount) Chaplin and Sir Frederic Johnstone, Bart., out onto the buffalo plains of what is now western Canada. With the redoubtable James McKay as guide, the party penetrated as yet unmapped country. This is Rae's account of the expedition, which has recently come to light. He made astronomical observations, and commented on the country, wildlife, Indians, and Red River settlers as he saw them in a critical period of change. He analysed the problems that would be encountered in attempts to colonize the Saskatchewan Valley and calculated that to reach the Pacific Coast would cost more and take longer by the proposed overland route than by the existing Panama Isthmus route."   J

2953. Strum, Harvey.   PROPHET OF RIGHTEOUSNESS. *Alberta Hist. [Canada] 1975 23(4): 21-27.* In 1909 William Jennings Bryan made a speaking tour of western Canada as a fund-raising effort for the Young Men's Christian Organization (YMCA). He began at Victoria, B.C., then moved across the prairie provinces. He spoke either on the YMCA movement, or delivered his famous "Prince of Peace" speech. He surprised many Canadians favorably; they were familiar with his role as political leader, but not moral reformer. His political views were especially popular in western Canada as he campaigned against trusts and the plutocracy in general. 3 photos, 34 notes.   D. Chaput

2954. Taylor, John H.   THE WESTERN CANADIAN URBAN HISTORY CONFERENCE: A REPORT. *Urban Hist. Rev. [Canada] 1974 74(2): 19-21.* Synopses of papers offered at the Western Canadian Urban History Conference held 24-26 October 1974 at the University of Winnipeg.

2955. Taylor, Murray W.   SOURCES AND LITERATURE FOR WESTERN AMERICAN HISTORY: A LIST OF DISSERTATIONS. *Western Hist. Q. 1975 6(3): 303-314.* Lists doctoral dissertations on subjects related to the history of the Canadian and American West as cited in volumes 34-35, *Dissertation Abstracts International*, January 1974-January 1975. Classified under 17 headings.   D. L. Smith

2956. Vernon, Howard A.   THE JOURNAL OF J. DUFAUT. *Beaver [Canada] 1974 305(2): 23-27.* J. Dufaut's journal describes the daily life and transactions of a fur trader for the XY Company during the winter of 1803-04. Dufaut recorded the weather, game caught, and goods traded with the Indians, as well as notes on life in the bush of Prince Rupert's Land. 5 illus.   D. Heermans

2957. Voisey, Paul.   THE URBANIZATION OF THE CANADIAN PRAIRIES, 1871-1916. *Social Hist. [Canada] 1975 8(15): 77-101.* The urbanization of the Canadian prairies began in the late 1870's and early 1880's with feverish and corrupt real estate speculation and promotion stimulated by the coming of the railroad. The boom declined when the flow of agricultural migrants was less than expected, but began again after 1900, following the same speculative pattern. Includes five major cities: Calgary, Edmonton, Saskatoon, Regina, and Winnipeg. Their prominence was due to the work of their City Councils and Boards of Trade in getting railway lines built to them, in advertising the city and its hinterland to migrants, and in garnering universities and seats of government. The even spacing of towns of the same size across the prairie shows their functional relationship with the agricultural economy. The economic downturn of 1913 ended the urban boom. Based on newspapers, published primary sources, and secondary sources; 4 maps, 3 tables, 12 notes.   W. K. Hobson

2958. Voisey, Paul.   THE "VOTES FOR WOMEN" MOVEMENT. *Alberta Hist. 1975 23(3): 10-23.* Study of the suffrage movement in the Prairie Provinces, especially Manitoba. The movement began around the turn of the century, largely related to curtailing alcoholism, gambling, and prostitution. Leadership changed over the years, but Anglo-Saxon Protestant women dominated the movement. World War I brought many changes, as more women were employed, and the immigrant population rose considerably. Examines the power structures in the three provinces, their stakes in suffrage, and the eventual women's victory in 1916. 6 illus., 78 notes.   D. Chaput

2959. Ward, Norman.   THE POLITICS OF PATRONAGE: JAMES GARDINER AND APPOINTMENTS IN THE WEST, 1935-57. *Can. Hist. Rev. [Canada] 1977 58(3): 294-310.* Studies political patronage in the West during the incumbency of James Garfield Gardiner as Agriculture Minister in the Liberal cabinet of William Lyon Mackenzie King during 1935-57. Although he was concerned about observing proprieties, he ran a "tight ship," and achieved a great advantage for the Liberal Party. Though his authority was not absolute, the actual appointments being subject to approval, his influence was enormous. However, under wartime conditions, when a good deal of nonpartisanship was demanded, the system suffered considerable erosion. 34 notes.   R. V. Ritter

2960. Williams, Glyndwr.   GOVERNOR GEORGE SIMPSON'S CHARACTER BOOK. *Beaver [Canada] 1975 306(1): 4-18.* George Simpson wrote this character book in 1832, a personal evaluation of 157 people associated with the Hudson's Bay Company in that year: 25 chief factors, 25 chief traders, 88 clerks, 19 postmasters. The book is the most widely used and quoted item in the Company Archives, yet has only been published this year (as part of Vol. XXX, Hudson's Bay Record Society series). The individual comments are rich, personal, and often damning. Some of the key figures analyzed by Simpson are John Stuart, Colin Robertson, John Rowland, Angus Cameron, and Francis Ermatinger. 20 illus.   D. Chaput

2961. Woywitka, Anne B. RECOLLECTIONS OF A UNION MAN. *Alberta Hist. [Canada] 1975 23(4): 6-20.* Peter Kyforuk, a Ukrainian immigrant, came to Canada in 1912 at the age of 18. In the next decades he worked as a woodsman and railroad hand from Ontario to British Columbia. In the 1920's he became active in the Ukrainian Labour-Farmer Association in Manitoba. Later active in Farmers Unity League, he played a key role in the Hunger March on Edmonton in December 1932 and with many other leaders was arrested. By the mid-1930's Kyforuk had settled in Alberta, became a successful farmer, and remained active in the Farmer's Union of Alberta. 8 photos.   D. Chaput

2962. Young, Walter D. M. J. COLDWELL, THE MAKING OF A SOCIAL DEMOCRAT. *J. of Can. Studies 1974 9(3): 50-60.* After beginning as a High Anglican and Tory in England, Major J. Coldwell went from Progressivism to Social Democracy in Western Canada. As a teacher, a school principal, and a Regina alderman, he became involved in urban and rural prairie life. This experience made it possible for him to emerge as leader of the Farmer Labor party in 1932. Based on interviews, newspapers, secondary works; 33 notes.   G. E. Panting

2963. Zink, Ella. CHURCH AND IMMIGRATION: THE SISTERS OF SERVICE, ENGLISH CANADA'S FIRST MISSIONARY CONGREGATION OF SISTERS, 1920-1930. *Study Sessions: Can. Catholic Hist. Assoc. [Canada] 1976 43: 23-38.* Sketches the broad background against which the Sisters of Service were founded and developed, beginning in Toronto, and working especially among the largely Protestant populations of new settlers in Western Canada.

2964. —. [FARMING THE GREAT PLAINS AND THE CANADIAN PRAIRIES]. *Agric. Hist. 1977 51(1): 78-108.*
Drache, Hiram. THOMAS D. CAMPBELL—THE PLOWER OF THE PLAINS, *pp. 78-91.* Thomas D. Campbell was one of the first successful large-scale farmers. With capital from Eastern bankers he established a huge wheat farm in Montana using big machines. Assuming ownership of the farm in 1921, Campbell proved the economies of scale in large, mechanized farming by succeeding in a decade of low wheat prices. Campbell pioneered in the use of windrow harvesting, motorized wagon trains, soil conservation, and enlightened labor practices. 18 notes.
Ankli, Robert E. FARM INCOME ON THE GREAT PLAINS AND CANADIAN PRAIRIES, 1920-1940, *pp. 92-103.* Farm income in the American Great Plains and Canadian Prairie Provinces fell after World War I, recovered some in the mid-1920's, and dropped sharply during the 1930's. Declining yields from drought were at least as responsible for this as falling prices. Large farms and those in areas less affected by drought suffered least. Diversifying from wheat to cattle would have had little effect on income. Table, 40 notes.
Anderson, Terry L. BONANZA FARMERS AND SUBSISTENCE: A RESPONSE, *pp. 104-108.* Campbell's improved technology, as discussed by Drache, did little to help small farmers. As one of the first users of this technology, Campbell benefited from the lack of competition, but he was also fortunate in acquiring his capital at a low cost. Ankli presents useful new data on wheat production and farm income but draws few conclusions and doesn't make allowance for the changing exchange rate between US and Canadian dollars. Both papers have overlooked the effect of government policies.   D. E. Bowers

Manitoba

2965. Arnold, A. J. THE EARLIEST JEWS IN WINNIPEG 1874-1882. *Beaver [Canada] 1974 305(2): 4-11.* Describes the settlement of Russian Jews in Winnipeg. Disappointed at first because most failed to receive land grants or find employment, many eventually moved out of the city to find or create employment opportunities. For those who stayed, the city offered closer ties with Jewish cultural institutions. 11 illus.   D. Heermans

2966. Artibise, A. F. J. MAYOR ALEXANDER LOGAN OF WINNIPEG. *Beaver [Canada] 1974 304(4): 4-12.* Relates the life and public career of Alexander Logan (1841-94) who served four terms as mayor of Winnipeg in the 1870's and 1880's.   S

2967. Artibise, Alan F. J. PATTERNS OF POPULATION GROWTH AND ETHNIC RELATIONSHIPS IN WINNIPEG, 1874-1974. *Social Hist. [Canada] 1976 9(18): 297-335.* Winnipeg's population growth can be divided into five major periods during 1874-1974. During the formative years, 1874-99, Anglo-Canadian migration set the enduring character and tone of Winnipeg society. During 1900-13, the population more than tripled because of an influx of Slavic and Jewish immigrants. Anglo-Canadians expressed bigotry toward the immigrants and used the schools in an attempt to Anglicize them. During 1914-20, ethnic conflict escalated and left social scars that took decades to heal. After 1921 the growth rate slowed and Winnipegers searched for ways to create more harmonious relationships between ethnic groups. After 1960, a period of stability and maintenance of earlier trends can be identified. Based on newspapers, other primary sources, and secondary sources; 2 maps, 12 tables, 96 notes.   W. K. Hobson

2968. Artibise, Alan F. J. WINNIPEG, 1874-1914. *Urban Hist. Rev. [Canada] 1975 75(1): 43-50.* During 1874-1914, economic growth and urbanization in Winnipeg, Manitoba, was based not on geographical advantage, but on the presence of able and dynamic political leaders and businessmen; one of eight articles in this issue on the Canadian city in the 19th century.

2969. Astrachan, Anthony. ON THE BROAD PRAIRIE: IN WINNIPEG, MANITOBA: A JEWISH PHENOMENON. *Present Tense 1975 2(4): 31-35.* History and description of the flourishing Jewish community in Winnipeg, Manitoba.   S

2970. Backeland, Lucille and Frideres, James S. FRANCO-MANITOBANS AND CULTURAL LOSS: A FOURTH GENERATION. *Prairie Forum [Canada] 1977 2(1): 1-18.* French Manitobans have maintained their cultural identity, although some loss is noted; corroborates Frank Vallee's hypothesis concerning the necessity of regional research.

2971. Beckman, M. Dale. THE PROBLEM OF COMMUNICATING PUBLIC POLICY EFFECTIVELY: BILL C-256 AND WINNIPEG BUSINESSMEN. *Can. J. of Pol. Sci. 1975 8(1): 138-143.* Winnipeg businessmen were not fully aware of an important federal bill (1971) designed to revamp competition policy. Based on questionnaires and telephone interviews. 6 tables, 2 notes.   R. V. Kubicek

2972. Booy, Cass. DEATH OF A RIVER. *Can. Dimension [Canada] 1973 9(6): 19-26.* Questions the ecological necessity of the destruction of the Churchill River due to hydroelectric development in northern Manitoba, 1966-70's.

2973. Bredin, Thomas F. THE RED RIVER ACADEMY. *Beaver [Canada] 1974 305(3): 10-17.* The Red River Academy opened in 1832 in Winnipeg, but there had been earlier efforts towards education beginning with the early 1820's. Though discipline was harsh, attendance was good; it was not, however, a financial success. Most of the students were children of Hudson's Bay Company employees and the school performed essential education until the late 1850's. By that time most parents preferred to send their children to schools in eastern Canada, England, or the United States. 8 illus., map.   D. Chaput

2974. Choquette, Robert. ADÉLARD LANGEVIN ET L'ÉREC-TION DE L'ARCHIDIOCÈSE DE WINNIPEG [Adélard Langevin and the establishment of the archdiocese of Winnipeg]. *Rev. d'Hist. de l'Amérique Française [Canada] 1974 28(2): 187-208.* Recounts the conflicts which arose after 1905 in Winnipeg between French Catholics and English-speaking Catholics over the administration of Monsignor Adélard Langevin.

2975. Crossin, Alan L. A MANITOBA MEMORIAL. *Manitoba Pageant 1973 18(2): 2-4.* Canadian Memorial Chapel in Vancouver was dedicated 9 November 1928. The first minister, Reverend George Fallis, helped raise funds for 10 stained-glass windows in memory of Canadians killed in World War I. Manitoba is represented by a panel depicting the founding of upper Fort Garry.   D. M. Dean

2976. Daniel, Forrest W. WM. A. ROGERS: THE ARTIST WHO PLAYED "HOOKY." *North Dakota Hist. 1976 43(3): 4-13.* William A. Rogers, an illustrator of wood engravings with *Harper's Weekly,* spent three months in late 1878 in and around Dakota Territory, producing memorable sketches of various scenes including Standing Rock Indian Reservation, Fort Garry in Manitoba, prairie fires, etc. His written descriptions of his trip in his autobiography and elsewhere include accounts of episodes in Bismarck, involvement in prairie fires on the Red River and on the plains, and anecdotes of life in Fargo. Based on primary and secondary sources; illus.   N. Lederer

2977. Driedger, Leo. ETHNIC BOUNDARIES: A COMPARISON OF TWO URBAN NEIGHBORHOODS. *Sociol. and Social Res. 1978 62(2): 193-211.* This study in metropolitan Winnipeg shows that St. Boniface and the North End represent two "natural ethnic areas" (Park and Burgess, 1967), with distinct urban boundaries (Suttles, 1968). Territory, institutions and culture were important boundary maintenance factors. The community of the North End, originally dominated by East European Jews, Ukrainians, and Poles is experiencing the process of invasion and succession as has been demonstrated in many other urban community studies. The Jews have moved to the suburbs taking their culture and institutions with them; the Ukrainians and Poles are also changing and adjusting to newcomers. The East European ethnic boundaries are giving way to a more heterogeneous, multi-ethnic invasion by native Indian and south European newcomers. In contrast, the community of north St. Boniface has remained essentially a French urban neighborhood for 160 years. The urban French community by means of residential segregation, with limited out mobility, has maintained a French culture within a fairly complete ethnic institutional framework. The unique French St. Boniface urban community does not follow the numerous other invasion-succession patterns which have been reported This paper explores possible reasons for the two differential community change patterns within the same metropolitan area.   J

2978. Driedger, Leo and Church, Glenn. RESIDENTIAL SEGRE-GATION AND INSTITUTIONAL COMPLETENESS: A COMPAR-ISON OF ETHNIC MINORITIES. *Can. R. of Sociol. and Anthrop. 1974 11(1): 30-52.* "The importance of residential segregation for the maintenance of institutional completeness is clearly demonstrated by this study of six ethnic groups in Winnipeg. The French community maintainers follow Joy's Quebec core area pattern in St. Boniface with extensions of their ethnic belt adjacent to the core and extensive intra-area mobility. On the other hand, the Scandinavians were never able to establish a very complete ethnic institutional base in a segregated ecological area, so they scattered as assimilationists would predict. Contrary to Joy's prediction, extensive Jewish mobility into their West Kildonan and River Heights suburban extended belt areas resulted in the establishment of two new segregated Jewish communities where they have created new complexes of ethnic institutions, leaving the original North End Jewish core area almost entirely."   J

2979. Fraser, Don. WINNIPEG'S POST OFFICES. *Manitoba Pageant [Canada] 1974 19(3): 12-15.* Discusses, with physical descriptions, the evolution of Winnipeg's post office buildings from 1855 to the present. 5 illus.   D. M. Dean

2980. Fuga, Olga. NEW WINNIPEG GOVERNMENT IS UNIQUE URBAN EXPERIMENT. *Natl. Civic R. 1973 62(4): 189-192.* "Winnipeg, not a large urban center by U.S. standards, is large

enough to be experiencing typical urban problems. Since January 1972 it has been governed under a new law accepting the thesis that the city is one in community in the social and economic sense and should be one for the purposes of government. Poor financial power is the major drawback to the new structure and administration as it was for the old."   J

2981. Gibbons, Lillian and McDowell, D. "ON WITH THE DANCE..."—HISTORIC BALLS IN MANITOBA. *Manitoba Pageant [Canada] 1976 21(4): 1-3.* Discusses two historic balls in Manitoba during 1892-1913. The Manitoba Historical Society recreated the ambiance of these social occasions at its first annual Dalnavert Ball 24 October 1975.   B. J. Lo Bue

2982. Gonick, Cy W. THE MISSING CHAPTER OF THE CFI REPORT. *Can. Dimension 1974 10(5): 13-18.* Reveals the details of the Churchill Forest Industry's attempt to defraud the people of Manitoba of $29 million.   S

2983. Grant, H. Roger. FRANK A. SEIBERLING AND THE FORMATIVE YEARS OF THE MIDLAND CONTINENTAL RAIL-ROAD 1912-1920. *North Dakota Hist. 1976 43(4): 28-36.* Frank A. Seiberling assumed ownership of the Midland Construction Company in 1912, probably through his acceptance of the company's notes as collateral for a personal loan to a friend. The company was trying to build a transcontinental railroad connecting the Gulf ports of Galveston and Corpus Christi, Texas, with Winnipeg, Manitoba. This route would provide a direct Gulf outlet for Great Plains farmers. The few miles of the railroad actually constructed lay in North Dakota and were used primarily as feeder lines to already existing railroads operating in an east-west direction. Seiberling maintained considerable interest in the well-being of his railroad. Through the appointment of able subordinates he managed to make the line profitable. Based on oral interviews and on primary and secondary sources.   N. Lederer

2984. Hall, Frank. CITY OF WINNIPEG—OFFSPRING OF CON-FLICTING PASSIONS. *Manitoba Pageant [Canada] 1974 19(3): 2-9.* In 1873, recent immigrants from Ontario favored the incorporation of Winnipeg while their opponents—wealthy landowners, retired fur traders, and the Hudson's Bay Company—fought the establishment of municipal government and subsequent taxation for public works. On November 8, after months of debate and some violence, the Legislative Council and the Legislative Assembly passed a Bill of Incorporation. 2 illus.   D. M. Dean

2985. Hall, Frank. MANITOBA'S OWN MOUNTIES. *Manitoba Pageant 1973 19(1): 4-9.* During the winter of 1873-74 the first detachment of the Northwest Mounted Police was mustered at Lower Garry, Manitoba. Their primary job was to stop the liquor traffic and gain the respect and confidence of the Indians. In July 1874, a column of troops marched from Fort Dufferin to Fort Whoop-Up to bring law and order to Western Canada. 2 illus.   D. M. Dean

2986. Inkster, Anne Ellen. MEMORIES FROM FORT CHURCHILL. *Manitoba Pageant [Canada] 1975 20(2): 2-5.* Author reminisces about growing up, 1885-93, in Churchill, Manitoba.

2987. Jackson, James A. RAILWAYS AND THE MANITOBA SCHOOL QUESTION. *Tr. of the Hist. and Sci. Soc. of Manitoba [Canada] 1973-74 (30): 81-87.* Examines the Railway Disallowance Question and how this issue accelerated and intensified Manitoba's controversial School Question of the 1890's. Liberal Party legislator Thomas Greenway and his Attorney-General Joseph Martin, in an effort to rally Manitobans' support in a period when they were accused of corrupt bargaining with the Northern Pacific Railway after achieving the withdrawal of the Canadian Pacific Railway monopoly through Manitoba, reintroduced the issue of abolishing French-English school segregation which had a history of long dissatisfaction. The school question was a huge success and "the Liberal party held a monolithic control of the government of Manitoba." Primary and secondary works; 16 notes.   S. R. Quéripel

2988. Kerri, James N. A SOCIAL ANALYSIS OF THE HUMAN ELEMENT IN HOUSING: A CANADIAN CASE. *Human Organization 1975 36(2): 173-185.* The Remote Housing Program is a joint federal-provincial venture in the Canadian province of Manitoba. Its purpose was to provide low cost single family housing to low income families. This paper evaluates the first two years of the program, including its economic and cultural implications. The rationale for the program is given and the extent to which its objectives have been realized is discussed.   J

2989. Kinghorn, Norton D. MARK TWAIN IN THE RED RIVER VALLEY OF THE NORTH. *Minnesota Hist. 1977 45(8): 321-328.* In 1895, as a means through which to recoup his fortunes, Mark Twain embarked on a lecture tour which took him to Winnipeg, Manitoba and Crookston, Minnesota. He attracted large audiences at both places for his seriocomedic readings. Newspaper reporters in both cities lauded his lectures. The reporter for the *Crookston Times* displayed in his review a greater appreciation of the serious underpinnings of Twain's humor than the reporter for the *Winnipeg Daily Tribune.* The latter primarily emphasized the entertainment of Twain's performance. Based on contemporary newspaper accounts.   N. Lederer

2990. Lightbody, James. ELECTORAL REFORM IN LOCAL GOVERNMENT: THE CASE OF WINNIPEG. *Can. J. of Pol. Sci. [Canada] 1978 11(2): 307-332.* Reform of this city's election system, i.e., extension of the ward system, has only marginally extended working class power in local politics. 2 maps, 7 tables, 98 notes.
R. V. Kubicek

2991. Loudfoot, Raymonde. THE NUYTTENS OF BELGIAN TOWN. *Manitoba Pageant [Canada] 1974 19(3): 15-18.* Discusses Edmund and Octavia Nuytten and other Belgian immigrants who settled in the East St. Boniface area of Winnipeg. Appended is a list of over 300 Belgian families who arrived in Winnipeg, 1880-1914. Illus.
D. M. Dean

2992. McKillop, A. B. SOCIALIST AS CITIZEN: JOHN QUEEN AND THE MAYORALTY OF WINNIPEG, 1935. *Tr. of the Hist. and Sci. Soc. of Manitoba [Canada] 1973-74 (30): 61-80.* Discusses the political involvement of socialist John Queen from the time he arrived in Winnipeg in 1909 through his mayoralty of Winnipeg (1935-42), concentrating on the issues faced and reforms sought by his administration. After his initial campaign to readjust the tax base of the city, much of his time was spent in the provincial legislature or in Ottawa making known "the urgency of Constitutional adjustments and provincial and federal legislation necessary for the coming into being of a full measure of social justice." Primary and secondary works; 69 notes, appendix.
S. R. Quéripel

2993. McKillop, Brian. A COMMUNIST IN CITY HALL. *Can. Dimension 1974 10(1): 41-50.* The political battles between Ralph Webb and Jacob Pennir epitomized Winnipeg's economic, ideological, and ethnic divisions in the 1930's.   S

2994. Medovy, Harry. THE EARLY JEWISH PHYSICIANS IN MANITOBA. *Tr. of the Hist. and Sci. Soc. of Manitoba 1972/73 Series 3(29): 23-39.* Discusses the development of medical practice among Jewish doctors in Manitoba. Thirteen doctors are described in biographical sketches which include anecdotal material. These were men who "helped the community come of age."   J. A. Casada

2995. Melnyk, George. WINNIPEG REVISITED: NOTES OF AN IMMIGRANT SON. *Can. Dimension [Canada] 1977 12(4-5): 31, 34-35.* The author discusses his impressions of Winnipeg, Manitoba; he moved there as an immigrant in 1949.

2996. Ogmundson, Rick. A SOCIAL PROFILE OF MEMBERS OF THE MANITOBA LEGISLATURE: 1950, 1960, 1970. *J. of Can. Studies [Canada] 1977 12(4): 79-84.* Studies the religious, ethnic, and occupational makeup of the legislative contingents of the three major Manitoba political parties in 1950 when the Liberals were in power, in 1960 when the Progessive Conservatives held office, and in 1970 after the surprise 1969 victory of the New Democratic Party. Tests the validity of popular views about the composition of each of these parties. The NDP, despite its working-class rhetoric, is now represented mainly by members of the professional class. Concludes that systematic scrutiny of this kind is useful, because several widely accepted ideas on this subject were not

supported. Based on the *Parliamentary Guide* and secondary sources; 5 tables, 6 notes.   L. W. Van Wyk

2997. O'Malley, Martin. HOW ONTARIO SUPPLIES WINNIPEG'S WATER. *Can. Geographical J. 1975 91(3): 28-31.* History (1912-75) of the aqueduct flowing from Ontario's Lake of the Woods to Winnipeg to supply the city with water.   S

2998. Penner, Norman. RECOLLECTIONS OF THE EARLY SOCIALIST MOVEMENT IN WINNIPEG, BY JACOB PENNER. *Social Hist. [Canada] 1974 7(14): 366-378.* Recollections of Jacob Penner (1880-1965), a Communist member of the Winnipeg City Council, 1933-60, except for a two-year period when jailed during World War II. Covers his youth and early manhood in Russia where he developed a Marxist consciousness, his migration to Canada in 1904, and the development of the Socialist movement in Winnipeg between 1906 and the General Strike of 1919. 10 notes.   W. K. Hobson

2999. Pinczuk, J. R. MANITOBA—CENTRE OF UKRAINIAN STUDIES. *Ukrainian R. [Great Britain] 1974 21(4): 85-95.*

3000. Reifschneider, John Charles. RECOLLECTIONS OF BEAUSEJOUR AND THE MANITOBA GLASS WORKS 1909-1911. *Manitoba Pageant [Canada] 1976 21(4): 4-13.* During 1909-11 the Manitoba Glass Works converted from the European method of making freeblown bottles to a semi-automated process. Amber and green beer and soda bottles were the principal product. Living conditions in Beausejour were harsh, and most factory workers did not bring their families with them. Recreation tended to be unorganized, but the factory did have a baseball team. Working conditions were difficult because of the extreme heat. The work force was divided into shops, and each shop was a complete production unit. 5 illus.   B. J. LoBue

3001. Richtik, James and Hutch, Danny. WHEN JEWISH SETTLERS FARMED IN MANITOBA'S INTERLAKE AREA. *Can. Geographical J. [Canada] 1977 95(1): 32-35.* Discusses settlements comprised primarily of Jewish immigrants in the Prairie Provinces, focusing on Bender Hamlet, Manitoba, an agricultural community, 1910-49.

3002. Riegert, P. W. A CENTURY OF LOCUSTS AND MORTGAGES. *Prairie Forum [Canada] 1977 2(2): 121-126.* Devastation of seed grain and food resources caused by an infestation of locusts in Manitoba, 1875-76, brought about the mortgaging of homesteads in the area and bills which were still being paid in 1941.

3003. Rostecki, Randy R. THE EARLY HISTORY OF THE CAUCHON BLOCK, LATER THE EMPIRE HOTEL. *Manitoba Pageant [Canada] 1976 21(3): 10-17.* Lieutenant-Governor Cauchon purchased the land in Winnipeg in late 1880, and the building opened in February 1883. It is one of only a few cast iron-fronted buildings ever built in Canada. Expected rental income did not materialize, and in 1884 the firm of Dunn and Price converted the building into apartments. In 1904 the building was converted into the Empire Hotel. Based on primary and secondary sources; illus., 54 notes.   B. J. LaBue

3004. Rostecki, R. R. SOME OLD WINNIPEG BUILDINGS. *Tr. of the Hist. and Sci. Soc. of Manitoba [Canada] 1972/73 Series 3(29): 5-22.* A chronological coverage "of some of the treasures to be found among Winnipeg's old buildings." Thirty-five buildings are described and historical sketches of each one presented. Based on printed and manuscript sources; 17 notes, biblio.   J. A. Casada

3005. Sawatzky, H. L. MANITOBA MENNONITES PAST AND PRESENT. *Mennonite Life 1974 29(1/2): 42-46.* Covers Mennonites in Manitoba 1870-1900.

3006. Selwood, H. John. URBAN DEVELOPMENT AND THE STREETCAR: THE CASE OF WINNIPEG, 1881-1913. *Urban Hist. Rev. [Canada] 1978 (3): 34-41.* Traces the growth of the streetcar system in Winnipeg through a series of four maps, and concludes that the streetcar system was shaped by the developing city and not vice versa. Primary and secondary sources; 4 maps, 13 notes.   C. A. Watson

3007. Shack, Sybil. THE IMMIGRANT CHILD IN THE MANITOBA SCHOOLS IN THE EARLY TWENTIETH CENTURY. *Tr. of the Hist. and Sci. Soc. of Manitoba [Canada] 1973-74 (30): 17-32.* Discusses the history of the public schools in Winnipeg during 1900-20, concentrating on the educational difficulties of Jewish Central European immigrant children. Examines the school attendance records. The lack of incentive was due in part to the academic program reflecting a strong Protestant British tradition taught by English-speaking teachers who paid little attention to the children's heritage, and to the clash with the impoverished home situation. Primary and secondary works; 14 notes.

S. R. Quéripel

3008. Siemens, Nettie. HISTORY OF THE DEVELOPMENT OF PUBLIC LIBRARIES IN MANITOBA. *Can. Lib. J. 1974 31(3): 206-211, 213.*

3009. Smith, Helen Pollitt. DR. CHARLOTTE W. ROSS— MANITOBA'S PIONEER WOMAN DOCTOR. *Manitoba Pageant 1975 21(1): 9-12.* Dr. Ross was Manitoba's first woman doctor. She officially practiced medicine from 1881-1910.   B. J. LaBue

3010. Smith, Helen Pollitt. OLD PINAWA. *Manitoba Pageant [Canada] 1976 21(3): 5-9.* The Winnipeg Electrical Street Railway Co. began land purchase for a hydroelectric plant in 1897 in the Seven Portages area of the Winnipeg River. The actual site selected was the Pinawa Channel because of its year-round water flow. To increase the amount of water a diversion dam was built. Construction began in April 1903 and the dam was completed 29 May 1906. The plant closed 21 September 1951. Illus.   B. J. LaBue

3011. Smith, Helen Pollitt. THE SOLOMON OF THE TRAPLINES. *Manitoba Pageant [Canada] 1976 21(2): 1-5.* In 1940 Harold Wells, an employee of the Department of Mines and Natural Resources, devised a plan for allocating trapping areas. The resulting Registered Trap Lines system has been credited with eliminating many of the abuses of industry, increasing the harvest, and saving the beaver from extinction in Manitoba. Illus.   B. J. LaBue

3012. Smith, Shirley A. THE STEWARD'S YARN. *Beaver [Canada] 1978 308(4): 20-23.* Retired traders, soldiers, and other frontiersmen, often told yarns of earlier adventures, exaggerated to include cannibalism tales. In 1844, Henry F. J. Jackson recorded a yarn of John Molden, a steward, of an event that happened in 1833. He was on a ship that stopped at Fort Churchill in December. Since the fort could not accommodate more people, most of the crew went overland to Fort York. According to Molden, they were inexperienced, the weather was fierce, one man was left to die, they were low on food, and his companion suggested killing one of the young apprentices for food. The Hudson's Bay Company Archives accounts verify much of the yarn, including the salvation of the party by an Indian who had hundreds of birds and other food that he shared for days with the starved group. The records suggest that, although there is no report of cannibalism, the event was full of hardship and sadness, and the yarn needed no exaggeration. 3 illus., map.

D. Chaput

3013. Spector, David. THE 1884 FINANCIAL SCANDALS AND ESTABLISHMENT OF BUSINESS GOVERNMENT IN WINNIPEG. *Prairie Forum [Canada] 1977 2(2): 167-178.* A business-minded city government in Winnipeg, Manitoba, sought efficient bookkeeping, limited services, and low taxes to promote effective administration for urbanization during the 1880's.

3014. Taylor, K. W. and Wiseman, N. CLASS AND ETHNIC VOTING IN WINNIPEG: THE CASE OF 1941. *Can. Rev. of Sociol. and Anthrop. [Canada] 1977 14(2): 174-187.* A unique opportunity to assess the relative strengths of class versus ethnic determinants of voting in provincial elections was offered by the historical development of class and ethnic relations in Winnipeg and the fact that the entire city was a multiple-member constituency for purposes of representation in the provincial legislature. Data analyses were carried out on areal units using census social area data, poll-by-poll voting results, and party and campaign literature. Class factors were found to be only marginally less important than ethnic factors in accounting for voting patterns despite a Liberal/Conservative/CCF party coalition and the lowest voter turnout in a provincial election historically recorded in Manitoba—factors which would tend to minimize class factors in voting. These results were corroborated by an analysis of transferable ballot data. Apart from minor differences in the relative weighting of class and ethnic factors, these results support the conclusions of an earlier similar study of Winnipeg voting patterns in the 1945 provincial election.

J

3015. Tweed, Tommy. ON THE TRAIL OF MR. O'B. *Alberta Hist. [Canada] 1975 23(2): 4-13.* An account of the scholarly hitch-hiker Eugene Francis O'Beirne from Ireland, who went to the Red River country in 1863 after wearing out his welcome in Wisconsin and Minnesota. O'Beirne figures prominently in travel narratives of the time as a fraud, interesting conversationalist, and alcoholic. Recent research in archives in Ireland confirms his background as a youth expelled from school and a young adult who gave inflammatory anti-Catholic lectures. After his Red River experiences, O'Beirne went to Queensland, Australia. 5 illus.

D. Chaput

3016. Unsigned. PUBLIC SERVICE BARGAINING IN MANITOBA. *Can. Labour 1974 19(4): 5-12.*

3017. Vernon, Donald E. INTEGRATING SOCIAL SERVICES IN MANITOBA. *Public Welfare 1973 31(3): 2-6.*

3018. Williamson, Norman J. LANSDOWNE COLLEGE: A PRODUCT OF THE DEPRESSION OF 1885. *Manitoba Pageant [Canada] 1976 21(4): 15-17.* In 1882 the Collegiate Institute began as a part of the Portage la Prairie school. As an economy measure on 12 June 1885 all first class teachers were fired. Two days later the Collegiate Institute closed. In 1887 the Reverend B. Franklin planned and organized his private college named after Marquis of Lansdowne, the Governor General of Canada. Unable to compete successfully with older, established colleges, Lansdowne College ceased operations in 1893.

B. J. LoBue

3019. Williamson, Norman J. PROSPECT SCHOOL 1876-1880. *Manitoba Pageant [Canada] 1976 21(2): 13-16.* The Prospect school district on the Portage Plains was organized in 1876. The selection of a rental site created a rift between families on the east and west side of the district. The selection of a permanent site in 1879 resulted in the district splitting into the East and West Prospect school districts. Based on the "secretary's book."

B. J. LaBue

3020. Wilson, John. THE DECLINE OF THE LIBERAL PARTY IN MANITOBA POLITICS. *J. of Can. Studies 1975 10(1): 24-44.* Because of the movement from a preindustrial to an advanced industrial society, a new kind of political polarization emerged in the Manitoba election of 1973. The Liberal Party, in decline since 1953, is no longer regarded as a serious political contender, even by supporters. Its working-class voters are tending to shift to the ruling New Democratic Party, while its middle-class voters look favorably upon the Progressive Conservative Party. Based on primary and secondary sources; 22 tables, 12 notes.

G. E. Panting

3021. Winkler, H. W. THE POLITICAL MEMOIRS OF H. W. WINKLER. *Manitoba Pageant 1972 18(1): 12-13, 24, 1973 (2): 8-11, (3): 16-21.* Continued from a previous article. Part III. The author discusses J. L. Brown's Liberal campaign for M.P. for Lisgar in 1926. Mennonites were shown that section 98 of the Criminal Code (an act giving Royal Canadian Mounted Police unlimited power in an emergency) could be repealed without hurting any anti-Communist movement. The author notes opposition from his party's "establishment" (T. A. Crerar, John Dafue, and John Bracken) until his retirement from politics in 1953. Part IV. Events in 1935 enabled the author to replace J. L. Brown as the Liberal-Progressive nominee for Parliament from Lisgar. His selection by a Liberal convention led to factionalism and disgust among many party members, especially officials of the Manitoba Liberal Association. Part V. The author discusses political campaigns and activities between his first election in 1935 as a Liberal M. P. from Lisgar until his retirement in 1952. Mentions election tactics, rival personalities, and the ingredients for a successful politician—time, qualifications, and luck.

D. M. Dean

3022. Wiseman, Nelson. THE CCF AND THE MANITOBA "NON-PARTISAN" GOVERNMENT OF 1940. *Hist. R. 1973 54(2): 175-193.* Traces the only case of participation in a Manitoba coalition government by Canada's Social Democratic Party. Reconstructs the debate within the party which led it to join the government and have its leader become minister of labor, the first socialist minister in Canada. Points to the dilemma faced by such parties operating in a parliamentary context, different only in degree, not in kind, from its competitors. Based on unpublished records of the Co-operative Commonwealth Federation in the national and Manitoba archives, primary and secondary sources.
J

3023. Wiseman, Nelson and Taylor, K. W. ETHNIC VS CLASS VOTING: THE CASE OF WINNIPEG, 1945. *Can. J. of Pol. Sci. 1974 7(2): 314-328.* Based on census and electoral returns and using multiple regression analyses, shows class voting to be exceptionally high and ethnicity a confounding factor disguising class voting behavior. 6 tables, fig, 33 notes.
R. V. Kubicek

Saskatchewan

3024. Appleblatt, Anthony. THE SCHOOL QUESTION IN THE 1929 SASKATCHEWAN ELECTION. *Study Sessions: Can. Catholic Hist. Assoc. [Canada] 1976 43: 75-90.* Summarizes the historical background of the school question in the 1929 provincial election, examines the impact and implications of separate school legislation in Saskatchewan, and outlines and analyzes the issues, especially heated Ku Klux Klan anti-Catholicism and campaigning.

3025. Arthur, Elizabeth. DUEL AT ILE-À-LA-CROSSE. *Saskatchewan Hist. [Canada] 1974 27(2): 41-50.* Deals with the conflicting details of a duel that may have occurred at Fort Chipewyan in October 1816 between two men named McVicar and McNeil. The problem arises when the two are cited variously as John, James, or Robert McVicar as well as Hector McNeil or McNeal. The matter is further complicated by either being located at Ile-à-la-Crosse or at Fort Chipewyan, and in 1815 or 1816. Attempts to clear up the confusion by examining a number of Hudson's Bay and North West Company sources. 47 notes.
C. Held

3026. Barnett, Le Roy. HOW BUFFALO BONES BECAME BIG BUSINESS. *Can. Geographical J. 1974 89(1/2): 20-25.* Traces the development in the late 19th century of the buffalo-bone trade into a major industry across the Prairie Provinces, especially in Saskatchewan. S

3027. Becker, A. THE LAKE GENEVA MISSION: WAKAW, SASKATCHEWAN. *Saskatchewan Hist. [Canada] 1976 29(2): 51-64.* In 1903 when the Presbyterian Church of Canada decided to establish a medical mission to serve the Dukhobors and Galicians of Western Canada they selected the Reverend George Arthur, originally from Hazel Grove, Prince Edward Island. He served in that position at the Lake Geneva Mission on Crooked Lake until 1908 when he was replaced by Reverend Robert George Scott, M.D., who served until the hospital and mission closed in 1942. A description of hospital problems during World War I and the Depression in Western Canada provides the bulk of the article. 6 photos, 34 notes.
C. Held

3028. Betke, Carl. THE MOUNTED POLICE AND THE DOUK-HOBORS IN SASKATCHEWAN, 1899-1909. *Saskatchewan Hist. [Canada] 1974 27(1): 1-14.* Following the initial need for the Royal Canadian Mounted Police to safeguard the province from the Indians, the force faced the necessity of being drastically reduced or changing its mission. The latter was the case and many new kinds of services were given by the officers to the settlers in the prairie West. Police comments on the suitability of certain ethnic groups for agricultural pursuits were not required but were made by the constables in their reports. These reports shed light upon the social and economic problems of the period. Personal antipathy toward certain ethnic groups was often overcome if they were successful as farmers. This was true in the case of the Galicians, Mennonites, and Mormons, and particularly the Doukhobors. The Doukhobors' tradition to "submit to no human authority" sorely tried the tolerance of the Mounted Police during their first decade in Canada. The

major reason for the problems that did exist is the change in policy toward the Doukhobor settlement, by the federal government. 2 illus., 60 notes.
C. Held

3029. Bohi, Charles W. and Grant, H. Roger. THE STANDARD-IZED RAILROAD STATION IN SASKATCHEWAN: THE CASE OF THE CANADIAN PACIFIC. *Saskatchewan Hist. [Canada] 1978 31(3): 81-96.* The railway depot was very much a part of the economic and social life of the communities through which the railroads passed. This was especially true for the Canadian Pacific Railway towns because so many were founded by the company. Because its lines were older and later had to develop different styles of architecture to compete with the Canadian National Lines, a large number of styles are characteristic of the CP stations. Map, 17 photos, 10 notes.
C. H. Held

3030. Bohi, Charles W. and Grant, H. Roger. THE STANDARD-IZED RAILROAD STATION IN SASKATCHEWAN: THE CASE OF THE CANADIAN NATIONAL SYSTEM. *Saskatchewan Hist. [Canada] 1976 29(3): 81-102.* Because the CN as it passes through Saskatchewan is made up of the former Canadian Northern and Grand Trunk Pacific lines it has inherited a number of different architectural styles and grades of quality in its stations. Some were town showpieces and others barely functional. Of the more than 200 standing in the early 1970's most were built between 1890 and 1914. 25 photos, 15 notes.
C. Held

3031. Brennan, J. W. PRESS AND PARTY IN SASKATCHE-WAN, 1914-1929. *Saskatchewan Hist. [Canada] 1974 27(3): 81-94.* The history of journalism in Saskatchewan is similar to that of many Canadian provinces from the late 19th century to the first third of the 20th century. Towns with many highly partisan small papers in the early years gradually evolved toward one-newspaper towns. Many newspapers were owned by large chains. Mentions Walter Scott, W. F. Herman, and George M. Bell, and more than 20 newspapers. 125 notes.
C. Held

3032. Bronson, H. E. THE SASKATCHEWAN MEAT PACKING INDUSTRY: SOME HISTORICAL HIGHLIGHTS. *Saskatchewan Hist. 1973 26(1): 24-37.* Although livestock production in Saskatchewan began in 1879 when range cattle were imported to supply the buffalo-deprived Indians, larger-than-local slaughterhouse processing did not begin until after 1900. Because changing international priorities, economic upheaval, and wars make the demand for meat products volatile and unpredictable, supplies of livestock to processors are generally undependable and inadequate. Mounting opposition to continentalism and favor to regional diversification may change this situation. 58 notes.
D. L. Smith

3033. Calderwood, William. RELIGIOUS REACTIONS TO THE KU KLUX KLAN IN SASKATCHEWAN. *Saskatchewan Hist. 1973 26(3): 103-114.* By 1926 the Ku Klux Klan was organized in most of the Canadian provinces. It fed on long-standing prejudices, but never had spectacular success. Its greatest impact was felt in Saskatchewan in 1927-30 where the prominent political issues of language, sectarianism, immigration, and control of natural resources could all be associated with a "Catholic plot." Evidence is strong that many conservative Protestants embraced and supported the principles of the KKK. 57 notes.
D. L. Smith

3034. Ching, Donald. SASKATCHEWAN'S OCCUPATIONAL HEALTH ACT. *Can. Labour 1973 18(4-6): 7-9, 41.*

3035. Choquette, Robert. OLIVIER-ELZÉAR MATHIEU ET L'É-RECTION DU DIOCÈSE DE REGINA, SASKATCHEWAN [Olivier-Elzear Mathieu and the establishment of the diocese of Regina, Saskatchewan]. *R. de l'U. d'Ottawa 1975 45(1): 101-116.* Discusses the conflict between Anglophiles and Francophiles in Saskatchewan and Mathieu's attempt to reconcile the two groups. Based on primary and secondary sources; 58 notes.
M. L. Frey

3036. Christensen, Deanna. "STEAMBOAT BILL" OF CUMBER-LAND HOUSE. *Beaver [Canada] 1974 305(3): 28-31.* Reminiscences of Bill McKenzie, born in 1901 at Cumberland House, where his father was a crew member on various steamwheelers plying the Saskatchewan and Bigstone rivers. Recalls boat stops, cargo, rates, shipping problems, personalities, and corporate competition. Copper discoveries in 1916-17 led to increased use of steamboats, but in 1925 a railroad extending from The Pas to Flin Flon led to their demise. 5 illus.   D. Chaput

3037. Church, G. C.   GOVERNMENT ASSISTANCE TO THE DAIRY INDUSTRY IN SASKATCHEWAN 1906-1917. *Saskatchewan Hist. [Canada] 1978 31(3): 97-110.* The attempt to establish and maintain a viable dairy industry in what was essentially a wheat growing area proved to be difficult for W. A. Wilson, Superintendent of Dairying in Saskatchewan, 1906-17, and for the Minister of Agriculture, W. R. Motherwell. Discusses many examples of cooperative creameries and other dairying enterprises. The original role of the government was to be advisory and educative, but this role was expanded on several fronts until disputes with private creamery operators brought Wilson's resignation. 64 notes.   C. H. Held

3038. Courtney, John C.   MACKENZIE KING AND PRINCE ALBERT CONSTITUENCY: THE 1933 REDISTRIBUTION. *Saskatchewan Hist. [Canada] 1976 29(1): 1-13.* Prince Albert, Saskatchewan, was William Lyon Mackenzie King's constituency since just after his defeat in North York in 1925. R. B. Bennett's Redistribution Bill of 1933 looked like a deliberate attempt to insure the opposition leader's defeat during the next election. King was offered an alternative to having his seat badly gerrymandered, but it involved losing W. R. Motherwell's constituency. King fought hard publicly to keep Prince Albert unchanged, but finally accepted a compromise which nevertheless gave him private concern for his safe seat. The 1935 election proved all concern to have been unnecessary. 2 maps, 24 notes.   C. Held

3039. Courville, L. D.   THE CONSERVATISM OF THE SASKATCHEWAN PROGRESSIVES. *Can. Hist. Assoc. Hist. Papers 1974: 157-181.* Discusses the underlying social and political conservatism of agrarian progressivism in Saskatchewan in the 1920's.

3040. Crone, Ray H.   AVIATION PIONEERS IN SASKATCHEWAN. *Saskatchewan Hist. [Canada] 1975 28(1): 9-28.* Discusses aviation in Saskatchewan from the first flight, by balloon, in 1908 by an unknown aeronaut, to the appearance of Katharine Stinson in Regina in the summer of 1918. Mentions W. W. Gibson, Don and Jim Brown, George and Ace Pepper, Bob St. Henry, Glenn L. Martin, Jimmy Ward, and Alfred Blakley. 7 photos, 47 notes.   C. Held

3041. Cullity, Emmet K.   RECOLLECTIONS AND REMINISCENCES: GOLD MINING CLAIMS. *Saskatchewan Hist. [Canada] 1974 27(1): 29-33.* A brief memoir of an engineer who embarked upon a gold seeking expedition at Beaver (Amisk) Lake in northern Saskatchewan in the spring of 1915. The gold strike grew as rich samples of ore were brought in from Flin Flon, derived from the mythical prospector Flintabatty Flonatin. Names Cullity's many acquaintances. His association with the area ended by 1927.   C. Held

3042. de Valk, Alphonse.   INDEPENDENT UNIVERSITY OR FEDERATED COLLEGE?: THE DEBATE AMONG ROMAN CATHOLICS DURING THE YEARS 1918-1921. *Saskatchewan Hist. [Canada] 1977 30(1): 18-32.* Deals with the complicated and often quarrelsome discussions of English-speaking Western Canadian Catholics attempting to establish a location for a college with degree-granting powers in Saskatchewan. The struggle centered on Regina and Saskatoon with the eventual victory going to Saskatoon through the federated college of St. Thomas More and the university there. J. J. Leddy, Father Henry Carr, President Murray (University of Saskatchewan), Archbishop Mathieu, Father Daly, and Father MacMahon played prominent roles in the eventual establishment of the federated college in Saskatoon. 54 notes.   C. Held

3043. Dojcsak, G. V.   THE MYSTERIOUS COUNT ESTERHAZY. *Saskatchewan Hist. 1973 26(2): 63-72.* The Saskatchewan town of Esterhazy bears the name of Count Paul O. d'Esterhazy (1831-1912), who founded a colony of Hungarian immigrants in 1886. This Esterhazy, however, was born as, and for his first 35 years was known as, Johan Baptista Packh. Illus., 30 notes.   D. L. Smith

3044. Driedger, Leo.   MENNONITE CHANGE: THE OLD COLONY REVISITED, 1955-1977. *Mennonite Life 1977 32(4): 4-12.* Com-

parison of studies of the Hague-Osler area of Saskatchewan shows that six of the original 15 villages disappeared between 1955 and 1977, and that six more are in decline. The role of the village committee and *Schultze* has been downgraded and Pentecostal evangelism has altered the old conservative religion. Other changes: consolidation of small schools, smaller families, more frequent use of English, more modern and colorful clothing, and introduction of nontraditional foods. Four processes have caused the changes: migration out of the area by the most conservative Mennonites, improved transportation to Saskatoon, influence of industrialization and capitalism, and a general liberalization in education and religion. 9 photos, map, 2 notes, biblio.   B. Burnett

3045. Goodwin, Theresa.   RECOLLECTIONS AND REMINISCENCES OF AN ENGLISH SCHOOL MARM IN SASKATCHEWAN. *Saskatchewan Hist. [Canada] 1974 27(2): 103-107.* The author writes of her teaching experiences in Chaplin and Duval, 1912-13. Photo.   C. Held

3046. Hall, D. J.   T. O. DAVIS AND FEDERAL POLITICS IN SASKATCHEWAN, 1896. *Saskatchewan Hist. [Canada] 1977 30(2): 56-62.* One of the roughest and readiest politicians, in an area known for such kinds, was Thomas O. Davis. In 1896 Wilfred Laurier was elected to both the Saskatchewan riding and Quebec East. A bye-election had to be held in Saskatchewan when he accepted the Quebec East seat. This was cause for a rough election and involved such figures as H. W. Newlands, A. E. Forget, Clifford Sifton, and Arthur L. Sifton as well as the successful T. O. Davis himself. The Liberal Party split, but not for long. Once in power the Liberal hold in Saskatchewan was not shaken for many years. 39 notes.   C. Held

3047. Hoffman, George.   THE ENTRY OF THE UNITED FARMERS OF CANADA, SASKATCHEWAN SECTION INTO POLITICS: A REASSESSMENT. *Saskatchewan Hist. [Canada] 1977 30(3): 99-109.* The usual interpretation of the relationship between North American agrarian movements and politics is that during economic hard times farm organizations resort to direct political action, while in more prosperous years they act as pressure groups. There is some evidence to support this, but the movement in Saskatchewan was more complex than that. Through the activities of George Edwards, J. S. Stoneman, George Williams, and others, the conservative wing of the movement advocated direct political involvement and later became leaders in the Co-operative Commonwealth Federation (CCF). Covers the period 1930-45. 72 notes.   C. Held

3048. Hoffman, George.   THE SASKATCHEWAN FARMER-LABOR PARTY, 1932-1934: HOW RADICAL WAS IT AT ITS ORIGIN? *Saskatchewan Hist. [Canada] 1975 28(2): 52-64.* While socialist and radical to some degree, in its early years the Farmer-Labor Party was moderated by the leadership of such persons as Tom Johnson, Mrs. A. Hollis of Shaunavon, Violet McNaughton, and M. J. Coldwell. There was considerable rank and file support for the social credit ideas of Major C. H. Douglas as well. "The generally held theory that the radical fathers of the party substantially moderated and compromised their ideas after 1934 needs to be seriously reassessed." 77 notes.   C. Held

3049. Huel, Raymond.   ADRIEN-GABRIEL MORICE, O.M.I., AND THE UNIVERSITY OF SASKATCHEWAN. *R. de l'U. d'Ot tawa [Canada] 1973 43(2): 195-204.* Discusses the scholarly career and contributions of Father Morice (1859-1938) in history, particularly at the University of Saskatchewan. Based on primary and secondary sources; 38 notes.   M. L. Frey

3050. Huel, Raymond.   THE ANDERSON AMENDMENTS AND THE SECULARIZATION OF SASKATCHEWAN PUBLIC SCHOOLS. *Study Sessions: Can. Catholic Hist. Assoc. [Canada] 1977 44: 61-76.* Dedicated to educational reform, Premier James T. M. Anderson advanced two major amendments to Saskatchewan's School Act which prohibited religious garb and symbols in the public schools (1930) and suppressed the French language in grade one (1931). These actions occurred in a climate of anti-Catholicism and spurred nationalism among French-speaking Catholics, including those in Quebec. Covers 1929-34.   G. A. Hewlett

3051. Kojder, Apolonja Maria. THE SASKATOON WOMEN TEACHERS' ASSOCIATION: A DEMAND FOR RECOGNITION. *Saskatchewan Hist. [Canada] 1977 30(2): 63-74.* Women educators in Saskatchewan can point to 1918 as the date when they first demonstrated their professional responsibility and integrity with the founding of the Saskatoon Women Teachers' Association (SWTA). Because the status of elementary teachers was very low, a positive self-image was necessary. The leaders in this early movement were Victoria "Tory" Miners and Hattie Wolfe. Later important figures were Ethel Coppinger and Caroline Robins. Great strides in improving conditions and wages for all teachers were made and the influence of the SWTA was widespread. 12 notes.
C. Held

3052. Kreider, Robert. 1923: THE YEAR OF OUR DISCONTENT, THE YEAR OF OUR PROMISE. *Mennonite Life 1973 28(4): 99-101.* Describes the immigration of 408 Russian Mennonites to Rosthern, Saskatchewan, in 1923, focusing on the prevailing social conditions in Canada at that time.

3053. Kupsch, Walter O. POWER OR WILD LIFE, LAND, RECREATION? *Can. Geographical J. 1974 89(4): 24-29.* Ecologists are concerned with the development of power plants in the Churchill River area of Saskatchewan.
S

3054. Lambert, Augustine. LIFE ON THE FARM. *Beaver [Canada] 1975 306(1): 19-23.* The 13 sketches and accompanying description were done by Augustine Lambert in 1913-14, while he farmed at Arelee, northwest of Saskatoon. The materials were then sent to his family in England. Lambert drew animals, wagons, harvesting and loading scenes, and social views such as Sunday church services and the family gathered around the pot-bellied stove. Lambert then joined the First Canadian Mounted Rifles and was killed at Vimy Ridge in 1917. Map, 13 illus.
D. Chaput

3055. Lander, Clara. SASKATCHEWAN MEMORIES OR HOW TO START A JEWISH CEMETERY. *Am. Jewish Arch. 1975 27(1): 5-7.*

3056. Makahonuk, Glen. TRADE UNIONS IN THE SASKATCHEWAN COAL INDUSTRY, 1907-1945. *Saskatchewan Hist. [Canada] 1978 31(2): 51-68.* The United Mine Workers of America, District 18, was organized in 1903. By 1907 it was active in Saskatchewan. The first strike occurred in 1908 and was considered marginally successful when only one large company recognized the union. A large, serious attempt at unionization was not mounted until the One Big Union (OBU) of 1919. This too was only temporarily successful. In 1931 the Mine Workers Union of Canada (MWUC) under J. Sloan made a more determined attempt. While not totally successful, it brought unionization much closer than ever before. Details numerous attempts to organize from 1931 to the Trade Union Act (1944), which finally made unionization possible in the mines of western Canada. 3 photos, 90 notes.
C. H. Held

3057. McLaren, Robert I. MANAGEMENT OF FOREIGN AFFAIRS REFLECTS PROVINCIAL PRIORITIES: THE CASE OF SASKATCHEWAN. *Int. Perspectives [Canada] 1978 (Sept.-Oct.): 28-30.* The provincial government of Saskatchewan, unlike the Federal Government of Canada, has no central machinery for the management of its international affairs, nor any general policy governing the international activities of its public servants. With the exceptions of Alberta and Quebec, the other provinces share the same approach to foreign relations, which consumes only five percent of the time of provincial officials. Although the Canadian provinces are involved in international affairs (mainly economic), the involvement is comparatively insignificant.
E. S. Palais

3058. O'Neill, P. B. D'OYLE CARTE V. DENNIS ET AL. *Saskatchewan Hist. [Canada] 1976 29(3): 114-117.* A landmark case for copyright was centered on the Regina Musical Society when it presented "The Pirates of Penzance" in December 1899. The resulting legal action required them to pay a fee that many felt would be the death of the theater in the Canadian West. It was not to be so. 13 notes.
C. Held

3059. O'Neill, P. B. REGINA'S GOLDEN AGE OF THEATER: HER PLAYHOUSES AND PLAYERS. *Saskatchewan Hist. [Canada]* *1975 28(1): 29-37.* The "Golden Age" of theater in North America, including Regina, was 1900-14. Mentions nearly a dozen theaters and several well-known performers, including Melba, Madame Albani, Minnie Maddern Fiske, Sophie Tucker, Lewis Waller, and Sir Johnston Forbes-Robertson. 3 photos, 35 notes.
C. Held

3060. Powell, T. J. D. NORTHERN SETTLEMENT, 1929-1935. *Saskatchewan Hist. [Canada] 1977 30(3): 81-98.* "Back to the land" movements have occurred several times in Canadian history, but the one which took place from 1929 to 1935 in the pioneer region of Saskatchewan had the most governmental support and perhaps the most problems. It arose naturally from the economic hard times of the period and was supported by the hard pressed city governments in the southern part of Saskatchewan as well as the Provincial and Dominion governments. The Conservative administration of J. T. M. Anderson took most of the blame for the general failure of the movement which came about mostly because of the haste and lack of supervision which allowed unsuitable lands to be opened up. This was only partially relieved by the Liberal Gardiner administration with the Land Utilization Board and the Northern Settlers' Reestablishment Branch. Map, photo, 90 notes.
C. Held

3061. Rees, R. THE "MAGIC CITY ON THE BANKS OF THE SASKATCHEWAN": THE SASKATCHEWAN REAL ESTATE BOOM 1910-1913. *Saskatchewan Hist. [Canada] 1974 27(2): 51-59.* By 1909 Saskatoon had acquired the basic functions which were to form the basis for its subsequent economic growth, the Canadian Pacific Railway, Canadian Northern, The Grand Trunk, and the University of Saskatchewan. The boom psychology was endemic throughout the prairie West and was served in Saskatoon by 257 real estate firms at its height in 1912. At its peak such things as the promotional group, the Industrial League, industrial cities named Factoria and Cordage Park, and a labor providing company with the Dickensian title of Toil Corporation Limited lent concepts to the boom, as did the adoption of Henry George's "single tax." J. C. Yorath, appointed city commissioner in 1913, gave some physical reality to Saskatoon with his city planning and famous map. Map, 30 notes.
C. Held

3062. Richards, John. SOCIAL DEMOCRACY VS. BUSINESS UNIONISM IN SASKATCHEWAN. *Can. Dimension 1975 10(7): 10-12.* Discusses conflicting labor relations in Saskatchewan involving the trade union movement.
S

3063. Richards, Mary Helen. CUMBERLAND HOUSE: TWO HUNDRED YEARS OF HISTORY. *Saskatchewan Hist. [Canada] 1974 27(3): 108-114.* A brief, chronologically arranged history of the oldest continuously occupied settlement west of Ontario. It was founded in 1774 by the Hudson's Bay Company, which is still operating in the community in 1974. Photo.
C. Held

3064. Riddell, W. A. POTASH: NEW WEALTH FOR SASKATCHEWAN. *Can. Geographical J. 1974 89(3): 16-23.* Describes deposit locations and mining projects.
S

3065. Robertson, D. F. THE SASKATCHEWAN PROVINCIAL POLICE, 1917-1928. *Saskatchewan Hist. [Canada] 1978 31(1): 1-11.* The Royal North West Mounted Police (RNWMP) were the policing authority in Saskatchewan and its territorial predecessor until 1916. Then, by mutual agreement, the "Force" was replaced by a provincial police force. The new police had the support of the Liberal Party but the Conservative Party favored retention of the old agreement. The question of politics concerning the changed policing arrangements is documented with many quotes from newspapers and speeches from 1916-28. Reasons given for the withdrawal of the RNWMP include war-caused shortages of men, need to concentrate on federal laws, and reluctance to enforce provincial liquor laws. By 1928 the political disadvantages of a provincial police became too great. Many official reasons were given, but the return to federal policing was heavily political. 2 photos, 41 notes.
C. Held

3066. Sinclair, Peter R. THE SASKATCHEWAN C.C.F. AND THE COMMUNIST PARTY IN THE 1930'S. *Saskatchewan Hist. 1973 26(1): 1-10.* The pragmatism of the Cooperative Commonwealth Federation in its programs and relations with other political organizations demonstrated that it was a political party rather than a social movement. The

C.C.F. efforts in the 1930's in the Meadow Lake constituency of Saskatchewan presented a united front of opposition supporters, including the Communist Party, to the governing Liberal Party. 41 notes.
D. L. Smith

3067. Sinclair, Peter R. THE SASKATCHEWAN CCF: ASCENT TO POWER AND THE DECLINE OF SOCIALISM. *Can. Hist. R. 1973 54(4): 419-433.* Examines the transformation of the Cooperative Commonwealth Federation's socialist policy, especially on land ownership, in order to appeal to a rural petit bourgeois electorate. Contributes to literature on the dilemma of parties which desire social change by electoral means. Based primarily on unpublished CCF party papers and newspapers in the Archives of Saskatchewan.   A

3068. Steck, Warren F. and Sarjeant, William A. S. A LOCAL SOCIETY IN URBAN AND PROVINCIAL AFFAIRS: THE HISTORY AND ACHIEVEMENTS OF THE SASKATOON ENVIRONMENTAL SOCIETY. *Urban Hist. Rev. [Canada] 1977 (2): 33-54.* Two members describe the formation and activities of the Saskatoon Environmental Society. As the leading private environmental group in Saskatoon, Saskatchewan, the S.E.S. became a major influence on environmental issues in and around the municipality. The S.E.S. decided to remain local in scope, urging the formation of similar groups in other Saskatchewan municipalities. 2 maps, 15 ref.   C. A. Watson

3069. Thomas, Lewis H. WELSH SETTLEMENT IN SASKATCHEWAN, 1902-1914. *Western Hist. Q. 1973 4(4): 435-449.* Part of a Welsh settlement in southern Argentina migrated to east-central Saskatchewan in 1902. Some 200 immigrants were closely knit by language, Protestantism, and customs, but they had no illusion that they could maintain their national identity. Previous experience on the Argentine pampas helped them to adjust rapidly and successfully to farming the prairies. 37 notes.   D. L. Smith

3070. Thomson, Colin A. DOC SHADD. *Saskatchewan Hist. [Canada] 1977 30(2): 41-55.* Alfred Schmitz Shadd, a black man from Ontario, moved to the Carrot River Valley in 1896. His ancestors, fugitive slaves, had long been activists who strove for equality for Canadian blacks. Deals with the black community around Chatham, Ontario, from the 1850's to about 1900. Shadd attended medical school in Toronto before moving to the North-West Territories where he became a school teacher and a "practical" doctor until he returned briefly to Toronto to complete his medical studies. From 1898 until his early death in 1915, Shadd's contributions to early Saskatchewan are well documented. Photo, 51 notes.
C. Held

3071. Tiessen, Hugo. MINING PRAIRIE COAL AND HEALING THE LAND. *Can. Geographical J. 1975 90(1): 29-37.* Looks at the history of strip coal mining in Saskatchewan's Estevan region since the 1850's, and the growing concern about the environmental effects of strip mining.   S

3072. Tiessen, Hugo. OLD-STYLE PRAIRIE RANCHING GIVES WAY TO INTENSIVE CROP-AND-CATTLE FARMING. *Can. Geographical J. 1974 88(4): 4-11.*

3073. Tiessen, Hugo. SASKATOON, SASKATCHEWAN. *Can. Geographical J. 1973 86(2): 54-61.*

3074. Trevena, J. E. OCAW MEMBERS SERVE CO-OP REFINERY. *Can. Labour 1973 18(7-9): 10-12, 43.*

3075. Unsigned. CUMBERLAND HOUSE, 1774-1794. *Beaver [Canada] 1974 305(3): 24-27.* Discusses the first days at Cumberland House on the Saskatchewan River, built by the Samuel Hearne party in 1774. 11 illus., map.   D. Chaput

3076. Wagner, Jonathan F. HEIM INS REICH: THE STORY OF LOON RIVER'S NAZIS. *Saskatchewan Hist. [Canada] 1976 29(2): 41-50.* Describes a group of 20 German families who settled in the Loon River area of Saskatchewan in 1929 and returned to Germany in 1939. Explores the difficulties they encountered in the Depression/Drought period of Western Canadian history, the role of the *Deutscher Bund Canada*, and the resultant reaction of anti-German neighbors. Hugo von

Schilling's letters and articles provide source material. 3 photos, 53 notes.
C. Held

3077. Wagner, Jonathan F. TRANSFERRED CRISIS: GERMAN VOLKISH THOUGHT AMONG RUSSIAN MENNONITE IMMIGRANTS TO WESTERN CANADA. *Can. Rev. of Studies in Nationalism [Canada] 1974 1(2): 202-220.* In 1917, a group of German Mennonite settlers left Russia to relocate in Saskatchewan, western Canada. In 1924, they established *Der Bote*, a German-language newspaper to inform and thus bind the Mennonite community more closely together. *Der Bote* enthusiastically supported Hitler after his advent to power in 1933. Earlier research has largely ignored this sympathy, and has emphasized instead the Mennonites' religious and ethnic diversity, or their contribution to the Canadian mosaic. This revision clears up the Mennonites' Nazi affinities by explaining their devotion to German völkisch thought, actually a mark of insecurity and a revolt against the chaotic conditions of modern living as well as a result of Mennonite hostility to the USSR, which had persecuted them. 55 notes.   T. Spira

3078. Ward, Norman. GARDINER AND ESTEVAN, 1929-34. *Saskatchewan Hist. [Canada] 1974 27(2): 60-65.* The election of 6 June 1929 led to a minority government by J. T. M. Anderson, a Conservative with support from Progressives and Independents. The opposition Liberal leader, James G. Gardiner, led a spirited by-election held in Estevan on 23 December 1930. The two contestants, David McKnight, Conservative, and Norman McLeod, Liberal, were over-shadowed by the big names from both parties who came to the district. The situation was very confused, as a recount and several court cases resulted in neither man sitting in the legislature. When the area was redistricted in 1932 both seats remained empty until 1934 when the Liberals won two newly created seats, Bromhead and Souris-Estevan. Portrait, 31 notes.   C. Held

3079. Ward, Norman. RT. HON. J. G. GARDINER AND 1905. *Saskatchewan Hist. [Canada] 1975 28(3): 111-117.* Memoir of James G. Gardiner which relates his experiences with the establishment of Saskatchewan as a province, 1905.

3080. White, C. O. THE HUMBOLDT MUNICIPAL ELECTRICAL UTILITY: A GRASSROOTS FEATURE OF THE SASKATCHEWAN POWER CORPORATION. *Saskatchewan Hist. [Canada] 1976 29(3): 103-113.* The electrical utility at Humboldt deserves attention because it became the first unit of the provincial electrical system on 1 November 1929, having been a small municipal system since 1907. Financial and operational problems occurred almost from the beginning, and the necessity of joining a larger system climaxed early in 1929. The choice of whether to sell out to the private Dominion Electric or join the new and untried Saskatchewan Power Corporation was finally decided in the latter's favor due to the work of such prominent local leaders as Frank H. Bence, Charles Cutting, Dr. Harry Fleming, Robert Telfer, and Father Dominic Hoffman. 58 notes.   C. Held

3081. White, Clinton O. THE QU' APPELLE ELECTRICAL UTILITY 1906-1927. *Saskatchewan Hist. [Canada] 1975 28(1): 1-8.* In the early 20th century electricity in Saskatchewan was produced by provincially, municipally, or privately sponsored companies. The electric utility at Qu'Appelle represents the latter origin. From 1906-27 the power plant of the Qu'Appelle Flour Mill, and its successors, provided the city with electricity. In 1927 the Montreal Engineering Company bought out the system, and the beginning of province-wide service lay on the horizon. 51 notes.   C. Held

3082. Wilson, L. J. EDUCATING THE SASKATCHEWAN FARMER: THE EDUCATIONAL WORK OF THE SASKATCHEWAN GRAIN GROWERS' ASSOCIATION. *Saskatchewan Hist. [Canada] 1978 31(1): 20-33.* The motto of the Saskatchewan Grain Growers' Association (SGGA), one of the oldest of the Canadian farm organizations, was: "Organization, Education and Co-operation Will Bring the Farmer Into His Own." Education was given high priority by George Edwards, the last president of the SGGA. The work of the association was complicated by the aggressive provincial educational programs fostered by W. R. Motherwell, former Provincial Minister of Agriculture and one of the founders of SGGA. Two women active on the Education Committee were Mrs. Violet McNaughton and Mrs. Annie Hollis. Much of the work mentioned occurred from the end of World War I to about the mid-

1920's. Education more than ideology was the hallmark of the SGGA. 53 notes.   C. Held

3083. —. AGRARIAN SOCIALISM. *Agric. Hist. 1977 51(1): 173-199.*
Burbank, Garin. AGRARIAN SOCIALISM IN SASKATCHEWAN AND OKLAHOMA: SHORT-RUN RADICALISM, LONG-RUN CONSERVATISM. *pp. 173-180.* Agrarian socialists in Oklahoma and Saskatchewan ca. 1900-45 did not want to replace capitalism with collective ownership of the land. The farmers and tenants who supported socialism wanted to better their lot rather than change the social order. 12 notes.
Calvert, Robert A. A. J. ROSE AND THE GRANGER CONCEPT OF REFORM. *pp. 181-196.* The leadership of the Texas Grange reflected southern conservatism in its stands on unions, railroad regulation, and the tariff. Like other Granges its organization was decentralized and divided. The most important Texas Granger, A. J. Rose, sought to keep the Grange out of politics. Rose emphasized educational and social activities and cooperatives along the Rochdale model which tried to avoid antagonizing merchants. When cooperatives failed, Grange membership declined and farmers turned to more radical groups such as the Alliance. 68 notes.
Hadwiger, Donald. AGRARIAN POLITICS IN THE GREAT PLAINS: A RESPONSE. *pp. 197-199.* The Saskatchewan Cooperative Commonwealth Federation and the Oklahoma Socialist Party had better success than the Texas Grangers in giving vent to frustration through political action. The Grange, on the other hand, did a better job of developing a sense of community among farmers. All three organizations may have had more influence on agrarian radicalism than Calvert or Burbank believe.   D. E. Bowers

Alberta

3084. Ajao, Adenihun O. and Barr, Brenton M. ENTREPRENEURIAL ASSESSMENT OF GOVERNMENTAL PROGRAMS TO ENCOURAGE ALBERTA'S FOREIGN TRADE. *Prairie Forum [Canada] 1977 2(2): 153-165.* Examines 60 businesses in Alberta involved in international trade and assesses how Canada's federal government can encourage Alberta business through incentives.

3085. Baldwin, Alice Sharples. THE SHARPLES. *Alberta Hist. R. 1973 21(1): 12-17.* Describes homesteading of horsemen Charles and William Sharples in southern Alberta, 1870's-1902. 2 illus.
                                                                D. L. Smith

3086. Baureiss, Gunter. THE CHINESE COMMUNITY IN CALGARY. *Alberta Hist. R. 1974 22(2): 1-8.* Traces the history of Calgary's Chinese community. The first Chinese came in 1886 when the coolie work force was no longer needed for railway construction in the Rockies. Through years of prejudice and discrimination a closely knit subcommunity has been formed. Today perpetuation of ethnic cultures and communities is official policy. 3 illus., table, 16 notes.
                                                                D. L. Smith

3087. Bicha, Karel D. JOHN W. LEEDY: CONTINENTAL COMMONER. *Alberta Hist. R. [Canada] 1974 22(3): 13-23.* Examines the career of John Whitnah Leedy (1849-1935), representative of a regional political type known as a "prairie radical," who had served as state senator and governor of Kansas before moving to Alberta.   S

3088. Boudreau, Joseph A. THE MEDIUM AND THE MESSAGE OF WILLIAM ABERHART. *Am. Rev. of Can. Studies 1978 8(1): 18-30.* William Aberhart, evangelist and first Social Credit premier of Alberta, used the radio effectively to promote his program of economic reform among his rural constituents. He spoke eloquently on political, social, and religious matters, often employing music and drama to heighten effect. Among his major themes were the evils of banks and the domination of the West by Eastern interests. Contrary to the popular view of Aberhart as a political opportunist, his radio broadcasts present him as a sincere, but naive, crusader. Primary and secondary sources, particularly recordings of Aberhart's radio broadcasts; 30 notes.
                                                                G.-A. Patzwald

3089. Breen, David H. CALGARY: THE CITY AND THE PETROLEUM INDUSTRY SINCE WORLD WAR TWO. *Urban Hist. Rev. [Canada] 1977 (2): 55-71.* Suggests that the oil economy of Calgary, Alberta, begun in 1914, but now based on the Leduc area discovered in 1947, fit nicely into the social-cultural milieu of the city's beef economy of the 19th and early 20th centuries. Calgary is compared with other prairie cities in terms of the oil industry and demographic change. Secondary works; 4 tables, 18 notes.   C. A. Watson

3090. Buchanan, Carl J. BY THE SEAT OF THE PANTS. *Beaver [Canada] 1977 308(3): 11-15.* In 1940 an eight-passenger Canadian Airways plane landed on the ice north of Edmonton. The author, a young boy, provided the necessary gasoline and was rewarded with his first airplane flight, a one-way trip to Edmonton. 4 illus.
                                                                D. Chaput

3091. Buchanan, Carl J. A WINTER'S DAY ON THE HOMESTEAD. *Beaver [Canada] 1976 307(3): 4-9.* Presents reminiscences of a typical winter day near Waskatenau, Alberta, northeast of Edmonton in the 1930's. Discusses chores, feeding animals, diet, weather, family activities, schooling, card games, and dancing. 6 illus.   D. Chaput

3092. Burles, Gordon. BILL PEYTO. *Alberta Hist. [Canada] 1976 24(1): 5-11.* Bill Peyto, an English immigrant, came to Alberta in 1887. From 1895 until his retirement in 1933 he was an explorer, guide, miner, and hunter in the Banff Park vicinity; he also participated in the Boer War and World War I. He was one of the pioneer guides near Banff and led major exploring and scientific expeditions to Mt. Assiniboine, Bow Glacier, Lake Louise, and Mt. Athabasca. 3 illus., 3 notes.   D. Chaput

3093. Carpenter, David C. ALBERTA IN FICTION: THE EMERGENCE OF A PROVINCIAL CONSCIOUSNESS. *J. of Can. Studies 1975 10(4): 12-23.* Discusses the portrayal of Alberta in fiction in the 20th century, emphasizing the works of W. O. Mitchell and Sinclair Ross.

3094. Chalmers, John W. SEASON'S GREETINGS FROM FORT CHIP. *Alberta Hist. [Canada] 1976 24(1): 1-4.* L. H. Lefroy, a British army officer at Fort Chipewyan and environs in 1843-44, wrote Christmas letters and poetry to friends and relatives in England. He included data on officers, fur company executives, and the Métis and other traders. 3 illus., 8 notes.   D. Chaput

3095. Choquette, Robert. JOHN THOMAS MCNAILLY ET L'ERECTION DU DIOCÈSE DE CALGARY [John Thomas McNailly and the establishment of the diocese of Calgary]. *Rev. de l'U. d'Ottawa [Canada] 1975 45(4): 401-416.* John Thomas McNailly (1871-1952), the first bishop of Calgary, was an anglophone who defended the interests of the Catholic anglophiles in Calgary, particularly the Irish. The Pope, in selecting McNailly, believed that western Canada was English in both language and culture. Provides brief sketch of McNailly's life and accomplishments and discusses his problems as bishop, particularly with the French Canadians. Primary and secondary sources; 84 notes.
                                                                M. L. Frey

3096. Comfort, D. J. TOM DRAPER: OIL SANDS PIONEER. *Alberta Hist. [Canada] 1977 25(1): 25-29.* In the 1920's, Tom Draper obtained leases to extract bitumen from the sands around Ft. McMurray, Alberta. Although the production of oil was part of the program, Draper emphasized the use of the sands as a paving substitute for asphalt. Transportation as well as leasing problems led to the abandonment of the project by the 1930's. 3 illus., 3 notes.   D. Chaput

3097. Corbet, Elise A. WOMAN'S CANADIAN CLUB OF CALGARY. *Alberta Hist. [Canada] 1977 25(3): 29-36.* The Woman's Canadian Club of Calgary was founded in 1911 as part of the elitism prominent at the turn of the century. Prior to World War I, the group was active in community affairs and patriotic activities. During the war, the club's efforts supported defense efforts. In postwar years, the group emphasized nationalism, integrating immigrants, and encouraging music and the arts. By the end of the 1920's, the group primarily was concerned with fostering a Canadian identity. Based on executive minutes and other organizational sources; 2 illus., 43 notes.   D. Chaput

3098. Corzyn, Jeni. EVERGREEN SUMMER, 1921: READINGS FROM A BIOGRAPHY BY EARLE BIRNEY. *Sound Heritage [Canada] 1977 6(3): 37-47.* Birney recounts his experiences as an axe man working with a survey party in Waterton Lakes National Park, Alberta, 1921.

3099. Court, Thomas. A SEARCH FOR OIL. *Alberta Hist. R. 1973 21(2): 10-12.* Describes three early attempts to tap supposed vast oil reserves under the oil sands of Alberta. 2 illus., biblio.
                                                        D. L. Smith

3100. Dempsey, Hugh A. GLENBOW CENTRE: CALGARY'S NEW MUSEUM. *Can. Geographical J. [Canada] 1977 94(2): 46-53.* Traces the history of the Glenbow-Alberta Institute from its beginnings in 1954 as the Glenbow Foundation, founded by Eric L. Harvie, to the 1976 opening of Glenbow Centre which houses the institute's museum collections, art gallery, library, and archives.

3101. Dempsey, Hugh A. A HISTORY OF ROCKY MOUNTAIN HOUSE. *Can. Historic Sites 1973 (6): 8-53.* "The history of Rocky Mountain House, a fur-trading post on the North Saskatchewan River in Alberta, . . . [and] contemporary accounts of the fort's appearance. An attempt is made to identify by historical evidence the sites of the three forts called 'Rocky Mountain House.' Seven lists from 19th-century invoices and inventories show the kinds of goods shipped to the West for the Indian trade and other uses."   J

3102. Dempsey, Hugh A. A LETTER FROM BISHOP GRANDIN. *Alberta Hist. R. 1973 21(1): 8-11.* Text of an 1876 letter of Vital Grandin (1829-1902), Bishop of St. Albert, which describes the Mounted Police, Fort Macleod, and Fort Calgary. 2 illus.   D. L. Smith

3103. Dempsey, Hugh A., ed. WHERE THE WEATHER COMES FROM. *Alberta Hist. [Canada] 1976 24(3): 28-30.* Based on an 1899 newspaper story from St. Paul, examines the role of Medicine Hat as a weather barometer for Canada and the United States. Details the gathering and reporting of weather information in Medicine Hat by a group headed by Col. James Beverly. Illus.   D. Chaput

3104. Den Otter, A. A. URBAN PIONEERS OF LETHBRIDGE. *Alberta Hist. [Canada] 1977 25(1): 15-24.* Lethbridge, founded in the early 1880's as a dreary coal mining village in Alberta, became a major urban center. The development of transportation and industry, as well as the city's educational, social, recreational, religious, and professional life are examined until 1890, when a municipal council was elected. 27 notes. 6 illus.   D. Chaput

3105. Easton, Carol. HISTORY AT PEACE. *Westways 1976 68(6): 32-35, 62-63.* Discusses the North Peace Country of Western Canada, focusing on homesteaders and the stories of pioneers, 1914-76.

3106. Elliott, David R. ANTITHETICAL ELEMENTS IN WILLIAM ABERHART'S THEOLOGY AND POLITICAL IDEOLOGY. *Can. Hist. Rev. [Canada] 1978 59(1): 38-58.* Close examination of the Social Credit ideology of William Aberhart, Alberta's premier from 1935-1943, indicates that it was clearly antithetical to his previous theology, which was highly sectarian, separatist, apolitical, other-worldly, and eschatologically oriented. Special attention has been paid to document collections which have not been used in previous studies: the Minutes of the Calgary School Board, the Minutes of Westbourne Baptist Church, the Minutes of the Bible Institute Baptist Church, the financial records of the Calgary Prophetic Bible Institute, the W. Norman Smith Papers, and the private collections of Mrs. Iris Miller and Mrs. Irene Barrett. Also used were the Premiers' Papers, Professor J. A. Irving's Papers, the Aberhart Papers, and the Calgary Prophetic Bible Institute Papers, which have been used very slightly by other scholars. This study challenges the statements of Mann (1955) and Irving (1959) that there was a definite connection between Aberhart's theology and political program. Further, Aberhart's political support did not come from the sectarian groups as Mann and Irving suggest, but rather it came from the members of established churches and those with marginal religious commitment.   A

3107. Flanagan, Thomas. STABILITY AND CHANGE IN ALBERTA PROVINCIAL ELECTIONS. *Alberta Hist. R. 1973 21(4):* *1-8.* Delineates three significant eras of provincial politics in Alberta: Liberal Party domination, 1905-21; United Farmers of Alberta control, 1921-35; Social Credit League leadership, 1935-73. A fourth period seems to be emerging. Points out numerous parallels and consistent patterns in each era. 2 illus., 3 tables, 6 notes, biblio.   D. L. Smith

3108. Foran, Max. BOB EDWARDS & SOCIAL REFORM. *Alberta Hist. R. 1973 21(3): 13-17.* Robert C. "Bob" Edwards, editor of *The Eye Opener,* a small newspaper published intermittently from 1904 to 1922, advocated social reform. He believed that the ills of society were caused by institutions which had outlived their usefulness. He was a populist, but lacked the characteristic evangelical strident clamor. 2 illus., 39 notes.   D. L. Smith

3109. Friedmann, Karl A. THE PUBLIC AND THE OMBUDSMAN: PERCEPTIONS AND ATTITUDES IN BRITAIN AND IN ALBERTA. *Can. J. of Pol. Sci. [Canada] 1977 10(3): 497-525.* Empirical study indicates that the general public, though very well disposed to the ombudsman, is not well informed on his functions. Data used from surveys in 1969 and 1971 in Alberta and in 1967 in Great Britain; 15 tables, 32 notes, appendix.   R. V. Kubicek

3110. Grayson, J. Paul and Grayson, L. M. THE SOCIAL BASE OF INTERWAR POLITICAL UNREST IN URBAN ALBERTA. *Can. J. of Pol. Sci. 1974 7(2): 289-313.* A statistical analysis based on census returns and reports of electoral officers. Provides a set of empirical generalizations which are used to test the conventional wisdom using different methods and sources about political protest movements. 3 tables, 41 notes.   R. V. Kubicek

3111. Hannant, Larry. FT. MC MURRAY'S PROBLEMS ARE GOING TO GET WORSE. *Can. Dimension 1975 10(7): 13-16.* Describes problems at the Great Canadian Oil Sands' Syncrude project.   S

3112. Holmgren, Eric J. EDMONTON'S REMARKABLE HIGH LEVEL BRIDGE. *Alberta Hist. [Canada] 1978 26(1): 1-9.* In 1891, the Calgary and Edmonton Railway reached north to the North Saskatchewan River; across the river was Edmonton, still without any rail connection to the south. Construction of a high-level bridge was begun in 1910, and the bridge first saw service on 2 June 1913. Discusses bridge-building, as well as motives of competing railway lines, attitudes of citizens of Edmonton, and workings of the city council and other city agencies, who had conflicting views about the bridge's location. Based on newspapers and legal documents; 4 illus.   D. Chaput

3113. Holtslander, Dale. RAILWAY TO ATHABASCA. *Alberta Hist. [Canada] 1978 26(1): 25-28.* In 1912, the Canadian Northern Railway line from Edmonton to Athabasca Landing was completed. Reprints a news story from the *Edmonton Bulletin* regarding the towns, bridges, and scenery along the route in 1912. Discusses changes viewed in a 1977 automobile trip along the route of the abandoned railway. Comments on the growth and demise of villages, especially related to the railway and subsequent highway developments.   D. Chaput

3114. Hurlburt, William H. THE UNIFIED BAR, ALBERTA STYLE. *Judicature 1974 57(6): 256-261.*

3115. Jameson, Sheilagh S. THE ARCHIVES OF THE GLENBOW-ALBERTA INSTITUTE (CALGARY). *Urban Hist. Rev. [Canada] 1978 (3): 69-79.* The Chief Archivist describes the history of the Glenbow-Alberta Institute, Calgary, from its beginnings in 1955 to the opening of its new building in 1976. Lists information for researchers.
                                                        C. A. Watson

3116. Johnson, Arthur H. COMING TO ALBERTA. *Alberta Hist. [Canada] 1976 24(1): 23-27.* Discusses turn-of-the-century homesteading near Red Deer-Halrirk by a family of North Dakota farm boys. Examines means of acquiring land, type and use of tools, neighborhood work sessions to harvest and plant, and early adjustments to the Alberta frontier. 2 illus.   D. Chaput

3117. Johnson, Ronald C. RESORT DEVELOPMENT AT BANFF. *Alberta Hist. [Canada] 1975 23(1): 18-24.* Traces governmental exploitation of the mineral hot springs at Rocky Mountain Park in the late nineteenth century.   S

3118. Kellas, James G. OIL, FEDERALISM AND DEVOLUTION: A CANADIAN-BRITISH COMPARISON. *Round Table [Great Britain] 1975 (259): 273-280.* Examines the similarities between the Scottish and Alberta devolution issues, their respective control over oil resources, and relationships with the federal and national government.

C. Anstey

3119. Keywan, Zonia. MARY PERCY JACKSON: PIONEER DOCTOR. *Beaver [Canada] 1977 308(3): 41-47.* In 1929, Dr. Mary Percy left England to practice medicine in northern Alberta. She began near Manning, among new immigrants from Eastern Europe who knew little English. After her marriage to Frank Jackson, they moved to the farm near Keg River. Most of her service here was with local Indians and Métis. With few medical supplies, inadequate transportation, and rarely any income from patients, she continued to provide medical service to the local population until her retirement in 1974. In the past few decades she has become a nationally known spokeswoman for Indian and Métis causes. 6 illus.

D. Chaput

3120. Klassen, Henry C. BICYCLES AND AUTOMOBILES IN EARLY CALGARY. *Alberta Hist. [Canada] 1976 24(2): 1-8.* The bicycle and automobile as modes of transportation in Calgary developed in a similar fashion to other North American cities, though the impact of the bicycle was slightly less in Calgary because of the cost. Examines impact of the bicycle and automobile on social habits, law, economy, and general community life. Impact on the livery stables was particularly harsh. 5 illus.

D. Chaput

3121. Klassen, Henry C. THE MENNONITES OF THE NAMAKA FARM. *Mennonite Life 1975 30(4): 8-14.* Describes farming on the Namaka Farm, a 13,000-acre communal Mennonite settlement east of Calgary, 1920's-40's.

3122. Klassen, Henry C. SOCIAL TROUBLES IN CALGARY IN THE MID-1890'S. *Urban Hist. Rev. [Canada] 1974 74(3): 8-16.* During 1894-96 the city government of Calgary, Alberta, was forced to deal with myriad social problems: poverty, public housing, unemployment, crime, sanitation, and disease.

3123. Koch, Agnes and Labovitz, Sanford. INTERORGANIZATIONAL POWER IN A CANADIAN COMMUNITY: A REPLICATION. *Sociol. Q. 1976 17(1): 3-15.* The Perrucci and Pilisuk community power study of a medium-sized midwestern U.S. city is replicated on a small Prairie Canadian resort town [Banff, Alberta]. The interorganizational basis for power, derived from overlapping executive memberships, is the perspective followed in both studies. Essentially the same results are found in both places. A well-defined elite structure exists capable of mobilizing interorganizational power resources.

J

3124. Koester, Mavis Addie. CHILDHOOD RECOLLECTIONS OF LUNDBRECK. *Alberta Hist. [Canada] 1978 26(4): 23-30.* The author and her sister came to Lundbreck, Alberta, in 1905 because her father, William Addie, became the manager of the coal mine at Lundbreck. Discusses loneliness, attempts to adjust to community, infrequent relations with the Indians, and occasional visits with the few other residents, 1905-08. 3 illus.

D. Chaput

3125. Lapul, David. THE BOBTAIL LAND SURRENDER. *Alberta Hist. [Canada] 1978 26(1): 29-39.* The Bobtail Cree Reserve was near Ponoka, on the Calgary-Edmonton Trail. Around 1900, the government acceded to pressure from settlers to permit more land to come into non-Indian ownership. A typical policy statement was: "The land is needed by better men." By 1909, most of the land had been sold, after surveys, agreements with several chiefs, and due process which led to investigations and policy statements by the Canadian government. The sales price per acre was not what the Cree had originally agreed to, which led to distrust and disillusionment. Based primarily on manuscripts in the Interior Department's Public Archives of Canada; 4 illus., map, 70 notes.

D. Chaput

3126. LaRose, Helen. THE CITY OF EDMONTON ARCHIVES. *Urban Hist. Rev. [Canada] 1974 74(3): 2-7.* Chronicles the Edmonton, Alberta, city archives, 1938-74, and discusses collection holdings and plans for the facility.

3127. Lehr, John C. CHANGING UKRAINIAN HOUSE STYLES. *Alberta Hist. [Canada] 1975 23(1): 25-29.* Transformation of immigrant architecture as a reflection of Anglo-Canadian assimilation from the late 19th century to the present.

S

3128. Lehr, John C. UKRAINIAN HOUSES IN ALBERTA. *Alberta Hist. R. 1973 21(4): 9-15.* Ukrainian pioneer cottages in Alberta are distinctive cultural expressions of generations of practical experience of the homeland. The Ukrainian area of settlement in Alberta became distinctive visually as well as culturally. 3 illus., 15 notes.

D. L. Smith

3129. Long, J. Anthony and Slemko, Brian. THE RECRUITMENT OF LOCAL DECISION-MAKERS IN FIVE CANADIAN CITIES: SOME PRELIMINARY FINDINGS. *Can. J. of Pol. Sci. 1974 7(3): 550-559.* Uses data from aldermen in five Alberta cities obtained through extensive interviews in 1971. Notes importance of service groups with no formalized political function in the recruitment process. 4 tables, 24 notes.

R. V. Kubicek

3130. Lund, Rolf T. THE DEVELOPMENT OF SKIING IN BANFF. *Alberta Hist. [Canada] 1977 25(4): 26-30.* Skiing began in the region in the 1890's and received its main impetus with the winter carnival in 1916. In the next decades the carnival became popular; ski jumping and cross-country races led to much publicity. By 1940, Banff had become one of Canada's leading skiing centers. 24 notes.

D. Chaput

3131. Lund, Rolf T. RECREATIONAL SKIING IN THE CANADIAN ROCKIES. *Alberta Hist. 1978 26(2): 30-34.* Recreational skiing began in the 1920's, through the efforts of the Banff Ski Club and the Canadian Pacific Railway. The Sunshine ski area was opened in 1933, and Mount Temple's chalet was opened in 1939. Snow Dome was the first major mountain peak to be climbed on skis in Canada, in March of 1930. Based on interviews, published guides, correspondence, and materials in the Provincial Archives of Alberta. 2 illus., 16 notes.

D. Chaput

3132. Mackie, Marlene. OUTSIDERS' PERCEPTION OF THE HUTTERITES. *Mennonite Q. Rev. 1976 50(1): 58-65.* Asks "How is a sacred community perceived by members of the containing society?" and "Do outsiders withhold acceptance of a people which refuses to be integrated?" The study is based on a sample of 590 persons around Edmonton, Alberta. The conclusions are that most appreciate Hutterite uniqueness. Social distance is not based on stereotyped prejudice. 4 tables, 12 notes.

E. E. Eminhizer

3133. Mansbridge, Stanley H. OF SOCIAL POLICY IN ALBERTA: ITS MANAGEMENT, ITS MODIFICATIONS, ITS EVALUATION AND ITS MAKING. *Can. Public Administration [Canada] 1978 21(3): 311-323.* Discusses policy formation, management, and modification in Alberta's Department of Social Services and Community Health in the 1970's, including the role of the minister in relation to the legislature, budgetary processes, and the structure of important committees.

3134. Masson, Jack K. DECISION-MAKING PATTERNS AND FLOATING COALITIONS IN AN URBAN CITY COUNCIL. *Can. J. of Pol. Sci. 1975 8(1): 128-137.* Edmonton city councillors who have campaigned together as an electoral party or slate do not regularly vote together on issues before the municipal government. 4 tables, 32 notes.

R. V. Kubicek

3135. McClellan, George B. PERSONAL EXPERIENCES OF AN R.C.M.P. OFFICER. *Can. Geographical J. 1973 86(5): 182-191.*

3136. McCormack, Martin. ALBERTA'S FIGHT TO REDUCE HAIL DAMAGE. *Can. Geographical J. 1974 89(1/2): 30-39.* Discusses Alberta's cloud-seeding program to suppress damage caused by hailstorms.

S

3137. McDougall, John. THROUGH THE FOOTHILLS. *Alberta Hist. [Canada] 1975 23(2): 1-3.* Reprint of a 1902 newspaper article by Methodist missionary John McDougall regarding his travels from Calgary to Banff. The author had crossed the same terrain many times since 1873. 2 illus.

D. Chaput

3138. McGinnis, J. P. Dickin. A CITY FACES AN EPIDEMIC. *Alberta Hist. [Canada] 1976 24(4): 1-11.* Examines the impact of the influenza epidemic of 1918-19 on Calgary. Dr. Cecil S. Mahood, city health officer, coordinated the programs, often leading to controversies regarding school closings and quarantine regulations. Calgary lacked doctors and nurses, many of whom were still in Europe with the armed forces. Based mostly on newspaper accounts; 4 illus., 27 notes.
D. Chaput

3139. McLeod, Evelyn Slater. RESTLESS PIONEERS. *Beaver [Canada] 1976 307(1): 34-41.* As a six-year-old, the author arrived at Stettler, Alberta, with her North Dakota family. Relates pioneer experiences such as building a sod-house, farming, gopher problems, and schooling. 10 illus.
D. Chaput

3140. Nearing, Peter. REV. JOHN R. MAC DONALD, ST. JOSEPH'S COLLEGE AND THE UNIVERSITY OF ALBERTA. *Study Sessions: Can. Catholic Hist. Assoc. 1975 42: 70-90.* John Roderick MacDonald (b. 1891), a Basilian Father, undertook Archbishop O'-Leary's 1922-23 project of organizing a Catholic university in Edmonton, thus working toward the evangelization of the large immigrant population of the West, despite his own failing health.

3141. Newinger, Scott. THE STREET CARS OF CALGARY. *Alberta Hist. R. [Canada] 1974 22(3): 8-12.*

3142. North, John. TOWARDS DECENTRALIZATION: THE LEARNING RESOURCE CENTRE OF MOUNT ROYAL COLLEGE. *Can. Lib. J. 1973 30(3): 236-242.*

3143. Orrell, John. EDMONTON THEATRES OF ALEXANDER W. CAMERON. *Alberta Hist. [Canada] 1978 26(2): 1-10.* In 1906, Alexander W. Cameron brought vaudeville to Edmonton at the Empire Theater. Until 1913, Cameron was the driving force in this aspect of Edmonton's cultural life. He was either the main investor, or planner, of the Edmonton Opera House, the Kevin, Orpheum, and Lyric Theaters. Cameron was innovative. When attendance dropped at the opera house, he converted the building into a roller skating rink during the weekdays. Cameron left the Edmonton area around 1913. Based on newspaper accounts and government documents. 4 illus., 16 notes.
D. Chaput

3144. Palmer, Howard. NATIVISM IN ALBERTA, 1925-1930. *Can. Hist. Assoc. Hist. Papers 1974: 183-212.* Discusses attitudes toward immigration and ethnic minorities in Alberta society 1925-30.

3145. Regehr, Ted D. MENNONITE CHANGE: THE RISE AND DECLINE OF MENNONITE COMMUNITY ORGANIZATIONS AT COALDALE, ALBERTA. *Mennonite Life 1977 32(4): 13-22.* Russian German immigrants settled Coaldale, Alberta, 1920-30, but because they came as individuals rather than as a colony, they were subject to Canadian regulations and could not transplant distinctly Mennonite institutions and social structures. Organizations evolving from the settlement included churches, a German library, a language preservation society, and Saturday schools. Settlers founded a cooperative cheese factory, a Savings and Credit Union, and a society to provide medical care. Although prosperous, Mennonites at Coaldale had become assimilated into the larger Canadian society by 1976, largely because of the decline of the German language, economic consolidation, superiority of government welfare services, and internal divisions involving religious splits and inadequate leadership. Primary sources; 13 photos.
B. Burnett

3146. Schrumm, J. R. VALLEY OF GOLD. *Alberta Hist. [Canada] 1974 22(4): 14-25.* Describes the activities of gold seekers during an 1897 gold rush on the upper Saskatchewan River in Alberta.
S

3147. Schwermann, Albert H. MY DEBT OF GRATITUDE TO THE U.S.A. *Concordia Hist. Inst. Q. 1977 50(1): 23-31.* The author was born in Jefferson City, Missouri, in 1891. He became a Lutheran minister in 1913 and served in Mellowdale, Alberta, before becoming the president and a faculty member of Concordia College in Edmonton. His career at Concordia spanned 42 years. Expresses gratitude for the upbringing and educational experiences he enjoyed in the United States. 6 notes.
W. T. Walker

3148. Serfaty, Meir. THE UNITY MOVEMENT IN ALBERTA. *Alberta Hist. R. 1973 21(2): 1-9.* Analyzes the failure of the unity movement, which was an effort to unite opposition parties under a single nonpartisan banner, a protest movement to upset the Social Credit Party that gained power in Alberta in 1935. Its importance was in demonstrating that only a provincially inspired and organized party could hope for electoral victory. 3 illus., 35 notes.
D. L. Smith

3149. Silverman, Elaine Leslau. PRELIMINARIES TO A STUDY OF WOMEN IN ALBERTA, 1890-1929. *Can. Oral Hist. Assoc. J. [Canada] 1978 3(1): 22-26.* Discusses 130 interviews with women who migrated to or were born in rural Alberta during 1890-1929, in order to assess the importance of oral history; concludes that history of exceptional women does not represent the cross section, that social hierarchy which related men to each other separated women from one another, that historical assessments of men's lives does not necessarily pertain to women's lives, and that historical periodization formed by men does not hold true for women.

3150. Spragins, F. K. SYNCRUDE: FULL STEAM AHEAD. *Can. Geographical J. 1975 90(2): 46-49.* The project to develop the Athabasca tar sands of northern Alberta continues.
S

3151. Stanley, George F. G. THE NAMING OF CALGARY. *Alberta Hist. 1975 23(3): 7-9.* When he founded Fort Brisbois as a Mounted Police post in 1875, the inspector first named the place after himself. The following year the name Calgary was adopted, supposedly meaning "clear running water." Examines Gaelic sources, and concludes that the site was named for a place on the Isle of Mull in the Hebrides, Scotland. Gaelic authorities conclude that the correct meaning is "bay farm." Illus., 7 notes.
D. Chaput

3152. Thomson, Colin A. "DARK SPOTS IN ALBERTA." *Alberta Hist. [Canada] 1977 25(4): 31-36.* In 1911, blacks from Oklahoma decided to homestead in western Canada. Local opposition in Alberta took many forms, including resolutions by various unions, editorials, and petitions to Prime Minister Laurier. Around 1,000 blacks settled in Alberta in 1912, and were carefully scrutinized for health problems and financial ability. The "invasion" never happened, as the blacks dispersed in the province and adjusted reasonably well. 2 illus., 30 notes.
D. Chaput

3153. Thomson, Theresa E. ONE THOUSAND CLIMBS TO BREAKFAST. *Alberta Hist. R. 1974 22(1): 12-17.* Biographical sketch of Riel Rebellion veteran Norman Bethune Sanson (1862-1949) who was curator of the Banff museum and a meteorologist. He put the weather observatory atop a nearly 9,000-foot peak and made more than 1,000 ascents to record data. 2 illus.
D. L. Smith

3154. Turner, A. E. THE CALGARY CO-OP. *Can. Labour 1973 18(7-9): 16-18, 42.*

3155. Unsigned. THE SOUTH FORK RANCH. *Alberta Hist. R. 1974 22(1): 28-29.* Anonymous account from the *Calgary Herald,* 26 August 1897, of a visit to F. W. Godsal's South Fork Ranch.
D. L. Smith

3156. Villa-Arce, José. ALBERTA PROVINCIAL POLICE. *Alberta Hist. R. 1973 21(4): 16-19.* Traces the history of the Alberta Provincial Police, 1917-32. 2 illus.
D. L. Smith

3157. Ward, Norman. HON. JAMES GARDINER AND THE LIBERAL PARTY OF ALBERTA, 1935-40. *Can. Hist. R. 1975 56(3): 303-322.* Previous studies of the Social Credit era in Alberta have virtually ignored other parties and their attempts to defeat Social Credit. Based almost entirely on the papers of Rt. Hon. J. G. Gardiner, who was the minister in charge of the Liberal Party in Alberta from 1935 to 1939, the article establishes that that party and others were indeed active in the period, and a loose coalition of them came close to winning the provincial election of 1940. A major question for the Liberals was whether to join that coalition or fight alone, as Gardiner desired. Gardiner believed coalition meant destruction for the Liberals.
A

3158. Ward, Norman. WILLIAM ABERHART IN THE YEAR OF THE TIGER. *Dalhousie R. [Canada] 1974 54(3): 473-479.* Seldom has the traditional honeymoon between politicians and the electorate been shorter than that enjoyed by William Aberhart of the Social Credit Party. Probably the greatest contributing cause outside the depression, which hit Alberta particularly hard, was the venture into a newspaper (The Calgary *Albertan*) and radio station (CJCJ). Many small investors in the projects had risked much based on Aberhart's advice, and when by 1938 the stock was worthless he could only be apologetic. His worst problem in 1938 was his near dismissal as provincial prime minister by lieutenant governor John C. Bowen, caused by disillusionment among some of his own supporters who urged the lieutenant governor to dismiss Aberhart. This plus the rather crude and bungling ouster of Governor Bowen from Government House nearly led to the dismissal of the prime minister. It was politically dangerous for the federal Liberals, however, and following much fuming but little action the issue eventually passed away. 10 notes.
C. Held

3159. Weaver, John C. EDMONTON'S PERILOUS COURSE 1904-1929. *Urban Hist. Rev. [Canada] 1977 (2): 20-32.* Describes the boom and bust years of Edmonton, Alberta. Huckster elements promoted Edmonton after its incorporation in 1904 and it gained a reputation as a progressive municipality. After the crash of 1913, however, its earlier corruption and lack of a solid financial base led to a very difficult 15 years. Based on Edmonton city records and secondary works; 38 notes.
C. A. Watson

3160. Williamson, David T. TOM KERR: A MIGHTY TRADER WAS HE. *Alberta Hist. [Canada] 1977 25(3): 23-28.* Tom Kerr was born in Scotland in 1861 and, lured by the fur trade, came to Canada in 1878. For the next 30 years Kerr served at many of the Hudson's Bay Company's posts, including Peace River, Fort St. John, Fort Dunvegan, Fond Du Lac, and Little Red River. In 1901 Kerr returned briefly to Scotland to marry, then went to Little Red River. In 1911 Kerr settled at Sturgeon Lake where he headed the Hudson's Bay Company's post. He lived there until his death in 1946. Based on childhood memories of the author, who knew Kerr at Sturgeon Lake; 3 illus.
D. Chaput

3161. Wilson, L. J. EDUCATIONAL ROLE OF THE UNITED FARM WOMEN OF ALBERTA. *Alberta Hist. [Canada] 1977 25(2): 28-36.* Traces the history of the United Farm Women of Alberta from its founding in 1915 until the Depression. Examines the development of library services, youth programs, folk school movements, and social services. The organization emphasized practical rather than theoretical approaches. Though its philosophy altered during the 1920's, the organization effectively served thousands. Its collapse was due to the Depression, not to any organizational shortcomings. 3 illus., 30 notes.
D. Chaput

3162. Wood, C. E. D. ON THE ROAD TO BANFF, 1890. *Alberta Hist. [Canada] 1977 25(3): 1-12.* Reprints an article by the author, editor of the Macleod *Gazette,* who visited Calgary and Banff with three companions. Examines the changes of a few years in Calgary: new officials, new building construction, new industries. Also comments on young communities along the way. Describes the Canadian Pacific Railway's hotel at Banff, and locations such as Devil's Lake and Sheep Creek. Comments on recreation and future use of the area as a National Park. 7 illus.
D. Chaput

3163. Woywitka, Anne B. DRUMHELLER STRIKE OF 1919. *Alberta Hist. R. 1973 21(1): 1-7.* The Alberta government, the mine companies, and the United Mine Workers of America allied to combat the threat of the One Big Union to the U.M.W.A. as the legal bargaining agent of mine workers in the Drumheller Valley. 4 illus.
D. L. Smith

3164. Woywitka, Anne B. A PIONEER WOMAN IN THE LABOUR MOVEMENT. *Alberta Hist. [Canada] 1978 26(1): 10-16.* Teklia Chaban was born in the Ukraine. She moved to Alberta in 1914, the year of her marriage. Her husband worked in the Cardiff coal mines, 15 miles north of Edmonton. Follows the family for the next 10 years, with agitation for a labor organization, dealings with the United Mine Workers of America, and strikes and violence in the early 1920's. She was active in Ukrainian cultural movements that were part of the labor efforts. In the

mid-1920's the family moved to Edmonton, and again was involved in agitation for labor recognition, spending some time in jail and suffering periodic unemployment for their efforts. 2 illus.
D. Chaput

3165. Woywitka, Anne B. A ROUMANIAN PIONEER. *Alberta Hist. R. 1973 21(4): 20-27.* Recounts the struggles of pioneer Rumanian homesteaders in Alberta, particularly of Mrs. Veronia Kokotailo (b. 1894) whose family migrated in 1898. 3 illus.
D. L. Smith

3166. Woywitka, Anne B. WAUGH HOMESTEADERS AND THEIR SCHOOL. *Alberta Hist. [Canada] 1975 23(1): 13-17.*

3167. Young, John J. A VISIT TO THE COCHRANE RANCHE. *Alberta Hist. R. [Canada] 1974 22(3): 26-30.* Section of a story written by the editor of the *Calgary Herald* about his 1902 visit to the Cochrane ranch.
S

3168. —. HARVEST TIME: A PICTURE STORY. *Alberta Hist. [Canada] 1978 26(4): 15-22.* Fourteen photographs of wheat harvests, wagons and other equipment, men at lunch, impact of the weather on harvest, and other agricultural views, during 1910-20, in Alberta, Canada.
D. Chaput

3169. —. HUGH BEYNON BIGGS: RANCH PHOTOGRAPHER. *Alberta Hist. [Canada] 1978 26(3): 13-20.* Biggs, born in India, settled at Rosebud Creek, Alberta, in 1892. He was an active amateur photographer whose glass plate negatives are now in the Glenbow Archives, Calgary. Reprints 12 photos, mostly agricultural, with Indian and railroad construction scenes, 1890's-1920's.
D. Chaput

3170. —. A SPORTING LIFE. *Alberta Hist. 1978 26(2): 13-20.* Fifteen photographs from the Provincial Archives, Edmonton, of sports events in the early 1900's. Pictures and comments on harness racing, ski jumping, sailing, fishing, hunting, hockey, curling, football, polo, and basketball.
D. Chaput

3171. —. W. HANSON BOORNE: PHOTOGRAPHIC ARTIST. *Alberta Hist. [Canada] 1977 25(2): 15-22.* The firm of Boorne and May was prominent in the west 1886-93. W. Hanson Boorne opened a studio in Calgary in 1886 and one in Edmonton in 1891. In 1893 he returned to England. Most of his negatives are in the Provincial Archives, Edmonton. Boorne is noted for his outstanding scenic views and for his views of the Blood Indian self-torture ritual. 13 illus.
D. Chaput

British Columbia

3172. Achtenberg, Ben. BC: THREE YEARS LATER. *Working Papers for a New Soc. 1976 3(4): 12-20.* Discusses politics, labor, housing, and the fishing industry in Vancouver, British Columbia, during the 1970's.

3173. Alper, Donald. THE EFFECTS OF COALITION GOVERNMENT ON PARTY STRUCTURE: THE CASE OF THE CONSERVATIVE PARTY. *BC Studies [Canada] 1977 (33): 40-49.* The Liberal-Conservative coalition government, 1941-52, was formed to prevent another wartime election and to block the socialist Co-operative Commonwealth Federation from coming to power in British Columbia. It allowed the Conservatives to reach positions of power which were not otherwise possible. It also had a disintegrative affect on the caucus and organizational structures of the Conservative Party. Chart, 24 notes.
D. L. Smith

3174. Andrews, Margaret W. EPIDEMIC AND PUBLIC HEALTH: INFLUENZA IN VANCOUVER, 1918-1919. *BC Studies [Canada] 1977 (34): 21-44.* The influenza pandemic during 1918-19 struck one-fourth of the world's population and was the greatest short term killer of any kind in human history. In Vancouver, British Columbia, the threat of a breakdown in delivery of crucial public health services and the high level of public concern temporarily weakened public confidence in public health authorities. As a whole, the epidemic experience was remarkably ephemeral and the long term trends of centralization, specialization, and bureaucratization of public health matters quickly resumed. Table, 6 graphs, 76 notes.
D. L. Smith

3175. Atherton, Jay. THE BRITISH COLUMBIA ORIGINS OF THE FEDERAL DEPARTMENT OF LABOUR. *BC Studies [Canada] 1976-77 (32): 93-105.* Traces the British Columbia antecedents in the 1800's and 1890's that led to the passage of the federal Conciliation Act in 1900. This act created the Department of Labour and established the foundations for the Canadian system of industrial relations. 46 notes.
D. L. Smith

3176. Begg, Hugh M. RESOURCE ENDOWMENT AND ECONOMIC DEVELOPMENT: THE CASE OF THE GULF ISLANDS OF BRITISH COLUMBIA. *Scottish Geographical Mag. [Great Britain] 1973 89(2): 119-130.* Examines the relations between human settlement and the environment on the Gulf Islands, 1858-1973.

3177. Bernard, Elaine. A UNIVERSITY AT WAR: JAPANESE CANADIANS AT UBC DURING WORLD WAR II. *BC Studies [Canada] 1977 (35): 36-55.* The impact of World War II on the University of British Columbia must be considered in the context of race relations in the province and national policy. The 1940 National Resources Mobilization Act meant compulsory military training on the campus in the Canadian Officers' Training Corps, including the Canadian students of Japanese descent. The Japanese Canadians were abruptly discharged from the service, however, after Pearl Harbor. Eventually some 70 "Japanese" students were forced out of the university and the coastal area. 30 notes, 4 appendixes.
D. L. Smith

3178. Bradbury, J. H. CLASS STRUCTURES AND CLASS CONFLICTS IN "INSTANT" RESOURCE TOWNS IN BRITISH COLUMBIA: 1965 TO 1972. *BC Studies [Canada] 1978 (37): 3-18.* The provincial government of British Columbia cooperated with multinational resource extraction companies, 1965-72, to create new "instant" towns to replace company towns. The promoters hoped that this would eliminate some of the class conflicts and industrial strikes present in the older towns. Such was not the case. 3 tables, graph, 27 notes.
D. L. Smith

3179. Brooks, G. W. S. EDGAR CROW BAKER: AN ENTREPRENEUR IN EARLY BRITISH COLUMBIA. *BC Studies [Canada] 1976 (31): 23-43.* Edgar Crow Baker (d. 1920) was a representative entrepreneur in Victoria when that city was the social, business, and political center of British Columbia. Although he came to Victoria as an employee, he had ideas and ambitions, a valuable family connection, and fraternal affiliations that allowed him into the business life of the city. Baker was involved in almost every major economic activity in the province: land, lumber, railroads, coal, shipping, public utilities. He was also active in municipal, provincial, and federal politics. 51 notes.
D. L. Smith

3180. Cain, Louis P. WATER AND SANITATION SERVICES IN VANCOUVER. AN HISTORICAL PERSPECTIVE. *BC Studies [Canada] 1976 (30): 27-43.* Traces the origin and development of the water supply, sewage-disposal and drainage practices of Vancouver, British Columbia. The evolution of these strategies have been analogous to those of other salt-water cities. Its relative youth enabled Vancouver to benefit from the mistakes of other cities and to adopt the best modern practices. 30 notes.
D. L. Smith

3181. Carey, Betty. SALVAGE FROM THE *KENNECOTT*. *Alaska J. 1973 3(1): 56-61.* Discusses the wrecking of Alaska Steamship Company motorship *Kennecott* on British Columbia's Queen Charlotte Islands in 1923.

3182. Carey, Neil G. QUEEN CHARLOTTES: RECOVERY, REDISCOVERY. *Can. Geographical J. 1974 89(4): 4-16.* Pictorial essay of the Queen Charlotte Islands of northern British Columbia.
S

3183. Carter, Margaret. BENNETT: TOWN OR ILLUSION? *Alaska J. 1978 8(1): 52-59.* A history of the town of Bennett, British Columbia. With the discovery of gold at Bonanza Creek, Yukon Territory, in 1896, White Pass and Chilkoot Pass became the leading routes to the Yukon interior. Both trails led from Taiya Inlet to the upper end of Lake Bennett, where the town of Bennett soon sprang up. It was prosperous because there travelers and freight exchanged land transport for water transport. At first it was a center for boat building; later, with the advent of stern-wheeler service north to Whitehorse, it became a center for warehousing. When the railroad through White Pass arrived in 1899, Bennett's prosperity seemed assured, but the railroad continued on to Whitehorse, and the town all but disappeared. Based on contemporary newspaper accounts, archival materials, and secondary sources; 3 illus., map, 29 notes.
L. W. Van Wyk

3184. Carter, Norman M. JOHNNY HARRIS OF SANDON. *Beaver [Canada] 1976 306(4): 42-49.* Sandon, in southeast British Columbia, was an important mining zone at the turn of the century, and Harris quickly had control of the best real estate. He ran hotels, saloons, shops, and gambling houses, and for several decades was the most important of the entrepreneurs in the area. Harris was hurt by investments in wheat futures at the time of the Depression. Based on reminiscences of the author, whose father was a dentist in Sandon; 9 illus.
D. Chaput

3185. Chapman, Peter, ed. NAVIGATING THE COAST: A HISTORY OF THE UNION STEAMSHIP COMPANY. *Sound Heritage [Canada] 1977 6(2): 1-77.* Interviews with former employees of the Union Steamship Company, 1889-1959, which operated along the coast of British Columbia; consists of individual statements and essays on crews, fishing, logging, navigation, working conditions, daily life, local people, and geography.

3186. Clemson, Donovan. CANYON CROSSINGS OF THE FRASER. *Can. Geographical J. 1973 86(2): 36-43.* Surveys bridges and ferries across Fraser Canyon.
S

3187. Cleveland, John and Packlington, Guy. THE N.D.P. DIDN'T SNEAK INTO POWER IN B.C.—IT WAS PUSHED. *Can. Dimension 1973 9(2/3): 13-18, 63.* Analyzes the results of the 1972 British Columbia provincial elections. The victory of the New Democratic Party (NDP) over the right-wing parties was due largely to labor discontent with the economy, unemployment, and "anti-union" activities such as compulsory arbitration. Some pre-election cooperation between unions and organizations of the unemployed contributed to a sharp leftward swing in the blue-collar vote. Public disputes and evident disorganization within the right-wing parties antagonized some voters. Illus.
W. B. Whitham

3188. Cole, Douglas. EARLY ARTISTIC PERCEPTIONS OF THE BRITISH COLUMBIA FOREST. *J. of Forest Hist. 1974 18(4): 128-131.* British explorers and colonizers of the 18th and 19th centuries thought coniferous forests uninteresting and unpleasant. Few artists painted the flora of the British Columbia coast until the 1930's. 10 notes.
L. F. Johnson

3189. Cole, Douglas. PAINTING IN BRITISH COLUMBIA: A REVIEW ARTICLE. *BC Studies [Canada] 1974 (23): 50-53.* Reviews three works on Canadian paintings: *A Concise History of Canadian Painting* by Dennis Reid (Toronto: Oxford U. Press, 1973), *Images of Canada* by the Public Archives of Canada (Ottawa: Information Canada, 1972), and *Impressionism in Canada, 1895-1913* by Joan Murray (Toronto: Art Gallery of Ontario, 1973). The British Columbia content is stressed. Secondary sources; 4 notes.
W. L. Marr and S

3190. Cuthbertson, Shirley. THE NEW LOOK OF B.C.'S PROVINCIAL MUSEUM. *Can. Geographical J. [Canada] 1978 96(1): 38-45.* The displays at the British Columbia Provincial Museum in Victoria range from archaeology to modern history.

3191. Dahlie, Jorgan. THE JAPANESE CHALLENGE TO PUBLIC SCHOOLS IN SOCIETY IN BRITISH COLUMBIA. *J. of Ethnic Studies 1974 2(1): 10-23.* Reviews the history of the Japanese communities of British Columbia from 1900 until sweeping evacuation orders in 1942 shipped thousands into camps in the province's interior. Ever since the beginning of the century prejudice and discrimination were overt and thinly disguised, based on "economic, political, and social rationalizations." The constant theme was that of non-assimilability, and by the interwar years the "Oriental Menace" was a threat to a white British Columbia. The maintenance of separate Japanese-language schools and Buddhist religious centers added to the discriminatory feeling, and by the 1940's their dual nationality automatically meant fifth column activities. Paradoxically most of the Issei and Nisei coped extremely well with the restrictions and persecutions, both official and unofficial, which they experienced. The only bright spot was the work of various Christian missionary groups among the Japanese children and in the relocation camps. Since World War II conditions for minorities have improved markedly in British Columbia with the establishment of a policy of multiculturalism. Based on contemporary sources; 58 notes.

G. J. Bobango

3192. Devlin, T. P. HOMESTEADING IN NORTHERN BRITISH COLUMBIA. *Mennonite Life 1976 31(4): 21-27.* In the late 1930's drought conditions in southern Saskatchewan forced many farm families on government relief. The Canadian government assisted relocation of some families to an area approximately 65 miles south of Burns Lake, British Columbia. Twenty-five families and 17 carloads of effects arrived in Burns Lake by rail on 7 May 1940. They proceeded by trucks and ferries to the homestead area, where they build log houses at an average cost of $15 and planted crops. Twenty-five additional families joined the settlers in 1941. All the families were self-sufficient by 1942. The successful program would have continued, but World War II intervened. 13 photos.

B. Burnett

3193. Elkins, David. POLITICS MAKES STRANGE BEDFELLOWS: THE B.C. PARTY SYSTEM IN THE 1952 AND 1953 PROVINCIAL ELECTIONS. *BC Studies [Canada] 1976 (30): 3-26.* The 1952 and 1953 elections in British Columbia were among the most significant elections in the 20th century. They marked the decline of the provincial Liberal and Conservative parties and the rise of Social Credit. In 1952 and 1953 voters were asked to rank all of the candidates in their riding. From this data the transferable vote system reveals the voters' collective perceptions as to which parties were distant from each other and which were close to each other. Tests two alternative hypotheses about rankings of the parties in the left-right spectrum. 5 tables, 3 figs., 31 notes.

D. L. Smith

3194. Esselmont, Harriet A. E. ALEXANDER JOHN DOULL: AN APPRECIATION. *J. of the Can. Church Hist. Soc. [Canada] 1976 18(4): 98-108.* Traces the life and career of Alexander John Doull, the first bishop of Kootenay in the Okanagan Valley, British Columbia. Born in Nova Scotia of a Church of Scotland family, Doull was an orphaned only child. Reared by relatives, he received his advanced education in the British Isles where he converted to Anglicanism and became a priest. After he returned to Canada, Doull served churches in Montreal and Victoria before he became the youngest bishop of the Church of England in Canada. A man of strong convictions, he took active positions on the issues of the day and worked to increase the strength of Anglicanism in his diocese. When he died in 1937, the *Canadian Churchman* declared, "His character was that beautiful combination of strength and beauty, grace and truth which the Apostles found in the Saviour." 25 notes.

J. A. Kicklighter

3195. Fleischman, Harry. A REPORT FROM BRITISH COLUMBIA. *Dissent 1975 22(3): 287-290.* Describes the goals of the New Democratic Party government in British Columbia and of its leader, David Barret.

S

3196. Forward, Charles N. RELATIONSHIPS BETWEEN ELDERLY POPULATION AND INCOME SOURCES IN THE URBAN ECONOMIC BASES OF VICTORIA AND VANCOUVER. *BC Studies [Canada] 1977-78 (36): 34-46.* The British Columbia cities of Victoria and Vancouver are widely known as leading Canadian retirement centers. Of 20 Canadian metropolitan areas, Victoria has the lowest proportion of income from employment and the highest from both investments and pensions. Vancouver's proportion of people 65 and older is second only to Victoria, but its income characteristics tend to resemble those of the average Canadian city. These conclusions are derived from taxation statistics, ordinarily overlooked in studies of urban functional characteristics. Future studies of the economic base of any area should include this source of income data. 2 tables, 7 graphs, 7 notes.

D. L. Smith

3197. Gough, Barry M. KEEPING BRITISH COLUMBIA BRITISH: THE LAW-AND-ORDER QUESTION ON A GOLD MINING FRONTIER. *Huntington Lib. Q. 1975 38(3): 269-280.* The 1858 gold rush in British Columbia brought an influx of people, causing a fear of

lawlessness. Colonial officials, particularly James Douglas, governor of the colony, succeeded in maintaining British law and administration. Primary and secondary sources; 44 notes.

S. R. Smith

3198. Gough, Barry M. SEA POWER AND THE HISTORY OF WESTERN CANADA. *J. of Can. Studies 1973 8(2): 50-59.* Chronicles the necessity for naval strength along Canada's western coast, 1790-1973.

3199. Greer, David M. REDISTRIBUTION OF SEATS IN THE BRITISH COLUMBIA LEGISLATURE, 1952-1978. *BC Studies [Canada] 1978 (38): 24-46.* Redistribution of legislative seats to reflect shifts in population growth usually creates turmoil and unhappiness. Reallocations of seats in the British Columbia legislature in 1955, 1966, and 1978 were no exception. During this period, however, the principle of having redistribution determined by independent commissions came to be accepted. Legislature tampering with commission recommendations and the political motivations of a commissioner turned the three commissions' efforts into partisanship. 2 tables, 89 notes.

D. L. Smith

3200. Harrington, Richard. TREKKING THE TRAIL OF 1898. *Can. Geographical J. 1974 89(1/2): 14-19.* Retraces the route traveled by gold miners over the Coast Range from Skagway, Alaska, to Lake Bennett, British Columbia, during the Klondike Stampede.

S

3201. Harris, Barbara P. and Kess, Joseph F. SALMON FISHING TERMS IN BRITISH COLUMBIA. *Names 1975 23(2): 61-66.*

3202. Harris, R. Cole. LOCATING THE UNIVERSITY OF BRITISH COLUMBIA. *BC Studies [Canada] 1976-77 (32): 106-125.* Location of the University of British Columbia was debated from 1885 to 1910. The debate involved newspapers, boards of trade, and businessmen. The controversy was caused largely by sectionalism, concern for growth and development, as manifested in the bidding for commercial and numerical preeminence and by concern for the quality of life the competitors offered to a university. 72 notes.

D. L. Smith

3203. Hatfield, H. R. ON THE BRIGADE TRAIL. *Beaver [Canada] 1974 305(1): 38-43.* The author, a retired engineer, in 1967 began to trace and mark the old Brigade Trail from Ft. Hope to Thompson's River, British Columbia, the major trail used by the Hudson's Bay Company in the mid-1800's. Relates each portion of the trail to persons who used it. Includes quotes from Hudson's Bay Company Archives and other sources. 6 illus., map.

D. Chaput

3204. Haworth, Kent M. and Maier, Charles R. *"NOT A MATTER OF REGRET": GRANVILLE'S RESPONSE TO SEYMOUR'S DEATH. BC Studies [Canada] 1975 (27): 62-66.* A letter from Lord Granville to Queen Victoria, June 1869, is presented to show that he recommended the appointment of Anthony Musgrave as governor of British Columbia after Frederick Seymour's death because he desired to unite British Columbia with Canada in Confederation. Secondary sources; 20 notes.

W. L. Marr

3205. Hawthorn, Audrey. UBC'S NEW MUSEUM OF ANTHROPOLOGY. *Can. Geographical J. 1976 93(2): 52-57.* Outlines the history and artifacts of the Museum of Anthropology at the University of British Columbia, 1947-70's, including archaeological exhibits.

3206. Hendrickson, James E. TWO LETTERS FROM WALTER COLQUHOUN GRANT. *BC Studies [Canada] 1975 (26): 3-15.* After giving a biography of Walter C. Grant, an early colonizer of Vancouver Island, two of his letters are reproduced, one dated 1851 and the other undated. Primary and secondary sources.

W. L. Marr

3207. Hitchman, James H. THE ORIGINS OF YACHT RACING IN BRITISH COLUMBIA AND WASHINGTON, 1870-1914. *Am. Neptune 1976 36(4): 231-250.* Describes the development of organized yacht racing in the Puget Sound area from its origins in the 1870's until World War I, when racing temporarily ceased. Focuses on US-Canadian competitions and the role of the Northwestern International Yachting Association. Based on published sources; 6 photos, map, table, 38 notes.

G. H. Curtis

3208. Houde, Serge. WHITE BEARS OF THE WEST COAST. *Can. Geographical J. [Canada] 1977 95(1): 10-17.* Chronicles the historical presence of the white black bear in British Columbia during the 20th century.

3209. Howard, Victor. THE VANCOUVER RELIEF CAMP STRIKE OF 1935: A NARRATIVE OF THE GREAT DEPRESSION. *Can.: An Hist. Mag. 1974 1(3): 9-16, 26-33.*

3210. Inkster, Tom H. FORT LANGLEY: MAINLAND B.C.'S BIG TOWN, 1827-58. *Can. Geographical J. [Canada] 1977 95(1): 48-53.* An historical restoration of Fort Langley, British Columbia (built by the Hudson's Bay Company in 1827), has just been completed; chronicles the settlement's importance strategically, economically, and politically, 1827-58.

3211. Irby, Charles C. THE BLACK SETTLERS ON SALT-SPRING ISLAND IN THE NINETEENTH CENTURY. *Phylon 1974 35(4): 368-374.* Negroes who settled on Saltspring Island, British Columbia, in the late 1850's and early 1860's did not, contrary to popular myth, establish a separate black colony; rather they were dispersed over the island like the other immigrant groups. The early settlement of the island created a mosaic of nationalities, and partly because of pressure from Native Americans, a degree of social cohesion developed among this mixed group of settlers. Portrays the antecedents of the settlement, and describes the roles and positions of blacks in the colonial society. Black settlement on the island involved four salient factors: 1) they immigrated via Vancouver Island, 2) they immigrated over a period of years, 3) they were a free black population, and 4) their hopes, desires, fears, and frustrations were the same as those of their nonblack neighbors. Based on primary and secondary sources; 28 notes. B. A. Glasrud

3212. Koenig, Daniel J.; Martin, Marlene; Martin, Gary R.; and Goudy, H. G. THE YEAR THAT BRITISH COLUMBIA WENT NDP: NDP VOTER SUPPORT PRE- AND POST- 1972. *BC Studies [Canada] 1974/75 (24): 65-86.* Voter support in British Columbia for the New Democratic Party is analyzed by various socioeconomic characteristics, 1968-74. Primary and secondary sources; 6 tables, 4 notes. W. L. Marr

3213. Kolehmainen, John I. THE LAST DAYS OF MATTI KURIKKA'S UTOPIA: A HISTORICAL VIGNETTE. *Turun Hist. Arkisto [Finland] 1976 31: 388-396.* The collapse of the Finnish American utopian colony at Harmony Island, British Columbia, active 1901-05, was due largely to the unrealistic ideas of its founder, Matti Kurikka (1863-1913). R. G. Selleck

3214. Kristianson, Gerry L. THE NON-PARTISAN APPROACH TO B.C. POLITICS: THE SEARCH FOR A UNITY PARTY—1972-1975. *BC Studies [Canada] 1977 (33): 13-29.* The depression of the 1930's and the extraordinary circumstances of World War II promoted appeals to British Columbian politicians to transcend party lines and unite. At various times since 1906 fear of a socialist electoral victory has brought similar demands. Soon after the collapse of W. A. C. Bennett's antisocialist coalition in the 1972 election and the accession of a socialist government, efforts began to forestall a repetition of this development in the next election. Most interest focuses on combining the three opposition parties into a single force. Discusses the efforts of the Majority Movement and of the politicians during 1972-75 and speculates whether the unity theme will have another resurgence. 38 notes. D. L. Smith

3215. Lai, Chuen-Yan David. A FENG SHUI MODEL AS A LOCATION INDEX. *Ann. of the Assoc. of Am. Geographers 1974 64(4): 506-513.* Use of the concept Feng Shui and an examination of topographical surveys suggests the location of a Chinese cemetery near Swan Lake, British Columbia. S

3216. Langan, Joy. BCFL WOMEN'S RIGHTS COMMITTEE. *Can. Labour 1975 20(2): 11-12, 34.* Discusses the British Columbia Federation of Labour's Committee for Women's Rights since 1970. S

3217. Lappage, Ronald S. BRITISH COLUMBIA'S CONTRIBUTION TO THE DOMINION-PROVINCIAL YOUTH TRAINING PROGRAM THROUGH PROVINCIAL-RECREATION PRO-GRAM. *Can. J. of Hist. of Sport and Physical Educ. [Canada] 1978 9(1): 86-92.* The Recreational and Physical Education Branch of British Columbia's Education Department provided physical training and recreational activity for unemployed youth during 1934-40.

3218. Lawrence, Joseph C. THE FOREST AND THE TREES: A REVIEW ARTICLE. *BC Studies [Canada] 1976 (30): 77-82.* Evaluates six recent, 1974-75, publications. Chides the Canadian forest industry for its reluctance to make its records safe and available for the use of historians. Contrasts the paucity of British Colombia records with the considerable volume of materials available to American scholars. D. L. Smith

3219. Layton, Monique. MAGICO-RELIGIOUS ELEMENTS IN THE TRADITIONAL BELIEFS OF MAILLARDVILLE, B. C. *BC Studies [Canada] 1975 (27): 50-61.* The magico-religious elements in the traditional beliefs of the people of Maillardville, British Columbia, are reviewed: remedies, weather, religious symbols, animals, gardening, games. Primary and secondary sources; 19 notes. W. L. Marr

3220. Lee, Carol F. THE ROAD TO ENFRANCHISEMENT: CHINESE AND JAPANESE IN BRITISH COLUMBIA. *BC Studies [Canada] 1976 (30): 44-76.* Traces the issue of Chinese and Japanese enfranchisement in British Columbia from 1935-49. Considers the events, trends, and concepts which finally eroded the long standing provincial hostility to Orientals. Enfranchisement symbolized a significant change in public attitudes and reflected a change in the prevailing conceptions of the nature of citizenship and political rights in Canada. 64 notes. D. L. Smith

3221. Lillard, Charles. LOGGING FACTS AND FICTION: A BIBLIOGRAPHY. *Sound Heritage [Canada] 1977 6(3): 73-77.* Alphabetical listing of books (both fiction and nonfiction) on the logging industry in the Pacific Northwest and British Columbia, 1890's-1960's.

3222. MacDonald, Norbert. THE CANADIAN PACIFIC RAILWAY AND VANCOUVER'S DEVELOPMENT TO 1900. *BC Studies [Canada] 1977 (35): 3-35.* The Canadian Pacific Railway played a critical role in shaping the overall development of Vancouver, British Columbia, in the 19th century, especially in the late 1880's and early 1890's. Its impact was clearly evident in the city's waterfront area, residential districts, street layout, parks, real estate prices, economy, politics, and social clubs. The CPR boom ended with the depression of 1893. When Vancouver began to recover with the Klondike gold rush in the late 1890's the CPR still played an important role, but the "utter dependence" of former years was over. 4 maps, 3 tables, 81 notes. D. L. Smith

3223. MacDonald, Norbert. VANCOUVER IN THE NINETEENTH CENTURY. *Urban Hist. Rev. [Canada] 1975 75(1): 51-54.* Geographical and natural resources aided in parallel growth of the economy and population in Vancouver, British Columbia, during the 19th century; one of eight articles in this issue on the Canadian city in the 19th century.

3224. MacLachlan, Morag. THE SUCCESS OF THE FRASER VALLEY MILK PRODUCERS' ASSOCIATION. *BC Studies [Canada] 1974/75 (24): 52-64.* After tracing the history of dairying in British Columbia before 1917, the activities of the Fraser Valley Milk Producers' Association, with respect to market stability after 1917, are examined. Primary and secondary sources; 20 notes. W. L. Marr

3225. Marchak, Patricia. WOMEN WORKERS AND WHITE-COLLAR UNIONS. *Can. R. of Sociol. and Anthrop. 1973 10(2): 134-147.* "A survey of white-collar workers in British Columbia revealed that union potential is higher among women than among men and is directly related to income and levels of job control. Union members provided an opposite response pattern to that of non-union workers in similar jobs. Men were more supportive of their union than were women, and their support was greater as their control and income levels increased. The descriptive data show that women have low incomes regardless of job control, education, or union status, that most have low job control regardless of education or union status, and that their hopes for promotion are small compared to those of men. The income and control allocations strongly suggest that existing white-collar unions do not benefit women workers."   J

3226. McDermott, John. MYSTERY MAN OF QUATSINO SOUND: THE SECOND LIFE OF WILLIAM CLARKE QUANTRILL. *Am. West 1973 10(2): 12-16, 63.* Argues that Quantrill apparently died in 1907, not in 1865 as formerly thought. By the Civil War Quantrill was a famous outlaw leader. His band included Jesse and Frank James. During the war "Quantrill's Raiders," operating independently, conducted raids and guerrilla warfare under the Confederate flag. They ransacked Lawrence, Kansas, and killed 150 people. Left for dead in a barnyard shootout with Union troops near Louisville, Kentucky, Quantrill recovered and escaped to South America. He returned, alias John Sharp, to Oregon, moved in 1882 to British Columbia, and after serving a jail sentence for mail robbery, became a coal mine watchman at a small town on Quatsino Sound. He bragged of former exploits while drinking. News of his identity reached American newspapers in 1907. After the story of his Lawrence raid was republished, two Lawrence men came to Quatsino Sound and beat him. He died the next day. 6 illus.
                                                                    D. L. Smith

3227. McKee, Bill. THE RESOURCES OF THE VANCOUVER CITY ARCHIVES. *Urban Hist. Rev. [Canada] 1977 (2): 3-9.* Discusses the public and private records at the Vancouver City Archives and suggests topics that urban historians can research there.
                                                                    C. A. Watson

3228. McLean, Bruce. B.C. GOVERNMENT EMPLOYEES UNION. *Can. Labour 1973 18(3): 10-15.* Covers the period 1944-73.
                                                                    S

3229. Miles, Walter K. 1770'S ANCESTOR A FUR TRADER: HOWSE PASS IN BRITISH COLUMBIA NAMED FOR HIM. *Pacific Northwesterner 1977 21(1): 1-9.* Genealogy of the author, dating from ancestors in England, 1602, to present-day inhabitants of British Columbia.

3230. Miller, Fern. VANCOUVER CIVIC POLITICAL PARTIES: DEVELOPING A MODEL OF PARTY-SYSTEM CHANGE AND STABILIZATION. *BC Studies [Canada] 1975 (25): 3-31.* Surveys the appearance and disappearance of political groups in Vancouver elections since 1937. A model is proposed and tested to explain the dominance of one group until 1965, the appearance of new groups after 1965, and the unpopularity of political parties at higher levels of government. Secondary sources; 43 notes.
                                                                    W. L. Marr

3231. Morley, John T. COMMENT: THE 1974 FEDERAL GENERAL ELECTION IN BRITISH COLUMBIA. *BC Studies [Canada] 1974 (23): 34-46.* Tests hypotheses about the 1974 federal general election in British Columbia. The Liberals captured working-class votes, the New Democratic Party's showing was disastrous, racism was present in Okanajan-Kootenay, and the Conservatives successfully captured the Social Credit vote. Primary sources; 4 tables.
                                                                    W. L. Marr

3232. Morley, Terence. LABOUR IN BRITISH COLUMBIA POLITICS. *Queen's Q. [Canada] 1976 83(2): 291-298.* Examines the volatile labor situation in British Columbia, where a large percent of the workers belong to unions, from the standpoint of its impact on politics in the province. Critics have correctly noted that the labor movement has had relatively little success as a pressure group, but it has played a significant role "in providing opposition to the economic policies espoused by the Government of the day." Such confrontations could be of great importance in the future. 6 notes.
                                                                    J. A. Casada

3233. Nikitiuk, Costia. EMERGENCY AND ORGANIZATIONAL LEGITIMACY: THE DILEMMA OF EMERGENCY PLANNING IN B.C. *BC Studies [Canada] 1978 (38): 47-64.* The British Columbia Provincial Civil Defence was created in 1951 in response to the threat posed by the Soviet Union's acquisition of nuclear capability and the Cold War. By the 1960's it had lost its organizational legitimacy as public interest receded with the threat of war. Caught up in a program of sweeping administrative reform in 1974, the provincial government reconstituted the PCD as the Provincial Emergency Programme. With a new sense of direction and emphasis, the PEP was community-oriented. It was designed to bring each community to a state of optimum emergency preparedness and to coordinate activities throughout the province. Suffering from a declining economy and lacking disaster to give it high visibility, the PEP has not reemerged as a legitimate organization. Biblio., 23 notes.
                                                                    D. L. Smith

3234. Norris, John. MARGARET ORMSBY. *BC Studies [Canada] 1976-77 (32): 11-27.* "No major historian in English-speaking Canada has been more identified with the personality and history of a province than Margaret Ormsby with that of British Columbia." A native of the province, Ormsby took undergraduate training, and spent most of her professional career, at the University of British Columbia. Her research and writing were concerned with the evolution of cultural life in the province as an alteration between two forces: the generality of a Canadian nationality based on the continent-wide influence of North American mores, and the particularity of a British community rooted in the large cosmopolitan civilization of a world-wide empire. 30 notes.
                                                                    D. L. Smith

3235. North, M.; Holdsworth, D.; and Teversham, J. A BRIEF GUIDE TO THE USE OF LAND SURVEYORS' NOTEBOOKS IN THE LOWER FRASER VALLEY, B.C., 1859-1890. *BC Studies [Canada] 1977 (34): 45-60.* Most of the Lower Fraser Valley of British Columbia was surveyed for settlement during 1859-90. As an archival source, the Land Surveyors' Notebooks of these five surveys yield detailed and specific information about the physical landscape that confronted early pioneer settlers. The problems of interpretation of these field observation records are complex but can be surmounted. 7 maps, 8 notes.
                                                                    D. L. Smith

3236. Ogden, R. Lynn. VANCOUVER CITY ARCHIVES: A NEW RESOURCE. *Urban Hist. Rev. [Canada] 1974 74(1): 20-23.* Examines the facilities, staff, and collections of the Vancouver, British Columbia, city archives, 1970-74.

3237. Persky, Stan and Brunet, Michele. HOW THE NDP'S DENNIS COCKE TOOK THE COMMUNITY OUT OF COMMUNITY MENTAL HEALTH . . . AND WHY. *Can. Dimension 1974 10(3): 32-41.* "A case study of the relationship between social democracy and the political economy of psychiatry in B.C.", describes failure of an attempt to create community psychiatric services.
                                                                    S

3238. Persky, Stan. SON OF SOCRED. *Can. Dimension [Canada] 1977 12(7): 9-14.* Discusses politics and legislation in British Columbia, 1977, including a local fight against pornography, legislative attempts at securing nonpublic education, a fight against community control of social services, and conflict with local labor unions.

3239. Ralston, H. Keith. JOHN SULLIVAN DEAS: A BLACK ENTREPRENEUR IN BRITISH COLUMBIA SALMON CANNING. *BC Studies [Canada] 1976-77 (32): 64-78.* In 1862 black tinsmith John Sullivan Deas migrated from California to Victoria, British Columbia. In 1871 he was engaged to make cans for the new salmon industry on the Fraser River, and he soon became the owner of a cannery supplying an English market. His seven continuous and successful seasons established Deas as one of the founders of the canning industry in the province. 75 notes.
                                                                    D. L. Smith

3240. Reid, David J. COMPANY MERGERS IN THE FRASER RIVER SALMON CANNING INDUSTRY, 1885-1902. *Can. Hist. R. 1975 56(3): 282-302.* Examines the reasons for the merger activity in the Fraser River salmon canning industry during 1885-1902. The analysis suggests that merger activity was motivated by the desire to gain control of the markets for labor and fish, rather than to take advantage of economies of large-scale production. Based on unpublished documents known as the Doyle Papers housed in the Special Collections Division of the University of British Columbia Library and documents published in Canada Government, Sessional Papers, 1889 to 1902.
                                                                    A

3241. Resnick, Philip. SOCIAL DEMOCRACY IN POWER: THE CASE OF BRITISH COLUMBIA. *BC Studies [Canada] 1977 (34): 3-20.* The New Democratic Party (NDP), Canada's principal left party, has been largely regional in its success. During 1972-75, the NDP government in British Columbia furnished a test case for the study of social democracy in practice in Canada. The NDP stood for a mixed economy, with increased government involvement in some sectors and tighter regulation and taxation in the area of natural resources. After instituting reforms in labor's favor, the NDP passed back-to-work and cooling-off-before-strikes legislation for "essential services." Programs in social policy ranged from achieving essential reform in some areas to "fundamental bankruptcy" and bungling in others. In performance, the NDP left "a trail of disappointment. Social democracy is not the easy road to socialism." 4 tables, 2 graphs, 29 notes.   D. L. Smith

3242. Robinson, J. Lewis. HOW VANCOUVER HAS GROWN AND CHANGED. *Can. Geographical J. 1974 89(4): 40-48.*

3243. Roueche, Leonard R. PUBLIC ENTERPRISE PRICING. *BC Studies [Canada] 1977 (33): 30-39.* Public debate in British Columbia is concerned with the pricing policies of provincial-operated enterprises such as ferries, hydroelectric power, health insurance, and public transit. Attempts to put the economic jargon of the pricing policies into language that can easily be understood by the layman and aims to raise the level of sophistication of the public debate on the key issues and to avoid discussion of the "irrelevant" ones. 2 graphs, 4 notes.
D. L. Smith

3244. Roy, Patricia E. 'THE COMPANY PROVINCE' AND ITS CENTENNIALS: A REVIEW OF RECENT BRITISH COLUMBIA HISTORIOGRAPHY. *Acadiensis [Canada] 1974 4(1): 148-159.* Comments on historical works concerning British Columbia, concentrating on Martin Robin's *The Company Province* (Toronto: McClelland and Stewart, 1972/73). Robin's thesis is that entrepreneurs acting through companies, and with governmental cooperation, carved out large economic empires in British Columbia by acquiring land, mineral, and timber resources to the detriment of the lower class workers. Notes examples of inadequate research and distorted evidence, which makes the book provocative but not always accurate. Secondary sources; 38 notes.
E. A. Churchill

3245. Roy, Patricia E. DIRECT MANAGEMENT FROM ABROAD: THE FORMATIVE YEARS OF THE BRITISH COLUMBIA ELECTRIC RAILWAY. *Business Hist. R. 1973 47(2): 239-259.* Unlike most Canadian business organizations, the British Columbia Electric Railway, headed by Robert M. Horne-Payne, a London financier, was directed by an English absentee management team with good results. The railway was able to "consider its financial security first and the wants of British Columbia second and, in the long run, to satisfy both." Based on company records; 43 notes.   C. J. Pusateri

3246. Roy, Patricia. THE ILLUMINATION OF VICTORIA: LATE NINETEENTH-CENTURY TECHNOLOGY AND MUNICIPAL ENTERPRISE. *BC Studies [Canada] 1976-77 (32): 79-92.* Following considerable debate about monopoly privileges and prices, the privately owned Victoria Gas Company was incorporated in 1863. It did not get a street lighting contract for another decade. Hostility to the policies and services of the gas company and Victoria's growth and ambition to remain the leading Canadian Pacific Coast city made Victorians receptive to a new lighting medium, electricity. By the mid-1890's Victoria had adopted electricity and made it a municipal enterprise. 32 notes.
D. L. Smith

3247. Roy, Patricia E. THE PRESERVATION OF THE PEACE IN VANCOUVER: THE AFTERMATH OF THE ANTI-CHINESE RIOT OF 1887. *BC Studies [Canada] 1976 (31): 44-59.* The Vancouver, British Columbia, riot of 1887 brought unprecedented anti-Chinese violence and a press war between that city and Victoria. It did show the determination of the provincial government to act decisively to preserve peace, justice, and the reputation of the province. The young city had not done as well for itself. 45 notes.   D. L. Smith

3248. Roy, R. H. MAJOR-GENERAL G. R. PEARKES AND THE CONSCRIPTION CRISIS IN BRITISH COLUMBIA, 1944. *BC Studies [Canada] 1975/76 (28): 53-72.* Shows the background of the conscription crisis of 1944 in British Columbia. Pearkes, instead of dragging his feet (as some historians write), really worked to implement the government's policies. Based on primary and secondary sources; 34 notes.
W. L. Marr

3249. Ruff, Norman J. PARTY DETACHMENT AND VOTING PATTERNS IN A PROVINCIAL TWO-MEMBER CONSTITUENCY: VICTORIA, 1972. *BC Studies [Canada] 1974 (23): 3-24.* Examines the Victoria, British Columbia, provincial election of 1972 for split voting. Candidate appeal appears to have been of major importance to the election's outcome. Primary and secondary sources; 12 tables, fig., 24 notes.   W. L. Marr

3250. Schultz, J. A. CANADIAN ATTITUDES TOWARD EMPIRE SETTLEMENT, 1919-1930. *J. of Imperial and Commonwealth Hist. [Great Britain] 1973 1(2): 237-251.* Analyzes Canadian attitudes towards immigration into British Columbia after World War I. Fear of American growth, a renewed closeness with Great Britain, and altered public opinion all contributed to a pervasive sentiment which encouraged Britons to come to Canada. The details of various settlement schemes and the impact of the movement, which attracted relatively few British immigrants, are described. Based on printed and manuscript sources; 67 notes.
J. A. Casada

3251. Shewchuk, Murphy. GOLD MINING DAYS IN BRIDGE RIVER VALLEY. *Can. Geographical J. 1977 94(2): 66-71.* Traces the history of gold mining and describes the current physical geography and economic conditions in British Columbia's Bridge River Valley.

3252. Shi, David E. SEWARD'S ATTEMPT TO ANNEX BRITISH COLUMBIA, 1865-1869. *Pacific Hist. Rev. 1978 47(2): 217-238.* When Secretary of State William H. Seward negotiated the purchase of Alaska in 1867, he intended it as the first step in a comprehensive plan to gain control of the entire northwest Pacific Coast. Seward was a firm believer in Manifest Destiny, primarily for its commercial advantages to the United States. Seward expected British Columbia to ask for annexation and Britain to accept this in exchange for the *Alabama* claims. Growing Canadian nationalist sentiment in British Columbia, American preoccupation with Reconstruction, and American lack of interest in territorial expansion or in funding a transcontinental railroad link to British Columbia, combined to doom the plan in 1868. Based on American, Canadian, and British unpublished private and diplomatic papers and on newspapers; 90 notes.   W. K. Hobson

3253. Sinclair, James M. ST. ANDREWS CHURCH, LAKE BENNETT. *Alaska J. 1974 4(4): 242-250.* Discusses the construction of St. Andrews Church, a Presbyterian Church in Bennett, British Columbia, built in 1898 during the Klondike gold rush.

3254. Smith, Dorothy Blakey. "POOR GAGGIN": IRISH MISFIT IN THE COLONIAL SERVICE. *BC Studies [Canada] 1976-77 (32): 41-63.* John Boles Gaggin sailed from Ireland in 1859 to seek his fortune in newly established British Columbia. He served as a minor cog in the civil service machine. He always gave his colleagues concern and eventually provoked a confrontation with the governor of the colony. 78 notes.
D. L. Smith

3255. Smith, Howie. LOGGING CAMP CHARACTERS: INTERVIEW WITH AL PARKIN. *Sound Heritage [Canada] 1977 6(3): 31-33.* Parkin recalls unique personalities in lumber camps, 1910's-30's, in British Columbia.

3256. Tanti, Spiro. W. F. HERRE'S SUBSCRIPTION READING-ROOM—VICTORIA'S FIRST PUBLIC LIBRARY. *Can. Lib. J. 1973 30(4): 364-368.*

3257. Thompson, Mark and Cairnie, James. COMPULSORY ARBITRATION: THE CASE OF BRITISH COLUMBIA TEACHERS. *Industrial and Labor Relations R. 1973 27(1): 3-17.* "The increasing use of compulsory arbitration in the public sector makes particularly timely this study of an arbitration system that has been in effect since 1937 and has resulted in over 500 awards in teacher salary disputes. The authors analyze trends in the proportion of negotiations ending in arbitration under this system, and they compare the record of teacher strikes and salaries in British Columbia with the record in other provinces. They conclude that this case demonstrates that compulsory arbitration can prevent strikes without demolishing collective bargaining and without producing wage awards that are far above or below the level of negotiated settlements."   J

3258. Tippett, Maria and Cole, Douglas. ART IN BRITISH CO-
LUMBIA—THE HISTORICAL SOURCES. *BC Studies [Canada]*
1974 (23): 25-33. Describes source material on various aspects of British
Columbia's art history from 1780 to the present, stating its location.
Primary and secondary sources; 30 notes.   W. L. Marr

3259. Tippett, Maria. CHARLES JOHN COLLINS: "THE RE-
CLUSE OF THE ROCKIES." *Beaver [Canada] 1975 306(2): 4-7.*
Charles John Collins was a London clerk with little art training when he
moved his family to British Columbia in 1910. There he developed a style
of water color art based on Japanese and English techniques, emphasizing
natural scenes. Some of his exhibitions were held in England, but he has
remained relatively unknown in Canada until recently. Examines the
development of the painting techniques and his artistic philosophy. 5 illus.
                                                            D. Chaput

3260. Tippett, Maria. EMILY CARR'S FOREST. *J. of Forest Hist.*
1974 18(4): 133-137. Emily Carr's paintings of British Columbia forests
and Indian villages placed her among Canada's finest artists. 20 notes.
                                                            L. F. Johnson

3261. Trower, Peter. SAGA OF A WEST COAST LOGGER: IN-
TERVIEW WITH GEORGE MC INNIS, 101-YEAR OLD LOGGER.
Sound Heritage [Canada] 1977 6(3): 13-15. McInnis recounts events in
his logging career in Maine, Washington, and British Columbia, 1894-
1949.

3262. Ujimoto, K. Victor. CONTRASTS IN THE PREWAR AND
POSTWAR JAPANESE COMMUNITY IN BRITISH COLUMBIA:
CONFLICT AND CHANGE. *Can. Rev. of Soc. and Anthrop. 1976*
13(1): 80-89. This paper explores and attempts to explain selected variations between the Japanese community in Vancouver as it existed prior
to the Second World War and the present Japanese "community." The
prewar Japanese community existed within a specific geographic area and
consisted of a highly systematized and interdependent social network.
Factors which contributed to the development of the cohesive and well-
unified collectivity are described. In contrast, the postwar Japanese collectivity was not able to develop the same degree of social organization.
Several factors are discussed to account for this major difference.   J

3263. Wilson, Maureen, comp. SELECTED MAPS OF BRITISH
COLUMBIA PUBLISHED DURING 1976 AND 1977. *BC Studies*
[Canada] 1977-78 (36): 89-94. Lists provincial, regional, provincial parks,
and municipalities maps issued in 1976 and 1977. Includes title, scale,
office or place of publication, date, and some annotation.
                                                            D. L. Smith

3264. Woodward, Frances M., comp. BIBLIOGRAPHY OF BRIT-
ISH COLUMBIA. *BC Studies [Canada] 1976 (29): 52-67.* A bibliography of books, government publications, and articles, with 1968-76 imprint
dates.   D. L. Smith

3265. Woodward, Frances M. BIBLIOGRAPHY OF BRITISH CO-
LUMBIA. *BC Studies [Canada] 1975/76 (28): 80-92.* Lists books, government publications, and articles on British Columbia written during the
1970's. 3 notes.   W. L. Marr

3266. Woodward, F. M. THE INFLUENCE OF THE ROYAL EN-
GINEERS ON THE DEVELOPMENT OF BRITISH COLUMBIA.
British Columbia Studies [Canada] 1974/75 (24): 3-51. Discusses the
significance of the various groups of Royal Engineers and their unique
relationship to British Columbia. Secondary sources; 8 tables, 65 notes.
                                                            W. L. Marr

3267. Woodward, Frances M. THESES IN BRITISH COLUMBIA
HISTORY AND RELATED SUBJECTS COMPLETED IN 1974.
BC Studies 1975/76 (28): 93-99. Lists theses relating to British Columbia
and finished in 1974. Gives author, title, and university where written.
                                                            W. L. Marr

3268. Woodward, Frances M., comp. THESES IN BRITISH CO-
LUMBIA HISTORY AND RELATED SUBJECTS COMPLETED IN
1975. *BC Studies [Canada] 1977 (33): 80-86.* Cites 72 essays and theses
concerning the history of British Columbia. Provides "Canadian thesis on
microfiche" numbers.   D. L. Smith

3269. Woodward, Frances M., comp. THESES IN BRITISH CO-
LUMBIA AND RELATED SUBJECTS COMPLETED IN 1976.
BC Studies [Canada] 1977-78 (36): 81-88. Lists 84 undergraduate essays
and graduate theses for 1976 on British Columbia and related subjects in
a wide range of disciplines. Includes author, title, institution, discipline,
date, pagination data, and Canadian thesis on microfiche number.
                                                            D. L. Smith

3270. Yankel, Reb. B.C.'S NORTHWEST QUESTION—THE
HORDES ARE AT THE NDP'S GATES. *Can. Dimension 1974 10(4):*
12-18. Northwest development in British Columbia poses a dilemma for
the National Democratic Party, which was elected on a platform of
"rational resource use."   S

3271. Young, Walter D. IDEOLOGY, PERSONALITY AND THE
ORIGIN OF THE CCF IN BRITISH COLUMBIA. *BC Studies [Can-*
ada] 1976-77 (32): 139-162. Between the Winnipeg General Strike of 1919
and the Cooperative Commonwealth Federation of 1932, British Columbia endured the power struggles of individual socialists who sought to use
their left wing ideology as a vehicle for fulfillment of personal ambitions.
For many, their doctrine was "a vehicle for personal salvation as well as
for social salvation." 94 notes.   D. L. Smith

3272. —. [CLASS, REGION, INSTITUTION, AND PARTY IN
BRITISH COLUMBIA].
Marchak, Patricia. CLASS, REGIONAL, AND INSTITUTIONAL
    SOURCES OF SOCIAL CONFLICT IN B.C. *BC Studies [Can-*
    ada] 1975 (27): 30-49. Three dimensions of social structure in Brit-
    ish Columbia are explored: class structure, regional structure, and
    institutional structure. Economic interests of classes may conflict
    with economic interests of the same population located in a differ-
    ent regional and institutional setting. Secondary sources, 3 tables,
    2 figs., 24 notes.
Koenig, Daniel J. and Proverbs, Trevor B. CLASS, REGIONAL AND
    INSTITUTIONAL SOURCES OF PARTY SUPPORT WITHIN
    BRITISH COLUMBIA. *BC Studies [Canada] 1976 (29): 19-28.*
    Examines some of the issues raised by Marchak. Concludes that the
    best single predictors of party support are various indicators of
    class. Confirms Marchak's speculation that party support in British
    Columbia varies by institutional sector within a class.
                                        W. L. Marr and D. L. Smith

3273. —. ENGINEERING AND BALLADEERING IN THE
WESTERN WOODS: AN INTERVIEW WITH ROBERT SWAN-
SON. *Sound Heritage [Canada] 1977 6(3): 3-9.* An engineer on logging
railroads in British Columbia describes his life in the logging industry and
how it inspired his poetry.

The Territories

General

3274. Barry, P. S. THE PROLIFIC PIPELINE: GETTING CANOL
UNDER WAY. *Dalhousie Rev. [Canada] 1976 56(2): 252-267.* The
Canol project of World War II was called prolific because its originally
projected 600-mile length from Norman Wells to Whitehorse grew to
1600 miles with branches to Skagway and Fairbanks, Alaska. There is
much to be learned by studying the history of Canol's construction in the
early 1940's in the Mackenzie River basin by the planners and builders
of the current Mackenzie Valley project. The Berger Commission, established to look into the impact of this current project, would also be greatly
instructed by the resurrection of Canol's history. Costs mounted from an
original estimate of $30 million to $300 million, and manpower from
8,000 to 25,000. Roads were an important but useful proliferation. Illus.,
map, 31 notes.   C. Held

3275. Bone, Robert M. CANADA'S LAST FRONTIER: THE
NORTH. *Current Hist. 1974 66(392): 161-164, 184.* Discusses the
problem of developing the Canadian North.   S

3276. Cayouette, Gilles and Hamelin, Louis-Edmond. L'EVOLU-TION DU NOMBRE DES HABITANTS DU NORD CANADIEN DE 1966 A 1971 [Population growth in the Canadian North from 1966 to 1971]. *Cahiers de Géographie de Québec [Canada] 1973 17(40): 200-209.* The Canadian North has 253,559 inhabitants, 1.2% of the Canadian total. During 1966-71 the North grew at a slightly faster rate than southern Canada. It appears that the development of natural resources and of territorial administration remains the most important factor in the growth of the Canadian North. Based on secondary sources; 5 tables, 2 figs., 7 notes, biblio.
A. E. LeBlanc

3277. Davies, Ivor. THE DEVELOPMENT OF CANADA'S NORTH. *Scottish Geographical Mag. [Great Britain] 1973 89(1): 36-43.* Various criteria by which the Canadian Northlands may be delimited are reviewed and the writer advances a delimitation based on residents' senses of northness. Three types of northern development, massive economic, moderate economic and social, are evaluated and the responsibilities of northern and southern Canada to each other are indicated.
J

3278. Dunbar, M. J. CLIMATIC CHANGE AND NORTHERN DEVELOPMENT. *Arctic [Canada] 1976 29(4): 183-193.* Examines the climatic changes effected by ocean currents along the northern coast of Canada and their influence on economic and cultural development, 1925-76.

3279. Grant, Francis W. GEORGE MAC KENZIE: NORTHERN PIONEER. *Nova Scotia Hist. Q. [Canada] 1974 4(2): 155-165.* George Patton MacKenzie (1873-1953) was a school teacher, prospector, Gold Commissioner of the Yukon Territory, Arctic explorer, administrator, and lecturer.
H. M. Evans

3280. Hemstock, R. A. TRANSPORTING PETROLEUM IN THE NORTH. *Can. Geographical J. 1975 90(4): 42-49.* Discusses Canada's efforts to create a land-use plan for the development of its vast northern petroleum resources.
S

3281. Hochbaum, H. Albert. ARCTIC STEEPLES. *Beaver [Canada] 1977 308(3): 28-35.* Descriptive detail, artistic renderings, and brief historical sketches of churches in the central and western Arctic. Fur trading and missionary work did not begin in this section until the 20th century. Catholic and Anglican missions are scattered about the land, serving the few merchants and the Eskimo-Indian communities. 11 illus.
D. Chaput

3282. Hudson, Heather E. THE ROLE OF RADIO IN NORTHERN CANADA. *J. of Communication 1977 27(4): 130-139.* Describes the radio system in the Canadian north and its efforts to provide national, international, and local information, also discusses the results of a survey of short wave radio operators conducted by the Canadian Broadcasting Corporation, Northern Service.

3283. Judd, D. A. W. DEVELOPMENTS IN FEDERAL POLICIES AND REGULATIONS FOR NORTHERN CANADA, 1968-72. *Polar Record [Great Britain] 1973 16(103): 583-590.* The Prudhoe Bay oil find has been followed by the formation of Federal Task Forces, legislation emphasizing pollution control, and studies on a northern pipeline, a northern railway, Arctic oil and iron ore shipping terminals, and 45 percent federal participation in an Arctic oil consortium. Based on government publications.
L. L. Hubbard

3284. Keith, Robert F. and Fischer, David W. ASSESSING THE DEVELOPMENT DECISION-MAKING PROCESS: A CASE STUDY OF CANADIAN FRONTIER PETROLEUM DEVELOPMENT. *Am. J. of Econ. and Sociol. 1977 36(2): 147-164.* Based upon the concept of a "technology assessment system," an examination is made of the decision-making process surrounding petroleum development in the Canadian Arctic. The roles of various actors, the nature of information processes, the decisions taken and the issues perceived point to additional problems inherent in the assessment system itself. The degree of involvement of various actors along with information and decision strategies often preclude comprehensive, balanced and timely assessments. In conclusion a number of general issues emerged. The lack of an overall policy mechanism, unresponsiveness to change, lack of coordinated data systems and unsatisfactory inter-actor coordinating mechanisms are seen to be important limitations to the assessment process.
J

3285. Krech, Shepard, III. THE EASTERN KUTCHIN AND THE FUR TRADE, 1800-1860. *Ethnohistory 1976 23(3): 213-235.* Analyzes fur trade between the Athapaskan Eastern Kutchin Indians and Eurocanadians during 1800-60 in the Mackenzie District and Yukon Territory.

3286. Lindsey, G. R. STRATEGIC ASPECTS OF THE POLAR REGIONS. *Behind the Headlines [Canada] 1977 35(6): 1-24.* The Canadian Arctic is a strategic problem, while Norway, Iceland, and Greenland's polar regions play a vital role in global military strategy; through NATO, Canada hopes to secure these areas as well as its own north coast; chronicles economic and strategic activities in the Canadian Arctic during 1945-77.

3287. Loftus, D. S. COMMUNICATIONS IN THE CANADIAN NORTH. *Polar Record [Great Britain] 1973 16(104): 675-682.* Communication has been limited to shortwave radio broadcasts, telephone connections to some communities, and some local TV stations. The Anik satellite, launched in 1972, will allow areas previously unserved to receive TV and telephone service. 2 maps.
L. L. Hubbard

3288. Miles, P. and Wright, N. J. R. AN OUTLINE OF MINERAL EXTRACTION IN THE ARCTIC. *Polar Record [Great Britain] 1978 19(118): 11-38.* Discusses mining in the Arctic Circle in the USSR, Scandinavia, Canada, and Alaska, 1917-78.

3289. Naysmith, John. CHANGING LAND-USE PATTERNS IN THE NORTH. *Can. Geographical J. 1975 90(1): 11-18.* Examines the land-use patterns of northern Canada (1670-1975), including hunting, trapping, mineral and petroleum exploration and production, and considers potential expansion in terms of hydro power, forestry, and recreation.
S

3290. Noble, Dennis L. and Strobridge, Truman R. THE ARCTIC ADVENTURES OF THE *THETIS*. *Arctic [Canada] 1977 30(1): 3-12.* The arctic voyages of the steam whaler *Thetis* include the rescue of the Greely party in 1884, the importation of reindeer from Siberia to Alaska between 1899 and 1906, and the Bering Sea Patrol from 1905 to 1913 as sister ship to the *Bear* in the US Revenue Cutter Service. *Thetis* was sold by the US Coast Guard in 1916 and was used as a Newfoundland sealer until 1950 when she was scrapped.
P. J. Anderson

3291. Ørvik, Nils. TOWARD A THEORY OF NORTHERN DEVELOPMENT. *Queen's Q. [Canada] 1976 83(1): 98-102.* Argues that the growth of northern studies, the many problems arising from increased northern development, and the region's future potential all indicate the need for a carefully thought out theory on the approach to be taken. Both modernization and respect for native societies must be prime considerations in the formulation of a theory for development.
J. A. Casada

3292. Peake, Frank A. ROBERT MCDONALD (1829-1913): THE GREAT UNKNOWN MISSIONARY OF THE NORTHWEST. *J. of the Can. Church Hist. Soc. 1975 17(3): 54-72.* Summarizes the career of this Anglican missionary in the Yukon and Mackenzie River valley. Robert McDonald differed from his fellow missionaries in several respects. First, he was of mixed blood; and though he was reared to identify himself with the Protestant, English-speaking society, they never considered him a part of their group. This helps explain why McDonald never became a bishop and why in later life he married a young Indian. Most importantly, his background was a factor in his efforts to understand the culture of the Indians he served. Learning the Tukudh language, McDonald translated the Apostle's Creed, the decalogue, and some hymns. He also learned to preach to the Indians in their own language. Showing appreciation for Indian culture, McDonald selected and trained certain of his converts to direct the others when he was absent. Primary and secondary sources; 23 notes; appendix.
J. A. Kicklighter

3293. Reeves, Randall. BOWHEAD WHALES: MARINE GIANTS IN OUR ARCTIC. *Can. Geographical J. 1976/77 93(3): 38-45.* Discusses the history of whaling of bowhead whales and more recent efforts to conserve the huge beasts who live in Canada's arctic areas, prehistory-1976.

3294. Ross, W. Gillies. CANADIAN SOVEREIGNTY IN THE ARCTIC: THE *NEPTUNE* EXPEDITION, 1903-04. *Arctic [Canada] 1976 29(2): 87-104.* Examines the first effort on the part of the Canadian government, 1903-04, with the expedition of the *Neptune,* to assert sovereignty over the eastern Arctic regions; examines customs stations, police posts, trade and hunting regulations, and cultural connections made with the Eskimos in the area.

3295. Scotter, George W. HOW ANDY BAHR LED THE GREAT REINDEER HERD FROM WESTERN ALASKA TO THE MACKENZIE DELTA. *Can. Geographic [Canada] 1978 97(2): 12-19.* Hired in 1928 to herd 3,000 reindeer from western Alaska to the Mackenzie River Delta to ensure against their extinction, Andrew Bahr, a Lapp herder, worked until 1934 relocating the herds.

3296. Snyder, Marsha. THOMAS VINCENT, THE ARCHDEACON OF MOOSONEE. *Ontario Hist. [Canada] 1976 68(2): 119-135.* Presents a biography of Archdeacon Thomas Vincent and attempts to assess his work for the Anglican Church and the Church Missionary Society in northern Canada. Vincent was born in the North and returned there after his education in the South. He was involved in missionary work before his ordination and thereafter made it his career. Discusses the relationship between the Church Missionary Society and the Hudson's Bay Company, and comments on the impact of Vincent's efforts during his 50 years of service. Remarks on his relationships with colleagues and others, and shows that some of the problems he faced derived, in part, from his intense evangelicism. 98 notes.   W. B. Whitham

3297. Wallace, A. I. and Williams, P. J. PROBLEMS OF BUILDING ROADS IN THE NORTH. *Can. Geographical J. 1974 89(1/2): 40-47.* Analyzes the role of road transport in northern Canada, and discusses effects of climate and terrain on highway construction.   S

Arctic Exploration

3298. Barratt, Glynn. RAE'S FORT HOPE. *Beaver [Canada] 1976 306(4): 33-39.* Brief biography of Dr. John Rae (1813-93) of the Hudson's Bay Company, and his explorations in the 1840's. Emphasizes the fort he built in 1846-47 in the Arctic, 60 miles north of Southampton Island. Provides construction details, enumeration of the party and their roles, and Rae's instructions in the Arctic, provided by Sir George Simpson. There are still remains at Fort Hope, but vandalism and weather have caused rapid deterioration in the past decade. 7 illus.   D. Chaput

3299. Barratt, Glynn R. THE RUSSIAN INTEREST IN ARCTIC NORTH AMERICA: THE KRUZENSHTERN-ROMANOV PROJECTS, 1819-1823. *Slavonic and East European R. [Great Britain] 1975 53(130): 27-43.* Captain-Commodore Ivan Fedorovich Kruzenshtern and Lieutenant Vladmir Pavlovich Romanov belonged to a group of naval officers who promoted scientific exploration of Arctic America between the Bering Strait and Hudson's Bay. In the early 1820's Romanov prepared for a voyage that would promise material benefits to the struggling Russian American Company. By 1825 political conditions had minimized any expansionist potential in the project, and it remained abortive. Based on Moscow naval archives; map, 45 notes.   R. E. Weltsch

3300. Barratt, Glynn R. WHALERS AND WEAVERS. *Beaver [Canada] 1977 308(3): 54-59.* The Royal Navy explored several portions of the Arctic Ocean in the early 1820's. This was an era of depression for the Navy, and for Britain. Naval strength was low, and technological changeovers throughout Great Britain led to mass unemployment, especially for those in textiles. However, these factors made recruiting for the Arctic voyages easier for the Navy. Aside from qualified seamen who applied, the Navy had the choice of many skilled weavers and experienced whalers. Double wages also helped in the recruiting drives. Weaving had little in common with sailing in the Arctic, but the weavers had work experience, toughness, and adaptability. Based on Admiralty papers recently obtained in Ottawa; 3 illus., table.   D. Chaput

3301. Finnie, Richard. FAREWELL VOYAGES: BERNIER AND THE *ARCTIC.* *Beaver [Canada] 1974 305(1): 44-54.* Based on the

1924 and 1925 voyages to the Arctic of Captain J. E. Bernier on the *Arctic*, a 165-foot barquentine. Bernier, an experienced seaman, was instructed by the government to plant the Canadian flag on all islands he could reach in the Eastern Arctic Archipelago. During the first voyage, the ship stopped at Baffin Island, Godhavn (Greenland), and Devon Island. For the 1925 trip, the *Arctic* again went to Baffin Island and Greenland, but Bernier made several sailing errors. Also explains the circumstances of Admiral Richard E. Byrd's flight over Canadian territory; he was the first to fly over and land on Canada's Arctic islands. 14 illus., map.   D. Chaput

3302. Finnie, Richard Sterling. MY FRIEND STEFANSSON. *Alaska J. 1978 8(1): 18-25, 84-85.* In 1931 the author met Vilhjalmur Stefansson (1879-1962), Canadian-born Arctic explorer and researcher. The author worked under him during World War II for the Office of the Coordinator of Information, which later became the OSS and much later the CIA. Having a brilliant intellect, Stefansson finished a four-year arts program at the State University of Iowa in one year, and later developed the very rare skill of speaking one of the Eskimo languages correctly as well as fluently. He made a few enemies, for example Roald Amundsen, who denounced him as a charlatan, but in general he was and is highly respected as an Arctic expert and pioneer. 8 illus., map.   L. W. Van Wyk

3303. Fischer, Lawrence J. HORSE SOLDIERS IN THE ARCTIC: THE GARLINGTON EXPEDITION OF 1883. *Am. Neptune 1976 36(2): 108-124.* An army expedition commanded by Lieutenant Ernest A. Garlington set out in 1883 to rescue Lieutenant Adolphus W. Greely's expedition to establish a polar observatory on Ellesmere Island, Canada. Garlington's expedition did not effect the rescue, because of severe hardship faced when its ship, *Proteus*, sank. The failure was primarily due to the poor planning of General William B. Hazen who directed the overall operation. Based on newspaper accounts and inquiry proceedings; 41 notes.   G. H. Curtis

3304. Francis, Daniel. STAKING CANADA'S CLAIM TO THE ARCTIC ISLANDS. *Can. Geographical J. [Canada] 1977 95(1): 60-69.* Chronicles an Arctic expedition led by William Wakeham in 1897 to prove the navigability of the Hudson Strait and to claim Baffin's Land and all the surrounding islands and dependencies as part of the Dominion of Canada.

3305. Frisch, Jack A. THE IROQUOIS INDIANS AND THE 1855 FRANKLIN SEARCH EXPEDITION IN THE ARCTIC. *Indian Hist. 1975 8(1): 27-30.* Three Iroquois Indians accompanied James Anderson of the Hudson Bay Company in an overland expedition attempting to locate the fate of Sir John Franklin's disastrous Arctic expedition. Questions the use of Iroquois instead of more northerly tribesmen and finds the answer in their excellent woodsmanship and canoe handling. Also notes that the Iroquois choice of vocations such as riverboating and ironwork construction reflects their love of dangerous occupations that take them away from home, just as their tribal ancestors spent much of their time in dangerous hunting and warring expeditions. Biblio.   E. D. Johnson

3306. Hensen, Steven. THE JOURNALS OF SIR JOHN HENRY LEFROY. *Yale U. Lib. Gazette 1974 48(3): 183-191.* Recently found in a vast collection of scientific-related archives of the Loomis-Wilder family, given to the Yale Library by Millicent Todd Bingham, were two important scientific journals labelled simply "Journal 1843" and "Journal 1844." These notebooks were kept by John Henry Lefroy (1817-90), a young British officer, on a magnetic surveying expedition into the Canadian Northwest, during April 1843-November 1844. George F. C. Stanley published Lefroy's letters under the title *In Search of the Magnetic North; A Soldier-Surveyor's Letters from the North-West, 1843-1844* (Toronto, 1955), in which reference was made to the lost journals.   D. A. Yanchisin

3307. Hodgson, Maurice. BELLOT AND KENNEDY: A CONTRAST IN PERSONALITIES. *Beaver [Canada] 1974 305(1): 55-58.* In 1851, Joseph René Bellot, a lieutenant in the French Marines, and William Kennedy, a *métis* from Rupert's Land, led an expedition to the Arctic on the *Prince Albert* to search for Sir John Franklin. Bellot was an educated Roman Catholic Frenchman, inexperienced in Arctic travel, whereas Kennedy was an intolerant Protestant, well-schooled in frontier life. They eventually found mutual respect and completed an amazing sled journey of 1,100 miles, traveling west of Prince of Wales Island, north to Cape Walker, around North Somerset, then to quarters at Batty Bay. Claims that Bellot was more interested in glory and future promotion than in finding Franklin. 4 illus., map.   D. Chaput

3308. Houston, C. Stuart. THE JOURNAL AND PAINTINGS OF ROBERT HOOD. Arctic [Canada] 1974 27(4): 251-255. Robert Hood was a midshipman in Sir John Franklin's 1819-22 search for the Northwest Passage. Describes his journal and the paintings he made in the course of the expedition. Illus., biblio.   J. A. Casada

3309. Houston, C. Stuart. WITH THE FIRST FRANKLIN EXPEDITION, 1819-1821: THE JOURNALS AND SKETCHES OF ROBERT HOOD. Can.: An Hist. Mag. 1974 2(1): 1-14. Midshipman Robert Hood, age 22, accompanied Arctic explorer John Franklin on his first overland search for the Northwest Passage in 1819, as illustrator and record keeper. Franklin's party turned south after exploring 675 miles of the Arctic coastline; 11 of the original 20, including Hood, died on the return overland journey. Based on Hood's extant journals and published materials; 16 illus., map, 10 notes.   D. B. Smith

3310. Kenyon, Walter. "ALL IS NOT GOLDE THAT SHINETH." Beaver [Canada] 1975 306(1): 40-46. In the 1570's Martin Frobisher, the first Arctic explorer, made three expeditions to Frobisher Bay, in the vicinity of Countess of Warwick Island. He convinced London speculators that much gold could be found there. He took back to London tons of worthless mica, feldspar, and quartz. The Royal Ontario Museum revisited the site in 1974, found traces of Frobisher's activities, and brought back specimens for an exhibit on Arctic exploration. Map, 12 illus.   D. Chaput

3311. Lamont, James. TREKKING ACROSS MOUNTAINOUS BYLOT ISLAND. Can. Geographic [Canada] 1978 97(2): 52-59. Chronicles exploration of Bylot Island, 1818-63, and describes a 1977 traversal, making note of historical, archaeological, and biological points.

3312. MacInnis, Joseph B. FIRE ON THE ICE: MEN OF THE EREBUS AND TERROR. Can. Geographical J. [Canada] 1978 96(2): 52-59. The 1845-48 Arctic expedition led by Sir John Franklin, a British naval captain, set out to explore the Canadian Arctic but became icelocked; after 578 days the ships were crushed and the crew perished from starvation and exposure.

3313. Mauro, R. G. DILLON WALLACE OF LABRADOR. Beaver [Canada] 1975 306(1): 50-57. In 1903 Leonidas Hubbard and Dillon Wallace set out to explore the northeast section of Labrador. Accompanied only by one guide, the party suffered from weather and lack of food. Hubbard froze to death. In 1905 Wallace, feeling a debt to Hubbard, decided to complete the expedition. However, he was competing with Hubbard's widow, who set out with her own party. She won the race, and both explorers published results of their trips. She suspected that Wallace knew more about her husband's death than he had revealed. Critics praised both works, pointing out the professional maps and diagrams in the widow's book, while granting to Wallace the better interpretation of the expedition trials. 22 illus., 2 maps.   D. Chaput

3314. Neatby, Leslie H. HANTZSCH OF BAFFIN ISLAND. Beaver [Canada] 1975 306(3): 4-13. In 1910-11 Bernard Adolf Hantzsch, German ornithologist, made a trip overland on Baffin Island that was significant for natural discoveries as well as for his journals portraying Eskimo life. He died as a result of trichinosis caused by eating bear's flesh. His scientific collections and journals can be found in the Museum Fuer Voelkerkunde, Berlin, and in the Public Archives of Canada. Hantzsch made little impact on the scientific-academic community, as his discoveries were overshadowed by Cook-Peary arguments regarding the North Pole, and the exploits of Amundsen and Scott at the South Pole. The eruption of World War I also shifted attention from his exploits. 7 illus., map.   D. Chaput

3315. Richards, R. L. RAE OF THE ARCTIC. Medical Hist. [Great Britain] 1975 19(2): 176-193. Dr. John Rae (1813-93) was one of the great 19th-century Arctic explorers. Rae became an explorer after a decade as surgeon at Moose Factory in Hudson Bay. Over the next ten years, he traveled some 23,000 miles in the Arctic, mostly on foot, and he surveyed from 1,700 to 1,800 miles of coastline. He was the first to ascertain the fate of Sir John Franklin's expedition which had been missing for seven years. His life and explorations are described, and his medical work is analyzed. Illus., 62 notes.   M. Kaufman

3316. Rowley, G. BERNHARD HANTZSCH: THE PROBABLE CAUSE OF HIS DEATH IN BAFFIN ISLAND IN 1911. Polar Record [Great Britain] 1977 18(117): 593-596. Through examination of the diary of Bernhard Hantzsch, 1911, determines that the cause of his death while exploring Baffin Island with a group of Eskimos was trichinosis.

3317. Soper, J. Dewey. BAFFIN ISLAND; THE MYSTERIOUS WEST COAST. Beaver [Canada] 1974 305(2): 54-59. An account of J. Dewey Soper's 1929 expedition along the western coast of Baffin Island. Except for the Bernard Hantzsch expedition (1910), most of the western coast was unexplored. Soper, a scientist, made a detailed study of the area. 6 illus., map.   D. Heermans

3318. Soper, J. Dewey. THE CONQUEST OF PANGNIRTUNG PASS. Beaver [Canada] 1973 303(4): 40-48. Early in 1925 Dr. Soper and several Eskimos explored this pass on the Cumberland Peninsula, Baffin Island. They encountered many glaciers, icefalls, sand flats, temperatures often -40 degrees, and no animals. The difficulties of travel convinced Soper and others that the best way to reach the east coast of Baffin Island was still the Kingnait Pass, favored by the Eskimos. 9 illus., map.   D. Chaput

3319. Theberge, C. B. and Theberge, Henry. HIGH ADVENTURE IN THE HIGH ARCTIC. Canada 1975 2(3): 44-57. Vilhjalmur Steffansson (1879-1962) spent his youth exploring the Canadian Arctic and attempting to advertise its wealth and its ability to sustain human life. A single disastrous expedition to Wrangel Island defeated his plans, but time has vindicated his theories. 7 photos, map, biblio., 9 notes.   W. W. Elison

3320. Verby, John and Buetow, Dave. ACROSS BAFFIN ISLAND BY CANOE. Beaver [Canada] 1974 305(2): 32-38. Traces the canoe journey of three Americans from Takuirbing Lake to Frobisher Bay in August, 1973. During their trip the three men observed and recorded the flora and fauna and compared what they saw with the journals of other expeditions in the area of Baffin Island. 13 illus., map.   D. Heermans

3321. Wright, Charles. SIR RAYMOND PRIESTLEY: AN APPRECIATION. Polar Record [Great Britain] 1974 17(108): 215-220. Discusses the historical writings and explorations of Great Britain's Sir Raymond Priestley in New Zealand, Australia, Canada, and the Antarctic, 1912-74.

Yukon Territory

3322. Alberts, Laurie. PETTICOATS AND PICKAXES. Alaska J. 1977 7(3): 146-159. Women were a part of the gold rush, 1897-99. Describes the kind of women who went north, their reasons for doing so, and their lives in the area. 11 photos, 53 notes, biblio.   E. E. Eminhizer

3323. Bearss, Edwin C. and White, Bruce M. GEORGE BRACKETT'S WAGON ROAD: MINNESOTA ENTERPRISE ON A NEW FRONTIER. Minnesota Hist. 1976 45(2): 42-57. Minnesota-based capitalist and business entrepreneur George Brackett emerged from retirement in 1897 to help facilitate land transportation between Skagway (Alaska) and the Yukon gold fields. The planned construction of a wagon road over treacherous terrain was organized by a syndicate of businessmen in which Brackett shortly became the leading figure: he involved much of his own money. The effort was plagued by continual monetary shortfalls, which Brackett partly alleviated through loans from prominent American businessmen including railroad magnate James J. Hill. Brackett's reputation for business probity stood him in good stead. With the

eventual opening of the road in 1898, Brackett was able, over strenuous protests from Alaskan shippers, to levy a toll on transportation over the road under the jurisdiction of the War Department. Fearing ruinous competition from a Canadian railroad, Brackett sold his interests in 1898.
                                                                    N. Lederer

3324. Bennett, Peter H. THE KLONDIKE GOLD RUSH HISTORIC PARK. *Can. Geographical J. 1974 89(5): 32-39.* A park has been created in the territory of the Klondike gold rush of 1897-98.
                                                                              S

3325. Bucksar, Richard G. THE ALASKA HIGHWAY DEVELOPMENT. *Arctic [Canada] 1974 27(1): 74-80.* Discusses the history of the Alaska Highway and recent political steps to pave its major unpaved sections. Analyzes alternative routes and proposals. Based on printed sources; map, 12 notes.
                                                                    J. A. Casada

3326. Bucksar, Richard G. THE WHITE PASS AND YUKON RAILWAY: PAST, PRESENT, AND FUTURE. *Michigan Academician 1973 5(3): 315-323.*

3327. Bush, Edward F. COMMISSIONERS OF THE YUKON, 1897-1918. *Can. Historic Sites 1974 10: 98-158.* "After a brief description of the opening of the Yukon Territory and the institution of territorial government, the tenures in office and characters of each of the commissioners or chief executives are traced in turn against the background of the politics and social life of the period. The abolition of the office of commissioner and re-organization of the territorial government in March 1918 is followed by a sketch of post-1918 Yukon history up to the time of the transferral of the territorial capital from Dawson to Whitehorse in 1954. An appendix lists the names of the commissioners and succeeding chief executives from 1897 to 1966."
                                                                              J

3328. Bush, Edward F. THE NORTH WEST MOUNTED IN KLONDIKE DAYS. *Can. Geographical J. 1976 92(1): 22-27.* Describes Fort Herchmer, a post on the Yukon River at Dawson, used by the North West Mounted Police from 1896 to approximately 1905.

3329. Finnie, Richard. BY CRUISE SHIP AND TRAIN TO THE YUKON. *Can. Geographical J. 1976 92(2): 62-69.* Discusses routes of travel by ships and railroads for tourists in Canada's Yukon Territory in the 20th century.

3330. Harbottle, Jeanne. CLYDE WANN, FATHER OF YUKON AVIATION. *Alaska J. 1973 3(4): 237-245.* Discusses airmail flights of aviator Clyde Wann in Canada's Yukon Territory, 1927-35.

3331. Harbottle, Jeanne. WHITE PASS AVIATION AND ITS RIVALS. *Alaska J. 1974 4(4): 232-241.* Discusses the pioneer air service of White Pass Aviation for mail as well as passengers from population centers in Alaska to the Yukon, 1934-40.

3332. Livermore, Carol. PERCY DE WOLFE: "IRON MAN OF THE YUKON." *Beaver [Canada] 1977 308(2): 16-20.* Percy DeWolfe, an ex-prospector, in 1915 became the government mail carrier between Dawson (Yukon Territory) and Eagle (Alaska). He performed this winter service until 1950, the year before his death. Summarizes the hardships of travel, nonmail functions of the carrier, and his reliability and integrity over the decades. In 1935 King George V awarded DeWolfe a silver medal for his services. 4 illus., map.
                                                                    D. Chaput

3333. McCollom, Pat. KLONDIKE OUTPOST. *Westways 1977 69(4): 20-23, 72.* Provides reminiscences about the gold rush in the Klondike, 1898-1913, by residents of its former capital, Dawson City.

3334. Mills, Thora McIlroy. THE CONTRIBUTION OF THE PRESBYTERIAN CHURCH TO THE YUKON DURING THE GOLD RUSH, 1897-1910. *Bull. of the United Church of Can. [Canada] 1976 (25): 5-94.*

3335. Morrison, W. R. THE NORTH-WEST MOUNTED POLICE AND THE KLONDIKE GOLD RUSH. *J. of Contemporary Hist. [Great Britain] 1974 9(2): 93-106.* A study of the philosophy and methods of the North-West Mounted Police in the Yukon during the Klondike

Stampede. Their flexibility and adjustment to the needs of an unusual situation coupled with a firm but fair manner gave them a well-deserved reputation and brought a level of law and order not known in American mining communities across the borders. Supplies numerous illustrations of their methods. 20 notes.
                                                                    R. V. Ritter

3336. Newell, Dianne. KLONDIKE PHOTOGRAPHER'S LODE. *Historic Preservation 1977 29(2): 14-21.* The 1897-98 Klondike gold rush to Canada's Yukon Territory was possibly "the most photographed event from the time of the invention of the camera" and influenced contemporary thinking. The photographs are now "the basis for an ambitious Klondike restoration project." 12 photos.
                                                                    R. M. Frame III

3337. Quinlan, Thomas A. THE LAST STAMPEDE: LETTERS FROM THE KLONDIKE. *Am. Hist. Illus. 1975 10(7): 10-21.* Five letters written by Thomas A. Quinlan to his cousin between 1898 and 1904 describe Quinlan's participation in the gold rush.

3338. Remley, David A. CROOKED ROAD: ORAL HISTORY OF THE ALASKAN HIGHWAY. *Alaska J. 1974 4(2):113-121.* Prints 13 short essays about the Alaskan Highway and discusses the difficulties incurred while it was being constructed as a corridor for military supplies through Alaska and the Yukon Territory in 1942-43.

3339. Schanz, A. B.; Wells, E. H.; and Sherman, Ro, ed. FROM KLUKMAN TO THE YUKON. *Alaska J. 1974 4(3): 169-180.* Reprints an 1890 account of the first overland expedition from Klukman, Alaska, to the Yukon via Chilkoot Pass achieved by white men—a team of three newspaper reporters, A. B. Schanz, E. H. Wells, and E. J. Grave.

3340. Tetrault, Gregory. A CARNEGIE LIBRARY FOR DAWSON CITY. *Beaver [Canada] 1974 305(3): 47-50.* A. Nicol appealed from this Yukon city of about 30,000 in 1902 to Andrew Carnegie for library funds; Nicol had family connections who were personally acquainted with Carnegie. A substantial construction and maintenance gift was provided, and the library opened in the fall of 1903. The library was crucial for Dawson's citizens during the long, cold winters. By 1920 the population of Dawson was down to 1,000, the library was soon sold to a local lodge, and the books were deposited in the public school. Includes details on community attitudes towards the Carnegie grant, along with various construction and labor information. 2 photos, diagram.
                                                                    D. Chaput

3341. Usherwood, Stephen. FLORA SHAW ON THE KLONDIKE, 1898. *Hist. Today [Great Britain] 1977 27(7): 445-451.* Discusses Flora Shaw, a female journalist who covered news in the Klondike for the *Times of London* during the gold rush in 1898.

3342. Warren, Iris. TAYLOR & DRURY, LTD., YUKON MERCHANTS. *Alaska J. 1975 5(2): 74-80.* Describes the founding, growth, and development of Taylor and Drury, Ltd., the largest merchandising firm in the Yukon. Founded in 1898 by Isaac Taylor and William Drury with a 12 by 14-foot tent and $200, it developed gross sales of over $183 million. 12 photos.
                                                                    E. E. Eminhizer

Northwest Territories

3343. Berger, Thomas R. THE MACKENZIE VALLEY PIPELINE INQUIRY. *Queen's Q. [Canada] 1976 83(1): 1-12.* Examines the issues at stake in the Mackenzie Valley Pipeline Inquiry and suggests that they "are unique in Canadian experience." The entire future of the river valley and its peoples hinges on the decision of whether or not to allow the building of a pipeline. Makes no final judgment on whether the pipeline should be constructed but concludes that "it is our responsibility to see that the north and its peoples are not the losers" in the Inquiry's ultimate decision.
                                                                    J. A. Casada

3344. Boyd, Josephine W. ON SOME WHITE WOMEN IN THE WILDS OF NORTHERN NORTH AMERICA. *Arctic [Canada] 1974 27(3): 167-174.* Describes the activities of the first white women in the northern Arctic, their role and lives there from the late 19th century to the present. Special emphasis is placed on Mollie Ward Greist, a pioneering nurse. Illus., biblio.
                                                                    J. A. Casada

3345. Buetow, David. THE DISMAL LAKES. *Beaver [Canada] 1978 309(1): 36-41.* These two large lakes are northwest of the Coppermine River. The lakes appear to have been discovered in the 1820's; presents data from Hudson's Bay Company publications and travel narratives that mention the lakes. Eskimos from the Hudson's Bay region still fish there in the summer. 7 illus., map.   D. Chaput

3346. Common, Robert. SOVIET SATELLITE DEBRIS HITS HISTORIC AREA AND RECALLS TRAGIC HORNBY DRAMA. *Can. Geographic [Canada] 1978 97(1): 8-17.* During the winter of 1926-27 three companions, John Hornby, Edgar Christian, and Harold Adlard, wintered at Hornby Point on the Thelon River in the Northwest Territories and starved to death after running out of provisions. Also discusses a 1976 trip made by a number of scientists to the same area in search of the debris of a Soviet satellite, COSMOS, which crashed there.

3347. Connelly, Dolly. MACKENZIE RIVER CRUISE. *Beaver [Canada] 1973 303(4): 24-29.* Describes a 15-day cruise on the Mackenzie River from Inuvik to the Arctic Ocean on the *Norweta.* Accompanied by photos of flora, Eskimos, and river scenes. 13 illus., map.   D. Chaput

3348. Copland, A. Dudley. HARVESTING THE NORTHERN SEAS. *Beaver [Canada] 1974 305(3): 40-46.* Reminiscences of the activities of the Hudson's Bay Company from 1909 to the 1930's by a long-time employee, with emphasis on Hudson Bay and Baffin Island. Includes views of the fur trade, Eskimo life, walrus trade, working-living conditions of hunting parties, international meat-fur markets, and the fish, skin, and ivory trade. 10 illus., map.   D. Chaput

3349. Cox, Bruce. CHANGING PERCEPTIONS OF INDUSTRIAL DEVELOPMENT IN THE NORTH. *Human Organization 1975 34(1): 27-33.* Discusses the industrialization of the Mackenzie River region of Canada.   S

3350. Dewar, Kenneth M. I FOUND THE BODIES OF THE HORNBY PARTY. *Can. Geographic [Canada] 1978 97(1): 18-23.* Recounts participating in a backwoods expedition in the Northwest Territories, 1928, which found the bodies of John Hornby, Harold Adlard, and Edgar Christian, all of whom had perished the previous year of starvation while participating in a similar expedition; discusses the contents of a diary kept by Adlard.

3351. Douglas, W. O. THE WRECK OF THE *FINBACK. Beaver [Canada] 1977 307(4): 16-21.* Reminiscences of W. O. Douglas who, in 1919, was a sergeant in the NWMP serving at Chesterfield Inlet. The *Finback,* a New England whaler, was wrecked 80 miles to the north. In the ensuing months, Douglas took care of the crew and its colorful, aged captain, George Comer. The wreck was auctioned, and Douglas was low bidder. Eskimos helped him salvage food, equipment, and firearms. Contains details about Comer, the last skipper in the Arctic to use shanghaied crews; 9 illus.   D. Chaput

3352. Hamelin, Louis-Edmond. DEVELOPPEMENT NORDIQUE ET HARMONIE [Northern development and harmony]. *Cahiers de Géographie de Québec [Canada] 1974 18(44): 337-346.* Development of the Northwest Territories must be accompanied by administrative and political change in order to meet regional needs.   S

3353. Hamelin, Louis-Edmond. LE FACIES DES AFFAIRES DANS LES TERRITOIRES-DU-NORD-OUEST DU CANADA

[Big and small business in the Northwest Territories of Canada]. *Cahiers de Géographie de Québec [Canada] 1973 17(40): 51-68.* Per capita business volume in the Northwest Territories is extremely high. Reliance on government spending keeps the North in a state of colonial dependence on the South and puts a massive drain on public finances. The small Eskimo community of Pelly Bay, for example, requires investments on the order of $1,500,000. Comprehensive planning is lacking for the region. Map, 6 tables, 24 notes, biblio.   A. E. LeBlanc

3354. Heinke, G. W. and Deans, B. SUPPLY AND WASTE DISPOSAL SYSTEMS FOR ARCTIC COMMUNITIES. *Arctic 1973 26(2): 149-159.* Discusses water supply and sewage-garbage disposal in Arctic areas. Present methods are a trucked and a piped system. Suggests improvements. Based on a detailed study of the systems used in the Frobisher Bay Community, Northwest Territories; fig., 8 tables, biblio.   J. A. Casada

3355. Hindle, Walter. PIPING ARCTIC GAS SOUTH VIA HUDSON BAY. *Can. Geographical J. 1975 90(6): 14-19.* Technical, economic and environmental aspects of the Polar Gas Project to move natural gas from Melville and King Christian Islands in the Northwest Territories to Canadian and US markets.   S

3356. Johnson, Lionel. THE GREAT BEAR LAKE: ITS PLACE IN HISTORY. *Arctic [Canada] 1975 28(4): 231-244.* Chronicles the history, ethnography, and geology of Canada's Great Bear Lake, prehistory-1972.

3357. Karamanski, Theodore J. LIFE IN THE SERVICE OF THE HUDSON'S BAY COMPANY, THE MACKENZIE DISTRICT. *Alaska J. 1977 7(3): 166-173.* Details the struggle for food by the fur traders of the Hudson's Bay Company in the Mackenzie River Valley in the winter. In this area, the company did not supply all needs. Emphasizes the winter of 1841-42. 9 illus., 27 notes, biblio.
                                                          E. E. Eminhizer

3358. Kuo, Chun-Yan. THE EFFECT OF EDUCATION ON THE EARNINGS OF INDIAN, ESKIMO, MÉTIS, AND WHITE WORKERS IN THE MACKENZIE DISTRICT OF NORTHERN CANADA. *Econ. Development and Cultural Change 1976 24(2): 387-398.* Discusses the impact of education and vocational training on the income of Indians, Eskimos, Métis, and white workers, 1969-70.

3359. Purdy, Harriet and Gagan, David, eds. PIONEERING IN THE NORTHWEST TERRITORIES: HARRIET JOHNSON NEVILLE. *Canada 1975 2(4): 3-63.* Chronicles pioneer life in the Northwest Territories through the life of Anthony Neville and his wife Harriet Johnson Neville, 1882-1905.

3360. Rivett-Carnac, Charles. THE ESTABLISHMENT OF THE R.C.M.P. PRESENCE IN THE NORTHWEST TERRITORIES AND THE ARCTIC. *Can. Geographical J. 1973 86(5): 155-167.*

3361. Stevenson, A. THE HIGH ARCTIC. *Beaver [Canada] 1974 304(1): 26-32.* Relates the author's experiences on his trip to the High Arctic in Spring 1973.   S

3362. White, Gavin. CAPTAIN W. J. JACKSON OF BAFFIN ISLAND. *Polar Record [Great Britain] 1975 17(109): 375-382.* Surveys the colorful career of Walter John Jackson (1856-1922), producer, dealer, free trader of Baffin Island, and owner of a third share in Arctic Enterprises Ltd.

SUBJECT INDEX

Subject Profile Index (ABC-SPIndex) carries both generic and specific index terms. Begin a search at the general term but also look under more specific or related terms. Cross-references are included.

Each string of index descriptors is intended to present a profile of a given article; however, no particular relationship between any two terms in the profile is implied. Terms within the profile are listed alphabetically after the leading term. The variety of punctuation and capitalization reflects production methods and has no intrinsic meaning; e.g., there is no difference in meaning between "History, study of" and "History (study of)."

Cities, towns, and counties are listed following their respective states or provinces; e.g., "Ohio (Columbus)." Terms beginning with an arabic numeral are listed after the letter Z. The chronology of the bibliographic entry follows the subject index descriptors. In the chronology, "c" stands for "century"; e.g., "19c" means "19th century."

Note that "Canada" is not used as a leading index term; if no country is mentioned, the index entry refers to Canada alone. When an entry refers to both Canada and the United States, "USA" appears in the string of index descriptors, but neither "USA" nor "Canada" is a leading term. When an entry refers to any other country and Canada, only the other country is indexed.

The last number in the index string, in italics, refers to the bibliographic entry number.

A

Aberhart, William. Alberta. Bowen, John C. Provincial Government. Social Credit Party. 1937-38. *3158*

—. Alberta. Economic reform. Politics. Radio. Religion. 1934-37. *3088*

—. Alberta. Ideology. Provincial Government. Social Credit Party. Theology. 1935-43. *3106*

Abnaki Indians, Western. Myths and Symbols. Transformer figures. ca 1840-1976. *369*

. New England. Quebec. Tufts, Henry. 1772-75. *368*

Abolition Movement *See also* Antislavery Sentiments.

—. Anderson, John. Foreign Relations. Great Britain. Politics. USA. 1860-61. *883*

—. Brown, John. Civil War (antecedents). Harpers Ferry (raid, 1859). Sanborn, Franklin Benjamin. 1854-60. *875*

Aborigines Protection Society. Australia. Great Britain. Indians. USA. ca 1830-50. *464*

Abortion. Birth control. 1870-1920. *929*

—. Press. Public opinion. Social Change. 1960's-74. *1375*

Abstract Index to Deeds. Land. Law. Ontario (Malden Township). 18c-1865. 1978. *778*

Academia. Archives. Journalism. Oral history. 1960-75. *1311*

Academic exchange programs. Canadian studies. Five-Year Cultural Plan. Government funding. 1970's. *1798*

Academic responsibility. Canadian studies. Colleges and Universities. Social responsibility. 1970's. *1360*

Acadia. Copper kettles. Micmac Indians. Mobility. Settlement. 17c. *424*

—. France. New England. Phips, William. War. 1689-1713. *597*

Acadian townsite. Excavations. Glassware. Nova Scotia (Beaubassin). Settlement. ca 1670-1800's. *2274*

Acadians. Acculturation. Exiles. France. Great Britain. Nova Scotia. 18c. *606*

—. Assimilation. Emigration. Minorities in Politics. New Brunswick (Moncton). 1871-1971. *2385*

—. Assimilation. Massachusetts (Gloucester). Nova Scotia (Arichat region). 1850's-1900. *2364*

—. Catholic Church. Discrimination. Irish. New Brunswick. 1860-1900. *2402*

. Catholic Church. English Canadians. Maritime Provinces. Social Conditions. 1763-1977. *2171*

—. Catholic Church. Irish Canadians. New Brunswick. Politics. Quebec. Schools. Taxation. 1871-73. *1067*

—. Colonial Government. Great Britain. Land tenure. Nova Scotia. Oath of allegiance. 11c-1755. *594*

—. Daily Life. Harley, William. New Brunswick, northeastern. Surveying. 1829. *2381*

—. Emigration. 1605-1800. *524*

—. Exiles. Great Britain. Nova Scotia. 1710-55. *614*

—. Institutions. Nationalism. Nova Scotia. Social Organization. 1700's-1970. *2281*

—. Louisiana. North America. 17c-20c. *580*

—. Nova Scotia. St. Lawrence, Gulf of. 1756-95. *622*

Accident prevention. International Longshoremen's and Warehousemen's Union. Working Conditions. 1973. *1601*

—. Management theories. Working Conditions. 20c. *87*

Accountability. Decisionmaking. Environment. Federal government. Science and Government. 1950's-70's. *1725*

—. Education. 1970-73. *1384*

—. Foreign policy. Voting and Voting Behavior. 1950's-74. *1872*

Accreditation. Construction industry. Labor legislation. 1973. *1603*

Acculturation *See also* Assimilation.

—. Acadians. Exiles. France. Great Britain. Nova Scotia. 18c. *606*

—. Bibliographies. French Americans. French Canadians. New England. 1755-1973. *2566*

—. Boardinghouses. Immigrants. Italian Canadians. Ontario (Toronto). 20c. *2782*

—. Cree Indians. Eskimos (Inuit). Race Relations. 1970-74. *284*

—. Cree Indians. Indian-White Relations. Quebec (James Bay). 1970's. *345*

—. Cultural alienation. French-speakers. Quebec. 1950-73. *2569*

—. Cultural preservation. Drama. Indians. 1606-1974. *414*

—. Ethnic identity. Jews. USA. 1961-74. *1486*

—. Ethnic studies. Sociology. 1960's-70's. *1409*

—. Federal Policy. Indians. Sifton, Clifford. 1896-1905. *395*

. French Canadians. Language. 1971. *1342*

—. French Canadians. Nationalism. New England. ca 1610-1975. *2704*

—. Immigrants. Ontario (Toronto). 1950's-70's. *2785*

—. Immigrants. Polish Canadians. 1945-75. *1436*

—. Immigration. Settlement. Slovak Canadians. 1885-1970's. *113*

—. Indian-White Relations. 1838-1976. *381*

—. Indian-White Relations (review article). USA. 1800-1977. 1976-77. *445*

Act of Confederation (1867). Papineau, Louis-Joseph. Political Theory. Quebec, battle of. 1759-1867. *896*

Act of Quebec (1774). French language. Quebec. Sovereignty. 1774-1974. *2673*

Act of Sexual Sterilization (Alberta, 1928). Alberta. Eugenics. Immigration. Press. Woodsworth, James S. 1900-28. *2906*

Action Catholique. Catholic Church. Courchesne, Georges. Quebec (Rimouski). 1940-67. *2466*

Action Catholique (newspaper). Catholic Church. Communist Parties and Movements. Nazism. Quebec. 1917-39. *1411*

Action Nationale (periodical). French Canadians. Minville, Esdras. Quebec. 1933. *2688*

Activity levels. Ontario. Population. Spatial structure. 1941-71. *2733*

Actors and Actresses. Saskatchewan (Regina). Theater. 1900-14. *3059*

Actors and Actresses (American). Nova Scotia (Halifax). Theater. 1768. *2213*

Adachi, Ken (review article). Immigration. Japanese Canadians. Racism. 1877-1976. *123*

Adams, Ian (interview). Intelligence Service. Royal Canadian Mounted Police. 1960's-70's. *1731*

Adams, John Quincy. Diplomacy. Fishing. Great Britain. Monroe, James. Newfoundland banks. USA. 1815-18. *782*

Adamson, John. Cholera cures, ineffective. Medicine (practice of). Nova Scotia (Halifax). 1834. *2219*

Adlard, Harold. Christian, Edgar. COSMOS (satellite). Hornby, John. Northwest Territories (Thelon River, Hornby Point). 1926-27. 1976. *3346*

— Christian, Edgar. Dewar, Kenneth M. (reminiscences). Diaries. Hornby, John. Northwest Territories (Thelon River, Hornby Point). 1928. *3350*

Administrative structure. International law. Organization of American States. Rio Treaty. San José resolution. 1945-75. *1892*

Adolescence *See also* Youth.

—. Boys. Protestantism. USA. Young Men's Christian Association. 1870-1920. *927*

—. Dependency. Employment. Frontier and Pioneer Life. Ontario (Orillia). Social change. 1861-71. *2769*

Adoption. Alberta. Blackfoot Indians. 1939. *413*

—. Belgium. France. Law. 1974. *1393*

Adult education. Colonial Government. Nova Scotia. ca 1820-35. *2289*

—. Denmark. Folk school concept. 1919-50. *1136*

—. Educators. Howe, Joseph. Nova Scotia. 1827-66. *2290*

—. Great Britain. 1516-1977. *105*

—. Halifax Mechanics' Institute. Middle Classes. Nova Scotia. Working class. 1830's-40's. *2291*

—. Libraries. Middle classes. Social Organization. Working class. 19c. *104*

—. Manpower training programs. Public Finance. 1967-77. *1699*

Aeronautics *See also* Air Lines; Space.

—. 20c. *207*

—. Saskatchewan. 1908-18. *3040*

Aeronautics (history). Archival Catalogs and Inventories. Hitchins, Fred H. Western Ontario, University of, D. B. Weldon Library (Hitchins Collection). 20c. *94*

—. Dirigibles (R-100). England. 1930. *1215*

—. Junker monoplanes. 1920-29. *1172*

Aeronautics, Military *See also* Air Warfare; Airplanes, Military.

. Burgess-Dunne Seaplane. Canadian Aviation Corps. Janney, Ernest L. 1914-15. *1155*

—. Ontario (Long Branch). Royal Canadian Air Force (Flying School). 1915-16. *1153*

Africa. Foreign aid. International Trade. 1970-75. *1864*

—. Foreign relations. France. French-speaking nations. Quebec. 1950's-70's. *1845*

—. Literature, African. 1973. *110*

—. Operation Crossroads Africa. Robinson, James H. Students. USA. 1958-73. *1749*

Africa, French-speaking. Belgium. Foreign Relations. France. French-speaking institutions. 1960-74. *1769*

—. Belgium. France. International cooperation. Quebec. 1964-74. *2718*

—. Foreign Aid. 1968-74. *1800*

Africa, southern. Foreign Policy. Peacekeeping Forces. Trudeau, Pierre Elliott. UN Conference on the Law of the Sea. 1968-78. *1775*

Africa, West. American Revolution. Emigration. Fugitive slaves. Great Britain. Nova Scotia. 1776-1820. *737*

Africans *See also* Negroes.

—. Asians. Indians. North America. Racism. Whites. 1600-1900. *10*

Africoids. Americas (North and South). Anthropological evidence. Discovery and Exploration. Prehistory. *293*

Afro-Americans. *See* Negroes.

Age. Political Participation. Voting and Voting Behavior. 1968. *1650*

—. Sex. Unemployment. 1957-70. *1606*

Aged *See also* Pensions; Public Welfare.

—. British Columbia (Vancouver, Victoria). Income. Population. Taxation. 1951-74. *3196*

—. Labor Unions and Organizations. Pensions. United Automobile Workers (Canadian Region). 1973. *1580*

—. Minority group concept. Sociology. Women. 1970's. *1339*

—. National Pensioners and Senior Citizens' Federation. 1954-73. *1570*

—. Pensions. Social security. -1973. *1505*

Agent general, office of. Great Britain (London). Intergovernmental Relations. 18c-20c. *212*

Agnosticism. Catholic Church. Quebec. Students. 1970-78. *2455*

Agricultural colonies. Bee, William. Methodists, Primitive. Saskatchewan (Grenfell). 1882. *949*

Agricultural commodities. Banking. Foreign Investments. Public services. Puerto Rico. 1800-1977. *180*

Agricultural Cooperatives. Coopérative Fédérée de Québec. Quebec. 1971-73. *2597*

Agricultural crisis. Historiography. Ouellet, Fernand. Paquet, Gilles. Quebec (Lower Canada). Wallot, J.-P. 1802-12. 1963-73. *789*

—. Historiography. Quebec (Lower Canada). 1802-12. *806*

Agricultural development. Boserup, Ester. China. North America. Russia. South. 18c-19c. *801*

—. Deforestation. Ecology. Ontario. 1880-1900. *275*

—. Models. Prairie Provinces. Settlement. 1870-1911. *1037*

—. Prairie Provinces. Settlement. 1872-1930. *1012*

Agricultural journals. Animal husbandry. Ontario (Canada West). 1835-55. *792*

Agricultural policy. Elections. Provincial government. Quebec. 1960-73. *2601*

Agricultural production. Cereals. Farmers. World War I. 1911-21. *1164*

—. Climate. Energy shortages. Food supply. Urbanization. 1956-74. *1511*

Agricultural Technology and Research. Prairie Provinces. Steam tractors. Western States. 1890-1925. *2913*

Agriculture *See also* Conservation of Natural Resources; Country Life; Crops; Dairying; Farms; Food Industry; Forests and Forestry; Land; Land Tenure; Rural Development; Soil Conservation; Winemaking.

—. Alberta (Rosebud Creek). Biggs, Hugh Beynon. Photography. Ranches. 1892-1941. *3169*

—. Business. Distribution system. Machinery. Manitoba. 1974. *2923*

—. Capitalism. Peasants. Quebec. 1600-1970's. *2595*

—. Economic conditions. Prairies. Railroads. Urbanization. 1871-1916. *2957*

—. Europe. Industrialization. Market economy. North America. Peasant movements (colloquium). ca 1875-1975. *13*

—. Federal Government. Income. 1973-76. *1621*

—. Federalism. Forests and Forestry. Industrialization. Natural resources. Quebec. 20c. *2646*

—. Hutterites. North America. Social Customs. Technology. 18c-20c. *2896*

—. Industry. Quebec (Saguenay region). Social Conditions. 1840-1972. *2472*

—. Jews. Prairie Provinces. Settlement. 1884-1920's. *2950*

—. Ontario. Political Attitudes. Quebec. Social change. 1850-1970. *2132*

Agriculture and Government. Elections. Ontario (Manitoulin). Political Protest. 1914-18. *2775*

Agriculture Minister. Gardiner, James G. Liberal Party. Patronage. 1935-57. *2959*

Air Lines. Alaska. White Pass Aviation. Yukon Territory. 1934-40. *3331*

Air mail flights. Wann, Clyde. Yukon Territory. 1927-35. *3330*

Air Mail Service. New Brunswick (Rimouski). Quebec (Montreal). 1920's-30's. *1179*

Air pollution. Political structures. Sweden. USA. 1974. *1691*

Air Warfare *See also* Airplanes, Military; Atomic Warfare.

—. Army Air Corps. Beeson, Duane. Idaho (Boise). World War II. 1941-45. *1222*

Airplanes *See also* names of airplanes, e.g. B-52 (aircraft); Aeronautics.

—. Alberta (Edmonton). Buchanan, Carl J. (reminiscences). Canadian Airways. 1940. *3090*

Airplanes, Military (training). China. Fraser, Douglas. Nationalism. Saskatchewan (Saskatoon). 1919-22. *1169*

Akins, Thomas Beamish. Nova Scotia. Public Records. 1857-91. *2246*

Alabama *See also* South Central and Gulf States.

—. Alcohol. Florida. Nova Scotia. Pentz, Gabriel. Smuggling. 20c. *2249*

Alabama (Florence). Freedmen. Rapier, John H., Sr. (biography). 1830-60. *886*

Alabama (Mobile). France (Paris). Iberville, Pierre Le Moyne d'. Immigration. Population. Women. 1702-04. *582*

Alaska. Air Lines. White Pass Aviation. Yukon Territory. 1934-40. *3331*

—. Anián, strait of. British Columbia. Cook, James. Discovery and Exploration. Northwest Passage. Voyages. 1778. *675*

—. Arctic. Mining. Scandinavia. USSR. 1917-78. *3288*

—. Artifacts. Emmons, George Thornton. Ethnology. Tlingit Indians. 1852-1945. *417*

—. British Columbia. China (Macao). Cook, James. Fur trade. Pacific Area. 1778-79. *784*

—. Discovery and Exploration. Lapérouse, Jean François. Ledyard, John. Pacific Area. Pacific Northwest. Russia (Siberia). 1778-1806. *652*

—. Economic Growth. Greenland. Population. Scandinavia. 1970's. *281*

—. Eskimos. Indians. Land claim settlements. 1958-77. *288*

—. Eskimos. Sleep paralysis. Prehistory-1976. *315*

—. Gold Rushes. Klondike Stampede. Women. Yukon Territory. 1897-99. *3322*

—. Haida Indians. Indians. Tlingit Indians. Tsimshian Indians. 1649-1973. *430*

—. Railroads. USSR. World War II. 1942-43. *1248*

Alaska (Eagle). DeWolfe, Percy. Mail carrier. Yukon Territory (Dawson). 1915-50. *3332*

Alaska (Klukman). Discovery and Exploration. Yukon Territory. 1890. *3339*

Alaska Land Settlement of 1971. Eskimos. Minorities. Politics. 1960-73. *318*

Alaska (Metlakahtla). British Columbia. Duncan, William. Missions and Missionaries. Tsimshian Indians. 1857-1974. *373*

Alaska pipeline. Economic competition. Oil Industry and Trade. USA. 1973-75. *2041*

Alaska (Skagway). Brackett, George. Entrepreneurs. Gold Rushes. Roads. Yukon Territory. 1897-98. *3323*

—. British Columbia (Lake Bennett). Gold miners. Klondike Stampede. 1896-99. 1960-73. *3200*

Alaska Steamship Company. British Columbia (Queen Charlotte Islands). *Kennecott* (vessel). Salvage. Shipwrecks. 1923. *3181*

Alaska, western. Bahr, Andrew. Northwest Territories (Mackenzie River Delta). Reindeer. 1928-34. *3295*

Alaska-British Columbia-Yukon Conferences. British Columbia. Economic development. Regional Planning. Yukon Territory. 1930-64. *2133*

Alaskan Coast. Bernard, Joseph Francis. Eskimos. Siberian Coast. Traders. 1903-29. *314*

Alaskan Highway. British Columbia. Highways. Yukon Territory. 1974. *3325*

—. Highway Engineering. Logistics. World War II. Yukon Territory. 1942-43. *3338*

Alberta *See also* Prairie Provinces.

—. Aberhart, William. Bowen, John C. Provincial Government. Social Credit Party. 1937-38. *3158*

—. Aberhart, William. Economic reform. Politics. Radio. Religion. 1934-37. *3088*

—. Aberhart, William. Ideology. Provincial Government. Social Credit Party. Theology. 1935-43. *3106*

—. Act of Sexual Sterilization (Alberta, 1928). Eugenics. Immigration. Press. Woodsworth, James S. 1900-28. *2906*

—. Adoption practices. Blackfoot Indians. 1939. *413*

—. Architecture. Assimilation. Ukrainians. 1891-1970's. *3127*

—. Athabasca Pass. British Columbia. Ritual toasts. 1811-1974. *694*

—. Bachelors. Calgary *Herald*, newspaper. Frontier. Marriage. 1895. *956*

—. Banff Park. Explorers. Peyto, Bill. Scientific expeditions. 1887-1933. *3092*

—. Birney, Earle (reminiscences). Surveying. Waterton Lakes National Park. 1921. *3098*

—. Blackfoot Indians. Church of England. Cree Indians. Missions and Missionaries. Trivett, Samuel. 1878-91. *360*

—. Blackfoot Indians. Cree Indians. Meteorite. 1810-1973. *442*

—. Blackfoot Indians. Indians. Wolf Collar (shaman). 1870-1928. *356*

—. Blackfoot Indians. Manhood ceremonies. Rites and Ceremonies. Shaw, P. C. (personal account). 1894. *447*

—. Bobtail Cree Reserve. Cree Indians. Indians. Land. 1900-09. *3125*

—. Boorne, W. Hanson. Photography. 1886-93. *3171*

—. British Columbia. Coal Mines and Mining. Depressions. Pass Strike of 1932. 1920's-30's. *1209*

—. Bureaucratization. Criminal sentencing. Indians. Urbanization. 1973. *1663*

—. Business. Federal Programs. International trade. 1977. *3084*

—. Canadian Shield. Natural resources. 1977. *273*

—. Cattle Raising. Cochrane ranch. 1881-1905. *3167*

—. Cities. Local Government. Political Recruitment. 1971. *3129*

—. Cities. Political protest. Social Conditions. 1918-39. *3110*

—. Cloud-seeding program. Hail damage. Storms. 1955-74. *3136*

—. Construction. Housing. Settlement. Sod. Williams, Wesley. 1909. *1004*

—. Cowboys. Farmers. Ranchers. Round-ups. 1911-19. *2932*

—. Cree Indians. Fuller, Richard. Hudson's Bay Company. Telegraph. Treaties. 1870's. *1020*

—. Cypress Hills Provincial Park. Saskatchewan. 1859-1973. *2914*

—. Daughters. Mothers. Oral history. Pioneers. 1890-1929. *1025*

—. Department of Social Services and Community Health. Provincial Government. Social policy. 1970's. *3133*

—. Depressions. Educational role. United Farm Women of Alberta. 1915-30. *3161*

—. Devolution. Federalism. Oil rights. Scotland. 1970's. *3118*

—. Edwards, Robert C. "Bob". *Eye Opener* (newspaper). Populists. 1904-22. *3108*

—. Elections, provincial. Liberal Party. Social Credit League. United Farmers of Alberta. 1905-73. *3107*

—. Farmers. Political parties. Provincial Legislatures. 1920's-30's. *2944*

—. Farming. Mennonites. Namaka Farm. 1920's-40's. *3121*

—. Fiction. Mitchell, W. O. Provincial consciousness. Ross, Sinclair. 20c. *3093*

—. Fort Chipewyan. Fur Trade. Lefroy, L. H. 1843-44. *3094*

—. Fur trade. Hudson's Bay Company. Kerr, Tom. 1861-1946. *3160*

—. Gardiner, James G. Liberal Party. Social Credit Party. 1935-39. *3157*

—. Godsal, F. W. Ranches. South Fork Ranch. 1897. *3155*

—. Grandin, Vital (letter). 1876. *3102*

—. Great Britain. Ombudsmen. Public Opinion. 1969-71. *3109*

—. Harvests. Photographs. Wheat. 1910-20. *3168*

—. Homesteading and Homesteaders. Immigration. Negroes. Race Relations. 1911-12. *3152*

—. Homesteading and Homesteaders. Kokotailo, Veronia. Rumanians. 1898- . *3165*

—. Homesteading and Homesteaders. Peace River country. Ukrainians. Zahara, Dominka Roshko. 1900-30. *1034*

—. Horses. 1870-90. *1000*

—. Houses. Ukrainians. 1890's-1915. *3128*

—. Immigration. Minorities. Nativism. 1925-30. *3144*

—. Indians. Ogilvie, William (field notes). Surveying. 1878-79. *433*
—. Johnson, Pauline (Tekahionwake). Mohawk Indians. Poetry. 1895-1913. *363*
—. Kansas. Leedy, John Whitnah. Politics. Prairie radical. Radicals and Radicalism. 1880's-1935. *3087*
—. Law Reform. 1939-74. *3114*
—. Military Medicine. North West Rebellion. Pennefather, John P. (reminiscences). Winnipeg Light Infantry. 1885. *1016*
—. Oil exploration. 1890's-1910's. *3099*
—. Oral history. Rural Settlements. Women. 1890-1929. *3149*
—. Police (provincial). 1917-32. *3156*
—. Political Parties. Unity movement. 1935-45. *3148*
—. Recreation. Rocky Mountains. Skiing. 1920's-30's. *3131*
—. Rocky Mountains. Tupper, William Johnston (letters). 1885. *964*
Alberta (Athabasca Landing). Canadian Northern Railway. *Edmonton Bulletin* (newspaper). Railroads. Villages. 1912-77. *3113*
Alberta (Athabasca River). Bitumen. Oil and Petroleum Products. Syncrude oil Project. 1974-75. *3150*
—. Oil Industry and Trade. Syncrude oil project. USA. 1975. *2036*
Alberta (Banff). Elites. Midwest. Power, interorganizational. 1960's-70's. *3123*
—. Macdonald, John A. National Parks and Reserves. Natural resources. Tourism. 1885-1978. *1040*
—. Meteorology. Sanson, Norman Bethune (biography). 1896-99. *3153*
—. Natural Resources. Resorts. Rocky Mountain Park. 1882-1909. *3117*
—. Skiing. 1890-1940. *3130*
Alberta (Banff, Calgary). McDougall, John. Travel. 1873-1902. *3137*
—. Recreation. Urbanization. 1890. *3162*
Alberta (Calgary). Archives. Glenbow-Alberta Institute. 1955-76. *3115*
—. Automobiles. Bicycles. Daily Life. 1880-1914. *3120*
—. Cattle Raising. Economic Conditions. Oil Industry and Trade. 19c-20c. *3089*
—. Chinese community. 1886-1974. *3086*
—. City government. Social problems. 1894-96. *3122*
—. Co-op. Labor Unions and Organizations. 1956-73. *3154*
—. Fort Brisbois. Toponymy. 1875-76. *3151*
—. Glenbow Centre. Harvie, Eric L. Museums. 1954-76. *3100*
—. Influenza epidemic. Mahood, Cecil S. 1918-19. *3138*
—. Libraries (decentralization) Mount Royal College (Learning Resource Center). 1973. *3142*
—. Models. Nationalism. Political ideologies. Regionalism. 1974. *2921*
—. News diffusion. Trudeau, Pierre Elliott. 1971. *1385*
—. Political Participation. Woman's Canadian Club. 1911-20's. *3097*
—. Public Transportation. Streetcars. 1907-50. *3141*
Alberta (Calgary Diocese). Catholic Church. French Canadians. Irish Canadians. McNailly, John Thomas. 1871-1952. *3095*
Alberta (Calgary, Edmonton). Williams, W. H. (travel account). 1881. *1031*
Alberta (Calgary, Mona Lisa Site). Artifacts. Bison kill. Stratigraphy. ca 8080 BP. 1968-74. *310*
Alberta (Cardiff, Edmonton). Chaban, Teklia. Coal Mines and Mining. Labor Unions and Organizations. Ukrainian Canadians. 1914-20's. *3164*
Alberta (Coaldale). Community organizations. Germans, Russian. Mennonites. Social Change. 1920-76. *3145*
Alberta (Cochrane). British American Ranche Company. Cattle Raising. Cochrane Ranch. Red River of the North. 1881-1905. *1010*
Alberta (De Winton). Indians. Prehistory. 1972. *295*
Alberta (Drumheller Valley). Labor disputes. One Big Union. United Mine Workers of America. 1919. *3163*
Alberta (Edmonton). Airplane flights. Buchanan, Carl J. (reminiscences). Canadian Airways. 1940. *3090*
—. Archives, city. 1938-74. *3126*
—. Bridges. Calgary and Edmonton Railway. City Government. Railroads. 1910-13. *3112*

—. Cameron, Alexander W. Theater. 1906-13. *3143*
—. Canadian Pacific Railway. Local Politics. Railroads. 1891-1914. *955*
—. Catholic Church. Colleges and Universities. MacDonald, John Roderick. St. Joseph's College (Alberta). 1922-23. *3140*
—. Church of England. Newton, William. 1875-1900. *983*
—. City councillors. Decisionmaking. Municipal government. Voting and Voting Behavior. 1966-72. *3134*
—. Depressions. 1904-29. *3159*
—. Farmer's Union of Alberta. Kyforuk, Peter. Manitoba. Ukrainian Labour-Farmer Association. 1912-30's. *2961*
—. Homesteading and Homesteaders. Rural Schools. Waugh School District. 1901-40's. *3166*
—. Hutterites. Public Opinion. Social distance. 1966-75. *3132*
—. McClellan, George B. (reminiscences). Royal Canadian Mounted Police. 1932-63. *3135*
—. Photographs. Sports. 1900's. *3170*
Alberta (Edmonton, Mellowdale). Concordia College. Lutheran Church. Schwermann, Albert H. (reminiscences). USA. 1891-1976. *3147*
Alberta (Fort McMurray). Draper, Tom. Oil sands. 1920's-30's. *3096*
—. Great Canadian Oil Sands. Oil Industry and Trade. Syncrude oil project. 1975. *3111*
Alberta (Lac la Biche). Beaver Indians. Hudson's Bay Company. North West Rebellion. Pruden, Patrick. Trading posts. 1885. *1026*
—. Erasmus, Peter. Faraud, Bishop. North West Rebellion. 1885. *1021*
Alberta (Lethbridge). Coal Mines and Mining. Galt, Alcander. 1885-1905. *958*
—. Coal Mines and Mining. Galt, Alexander. Government. Settlement. 1879-93. *960*
—. Culture. Industry. Pioneers. Transportation. 1880's. *3104*
Alberta (Lundbreck). Coal Mines and Mining. Daily Life. Koester, Mavis Addie (reminiscences). 1905-08. *3124*
Alberta (Medicine Hat). Beverly, James. Weather. 1899. *3103*
Alberta (Mount Alberta). Explorers. Hirohito, Emperor. Japanese. Mountain climbing party. 1925-48. *2924*
Alberta (North Saskatchewan River). Fur Trade. Rocky Mountain House. 19c. *3101*
Alberta, northern. Indians. Jackson, Mary Percy. Métis. Physicians. 1929-70's. *3119*
Alberta (Red Deer-Halkirk). Farms. Homesteading and Homesteaders. 1900-15. *3116*
Alberta (Rosebud Creek). Agriculture. Biggs, Hugh Beynon. Photography. Ranches. 1892-1941. *3169*
Alberta (Saskatchewan River). Gold rushes. 1897. *3146*
Alberta, southern. Boundary Waters Treaty. Irrigation. USA. 1885-1909. *962*
—. British Columbia. Japanese Canadians. World War II. 1941-45. *1233*
—. Homesteading and Homesteaders. Sharples (family). 1870's-1902. *3085*
Alberta (Stettler). Frontier and Pioneer Life. McLeod, Evelyn Slater (reminiscences). 1900's. *3139*
Alberta (Waskatenau). Buchanan, Carl, Jr. (reminiscences). Daily Life. Homesteading and Homesteaders. 1930's. *3091*
Alberta (Writing-On-Stone, Milk River). Indians. Law Enforcement. Military Camps and Forts. North West Mounted Police. 1887-1918. *957*
Albert-Westmorland-Kent Regional Library. Libraries. New Brunswick (Moncton). 1911-73. *2398*
Albion mines. Coal Mines and Mining. Nova Scotia (Pictou County). 1767-1881. *2226*
Alcan Aluminium, Ltd. Bauxite industry. Guyana. Multinational corporations. Nationalization. 1960-75. *1852*
Alcohol. Alabama. Florida. Nova Scotia. Pentz, Gabriel. Smuggling. 20c. *2249*
Alcoholism. Cultural influences. Quebec (Montreal). Social performance. 1973. *1443*
Aleutian campaign. USA. World War II. 1938-45. *1231*
Alexander I. Foreign policy. North America. Pacific Area. Russian-American Company. 1799-1824. *678*

Alexander I (ukase). Foreign Relations. Great Britain. Noncolonization principle. Pacific Northwest. Russo-American Convention of 1824. 1821-25. *627*
Algonkin Indians. Historical Sites and Parks. Iroquois Indians. Missions and Missionaries. Quebec (Oka). Sulpicians. 1700's-1800's. *521*
—. Indians. Maine. Maritime Provinces. Missions and Missionaries. Social change. 1610-1750. *516*
Algonquin College Resource Centre. Bibliography, regional. Methodology. Ontario (Ottawa). 1974-78. *2142*
Alienation. Acculturation. Francophones. Quebec. 1950-73. *2569*
—. Automation. Working Conditions. 1973. *1557*
—. Business education. Quebec. USA. 1972. *2034*
—. Charities. Government. Quebec (Quebec; Lower Town). Social Problems. Working Class. 1896-1914. *2637*
—. Hamilton, Pierce Stevens (memoirs). Morality. Social Conditions. 1826-93. *2335*
—. Ontario. Socialization. Student activism. Western Ontario, University of. 1970. *2773*
Aliens *See also* Immigration.
—. Austrians. Internment camps. World War I. 1914-19. *1150*
All in the Family (program). Television. USA. 1972-73. *1479*
Alliance Laurentienne. Barbeau, Raymond. Guillemette, Pierre. Independence Movements. Quebec. 1960's-75. *2674*
—. Federalism. Quebec. Separatism. 1957-70's. *2681*
Alliances *See also* International Relations (discipline); Treaties.
—. Chickasaw Indians. Choctaw Indians. France. Indians. South Central and Gulf States. Tonti, Henri de. 1702. *581*
Alline, Henry. Charisma. Nova Scotia. 1776-83. *732*
Alpine Club of Canada. Himalayas. Mountain climbers. Pumori (mountain). 1977. *1260*
Alta California. See California.
Aluminum industry. Hydroelectric power. 1900-76. *65*
Amazon River. Americas (North and South). Environment. Northwest Territories (Mackenzie River). Rivers. 1977. *268*
American Federation of Labor. Babcock, Robert H. (review article). Gompers, Samuel. USA. 1897-1914. *1078*
—. Canadian Labour Congress. Labor Unions and Organizations. Strong, Cyril. 1949-77. *1525*
—. French Canadians. Gompers, Samuel. Quebec. 1900-14. *2588*
—. Industrial Workers of the World. One Big Union. Washington. 1919. *1167*
American Institute of the History of Pharmacy. Canadian Academy of the History of Pharmacy. Pharmacy, History of. Stieb, Ernst W. (account). 1940's-70's. *2059*
American Revolution *See also* Treaty of Paris (1783); Fourth of July; Loyalists.
—. Africa, West. Emigration. Fugitive slaves. Great Britain. Nova Scotia. 1776-1820. *737*
—. Amphibious operations. Marines. Naval expeditions. Nova Scotia. 1654-1798. *724*
—. Arnold, Benedict. Carleton, Guy. Fort Ticonderoga. Lake Champlain. 1776. *722*
—. Attitudes. Carleton, Guy. Military Occupation. Peasants. Quebec. 1775-76. *717*
—. Bailey, Jacob. Church of England. Letters. Nova Scotia. 1784. *726*
—. Bennington (battle). Burgoyne, John. Stark, John. Vermont. 1777. *730*
—. British Army. Carleton, Guy. Logistics. Quebec. 1776. *714*
—. Business. Fort Niagara. New York. 1775-83. *736*
—. Colonies. France. Heraldry. Knights of Malta. 1600's-1976. *172*
—. Colonization. Loyalists. New Brunswick. Saunders, John. Virginia. 1774-1834. *740*
—. Congress. Hazen, Moses. Military. 1776-1803. *734*
—. Crèvecoeur, Michel (pseud. J. Hector St. John). France. Great Britain. 1755-1813. *618*
—. Economic Conditions. Great Britain. Quebec. 1770's. *731*
—. Economic Policy. Federalism. USA. 1776-1976. *202*
—. Fishing. Nova Scotia (Lockport). Privateers. 18c. *720*

—. Florida (St. Augustine). Loyalists. ca 1775-85. *752*
—. France. 1776. *716*
—. France. Protestants. Settlement. USA. Whaling industry and Trade. 17c-20c. *1287*
—. French Canadians. French Revolution. Quebec (Lower Canada). Reform. 1773-1815. *712*
—. French Revolution. Ideology. Popular movements. 1775-1838. *819*
—. Friends, Society of. Great Britain. Ireland. Pennsylvania (Philadelphia). Relief funds. 1778-97. *739*
—. Friends, Society of. Massachusetts (Nantucket Island). Whaling Industry and Trade. 1750's-1800. *733*
—. Gates, Horatio. Military strategy. 1777-80. *721*
—. Great Britain. Great Lakes. Old Northwest. Peace of Paris (1783). Shelburne, 2d Earl of (William Petty). 1783. *727*
—. Great Britain. Smith, Adam. 1770-76. *728*
—. Language. Loyalists. Settlement. 1774-84. *746*
—. Loyalists. 1782-90's. *738*
—. Morgan, Daniel. Riflemen. ca 1735-1802. *719*
—. USA. War of 1812. 1759-20c. *634*
American Revolution (antecedents). Georgia. Great Britain. Immigrants. Military. Nova Scotia. 1765-75. *729*
Americanism. Lemelin, Roger *(Les Plouffe)*. Nationalism. Quebec. 1938-45. *2722*
Americanization. Criminal Law. Laskin, Bora. Supreme Court (Canada). 1973-74. *2068*
—. Historiography. Moffett, Samuel E. 1867-1974. *162*
—. Popular Culture. USA. 1921-75. *1979*
Americas (North and South). Africoids. Anthropological evidence. Discovery and Exploration. Prehistory. *293*
—. Amazon River. Environment. Northwest Territories (Mackenzie River). Rivers. 1977. *268*
—. Discovery and Exploration. Europe, Eastern. Pacific Area. 16c-19c. *175*
—. Foreign relations. Human rights. 1945-75. *1843*
—. Human rights. 19c-20c. *163*
—. Indians. International law. Organization of American States. UN. 19c-1974. *367*
Amherst, Jeffrey. French and Indian War. Iroquois Indians. Military History. New France. Pontiac's Rebellion. 1760-65. *612*
Amish. Dukhobors. Hutterites. Mennonites. Molokans. North America. ca 1650-1977. *184*
Amnesty International. Political prisoners. 1961-75. *1831*
Amphibious operations. American Revolution. Marines. Naval expeditions. Nova Scotia. 1654-1798. *724*
Anatomy, morbid. Dreams. Medicine (practice of). Osler, William. USA. 1872-1919. *908*
Ancient, William J. *Atlantic* (vessel). Heroes. Nova Scotia (Terence Bay). Shipwrecks. 1873. *2225*
Anderson, James. Arctic. Expedition, search. Franklin, John. Iroquois Indians. Woodsmanship. 1855. *3305*
—. Hudson's Bay Company. Quebec (Eastmain River). Rivers. Whaling Industry and Trade. 1850's-70. *847*
Anderson, James T. M. Anti-Catholicism. Public schools. Saskatchewan. School Act (amended). Secularization. 1929-34. *3050*
—. Elections. Gardiner, James G. Provincial Legislatures. Saskatchewan (Estevan). 1929-30. *3078*
Anderson, John. Abolition Movement. Foreign Relations. Great Britain. Politics. USA. 1860-61. *883*
Anderson, William J. House of Representatives. Negroes. Political Leadership. Vermont (Montpelier, Shoreham). 1900-40's. *2565*
Anglican Communion *See also* Church of England; Episcopal Church, Protestant.
—. Cree Indians. Faries, Richard. Missions and Missionaries. Ontario (York Factory). 1896-1961. *379*
—. Manitoba (Red River). Missionary wives. Missions and Missionaries. Women. 1820-37. *462*
Anglicization. French Canadians. French language. Grignon, Claude Henri. 20c. *135*
—. French Canadians. Immigration. MacDonald, John A. 1860-1900. *705*
—. Language. Quebec. Social classes. 1971. *2461*

Anglin, Timothy Warren. Baker, W. M. Fenians. Irish Canadians (review article). Neidhardt, W. S. 19c. 1970's. *1073*
—. Catholic Church. Confederation. Fenians. New Brunswick. 1866. *890*
—. Catholic Church. Irish Canadians. New Brunswick. Saint John *Freeman* (newspaper). 1849-83. *2373*
—. Fenians. Irish Canadians. McGee, D'Arcy. Political debates. 1863-68. *891*
—. Parliaments. 1874-78. *1039*
Anglo-Japanese Treaty of Alliance (1902). Asiatic Exclusion League. British Columbia (Vancouver). Japan. USA. 1907-22. *1108*
Anglophiles. Francophiles. Mathieu, Olivier-Elzéar. Saskatchewan (Regina). 1905-30. *3035*
Anglophobia. Aroostook War (1839). Boundary dispute. Great Britain. USA. 1837-39. *654*
Anglophones. Ethnicity. French-speakers. Historical traditions. 1464
—. French-speakers. Income. 1961-74. *1564*
—. Language. Quebec. 1830-1976. *2714*
—. National identification. Political Attitudes. Quebec. Separatist Movements. 1970's. *2120*
Anián, strait of. Alaska. British Columbia. Cook, James. Discovery and Exploration. Northwest Passage. Voyages. 1778. *675*
Anik Satellite. Communications. Northwest Territories. Satellites. 1972. *3287*
Animal husbandry. Agricultural journals. Ontario (Canada West). 1835-55. *792*
—. Frontier. Meat (sources). Prince Rupert's Land. 18c-20c. *2942*
Annan, Ebenezer (letters). Daily Life. Immigration. Nova Scotia (Halifax). 1842. *2220*
Annexation. British Columbia. Foreign Policy. Seward, William H. 1865-69. *3252*
—. Confederation. Newfoundland. Outports. Poverty. Social Customs. 1920-48. *2200*
—. Foreign Relations. USA. 1760-1971. *40*
—. Public Opinion. USA. 1956-71. *1970*
—. Trade. USA. 1911. *1084*
Antarctic *See also* Polar Exploration.
—. Australia. Explorers. Great Britain. Priestley, Raymond. 1912-74. *3321*
Anthropological evidence. Africoids. Americas (North and South). Discovery and Exploration. Prehistory. *293*
Anthropological studies. 1850-1910. *282*
Anthropologists. Social reform. 1974. *1388*
Anthropology *See also* Acculturation; Archaeology; Ethnology; Language; Linguistics; Race Relations; Social Change.
—. Archives. Indians. Subarctic. 1975. *347*
—. Art. British Columbia. Duff, Wilson. Pacific Northwest. 1950-76. *280*
—. Authority. Ecology. Eskimos, Central. Social organization. 1970's. *322*
—. Cultural. Myths and Symbols. Pacific Northwest. Tsimshian Indians. Prehistory-20c. *456*
Anthropology, Physical. Craniology. Eskimos. Prehistory. 1971. *313*
Anti-Americanism. Anti-Continentalism. Capitalism. Nationalism. 1960's-74. *2045*
—. Attitudes. National Characteristics. USA. 1972. *1969*
—. Loyalist tradition. New Brunswick. Political Attitudes. 1825-1914. *2375*
—. Ontario (Upper Canada). Rebellion of 1837. Sectarianism. 1837. *817*
—. USA. 18c-20c. *107*
Anti-Canadianism. Civil War. New York City. Press. 1861-65. *864*
Anti-Catholicism. Anderson, James T. M. Public schools. Saskatchewan. School Act (amended). Secularization. 1929-34. *3050*
—. Elections (provincial). Ku Klux Klan. Saskatchewan. Separate school legislation. 1929. *3024*
—. Ku Klux Klan. Protestants. Saskatchewan. 1927-30. *3033*
—. New Brunswick. Pitts, Herman H. Religion in the Public Schools. 1871-90. *2388*
Anticlericalism. Boycotts. *Canada-Revue* (newspaper). Catholic Church. Freedom of the press. Quebec (Montreal). 1890-94. *2484*
Anti-Communist movements. Anti-Semitism. Freedom of speech. Immigration. National self-image. Ontario (Toronto). 1928-29. *2791*
Anti-Confucius Campaign. China. Students. 1973-74. *1783*
Anti-Continentalism. Anti-Americanism. Capitalism. Nationalism. 1960's-74. *2045*
Anti-discrimination legislation. Anti-Semitism. Nazism. 1930's. *1196*
Antigonish Movement. Atlantic Provinces. Cooperatives. 1900-45. *2165*

—. Catholic Church. Nova Scotia. Rural Development. Social change. ca 1928-73. *2297*
—. Cooperatives. Economic Development. Nova Scotia, eastern. Social Classes. 1920's-30's. *2338*
—. Cooperatives. Maritime Provinces. Social economics. 1920's-40's. *2169*
Anti-Inflation Act. Canadian Labour Congress. Economic Conditions. Income. 1970's. *1572*
—. Emergency powers. Peacetime. Supreme Court (Canada). Wages. 1976. *1607*
—. Parliaments. Supreme Court, Canada. 1975-76. *1685*
Anti-Inflation Board. Collective bargaining. Labor Unions and Organizations. Wages. 1975. *1630*
Anti-inflation program. Public relations. Trudeau, Pierre Elliott. 1976. *1656*
Antilabor sentiments. Elections, local. Immigration policy. Ku Klux Klan. 1921-30's. *2925*
—. Holmes Foundry. Immigrants. Ontario. Strikes. 1935-40. *1210*
Anti-Semitism *See also* Jews.
—. 1942-72. *2912*
—. Anti-Communist movements. Freedom of speech. Immigration. National self-image. Ontario (Toronto). 1928-29. *2791*
—. Anti-discrimination legislation. Nazism. 1930's. *1196*
—. French Language Charter. Nationalism. Quebec. 1977. *2421*
Antislavery Sentiments *See also* Abolition Movement.
—. Negroes. Newspapers. Ontario. *Provincial Freeman* (newspaper). Shadd, Mary Ann. 1852-93. *1046*
Antitrust. Corporations. Public Policy. 1889-1910. *1081*
Apple industry. Calkin(s) family. Halliburton, Robert Grant. Inglis, Charles. Nova Scotia. Starr family. 19c. *2279*
—. Crops. Genealogy. Nova Scotia. Prescott, Charles Ramage. 1772-1970's. *2280*
Apportionment. British Columbia. Partisanship. Provincial Legislatures. 1952-78. *3199*
—. British North America Act (1867). Nova Scotia. 1971-72. *2336*
—. Constitutional amendment. 1971. *2108*
—. King, William Lyon Mackenzie. Parliaments. Saskatchewan (Prince Albert). 1925-35. *3038*
Arab States. Economic Aid. International Trade. Oil Industry and Trade. 1960's-70's. *1770*
Arbitration, compulsory. British Columbia. Teachers. 1937-73. *3257*
Arbitration, Industrial *See also* Collective Bargaining; Strikes.
—. Armaments Industry. Imperial Munitions Board. Labor Unions and Organizations. 1900-20. *1080*
—. Canadian Industrial Disputes Investigation Act (1907). Industrial Relations. USA. 1907. *1101*
—. Civil Service. Legislation. 1967. *1497*
Archaeological research. British Columbia (Alberni Valley). Ethnography. Indians. Prehistory. 1973. *301*
Archaeology *See also* Anthropology; Artifacts; Excavations; Indians; Museums; Pottery.
—. Boulder configurations. Indians. Saskatchewan. Solstices. Sun Dance structures. Prehistory. 1975. *406*
—. British Columbia. Duff, Wilson. Indians. 1950-76. *292*
—. British Columbia (Prince Rupert area). Tsimshian Indians. ca 3,000 BC. *297*
Archaeology (amateur). *Chicora* (vessel). Great Lakes. Ontario (Sault Ste. Marie, St. Joseph's Island). Scuba diving. 1961-62. *585*
Archaeology, industrial. Education. Great Britain. History, study of. USA. 1955-70. *1302*
Archambeault, Louis. Politics. 1815-90. *898*
Architects. Ontario (Toronto). 1834-90's. *2740*
Architectural drawings. Fortification. Historical Sites and Parks. Louisbourg, Fortress of. Nova Scotia (Cape Breton Island). 1707-58. *603*
Architectural surveys. Ontario (Rideau Corridor). -1880. 1969-74. *2793*
Architecture *See also* Buildings; Construction.
—. Alberta. Assimilation. Ukrainians. 1891-1970's. *3127*
—. British Columbia Mills, Timber, and Trading Company. Canadian Bank of Commerce. Prairie Provinces. 1904-22. *2926*
—. Canadian National Railroad System. Railroads. Saskatchewan. 1890-1970's. *3030*

—. Canadian Pacific Railway. Railroads. Saskatchewan. 20c. *3029*
—. Capitol Theatre. Entertainment. Movie palaces. Ontario (Ottawa). Vaudeville. 1920-70. *1138*
—. Catholic Church. New France. 1600-1760. *553*
—. City planning. Mutual Advisory Committee. Ontario (London). Politics. Preservation. 1970-77. *2727*
—. Europe. North America. Subways. 1940's-70's. *1307*
—. France. Guardhouses. Louisbourg, Fortress of. Military Camps and Forts. Nova Scotia. 1713-68. *616*
—. Historical Sites and Parks. Nova Scotia (Halifax). Waterfront. 1815-1973. *2229*
—. Houses. Wood carving. Woodland, George. 1867-1969. *2264*
—. Manitoba (Winnipeg). Post offices. 1855-1974. *2979*
—. Martello towers. Military Camps and Forts. USA. 19c. *188*
—. Nova Scotia (Halifax). 1749-1973. *2239*
—. Ontario. Rideau Canal. 1820's-1971. *2794*
Architecture, Victorian. Industrialization. New Brunswick (Saint John). Urban Renewal. 17c-1966. *2399*
Archival Catalogs and Inventories. Aeronautics (history). Hitchins, Fred H. Western Ontario, University of, D. B. Weldon Library (Hitchins Collection). 20c. *94*
Archives *See also* names of individual archives, e.g. Georgetown University Archives; Documents; Public Archives of Canada; Public Records.
—. Academia. Journalism. Oral history. 1960-75. *1311*
—. Alberta (Calgary). Glenbow-Alberta Institute. 1955-76. *3115*
—. Anthropology. Indians. Subarctic. 1975. *347*
—. Basques. Labrador (Red Bay). *San Juan* (vessel). Shipwrecks. Spain. 1565. 1978. *558*
—. Bibliographies. Canadian Institute of Montreal. Quebec. 1844-1900. *120*
—. Bishops. Catholic Church. Church History. Kingston, Archdiocese of. Ontario. 1800-1966. *2847*
—. City Government. Ontario (Ottawa). 19c-1976. *2886*
—. Culture. Education. France. 1977. *215*
—. Ethnic Groups. 1970's. *160*
—. Immigrants. Ontario (Toronto). Photographs. 1900-30. 1974. *2877*
—. Mennonite history resources. 19c-1975. *39*
—. Methodist Church. Presbyterian Church. United Church of Canada. 18c 1973. *233*
—. Newfoundland. Provincial government. 1825-1973. *2185*
—. Oral history. Public Archives of Canada. 1976. *1265*
—. Quebec (Montreal). Radio. Radio Canada Archives. Television. 1959-75. *1351*
—. USA. 1977. *229*
Archives, city. Alberta (Edmonton). 1938-74. *3126*
—. British Columbia (Vancouver). 19c-20c. *3227*
—. British Columbia (Vancouver). 1970-74. *3236*
—. Ontario (Toronto). 1959-73. *2797*
—. Quebec (Montreal). 1913-74. *2434*
—. Quebec (Quebec). 1924-70's. *2430*
Arctic *See also* Polar Exploration.
—. Alaska. Mining. Scandinavia. USSR. 1917-78. *3288*
—. Anderson, James. Expedition, search. Franklin, John. Iroquois Indians. Woodsmanship. 1855. *3305*
—. Bellot, Joseph René. Franklin, John. Kennedy, William. *Prince Albert* (vessel). Voyages. 1851. *3307*
—. Berthe, Jean. Eskimos. Fur trade. Quebec. Stevenson, A. (account). 1930's. *2663*
—. Churches. Fur Trade. Missions and Missionaries. 20c. *3281*
—. Colonization. Eskimos. Social Change. 1930-60. *317*
—. Daily life. Hare Indians. Indians. Northwest Territories. Oil exploration. 1859-1974. *358*
—. Decisionmaking. Oil development. Technology. 1970's. *3284*
—. Discovery and Exploration. Finnie, Richard Sterling (account). North America. Office of the Coordinator of Information. Stefansson, Vilhjalmur. 1931-62. *3302*
—. Discovery and Exploration. Fort Hope. Hudson's Bay Company. Northwest Territories. Rae, John. 1840's. *3298*

—. Discovery and Exploration. Franklin, John. Great Britain. Northwest Territories (Beechey Island). 1845-48. *3312*
—. Discovery and Exploration. Franklin, John. Hood, Robert (journal). Northwest Territories. 1819-21. *3309*
—. Discovery and Exploration. Hantzsch, Bernard. Northwest Territories (Baffin Island). Trichinosis. 1911. *3316*
—. Eskimos. Federal government. Mass Media. Satellite service. 1972. *329*
—. Eskimos. Inkshuks (monuments). Prehistory-1978. *319*
—. Eskimos, Inuit. Living conditions. 1950-75. *325*
—. Explorers. Frobisher, Martin. Gold. Great Britain (London). Northwest Territories (Frobisher Bay). 1570's. *3310*
—. Explorers. Physicians. Rae, John. 1835-93. *3315*
—. Explorers. Stefansson, Vilhjalmur. 1915-24. *3319*
—. Federal Government. *Neptune* (vessel). Sovereignty. 1903-04. *3294*
—. Hunting. Ringed seals. Seals. Wildlife Conservation. 1966-73. *335*
—. Kruzenshtern, Ivan Fedorovich. Romanov, Vladmir Pavlovich. Russia. Scientific Expeditions. USA. 1819-25. *3299*
—. Military strategy. 1945-77. *3286*
—. Natural gas. Northwest Territories (Melville, King Christian Islands). Polar Gas Project. USA. 1972-75. *3355*
—. Northwest Territories. Royal Canadian Mounted Police. 1890-1929. *3360*
—. Northwest Territories (Frobisher Bay). Waste disposal. Water supply. 1973. *3354*
—. Stevenson, A. (account). 1973. *3361*
—. *Thetis* (vessel). Voyages. Whaling vessels (converted). 1881-1950. *3290*
—. Whales, bowhead. Whaling Industry and Trade. Wildlife Conservation. Prehistory-1976. *3293*
Arctic islands. Discovery and Exploration. Hudson Strait (navigability). Wakeham, William. 1897. *3304*
Arctic, northern. Greist, Mollie Ward. Pioneers. Women. ca 1850-1970's. *3344*
Arctic Ocean. Eskimos. Mackenzie Bay (Herschel Island). Polar exploration. Whaling Industry and Trade. 1826-1972. *339*
—. Great Britain. Navies. Weavers. Whalers. 1818-25. *3300*
Arctic (vessel). Bernier, Joseph E. Byrd, Richard E. Discovery and Exploration. 1924-25. *3301*
Arès, Richard. French tradition. Minville, Esdras. Quebec. Tremblay Commission. 1953-56. *2676*
Aristocracy *See also* Nobility; Upper Classes.
—. Estate ownership. France. Meyer, Rudolf. Roffignac, Yves de. Saskatchewan (Eastern Assiniboia; Whitewood). 1885-1900. *982*
—. France. Meyer, Rudolf. Saskatchewan (Pipestone Creek, Whitewood). Settlement. 1880's. *985*
Armaments *See also* Aeronautics, Military.
—. Cannons. Fur trade. 1600's-1800's. *141*
Armaments Industry. Arbitration, Industrial. Imperial Munitions Board. Labor Unions and Organizations. 1900-20. *1080*
Armed Forces. *See* Military.
Armenians. Immigration. Quebec (Montreal). 1900-66. *28*
Armies *See also* Confederate Army; Volunteer Armies.
—. American Revolution. Carleton, Guy. Great Britain. Logistics. Quebec. 1776. *714*
—. Defense. International relations. Self-determination. 1970's. *1778*
—. Desertion. France. New France. 1700-63. *530*
—. Fort Niagara (battle). French and Indian War. Great Britain. 1759. *600*
—. Great Britain. Kent, Duke of (Edward). Lyons, Charles (family). Nova Scotia (Halifax). 1812-63. *2273*
—. Indians. Royal Canadian Mounted Police. Settlement. USA. 1870-1900. *1008*
—. Larsen, Lawrence W. (paper). Military Strategy. North Dakota. 1919. 1975. *1157*
Armour, John. Letters. Ontario (Dunnville). 1829-81. *768*
Arms. *See* Weapons.
Armstrong, E. H. Nova Scotia. Politics. 1923-24. *2367*
Armstrong, Frederick H. Mackenzie, William Lyon. Mayors. Ontario (Toronto). 1835-37. 1967. *2854*

Army Air Corps. Air Warfare. Beeson, Duane. Idaho (Boise). World War II. 1941-45. *1222*
Army Corps of Engineers. Boundary protection. North Dakota. Sherrill, Clarence O. 1919. *1158*
Arnold, Benedict. American Revolution. Carleton, Guy. Fort Ticonderoga. Lake Champlain. 1776. *722*
—. Arnold, Peggy. Great Britain. New Brunswick. West Indies. 1781-1801. *2374*
Arnold, Peggy. Arnold, Benedict. Great Britain. New Brunswick. West Indies. 1781-1801. *2374*
Aroostook War (1839). Anglophobia. Boundary dispute. Great Britain. USA. 1837-39. *654*
Art *See also* Architecture; Artists; Folk Art; Landscape Painting; Painting; Sculpture.
—. Anthropology. British Columbia. Duff, Wilson. Pacific Northwest. 1950-76. *280*
—. Artifacts. Canadian Conservation Institute. Ontario (Ottawa). Preservation. 1978. *31*
—. Atlantic Provinces. Micmac Indians. 17c-1974. *420*
—. British Columbia. Collins, Charles John. 1900-30. *3259*
—. British Columbia (Hazelton). Gitksan Indians. 'Ksan Historic Indian Village. 1973. *434*
—. British Empire Exhibition (1923). National Gallery of Canada. Royal Canadian Academy. Wembley controversy. 1877-1933. *1170*
—. Bucke, Richard M. (*Cosmic Consciousness*). Harris, Lawren. Theosophy. 1920's. *1181*
—. Buffalo. Central America. North America. Prehistory-20c. *265*
—. Canadian studies. Symons, T. H. B. (report). 1960's-77. *1495*
—. Chabert, Joseph. Education. National Institute for Arts and Crafts. Quebec (Montreal). Teachers. Working Class. 1861-94. *1053*
—. Chippewa Indians. Cree Indians. Métis. Prairie Provinces. 1750's-1850's. *357*
—. Cultural relations. Mass Media. Poland. USA. 1940-74. *1953*
—. Eskimos. Northwest Territories (Frobisher Bay). 1969. *316*
—. Fraktur. German Canadians. Ontario. 1976. *2741*
—. History. Illustrators. Jeffreys, Charles William. Textbooks. 1920's-50. *1119*
—. Language. Politics. Regionalism. 1978. *2123*
—. Proch, Don. Ukrainian Canadians. 1970's. *1403*
Art Galleries and Museums *See also* names of particular galleries and museums, e.g. Boston Museum of Fine Arts, etc.
—. Légaré, Joseph. Painting. Quebec. 1824-1933. *2544*
Art history. Bourassa, Napoléon. Oral History. 1800-1930. *241*
—. British Columbia. 1780-1974. *3258*
—. Hill, Charles C. (account). Oral history. 1975. *1400*
Art History (review article). British Columbia. Murray, Joan. Paintings. Reid, Dennis. 1778-1935. *3189*
Art (romantic; review article). Bartlett, William Henry. Indians. Miller, Alfred J. ca 1840-70. *659*
Artifacts *See also* Excavations.
—. Alaska. Emmons, George Thornton. Ethnology. Tlingit Indians. 1852-1945. *417*
—. Alberta (Calgary, Mona Lisa Site). Bison kill. Stratigraphy. ca 8080 BP. 1968-74. *310*
—. British Columbia, University of. Museum of Anthropology. 1947-70's. *3205*
—. Art. Canadian Conservation Institute. Ontario (Ottawa). Preservation. 1978. *31*
—. Eskimos. Europeans. Labrador. Quebec. Ungava Peninsula. ca 400-18c. *300*
Artillery. British Columbia. Coast defenses. World War II. 1862-1941. *1232*
—. Martello towers. Military Capability. 1796-1871. *198*
Artisans. Construction. Labor Unions and Organizations. Ontario (Toronto). Politics. 1896-1914. *1103*
—. French Canadians. Organizations. Quebec. 17c-18c. *533*
Artists. Chippewa Indians. Cree Indians. Indians. Legend painting. Manitoba. Ontario. 1960's-70's. *470*
—. Cleveland, Xenophon. Massachusetts. New Brunswick. Stencils. 1839-99. *2379*
—. Clymer, John. North America. West. 1960's-70's. *1460*
—. Cultural trends. USA. 1970's. *1390*

—. Dakota Territory. Frontier and Pioneer Life. *Harper's Weekly* (periodical). Rogers, William A. 1878. *2976*
—. Great Lakes. Nickerson, Vincent D. Norton, Charles W. Ships. Sprague, Howard F. Whipple, Seth A. 1844-1901. *2861*
—. Painting. Rand, Paul. 1930's-50's. *1118*
Arts programs. Ontario (Toronto). 1978. *2764*
Asia. Colleges and Universities. Protestant Churches. USA. 1850-1971. *5*
—. Foreign Policy. Trudeau, Pierre Elliott. 1968-78. *1907*
Asian Canadians. British Columbia. Immigration. Politics. Racism. 1850-1914. *900*
—. Ontario (Toronto). Political Protest. 1970's. *2795*
Asians *See also* East Indians.
—. Africans. Indians. North America. Racism. Whites. 1600-1900. *10*
Asiatic Exclusion League. Anglo-Japanese Treaty of Alliance (1902). British Columbia (Vancouver). Japan. USA. 1907-22. *1108*
Assimilation *See also* Acculturation.
—. Acadians. Emigration. Minorities in Politics. New Brunswick (Moncton). 1871-1971. *2385*
—. Acadians. Massachusetts (Gloucester). Nova Scotia (Arichat region). 1850's-1900. *2364*
—. Alberta. Architecture. Ukrainians. 1891-1970's. *3127*
—. British Colonial Office. Indians. 1760-1830. *469*
—. British Columbia (Saltspring Island). Immigration. Negroes. 1850-1900. *3211*
—. Catholic Church. French Americans. Vermont (Winooski). 1867-1900. *2469*
—. Choquette, Robert. French Canadians (review article). Joy, Richard. Maxwell, Thomas R. 18c-20c. 1970's. *218*
—. Cultural autonomy. Italians. Mass media. Ontario (Toronto). 1970's. *2735*
—. Employment. Immigrants. Language training. Ontario (Toronto). 1968-70. *1625*
—. Ethnic groups. Europe. Race Relations. USA. 20c. *15*
—. Ethnicity. Technology. USA. 20c. *1408*
—. Fitzpatrick, Alfred. Frontier College. Immigration. Labor. 1899-1922. *1086*
—. French Canadians. Language. 1961-71. *1364*
—. French Canadians. Prairie Provinces. 1871-1975. *2897*
—. Immigrants. Macedonians. Ontario (Toronto). 1900-20. *2840*
—. Immigrants. Multiculturalism. Psychology. 1970's. *1424*
—. Immigration. Mining. Quebec. 1941-71. *2639*
—. Jews. Ontario (Toronto). Presbyterian Church. 1912-18. *2776*
Assiniboin Indians. Cree Indians. Montana. Prairie Provinces. Social organization. ca 1640-1913. *446*
—. Cypress Hills Massacre. Historiography. Saskatchewan, southwestern. 1873. *978*
Assiniboine and Saskatchewan Exploring Expedition. Discovery and Exploration. Hime, Humphrey Lloyd. Photography. Prairie Provinces. 1858. *863*
Association of Commercial and Technical Employees. Canadian Labour Congress. Labor Reform. Ontario (Toronto). White-collar employees. 1972. *2724*
Association of Southeast Asian Nations. Foreign Relations. 1967-77. *1912*
Astrolabe, Cobden. Champlain, Samuel de. Discovery and Exploration. 1613. *506*
Astronomy. British Columbia. Calendars. Indians. Northwest Coast Indians. Prehistory. 1975. *303*
Asylum, right of. Latin America. 1973. *1735*
Asylums. Mental Illness. New Brunswick. Nova Scotia. 1749-1900. *2159*
Athabasca Pass. Alberta. British Columbia. Ritual toasts. 1811-1974. *694*
Athapascan Indians. Ethnographers. Subarctic. 1900-65. *449*
Athens (battle). Civil War. Missouri. 1861. *834*
Athletes. Hanlan, Edward "Ned". Professionalism. Sports. 1870's-80's. *1042*
Athletics. *See* Physical Education and Training; Sports.
Atlantic Coast. Blockade-running. Civil War. Letters. Nova Scotia. Wade, Norman. 1859-62. *841*
—. Discovery and Exploration. Historical Sites and Parks. North America. Vikings. 10c-14c. 20c. *483*

Atlantic Provinces *See also* Acadia; Labrador; Maritime Provinces; New Brunswick; Newfoundland; Nova Scotia; Prince Edward Island.
—. Antigonish Movement. Cooperatives. 1900-45. *2165*
—. Art. Micmac Indians. 17c-1974. *420*
—. Bargaining rights. Fisheries. Legislation. Nova Scotia. 1975. *2351*
—. Bibliographies. Economic development. Politics. Social classes. 1920's-70's. *2161*
—. Boardinghouses. Government. Labor. Merchant Marine. Social reform. ca 1850's-90's. *916*
—. Capital. Social classes. Unemployment. 1972-77. *2172*
—. Catholic Church. Diaries. Plessis, Joseph-Octave. Quebec Archdiocese. 1812-15. *2155*
—. Dun and Bradstreet (records). 1842-1968. *2166*
—. Economic conditions. Immigration. Kennedy, Albert J. Massachusetts (Boston). 1910's. *2162*
—. Economic interests. International Trade. Provincial government. USA. 1960's-70's. *2013*
—. Historiography. Nationalism. Regionalism. 19c-20c. *2160*
—. Maritime Rights Movement. Reform. Regionalism. 1900-25. *2158*
—. Mennonites. Settlement. 1950-70. *2168*
Atlantic Provinces (review article). France. Historiography. Missions and Missionaries. New France. Politics. 1000-1770. 19c. *67*
Atlantic region. Buchan, Alastair. Foreign Relations. Institute of Strategic Studies. Military Strategy. 1958-75. *1913*
Atlantic (vessel). Ancient, William J. Heroes. Nova Scotia (Terence Bay). Shipwrecks. 1873. *2225*
Atomic Energy *See also* Nuclear Arms; Nuclear Science and Technology.
—. Nuclear proliferation. 1945-75. *1328*
Atomic Warfare *See also* Air Warfare; Nuclear Arms.
—. Diaries. King, William Lyon MacKenzie. Racism. 1921-48. *1139*
Atsina Indians. "Fall" Indians. Indians. "Rapid" Indians. Saskatchewan, southcentral. 18c. *405*
Attitudes *See also* Political Attitudes; Public Opinion; Values.
—. American Revolution. Carleton, Guy. Military Occupation. Peasants. Quebec. 1775-76. *717*
—. Anti-Americanism. National Characteristics. USA. 1972. *1969*
—. Behavior. Labor. 20c. *1599*
—. Body painting. Europeans. Indians. 1497-1684. *388*
—. British officials. Negroes. 1830-65. *668*
—. Business community. Canadian Labour Congress. Federal government. Tripartism. 1977. *1295*
—. Cather, Willa (*Shadows on the Rock*). Idealism. 1920's-31. *1177*
—. Citizenship. Japanese. USA. World War II. 1941-58. *1261*
—. Conservatism. USA. 1966-77. *1721*
—. Economic nationalism. Elites. Foreign investments. Legislatures. 1973-74. *2147*
—. English Canadians. Race. Sex. Woman Suffrage. ca 1877-1918. *902*
—. Ethnic Groups. Social Status. 1968. *1374*
—. Foreign Relations. USA. ca 1776-1976. *93*
—. French Canadians. Slander. 1712-48. *531*
—. Geographic Space. Language. National Development. 1776-1976. *56*
—. Immigration. Ireland. Ontario (Canada West). Potato famine. 1845-50. *797*
—. Industrial relations. Management. 1970's. *1614*
—. Industrialization. Labor Unions and Organizations. Radicals and Radicalism. Working class. 1897-1919. *2899*
—. Industrialization. Work ethic. Youth. 1950's-73. *1455*
—. Intellectual traditions. National self-image. Science. Technology. 1970's. *1327*
—. Legislatures. Models. Ontario. Political Parties. 1957-74. *2890*
—. Migration, Internal. Rural-Urban Studies. Urbanization. 1955-75. *1366*
—. Military planning. USA. 1776-1976. *178*
—. Political culture. Regionalism. 1965. *2143*
—. Television. USA. 1975-76. *2056*

Attorney General of Canada v. *Lavell* (Canada, 1973). Indians. Lavell, Jeannette (Wikwemikong Indian). Sex Discrimination. Supreme Court. Women. 1973-74. *473*
Aubert de la Chesnaye, Charles. Fur trade. Netherlands. 1695-98. *568*
Auditors General. Provincial government. Public Accounts committees. Public spending. 1970-75. *1694*
Australia. Aborigines Protection Society. Great Britain. Indians. ca 1830-50. *464*
—. Antarctic. Explorers. Great Britain. Priestley, Raymond. 1912-74. *3321*
—. Business. English-language culture. Foreign Relations. 1975. *1949*
—. Cabinet. Great Britain. Netherlands. Political recruitment. USA. 1940's-60's. *1666*
—. Constitutional conferences. Federalism. 1965-74. *2092*
—. Federal grants. USA. 1787-1974. *1693*
—. Federal Policy. Immigration. Population. 1967-75. *1466*
—. Federalism. Suffrage. USA. 19c-20c. *179*
—. Germany. Middle powers. Political integration. South Africa. 1850-1900. *903*
—. Government policy. New Zealand. Nonwhites. Race politics. South Africa. 1900-73. *1926*
Australia (Victoria). California, northern. Frontier thesis. Turner, Frederick Jackson. 1850-1900. *247*
Austria-Hungary. *See* Habsburg Empire.
Austrians. Aliens. Internment camps. World War I. 1914-19. *1150*
Auteuil, Denis-Joseph Ruette d' (estate). Inventories. Property. Quebec. 1661-80. *528*
Authority. Anthropology. Ecology. Eskimos, Central. Social organization. 1970's. *322*
—. Government. Trudeau, Pierre Elliott. 1950's-70's. *2111*
Authors *See also* names of individual authors; Poets.
—. Educators. Mount Allison University. New Brunswick (Sackville). Webster, John Clarence. 1882-1950. *2404*
—. Pastoral vision. 18c-19c. *259*
Autobiography and Memoirs *See also* names of individuals with the subdivision reminiscences, e.g. Franklin, Benjamin (reminiscences); Biography; Diaries.
—. Baptist Church. Crandall, Joseph. New Brunswick. 1795-1810. *2378*
—. Biography. Political Leadership (review article). 19c-20c. *242*
Autobiography and Memoirs (review article). Behavior. Political leadership. 1914-70. *1661*
Autocovariance procedures. Metropolitan Areas. Ontario, southern. Population. 1871-1975. *2732*
Automation. Alienation. Working Conditions. 1973. *1557*
—. Employment. International Longshoremen's and Warehousemen's Union. Labor Disputes. 1973. *1600*
Automobiles. Alberta (Calgary). Bicycles. Daily Life. 1880-1914. *3120*
—. Conestoga wagons. Driving. Social Customs. USA. 1755-20c. *174*
—. Legislation. Nova Scotia. 1899-1913. *2300*
—. Mass transit. Motoring, urban. North America. Travel. 1960-75. *2758*
Automobile Industry and Trade. International Trade. USA. 1960's-70's. *2057*
—. Market structure. USA. -1973. *2027*
Autopsies. Medical Research. Osler, William. ca 1876-1900. *2552*
Aviation. *See* Aeronautics.

B

Babcock, Robert H. (review article). American Federation of Labor. Gompers, Samuel. USA. 1897-1914. *1078*
Bachelors. Alberta. Calgary *Herald*, newspaper. Frontier. Marriage. 1895. *956*
Bachman, John Baptist (and descendants). Nova Scotia (Lunenburg Township). 1752-1952. *2218*
Baerg, Anna (diary). Immigration. Mennonites. Russian Revolution. 1917-23. *1171*
Baggataway (Indian game). Lacrosse. 1840-1931. *240*
Bahr, Andrew. Alaska, western. Northwest Territories (Mackenzie River Delta). Reindeer. 1928-34. *3295*
Bailey, Jacob. American Revolution. Church of England. Letters. Nova Scotia. 1784. *726*

Baker, Edgar Crow. British Columbia (Victoria). Entrepreneurs. 1872-98. *3179*

Baker, W. M. Anglin, Timothy Warren. Fenians. Irish Canadians (review article). Neidhardt, W. S. 19c. 1970's. *1073*

Bakewell, Robert. Coal Mines and Mining. Howe, Joseph. Nova Scotia (Pictou County; Stellarton). 1798-1881. *2227*

Balance of power. Defense Policy. North America. Quebec. Separatist Movements. 1970's. *1921*

Baldwin, William Warren. Duels. McDonnell, John. Ontario (Upper Canada). 1812. *2842*

Ball, George P. M. Business records. Depressions. Economic change. Ontario (Upper Canada). Rural Settlements. 1825-60. *672*

Ballads. French and Indian War. New England. Quebec. Rogers' Rangers (retreat). 1759. *591*

—. Prairie provinces. Ukranian Canadians. 1900-74. *2934*

Balloons (hot air). Haddock, John A. LaMountain, John. Quebec. USA. 1859. *845*

Baltic Area *See also* USSR.

—. Immigrants. Lutheran Church. 1947-55. *1492*

Baltimore (vessel). Buckler, Susannah. Nova Scotia (Chebogue). 1735. *2314*

Banff National Park. Alberta. Explorers. Peyto, Bill. Scientific expeditions. 1887-1933. *3092*

Banking *See also* Investments.

—. Agricultural commodities. Foreign Investments. Public services. Puerto Rico. 1800-1977. *180*

—. Business. Industry. Naylor, R. T. (review article). 1867-1914. *928*

—. Finance. Government regulation. 1963-73. *1697*

—. Illinois (Chicago). Immigration. Swedish Americans. 1892-1974. *1093*

—. International Power and Paper Company. Newsprint industry. USA. 1914-33. *1186*

—. Nova Scotia (Pictou). 1872-85. *2232*

Banking (central). Bureaucracies. 1960's-70's. *1522*

Banking (international). France (Paris). Great Britain (London). Morton, Levi Parsons. USA. 1860's. *853*

Banking (locations). Quebec (Montreal). Urbanization. 1966-71. *2654*

Banks, Joshua. Banks, Moses. Genealogy. Nova Scotia (Granville). 1739-1843. *2308*

Banks, Moses. Banks, Joshua. Genealogy. Nova Scotia (Granville). 1739-1843. *2308*

Baptista de Lima, Manuel C. (research). Discovery and Exploration. Pinheiro, Diogo (voyages). Pinheiro, Manoel (voyages). Portugal (Barcelos). 1521-98. *508*

Baptists. Christian Biography. McMaster, Susan Moulton Fraser. Ontario (Toronto). 1819-1916. *2750*

—. Crandall, Joseph. Memoirs. New Brunswick. 1795-1810. *2378*

—. Fundamentalist-Modernist controversy. Jarvis Street Church. Ontario (Toronto). Religious factionalism. Social Classes. 1895-1934. *2762*

—. Language. Micmac Indians. Missions and Missionaries. Nova Scotia. Rand, Silas Tertius. 1830-89. *422*

Barbeau, Marius. Harris, Kenneth B. Indians (review article). 1928. 1974. *421*

Barbeau, Raymond. Alliance Laurentienne. Guillemette, Pierre. Independence Movements. Quebec. 1960's-75. *2674*

Barbel, Marie-Anne. Business. New France. Women. 18c. *575*

Barber, James David. King, William Lyon Mackenzie. Political leadership. Prime ministers. 1920's-40's. 1972-76. *1147*

Barns. Bibliographies. USA. 1864-1977. *25*

Barracks. Historical Sites and Parks. Louisbourg, Fortress of. Nova Scotia. 1716-39. 1969. *590*

Barret, David. British Columbia. Federal Government. New Democratic Party. 1959-75. *3195*

Barrington and Cape Island Steam Ferry Company. Ferries. Nova Scotia (Cape Sable Island). 1847-1949. *2216*

Bartlett, William Henry. Art (romantic, review article). Indians. Miller, Alfred J. ca 1840-70. *659*

Baskets. Indians. Pacific Northwest. Photographs. 1880's-1900's. 1978. *415*

Basque language. Documents. Labrador. 1572-77. *559*

Basques. Archives. Labrador (Red Bay). *San Juan* (vessel). Shipwrecks. Spain. 1565. 1978. *558*

—. Labrador. Whaling Industry and Trade. 16c. *557*

Bauxite industry. Alcan Aluminium, Ltd. Guyana. Multinational corporations. Nationalization. 1960-75. *1852*

Bear River. Bridges. Nova Scotia (Annapolis, Digby counties). 1853-66. *2323*

Beardy, Q. P. Jackson. Indian-White Relations. Ojibwa Indians. Painting. 1944-75. *401*

Beaudry Report. Ham Report. Industry. Ontario. Quebec. Working Conditions. 1972-74. *1536*

Beauty shops. Hair care. Harper, Martha Matilda. Ontario (Oakville). 1857-93. *2874*

Beaver Indians. Alberta (Lac la Biche). Hudson's Bay Company. North West Rebellion. Pruden, Patrick. Trading posts. 1885. *1026*

Beaverbrook, 1st Baron. British Empire. Free trade movement. Great Britain. Publishers and Publishing. 1900-31. *24*

Bédard, Pierre (discourse). Dionne, Narcisse-Eutrope. Language, official. Quebec (Lower Canada). 1792-1809. 1909. *699*

Bee, William. Agricultural colony. Methodists, Primitive. Saskatchewan (Grenfell). 1882. *949*

Beeson, Duane. Air Warfare. Army Air Corps. Idaho (Boise). World War II. 1941-45. *1222*

Behavior. Alcoholism. Social customs. Quebec (Montreal). 1973. *1443*

—. Attitudes. Labor. 20c. *1599*

—. Autobiography and Memoirs (review article). Political leadership. 1914-70. *1661*

—. Hockey. Ontario (Toronto). Sports. Violence. 1972. *2862*

Behaviorism. Political geography. Quebec (Saguenay County). Spatial perception. Territorialism. 1969-74. *2448*

Behuncik, Edward J. (speech). Canadian Slovak League. Slovak World Congress. 1970-72. *1740*

Belaney, Archibald S. (Grey Owl). Conservation movements. Great Britain. 1906-38. *1140*

Bélanger Report. Quebec. Taxation. 1966-76. *2419*

Belcher, Jonathan. Grand jury. Law. Nova Scotia. 1754. *2362*

Belgian families. Immigration. Manitoba (Winnipeg, East St. Boniface). Nuytten, Edmund. Nuytten, Octavia. 1880-1914. *2991*

Belgium. Adoption. France. Law. 1974. *1393*

—. Africa, French-speaking. Foreign Relations. France. French-speaking institutions. 1960-74. *1769*

—. Africa, French-speaking. France. International cooperation. Quebec. 1964-74. *2718*

—. Ethnicity. Nationalism. Quebec. Social Classes. 1970's. *2702*

Bell, Alexander Graham. Communications. Field, Cyrus Fleming, Sandford. Gisborne, F. N. Nova Scotia. 1749-1964. *2260*

—. Deaf. Library of Congress, Gilbert J. Grosvenor Collection. Photographs. 1870-1922. *2228*

Bellot, Joseph René. Arctic. Franklin, John. Kennedy, William. *Prince Albert* (vessel). Voyages. 1851. *3307*

Bengough, John Wilson. City government. *Grip* (periodical). Ontario (Toronto). Political Reform. Protestantism. 1873-1910. *2807*

Bennett, Richard Bedford. Communist Party. Conservative Party. 1930-35. *1207*

—. Foreign Relations. Hoover, Herbert C. USA. 1930-31. *1205*

Bennington (battle). American Revolution. Burgoyne, John. Stark, John. Vermont. 1777. *730*

Beothuk Indians. Indian-White Relations. Newfoundland. 1500-1848. *466*

Beothuk Indians (review article). Howley, J. P. Indian-White Relations. Newfoundland. Rowe, F. W. Prehistory-1830. 1977. *290*

Berger, Carl (review article). English Canadians. Historiography. Nationalism. 1900-76. *232*

Bergeron, Léandre (review article). Historiography. Marxism. Quebec. 1970-75. *2618*

Bergson, Henri. Creativity. Federal government. Intergovernmental Relations. Quebec. 1970's. *2109*

Bermuda. Education. Political Factions. Religion. 1800-1977. *136*

Bernard, Joseph Francis. Alaskan Coast. Eskimos. Siberian Coast. Traders. 1903-29. *314*

Bernard, Joseph-Fidèle (diary). Chukchi natives. Firearms. Trade. USSR. 1921-22. *1166*

Bernier, Joseph E. *Arctic* (vessel). Byrd, Richard E. Discovery and Exploration. 1924-25. *3301*

Bernou, Claude. France. LeClercq, Crestien. *Premier Établissement de la Foy dans la Nouvelle France* (book). Renaudot, Eusèbe. 1691. *548*

Berthe, Jean. Arctic. Eskimos. Fur trade. Quebec. Stevenson, A. (account). 1930's. *2663*

Beruson, David J. (review article). General Strike. Industrial relations. Manitoba (Winnipeg). Social organization. 1919. 1975. *1165*

Bethune, Angus. China (Canton). International Trade. North America. North West Company. 1812-17. *802*

Bethune, Donald. Finance. Ontario (Upper Canada). Steamboat business. 19c. *837*

Beverly, James. Alberta (Medicine Hat). Weather. 1899. *3103*

Bibb, Henry. Emigration. Negroes. Separatism. USA. 1830-60. *858*

Bible. Catholic Church. Politics. Prince Edward Island. Protestants. Public Schools. 1856-60. *2207*

—. Indians. Missions and Missionaries. Myths and Symbols. Pacific Northwest. 1830-50. *438*

Bibliographies. 16c-1975. *12*

—. Acculturation. French Americans. French Canadians. New England. 1755-1973. *2566*

—. Archives. Canadian Institute of Montreal. Quebec. 1844-1900. *120*

—. Atlantic Provinces. Economic development. Politics. Social classes. 1920's-70's. *2161*

—. Barns. USA. 1864-1977. *25*

—. Biculturalism. Bilingualism. Research. 1964-67. *1340*

—. British Columbia. 1968-76. *3264*

—. British Columbia. 18c-20c. 1970's. *3265*

—. British Columbia. Essays. Theses. 1976. *3269*

—. British Columbia. Lumber and Lumbering. Pacific Northwest. 1890's-1960's. *3221*

—. British Columbia. Maps. 1976-77. *3263*

—. British Columbia. Theses. 12c-20c. 1974. *3267*

—. British Columbia. Theses. 1975. *3268*

—. Brouillette, Benoit. Geography. Quebec (Montreal). 1903-73. *2496*

—. Catholic Church. Church history. 17c-1973. *80*

—. Catholic Church. Church history. ca 1800-1976. *91*

—. Church history. 17c-20c. *92*

—. City planning. Research. 1890-1939. *237*

—. *Dissertation Abstracts*. Western States. 1973. *2903*

—. Dissertations. Western States. 1974-75. *2955*

—. East Indians. Immigration. 1900-77. *1358*

—. Economic Theory. Minville, Esdras. Quebec. 20c. *2467*

—. Editorials. French Canadians. Latin America. Newspapers. Quebec. 1959-73. *2433*

—. Education. 17c-20c. 1973-74. *64*

—. Eskimos. Explorers. Greenland. 16c-19c. *331*

—. Eskimos. Indians. Métis. 1975. *283*

—. Ethnic Groups. Multiculturalism. Public Policy. 1967-76. *98*

—. Europe. Folk religion. North America. 1900-74. *256*

—. Europe. Literary associations (French-language). Quebec. USA. Voluntary associations. 1840-1900. *2524*

—. Feminism. Publishers and Publishing. 1968-76. *255*

—. Foreign relations. Interdependence. USA. 1900-74. *2084*

—. French Americans. French Canadians. Vermont Historical Society Library. 1609-1975. *504*

—. French Canadians. Literature. 1606-1977. *2581*

—. Historiography. Protestant churches. 1825-1973. *130*

—. Indians. Music. 20c. *354*

—. Indians. Music. Pacific Northwest. 1888-1976. *353*

—. Indians. Northwest Coast Indians. 1975. *352*

—. Lake Erie. North Central States. Pollution. 1872-1965. *2730*

—. Legislative Library. Nova Scotia. 1976. *2371*

—. Management. Women. 1970-73. *1523*

—. Nationalism. 1949-76. *46*

—. Nova Scotia. 1974. *2370*

—. Onomastics. Toponymy. USA. 1964-75. *203*

—. Scandinavia. USA. 1972. *230*

—. Toponymy. USA. 1971-74. *1263*

—. Urban history. 19c-20c. *221*

Bibliography *See also* Archives; Books; Information Storage and Retrieval Systems; Printing.
—. Algonquin College Resource Centre. Methodology. Ontario (Ottawa). 1974-78. *2142*
—. *Canadiana* (bibliography). National Library of Canada. 1950-77. *249*
Bicentennial Celebrations. *See* Centennial Celebrations.
Biculturalism. Bibliographies. Bilingualism. Research. 1964-67. *1340*
—. Confederation, Fathers of. Diversity, doctrine of. Nationalism. 1860's-1970's. *154*
—. English Canadians. Federalism. French Canadians. Quebec. 20c. *1354*
Bicycle industry. Labor. Mexico. Production. USA. 1972-76. *1906*
Bicycles. Alberta (Calgary). Automobiles. Daily Life. 1880-1914. *3120*
Big Bear. Métis. North West Rebellion. Poundmaker. Trials. 1885. *948*
Biggs, Hugh Beynon. Agriculture. Alberta (Rosebud Creek). Photography. Ranches. 1892-1941. *3169*
Bighorn River. Discovery and Exploration. Indians. Montana. Wyoming. Prehistory-1965. *444*
Bilateral commissions. Judicial organizations, international. Mexico. USA. 19c-1974. *262*
Bilingual districts. Federal Policy. Quebec. 1969-76. *2480*
Bilingual Education. French Canadians. Ontario. Postsecondary schools. 1946-73. *1499*
Bilingualism. Bibliographies. Biculturalism. Research. 1964-67. *1340*
—. Ethnic Groups. French language. 1970-73. *1427*
—. Gendron Report. Quebec. Schools. 1973. *2504*
—. National self-identity. USA. 1760-1974. *1*
—. Occupations. Puerto Rico. 1970. *2587*
Bill C-256. Businessmen. Communications. Federal Regulation. Manitoba (Winnipeg). Public policy. 1971-72. *2971*
Bill C-58. Nationalism. Protectionism. *Reader's Digest* (periodical). Taxation. *Time* (periodical). 1922-76. *2017*
Bill of Incorporation (1873). City Government. Manitoba (Winnipeg). Taxation. 1873. *2984*
Bill of Rights *See also* Civil Rights; Freedom of Speech; Freedom of the Press; Religious Liberty.
—. Civil Rights. Supreme Court. 1960-75. *2089*
Biography *See also* names of persons for biographies of individuals; Autobiography and Memoirs; Christian Biography; Genealogy; Military Biography.
—. Autobiography and Memoirs. Political Leadership (review article). 19c-20c. *242*
—. Crampton, Esmé (account). Dance. Lloyd, Gweneth. Oral History. 1969-75. *1371*
Birch, Arthur N. (letter). British Columbia (New Westminster). Local government. Social Conditions. 1864. *870*
Birchbark. Containers. Indians. Northeastern or North Atlantic States. Prehistory-1978. *471*
Bird, Lilah Smith (recollections). Daily Life. Nova Scotia (Cape Breton; Port Hood Island). ca 1907-70. *2221*
Birds. Discovery and Exploration. Hood, Robert. Painting. Saskatchewan River. 1819-21. *2928*
—. Indians. Mammals. Names. 1973. *399*
Birds, migratory. Federal government. International Migratory Bird Treaty (1916). USA. Wildlife conservation. 1883-1917. *920*
Birney, Earle (reminiscences). Alberta. Surveying. Waterton Lakes National Park. 1921. *3098*
Birth Control *See also* Abortion; Birth Rate.
—. Abortion. 1870-1920. *929*
—. Demography. India. USA. 1970's. *1444*
Birth Rate *See also* Birth Control; Fertility; Population.
—. Demography. 1961-71. *1453*
—. Demography. Ethnic variations. Immigrants. Marriage. 1871. *1072*
—. Demography. Family size. 1961. *1426*
—. French language. 1960-75. *2464*
Bishops. Archives. Catholic Church. Church History. Kingston, Archdiocese of. Ontario. 1800-1966. *2847*
—. Catholic Church. Chicoutimi, Séminaire de. Church History. Quebec (Saguenay). 1873-1973. *2542*
—. Catholic Church. Church of England. Liberal government. Newfoundland. 1860-62. *2187*
—. Christian Biography. Church History. Quebec (Sherbrooke). 1868-72. *2579*

—. Church of England. Fulford, Francis. Quebec (Montreal). 1850-68. *874*
Bison kill. Alberta (Calgary, Mona Lisa Site). Artifacts. Stratigraphy. ca 8080 BP. 1968-74. *310*
Bitumen. Alberta (Athabasca River). Oil and Petroleum Products. Syncrude oil Project. 1974-75. *3150*
Black bear, white. British Columbia. 20c. *3208*
Black Capitalism. British Columbia. Canning industry. Deas, John Sullivan. Salmon. 1862-78. *3239*
Black, Conrad. Duplessis, Maurice. Historiography. Political Leadership. Quebec. Rumilly, Robert. 1936-59. *2684*
Blackfoot Indians. Adoption practices. Alberta. 1939. *413*
—. Alberta. Church of England. Cree Indians. Missions and Missionaries. Trivett, Samuel. 1878-91. *360*
—. Alberta. Cree Indians. Meteorite. 1810-1973. *442*
—. Alberta. Indians. Wolf Collar (shaman). 1870-1928. *356*
—. Alberta. Manhood ceremonies. Rites and Ceremonies. Shaw, P. C. (personal account). 1894. *447*
—. Dance. Indian Days. Oklahoma. 19c-20c. *437*
—. Fur trade. Indian-White Relations. 1810-40. *376*
—. Identity. Indians. Menominee Indians. Militancy. 1950's-60's. *457*
Blacks. *See* Negroes.
Blair, Duncan Black. Gaelic language, Scots. Nova Scotia (Pictou County). Poetry. Scholars. Scotland. 1846-93. *2346*
Blake, Edward (career). Politics. Psychological problems. 1850-1900. *926*
Blakiston, Thomas Wright. British North American Exploring Expedition. Explorers. North America. Ornithology. Palliser, John. 1857-91. *859*
Blakiston, Thomas Wright (letters). Ornithology. Saskatchewan River. 1857-59. *860*
Bland, Salem. Methodism. Theology. 1880-86. *1038*
Blau-Duncan model. Social mobility. Stratification. 1972. *1373*
Blockade-running. Atlantic Coast. Civil War. Letters. Nova Scotia. Wade, Norman. 1859-62. *841*
Blockades. Civil War. Letters. Nova Scotia. Wade, Norman. 1861-62. *889*
Blue-collar workers. Company satisfaction and commitment. Labor. 1970. *1503*
Board of Commerce of Canada. Price control. Sugar refining industry. 1919-20. *1192*
Boardinghouses. Acculturation. Immigrants. Italian Canadians. Ontario (Toronto). 20c. *2782*
—. Atlantic Provinces. Government. Labor. Merchant Marine. Social reform. ca 1850's-90's. *916*
Boats *See also* Ships; Steamboats.
—. Folklore. New York. St. Lawrence River Skiff. 1860-1973. *133*
Bobtail Cree Reserve. Alberta. Cree Indians. Indians. Land. 1900-09. *3125*
Body painting. Attitudes. Europeans. Indians. 1497-1684. *388*
Boer War. English Canadians. 1899-1902. *1098*
—. Military service, British. Patriotism. Socioeconomic characteristics. Volunteers. 1899-1902. *1099*
Bombings. Clan-na-Gael. Dillon, Luke. Irish Americans. Ontario (Thorold). Welland Canal. 1900-14. *1083*
Bonaparte, Jerome Napoleon. France. North America. Travel. 1861. *839*
Bonds. *See* Stocks and Bonds.
Bone tools. Indians. Man, presence of. Yukon Territory. ca 25,000 BC. *296*
Book Industries and Trade. Copyright Act (Canada, 1900). Publishers and Publishing. 1872-1900. *934*
—. Copyright violations. Ontario (Toronto). Publishers and Publishing. Robertson, John Ross. 1877-90. *2815*
Books *See also* Authors; Bibliography; Copyright; Libraries; Literature; Press; Printing; Publishers and Publishing; Textbooks.
—. Catholic Church. Clergy. France. French Canadians. 1850-1914. *2564*
—. Catholic Church. Clergy. *Index* (legitimacy of). 1862. *844*
Boomtowns. British Columbia (Bennett). Gold Rushes. Yukon Territory. 1896-99. *3183*

—. Iron Industry. Nova Scotia (Bay of Fundy, Londonderry). Steel industry. 1844-98. *2352*
Boorne, W. Hanson. Alberta. Photography. 1886-93. *3171*
Boosterism. Capital, national. Ontario (Ottawa). 1822-59. *865*
—. New Brunswick (Saint John). Population. Railroads. 1851-80. *2410*
Borden, F. W. Physical Education and Training. Strathcona Trust fund. ca 1900-10. *1104*
Borden, Frederick W. Business. Family. Liberal Party. Nova Scotia (King's County). Parliaments. 1874-96. *2316*
Borden, Robert. British Empire. Economic cooperation. Tariff. 1912-18. *1151*
—. Nationalization. Railroads. 1915-19. *1154*
Border problems. USA. 1970's. *2069*
Boserup, Ester. Agricultural growth. China. North America. Russia. South. 18c-19c. *801*
Bossism. Houde, Camillien. Local government. Martin, Médéric. Quebec (Montreal). 1923-29. *2446*
Botany. Burke, Joseph. Hudson's Bay Company. Manitoba. Northwest Territories. Royal Botanic Gardens. 1843-45. *2922*
—. Douglas, David. Horticulture. North America. Scientific Expeditions. 1823-34. *650*
—. Ontario (Peterborough). Traill, Catherine Parr. 1830's-99. *2819*
Bote (newspaper). Germans, Russian. Mennonites. Nazism. Saskatchewan. USSR. Völkisch thought. 1917-39. *3077*
Bothwick, J. Douglas *(History and Biographical Gazetteer of Montreal to the Year 1892)*. Elites. Quebec (Montreal). Social stratification. 19c. *2550*
Boucherville, Charles Eugène Boucher de. Federalism. Joly, Henri-Gustave. Liberal Party. Political Campaigns. Provincial government. Quebec. 1878. *2452*
Boulder configurations. Archaeology. Indians. Saskatchewan. Solstices. Sun Dance structures. Prehistory. 1975. *406*
Boundaries *See also* Annexation; Geopolitics; International Waters.
—. Environmental control. International Boundary and Water Commission. International Joint Commission. Mexico. USA. 1973. *2053*
—. Ethnic Groups. Manitoba (Winnipeg; North End, St. Boniface). Neighborhoods. 19c-1978. *2977*
—. Fishing. Foreign Relations. Territorial Waters. 1977. *1933*
—. Fulford, Frederick M. J. (personal account). Monument setter. USA. 1908-12. *1091*
—. Gibbons, George Christie. Maritime law disputes. USA. Water resources. 1905-10. *1113*
—. Great Britain. International Trade. Vermont. 1763-1815. *630*
—. Great Britain. Lake of the Woods. Paris, Treaty of (1783). USA. 1755-1925. *723*
—. Quebec. Vermont. 1684-1933. *662*
—. USA. 49th parallel. 18c-19c. *661*
Boundary disputes. Anglophobia. Aroostook War (1839). Great Britain. USA. 1837-39. *654*
—. Diplomacy. Great Britain. Oregon. Polk, James K. USA. 1845-46. *835*
Boundary protection. Army Corps of Engineers. North Dakota. Sherrill, Clarence O. 1919. *1158*
Boundary survey incident. Great Lakes. Lee, Robert E. USA. 1835. *674*
Boundary Waters Treaty. Alberta, southern. Irrigation. USA. 1885-1909. *962*
—. British Columbia (Cabin Creek). Coal explorations. Ecology. Montana. USA. 1909. 1973-75. *2035*
—. Foreign Relations. Niagara Falls. USA. 1899-1911. *1088*
—. Gibbons, George Christie. International Waters. USA. 1905-11. *1114*
Bourassa, Henri. Divorce. Feminism. Woman suffrage. 1913-25. *1142*
—. Parliaments. Progressives. 1926. *1182*
Bourassa, Napoléon. Art history. Oral History. 1800-1930. *241*
Bourassa, Robert. Liberal Party. Political patronage. Quebec. 1970-75. *2440*
Bourgeoisie. *See* Middle Classes.
Bourget, Ignace. Catholic Church. Colleges and Universities. Laval University. Quebec (Quebec). 1840's-50's. *2523*
Bournot, John (impressions). Nova Scotia (Cape Breton). 1867. *2358*

Bowen, John C. Aberhart, William. Alberta. Provincial Government. Social Credit Party. 1937-38. *3158*

Boxing. Langford, Sam ("Boston Tarbaby"). Race Relations. 1886-1956. *2369*

Boycotts. Anticlericalism. *Canada-Revue* (newspaper). Catholic Church. Freedom of the press. Quebec (Montreal). 1890-94. *2484*

Boys. Adolescence. Protestantism. USA. Young Men's Christian Association. 1870-1920. *927*

—. Charities. Great Britain. Hudson's Bay Company. Schools. 18c-19c. *684*

Brackett, George. Alaska (Skagway). Entrepreneurs. Gold Rushes. Roads. Yukon Territory. 1897-98. *3323*

Bradstreet, John. Great Britain. Louisbourg, Fortress of. Military Biography. Nova Scotia. 1739-74. *604*

Brain drain. British West Indies. Immigration policy. Racism. 1946-77. *1742*

—. Developing Nations. Economic Conditions. Immigration policy. 1962-74. *1931*

Brant, Joseph (Thayendanegea, Mohawk chief). Indians. Iroquois Indians. Ontario (Grand River). 1742-1807. *440*

Brant, Joseph (Thayendanegea, Mohawk chief; interview). Iroquois Indians. Norton, John (interview). 1801. *351*

Brendan, Saint. Discovery and Exploration. Ireland. North America. Voyages. 500-85. 1976-77. *488*

Brethren in Christ. Engel, Jacob. Pennsylvania (Lancaster County). Sects, Religious. 1775-1964. *250*

—. North Central States. Wesleyan Holiness. 1910-50. *1145*

Bricklin (automobile). Music. New Brunswick. Popular culture. Russell, Charlie. Satire. 1970's. *2401*

Bridges *See also* names of bridges, e.g. Golden Gate Bridge, etc.

—. Alberta (Edmonton). Calgary and Edmonton Railway. City Government. Railroads. 1910-13. *3112*

—. Bear River. Nova Scotia (Annapolis, Digby counties). 1853-66. *2323*

—. British Columbia (Fraser Canyon). Ferries. 1863-1973. *3186*

—. Quebec (Abitibi County). 1820-1950's. *2438*

Brigade Trail. British Columbia. Hudson's Bay Company. Trade Routes. 1849-60. 1967-73. *3203*

Britannic Idealism (concept). Imperialism. Nationalism. Parkin, George R. 1871-1922. *912*

British American Ranche Company. Alberta (Cochrane). Cattle Raising. Cochrane Ranch. Red River of the North. 1881-1905. *1010*

British Colonial Office. Assimilation. Indians. 1760-1830. *469*

British Columbia. Alaska. Anián, strait of. Cook, James. Discovery and Exploration. Northwest Passage. Voyages. 1778. *675*

—. Alaska. China (Macao). Cook, James. Fur trade. Pacific Area. 1778-79. *784*

—. Alaska Highway. Highways. Yukon Territory. 1974. *3325*

—. Alaska (Metlakahtla). Duncan, William. Missions and Missionaries. Tsimshian Indians. 1857-1974. *373*

—. Alaska-British Columbia-Yukon Conferences. Economic development. Regional Planning. Yukon Territory. 1930-64. *2133*

—. Alberta. Athabasca Pass. Ritual toasts. 1811-1974. *694*

—. Alberta. Coal Mines and Mining. Depressions. Pass Strike of 1932. 1920's-30's. *1209*

—. Alberta, southern. Japanese Canadians. World War II. 1941-45. *1233*

—. Annexation. Foreign Policy. Seward, William H. 1865-69. *3252*

—. Anthropology. Art. Duff, Wilson. Pacific Northwest. 1950-76. *280*

—. Apportionment. Partisanship. Provincial Legislatures. 1952-78. *3199*

—. Arbitration, compulsory. Teachers. 1937-73. *3257*

—. Archaeology. Duff, Wilson. Indians. 1950-76. *292*

—. Art. Collins, Charles John. 1900-30. *3259*

—. Art history. 1780-1974. *3258*

—. Art History (review article). Murray, Joan. Paintings. Reid, Dennis. 1778-1935. *3189*

—. Artillery. Coast defenses. World War II. 1862-1941. *1232*

—. Asian Canadians. Immigration. Politics. Racism. 1850-1914. *900*

—. Astronomy. Calendars. Indians. Northwest Coast Indians. Prehistory. 1975. *303*

—. Barret, David. Federal Government. New Democratic Party. 1959-75. *3195*

—. Bibliographies. 1968-1976. *3264*

—. Bibliographies. 18c-20c. 1970's. *3265*

—. Bibliographies. Essays. Theses. 1976. *3269*

—. Bibliographies. Lumber and Lumbering. Pacific Northwest. 1890's-1960's. *3221*

—. Bibliographies. Maps. 1976-77. *3263*

—. Bibliographies. Theses. 12c-20c. 1974. *3267*

—. Bibliographies. Theses. 1975. *3268*

—. Black bear, white. 20c. *3208*

—. Black Capitalism. Canning industry. Deas, John Sullivan. Salmon. 1862-78. *3239*

—. Brigade Trail. Hudson's Bay Company. Trade Routes. 1849-60. 1967-73. *3203*

—. Business History. Economic Development. Historiography. Robin, Martin (review article). 19c-20c. 1974. *3244*

—. California. Discrimination. Gold Rushes. Negroes. Race Relations. 1849-66. *846*

—. Carr, Emily. Forests and Forestry. Indians. Paintings. 1904-45. *3260*

—. Chinese. Immigration. Japanese. Suffrage. 1935-49. *3220*

—. Chinese. Japanese Canadians. Military Service. World War II. 1939-45. *1242*

—. Chinese, overseas. Clan origins. Home county. 1880-85. *1052*

—. Chinook jargon. Pacific Northwest. 1830's-1976. *412*

—. Civil Defense. Emergencies. Planning. Provincial Government. 1951-76. *3233*

—. Civil service. Gaggin, John Boles. 1859-66. *3254*

—. Coalition government. Conservative Party. Cooperative Commonwealth Federation. 1941-52. *3173*

—. Colonial Government. Granville, George, 2d earl (letter). Great Britain. Musgrave, Anthony. Seymour, Frederick (death). 1869. *3204*

—. Conciliation Act (1900; antecedents). Industrial relations. Labour, Department of. 1880's-1900. *3175*

—. Conscription, Military. Pearkes, G. R. World War II. 1943-44. *3248*

—. Cooperative Commonwealth Federation (origins). Ideology. Power struggles. Socialists. 1919-32. *3271*

—. Cultural History. Ormsby, Margaret. 1930's-74. *3234*

—. Daily life. Dukhobors. Immigration. Russia. 1880's-1976. *1035*

—. Daily Life. Lumber camps. Parkin, Al (interview). 1910's-30's. *3255*

—. Daily life. Union Steamship Company. 1889-1959. *3185*

—. Dairying. Economic History. Fraser Valley Milk Producers' Association. 1867-1969. *3224*

—. Depressions. Education Department (Recreational and Physical Education Branch). Sports. Youth. 1934-40. *3217*

—. Douglas, James. Frontier and Pioneer Life. Gold rushes. Law Enforcement. 1858. *3197*

—. Dukhobors. Russian Canadians. Saskatchewan. 1652-1976. *152*

—. Economic Development. Royal Engineers. 1845-1910. *3266*

—. Elections (federal). Political Parties. Voting and Voting Behavior. 1974. *3231*

—. Elections, provincial. New Democratic Party. 1970-73. *3187*

—. Elections, provincial. Social Credit. 1952-53. *3193*

—. Engineering. Lumber and Lumbering. Poetry. Railroads. Swanson, Robert (interview). 20c. *3273*

—. Evacuation, forced. Federal government. Japanese. Public opinion. World War II. 1937-42. *1247*

—. Explorers. Fraser River. Mackenzie, Alexander. 1793. *646*

—. Fiction. Greater Victoria Public Library. 1968. *8*

—. Foreign investments. Jurisdictional law. Land ownership. Washington (Whatcom County). 1970's. *2047*

—. Forests and Forestry. Landscape Painting. 1700-1950. *3188*

—. Fort Langley. Hudson's Bay Company. Restorations. 1827-58. 1976-77. *3210*

—. Frontier process. Great Britain. Imperial administration. 1846-71. *979*

—. Government. Political Parties. Socialism. 1972-75. *3214*

—. Government Enterprise. Pricing policies. 1977. *3243*

—. Great Britain. Gunboats. Indians. Liquor. Slave trade, Indian. 1860's. *390*

—. Great Britain. Immigration. Public opinion. 1919-30. *3250*

—. Great Britain. Miles, Walter K. (and ancestors). 1602-1977. *3229*

—. Great Britain. Nootka Sound controversy. Spain. Territorial rights. 1790. *691*

—. Homesteading and Homesteaders. Immigration. Prairie Provinces. Scandinavian Canadians. 1850's-1970's. *1032*

—. Indians. Land policies. Provincial government. 1875-80. *383*

—. Indians (reservations). Socioeconomic characteristics. Urban Residents. 1971. *458*

—. Japanese communities. Minorities. Public schools. 1900-72. *3191*

—. Labor Unions and Organizations. Politics. 1976. *3232*

—. Labor Unions and Organizations. Women. 1973. *3225*

—. Legislation. New Democratic Party. Public Policy. Social Democracy. 1972-75. *3241*

—. Legislation. Politics. Provincial Government. 1977. *3238*

—. Lumber and Lumbering. Maine. McInnis, George (interview). Washington. 1894-1949. *3261*

—. Multinational Corporations. Natural Resources. Provincial government. Social Classes. Towns, "instant". 1965-72. *3178*

—. New Democratic Party. Political Indicators. Voting and Voting Behavior. 1968-74. *3212*

—. Northwestern International Yachting Association. Washington (Puget Sound area). Yacht racing, organized. 1870-1914. *3201*

—. Nova Scotia (Pictou County). Politics. Tupper, Charles Hibbert. 1882-1904. *2140*

—. Okanagan Indians. Saunas. 1973. *448*

—. Political Parties. Social Classes. 1971-73. *3272*

—. Public Utilities. Victoria Gas Company. 1860's-90's. *3246*

—. Vancouver City Archives. 19c-20c. *3227*

British Columbia (Alberni Valley). Archaeological research. Ethnography. Indians. Prehistory. 1973. *301*

British Columbia (Anthony, Queen Charlotte Islands). Haida Indians. Totem poles. Prehistory-1795. *375*

British Columbia (Bennett). Boomtowns. Gold Rushes. Yukon Territory. 1896-99. *3183*

—. Presbyterian Church. St. Andrews Church, construction of. 1898. *3253*

British Columbia (Bridge River Valley). Economic conditions. Gold Mines and Mining. Physical geography. 19c-1970's. *3251*

British Columbia (Cabin Creek). Boundary Waters Treaty. Coal explorations. Ecology. Montana. USA. 1909. 1973-75. *2035*

British Columbia Electric Railway. Management. Railroads. 1890-1920. *3245*

British Columbia Federation of Labour. Labor Unions and Organizations. Women's rights. 1970-75. *3216*

British Columbia (Fraser Canyon). Bridges. Ferries. 1863-1973. *3186*

British Columbia (Fraser River). Canning industry. Labor. Mergers. Salmon. 1885-1902. *3240*

British Columbia Government Employees Union. Labor Unions and Organizations. Public Employees. 1944-73. *3228*

British Columbia (Gulf Islands). Economic development. Environment. Resource endowment. 1858-1973. *3176*

British Columbia (Harmony Island). Finnish Americans. Kurikka, Matti. Utopias. 1901-05. *3213*

British Columbia (Hazelton). Art. Gitksan Indians. 'Ksan Historic Indian Village. 1973. *434*

British Columbia (Kitsilano). Community services. Mental health. Politics. Psychiatry. 1973-74. *3237*

British Columbia (Kootenay). Church of England. Doull, Alexander John. 1870-1937. *3194*

British Columbia (Lake Bennett). Alaska (Skagway). Gold miners. Klondike Stampede. 1896-99. 1960-73. *3200*

British Columbia (Louise Island, Koona village). Haida Indians. Indians. 1830-90. *454*

British Columbia (Lower Fraser Valley). Landscape, physical. Pioneers. Surveyors. 1859-90. *3235*

British Columbia (Maillardville). Folklore. Magico-religious elements. 1973-74. *3219*

British Columbia Mills, Timber, and Trading
Company. Architecture. Canadian Bank of
Commerce. Prairie Provinces. 1904-22. *2926*
—. Buildings. Housing. 1904-10. *2941*
British Columbia (New Westminster). Birch, Arthur
N. (letter). Local government. Social
Conditions. 1864. *870*
British Columbia (northern). Government relief.
Homesteading and Homesteaders. Resettlement.
1940-42. *3192*
British Columbia (northwest). Economic Growth.
National Democratic Party. Natural Resources.
1973-74. *3270*
British Columbia (Port Simpson). Potlatches.
Tsimshian Indians. 1788-1862. *393*
British Columbia (Prince Rupert). Coastal defense.
Diaries. Thistle, R. World War II. 1941-42.
1243
British Columbia (Prince Rupert area).
Archaeological findings. Tsimshian Indians.
ca 3,000 BC. *297*
British Columbia Provincial Museum. Museums.
1978. *3190*
British Columbia (Quatsino Sound). Civil War.
Outlaws. Quantrill, William Clarke. 1861-1907.
3226
British Columbia (Queen Charlotte Islands).
1787-1974. *3182*
—. Alaska Steamship Company. *Kennecott*
(vessel). Salvage. Shipwrecks. 1923. *3181*
—. Fishing gear. Haida Indians. Indians. Wood.
Prehistory. *287*
—. Haida Indians. Missions and Missionaries.
Protestantism. Settlement. Subsistence patterns.
1876-1920. *398*
—. Haida Indians. Preservation. Totem poles.
1700's-1800's. 1957. *453*
British Columbia (Saltspring Island). Assimilation.
Immigration. Negroes. 1850-1900. *3211*
British Columbia (Sandon). Entrepreneurs. Harris,
Johnny. 1890's-1950's. *3184*
British Columbia (southern). Fishing. Vocabulary.
1975. *3201*
British Columbia, southwestern. Indians. Lillooet
Indians. Oral tradition. Prehistory-1976.
289
—. Indians. Lillooet Indians. Oral tradition.
Prehistory-1976. *291*
British Columbia (Swan Lake). Cemeteries.
Chinese. Feng Shui, concept. Geography.
1974. *3215*
British Columbia, University of. Archaeological
exhibits. Artifacts. Museum of Anthropology.
1947-70's. *3205*
—. Japanese Canadians. Race relations. World
War II. 1939-42. *3177*
—. Sectionalism. 1885-1910. *3202*
British Columbia (Vancouver). Anglo-Japanese
Treaty of Alliance (1902). Asiatic Exclusion
League. Japan. USA. 1907-22. *1108*
—. Archives, city. 1970-74. *3236*
—. Canadian Memorial Chapel (Manitoba memorial
window). 1928. *2975*
—. Canadian Pacific Railway. Economic
Development. 1880's-93. *3222*
—. Depressions. Relief Camp Workers Union.
Strikes. 1935. *3209*
—. Diplomacy. France (Paris). Great Britain.
Nootka Sound Controversy. Spain. 1789-90.
636
—. Economic Growth. Natural resources.
Population. 19c. *3223*
—. Elections. Models. Political parties. 1937-74.
3230
—. Epidemics. Influenza. Public health services.
1918-19. *3174*
—. Fishing industry. Housing. Labor. Politics.
1970's. *3172*
—. Ideology. Manitoba (Winnipeg). Methodology.
Political Parties. 1967-69. *1727*
—. Japanese community. Social Change. 20c.
3262
—. Law Enforcement. Provincial government.
Riots (anti-Chinese). 1887. *3247*
—. Sanitation. Water supply. 1886-1976. *3180*
—. Urbanization. 1871-1974. *3242*
British Columbia (Vancouver Island). Colonization.
Grant, Walter C. (letters). 1851. *3206*
—. *Columbia Rediviva* (vessel). Fourth of July.
Kendrick, John. Nootka Sound controversy.
1789. *647*
—. Cook, James. Discovery and Exploration.
Great Britain. Nootka Sound controversy.
Spain. 1778-94. *695*
—. Fishing rights. International Pacific Salmon
Fisheries Commission. Pacific Northwest.
Salmon. Treaties. 1970's. *2018*

British Columbia (Vancouver Island, Nootka
Sound). *Columbia* (vessel). Discovery and
Exploration. Fur trade. Ingraham, Joseph
(travel account). 1774-89. *655*
British Columbia (Vancouver, Victoria). Aged.
Income. Population. Taxation. 1951-74.
3196
British Columbia (Victoria). Baker, Edgar Crow.
Entrepreneurs. 1872-98. *3179*
—. British Empire. Espionage. Neutrality.
Spanish-American War. 1898. *1105*
—. Elections (provincial). Voting and Voting
Behavior. 1972. *3249*
—. Herre, W. F. Libraries. Reading-rooms.
1858-63. *3256*
—. Navy-yards and Naval Stations. Nova Scotia
(Halifax). Provincial capitals. 1749-1971.
2126
—. Pit houses. Provincial Museum. Salish
(Flathead) Indians. Shuswap Lake Park. 1972.
455
British Commonwealth *See also* Great Britain.
—. 1945-74. *1828*
—. 1944-73. *1914*
—. Economic development. Sugar Agreement.
1949-51. *1870*
—. Foreign Policy. Trudeau, Pierre Elliott. 1970's.
1842
—. Foreign Relations. Ireland. Neutrality. World
War II. 1939-45. *1237*
British Empire *See also* Great Britain.
—. Beaverbrook, 1st Baron. Free trade movement.
Great Britain. Publishers and Publishing.
1900-31. *24*
—. Borden, Robert. Economic cooperation. Tariff.
1912-18. *1151*
—. British Columbia (Victoria). Espionage.
Neutrality. Spanish-American War. 1898.
1105
—. Catholic Church. Ideology. Imperialism.
Quebec. 19c-20c. *2560*
—. Confederation. *Le Canadien* (newspaper).
Parent, Étienne. 1831-52. *830*
—. Defense Policy. 1930's. *1199*
—. Ellice, Edward. Self-government. 1838-40.
826
—. Foreign relations. France. Tariff. Treaties.
1901-09. *1106*
—. Foster, George. Free trade policy. Tariff.
1912-17. *1152*
—. Governors-general. 1867-1952. *111*
—. High commissioner (appointment of). 1920's.
1180
—. International trade. Reciprocity. Sovereignty.
USA. 1909-11. *1107*
British Empire Exhibition (1923). Art (Wembley
controversy). National Gallery of Canada.
Royal Canadian Academy. 1877-1933. *1170*
British Empire Steel Corporation. Coal industry.
Economic Development. Nova Scotia (Cape
Breton Island). 1910's-20's. *1175*
British influences. Constitutions. Legal systems.
USA. 18c-20c. *124*
British Library (Townshend archive). French and
Indian War. Great Britain. Maps. Quebec
(battle of). 1759. *609*
British North America *See also* North America;
USA.
—. British West Indies. Economic Conditions.
International Trade. ca 1609-1800. *715*
—. Colonial Government. Frontier. Indian Affairs
Department. 1755-1830. *623*
—. Colonial Government. Pepperrell, William.
ca 1715-59. *601*
—. Droz, Pierre-Frédéric. Europe. Travel.
Watchmakers. 1768-70. *685*
—. Fur Trade. Garrison towns. Michigan
(Detroit). Military Camps and Forts. Quebec
(Montreal). 1760-75. *637*
—. Fur Trade. Hudson's Bay Company (review
article). 1670-1870. 1970's. *97*
—. Great Britain. Indian Affairs Department.
Uniforms. 1755-1823. *632*
—. Public schools. Teaching. Women. 1845-75.
880
British North America Act (1867). Apportionment.
Nova Scotia. 1971-72. *2336*
—. Constitutional amendments. Great Britain.
Parliaments. Trudeau, Pierre Elliott.
1867-1970's. *1249*
—. Federalism. Intergovernmental relations.
1930's-74. *2091*
British North America Act (1929). Woman
Suffrage. 1870's-1940's. *72*
British North American Exploring Expedition.
Blakiston, Thomas Wright. Explorers. North
America. Ornithology. Palliser, John. 1857-91.
859

British West Indies *See also* West Indies.
—. Brain drain. Immigration policy. Racism.
1946-77. *1742*
—. British North America. Economic Conditions.
International Trade. ca 1609-1800. *715*
—. Political Factions. 1884-1921. *196*
British-Canadian Symposium, 2d. Geography.
1977. *1761*
Broadcasting. Canadian Radio-Television
Commission. Federal Regulation. 1968-75.
1634
Bromley, Walter. Micmac Indians. Nova Scotia.
Self-help. Urban poor. 1813-25. *2258*
Brotherhood of the Holy Family. Catholic Church.
Chaumonot, Joseph-Marie-Pierre. Elites.
Laval, François de. Quebec (Montreal).
1663-1760. *547*
Brougham, Henry Peter. Canadian Rebellion Losses
Bill. Gladstone, William Ewart. Great Britain.
Political Theory. 1849. *814*
Brouillette, Benoit. Bibliographies. Geography.
Quebec (Montreal). 1903-73. *2496*
Brown, George. Congress. Diplomacy. Reciprocity
treaty (proposed). USA. 1870-80. *1071*
—. Labor Unions and Organizations. Ontario.
Publishers and Publishing. Toronto *Globe*
(newspaper). Toronto Typographical Union.
1843-72. *2893*
Brown, J. L. Liberal Party. Manitoba (Lisgar).
Parliaments. Winkler, H. W. (career). 1926-53.
3021
Brown, John. Abolition Movement. Civil War
(antecedents). Harpers Ferry (raid, 1859).
Sanborn, Franklin Benjamin. 1854-60. *875*
Brubacher brothers. Letters. Mennonites. Ontario.
Pennsylvania. 1817-46. *786*
Bryan, William Jennings. Fund-raising. Lectures.
Prairie Provinces. Young Men's Christian
Association. 1909. *2953*
Buchan, Alastair. Atlantic region. Foreign
Relations. Institute of Strategic Studies.
Military Strategy. 1958-75. *1913*
Buchan, John. Governors-General. Lascelles, Alan
(memorandum). 1935. *1217*
Buchanan, Carl J. (reminiscences). Airplane flights.
Alberta (Edmonton). Canadian Airways.
1940. *3090*
Buchanan, Carl, Jr. (reminiscences). Alberta
(Waskatenau). Daily Life. Homesteading and
Homesteaders. 1930's. *3091*
Buchanan, Isaac. Buchanan, Peter. Commercial
crisis. Grain trade. 1840's. *790*
Buchanan, Peter. Buchanan, Isaac. Commercial
crisis. Grain trade. 1840's. *790*
Bucke, Richard M. Ontario (London). Whitman,
Walt (interview). 1880. *1055*
Bucke, Richard M. (*Cosmic Consciousness*). Art.
Harris, Lawren. Theosophy. 1920's. *1181*
Buckler, Susannah. *Baltimore* (vessel). Nova Scotia
(Chebogue). 1735. *2314*
Buffalo. Art. Central America. North America.
Prehistory-20c. *265*
Buffalo bones. Industry. Saskatchewan. 1884-93.
3026
Buffalo migrations. Fur trade. Plains Indians.
Prairie Provinces. 1770-1869. *429*
Buies, Arthur. Catholic Church. 1880's-1901.
1074
Building plans. Insurance. Land use atlases.
Research. Urban historians. 1696-1973. *86*
Buildings *See also* Architecture.
—. British Columbia Mills, Timber, and Trading
Company. Housing. 1904-10. *2941*
—. Cast iron fronts. Cauchon Block. Manitoba
(Winnipeg). 1880-1920. *3003*
—. Cumberland House. Hearne, Samuel.
Saskatchewan. 1794-1800's. *3075*
—. Halifax Historic Properties. Nova Scotia.
Restorations. 1825-1905. 1978. *2255*
—. Historical Sites and Parks. Louisbourg,
Fortress of. Nova Scotia (Cape Breton Island).
1713-58. *529*
—. Manitoba (Winnipeg). 19c-1973. *3004*
—. Quebec (Lower Town Place Royale).
Restorations. 17c. 1975. *515*
—. Research. 19c-20c. *19*
Bulgaria. Great Powers. Hungary. Rumania.
UN. 1947-55. *1927*
Burchard, Jedediah. Protestants. Revivals. Social
Conditions. Vermont. 1835-36. *815*
Bureaucracies. Banking (central). 1960's-70's.
1522
—. Capitalism. Government. Institutions. North
America. Social change. 1750's-1850's. *656*
—. Citizen participation. Great Britain. Political
Reform. USA. 1973. *1667*
—. Civil Service. English Canadians. French
Canadians. 1944-75. *1706*

—. Democracy. Legislators. 1968-72. *1712*

—. Foreign Relations. International Organizations. USA. 1909-74. *1996*

—. Personnel management. Scientific management. USA. -1973. *1489*

Bureaucratization. Alberta. Criminal sentencing. Indians. Urbanization. 1973. *1663*

Burge family. Friendship. Letters. Ontario (Upper Canada). Simcoe family. 1790-1820. *669*

Burgess-Dunne Seaplane. Aeronautics, Military. Canadian Aviation Corps. Janney, Ernest L. 1914-15. *1155*

Burgoyne, John. American Revolution. Bennington (battle). Stark, John. Vermont. 1777. *730*

Burke, Joseph. Botany (specimens). Hudson's Bay Company. Manitoba. Northwest Territories. Royal Botanic Gardens. 1843-45. *2922*

Burns family. Immigration. Ireland. Nova Scotia (Annapolis County; Wilmot Township). 1764-20c. *2305*

Burry, Thomas. Gold rushes. Klondike Stampede. 1897. *2124*

Business *See also* Banking; Consumers; Corporations; Management; Manufactures; Marketing; Multinational Corporations.

—. Agriculture. Distribution system. Machinery. Manitoba. 1974. *2923*

—. Alberta. Federal Programs. International trade. 1977. *3084*

—. American Revolution. Fort Niagara. New York. 1775-83. *736*

—. Australia. English-language culture. Foreign Relations. 1975. *1949*

—. Banks. Industry. Naylor, R. T. (review article). 1867-1914. *928*

—. Barbel, Marie-Anne. New France. Women. 18c. *575*

—. Borden, Frederick W. Family. Liberal Party. Nova Scotia (King's County). Parliaments. 1874-96. *2316*

—. California (Fort Bragg). Jews. Russia. Shafsky family. 1889-1976. *1077*

—. Civil service. Middle Classes. Quebec. Technocracy. 1939-75. *2451*

—. Cooperative movement. Public opinion. Quebec. 1970's. *2643*

—. Council on Foreign Relations (publications). Government. USA. 1971-74. *1966*

—. Economic growth. Manitoba (Winnipeg). Political Leadership. Urbanization. 1874-1914. *2968*

—. Economic history. Historiography. Laurentian thesis. 1960-73. *1592*

—. Electric Power. Nova Scotia (Guysborough). 1927. *2268*

—. Elites. Law. Social institutions, stratifying. 19c-1974. *211*

—. Elites. Ontario (Toronto). Upper Canada Club. 1835-40. *812*

—. Ethics. 1867-1914. 1976-77. *944*

—. Federal Government. Indians (reservations). Missions and Missionaries. Ontario (Manitoulin Island). 1830-60. *350*

—. Legislative investigations. Oliver, Adam. Ontario (Ingersoll, Thunder Bay). Provincial Politics. 1820-85. *2763*

—. Northwest Territories. Public finance. 1947-73. *3353*

—. Quebec (Montreal). 1825. *2594*

Business Administration. French Canadians. Students. 1973. *2585*

Business education. Cultural alienation. Quebec. USA. 1972. *2034*

Business History. British Columbia. Economic Development. Historiography. Robin, Martin (review article). 19c-20c. 1974. *3244*

—. Economic policy. Local Government. Ontario. Property, private. 1898-1911 *1100*

—. Maritime Provinces. 1800-1950. *2173*

—. Marketing (wholesale). Ontario (Hamilton). 1840-75. *2823*

—. Methodology. Naylor, R. T. (*A History of Canadian Business, 1867-1914*). 1867-1914. *933*

Business records. Ball, George P. M. Depressions. Economic change. Ontario (Upper Canada). Rural Settlements. 1825-60. *672*

Business unionism. Labor relations. Saskatchewan. Social democracy. 1974-75. *3062*

Businessmen *See also* Entrepreneurs; Merchants.

—. Attitudes. Canadian Labour Congress. Federal goverment. Tripartism. 1977. *1295*

—. Bill C-256. Communications. Federal Regulation. Manitoba (Winnipeg). Public policy. 1971-72. *2971*

—. Nationalism. Parti Québécois. Quebec. Working class. 1970's. *2690*

—. Ontario (Thunder Bay). Voting and Voting Behavior. 1968-71. *2829*

Buttons, Phoenix. Haiti. Indians. Pacific Northwest. Trade. Uniforms, Military. 1812-30. 20c. *460*

Byng of Vimy, Julian Hedworth George (Viscount). King, William Lyon Mackenzie. Psychohistory. 1919-26. *1174*

Byrd, Richard E. *Arctic* (vessel). Bernier, Joseph E. Discovery and Exploration. 1924-25. *3301*

C

Cabinet *See also* individual portfolios, e.g. Popular Culture, Ministry of; Prime Minister; individual names of cabinet members and presidents.

—. Australia. Great Britain. Netherlands. Political recruitment. USA. 1940's-60's. *1666*

—. Howe, Clarence Decatur. 1935-57. *18*

—. Nova Scotia (Pictou County). Politics. Tupper, Charles H. 1882-1904. *2321*

Cable, George Washington. Kentucky. Lectures. Twain, Mark. 1884-85. *1076*

Cable relay point. Great Britain. Hawaii. USA. 1894-96. *1051*

Cabot, John. Day, John (letter). Morison, Samuel Eliot. Newfoundland (Cape Bonavista). Voyages. 1497-98. *486*

Cadieux, Lorenzo (obituary). Jesuits. Ontario, northern. Scholarship. 1903-76. *2772*

Cahan, Charles H. (address). Japan. League of Nations Covenant. Manchuria. 1932-33. *1211*

Cairns, Alan C. (views). Federalism. ca 1930-77. *1642*

Caisses Populaires Desjardins. Credit unions. Quebec. 1912-73. *2598*

Calcium carbide, manufacture of. Electrochemistry. Inventions. Willson, Thomas Leopold "Carbide". 1860-1915. *939*

Caldwell, Billy. Frontier and Pioneer Life. Great Britain. Great Lakes. Indians. Trade. 1797-1841. *365*

Calendars. Astronomy. British Columbia. Indians. Northwest Coast Indians. Prehistory. 1975. *303*

Calgary and Edmonton Railway. Alberta (Edmonton). Bridges. City Government. Railroads. 1910-13. *3112*

Calgary *Herald*, newspaper. Alberta. Bachelors. Frontier. Marriage. 1895. *956*

California. British Columbia. Discrimination. Gold Rushes. Negroes. Race Relations. 1849 66. *846*

—. *Design for Development* (Ontario, 1966). Ontario. Regional planning. 1965-74. *2873*

—. Discovery and Exploration. Drake, Francis. *Golden Hinde* (vessel). Nova Albion (location of). 1579. *505*

California (Fort Bragg). Business. Jews. Russia. Shafsky family. 1889-1976. *1077*

California, northern. Australia (Victoria). Frontier thesis. Turner, Frederick Jackson. 1850-1900. *247*

California (San Francisco). Hudson's Bay Company. Ice trade. Pacific Area. Russian-American Company. 1850's. *878*

Calkin(s) family. Apple industry. Halliburton, Robert Grant. Inglis, Charles. Nova Scotia. Starr family. 19c. *2279*

Calonne, Abbot de (letters). Catholic Church. Clergy. Public schools. 1819-20. *706*

Calvert, George (1st Lord Baltimore). Catholic Church. Colonization. Newfoundland (Avalon Peninsula). Religious Liberty. 1620's. *551*

—. Colonization. Great Britain. Newfoundland (Avalon Peninsula). 1609-32. *2182*

Cameron, Alexander W. Alberta (Edmonton). Theater. 1906-13. *3143*

Cameron, John Hillyard. Conservatism. Ontario (Canada West). Political Leadership. 1854-56. *855*

Camp Wanapitei. Ontario (Sandy Inlet, Lake Temagami). Paradis, Charles. Settlement. 1895-1970's. *2789*

Campaign Finance *See also* Election Expenses Act.

—. Elections. 1972. *1701*

—. Manitoba. Political success. Quebec. Voting and Voting Behavior. 1975. *1728*

Campaigns, Military. *See* Military Campaigns.

Campaigns, Political. *See* Political Campaigns.

Campbell, Thomas D. Droughts. Farm income. Great Plains. Prairie Provinces. Wheat. 1915-1940. *2964*

Canada. *See* individual provinces; Atlantic Provinces; British North America; Acadia; Labrador; Maritime Provinces; Northwest Territories; North America; Prairie Provinces; Yukon Territory.

Canada Assistance Plan. Federal government. Federalism. Provincial government. 1966. *1652*

Canada Company. Galt, John. Hibernia colony (proposed). Quebec (Lower Canada). Settlement. 1825-35. *774*

Canada First (group). Expansionism. Mair, Charles. Red River Rebellion. Riel, Louis. 1869-70. *1009*

Canada-Revue (newspaper). Anticlericalism. Boycotts. Catholic Church. Freedom of the press. Quebec (Montreal). 1890-94. *2484*

Canadian Academy of the History of Pharmacy. American Institute of the History of Pharmacy. Pharmacy, History of. Stieb, Ernst W. (account). 1940's-70's. *2059*

Canadian Airways. Airplane flights. Alberta (Edmonton). Buchanan, Carl J. (reminiscences). 1940. *3090*

Canadian Armed Forces Command and Staff College. Military Education. Ontario (Toronto). 1966-74. *1312*

Canadian Aviation Corps. Aeronautics, Military. Burgess-Dunne Seaplane. Janney, Ernest L. 1914-15. *1155*

Canadian Bank of Commerce. Architecture. British Columbia Mills, Timber, and Trading Company. Prairie Provinces. 1904-22. *2926*

Canadian Broadcasting Corporation. Drama. Fink, Howard (account). Radio. 1940's-50's. 1976. *1386*

—. News. Radio. USA. 1975-76. *2031*

Canadian Catholic Historical Association. Catholic Church. Ontario (Toronto). 1933-73. *1318*

Canadian Conservation Institute. Art. Artifacts. Ontario (Ottawa). Preservation. 1978. *31*

Canadian Expeditionary Force. English Canadians. French Canadians. Hughes, Samuel. Imperialist sentiment. World War I. 1853-1921. *245*

Canadian Expeditionary Force, 41st Battalion. French Canadians. World War I. 1914-15. *1160*

Canadian Forum (periodical). Depressions. Poetry. 1929-39. *1213*

Canadian Industrial Disputes Investigation Act (1907). Arbitration. Industrial Relations. USA. 1907. *1101*

Canadian Institute of International Affairs. Colleges and Universities. External Affairs Department. Foreign Policy. Soward, F. H. (account). 1926-66. *217*

Canadian Institute of Longueuil. Voluntary Associations. 1857-60. *2525*

Canadian Institute of Montreal. Archives. Bibliographies. Quebec. 1844-1900. *120*

—. Quebec (Montreal). Social history. 1845-73. *2509*

Canadian International Development Agency. Higher Education. Manitoba, University of. Thailand. 1964-74. *1911*

Canadian Inventory of Historic Buildings. Historical Sites and Parks. 1968-73. *1289*

Canadian Labour Congress. American Federation of Labor. Labor Unions and Organizations. Strong, Cyril. 1949-77. *1525*

—. Anti-Inflation Act. Economic Conditions. Income. 1970's. *1572*

—. Association of Commercial and Technical Employees. Labor Reform. Ontario (Toronto). White-collar employees. 1972. *2724*

—. Attitudes. Business community. Federal government. Tripartism. 1977. *1295*

—. Communist Party. Labor. 1974. *1575*

—. Conference on Equal Opportunity and Treatment for Women Workers. Employment. Equal opportunity. Women. 1978. *1558*

—. Federal government. Political protest. Wages. 1976. *1563*

—. Income. Inflation. 1975. *1616*

—. Labor Unions and Organizations. Rehabilitation. 1973. *1584*

—. Leadership. Morris, Joe (interview). 1930's-78. *1527*

Canadian Labour Congress Executive Council. Unemployment insurance. 1974-75. *1619*

Canadian Labour Council. Labour Manifesto (1976). 1976. *1549*

Canadian League for Socialist Action. Trotskyism. 1973. *2040*

Canadian Library Association Committee on the Status of Women. Cheda, Sherrill. Feminism. Librarians. 1973-74. *1418*

Canadian Memorial Chapel (Manitoba memorial window). British Columbia (Vancouver). 1928. *2975*

Canadian National Railroad System. Architecture. Railroads. Saskatchewan. 1890-1970's. *3030*

Canadian Northern Railway. Alberta (Athabasca Landing). *Edmonton Bulletin* (newspaper). Railroads. Villages. 1912-77. *3113*

—. Canadian Pacific Railway. Railroads (review article). 19c-20c. 1968-77. *915*

Canadian Pacific Railway. Alberta (Edmonton). Local Politics. Railroads. 1891-1914. *955*

—. Architecture. Railroads. Saskatchewan. 20c. *3029*

—. British Columbia (Vancouver). Economic Development. 1880's-93. *3222*

—. Canadian Northern Railway. Railroads (review article). 19c-20c. 1968-77. *915*

—. Capital alliances. Morton, Bliss & Company. Railroads. St. Paul & Pacific Railroad. Stephen, George. USA. 1860-70's. *980*

—. Construction crews. Manitoba (Virden). McLeod, Finlay J. C. (reminiscences). Presbyterian Church. 1881-82. *1005*

—. Engineers, locomotive. Labor Unions and Organizations. Prairie Provinces. Strikes. 1883. *1066*

Canadian Permanent Commission on Geographic Names. Toponymy. 1973. *1336*

Canadian Psychological Associations. Oral history. Psychology. 1970-75. *1442*

Canadian Radio-Television Commission. Broadcasting. Federal Regulation. 1968-75. *1634*

Canadian Railway Labour Association. Employment. Railroads. Technology. Working Conditions. 1973. *1620*

Canadian Railway Museum. Japan. *John Molson* (locomotive, replica). Locomotives. Scotland. 1849. 1969. *877*

—. Quebec (St. Constant). Railroads. 1940's-77. *1305*

Canadian Rebellion Losses Bill. Brougham, Henry Peter. Gladstone, William Ewart. Great Britain. Political Theory. 1849. *814*

Canadian Seamen's Union. Communists. Syndicalism. 1936-49. *1197*

Canadian Shield. Alberta. Natural resources. 1977. *273*

Canadian Slovak League. Behuncik, Edward J. (speech). Slovak World Congress. 1970-72. *1740*

Canadian studies. Academic exchange programs. Five-Year Cultural Plan. Government funding. 1970's. *1798*

—. Academic responsibility. Colleges and Universities. Social responsibility. 1970's. *1360*

—. Art. Symons, T. H. B. (report). 1960's-77. *1495*

—. French civilization. Royal Society of Canada (Letters and Social Sciences Section). 1952-72. *1344*

—. Higher education. Symons report. 1970's. *1368*

Canadian Union of Public Employees. Labor Unions and Organizations. MacMillan, John F. "Lofty". Public Employees. 1935-73. *1504*

—. Public Employees. Sex discrimination. Women. 1975. *1617*

Canadian Urban History Conference. Urban history. 1977. *116*

—. Urban history. 19c-20c. 1977. *220*

Canadian Voltiguer Regiment. Glengarry Light Infantry Fencible Regiment. Uniforms, Military. War of 1812. 1812-16. *755*

Canadiana (bibliography). Bibliography, national. National Library of Canada. 1950-77. *249*

Canals *See also* names of canals, e.g. Rideau Canal, etc.

—. Erie Canal. Freight capacity and utilization. Great Lakes. 1810-50. *791*

—. Geographic space. International Trade. National Development. Politics. Railroads. 1818-1930. *54*

—. Imperial funds (diversion). Military. Ottawa-Rideau military canal. 1815-25. *799*

—. Nova Scotia. Shubenacadie Canal. 1791-1974. *2270*

—. Ontario (Georgian Bay). Public Finance. Railroads. 1850-1915. *925*

—. St. Lawrence Seaway. 1760-1973. *787*

Cannibalism tales. Fort Churchill. Fort York. Manitoba. Molden, John. Shipwrecks. 1833. *3012*

Canning industry. Black Capitalism. British Columbia. Deas, John Sullivan. Salmon. 1862-78. *3239*

—. British Columbia (Fraser River). Labor. Mergers. Salmon. 1885-1902. *3240*

Cannons. Armaments. Fur trade. 1600's-1800's. *141*

Canoe trips. Discovery and Exploration. Rupert's Land. Tyrrell, Joseph Burr. 1893. *975*

—. Frobisher Bay. Northwest Territories (Baffin Island, Takuirbing Lake). Travel. 1973. *3320*

—. MacKenzie, A. Stanley (journal). Nova Scotia. 1885. *2269*

Canoeing. Ontario. Recreation. 1888-1914. *2738*

—. Recreation. 16c-20c. *157*

Canoes, development of. Indians. Prehistory. 1977. *294*

Canol Project. Foster, W. W. Oil Industry and Trade. USA. War Department. 1942-45. *1219*

—. Northwest Territories (Mackenzie Valley). Oil Industry and Trade. Pipelines. Planning. World War II. 1942-45. *3274*

Capital *See also* Banking; Capitalism; Investments; Labor; Monopolies.

—. Atlantic Provinces. Social classes. Unemployment. 1972-77. *2172*

—. Economic activity. Financial institutions. 1947-72. *1581*

—. Employment. Manufacturing. 1949-72. *1608*

Capital alliances. Canadian Pacific Railroad. Morton, Bliss & Company. Railroads. St. Paul & Pacific Railroad. Stephen, George. USA. 1860-70's. *980*

Capital (export). Foreign investments. 1900-73. *1792*

Capital flow restrictions. Economic Policy. Foreign relations. USA. 1960's-71. *2080*

Capital investment, American. Economic Policy. Quebec. 1970's. *2067*

Capitals, national. Boosterism. Ontario (Ottawa). 1822-59. *865*

Capitalism *See also* Capital; Socialism.

—. Agriculture. Peasants. Quebec. 1600-1970's. *2595*

—. Anti-Americanism. Anti-Continentalism. Nationalism. 1960's-74. *2045*

—. Bureaucracies. Government. Institutions. North America. Social change. 1750's-1850's. *656*

—. Economic Regulations. Quebec. 1870-1900. *2650*

—. Imperialism. Socialism. Women. ca 1870-1975. *139*

—. Quebec. Revolution. USA. 1920-40. 1960's. *2431*

—. Quebec (Montreal). Research Group on Montreal Society. Social History. 19c. *2642*

Capitalists. Laurentide Company. Newsprint. Quebec. 1887-1928. *161*

Capitol Theatre. Architecture. Entertainment. Movie palaces. Ontario (Ottawa). Vaudeville. 1920-70. *1138*

Career patterns. Entrepreneurial behaviour. Quebec (Montreal). Real estate agents, residential. -1974. *2634*

Carey, Henry C. Nationalism. Protectionism. Reciprocity Treaty, proposed. USA. 1871-75. *1060*

Cargo. France. French and Indian War. Glass. *Machault* (vessel). 1760. *532*

Caribbean Region. Garrison duty. Great Britain. Military. 1914-45. *1131*

Caribou. Quebec. Wildlife Conservation. 20c. *267*

Carleton, Guy. American Revolution. Arnold, Benedict. Fort Ticonderoga. Lake Champlain. 1776. *722*

—. American Revolution. Attitudes. Military Occupation. Peasants. Quebec. 1775-76. *717*

—. American Revolution. British Army. Logistics. Quebec. 1776. *714*

Carman, William Bliss (letters). Guiney, Louise Imogen. Poets. 1887-98. *1045*

Carnegie, Andrew. Libraries. Nicol, A. Yukon Territory (Dawson). 1902-20's. *3340*

Carr, Emily. British Columbia. Forests and Forestry. Indians. Paintings. 1904-45. *3260*

—. Indians. Painting. 1888-1972. *362*

Cartography. *See* Maps.

Cary, James. Exiles. Great Britain. Jamaica. Loyalists. Nova Scotia. 1781-1804. *744*

Cast Iron. Stoves, cooking. VanNorman, Joseph. 1820-80's. *195*

Cast iron fronts. Buildings. Cauchon Block. Manitoba (Winnipeg). 1880-1920. *3003*

Castonguay, Claude (interview). Federalism. Nationalism. Quebec. 1917-73. *63*

Casualty rates. Currie, Arthur. Hughes, Sam. Military General Staff. World War I. 1914-30. *1156*

Cather, Willa (*Shadows on the Rock*). Attitudes. Idealism. 1920's-31. *1177*

Catholic Church *See also* religious orders by name, e.g. Franciscans, Jesuits, etc.

—. Acadians. Discrimination. Irish. New Brunswick. 1860-1900. *2402*

—. Acadians. English Canadians. Maritime Provinces. Social Conditions. 1763-1977. *2171*

—. Acadians. Irish Canadians. New Brunswick. Politics. Quebec. Schools. Taxation. 1871-73. *1067*

—. Action Catholique. Courchesne, Georges. Quebec (Rimouski). 1940-67. *2466*

—. *Action Catholique* (newspaper). Communist Parties and Movements. Nazism. Quebec. 1917-39. *1411*

—. Agnosticism. Quebec. Students. 1970-78. *2455*

—. Alberta (Calgary Diocese). French Canadians. Irish Canadians. McNailly, John Thomas. 1871-1952. *3095*

—. Alberta (Edmonton). Colleges and Universities. MacDonald, John Roderick. St. Joseph's College (Alberta). 1922-23. *3140*

—. Anglin, Timothy Warren. Confederation. Fenians. New Brunswick. 1866. *890*

—. Anglin, Timothy Warren. Irish Canadians. New Brunswick. Saint John *Freeman* (newspaper). 1849-83. *2373*

—. Anticlericalism. Boycotts. *Canada-Revue* (newspaper). Freedom of the press. Quebec (Montreal). 1890-94. *2484*

—. Antigonish Movement. Nova Scotia. Rural Development. Social change. ca 1928-73. *2297*

—. Architecture. New France. 1600-1760. *553*

—. Archives. Bishops. Church History. Kingston, Archdiocese of. Ontario. 1800-1966. *2847*

—. Assimilation. French Americans. Vermont (Winooski). 1867-1900. *2469*

—. Atlantic Provinces. Diaries. Plessis, Joseph-Octave. Quebec Archdiocese. 1812-15. *2155*

—. Bible-reading. Politics. Prince Edward Island. Protestants. Public Schools. 1856-60. *2207*

—. Bibliographies. Church history. 17c-1973. *80*

—. Bibliographies. Church history. ca 1800-1976. *91*

—. Bishops. Chicoutimi, Séminaire de. Church History. Quebec (Saguenay). 1873-1973. *2542*

—. Bishops. Church of England. Liberal government. Newfoundland. 1860-62. *2187*

—. Books. Clergy. France. French Canadians. 1850-1914. *2564*

—. Books. Clergy. *Index* (legitimacy of). 1862. *844*

—. Bourget, Ignace. Colleges and Universities. Laval University. Quebec (Quebec). 1840's-50's. *2523*

—. British Empire. Ideology. Imperialism. Quebec. 19c-20c. *2560*

—. Brotherhood of the Holy Family. Chaumonot, Joseph-Marie-Pierre. Elites. Laval, François de. Quebec (Montreal). 1663-1760. *547*

—. Buies, Arthur. 1880's-1901. *1074*

—. Calonne, Abbot de (letters). Clergy. Public schools. 1819-20. *706*

—. Calvert, George (1st Lord Baltimore). Colonization. Newfoundland (Avalon Peninsula). Religious Liberty. 1620's. *551*

—. Canadian Catholic Historical Association. Ontario (Toronto). 1933-73. *1318*

—. Census. Clergy. 1761-90. *660*

—. Chicoutimi, Petit-Séminaire de. Quebec (Saguenay). Religious Education. Students. 1873-1930. *2562*

—. Chicoutimi, Séminaire de. Church and State. Simard, Ovide-D. (personal account). 1873-1973. *2563*

—. Chippewa Indians. Hudson's Bay Company. Métis. Provencher, John N. (memoir). Quebec. Red River Settlement. 1812-36. *2948*

—. Church and State. Europe, Western. North America. Politics. 1870-1974. *246*

—. Church and State. Provincial Government. Public Charities Act (1921). Quebec. Recessions. 1921-26. *2578*

—. Church and State. Quebec. 18c-20c. *2699*

—. Church Finance. Economic Development. LaRocque, Paul. Quebec (Sherbrooke). 1893-1926. *2636*

—. Church History. Ontario (Kingston). St. Mary's Cathedral of the Immaculate Conception. 1843-1973. *2765*

—. Church Schools. Manitoba. McCarthy, D'Alton. Provincial legislatures. 1870-90. *931*

—. Cistercians. Mistassini, monastery of. Quebec. Trappists. 1900-03. *2482*

—. Clergy. 1790's-1830's. *664*

—. Clergy. Craig, James Henry. French Canadian nationalism. Government repression. Quebec (Lower Canada). 1810. *711*

—. Congregation of Notre Dame (Sisters). Ontario (Kingston). Religious education. Women. 1841-48. *2737*

—. Cults, Liturgical. Devotions, popular. Quebec (Lac-Saint-Jean, Portneuf Counties). 1970's. *2561*

—. D'Aquin, Marie Thomas. Joan of Arc Institute. Ontario (Ottawa). Social Work. Women. 1903-19. *2746*

—. Devotions, popular. Quebec (La Beauce County). Shrines, roadside. Social customs. 1970's. *2514*

—. Discrimination. Normal school issue. Prairie Provinces. 1884-1900. *2947*

—. École Sociale Populaire. Labor unions and Organizations. Quebec. Social Change. 1911-75. *2500*

—. Education (British, US). Newspapers. Ontario. 1851-1948. *2833*

—. Educational system. French Canadians. Parent-youth conflict. Quebec. Social change. 1960-70. *2516*

—. Episcopal nominations. French Canadians. Irish Canadians. 1900-75. *2930*

—. Ethnic groups. Evangelists. Protestantism. Quebec (Lower Canada). Rebellion of 1837. 1766-1865. *811*

—. Eudists. Industrialization. Quebec (Chicoutimi Basin). Working class. 1903-30. *2475*

—. Fédération Nationale Saint-Jean-Baptiste. Feminism. Gérin-Lajoie, Marie. Quebec. 1907-33. *1128*

—. France (Paris). Quebec (Montreal). Reading rooms. Social Customs. 19c. *2531*

—. French Canadians. Guigues, Joseph-Eugène. Ontario (Ottawa Diocese). 1848-74. *2747*

—. French Canadians. Migration, Internal. Parishes. Quebec (Compton County). Rural-Urban Studies. 1851-91. *2534*

—. French Canadians. Minnesota (Gentilly). Settlement. Theillon, Elie. 1870's-1974. *946*

—. French Canadians. Minville, Esdras. Quebec. 1975. *2459*

—. French language. *Patriote de l'Ouest* (newspaper). Saskatchewan. 1910-41. *2929*

—. General Hospital. Mental Illness. Quebec. 1692-1845. *2543*

—. Geographic Space. Regionalism. 1615-1851. *3*

—. German Alsatians. Gravemarkers. Iron work. Ontario (Bruce County; Waterloo). 1850-1910. *2837*

—. Gibbons, James. Knights of Labor. Social thought. Taschereau, Elzéar-Alexandre. 1880's. *1068*

—. Government. Parish registers. Quebec. 1539-1913. *526*

—. Governors, provincial. Laval, François de. New France (Sovereign Council). 1659-84. *546*

—. Harris, William Richard (biography). Ontario (Toronto). 1846-1923. 1974. *2858*

—. Hospitals. Hôtel-Dieu. Indian-White Relations. Quebec. 1635-98. *552*

—. Ideas, History of. Laval, François de. Quebec. 17c. *549*

—. Immigration. Mathieu, Olivier-Elzéar. Regina Archdiocese. Saskatchewan. 1911-31. *2936*

—. Immigration. Missions and Missionaries. Sisters of Service. 1920-30. *2963*

—. Indians. Louisiana. Missions and Missionaries. 18c-20c. *587*

—. Irish Canadians. McMahon, Patrick. Poor. Quebec (Quebec). St. Bridget's Home. 1847-1972. *2541*

—. Journalism. Social thought. Somerville, Henry. 1915-53. *1115*

—. Knights of Labor. Labor Unions and Organizations. Taschereau, Elzéar-Alexandre. 1884-94. *1069*

—. Lamarche, Gustave. Political philosophy. Quebec. Separatist Movements. 1922-75. *2705*

—. Macdonald, John. Voting and Voting Behavior. 1850's-91. *1059*

—. New Brunswick (Saint John). Sisters of Charity of the Immaculate Conception. 1854-64. *2392*

—. Ontario (Toronto). St. Basil's Seminary. Vatican Council II. 1962-67. *2806*

—. Ontario (Toronto). Saints Cyril and Methodius Parish. Slovak Canadians. 1934-77. *2894*

—. Parish registers. Population. Quebec. 1616-1700. *540*

—. Quebec (Gaspé). Ross, François Xavier. Social Conditions. 1923-45. *2532*

—. Quebec (Hébertville, Lake Saint John). Settlement. ca 1840-1900. *2558*

Catholic parishes. Slovak Canadians. 1900-77. *114*

Catholicism. Church History. Colonization. Quebec (Eastern Townships). Settlement. 1800-60. *704*

—. French Canadians. Lévesque, Georges-Henri (personal account). Nationalism. Quebec. Youth movements. 1930's. *2700*

Catholics. Church History. Discipline, ecclesiastical. Morality. Prairie Provinces. 1900-30. *2907*

—. Colleges and Universities. St. Thomas More College. Saskatchewan (Regina, Saskatoon). 1918-21. *3042*

—. Emigration (Scottish). Glengarry Highlanders. Great Britain. Macdonnell, Alexander. Ontario. 1770's-1814. *805*

—. Langevin, Adélard. Manitoba (Winnipeg Archdiocese). 1905. *2974*

Catlin, George. Chippewa Indians. Europe. Maungwudaus (George Henry). Ontario. Theater. 1840's. *450*

Cattle disease. Nova Scotia. Ragwort weed. 1850-1910. *2299*

Cattle Raising. Alberta. Cochrane ranch. 1881-1905. *3167*

—. Alberta (Calgary). Economic Conditions. Oil Industry and Trade. 19c-20c. *3089*

—. Alberta (Cochrane). British American Ranche Company. Cochrane Ranch. Red River of the North. 1881-1905. *1010*

—. Farming. Ranching. Saskatchewan (southwestern). 1872-1974. *3072*

—. Prairie Provinces. Western States. 1880's-1900. *968*

Cauchon Block. Buildings. Cast iron fronts. Manitoba (Winnipeg). 1880-1920. *3003*

Cavalry. Frontier. Quebec (Montreal). 1837-50. *820*

Cemeteries. British Columbia (Swan Lake). Chinese. Feng Shui, concept. Geography. 1974. *3215*

—. Frontier society. Mortality. Ontario (Upper Canada, Midland District). 1783-1851. *749*

—. Jews. Saskatchewan. 1975. *3055*

Censorship See also Freedom of Speech; Freedom of the Press.

—. Films. National Film Board. Quebec. 1971. *1406*

Census See also Statistics.

—. 1852. 1861. *848*

—. Catholic Church. Clergy. 1761-90. *660*

—. Construction. Irish Canadians. Migrant labor. Quebec (Sherbrooke area). Railroads. 1851-53. *2520*

—. Documents. Literacy. Methodology. 1861. *852*

—. Economic conditions. New Brunswick. Social Conditions. 1861. *2377*

—. German Canadians. Population. 1891-1931. *2898*

—. History. Privacy. Research. 1918-77. *57*

—. Household structure. Ontario (Hamilton). 1851-71. *2759*

—. Literacy. Methodology. Ontario (Peel, Hamilton Counties). Social organization. 19c. *2822*

—. Methodology. New Brunswick (Saint John). Social organization. 1871. 1974. *2400*

—. Methodology. Population. Quebec (Quebec). 1795-1805. 1974-76. *2584*

—. Nova Scotia (Halifax). 1838. *2327*

—. Research. Urbanization. 1950's-78. *1353*

Centennial Celebrations. Great Britain. Indians. Treaty Seven. 1877-1977. *370*

Central America. Art. Buffalo. North America. Prehistory-20c. *265*

Central Place System. Ontario (Guelph area). Quantitative Methods. Urbanization. 1851-1970. *2753*

Centralization. Political stability. Quebec. Separatist movements. 1960-75. *1695*

Centre de documentation en civilisation traditionelle. French Canadian identity. Quebec. University of. Séguin, Robert-Lionel (writings). 1959-75. *494*

Centre for Urban and Community Studies. Ontario (Toronto). Rural-Urban Studies. Urban history. 1965-78. *1352*

Cereals. Agricultural production. Farmers. World War I. 1911-21. *1164*

Chaban, Teklia. Alberta (Cardiff, Edmonton). Coal Mines and Mining. Labor Unions and Organizations. Ukrainian Canadians. 1914-20's. *3164*

Chabert, Joseph. Art. Education. National Institute for Arts and Crafts. Quebec (Montreal). Teachers. Working Class. 1861-94. *1053*

Challenger (vessel). Expedition. Honeyman, David. Nova Scotia (Halifax). Oceanography. 1872-76. *2317*

Champlain, Samuel de. Astrolabe, Cobden. Discovery and Exploration. 1613. *506*

—. L'Ordre de Bon Temps. Nova Scotia. Social Organizations. 1606-07. *543*

—. L'Ordre de Bon Temps. Nova Scotia (Port Royal). Social Organizations. 1606. *542*

—. Maine. Military Camps and Forts. Monts, Sieur de. New Brunswick. St. Croix Island. 1603-05. *507*

Chapais, Thomas (and ancestors). Historians. 1640-1960. *126*

Character books. Hudson's Bay Company. Simpson, George. 1832. *2960*

Charbonneau, Hubert. Dechêne, Louise (review article). Family structure. Migration. Quebec. Vital Statistics. 1660-1713. 1974-75. *527*

Charisma. Alline, Henry. Nova Scotia. 1776-83. *732*

Charities See also Philanthropy; Public Welfare.

—. Alienation. Government. Quebec (Quebec; Lower Town). Social Problems. Working Class. 1896-1914. *2637*

—. Boys. Great Britain. Hudson's Bay Company. Schools. 18c-19c. *684*

—. Cities. Poverty. Unemployment. 1815-60. *2157*

Charles I. Colonization. France. Great Britain. Nova Scotia (Port Royal). Scotland. 1629-32. *501*

Charpentier, Alfred. Confederation of Catholic Workers of Canada. Industrial Relations. Provincial government. Quebec. 1935-46. *2609*

Charte du Français. French language. Minorities. Quebec. 1913-77. *2503*

Châteauguay (battle). Quebec. War of 1812. 1813. *763*

Chaumonot, Joseph-Marie-Pierre. Brotherhood of the Holy Family. Catholic Church. Elites. Laval, François de. Quebec (Montreal). 1663-1760. *547*

Cheda, Sherrill. Canadian Library Association Committee on the Status of Women. Feminism. Librarians. 1973-74. *1418*

Chemistry See also Pharmacy.

Chesapeake (vessel). Civil War. Confederate States of America. Nova Scotia (Bay of Fundy). 1863. *872*

Chesterton, G. K. (lectures). Intellectuals. Poets. 1921. 1930. *1184*

Chesterton, G. K. (principles). Social Organization. 1973-75. *1405*

Chickasaw Indians. Alliances. Choctaw Indians. France. Indians. South Central and Gulf States. Tonti, Henri de. 1702. *581*

Chicopee Manufacturing Company. Immigration. Irish Americans. Massachusetts (Chicopee). Mills. Nativism. 1830-75. *635*

Chicora (vessel). Archaeology (amateur). Great Lakes. Ontario (Sault Ste. Marie, St. Joseph's Island). Scuba diving. 1961-62. *585*

Chicoutimi, Petit-Séminaire de. Catholic Church. Quebec (Saguenay). Religious Education. Students. 1873-1930. *2562*

Chicoutimi, Séminaire de. Bishops. Catholic Church. Church History. Quebec (Saguenay). 1873-1973. *2542*

—. Catholic Church. Church and State. Simard, Ovide-D. (personal account). 1873-1973. *2563*

Chief Justices. See Judges; Supreme Court.

Chignecto Ship Railway. Construction. Ketchum, Henry George Clepper. Nova Scotia. 1888-91. *2353*

Children See also Birth Rate; Education; Youth.

—. Education. Fur trade. Hudson's Bay Company. Métis. 1820's-60's. *628*

—. Education. Nova Scotia (Guysborough). Welsh, Matthew. Wills. 19c. *2267*

—. Federal government. New York (Watertown). Ontario (Belleville). Political structures. Provincial government. 1977. *1423*

—. Government. Political socialization. Quebec. 1970-71. *2549*

—. Great Britain. Immigration. Ontario. Poor. Press. Rye, Miss. 1865-1925. *2879*

—. Identification, racial and cultural. Indians. 1972-73. *392*

—. Immigration. Jews. Manitoba (Winnipeg). Public schools. 1900-20. *3007*

—. Inequality (perceived). Ontario (Toronto area). Public schools. Social Classes. Values. 1977. *1345*

—. Inkster, Anne Ellen (reminiscences). Manitoba (Churchill). 1885-93. *2986*

—. Nationalism. USA. 1971-72. *1463*

—. Nova Scotia (Halifax). Orphan House. 1752-87. *2262*

—. Population. Quebec (Quebec). 1951-71. *2508*

Chile. Churches. Loans. Royal Bank of Canada. South Africa. 1976. *1951*

China. Agricultural growth. Boserup, Ester. North America. Russia. South. 18c-19c. *801*

—. Airplanes, Military (training). Fraser, Douglas. Nationalism. Saskatchewan (Saskatoon). 1919-22. *1169*

—. Anti-Confucius Campaign. Students. 1973-74. *1783*

—. Church of England. Missionary Society of the Canadian Church. Scovil, G. C. Coster (reminiscences). 1946-47. *1262*

—. Davis, Thomas Clayton (letters). Diplomacy. 1946-49. *1943*

—. Developing nations. Foreign relations. USA. USSR. 1950-75. *1824*

—. Diplomacy. Odlum, Victor Wentworth. 1943-46. *1877*

—. Diplomatic recognition. Foreign Relations. Trudeau, Pierre Elliott. 1968-73. *1807*

—. Diplomatic relations. International claims, settlement of. 1946-75. *1759*

—. Diplomatic trips. Trudeau, Pierre Elliott. 1973. *1934*

—. Foreign Relations. International Trade. USA. USSR. 1969-72. *1853*

—. Foreign relations. Wheat. 1970-77. *1817*

—. Fur Trade. North West Company. Oregon (Astoria). 1760's-1821. *785*

—. Hurford, Grace Gibberd (reminiscences). Missions and Missionaries. Teaching. World War II. 1928-45. *1122*

—. International Trade. North West Company. 1784-1821. *783*

China (Canton). Bethune, Angus. International Trade. North America. North West Company. 1812-17. *802*

China (Macao). Alaska. British Columbia. Cook, James. Fur trade. Pacific Area. 1778-79. *784*

Chinese. British Columbia. Clan origins. Home county. 1880-85. *1052*

—. British Columbia. Immigration. Japanese. Suffrage. 1935-49. *3220*

—. British Columbia (Vancouver). Law Enforcement. Provincial Government. Riots. 1887. *3247*

—. Ontario (Toronto). Racism. 1881-1912. *2838*

Chinese Canadians. Alberta (Calgary). 1886-1974. *3086*

—. British Columbia. Japanese Canadians. Military Service. World War II. 1939-45. *1242*

—. British Columbia (Swan Lake). Cemeteries. Feng Shui, concept. Geography. 1974. *3215*

Chinook jargon. British Columbia. Pacific Northwest. 1830's-1970's. *412*

Chipewyan Indians. Cree Indians. Expansionism. Fur Trade. Indian-White Relations. Northwest Territories (Mackenzie District, eastern). Prairie Provinces. 1680's-18c. *476*

Chipman, George. Editors and Editing. *Grain Growers' Guide* (periodical). Prairie Provinces. Teaching. 1903-05. *2938*

Chippewa Indians. Art. Cree Indians. Métis. Prairie Provinces. 1750's-1850's. *357*

—. Artists. Cree Indians. Indians. Legend painting. Manitoba. Ontario. 1960's-70's. *470*

—. Catholic Church. Hudson's Bay Company. Métis. Provencher, John N. (memoir). Quebec. Red River Settlement. 1812-36. *2948*

—. Catlin, George. Europe. Maungwudaus (George Henry). Ontario. Theater. 1840's. *450*

—. Cree Indians. Fishing. Indians. Lakes. Ontario, northern. 19c-1978. *341*

—. Cree Indians. Fur Trade. Saskatchewan. Thanadelthur ("Slave Woman," Chippewa Indian). 1715-17. *577*

—. Cree Indians. Health services. Ontario (Sioux Lookout Zone). 1900-73. *427*

—. Folklore. Indians. Nanabozho (mythical character). Ottawa Indians. 19c-20c. *397*

—. Grey Owl (Archie Belaney). Myths and Symbols. Ontario. 1880-1938. *372*

—. Immigration. Manitoba. Mennonites, Russian. Métis. 1872-73. *990*

—. Indians. Mississauga Indians. 1650-1975. *452*

—. Indians. Ontario (Kenora, Anicinabe Park). 1950's-74. *389*

Chloroform. Fraser, James Daniel Bain. Medicine (practice of). Nova Scotia (Pictou). Pharmacy. 1807-69. *2247*

Choctaw Indians. Alliances. Chickasaw Indians. France. Indians. South Central and Gulf States. Tonti, Henri de. 1702. *581*

Cholera. Adamson, John. Medicine (practice of). Nova Scotia (Halifax). 1834. *2219*

—. City Government. Epidemic. New Brunswick (Saint John). 1854. *2386*

—. Medicine (practice of). Quebec (Lower Canada). 1832. *770*

Choquette, Robert. Assimilation. French Canadians (review article). Joy, Richard. Maxwell, Thomas R. 18c-20c. 1970's. *218*

Christian Biography *See also* Missions and Missionaries.

—. Baptist. McMaster, Susan Moulton Fraser. Ontario (Toronto). 1819-1916. *2750*

—. Bishops. Church History. Quebec (Sherbrooke). 1868-72. *2579*

Christian, Edgar. Adlard, Harold. COSMOS (satellite). Hornby, John. Northwest Territories (Thelon River, Hornby Point). 1926-27. 1976. *3346*

—. Adlard, Harold. Dewar, Kenneth M. (reminiscences). Diaries. Hornby, John. Northwest Territories (Thelon River, Hornby Point). 1928. *3350*

Christianity *See also* Catholic Church; Missions and Missionaries; Protestantism; Theology.

—. Church and state. USA. 18c-20c. *171*

—. Cultural transmission. Maritime Provinces. Micmac Indians. Western civilization. 1970's. *344*

—. Fiction. Social gospel. 1890's. *1112*

—. Missions and Missionaries. Sex roles. Women. 1815-99. *923*

Christianization. Indian-White Relations. Micmac Indians. New Brunswick. Nova Scotia. 1803-60. *465*

Chukchi natives. Bernard, Joseph-Fidèle (diary). Firearms. Trade. USSR. 1921-22. *1166*

Church and State *See also* Religion in the Public Schools; Religious Liberty.

—. Catholic Church. Chicoutimi, Séminaire de. Simard, Ovide-D. (personal account). 1873-1973. *2563*

—. Catholic Church. Europe, Western. North America. Politics. 1870-1974. *246*

—. Catholic Church. Provincial Government. Public Charities Act (1921). Quebec. Recessions. 1921-26. *2578*

—. Catholic Church. Quebec. 18c-20c. *2699*

—. Christianity. USA. 18c-20c. *171*

—. Church of England. King's College, York (charter). Ontario (Toronto). Scotland. Strachan, John. 1815-43. *625*

—. Elections (1890). Equal Rights Association. Ontario reaction. Quebec. 1885-95. *2827*

—. Mennonite Conference of 1970 (leaders). Social issues. Students. 1917-74. *1381*

—. Political Parties. Prince Edward Island. Prince of Wales College Act (1860). School Boards. 1860-63. *2208*

Church Finance. Catholic Church. Economic Development. LaRocque, Paul. Quebec (Sherbrooke). 1893-1926. *2636*

Church history. 1976. *1461*

—. Archives. Bishops. Catholic Church. Kingston, Archdiocese of. Ontario. 1800-1966. *2847*

—. Bibliographies. 17c-20c. *92*

—. Bibliographies. Catholic Church. 17c-1973. *80*

—. Bibliographies. Catholic Church. ca 1800-1976. *91*

—. Bishops. Catholic Church. Chicoutimi, Séminaire de. Quebec (Saguenay). 1873-1973. *2542*

—. Bishops. Christian Biography. Quebec (Sherbrooke). 1868-72. *2579*

—. Catholic Church. Ontario (Kingston). St. Mary's Cathedral of the Immaculate Conception. 1843-1973. *2765*

—. Catholicism. Colonization. Quebec (Eastern Townships). Settlement. 1800-60. *704*

—. Catholics. Discipline, ecclesiastical. Morality. Prairie Provinces. 1900-30. *2907*

—. Ecumenism. United Church of Canada. 1920-76. *29*

Church Missionary Society. Church of England. Eskimos. Hudson's Bay Company. Missions and Missionaries. Northwest Territories (Baffin Island). Peck, E. J. Trade. 1894-1913. *340*

Church names, origin of. Quebec. Religion. Toponymy. 1600-1925. *2557*

Church of England. Alberta. Blackfoot Indians. Cree Indians. Missions and Missionaries. Trivett, Samuel. 1878-91. *360*

—. Alberta (Edmonton). Newton, William. 1875-1900. *983*

—. American Revolution. Bailey, Jacob. Letters. Nova Scotia. 1784. *726*

—. Bishops. Catholic Church. Liberal government. Newfoundland. 1860-62. *2187*

—. Bishops. Fulford, Francis. Quebec (Montreal). 1850-68. *874*

—. British Columbia (Kootenay). Doull, Alexander John. 1870-1937. *3194*

—. China. Missionary Society of the Canadian Church. Scovil, G. C. Coster (reminiscences). 1946-47. *1262*

—. Church and State. King's College, York (charter). Ontario (Toronto). Scotland. Strachan, John. 1815-43. *625*

—. Church Missionary Society. Eskimos. Hudson's Bay Company. Missions and Missionaries. Northwest Territories (Baffin Island). Peck, E. J. Trade. 1894-1913. *340*

—. Clergy. Diocesan Theological Institute. Frontier and Pioneer Life. Ontario (Cobourg). Strachan, John. 1840-55. *679*

—. Clergy. Feild, Edward. Great Britain. Newfoundland. 1826-44. *2190*

—. Clergy. McMurray, William. 1810-94. *665*

—. Documents. 1850-52. *873*

—. Domestic and Foreign Missionary Society. Japan. Missions and Missionaries. 1883-1902. *932*

—. Ecumenism. Symonds, Herbert. 1897-1921. *194*

—. Feild, Edward. Newfoundland. Sects, Religious. 1765-1852. *2188*

—. Hudson's Bay Company. Hunter, James. Missions and Missionaries. 1844-64. *2946*

—. Indians. McDonald, Robert. Missions and Missionaries. Northwest Territories. Yukon Territory. 1850's-1913. *3292*

—. Indians. Missions and Missionaries. Ontario (Algoma, Huron). Wilson, Edward F. 1868-93. *432*

—. Land endowment. Ontario (Upper Canada). Rolph, John. Strachan, John. Toronto, University of. 1820-70. *809*

—. Letters. Ontario (Ottawa). Politics. Thompson, Annie Affleck. Thompson, John S. D. 1867-94. *1075*

—. Loyalists. Nova Scotia. Society for the Propagation of the Gospel. 1783. *751*

—. Medley, John (letters). New Brunswick (Fredericton). Oxford Movement. Pusey, Edward Bouverie. ca 1840-44. *2389*

—. Missions and Missionaries. Nova Scotia (Halifax). St. Paul's Church. Society for the Propagation of the Gospel. Tutty, William. 1749-52. *2359*

—. Missions and Missionaries. Ontario (Moosonee). Vincent, Thomas. 1835-1910. *3296*

—. Missions and Missionaries. Quebec (Three Rivers). Wood, Samuel. 1822-68. *658*

—. Morris, William. Ontario (Kingston). Presbyterians. Queen's College. Scots. 1836-42. *2831*

—. Ontario (Toronto). Strachan, John. 1802-67. *2834*

—. Religion. Tractarians. 1840-68. *857*

Church Schools *See also* Religious Education.

—. Catholic Church. Manitoba. McCarthy, D'Alton. Provincial legislatures. 1870-90. *931*

—. East Indians. Missions and Missionaries. Presbyterian Church. Trinidad and Tobago. 1868-1912. *2319*

Churches. Arctic. Fur Trade. Missions and Missionaries. 20c. *3281*

—. Chile. Loans. Royal Bank of Canada. South Africa. 1976. *1951*

Churchill River. Ecology. Hydroelectric development. Manitoba, northern. 1966-70's. *2972*

Cistercians. Catholic Church. Mistassini, monastery of. Quebec. Trappists. 1900-03. *2482*
Cities *See also* headings beginning with the word city and the word urban; names of cities and towns by state; Housing; Metropolitan Areas; Neighborhoods; Rural-Urban Studies; Sociology; Suburbs; Urban Renewal; Urbanization.
—. 19c. *223*
—. Alberta. Local Government. Political Recruitment. 1971. *3129*
—. Alberta. Political protest. Social Conditions. 1918-39. *3110*
—. Automobiles. Mass transit. North America. Travel. 1960-75. *2758*
—. British Columbia. Indians (reservations). Social conditions. 1971. *458*
—. Bromley, Walter. Micmac Indians. Nova Scotia. Poor. Self-help. 1813-25. *258*
—. Charities. Poverty. Unemployment. 1815-60. *2157*
—. Conservative Party. Ontario, southern. Voting and Voting Behavior. 1908-19. *2844*
—. Demography. Economic diversity. 1961-73. *1434*
—. Employment. Ethnic Groups. Property ownership. Social Classes. 19c. *90*
—. Foreign Investments. Real Estate. USA. 1960's-75. *1766*
—. France. International trade. 1730-60. *572*
—. Housing costs. Land banks. ca 1970-81. *1524*
—. Information Storage and Retrieval Systems. Ontario. Public Records. 1974. *2859*
—. Population. Quebec (Montreal). 18c. *510*
—. Social scientists. -1974. *68*
—. USA. Voting and Voting Behavior. 1952-68. *1649*
Citizen participation. Bureaucracies. Great Britain. Political Reform. USA. 1973. *1667*
Citizenship *See also* Patriotism; Suffrage.
—. Attitudes. Japanese. USA. World War II. 1941-58. *1261*
—. Great Britain. Riel, Louis. Treason. USA. 1885. *951*
City councillors. Alberta (Edmonton). Decisionmaking. Municipal government. Voting and Voting Behavior. 1966-72. *3134*
City Government *See also* Cities; City Politics; Public Administration.
—. Alberta (Calgary). Social problems. 1894-96. *3122*
—. Alberta (Edmonton). Bridges. Calgary and Edmonton Railway. Railroads. 1910-13. *3112*
—. Archives. Ontario (Ottawa). 19c-1976. *2886*
—. Bengough, John Wilson. *Grip* (periodical). Ontario (Toronto). Political Reform. Protestantism. 1873-1910. *2807*
—. Bill of Incorporation (1873). Manitoba (Winnipeg). Taxation. 1873. *2984*
—. Cholera. Epidemic. New Brunswick (Saint John). 1854. *2386*
—. Compensation, municipal. Ontario (Toronto). 1858-70. *2798*
—. Economic growth. Public Administration. Quebec (Montreal). Social Conditions. Urbanization. 1850-1914. *2441*
—. Libraries. Metropolitan Areas. 1950-71. *1361*
—. Logan, Alexander. Manitoba (Winnipeg). 1870's-80's. *2966*
—. Manitoba (Winnipeg). 1972-73. *2980*
—. Manitoba (Winnipeg). Political Corruption. Public Administration. Urbanization. 1884-85. *3013*
—. Municipal limits. Quebec (Quebec). 1831-1972. *2426*
—. Newfoundland (St. John's). Political Reform. 1888-92. *2180*
—. Ontario (Hamilton). Pressure groups. Public Utilities. 1900-25. *2817*
—. Ontario (Toronto). Political Corruption. Pressure Groups. Reform. 1890-1900. *2884*
—. Ontario (Toronto). Progressivism. Wickett, Samuel Morley. 1900-15. *2885*
—. Political Reform. 1890-1920. *158*
—. Political Reform. 1875-1976. *243*
—. Public housing. Quebec (Hull). 1968-74. *2456*
City Life. Immigration. Jews, Russian. Manitoba (Winnipeg). 1874-82. *2965*
City Planning *See also* Housing; Regional Planning; Social Surveys; Urban Renewal.
—. Architecture. Mutual Advisory Committee. Ontario (London). Politics. Preservation. 1970-77. *2727*
—. Bibliographies. Research. 1890-1939. *237*

—. Economic growth. Real estate. Saskatchewan (Saskatoon). Yorath, J. C. 1909-13. *3061*
—. Environment. Housing. Suburbs. 1893-1930. *236*
—. Geographical studies. Settlement. USA. 19c-20c. *127*
—. Hudson's Bay Company. Manitoba (Selkirk). 1869-79. *1023*
—. Ontario (Toronto). 1970's. *2804*
City Politics *See also* City Government; Minorities in Politics.
—. Manitoba (Winnipeg). Penner, Jacob. Webb, Ralph. 1919-34. *2993*
Civil Defense. British Columbia. Emergencies. Planning. Provincial Government. 1951-76. *3233*
Civil Liberty. *See* Civil Rights.
Civil Rights *See also* Freedom of Speech; Freedom of the Press; Human Rights; Religious Liberty.
—. Bill of Rights (Canada, 1958). Supreme Court, Canada. 1960-75. *2089*
—. Constitutional reform. Ethnic groups. 1972. *2121*
—. Internal security. Royal Canadian Mounted Police. 1970's. *1708*
—. Law. Mexico. USA. Violence. 18c-1974. *52*
Civil Service *See also* Federal Government; Public Administration; Public Employees.
—. Arbitration, Industrial. Legislation. 1967. *1497*
—. British Columbia. Gaggin, John Boles. 1859-66. *3254*
—. Bureaucracies. English Canadians. French Canadians. 1944-75. *1706*
—. Business. Middle Classes. Quebec. Technocracy. 1939-75. *2451*
—. Committee of Imperial Defence. Defense policy. Great Britain. War Office. 1896-1914. *1092*
—. Quebec. USA. Wages. 1970's. *2599*
Civil Service Commission. Organization and Methods Development. 1946-76. *1660*
Civil War *See also* battles and campaigns by name; Confederate Army; Confederate States of America.
—. Anti-Canadianism. New York City. Press. 1861-65. *864*
—. Athens (battle). Missouri. 1861. *834*
—. Atlantic Coast. Blockade-running. Letters. Nova Scotia. Wade, Norman. 1859-62. *841*
—. Blockades. Letters. Nova Scotia. Wade, Norman. 1861-62. *889*
—. British Columbia (Quatsino Sound). Outlaws. Quantrill, William Clarke. 1861-1907. *3226*
—. *Chesapeake* (vessel). Confederate States of America. Nova Scotia (Bay of Fundy). 1863. *872*
—. Fenians (raid). Foreign Relations. St. Albans Raid. USA. 1861-66. *887*
—. Great Britain. Military. Williams, William Fenwick. 1859-67. *881*
—. Letters. Navies. Nova Scotia. Wade, Norman. 1859-62. *842*
Civil War (antecedents). Abolition Movement. Brown, John. Harpers Ferry (raid, 1859). Sanborn, Franklin Benjamin. 1854-60. *875*
"Civility" (measured). Gouzenko, Igor. Political culture. USA. 1953-54. *1941*
Clan origins. British Columbia. Chinese, overseas. Home county. 1880-85. *1052*
Clan-na-Gael. Bombings. Dillon, Luke. Irish Americans. Ontario (Thorold). Welland Canal. 1900-14. *1083*
Clark, Arthur Hill (obituary). Literature. 1911-75. *1440*
Clark, Septimus Alfred. Frontier and Pioneer Life. Great Britain. Letters. Radcliffe, Mary. Saskatchewan (Regina). 1884-1909. *967*
Class structure. Ontario (Toronto). Public schools. 1851. 1964-74. *1445*
Class struggle. Equality. French-speaking community. Intellectuals. Nationalism. Quebec. 1960's-70's. *2677*
—. Quebec. Socialists. 1970's. *2670*
Clay belt. Colonization. Ontario. Quebec. 1900-30. *274*
Clays, sensitive. Geology. Ontario (Ottawa). Soil Conservation. 1648-1971. *276*
Clemens, Samuel Langhorne. *See* Twain, Mark.
Clergy *See also* specific denominations by name.
—. Books. Catholic Church. France. French Canadians. 1850-1914. *2564*
—. Books. Catholic Church. *Index* (legitimacy of). 1862. *844*
—. Calonne, Abbot de (letters). Catholic Church. Public schools. 1819-20. *706*
—. Catholic Church. 1790's-1830's. *664*

—. Catholic Church. Census. 1761-90. *660*
—. Catholic Church. Craig, James Henry. French Canadian nationalism. Government repression. Quebec (Lower Canada). 1810. *711*
—. Church of England. Diocesan Theological Institute. Frontier and Pioneer Life. Ontario (Cobourg). Strachan, John. 1840-55. *679*
—. Church of England. Feild, Edward. Great Britain. Newfoundland. 1826-44. *2190*
—. Church of England. McMurray, William. 1810-94. *665*
—. New France. Trade. 1627-1760. *563*
—. Nova Scotia (Springhill). Presbyterian Church. 1874-1925. *2234*
—. Quebec (Nicolet, Trois-Rivières dioceses). 1852-85. *2580*
Cleveland, Xenophon. Artists. Massachusetts. New Brunswick. Stencils. 1839-99. *2379*
Climate *See also* Weather.
—. Agricultural Production. Energy shortages. Food supply. Urbanization. 1956-74. *1511*
—. Cultural development. Economic development. Ocean currents. 1925-76. *3278*
—. Environment. Indians. North America. Settlement. Prehistory. 1956-78. *309*
—. Highway construction. Physical Geography. Roads. 1949-73. *3297*
—. Ice caps. Scientific Experiments and Research. 1954-77. *271*
Clothing industries. Locational clustering. Ontario (Toronto). Publishers and Publishing. Quebec (Montreal). 1949-67. *1611*
Cloud-seeding program. Alberta. Hail damage. Storms. 1955-74. *3136*
Clymer, John. Artists. North America. West. 1960's-70's. *1460*
Coal *See also* Mineral Resources.
—. Energy. 1892-1978. *170*
—. Environmental effects. Saskatchewan (Estevan region). Strip mining. 1850's-1975. *3071*
Coal explorations. Boundary Waters Treaty. British Columbia (Cabin Creek). Ecology. Montana. USA. 1909. 1973-75. *2035*
Coal industry. British Empire Steel Corporation. Economic Development. Nova Scotia (Cape Breton Island). 1910's-20's. *1175*
Coal Mines and Mining. Alberta. British Columbia. Depressions. Pass Strike of 1932. 1920's-30's. *1209*
—. Alberta (Cardiff, Edmonton). Chaban, Teklia. Labor Unions and Organizations. Ukrainian Canadians. 1914-20's. *3164*
—. Alberta (Lethbridge). Galt, Alexander. 1885-1905. *958*
—. Alberta (Lethbridge). Galt, Alexander. Government. Settlement. 1879-93. *960*
—. Alberta (Lundbreck). Daily Life. Koester, Mavis Addie (reminiscences). 1905-08. *3124*
—. Albion mines. Nova Scotia (Pictou County). 1767-1881. *2226*
—. Bakewell, Robert. Howe, Joseph. Nova Scotia (Pictou County; Stellarton). 1798-1881. *2227*
—. Disasters. Nova Scotia (Pictou). 1832-1957. *2231*
—. Economic Development. Europeans. Immigrants. Kansas. 1870-1940. *1062*
—. Labor Unions and Organizations. One Big Union. Saskatchewan. 1907-45. *3056*
Coalition government. British Columbia. Conservative Party. Cooperative Commonwealth Federation. 1941-52. *3173*
Coast defenses. Artillery. British Columbia. World War II. 1862-1941. *1232*
—. British Columbia (Prince Rupert). Diaries. Thistle, R. World War II. 1941-42. *1243*
Coasting trade. Economic Growth. Employment. Natural Resources. 1931-73. *1579*
Cobb, Sylvanus. Fundy, Bay of. Nova Scotia. Ships. Trade. *York* (vessel). 1755. *2163*
Cobbett, William. Military Service. New Brunswick. 1785-91. *629*
Cobequid (vessel). Nova Scotia (Halifax). Rescue operations. Shipwrecks. 1914. *2322*
Cocagne Academy. New Brunswick. Theal, George McCall (recollections). 1840-94. *2405*
Cochran, William. Education. Enlightenment. Nova Scotia. 1789. *745*
Cochrane ranch. Alberta. Cattle Raising. 1881-1905. *3167*
—. Alberta (Cochrane). British American Ranche Company. Cattle Raising. Red River of the North. 1881-1905. *1010*
Cod. Fisheries. Netherlands. Newfoundland. 1589-1670. *570*
CODOC (system). Documents. Government. Information Storage and Retrieval Systems. Libraries. USA. 1960's-70's. *177*
Cold War *See also* Detente.

—. Diplomacy. USSR. 1946-47. *1885*
—. Foreign Relations. Pearson, Lester B. 1948-57. *1821*
Coldwell, Major J. Farmer Labor party. Political Leadership. Progressivism. Social Democracy. 1907-32. *2962*
Colebrook, William. Indians. New Brunswick. Perley, Moses H. 1840's. *2408*
Collective Bargaining *See also* Arbitration, Industrial; Labor Unions and Organizations; Strikes.
—. Anti-Inflation Board. Labor Unions and Organizations. Wages. 1975. *1630*
—. Atlantic Provinces. Fisheries. Legislation. Nova Scotia. 1975. *2351*
—. Crown Employees Collective Bargaining Act. Labor. Law. Ontario. 1970-74. *2745*
—. Federal Government. Public Employees. 1940's-60's. *1500*
—. Industrial Relations. 1975. *1520*
—. Industrial relations. Labor Unions and Organizations (international). Multinational corporations. 1974. *1763*
—. *McGavin Toastmaster Limited* v. *Ainscough et al.* (Canada, 1975). Strikes. Supreme Court. 1975-77. *1529*
—. Ontario (Toronto). Organizational Theory. Printing. 19c. *2892*
—. Prince Edward Island. Public Employees. Teachers. 1970-74. *2204*
—. Professionals. 1940's-70's. *1496*
—. Public Employees. 1920-73. *118*
—. Public employees. Quebec. 1964-72. *2602*
—. Public Employees. Quebec. 1966-75. *2632*
—. Public Employees. Wages. 1960-70's. *1538*
—. Public sector. 1964-73. *1628*
Colleges and Universities *See also* names of individual institutions; Dissertations; Higher Education; Students.
—. Academic responsibility. Canadian studies. Social responsibility. 1970's. *1360*
—. Alberta (Edmonton). Catholic Church. MacDonald, John Roderick. St. Joseph's College (Alberta). 1922-23. *3140*
—. Asia. Protestant Churches. USA. 1850-1971. *5*
—. Bourget, Ignace. Catholic Church. Laval University. Quebec (Quebec). 1840's-50's. *2523*
—. Canadian Institute of International Affairs. External Affairs Department. Foreign Policy. Soward, F. H. (account). 1926-66. *217*
—. Catholics. St. Thomas More College. Saskatchewan (Regina, Saskatoon). 1918-21. *3042*
—. Collegiate Institute. Depressions. Lansdowne College. Manitoba (Portage la Prairie). 1882-93. *3018*
—. Commission on Post-Secondary Education (report). 1967-72. *2860*
—. Curricula. Economic returns. Labor market. 1961-72. *1582*
—. Dalhousie University. Mackenzie, Arthur Stanley. Nova Scotia. Stanley, Carleton. 1911-45. *2282*
—. Employment. Ontario. Social Status. 1960-71. *2787*
—. Federal Aid to Education. 1966-70. *1471*
—. Federal Aid to Education. Massey Commission. National Conference of Canadian Universities. 1951-66. *1476*
—. French Canadians. Historiography. Quebec. 1947-72. *2449*
—. French Canadians. Quebec. Sociology. 1960-74. *2499*
—. Graduate students. History. 1966-75. *1281*
—. Graduates. Occupational attainment. Ontario. Social mobility. Women. 1960-75. *2821*
—. Historiography. Nationalism. 1810-1967. *165*
—. International Relations, teaching of. USA. 1945-73. *2073*
—. Labor education. 1960's-1970's. *1627*
—. Labor Unions and Organizations. Professors. Quebec. 1972-74. *2417*
—. Libraries. 1970's. *1347*
—. Libraries. Nordic area studies. 1970-73. *1343*
—. Mate selection preferences. Sex status. Students. USA. 1970's. *1482*
—. North America. Publishers and Publishing. Scholarship. 1920's-70's. *206*
—. Politics. Public opinion. Students. 1974. *1432*
—. Social organization. Sociology (teaching of). 1940-70. *1398*
—. Social Problems. 1972. *1370*
—. Sociology. 1972. *1363*

—. Teaching. USA. 1973. *2009*
Collegiate Institute. Colleges and Universities. Depressions. Lansdowne College. Manitoba (Portage la Prairie). 1882-93. *3018*
Collins Bay Penitentiary. Libraries. Ontario (Kingston). Prisons. Resocialization. 1963-73. *2851*
Collins, Charles John. Art. British Columbia. 1900-30. *3259*
Colombo Plan. Foreign aid policy. International Development Agency. 1950-69. *1736*
Colonial Government *See also* Imperialism.
—. Acadians. Great Britain. Land tenure. Nova Scotia. Oath of allegiance. 11c-1755. *594*
—. Adult education. Nova Scotia. ca 1820-35. *2289*
—. Attitudes. Negroes. 1830-65. *668*
—. British Columbia. Granville, George, 2d earl (letter). Great Britain. Musgrave, Anthony. Seymour, Frederick (death). 1869. *3204*
—. British North America. Frontier. Indian Affairs Department. 1755-1830. *623*
—. British North America. Pepperrell, William. ca 1715-59. *601*
—. France. Great Britain. New England. Nova Scotia (Canso, Cape Breton). 1710-21. *492*
—. France. Louisiana Territory. Mississippi River Valley. New France. 1683-1762. *584*
—. Frégault, Guy. Historiography. New France. Rioux, Marcel. 1615-1763. 1957-60's. *491*
—. Great Britain. Political oppression. Quebec (Lower Canada). 1831. *697*
Colonial policy. Emigrant guides. Great Britain. Land grants (proposed). Ontario (Peterborough). Traill, Catherine Parr. 19c. *869*
Colonial policy (review article). Eccles, William J. France. New France. Seignelay, Marquis de. ca 1663-1701. 1962-64. *499*
Colonial Stock Act (1900). Great Britain. Imperialism. Laurier, Wilfrid. 1890's-1900. *1095*
Colonialism *See also* Imperialism.
—. Cultural change. Fur trade. Indians. North America. Prehistory-1900. *286*
—. France. Immigration. Louisiana. 1718-21. *578*
—. French Canadians. Great Britain. Social Classes. 18c. *707*
Colonies. American Revolution. France. Heraldry. Knights of Malta. 1600's-1976. *172*
—. France. Great Britain. Historiography. Italy. North America. 1663-1763. *598*
Colonization *See also* Settlement.
—. American Revolution. Loyalists. New Brunswick. Saunders, John. Virginia. 1774-1834. *740*
—. Arctic. Eskimos. Social Change. 1930-60. *317*
—. British Columbia (Vancouver Island). Grant, Walter C. (letters). 1851. *3206*
—. Calvert, George (1st Lord Baltimore). Catholic Church. Newfoundland (Avalon Peninsula). Religious Liberty. 1620's. *551*
—. Calvert, George (1st Lord Baltimore). Great Britain. Newfoundland (Avalon Peninsula). 1609-32. *2182*
—. Catholicism. Church History. Quebec (Eastern Townships). Settlement. 1800-60. *704*
—. Charles I. France. Great Britain. Nova Scotia (Port Royal). Scotland. 1629-32. *501*
—. Commerce. Ships. 19c. *144*
—. Cornwallis, Edward. Nova Scotia (Halifax area). 1749-52. *2217*
—. Defoe, Daniel. Hudson's Bay Company. Publicity. Rupert's Land. Sergeant, Henry. 1680's. *502*
—. France. Great Britain. North America. 1670's-1760. *512*
—. Frobisher, Martin. Great Britain. Hall, Charles Francis. Northwest Territories (Baffin Island). Pottery. 1578. 1862-1974. *513*
—. Great Britain. Indian Affairs Department. Indians. USA. 1755-1830. 1800H. *624*
—. Great Clay Belt. Ontario. Quebec. 1900-30. *274*
—. Industrialization. Quebec (Herbertville). 1844-1900. *2657*
—. Nova Scotia (Sable Island). Rescue stations. Shipwrecks. 1759-1801. *2235*
—. Pearson, William (reminiscences). Real Estate. Saskatchewan. 1903-13. *1015*
Colonization companies. Economic growth. Railroads. Saskatchewan (Yorkton). 1882-1905. *1002*
Colonization literature. Ontario (Great Clay Belt). Settlement. 1900-31. *2848*
Colorado *See also* Western States.

—. Daily Life. Frontier and Pioneer Life. Nebraska. Ouren, Hogan (reminiscences). 1861-66. *851*
Columbia Rediviva (vessel). British Columbia (Vancouver Island). Fourth of July. Kendrick, John. Nootka Sound controversy. 1789. *647*
Columbia River Treaty. Foreign policy. Neuberger, Richard. USA. 1955-61. *2071*
Columbia (vessel). British Columbia (Vancouver Island, Nootka Sound). Discovery and Exploration. Fur trade. Ingraham, Joseph (travel account). 1774-89. *655*
Comer, George. Douglas, W. O. (reminiscences). *Finback* (whaler). Northwest Territories (Chesterfield Inlet). Shipwrecks. 1919. *3351*
Commerce *See also* Banking; Business; International Trade; Monopolies; Prices; Statistics; Stocks and Bonds; Tariff; Trade; Trade Routes; Transportation.
—. Colonization. Ships. 19c. *144*
—. France. Fur trade. Great Britain. Middle classes. Quebec (Montreal). 1750-92. *702*
—. Hudson's Bay Company. 1683-1852. *663*
—. Immigration. Italians. USA. 1870-1977. *83*
—. International Trade. Quebec (Lower Canada). Social Classes. 1792-1812. *796*
Commerce Department. Foreign policy. State Department. USA. 1927-41. *1124*
Commercial crisis. Buchanan, Isaac. Buchanan, Peter. Grain trade. 1840's. *790*
Commission on Industrial Accidents. Industry. Provincial Government. Quebec. Workmen's Compensation. 1890-1978. *2623*
Commission on International Development. Pearson, Lester B. 1968-69. *1806*
Commission on Post-Secondary Education (report). Colleges and Universities. 1967-72. *2860*
Commissioners, territorial. Territorial government. Yukon Territory. 1897-1954. *3327*
Committee of Imperial Defence. Civil service. Defense policy. Great Britain. War Office. 1896-1914. *1092*
Committee on the Challenges of Modern Society. Environmentalism. Foreign Policy. NATO. USA. 1969-77. *1838*
Commodities. Economic Policy. International Organizations. Natural Resources. USA. 1974-76. *1945*
Common Market. *See* European Economic Community.
Communalism *See also* Communes.
—. Dukhobors. Saskatchewan. 1904. *1001*
Communes *See also* names of individual communes; Counter Culture; Utopias.
—. Hutterites. USA. 1870's-1970. *987*
Communications *See also* Language; Mass Media; Newspapers.
—. Anik Satellite. Northwest Territories. Satellites. 1972. *3287*
—. Bell, Alexander Graham. Field, Cyrus. Fleming, Sandford. Gisborne, F. N. Nova Scotia. 1749-1964. *2260*
—. Bill C-256. Businessmen. Federal Regulation. Manitoba (Winnipeg). Public policy. 1971-72. *2971*
—. Ethnic groups. Geographic Space. Great Britain. Regionalism. 1976. *2139*
—. Frontier and Pioneer Life. Hutterites. West. 1874-1977. *1022*
—. Nova Scotia. Prehistory-1977. *2261*
—. Quebec. St. Lawrence Seaway. 16c-20c. *2582*
Communications (international, theory of). Hecksher-Ohlin theory. Ontario. Quebec. 1974. *2148*
Communications (Transcontinental). Railroads. Telegraph. Watkin, Edward. 1860-65. *884*
Communism *See also* Anti-Communist Movements; Leftism; Maoism; Marxism; Socialism; Trotskyism.
—. Congress. Espionage. Norman, E. Herbert. USA. 1945-57. *2070*
—. Czechoslovakia. Jesuits. Refugees. Religious communities, dissolution of. 1950. *1416*
—. Europe, Eastern. Historiography. Public administration. USA. USSR. ca 1850-1975. *1316*
Communist Countries *See also* Western Nations.
Communist Parties and Movements *See also* specific parties by country.
—. *Action Catholique* (newspaper). Catholic Church. Nazism. Quebec. 1917-39. *1411*
Communist Party. Bennett, Richard Bedford. Conservative Party. 1930-35. *1207*
—. Canadian Labour Congress. Labor. 1974. *1575*

—. Cooperative Commonwealth Federation. Elections (provincial). Saskatchewan. 1930's. 3066
—. Elections. 1972-73. 1677
—. Evans, Arthur. Labor. 1930's. 2945
—. Germany (Berlin). Olympic Games. People's Olympic Games. Spain (Barcelona). 1936. 1202
—. Intellectuals. 1971-73. 1658
Communist Party (21st convention). Elections, federal. 1972-73. 1676
Communists. Canadian Seamen's Union. Syndicalism. 1936-49. 1197
—. New Democratic Party. 1961-73. 1719
Community involvement. Libraries. Public Schools. 1973. 1396
Community organizations. Alberta (Coaldale). Germans, Russian. Mennonites. Social Change. 1920-76. 3145
Community services. British Columbia (Kitsilano). Mental health. Politics. Psychiatry. 1973-74. 3237
Company satisfaction and commitment. Blue-collar workers. Labor. 1970. 1503
Compensation, municipal. City Government. Ontario (Toronto). 1858-70. 2798
Competition. Federal Regulation. Industry. 1970's. 1597
Competitiveness. Corporations. Productivity. Wages. 1970-77. 1622
Conciliation Act (1900; antecedents). British Columbia. Industrial relations. Labour, Department of. 1880's-1900. 3175
Concordia College. Alberta (Edmonton, Mellowdale). Lutheran Church. Schwermann, Albert H. (reminiscences). USA. 1891-1976. 3147
Conestoga wagons. Automobiles. Driving. Social Customs. USA. 1755-20c. 174
Confederate Army See also Confederate States of America.
—. Kennedy, Robert C. New York City. Saboteurs. 1861-65. 843
—. St. Albans (raid). Vermont. Young, Bennett H. 1864. 868
Confederate States of America See also names of individual states; Confederate Army.
—. Chesapeake (vessel). Civil War. Nova Scotia (Bay of Fundy). 1863. 872
Confederation See also Political Integration.
—. Anglin, Timothy Warren. Catholic Church. Fenians. New Brunswick. 1866. 890
—. Annexation. Newfoundland. Outports. Poverty. Social Customs. 1920-48. 2200
—. British Empire. Le Canadien (newspaper). Parent, Étienne. 1831-52. 830
—. Creighton, D. G. English Canadians. French Canadians. Heintzman, Ralph. Minorities in Politics. 1850's-90's. 922
—. Derby, 15th Earl of. Great Britain. Head, Edmund Walker. Letters. Political Attitudes. 1858. 894
—. Doyle, Hastings. Federal government. Local government. Nova Scotia. 1867-68. 895
—. Federalism. Quebec. 19c-20c. 2105
—. French Canadians. Ontario. Provincial Government. Quebec. 1867-1937. 155
—. Howe, Joseph. Nova Scotia. 1832-69. 892
Confederation, Fathers of. Biculturalism. Diversity, doctrine of. Nationalism. 1860's-1970's. 154
Confederation of Catholic Workers of Canada. Charpentier, Alfred. Industrial Relations. Provincial government. Quebec. 1935-46. 2609
Confederation of National Trade Unions. Labor Unions and Organizations (leaders). 1966-75. 1562
Conference of Historic Peace Churches. Mennonites. World War II. ca 1914-45. 1235
Conference on Equal Opportunity and Treatment for Women Workers. Canadian Labour Congress. Employment. Equal opportunity. Women. 1978. 1558
Conference on Security and Cooperation in Europe. Europe. International Security. 1950-73. 1794
—. Europe. USA. 1973-74. 1840
Conference on the Historical Urbanization of North America. North America. Urban history. 1973. 117
Conflict and Conflict Resolution. Federal Government. Labor Disputes. Public Employees. 1967-76. 1718
—. Institutions. Quebec. Regional autonomy. Separatist movements. South. 19c-1970. 2101
—. Foreign Relations. USA. 1920's-70's. 2029

Congregation of Notre Dame (Sisters). Catholic Church. Ontario (Kingston). Religious education. Women. 1841-48. 2737
Congress See also House of Representatives.
—. American Revolution. Hazen, Moses. Military. 1776-1803. 734
—. Brown, George. Diplomacy. Reciprocity treaty (proposed). USA. 1870-80. 1071
—. Communism. Espionage. Norman, E. Herbert. USA. 1945-57. 2070
—. Foreign relations. USA. 1950's-73. 1974
—. Jackson, John George. Nationalism. Republicanism. Virginia. War of 1812. 1813-17. 754
Conscription, Military See also Military Recruitment.
—. British Columbia. Pearkes, G. R. World War II. 1943-44. 3248
—. Elections. King, William Lyon Mackenzie. Ligue pour la Défense du Canada. Quebec. World War II. 1942-44. 1226
Conservation movements. Belaney, Archibald S. (Grey Owl). Great Britain. 1906-38. 1140
—. Federal Regulation. Lumber industry. Ontario (Ottawa). "Robber Barons.". 1873-1914. 2774
Conservation of Natural Resources See also types of resource conservation, e.g. Soil Conservation, Water Conservation, Wildlife Conservation, etc.; Ecology; Environment; Forests and Forestry; Nature Conservation.
—. Foreign Relations. Maritime Law. Navigation. USA. 1975. 2052
—. International regulation. North America. Pollution. Water quality. 1960's-74. 1982
—. Nova Scotia. Smith, Titus. Surveying. 1801. 2328
Conservatism. 1850-1970. 32
—. Attitude scale. USA. 1966-77. 1721
—. Cameron, John Hillyard. Ontario (Canada West). Political Leadership. 1854-56. 855
—. France. French Canadians. Groulx, Lionel. Maurras, Charles. Nationalism. 1910-40. 1141
—. Hartz, Louis. Liberalism. Politics. Socialism. USA. 1955-78. 1668
—. LeSage, Simeon. Nationalism. Quebec. Riel, Louis. 1867-1909. 2717
—. Liberalism. Mennonites. Ontario (Waterloo County). 1977. 2767
—. Progressivism. Saskatchewan. 1920's. 3039
Conservative Party. Bennett, Richard Bedford. Communist Party. 1930-35. 1207
—. British Columbia. Coalition government. Cooperative Commonwealth Federation. 1941-52. 3173
—. Cities. Ontario, southern. Voting and Voting Behavior. 1908-19. 2844
—. Diefenbaker, John. Political Parties. 1956-67. 1672
—. Drew, George. Ontario (Guelph). Political Campaigns. 1890-1925. 2736
—. Elections. Liberal Party. New Democratic Party. 1972. 1675
—. Liberal Party. Manitoba. New Democratic Party. Voting and Voting Behavior. 1953-73. 3020
—. Liberal Party. Newfoundland. Politics. 1908-72. 2195
Constituency services. Political parties. Provincial legislatures. 1972. 1647
Constitutional Amendments See also specific amendments, e.g. Constitutional Amendment (14th).
—. Apportionment. 1971. 2108
—. British North America Act (1867). Great Britain. Parliaments. Trudeau, Pierre Elliott. 1867-1970's. 1249
Constitutional conferences. Australia. Federalism. 1965-74. 2092
Constitutional History See also Democracy; Government; Political Science.
—. Great Britain. Quebec. 1791-1814. 2694
Constitutional Law See also Citizenship; Civil Rights; Democracy; Federal Government; Legislation; Political Science; Referendum; Suffrage.
—. Federalism. Political Reform. 1968-77. 2118
—. Licensing procedures. Provinces. States. USA. 1970's. 2063
Constitutional reform. Civil Rights. Ethnic groups. 1972. 2121
Constitutions. British influences. Legal systems. USA. 18c-20c. 124
—. Economic Conditions. Quebec. Separatist Movements. 1973. 2115
—. Economic Regulations. Federal government. Provincial Government. 1856-1975. 60

—. Ethnic groups. Joint Committee of the Canadian Senate and House of Commons. Language, official. 1970's. 1947
—. Federal Government. Provincial Government. Quebec. Separatist Movements. 1968-76. 2117
—. Judicial Administration. USA. 1970's. 1633
—. Macdonald, John A. 1867. 893
—. Nationalism. Supreme Court. USA. 1875-1973. 238
—. Parliamentary government. Quebec (Lower Canada). 1791. 710
Construction See also Architecture; Engineering.
—. Alberta. Housing. Settlement. Sod. Williams, Wesley. 1909. 1004
—. Artisans. Labor Unions and Organizations. Ontario (Toronto). Politics. 1896-1914. 1103
—. Census. Irish Canadians. Migrant labor. Quebec (Sherbrooke area). Railroads. 1851-53. 2520
—. Chignecto Ship Railway (proposed). Ketchum, Henry George Clepper. Nova Scotia. 1888-91. 2353
—. Contracts. Housing. Population. Quebec (Quebec). 1810-20. 2596
—. Farms. Fence patterns. 17c-19c. 182
—. France. Lime preparation. Louisbourg, Fortress of. Military Camps and Forts. Nova Scotia. 1725-58. 615
Construction crews. Canadian Pacific Railway. Manitoba (Virden). McLeod, Finlay J. C. (reminiscences). Presbyterian Church. 1881-82. 1005
Construction industry. Accreditation. Labor legislation. 1973. 1603
—. Labor. Office de la construction du Québec. Quebec. 1960's-70's. 2647
Construction Industry Labour Relations Act. Labor relations. Quebec. 1973. 2631
Construction Labour Relations Association of British Columbia. Industrial Relations. 1960's-70's. 1604
Consular Service. 1977. 1750
Consulates. Diplomacy. USA. 1833-1977. 226
—. Economic cooperation. Foreign relations. USA. 1941-70's. 2033
Consumers. Attitudes. Public housing projects. 1974. 1587
—. Middle classes. Newspapers. Ombudsmen. 1970's. 1299
—. Negroes. 1970's. 1556
—. Ontario (Toronto). Population. Shopping centers. 1974. 2835
Consumers Cooperative Refineries Ltd. Co-op. Oil, Chemical, and Atomic Workers International Union. Saskatchewan. 1934-73. 3074
Containerization. Employment. International Longshoremen's and Warehousemen's Union. Labor Disputes. 1973. 1593
—. Nova Scotia (Halifax). Ports. 1971-73. 2296
—. Ports. Shipping. 1970's. 2072
Containers. Birchbark. Indians. Northeastern or North Atlantic States. Prehistory-1978. 471
Contracts. Construction. Housing. Population. Quebec (Quebec). 1810-20. 2596
—. McDonald, Alexander N. Nova Scotia (Sherbrooke). Shipbuilding. Sutherland, Peter. 1873-74. 2265
Conventions, International. See Treaties.
Convict transportation. Great Britain. Ireland. Newfoundland. 1789. 2192
Cook, James. Alaska. Anián, strait of. British Columbia. Discovery and Exploration. Northwest Passage. Voyages. 1778. 675
—. Alaska. British Columbia. China (Macao). Fur trade. Pacific Area. 1778-79. 784
—. British Columbia (Vancouver Island). Discovery and Exploration. Great Britain. Nootka Sound controversy. Spain. 1778-94. 695
—. Fisheries. Great Britain. Newfoundland. 1763-67. 2203
Cooke, Willie. Custer, George A. Little Big Horn (battle). Ontario (Hamilton). 1860's-70's. 2878
Cooking. Food. Pioneers. 1750-1850. 803
Cooperative Commonwealth Federation. British Columbia. Coalition government. Conservative Party. 1941-52. 3173
—. British Columbia. Ideology. Power struggles. Socialists. 1919-32. 3271
—. Communist Party. Elections (provincial). Saskatchewan. 1930's. 3066
—. Defense policy. New Democratic Party. 1932-75. 234
—. Labor. National Democratic Party. Socialism. 1933-75. 1294

—. League for Social Reconstruction. Regina Manifesto. Saskatchewan. Underhill, Frank. 1933. *2927*
—. Manitoba. Provincial Government. Social Democratic Party. Socialism. ca 1940. *3022*
—. Political Participation. Saskatchewan. United Farmers of Canada. 1930-45. *3047*
—. Political Parties. Saskatchewan. Socialism. 1928-44. *3067*
Coopérative Fédérée de Québec. Agricultural Cooperatives. Quebec. 1971-73. *2597*
Cooperative movement. Business. Public opinion. Quebec. 1970's. *2643*
Co-operative Union of Canada. Labor Unions and Organizations. Politics. 1909-31. *1129*
Cooperatives *See also* Agricultural Cooperatives.
—. Alberta (Calgary). Labor Unions and Organizations. 1956-73. *3154*
—. Antigonish Movement. Atlantic Provinces. 1900-45. *2165*
—. Antigonish Movement. Economic Development. Nova Scotia, eastern. Social Classes. 1920's-30's. *2338*
—. Antigonish movement. Maritime Provinces. Social economics. 1920's-40's. *2169*
—. Consumers Cooperative Refineries Ltd. Oil, Chemical, and Atomic Workers International Union. Saskatchewan. 1934-73. *3074*
—. Economic Growth. Nova Scotia (Cape Breton Island). 1906-73. *2237*
—. English Canadians. French Canadians. 19c. *37*
—. Fishing. Pêcheurs-Unis. Quebec (Gaspé Peninsula). World War II. 1939-48. *2638*
—. Maritime Provinces. Prairie Provinces. 1900-55. *2136*
Cooperativism. Quebec. Syndicalism. 1972-77. *2648*
Cooprix supermarkets. Supermarkets. 1960-73. *1551*
Copper kettles. Acadia. Micmac Indians. Mobility. Settlement. 17c. *424*
Copyright *See also* Books; Publishers and Publishing.
—. Book Industries and Trade. Ontario (Toronto). Publishers and Publishing. Robertson, John Ross. 1877-90. *2815*
—. *D'Oyle Carte* v. *Dennis et al.* (Canada, 1899). Saskatchewan (Regina). Theater. 1899-1900's. *3058*
Copyright Act (Canada, 1900). Book Industries and Trade. Publishers and Publishing. 1872-1900. *934*
Copyright law. Oral history. Oral Institute for Studies in Education. Publishers and Publishing. 1960's-75. *1313*
Corbett, Griffiths Owen. Half-breeds (English). Manitoba. Métis. Red River Rebellion. 1863-70. *1014*
Cornwallis, Edward. Colonization. Nova Scotia (Halifax area). 1749-52. *2217*
Corporation Law *See also* Cooperatives; Public Utilities.
—. Professionalism. Quebec. 1840's-1970's. *2615*
Corporations *See also* Multinational Corporations; Public Utilities.
—. Antitrust. Public Policy. 1889-1910. *1081*
—. Competitiveness. Productivity. Wages. 1970-77. *1622*
—. Social Mobility. Upper classes. 1951-72. *1369*
Corundum mining. Ontario (Craigmont). 1900-13. *2812*
COSMOS (satellite). Adlard, Harold. Christian, Edgar. Hornby, John. Northwest Territories (Thelon River, Hornby Point). 1926-27. 1976. *3346*
Cotton mills. French Canadians. Immigration. Massachusetts (Springfield). Statistics. 1870. *2607*
Coubertin, Pierre de. Nationalism. Olympic Games. Quebec (Montreal). 1900-76. *2414*
Coughlin, Lawrence. Methodism. Newfoundland. 1765-1815. *2191*
Council of Assiniboia. French Canadians. Manitoba. Métis. 1860-71. *2910*
Council of Europe. Foreign relations. International law. Political systems. 1965-70's. *1801*
Council of Maritime Premiers. Maritime Provinces. Regional Government. 1971-76. *2164*
Council on Foreign Relations (publications). Business. Government. USA. 1971-74. *1966*
Councillors. Local government. Public policy. 1968-75. *1632*
Counter Culture *See also* Communes.
—. Great Britain. Press. USA. 1957-72. *1475*

Counterintelligence (US). Gage, Lyman. Quebec (Montreal). Spanish-American War. Spy ring, Spanish. Wilkie, John. 1898. *1094*
Counties. Health care services. Quebec. Regions, homogeneous. Socioeconomic development, planning of. 1974. *2428*
Country Life *See also* Rural Settlements.
—. Depressions. Fiction. Literary themes. Prairie Provinces. 1930's. *2918*
—. Fiction. Munro, Alice. Ontario. South. 1940's-70's. *2869*
—. Lambert, Augustine. Saskatchewan (Arelee). Sketches. 1913-14. *3054*
County Government *See also* Local Government.
—. Local Government. Municipalities, rural. New Brunswick. 1967-77. *2384*
Courchesne, Georges. Action Catholique. Catholic Church. Quebec (Rimouski). 1940-67. *2466*
Courtney, Charles. Hanlan, Edward "Ned". Rowing. 1870's-80's. *1043*
Courts *See also* Judges; Judicial Administration; Judicial Process; Supreme Court.
—. Nova Scotia (Pictou County). Trials. 1813. *2341*
—. Ontario. Rape. 19c. *676*
Courtship. Field, Eliza. Great Britain (London). Indians. Jones, Peter. Methodism. New York. 1820's-33. *451*
Cowboys. Alberta. Farmers. Ranchers. Round-ups. 1911-19. *2932*
Cox, Ebenezer. Nova Scotia (Kingsport). Shipbuilding. ca 1840-1915. *2250*
Craig, James Henry. Catholic Church. Clergy. French Canadian nationalism. Government repression. Quebec (Lower Canada). 1810. *711*
Crampton, Esmé (account). Biography. Dance. Lloyd, Gweneth. Oral History. 1969-75. *1371*
Crandall, Joseph. Autobiography and memoirs. Baptist Church. New Brunswick. 1795-1810. *2378*
Craniology. Anthropology, Physical. Eskimos. Prehistory. 1971. *313*
Creativity. Bergson, Henri. Federal government. Intergovernmental Relations. Quebec. 1970's. *2109*
Credit unions *See also* Banking; Loans.
—. Caisses Populaires Desjardins. Quebec. 1912-73. *2598*
Créditiste movement. French Canada. Pinard, Maurice (review article). Quebec. Stein, Michael (review article). 1971-74. *2447*
Cree Indians. Acculturation. Eskimos (Inuit). Race Relations. 1970-74. *284*
—. Acculturation. Indian-White Relations. Quebec (James Bay). 1970's. *345*
—. Alberta. Blackfoot Indians. Church of England. Missions and Missionaries. Trivett, Samuel. 1878-91. *360*
—. Alberta. Blackfoot Indians. Meteorite. 1810-1973. *442*
—. Alberta. Bobtail Cree Reserve. Indians. Land. 1900-09. *3125*
—. Alberta. Fuller, Richard. Hudson's Bay Company. Telegraph. Treaties. 1870's. *1020*
—. Anglican Communion. Faries, Richard. Missions and Missionaries. Ontario (York Factory). 1896-1961. *379*
—. Art. Chippewa Indians. Métis. Prairie Provinces. 1750's-1850's. *357*
—. Artists. Chippewa Indians. Indians. Legend painting. Manitoba. Ontario. 1960's-70's. *470*
—. Assiniboin Indians. Montana. Prairie Provinces. Social organization. ca 1640-1913. *446*
—. Chipewyan Indians. Expansionism. Fur Trade. Indian-White Relations. Northwest Territories (Mackenzie District, eastern). Prairie Provinces. 1680's-18c. *476*
—. Chippewa Indians. Fishing. Indians. Lakes. Ontario, northern. 19c-1978. *341*
—. Chippewa Indians. Fur Trade. Saskatchewan. Thanadelthur ("Slave Woman," Chippewa Indian). 1715-17. *577*
—. Chippewa Indians. Health services. Ontario (Sioux Lookout Zone). 1900-73. *427*
—. Crooked Lakes Reserves. Rations policies. Saskatchewan (Qu'Appelle Valley). Yellow Calf (chief). 1884. *343*
—. Evans, James. Methodist Church. Missions and Missionaries. 1833-46. *651*
—. Fertility. Modernization. 1968. *441*
—. Fisheries. James Bay. 1972-75. *346*
—. Fort Albany. Henley House Massacres. Hudson's Bay Company. Ontario. Woudbee (chief). 1750's. *348*

—. Fort Pitt. Frenchman's Butte, Battle of. Indians. Manitoba. McLean, W. J. (diary). 1885. *1003*
—. Indians. Names (assignation). Values. 20c. *355*
—. Maskipiton (identity). Prairie Provinces. 1830's-50's. *443*
Cree Treaty of 1876. Government. Indians. Land rights. 1876-1970's. *364*
Creek Indians. Manitoba (Camperville, Duck Bay). Missions and Missionaries. 1600-1938. *435*
Creighton, D. G. Confederation. English Canadians. French Canadians. Heintzman, Ralph. Minorities in Politics. 1850's-90's. *922*
Creighton, Donald. Family. Macdonald, John A. (biography). Women. 1843-91. *1063*
Crerar family. Nova Scotia (Pictou). Shipping. 1840's-50's. *2344*
Crèvecoeur, Michel (pseud. J. Hector St. John). American Revolution. France. Great Britain. 1755-1813. *618*
Cricket (game). Nova Scotia. 19c. *2318*
Criddle, Percy. Diaries. Homesteading and Homesteaders. Manitoba (Aweme). 1882-1900's. *954*
Crime and Criminals *See also* names of crimes, e.g. Murder, etc.; Criminal Law; Juvenile Delinquency; Outlaws; Police; Political Crimes; Prisons; Riots; Treason; Trials; Violence.
—. Depression of 1857. Embezzlement. Land speculation. Street, William Warren. 1830-70. *2799*
—. Ethnicity. Illiteracy. Ontario (Middlesex County). Sex. Social Status. 1867-68. *1044*
—. Ontario (Middlesex County). Quantitative Methods. 19c-20c. *74*
—. Smith, Henry Moore. 1812-35. *641*
Crimean War. Great Britain. Howe, Joseph. Military recruitment. USA. 1854-56. *867*
Criminal Justice System. Ontario (Upper Canada). Prisons. Reform. 1835-50. *769*
Criminal Law *See also* Trials.
—. Americanization. Laskin, Bora. Supreme Court (Canada). 1973-74. *2068*
—. Justice. 1648-1748. *536*
Criminal sentencing. Alberta. Bureaucratization. Indians. Urbanization. 1973. *1663*
Criminology. Economic Conditions. 1971-72. *1332*
—. Royal Canadian Mounted Police. 1873-1973. *106*
Cris Indians. Ethnomusicology. Leden, Christian. Phonograph. Songs. 1911. *387*
Cromwell, James. Garrettson, Freeborn. Methodist Episcopal Church. Missions and Missionaries. Nova Scotia. USA. 1785-1800. *2315*
Crooked Lakes Reserves. Cree Indians. Rations policies. Saskatchewan (Qu'Appelle Valley). Yellow Calf (chief). 1884. *343*
Crops *See also* names of crops and farm products, e.g. Hay, Corn, etc.
—. Apple industry. Genealogy. Nova Scotia. Prescott, Charles Ramage. 1772-1970's. *2280*
Crown Employees Collective Bargaining Act. Collective bargaining. Labor. Law. Ontario. 1970-74. *2745*
Cuba. Foreign relations. International Trade. 1975-76. *1867*
—. Foreign Relations. International Trade. USA. ca 1960's-70's. *1879*
Cullity, Emmet K. (memoir). Gold Mines and Mining. Saskatchewan (Beaver Lake). 1915-27. *3041*
Cults, Liturgical. Catholic Church. Devotions, popular. Quebec (Lac-Saint-Jean, Portneuf Counties). 1970's. *2561*
Cultural autonomy. Assimilation. Italians. Mass media. Ontario (Toronto). 1970's. *2735*
Cultural change. Colonialism. Fur trade. Indians. North America. Prehistory-1900. *286*
—. Eskimos. Indians. 1970's. *408*
Cultural cleavages. Models. Occupational categories. Voting and Voting Behavior. 1965-71. *1470*
Cultural development. Climate. Economic development. Ocean currents. 1925-76. *3278*
Cultural ecology. European contact. Micmac Indians. 15c-18c. *423*
Cultural exchange programs. Diplomacy. Foreign policy. 1963-70's. *1932*
Cultural heritage. Ethnic Groups. Slovaks. USA. 19c-20c. *1449*
—. Ethnic Groups. Political attitudes. Quebec. 1974. *2548*
Cultural History. British Columbia. Ormsby, Margaret. 1930's-74. *3234*

—. Ontario. Protestantism. Victorian era. 1840's-1900. *913*
Cultural identity. Economic Conditions. USA. 1973. *1998*
—. Quebec. Regionalism. 1973. *2672*
Cultural Interdependence. USA. 1976. *2061*
Cultural relations. Art. Mass Media. Poland. USA. 1940-74. *1953*
—. Europe, Western. Foreign policy. USA. ca 1850's-20c. *34*
—. France. International Trade. 1760-1870. *879*
Cultural transmission. Christianity. Maritime Provinces. Micmac Indians. Western civilization. 1970's. *344*
Culture *See also* Education; Popular Culture; Scholarship.
—. Alberta (Lethbridge). Industry. Pioneers. Transportation. 1880's. *3104*
—. Archives. Education. France. 1977. *215*
—. Artists. USA. 1970's. *1390*
—. Economic Growth. Ontario (Toronto). Urbanization. 1850-1914. *2863*
—. Economic independence. Foreign Relations. Nationalism. USA. 1948-75. *2081*
—. Ethnic groups. USA. 1776-1976. *79*
—. Indians. Manitoba, southwestern. Natural Resources. Pottery. Prehistory-18c. 1970's. *307*
—. Revolution. USA. Violence. 1776-1976. *61*
Cumberland House. Buildings. Hearne, Samuel. Saskatchewan. 1794-1800's. *3075*
—. Hudson's Bay Company. Saskatchewan. 1774-1974. *3063*
Curricula. Colleges and Universities. Economic returns. Labor market. 1961-72. *1582*
—. Fenton, Edwin. High schools. Historical thinking. 1975. *1346*
—. Higher Education. Teaching. Women's history. 1940-73. *1387*
—. Ontario. Physical education and training. Public schools. Strathcona Trust fund. 1919-39. *1130*
Currie, Arthur. Casualty rates. Hughes, Sam. Military General Staff. World War I. 1914-30. *1156*
Curtis, Edward S. Indians. Morgan, J. P. Photographs. 1868-1952. *472*
—. Indians. Photographs. 1892-1932. *403*
Custer, George A. Cooke, Willie. Little Big Horn (battle). Ontario (Hamilton). 1860's-70's. *2878*
Cyclones *See also* Storms.
—. Legislation. Ontario. Sex Discrimination. Wages. Wages. 1946-71. *2777*
Cypress Hills Massacre. Assiniboin Indians. Historiography. Saskatchewan, southwestern. 1873. *978*
Cypress Hills Provincial Park. Alberta. Saskatchewan. 1859-1973. *2914*
Czechoslovakia *See also* Europe, Eastern; Hungary.
—. Communism. Jesuits. Refugees. Religious communities, dissolution of. 1950. *1416*

D

Daily Life *See also* Popular Culture.
—. Acadians. Harley, William. New Brunswick, northeastern. Surveying. 1829. *2381*
—. Alberta (Calgary). Automobiles. Bicycles. 1880-1914. *3120*
—. Alberta (Lundbreck). Coal Mines and Mining. Koester, Mavis Addie (reminiscences). 1905-08. *3124*
—. Alberta (Waskatenau). Buchanan, Carl, Jr. (reminiscences). Homesteading and Homesteaders. 1930's. *3091*
—. Annan, Ebenezer (letters). Immigration. Nova Scotia (Halifax). 1842. *2220*
—. Arctic. Hare Indians. Indians. Northwest Territories. Oil exploration. 1859-1974. *358*
—. Bird, Lilah Smith (recollections). Nova Scotia (Cape Breton; Port Hood Island). ca 1907-70. *2221*
—. British Columbia. Dukhobors. Immigration. Russia. 1880's-1976. *1035*
—. British Columbia. Lumber camps. Parkin, Al (interview). 1910's-30's. *3255*
—. British Columbia. Union Steamship Company. 1889-1959. *3185*
—. Colorado. Frontier and Pioneer Life. Nebraska. Ouren, Hogan (reminiscences). 1861-66. *851*
—. Dufaut, J. (diary). Fur trade. Indians. Ontario (Prince Rupert's Land). XY Company. 1803-04. *2956*

—. Great Lakes. Indians. Kane, Paul. Paintings. 1845-46. *384*
—. Historical Sites and Parks. Louisbourg, Fortress of. Nova Scotia (Cape Breton Island). Social classes. 1713-50. *537*
—. Historiography. Oral history. Popular thought. 20c. *1320*
—. Hudson's Bay Company. Trading posts. ca 1850. *862*
—. Humphrys, James (and family). Saskatchewan (Cannington Manor). 1880's-1908. *986*
—. Morton, Sydney (diary). Nova Scotia (Liverpool, Halifax). 1874. *2294*
—. Nova Scotia. Pioneers. 19c-1910. *2311*
—. Nova Scotia (Glenwood). Ricker, Helen S. (reminiscences). 1895-1909. *2334*
—. Nova Scotia (Pictou Island). ca 1930-75. *2342*
Dairying. British Columbia. Economic History. Fraser Valley Milk Producers' Association. 1867-1969. *3224*
—. Government. Motherwell, W. R. Saskatchewan. Subsidies. Wilson, W. A. 1906-17. *3037*
Dakota Indians. *See* Sioux Indians.
Dakota Territory. Artists. Frontier and Pioneer Life. *Harper's Weekly* (periodical). Rogers, William A. 1878. *2976*
Dalhousie University. Colleges and Universities. Mackenzie, Arthur Stanley. Nova Scotia. Stanley, Carleton. 1911-45. *2282*
—. McCulloch, Thomas. Missions and Missionaries. Nova Scotia. Pictou Academy. Presbyterian Church. ca 1803-42. *2215*
Dalnavert Ball. Dance. Manitoba Historical Society. 1892 1913. 1975. *2981*
Dams *See also* names of dams, e.g. Hoover Dam, etc.
—. Energy crisis. Farms. Ontario (Osceola). Water power. 1902 05. *2813*
Dance. Biography. Crampton, Esmé (account). Lloyd, Gweneth. Oral History. 1969-75. *1371*
—. Blackfoot Indians. Indian Days. Oklahoma. 19c-20c. *437*
—. Dalnavert Ball. Manitoba Historical Society. 1892-1913. 1975. *2981*
D'Aquin, Marie Thomas. Catholic Church. Joan of Arc Institute. Ontario (Ottawa). Social Work. Women. 1903-19. *2746*
Daughters. Alberta. Mothers. Oral history. Pioneers. 1890-1929. *1025*
Davis, Jefferson. Lincoln, Abraham. Peace mission. Virginia (Richmond). 1864. *838*
Davis, Thomas Clayton (letters). China. Diplomacy. 1946-49. *1943*
Davis, Thomas O. Elections. Liberal Party. Saskatchewan. 1896. *3046*
Davis, William. Ontario. Politics. Quebec. Separatist Movements. 1976-77. *1280*
Dawson, John William. Grant, George Monro. Higher education. Scotland. 19c. *2*
Day, John (letter). Cabot, John. Morison, Samuel Eliot. Newfoundland (Cape Bonavista). Voyages. 1497-98. *486*
Deaf. Bell, Alexander Graham. Library of Congress. Gilbert J. Grosvenor Collection. Photographs. 1870-1922. *2228*
Deas, John Sullivan. Black Capitalism. British Columbia. Canning industry. Salmon. 1862-78. *3239*
Death and Dying. Quebec. Social Classes. 1934-74. *2468*
Decentralization. Europe. Industrial relations. Labor. USA. 1960's-70's. *1626*
Dechêne, Louise (review article). Charbonneau, Hubert. Family structure. Migration. Quebec. Vital Statistics. 1660-1713. 1974-75. *527*
Decisionmaking *See also* Elites; Foreign Policy.
—. Accountability. Environment. Federal government. Science and Government. 1950's-70's. *1725*
—. Alberta (Edmonton). City councillors. Municipal government. Voting and Voting Behavior. 1966-72. *3134*
—. Arctic. Oil development. Technology. 1970's. *3284*
—. Federal government. Public Policy. 1970's. *1636*
—. Foreign policy. Nuclear Arms. 1950's-60's. *1847*
—. Government. ca 1867-1970's. *1707*
—. Grosman, Brian A. (review article). Law Enforcement. Police politics. 1975. *1674*
—. Public policy. 1950's-70's. *1680*
Declaration of Atlantic Principles. NATO. 1974. *1862*
—. NATO. 1974. *1948*

—. NATO. USA. 1974. *1818*
Defense. Armies. International relations. Self-determination. 1970's. *1778*
—. Great Britain. USA. War of 1812. 1812-14. *767*
Defense Policy *See also* National Security.
—. Balance of power. North America. Quebec. Separatist Movements. 1970's. *1921*
—. British Empire. 1930's. *1199*
—. Civil service. Committee of Imperial Defence. Great Britain. War Office. 1896-1914. *1092*
—. Cooperative Commonwealth Federation. New Democratic Party. 1932-75. *234*
—. Economic Conditions. Government. Military strategy. NATO. 1973-76. *1863*
—. Expansionism. Great Britain. Pacific Area (north). 1850-1914. *919*
—. Force, attitudes toward. Military strategy. 1970's. *1278*
—. Foreign policy. Nationalism. 1971-75. *1857*
—. Foreign policy. NATO. North American Air Defense Command. USA. 1950's-70's. *1986*
—. Foreign Relations. USA. 1974. *1968*
—. Hartford Convention. Militia. New England. War of 1812. 1812-15. *757*
—. Interdependence. USA. 1940's-70's. *2062*
—. Maritime Law. UN Conference on the Law of the Sea. 1977. *1764*
—. Military Strategy. 1957-77. *1291*
—. Military strategy. North American Air Defense Command. USA. 1930's-70's. *1988*
—. Military structure. USA. 1963-70's. *2004*
—. NATO. Peacekeeping Forces. Trudeau, Pierre Elliott. 1968-78. *1752*
—. Weapons. 1976-78. *1285*
Defense Policy (review article). 1970-78. *2038*
Defense Policy (white paper). 1971-77. *1258*
Defoe, Daniel. Colonization (supposed). Hudson's Bay Company. Publicity. Rupert's Land. Sergeant, Henry. 1680's. *502*
Deforestation. Agricultural development. Ecology. Ontario. 1880-1900. *275*
deGaulle, Charles (attitudes). France. French Canadians. Quebec. 1940-67. *2685*
delaRoche, Mazo. Loyalist myth. Novels. USA. 1780's. 1920's-40's. *742*
Delinquency. *See* Juvenile Delinquency.
Demers, Jerôme. Philosophy. Quebec. Science. Teaching. 1765-1835. *2502*
Democracy *See also* Federal Government; Middle Classes; Referendum; Socialism; Suffrage.
—. Bureaucracies. Legislators. 1968-72. *1712*
—. Dissent. Political stability. Quebec. 1960's-70's. *2489*
—. Foreign policy. Mass media. Totalitarianism. 1960-76. *1924*
—. Foreign Relations. France. Immigration. 1855. *836*
—. Government. 1867-1977. *142*
—. Humanism. MacPherson, C. B. Marxism. Political Theory. 1976. *1338*
Democratic Union Central. Labor Unions and Organizations. Quebec. 1968-74. *2621*
Democrats (writings). Political Commentary. Social thought. 19c. *235*
Demography *See also* Birth Control; Birth Rate; Geopolitics; Mortality; Population; Vital Statistics.
—. Birth Control. India. USA. 1970's. *1444*
—. Birth rate. Ethnic variations. Immigrants. Marriage. 1871. *1072*
—. Birth Rate (decline). Family size. 1961. *1426*
—. Birth Rate (decline analysis). 1961-71. *1453*
—. Cities. Economic diversity. 1961-73. *1434*
—. Epidemics. Fur trade. Indians. Wildlife diseases. 15c-18c. *425*
—. Ethnic groups. Quebec (Quebec). 1795-1805. *2512*
—. Family reconstitution studies. Methodology. Migration, Internal. Quebec (Laterrière). 1855-1970. *2474*
—. Family size. Social Surveys. 1945-74. *1355*
—. Federal Government. Immigration policy. Local government. 1970's. *1811*
—. Francisation. Quebec (Rawdon). Rural Settlements. 1791-1970. *2575*
—. French Canadians. Quebec. Social Organization. 1974. *2481*
—. Indians. North America. 15c-1600. *298*
—. Ontario. Peel County History Project. Population. Social History. 1840-80. 1973. *2770*
—. Population. Trudel, Marcel (review article). 1663. 1973. *509*
—. Quebec. St. Lawrence River (St. Ignace, Dupas islands). Settlement. 1648-1973. *2486*
Denmark *See also* Scandinavia.

—. Adult education. Folk school concept. 1919-50. *1136*

Densmore, Frances. Ethnology. Indians. Musicology. 1918-57. *400*

Dependency. Adolescence. Employment. Frontier and Pioneer Life. Ontario (Orillia). Social change. 1861-71. *2769*

Depressions *See also* Recessions.

—. 1930's. *1214*

—. Alberta. British Columbia. Coal Mines and Mining. Pass Strike of 1932. 1920's-30's. *1209*

—. Alberta. Educational role. United Farm Women of Alberta. 1915-30. *3161*

—. Alberta (Edmonton). 1904-29. *3159*

—. Ball, George P. M. Business records. Economic change. Ontario (Upper Canada). Rural Settlements. 1825-60. *672*

—. British Columbia. Education Department (Recreational and Physical Education Branch). Sports. Youth. 1934-40. *3217*

—. British Columbia (Vancouver). Relief Camp Workers Union. Strikes. 1935. *3209*

—. *Canadian Forum* (periodical). Poetry. 1929-39. *1213*

—. Colleges and Universities. Collegiate Institute. Lansdowne College. Manitoba (Portage la Prairie). 1882-93. *3018*

—. Country Life. Fiction. Literary themes. Prairie Provinces. 1930's. *2918*

—. Crime and Criminals. Embezzlement. Land speculation. Street, William Warren. 1830-70. *2799*

—. Emigration. Maritime Provinces. Massachusetts (Boston). New England. 1860-1900. *2154*

—. Middle classes. 1930's. *1201*

Derby, 15th Earl of. Confederation. Great Britain. Head, Edmund Walker. Letters. Political Attitudes. 1858. *894*

Desertion. Armies. France. New France. 1700-63. *530*

Design for Development (Ontario, 1966). California. Ontario. Regional planning. 1965-74. *2873*

Desjardins cooperative movement. Government. Interest groups. Quebec. 18c-1973. *2415*

Detente *See also* Balance of Power.

—. Foreign Policy. USA. USSR. 1947-75. *1925*

Deutscher Bund Canada. German Canadians. Immigration. Saskatchewan (Loon River area). 1929-39. *3076*

—. German Canadians. Nazism. Propaganda. 1934-39. *1216*

—. German Canadians. Nazism. Saskatchewan. 1934-39. *1246*

Developing Nations *See also* Industrialized Countries.

—. Brain drain. Economic Conditions. Immigration policy. 1962-74. *1931*

—. China. Foreign relations. USA. USSR. 1950-75. *1824*

—. Economic aid. Foreign policy. 1970's. *1793*

—. Economic Aid. Trudeau, Pierre Elliott. 1968-78. *1816*

—. Economic Policy. Mineral Resources. Mines. 1960-77. *1779*

—. Energy-environment policy. Environment. 1975. *1274*

—. Europe. Foreign policy. Japan. USA. 1950-75. *1741*

—. Food. Foreign aid. 1975. *2048*

—. Foreign aid. 1960's-70's. *1748*

—. Foreign policy. Trudeau, Pierre Elliott. 1968-78. *1929*

—. Foreign Relations (review article). Ismael, T. Y. Lyon, P. V. Ogelsby, J. C. M. USA. 1860's-1976. *239*

—. Humanitarian attitudes. Poverty. UN Security Council. 1970's. *1796*

—. Immigration policy. Refugees. 1950's-70's. *1747*

—. International Development Research Centre (projects). 1970-74. *1904*

—. International law. UN. Violence. 1945-75. *1739*

Development *See also* Economic Development; National Development.

—. Northwest Territories. 1976. *3291*

Devit, Charles. M'Grath, Michael. Nova Scotia (Halifax). Trials. Westmacott, John (murder of). 1816. *2243*

Devolution. Alberta. Federalism. Oil rights. Scotland. 1970's. *3118*

Devotions, popular. Catholic Church. Cults, Liturgical. Quebec (Lac-Saint-Jean, Portneuf Counties). 1970's. *2561*

—. Catholic Church. Quebec (La Beauce County). Shrines, roadside. Social customs. 1970's. *2514*

Dewar, Kenneth M. (reminiscences). Adlard, Harold. Christian, Edgar. Diaries. Hornby, John. Northwest Territories (Thelon River, Hornby Point). 1928. *3350*

DeWolfe, Percy. Alaska (Eagle). Mail carrier. Yukon Territory (Dawson). 1915-50. *3332*

Dialects *See also* Linguistics.

—. Language. Survey of Canadian English. Youth. 1972. *1484*

Diaries. Adlard, Harold. Christian, Edgar. Dewar, Kenneth M. (reminiscences). Hornby, John. Northwest Territories (Thelon River, Hornby Point). 1928. *3350*

—. Atlantic Provinces. Catholic Church. Plessis, Joseph-Octave. Quebec Archdiocese. 1812-15. *2155*

—. Atomic Warfare. King, William Lyon MacKenzie. Racism. 1921-48. *1139*

—. British Columbia (Prince Rupert). Coastal defense. Thistle, R. World War II. 1941-42. *1243*

—. Criddle, Percy. Homesteading and Homesteaders. Manitoba (Aweme). 1882-1900's. *954*

—. Hurricanes. Marshall, John George. Nova Scotia (Guysborough County). 1811. *2223*

Diefenbaker, John. Conservative Party. Political Parties. 1956-67. *1672*

—. Oral history. Stursberg, Peter (reminiscences). 1957-75. *1264*

Dieppe (air battle). Great Britain. Leigh-Mallory, Trafford. Royal Canadian Air Force. World War II. 1942. *1220*

Diffusion theories. Civilization (review article). Geography. Gordon, Cyrus H. Riley, Carroll. Transoceanic contacts. Prehistory-1492. *304*

—. Mechanization. Ontario. Reaping. Technology. 1850-70. *2846*

Dillon, Luke. Bombings. Clan-na-Gael. Irish Americans. Ontario (Thorold). Welland Canal. 1900-14. *1083*

Diocesan Theological Institute. Church of England. Clergy. Frontier and Pioneer Life. Ontario (Cobourg). Strachan, John. 1840-55. *679*

Dionne, Narcisse-Eutrope. Bédard, Pierre (discourse). Language, official. Quebec (Lower Canada). 1792-1809. 1909. *699*

Diplomacy *See also* Treaties.

—. 1973. *1734*

—. 1970's. *1899*

—. Adams, John Quincy. Fishing. Great Britain. Monroe, James. Newfoundland banks. USA. 1815-18. *782*

—. Boundary dispute. Great Britain. Oregon. Polk, James K. USA. 1845-46. *835*

—. British Columbia (Vancouver). France (Paris). Great Britain. Nootka Sound Controversy. Spain. 1789-90. *636*

—. Brown, George. Congress. Reciprocity treaty (proposed). USA. 1870-80. *1071*

—. China. Davis, Thomas Clayton (letters). 1946-49. *1943*

—. China. Odlum, Victor Wentworth. 1943-46. *1877*

—. Cold War. USSR. 1946-47. *1885*

—. Consulates, Canadian. USA. 1833-1977. *226*

—. Cultural exchange programs. Foreign policy. 1963-70's. *1932*

—. Economic Conditions. International trade. USA. 1945-76. *2008*

—. External Affairs Department. Travelers. 1973-74. *1865*

—. Great Britain. International meetings. Pearson, Lester B. USA. 1935-72. *1910*

—. Great Britain. Nuclear technology. 1973-74. *1888*

—. Korean War. Pearson, Lester B. Self-determination. UN. 1950-72. *1768*

—. Korean War. Stairs, Denis (review article). USA. 1950-53. *1881*

—. Maritime Law. Pacific Area, North. Territorial Waters. 1958-75. *1826*

—. Monroe Doctrine. Pacific Northwest. Russia. 1812-23. *657*

—. Nuclear Arms. Pearson, Lester B. 1957-59. *1832*

—. Pearson, Lester B. 1948-57. *1918*

—. Pearson, Lester B. St. Lawrence Seaway. USA. 1949-66. *1758*

—. Pearson, Lester B. Suez crisis (1956). UN. 1956. *1873*

—. Sharp, Mitchell. USSR. 1973. *1813*

—. Sharp, Mitchell. USSR. 1973. *1848*

—. Travel. Trudeau, Pierre Elliott. 1973. *1934*

—. USA. 1970's. *2026*

—. USA. 1927-73. *2065*

Diplomatic recognition. China. Foreign Relations. Trudeau, Pierre Elliott. 1968-73. *1807*

Diplomatic relations. China. International claims, settlement of. 1946-75. *1759*

—. Foreign Policy. Mexico. USA. 1945-74. *1860*

—. Heeney, Arnold D. P. (memoirs). Pearson, Lester B. USA. 1897-1972. *1975*

Diplomats. Equal employment. External Affairs Department. Women. 1909-75. *82*

—. Foreign affairs. -1973. *1894*

—. Political scientists. Public Policy. 1970's. *1703*

Dirigibles (R-100). Aeronautics (history). England. 1930. *1215*

Disaster relief. Fire. New Brunswick (Saint John). Nova Scotia. 1877. *2397*

Disasters *See also* names of particular disasters, e.g. San Francisco Earthquake and Fire (1906); Earthquakes; Storms.

—. Coal Mines and Mining. Nova Scotia (Pictou). 1832-1957. *2231*

—. *Imo* (vessel). *Mont Blanc* (vessel). Nova Scotia (Halifax). 1917. *2332*

Disciples of Christ. Nova Scotia (Cornwallis Township). 1812-1910. *2251*

Discipline, ecclesiastical. Catholics. Church History. Morality. Prairie Provinces. 1900-30. *2907*

Discovery and Exploration *See also* Explorers; Polar Exploration; Scientific Expeditions; Westward Movement.

—. Africoids. Americas (North and South). Anthropological evidence. Prehistory. *293*

—. Alaska. Anián, strait of. British Columbia. Cook, James. Northwest Passage. Voyages. 1778. *675*

—. Alaska. Lapérouse, Jean François. Ledyard, John. Pacific Area. Pacific Northwest. Russia (Siberia). 1778-1806. *652*

—. Alaska (Klukman). Yukon Territory. 1890. *3339*

—. Americas (North and South). Europe, Eastern. Pacific Area. 16c-19c. *175*

—. Arctic. Finnie, Richard Sterling (account). North America. Office of the Coordinator of Information. Stefansson, Vilhjalmur. 1931-62. *3302*

—. Arctic. Fort Hope. Hudson's Bay Company. Northwest Territories. Rae, John. 1840's. *3298*

—. Arctic. Franklin, John. Great Britain. Northwest Territories (Beechey Island). 1845-48. *3312*

—. Arctic. Franklin, John. Hood, Robert (journal). Northwest Territories. 1819-21. *3309*

—. Arctic. Hantzsch, Bernard. Northwest Territories (Baffin Island). Trichinosis. 1911. *3316*

—. Arctic islands. Hudson Strait (navigability). Wakeham, William. 1897. *3304*

—. *Arctic* (vessel). Bernier, Joseph E. Byrd, Richard E. 1924-25. *3301*

—. Assiniboine and Saskatchewan Exploring Expedition. Hime, Humphrey Lloyd. Photography. Prairie Provinces. 1858. *863*

—. Astrolabe, Cobden. Champlain, Samuel de. 1613. *506*

—. Atlantic Coast. Historical Sites and Parks. North America. Vikings. 10c-14c. 20c. *483*

—. Baptista de Lima, Manuel C. (research). Pinheiro, Diogo (voyages). Pinheiro, Manoel (voyages). Portugal (Barcelos). 1521-98. *508*

—. Bighorn River. Indians. Montana. Wyoming. Prehistory-1965. *444*

—. Birds. Hood, Robert. Painting. Saskatchewan River. 1819-21. *2928*

—. Brendan, Saint. Ireland. North America. Voyages. 500-85. 1976-77. *488*

—. British Columbia (Vancouver Island). Cook, James. Great Britain. Nootka Sound controversy. Spain. 1778-94. *695*

—. British Columbia (Vancouver Island, Nootka Sound). *Columbia* (vessel). Fur trade. Ingraham, Joseph (travel account). 1774-89. *655*

—. California. Drake, Francis. *Golden Hinde* (vessel). Nova Albion (location of). 1579. *505*

—. Canoe trips. Rupert's Land. Tyrrell, Joseph Burr. 1893. *975*

—. Environmental determinism. Mississippi River. Natural resources. North America. St. Lawrence River. 17c-19c. *270*

—. Eskimo life. Hantzsch, Bernard. Naturalists. Northwest Territories (Baffin Island). 1910-11. *3314*

—. Excavations. Newfoundland (L'Anse aux Meadows). Vikings. 1000. 1961-68. *480*

—. Forgeries. North America. Vikings. Vinland map. 15c. 1957. *482*

—. France. Mississippi River Valley. Spain. 16c-17c. *588*

—. Fur Trade. Hudson's Bay Company. Ogden, Peter Skene. 1811-54. *688*

—. Geographical ideas, history of. Maps. Vinland Map. 1974. *484*

—. Great Britain. Jameson, Robert. North America. Northwest Passage. 1804-54. *689*

—. Great Britain. Netherlands. North America. Vancouver, George. 1778-98. *666*

—. Hantzsch, Bernard. Northwest Territories (Baffin Island). Soper, J. Dewey. 1929. *3317*

—. Hudson's Bay Company. Simpson, George. 1787-1860. *639*

—. Inscriptions. Ireland. Newfoundland. Ogham alphabet. St. Lunaire boulder. ca 5c-1977. *487*

—. Mackenzie, Alexander. Overland Journeys to the Pacific. Trade Routes. 1789-93. *2134*

—. North America. Vikings. Voyages. 985-1975. *477*

—. Northwest Territories (Bylot Island). 1818-1977. *3311*

—. Romanticism. Western history. 1540-1800. *579*

Discrimination *See also* Civil Rights; Minorities; Racism; Segregation; Sex Discrimination.

—. Acadians. Catholic Church. Irish. New Brunswick. 1860-1900. *2402*

—. British Columbia. California. Gold Rushes. Negroes. Race Relations. 1849-66. *846*

—. Catholic Church. Normal school issue. Prairie Provinces. 1884-1900. *2947*

—. Economic Conditions. Ontario (Toronto). West Indians. 1971. *2168*

—. Ethnic groups. Immigrants. Manitoba (Winnipeg). Population. 1874-1974. *2967*

—. Historiography. Negroes. 1776-1976. *252*

—. Human rights. Language. USA. 1960's. *1481*

—. International organizations. Women. 1960's-70's. *1447*

Discrimination, Educational. Ontario. School attendance. Social Classes. Women. 1851-71. *2754*

Discrimination, Employment. Immigrants. Ontario (Toronto). Social Status. West Indians. 1972. *2849*

Diseases *See also* names of diseases, e.g. diphtheria, etc.; Epidemics; Medicine (practice of).

—. Indians. Micmac Indians. Population. 16c-17c. *302*

—. Leprosy. Massachusetts. New Brunswick. Social stigma. 1844-80. 1904-21. *2391*

Diseases, diffusion of. Folk medicine. USA. 20c. *1298*

—. Fur Trade. Hudson's Bay Company. Indians. 1830-50. *2949*

Diseases, industrial. Working Conditions. 1970-73. *1578*

Dissent. Democracy. Political stability. Quebec. 1960's-70's. *2489*

Dissertation Abstracts International. Bibliographies. Western States. 1973. *2903*

Dissertations. Bibliographies. Western States. 1974-75. *2955*

—. Economic History Association (37th annual meeting). Industrialization. Labor. 19c-20c. 1977. *263*

Distilling industry. Whiskey. 1668-1976. *181*

Distribution system. Agriculture. Business. Machinery. Manitoba. 1974. *2923*

Disturnell, John (*The Great Lakes, or 'Inland Seas' of America*). Great Lakes. Handbooks. Travel. 1862. *882*

Divorce *See also* Family; Marriage.

—. Bourassa, Henri. Feminism. Woman suffrage. 1913-25. *1142*

Divorce rates. Law and Society. Legal access. 1867-1973. *1451*

Doane, Elizabeth O. M. P. (memoirs). Nova Scotia (Barrington). Payne, John Howard. 1715-98. *2224*

Dobbins, Daniel. Lake Erie (battle of). Madison, James. Perry, Oliver Hazard. War of 1812. Warships. 1812-13. *762*

Documents. Basque language. Labrador. 1572-77. *559*

—. Census. Literacy. Methodology. 1861. *852*

—. Church of England. 1850-52. *873*

—. CODOC (system). Government. Information Storage and Retrieval Systems. Libraries. USA. 1960's-70's. *177*

—. Forests and Forestry. 1974-75. *3218*

—. New France. Occupations. Social status. 1640's-1740's. *534*

Dollar standard. International exchange. USA. 1945-. *1629*

Domestic and Foreign Missionary Society. Church of England. Japan. Missions and Missionaries. 1883-1902. *932*

Domestic Policy *See also* Federal Policy.

—. Economic History. Government. ca 1865-1975. *209*

—. Foreign relations. Newspapers. Nova Scotia. USA. 1827-40. *2312*

Domestics. Social Mobility. Social networks. West Indies (Montserrat). Women. 1960's-75. *1935*

Douglas, David. Botany. Horticulture. North America. Scientific Expeditions. 1823-34. *650*

Douglas, James. British Columbia. Frontier and Pioneer Life. Gold rushes. Law Enforcement. 1858. *3197*

Douglas, W. O. (reminiscences). Comer, George. *Finback* (whaler). Northwest Territories (Chesterfield Inlet). Shipwrecks. 1919. *3351*

—. Northwest Territories (Baker Lake District). Quangwak (Eskimo). Royal Canadian Mounted Police. 1919-20's. *323*

Doull, Alexander John. British Columbia (Kootenay). Church of England. 1870-1937. *3194*

D'Oyle Carte v. *Dennis et al.* (Canada, 1899). Copyright. Saskatchewan (Regina). Theater. 1899-1900's. *3058*

Doyle, Hastings. Confederation. Federal government. Local government. Nova Scotia. 1867-68. *895*

Drake, Francis. California. Discovery and Exploration. *Golden Hinde* (vessel). Nova Albion (location of). 1579. *505*

Drama *See also* Films; Theater.

—. Acculturation. Cultural preservation. Indians. 1606-1974. *414*

—. Canadian Broadcasting Corporation. Fink, Howard (account). Radio. 1940's-50's. 1976. *1386*

Drapeau, Jean. Montreal Citizens' Movement. Quebec. 1957-76. *2649*

—. Olympic Games. Quebec (Montreal). Sports. 1970-76. *2521*

Draper, Tom. Alberta (Ft. McMurray). Oil sands. 1920's-30's. *3096*

Dreams. Anatomy, morbid. Medicine (practice of), Osler, William. USA. 1872-1919. *908*

Drew, George. Conservative Party. Ontario (Guelph). Political Campaigns. 1890-1925. *2736*

Driving. Automobiles. Conestoga wagons. Social Customs. USA. 1755-20c. *174*

Droughts. Campbell, Thomas D. Farm income. Great Plains. Prairie Provinces. Wheat. 1915-1940. *2964*

Droz, Pierre-Frédéric. British North America. Europe. Travel. Watchmakers. 1768-70. *685*

Drug Abuse *See also* Crime and Criminals; Juvenile Delinquency; Pharmacy.

—. Prairie Provinces. 1860's-1919. *2905*

Drug abuse programs. International cooperation. North America. 1960's-74. *1417*

Drugs. Food. Fur Trade. Indians. 17c-19c. *187*

Drummond County Mechanics Institute. Farmers. Labor Unions and Organizations. Quebec (Drummond County). 1856-90. *2537*

Dry farming. Economic Conditions. Grain production. Prairie Provinces. 1870-1930. *2943*

Dubuc family papers. Paper Industry. Quebec (Saguenay River, Lake St. John). 1892-1963. *2612*

Duels. Baldwin, William Warren. McDonnell, John. Ontario (Upper Canada). 1812. *2842*

—. Saskatchewan (Ile-à-La-Crosse, Fort Chipewyan). ca 1815-16. *3025*

Dufaut, J. (diary). Daily life. Fur trade. Indians. Ontario (Prince Rupert's Land). XY Company. 1803-04. *2956*

Duff, Wilson. Anthropology. Art. British Columbia. Pacific Northwest. 1950-76. *280*

—. Archaeology. British Columbia. Indians. 1950-76. *292*

Dufferin and Ava, 1st Marquis of (visit). Icelandic community. Manitoba (Gimli). 1877. *969*

Duguid, Archer Fortescue (obituary). Heraldry Society of Canada. Historians. 1910-76. *1133*

Duke University (Lionel Stevenson Collection). Letters. Literature. Stevenson, Lionel. 1860's-1960's. *4*

Dukhobors. Amish. Hutterites. Mennonites. Molokans. North America. ca 1650-1977. *184*

—. British Columbia. Daily life. Immigration. Russia. 1880's-1976. *1035*

—. British Columbia. Russian Canadians. Saskatchewan. 1652-1976. *152*

—. Communalism. Saskatchewan. 1904. *1001*

—. Ethnic groups. Royal Canadian Mounted Police. Saskatchewan. Settlement. 1899-1909. *3028*

—. Galicians. Lake Geneva Mission. Missions and Missionaries. Presbyterian Church. Saskatchewan (Wakaw). 1903-42. *3027*

—. Immigration. Religious persecution. Russia. Sects, Religious. 1654-1902. *1033*

—. Immigration. Russia. 1652-1908. *996*

Dun and Bradstreet (records). Atlantic Provinces. 1842-1968. *2166*

Duncan, Sara Jeanette (*The Imperialist*). Imperialism. Novels. 1902-04. *1109*

Duncan, William. Alaska (Metlakahtla). British Columbia. Missions and Missionaries. Tsimshian Indians. 1857-1974. *373*

Duplessis, Maurice. Black, Conrad. Historiography. Political Leadership. Quebec. Rumilly, Robert. 1936-59. *2684*

Durham, 1st Earl of. Great Britain. Whigs. 1838-40. *829*

—. Penal transportation. Political prisoners. Public opinion. 1835-50. *827*

Durrell, Philip (and descendants). New England. 17c-18c. *491*

E

Earthquakes. Nova Scotia (Cape Breton). 1882. 1909. 1929. *278*

East Indians *See also* Asians.

—. Bibliographies. Immigration. 1900-77. *1358*

—. Church Schools. Missions and Missionaries. Presbyterian Church. Trinidad and Tobago. 1868-1912. *2319*

Eby, Ezra E. Immigration. Loyalists. Mennonites. Pennsylvania. 18c-1835. *743*

Eccles, William J. Colonial policy (review article). France. New France. Seignelay, Marquis de. ca 1663-1701. 1962-64. *499*

Ecclesiastical authority. Protestantism. United Church of Canada. 1925-71. *1101*

École des Hautes Études Commerciales. Economics. Educators. Minville, Esdras. Quebec (Montreal). 20c. *2457*

École Sociale Populaire. Catholic Church. Labor unions and Organizations. Quebec. Social Change. 1911-75. *2500*

Ecology *See also* Conservation of Natural Resources; Environment; Nature Conservation; Pollution.

—. Agricultural development. Deforestation. Ontario. 1880-1900. *275*

—. Anthropology. Authority. Eskimos, Central. Social organization. 1970's. *322*

—. Boundary Waters Treaty. British Columbia (Cabin Creek). Coal explorations. Montana. USA. 1909. 1973-75. *672*

—. Churchill River. Hydroelectric development. Manitoba, northern. 1966-70's. *2972*

—. Fisheries. 1945-74. *1786*

—. Land (use, planning). 1973. *1271*

—. North American Water and Power Alliance. USA. Water management. 1968-71. *1961*

—. Snowmobiles. 1950-74. *1276*

Economic Aid. Arab States. International Trade. Oil Industry and Trade. 1960's-70's. *1770*

—. Developing nations. Foreign policy. 1970's. *1793*

—. Developing Nations. Trudeau, Pierre Elliott. 1968-78. *1816*

Economic blocs. Foreign policy. Industrialized Countries. 1944-74. *1896*

Economic change. Ball, George P. M. Business records. Depressions. Ontario (Upper Canada). Rural Settlements. 1825-60. *77*

Economic competition. Alaska pipeline. Oil Industry and Trade. USA. 1973-75. *2041*

—. Great Britain. USA. Wheat. 1900-14. *1102*

Economic Conditions *See also* terms beginning with Economic; Natural Resources; Statistics.

—. Alberta (Calgary). Cattle Raising. Oil Industry and Trade. 19c-20c. *3089*

—. American Revolution. Great Britain. Quebec. 1770's. *731*
—. Anti-Inflation Act. Canadian Labour Congress. Income. 1970's. *1572*
—. Atlantic Provinces. Immigration. Kennedy, Albert J. Massachusetts (Boston). 1910's. *2162*
—. Brain drain. Developing Nations. Immigration policy. 1962-74. *1931*
—. British Columbia (Bridge River Valley). Gold Mines and Mining. Physical geography. 19c-1970's. *3251*
—. British North America. British West Indies. International Trade. ca 1609-1800. *715*
—. Capital market. Financial institutions. 1947-72. *1581*
—. Census. New Brunswick. Social Conditions. 1861. *2377*
—. Cities. Demography. 1961-73. *1434*
—. Constitutions. Quebec. Separatist Movements. 1973. *2115*
—. Criminology. 1971-72. *1332*
—. Cultural identity. USA. 1973. *1998*
—. Defense policy. Government. Military strategy. NATO. 1973-76. *1863*
—. Diplomacy. International trade. USA. 1945-76. *2008*
—. Discrimination. Ontario (Toronto). West Indians. 1977. *2768*
—. Dry farming. Grain production. Prairie Provinces. 1870-1930. *2943*
—. Employment. Immigration policy. 1962-74. *1448*
—. Employment. New Brunswick. Nova Scotia. Rural Settlements. 1961-76. *2293*
—. English Canadians. French Canadians. New Brunswick. Working class. -1973. *2393*
—. Ethnic Groups. Industrialization. Labor law. Quebec. 1865-88. *2627*
—. Exports. Fishing. Foreign investments. Newfoundland. 1600-1934. *2178*
—. Federalism. Regionalism. 1960's-70's. *2096*
—. Fishing industry. Newfoundland. 1880-1970. *2177*
—. Foreign investments. Natural resources. 1950-75. *1903*
—. Foreign policy. Race relations. USA. Vietnam War. 1970's. *2078*
—. Foreign relations. International Trade. USA. 1950's-70's. *1964*
—. Foreign Relations. Politics. USA. 1970's. *1995*
—. Foreign Relations. USA. 1950-74. *1980*
—. French language. Parti Québécois. Politics. Quebec. Social Customs. 1973-78. *2696*
—. Fur trade. New France. Quebec. 1760-90. *574*
—. GNP. Statistics. USA. 1960-69. *1530*
—. Great Awakening. Nova Scotia (Yarmouth). Social Conditions. 1760's-70's. *2354*
—. Immigration (theory). 1940's-70's. *1329*
—. Industrial structure. Quebec (Montreal). 17c-1971. *2610*
—. Industry. Western Nations. 1969-71. *1561*
—. Interdependence. Nationalism. USA. ca 1910-73. *1990*
—. King George's War. Louisbourg, fortress of. New England. Nova Scotia. 1745-50. *607*
—. Labor. Management. 1974. *1942*
—. Men. Unemployment. USA. Women. 1950-73. *1533*
—. Migration, Internal. USA. 1960's-70's. *1415*
—. Mining. Railroads. 1960's-70's. *1623*
—. Monetary systems. 1973. *1537*
—. Nationalism. Social Classes. 1968-76. *1567*
—. Ontario. Quebec. Social Change. Violence. 1963-73. *2127*
—. Politics. 1970's. *1314*
—. Unemployment. 1975. *1518*
Economic cooperation. Borden, Robert. British Empire. Tariff. 1912-18. *1151*
—. Consulates. Foreign relations. USA. 1941-70's. *2033*
—. Foreign Investments. Multinational corporations. USA. 1945-74. *1962*
Economic Council of Canada (annual review). 1973. *1541*
Economic Council of Canada. Industrial policy. 1974. *1256*
Economic dependence. Foreign investments. Multinational corporations. USA. 1970's. *2060*
Economic Development See also National Development.
—. Alaska-British Columbia-Yukon Conferences. British Columbia. Regional Planning. Yukon Territory. 1930-64. *2133*

—. Antigonish Movement. Cooperatives. Nova Scotia, eastern. Social Classes. 1920's-30's. *2338*
—. Atlantic Provinces. Bibliographies. Politics. Social classes. 1920's-70's. *2161*
—. British Columbia. Business History. Historiography. Robin, Martin (review article). 19c-20c. 1974. *3244*
—. British Columbia. Royal Engineers. 1845-1910. *3266*
—. British Columbia (Gulf Islands). Environment. Resource endowment. 1858-1973. *3176*
—. British Columbia (Vancouver). Canadian Pacific Railway. 1880's-93. *3222*
—. British Commonwealth. Sugar Agreement. 1949-51. *1870*
—. British Empire Steel Corporation. Coal industry. Nova Scotia (Cape Breton Island). 1910's-20's. *1175*
—. Catholic Church. Church Finance. LaRocque, Paul. Quebec (Sherbrooke). 1893-1926. *2636*
—. Climate. Cultural development. Ocean currents. 1925-76. *3278*
—. Coal Mines and Mining. Europeans. Immigrants. Kansas. 1870-1940. *1062*
—. Emigration. French Canadians. Quebec. 1837-1930. *2616*
—. Energy. Politics. Public Policy. 1945-76. *1571*
—. Family structure. Geographic mobility. Quebec (Laterrière). 1851-1935. *2471*
—. Federal government. Provinces. States. USA. 1950's-70's. *2012*
—. Federal Regulation. Population. Transportation. 1945-77. *1273*
—. Federalism. Independence Movements. Quebec. 1867-1973. *2085*
—. Foreign Relations. USA. 1973. *1977*
—. Forests and Forestry. Minville, Esdras. Multinational corporations. Quebec. USA. 1923-36. *2629*
—. Government. Quebec (Lower Canada). Social classes. Ultramontanism. 19c. *698*
—. Harbors. Nova Scotia (Cape Breton Island, Canso Causeway). 1955-73. *2320*
—. Industrial Revolution. New Brunswick (Saint John). Railroads. Transportation. 1867-1911. *2395*
—. Land tenure. Seigneurial system. 1700-1854. *798*
—. Northwest Territories. Political change. 19c-. *3352*
—. Northwest Territories. Public Opinion. Regionalism. 1970-73. *3277*
—. Ontario. Quebec. 1951-78. *2150*
—. Ontario (Credit River Valley). Population. 1820's-1976. *2824*
—. Planning. Social Conditions. Sweden. 20c. *1310*
—. Provincial Government. 1960's-70's. *2919*
—. Quebec. USA. 1960-73. *1983*
—. Quebec (Saguenay). Settlement. 1840-1900. *2658*
Economic Growth See also Business History; Economic History; Economic Policy; Foreign Aid; GNP; Industrialization; Modernization.
—. 1945-76. *1517*
—. Alaska. Greenland. Population. Scandinavia. 1970's. *281*
—. British Columbia (northwest). National Democratic Party. Natural Resources. 1973-74. *3270*
—. British Columbia (Vancouver). Natural resources. Population. 19c. *3223*
—. Business. Manitoba (Winnipeg). Political Leadership. Urbanization. 1874-1914. *2968*
—. City Government. Public Administration. Quebec (Montreal). Social Conditions. Urbanization. 1850-1914. *2441*
—. City planning. Real estate. Saskatchewan (Saskatoon). Yorath, J. C. 1909-13. *3061*
—. Coasting trade. Employment. Natural Resources. 1931-73. *1579*
—. Colonization companies. Railroads. Saskatchewan (Yorkton). 1882-1905. *1002*
—. Co-op development. Nova Scotia (Cape Breton Island). 1906-73. *2237*
—. Culture. Ontario (Toronto). Urbanization. 1850-1914. *2863*
—. Elites. Ideology. Laval University. Quebec. Social sciences. 1930's-70's. *2527*
—. Energy crisis. Oil and Petroleum Products. Quebec (Montreal). 1960-80. *2644*
—. Federal Government. Free trade. Mathias, Philip. 1973. *1266*
—. Federal policy. Maritime Union Movement. Nova Scotia. Regional development. 1783-1974. *2167*

—. Foreign investments. Nationalism. USA. 1961-74. *1987*
—. Foreign ownership. Industry. 1973. *1936*
—. Fur Trade. Hudson's Bay Company. Lake, Bibye. 1684-1743. *503*
—. Industry. Pollution. Quebec (Saint-Georges Est, Chaudière River). Tourism. 1973. *2652*
—. Maritime Provinces. Newfoundland. 1880-1940. *2151*
—. New Brunswick (Saint John). Social Conditions. 19c. *2411*
—. Northwest Territories. 1970-74. *3275*
—. Nova Scotia (Halifax). Urbanization. 1815-1914. *2356*
—. Ontario (Ottawa). Urbanization. 19c. *2872*
—. Pacific Area. Trade Regulations. 1970-73. *1830*
—. Quebec. 1974. *2656*
—. Quebec. Service activities. 1968-72. *2141*
—. Quebec (Havre, Saint Pierre). Roads. 1685-1973. *2626*
—. Quebec (Montreal). Regional accounting. 1951-66. *2635*
Economic History. British Columbia. Dairying. Fraser Valley Milk Producers' Association. 1867-1969. *3224*
—. Business. Historiography. Laurentian thesis. 1960-73. *1592*
—. Domestic Policy. Government. ca 1865-1975. *209*
—. Industrialization. Iron mining. Newfoundland (Conception Bay; Bell Island). Social History. 1870's-1966. *2199*
—. Mining. Quebec (Abitibi-Témiscamingue). 1885-1950. *2625*
Economic History Association (37th annual meeting). Dissertations. Industrialization. Labor. 19c-20c. 1977. *263*
Economic imperialism. Tariff. USA. 1870-1945. *199*
Economic independence. Culture. Foreign Relations. Nationalism. USA. 1948-75. *2081*
—. Europe, Western. "Third Option" policy. 1970's. *1777*
—. Parti Québécois. Quebec. USA. 1972-73. *1267*
Economic Integration See also Foreign Relations; Tariff.
—. Foreign Relations. International Trade. USA. 1929-33. *1218*
—. Foreign Relations. National self-image. Sharp, Mitchell. USA. -1973. *2083*
Economic interdependence. Foreign investments. Foreign policy. NORAD treaty. USA. 1970's. *1973*
—. Foreign Policy. USA. 1970-74. *2066*
Economic issues. French-speakers. Minorities. Quebec. Separatist Movements. 1976. *2689*
Economic nationalism. Attitudes. Elites. Foreign investments. Legislatures. 1973-74. *2147*
Economic opportunities. Political Protest. Social Classes. USA. 1960-74. *1365*
Economic organizations. Free Trade Area (proposed). International Trade. Pacific area. 1975. *1837*
Economic Policy See also Agricultural Policy; Foreign Aid; Free Trade; Industrialization; International Trade; Modernization; Protectionism; Tariff.
—. American Revolution. Federalism. USA. 1776-1976. *202*
—. Atlantic Provinces. International Trade. Provincial government. USA. 1960's-70's. *2013*
—. Business History. Local Government. Ontario. Property, private. 1898-1911. *1100*
—. Capital flow restrictions. Foreign relations. USA. 1960's-71. *2080*
—. Capital investment, American. Quebec. 1970's. *2067*
—. Commodities. International Organizations. Natural Resources. USA. 1974-76. *1945*
—. Developing nations. Mineral Resources. Mines. 1960-77. *1779*
—. Employment. Inflation. Price stability. 1954-72. *1965*
—. Europe. Foreign Relations. USA. 1974. *1916*
—. European Economic Community. 1960-76. *1858*
—. European Economic Community. Foreign policy. Treaties. 1958-76. *1891*
—. Fishing Industry. International Trade. Newfoundland. 1934-60's. *2175*
—. Foreign Investments. USA. 1975. *1773*
—. Foreign policy. Nationalism. Trudeau, Pierre Elliott. 1968-78. *1772*

—. Foreign Policy. Robertson, Norman Alexander. 1929-68. *1234*
—. Foreign Relations. Japan. 1974-75. *1814*
—. Foreign relations. Prime ministers. Trudeau, Pierre Elliott. USA. 1960's-70's. *2006*
—. Industry. Regionalism. 1965-75. *2129*
—. Industry. USA. 1971-75. *2007*
—. Quebec. 1974. *2667*
—. Quebec. Water use (theories). 1970's. *1324*
Economic power. French Canadians. Quebec. Separatist movements. 1960's-70's. *2679*
Economic progression. Education. Immigration. Political autonomy. Professions. 1945-75. *1425*
Economic prosperity. International Trade. Natural resources. 1950's-70's. *1833*
Economic rationality. Nationalism. 1900's-60's. *1126*
Economic reform. Aberhart, William. Alberta. Politics. Radio. Religion. 1934-37. *3088*
Economic Regulations *See also* Federal Regulation; Trade Regulations.
—. Capitalism. Quebec. 1870-1900. *2650*
—. Constitutions. Federal government. Provincial Government. 1856-1975. *60*
—. Natural resources. 1972-75. *1508*
Economic relations. Energy policy. USA. 1950's-74. *1958*
—. European Economic Community. 1976. *1753*
—. European Economic Community. 1973. *1835*
—. European Economic Community. 1976. *1893*
—. European Economic Community. Foreign policy. Press. 1974-75. *1820*
—. Foreign policy. Great Britain. USA. 1873-1973. *17*
—. Heeney-Merchant Report (1965). USA. 1973-. *1967*
—. Industrial strategy. USA. 1970's. *1978*
Economic returns. Colleges and Universities. Curricula. Labor market. 1961-72. *1582*
Economic security. Families, low-income. Poverty. Public Welfare. Quebec. Social Aid Act (1969). 1969-75. *2668*
Economic Structure. Unemployment. 1971-74. *1528*
Economic Theory. Bibliographies. Minville, Esdras. Quebec. 20c. *2467*
—. French Canadians. Minville, Esdras. Quebec. 20c. *2586*
—. Income. Inflation. Investments. Keynes, John Maynard. 1974. *1548*
—. Mining. Vertical integration. 1960's-70's. *1513*
Economic viability. Technology. USA. 1900's-70's. *121*
Economics *See also* Business; Capital; Commerce; Depressions; Finance; Income; Industry; Labor; Land; Monopolies; Political Economy; Population; Prices; Property; Trade.
—. École des Hautes Études Commerciales. Educators. Minville, Esdras. Quebec (Montreal). 20c. *2457*
—. Employment. Immigration. Wages. 1970's. *1588*
—. Foreign policy. Military. Politics. 1950's-70's. *1856*
—. Foreign Relations. Politics. USA. 1945-74. *1253*
—. Industrialization. Natural resources. 1950's-70's. *1765*
—. Minville, Esdras. Periodicals. Quebec (Montreal). 1922-28. *2533*
—. Nationalism. Popular Culture. USA. 1776-1976. *725*
Ecumenism. Church History. United Church of Canada. 1920-76. *29*
—. Church of England. Symonds, Herbert. 1897-1921. *194*
—. Patrick, William. Presbyterian Church. 1900-11. *1085*
Editorials. Bibliographies. French Canadians. Latin America. Newspapers. Quebec. 1959-73. *2433*
—. Elections. Foreign Relations. Newspapers. 1972-74. *1917*
—. Federal systems. Political Campaigns. USA. 1972. *1715*
—. Newspapers. Political campaigns. 1972. *1722*
Editors and Editing *See also* Press; Reporters and Reporting.
—. Chipman, George. *Grain Growers' Guide* (periodical). Prairie Provinces. Teaching. 1903-05. *2938*
—. Grove, Frederick Philip (letters). Literature. Pacey, Desmond. 1912-48. 1976. *1135*

Edmonton Bulletin (newspaper). Alberta (Athabasca Landing). Canadian Northern Railway. Railroads. Villages. 1912-77. *3113*
Education *See also* headings beginning with education and educational; Adult Education; Bilingual Education; Colleges and Universities; Curricula; Discrimination, Educational; Elementary Education; Higher Education; Illiteracy; Military Education; Physical Education and Training; Religious Education; Scholarship; Schools; Teaching; Textbooks.
—. Accountability. 1970-73. *1384*
—. Archaeology, industrial. Great Britain. History, study of. USA. 1955-70. *1302*
—. Archives. Culture. France. 1977. *215*
—. Art. Chabert, Joseph. National Institute for Arts and Crafts. Quebec (Montreal). Teachers. Working Class. 1861-94. *1053*
—. Bermuda. Political Factions. Religion. 1800-1977. *136*
—. Bibliographies. 17c-20c. 1973-74. *64*
—. Children. Fur trade. Hudson's Bay Company. Métis. 1820's-60's. *628*
—. Children. Nova Scotia (Guysborough). Welsh, Matthew. Wills. 19c. *2267*
—. Cochran, William. Enlightenment. Nova Scotia. 1789. *745*
—. Economic progression. Immigration. Political autonomy. Professions. 1945-75. *1425*
—. Employment. Hudson Bay. Hudson's Bay Company. Métis. 1790's-1820's. *771*
—. Eskimos. Indians. Métis. Northwest Territories (Mackenzie District). Whites. 1969-70. *3358*
—. Farmers. Saskatchewan Grain Growers' Association. ca 1918-25. *3082*
—. Federal government. Indians. Métis. 1940-70. *361*
—. French Canadians. Literary associations. Quebec (Lower Canada). Social Problems. 1840-67. *2526*
—. Great Britain. Missions and Missionaries. Protestantism. Sudan Interior Mission. 1937-55. *197*
—. Immigrants. Labor. Social Classes. 1973. *2149*
—. Immigration. Jews. Russia. Segal, Beryl (reminiscences). USA. 1900-70's. *204*
—. Income. Personal growth. Scandinavia. USA. 1975. *1450*
—. Indians. 19c-20c. *385*
—. Manitoba (Winnipeg). Red River Academy. 1820's-50's. *2973*
—. McCulloch, Thomas. Nova Scotia. Pictou Grammar School. 19c. *2337*
—. New Brunswick. Socialism. Stuart, Henry Harvey. 1873-1952. *2380*
Education (British, US). Catholic Church. Newspapers. Ontario. 1851-1948. *2833*
Education Department (Recreational and Physical Education Branch). British Columbia. Depressions. Sports. Youth. 1934-40. *3217*
Education (review article). Historiography. Social Change. 19c-20c. *248*
Educational Policy. Goggin, David James. Manitoba. Northwest Territories. Teaching. ca 1890's. *2904*
Educational Reform *See also* Education; Educators.
—. Parent Commission. Quebec. 1944-66. *2416*
Educational role. Alberta. Depressions. United Farm Women of Alberta. 1915-30. *3161*
Educational system. Catholic Church. French Canadians. Parent-youth conflict. Quebec. Social change. 1960-70. *2516*
—. Ideological structures. Sex Discrimination. Sociology. Women. 1970's. *1474*
Educators *See also* Teachers.
—. Adult education. Howe, Joseph. Nova Scotia. 1827-66. *2290*
—. Authors. Mount Allison University. New Brunswick (Sackville). Webster, John Clarence. 1882-1950. *2404*
—. École des Hautes Études Commerciales. Economics. Minville, Esdras. Quebec (Montreal). 20c. *2457*
—. Forrester, Alexander. Nova Scotia (Truro). ca 1848-69. *2277*
Edward VIII (tour). Great Britain. 1919. *1163*
Edwards, Robert C. "Bob". Alberta. *Eye Opener* (newspaper). Populists. 1904-22. *3108*
Egalitarianism. Social Organization. Women. Prehistory-1977. *409*
Election Expenses Act (Canada, 1973). Legislation. 1973. *1665*
Elections *See also* Campaign Finance; Political Campaigns; Referendum; Suffrage; Voting and Voting Behavior.

—. Agricultural policy. Provincial government. Quebec. 1960-73. *2601*
—. Agriculture and Government. Ontario (Manitoulin). Political Protest. 1914-18. *2775*
—. Anderson, James T. M. Gardiner, James G. Provincial Legislatures. Saskatchewan (Estevan). 1929-30. *3078*
—. British Columbia (Vancouver). Models. Political parties. 1937-74. *3230*
—. Campaign Finance. 1972. *1701*
—. Church and State. Equal Rights Association. Ontario. Quebec. 1885-95. *2827*
—. Communist Party. 1972-73. *1677*
—. Conscription, Military. King, William Lyon Mackenzie. Ligue pour la Défense du Canada. Quebec. World War II. 1942-44. *1226*
—. Conservative Party. Liberal Party. New Democratic Party. 1972. *1675*
—. Davis, Thomas O. Liberal Party. Saskatchewan. 1896. *3046*
—. Editorials. Foreign Relations. Newspapers. 1972-74. *1917*
—. Farmers. Orange Order. Political Attitudes. United Farmers of Ontario. 1920-25. *2839*
—. Fielding, William Stevens. Liberal Party. Nova Scotia. 1891-96. *2313*
—. France. Language. Parliaments. Quebec. 1792-1810. *700*
—. Geopolitics. 1921-74. *100*
—. Independence issue. Liberals. Parti Québécois. Quebec. 1973-76. *2707*
—. Labor Unions and Organizations. Parti Québécois. Quebec. 1970-77. *2591*
—. Legislative Assembly. Political Factions. Propaganda. 1792. *708*
—. Liberal Government. Trudeau, Pierre Elliott. 1968-72. *1638*
—. Maoism. 1971 73. *1331*
—. New Brunswick (Northumberland County). Street, John Ambrose. Violence. 1842. *2403*
—. Newfoundland (St. John's). Political Reform. Representative government. 1815-32. *2194*
—. Ontario (Lennox and Addington). Political Change. 1836. *823*
—. Parti Québécois. Quebec. 1973-76. *2693*
—. Parti Québécois. Quebec. 1976. *2695*
—. Political Parties. 1965. 1968. *1653*
—. Quebec. 1867-86. *2425*
Elections (federal). 1925-72. *1690*
—. British Columbia. Political Parties. Voting and Voting Behavior. 1974. *3231*
—. Communist Party (21st convention). 1972-73. *1676*
—. Government, majority. Public Opinion. Voting and Voting behavior. 1965-74. *1686*
—. Municipalities, redistributing. Political Parties. Quebec. Voting and Voting Behavior. 1968. *2422*
—. Occupations. Parliaments. Political candidates. 1974. *1657*
—. Voting and Voting Behavior. 1974. *1702*
Elections, local. Antilabor sentiments. Immigration policy. Ku Klux Klan. 1921-30's. *2925*
Elections (municipal, provincial). Ontario (Kitchener). Urban Renewal. 1967-71. *2889*
Elections, provincial. Alberta. Liberal Party. Social Credit League. United Farmers of Alberta. 1905-73. *3107*
—. Anti-Catholicism. Ku Klux Klan. Saskatchewan. Separate school legislation. 1929. *3024*
—. British Columbia. New Democratic Party. 1970-73. *3187*
—. British Columbia. Social Credit. 1952-53. *3193*
—. British Columbia (Victoria). Voting and Voting Behavior. 1972. *3249*
—. Communist Party. Cooperative Commonwealth Federation. Saskatchewan. 1930's. *3066*
—. Jews. Parti Québécois. Quebec. Separatist Movements. 1976. *2721*
—. Nationalism. Quebec. Social issues. 1973. *2099*
Electoral systems. Models. 1867-1970. *1709*
Electric Power. Business. Nova Scotia (Guysborough). 1927. *2268*
—. Energy. Fundy, Bay of. Passamaquoddy Bay. Tides. 1919-64. 1975. *115*
—. Environment. Federal regulation. Niagara Falls. USA. 1895-1906. 1960's-70's. *2075*
—. Manitoba. Ontario. Public Utilities. 1905-30. *2138*
—. Saskatchewan (Humboldt). Saskatchewan Power Corporation. 1907-29. *3080*
Electricity and Electronics. Energy crisis. James Bay. Quebec. 1960-70's. *1292*

—. Private enterprise. Qu'Appelle Flour Mill. Saskatchewan. 1906-27. *3081*

Electrochemistry. Calcium carbide, manufacture of. Inventions. Willson, Thomas Leopold "Carbide". 1860-1915. *939*

Elementary education. Ontario (Upper Canada). 1810-45. *780*

Elites *See also* Decisionmaking; Social Classes; Social Status.
—. Alberta (Banff). Midwest. Power, interorganizational. 1960's-70's. *3123*
—. Attitudes. Economic nationalism. Foreign investments. Legislatures. 1973-74. *2147*
—. Bothwick, J. Douglas (*History and Biographical Gazetteer of Montreal to the Year 1892*). Quebec (Montreal). Social stratification. 19c. *2550*
—. Brotherhood of the Holy Family. Catholic Church. Chaumonot, Joseph-Marie-Pierre. Laval, François de. Quebec (Montreal). 1663-1760. *547*
—. Business. Law. Social institutions, stratifying. 19c-1974. *211*
—. Business. Ontario (Toronto). Upper Canada Club. 1835-40. *812*
—. Economic growth. Ideology. Laval University. Quebec. Social sciences. 1930's-70's. *2527*
—. Entrepreneurs. Ontario (Hamilton). 1850's. *2801*
—. Ethnic values. Protestant ethic. Rationality. Senators. 1971. *1645*
—. Foreign Policy. International system. 1975-76. *1751*
—. Government. Ontario (Upper Canada; Toronto). Simcoe, John Graves. Strachan, John. 1793-1818. *773*
—. Great Britain. Pressure Groups (review article). USA. 1960's-70's. *1325*
—. Management. Social mobility. 1880-85. 1905-10. *899*
—. Quebec. Science. 1824-44. *2515*

Ellice, Edward. British Empire. Self-government. 1838-40. *826*

Embezzlement. Crime and Criminals. Depression of 1857. Land speculation. Street, William Warren. 1830-70. *2799*

Emergencies. British Columbia. Civil Defense. Planning. Provincial Government. 1951-76. *3233*

Emergency powers. Anti-Inflation Act. Peacetime. Supreme Court (Canada). Wages. 1976. *1607*

Emigrant guides. Colonial policy. Great Britain. Land grants (proposed). Ontario (Peterborough). Traill, Catherine Parr. 19c. *869*

Emigration *See also* Demography; Immigration; Population; Race Relations; Refugees.
—. Acadians. 1605-1800. *524*
—. Acadians. Assimilation. Minorities in Politics. New Brunswick (Moncton). 1871-1971. *2385*
—. Africa, West. American Revolution. Fugitive slaves. Great Britain. Nova Scotia. 1776-1820. *737*
—. Bibb, Henry. Negroes. Separatism. USA. 1830-60. *858*
—. Catholics. Glengarry Highlanders. Great Britain. Macdonnell, Alexander. Ontario. 1770's-1814. *805*
—. Depressions. Maritime Provinces. Massachusetts (Boston). New England. 1860-1900. *2154*
—. Economic Development. French Canadians. Quebec. 1837-1930. *2616*
—. Epp, Johann (letter). Mennonites. North America. Russia. 1875. *981*
—. Foreign Relations. France. Quebec (Sherbrooke). Trappists. 1903-14. *2529*
—. Great Britain (Sussex). Ontario (Upper Canada, York). Petworth Emigration Committee. 1830-40. *775*
—. Jews. Morocco. Quebec (Montreal). 1960's-70's. *2517*
—. Population. 1961-71. *1413*

Emmons, Ebenezer. Geology. New York (Taconic Mountains). Scientific Discoveries. 1840-1900. *277*

Emmons, George Thornton. Alaska. Artifacts. Ethnology. Tlingit Indians. 1852-1945. *417*

Empire Day celebrations. Great Britain. Imperialism. Nationalism. Ontario. Public Schools. 1890-1930's. *2864*

Employers' groups. Quebec. 1967-73. *2592*

Employment *See also* Discrimination, Employment; Occupations; Unemployment.
—. Adolescence. Dependency. Frontier and Pioneer Life. Ontario (Orillia). Social change. 1861-71. *2769*

—. Assimilation. Immigrants. Language training. Ontario (Toronto). 1968-70. *1625*
—. Automation. International Longshoremen's and Warehousemen's Union. Labor Disputes. 1973. *1600*
—. Canadian Labour Congress. Conference on Equal Opportunity and Treatment for Women Workers. Equal opportunity. Women. 1978. *1558*
—. Canadian Railway Labour Association. Railroads. Technology. Working Conditions. 1973. *1620*
—. Capital. Manufacturing. 1949-72. *1608*
—. Cities. Ethnic Groups. Property ownership. Social Classes. 19c. *90*
—. Coasting trade. Economic Growth. Natural Resources. 1931-73. *1579*
—. Colleges and Universities. Ontario. Social Status. 1960-71. *2787*
—. Containerization. International Longshoremen's and Warehousemen's Union. Labor Disputes. 1973. *1593*
—. Economic Conditions. Immigration policy. 1962-74. *1448*
—. Economic Conditions. New Brunswick. Nova Scotia. Rural Settlements. 1961-76. *2293*
—. Economic policy. Inflation. Price stability. 1954-72. *1965*
—. Economics. Immigration. Wages. 1970's. *1588*
—. Education. Hudson Bay. Hudson's Bay Company. Métis. 1790's-1820's. *771*
—. Families (low-income). Methodology. Models. 1974. *1510*
—. Fiscal Policy. Income. Labor Unions and Organizations. Monetary policy. 1975. *1624*
—. Fringe benefits (economic effects). Overtime. 1957-67. *1552*
—. Immigrants. Italians. Ontario (Toronto). 1885-1915. *2783*
—. Immigration Bill, 1976. Management. 1976. *1394*
—. Industry. Worker tenure. 1974. *1555*
—. Labor cost, non-wage. Overtime. 1973. *1566*
—. Manufacturing. Trade. 1949-70. *2145*

Energy *See also* Fuel; Power Resources.
—. 1973. *1900*
—. Coal. 1892-1978. *170*
—. Development. Imperial Oil Company. Public ownership. 1970's. *1841*
—. Economic conditions. Fuel. Quebec. 1974-. *2432*
—. Economic development. Politics. Public Policy. 1945-76. *1571*
—. Electric power. Fundy, Bay of. Passamaquoddy Bay. Tides. 1919-64. 1975. *115*
—. USA. 1973-75. *1333*

Energy Crisis. Agricultural Production. Climate. Food supply. Urbanization. 1956-74. *1511*
—. Dams. Farms. Ontario (Osceola). Water power. 1902-05. *2813*
—. Economic growth. Oil and Petroleum Products. Quebec (Montreal). 1960-80. *2644*
—. Electricity and Electronics. James Bay. Quebec. 1960-70's. *1292*
—. North America. 1960's-70's. *1908*
—. Oil Industry and Trade. USA. 1947-48. *2032*
—. Public ownership. USA. 1970-73. *1286*
—. Taxation. USA. 1973-75. *1643*

Energy policy. Commercial relations. USA. 1950's-74. *1958*
—. Developing nations. Environment. 1975. *1274*
—. Federal Government. Provincial Government. Trudeau, Pierre Elliott. 1950-77. *2093*

Engel, Jacob. Brethren in Christ. Pennsylvania (Lancaster County). Sects, Religious. 1775-1964. *250*

Engineering *See also* Aeronautics; Highway Engineering; Marine Engineering.
—. British Columbia. Lumber and Lumbering. Poetry. Railroads. Swanson, Robert (interview). 20c. *3273*
—. Keefer, Thomas Coltrin. Ontario (Upper Canada). Railroads. 1821-1915. *909*

Engineers. Ethnic groups. Occupational preferences and values. Quebec (Montreal). -1974. *2559*

Engineers, locomotive. Canadian Pacific Railway. Labor Unions and Organizations. Prairie Provinces. Strikes. 1883. *1066*

English Canadians. Acadians. Catholic Church. Maritime Provinces. Social Conditions. 1763-1977. *2171*
—. Attitudes. Race. Sex. Woman Suffrage. ca 1877-1918. *902*

—. Berger, Carl (review article). Historiography. Nationalism. 1900-76. *232*
—. Biculturalism. Federalism. French Canadians. Quebec. 20c. *1354*
—. Boer War. 1899-1902. *1098*
—. Bureaucracies. Civil Service. French Canadians. 1944-75. *1706*
—. Canadian Expeditionary Force. French Canadians. Hughes, Samuel. Imperialismo. World War I. 1853-1921. *245*
—. Confederation. Creighton, D. G. French Canadians. Heintzman, Ralph. Minorities in Politics. 1850's-90's. *922*
—. Continental dimension. Cultural environment. National Self-image. North America. 1840's-1960's. *210*
—. Cooperatives. French Canadians. 19c. *37*
—. Economic environment, bicultural. French. New Brunswick. Worker attitudes. -1973. *2393*
—. Family. Woman suffrage. 1877-1918. *901*
—. French Canadians. Laurendeau, André. Nationalism. Quebec. 1945-66. *2556*
—. French Canadians. Multiculturalism. Quebec. 1970's. *1303*
—. French Canadians. Political power. Press. Quebec. 1864-67. *2572*
—. French Canadians. Quebec. 17c-20c. *33*
—. English Canadians. French Canadians. Social Customs. 1922-76. *102*
—. Nationalism. Oil Industry and Trade. ca 1950-75. *1976*

English language. French Quebec Movement. Official Language Act (Quebec, 1974). Quebec. 1974. *2460*
—. Australia. Business. Foreign Relations. Social Customs. 1975. *1949*

Enlightenment. Cochran, William. Education. Nova Scotia. 1789. *745*
—. Ideas, diffusion of. Newspapers. 1764-1810. *648*

Entertainment. Architecture. Capitol Theatre. Movie palaces. Ontario (Ottawa). Vaudeville. 1920-70. *1138*

Entrepreneurial behaviour. Career patterns. Quebec (Montreal). Real estate agents, residential. -1974. *2634*

Entrepreneurs. Alaska (Skagway). Brackett, George. Gold Rushes. Roads. Yukon Territory. 1897-98. *3323*
—. Baker, Edgar Crow. British Columbia (Victoria). 1872-98. *3179*
—. British Columbia (Sandon). Harris, Johnny. 1890's-1950's. *3184*
—. Elites. Ontario (Hamilton). 1850's. *2801*
—. Jackson, Walter John. Northwest Territories (Baffin Island). ca 1875-1922. *3362*

Entropy concept. Information theory. Political Parties. Voting and Voting Behavior. 1962-69. *1683*

Environment *See also* Conservation of Natural Resources; Ecology; Nature Conservation.
—. Accountability. Decisionmaking. Federal government. Science and Government. 1950's-70's. *1725*
—. Amazon River. Americas (North and South). Northwest Territories (Mackenzie River). Rivers. 1977. *268*
—. British Columbia (Gulf Islands). Economic development. Resource endowment. 1858-1973. *3176*
—. City planning. Housing. Suburbs. 1893-1930. *236*
—. Climate. Indians. North America. Settlement. Prehistory. 1956-78. *309*
—. Coal. Saskatchewan (Estevan region). Strip mining. 1850's-1975. *3071*
—. Developing nations. Energy-environment policy. 1975. *1274*
—. Electric power. Federal regulation. Niagara Falls. USA. 1895-1906. 1960's-70's. *2075*
—. Fisheries. USA. ca 1900-72. *2049*

Environmentalism. Committee on the Challenges of Modern Society. Foreign Policy. NATO. USA. 1969-77. *1838*
—. Foreign Relations. USA. 1965-75. *2011*
—. Indians. Labrador. Quebec. Religion. Social organization. 17c-20c. *428*
—. Saskatchewan. Saskatoon Environmental Society. 1970-77. *3068*

Environment Department. Government. 1970-73. *1288 1288*

Environmental policy. Boundaries. International Boundary and Water Commission. International Joint Commission. Mexico. USA. 1973. *2053*
—. Foreign Relations. USA. 1960's-70's. *2000*

—. Discovery and exploration. Mississippi River. Natural resources. North America. St. Lawrence River. 17c-19c. *270*

Epidemics *See also* names of contagious diseases, e.g. Smallpox, etc.

—. Alberta (Calgary). Influenza. Mahood, Cecil S. 1918-19. *3138*

—. British Columbia (Vancouver). Influenza. Public health services. 1918-19. *3174*

—. Cholera. City Government. New Brunswick (Saint John). 1854. *2386*

—. Demography. Fur trade. Indians. Wildlife diseases. 15c-18c. *425*

—. Fur Trade. Hunt, George T. *(The Wars of the Iroquois)*. Indians. Iroquois Indians. 1609-53. *523*

Episcopal Church, Protestant. Hudson's Bay Company. Indians. Missions and Missionaries. Pacific Northwest. 1825-75. *402*

—. Ontario (Algoma Diocese). 1873-1973. *2880*

Episcopal nominations. Catholic Church. French Canadians. Irish Canadians. 1900-75. *2930*

Epp, Johann (letter). Emigration. Mennonites. North America. Russia. 1875. *981*

Equal employment. Diplomats. External Affairs Department. Women. 1909-75. *82*

Equal opportunity. Canadian Labour Congress. Conference on Equal Opportunity and Treatment for Women Workers. Employment. Women. 1978. *1558*

—. Hutterites. Leadership succession. Population. Prairie Provinces. Social Organization. 1940's-70's. *2908*

Equal Rights Association. Church and state. Elections (1890). Ontario reaction. Quebec. 1885-95. *2827*

Equality. Class struggle. French-speaking community. Intellectuals. Nationalism. Quebec. 1960's-70's. *2677*

—. Women. 1966-76. *1349*

Erasmus, Peter. Alberta (Lac la Biche). Faraud, Bishop. North West Rebellion. 1885. *1021*

Erie Canal. Canals. Freight capacity and utilization. Great Lakes. 1810-50. *791*

Eskimos. Acculturation. Cree Indians. Race Relations. 1970-74. *284*

—. Alaska. Indians. Land claim settlements. 1958-77. *288*

—. Alaska. Sleep paralysis. Prehistory-1976. *315*

—. Alaska Land Settlement of 1971. Minorities. Politics. 1960-73. *318*

—. Alaskan Coast. Bernard, Joseph Francis. Siberian Coast. Traders. 1903-29. *314*

—. Anthropology, Physical. Craniology. Prehistory. 1971. *313*

—. Arctic. Berthe, Jean. Fur trade. Quebec. Stevenson, A. (account). 1930's. *2663*

—. Arctic. Colonization. Social Change. 1930-60. *317*

—. Arctic. Federal government. Mass Media. Satellite service. 1972. *329*

—. Arctic. Inkshuks (monuments). Prehistory-1978. *319*

—. Arctic. Living conditions. 1950-75. *325*

—. Arctic Ocean. Mackenzie Bay (Herschel Island). Polar exploration. Whaling Industry and Trade. 1826-1972. *339*

—. Art. Northwest Territories (Frobisher Bay). 1969. *316*

—. Artifacts. Europeans. Labrador. Quebec. Ungava Peninsula. ca 400-18c. *300*

—. Bibliographies. Explorers. Greenland. 16c-19c. *331*

—. Bibliographies. Indians. Métis. 1975. *283*

—. Church Missionary Society. Church of England. Hudson's Bay Company. Missions and Missionaries. Northwest Territories (Baffin Island). Peck, F. J. Trade. 1894-1913. *340*

—. Cultural change. Indians. 1970's. *408*

—. Daily life. Discovery and Exploration. Hantzsch, Bernard. Naturalists. Northwest Territories (Baffin Island). 1910-11. *3314*

—. Daily life. Fur trade. Hudson's Bay Company. Northwest Territories (Hudson Bay, Baffin Island). 1909-30's. *3348*

—. Education. Indians. Métis. Northwest Territories (Mackenzie District). Whites. 1969-70. *3358*

—. Ethnology. Indians. Pacific Basin. Polynesians. Prehistory-1976. *285*

—. Excavations. Grizzly bear skull. Labrador. 18c-19c. *336*

—. Expedition. Geological Survey of Canada. Tyrrell, J. W. (travel diary). 1890's. *337*

—. Eye diseases. Ophthalmology. 1974. *312*

—. Family. Personality. Values. 1974. *333*

—. Hudson Bay. Mina (Eskimo woman). Religion. 1940's-50's. *326*

—. Hudson's Bay Company. Northwest Territories (Baffin Island, Devon Island). Russell, Chesley (account). Settlement. 1934-36. *332*

—. Industrial expansion. Land use (control). Oil Industry and Trade. Pollution. 1975. *338*

—. Masak (personal account). Northwest Territories (Aklavik). Socialization. 1930's. *324*

—. Northwest Territories (Baffin Island). Radio. Television. 1972-73. *321*

—. Northwest Territories (Baffin Island). Social customs. Television. 1972-74. *320*

—. Television. Values. 1976-77. *330*

Eskimos (Aivilik). Northwest Territories (Roes Welcome Sound). Witchcraft. 1953-73. *327*

Eskimos, Central. Anthropology. Authority. Ecology. Social organization. 1970's. *322*

Eskimos, Sadlermiut. Gibbons, Jimmy (interview). Housing. Marsh, Donald B. (reminiscences). Northwest Territories (Southampton Island). ca 1900. *328*

Eskimos, Thule culture. Excavations. Houses, communal. Labrador (Saglek Bay). 1650-1700. *334*

Espionage. British Columbia (Victoria). British Empire. Neutrality. Spanish-American War. 1898. *1105*

—. Communism. Congress. Norman, E. Herbert. USA. 1945-57. *2070*

—. Leftism. Rosenberg Case. USA. 1940's-50's. *1682*

Essays. Bibliographies. British Columbia. Theses. 1976. *3269*

Estate ownership. Aristocracy. France. Meyer, Rudolf. Roffignac, Yves de. Saskatchewan (Eastern Assiniboia; Whitewood). 1885-1900. *982*

Esterhazy, Paul O. d' (Johan Baptista Packh). Hungarian immigrants. Saskatchewan (Esterhazy). 1831-1912. *3043*

Ethics *See also* Morality; Values.

—. Business. 1867-1914. 1976-77. *944*

Ethnic Groups *See also* Minorities.

—. Archives. 1970's. *160*

—. Assimilation. Europe. Race Relations. USA. 20c. *15*

—. Attitudes. Social Status. 1968. *1374*

—. Bibliographies. Multiculturalism. Public Policy. 1967-76. *98*

—. Bilingualism. French language. 1970-73. *1427*

—. Birth rate. Demography. Immigrants. Marriage. 1871. *1072*

—. Boundaries. Manitoba (Winnipeg; North End, St. Boniface). Neighborhoods. 19c-1978. *2977*

—. Catholic Church. Evangelists. Protestantism. Quebec (Lower Canada). Rebellion of 1837. 1766-1865. *811*

—. Cities. Employment. Property ownership. Social Classes. 19c. *90*

—. Civil Rights. Constitutional reform. 1972. *2121*

—. Communications. Geographic Space. Great Britain. Regionalism. 1976. *2139*

—. Constitutions. Joint Committee of the Canadian Senate and House of Commons. Language, official. 1970's. *1947*

—. Cultural heritage. Slovaks. USA. 19c-20c. *1449*

—. Cultural membership. Political attitudes. Quebec. 1974. *2548*

—. Culture. USA. 1776-1976. *79*

—. Demography. Quebec (Quebec). 1795-1805. *2512*

—. Discrimination. Immigrants. Manitoba (Winnipeg). Population. 1874-1974. *2967*

—. Dukhobors. Royal Canadian Mounted Police. Saskatchewan. Settlement. 1899-1909. *3028*

—. Economic Conditions. Industrialization. Labor law. Quebec. 1865-88. *2627*

—. Elites. Rationality. Senators. Work ethic. 1971. *1645*

—. Engineers. Occupational preferences and values. Quebec (Montreal). -1974. *2559*

—. Ethnic Serials Project. National Library of Canada. Newspapers. 18c-20c. *51*

—. Europe. Immigration. Occupations. Ontario (Toronto). Social Status. 1940's-70's. *2814*

—. French Canadians. Geographic space. Multiculturalism. Quebec. Regionalism. Urbanization. 1930-73. *2715*

—. Identity. Nationalism. Regionalism. Students. 1960-77. *2915*

—. Indian-White Relations. Sex Discrimination. 1972-73. *1420*

—. Interpersonal Relations. Students. -1973. *1435*

—. Manitoba (Winnipeg). Social Classes. Voting and Voting Behavior. 1941. *3014*

—. Manitoba (Winnipeg). Social Classes. Voting and Voting Behavior. 1945-46. *3023*

—. Maps. Methodology. North America. 1900-78. *1457*

—. Meisel, John (review). Politics. Simeon, Richard (review). 1960-68. *1713*

—. Multiculturalism. Public Policy. 1970's. *1494*

—. National Conference on Canadian Culture and Ethnic Groups. 1973. *1356*

—. Occupations. Ontario (London). 1871. *2744*

—. Ontario (Holland Marsh). Rural settlements. 1930's-76. *2881*

Ethnic Serials Project. Ethnic groups. National Library of Canada. Newspapers. 18c-20c. *51*

Ethnic stigmas. Impression management. Indian-White Relations. Migrants. 1967-68. *371*

Ethnic studies. Immigrant adjustment. Sociology. 1960's-70's. *1409*

Ethnic tension. Immigration policy. Radicals and Radicalism. 1896-1919. *1079*

Ethnicity. Acculturation. Jews. USA. 1961-74. *1486*

—. Anglophones. French-speakers. Historical traditions. 1974. *1464*

—. Assimilation. Technology. USA. 20c. *1408*

—. Belgium. Nationalism. Quebec. Social Classes. 1970's. *2702*

—. Crime and Criminals. Illiteracy. Ontario (Middlesex County). Sex. Social Status. 1867-68. *1044*

—. Greek Canadians. Immigration. Ontario (Toronto). Private Schools. 1900-40. *2845*

—. Immigration. North America. 1974. *1407*

—. Immigration policy. USA. 1867-1975. *168*

—. National self-identity. Regionalism. USA. 1974. *2146*

—. Students. 1971. *1380*

Ethnicity (review article). Polish Canadians. Portuguese Canadians. Scottish Canadians. 18c-20c. 1976. *201*

Ethnographers. Athapascan Indians. Subarctic. 1900-65. *449*

—. Indians. Labrador. 1908-68. *436*

Ethnography. Archaeological research. British Columbia (Alberni Valley). Indians. Prehistory. 1973. *301*

Ethnohistory. Quebec. St. Lawrence estuary. 20c. *2491*

Ethnology *See also* Acculturation; Anthropology; Folklore; Language; Negroes; Race Relations.

—. Alaska. Artifacts. Emmons, George Thornton. Tlingit Indians. 1852-1945. *417*

—. Densmore, Frances. Indians. Musicology. 1918-57. *400*

—. Eskimos. Indians. Pacific Basin. Polynesians. Prehistory-1976. *285*

Ethnomusicology. Cris Indians. Leden, Christian. Phonograph. Songs. 1911. *387*

Eucharistic worship. Protestantism. Religion. United Church of Canada. 1952-72. *1452*

Eudists. Catholic Church. Industrialization. Quebec (Chicoutimi Basin). Working class. 1903-30. *2475*

Eugenics *See also* Birth Control.

—. Act of Sexual Sterilization (Alberta, 1928). Alberta. Immigration. Press. Woodsworth, James S. 1900-28. *2906*

Europe *See also* Europe, Eastern; Europe, Western.

—. Agriculture. Industrialization. Market economy. North America. Peasant movements (colloquium). ca 1875-1975. *13*

—. Architecture. North America. Subways. 1940's-70's. *1307*

—. Assimilation. Ethnic groups. Race Relations. USA. 20c. *15*

—. Bibliographies. Folk religion. North America. 1900-74. *256*

—. Bibliographies. Literary associations (French-language). Quebec. USA. Voluntary associations. 1840-1900. *2524*

—. British North America. Droz, Pierre-Frédéric. Travel. Watchmakers. 1768-70. *685*

—. Catlin, George. Chippewa Indians. Maungwudaus (George Henry). Ontario. Theater. 1840's. *450*

—. Conference on Security and Cooperation in Europe. International Security. 1950-73. *1794*

—. Conference on Security and Co-operation in Europe. USA. 1973-74. *L'Anse* 1840
—. Decentralization. Industrial relations. Labor. USA. 1960's-70's. 1626
—. Developing Nations. Foreign policy. Japan. USA. 1950-75. 1741
—. Economic Policy. Foreign Relations. USA. 1974. 1916
—. Ethnic Groups. Immigration. Occupations. Ontario (Toronto). Social Status. 1940's-70's. 2814
—. Flint. Gunflints. Indians. Quebec (Chicoutimi). Travel. 17c. 20c. 349
—. Foreign Policy. Trudeau, Pierre Elliott. 1968-78. 1946
—. Foreign Relations. 1974. 1846
—. Foreign Relations. USA. 1945-73. 1827
—. Ideas, history of. Quebec. Social Classes. 1960-75. 2501
—. Industrial plant size. North America. 1963-67. 1609
—. Military operations. Politics. World War II. 1939-45. 1244
—. North America. Physical achievement. Sports. 1740-1975. 131
—. Quebec. Separatist Movements. USA. 1977. 1920
Europe, Eastern. Americas (North and South). Discovery and Exploration. Pacific Area. 16c-19c. 175
—. Communism. Historiography. Public administration. USA. USSR. ca 1850-1975. 1316
Europe (Eastern, Southern). Immigration. Legislation. Physicians. Racism. 1920's. 1178
Europe, Western. Catholic Church. Church and State. North America. Politics. 1870-1974. 246
—. Cultural relations. Foreign policy. USA. ca 1850's-20c. 34
—. Economic independence. "Third Option" policy. 1970's. 1777
European Economic Community. Economic Policy. 1960-76. 1858
—. Economic Policy. Foreign policy. Treaties. 1958-76. 1891
—. Economic relations. 1976. 1753
—. Economic relations. 1973. 1835
—. Economic relations. 1976. 1893
—. Economic relations. Foreign policy. Press. 1974-75. 1820
—. Foreign policy. Models. USA. 1957-77. 1890
—. Foreign Relations. 1974. 1839
—. Foreign Relations. 1970-77. 1939
—. Foreign Relations. Trudeau, Pierre Elliott. USA. 1968-74. 1922
—. Framework Agreement for Commercial and Economic Co-operation. International Trade. 1976. 1745
Europeans. Artifacts. Eskimos. Labrador. Quebec. Ungava Peninsula. ca 400-18c. 300
—. Attitudes. Body painting. Indians. 1497-1684. 388
—. Coal Mines and Mining. Economic Development. Immigrants. Kansas. 1870-1940. 1062
—. Cultural ecology. Micmac Indians. 15c-18c. 423
Evangelism. Holiness Movement Church. Horner, Ralph Cecil. Methodist Church. 1887-1921. 1064
—. Holiness Movement Church. Horner, Ralph Cecil. Methodist Church. 1887-1921. 1065
—. Hospitals. Indians. Quebec. 1633-1703. 539
—. Methodism. United Church of Canada. 18c-20c. 85
—. Osgood, Thaddeus. Religious Education. 1807-52. 673
Evangelists. Catholic Church. Ethnic groups. Protestantism. Quebec (Lower Canada). Rebellion of 1837. 1766-1865. 811
Evans, Arthur. Communist Party. Labor. 1930's. 2945
Evans, James. Cree Indians. Methodist Church. Missions and Missionaries. 1833-46. 651
—. Missions and Missionaries. Ontario (Lake Superior). Voyages. Wesleyan Methodist Church. 1837-38. 2810
Excavations See also Artifacts.
—. Acadian townsite. Glassware. Nova Scotia (Beaubassin). Settlement. ca 1670-1800's. 2274
—. British colonial materials. Military installations. Newfoundland (Signal Hill National Historic Park). 1800-60. 1965-66. 2186

—. Discovery and Exploration. Newfoundland (L'Anse aux Meadows). Vikings. 1000. 1961-68. 480
—. Eskimos. Grizzly bear skull. Labrador. 18c-19c. 336
—. Eskimos, Thule culture. Houses, communal. Labrador (Saglek Bay). 1650-1700. 334
—. Fort Amherst. Glass. Prince Edward Island. 1758-71. 1970's. 2206
—. Glassware. New Brunswick (Fort Gaspereau). 1751-56. 2387
—. Gunflints. Louisbourg, Fortress of. Military Camps and Forts. Nova Scotia. 1720-60. 608
—. Hudson's Bay Company. Ontario (Charlton Island, James Bay). 1680's. 1972-73. 566
—. Indians. Manitoba, southeastern. ca 8100-7600 BC. 305
—. Indians. Manitoba, southwestern (Site DgMg-15). Refuse pit. ca 1480-1740. 306
—. Martello towers. Ontario (Kingston, Market Shoal). 19c. 1972. 856
—. Vikings. Quebec (Ungava Peninsula). Prehistory. 1965. 479
Executive Behavior. Occupational and career patterns. -1973. 1583
Executives, high-level. 1900-30. 173
Exiles See also Asylum, Right of.
—. Acadians. Acculturation. France. Great Britain. Nova Scotia. 18c. 606
—. Acadians. Great Britain. Nova Scotia. 1710-55. 614
—. Cary, James. Great Britain. Jamaica. Loyalists. Nova Scotia. 1781-1804. 744
—. Loyalists. McDowall, Robert James. Missions and Missionaries. Ontario (Upper Canada). Reformed Dutch Church. 1790-1819. 747
Expansionism See also Imperialism.
—. Canada First (group). Mair, Charles. Red River Rebellion. Riel, Louis. 1869-70. 1009
—. Chipewyan Indians. Cree Indians. Fur Trade. Indian-White Relations. Northwest Territories (Mackenzie District, eastern). Prairie Provinces. 1680's-18c. 476
—. Defense Policy. Great Britain. Pacific Area (north). 1850-1914. 919
Explorers See also Discovery and Exploration; Voyages.
—. Alberta. Banff Park. Peyto, Bill. Scientific expeditions. 1887-1933. 3092
—. Alberta (Mount Alberta). Hirohito, Emperor. Japanese. Mountain climbing party. 1925-48. 2924
—. Antarctic. Australia. Great Britain. Priestley, Raymond. 1912-74. 3321
—. Arctic. Frobisher, Martin. Gold. Great Britain (London). Northwest Territories (Frobisher Bay). 1570's. 3310
—. Arctic. Physicians. Rae, John. 1835-93. 3315
—. Arctic. Stefansson, Vilhjalmur. 1915-24. 3319
—. Bibliographies. Eskimos. Greenland. 16c-19c. 331
—. Blakiston, Thomas Wright. British North American Exploring Expedition. North America. Ornithology. Palliser, John. 1857-91. 859
—. British Columbia. Fraser River. Mackenzie, Alexander. 1793. 646
—. France. West. 18c. 586
—. Franklin, John. Hood, Robert (journal, paintings). Northwest Passage. 1819-22. 3308
—. Hubbard, Leonidas. Labrador (northeast). Wallace, Dillon. 1903-05. 3313
—. Northwest Territories (Baffin Island, Pangnirtung Pass). Soper, J. Dewey (journal). 1925. 3318
—. Pond, Peter (biography). 1773-90. 2909
—. Rae, John (travel account). 1861. 2952
Exports. Economic conditions. Fishing. Foreign investments. Newfoundland. 1600-1934. 2178
—. Horst, Thomas (review article). Tariff. Trade Regulations. USA. 1970's. 1882
—. Quantitative methods. Quebec. Regional Planning. 1969. 1254
External Affairs Department. Canadian Institute of International Affairs. Colleges and Universities. Foreign Policy. Soward, F. H. (account). 1926-66. 217
—. Diplomacy. Travelers. 1973-74. 1865
—. Diplomats. Equal employment. Women. 1909-75. 82
—. Foreign relations. National security. Skelton, O. D. 1925-41. 1120
—. Press. 1942-76. 1789

External Affairs Department (Historical Division). Oral history. Videotaping. 1971-76. 1255
External Affairs Department (Policy Analysis Group). Foreign Policy. Planning. 1969-77. 1889
Extinction, threatened. Hunting. Pacific Area (north). Seals. USA. 1886-1910. 936
Extraparliamentarism. Political theory. 1840-1972. 186
Eye diseases. Eskimos. Ophthalmology. 1974. 312
Eye Opener (newspaper). Alberta. Edwards, Robert C. "Bob". Populists. 1904-22. 3108

F

Fabyan, Horace. Hotel trade. New Hampshire (Portland). White Mountain Grand Hotel. 1807-81. 772
Fairbairn, R. Edis. Pacifism. Protestantism. United Church of Canada. World War II. 1939. 1241
Fairy Queen (vessel). Nova Scotia (Charlottetown, Pictou). Shipwrecks. 1853. 2170
"Fall" Indians. Atsina Indians. Indians. "Rapid" Indians. Saskatchewan, southcentral. 18c. 405
Family See also Divorce; Marriage; Women.
—. Borden, Frederick W. Business. Liberal Party. Nova Scotia (King's County). Parliaments. 1874-96. 2316
—. Creighton, Donald. Macdonald, John A. (biography). Women. 1843-91. 1063
—. Economic security. Poverty. Public Welfare. Quebec. Social Aid Act (1969). 1969-75. 2668
—. Employment. Methodology. Models. Poor. 1974. 1510
—. English Canadians. Woman suffrage. 1877-1918. 901
—. Eskimos, Inuit. Personality. Values. 1974. 333
—. Feminism. Ontario. Social reform. 1875-1900. 2830
—. France. Protestantism. Quebec. Trade. 1740-60. 593
—. Generations. Immigrants. Italians. 20c. 1493
—. Indians. Kin terminologies. Language. Plains Indians. Social Organization. Prehistory-19c. 426
—. Italian Canadians. Ontario (Toronto). Social Mobility. 1935-60. 2870
—. Katz, Michael B. (review article). Ontario (Hamilton). Social Classes. 1850-80. 2725
—. Marriage. North America. Sociology. Women. 1974. 1469
—. Ontario. Social Conditions. 1820-60. 2771
Family compact. Government, responsible. Political attitudes. 19c. 831
—. McNab, Allan. Political reform. 1838-44. 825
Family Histories. See Genealogy.
Family reconstitution studies. Demography. Methodology. Migration, Internal. Quebec (Laterrière). 1855-1970. 2474
Family size. Birth Rate (decline). Demography. 1961. 1426
—. Demography. Social Surveys. 1945-74. 1355
—. Ontario (Wentworth County). Rural-Urban Studies. Social Surveys. 1871. 2757
Family structure. Charbonneau, Hubert. Dechêne, Louise (review article). Migration. Quebec. Vital Statistics. 1660-1713. 1974-75. 527
—. Economic development. Geographic mobility. Quebec (Laterrière). 1851-1935. 2471
Faraud, Bishop. Alberta (Lac la Biche). Erasmus, Peter. North West Rebellion. 1885. 1021
Faries, Richard. Anglican Communion. Cree Indians. Missions and Missionaries. Ontario (York Factory). 1896-1961. 379 Prairie Provinces. Wheat. 1915-1940. 2964
Farmer Labor party. Coldwell, Major J. Political Leadership. Progressivism. Social Democracy. 1907-32. 2962
—. Political Leadership. Radicals and Radicalism. Saskatchewan. Socialism. 1932-34. 3048
Farmers See also Peasants.
—. Agricultural production. Cereals. World War I. 1911-21. 1164
—. Alberta. Cowboys. Ranchers. Round-ups. 1911-19. 2932
—. Alberta. Political parties. Provincial Legislatures. 1920's-30's. 2944
—. Drummond County Mechanics Institute. Labor Unions and Organizations. Quebec (Drummond County). 1856-90. 2537

—. Education. Saskatchewan Grain Growers' Association. ca 1918-25. *3082*
—. Elections. Orange Order. Political Attitudes. United Farmers of Ontario. 1920-25. *2839*
—. French Canadians. Kansas. Mennonites. Swedish Americans. 1875-1925. *150*
—. Grange. Oklahoma. Saskatchewan. Socialism. Texas. 1900-45. *3083*
—. Inheritance. Land. Ontario. 19c. *807*
—. Maoism. National Farmers Union (convention, 1972). 1972-73. *1507*
Farmer's Union of Alberta. Alberta (Edmonton). Kyforuk, Peter. Manitoba. Ukrainian Labour-Farmer Association. 1912-30's. *2961*
Farming. Alberta. Mennonites. Namaka Farm. 1920's-40's. *3121*
—. Cattle Raising. Ranching. Saskatchewan (southwestern). 1872-1974. *3072*
—. Quebec (Gatineau Valley). 1800-1975. *2651*
Farmlands (preservation of). Population. 1974. *1589*
Farms. Alberta (Red Deer-Halrirk). Homesteading and Homesteaders. 1900-15. *3116*
—. Campbell, Thomas D. Droughts. Great Plains. Income. Prairie Provinces. Wheat. 1915-40. *2964*
—. Construction. Fence patterns. 17c-19c. *182*
—. Dams. Energy crisis. Ontario (Osceola). Water power. 1902-05. *2813*
—. Immigrants. Manitoba (Brandon). Railroads. Wheat. 1880-87. *961*
—. Land use. Markets. Quebec. 1908-71. *2661*
—. Murder. Nova Scotia (Cumberland County). 1838. *2349*
Federal Aid to Education. Colleges and Universities. 1966-70. *1471*
—. Colleges and Universities. Massey Commission. National Conference of Canadian Universities. 1951-66. *1476*
—. Mobility. Students. 1960-. *1421*
Federal Government *See also* names of individual agencies, bureaus, and departments, e.g. Bureau of Indian Affairs, Office of Education, but Education Department, External Affairs Department, etc.; Civil Service; Congress; Constitutions; Government; Legislation; Parliaments; Supreme Court.
—. Accountability. Decisionmaking. Environment. Science and Government. 1950's-70's. *1725*
—. Agriculture. Income. 1973-76. *1621*
—. Arctic. Eskimos. Mass Media. Satellite service. 1972. *329*
—. Arctic. *Neptune* (vessel). Sovereignty. 1903-04. *3294*
—. Attitudes. Business community. Canadian Labour Congress. Tripartism. 1977. *1295*
—. Barret, David. British Columbia. New Democratic Party. 1959-75. *3195*
—. Bergson, Henri. Creativity. Intergovernmental Relations. Quebec. 1970's. *2109*
—. Birds, migratory. International Migratory Bird Treaty (1916). USA. Wildlife conservation. 1883-1917. *920*
—. British Columbia. Evacuation, forced. Japanese. Public opinion. World War II. 1937-42. *1247*
—. Business. Indians (reservations). Missions and Missionaries. Ontario (Manitoulin Island). 1830-60. *350*
—. Canada Assistance Plan. Federalism. Provincial government. 1966. *1652*
—. Canadian Labour Congress. Political protest. Wages. 1976. *1563*
—. Children. New York (Watertown). Ontario (Belleville). Political structures. Provincial government. 1977. *1423*
—. Collective bargaining. Public Employees. 1940's-60's. *1500*
—. Confederation. Doyle, Hastings. Local government. Nova Scotia. 1867-68. *895*
—. Conflict and Conflict Resolution. Labor Disputes. Public Employees. 1967-76. *1718*
—. Constitutions. Economic Regulations. Provincial Government. 1856-1975. *60*
—. Constitutions. Provincial Government. Quebec. Separatist Movements. 1968-76. *2117*
—. Decisionmaking. Public Policy. 1970's. *1636*
—. Demographic research. Immigration policy. Local government. 1970's. *1811*
—. Economic development. Provinces. States. USA. 1950's-70's. *2012*
—. Economic Growth. Free trade. Mathias, Philip. 1973. *1266*
—. Education. Indians. Métis. 1940-70. *361*
—. Empire, establishment of. Mississippi River. St. Lawrence River. USA. 1760's-1860's. *631*

—. Energy policy. Provincial Government. Trudeau, Pierre Elliott. 1950-77. *2093*
—. Fiscal policy. Income. Income Tax. Inflation. Quebec. Regional Government. 1970-74. *1573*
—. Fiscal Policy. Investments. Manufactures. 1965-74. *1569*
—. Fiscal policy. Public employees. 1950-. *1532*
—. Foreign Investments. 1970's. *1851*
—. Foreign investments. Multinational corporations. 1972. *1874*
—. French Canadians. Public Policy. Quebec. Separatist Movements. 1976. *1306*
—. Glassco Commission. Public finance. 1960's-70's. *1717*
—. Government control. Sports. ca 1930-70. *1468*
—. Hepburn, Mitchell F. King, William Lyon Mackenzie. Lieutenant governors. Ontario. Provincial government. 1937. *1208*
—. Labor Disputes. Ontario, southern. Unemployment. 1901-20's. *89*
—. Labor Unions and Organizations. Multinational Corporations. 1970's. *1268*
—. Language equality. Official Language Act (Quebec, 1974). Quebec. 1960-76. *1438*
—. Language policy. Middle Classes. Modernization. Provincial government. Quebec. 1960-76. *2090*
—. Multinational corporations. USA. 1945-71. *2014*
—. New Democratic Party. Parti Québécois. Quebec. Separatist Movements. 1960's-70's. *2102*
—. Parti Québécois. Provincial Government. Quebec. Social Change. 1960-77. *2420*
—. Parti Québécois. Quebec. Separatist Movements. 1976-77. *2112*
—. Personnel management. Quebec. 1972-74. *2435*
—. Physical Education and Training. 1850-1972. *62*
—. Physical Education and Training. Sports. 1909-54. *1144*
—. Provincial Government. 1940-74. *2113*
—. Provincial Government. Public Employees. Regulatory agencies. 1974. *1639*
—. Public Administration. 1940's-78. *1678*
—. Quebec. Separatist Movements. 1960-77. *2710*
—. Quebec. Separatist Movements. 1976-77. *2087*
—. Research. Social sciences. 1976. *1467*
—. Social policy. Unemployment. 1918-21. *1190*
—. Taxation. Unemployment. Wealth distribution. 1977. *1635*
—. Violence. 1869-1935. *231*
Federal grants. Australia. USA. 1787-1974. *1693*
Federal Policy *See also* Domestic Policy.
—. Acculturation. Indians. Sifton, Clifford. 1896-1905. *395*
—. Australia. Immigration. Population. 1967-75. *1466*
—. Australia. New Zealand. Politics. Race. South Africa. 1900-73. *1926*
—. Bilingual districts. Quebec. 1969-76. *2480*
—. Economic growth. Maritime Union Movement. Nova Scotia. Regional development. 1783-1974. *2167*
—. Guaranteed annual income. Poverty. 1974. *1509*
—. Immigration. Migration, internal. 1896-1973. *99*
—. Immigration. Unemployment. 1950-77. *1410*
—. Indian-white relations. USA. 17c-20c. *394*
—. Oil Industry and Trade. 1968-72. *3283*
—. Prairie Provinces. Settlements. USA. 1870-80. *1018*
—. Unemployment. 1978. *1526*
Federal Programs. Alberta. Business. International trade. 1977. *3084*
Federal Regulation *See also* Economic Regulations.
—. Banking. Finance. 1963-73. *1197*
—. Bill C-256. Businessmen. Communications. Manitoba (Winnipeg). Public policy. 1971-72. *2971*
—. Broadcasting. Canadian Radio-Television Commission. 1968-75. *1634*
—. Competition. Industry. 1970's. *1597*
—. Conservation movements. Lumber industry. Ontario (Ottawa). "Robber Barons." 1873-1914. *2774*
—. Economic development. Population. Transportation. 1945-77. *1273*
—. Electric power. Environment. Niagara Falls. USA. 1895-1906. 1960's-70's. *2075*

—. Foreign investments. Manufacturing. USA. 1950-75. *1782*
—. Inflation. 1970-76. *1559*
—. Parliaments. 1970's. *1659*
—. Quebec. Radio-Québec. Television. 1969-76. *2478*
—. Sports. ca 1930-70. *1468*
—. Television. 1959-76. *1901*
Federal systems. Editorials. Political Campaigns. USA. 1972. *1715*
Federalism *See also* Federal Government; Revenue Sharing.
—. Agriculture. Forests and Forestry. Industrialization. Natural resources. Quebec. 20c. *2646*
—. Alberta. Devolution. Oil rights. Scotland. 1970's. *3118*
—. Alliance Laurentienne. Quebec. Separatism. 1957-70's. *2681*
—. American Revolution. Economic Policy. USA. 1776-1976. *202*
—. Australia. Constitutional conferences. 1965-74. *2092*
—. Australia. Suffrage. USA. 19c-20c. *179*
—. Biculturalism. English Canadians. French Canadians. Quebec. 20c. *1354*
—. Boucherville, Charles Eugène Boucher de. Joly, Henri-Gustave. Liberal Party. Political Campaigns. Provincial government. Quebec. 1878. *2452*
—. British North America Act (1867). Intergovernmental relations. 1930's-74. *2091*
—. Cairns, Alan C. (views). ca 1930-77. *1642*
—. Canada Assistance Plan. Federal government. Provincial government. 1966. *1652*
—. Castonguay, Claude (interview). Nationalism. Quebec. 1917-73. *63*
—. Confederation. Quebec. 19c-20c. *2105*
—. Constitutional Law. Political Reform. 1968-77. *2118*
—. Economic Conditions. Regionalism. 1960's-70's. *2096*
—. Economic expansion. Independence Movements. Quebec. 1867-1973. *2085*
—. Foreign policy. 1960-74. *1886*
—. French Canadians. Political systems. 1763-1973. *690*
—. French Canadians. Quebec. 1970's. *2103*
—. French Canadians. Quebec. Social Change. 1968-77. *2114*
—. French Canadians. Quebec. Sovereignty. Territorialization. 1760-1977. *167*
—. Government, federal and provincial. Political Systems. 1867-1974. *219*
—. Lamontagne, Maurice (views). Quebec. Separatist Movements. 1867-1976. *2097*
—. Provincial Government. Public Policy. 1867-1977. *30*
—. Quebec. Separatist Movements. 1759-1977. *69*
Federation. *See* Confederation.
Fédération Nationale Saint-Jean-Baptiste. Catholic Church. Feminism. Gérin-Lajoie, Marie. Quebec. 1907-33. *1128*
Feild, Edward. Church of England. Clergy. Great Britain. Newfoundland. 1826-44. *2190*
—. Church of England. Newfoundland. Sects, Religious. 1765-1852. *2188*
Fellows family. Genealogy. Massachusetts. Nova Scotia (Granville). 1635-1977. *2240*
Feminism *See also* Women's Liberation Movement.
—. Bibliographies. Publishers and Publishing. 1968-76. *255*
—. Bourassa, Henri. Divorce. Woman suffrage. 1913-25. *1142*
—. Canadian Library Association Committee on the Status of Women. Cheda, Sherrill. Librarians. 1973-74. *1418*
—. Catholic Church. Fédération Nationale Saint-Jean-Baptiste. Gérin-Lajoie, Marie. Quebec. 1907-33. *1128*
—. Family. Ontario. Social reform. 1875-1900. *2830*
—. Law Enforcement. Ontario (Toronto). Prostitution. Rape. 1975-78. *2825*
—. Literature. McClung, Nellie L. Politics. Reform. 1873-1930's. *1189*
—. McClung, Nellie (review article). 1902-15. *1097*
—. National Council of Women of Canada. 1893-1929. *225*
—. Research. Sociology. 1600-1975. *49*
Fence patterns. Construction. Farms. 17c-19c. *182*
Feng Shui, concept. British Columbia (Swan Lake). Cemeteries. Chinese. Geography. 1974. *3215*

Fenians. Anglin, Timothy Warren. Baker, W. M. Irish Canadians (review article). Neidhardt, W. S. 19c. 1970's. *1073*

—. Anglin, Timothy Warren. Catholic Church. Confederation. New Brunswick. 1866. *890*

—. Anglin, Timothy Warren. Irish Canadians. McGee, D'Arcy. Political debates. 1863-68. *891*

—. Foreign Relations. Irish Americans. Trials. USA. 1865-70. *876*

Fenians (raid). Civil War. Foreign Relations. St. Albans Raid. USA. 1861-66. *887*

Fenton, Edwin. Curricula. High schools. Historical thinking. 1975. *1346*

Ferries. Barrington and Cape Island Steam Ferry Company. Nova Scotia (Cape Sable Island). 1847-1949. *2216*

—. Bridges. British Columbia (Fraser Canyon). 1863-1973. *3186*

Fertility. Cree Indians. Modernization. 1968. *441*

Festschriften publications. Kniffen, Fred B. Mayo, Bernard. Morris, Richard B. Talman, James J. 1863-1974. *109*

Feudal law. New France (Notre Dame des Anges). Provost Court of Quebec. 1626-1750. *554*

Feudalism. Quebec. 1774-1971. *16*

Fiction See also Novels.

—. Alberta. Mitchell, W. O. Provincial consciousness. Ross, Sinclair. 20c. *3093*

—. British Columbia. Greater Victoria Public Library. 1968. *8*

—. Christian responsibility. Labor. Social gospel. 1890's. *1112*

—. Country Life. Depressions. Literary themes. Prairie Provinces. 1930's. *2918*

—. Country Life. Munro, Alice. Ontario. South. 1940's-70's. *2869*

—. Periodicals. Social Organization. 1930's-70's. *260*

Field, Cyrus. Bell, Alexander Graham. Communications. Fleming, Sandford. Gisborne, F. N. Nova Scotia. 1749-1964. *2260*

Field, Eliza. Courtship. Great Britain (London). Indians. Jones, Peter. Methodism. New York. 1820's-33. *451*

Fielding, William Stevens. Elections. Liberal Party. Nova Scotia. 1891-96. *2313*

Films See also Actors and Actresses.

—. Censorship. National Film Board. Quebec. 1971. *1406*

—. Television. 1960's-70's. *1348*

Finance See also subjects with the subdivision finance, e.g. Education (finance); Business; Campaign Finance; Commerce; Economics; Public Finance.

—. Banking. Government regulation. 1963-73. *1697*

—. Bethune, Donald. Ontario (Upper Canada). Steamboat business. 19c. *837*

Financial Administration Act (1951). Government Enterprise. 1950's-70's. *1560*

Financial institutions. Capital market. Economic activity. 1947-72. *1581*

Finback (whaler). Comer, George. Douglas, W. O. (reminiscences). Northwest Territories (Chesterfield Inlet). Shipwrecks. *3351*

Fink, Howard (account). Canadian Broadcasting Corporation. Drama. Radio. 1940's-50's. 1976. *1386*

Finkelman report. Labor Relations. Public Service Staff Relations Act. 1965-74. *1542*

Finnie, Richard Sterling (account). Arctic. Discovery and Exploration. North America. Office of the Coordinator of Information. Stefansson, Vilhjalmur. 1931-62. *3302*

Finnish Americans. British Columbia (Harmony Island). Kurikka, Matti. Utopias. 1901-05. *3213*

Finns. Immigrants. Labor Unions and Organizations. Radicals and Radicalism. USA. 1918-26. *1183*

Fire See also Fuel; Heating.

—. Disaster relief. New Brunswick (Saint John). Nova Scotia. 1877. *2397*

Fire Departments. Nova Scotia (Bedford). 1921-22. *2360*

Fire fighting. Forest fires. Great Idaho Fire. Idaho. Montana. 1910. *1082*

Firearms. Bernard, Joseph-Fidèle (diary). Chukchi natives. Trade. USSR. 1921-22. *1166*

—. Indians. Pacific Northwest. 1774-1825. *382*

Fires, prairie. Fur trade. Hudson's Bay Company. Indians. Saskatchewan. 1790-1840. *461*

Fiscal Policy. Employment. Income. Labor Unions and Organizations. Monetary policy. 1975. *1624*

—. Federal government. Income. Income Tax. Inflation. Quebec. Regional Government. 1970-74. *1573*

—. Federal government. Investments. Manufactures. 1965-74. *1569*

—. Federal Government. Public employees. 1950-. *1532*

—. Inflation. Politics. 1945-75. *1596*

Fisheries. Atlantic Provinces. Bargaining rights. Legislation. Nova Scotia. 1975. *2351*

—. Cod. Netherlands. Newfoundland. 1589-1670. *570*

—. Cook, James. Great Britain. Newfoundland. 1763-67. *2203*

—. Cree Indians. James Bay. 1972-75. *346*

—. Ecology. 1945-74. *1786*

—. Environmental protection. USA. ca 1900-72. *2049*

—. Hudson's Bay Company. Salmon. Ungava Bay region. 1830's-1939. *2653*

Fishermen, commercial. 1972-73. *1602*

Fishing See also Whaling Industry and Trade.

—. Adams, John Quincy. Diplomacy. Great Britain. Monroe, James. Newfoundland banks. USA. 1815-18. *782*

—. American Revolution. Nova Scotia (Lockport). Privateers. 18c. *720*

—. Boundaries. Foreign Relations. Territorial Waters. 1977. *1933*

—. British Columbia (southern). Vocabulary. 1975. *3201*

—. Chippewa Indians. Cree Indians. Indians. Lakes. Ontario, northern. 19c-1978. *341*

—. Cooperatives. Pêcheurs-Unis. Quebec (Gaspé Peninsula). World War II. 1939-48. *2638*

—. Economic conditions. Exports. Foreign investments. Newfoundland. 1600-1934. *2178*

—. Foreign policy. 1972-74. *1785*

—. Foreign Relations. Mitchell, Peter. New England. 1866-70's. *1070*

—. Indians. Ontario (Sault Ste. Marie). Trade. 17c-1920. *419*

—. Territorial Waters. 1977. *1854*

Fishing gear. British Columbia (Queen Charlotte Islands). Haida Indians. Indians. Wood. Prehistory. *287*

Fishing industry. British Columbia (Vancouver). Housing. Labor. Politics. 1970's. *3172*

—. Economic conditions. Newfoundland. 1880-1970. *2177*

—. Economic Policy. International Trade. Newfoundland. 1934-60's. *2175*

—. France (Poitou; Les Sables d'Olonne). Huart, Christophe-Albert-Alberic d'. Louisbourg, Fortress of. Nobility. Nova Scotia (Cape Breton Island). 1750-75. *560*

—. Government. Newfoundland. Political economy. 1949-75. *2179*

—. Historical Sites and Parks. Louisbourg, Fortress of. Nova Scotia (Cape Breton Island, Isle Royale). 1705-50. *573*

—. King William's War. New England. Privateers. Queen Anne's War. Shipping. 1689-1713. *596*

—. Maritime Fishermen's Union. Nova Scotia. 1977. *2366*

—. Newfoundland. Provincial government. 1972-77. *2196*

—. Newfoundland Fishermen, Food, and Allied Workers. 1970-77. *2197*

Fishing Rights See also Maritime Law.

—. British Columbia (Vancouver Island). International Pacific Salmon Fisheries Commission. Pacific Northwest. Salmon. Treaties. 1970's. *2018*

—. Great Britain. Newfoundland. USA. 1905-12. *2184*

—. International cooperation. 1977-78. *1871*

—. Labrador. Newfoundland. Public Administration. Quebec. 1763-83. *735*

Fitzpatrick, Alfred. Assimilation. Frontier College. Immigration. Labor. 1899-1922. *1086*

Five-Year Cultural Plan. Academic exchange programs. Canadian studies. Government funding. 1970's. *1798*

Flags. Military museum (collection). North America. Volunteers. Yugoslavia (Belgrade). 1917-18. 1974. *1162*

Fleming, Sandford. Bell, Alexander Graham. Communications. Field, Cyrus. Gisborne, F. N. Nova Scotia. 1749-1964. *2260*

Flint. Europe. Gunflints. Indians. Quebec (Chicoutimi). Travel. 17c. 20c. *349*

Florida See also Southeastern States.

—. Alabama. Alcohol. Nova Scotia. Pentz, Gabriel. Smuggling. 20c. *2249*

Florida (St. Augustine). American Revolution. Loyalists. ca 1775-85. *752*

Folk Art See also Art; Legend Painting.

—. Fraktur. Mennonites. Ontario (Waterloo County). Weber, Anna. 1825-88. *2836*

Folk Art (review article). Harper, Russell. Lipman, Jean. USA. Winchester, Alice. 19c. *149*

Folk high schools. Adult education. Denmark. 1919-50. *1136*

Folk medicine. Diseases, diffusion of. USA. 20c. *1298*

Folk music. Political protest. Social change. Values. 1776-1976. *1377*

Folk religion. Bibliographies. Europe. North America. 1900-74. *256*

Folk Songs. Music. Patriotism. "Yankee Doodle" (song; origins). 1730-1820. *2295*

—. Newfoundland (Calvert). Sex roles. Social status. 1916-74. *2201*

Folklore See also Folk Medicine; Folk Songs; Myths and Symbols.

—. Boats. New York. St. Lawrence River Skiff. 1860-1973. *133*

—. British Columbia (Maillardville). Magico-religious elements. 1973-74. *3219*

—. Chippewa Indians. Indians. Nanabozho (mythical character). Ottawa Indians. 19c-20c. *397*

—. Immigration. Ukrainians. 1945-75. *2933*

—. Kealey, James (and family). Oral history. Quebec (Hull). 1974-75. *2492*

—. Nova Scotia. Oral tradition. 20c. *2357*

Folklore studies. Scholarship. Sociopolitical milieu. ca 1900-75. *88*

Food. Cooking. Pioneers. 1750-1850. *803*

—. Developing nations. Foreign aid. 1975. *2048*

—. Drugs. Fur Trade. Indians. 17c-19c. *187*

—. Prices. Wages. 1961-73. *1535*

Food industry. Provigo (corporation). Quebec. 20c. *2620*

Food Supply. 1976. *1781*

—. Agricultural Production. Climate. Energy shortages. Urbanization. 1956-74. *1511*

—. Fur trade. Hudson's Bay Company. Mackenzie River Valley. Northwest Territories. Winter. 19c. *3357*

—. Gardening. Hudson's Bay Company. 1670-1760's. *497*

Ford, Gerald R. Foreign Relations. Trudeau, Pierre Elliott. USA. 1974-76. *2064*

Ford Motor Company of Canada. Labor Law. Ontario (Windsor). Rand formula. United Automobile Workers (Canadian Region). 1945-46. *1534*

—. Labor Law. Ontario (Windsor). Rand formula. United Automobile Workers (Canadian Region). 1946. *1595*

Foreign Aid See also Economic Aid; Industrialization; Modernization.

—. Africa. International Trade. 1970-75. *1864*

—. Africa, French-speaking. 1968-74. *1800*

—. Colombo Plan. International Development Agency. 1950-69. *1736*

—. Developing nations. 1960's-70's. *1748*

—. Developing nations. Food. 1975. *2048*

—. USA. Vietnam. War damage repair agency. 1972. *1760*

Foreign influences. National self-identity. Poland. Quebec. 1970's. *2675*

Foreign Investments. Agricultural commodities. Banking. Public services. Puerto Rico. 1800-1977. *180*

—. Attitudes. Economic nationalism. Elites. Legislatures. 1973-74. *2147*

—. British Columbia. Jurisdictional law. Land ownership. Washington (Whatcom County). 1970's. *2047*

—. Capital (export). 1900-73. *1792*

—. Cities. Real Estate. USA. 1960's-75. *1766*

—. Economic conditions. Exports. Fishing. Newfoundland. 1600-1934. *2178*

—. Economic Conditions. Natural resources. 1950-75. *1903*

—. Economic cooperation. Multinational corporations. USA. 1945-74. *1962*

—. Economic dependence. Multinational corporations. USA. 1970's. *2060*

—. Economic growth. Nationalism. USA. 1961-74. *1987*

—. Economic interdependence. Foreign policy. NORAD treaty. USA. 1970's. *1973*

—. Economic Policy. USA. 1975. *1773*

—. Federal Government. 1970's. *1851*

—. Federal Government. Multinational corporations. 1972. *1874*

—. Federal regulation. Manufacturing. USA. 1950-75. *1782*

—. Foreign policy. Public opinion. USA. 1973-75. *2010*

—. Great Britain. Hudson's Bay Company. International Financial Society. Railroads. 1863. *840*
—. Great Britain. Manufacturing. 1970-74. *1756*
—. Income. Income Tax. Interest groups. Periodicals. USA. ca 1930-74. *2016*
—. International Trade. Multinational corporations. 1973-76. *1895*
—. Multinational corporations. Oil Industry and Trade. Social organization. 1970's. *1819*
—. Nationalism. Social Classes. USA. 1960's-70's. *2082*
—. Natural resources. Prince Edward Island. 1970's. *2205*
—. Natural Resources. USA. 1920-55. *1125*
—. Natural resources. USA. 1960's-70's. *1971*
Foreign ownership. Economic Growth. Industry. 1973. *1936*
Foreign Policy *See also* Defense Policy; Detente; International Relations (discipline).
—. 1945-76. *1897*
—. Accountability. Voting and Voting Behavior. 1950's-74. *1872*
—. Africa, southern. Peacekeeping Forces. Trudeau, Pierre Elliott. UN Conference on the Law of the Sea. 1968-78. *1775*
—. Alexander I. North America. Pacific Area. Russian-American Company. 1799-1824. *678*
—. Annexation. British Columbia. Seward, William H. 1865-69. *3252*
—. Asia. Trudeau, Pierre Elliott. 1968-78. *1907*
—. British Commonwealth. Trudeau, Pierre Elliott. 1970's. *1842*
—. Canadian Institute of International Affairs. Colleges and Universities. External Affairs Department. Soward, F. H. (account). 1926-66. *217*
—. Columbia River Treaty. Neuberger, Richard. USA. 1955-61. *2071*
—. Commerce Department. State Department. USA. 1927-41. *1124*
—. Committee on the Challenges of Modern Society. Environmentalism. NATO. USA. 1969-77. *1838*
—. Cultural exchange programs. Diplomacy. 1963-70's. *1932*
—. Cultural relations. Europe, Western. USA. ca 1850's-20c. *34*
—. Decisionmaking. Nuclear Arms. 1950's-60's. *1847*
—. Defense policy. Nationalism. 1971-75. *1857*
—. Defense Policy. NATO. North American Air Defense Command. USA. 1950's-70's. *1986*
—. Democracy. Mass media. Totalitarianism. 1960-76. *1924*
—. Detente. USA. USSR. 1947-75. *1925*
—. Developing nations. Economic aid. 1970's. *1793*
—. Developing Nations. Europe. Japan. USA. 1950-75. *1741*
—. Developing nations. Trudeau, Pierre Elliott. 1968-78. *1929*
—. Diplomatic relations. Mexico. USA. 1945-74. *1860*
—. Economic blocs. Industrialized Countries. 1944-74. *1896*
—. Economic conditions. Race relations. USA. Vietnam War. 1970's. *2078*
—. Economic interdependence. Foreign investments. NORAD treaty. USA. 1970's. *1973*
—. Economic interdependence. USA. 1970-74. *2066*
—. Economic Policy. European Economic Community. Treaties. 1958-76. *1891*
—. Economic Policy. Nationalism. Trudeau, Pierre Elliott. 1968-78. *1772*
—. Economic Policy. Robertson, Norman Alexander. 1929-68. *1234*
—. Economic relations. European Economic Community. Press. 1974-75. *1820*
—. Economic relations. Great Britain. USA. 1873-1973. *17*
—. Economics. Military. Politics. 1950's-70's. *1856*
—. Elites. International system. 1975-76. *1751*
—. Europe. Trudeau, Pierre Elliott. 1968-78. *1946*
—. European Economic Community. Models. USA. 1957-77. *1890*
—. External Affairs Department (Policy Analysis Group). Planning. 1969-77. *1889*
—. Federalism. 1960-74. *1886*
—. Fishing. 1972-74. *1785*
—. Foreign Investments. Public opinion. USA. 1973-75. *2010*

—. France. 1882-1972. *42*
—. Free trade. USA. 1970-74. *2079*
—. French Canadians. Nationalism. Quebec. USA. 1945-76. *2044*
—. Gauvin, Michel (speech). International Commission for Supervision and Control. Sharp, Mitchell. Vietnam War. 1973. *1950*
—. Great Britain. King, William Lyon Mackenzie. USA. 1935-39. *1198*
—. Great Britain. USA. World War II. 1939-45. *1225*
—. Immigration. Labor. Population. Refugees. 1950's-70's. *1887*
—. Independence. 19c-1970's. *254*
—. International interdependence. USA. 1970. *2039*
—. International relations (discipline). 1974. *1776*
—. International Trade. Rhodesia. South Africa. 1960's-76. *1905*
—. Japan. Trudeau, Pierre Elliott. 1968-78. *1880*
—. Latin America. Trudeau, Pierre Elliott. 1968-77. *1803*
—. Latin America. Trudeau, Pierre Elliott. 1940-76. *1804*
—. Latin America. Trudeau, Pierre Elliott. 1968-78. *1878*
—. Mass media. 19c-20c. *1743*
—. National Characteristics. 1973. *1737*
—. National self-image. USA. 18c-20c. *11*
—. Nationalism. Public opinion. 1972-75. *1875*
—. NATO. Peacekeeping Forces. UN. 1956-77. *1861*
—. Newspapers. Press. ca 1970's. *1919*
—. North American Air Defense Command. 1973. *1991*
—. Nuechterlein, Donald E. (views). USA. 1972-78. *2028*
—. Oral history. 1970-75. *1744*
—. Pacific Area. 1969-73. *1829*
—. Parti Québécois. Trudeau, Pierre Elliott. 1968-78. *1836*
—. Planning. World War II. 1943-45. *1238*
—. Prime ministers. 1948-70's. *1930*
—. Provincial government. 1970's. *1866*
—. Quebec. 1977. *2706*
—. Quebec. Separatist Movements. 1690-1976. *2680*
—. Trudeau, Pierre Elliott. 1968-74. *1787*
—. Trudeau, Pierre Elliott. 1968-78. *1815*
—. Trudeau, Pierre Elliott. 1968-78. *1923*
—. Trudeau, Pierre Elliott. 1968-78. *1940*
—. UN General Assembly, 30th. 1975. *1825*
—. USA. 1974-77. *1928*
Foreign Relations *See also* Boundaries; Detente; Diplomacy; Geopolitics; International Relations (discipline); Tariff; Treaties.
—. 1970's. *1960*
—. Abolition Movement. Anderson, John. Great Britain. Politics. USA. 1860-61. *883*
—. Africa. France. French-speaking nations. Quebec. 1950's-70's. *1845*
—. Africa, French-speaking. Belgium. France. French-speaking institutions. 1960-74. *1769*
—. Alexander I (ukase). Great Britain. Noncolonization principle. Pacific Northwest. Russo-American Convention of 1824. 1821-25. *627*
—. Americas (North and South). Human rights. 1945-75. *1843*
—. Annexation. USA. 1760-1971. *40*
—. Association of Southeast Asian Nations. 1967-77. *1912*
—. Atlantic region. Buchan, Alastair. Institute of Strategic Studies. Military Strategy. 1958-75. *1913*
—. Attitudes. USA. ca 1776-1976. *93*
—. Australia. Business. English-language culture. 1975. *1949*
—. Bennett, Richard Bedford. Hoover, Herbert C. USA. 1930-31. *1205*
—. Bibliographies. Interdependence. USA. 1900-74. *2084*
—. Boundaries. Fishing. Territorial Waters. 1977. *1933*
—. Boundary Waters Treaty. Niagara Falls. USA. 1899-1911. *1088*
—. British Commonwealth. Ireland. Neutrality. World War II. 1939-45. *1237*
—. British Empire. France. Tariff. Treaties. 1901-09. *1106*
—. Bureaucracies. International Organizations. USA. 1909-74. *1996*
—. Capital flow restrictions. Economic Policy. USA. 1960's-71. *2080*
—. China. Developing nations. USA. USSR. 1950-75. *1824*

—. China. Diplomatic recognition. Trudeau, Pierre Elliott. 1968-73. *1807*
—. China. International Trade. USA. USSR. 1969-72. *1853*
—. China. Wheat. 1970-77. *1817*
—. Civil War. Fenians (raid). St. Albans Raid. USA. 1861-66. *887*
—. Cold War. Pearson, Lester B. 1948-57. *1821*
—. Conflicts, interstate. USA. 1920's-70's. *2029*
—. Congress. USA. 1950's-73. *1974*
—. Conservation of Natural Resources. Maritime Law. Navigation. USA. 1975. *2052*
—. Consulates. Economic cooperation. USA. 1941-70's. *2033*
—. Council of Europe. International law. Political systems. 1965-70's. *1801*
—. Cuba. International Trade. 1975-76. *1867*
—. Cuba. International Trade. USA. ca 1960's-70's. *1879*
—. Culture. Economic independence. Nationalism. USA. 1948-75. *2081*
—. Defense Policy. USA. 1974. *1968*
—. Democracy. France. Immigration. 1855. *836*
—. Diplomats. -1973. *1894*
—. Domestic Policy. Newspapers. Nova Scotia. USA. 1827-40. *2312*
—. Economic Conditions. International Trade. USA. 1950's-73. *1964*
—. Economic conditions. Politics. USA. 1970's. *1995*
—. Economic Conditions. USA. 1950-74. *1980*
—. Economic Development. USA. 1973. *1977*
—. Economic goals. Japan. 1974-75. *1814*
—. Economic integration. International Trade. USA. 1929-33. *1218*
—. Economic integration. National self-image. Sharp, Mitchell. USA. -1973. *2083*
—. Economic Policy. Europe. USA. 1974. *1916*
—. Economic policy. Prime ministers. Trudeau, Pierre Elliott. USA. 1960's-70's. *2006*
—. Economics. Politics. USA. 1945-74. *1253*
—. Editorials. Elections. Newspapers. 1972-74. *1917*
—. Emigration. France. Quebec (Sherbrooke). Trappists. 1903-14. *2529*
—. Environment. USA. 1965-75. *2011*
—. Environmental policy. USA. 1960's-70's. *2000*
—. Europe. 1974. *1846*
—. Europe. USA. 1945-73. *1827*
—. European Economic Community. 1974. *1839*
—. European Economic Community. 1970-77. *1939*
—. European Economic Community. Trudeau, Pierre Elliott. USA. 1968-74. *1922*
—. External Affairs Department. National security. Skelton, O. D. 1925-41. *1120*
—. Fenians. Irish Americans. Trials. USA. 1865-70. *876*
—. Fishing. Mitchell, Peter. New England. 1866-70's. *1070*
—. Ford, Gerald R. Trudeau, Pierre Elliott. USA. 1974-76. *2064*
—. France. Pearson, Lester B. 1955-65. *1250*
—. France. Quebec. 1967-75. *1952*
—. France. Quebec. 1763-1976. *2686*
—. Geography. National characteristics. USA. 19c-20c. *269*
—. Great Britain. Japan. Versailles Treaty (Article X). 1919-21. *1168*
—. Great Britain. Pearson, Lester B. 1936-72. *1791*
—. Haiti. 20c. *1784*
—. Hoover, Herbert C. St. Lawrence Seaway Treaty of 1932. USA. 1932. *1884*
—. Hoover, Herbert C. Smoot-Hawley Tariff. USA. 1929-33. *1203*
—. Idealism. USA. 1904-32. *1884*
—. Independence. Quebec. USA. 1950's-73. *2005*
—. Interdependence. Politics. USA. 1960's-70's. *2002*
—. Interdependence. USA. 1900-74. *1985*
—. King, William Lyon Mackenzie. USA. World War II. 1939-45. *1223*
—. Latin America. 1970's. *1808*
—. Latin America. 1970-76. *1834*
—. Latin America. Pan-American Union. USA. World War II. 1939-44. *1239*
—. Mexico. 1944-73. *1754*
—. Multinational corporations. Politics. UN. 1970's. *1868*
—. Multinational corporations. USA. 1960's-70's. *2015*
—. Nationalism. USA. 1945-75. *2037*
—. New England. USA. 1850's-1970's. *77*

—. Nongovernmental subsystems. USA. 1775-1976. *185*
—. Nuclear arms. Pearson, Lester B. USA. 1945. *2024*
—. Pakistan. 1973. *1733*
—. Parti Québécois. Quebec. Separatist Movements. USA. 1973-77. *1993*
—. Pearson, Lester B. 1948-57. *1855*
—. Political attitudes. USA. 1975-76. *2020*
—. Power Resources. USA. 1973. *1984*
—. Provincial government. Saskatchewan. 1963-78. *3057*
—. Public opinion. USA. 1950's-73. *2050*
—. Public Policy. Scandinavia. Transgovernmental politics. USA. 1970's. *1771*
—. Quebec. Separatist Movements. 1960-76. *2711*
—. Trudeau, Pierre Elliott. USA. 1968-78. *2058*
—. USA. 1975-77. *1959*
—. USA. 1939-76. *1981*
—. USA. 1972-75. *1997*
—. USA. 1965-78. *2025*
—. USA. 1967-73. *2046*
—. USA. USSR. 1970-73. *1898*
—. USA. Wrong, Hume (views). 1927-51. *1146*
—. USSR. Working class. 1917-73. *1944*
Foreign Relations (review article). Developing nations. Ismael, T. Y. Lyon, P. V. Ogelsby, J. C. M. USA. 1860's-1976. *239*
—. History, uses of. USA. 1923-73. *253*
Foreign Trade. *See* International Trade.
Forest fires. Fire fighting. Great Idaho Fire. Idaho. Montana. 1910. *1082*
Forestry museums. USA. -1973. *1531*
Forests and Forestry *See also* Lumber and Lumbering; Wood.
—. Agriculture. Federalism. Industrialization. Natural resources. Quebec. 20c. *2646*
—. British Columbia. Carr, Emily. Indians. Paintings. 1904-45. *3260*
—. British Columbia. Landscape Painting. 1700-1950. *3188*
—. Documents. 1974-75. *3218*
—. Economic development. Minville, Esdras. Multinational corporations. Quebec. USA. 1923-36. *2629*
—. Fraud. Manitoba (Churchill area). Political crimes. ca 1965-74. *2982*
—. Great Britain. Kennebeck Purchase Company. Mast policy, royal. New England. Wentworth, John. 1769-78. *718*
—. Lumberers. New Brunswick. Surveyors. 1820's-44. *2412*
Forgeries. Discovery and Exploration. North America. Vikings. Vinland map. 15c. 1957. *482*
Forman, George. Lewis, Henry. Logging. Mississippi River. Shipping. 1849-54. 1883. *2755*
Forrester, Alexander. Educators. Nova Scotia (Truro). ca 1848-69. *2277*
Fort Albany. Cree Indians. Henley House Massacres. Hudson's Bay Company. Ontario. Woudbee (chief). 1750's. *348*
Fort Amherst. Excavations. Glass. Prince Edward Island. 1758-71. 1970's. *2206*
Fort Brisbois. Alberta (Calgary). Toponymy. 1875-76. *3151*
Fort Chipewyan. Alberta. Fur Trade. Lefroy, L. H. 1843-44. *3094*
Fort Churchill. Cannibalism tales. Fort York. Manitoba. Molden, John. Shipwrecks. 1833. *3012*
Fort Frontenac. Indian-White Relations. Iroquois Indians. Missions and Missionaries. Quinte Mission. Sulpicians. 1665-80. *522*
Fort George. Ontario (Upper Canada). 1796-1969. *753*
Fort Herchmer. Gold Rushes. Klondike Stampede. Royal Canadian Mounted Police. Yukon Territory (Dawson). 1896-1905. 1972-76. *3328*
Fort Hope. Arctic. Discovery and Exploration. Hudson's Bay Company. Northwest Territories. Rae, John. 1840's. *3298*
Fort Langley. British Columbia. Hudson's Bay Company. Restorations. 1827-58. 1976-77. *3210*
Fort McMurray. McMurray, William. Moberly, Henry John. Trading posts. 1870's. *953*
Fort Meigs. Harrison, William Henry. Ohio. Virginia (Petersburg). Volunteer Armies. War of 1812. 1812-13. *765*
Fort Niagara. American Revolution. Business. New York. 1775-83. *736*
Fort Niagara (battle). Armies. French and Indian War. Great Britain. 1759. *600*

Fort Pitt. Cree Indians. Frenchman's Butte, Battle of. Indians. Manitoba. McLean, W. J. (diary). 1885. *1003*
Fort Ticonderoga. American Revolution. Arnold, Benedict. Carleton, Guy. Lake Champlain. 1776. *722*
Fort Vancouver. Fur trade. Hudson's Bay Company. McLoughlin, John. Pacific Northwest. 1825-60. *861*
Fort York. Cannibalism tales. Fort Churchill. Manitoba. Molden, John. Shipwrecks. 1833. *3012*
Fortification *See also* Military Camps and Forts.
—. Architectural drawings. Historical Sites and Parks. Louisbourg, Fortress of. Nova Scotia (Cape Breton Island). 1707-58. *603*
Forts. *See* Military Camps and Forts.
Foster, George. British Empire. Free trade policy. Tariff. 1912-17. *1152*
Foster, W. W. Canol Project. Oil Industry and Trade. USA. War Department. 1942-45. *1219*
Fourth of July. British Columbia (Vancouver Island). *Columbia Rediviva* (vessel). Kendrick, John. Nootka Sound controversy. 1789. *647*
Fraktur. Art. German Canadians. Ontario. 1976. *2741*
—. Folk Art. Mennonites. Ontario (Waterloo County). Weber, Anna. 1825-88. *2836*
Framework Agreement for Commercial and Economic Co-operation. European Economic Community. International Trade. 1976. *1745*
France *See also* French Revolution.
—. Acadia. New England. Phips, William. War. 1689-1713. *597*
—. Acadians. Acculturation. Exiles. Great Britain. Nova Scotia. 18c. *606*
—. Adoption. Belgium. Law. 1974. *1393*
—. Africa. Foreign relations. French-speaking nations. Quebec. 1950's-70's. *1845*
—. Africa, French-speaking. Belgium. Foreign Relations. French-speaking institutions. 1960-74. *1769*
—. Africa, French-speaking. Belgium. International cooperation. Quebec. 1964-74. *2718*
—. Alliances. Chickasaw Indians. Choctaw Indians. Indians. South Central and Gulf States. Tonti, Henri de. 1702. *581*
—. American Revolution. 1776. *716*
—. American Revolution. Colonies. Heraldry. Knights of Malta. 1600's-1976. *172*
—. American Revolution. Crèvecoeur, Michel (pseud. J. Hector St. John). Great Britain. 1755-1813. *618*
—. American Revolution. Protestants. Settlement. USA. Whaling industry and Trade. 17c-20c. *1287*
—. Architecture. Guardhouses. Louisbourg, Fortress of. Military Camps and Forts. Nova Scotia. 1713-68. *616*
—. Archives. Culture. Education. 1977. *215*
—. Aristocracy. Estate ownership. Meyer, Rudolf. Roffignac, Yves de. Saskatchewan (Eastern Assiniboia; Whitewood). 1885-1900. *982*
—. Aristocracy. Meyer, Rudolf. Saskatchewan (Pipestone Creek, Whitewood). Settlement. 1880's. *985*
—. Armies. Desertion. New France. 1700-63. *530*
—. Atlantic Provinces (review article). Historiography. Missions and Missionaries. New France. Politics. 1000-1770. 19c. *67*
—. Bernou, Claude. LeClercq, Crestien. *Premier Établissement de la Foy dans la Nouvelle France* (book). Renaudot, Eusèbe. 1691. *548*
—. Bonaparte, Jerome Napoleon. North America. Travel. 1861. *839*
—. Books. Catholic Church. Clergy. French Canadians. 1850-1914. *2564*
—. British Empire. Foreign relations. Tariff. Treaties. 1901-09. *1106*
—. Cargo. French and Indian War. Glass. *Machault* (vessel). 1760. *532*
—. Charles I. Colonization. Great Britain. Nova Scotia (Port Royal). Scotland. 1629-32. *501*
—. Cities. International trade. 1730-60. *572*
—. Colonial Government. Great Britain. New England. Nova Scotia (Canso, Cape Breton). 1710-21. *492*
—. Colonial Government. Louisiana Territory. Mississippi River Valley. New France. 1683-1762. 19c. *499*
—. Colonial policy (review article). Eccles, William J. New France. Seignelay, Marquis de. ca 1663-1701. 1962-64. *499*
—. Colonialism. Immigration. Louisiana. 1718-21. *578*

—. Colonies. Great Britain. Historiography. Italy. North America. 1663-1763. *598*
—. Colonization. Great Britain. North America. 1670's-1760. *512*
—. Commerce. Fur trade. Great Britain. Middle classes. Quebec (Montreal). 1750-92. *702*
—. Conservatism. French Canadians. Groulx, Lionel. Maurras, Charles. Nationalism. 1910-40. *1141*
—. Construction. Lime preparation. Louisbourg, Fortress of. Military Camps and Forts. Nova Scotia. 1725-58. *615*
—. Cultural relations. International Trade. 1760-1870. *879*
—. deGaulle, Charles (attitudes). French Canadians. Quebec. 1940-67. *2685*
—. Democracy. Foreign Relations. Immigration. 1855. *836*
—. Discovery and Exploration. Mississippi River Valley. Spain. 16c-17c. *588*
—. Elections. Language. Parliaments. Quebec. 1792-1810. *700*
—. Emigration. Foreign Relations. Quebec (Sherbrooke). Trappists. 1903-14. *2529*
—. Explorers. West. 18c. *586*
—. Family. Protestantism. Quebec. Trade. 1740-60. *593*
—. Foreign policy. 1882-1972. *42*
—. Foreign Relations. Pearson, Lester B. 1955-65. *1250*
—. Foreign Relations. Quebec. 1967-75. *1952*
—. Foreign relations. Quebec. 1763-1976. *2686*
—. French and Indian War. Great Britain. New Brunswick. Restigouche River (battle). 1760. *592*
—. French and Indian War. Ports. Trade. 1750's-60's. *562*
—. Gentry, small landowning. Great Britain. 1763-1815. *709*
—. Great Britain. Indian-White Relations. Micmac Indians. Prince Edward Island. 1763-1873. *468*
—. Great Britain. Jews. Poverty. Uruguay. 1975. *1389*
—. Great Britain. Multinational corporations. 1960's-70's. *1850*
—. Great Britain. New England. Nova Scotia (Canso). Territorial rivalry. 1710-21. *595*
—. Huguenots. New France. Protestantism. 1541-1760. *550*
—. Huron Indians. Indians (review article). Jaenen, Cornelius J. Trigger, Bruce G. Values. 1600-60. 1976. *520*
—. Immigration. Nova Scotia (Port Royal). Settlement. 1650-1755. *511*
—. King George's War. Louisbourg, Fortress of. Mutinies. Nova Scotia. 1744-45. *605*
—. Lamaletie, Jean-André. Quebec. Trading circles. 1741-63. *561*
—. Langille family. Nova Scotia. 1718-1804. *2230*
—. Legislation. North America. Psychiatric care. Quebec. 1973. *2546*
—. Quebec. Sociology. USA. 1970's. *2551*
France (Paris). Alabama (Mobile). Iberville, Pierre Le Moyne d'. Immigration. Population. Women. 1702-04. *582*
—. Banking (international). Great Britain (London). Morton, Levi Parsons. USA. 1860's. *853*
—. British Columbia (Vancouver). Diplomacy. Great Britain. Nootka Sound Controversy. Spain. 1789-90. *636*
—. Catholic Church. Quebec (Montreal). Reading rooms. Social Customs. 19c. *2531*
France (Poitou; Les Sables d'Olonne). Fishing company. Huart, Christophle-Albert-Alberic d'. Louisbourg, Fortress of. Nobility. Nova Scotia (Cape Breton Island). 1750-75. *560*
Franchise. *See* Citizenship; Suffrage.
Franco-Americans. Immigration. Maine. ca 1870-20c. *2152*
Francophiles. Anglophiles. Mathieu, Olivier-Elzéar. Saskatchewan (Regina). 1905-30. *3035*
Franklin, John. Anderson, James. Arctic. Expedition, search. Iroquois Indians. Woodsmanship. 1855. *3305*
—. Arctic. Bellot, Joseph René. Kennedy, William. *Prince Albert* (vessel). Voyages. 1851. *3307*
—. Arctic. Discovery and Exploration. Great Britain. Northwest Territories (Beechey Island). 1845-48. *3312*
—. Arctic. Discovery and Exploration. Hood, Robert (journal). Northwest Territories. 1819-21. *3309*
—. Explorers. Hood, Robert (journal, paintings). Northwest Passage. 1819-22. *3308*

Fraser, Douglas. Airplanes, Military (training). China. Nationalism. Saskatchewan (Saskatoon). 1919-22. *1169*

Fraser, James Daniel Bain. Chloroform. Medicine (practice of). Nova Scotia (Pictou). Pharmacy. 1807-69. *2247*

Fraser River. British Columbia. Explorers. Mackenzie, Alexander. 1793. *646*

Fraser Valley Milk Producers' Association. British Columbia. Dairying. Economic History. 1867-1969. *3224*

Fraud. Churchill Forest Industry. Manitoba. Political Crimes. ca 1965-74. *2982*

Frederick House Massacre. Fur Trade. Hudson's Bay Company. Indian-White Relations. Ontario. 1812-13. *2828*

Free Trade *See also* Tariff.
—. Economic Growth. Federal Government. Mathias, Philip. 1973. *1266*
—. Economic organizations. International Trade. Pacific area. 1975. *1837*
—. Foreign Policy. USA. 1970-74. *2079*

Free trade movement. Beaverbrook, 1st Baron. British Empire. Great Britain. Publishers and Publishing. 1900-31. *24*

Free trade policy. British Empire. Foster, George. Tariff. 1912-17. *1152*

Free World. *See* Western Nations; Industrialized Countries.

Freedmen. Alabama (Florence). Rapier, John H., Sr. (biography). 1830-60. *886*

Freedom of Speech *See also* Freedom of the Press.
—. Anti-Communist movements. Anti-Semitism. Immigration. National self-image. Ontario (Toronto). 1928-29. *2791*

Freedom of the press. Anticlericalism. Boycotts. *Canada-Revue* (newspaper). Catholic Church. Quebec (Montreal). 1890-94. *2484*

Frégault, Guy. Colonial Government. Historiography. New France. Rioux, Marcel. 1615-1763. 1957-60's. *491*
—. Historiography. Quebec (Montreal). 17c. 1950-60. *490*

Freight and Freightage *See also* Aeronautics; Railroads.
—. Canals. Erie Canal. Great Lakes. 1810-50. *791*
—. Leeson & Scott (firm). Prairie Provinces. 1883-1909. *1027*

French. Culture contacts. Indians. Social Customs. 17c. *519*

French Americans. Acculturation. Bibliographies. French Canadians. New England. 1755-1973. *2566*
—. Assimilation. Catholic Church. Vermont (Winooski). 1867-1900. *2469*
—. Bibliographies. French Canadians. Vermont Historical Society Library. 1609-1975. *504*
—. Historiography. Research. Vermont. 1609-1976. *2583*

French and Indian War. Amherst, Jeffrey. Iroquois Indians. Military History. New France. Pontiac's Rebellion. 1760-65. *612*
—. Armies. Fort Niagara (battle). Great Britain. 1759. *600*
—. Ballads. New England. Quebec. Rogers' Rangers (retreat). 1759. *591*
—. British Library (Townshend archive). Great Britain. Maps. Quebec (battle of). 1759. *609*
—. Cargo. France. Glass. *Machault* (vessel). 1760. *532*
—. France. Great Britain. New Brunswick. Restigouche River (battle). 1760. *592*
—. France. Ports. Trade. 1750's-60's. *562*
—. Great Britain. Nova Scotia (Halifax). Pringle, Henry (letters). 1757. *617*
—. New England. Rhetoric. War. 1754-60. *620*
—. New England. Rogers, Robert. 1755-60. *599*
—. Quebec (Battle of). Wolfe, James. 1759. *621*

French Canadians. 1970's. *1399*
—. 1871-1971. *2462*
—. *2463*
—. Acculturation. Bibliographies. French Americans. New England. 1755-1973. *2566*
—. Acculturation. Language. 1971. *1342*
—. Acculturation. Nationalism. New England. ca 1610-1975. *2704*
—. *Action Nationale* (periodical). Minville, Esdras. Quebec. 1933. *2688*
—. Alberta (Calgary Diocese). Catholic Church. Irish Canadians. McNailly, John Thomas. 1871-1952. *3095*
—. American Federation of Labor. Gompers, Samuel. Quebec. 1900-14. *2588*

—. American Revolution. French Revolution. Quebec (Lower Canada). Reform. 1773-1815. *712*
—. Anglicization. French language. Grignon, Claude Henri. 20c. *135*
—. Anglicization. Immigration. MacDonald, John A. 1860-1900. *705*
—. Arès, Richard. Minville, Esdras. Quebec. Social Customs. Tremblay Commission. 1953-56. *2676*
—. Assimilation. Language. 1961-71. *1364*
—. Assimilation. Prairie Provinces. 1871-1975. *2897*
—. Assiniboia, Council of. Manitoba. Métis. 1860-71. *2910*
—. Attitudes. Slander. 1712-48. *531*
—. Bibliographies. Editorials. Latin America. Newspapers. Quebec. 1959-73. *2433*
—. Bibliographies. French Americans. Vermont Historical Society Library. 1609-1975. *504*
—. Bibliographies. Literature. 1606-1977. *2581*
—. Biculturalism. English Canadians. Federalism. Quebec. 20c. *1354*
—. Bilingual Education. Ontario. Postsecondary schools. 1946-73. *1499*
—. Books. Catholic Church. Clergy. France. 1850-1914. *2564*
—. Bureaucracies. Civil Service. English Canadians. 1944-75. *1706*
—. Business Administration. Students. 1973. *2585*
—. Canadian Expeditionary Force. English Canadians. Hughes, Samuel. Imperialism. World War I. 1853-1921. *245*
—. Canadian Expeditionary Force, 41st Battalion. World War I. 1914-15. *1160*
—. Catholic Church. Clergy. Craig, James Henry. Government repression. Nationalism. Quebec (Lower Canada). 1810. *711*
—. Catholic Church. Educational system. Parent-youth conflict. Quebec. Social change. 1960-70. *2516*
—. Catholic Church. Episcopal nominations. Irish Canadians. 1900-75. *2930*
—. Catholic Church. Guigues, Joseph-Eugène. Ontario (Ottawa Diocese). 1848-74. *2747*
—. Catholic Church. Migration, Internal. Parishes. Quebec (Compton County). Rural-Urban Studies. 1851-91. *2534*
—. Catholic Church. Minnesota (Gentilly). Settlement. Theillon, Elie. 1870's-1974. *946*
—. Catholic Church. Minville, Esdras. Quebec. 1975. *2459*
—. Catholicism. Lévesque, Georges-Henri (personal account). Nationalism. Quebec. Youth movements. 1930's. *2700*
—. Centre de documentation en civilisation traditionelle. Identity. Quebec, University of. Séguin, Robert-Lionel. 1959-75. *494*
—. Colleges and Universities. Historiography. Quebec. 1947-72. *2449*
—. Colleges and Universities. Quebec. Sociology. 1960-74. *2499*
—. Colonialism. Great Britain. Social Classes. 18c. *707*
—. Confederation. Creighton, D. G. English Canadians. Heintzman, Ralph. Minorities in Politics. 1850's-90's. *922*
—. Confederation. Ontario. Provincial Government. Quebec. 1867-1937. *155*
—. Conservatism. France. Groulx, Lionel. Maurras, Charles. Nationalism. 1910-40. *1141*
—. Cooperatives. English Canadians. 19c. *37*
—. Cotton mills. Immigration. Massachusetts (Springfield). Statistics. 1870. *2607*
—. Craftsmen's associations. Quebec. 17c-18c. *533*
—. Créditiste movement (review article). Pinard, Maurice. Quebec. Stein, Michael. 1971-74. *2447*
—. deGaulle, Charles (attitudes). France. Quebec. 1940-67. *2685*
—. Demography. Quebec. Social Organization. 1974. *2481*
—. Demography. Quebec (Rawdon). Rural Settlements. Social customs. 1791-1970. *2575*
—. Economic Development. Emigration. Quebec. 1837-1930. *2616*
—. Economic conditions. English Canadians. New Brunswick. Labor attitudes. -1973. *2393*
—. Economic power. Quebec. Separatist movements. 1960's-70's. *2679*
—. Economic Theory. Minville, Esdras. Quebec. 20c. *2586*

—. Education. Literary associations. Quebec (Lower Canada). Social Problems. 1840-67. *2526*
—. English Canadians. Laurendeau, André. Nationalism. Quebec. 1945-66. *2556*
—. English Canadians. Multiculturalism. Quebec. 1970's. *1303*
—. English Canadians. Political power. Press. Quebec. 1864-67. *2572*
—. English Canadians. Quebec. 17c-20c. *33*
—. English Canadians. Social Customs. 1922-76. *102*
—. Ethnic groups. Geographic space. Multiculturalism. Quebec. Regionalism. Urbanization. 1930-73. *2715*
—. Farmers. Kansas. Mennonites. Swedish Americans. 1875-1925. *150*
—. Federal government. Public Policy. Quebec. Separatist Movements. 1976. *1306*
—. Federalism. Political systems. 1763-1973. *690*
—. Federalism. Quebec. 1970's. *2103*
—. Federalism. Quebec. Social Change. 1968-77. *2114*
—. Federalism. Quebec. Sovereignty. Territorialization. 1760-1977. *167*
—. Foreign Policy. Nationalism. Quebec. USA. 1945-76. *2044*
—. Genealogy. Page Family. Quebec (Laprairie). 1763-1967. *2530*
—. Grey, Albert Henry George, 4th Earl. Quebec (Quebec). 1903-06. *2691*
—. Groulx, Lionel. Historians. Nationalism. Nonviolence. Quebec. 1917-30. *489*
—. Historiography. Quebec. 1660-1976. *495*
—. Hume, David (writings). Literature, moralistic. Luxury, concept of. Quebec. 1849-1900. *2617*
—. Immigration. Massachusetts (Holyoke). Proulx, Nicholas. Working Class. 1850-1900. *2600*
—. Independence. Monetary Systems. Parti Québécois. Quebec. 1974. *2424*
—. Independence Movements. Lévesque, René (views). Nationalism. Quebec. 1763-1976. *2701*
—. Industry. Quebec. 20c. *2665*
—. Industry. Quebec. 1961-75. *2669*
—. Jews. Quebec. Separatist movements. Social Conditions. 1976-77. *2723*
—. Lawyers. LeSage, Simeon. Provincial Government. Quebec. 1835-1909. *2570*
—. Liberal Party. Parti Québécois. 1978. *1716*
—. Literacy. Quebec. 1745-1899. *2507*
—. Literary characters. Novels. Ontario (Glengarry County). 1925-75. *2857*
—. Manitoba. Settlement. 1870-1920. *1013*
—. Manitoba. Social Customs. Vallee, Frank. 1970-74. *2970*
—. Military Service. World War II. 1939-45. *1228*
—. Minorities. Social Organization. Ukrainian Canadians. 1970's. *1458*
—. National Characteristics (US). 1837-1973. *2483*
—. Nationalism. Official Language Act (Quebec, 1974). Quebec. USA. 1970's. *2517*
—. Newspapers. Quebec (St. Francis District). Rebellion of 1837. 1823-45. *813*
—. Novels. Quebec. USA. 1960's-70's. *2074*
—. Population. 1604-1971. *2156*
—. Quebec. Separatism. 1974-76. *2683*
—. Quebec. Separatist Movements. 1774-1975. *2719*
—. Quebec (Montreal). Richelieu Company. 1845-54. *2666*

French Canadians (review article). Assimilation. Choquette, Robert. Joy, Richard. Maxwell, Thomas R. 18c-20c. 1970's. *278*
—. Great Britain. Ideology. 1867-1936. *2708*

French civilization. Canadian studies. Royal Society of Canada (Letters and Social Sciences Section). 1952-72. *1344*

French language. Act of Quebec (1774). Quebec. Sovereignty. 1774-1974. *2673*
—. Anglicization. French Canadians. Grignon, Claude Henri. 20c. *135*
—. Bilingualism. Ethnic Groups. 1970-73. *1427*
—. Birth rates. 1960-75. *2464*
—. Catholic Church. *Patriote de l'Ouest* (newspaper). Saskatchewan. 1910-41. *2929*
—. *Charte du Français* (proposed). Minorities. Quebec. 1913-77. *2503*
—. Economic Conditions. Parti Québécois. Politics. Quebec. Social Customs. 1973-78. *2696*
—. Linguistics. Quebec. 1971. *2576*

—. Official Language Act (Quebec, 1974). Quebec. 1974. *2458*

—. Official Language Act (Quebec, 1974). Quebec. 1974. *2465*

—. Provincial Government. 19c-20c. *47*

—. Quebec. Regionalism. Social Customs. 1977. *2716*

French Language Charter. Anti-Semitism. Nationalism. Quebec. 1977. *2421*

French Quebec Movement. English language. Official Language Act (Quebec, 1974). Quebec. 1974. *2460*

French Revolution. American Revolution. French Canadians. Quebec (Lower Canada). Reform. 1773-1815. *712*

—. American Revolution. Ideology. Popular movements. 1775-1838. *819*

Frenchman's Butte, Battle of. Cree Indians. Fort Pitt. Indians. Manitoba. McLean, W. J. (diary). 1885. *1003*

French-speakers. Acculturation. Cultural alienation. Quebec. 1950-73. *2569*

—. Anglophones. Ethnicity. Historical traditions. 1974. *1464*

—. Anglophones. Income. 1961-74. *1564*

—. Class struggle. Equality. Intellectuals. Nationalism. Quebec. 1960's-70's. *2677*

—. Economic issues. Minorities. Quebec. Separatist Movements. 1976. *2689*

—. Quebec. Separatism. Social-class levels. 1968. *2682*

French-speaking institutions. Africa, French-speaking. Belgium. Foreign Relations. France. 1960-74. *1769*

French-speaking nations. Africa. Foreign relations. France. Quebec. 1950's-70's. *1845*

Friends, Society of. American Revolution. Great Britain. Ireland. Pennsylvania (Philadelphia). Relief funds. 1778-97. *739*

—. American Revolution. Massachusetts (Nantucket Island). Whaling Industry and Trade. 1750's-1800. *733*

—. Ontario, southern. 19c. *2792*

Friendship. Burge family. Letters. Ontario (Upper Canada). Simcoe family. 1790-1820. *669*

Fringe benefits. Employment. Overtime. 1957-67. *1552*

—. Wages. Working Conditions. 1973. *1586*

Frobisher Bay. Canoe trips. Northwest Territories (Baffin Island, Takuirbing Lake). Travel. 1973. *3320*

Frobisher, Martin. Arctic. Explorers. Gold. Great Britain (London). Northwest Territories (Frobisher Bay). 1570's. *3310*

—. Colonization. Great Britain. Hall, Charles Francis. Northwest Territories (Baffin Island). Pottery. 1578. 1862-1974. *513*

Frontier and Pioneer Life *See also* Cowboys; Homesteading and Homesteaders; Indians; Overland Journeys to the Pacific; Pioneers.

—. Adolescence. Dependency. Employment. Ontario (Orillia). Social change. 1861-71. *2769*

—. Alberta. Bachelors. Calgary *Herald*, newspaper. Marriage. 1895. *956*

—. Alberta (Stettler). McLeod, Evelyn Slater (reminiscences). 1900's. *3139*

—. Animal husbandry. Meat (sources). Prince Rupert's Land. 18c-20c. *2942*

—. Artists. Dakota Territory. *Harper's Weekly* (periodical). Rogers, William A. 1878. *2976*

—. British Columbia. Douglas, James. Gold rushes. Law Enforcement. 1858. *3197*

—. British Columbia. Great Britain. Imperial administration. 1846-71. *979*

—. British North America. Colonial Government. Indian Affairs Department. 1755-1830. *623*

—. Caldwell, Billy. Great Britain. Great Lakes. Indians. Trade. 1797-1841. *365*

—. Cemeteries. Mortality. Ontario (Upper Canada; Midland District). 1783-1851. *749*

—. Cavalry. Quebec (Montreal). 1837-50. *820*

—. Church of England. Clergy. Diocesan Theological Institute. Ontario (Cobourg). Strachan, John. 1840-55. *679*

—. Clark, Septimus Alfred. Great Britain. Letters. Radcliffe, Mary. Saskatchewan (Regina). 1884-1909. *967*

—. Colorado. Daily Life. Nebraska. Ouren, Hogan (reminiscences). 1861-66. *851*

—. Communications. Hutterites. West. 1874-1977. *1022*

—. Gold Mines and Mining. Ontario (Casummit Lake). William, Eileen (recollections). 1930's. *2888*

—. Letters. Ontario (Upper Canada). Painting. Simcoe, Elizabeth. Values. 1790-1800. *638*

—. Manitoba (Red River region). North West Mounted Police. Sitting Bull (chief). Walsh, James. 1873-1905. *1030*

—. Methodist Church. Missions and Missionaries. 1840-1925. *950*

—. Neville, Anthony. Neville, Harriet Johnson. Northwest Territories. 1882-1905. *3359*

—. North West Mounted Police. Potts, Jerry. ca 1860-96. *1006*

—. Women. 1794-1899. *191*

Frontier College. Assimilation. Fitzpatrick, Alfred. Immigration. Labor. 1899-1922. *1086*

Frontier College history project. Public Archives of Canada. 1974-75. *1282*

Frontier thesis. Australia (Victoria). California, northern. Turner, Frederick Jackson. 1850-1900. *247*

Frye, Northrop. Levi-Strauss, Claude. Primitivism. Shadbolt, Jack. 1977. *251*

Fuel *See also* Coal; Energy; Heating; Oil and Petroleum Products; Wood.

—. Energy situation (consumption, price). Quebec. 1974-. *2432*

Fuga, Francis J. Ontario (Hamilton). Shrine of Our Lady of Klococov. Slovak Canadians. Uniates. 1952-77. *2895*

Fugitive slaves. Africa, West. American Revolution. Emigration. Great Britain. Nova Scotia. 1776-1820. *737*

—. Land. New Brunswick. Settlement. USA. 1815-36. *804*

Fulford, Francis. Bishops. Church of England. Quebec (Montreal). 1850-68. *874*

Fulford, Frederick M. J. (personal account). Boundaries. Monument setter. USA. 1908-12. *1091*

Fuller, Richard. Alberta. Cree Indians. Hudson's Bay Company. Telegraph. Treaties. 1870's. *1020*

Fundamentalist-Modernist controversy. Baptists. Jarvis Street Church. Ontario (Toronto). Religious factionalism. Social Classes. 1895-1934. *2762*

Fund-raising. Bryan, William Jennings. Lectures. Prairie Provinces. Young Men's Christian Association. 1909. *2953*

Fundy, Bay of. Cobb, Sylvanus. Nova Scotia. Ships. Trade. *York* (vessel). 1755. *2163*

—. Electric power. Energy. Passamaquoddy Bay. Tides. 1919-64. 1975. *115*

Fundy National Park. Lumber industry. New Brunswick. Settlement. 1820's-1976. *2383*

Funk, John F. Manitoba. Mennonites, Russian. Settlement. 1873. *993*

Fur trade. Alaska. British Columbia. China (Macao). Cook, James. Pacific Area. 1778-79. *784*

—. Alberta. Fort Chipewyan. Lefroy, L. H. 1843-44. *3094*

—. Alberta. Hudson's Bay Company. Kerr, Tom. 1861-1946. *3160*

—. Alberta (North Saskatchewan River). Rocky Mountain House. 19c. *3101*

—. Arctic. Berthe, Jean. Eskimos. Quebec. Stevenson, A. (account). 1930's. *2663*

—. Arctic. Churches. Missions and Missionaries. 20c. *3281*

—. Armaments. Cannons. 1600's-1800's. *141*

—. Aubert de la Chesnaye, Charles. Netherlands. 1695-98. *568*

—. Blackfoot Indians. Indian-White Relations. 1810-40. *376*

—. British Columbia (Vancouver Island, Nootka Sound). *Columbia* (vessel). Discovery and Exploration. Ingraham, Joseph (travel account). 1774-89. *655*

—. British North America. Garrison towns. Michigan (Detroit). Military Camps and Forts. Quebec (Montreal). 1760-75. *637*

—. British North America. Hudson's Bay Company (review article). 1670-1870. 1970's. *97*

—. Buffalo migrations. Plains Indians. Prairie Provinces. 1770-1869. *429*

—. Children. Education. Hudson's Bay Company. Métis. 1820's-60's. *628*

—. China market. North West Company. Oregon (Astoria). 1760's-1821. *785*

—. Chipewyan Indians. Cree Indians. Expansionism. Indian-White Relations. Northwest Territories (Mackenzie District, eastern). Prairie Provinces. 1680's-18c. *476*

—. Chippewa Indians. Cree Indians. Saskatchewan. Thanadelthur ("Slave Woman," Chippewa Indian). 1715-17. *577*

—. Colonialism. Cultural change. Indians. North America. Prehistory-1900. *286*

—. Commerce. France. Great Britain. Middle classes. Quebec (Montreal). 1750-92. *702*

—. Daily life. Dufaut, J. (diary). Indians. Ontario (Prince Rupert's Land). XY Company. 1803-04. *2956*

—. Demography. Epidemics. Indians. Wildlife diseases. 15c-18c. *425*

—. Discovery and Exploration. Hudson's Bay Company. Ogden, Peter Skene. 1811-54. *688*

—. Diseases, diffusion of. Hudson's Bay Company. Indians. 1830-50. *2949*

—. Drugs. Food. Indians. 17c-19c. *187*

—. Economic Conditions. New France. Quebec. 1760-90. *574*

—. Economic Growth. Hudson's Bay Company. Lake, Bibye. 1684-1743. *503*

—. Epidemics. Hunt, George T. *(The Wars of the Iroquois)*. Indians. Iroquois Indians. 1609-53. *523*

—. Eskimo life. Hudson's Bay Company. Northwest Territories (Hudson Bay, Baffin Island). 1909-30's. *3348*

—. Fires, prairie. Hudson's Bay Company. Indians. Saskatchewan. 1790-1840. *461*

—. Food Supply. Hudson's Bay Company. Mackenzie River Valley. Northwest Territories. Winter. 19c. *3357*

—. Fort Vancouver. Hudson's Bay Company. McLoughlin, John. Pacific Northwest. 1825-60. *861*

—. Frederick House Massacre. Hudson's Bay Company. Indian-White Relations. Ontario. 1812-13. *2828*

—. Genealogy. Godbout, Archange. New France. Population. Voyages. 1608-1763. *565*

—. Hudson's Bay Company. Indians. Trade. 17c-18c. *576*

—. Hudson's Bay Company. Mineral Resources. North America. 17c-20c. *258*

—. Hudson's Bay Company. New York. Sutherland, James. 1751-97. *687*

—. Indian-White Relations. Kutchin Indians. Eastern. Northwest Territories (Mackenzie District). Yukon Territory. 1800-60. *3285*

—. Indian-White Relations. Mississauga Indians. Ramsay, David. 1760-1810. *686*

—. Japan. Sea otters. Wildlife Conservation. 18c-20c. *257*

—. La Jonquière, Marquis de. Ontario (Toronto). 1750-1887. *564*

—. Manitoba. Registered Trap Lines system. Trapping. Wells, Harold. 1940-53. *3011*

—. Melyn, Cornelis. New England. Nova Scotia. 1633-52. *569*

—. Merchants. Quebec (Montreal). Social Classes. 1750-75. *703*

—. Railroads. Saskatchewan (Grand Rapids). Saskatchewan River. Tramways. 1877-1909. *997*

F2H-3 (aircraft). McDonnell Aircraft Corporation. Naval Air Forces. 1956-63. *1272*

G

Gaelic language, Scots. Blair, Duncan Black. Nova Scotia (Pictou County). Poetry. Scholars. Scotland. 1846-93. *2346*

Gage, Lyman. Counterintelligence (US). Quebec (Montreal). Spanish-American War. Spy ring, Spanish. Wilkie, John. 1898. *1094*

Gaggin, John Boles. British Columbia. Civil service. 1859-66. *3254*

Galicians. Dukhobors. Lake Geneva Mission. Missions and Missionaries. Presbyterian Church. Saskatchewan (Wakaw). 1903-42. *3027*

Galt, Alexander. Alberta (Lethbridge). Coal Mines and Mining. 1885-1905. *958*

—. Alberta (Lethbridge). Coal Mines and Mining. Government. Settlement. 1879-93. *960*

—. Jews. Kaplun, Alter (family). Russia. Saskatchewan. Settlement. 1880's-90's. *945*

Galt, Elliott. Indians. Letters. Prairie Provinces. Travel. 1879-80. *959*

Galt, John. Canada Company. Hibernia colony (proposed). Quebec (Lower Canada). Settlement. 1825-35. *774*

Galtung, Johan. Quebec. Separatism. Social change. 1961-75. *2712*

Galveston Plan. Immigration. Jews. Schiff, Jacob H. USA. 1907-14. *905*

Gardening. Food Supply. Hudson's Bay Company. 1670-1760's. *497*

Gardens. Nova Scotia. 1850-1900. *2345*

Gardiner, James G. Agriculture Minister. Liberal Party. Patronage. 1935-57. *2959*

—. Alberta. Liberal Party. Social Credit Party. 1935-39. *3157*
—. Anderson, James T. M. Elections. Provincial Legislatures. Saskatchewan (Estevan). 1929-30. *3078*
—. Provincial Government. Saskatchewan. 1905. *3079*
Garlington, Ernest A. Greely, Adolphus W. Hazen, William B. Northwest Territories (Ellesmere Island). Scientific Expeditions. 1881-83. *3303*
Garrettson, Freeborn. Cromwell, James. Methodist Episcopal Church. Missions and Missionaries. Nova Scotia. USA. 1785-1800. *2315*
Garrison duty. Caribbean Region. Great Britain. Military. 1914-45. *1131*
Garrison towns. British North America. Fur Trade. Michigan (Detroit). Military Camps and Forts. Quebec (Montreal). 1760-75. *637*
Garrisons. Great Britain. Quebec (Montreal). 1840's. *833*
Gasoline Licensing Act (1934). Marketing. Nova Scotia Board of Commissioners of Public Utilities. Provincial Government. 1960's-74. *2283*
Gates, Horatio. American Revolution. Military strategy. 1777-80. *721*
Gauvin, Michel (speech). Foreign Policy. International Commission for Supervision and Control. Sharp, Mitchell. Vietnam War. 1973. *1950*
Gendron Report. Bilingualism. Quebec. Schools. 1973. *2504*
Genealogy *See also* Heraldry.
—. Apple industry. Crops. Nova Scotia. Prescott, Charles Ramage. 1772-1970's. *2280*
—. Banks, Joshua. Banks, Moses. Nova Scotia (Granville). 1739-1843. *2308*
—. Fellows family. Massachusetts. Nova Scotia (Granville). 1635-1977. *2240*
—. French Canadians. Page Family. Quebec (Laprairie). 1763-1967. *2530*
—. Fur trade. Godbout, Archange. New France. Population. Voyages. 1608-1763. *565*
—. Great Britain. Massachusetts. Morris family. Nova Scotia. 18c-19c. *2242*
—. Harvie, John (and family). Nova Scotia. 1730-1945. *2276*
—. Howe, John (and family). Nova Scotia (Halifax). 18c-19c. *750*
—. Ireland (Waterford). Prime Ministers. Thompson, John S. D. 1796-1903. *1056*
—. LaVache family. Nova Scotia (Cape Breton; Arichat). 1774-20c. *2365*
—. Lewis, Waitsill (family). Methodology. Nova Scotia (Yarmouth). 1976. *2212*
—. Nova Scotia (Beaver River, Chebogue). Raymond, Daniel (family). Raymond, Jonathan (family). 1772-1869. *2331*
—. Nova Scotia (Cornwallis). Walton, Jacob (identity). ca 1811-1914. *2252*
—. Nova Scotia (Halifax, Lunenburg). West family. Wuest, Johann Wendel. 17c-20c. *2330*
—. Nova Scotia (Hants County). Weatherhead family. ca 1820-1946. *2272*
General Hospital. Catholic Church. Mental Illness. Quebec. 1692-1845. *2543*
General Strikes. Beruson, David J. (review article). Industrial relations. Manitoba (Winnipeg). Social organization. 1919. 1975. *1165*
—. Manitoba (Winnipeg). 1919-70. *1116*
Generation conflict. Catholic Church. Educational system. French Canadians. Quebec. Social change. 1960-70. *2516*
—. Identity. Quebec (Quebec). Social integration. 1968. *2487*
Generations. Family. Immigrants. Italians. 20c. *1493*
Gentry, small landowning. France. Great Britain. 1763-1815. *709*
Geographic Mobility *See also* Migration, Internal.
—. Acadia. Copper kettles. Micmac Indians. Settlement. 17c. *424*
—. Economic development. Family structure. Quebec (Laterrière). 1851-1935. *2471*
—. Federal Aid to Education. Students. 1960-. *1421*
—. Ontario. Rural Settlements. Social mobility. 19c. *849*
Geographic Space. Attitudes. Language. National Development. 1776-1976. *56*
—. Canals. International Trade. National Development. Politics. Railroads. 1818-1930. *54*
—. Catholic Church. Regionalism. 1615-1851. *3*

—. Communications. Ethnic groups. Great Britain. Regionalism. 1976. *2139*
—. Ethnic groups. French Canadians. Multiculturalism. Quebec. Regionalism. Urbanization. 1930-73. *2715*
Geographical studies. City planning. Settlement. USA. 19c-20c. *127*
Geography *See also* Boundaries; Ethnology; Maps; Physical Geography; Surveying; Voyages.
—. Bibliographies. Brouillette, Benoit. Quebec (Montreal). 1903-73. *2496*
—. British Columbia (Swan Lake). Cemeteries. Chinese. Feng Shui, concept. 1974. *3215*
—. British-Canadian Symposium, 2d. 1977. *1761*
—. Civilization (review article). Diffusion theories. Gordon, Cyrus H. Riley, Carroll. Transoceanic contacts. Prehistory-1492. *304*
—. History of ideas. Discovery and Exploration. Maps. Vinland Map. 1974. *484*
—. Foreign relations. National characteristics. USA. 19c-20c. *269*
—. Hudson's Bay Company. Societies. Wegg, Samuel. 1750-1800. *683*
—. Industrial decline. Quebec (Shawinigan). 1932-72. *2605*
—. Ontario. Urban history. Prehistory-1976. *1317*
—. Quebec (southern). Regional divisions. 1932-66. *2687*
—. Rural-Urban studies. 1900-73. *138*
Geological Survey of Canada. Eskimos. Expedition. Tyrrell, J. W. (travel diary). 1890's. *337*
Geological surveys. Photography. 1858-97. *266*
Geology *See also* Earthquakes; Mineral Resources; Oceanography; Physical Geography.
—. Clays, sensitive. Ontario (Ottawa). Soil Conservation. 1648-1971. *276*
—. Emmons, Ebenezer. New York (Taconic Mountains). Scientific Discoveries. 1840-1900. *277*
—. Great Britain. Jukes, Joseph Beete. Newfoundland. Travel. 19c. *2181*
—. Great Lakes. 1974. *272*
Geopolitics *See also* Boundaries; Demography; International Waters.
—. Elections. 1921-74. *100*
Georgia *See also* Southeastern States.
—. American Revolution (antecedents). Great Britain. Immigrants. Military. Nova Scotia. 1765-75. *729*
Gérin, Elzéar. Gérin-Lajoie, Antoine. Journalism. 1843-87. *2567*
Gérin-Lajoie, Antoine. Gérin, Elzéar. Journalism. 1843-87. *2567*
Gérin-Lajoie, Marie. Catholic Church. Fédération Nationale Saint-Jean-Baptiste. Feminism. Quebec. 1907-33. *1128*
German Alsatians. Catholic Church. Gravemarkers. Iron work. Ontario (Bruce County; Waterloo). 1850-1910. *2837*
German Canadians. Art. Fraktur. Ontario. 1976. *2741*
—. Census. Population. 1891-1931. *2898*
—. Deutscher Bund Canada. Immigration. Saskatchewan (Loon River area). 1929-39. *3076*
—. Deutscher Bund Canada. Nazism. Propaganda. 1934-39. *1216*
—. Deutscher Bund Canada. Nazism. Saskatchewan. 1934-39. *1246*
German South-West Africa. *See* Africa, Southern.
Germans. Immigrants. Nova Scotia. Protestants. 1749-52. *2259*
Germans, Russian. Alberta (Coaldale). Community organizations. Mennonites. Social Change. 1920-76. *3145*
—. *Der Bote* (newspaper). Mennonites. Nazism. Saskatchewan. USSR. Völkisch thought. 1917-39. *3077*
Germany *See also* component parts, e.g. Bavaria, Prussia, etc.
—. Australia. Middle powers. Political integration. South Africa. 1850-1900. *903*
—. Great Britain. Land prices. Taxation. 1890-1970's. *214*
Germany (Berlin). Communist Party. Olympic Games. People's Olympic Games. Spain (Barcelona). 1936. *1202*
Ghost Dance. Indians. Revitalization movements. Social Organization. 1889. *359*
Ghost ships. Myths and Symbols. Nova Scotia (Mahone Bay). War of 1812. *Young Teazer* (vessel). 1812-1976. *764*
Gibbons, George Christie. Boundaries. Maritime law disputes. USA. Water resources. 1905-10. *1113*
—. Boundary Waters Treaty. International Waters. USA. 1905-11. *1114*

Gibbons, James. Catholic Church. Knights of Labor. Social thought. Taschereau, Elzéar-Alexandre. 1880's. *1068*
Gibbons, Jimmy (interview). Eskimos, Sadlermiut. Housing. Marsh, Donald B. (reminiscences). Northwest Territories (Southampton Island). ca 1900. *328*
Gill, Valentine. Natural resources. Nova Scotia. Smith, Titus. Surveying. 1800-15. *2271*
Gisborne, F. N. Bell, Alexander Graham. Communications. Field, Cyrus. Fleming, Sandford. Nova Scotia. 1749-1964. *2260*
Gitksan Indians. Art. British Columbia (Hazelton). 'Ksan Historic Indian Village. 1973. *434*
Gladstone, William Ewart. Brougham, Henry Peter. Canadian Rebellion Losses Bill. Great Britain. Political Theory. 1849. *814*
Glass. Cargo. France. French and Indian War. *Machault* (vessel). 1760. *532*
—. Excavations. Fort Amherst. Prince Edward Island. 1758-71. 1970's. *2206*
Glassco Commission. Federal Government. Public finance. 1960's-70's. *1717*
Glassware. Acadian townsite. Excavations. Nova Scotia (Beaubassin). Settlement. ca 1670-1800's. *2274*
—. Excavations. New Brunswick (Fort Gaspereau). 1751-56. *2387*
Glassworks. Living conditions. Manitoba (Beausejour). Recreation. Working conditions. 1909-11. *3000*
Glenbow Centre. Alberta (Calgary). Harvie, Eric L. Museums. 1954-76. *3100*
Glenbow-Alberta Institute. Alberta (Calgary). Archives. 1955-76. *3115*
Glengarry Highlanders. Catholics. Emigration (Scottish). Great Britain. Macdonnell, Alexander. Ontario. 1770's-1814. *805*
Glengarry Light Infantry Fencible Regiment. Canadian Voltiguer Regiment. Uniforms, Military. War of 1812. 1812-16. *755*
GNP. Economic Conditions. Statistics. USA. 1960-69. *1530*
Godbout, Archange. Fur trade. Genealogy. New France. Population. Voyages. 1608-1763. *565*
Godsal, F. W. Alberta. Ranches. South Fork Ranch. 1897. *3155*
Goggin, David James. Educational Policy. Manitoba. Northwest Territories. Teaching. ca 1890's. *2904*
Gold *See also* Mineral Resources.
—. Arctic. Explorers. Frobisher, Martin. Great Britain (London). Northwest Territories (Frobisher Bay). 1570's. *3310*
—. Nova Scotia (Eastern shore). Roads. Travel. 19c. *2266*
Gold miners. Alaska (Skagway). British Columbia (Lake Bennett). Klondike Stampede. 1896-99. 1960-73. *3200*
Gold Mines and Mining. British Columbia (Bridge River Valley). Economic conditions. Physical geography. 19c-1970's. *3251*
—. Cullity, Emmet K. (memoir). Saskatchewan (Beaver Lake). 1915-27. *3041*
—. Frontier and Pioneer Life. Ontario (Casummit Lake). William, Eileen (recollections). 1930's. *2888*
—. Nova Scotia (Waverley). 1860-1976. *2275*
Gold Rushes. Alaska. Klondike Stampede. Women. Yukon Territory. 1897-99. *3322*
—. Alaska (Skagway). Brackett, George. Entrepreneurs. Roads. Yukon Territory. 1897-98. *3323*
—. Alberta (Saskatchewan River). 1897. *3146*
—. Boomtowns. British Columbia (Bennett). Yukon Territory. 1896-99. *3183*
—. British Columbia. California. Discrimination. Negroes. Race Relations. 1849-66. *846*
—. British Columbia. Douglas, James. Frontier and Pioneer Life. Law Enforcement. 1858. *3197*
—. Burry, Thomas. Klondike Stampede. 1897. *2124*
—. Fort Herchmer. Klondike Stampede. Royal Canadian Mounted Police. Yukon Territory (Dawson). 1896-1905. 1972-76. *3328*
—. Great Britain. Journalism. Klondike Stampede. Shaw, Flora. *Times of London* (newspaper). Yukon Territory. 1898. *3341*
—. Klondike Gold Rush Historic Park. National Parks and Reserves. Yukon Territory. 1897-98. 1974. *3324*
—. Klondike Stampede. Photography. Restorations. Yukon Territory. 1897-98. 1970's. *3336*
—. Klondike Stampede. Quinlan, Thomas A. (letters). Yukon Territory. 1898-1904. *3337*

—. Klondike Stampede. Royal Canadian Mounted Police. Yukon Territory. 1896-99. *3335*

—. Presbyterian Church. Yukon Territory. 1897-1910. *3334*

—. Yukon Territory (Klondike; Dawson City). 1898-1913. *3333*

Golden Hinde (vessel). California. Discovery and Exploration. Drake, Francis. Nova Albion (location of). 1579. *505*

Gompers, Samuel. American Federation of Labor. Babcock, Robert H. (review article). USA. 1897-1914. *1078*

—. American Federation of Labor. French Canadians. Quebec. 1900-14. *2588*

Goodwin, Theresa (reminiscences). Saskatchewan (Chaplin, Duval). Teaching. 1912-13. *3045*

Gordon, Cyrus H. Western Civilization (review article). Diffusion theories. Geography. Riley, Carroll. Transoceanic contacts. Prehistory-1492. *304*

Gospel Temperance Movement. Revivalism. Rine, D.I.K. 1877-82. *1041*

Gosselin, Auguste-Honoré (review article). Laval, François de. New France. School of Arts and Crafts of St. Joachim. 1668-1730. *535*

Gouzenko, Igor. "Civility" (measured). Political culture. USA. 1953-54. *1941*

Government *See also* Cabinet; City Government; Civil Service; Constitutions; County Government; Federal Government; Local Government; Political Science; Politics; Provincial Government; Public Administration; Public Employees; Regional Government.

—. Alberta (Lethbridge). Coal Mines and Mining. Galt, Alexander. Settlement. 1879-93. *960*

—. Alienation. Charities. Quebec (Quebec; Lower Town). Social Problems. Working Class. 1896-1914. *2637*

—. Atlantic Provinces. Boardinghouses. Labor. Merchant Marine. Social reform. ca 1850's-90's. *916*

—. Authority. Trudeau, Pierre Elliott. 1950's-70's. *2111*

—. British Columbia. Political Parties. Socialism. 1972-75. *3214*

—. Bureaucracies. Capitalism. Institutions. North America. Social change. 1750's-1850's. *656*

—. Business. Council on Foreign Relations (publications). USA. 1971-74. *1966*

—. Catholic Church. Parish registers. Quebec. 1539-1973. *526*

—. Children, English- and French-Canadian. Political socialization. Quebec. 1970-71. *2549*

—. CODOC (system). Documents. Information Storage and Retrieval Systems. Libraries. USA. 1960's-70's. *177*

—. Cree Treaty of 1876. Indians. Land rights. 1876-1970's. *364*

—. Dairying. Motherwell, W. R. Saskatchewan. Subsidies. Wilson, W. A. 1906-17. *3037*

—. Decisionmaking. ca 1867-1970's. *1707*

—. Defense policy. Economic Conditions. Military strategy. NATO. 1973-76. *1863*

—. Democracy. 1867-1977. *142*

—. Desjardins cooperative movement. Interest groups. Quebec. 18c-1973. *2415*

—. Domestic Policy. Economic History. ca 1865-1975. *209*

—. Economic Development. Quebec (Lower Canada). Social classes. Ultramontanism. 19c. *698*

—. Elites. Ontario (Upper Canada; Toronto). Simcoe, John Graves. Strachan, John. 1793-1818. *773*

—. Environment, Department of (Canada). 1970-73. *1288*

—. Federalism. Political Systems. 1867-1974. *219*

—. Fishing industry. Newfoundland. Political economy. 1949-75. *2179*

—. Great Plains. Hunting. Mississippi Flyway. North Central States. Spring shooting issue. Waterfowl. 1887-1913. *906*

—. Higher Education. Public Opinion. 1975. *1485*

—. Human rights agencies. Ontario. Racism. 1973-77. *2790*

—. Land. Saskatchewan. Settlement. 1929-35. *3060*

—. Nationhood. Quebec. 1960-76. *2698*

—. Politics. Regionalism. 1974. *2144*

—. Politics. Textbooks. 1607-1974. *1729*

—. Publications. 1977. *189*

—. Publishers and Publishing. 1791-1972. *81*

—. Quebec. 20c. *2098*

Government commissions. Indians. Land claims. Métis. Prairie Provinces. 1885-1900. *396*

Government Employees. *See* Civil Service; Public Employees.

Government Enterprise *See also* Nationalization.

—. British Columbia. Pricing policies. 1977. *3243*

—. Financial Administration Act (1951). 1950's-70's. *1560*

Government houses. 1605-1867. *95*

Government, majority. Elections, federal. Public Opinion. Voting and Voting behavior. 1965-74. *1686*

Government relief. British Columbia (northern). Homesteading and Homesteaders. Resettlement. 1940-42. *3192*

Government Reorganization Act of 1971. Ministers and Ministries Act. Parliamentary system. Presidential politics. 1966-74. *2106*

Government repression. Catholic Church. Clergy. Craig, James Henry. French Canadian nationalism. Quebec (Lower Canada). 1810. *711*

Government, responsible. Family compact. Political attitudes. 19c. *831*

Government secrecy. India. Nuclear Nonproliferation Treaty (1968). Nuclear Science and Technology. 1968-70's. *1844*

Governors. Catholic Church. Laval, François de. New France (Sovereign Council). 1659-84. *546*

—. Great Britain. Head, Francis Bond. Ontario (Upper Canada). 1835. *667*

Governors-general. British Empire. 1867-1952. *111*

—. Buchan, John. Lascelles, Alan (memorandum). 1935. *1217*

—. Political Leadership. 1915-72. *66*

Gowan, Ogle. Immigration. Irish influence. Ontario (Upper Canada). Orangeism. Politics. 1830-33. *821*

Graduate students. Colleges and Universities. History. 1966-75. *1281*

Graduates. Colleges and Universities. Occupational attainment. Ontario. Social mobility. Women. 1960-75. *2821*

Graham, Andrew. Hudson's Bay Company. Hutchins, Thomas. Natural history. Plagiarism. 1770's-1815. *692*

Graham, John (report). Higher education. 1974. *1498*

Grain *See also* Cereals.

—. Dry farming. Economic Conditions. Prairie Provinces. 1870-1930. *2943*

Grain Growers' Guide (periodical). Chipman, George. Editors and Editing. Prairie Provinces. Teaching. 1903-05. *2938*

Grain trade. Buchanan, Isaac. Buchanan, Peter. Commercial crisis. 1840's. *790*

Grand Jurors' Book. Local government. Nova Scotia (Yarmouth and Argyle). 1814-51. *2310*

Grand jury. Belcher, Jonathan. Law. Nova Scotia. 1754. *2362*

Grand Trunk Railway. Railroads. Strikes. 1896-1912. *1111*

Grandin, Vital (letter). Alberta. 1876. *3102*

Grange. Farmers. Oklahoma. Saskatchewan. Socialism. Texas. 1900-45. *3083*

Grant, George Monro. Dawson, John William. Higher education. Scotland. 19c. *2*

Grant, Walter C. (letters). British Columbia (Vancouver Island). Colonization. 1851. *3206*

Granville, George, 2d earl (letter). British Columbia. Colonial Government. Great Britain. Musgrave, Anthony. Seymour, Frederick (death). 1869. *3204*

Gravemarkers. Catholic Church. German Alsatians. Iron work. Ontario (Bruce County; Waterloo). 1850-1910. *2837*

Great Awakening. Economic Conditions. Nova Scotia (Yarmouth). Social Conditions. 1760's-70's. *2354*

Great Britain *See also* British Commonwealth; British Empire; Ireland; Scotland.

—. Abolition Movement. Anderson, John. Foreign Relations. Politics. USA. 1860-61. *883*

—. Aborigines Protection Society. Australia. Indians. USA. ca 1830-50. *464*

—. Acadians. Acculturation. Exiles. France. Nova Scotia. 18c. *606*

—. Acadians. Colonial Government. Land tenure. Nova Scotia. Oath of allegiance. 11c-1755. *594*

—. Acadians. Exiles. Nova Scotia. 1710-55. *614*

—. Adams, John Quincy. Diplomacy. Fishing. Monroe, James. Newfoundland banks. USA. 1815-18. *782*

—. Adult education. 1516-1977. *105*

—. Aeronautics (history). Dirigibles (R-100). 1930. *1215*

—. Africa, West. American Revolution. Emigration. Fugitive slaves. Nova Scotia. 1776-1820. *737*

—. Alberta. Ombudsmen. Public Opinion. 1969-71. *3109*

—. Alexander I (ukase). Foreign Relations. Noncolonization principle. Pacific Northwest. Russo-American Convention of 1824. 1821-25. *627*

—. American Revolution. Crèvecoeur, Michel (pseud. J. Hector St. John). France. 1755-1813. *618*

—. American Revolution. Economic Conditions. Quebec. 1770's. *731*

—. American Revolution. Friends, Society of. Ireland. Pennsylvania (Philadelphia). Relief funds. 1778-97. *739*

—. American Revolution. Great Lakes. Old Northwest. Peace of Paris (1783). Shelburne, 2d Earl of (William Petty). 1783. *727*

—. American Revolution. Smith, Adam. 1770-76. *728*

—. American Revolution (antecedents). Georgia. Immigrants. Military. Nova Scotia. 1765-75. *729*

—. Anglophobia. Aroostook War (1839). Boundary dispute. USA. 1837-39. *654*

—. Antarctic. Australia. Explorers. Priestley, Raymond. 1912-74. *3321*

—. Archaeology, industrial. Education. History, study of. USA. 1955-70. *1302*

—. Arctic. Discovery and Exploration. Franklin, John. Northwest Territories (Beechey Island). 1845-48. *3312*

—. Arctic Ocean. Navies. Weavers. Whalers. 1818-25. *3300*

—. Armies. Fort Niagara (battle). French and Indian War. 1759. *600*

—. Armies. Kent, Duke of (Edward). Lyons, Charles (family). Nova Scotia (Halifax). 1812-63. *2273*

—. Arnold, Benedict. Arnold, Peggy. New Brunswick. West Indies. 1781-1801. *2374*

—. Australia. Cabinet. Netherlands. Political recruitment. USA. 1940's-60's. *1666*

—. Beaverbrook, 1st Baron. British Empire. Free trade movement. Publishers and Publishing. 1900-31. *24*

—. Belaney, Archibald S. (Grey Owl). Conservation movements. 1906-38. *1140*

—. Boundaries. International Trade. Vermont. 1763-1815. *630*

—. Boundaries. Lake of the Woods. Paris, Treaty of (1783). USA. 1755-1925. *723*

—. Boundary dispute. Diplomacy. Oregon. Polk, James K. USA. 1845-46. *835*

—. Boys. Charities. Hudson's Bay Company. Schools. 18c-19c. *684*

—. Bradstreet, John. Louisbourg, Fortress of. Military Biography. Nova Scotia. 1739-74. *604*

—. British Columbia. Colonial Government. Granville, George, 2d earl (letter). Musgrave, Anthony. Seymour, Frederick (death). 1869. *3204*

—. British Columbia. Frontier process. Imperial administration. 1846-71. *979*

—. British Columbia. Gunboats. Indians. Liquor. Slave trade, Indian. 1860's. *390*

—. British Columbia. Immigration. Public opinion. 1919-30. *3250*

—. British Columbia. Miles, Walter K. (and ancestors). 1602-1977. *3229*

—. British Columbia. Nootka Sound controversy. Spain. Territorial rights. 1790. *691*

—. British Columbia (Vancouver). Diplomacy. France (Paris). Nootka Sound Controversy. Spain. 1789-90. *636*

—. British Columbia (Vancouver Island). Cook, James. Discovery and Exploration. Nootka Sound controversy. Spain. 1778-94. *695*

—. British garrison. Quebec (Montreal). 1840's. *833*

—. British Library (Townshend archive). French and Indian War. Maps. Quebec (battle of). 1759. *609*

—. British North America. Indian Affairs Department. Uniforms. 1755-1823. *632*

—. British North America Act (1867). Constitutional amendments. Parliaments. Trudeau, Pierre Elliott. 1867-1970's. *1249*

—. Brougham, Henry Peter. Canadian Rebellion Losses Bill. Gladstone, William Ewart. Political Theory. 1849. *814*

—. Bureaucracies. Citizen participation. Political Reform. USA. 1973. *1667*

—. Cable relay point. Hawaii. USA. 1894-96. *1051*

—. Caldwell, Billy. Frontier and Pioneer Life. Great Lakes. Indians. Trade. 1797-1841. *365*

—. Calvert, George (1st Lord Baltimore). Colonization. Newfoundland (Avalon Peninsula). 1609-32. *2182*

—. Caribbean Region. Garrison duty. Military. 1914-45. *1131*

—. Cary, James. Exiles. Jamaica. Loyalists. Nova Scotia. 1781-1804. *744*

—. Catholics. Emigration (Scottish). Glengarry Highlanders. Macdonnell, Alexander. Ontario. 1770's-1814. *805*

—. Centennial Celebrations. Indians. Treaty Seven. 1877-1977. *370*

—. Charles I. Colonization. France. Nova Scotia (Port Royal). Scotland. 1629-32. *501*

—. Children. Immigration. Ontario. Poor. Press. Rye, Miss. 1865-1925. *2879*

—. Church of England. Clergy. Feild, Edward. Newfoundland. 1826-44. *2190*

—. Citizenship. Riel, Louis. Treason. USA. 1885. *951*

—. Civil service. Committee of Imperial Defence. Defense policy. War Office. 1896-1914. *1092*

—. Civil War. Military. Williams, William Fenwick. 1859-67. *881*

—. Clark, Septimus Alfred. Frontier and Pioneer Life. Letters. Radcliffe, Mary. Saskatchewan (Regina). 1884-1909. *967*

—. Colonial Government. France. New England. Nova Scotia (Canso, Cape Breton). 1710-21. *492*

—. Colonial Government. Political oppression. Quebec (Lower Canada). USA. 1851. *697*

—. Colonial policy. Emigrant guides. Land grants (proposed). Ontario (Peterborough). Traill, Catherine Parr. 19c. *869*

—. Colonial Stock Act (1900). Imperialism. Laurier, Wilfrid. 1890's-1900. *1095*

—. Colonialism. French Canadians. Social Classes. 18c. *707*

—. Colonies. France. Historiography. Italy. North America. 1663-1763. *598*

—. Colonization. France. North America. 1670's-1760. *512*

—. Colonization. Frobisher, Martin. Hall, Charles Francis. Northwest Territories (Baffin Island). Pottery. 1578. 1862-1974. *513*

—. Colonization. Indian Affairs Department. Indians. USA. 1755-1830. 1800H. *624*

—. Commerce. France. Fur trade. Middle classes. Quebec (Montreal). 1750-92. *702*

—. Communications. Ethnic groups. Geographic Space. Regionalism. 1976. *2139*

—. Confederation. Derby, 15th Earl of. Head, Edmund Walker. Letters. Political Attitudes. 1858. *894*

—. Constitutional History. Quebec. 1791-1814. *2694*

—. Convict transportation. Ireland. Newfoundland. 1789. *2192*

—. Cook, James. Fisheries. Newfoundland. 1763-67. *2203*

—. Counter Culture. Press. USA. 1957-72. *1475*

—. Crimean War. Howe, Joseph. Military recruitment. USA. 1854-56. *867*

—. Defense. USA. War of 1812. 1812-14. *767*

—. Defense Policy. Expansionism. Pacific Area (north). 1850-1914. *919*

—. Dieppe (air battle). Leigh-Mallory, Trafford. Royal Canadian Air Force. World War II. 1942. *1220*

—. Diplomacy. International meetings. Pearson, Lester B. USA. 1935-72. *1910*

—. Diplomacy. Nuclear technology. 1973-74. *1888*

—. Discovery and Exploration. Netherlands. North America. Vancouver, George. 1778-98. *666*

—. Durham, 1st Earl of. Whigs. 1838-40. *829*

—. Economic competition. USA. Wheat. 1900-14. *1102*

—. Economic relations. Foreign policy. USA. 1873-1973. *17*

—. Education. Missions and Missionaries. Protestantism. Sudan Interior Mission. 1937-55. *197*

—. Edward VIII (tour). 1919. *1163*

—. Elites. Pressure Groups (review article). USA. 1960's-70's. *1325*

—. Empire Day celebrations. Imperialism. Nationalism. Ontario. Public Schools. 1890-1930's. *2864*

—. Exploration. Jameson, Robert. North America. Northwest Passage. 1804-54. *689*

—. Fishing Rights. Newfoundland. USA. 1905-12. *2184*

—. Foreign Investments. Hudson's Bay Company. International Financial Society. Railroads. 1863. *840*

—. Foreign Investments. Manufacturing. 1970-74. *1756*

—. Foreign policy. King, William Lyon Mackenzie. USA. 1935-39. *1198*

—. Foreign policy. USA. World War II. 1939-45. *1225*

—. Foreign Relations. Japan. Versailles Treaty (Article X). 1919-21. *1168*

—. Foreign Relations. Pearson, Lester B. 1936-72. *1791*

—. Forests and Forestry. Kennebeck Purchase Company. Mast policy, royal. New England. Wentworth, John. 1769-78. *718*

—. France. French and Indian War. New Brunswick. Restigouche River (battle). 1760. *592*

—. France. Gentry, small landowning. 1763-1815. *709*

—. France. Indian-White Relations. Micmac Indians. Prince Edward Island. 1763-1873. *468*

—. France. Jews. Poverty. Uruguay. 1975. *1389*

—. France. Multinational corporations. 1960's-70's. *1850*

—. France. New England. Nova Scotia (Canso). Territorial rivalry. 1710-21. *595*

—. French and Indian War. Nova Scotia (Halifax). Pringle, Henry (letters). 1757. *617*

—. French Canadians (review article). Ideology. 1867-1936. *2708*

—. Genealogy. Massachusetts. Morris family. Nova Scotia. 18c-19c. *2242*

—. Geology. Jukes, Joseph Beete. Newfoundland. Travel. 19c. *2181*

—. Germany. Land prices. Taxation. 1890-1970's. *214*

—. Gold rushes. Journalism. Klondike Stampede. Shaw, Flora. *Times of London* (newspaper). Yukon Territory. 1898. *3341*

—. Governors. Head, Francis Bond. Ontario (Upper Canada). 1835. *667*

—. Great Lakes. Navies. 1760-89. *680*

—. Halifax Citadel (fortress). Naval Strategy. Nova Scotia. 1825-60. *642*

—. Heeney, Arnold D. P. (review article). Pearson, Lester B. USA. 1920's-70's. *1790*

—. Hudson's Bay Company. Royal Society of Canada. Wegg, Samuel. 1753-1802. *082*

—. Hyde Park Declaration (1941). USA. World War II. 1939-41. *1224*

—. Imperial Shipping Committee. International Trade. Trade Regulations. 1918-63. *20*

—. India. Periodicals. Political science. 1970's. *1805*

—. International Trade. Lower, Arthur (review article). Lumber and Lumbering. 1763-1867. *781*

—. International Trade. USA. 1943-47. *1746*

—. Landscape Painting. Menzies, Archibald. Nature. Vancouver, George. ca 1775-1800. *633*

—. Lawrence, D. H. Novels. 1911-30. *1121*

—. Lefroy, John Henry (journals). Magnetic survey. Northwest Territories. Scientific Expeditions. 1843-44. *3306*

—. MacKinnon, Frank (review article). 19c-20c. *156*

—. Military Finance. World War II. 1943-45. *1227*

. National characteristics, British. Textbooks. USA. 1880-1930. *14*

—. Navies. Nova Scotia (Halifax). War of 1812. 1795-1815. *760*

—. Newfoundland. *Pegasus* (vessel). William IV (visit). 1786. *2193*

—. Nova Scotia. Public opinion. Reciprocity. Treaties. USA. 1846-54. *871*

—. Political Commentary. Social change. Socialism. Webb, Beatrice. Webb, Sidney James. 1911. *1090*

—. Prairie settlement. Public Opinion. 1840's-1860's. *2939*

—. Regionalism. 1969-77. *1762*

Great Britain (Liverpool). Industrial Insurance. Montreal Steamship Company. Mutual Benefit Societies. 19c. *2662*

Great Britain (London). Agent general, office of. Intergovernmental Relations. 18c-20c. *212*

—. Arctic. Explorers. Frobisher, Martin. Gold. Northwest Territories (Frobisher Bay). 1570's. *3310*

—. Banking (international). France (Paris). Morton, Levi Parsons. USA. 1860's. *853*

—. Courtship. Field, Eliza. Indians. Jones, Peter. Methodism. New York. 1820's-33. *451*

Great Britain (Sussex). Emigration. Ontario (Upper Canada, York). Petworth Emigration Committee. 1830-40. *775*

Great Lakes. American Revolution. Great Britain. Old Northwest. Peace of Paris (1783). Shelburne, 2d Earl of (William Petty). 1783. *727*

—. Archaeology (amateur). *Chicora* (vessel). Ontario (Sault Ste. Marie, St. Joseph's Island). Scuba diving. 1961-62. *585*

—. Artists. Nickerson, Vincent D. Norton, Charles W. Ships. Sprague, Howard F. Whipple, Seth A. 1844-1901. *2861*

—. Boundary survey incident. Lee, Robert E. USA. 1835. *674*

—. Caldwell, Billy. Frontier and Pioneer Life. Great Britain. Indians. Trade. 1797-1841. *365*

—. Canals. Erie Canal. Freight capacity and utilization. 1810-50. *791*

—. Daily life. Indians. Kane, Paul. Paintings. 1845-46. *384*

—. Disturnell, John (*The Great Lakes, or 'Inland Seas' of America*). Handbooks. Travel. 1862. *882*

—. Geology. 1974. *272*

—. Great Britain. Navies. 1760-89. *680*

—. Howell, William Maher (reminiscences). Ontario. Pennsylvania (Erie). Quebec. St. Lawrence Seaway. Travel. 1928. *2131*

—. Illinois (Chicago). Pollution. Sewage disposal. 1890-1940. *1117*

—. International Ship Masters Association. Shipping. 1886-1977. *1087*

—. Navigation. Shipping. 1948-74. *2876*

—. *North Land* (vessel). *North West* (vessel). Steamboats. 1888-1941. *937*

—. Oil and petroleum products. Ontario. St. Lawrence Seaway. Shipping. 1973. *1539*

—. Oil Industry and Trade. Shipping. ca 1700-1974. *2076*

—. Ontario (St. Catharines). Shickluna, Louis. Shipbuilding. 1835-80. *2882*

—. Ports. Quebec. St. Lawrence River (north shore). Shipping. 1937-70. *1565*

—. Shipping. Steamships. 1871-1976. *43*

—. Toponymy. USA. 1534-1974. *50*

Great Lakes Towing Company. Shipping. 1899-1901. *2826*

Great Plains. Campbell, Thomas D. Droughts. Farm income. Prairie Provinces. Wheat. 1915-1940. *2964*

—. Government. Hunting. Mississippi Flyway. North Central States. Spring shooting issue. Waterfowl. 1887-1913. *906*

—. Horses (Appaloosa). Nez Percé Indians. 1670-1877. *411*

—. Immigration. Manitoba. Mennonites. Russia. 1871-74. *994*

—. Pietism. Prairie Radicals. 1890-1975. *2901*

Great Pontack Inn. Inns, waterfront. Nova Scotia (Halifax). 1754-1837. *2303*

Great Powers. 1925-75. *1780*

—. Bulgaria. Hungary. Rumania. UN. 1947-55. *1927*

—. Lie, Trygve. Pearson, Lester B. UN. 1946. *1738*

Greater Victoria Public Library. British Columbia. Fiction. 1968. *8*

Greek Canadians. Ethnicity. Immigration. Ontario (Toronto). Private Schools. 1900-40. *2845*

Greely, Adolphus W. Garlington, Ernest A. Hazen, William B. Northwest Territories (Ellesmere Island). Scientific Expeditions. 1881-83. *3303*

Green Papers. Immigration policy. 1975. *1809*

Greenland. Alaska. Economic Growth. Population. Scandinavia. 1970's. *281*

—. Bibliographies. Eskimos. Explorers. 16c-19c. *331*

Greist, Mollie Ward. Arctic, northern. Pioneers. Women. ca 1850-1970's. *3344*

Grey, Albert Henry George, 4th Earl. French Canadians. Quebec (Quebec). 1903-06. *2691*

Grey Owl (Archie Belaney). Chippewa Indians. Myths and Symbols. Ontario. 1880-1938. *372*

Grignon, Claude Henri. Anglicization. French Canadians. French language. 20c. *135*

Grip (periodical). Bengough, John Wilson. City government. Ontario (Toronto). Political Reform. Protestantism. 1873-1910. *2807*

Grizzly bear skulls. Eskimos. Excavations. Labrador. 18c-19c. *336*

Grosman, Brian A. (review article). Decisionmaking. Law Enforcement. Police politics. 1975. *1674*

Gross Domestic Product. See GNP.

Gross National Product. See GNP.

Groulx, Lionel. Conservatism. France. French Canadians. Maurras, Charles. Nationalism. 1910-40. *1141*

—. French Canadians. Historians. Nationalism. Nonviolence. Quebec. 1917-30. *489*

Grove, Frederick Philip (letters). Editors and Editing. Literature. Pacey, Desmond. 1912-48. 1976. *1135*

Grove, Frederick Phillip (writings). Literature. Pastoral ideal. Technology. 1920-45. *38*

Guaranteed annual income. Federal Policy. Poverty. 1974. *1509*

Guardhouses. Architecture. France. Louisbourg, Fortress of. Military Camps and Forts. Nova Scotia. 1713-68. *616*

Guigues, Joseph-Eugène. Catholic Church. French Canadians. Ontario (Ottawa Diocese). 1848-74. *2747*

Guillemette, Pierre. Alliance Laurentienne. Barbeau, Raymond. Independence Movements. Quebec. 1960's-75. *2674*

Guiney, Louise Imogen. Carman, William Bliss (letters). Poets. 1887-98. *1045*

Gunboats. British Columbia. Great Britain. Indians. Liquor. Slave trade, Indian. 1860's. *390*

Gunflints. Europe. Flint. Indians. Quebec (Chicoutimi). Travel. 17c. 20c. *349*

—. Excavations. Louisbourg, Fortress of. Military Camps and Forts. Nova Scotia. 1720-60. *608*

Guyana. Alcan Aluminium, Ltd. Bauxite industry. Multinational corporations. Nationalization. 1960-75. *1852*

H

Haddock, John A. Balloons (hot air). LaMountain, John. Quebec. USA. 1859. *845*

Haida Indians. Alaska. Indians. Tlingit Indians. Tsimshian Indians. 1649-1973. *430*

—. British Columbia (Anthony, Queen Charlotte Islands). Totem poles. Prehistory-1795. *375*

—. British Columbia (Louise Island, Koona village). Indians. 1830-90. *454*

—. British Columbia (Queen Charlotte Islands). Fishing gear. Indians. Wood. Prehistory. *287*

—. British Columbia (Queen Charlotte Islands). Missions and Missionaries. Protestantism. Settlement. Subsistence patterns. 1876-1920. *398*

—. British Columbia (Queen Charlotte Islands). Preservation. Totem poles. 1700's-1800's. 1957. *453*

Haidasz, Stanley. Multiculturalism. Polish Canadians. 1975. *1412*

Hail damage. Alberta. Cloud-seeding program. Storms. 1955-74. *3136*

Hair care. Beauty shop. Harper, Martha Matilda. Ontario (Oakville). 1857-93. *2874*

Haiti. Buttons, Phoenix. Indians. Pacific Northwest. Trade. Uniforms, Military. 1812-30. 20c. *460*

—. Foreign Relations. 20c. *1784*

Half-breeds (English). Corbett, Griffiths Owen. Manitoba. Métis. Red River Rebellion. 1863-70. *1014*

Halifax Citadel (fortress). Great Britain. Naval Strategy. Nova Scotia. 1825-60. *642*

Halifax Historic Properties. Buildings. Nova Scotia. Restorations. 1825-1905. 1978. *2255*

Halifax Mechanics' Institute. Adult education. Middle Classes. Nova Scotia. Working class. 1830's-40's. *2291*

Hall, Charles Francis. Colonization. Frobisher, Martin. Great Britain. Northwest Territories (Baffin Island). Pottery. 1578. 1862-1974. *513*

Halliburton, Robert Grant. Apple industry. Calkin(s) family. Inglis, Charles. Nova Scotia. Starr family. 19c. *2279*

Ham Report. Beaudry Report. Industry. Ontario. Quebec. Working Conditions. 1972-74. *1536*

Hamilton, Pierce Stevens (memoirs). Alienation. Morality. Social Conditions. 1826-93. *2335*

Hammer, Armand. Historical Sites and Parks. New Brunswick. Roosevelt Campobello International Park. USA. 1959-74. *2077*

Handbooks. Disturnell, John (*The Great Lakes, or 'Inland Seas' of America*). Great Lakes. Travel. 1862. *882*

Hanlan, Edward "Ned". Athletes. Professionalism. Sports. 1870's-80's. *1042*

—. Courtney, Charles. Rowing. 1870's-80's. *1043*

Hantzsch, Bernard. Arctic. Discovery and Exploration. Northwest Territories (Baffin Island). Trichinosis. 1911. *3316*

—. Discovery and Exploration. Eskimo life. Naturalists. Northwest Territories (Baffin Island). 1910-11. *3314*

—. Discovery and Exploration. Northwest Territories (Baffin Island). Soper, J. Dewey. 1929. *3317*

Harbor Masters. Marine Engineering. Ontario (Toronto). Richardson, Hugh. 1821-70. *2726*

Harbors. Economic development. Nova Scotia (Cape Breton Island, Canso Causeway). 1955-73. *2320*

Hardy, Thomas. Literary Critics. 1870's-1900. *918*

Hare Indians. Arctic. Daily life. Indians. Northwest Territories. Oil exploration. 1859-1974. *358*

Harley, William. Acadians. Daily Life. New Brunswick, northeastern. Surveying. 1829. *2381*

Harper, Martha Matilda. Beauty shop. Hair care. Ontario (Oakville). 1857-93. *2874*

Harper, Russell. Folk Art (review article). Lipman, Jean. USA. Winchester, Alice. 19c. *149*

Harpers Ferry (raid, 1859). Abolition Movement. Brown, John. Civil War (antecedents). Sanborn, Franklin Benjamin. 1854-60. *875*

Harper's Weekly (periodical). Artists. Dakota Territory. Frontier and Pioneer Life. Rogers, William A. 1878. *2976*

Harris, John. Nova Scotia (Halifax, Annapolis). Provincial Government. Roads. 1816-30's. *2253*

Harris, Johnny. British Columbia (Sandon). Entrepreneurs. 1890's-1950's. *3184*

Harris, Kenneth B. Barbeau, Marius. Indians (review article). 1928. 1974. *421*

Harris, Lawren. Art. Bucke, Richard M. (*Cosmic Consciousness*). Theosophy. 1920's. *1181*

Harris, Robert Edward. Nova Scotia. Supreme Court. Townshend, Charles James. 1887-1931. *2286*

Harris, William Richard (biography). Catholic Church. Ontario (Toronto). 1846-1923. 1974. *2858*

Harrison, William Henry. Fort Meigs. Ohio. Virginia (Petersburg). Volunteer Armies. War of 1812. 1812-13. *765*

Hartford Convention. Defense Policy. Militia. New England. War of 1812. 1812-15. *757*

Hartz, Louis. Conservatism. Liberalism. Politics. Socialism. USA. 1955-78. *1668*

—. Historiography. Liberal consensus. ca 1760-1800. 1970's. *693*

Harvard University. Leverett, John. Massachusetts (Cambridge). Quebec Expedition. Speeches, Addresses, etc. 1711. *610*

Harvests. Alberta. Photographs. Wheat. 1910-20. *3168*

Harvie, Eric L. Alberta (Calgary). Glenbow Centre. Museums. 1954-76. *3100*

Harvie, John (and family). Genealogy. Nova Scotia. 1730-1945. *2276*

Hasidism. Judaism. Quebec (Montreal). 1942-71. *2510*

Hawaii. Cable relay point. Great Britain. USA. 1894-96. *1051*

Hazen, Moses. American Revolution. Congress. Military. 1776-1803. *734*

Hazen, William B. Garlington, Ernest A. Greely, Adolphus W. Northwest Territories (Ellesmere Island). Scientific Expeditions. 1881-83. *3303*

Head, Edmund Walker. Confederation. Derby, 15th Earl of. Great Britain. Letters. Political Attitudes. 1858. *894*

Head, Francis Bond. Governors. Great Britain. Ontario (Upper Canada). 1835. *667*

Health care. Health insurance. 1950's-70's. *1577*

Health care, national. 1972. *1439*

Health care programs. Legislative determinants. Social Conditions. 1945-65. *1383*

Health care services. Chippewa Indians. Cree Indians. Ontario (Sioux Lookout Zone). 1900-73. *427*

—. Counties (regrouping of). Quebec. Regions, homogeneous. Socioeconomic development, planning of. 1974. *2428*

—. Patient use (regional analysis). Quebec. 1974. *2540*

Health Insurance See also Insurance; Workmen's Compensation.

—. Health care. 1950's-70's. *1577*

Hearne, Samuel. Buildings. Cumberland House. Saskatchewan. 1794-1800's. *3075*

Heating See also Fuel.

—. Housing. Winter. 1958-77. *2485*

Hecksher-Ohlin theory. Communications (international, theory of). Ontario. Quebec. 1974. *2148*

Hector (vessel). Immigrants. Mackenzie, Alexander. Nova Scotia (Pictou Harbor). Passenger lists. Scotland. 1773. 1883. *2302*

—. Immigrants. Nova Scotia (Pictou Harbor). Scotland. Voyages. 1773. *2340*

Heeney, Arnold D. P. (memoirs). Diplomatic relations. Pearson, Lester B. USA. 1897-1972. *1975*

Heeney, Arnold D. P. (review article). Great Britain. Pearson, Lester B. USA. 1920's-70's. *1790*

Heeney-Merchant Report (1965). Economic relations. USA. 1973-. *1967*

Heintzman, Ralph. Confederation. Creighton, D. G. English Canadians. French Canadians. Minorities in Politics. 1850's-90's. *922*

Heir and Devisee Commission (2d, 1805). Land grants. Ontario (Upper Canada). 1800-45. *645*

Henley House. Hudson's Bay Company. York boats (prototypes). ca 1750's. *556*

Henley House Massacres. Cree Indians. Fort Albany. Hudson's Bay Company. Ontario. Woudbee (chief). 1750's. *348*

Hepburn, Mitchell F. Federal Government. King, William Lyon Mackenzie. Lieutenant governors. Ontario. Provincial government. 1937. *1208*

Heraldry. American Revolution. Colonies. France. Knights of Malta. 1600's-1976. *172*

Heraldry Society of Canada. Duguid, Archer Fortescue (obituary). Historians. 1910-76. *1133*

Heritage Act (1975). Local Architectural Conservation Advisory Committee. Ontario (London). Preservation. 1945-77. *2818*

Heritage Canada. Historical Sites and Parks. 1969-73. *1326*

Heroes. Ancient, William J. *Atlantic* (vessel). Nova Scotia (Terence Bay). Shipwrecks. 1873. *2225*

Herre, W. F. British Columbia (Victoria). Libraries. Reading-rooms. 1858-63. *3256*

Herty, Charles Holmes. Newsprint. Paper mills. Pine trees. Scientific Experiments and Research. Southeastern States. 1927-40. *1134*

Herzberg, Gerhard. Immigration policy. Murray, Walter. Scholars. 1935-37. *1212*

Hibernia colony (proposed). Canada Company. Galt, John. Quebec (Lower Canada). Settlement. 1825-35. *774*

Higgins, William (imprisonment). Ontario (Toronto). Political Corruption. 1834. *2853*

High commissioner (appointment of). British Empire. 1920's. *1180*

High schools. Curricula. Fenton, Edwin. Historical thinking. 1975. *1346*

Higher Education See also Adult Education; Colleges and Universities.

—. 1964-73. *1372*

—. Bilingual Education. French Canadians. Ontario. 1946-73. *1499*

—. Canadian International Development Agency. Manitoba, University of. Thailand. 1964-74. *1911*

—. Canadian studies. Symons report. 1970's. *1368*

—. Curricula. Teaching. Women's history. 1940-73. *1387*

—. Dawson, John William. Grant, George Monro. Scotland. 19c. *2*

—. Government. Public Opinion. 1975. *1485*

—. Graham, John (report). 1974. *1498*

—. Labor market. Social Conditions. 1960-74. *1446*

—. Nationalism. Quebec. Symons report. 1970's. *1472*

—. Quebec (Saguenay County). Students. 1975. *2498*

—. Quebec (Saguenay region). 1949-69. *2506*

—. Symons report. 1950's-70's. *1490*

Highway construction. Climate. Physical Geography. Roads. 1949-73. *3297*

Highway Engineering See also Roads.

—. Alaskan Highway. Logistics. World War II. Yukon Territory. 1942-43. *3338*

Highways. Alaska Highway. British Columbia. Yukon Territory. 1974. *3325*

Hill, Charles C. (account). Art history. Oral history. 1975. *1400*

Himalayas. Alpine Club of Canada. Mountain climbers. Pumori (mountain). 1977. *1260*

Hime, Humphrey Lloyd. Assiniboine and Saskatchewan Exploring Expedition. Discovery and Exploration. Photography. Prairie Provinces. 1858. *863*

Hirohito, Emperor. Alberta (Mount Alberta). Explorers. Japanese. Mountain climbing party. 1925-48. *2924*

Historians. Chapais, Thomas (and ancestors). 1640-1960. *126*

—. Duguid, Archer Fortescue (obituary). Heraldry Society of Canada. 1910-76. *1133*

—. French Canadians. Groulx, Lionel. Nationalism. Nonviolence. Quebec. 1917-30. *489*

—. Intellectual history. 20c. *101*

—. Japan. Norman, E. Herbert (review article). 1940-77. *176*

—. Morice, Adrien-Gabriel. Saskatchewan, University of. ca 1900-38. *3049*

—. Morison, Samuel Eliot (review article). Ocean Travel. Parkman, Francis. 1974. *485*

—. Ontario. Spragge, George Warburton (obituary). 1893-1976. *2731*

—. Quebec Act. 1774. 1974. *696*

Historical Sites and Parks *See also* Restorations.

—. Algonkin Indians. Iroquois Indians. Missions and Missionaries. Quebec (Oka). Sulpicians. 1700's-1800's. *521*

—. Architectural drawings. Fortification. Louisbourg, Fortress of. Nova Scotia (Cape Breton Island). 1707-58. *603*

—. Architecture. Nova Scotia (Halifax). Waterfront. 1815-1973. *2229*

—. Atlantic Coast. Discovery and Exploration. North America. Vikings. 10c-14c. 20c. *483*

—. Barracks. Louisbourg, Fortress of. Nova Scotia. 1716-39. 1969. *590*

—. Buildings. Louisbourg, Fortress of. Nova Scotia (Cape Breton Island). 1713-58. *529*

—. Canadian Inventory of Historic Building. 1968-73. *1289*

—. Daily life. Louisbourg, Fortress of. Nova Scotia (Cape Breton Island). Social classes. 1713-50. *537*

—. Fishing industry. Louisbourg, Fortress of. Nova Scotia (Cape Breton Island, Isle Royale). 1705-50. *573*

—. Hammer, Armand. New Brunswick. Roosevelt Campobello International Park. USA. 1959-74. *2077*

—. Heritage Canada. 1969-73. *1326*

—. Lighthouses. 1873-1970. *22*

—. Louisbourg, Fortress of. Nova Scotia (Cape Breton Island). Restorations. 18c. 1961-75. *602*

—. Quebec (Orléans Island). Urbanization. 1969-76. *2490*

Historical Society of Montreal. Lapierre, Eugène (obituary). Nationalism. Quebec. 1927-70's. *2450*

Historical thinking. Curricula. Fenton, Edwin. High schools. 1975. *1346*

Historical traditions. Anglophones. Ethnicity. French-speakers. 1974. *1464*

Historiography *See also* Historians; Quantitative Methods.

—. 1970-76. *78*

—. 17c-1973. 1945-69. *169*

—. Agricultural crisis. Ouellet, Fernand. Paquet, Gilles. Quebec (Lower Canada). Wallot, J.-P. 1802-12. 1963-73. *789*

—. Agricultural crisis. Quebec (Lower Canada). 1802-12. *806*

—. Americanization. Moffett, Samuel E. 1867-1974. *162*

—. Assiniboin Indians. Cypress Hills Massacre. Saskatchewan, southwestern. 1873. *978*

—. Atlantic Provinces. Nationalism. Regionalism. 19c-20c. *2160*

—. Atlantic Provinces (review article). France. Missions and Missionaries. New France. Politics. 1000-1770. 19c. *67*

—. Berger, Carl (review article). English Canadians. Nationalism. 1900-76. *232*

—. Bergeron, Léandre (review article). Marxism. Quebec. 1970-75. *2618*

—. Bibliographies. Protestant churches. 1825-1973. *130*

—. Black, Conrad. Duplessis, Maurice. Political Leadership. Quebec. Rumilly, Robert. 1936-59. *2684*

—. British Columbia. Business History. Economic Development. Robin, Martin (review article). 19c-20c. 1974. *3244*

—. Business. Economic history. Laurentian thesis. 1960-73. *1592*

—. Colleges and Universities. French Canadians. Quebec. 1947-72. *2449*

—. Colleges and Universities. Nationalism. 1810-1967. *165*

—. Colonial Government. Frégault, Guy. New France. Rioux, Marcel. 1615-1763. 1957-60's. *491*

—. Colonies. France. Great Britain. Italy. North America. 1663-1763. *598*

—. Communism. Europe, Eastern. Public administration. USA. USSR. ca 1850-1975. *1316*

—. Daily life. Oral history. Popular thought. 20c. *1320*

—. Discrimination. Negroes. 1776-1976. *252*

—. Education (review article). Social Change. 19c-20c. *248*

—. Frégault, Guy. Quebec (Montreal). 17c. 1950-60. *490*

—. French Americans. Research. Vermont. 1609-1976. *2583*

—. French Canadians. Quebec. 1660-1976. *495*

—. Hartz, Louis (thesis). Liberal consensus. ca 1760-1800. 1970's. *693*

—. Jesuits. New France. Parkman, Francis. 17c. 1840's-60's. *518*

—. Land Settlement. Prairie Provinces. 1880-1900. *2902*

—. Manufacturing. Merchants. 19c. 1975. *134*

—. Maritime Provinces. 1900-67. *59*

—. Morality. New France. 17c-18c. *525*

—. Oral history. Working Class (review article). 20c. *103*

—. Papineau, Louis-Joseph. Politics. Quebec. Rebellion of 1837. Rumilly, Robert (review article). 1791-1871. 1934. 1977. *822*

—. Prairie provinces. 1974. *2900*

—. Press. World War II (antecedents). 1938-39. *1236*

—. Psychology. 1977. *122*

—. Quebec. 1790-1890. 1950-78. *2453*

—. Quebec. Social Credit. 1936-65. *2619*

—. Quebec. Working class. 1897-1974. *2611*

—. Teachers. 19c-20c. *23*

—. Urbanization. 17c-1974. *222*

—. World War II. 1939-45. *1221*

—. World War II. 1939-78. *1230*

—. World War II. 1939-45. *1230*

History *See also* particular branches of history, e.g. business history, oral history, psychohistory, science, history of; Ideas, History of.

—. Archaeology, industrial. Education. Great Britain. USA. 1955-70. *1302*

—. Art. Illustrators. Jeffreys, Charles William. Textbooks. 1920's-50. *1119*

—. Census. Privacy. Research. 1918-77. *57*

—. Colleges and Universities. Graduate students. 1966-75. *1281*

History Teaching. Loyalism. Ontario (Upper Canada). Textbooks. 19c-20c. *741*

History, uses of. Foreign Relations (review article). USA. 1923-73. *253*

Hitchins, Fred H. Aeronautics (history). Archival Catalogs and Inventories. Western Ontario, University of, D. B. Weldon Library (Hitchins Collection). 20c. *94*

Hockey. Behavior (aggressive). Ontario (Toronto). Sports. Violence. 1972. *2862*

Holiness Movement. Brethren in Christ. North Central States. 1910-50. *1145*

Holiness Movement Church. Evangelism. Horner, Ralph Cecil. Methodist Church. 1887-1921. *1064*

—. Evangelism. Horner, Ralph Cecil. Methodist Church. 1887-1921. *1065*

Holmes Foundry. Antilabor sentiments. Immigrants. Ontario. Strikes. 1935-40. *1210*

Holy Ghost and Us Society. Nova Scotia. Sanford, Frank. Sects, Religious. Shipwrecks. 1910-48. *2333*

Home county. British Columbia. Chinese, overseas. Clan origins. 1880-85. *1052*

Homesteading and Homesteaders. Alberta. Immigration. Negroes. Race Relations. 1911-12. *3152*

—. Alberta. Kokotailo, Veronia. Rumanians. 1898- . *3165*

—. Alberta. Peace River country. Ukrainians. Zahara, Dominka Roshko. 1900-30. *1034*

—. Alberta (Edmonton). Rural Schools. Waugh School District. 1901-40's. *3166*

—. Alberta (Red Deer-Halrirk). Farms. 1900-15. *3116*

—. Alberta, southern. Sharples (family). 1870's-1902. *3085*

—. Alberta (Waskatenau). Buchanan, Carl, Jr. (reminiscences). Daily Life. 1930's. *3091*

—. British Columbia. Immigration. Prairie Provinces. Scandinavian Canadians. 1850's-1970's. *1032*

—. British Columbia (northern). Government relief. Resettlement. 1940-42. *3192*

—. Criddle, Percy. Diaries. Manitoba (Aweme). 1882-1900's. *954*

—. Locusts. Manitoba. Mortgages. 1875-1941. *3002*

Honeyman, David. *Challenger* (vessel). Expedition. Nova Scotia (Halifax). Oceanography. 1872-76. *2317*

Hood, Robert. Birds. Discovery and Exploration. Painting. Saskatchewan River. 1819-21. *2928*

Hood, Robert (journal). Arctic. Discovery and Exploration. Franklin, John. Northwest Territories. 1819-21. *3309*

Hood, Robert (journal, paintings). Explorers. Franklin, John. Northwest Passage. 1819-22. *3308*

Hoover, Herbert C. Bennett, Richard Bedford. Foreign Relations. USA. 1930-31. *1205*

—. Foreign Relations. St. Lawrence Seaway Treaty of 1932. USA. 1932. *1204*

—. Foreign Relations. Smoot-Hawley Tariff. USA. 1929-33. *1203*

Hornby, John. Adlard, Harold. Christian, Edgar. COSMOS (satellite). Northwest Territories (Thelon River, Hornby Point). 1926-27. 1976. *3346*

—. Adlard, Harold. Christian, Edgar. Dewar, Kenneth M. (reminiscences). Diaries. Northwest Territories (Thelon River, Hornby Point). 1928. *3350*

Horner, Ralph Cecil. Evangelism. Holiness Movement Church. Methodist Church. 1887-1921. *1064*

—. Evangelism. Holiness Movement Church. Methodist Church. 1887-1921. *1065*

Horse racing. Sports. 1830-65. *644*

Horses. Alberta. 1870-90. *1000*

Horses (Appaloosa). Great Plains. Nez Percé Indians. 1670-1877. *411*

Horst, Thomas (review article). Exports. Tariff. Trade Regulations. USA. 1970's. *1882*

Horticulture. Botany. Douglas, David. North America. Scientific Expeditions. 1823-34. *650*

Hospitals. Catholic Church. Hôtel-Dieu. Indian-White Relations. Quebec. 1635-98. *552*

—. Evangelism. Indians. Quebec. 1633-1703. *539*

Hotel trade. Fabyan, Horace. New Hampshire (Portland). White Mountain Grand Hotel. 1807-81. *772*

Hôtel-Dieu. Catholic Church. Hospitals. Indian-White Relations. Quebec. 1635-98. *552*

Houde, Camillien. Bossism. Local government. Martin, Médéric. Quebec (Montreal). 1923-29. *2446*

House of Commons. Legislation. 1958-72. *1669*

House of Representatives *See also* Legislation.

—. Anderson, William J. Negroes. Political Leadership. Vermont (Montpelier, Shoreham). 1900-40's. *2565*

Household structure. Census. Ontario (Hamilton). 1851-71. *2759*

Houses. Alberta. Ukrainians. 1890's-1915. *3128*

—. Architecture. Wood carving. Woodland, George. 1867-1969. *2264*

Houses, communal. Eskimos, Thule culture. Excavations. Labrador (Saglek Bay). 1650-1700. *334*

—. Pensions. 1971-73. *1297*

Housework. Politics. Wages. Women. 1970's. *1692*

Housing *See also* City Planning; Public Housing; Urban Renewal.

—. Alberta. Construction. Settlement. Sod. Williams, Wesley. 1909. *1004*

—. British Columbia Mills, Timber, and Trading Company. Buildings. 1904-10. *2941*

—. British Columbia (Vancouver). Fishing industry. Labor. Politics. 1970's. *3172*

—. City planning. Environment. Suburbs. 1893-1930. *236*

—. Construction. Contracts. Population. Quebec (Quebec). 1810-20. *2596*

—. Eskimos, Sadlermiut. Gibbons, Jimmy (interview). Marsh, Donald B. (reminiscences). Northwest Territories (Southampton Island). ca 1900. *328*
—. Heating. Winter. 1958-77. *2485*
—. Ontario (London). Prices. Railroads. 1972. *1591*
Housing costs. Cities. Land banks. ca 1970-81. *1524*
Housing (low-cost). Intergovernmental relations. Manitoba. Remote Housing Program. 1968-70. *2988*
Howe, Clarence Decatur. Cabinet. 1935-57. *18*
Howe, John (and family). Genealogy. Nova Scotia (Halifax). 18c-19c. *750*
Howe, Joseph. Adult education. Educators. Nova Scotia. 1827-66. *2290*
—. Bakewell, Robert. Coal Mines and Mining. Nova Scotia (Pictou County; Stellarton). 1798-1881. *2227*
—. Confederation. Nova Scotia. 1832-69. *892*
—. Crimean War. Great Britain. Military recruitment. USA. 1854-56. *867*
—. Journalism. Nova Scotia (Halifax). *Novascotian* (newspaper). 1824-38. *828*
—. Local Government. Nova Scotia (Halifax). Political Corruption. Trials. 1835. *808*
—. Nova Scotia (Lochaber). Rural Development. 1795-1880. *2285*
—. Nova Scotia (Upper Musquodoboit). 1845-47. *2355*
Howell, William Maher (reminiscences). Great Lakes. Ontario. Pennsylvania (Erie). Quebec. St. Lawrence Seaway. Travel. 1928. *2131*
Howells, William Dean. Quebec (Quebec). Travel. 1871-72. *2454*
Howley, J. P. Beothuk Indians (review article). Indian-White Relations. Newfoundland. Rowe, F. W. Prehistory-1830. 1977. *290*
Huart, Christophle-Albert-Alberic d'. Fishing company. France (Poitou; Les Sables d'Olonne). Louisbourg, Fortress of. Nobility. Nova Scotia (Cape Breton Island). 1750-75. *560*
Hubbard, Leonidas. Explorers. Labrador (northeast). Wallace, Dillon. 1903-05. *3313*
Hudson Bay. Education. Employment. Hudson's Bay Company. Métis. 1790's-1820's. *771*
—. Eskimos. Mina (Eskimo woman). Religion. 1940's-50's. *326*
Hudson Strait (navigability). Arctic islands. Discovery and Exploration. Wakeham, William. 1897. *3304*
Hudson's Bay Company. Alberta. Cree Indians. Fuller, Richard. Telegraph. Treaties. 1870's. *1020*
—. Alberta. Fur trade. Kerr, Tom. 1861-1946. *3160*
—. Alberta (Lac la Biche). Beaver Indians. North West Rebellion. Pruden, Patrick. Trading posts. 1885. *1026*
—. Anderson, James. Quebec (Eastmain River). Rivers. Whaling Industry and Trade. 1850's-70. *847*
—. Arctic. Discovery and Exploration. Fort Hope. Northwest Territories. Rae, John. 1840's. *3298*
—. Botany (specimens). Burke, Joseph. Manitoba. Northwest Territories. Royal Botanic Gardens. 1843-45. *2922*
—. Boys. Charities. Great Britain. Schools. 18c-19c. *684*
—. Brigade Trail. British Columbia. Trade Routes. 1849-60. 1967-73. *3203*
—. British Columbia. Fort Langley. Restorations. 1827-58. 1976-77. *3210*
—. California (San Francisco). Ice trade. Pacific Area. Russian-American Company. 1850's. *878*
—. Catholic Church. Chippewa Indians. Métis. Provencher, John N. (memoir). Quebec. Red River Settlement. 1812-36. *2948*
—. Character book. Simpson, George. 1832. *2960*
—. Children. Education. Fur trade. Métis. 1820's-60's. *628*
—. Church Missionary Society. Church of England. Eskimos. Missions and Missionaries. Northwest Territories (Baffin Island). Peck, E. J. Trade. 1894-1913. *340*
—. Church of England. Hunter, James. Missions and Missionaries. 1844-64. *2946*
—. City planning. Manitoba (Selkirk). 1869-79. *1023*
—. Colonization (supposed). Defoe, Daniel. Publicity. Rupert's Land. Sergeant, Henry. 1680's. *502*
—. Commerce. 1683-1852. *663*

—. Cree Indians. Fort Albany. Henley House Massacres. Ontario. Woudbee (chief). 1750's. *348*
—. Cumberland House. Saskatchewan. 1774-1974. *3063*
—. Daily Life. Trading posts. ca 1850. *862*
—. Discovery and Exploration. Fur Trade. Ogden, Peter Skene. 1811-54. *688*
—. Discovery and Exploration. Simpson, George. 1787-1860. *639*
—. Diseases, diffusion of. Fur Trade. Indians. 1830-50. *2949*
—. Economic Growth. Fur Trade. Lake, Bibye. 1684-1743. *503*
—. Education. Employment. Hudson Bay. Métis. 1790's-1820's. *771*
—. Episcopal Church, Protestant. Indians. Missions and Missionaries. Pacific Northwest. 1825-75. *402*
—. Eskimo life. Fur trade. Northwest Territories (Hudson Bay, Baffin Island). 1909-30's. *3348*
—. Eskimos. Northwest Territories (Baffin Island, Devon Island). Russell, Chesley (account). Settlement. 1934-36. *332*
—. Excavations. Ontario (Charlton Island, James Bay). 1680's. 1972-73. *566*
—. Fires, prairie. Fur trade. Indians. Saskatchewan. 1790-1840. *461*
—. Fisheries. Salmon. Ungava Bay region. 1830's-1939. *2653*
—. Food Supply. Fur trade. Mackenzie River Valley. Northwest Territories. Winter. 19c. *3357*
—. Food Supply. Gardening. 1670-1760's. *497*
—. Foreign Investments. Great Britain. International Financial Society. Railroads. 1863. *840*
—. Fort Vancouver. Fur trade. McLoughlin, John. Pacific Northwest. 1825-60. *861*
—. Frederick House Massacre. Fur Trade. Indian-White Relations. Ontario. 1812-13. *2828*
—. Fur trade. Indians. Trade. 17c-18c. *576*
—. Fur trade. Mineral Resources. North America. 17c-20c. *258*
—. Fur Trade. New York. Sutherland, James. 1751-97. *687*
—. Geography. Societies. Wegg, Samuel. 1750-1800. *683*
—. Graham, Andrew. Hutchins, Thomas. Natural history. Plagiarism. 1770's-1815. *692*
—. Great Britain. Royal Society of Canada. Wegg, Samuel. 1753-1802. *682*
—. Henley House. York boats (prototypes). ca 1750's. *556*
—. Northwest Territories (Marble Island). *Perseverance* (vessel). Whaling industry and Trade. 1866-67. 1892-97. *681*
Hudson's Bay Company (review article). British North America. Fur Trade. 1670-1870. 1970's. *97*
Hughes, Helen McGill. Sociology. USA. Women. 1916-77. *96*
Hughes, Sam. Anglo-French divisions. Canadian Expeditionary Force. Imperialist sentiment. World War I. 1853-1921. *245*
—. Casualty rates. Currie, Arthur. Military General Staff. World War I. 1914-30. *1156*
Hugo, Adèle. Nova Scotia (Halifax). 1863-66. *2278*
Huguenots. France. New France. Protestantism. 1541-1760. *550*
Human rights. Americas (North and South). 19c-20c. *163*
—. Americas (North and South). Foreign relations. 1945-75. *1843*
—. Discrimination. Language. USA. 1960's. *1481*
—. Freedoms. North America. Race relations. 1973. *1478*
—. Law. USA. 1930-73. *1963*
Human rights agencies. Government. Ontario. Racism. 1973-77. *2790*
Humanism. Democracy. MacPherson, C. B. Marxism. Political Theory. 1976. *1338*
Humanitarian attitudes. Developing nations. Poverty. UN Security Council. 1970's. *1796*
Hume, David (writings). French Canadians. Literature, moralistic. Luxury, concept of. Quebec. 1849-1900. *2617*
Humor *See also* Satire.

—. Identification classes. Students. *Vicarious superiority* theory. Windsor, University of. 1969-74. *2808*
—. New Brunswick (western). Social Customs. Wedding night pranks. 18c-1974. *2396*
Humphrys, James (and family). Daily Life. Saskatchewan (Cannington Manor). 1880's-1908. *986*
Hungarians. Esterhazy, Paul O. d' (Johan Baptista Packh). Immigrants. Saskatchewan (Esterhazy). 1831-1912. *3043*
Hungary. Bulgaria. Great Powers. Rumania. UN. 1947-55. *1927*
Hunt, George T. (*The Wars of the Iroquois*). Epidemics. Fur Trade. Indians. Iroquois Indians. 1609-53. *523*
Hunter, James. Church of England. Hudson's Bay Company. Missions and Missionaries. 1844-64. *2946*
Hunter, R. H. (reminiscences). Saskatchewan. Teaching. 1923-67. *2931*
Hunting *See also* Trapping.
—. Arctic. Ringed seals. Seals. Wildlife Conservation. 1966-73. *335*
—. Extinction, threatened. Pacific Area (north). Seals. USA. 1886-1910. *936*
—. Government. Great Plains. Mississippi Flyway. North Central States. Spring shooting issue. Waterfowl. 1887-1913. *906*
—. Indians. 17c. *571*
Hurford, Grace Gibberd (reminiscences). China. Missions and Missionaries. Teaching. World War II. 1928-45. *1122*
Huron Indians. France. Indians (review article). Jaenen, Cornelius J. Trigger, Bruce G. Values. 1600-60. 1976. *520*
Hurricanes *See also* names of particular hurricanes, e.g. New England Hurricane, 1938, etc.; Cyclones; Storms.
—. Diaries. Marshall, John George. Nova Scotia (Guysborough County). 1811. *2223*
Hutchins, Thomas. Graham, Andrew. Hudson's Bay Company. Natural history. Plagiarism. 1770's-1815. *692*
Hutterites. Agriculture. North America. Social Customs. Technology. 18c-20c. *2896*
—. Alberta (Edmonton). Public Opinion. Social distance. 1966-75. *3132*
—. Amish. Dukhobors. Mennonites. Molokans. North America. ca 1650-1977. *184*
—. Communes. USA. 1870's-1970. *987*
—. Communications. Frontier and Pioneer Life. West. 1874-1977. *1022*
—. Equal opportunity. Leadership succession. Population. Prairie Provinces. Social Organization. 1940's-70's. *2908*
—. Life-styles, alternative. South Dakota. 1874-1975. *977*
Hyde Park Declaration (1941). Great Britain. USA. World War II. 1939-41. *1224*
Hydroelectric development. Churchill River. Ecology. Manitoba, northern. 1966-70's. *2972*
Hydroelectric plants. Manitoba (Winnipeg River; Pinawa Channel). Winnipeg Electrical Street Railway Co. 1903-51. *3010*
Hydroelectric power. Aluminum industry. 1900-76. *65*
—. Nova Scotia (Halifax). Street railways. 1907-17. *2211*
—. Planning. Water. 1973. *1335*
Hydroelectric projects. 1971-74. *2130*
Hydrographic regions. Population. Quebec. Statistics. 1845-1971. *2488*

I

Iberville, Pierre Le Moyne d'. Alabama (Mobile). France (Paris). Immigration. Population. Women. 1702-04. *582*
Ice caps. Climate. Scientific Experiments and Research. 1954-77. *271*
Ice trade. California (San Francisco). Hudson's Bay Company. Pacific Area. Russian-American Company. 1850's. *878*
Iceland. Immigration. Ontario. 1872-75. *2761*
Icelandic Canadians. Dufferin and Ava, 1st Marquis of (visit). Manitoba (Gimli). 1877. *969*
Idaho. Fire fighting. Forest fires. Great Idaho Fire. Montana. 1910. *1082*
—. Indian Wars. MacDonald, Duncan. Nez Percé Indians. 1877. *418*
Idaho (Boise). Air Warfare. Army Air Corps. Beeson, Duane. World War II. 1941-45. *1222*
Ideal States. *See* Utopias.

Idealism. Attitudes. Cather, Willa (*Shadows on the Rock*). 1920's-31. *1177*
—. Foreign Relations. USA. 1904-32. *1884*
Ideas, diffusion of. Enlightenment. Newspapers. 1764-1810. *648*
Ideas, History of *See also* Intellectuals.
—. Catholic Church. Laval, François de. Quebec. 17c. *549*
—. Discovery and Exploration. Geography. Maps. Vinland Map. 1974. *484*
—. Europe, influence of. Quebec. Social Classes. 1960-75. *2501*
—. Political change. Social Change. 1780-1800. *795*
Identification classes. Humor. Students. *Vicarious superiority* theory. Windsor, University of. 1969-74. *2808*
Identification (cultural, racial). Children. Indians. 1972-73. *392*
Identity. Blackfoot Indians. Indians. Menominee Indians. Militancy. 1950's-60's. *457*
—. Ethnic Groups. Nationalism. Regionalism. Students. 1960-77. *2915*
—. Generation conflict, basis. Quebec (Quebec). Social integration. 1968. *2487*
Ideology. Aberhart, William. Alberta. Provincial Government. Social Credit Party. Theology. 1935-43. *3106*
—. Alberta (Calgary). Models. Nationalism. Regionalism. 1974. *2921*
—. American Revolution. French Revolution. Popular movements. 1775-1838. *819*
—. British Columbia. Cooperative Commonwealth Federation (origins). Power struggles. Socialists. 1919-32. *3271*
—. British Columbia (Vancouver). Manitoba (Winnipeg). Methodology. Political Parties. 1967-69. *1727*
—. British Empire. Catholic Church. Imperialism. Quebec. 19c-20c. *2560*
—. Economic growth. Elites. Laval University. Quebec. Social sciences. 1930's-70's. *2527*
—. Educational system. Sex Discrimination. Sociology. Women. 1970's. *1474*
—. French Canadians (review article). Great Britain. 1867-1936. *2708*
—. Research. Sociology of knowledge. Women's studies. 1970's. *1430*
Illinois *See also* North Central States.
Illinois (Chicago). Banking. Immigration. Swedish Americans. 1892-1974. *1093*
—. Great Lakes. Pollution. Sewage disposal. 1890-1940. *1117*
Illiteracy. Crime and Criminals. Ethnicity. Ontario (Middlesex County). Sex. Social Status. 1867-68. *1044*
Illness. *See* Diseases.
Illustrators. Art. History. Jeffreys, Charles William. Textbooks. 1920's-50. *1119*
Immigrants. Acculturation. Boardinghouses. Italian Canadians. Ontario (Toronto). 20c. *2782*
—. Acculturation. Ethnic studies. Sociology. 1960's-70's. *1409*
—. Acculturation. Ontario (Toronto). 1950's-70's. *2785*
—. Acculturation. Polish Canadians. 1945-75. *1436*
—. American Revolution (antecedents). Georgia. Great Britain. Military. Nova Scotia. 1765-75. *729*
—. Antilabor sentiments. Holmes Foundry. Ontario. Strikes. 1935-40. *1210*
—. Archives. Ontario (Toronto). Photographs. 1900-30. 1974. *2877*
—. Assimilation. Employment. Language training. Ontario (Toronto). 1968-70. *1625*
—. Assimilation. Macedonians. Ontario (Toronto). 1900-20. *2840*
—. Assimilation. Multiculturalism. Psychology. 1970's. *1424*
—. Baltic Area. Lutheran Church. 1947-55. *1492*
—. Birth rate. Demography. Ethnic variations. Marriage. 1871. *1072*
—. Coal Mines and Mining. Economic Development. Europeans. Kansas. 1870-1940. *1062*
—. Discrimination. Ethnic groups. Manitoba (Winnipeg). Population. 1874-1974. *2967*
—. Discrimination. Employment. Ontario (Toronto). Social Status. West Indians. 1972. *2849*
—. Education. Labor. Social Classes. 1973. *2149*
—. Employment. Italians. Ontario (Toronto). 1885-1915. *2783*

—. Esterhazy, Paul O. d' (Johan Baptista Packh). Hungarians. Saskatchewan (Esterhazy). 1831-1912. *3043*
—. Family. Generations. Italians. 20c. *1493*
—. Farms. Manitoba (Brandon). Railroads. Wheat. 1880-87. *961*
—. Finns. Labor Unions and Organizations. Radicals and Radicalism. USA. 1918-26. *1183*
—. Germans. Nova Scotia. Protestants. 1749-52. *2259*
—. *Hector* (vessel). Mackenzie, Alexander. Nova Scotia (Pictou Harbor). Passenger lists. Scotland. 1773. 1883. *2302*
—. *Hector* (vessel). Nova Scotia (Pictou Harbor). Scotland. Voyages. 1773. *2340*
—. Labor Unions and Organizations. Massachusetts (Fall River). Textile industry. 1890-1905. *2659*
—. Macedonians. Ontario (Toronto). Urban history. 20c. *2786*
—. Manitoba. Mennonites, Russian. Russians. Shantz, Jacob Y. 1873. *1024*
—. McDonald, Donald. Millenarianism. Prince Edward Island. Scottish Canadians. ca 1828-67. *2209*
—. Negroes. Nova Scotia. 1776-1815. *640*
—. North America. Occupations. Statistics. Women. 1964-71. *1516*
—. Ontario (Toronto). Stereotypes. Urban history. 19c-20c. *2784*
Immigration *See also* Assimilation; Demography; Emigration; Population; Race Relations; Refugees; Social Problems.
—. Acculturation. Settlement. Slovak Canadians. 1885-1970's. *113*
—. Act of Sexual Sterilization (Alberta, 1928). Alberta. Eugenics. Press. Woodsworth, James S. 1900-28. *2906*
—. Adachi, Ken (review article). Japanese Canadians. Racism. 1877-1976. *123*
—. Alabama (Mobile). France (Paris). Iberville, Pierre Le Moyne d'. Population. Women. 1702-04. *582*
—. Alberta. Homesteading and Homesteaders. Negroes. Race Relations. 1911-12. *3152*
—. Alberta. Minorities. Nativism. 1925-30. *3144*
—. Anglicization. French Canadians. MacDonald, John A. 1860-1900. *705*
—. Annan, Ebenezer (letters). Daily Life. Nova Scotia (Halifax). 1842. *2220*
—. Anti-Communist movements. Anti-Semitism. Freedom of speech. National self-image. Ontario (Toronto). 1928-29. *2791*
—. Armenians. Quebec (Montreal). 1900-66. *28*
—. Asian Canadians. British Columbia. Politics. Racism. 1850-1914. *900*
—. Assimilation. British Columbia (Saltspring Island). Negroes. 1850-1900. *3211*
—. Assimilation. Fitzpatrick, Alfred. Frontier College. Labor. 1899-1922. *1086*
—. Assimilation. Mining. Quebec. 1941-71. *2639*
—. Atlantic Provinces. Economic conditions. Kennedy, Albert J. Massachusetts (Boston). 1910's. *2162*
—. Attitudes. Ireland. Ontario (Canada West). Potato famine. 1845-50. *797*
—. Australia. Federal Policy. Population. 1967-75. *1466*
—. Baerg, Anna (diary). Mennonites. Russian Revolution. 1917-23. *1171*
—. Banking. Illinois (Chicago). Swedish Americans. 1892-1974. *1093*
—. Belgian families. Manitoba (Winnipeg, East St. Boniface). Nuytten, Edmund. Nuytten, Octavia. 1880-1914. *2991*
—. Bibliographies. East Indians. 1900-77. *1358*
—. British Columbia. Chinese. Japanese. Suffrage. 1935-49. *3220*
—. British Columbia. Daily life. Dukhobors. Russia. 1880's-1976. *1035*
—. British Columbia. Great Britain. Public opinion. 1919-30. *3250*
—. British Columbia. Homesteading and Homesteaders. Prairie Provinces. Scandinavian Canadians. 1850's-1970's. *1032*
—. Burns family. Ireland. Nova Scotia (Annapolis County; Wilmot Township). 1764-20c. *2305*
—. Catholic Church. Manitoba. Mathieu, Olivier-Elzéar. Regina Archdiocese. Saskatchewan. 1911-31. *2936*
—. Catholic Church. Missions and Missionaries. Sisters of Service. 1920-30. *2963*

—. Chicopee Manufacturing Company. Irish Americans. Massachusetts (Chicopee). Mills. Nativism. 1830-75. *635*
—. Children. Great Britain. Ontario. Poor. Press. Rye, Miss. 1865-1925. *2879*
—. Children. Jews. Manitoba (Winnipeg). Public schools. 1900-20. *3007*
—. Chippewa Indians. Manitoba. Mennonites, Russian. Métis. 1872-73. *990*
—. City Life. Jews, Russian. Manitoba (Winnipeg). 1874-82. *2965*
—. Colonialism. France. Louisiana. 1718-21. *578*
—. Commerce. Italians. USA. 1870-1977. *83*
—. Cotton mills. French Canadians. Massachusetts (Springfield). Statistics. 1870. *2607*
—. Democracy. Foreign Relations. France. 1855. *836*
—. Deutscher Bund Canada. German Canadians. Saskatchewan (Loon River area). 1929-39. *3076*
—. Dukhobors. Religious persecution. Russia. Sects, Religious. 1654-1902. *1033*
—. Dukhobors. Russia. 1652-1908. *996*
—. Eby, Ezra F. Loyalists. Mennonites. Pennsylvania. 18c-1835. *743*
—. Economic progression. Education. Political autonomy. Professions. 1945-75. *1425*
—. Economics. Employment. Wages. 1970's. *1588*
—. Education. Jews. Russia. Segal, Beryl (reminiscences). USA. 1900-70's. *204*
—. Ethnic Groups. Europe. Occupations. Ontario (Toronto). Social Status. 1940's-70's. *2814*
—. Ethnicity. Greek Canadians. Ontario (Toronto). Private Schools. 1900-40. *2845*
—. Ethnicity. North America. 1974. *1407*
—. Europe (Eastern, Southern). Legislation. Physicians. Racism. 1920's. *1178*
—. Federal Policy. Unemployment. 1950-77. *1410*
—. Folklore. Ukrainians. 1945-75. *2933*
—. Foreign policy. Labor. Population. Refugees. 1950's-70's. *1887*
—. France. Nova Scotia (Port Royal). Settlement. 1650-1755. *511*
—. Franco-Americans. Maine. ca 1870-20c. *2152*
—. French Canadians. Massachusetts (Holyoke). Proulx, Nicholas. Working Class. 1850-1900. *2600*
—. Galveston Plan. Jews. Schiff, Jacob H. USA. 1907-14. *905*
—. Government policy. Migration, Internal. 1896-1973. *99*
—. Gowan, Ogle. Irish influence. Ontario (Upper Canada). Orangeism. Politics. 1830-33. *821*
—. Great Plains. Manitoba. Mennonites. Russia. 1871-74. *994*
—. Iceland. Ontario. 1872-75. *2761*
—. Ireland. Poor Law Commissioners. Servants. Women. 1865. *888*
—. Italian Canadians. Ontario (Toronto). Population. 1946-72. *2875*
—. Jews. New York City. Vanger, Max. 1900-50. *1143*
—. Macedonians. Ontario (Toronto). Social Conditions. 1900-30. *2841*
—. Manitoba. Mennonites, Bergthaler. Stoesz, David. Ukraine. 1872-76. *988*
—. Manitoba. Mennonites, Russian. Russians. 1873. *989*
—. Manitoba. Shantz, Jacob Y. Ukraine. 1870's. *992*
—. Manitoba (Winnipeg). Melnyk, George (reminiscences). 1949. 1977. *2995*
—. Mennonites. Ukraine. 1922-23. *1173*
—. Mennonites (Russian). Passenger lists. Quebec. 1874-80. *966*
—. Mennonites, Russian. Saskatchewan (Rosthern). Social conditions. 1923. *3052*
—. Nationalism. Protestant churches. United Church of Canada. 1902-25. *1194*
—. Negroes. Ohio (Cincinnati). Ontario (Wilberforce). 1829-56. *626*
—. Ontario (Toronto). Wages. 1971. *2871*
—. Organizations. Slovak Americans. 1890-1964. *112*
—. Polish Canadians. 1900-65. *1419*
—. Prairie Provinces. Settlement. Ukrainians. 1910-31. *2937*
—. Public Policy. 1967-75. *1812*
Immigration Bill (1976). Employment. Management. 1976. *1394*
Immigration. DeLaGarza, E. (Kika). Mexico. Public Policy. USA. 1910-74. *1732*
Immigration policy. 1945-74. *1810*

—. Antilabor sentiments. Elections, local. Ku Klux Klan. 1921-30's. *2925*
—. Brain drain. British West Indies. Racism. 1946-77. *1742*
—. Brain drain. Developing Nations. Economic Conditions. 1962-74. *1931*
—. Demographic research. Federal Government. Local government. 1970's. *1811*
—. Developing nations. Refugees. 1950's-70's. *1747*
—. Economic Conditions. Employment. 1962-74. *1448*
—. Ethnic tension. Radicals and Radicalism. 1896-1919. *1079*
—. Ethnicity. USA. 1867-1975. *168*
—. Green Paper. 1975. *1809*
—. Herzberg, Gerhard. Murray, Walter. Scholars. 1935-37. *1212*
—. O'Connell, Martin. Public opinion. 1975. *1376*
—. Population. 1945-76. *1395*
Immigration (theory). Economic Conditions. 1940's-70's. *1329*
Imo (vessel). Disasters. *Mont Blanc* (vessel). Nova Scotia (Halifax). 1917. *2332*
Imperial administration. British Columbia. Frontier process. Great Britain. 1846-71. *979*
Imperial funds (diversion). Canals. Military. Ottawa-Rideau military canal. 1815-25. *799*
Imperial Munitions Board. Arbitration, Industrial. Armaments Industry. Labor Unions and Organizations. 1900-20. *1080*
Imperial Oil Company. Energy development. Public ownership. 1970's. *1841*
Imperial Shipping Committee. Great Britain. International Trade. Trade Regulations. 1918-63. *20*
Imperialism *See also* Colonialism; Expansionism.
—. Britannic Idealism (concept). Nationalism. Parkin, George R. 1871-1922. *912*
—. British Empire. Catholic Church. Ideology. Quebec. 19c-20c. *2560*
—. Capitalism. Socialism. Women. ca 1870-1975. *139*
—. Colonial Stock Act (1900). Great Britain. Laurier, Wilfrid. 1890's-1900. *1095*
—. Duncan, Sara Jeanette *(The Imperialist)*. Novels. 1902-04. *1109*
—. Empire Day celebrations. Great Britain. Nationalism. Ontario. Public Schools. 1890-1930's. *2864*
—. Federal government. Mississippi River. St. Lawrence River. USA. 1760's-1860's. *631*
Imperialism (review article). Leftism. Moore, Steve. Nationalism. Wells, Debi. 1960's-70's. *1269*
Imperialist sentiment. Anglo-French divisions. Canadian Expeditionary Force. Hughes, Samuel. World War I. 1853-1921. *245*
Inco, Ltd. Labor Disputes. Ontario (Sudbury). 1977. *2816*
Income *See also* Capital.
—. Aged. British Columbia (Vancouver, Victoria). Population. Taxation. 1951-74. *3196*
—. Agriculture. Federal Government. 1973-76. *1621*
—. Anglophones. French-speakers. 1961-74. *1564*
—. Anti-Inflation Act. Canadian Labour Congress. Economic Conditions. 1970's. *1572*
—. Canadian Labour Congress. Inflation. 1975. *1616*
—. Economic theory. Inflation. Investments. Keynes, John Maynard. 1974. *1548*
—. Education. Personal growth. Scandinavia. USA. 1975. *1450*
—. Employment. Fiscal Policy. Labor Unions and Organizations. Monetary policy. 1975. *1624*
—. Federal government. Fiscal policy. Income Tax. Inflation. Quebec. Regional Government. 1970-74. *1573*
—. Foreign investments. Income Tax. Interest groups. Periodicals. USA. ca 1930-74. *2016*
—. Wheat. 1901-11. 1966-75. *1096*
Income Tax. Federal government. Fiscal policy. Income. Inflation. Quebec. Regional Government. 1970-74. *1573*
—. Foreign investments. Income. Interest groups. Periodicals. USA. ca 1930-74. *2016*
Independence. Foreign policy. 19c-1970's. *254*
—. Foreign relations. Quebec. USA. 1950's-73. *2005*
—. French Canadians. Monetary Systems. Parti Québécois. Quebec. 1974. *2424*
Independence Movements *See also* Nationalism; Self-Determination; Separatist Movements.
—. Alliance Laurentienne. Barbeau, Raymond. Guillemette, Pierre. Quebec. 1960's-75. *2674*

—. Economic expansion. Federalism. Quebec. 1867-1973. *2085*
—. Elections. Liberals. Parti Québécois. Quebec. 1973-76. *2707*
—. French Canadians. Lévesque, René (views). Nationalism. Quebec. 1763-1976. *2701*
—. Political Attitudes. Quebec. 1960's-70's. *2100*
Index. Books. Catholic Church. Clergy. 1862. *844*
Indexing procedures. Newfoundland, Memorial University of (Maritime History Group). Shipping documents. 1863-1913. *2176*
India *See also* Pakistan.
—. Birth Control. Demography. USA. 1970's. *1444*
—. Government secrecy. Nuclear Nonproliferation Treaty (1968). Nuclear Science and Technology. 1968-70's. *1844*
—. Great Britain. Periodicals. Political science. 1970's. *1805*
Indian *See also* Indians.
Indian Affairs Department. British North America. Colonial Government. Frontier. 1755-1830. *623*
—. British North America. Great Britain. Uniforms. 1755-1823. *632*
—. Colonization. Great Britain. Indians. USA. 1755-1830. 1800H. *624*
—. Iroquois Indians. Law. Quebec. St. Regis Reservation. 1876-1918. *459*
Indian Days. Blackfoot Indians. Dance. Oklahoma. 19c-20c. *437*
Indian Wars. Idaho Territory. MacDonald, Duncan. Nez Percé Indians. 1877. *418*
—. Montana. Nez Percé Indians. Public sympathy. Settlers. 1877. *431*
—. Ontario (Ehwae). Seneca Indians. 1640-42. *517*
Indians *See also* terms beginning with the word Indian; names of Indian tribes, e.g. Delaware Indians; Acculturation; Asians; East Indians.
—. Aborigines Protection Society. Australia. Great Britain. USA. ca 1830-50. *464*
—. Acculturation. Cultural preservation. Drama. 1606-1974. *414*
—. Acculturation. Federal Policy. Sifton, Clifford. 1896-1905. *395*
—. Africans. Asians. North America. Racism. Whites. 1600-1900. *10*
—. Alaska. Eskimos. Land claim settlements. 1958-77. *288*
—. Alaska. Haida Indians. Tlingit Indians. Tsimshian Indians. 1649-1973. *430*
—. Alberta. Blackfoot Indians. Wolf Collar (shaman). 1870-1928. *356*
—. Alberta. Bobtail Cree Reserve. Cree Indians. Land. 1900-09. *3125*
—. Alberta. Bureaucratization. Criminal sentencing. Urbanization. 1973. *1663*
—. Alberta. Ogilvie, William (field notes). Surveying. 1878-79. *433*
—. Alberta (De Winton). Prehistory. 1972. *295*
—. Alberta, northern. Jackson, Mary Percy. Métis. Physicians. 1929-70's. *3119*
—. Alberta (Writing-On-Stone, Milk River). Law Enforcement. Military Camps and Forts. North West Mounted Police. 1887-1918. *957*
—. Algonkin Indians. Maine. Maritime Provinces. Missions and Missionaries. Social change. 1610-1750. *516*
—. Alliances. Chickasaw Indians. Choctaw Indians. France. South Central and Gulf States. Tonti, Henri de. 1702. *581*
—. Americas (North and South). International law. Organization of American States. UN. 19c-1974. *367*
—. Anthropology. Archives. Subarctic. 1975. *347*
—. Archaeological research. British Columbia (Alberni Valley). Ethnography. Prehistory. 1973. *301*
—. Archaeology. Boulder configurations. Saskatchewan. Solstices. Sun Dance structures. Prehistory. 1975. *406*
—. Archaeology. British Columbia. Duff, Wilson. 1950-76. *292*
—. Arctic. Daily life. Hare Indians. Northwest Territories. Oil exploration. 1859-1974. *358*
—. Armies. Royal Canadian Mounted Police. Settlement. USA. 1870-1900. *1008*
—. Art (romantic, review article). Bartlett, William Henry. Miller, Alfred J. ca 1840-70. *659*
—. Artists. Chippewa Indians. Cree Indians. Legend painting. Manitoba. Ontario. 1960's-70's. *470*

—. Assimilation. British Colonial Office. 1760-1830. *469*
—. Astronomy. British Columbia. Calendars. Northwest Coast Indians. Prehistory. 1975. *303*
—. Atsina Indians. "Fall" Indians. "Rapid" Indians. Saskatchewan, southcentral. 18c. *405*
—. Attitudes. Body painting. Europeans. 1497-1684. *388*
—. *Attorney General of Canada* v. *Lavell* (Canada, 1973). Lavell, Jeannette (Wikwemikong Indian). Sex Discrimination. Supreme Court. Women. 1973-74. *473*
—. Baskets. Pacific Northwest. Photographs. 1880's-1900's. 1978. *415*
—. Bible. Missions and Missionaries. Myths and Symbols. Pacific Northwest. 1830-50. *438*
—. Bibliographies. Eskimos. Métis. 1975. *283*
—. Bibliographies. Music. 20c. *354*
—. Bibliographies. Music. Pacific Northwest. 1888-1976. *353*
—. Bibliographies. Northwest Coast Indians. 1975. *352*
—. Bighorn River. Discovery and Exploration. Montana. Wyoming. Prehistory-1965. *444*
—. Birchbark. Containers. Northeastern or North Atlantic States. Prehistory-1978. *471*
—. Blackfoot Indians. Identity. Menominee Indians. Militancy. 1950's-60's. *457*
—. Bone tools. Man, presence of. Yukon Territory. ca 25,000 BC. *296*
—. Brant, Joseph (Thayendanegea, Mohawk chief). Iroquois Indians. Ontario (Grand River). 1742-1807. *440*
—. British Columbia. Carr, Emily. Forests and Forestry. Paintings. 1904-45. *3260*
—. British Columbia. Great Britain. Gunboats. Liquor. Slave trade, Indian. 1860's. *390*
—. British Columbia. Land policies. Provincial government. 1875-80. *383*
—. British Columbia (Louise Island, Koona village). Haida Indians. 1830-50. *454*
—. British Columbia (Queen Charlotte Islands). Fishing gear. Haida Indians. Wood. Prehistory. *287*
—. British Columbia, southwestern. Lillooet Indians. Oral tradition. Prehistory-1976. *289*
—. British Columbia, southwestern. Lillooet Indians. Oral tradition. Prehistory-1976. *291*
—. Buttons, Phoenix. Haiti. Pacific Northwest. Trade. Uniforms, Military. 1812-30. 20c. *460*
—. Caldwell, Billy. Frontier and Pioneer Life. Great Britain. Great Lakes. Trade. 1797-1841. *365*
—. Canoes, development of. Prehistory. 1977. *294*
—. Carr, Emily. Painting. 1888-1972. *362*
—. Catholic Church. Louisiana. Missions and Missionaries. 18c-20c. *587*
—. Centennial Celebrations. Great Britain. Treaty Seven. 1877-1977. *370*
—. Children. Identification, racial and cultural. 1972-73. *392*
—. Chippewa Indians. Cree Indians. Fishing. Lakes. Ontario, northern. 19c-1978. *341*
—. Chippewa Indians. Folklore. Nanabozho (mythical character). Ottawa Indians. 19c-20c. *397*
—. Chippewa Indians. Mississauga Indians. 1650-1975. *452*
—. Chippewa Indians. Ontario (Kenora, Anicinabe Park). 1950's-74. *389*
—. Church of England. McDonald, Robert. Missions and Missionaries. Northwest Territories. Yukon Territory. 1850's-1913. *3292*
—. Church of England. Missions and Missionaries. Ontario (Algoma, Huron). Wilson, Edward F. 1868-93. *432*
—. Climate. Environment. North America. Settlement. Prehistory. 1956-78. *309*
—. Colebrook, William. New Brunswick. Perley, Moses H. 1840's. *2408*
—. Colonialism. Cultural change. Fur trade. North America. Prehistory-1900. *286*
—. Colonization. Great Britain. Indian Affairs Department. USA. 1755-1830. 1800H. *624*
—. Courtship. Field, Eliza. Great Britain (London). Jones, Peter. Methodism. New York. 1820's-33. *451*
—. Cree Indians. Fort Pitt. Frenchman's Butte, Battle of. Manitoba. McLean, W. J. (diary). 1885. *1003*

—. Cree Indians. Names (assignation). Values. 20c. *355*

—. Cree Treaty of 1876. Government. Land rights. 1876-1970's. *364*

—. Cultural change. Eskimos. 1970's. *408*

—. Culture. Manitoba, southwestern. Natural Resources. Pottery. Prehistory-18c. 1970's. *307*

—. Curtis, Edward S. Morgan, J. P. Photographs. 1868-1952. *472*

—. Curtis, Edward S. Photographs. 1892-1932. *403*

—. Daily life. Dufaut, J. (diary). Fur trade. Ontario (Prince Rupert's Land). XY Company. 1803-04. *2956*

—. Daily life. Great Lakes. Kane, Paul. Paintings. 1845-46. *384*

—. Demography. Epidemics. Fur trade. Wildlife diseases. 15c-18c. *425*

—. Demography. North America. 15c-1600. *298*

—. Densmore, Frances. Ethnology. Musicology. 1918-57. *400*

—. Diseases. Micmac Indians. Population. 16c-17c. *302*

—. Diseases, diffusion of. Fur Trade. Hudson's Bay Company. 1830-50. *2949*

—. Drugs. Food. Fur Trade. 17c-19c. *187*

—. Education. 19c-20c. *385*

—. Education. Eskimos. Métis. Northwest Territories (Mackenzie District). Whites. 1969-70. *3358*

—. Education. Federal government. Métis. 1940-70. *361*

—. Environment. Labrador. Quebec. Religion. Social organization. 17c-20c. *428*

—. Epidemics. Fur Trade. Hunt, George T. (*The Wars of the Iroquois*). Iroquois Indians. 1609-53. *523*

—. Episcopal Church, Protestant. Hudson's Bay Company. Missions and Missionaries. Pacific Northwest. 1825-75. *402*

—. Eskimos. Ethnology. Pacific Basin. Polynesians. Prehistory-1976. *285*

—. Ethnographers. Labrador. 1908-68. *436*

—. Europe. Flint. Gunflints. Quebec (Chicoutimi). Travel. 17c. 20c. *349*

—. Evangelism. Hospitals. Quebec. 1633-1703. *539*

—. Excavations. Manitoba, southeastern. ca 8100-7600 BC. *305*

—. Excavations. Manitoba, southwestern (Site DgMg-15). Refuse pit. ca 1480-1740. *306*

—. Family. Kin terminologies. Language. Plains Indians. Social Organization. Prehistory-19c. *426*

—. Firearms. Pacific Northwest. 1774-1825. *382*

—. Fires, prairie. Fur trade. Hudson's Bay Company. Saskatchewan. 1790-1840. *461*

—. Fishing. Ontario (Sault Ste. Marie). Trade. 17c 1920. *419*

—. French culture. 17c. *519*

—. Fur trade. Hudson's Bay Company. Trade. 17c-18c. *576*

—. Galt, Elliott. Letters. Prairie Provinces. Travel. 1879-80. *959*

—. Ghost Dance. Revitalization movements. Social Organization. 1889. *359*

—. Government commissions. Land claims. Métis. Prairie Provinces. 1885-1900. *396*

—. Hunting. 17c. *571*

—. Indian-White Relations. Ontario (Sault Ste. Marie). Schools. Shingwauk Industrial Home. Wawanosh Home for Indian Girls. Wilson, E. F. 1871-93. *475*

—. Jay's Treaty (1794). USA. 1794-1974. *377*

—. Manitoba (Red River Valley). Mennonites. Métis. Saskatchewan River Valley. Settlement. 1869-95. *963*

—. Manitoba, southwestern. Tools. Weapons. ca 10,000 BC-1600 AD. *308*

—. McDougall, John. Missions and Missionaries. Prairie provinces. Wesleyan Methodist. 1860-1917. *386*

—. Métis. Smallpox. Traders. Vaccination program. 1837-38. *439*

—. Migration. USA. 1972. *407*

—. Montana (Dune Buggy Site, 24RV1). Pottery. Prehistory. 1947-70's. *299*

—. Names (mammal, bird). 1973. *399*

—. Nationalism. Nova Scotia (Cape Breton). Political socialization. Regionalism. Whites. 1860's-1970's. *2361*

—. Native Peoples' Caravan. Ontario (Ottawa). Political Protest. 1975. *463*

—. New World. Pottery. 4500-50 BC. *311*

—. North America. Sports. 16c-17c. *378*

—. Nova Scotia. Public Policy. 1783-1871. *467*

—. Pacific Northwest. -1973. *342*

—. Prairie Provinces. Public Opinion. Social Change. 1976. *2920*

—. Quebec (Caughnawaga, Sault St. Louis). Women. 1852. *374*

—. Royal Canadian Mounted Police. 1873-85. *1011*

—. Sacred pipe myth. Sioux Indians. Tipi covers. 1770-1975. *366*

—. Saskatchewan. Sioux Indians. 1880-1970. *404*

—. Sioux Indians. Sitting Bull (chief). USA. 1876-81. *1049*

—. Thlingchadinne Indians. Northwest Territories (Rae). Social Change. 1939. 1974. *380*

Indians (reservations). British Columbia. Socioeconomic characteristics. Urban Indians. 1971. *458*

—. Business. Federal Government. Missions and Missionaries. Ontario (Manitoulin Island). 1830-60. *350*

Indians (review article). Barbeau, Marius. Harris, Kenneth B. 1928. 1974. *421*

—. France. Huron Indians. Jaenen, Cornelius J. Trigger, Bruce G. Values. 1600-60. 1976. *520*

Indian-White Relations. Acculturation. 1838-1976. *381*

—. Acculturation. Cree Indians. Quebec (James Bay). 1970's. *345*

—. Beardy, Q. P. Jackson. Ojibwa Indians. Painting. 1944-75. *401*

—. Beothuk Indians. Newfoundland. 1500-1848. *466*

—. Beothuk Indians (review article). Howley, J. P. Newfoundland. Rowe, F. W. Prehistory-1830. 1977. *290*

—. Blackfoot Indians. Fur trade. 1810-40. *376*

—. Catholic Church. Hospitals. Hôtel-Dieu. Quebec. 1635-98. *552*

—. Chipewyan Indians. Cree Indians. Expansionism. Fur Trade. Northwest Territories (Mackenzie District, eastern). Prairie Provinces. 1680's-18c. *476*

—. Christianization. Micmac Indians. New Brunswick. Nova Scotia. 1803-60. *465*

—. Ethnic groups. Sex Discrimination. 1972-73. *1420*

—. Ethnic stigma. Impression management. Migrants. 1967-68. *371*

—. Federal Policy. USA. 17c-20c. *394*

—. Fort Frontenac. Iroquois Indians. Missions and Missionaries. Quinte Mission. Sulpicians. 1665-80. *522*

—. France. Great Britain. Micmac Indians. Prince Edward Island. 1763-1873. *468*

—. Frederick House Massacre. Fur Trade. Hudson's Bay Company. Ontario. 1812-13. *2828*

—. Fur trade. Kutchin Indians, Eastern. Northwest Territories (Mackenzie District). Yukon Territory. 1800-60. *3285*

—. Fur trade. Mississauga Indians. Ramsay, David. 1760-1810. *686*

—. Indians. Ontario (Sault Ste. Marie). Schools. Shingwauk Industrial Home. Wawanosh Home for Indian Girls. Wilson, E. F. 1871-93. *475*

—. Northwest Territories. Social Organization. 1940-76. *416*

—. Ontario. Schools. 1780-1841. *474*

—. Ontario (Manitoulin Island). Violence. 1860-65. *410*

Indian-White Relations (review article). Acculturation. USA. 1800-1977. 1976-77. *445*

Individualism. Values 1850-1914. *943*

Industrial councils. Massey-Harris plant. Ontario (Toronto). Public relations. 1919-29. *1188*

Industrial decline. Geography. Quebec (Shawinigan). 1932-72. *2605*

Industrial democracy. Labor. 20c. *70*

Industrial Insurance. Great Britain (Liverpool). Montreal Steamship Company. Mutual Benefit Societies. 19c. *2662*

Industrial plant size. Europe. North America. 1963-67. *1609*

Industrial policy. Economic Council of Canada. 1974. *1256*

—. Economic relations. USA. 1970's. *1978*

Industrial Relations *See also* Arbitration, Industrial; Collective Bargaining; Labor Unions and Organizations; Strikes.

—. Arbitration. Canadian Industrial Disputes Investigation Act (1907). USA. 1907. *1101*

—. Attitudes. Management. 1970's. *1614*

—. Beruson, David J. (review article). General Strike. Manitoba (Winnipeg). Social organization. 1919. 1975. *1165*

—. British Columbia. Conciliation Act (1900; antecedents). Labour, Department of. 1880's-1900. *3175*

—. Charpentier, Alfred. Confederation of Catholic Workers of Canada. Provincial government. Quebec. 1935-46. *2609*

—. Collective bargaining. 1975. *1520*

—. Collective bargaining. Labor Unions and Organizations (international). Multinational corporations. 1974. *1763*

—. Construction Labour Relations Association of British Columbia. 1960's-70's. *1604*

—. Decentralization. Europe. Labor. USA. 1960's-70's. *1626*

—. Labor Unions and Organizations. Management. USA. 1975. *1615*

Industrial Revolution. Economic Development. New Brunswick (Saint John). Railroads. Transportation. 1867-1911. *2395*

Industrial structure. Economic conditions. Quebec (Montreal). 17c-1971. *2610*

Industrial Workers of the World. American Federation of Labor. One Big Union. Washington. 1919. *1167*

—. Labor Unions and Organizations. Radicals and Radicalism. 1905-14. *2940*

Industrialization *See also* Economic Growth; Foreign Aid; Modernization.

—. Agriculture. Europe. Market economy. North America. Peasant movements (colloquium). ca 1875-1975. *13*

—. Agriculture. Federalism. Forests and Forestry. Natural resources. Quebec. 20c. *2646*

—. Architecture, Victorian. New Brunswick (Saint John). Urban Renewal. 17c-1966. *2399*

—. Attitudes. Labor Unions and Organizations. Radicals and Radicalism. Working class. 1897-1919. *2899*

—. Attitudes. Work ethic. Youth. 1950's-73. *1455*

—. Catholic Church. Eudists. Quebec (Chicoutimi Basin). Working class. 1903-30. *2475*

—. Colonization. Quebec (Herbertville). 1844-1900. *2657*

—. Dissertations. Economic History Association (37th annual meeting). Labor. 19c-20c. 1977. *263*

—. Economic Conditions. Ethnic Groups. Labor law. Quebec. 1865-88. *2627*

—. Economic History. Iron mining. Newfoundland (Conception Bay; Bell Island). Social History. 1870's-1966. *2199*

—. Economics. Natural resources. 1950's-70's. *1765*

—. Knights of Labor. Knights of St. Crispin. Labor Unions and Organizations. Ontario (Toronto). 1836-90. *1050*

—. Mineral Resources. Mining. USA. 1700-1977. *208*

—. Multinational Corporations. USA. 1879. 1961-74. *140*

—. National Self-image. Population. Utopias. 20c. *26*

—. Northwest Territories (Mackenzie River region). 1970-75. *3349*

—. Ontario (Hamilton). Public schools. Socialization. 19c. *2802*

—. Quebec. Urbanization. 1941-61. *2613*

—. Quebec (Montreal). Shoe industry. 1840-70. *2606*

Industrialized Countries *See also* Developing Nations; Western Nations.

—. Economic blocs. Foreign policy. 1944-74. *1896*

—. Unemployment. USA. 1974-76. *1585*

Industry *See also* individual industries, e.g. Iron Industry, etc.; Industrialization; Management; Manufactures.

—. Agriculture. Quebec (Saguenay region). Social Conditions. 1840-1972. *2472*

—. Alberta (Lethbridge). Culture. Pioneers. Transportation. 1880's. *3104*

—. Banks. Business. Naylor, R. T. (review article). 1867-1914. *928*

—. Beaudry Report. Ham Report. Ontario. Quebec. Working Conditions. 1972-74. *1536*

—. Buffalo bones. Saskatchewan. 1884-93. *3026*

—. Commission on Industrial Accidents. Provincial Government. Quebec. Workmen's Compensation. 1890-1978. *2623*

—. Competition. Federal Regulation. 1970's. *1597*

—. Economic Conditions. Western Nations. 1969-71. *1561*

—. Economic Growth. Foreign ownership. 1973. *1936*
—. Economic Growth. Pollution. Quebec (Saint-Georges Est, Chaudière River). Tourism. 1973. *2652*
—. Economic Policy. Regionalism. 1965-75. *2129*
—. Economic Policy. USA. 1971-75. *2007*
—. Employment. Worker tenure. 1974. *1555*
—. French Canadians. Quebec. 20c. *2665*
—. French Canadians. Quebec. 1961-75. *2669*
—. Market structure. Research. 1973. *1545*
—. Pollution. Working Conditions. 1973. *1296*
—. USA. 1965. *2030*
Inequality. Children. Ontario (Toronto area). Public schools. Social Classes. Values. 1977. *1345*
Inflation. Canadian Labour Congress. Income. 1975. *1616*
—. Economic conditions. 1972-74. *1546*
—. Economic policy. Employment. Price stability. 1954-72. *1965*
—. Economic theory. Income. Investments. Keynes, John Maynard. 1974. *1548*
—. Federal government. Fiscal policy. Income. Income Tax. Quebec. Regional Government. 1970-74. *1573*
—. Federal Regulation. 1970-76. *1559*
—. Fiscal policy. Politics. 1945-75. *1596*
—. Labor. Management. 1970's. *1521*
—. Quebec. Strikes. 1974. *2624*
—. British Columbia (Vancouver). Epidemics. Public health services. 1918-19. *3174*
Influenza. Alberta (Calgary). Epidemics. Mahood, Cecil S. 1918-19. *3138*
Information Storage and Retrieval Systems. Cities. Ontario. Public Records. 1974. *2859*
—. CODOC (system). Documents. Government. Libraries. USA. 1960's-70's. *177*
Information theory. Entropy concept. Political Parties. Voting and Voting Behavior. 1962-69. *1683*
Inglis, Charles. Apple industry. Calkin(s) family. Halliburton, Robert Grant. Nova Scotia. Starr family. 19c. *2279*
Ingraham, Joseph (travel account). British Columbia (Vancouver Island, Nootka Sound). *Columbia* (vessel). Discovery and Exploration. Fur trade. 1774-89. *655*
Inheritance *See also* Land Tenure; Wills.
—. Farmers. Land. Ontario. 19c. *807*
Inkshuks (monuments). Arctic. Eskimos. Prehistory-1978. *319*
Inkster, Anne Ellen (reminiscences). Children. Manitoba (Churchill). 1885-93. *2986*
Inns, waterfront. Great Pontack Inn. Nova Scotia (Halifax). 1754-1837. *2303*
Inoculation. *See* Vaccination.
Insanity. *See* Mental Illness.
Inscriptions. Discovery and Exploration. Ireland. Newfoundland. Ogham alphabet. St. Lunaire boulder. ca 5c-1977. *487*
Institute of History. Laval University. Quebec (Quebec). 1947. *2571*
Institute of Strategic Studies. Atlantic region. Buchan, Alastair. Foreign Relations. Military Strategy. 1958-75. *1913*
Institutional completeness. Manitoba (Winnipeg). Minorities. Segregation, residential. -1974. *2978*
Institutional orientations. Liberal democracy. Senators. 1970's. *1644*
Institutions. Acadians. Nationalism. Nova Scotia. Social Organization. 1700's-1970. *2281*
—. Bureaucracies. Capitalism. Government. North America. Social change. 1750's-1850's. *656*
—. Business. Elites. Law. Social Organization. 19c-1974. *211*
—. Conflict management. Quebec. Regional autonomy. Separatist movements. South. 19c-1970. *2101*
—. Legitimacy. Quebec. Radio-Québec. Television. 1969-74. *2477*
Insurance *See also* types of insurance, e.g. Automobile Insurance, Industrial Insurance, Unemployment Insurance, etc.
—. Building plans. Land use atlases. Research. Urban historians. 1696-1973. *86*
Intellectual history. Historians. 20c. *101*
—. National Self-image. Nationalism. 1974. *145*
—. Ontario (Upper Canada). Political theory. Reform. 1800-50. *832*
Intellectual traditions. Attitudes. National self-image. Science. Technology. 1970's. *1327*

Intellectuals. Chesterton, G. K. (lectures). Poets. 1921. 1930. *1184*
—. Class struggle. Equality. French-speaking community. Nationalism. Quebec. 1960's-70's. *2677*
—. Communist Party. 1971-73. *1658*
—. Libraries. New France. Royal intendants. 1663-1760. *555*
—. Smith, Goldwin. 1875-1933. *911*
Intelligence Service *See also* Espionage.
—. Adams, Ian (interview). Royal Canadian Mounted Police. 1960's-70's. *1731*
Intendants. Intellectuals. Libraries. New France. 1663-1760. *555*
Interdependence. Bibliographies. Foreign relations. USA. 1900-74. *2084*
—. Defense policy. USA. 1940's-70's. *2062*
—. Economic Conditions. Nationalism. USA. ca 1910-73. *1990*
—. Foreign Relations. Politics. USA. 1960's-70's. *2002*
—. Foreign relations. USA. 1900-74. *1985*
Interdisciplinary studies. Sociocultural history. 17c-20c. *166*
Interest Groups *See also* Political Factions; Pressure Groups.
—. Desjardins cooperative movement. Government. Quebec. 18c-1973. *2415*
—. Foreign investments. Income. Income Tax. Periodicals. USA. ca 1930-74. *2016*
—. Political Systems. Quebec. 1970's. *2429*
—. Public policy. USA. 20c. *1704*
Intergovernmental Relations. Agent general, office of. Great Britain (London). 18c-20c. *212*
—. Bergson, Henri. Creativity. Federal government. Quebec. 1970's. *2109*
—. British North America Act (1867). Federalism. 1930's-74. *2091*
—. Housing (low-cost). Manitoba. Remote Housing Program. 1968-70. *2988*
—. King, William Lyon Mackenzie. Newspapers. Public opinion. Taxation. 1945-46. *2119*
—. Law Enforcement. Legislation. Police jurisdiction. 1970's. *1711*
Intermarriage. Jewish community. 1957-69. *2128*
Internal Migration. *See* Migration, Internal.
Internal security. Civil rights. Royal Canadian Mounted Police. 1970's. *1708*
International Association of Machinists and Aerospace Workers. Pensions. Social Security. 1968-73. *1618*
International Boundary and Water Commission. Boundaries. Environmental control. Mexico. USA. 1973. *2053*
International claims. China. Diplomatic relations. 1946-75. *1759*
International Commission for Supervision and Control. Foreign Policy. Gauvin, Michel (speech). Sharp, Mitchell. Vietnam War. 1973. *1950*
—. Peacekeeping Forces. Vietnam War. 1954-73. *1774*
—. Peacekeeping Forces. Vietnam War. 1973. *1795*
—. Peacekeeping Forces. Vietnam War. 1973. *1938*
International cooperation. Africa, French-speaking. Belgium. France. Quebec. 1964-74. *2718*
—. Drug abuse programs. North America. 1960's-74. *1417*
—. Fishing Rights. 1977-78. *1871*
—. Marine pollution. 1967-78. *1869*
International Development Agency. Colombo Plan. Foreign aid policy. 1950-69. *1736*
International Development Research Centre. Developing nations. 1970-74. *1904*
International exchange. Dollar standard. USA. 1945-. *1629*
International Financial Society. Foreign Investments. Great Britain. Hudson's Bay Company. Railroads. 1863. *840*
International interdependence. Foreign Policy. USA. 1970. *2039*
International Ladies' Garment Workers' Union. Labor Unions and Organizations. Women. 1975. *1937*
—. Quebec (Montreal). 1937-77. *1512*
International Law *See also* Boundaries; International Relations (discipline); Maritime Law; Refugees; Slave Trade; Treaties; War.
—. Administrative structure. Organization of American States. Rio Treaty. San José resolution. 1945-75. *1892*
—. Americas (North and South). Indians. Organization of American States. UN. 19c-1974. *367*
Bilateral commissions. Mexico. USA. 19c-1974. *262*

—. Council of Europe. Foreign relations. Political systems. 1965-70's. *1801*
—. Developing nations. UN. Violence. 1945-75. *1739*
—. Labor Unions and Organizations (international). Latin America. Multinational corporations. North America. 1937-74. *1955*
—. Lawyers. 1974. *1788*
—. Oceans (national jurisdiction). Space. 1945-73. *1797*
International Law (review article). 1974. *1799*
International Longshoremen's and Warehousemen's Union. Accident prevention. Working Conditions. 1973. *1601*
—. Automation. Employment. Labor Disputes. 1973. *1600*
—. Containerization. Employment. Labor Disputes. 1973. *1593*
International meetings. Diplomacy. Great Britain. Pearson, Lester B. USA. 1935-72. *1910*
International Migratory Bird Treaty (1916). Birds, migratory. Federal government. USA. Wildlife conservation. 1883-1917. *920*
International Organizations *See also* specific organizations by name.
—. Bureaucracies. Foreign Relations. USA. 1909-74. *1996*
—. Commodities. Economic Policy. Natural Resources. USA. 1974-76. *1945*
—. Discrimination. Women. 1960's-70's. *1447*
—. Parliaments. 1969-74. *1849*
International Pacific Salmon Fisheries Commission. British Columbia (Vancouver Island). Fishing rights. Pacific Northwest. Salmon. Treaties. 1970's. *2018*
International Power and Paper Company. Banking. Newsprint industry. USA. 1914-33. *1186*
International Programme for Loyalist Studies. Local history. MacNutt, W. Stewart (obituary). New Brunswick, University of. 1935-76. *2174*
International regulation. Conservation of Natural Resources. North America. Pollution. Water quality. 1960's-74. *1982*
International relations. Armies. Defense. Self-determination. 1970's. *1778*
International Relations (discipline) *See also* Foreign Relations.
—. Colleges and universities. USA. 1945-73. *2073*
—. Foreign policy. 1974. *1776*
International Security. Conference on Security and Cooperation in Europe. Europe. 1950-73. *1794*
—. Peacekeeping Forces. UN. 1975. *1823*
International Ship Masters Association. Great Lakes. Shipping. 1886-1977. *1087*
International system. Elites. Foreign Policy. 1975-76. *1751*
International Trade *See also* Foreign Investments.
—. Africa. Foreign aid. 1970-75. *1864*
—. Alberta. Business. Federal Programs. 1977. *3084*
—. Arab States. Economic Aid. Oil Industry and Trade. 1960's-70's. *1770*
—. Atlantic Provinces. Economic interests. Provincial government. USA. 1960's-70's. *2013*
—. Automotive agreement. USA. 1960's-70's. *2057*
—. Bethune, Angus. China (Canton). North America. North West Company. 1812-17. *802*
—. Boundaries. Great Britain. Vermont. 1763-1815. *630*
—. British Empire. Reciprocity. Sovereignty. USA. 1909-11. *1107*
—. British North America. British West Indies. Economic Conditions. ca 1609-1800. *715*
—. Canals. Geographic space. National Development. Politics. Railroads. 1818-1930. *54*
—. China. Foreign Relations. USA. USSR. 1969-72. *1853*
—. China. North West Company. 1784-1821. *783*
—. Cities. France. 1730-60. *572*
—. Commerce. Quebec (Lower Canada). Social Classes. 1792-1812. *796*
—. Cuba. Foreign relations. 1975-76. *1867*
—. Cuba. Foreign Relations. USA. ca 1960's-70's. *1879*
—. Cultural relations. France. 1760-1870. *879*
—. Diplomacy. Economic Conditions. USA. 1945-76. *2008*
—. Economic Conditions. Foreign relations. USA. 1950's-70's. *1964*
—. Economic integration. Foreign Relations. USA. 1929-33. *1218*

—. Economic organizations. Free Trade Area (proposed). Pacific area. 1975. *1837*
—. Economic Policy. Fishing Industry. Newfoundland. 1934-60's. *2175*
—. Economic prosperity. Natural resources. 1950's-70's. *1833*
—. Energy resources. Power resources. USA. 1950's-73. *1992*
—. European Economic Community. Framework Agreement for Commercial and Economic Co-operation. 1976. *1745*
—. Foreign investments. Multinational corporations. 1973-76. *1895*
—. Foreign Policy. Rhodesia. South Africa. 1960's-76. *1905*
—. Great Britain. Imperial Shipping Committee. Trade Regulations. 1918-63. *20*
—. Great Britain. Lower, Arthur (review article). Lumber and Lumbering. 1763-1867. *781*
—. Great Britain. USA. 1943-47. *1746*
—. Iron Mining. 1939-70. *1506*
—. Latin America. Trudeau, Pierre Elliott. 1968-76. *1802*
—. Mexico. Tariff. USA. 1946-74. *1954*
—. Public opinion. USA. 1960's-70's. *2001*
—. Steel industry. 1973-80. *1767*
—. USA. 1970-75. *1859*
—. USA. 1970's. *1989*
International Waters *See also* Maritime Law; Territorial Waters.
—. Boundary Waters Treaty. Gibbons, George Christie. USA. 1905-11. *1114*
Internment camps. Aliens. Austrians. World War I. 1914-19. *1150*
Internment operations. Otter, William. World War I. 1914-20. *1161*
Interpersonal Relations. Ethnic groups. Students. -1973. *1435*
Inventions. Calcium carbide, manufacture of. Electrochemistry. Willson, Thomas Leopold "Carbide". 1860-1915. *939*
Inventories. Auteuil, Denis-Joseph Ruette d' (estate). Property. Quebec. 1661-80. *528*
Investments *See also* Mortgages; Securities; Stocks and Bonds.
—. Economic theory. Income. Inflation. Keynes, John Maynard. 1974. *1548*
—. Federal government. Fiscal Policy. Manufactures. 1965-74. *1569*
—. Monetary policy. 1950-73. *1605*
—. Nova Scotia (Yarmouth). Ports. Shipping. 1840-89. *2210*
Ireland *See also* Great Britain.
—. American Revolution. Friends, Society of. Great Britain. Pennsylvania (Philadelphia). Relief funds. 1778-97. *739*
—. Attitudes. Immigration. Ontario (Canada West). Potato famine. 1845-50. *797*
—. Brendan, Saint. Discovery and Exploration. North America. Voyages. 500-85, 1976-77. *488*
—. British Commonwealth. Foreign Relations. Neutrality. World War II. 1939-45. *1237*
—. Burns family. Immigration. Nova Scotia (Annapolis County; Wilmot Township). 1764-20c. *2305*
—. Convict transportation. Great Britain. Newfoundland. 1789. *2192*
—. Discovery and Exploration. Inscriptions. Newfoundland. Ogham alphabet. St. Lunaire boulder. ca 5c-1977. *487*
—. Immigration. Poor Law Commissioners. Servants. Women. 1865. *888*
Ireland (Waterford). Genealogy. Prime Ministers. Thompson, John S. D. 1796-1903. *1056*
Irish. Acadians. Catholic Church. Discrimination. New Brunswick. 1860-1900. *2402*
—. Gowan, Ogle. Immigration. Ontario (Upper Canada). Orangeism. Politics. 1830-33. *821*
Irish Americans. Bombings. Clan-na-Gael. Dillon, Luke. Ontario (Thorold). Welland Canal. 1900-14. *1083*
—. Chicopee Manufacturing Company. Immigration. Massachusetts (Chicopee). Mills. Nativism. 1830-75. *635*
—. Fenians. Foreign Relations. Trials. USA. 1865-70. *876*
Irish Canadians. Acadians. Catholic Church. New Brunswick. Politics. Quebec. Schools. Taxation. 1871-73. *1067*
—. Alberta (Calgary Diocese). Catholic Church. French Canadians. McNailly, John Thomas. 1871-1952. *3095*
—. Anglin, Timothy Warren. Catholic Church. New Brunswick. Saint John *Freeman* (newspaper). 1849-83. *2373*
—. Anglin, Timothy Warren. Fenians. McGee, D'Arcy. Political debates. 1863-68. *891*

—. Catholic Church. Episcopal nominations. French Canadians. 1900-75. *2930*
—. Catholic Church. McMahon, Patrick. Poor. Quebec (Quebec). St. Bridget's Home. 1847-1972. *2541*
—. Census. Construction. Migrant labor. Quebec (Sherbrooke area). Railroads. 1851-53. *2520*
—. McCabe, James (and descendants). Nova Scotia (Pictou). Pennsylvania (Philadelphia). ca 1743-1917. *2306*
—. Newfoundland. Politics. Religion. 19c. *2189*
—. Nova Scotia (Halifax). Tobin, Thomas (and descendants). ca 1759-1936. *2329*
Irish Canadians (review article). Anglin, Timothy Warren. Baker, W. M. Fenians. Neidhardt, W. S. 19c. 1970's. *1073*
Iron Industry *See also* Steel Industry.
—. Boomtowns. Nova Scotia (Bay of Fundy, Londonderry). Steel industry. 1844-98. *2352*
Iron mining. Economic History. Industrialization. Newfoundland (Conception Bay; Bell Island). Social History. 1870's-1966. *2199*
—. International Trade. 1939-70. *1506*
—. Natural resources. Newfoundland. Quebec (Fire Lake). SIDBEC (consortium). 1960's. *2622*
Ironwork. Catholic Church. German Alsatians. Gravemarkers. Ontario (Bruce County; Waterloo). 1850-1910. *2837*
Iroquois Indians. Algonkin Indians. Historical Sites and Parks. Missions and Missionaries. Quebec (Oka). Sulpicians. 1700's-1800's. *521*
—. Amherst, Jeffrey. French and Indian War. Military History. New France. Pontiac's Rebellion. 1760-65. *612*
—. Anderson, James. Arctic. Expedition, search. Franklin, John. Woodsmanship. 1855. *3305*
—. Brant, Joseph (Thayendanegea, Mohawk chief). Indians. Ontario (Grand River). 1742-1807. *440*
—. Brant, Joseph (Thayendanegea, Mohawk chief), interview. Norton, John (interview). 1801. *351*
—. Epidemics. Fur Trade. Hunt, George T. *(The Wars of the Iroquois)*. Indians. 1609-53. *523*
—. Fort Frontenac. Indian-White Relations. Missions and Missionaries. Quinte Mission. Sulpicians. 1665-80. *522*
—. Indian Affairs Department. Law. Quebec. St. Regis Reservation. 1876-1918. *459*
Irrigation *See also* Dams.
—. Alberta, southern. Boundary Waters Treaty. USA. 1885-1909. *962*
Ismael, T. Y. Developing nations. Foreign Relations (review article). Lyon, P. V. Ogelsby, J. C. M. USA. 1860's-1976. *239*
Italian Canadians. Acculturation. Boardinghouses. Immigrants. Ontario (Toronto). 20c. *2782*
—. Family. Ontario (Toronto). Social Mobility. 1935-60. *2870*
—. Immigration. Ontario (Toronto). Population. 1946-72. *2875*
Italians. Assimilation. Cultural autonomy. Mass media. Ontario (Toronto). 1970's. *2735*
—. Commerce. Immigration. USA. 1870-1977. *83*
—. Employment. Immigrants. Ontario (Toronto). 1885-1915. *2783*
—. Family. Generations. Immigrants. 20c. *1493*
Italy *See also* Tuscany, Venetian Republic, etc.
—. Colonies. France. Great Britain. Historiography. North America. 1663-1763. *598*

J

Jackman, Alonzo. Military Strategy. New York. Quebec. Travel. Vermont. 1838. *2443*
Jackson, Henry A. C. Mushrooms. Naturalists. Painting. 1870's-1950's. *228*
Jackson, John George. Congress. Nationalism. Republicanism. Virginia. War of 1812. 1813-17. *754*
Jackson, Mary Percy. Alberta, northern. Indians. Métis. Physicians. 1929-70's. *3119*
Jackson, Walter John. Entrepreneurs. Northwest Territories (Baffin Island). ca 1875-1922. *3362*
Jaenen, Cornelius J. France. Huron Indians. Indians (review article). Trigger, Bruce G. Values. 1600-60. 1976. *520*
Jamaica. Cary, James. Exiles. Great Britain. Loyalists. Nova Scotia. 1781-1804. *744*
James Bay. Cree Indians. Fisheries. 1972-75. *346*

—. Electricity and Electronics. Energy crisis. Quebec. 1960-70's. *1292*
Jameson, Robert. Exploration. Great Britain. North America. Northwest Passage. 1804-54. *689*
Janney, Ernest L. Aeronautics, Military. Burgess-Dunne Seaplane. Canadian Aviation Corps. 1914-15. *1155*
Japan. Anglo-Japanese Treaty of Alliance (1902). Asiatic Exclusion League. British Columbia (Vancouver). USA. 1907-22. *1108*
—. Cahan, Charles H. (address). League of Nations Covenant. Manchuria. 1932-33. *1211*
—. Canadian Railway Museum. *John Molson* (locomotive, replica). Locomotives. Scotland. 1849. 1969. *877*
—. Church of England. Domestic and Foreign Missionary Society. Missions and Missionaries. 1883-1902. *932*
—. Developing Nations. Europe. Foreign policy. USA. 1950-75. *1741*
—. Economic goals. Foreign Relations. 1974-75. *1814*
—. Foreign policy. Trudeau, Pierre Elliott. 1968-78. *1880*
—. Foreign Relations. Great Britain. Versailles Treaty (Article X). 1919-21. *1168*
—. Fur trade. Sea otters. Wildlife Conservation. 18c-20c. *257*
—. Historians. Norman, E. Herbert (review article). 1940-77. *176*
Japanese. Alberta (Mount Alberta). Explorers. Hirohito, Emperor. Mountain climbing party. 1925-48. *2924*
—. Attitudes. Citizenship. USA. World War II. 1941-58. *1261*
—. British Columbia. Chinese. Immigration. Suffrage. 1935-49. *3220*
—. British Columbia. Evacuation, forced. Federal government. Public opinion. World War II. 1937-42. *1247*
Japanese Canadians. Adachi, Ken (review article). Immigration. Racism. 1877-1976. *123*
—. Alberta, southern. British Columbia. World War II. 1941-45. *1233*
—. British Columbia. Chinese. Military Service. World War II. 1939-45. *1242*
—. British Columbia. Minorities. Public schools. 1900-72. *3191*
—. British Columbia (Vancouver). Social Change. 20c. *3262*
—. British Columbia, University of. Race relations. World War II. 1939-42. *3177*
—. Race Relations. Relocation, forced. World War II. 1890's-1940's. *1245*
Jarvis, Stinson. Ontario. Psychic phenomena. Watkins, Kathleen ("Kit of the Mail"). 1885-95. *2891*
Jarvis Street Church. Baptists. Fundamentalist-Modernist controversy. Ontario (Toronto). Religious factionalism. Social Classes. 1895-1934. *2762*
Jay's Treaty (1794). Indians. USA. 1794-1974. *377*
Jeffreys, Charles William. Art. History. Illustrators. Textbooks. 1920's-50. *1119*
Jesuits. Cadieux, Lorenzo (obituary). Ontario, northern. Scholarship. 1903-76. *2772*
—. Communism. Czechoslovakia. Refugees. Religious communities, dissolution of. 1950. *1416*
—. Historiography. New France. Parkman, Francis. 17c. 1840's-60's. *518*
—. Lacouture, Onésime. Quebec. 1931-50. *2493*
—. Land Tenure. Legislation. Mercier, Honoré. Protestant Churches. Quebec. 1886. *2645*
Jesuits' Estates Act. Political Protest. Protestants. 1880-90. *1058*
Jews *See also* Anti-Semitism; Judaism.
—. 1977. *1397*
—. Acculturation. Ethnic identity. USA. 1961-74. *1486*
—. Agriculture. Prairie Provinces. Settlement. 1884-1920's. *2950*
—. Assimilation. Ontario (Toronto). Presbyterian Church. 1912-18. *2776*
—. Business. California (Fort Bragg). Russia. Shafsky family. 1889-1976. *1077*
—. Cemetery. Saskatchewan. 1975. *3055*
—. Children. Immigration. Manitoba (Winnipeg). Public schools. 1900-20. *3007*
—. Education. Immigration. Russia. Segal, Beryl (reminiscences). USA. 1900-70's. *204*
—. Elections, provincial. Parti Québécois. Quebec. Separatist Movements. 1976. *2721*
—. Emigration. Morocco. Quebec (Montreal). 1960's-70's. *2517*

—. France. Great Britain. Poverty. Uruguay. 1975. *1389*

—. French Canadians. Quebec. Separatist movements. Social Conditions. 1976-77. *2723*

—. Galt, Alexander. Kaplun, Alter (family). Russia. Saskatchewan. Settlement. 1880's-90's. *945*

—. Galveston Plan. Immigration. Schiff, Jacob H. USA. 1907-14. *905*

—. Immigration. New York City. Vanger, Max. 1900-50. *1143*

—. Intermarriage. 1957-69. *2128*

—. Kalter, Bella Briansky (reminiscences). Ontario (Ansonville). Rural Settlements. 1929-40. *2800*

—. Manitoba. Physicians. 19c. *2994*

—. Manitoba (Bender Hamlet). Settlement. 1910-49. *3001*

—. Manitoba (Winnipeg). Pioneers. 1860's-1975. *2969*

—. USA. Vietnam War. 1969-73. *1252*

Jews, Russian. City Life. Immigration. Manitoba (Winnipeg). 1874-82. *2965*

Joan of Arc Institute. Catholic Church. D'Aquin, Marie Thomas. Ontario (Ottawa). Social Work. Women. 1903-19. *2746*

John Molson (locomotive; replica). Canadian Railway Museum. Japan. Locomotives. Scotland. 1849. 1969. *877*

Johnson, Pauline (Tekahionwake). Alberta. Mohawk Indians. Poetry. 1895-1913. *363*

Joint Committee of the Canadian Senate and House of Commons. Constitutions. Ethnic groups. Language, official. 1970's. *1947*

Joly, Henri-Gustave. Boucherville, Charles Eugène Boucher de. Federalism. Liberal Party. Political Campaigns. Provincial government. Quebec. 1878. *2452*

Jones, Peter. Courtship. Field, Eliza. Great Britain (London). Indians. Methodism. New York. 1820's-33. *451*

Journalism *See also* Editors and Editing; Films; Freedom of the Press; Newspapers; Periodicals; Press; Reporters and Reporting.

—. Academia. Archives. Oral history. 1960-75. *1311*

—. Catholic Church. Social thought. Somerville, Henry. 1915-53. *1115*

—. Gérin, Elzéar. Gérin-Lajoie, Antoine. 1843-87. *2567*

—. Gold rushes. Great Britain. Klondike Stampede. Shaw, Flora. *Times of London* (newspaper). Yukon Territory. 1898. *3341*

—. Howe, Joseph. Nova Scotia (Halifax). *Novascotian* (newspaper). 1824-38. *828*

—. Professionalism. 1973. *1491*

Journals. *See* Diaries; Periodicals.

Joy, Richard. Assimilation. Choquette, Robert. French Canadians (review article). Maxwell, Thomas R. 18c-20c. 1970's. *218*

Judaism *See also* Anti-Semitism; Jews.

—. Hasidism. Quebec (Montreal). 1942-71. *2510*

Judicial Administration. Constitutions. USA. 1970's. *1633*

Judicial Process. Supreme Court. 1875-1975. *125*

Judicial review. 20c. *1684*

Jukes, Joseph Beete. Geology. Great Britain. Newfoundland. Travel. 19c. *2181*

Junker monoplanes. Aeronautics (history). 1920-29. *1172*

Jurisdictional law. British Columbia. Foreign investments. Land ownership. Washington (Whatcom County). 1970's. *2047*

Justice. Criminal Law. 1648-1748. *536*

Juvenile Delinquency *See also* Children; Drug Abuse.

—. Legislation. Marxism. Social history. 1870's-1970's. *76*

K

Kalter, Bella Briansky (reminiscences). Jews. Ontario (Ansonville). Rural Settlements. 1929-40. *2800*

Kane, Paul. Daily life. Great Lakes. Indians. Paintings. 1845-46. *384*

Kansas *See also* Western States.

—. Alberta. Leedy, John Whitnah. Politics. Prairie radical. Radicals and Radicalism. 1880's-1935. *3087*

—. Coal Mines and Mining. Economic Development. Europeans. Immigrants. 1870-1940. *1062*

—. Farmers. French Canadians. Mennonites. Swedish Americans. 1875-1925. *150*

Kaplun, Alter (family). Galt, Alexander. Jews. Russia. Saskatchewan. Settlement. 1880's-90's. *945*

Katz, Michael B. (review article). Family. Ontario (Hamilton). Social Classes. 1850-80. *2725*

Kealey, James (and family). Folklore. Oral history. Quebec (Hull). 1974-75. *2492*

Keefer, Thomas Coltrin. Engineering. Ontario (Upper Canada). Railroads. 1821-1915. *909*

Kendrick, John. British Columbia (Vancouver Island). *Columbia Rediviva* (vessel). Fourth of July. Nootka Sound controversy. 1789. *647*

Kennebeck Purchase Company. Forests and Forestry. Great Britain. Mast policy, royal. New England. Wentworth, John. 1769-78. *718*

Kennecott (vessel). Alaska Steamship Company. British Columbia (Queen Charlotte Islands). Salvage. Shipwrecks. 1923. *3181*

Kennedy, Albert J. Atlantic Provinces. Economic conditions. Immigration. Massachusetts (Boston). 1910's. *2162*

Kennedy family. 18c-1973. *205*

Kennedy, Robert C. Confederate Army. New York City. Saboteurs. 1861-65. *843*

Kennedy, William. Arctic. Bellot, Joseph René. Franklin, John. *Prince Albert* (vessel). Voyages. 1851. *3307*

Kent, Duke of (Edward). Armies. Great Britain. Lyons, Charles (family). Nova Scotia (Halifax). 1812-63. *2273*

Kentucky *See also* South Central and Gulf States.

—. Cable, George Washington. Lectures. Twain, Mark. 1884-85. *1076*

Kerr, Tom. Alberta. Fur trade. Hudson's Bay Company. 1861-1946. *3160*

Ketchum, Henry George Clepper. Chignecto Ship Railway (proposed). Construction. Nova Scotia. 1888-91. *2353*

Keynes, John Maynard. Economic theory. Income. Inflation. Investments. 1974. *1548*

King George's War. Economic Conditions. Louisbourg, fortress of. New England. Nova Scotia. 1745-50. *607*

—. France. Louisbourg, Fortress of. Mutinies. Nova Scotia. 1744-45. *605*

King, William Lyon Mackenzie. Apportionment. Parliaments. Saskatchewan (Prince Albert). 1925-35. *3038*

—. Atomic Warfare. Diaries. Racism. 1921-48. *1139*

—. Barber, James David. Political leadership. Prime ministers. 1920's-40's. 1972-76. *1147*

—. Byng of Vimy, Julian Hedworth George (Viscount). Psychohistory. 1919-26. *1174*

—. Conscription, Military. Elections. Ligue pour la Défense du Canada. Quebec. World War II. 1942-44. *1226*

—. Federal Government. Hepburn, Mitchell F. Lieutenant governors. Ontario. Provincial government. 1937. *1208*

—. Foreign policy. Great Britain. USA. 1935-39. *1198*

—. Foreign Relations. USA. World War II. 1939-45. *1223*

—. Intergovernmental Relations. Newspapers. Public opinion. Taxation. 1945-46. *2119*

—. Liberal Party. Politics. Quebec. 1919-50. *1132*

King William's War. Fishing industry. New England. Privateers. Queen Anne's War. Shipping. 1689-1713. *596*

King's College, York (charter). Church and State. Church of England. Ontario (Toronto). Scotland. Strachan, John. 1815-43. *625*

Kingston, Archdiocese of. Bishops. Catholic Church. Church History. Ontario. 1800-1966. *2847*

Klondike Gold Rush Historic Park. Gold Rushes. National Parks and Reserves. Yukon Territory. 1897-98. 1974. *3324*

Klondike Stampede. Alaska. Gold Rushes. Women. Yukon Territory. 1897-99. *3322*

—. Alaska (Skagway). British Columbia (Lake Bennett). Gold miners. 1896-99. 1960-73. *3200*

—. Burry, Thomas. Gold rushes. 1897. *2124*

—. Fort Herchmer. Gold Rushes. Royal Canadian Mounted Police. Yukon Territory (Dawson). 1896-1905. 1972-76. *3328*

—. Gold rushes. Great Britain. Journalism. Shaw, Flora. *Times of London* (newspaper). Yukon Territory. 1898. *3341*

—. Gold Rushes. Photography. Restorations. Yukon Territory. 1897-98. 1970's. *3336*

—. Gold Rushes. Quinlan, Thomas A. (letters). Yukon Territory. 1898-1904. *3337*

—. Gold Rushes. Royal Canadian Mounted Police. Yukon Territory. 1896-99. *3335*

Kniffen, Fred B. Festschriften publications. Mayo, Bernard. Morris, Richard B. Talman, James J. 1863-1974. *109*

Knights of Labor. Catholic Church. Gibbons, James. Social thought. Taschereau, Elzéar-Alexandre. 1880's. *1068*

—. Catholic Church. Labor Unions and Organizations. Taschereau, Elzéar-Alexandre. 1884-94. *1069*

—. Industrialization. Knights of St. Crispin. Labor Unions and Organizations. Ontario (Toronto). 1856-90. *1050*

Knights of Malta. American Revolution. Colonies. France. Heraldry. 1600's-1976. *172*

Knights of St. Crispin. Industrialization. Knights of Labor. Labor Unions and Organizations. Ontario (Toronto). 1856-90. *1050*

Knollin, William Mortimer. Marshall, Samuel. Nova Scotia. Pioneers. Villiers, Charles E. 19c. *2309*

Koester, Mavis Addie (reminiscences). Alberta (Lundbreck). Coal Mines and Mining. Daily Life. 1905-08. *3124*

Kokotailo, Veronia. Alberta. Homesteading and Homesteaders. Rumanians. 1898- . *3165*

Korean War. Diplomacy. Pearson, Lester B. Self-determination. UN. 1950-72. *1768*

—. Diplomacy. Stairs, Denis (review article). USA. 1950-53. *1881*

Kruzenshtern, Ivan Fedorovich. Arctic. Romanov, Vladmir Pavlovich. Russia. Scientific Expeditions. USA. 1819-25. *3299*

'Ksan Historic Indian Village. Art. British Columbia (Hazelton). Gitksan Indians. 1973. *434*

Ku Klux Klan. Anti-Catholicism. Elections (provincial). Saskatchewan. Separate school legislation. 1929. *3024*

—. Anti-Catholicism. Protestants. Saskatchewan. 1927-30. *3033*

—. Antilabor sentiments. Elections, local. Immigration policy. 1921-30's. *2925*

Kurikka, Matti. British Columbia (Harmony Island). Finnish Americans. Utopias. 1901-05. *3213*

Kutchin Indians, Eastern. Fur trade. Indian-White Relations. Northwest Territories (Mackenzie District). Yukon Territory. 1800-60. *3285*

Kyforuk, Peter. Alberta (Edmonton). Farmer's Union of Alberta. Manitoba. Ukrainian Labour-Farmer Association. 1912-30's. *2961*

L

La Jonquière, Marquis de. Fur Trade. Ontario (Toronto). 1750-1887. *564*

Labor *See also* Arbitration, Industrial; Capitalism; Collective Bargaining; Communism; Employment; Industrial Insurance; Industrial Relations; Labor Law; Migrant Labor; Public Employees; Socialism; Strikes; Syndicalism; Unemployment; Unemployment Insurance; Wages; Working Class; Working Conditions.

—. Assimilation. Fitzpatrick, Alfred. Frontier College. Immigration. 1899-1922. *1086*

—. Atlantic Provinces. Boardinghouses. Government. Merchant Marine. Social reform. ca 1850's-90's. *916*

—. Attitudes. Behavior. 20c. *1599*

—. Attitudes. Economic conditions. English. French. New Brunswick. -1973. *2393*

—. Bicycle industry. Mexico. Production. USA. 1972-76. *1906*

—. Blue-collar workers. Company satisfaction and commitment. 1970. *1503*

—. British Columbia (Fraser River). Canning industry. Mergers. Salmon. 1885-1902. *3240*

—. British Columbia (Vancouver). Fishing industry. Housing. Politics. 1970's. *3172*

—. Canadian Labour Congress. Communist Party. 1974. *1575*

—. Christian responsibility. Fiction. Social gospel. 1890's. *1112*

—. Collective bargaining. Crown Employees Collective Bargaining Act. Law. Ontario. 1970-74. *2745*

—. Communist Party. Evans, Arthur. 1930's. *2945*

—. Construction industry. Office de la construction du Québec. Quebec. 1960's-70's. *2647*

—. Co-operative Commonwealth Federation. National Democratic Party. Socialism. 1933-75. *1294*

—. Decentralization. Europe. Industrial relations. USA. 1960's-70's. *1626*

—. Dissertations. Economic History Association (37th annual meeting). Industrialization. 19c-20c. 1977. *263*

—. Economic Conditions. Management. 1974. *1942*

—. Education. Immigrants. Social Classes. 1973. *2149*

—. Foreign policy. Immigration. Population. Refugees. 1950's-70's. *1887*

—. Industrial democracy. 20c. *70*

—. Inflation. Management. 1970's. *1521*

—. Lowry, Ira S. Migration, Internal. Models. Quebec. -1973. *2593*

—. Marxism. Women (review article). 19c-1976. *71*

—. Occupational segregation. Women. 1941-71. *1502*

—. Occupations. Quebec (Montreal). 1960's-70's. *1594*

—. Overtime. Prices. 1973. *1566*

—. Quebec (St. Jérôme). Textile workers. 1974. *2590*

—. Regression results (cross-section, time series). Unemployment. -1973. *1612*

—. Unemployment insurance. 1953-73. *1576*

—. Women. World War II. 1942-46. *1240*

Labor Disputes *See also* Strikes.

—. -1973. *1543*

—. Alberta (Drumheller Valley). One Big Union. United Mine Workers of America. 1919. *3163*

—. Automation. Employment. International Longshoremen's and Warehousemen's Union. 1973. *1600*

—. Conflict and Conflict Resolution. Federal Government. Public Employees. 1967-76. *1718*

—. Containerization. Employment. International Longshoremen's and Warehousemen's Union. 1973. *1593*

—. Federal Government. Ontario, southern. Unemployment. 1901-20's. *89*

—. Inco, Ltd. Ontario (Sudbury). 1977. *2816*

—. Militia. Nova Scotia (Cape Breton Island). 1920's. *2298*

—. Ontario (Peterborough). Textile Workers' Union of America. Tilco Plastics Strike (1965-67). 1965-70. *1610*

—. Public employees. 1973. *1547*

—. Public opinion. 1940's-70's. *1590*

Labor education. Colleges and Universities. 1960's-1970's. *1627*

Labor Law *See also* Arbitration, Industrial; Collective Bargaining; Labor Unions and Organizations; Strikes.

—. Accreditation. Construction industry. 1973. *1603*

—. Economic Conditions. Ethnic Groups. Industrialization. Quebec. 1865-88. *2627*

—. Ford Motor Company of Canada. Ontario (Windsor). Rand formula. United Automobile Workers (Canadian Region). 1945-46. *1534*

—. Ford Motor Company of Canada. Ontario (Windsor). Rand formula. United Automobile Workers (Canadian Region). 1946. *1595*

—. Women. 1951-71. *1544*

Labor market. Colleges and Universities. Curricula. Economic returns. 1961-72. *1582*

—. Higher education. Social Conditions. 1960-74. *1446*

—. USA. ca 1880's-1974. *35*

Labor movement. Quebec. Vaillancourt, Philippe (account). 1936-76. *2589*

—. Technology. 1970's. *1514*

Labor Reform. Regionalism. Socialism. 1918-19. *2917*

—. Royal Commission of Inquiry into the Relations between Capital and Labour. 1886-89. *1047*

Labor relations. Business unionism. Saskatchewan. Social democracy. 1974-75. *3062*

—. Construction Industry Labour Relations Act. Quebec. 1973. *2631*

—. Finkelman report. Public Service Staff Relations Act. 1965-74. *1542*

Labor Unions and Organizations *See also* names of labor unions and organizations, e.g. American Federation of Labor, United Automobile Workers, etc.; Arbitration, Industrial; Collective Bargaining; Labor Law; Strikes; Syndicalism.

—. 1911-70. *227*

—. Aged. Pensions. United Automobile Workers (Canadian Region). 1973. *1580*

—. Alberta (Calgary). Co-op. 1956-73. *3154*

—. Alberta (Cardiff, Edmonton). Chaban, Teklia. Coal Mines and Mining. Ukrainian Canadians. 1914-20's. *3164*

—. American Federation of Labor. Canadian Labour Congress. Strong, Cyril. 1949-77. *1525*

—. Anti-Inflation Board. Collective bargaining. Wages. 1975. *1630*

—. Arbitration, Industrial. Armaments Industry. Imperial Munitions Board. 1900-20. *1080*

—. Artisans. Construction. Ontario (Toronto). Politics. 1896-1914. *1103*

—. Attitudes. Industrialization. Radicals and Radicalism. Working class. 1897-1919. *2899*

—. British Columbia. Politics. 1976. *3232*

—. British Columbia. Women. 1973. *3225*

—. British Columbia Federation of Labour. Women's rights. 1970-75. *3216*

—. British Columbia Government Employees Union. Public Employees. 1944-73. *3228*

—. Brown, George. Ontario. Publishers and Publishing. Toronto *Globe* (newspaper). Toronto Typographical Union. 1843-72. *2893*

—. Canadian Labour Congress. Rehabilitation. 1973. *1584*

—. Canadian Pacific Railway. Engineers, locomotive. Prairie Provinces. Strikes. 1883. *1066*

—. Canadian Union of Public Employees. MacMillan, John F. "Lofty". Public Employees. 1935-73. *1504*

—. Catholic Church. École Sociale Populaire. Quebec. Social Change. 1911-75. *2500*

—. Catholic Church. Knights of Labor. Taschereau, Elzéar-Alexandre. 1884-94. *1069*

—. Coal Mines and Mining. One Big Union. Saskatchewan. 1907-45. *3056*

—. Colleges and Universities. Professors. Quebec. 1972-74. *2417*

—. Co-operative Union of Canada. Politics. 1909-31. *1129*

—. Democratic Union Central. Quebec. 1968-74. *2621*

—. Drummond County Mechanics Institute. Farmers. Quebec (Drummond County). 1856-90. *2537*

—. Elections. Parti Québécois. Quebec. 1970-77. *2591*

—. Employment. Fiscal Policy. Income. Monetary policy. 1975. *1624*

—. Federal Government. Multinational Corporations. 1970's. *1268*

—. Finns. Immigrants. Radicals and Radicalism. USA. 1918-26. *1183*

—. Immigrants. Massachusetts (Fall River). Textile industry. 1890-1905. *2659*

—. Industrial relations. Management. USA. 1975. *1615*

—. Industrial Workers of the World. Radicals and Radicalism. 1905-14. *2940*

—. Industrialization. Knights of Labor. Knights of St. Crispin. Ontario (Toronto). 1856-90. *1050*

—. International Ladies' Garment Workers' Union. Women. 1975. *1937*

—. Models. 1911-70. *7*

—. National Trades and Labour Congress. Ontario (Kitchener). Quebec. Trades and Labour Congress of Canada. 1892-1902. *2655*

—. Office and Professional Employees International Union. White-collar employees. 1973. *1515*

—. One Big Union. Radicals and Radicalism. Socialism. 1917-19. *1149*

—. Ontario (Toronto). Production control. 1860-92. *2803*

—. USA. 1970-73. *1972*

—. USA. 1930-73. *2043*

—. Working class. 1845-75. *866*

Labor Unions and Organizations (international). Collective bargaining. Industrial relations. Multinational corporations. 1974. *1763*

—. International Law. Latin America. Multinational corporations. North America. 1937-74. *1955*

Labor Unions and Organizations (leaders). Confederation of National Trade Unions. 1966-75. *1562*

—. Turnover rates. 1912-71. *27*

Labor unity. State-monopoly power. 1967-72. *1574*

Labor (white collar). Association of Commercial and Technical Employees. Canadian Labour Congress. Ontario (Toronto). 1972. *2724*

Labour Department. British Columbia. Conciliation Act (1900; antecedents). Industrial relations. 1880's-1900. *3175*

Labour Manifesto (1976). Canadian Labour Council. 1976. *1549*

Labrador *See also* Atlantic Provinces; Newfoundland.

—. Artifacts. Eskimos. Europeans. Quebec. Ungava Peninsula. ca 400-18c. *300*

—. Basque language. Documents. 1572-77. *559*

—. Basques. Whaling Industry and Trade. 16c. *557*

—. Environment. Indians. Quebec. Religion. Social organization. 17c-20c. *428*

—. Eskimos. Excavations. Grizzly bear skull. 18c-19c. *336*

—. Ethnographers. Indians. 1908-68. *436*

—. Fishing Rights. Newfoundland. Public Administration. Quebec. 1763-83. *735*

Labrador (northeast). Explorers. Hubbard, Leonidas. Wallace, Dillon. 1903-05. *3313*

Labrador (Red Bay). Archives. Basques. *San Juan* (vessel). Shipwrecks. Spain. 1565. 1978. *558*

Labrador (Saglek Bay). Eskimos, Thule culture. Excavations. Houses, communal. 1650-1700. *334*

Lacouture, Onésime. Jesuits. Quebec. 1931-50. *2493*

Lacrosse. Athletics (concept). Sports. 1840-89. *153*

—. Baggataway (Indian game). 1840-1931. *240*

Lake, Bibye. Economic Growth. Fur Trade. Hudson's Bay Company. 1684-1743. *503*

Lake Champlain. American Revolution. Arnold, Benedict. Carleton, Guy. Fort Ticonderoga. 1776. *722*

Lake Champlain (battle). Northeastern or North Atlantic States. War of 1812. 1814. *758*

Lake Erie. Bibliographies. North Central States. Pollution. 1872-1965. *2730*

Lake Erie (battle). Dobbins, Daniel. Madison, James. Perry, Oliver Hazard. War of 1812. Warships. 1812-13. *762*

Lake Geneva Mission. Dukhobors. Galicians. Missions and Missionaries. Presbyterian Church. Saskatchewan (Wakaw). 1903-42. *3027*

Lake Huron. Ontario (Georgian Bay). Ragueneau, Paul (letter). 1648. *589*

Lake Huron (Georgian Bay). Lumber industry. Ontario (Depot Harbour). Ports. 1900-28. *2742*

Lake of the Woods. Boundaries. Great Britain. Paris, Treaty of (1783). USA. 1755-1925. *723*

Lake Ontario. New York (Ogdensburg). Ontario (Kingston). Steamboating. Transportation. 1815-70. *653*

—. Shipwrecks. 1679-1890. *58*

Lake Superior. Shipwrecks. 1872-1919. *943*

Lakes. Chippewa Indians. Cree Indians. Fishing. Indians. Ontario, northern. 19c-1978. *341*

Lamaletie, Jean-André. France. Quebec. Trading circles. 1741-63. *561*

Lamarche, Gustave. Catholic Church. Political philosophy. Quebec. Separatist Movements. 1922-75. *2705*

Lambert, Augustine. Country Life. Saskatchewan (Arelee). Sketches. 1913-14. *3054*

Lamontagne, Maurice (views). Federalism. Quebec. Separatist Movements. 1867-1976. *2097*

LaMountain, John. Balloons (hot air). Haddock, John A. Quebec. USA. 1859. *845*

Land *See also* Agriculture; Land Tenure; Real Estate.

—. Abstract Index to Deeds. Law. Ontario (Malden Township). 18c-1865. 1978. *778*

—. Alberta. Bobtail Cree Reserve. Cree Indians. Indians. 1900-09. *3125*

—. Farmers. Inheritance. Ontario. 19c. *807*

—. Fugitive Slaves. New Brunswick. Settlement. USA. 1815-36. *804*

—. Government. Saskatchewan. Settlement. 1929-35. *3060*

—. Ontario (Essex County). Speculation. 1790-1900. *777*

—. Population. Social change. Westward Movement. 1850's-67. *850*

—. Population. Urbanization. 1970-74. *1483*

—. Real Estate. 1863-1973. *36*

Land banks. Cities. Housing costs. ca 1970-81. *1524*

Land claim settlements. Alaska. Eskimos. Indians. 1958-77. *288*

Land claims. Government commissions. Indians. Métis. Prairie Provinces. 1885-1900. *396*

Land endowment. Church of England. Ontario (Upper Canada). Rolph, John. Strachan, John. Toronto, University of. 1820-70. *809*

Land grants. Heir and Devisee Commission (2d, 1805). Ontario (Upper Canada). 1800-45. *645*

—. Military. Ontario (Upper Canada). Settlement. 1816-20. *788*

Land grants (proposed). Colonial policy. Emigrant guides. Great Britain. Ontario (Peterborough). Traill, Catherine Parr. 19c. *869*
Land ownership. British Columbia. Foreign investments. Jurisdictional law. Washington (Whatcom County). 1970's. *2047*
Land policies. British Columbia. Indians. Provincial government. 1875-80. *383*
Land prices. Germany. Great Britain. Taxation. 1890-1970's. *214*
Land rights. Cree Treaty of 1876. Government. Indians. 1876-1970's. *364*
Land Settlement. Historiography. Prairie Provinces. 1880-1900. *2902*
Land speculation. Crime and Criminals. Depression of 1857. Embezzlement. Street, William Warren. 1830-70. *2799*
—. Ontario (Essex County). 1790-1900. *777*
—. Ontario (Upper Canada). Rural land occupation. Settlers. Townships. 1782-1851. *793*
Land Tenure See also Peasants; Real Estate.
—. Acadians. Colonial Government. Great Britain. Nova Scotia. Oath of allegiance. 11c-1755. *594*
—. Economic development. Seigneurial system. 1700-1854. *798*
—. Jesuits. Legislation. Mercier, Honoré. Protestant Churches. Quebec. 1886. *2645*
—. Manors. St. Lawrence Valley. Social Classes. 1663-1840. 1840D 1800H. *538*
—. Methodology. Quebec (Saguenay County). 1840-1975. *2633*
Land use. Eskimos. Industrial expansion. Oil Industry and Trade. Pollution. 1975. *338*
—. Farm. Markets. Quebec. 1908-71. *2661*
Land use atlases. Building plans. Insurance. Research. Urban historians. 1696-1973. *86*
Land use patterns. 1670-1975. *3289*
Land (use, planning). Ecology. 1973. *1271*
—. Oil Industry and Trade. 1960's-70's. *3280*
Landscape. British Columbia (Lower Fraser Valley). Pioneers. Surveyors. 1859-90. *3235*
Landscape Painting. British Columbia. Forests and Forestry. 1700-1950. *3188*
—. Great Britain. Menzies, Archibald. Nature. Vancouver, George. ca 1775-1800. *633*
—. Lortie, Jocelyne. 1965-78. *2495*
—. Lynn, Washington Frank. Reporters and Reporting. USA. 1860's-70's. *947*
Langevin, Adélard. Catholics. Manitoba (Winnipeg Archdiocese). 1905. *2974*
Langford, Sam ("Boston Tarbaby"). Boxing. Race Relations. 1886-1956. *2369*
Langille family. France. Nova Scotia. 1718-1804. *2230*
Language See also Linguistics; Literature; Rhetoric.
—. Acculturation. French Canadians. 1971. *1342*
—. American Revolution. Loyalists. Settlement. 1774-84. *746*
—. Anglicization. Quebec. Social classes. 1971. *2461*
—. Anglophones. Quebec. 1830-1976. *2714*
—. Art. Politics. Regionalism. 1978. *2123*
—. Assimilation. French Canadians. 1961-71. *1364*
—. Attitudes. Geographic Space. National Development. 1776-1976. *56*
—. Baptists. Micmac Indians. Missions and Missionaries. Nova Scotia. Rand, Silas Tertius. 1830-89. *422*
—. Dialects. Survey of Canadian English. Youth. 1972. *1484*
—. Discrimination. Human rights. USA. 1960's. *1481*
—. Elections. France. Parliaments. Quebec. 1792-1810. *700*
—. Family. Indians. Kin terminologies. Plains Indians. Social Organization. Prehistory-19c. *426*
—. Minorities. Official Language Act (Quebec, 1974). Quebec. 1750's-1974. *2476*
—. Population. Representation Act (1974). 1974. *2104*
Language equality. Federal government. Official Language Act (Quebec, 1974). Quebec. 1960-76. *1438*
Language, official. Bédard, Pierre (discourse). Dionne, Narcisse-Eutrope. Quebec (Lower Canada). 1792-1809. 1909. *699*
—. Constitutions. Ethnic groups. Joint Committee of the Canadian Senate and House of Commons. 1970's. *1947*
Language policy. Federal government. Middle Classes. Modernization. Provincial government. Quebec. 1960-76. *2090*

Language training. Assimilation. Employment. Immigrants. Ontario (Toronto). 1968-70. *1625*
Lansdowne College. Colleges and Universities. Collegiate Institute. Depressions. Manitoba (Portage la Prairie). 1882-93. *3018*
Lapérouse, Jean François. Alaska. Discovery and Exploration. Ledyard, John. Pacific Area. Pacific Northwest. Russia (Siberia). 1778-1806. *652*
Lapierre, Eugène (obituary). Historical Society of Montreal. Nationalism. Quebec. 1927-70's. *2450*
LaRocque, Paul. Catholic Church. Church Finance. Economic Development. Quebec (Sherbrooke). 1893-1926. *2636*
Larsen, Lawrence W. (paper). Armies. Military Strategy. North Dakota. 1919. 1975. *1157*
Lascelles, Alan (memorandum). Buchan, John. Governors-General. 1935. *1217*
Laskin, Bora. Americanization. Criminal Law. Supreme Court (Canada). 1973-74. *2068*
Latin America. Asylum, right of. 1973. *1735*
—. Bibliographies. Editorials. French Canadians. Newspapers. Quebec. 1959-73. *2433*
—. Foreign policy. Trudeau, Pierre Elliott. 1968-77. *1803*
—. Foreign Policy. Trudeau, Pierre Elliott. 1940-76. *1804*
—. Foreign Policy. Trudeau, Pierre Elliott. 1968-78. *1878*
—. Foreign Relations. 1970's. *1808*
—. Foreign Relations. 1970-76. *1834*
—. Foreign Relations. Pan-American Union. USA. World War II. 1939-44. *1239*
—. International Law. Labor Unions and Organizations (international). Multinational corporations. North America. 1937-74. *1955*
—. International trade. Trudeau, Pierre Elliott. 1968-76. *1802*
Laurendeau, André. English Canadians. French Canadians. Nationalism. Quebec. 1945-66. *2556*
Laurentian thesis. Business. Economic history. Historiography. 1960-73. *1592*
Laurentide Company. Capitalists. Newsprint. Quebec. 1887-1928. *161*
Laurier, Wilfrid. Colonial Stock Act (1900). Great Britain. Imperialism. 1890's-1900. *1095*
LaVache family. Genealogy. Nova Scotia (Cape Breton; Arichat). 1774-20c. *2365*
Laval, François de. Brotherhood of the Holy Family. Catholic Church. Chaumonot, Joseph-Marie-Pierre. Elites. Quebec (Montreal). 1663-1760. *547*
—. Catholic Church. Governors, provincial. New France (Sovereign Council). 1659-84. *546*
—. Catholic Church. Ideas, History of. Quebec. 17c. *549*
—. Gosselin, Auguste-Honoré (review article). New France. School of Arts and Crafts of St. Joachim. 1668-1730. *535*
Laval University. Bourget, Ignace. Catholic Church. Colleges and Universities. Quebec (Quebec). 1840's-50's. *2523*
—. Economic growth. Elites. Ideology. Quebec. Social sciences. 1930's-70's. *2527*
—. Institute of History. Quebec (Quebec). 1947. *2571*
Lavell, Jeannette (Wikwemikong Indian). *Attorney General of Canada v. Lavell* (Canada, 1973). Indians. Sex Discrimination. Supreme Court. Women. 1973-74. *473*
Law See also Constitutional Law; Corporation Law; Courts; Criminal Law; International Law; Judges; Judicial Administration; Judicial Process; Lawyers; Legislation; Maritime Law; Police.
—. Abstract Index to Deeds. Land. Ontario (Malden Township). 18c-1865. 1978. *778*
—. Adoption. Belgium. France. 1974. *1393*
—. Belcher, Jonathan. Grand jury. Nova Scotia. 1754. *2362*
—. Business. Elites. Social institutions, stratifying. 19c-1974. *211*
—. Civil rights. Mexico. USA. Violence. 18c-1974. *52*
—. Collective bargaining. Crown Employees Collective Bargaining Act. Labor. Ontario. 1970-74. *2745*
—. Human rights. USA. 1930-73. *1963*
—. Indian Affairs Department. Iroquois Indians. Quebec. St. Regis Reservation. 1876-1918. *459*
—. Macdonald, Hugh John. Politics. 1870-1929. *921*
—. Parliaments. Political parties. 1920's-74. *1648*

Law and Society. Divorce rates. Legal access. 1867-1973. *1451*
Law Enforcement. Alberta (Writing-On-Stone, Milk River). Indians. Military Camps and Forts. North West Mounted Police. 1887-1918. *957*
—. British Columbia. Douglas, James. Frontier and Pioneer Life. Gold rushes. 1858. *3197*
—. British Columbia (Vancouver). Provincial government. Riots (anti-Chinese). 1887. *3247*
—. Decisionmaking. Grosman, Brian A. (review article). Police politics. 1975. *1674*
—. Feminism. Ontario (Toronto). Prostitution. Rape. 1975-78. *2825*
—. Intergovernmental Relations. Legislation. Police jurisdiction. 1970's. *1711*
—. Manitoba. North West Mounted Police. 1873-74. *2985*
—. Northwest Territories. Prohibition. Royal Canadian Mounted Police. 1874-91. *984*
—. USA. 1950's-76. *1664*
Law Reform. Alberta. 1939-74. *3114*
—. Obscenity. 1966-73. *1382*
Lawrence, D. H. Great Britain. Novels. 1911-30. *1121*
Lawson, Mary Jane Katzman. Literature. Nova Scotia. 1828-90. *2292*
Lawyers See also Judges.
—. French Canadians. LeSage, Simeon. Provincial Government. Quebec. 1835-1909. *2570*
—. International law. 1974. *1788*
—. McCaul, Charles Coursolles. 1883-1928. *1019*
Le Canadien (newspaper). British Empire. Confederation. Parent, Étienne. 1831-52. *830*
Leadership See also Political Leadership.
—. Canadian Labour Congress. Morris, Joe (interview). 1930's-78. *1527*
Leadership succession. Equal opportunity. Hutterites. Population. Prairie Provinces. Social Organization. 1940's-70's. *2908*
League for Social Reconstruction. Cooperative Commonwealth Federation. Regina Manifesto. Saskatchewan. Underhill, Frank. 1933. *2927*
League of Nations Covenant. Cahan, Charles H. (address). Japan. Manchuria. 1932-33. *1211*
LeClercq, Crestien. Bernou, Claude. France. *Premier Établissement de la Foy dans la Nouvelle France* (book). Renaudot, Eusèbe. 1691. *548*
Lectures See also Speeches, Addresses, etc.
—. Bryan, William Jennings. Fund-raising. Prairie Provinces. Young Men's Christian Association. 1909. *2953*
—. Cable, George Washington. Kentucky. Twain, Mark. 1884-85. *1076*
—. Manitoba (Winnipeg). Minnesota (Crookston). Twain, Mark. 1895. *2989*
—. Melville, Herman. Quebec (Montreal). 1857. *2519*
—. USA. Wilde, Oscar ("The House Beautiful"). 1882. *1061*
Leden, Christian. Cris Indians. Ethnomusicology. Phonograph. Songs. 1911. *387*
Ledyard, John. Alaska. Discovery and Exploration. Lapérouse, Jean François. Pacific Area. Pacific Northwest. Russia (Siberia). 1778-1806. *652*
Lee, Robert E. Boundary survey incident. Great Lakes. USA. 1835. *674*
Leedy, John Whitnah. Alberta. Kansas. Politics. Prairie radical. Radicals and Radicalism. 1880's-1935. *3087*
Leeson & Scott (firm). Freight and Freightage. Prairie Provinces. 1883-1909. *1027*
Lefroy, John Henry (journals). Great Britain. Magnetic survey. Northwest Territories. Scientific Expeditions. 1843-44. *3306*
Lefroy, L. H. Alberta. Fort Chipewyan. Fur Trade. 1843-44. *3094*
Leftism See also Communism; Radicals and Radicalism; Socialism.
—. Espionage. Rosenberg Case. USA. 1940's-50's. *1682*
—. Imperialism (review article). Moore, Steve. Nationalism. Wells, Debi. 1960's-70's. *1269*
—. Nationalism. Quebec. Social classes. 1970's. *2703*
Legal access. Divorce rates. Law and Society. 1867-1973. *1451*
Legal systems. British influences. Constitutions. USA. 18c-20c. *124*
Légaré, Joseph. Art Galleries and Museums (proposed). Painting. Quebec. 1824-1933. *2544*
Legend painting. Artists. Chippewa Indians. Cree Indians. Indians. Manitoba. Ontario. 1960's-70's. *470*

Legislation *See also* Congress; Law; Parliament.
—. Arbitration, Industrial. Civil Service. 1967. *1497*
—. Atlantic Provinces. Bargaining rights. Fisheries. Nova Scotia. 1975. *2351*
—. Automobiles. Nova Scotia. 1899-1913. *2300*
—. British Columbia. New Democratic Party. Public Policy. Social Democracy. 1972-75. *3241*
—. British Columbia. Politics. Provincial Government. 1977. *3238*
—. Cyclones. Ontario. Sex Discrimination. Wages. Wages. 1946-71. *2777*
—. Election Expenses Act (Canada, 1973). 1973. *1665*
—. Europe (Eastern, Southern). Immigration. Physicians. Racism. 1920's. *1178*
—. France. North America. Psychiatric care. Quebec. 1973. *2546*
—. Health care programs. Social Conditions. 1945-65. *1383*
—. House of Commons. 1958-72. *1669*
—. Intergovernmental Relations. Law Enforcement. Police jurisdiction. 1970's. *1711*
—. Jesuits. Land Tenure. Mercier, Honoré. Protestant Churches. Quebec. 1886. *2645*
—. Juvenile Delinquency. Marxism. Social history. 1870's-1970's. *76*
—. Price control. -1973. *1698*
Legislative Assembly. Elections. Political Factions. Propaganda. 1792. *708*
—. Quebec (Lower Canada). Voting and Voting Behavior. 1792-1814. *701*
Legislative investigations. Business. Oliver, Adam. Ontario (Ingersoll, Thunder Bay). Provincial Politics. 1820-85. *2763*
Legislative Library. Bibliographies. Nova Scotia. 1976. *2371*
Legislators. Bureaucracies. Democracy. 1968-72. *1712*
Legitimacy. Institutions. Quebec. Radio-Québec. Television. 1969-74. *2477*
Leigh-Mallory, Trafford. Dieppe (air battle). Great Britain. Royal Canadian Air Force. World War II. 1942. *1220*
Leisure *See also* Recreation.
—. Political Science. Politics. 1974. *1696*
Lemelin, Roger *(Les Plouffe)*. Americanism. Nationalism. Quebec. 1938-45. *2722*
Leprosy. Diseases. Massachusetts. New Brunswick. Social stigma. 1844-80. 1904-21. *2391*
LeSage, Simeon. Conservatism. Nationalism. Quebec. Riel, Louis. 1867-1909. *2717*
—. French Canadians. Lawyers. Provincial Government. Quebec. 1835-1909. *2570*
Letters. American Revolution. Bailey, Jacob. Church of England. Nova Scotia. 1784. *726*
—. Armour, John. Ontario (Dunnville). 1829-81. *768*
—. Atlantic Coast. Blockade running. Civil War. Nova Scotia. Wade, Norman. 1859-62. *841*
—. Blockades. Civil War. Nova Scotia. Wade, Norman. 1861-62. *889*
—. Brubacher brothers. Mennonites. Ontario. Pennsylvania. 1817-46. *786*
—. Burge family. Friendship. Ontario (Upper Canada). Simcoe family. 1790-1820. *669*
—. Church of England. Ontario (Ottawa). Politics. Thompson, Annie Affleck. Thompson, John S. D. 1867-94. *1075*
—. Civil War. Navies. Nova Scotia. Wade, Norman. 1859-62. *842*
—. Clark, Septimus Alfred. Frontier and Pioneer Life. Great Britain. Radcliffe, Mary. Saskatchewan (Regina). 1884-1909. *967*
—. Confederation. Derby, 15th Earl of. Great Britain. Head, Edmund Walker. Political Attitudes. 1858. *894*
—. Duke University (Lionel Stevenson Collection). Literature. Stevenson, Lionel. 1860's-1960's. *4*
—. Frontier. Ontario (Upper Canada). Painting. Simcoe, Elizabeth. Values. 1790-1800. *638*
—. Galt, Elliott. Indians. Prairie Provinces. Travel. 1879-80. *959*
Leverett, John. Harvard University. Massachusetts (Cambridge). Quebec Expedition. Speeches, Addresses, etc. 1711. *610*
Lévesque, Georges-Henri (personal account). Catholicism. French Canadians. Nationalism. Quebec. Youth movements. 1930's. *2700*
Lévesque, René. Newspapers. Parti Québécois. Provincial Government. Quebec (Montreal). 1976-77. *2423*
—. Parti Québécois. Quebec. Separatism. Trudeau, Pierre Elliott. 1970's. *2110*

—. Parti Québécois. Quebec. Separatist Movements. 1968-70's. *2713*
Lévesque, René (views). French Canadians. Independence Movements. Nationalism. Quebec. 1763-1976. *2701*
Levi-Strauss, Claude. Frye, Northrop. Primitivism. Shadbolt, Jack. 1977. *251*
Lewis, Henry. Forman, George. Logging. Mississippi River. Shipping. 1849-54. 1883. *2755*
Lewis, Waitsill (family). Genealogy. Methodology. Nova Scotia (Yarmouth). 1976. *2212*
Liberal consensus. Hartz, Louis (thesis). Historiography. ca 1760-1800. 1970's. *693*
Liberal democracy. Institutional orientations. Senators. 1970's. *1644*
Liberal Party. Agriculture Minister. Gardiner, James G. Patronage. 1935-57. *2959*
—. Alberta. Elections, provincial. Social Credit League. United Farmers of Alberta. 1905-73. *3107*
—. Alberta. Gardiner, James G. Social Credit Party. 1935-39. *3157*
—. Bishops. Catholic Church. Church of England. Newfoundland. 1860-62. *2187*
—. Borden, Frederick W. Business. Family. Nova Scotia (King's County). Parliaments. 1874-96. *2316*
—. Boucherville, Charles Eugène Boucher de. Federalism. Joly, Henri-Gustave. Political Campaigns. Provincial government. Quebec. 1878. *2452*
—. Bourassa, Robert. Political patronage. Quebec. 1970-75. *2440*
—. Brown, J. L. Manitoba (Lisgar). Parliaments. Winkler, H. W. (career). 1926-53. *3021*
—. Conservative Party. Elections. New Democratic Party. 1972. *1675*
—. Davis, Thomas O. Elections. Saskatchewan. 1896. *3046*
—. Elections. Fielding, William Stevens. Nova Scotia. 1891-96. *2313*
—. Elections. Trudeau, Pierre Elliott. 1968-72. *1638*
—. French Canadians. Parti Québécois. 1978. *1716*
—. King, William Lyon Mackenzie. Politics. Quebec. 1919-50. *1132*
—. Manitoba. New Democratic Party. Progressive Conservative Party. Voting and Voting Behavior. 1953-73. *3020*
—. Manitoba. Politics. Railroads. Schools. 1870's-90's. *2987*
—. Newfoundland. Politics. Progressive Conservative Party. 1908-72. *2195*
—. Ontario. Political participation. 1960's-70's. *2748*
—. Ridings. Voting and Voting Behavior. 1968. *1637*
Liberalism. Conservatism. Hartz, Louis. Politics. Socialism. USA. 1955-78. *1668*
—. Conservatism. Mennonites. Ontario (Waterloo County). 1977. *2767*
Liberals. Elections. Independence issue. Parti Québécois. Quebec. 1973-76. *2707*
Librarians. Canadian Library Association Committee on the Status of Women. Cheda, Sherrill. Feminism. 1973-74. *1418*
Libraries *See also* names of individual libraries; Archives; Museums.
—. Adult education. Middle classes. Social Organization. Working class. 19c. *104*
—. Albert-Westmorland-Kent Regional Library. New Brunswick (Moncton). 1911-73. *2398*
—. British Columbia (Victoria). Herre, W. F. Reading-rooms. 1858-63. *3256*
—. Carnegie, Andrew. Nicol, A. Yukon Territory (Dawson). 1902-20's. *3340*
—. City Government. Metropolitan Areas. 1950-71. *1361*
—. CODOC (system). Documents. Government. Information Storage and Retrieval Systems. USA. 1960's-70's. *177*
—. Colleges and Universities. 1970's. *1347*
—. Colleges and Universities. Nordic area studies. 1970-73. *1343*
—. Collins Bay Penitentiary. Ontario (Kingston). Prisons. Resocialization. 1963-73. *2851*
—. Community involvement. Public Schools. 1973. *1396*
—. Alberta (Calgary). Decentralization. Mount Royal College (Learning Resource Center). 1973. *3142*
—. Intellectuals. New France. Royal intendants. 1663-1760. *555*
—. Manitoba. 1847-1974. *3008*
—. Mechanics' Institute movement. Ontario (Napanee). Social Classes. 1850-1900. *914*

—. Montreal, University of, Melzack Collection. 18c-. *6*
—. Mount Allison University (Ralph Packard Bell Library). New Brunswick (Sackville). 1970-73. *2394*
—. National Library of Canada. 1953-78. *244*
—. National Library of Canada (Library Documentation Centre). 1970-73. *1488*
—. North America. 1972. *1378*
—. Nova Scotia. Strathbeg Reading Society. 1866-69. *2347*
Libraries, American. Literature. 1956-73. *1257*
Libraries (circulation). Newfoundland Regional Library System. 1942-68. *2198*
Library of Congress, Gilbert J. Grosvenor Collection. Bell, Alexander Graham. Deaf. Photographs. 1870-1922. *2228*
Licensing procedures. Constitutional law. Provinces. States. USA. 1970's. *2063*
Lie, Trygve. Great Powers. Pearson, Lester B. UN. 1946. *1738*
Lieutenant governors. Federal Government. Hepburn, Mitchell F. King, William Lyon Mackenzie. Ontario. Provincial government. 1937. *1208*
Lifesaving service. Nova Scotia (Sable Island). Wentworth, John. 1801. *2236*
Lifestyles. Newfoundland. Public identity. Sects, religious. Social Classes. 1949-75. *2183*
Lifestyles, alternative. Hutterites. South Dakota. 1874-1975. *977*
Lighthouses. 18c-1975. *21*
—. Historical Sites and Parks. 1873-1970. *22*
Ligue pour la Défense du Canada. Conscription, Military. Elections. King, William Lyon Mackenzie. Quebec. World War II. 1942-44. *1226*
Lillooet Indians. British Columbia, southwestern. Indians. Oral tradition. Prehistory-1976. *289*
—. British Columbia, southwestern. Indians. Oral tradition. Prehistory-1976. *291*
Lime kilns. Ontario. Pioneers. Technology. 1870-1917. *2850*
Lime preparation. Construction. France. Louisbourg, Fortress of. Military Camps and Forts. Nova Scotia. 1725-58. *615*
Lincoln, Abraham. Davis, Jefferson. Peace mission. Virginia (Richmond). 1864. *838*
Lindsay, James. Métis. Military Campaigns. Red River Expedition. 1869-70. *999*
Linguistics *See also* Dialects; Language.
—. French language. Quebec. 1971. *2576*
—. Race relations. -1973. *1437*
Lipman, Jean. Folk Art (review article). Harper, Russell. USA. Winchester, Alice. 19c. *149*
Lipset, Seymour Martin. Sociology. USA. 1963-73. *1304*
Liquor. British Columbia. Great Britain. Gunboats. Indians. Slave trade, Indian. 1860's. *390*
Literacy. Census. Documents. Methodology. 1861. *852*
—. Census. Methodology. Ontario (Peel, Hamilton Counties). Social organization. 19c. *2822*
—. French Canadians. Quebec. 1745-1899. *2507*
Literary associations. Education. French Canadians. Quebec (Lower Canada). Social Problems. 1840-67. *2526*
—. Bibliographies. Europe. French language. Quebec. USA. Voluntary associations. 1840-1900. *2524*
Literary characters. French Canadians. Novels. Ontario (Glengarry County). 1925-75. *2857*
Literary Criticism. Novels. Realism. 1920-30. *1176*
Literary Critics. Hardy, Thomas. 1870's-1900. *918*
Literary growth, theories of. Patriotism. 1864-1914. *904*
Literary themes. Country Life. Depressions. Fiction. Prairie Provinces. 1930's. *2918*
Literature *See also* Authors; Autobiography and Memoirs; Biography; Books; Drama; Fiction; Humor; Journalism; Language; Novels; Poetry; Satire.
—. 20c. *55*
—. Bibliographies. French Canadians. 1606-1977. *2581*
—. Clark, Arthur Hill (obituary). 1911-75. *1440*
—. Duke University (Lionel Stevenson Collection). Letters. Stevenson, Lionel. 1860's-1960's. *4*
—. Editors and Editing. Grove, Frederick Philip (letters). Pacey, Desmond. 1912-48. 1976. *1135*
—. Feminism. McClung, Nellie L. Politics. Reform. 1873-1930's. *1189*

—. Grove, Frederick Phillip (writings). Pastoral ideal. Technology. 1920-45. *38*
—. Lawson, Mary Jane Katzman. Nova Scotia. 1828-90. *2292*
—. Libraries, American. 1956-73. *1257*
—. McCulloch, Thomas (*Letters of Mephibosheth Stepsure*). Nova Scotia. Presbyterian Church. Satire. 1821-22. *2339*
—. Moodie, Susanna. National self-image. Social Classes. 1832-53. *670*
—. New Brunswick. 18c-1977. *2382*
—. Nova Scotia. Pictou Literature and Scientific Society. Science. 1834-54. *2248*
—. Periodicals. Quebec. 20c. *2505*
Literature, African. Africa. 1973. *110*
Literature, moralistic. French Canadians. Hume, David (writings). Luxury, concept of. Quebec. 1849-1900. *2617*
Little Big Horn (battle). Cooke, Willie. Custer, George A. Ontario (Hamilton). 1860's-70's. *2878*
Lloyd, Gweneth. Biography. Crampton, Esmé (account). Dance. Oral History. 1969-75. *1371*
Loans *See also* Investments.
—. Chile. Churches. Royal Bank of Canada. South Africa. 1976. *1951*
Lobbying *See also* Interest Groups; Political Factions.
—. Political science. Politics. 1975. *1651*
Lobsticks. Monuments. Trees. 1826-1973. *84*
Local Architectural Conservation Advisory Committee. Heritage Act (1975). Ontario (London). Preservation. 1945-77. *2818*
Local Government *See also* Local Politics; Public Administration.
—. Alberta. Cities. Political Recruitment. 1971. *3129*
—. Birch, Arthur N. (letter). British Columbia (New Westminster). Social Conditions. 1864. *870*
—. Bossism. Houde, Camillien. Martin, Médéric. Quebec (Montreal). 1923-29. *2446*
—. Business History. Economic policy. Ontario. Property, private. 1898-1911. *1100*
—. Confederation. Doyle, Hastings. Federal government. Nova Scotia. 1867-68. *895*
—. Councillors. Public policy. 1968-75. *1632*
—. County Government. Municipalities, rural. New Brunswick. 1967-77. *2384*
—. Demographic research. Federal Government. Immigration policy. 1970's. *1811*
—. Grand Jurors' Book. Nova Scotia (Yarmouth and Argyle). 1814-51. *2310*
—. Howe, Joseph. Nova Scotia (Halifax). Political Corruption. Trials. 1835. *808*
—. Manitoba (Assiniboia, Red River settlement). Métis. 1857-65. *2911*
—. Manitoba (Winnipeg). Political Reform. Working class. 1873-1971. *2990*
—. Manitoba (Winnipeg). Queen, John. Socialism. Taxation. 1909-42. *2992*
—. Models. Quebec (Montreal). 1911-71. *2445*
—. Nova Scotia (East Hants). 1861-1923. *2363*
—. Provincial government. Public Finance. Quebec. 1960-73. *2418*
Local history. International Programme for Loyalist Studies. MacNutt, W. Stewart (obituary). New Brunswick, University of. 1935-76. *2174*
Local Politics *See also* Local Government.
—. Alberta (Edmonton). Canadian Pacific Railway. Railroads. 1891-1914. *955*
Locational clustering. Clothing industries. Ontario (Toronto). Publishers and Publishing. Quebec (Montreal). 1949-67. *1611*
Locomotives. Canadian Railway Museum. Japan. *John Molson* (locomotive; replica). Scotland. 1849. 1969. *877*
Locomotives' rosters. Mexico. Railroads. USA. 1911-78. *48*
Locusts. Homesteading and Homesteaders. Manitoba. Mortgages. 1875-1941. *3002*
Logan, Alexander. City Government. Manitoba (Winnipeg). 1870's-80's. *2966*
Logging. Forman, George. Lewis, Henry. Mississippi River. Shipping. 1849-54. 1883. *2755*
Logistics *See also* Military Strategy; Naval Strategy.
—. Alaskan Highway. Highway Engineering. World War II. Yukon Territory. 1942-43. *3338*
—. American Revolution. British Army. Carleton, Guy. Quebec. 1776. *714*
L'Ordre de Bon Temps. Champlain, Samuel de. Nova Scotia (Port Royal). Social Organizations. 1606. *542*
—. Champlain, Samuel de. Nova Scotia. Social Organizations. 1606-07. *543*

Lord's Day Act (1906). Sabbath (observation). Sports. Sunday. 1906-77. *200*
Lortie, Jocelyne. Landscape Painting. 1965-78. *2495*
Lotteries. Provincial Government. Public Finance. Quebec. 1970-73. *2603*
Louisbourg, Fortress of. Architectural drawings. Fortification. Historical Sites and Parks. Nova Scotia (Cape Breton Island). 1707-58. *603*
—. Architecture. France. Guardhouses. Military Camps and Forts. Nova Scotia. 1713-68. *616*
—. Barracks. Historical Sites and Parks. Nova Scotia. 1716-39. 1969. *590*
—. Bradstreet, John. Great Britain. Military Biography. Nova Scotia. 1739-74. *604*
—. Buildings. Historical Sites and Parks. Nova Scotia (Cape Breton Island). 1713-58. *529*
—. Construction. France. Lime preparation. Military Camps and Forts. Nova Scotia. 1725-58. *615*
—. Daily life. Historical Sites and Parks. Nova Scotia (Cape Breton Island). Social classes. 1713-50. *537*
—. Economic Conditions. King George's War. New England. Nova Scotia. 1745-50. *607*
—. Excavations. Gunflints. Military Camps and Forts. Nova Scotia. 1720-60. *608*
—. Fishing company. France (Poitou; Les Sables d'Olonne). Huart, Christophle-Albert-Alberic d'. Nobility. Nova Scotia (Cape Breton Island). 1750-75. *560*
—. Fishing industry. Historical Sites and Parks. Nova Scotia (Cape Breton Island, Isle Royale). 1705-50. *573*
—. France. King George's War. Mutinies. Nova Scotia. 1744-45. *605*
—. Historical Sites and Parks. Nova Scotia (Cape Breton Island). Restorations. 18c. 1961-75. *602*
—. Military Camps and Forts. Nova Scotia. Restorations. 1654-1745. 1928-73. *613*
—. Nova Scotia (Cape Breton Island). Preservation. 1720-68. 1976. *619*
Louisiana *See also* South Central and Gulf States.
—. Acadians. North America. 17c-20c. *580*
—. Catholic Church. Indians. Missions and Missionaries. 18c-20c. *587*
—. Colonialism. France. Immigration. 1718-21. *578*
Louisiana Territory. Colonial Government. France. Mississippi River Valley. New France. 1683-1762. *584*
Lower, Arthur (review article). Great Britain. International Trade. Lumber and Lumbering. 1763-1867. *781*
Lowes, Ellen McFadden (diary). Manitoba (Elliott Settlement). Pioneers. 1882-83. *998*
Lowry, Ira S. Labor. Migration, Internal. Models. Quebec. -1973. *2593*
Loyalism. History Teaching. Ontario (Upper Canada). Textbooks. 19c-20c. *741*
Loyalist myth. delaRoche, Mazo. Novels. USA. 1780's. 1920's-40's. *742*
Loyalist tradition. Anti-Americanism. New Brunswick. Political Attitudes. 1825-1914. *2375*
Loyalists. American Revolution. 1782-90's. *738*
—. American Revolution. Colonization. New Brunswick. Saunders, John. Virginia. 1774-1834. *740*
—. American Revolution. Florida (St. Augustine). ca 1775-85. *752*
—. American Revolution. Language. Settlement. 1774-84. *746*
—. Cary, James. Exiles. Great Britain. Jamaica. Nova Scotia. 1781-1804. *744*
—. Church of England. Nova Scotia. Society for the Propagation of the Gospel. 1787-1864. *751*
—. Eby, Ezra E. Immigration. Mennonites. Pennsylvania. 18c-1835. *743*
—. Exiles. McDowall, Robert James. Missions and Missionaries. Ontario (Upper Canada). Reformed Dutch Church. 1790-1819. *747*
—. Nova Scotia (Cape Breton Island). Settlers. 1784-1820. *748*
Lumber and Lumbering. Bibliographies. British Columbia. Pacific Northwest. 1890's-1960's. *3221*
—. British Columbia. Engineering. Poetry. Railroads. Swanson, Robert (interview). 20c. *3273*
—. British Columbia. Maine. McInnis, George (interview). Washington. 1894-1949. *3261*
—. Conservation movements. Federal Regulation. Ontario (Ottawa). "Robber Barons". 1873-1914. *2774*

—. Fundy National Park. New Brunswick. Settlement. 1820's-1976. *2383*
—. Great Britain. International Trade. Lower, Arthur (review article). 1763-1867. *781*
—. Lake Huron (Georgian Bay). Ontario (Depot Harbour). Ports. 1900-28. *2742*
—. Photographs. Price, Vernon (interview). Quebec (Schyan River area). 1938-39. *2641*
—. Port Blakely Mill Company. Washington (Bainbridge Island). 1888-1903. *2257*
Lumber camps. British Columbia. Daily Life. Parkin, Al (interview). 1910's-30's. *3255*
Lumberers. Forests and Forestry. New Brunswick. Surveyors. 1820's-44. *2412*
Lutheran Church. Alberta (Edmonton, Mellowdale). Concordia College. Schwermann, Albert H. (reminiscences). USA. 1891-1976. *3147*
—. Baltic Area. Immigrants. 1947-55. *1492*
Lutheran Church, Missouri Synod. Manitoba (Township Berlin). Wagner, William. ca 1870. *1029*
Lutheran synods. Stuermer, Herbert. 1922. *1191*
Luxury. French Canadians. Hume, David (writings). Literature, moralistic. Quebec. 1849-1900. *2617*
Lynn, Washington Frank. Landscape Painting. Reporters and Reporting. USA. 1860's-70's. *947*
Lyon, Matthew (letter). Conquest (discouraged). Monroe, James. USA. War of 1812 (Antecedents). 1811. *756*
Lyon, P. V. Developing nations. Foreign Relations (review article). Ismael, T. Y. Ogelsby, J. C. M. USA. 1860's-1976. *239*
Lyons, Charles (family). Armies. Great Britain. Kent, Duke of (Edward). Nova Scotia (Halifax). 1812-63. *2273*

M

MacDonald, Duncan. Idaho Territory. Indian Wars. Nez Percé Indians. 1877. *418*
Macdonald, Hugh John. Law. Politics. 1870-1929. *921*
Macdonald, John. Catholic Church. Voting and Voting Behavior. 1850's-91. *1059*
Macdonald, John A. Alberta (Banff). National Parks and Reserves. Natural resources. Tourism. 1885-1978. *1040*
—. Anglicization. French Canadians. Immigration. 1860-1900. *705*
—. Constitution. 1867. *893*
Macdonald, John A. (biography). Creighton, Donald. Family. Women. 1843-91. *1063*
MacDonald, John Roderick. Alberta (Edmonton). Catholic Church. Colleges and Universities. St. Joseph's College (Alberta). 1922-23. *3140*
Macdonnell, Alexander. Catholics. Emigration (Scottish). Glengarry Highlanders. Great Britain. Ontario. 1770's-1814. *805*
Macedonians. Assimilation. Immigrants. Ontario (Toronto). 1900-20. *2840*
—. Immigrants. Ontario (Toronto). Urban history. 20c. *2786*
—. Immigration. Ontario (Toronto). Social Conditions. 1900-30. *2841*
MacGregor, James. Missions and Missionaries. Nova Scotia (Pictou). Presbyterian Church of Scotland. 1786-1830. *2343*
Machault (vessel). Cargo. France. French and Indian War. Glass. 1760. *532*
—. New Brunswick. Pottery. Restigouche River (battle). 1760. *2376*
Machinery *See also* Inventions.
—. Agriculture. Business. Distribution system. Manitoba. 1974. *2923*
MacKenzie, A. Stanley (journal). Canoe trip. Nova Scotia. 1885. *2269*
Mackenzie, Alexander. British Columbia. Explorers. Fraser River. 1793. *646*
—. Discovery and Exploration. Overland Journeys to the Pacific. Trade Routes. 1789-93. *2134*
—. *Hector* (vessel). Immigrants. Nova Scotia (Pictou Harbor). Passenger lists. Scotland. 1773. 1883. *2302*
Mackenzie, Arthur Stanley. Colleges and Universities. Dalhousie University. Nova Scotia. Stanley, Carleton. 1911-45. *2282*
Mackenzie Bay (Herschel Island). Arctic Ocean. Eskimos. Polar exploration. Whaling Industry and Trade. 1826-1972. *339*
MacKenzie, George Patton. 1890's-1953. *3279*
Mackenzie River Valley. Food Supply. Fur trade. Hudson's Bay Company. Northwest Territories. Winter. 19c. *3357*

Mackenzie Valley Pipeline Inquiry. Northwest Territories. Oil Industry and Trade. Pipelines. 1976. *3343*

Mackenzie, William Lyon. Armstrong, Frederick H. Mayors. Ontario (Toronto). 1835-37. 1967. *2854*

MacKinnon, Frank (review article). Great Britain. 19c-20c. *156*

MacLeod, Norman. Migration. Nova Scotia (St. Ann's). Presbyterian Church. Scotland. ca 1800-50's. *2244*

MacMillan, John F. "Lofty". Canadian Union of Public Employees. Labor Unions and Organizations. Public Employees. 1935-73. *1504*

MacNutt, W. Stewart (obituary). International Programme for Loyalist Studies. Local history. New Brunswick, University of. 1935-76. *2174*

MacPherson, C. B. Democracy. Humanism. Marxism. Political Theory. 1976. *1338*

Madison, James. Dobbins, Daniel. Lake Erie (battle of). Perry, Oliver Hazard. War of 1812. Warships. 1812-13. *762*

Magazines. *See* Periodicals.

Magico-religious elements. British Columbia (Maillardville). Folklore. 1973-74. *3219*

Magnetic survey. Great Britain. Lefroy, John Henry (journals). Northwest Territories. Scientific Expeditions. 1843-44. *3306*

Mahood, Cecil S. Alberta (Calgary). Influenza epidemic. 1918-19. *3138*

Mail carriers. Alaska (Eagle). DeWolfe, Percy. Yukon Territory (Dawson). 1915-50. *3332*

Maine *See also* New England; Northeastern or North Atlantic States.

—. Algonkin Indians. Indians. Maritime Provinces. Missions and Missionaries. Social change. 1610-1750. *516*

—. British Columbia. Lumber and Lumbering. McInnis, George (interview). Washington. 1094-1949. *3261*

—. Champlain, Samuel de. Military Camps and Forts. Monts, Sieur de. New Brunswick. St. Croix Island. 1603-05. *507*

—. Franco-Americans. Immigration. ca 1870-20c. *2152*

—. Massachusetts. Newfoundland. Runestones. Vikings. 986-1121. *481*

Mair, Charles. Canada First (group). Expansionism. Red River Rebellion. Riel, Louis. 1869-70. *1009*

Mammals. Birds. Indians. Names. 1973. *379*

Management *See also* Arbitration, Industrial; Collective Bargaining; Executive Behavior; Industrial Relations.

—. Accident prevention. Working Conditions. 20c. *87*

—. Attitudes. Industrial relations. 1970's. *1614*

—. Bibliographies. Women. 1970-73. *1523*

—. British Columbia Electric Railway. Railroads. 1890-1920. *3245*

—. Economic Conditions. Labor. 1974. *1942*

—. Elites. Social mobility. 1880-85. 1905-10. *899*

—. Employment. Immigration Bill, 1976. 1976. *1394*

—. Industrial relations. Labor Unions and Organizations. USA. 1975. *1615*

—. Inflation. Labor. 1970's. *1521*

Management, scientific. Bureaucracies. USA. -1973. *1489*

Manchuria. Cahan, Charles H. (address). Japan. League of Nations Covenant. 1932-33. *1211*

Manhood ceremonies. Alberta. Blackfoot Indians. Rites and Ceremonies. Shaw, P. C. (personal account). 1894. *447*

Manitoba *See also* Prairie Provinces.

—. Agriculture. Business. Distribution system. Machinery. 1974. *2923*

—. Alberta. Military Medicine. North West Rebellion. Winnipeg Light Infantry. Pennefather, John P. (reminiscences). 1885. *1016*

—. Alberta (Edmonton). Farmer's Union of Alberta. Kyforuk, Peter. Ukrainian Labour-Farmer Association. 1912-30's. *2961*

—. Artists. Chippewa Indians. Cree Indians. Indians. Legend painting. Ontario. 1960's-70's. *470*

—. Assiniboia, Council of. French Canadians. Métis. 1860-71. *2910*

—. Botany (specimens). Burke, Joseph. Hudson's Bay Company. Northwest Territories. Royal Botanic Gardens. 1843-45. *2922*

—. Campaign Finance. Political success. Quebec. Voting and Voting Behavior. 1975. *1728*

—. Cannibalism tales. Fort Churchill. Fort York. Molden, John. Shipwrecks. 1833. *3012*

—. Catholic Church. Church Schools. McCarthy, D'Alton. Provincial legislatures. 1870-90. *931*

—. Catholic Church. Immigration. Mathieu, Olivier-Elzéar. Regina Archdiocese. Saskatchewan. 1911-31. *2936*

—. Chippewa Indians. Immigration. Mennonites, Russian. Métis. 1872-73. *990*

—. Churchill Forest Industry. Fraud. Political Crimes. ca 1965-74. *2982*

—. Co-operative Commonwealth Federation. Provincial Government. Social Democratic Party. Socialism. ca 1940. *3022*

—. Corbett, Griffiths Owen. Half-breeds (English). Métis. Red River Rebellion. 1863-70. *1014*

—. Cree Indians. Fort Pitt. Frenchman's Butte, Battle of. Indians. McLean, W. J. (diary). 1885. *1003*

—. Educational Policy. Goggin, David James. Northwest Territories. Teaching. ca 1890's. *2904*

—. Electric power. Ontario. Public Utilities. 1905-30. *2138*

—. French Canadians. Settlement. 1870-1920. *1013*

—. French Canadians. Social Customs. Vallee, Frank. 1970-74. *2970*

—. Funk, John F. Mennonites, Russian. Settlement. 1873. *993*

—. Fur Trade. Registered Trap Lines system. Trapping. Wells, Harold. 1940-53. *3011*

—. Great Plains. Immigration. Mennonites. Russia. 1871-74. *994*

—. Homesteading and Homesteaders. Locusts. Mortgages. 1875-1941. *3002*

—. Housing (low-cost). Intergovernmental relations. Remote Housing Program. 1968-70. *2988*

—. Immigrants. Mennonites, Russian. Russians. Shantz, Jacob Y. 1873. *1024*

—. Immigration. Mennonites, Bergthaler. Stocsz, David. Ukraine. 1872-76. *988*

—. Immigration. Mennonites, Russian. Russians. 1873. *989*

—. Immigration. Shantz, Jacob Y. Ukraine. 1870's. *992*

—. Jews. Physicians. 19c. *2994*

—. Labor (government workers). 1974. *3016*

—. Law Enforcement. North West Mounted Police. 1873-74. *2985*

—. Liberal Party. New Democratic Party. Progressive Conservative Party. Voting and Voting Behavior. 1953-73. *3020*

—. Liberal Party. Politics. Railroads. Schools. 1870's-90's. *2987*

—. Libraries. 1847-1974. *3008*

—. Medicine (practice of). Ross, Charlotte W. 1865-1916. *3009*

—. Mennonites. 1870-1900. *3005*

—. Mennonites, Russian. Settlement. 1870-80. *991*

—. Métis. Political theory. Red River Rebellion. Riel, Louis. 1869. *972*

—. Ontario. Winnipeg River. 1730's-1960's. *2122*

—. Pioneers. Red River of the North. Sutherland, Catherine McPherson. 1814-71. *1028*

—. Public Welfare. Social services. 1973. *3017*

—. Thanksgiving. 1763-1957. *41*

—. Ukrainian studies. 1949-74. *2999*

Manitoba (Assiniboia, Red River settlement). Local Government. Métis. 1857-65. *2911*

Manitoba (Aweme). Criddle, Percy. Diaries. Homesteading and Homesteaders. 1882-1900's. *954*

Manitoba (Beausejour). Glass works. Living conditions. Recreation. Working conditions. 1909-11. *3000*

Manitoba (Bender Hamlet). Jews. Settlement. 1910-49. *3001*

Manitoba (Brandon). Farms. Immigrants. Railroads. Wheat. 1880-87. *961*

Manitoba (Camperville, Duck Bay). Creek Indians. Missions and Missionaries. 1600-1938. *435*

Manitoba (Churchill). Children. Inkster, Anne Ellen (reminiscences). 1885-93. *2986*

Manitoba (Elliott Settlement). Lowes, Ellen McFadden (diary). Pioneers. 1888. *998*

Manitoba (Flin Flon). Cullity, Emmet K. (memoir). Gold Mines and Mining. Saskatchewan (Beaver Lake). 1915-27. *3041*

Manitoba (Gimli). Dufferin and Ava, 1st Marquis of (visit). Icelandic community. 1877. *969*

Manitoba Historical Society. Dalnavert Ball. Dance. 1892-1913. 1975. *2981*

Manitoba (Lisgar). Brown, J. L. Liberal Party. Parliaments. Winkler, H. W. (career). 1926-53. *3021*

Manitoba, northern. Churchill River. Ecology. Hydroelectric development. 1966-70's. *2972*

Manitoba (Portage la Prairie). Colleges and Universities. Collegiate Institute. Depressions. Lansdowne College. 1882-93. *3018*

Manitoba (Red River). Anglican Communion. Missionary wives. Missions and Missionaries. Women. 1820-37. *462*

Manitoba (Red River country). O'Beirne, Eugene Francis. Travel. 1860's. *3015*

Manitoba (Red River region). Frontier and Pioneer Life. North West Mounted Police. Sitting Bull (chief). Walsh, James. 1873-1905. *1030*

Manitoba (Red River Valley). Indians. Mennonites. Métis. Saskatchewan River Valley. Settlement. 1869-95. *963*

Manitoba (Selkirk). City planning. Hudson's Bay Company. 1869-79. *1023*

Manitoba, southeastern. Excavations. Indians. ca 8100-7600 BC. *305*

Manitoba, southwestern. Culture. Indians. Natural Resources. Pottery. Prehistory-18c. 1970's. *307*

—. Indians. Tools. Weapons. ca 10,000 BC-1600 AD. *308*

Manitoba, southwestern (Site DgMg-15). Excavations. Indians. Refuse pit. ca 1480-1740. *306*

Manitoba (Township Berlin). Lutheran Church, Missouri Synod. Wagner, William. ca 1870. *1029*

Manitoba, University of. Canadian International Development Agency. Higher Education. Thailand. 1964-74. *1911*

Manitoba (Virden). Canadian Pacific Railway. Construction crews. McLeod, Finlay J. C. (reminiscences). Presbyterian Church. 1881-82. *1005*

Manitoba (Winnipeg). Architecture. Post offices 1855-1974. *2979*

—. Bercuson, David J. (review article). General Strike. Industrial relations. Social organization. 1919. 1975. *1165*

—. Bill C-256. Businessmen. Communications. Federal Regulation. Public policy. 1971-72. *2971*

—. Bill of Incorporation (1873). City Government. Taxation. 1873. *2984*

—. British Columbia (Vancouver). Ideology. Methodology. Political Parties. 1967-69. *1727*

—. Buildings. 19c-1973. *3004*

—. Buildings. Cast iron fronts. Cauchon Block. 1880-1920. *3003*

—. Business. Economic growth. Political Leadership. Urbanization. 1874-1914. *2968*

—. Catholic Church. Chippewa Indians. Hudson's Bay Company. Métis. Provencher, John (mission). Quebec. 1812-36. *2948*

—. Children. Immigration. Jews. Public schools. 1900-20. *3007*

—. City Government. 1972-73. *2980*

—. City Government. Logan, Alexander. 1870's-80's. *2966*

—. City government. Political Corruption. Public Administration. Urbanization. 1884-85. *3013*

—. City Life. Immigration. Jews, Russian. 1874-82. *2965*

—. City Politics. Penner, Jacob. Webb, Ralph. 1919-34. *2993*

—. Discrimination. Ethnic groups. Immigrants. Population. 1874-1974. *2978*

—. Education. Red River Academy. 1820's-50's. *2973*

—. Ethnic Groups. Social Classes. Voting and Voting Behavior. 1941. *3014*

—. Ethnic Groups. Social Classes. Voting and Voting Behavior. 1945-46. *3023*

—. General strikes. 1919-70. *1116*

—. Immigration. Melnyk, George (reminiscences). 1949. 1977. *2995*

—. Institutional completeness. Minorities. Segregation, residential. -1974. *2978*

—. Jews. Pioneers. 1860's-1975. *2969*

—. Lectures. Minnesota (Crookston). Twain, Mark. 1895. *2989*

—. Local government. Political Reform. Working class. 1873-1971. *2990*

—. Local Government. Queen, John. Socialism. Taxation. 1909-42. *2992*

—. Métis. Minnesota (St. Paul). Prairies. Red River of the North. Trade. Trails. 19c. *976*

—. Ontario (Lake of the Woods). Water supply. 1912-75. *2997*

—. Penner, Jacob. Russia. Socialist movement. 1900-65. *2998*

—. Streetcars. Urbanization. 1881-1913. *3006*

Manitoba (Winnipeg Archdiocese). Catholics. Langevin, Adélard. 1905. *2974*

Manitoba (Winnipeg, East St. Boniface). Belgian families. Immigration. Nuytten, Edmund. Nuytten, Octavia. 1880-1914. *2991*

Manitoba (Winnipeg; North End, St. Boniface). Boundaries. Ethnic Groups. Neighborhoods. 19c-1978. *2977*

Manitoba (Winnipeg River; Pinawa Channel). Hydroelectric plants. Winnipeg Electrical Street Railway Co. 1903-51. *3010*

Manors. Land Tenure. St. Lawrence Valley. Social Classes. 1663-1840. 1840D 1800H. *538*

Manpower Programs, Federal. 1960's-1973. *1554*

Manpower training programs. Adult education. Public Finance. 1967-77. *1699*

Manufactures *See also* names of articles manufactured, e.g. Furniture, etc.; names of industries, e.g. Steel Industry and Trade, etc.; Corporations; Machinery; Prices.

—. Federal government. Fiscal Policy. Investments. 1965-74. *1569*

—. Material linkages. Quebec (Montreal). 1927-71. *2604*

Manufacturing. Capital. Employment. 1949-72. *1608*

—. Employment. Trade. 1949-70. *2145*

—. Federal regulation. Foreign investments. USA. 1950-75. *1782*

—. Foreign Investments. Great Britain. 1970-74. *1756*

—. Historiography. Merchants. 19c. 1975. *134*

—. Monopolies. Multinational corporations. 1970's. *1757*

Maoism. Elections. 1971-73. *1331*

—. Farmers. National Farmers Union (convention, 1972). 1972-73. *1507*

Maps. Public Archives of Canada. Research. Urban history. 1865-1905. *917*

—. Bibliographies. British Columbia. 1976-77. *3263*

—. British Library (Townshend archive). French and Indian War. Great Britain. Quebec (battle of). 1759. *609*

—. Discovery and Exploration. Geographical ideas, history of. Vinland Map. 1974. *484*

—. Ethnic groups. Methodology. North America. 1900-78. *1457*

—. North America. 16c-18c. *498*

Marine Engineering. Harbor Master. Ontario (Toronto). Richardson, Hugh. 1821-70. *2726*

Marine pollution. International cooperation. 1967-78. *1869*

Marine Resources *See also* Fishing.

—. Pollution. UN Conference on the Law of the Sea. 1974. *1902*

Marines *See also* Amphibious Operations; Navies.

—. American Revolution. Amphibious operations. Naval expeditions. Nova Scotia. 1654-1798. *724*

Maritime Fishermen's Union. Fishing industry. Nova Scotia. 1977. *2366*

Maritime history. *Pewaukee* (vessel). Shipwrecks. *Two Friends* (vessel). Wisconsin (North Bay, Milwaukee). 1873-1913. *1048*

Maritime Law *See also* Fishing Rights; Freight and Freightage; International Waters; Merchant Marine; Territorial Waters.

—. Conservation of Natural Resources. Foreign Relations. Navigation. USA. 1975. *2052*

—. Defense Policy. UN Conference on the Law of the Sea. 1977. *1764*

—. Diplomacy. Pacific Area, North. Territorial Waters. 1958-75. *1826*

—. UN. USA. 1970's. *2022*

—. USA. 1958-73. *1994*

Maritime law disputes. Boundaries. Gibbons, George Christie. USA. Water resources. 1905-10. *1113*

Maritime Provinces *See also* Atlantic Provinces.

—. Acadians. Catholic Church. English Canadians. Social Conditions. 1763-1977. *2171*

—. Algonkin Indians. Indians. Maine. Missions and Missionaries. Social change. 1610-1750. *516*

—. Antigonish movement. Cooperatives. Social economics. 1920's-40's. *2169*

—. Business history. 1800-1950. *2173*

—. Christianity. Cultural transmission. Micmac Indians. Western civilization. 1970's. *344*

—. Cooperatives. Prairie Provinces. 1900-55. *2136*

—. Council of Maritime Premiers. Regional Government. 1971-76. *2164*

—. Depressions. Emigration. Massachusetts (Boston). New England. 1860-1900. *2154*

—. Economic growth. Newfoundland. 1880-1940. *2151*

—. Historiography. 1900-67. *59*

—. Politics. Prairie Provinces. Provincial Government. 1910-27. *2125*

—. Regionalism. 1960-74. *2135*

—. Regionalism. Self-perception. 1911-72. *2153*

Maritime Rights Movement. Atlantic Provinces. Reform. Regionalism. 1900-25. *2158*

Maritime Union Movement. Economic growth. Federal policy. Nova Scotia. Regional development. 1783-1974. *2167*

Markers. National Museum of Science and Technology. Surveying. 1765-19c. 1960-70. *129*

Market economy. Agriculture. Europe. Industrialization. North America. Peasant movements (colloquium). ca 1875-1975. *13*

Market structure. Auto replacements. Trade. USA. -1973. *2027*

—. Industry. Research. 1973. *1545*

Marketing. Gasoline Licensing Act (1934). Nova Scotia Board of Commissioners of Public Utilities. Provincial Government. 1960's-74. *2283*

Marketing (wholesale). Business History. Ontario (Hamilton). 1840-75. *2823*

Markets. Farm. Land use. Quebec. 1908-71. *2661*

Marriage *See also* Divorce; Family; Sex.

—. Alberta. Bachelors. Calgary *Herald*, newspaper. Frontier. 1895. *956*

—. Birth rate. Demography. Ethnic variations. Immigrants. 1871. *1072*

—. Family. North America. Sociology. Women. 1974. *1469*

Marsh, Donald B. (reminiscences). Eskimos, Sadlermiut. Gibbons, Jimmy (interview). Housing. Northwest Territories (Southampton Island). ca 1900. *328*

Marsh, Leonard *(Report)*. Social Security. Socialism. Welfare state. 1930-44. *1200*

Marshall, John George. Diaries. Hurricanes. Nova Scotia (Guysborough County). 1811. *2223*

—. Nova Scotia (Cape Breton). Roads. 1823-26. *2222*

Marshall, Samuel. Knollin, William Mortimer. Nova Scotia. Pioneers. Villiers, Charles E. 19c. *2309*

Martello towers. Architecture. Military Camps and Forts. USA. 19c. *188*

—. Artillery. Military Capability. 1796-1871. *198*

—. Excavations. Ontario (Kingston, Market Shoal). 19c. 1972. *856*

Martin, Méderic. Bossism. Houde, Camillien. Local government. Quebec (Montreal). 1923-29. *2446*

Marxism *See also* Class Struggle; Communism; Social Democratic Party; Socialism; Syndicalism.

—. Bergeron, Léandre (review article). Historiography. Quebec. 1970-75. *2618*

—. Democracy. Humanism. MacPherson, C. B. Political Theory. 1976. *1338*

—. Juvenile Delinquency. Legislation. Social history. 1870's-1970's. *76*

—. Labor. Women (review article). 19c-1976. *71*

—. Political Reform. Quebec. Revolution. 1960-65. *2640*

Maryland *See also* Southeastern States.

Masak (personal account). Eskimos. Northwest Territories (Aklavik). Socialization. 1930's. *324*

Maskipiton (identity). Cree Indians. Prairie Provinces. 1830's-50's. *443*

Mass Media *See also* Films; Newspapers; Radio; Television.

—. Arctic. Eskimos. Federal government. Satellite service. 1972. *329*

—. Art. Cultural relations. Poland. USA. 1940-74. *1953*

—. Assimilation. Cultural autonomy. Italians. Ontario (Toronto). 1970's. *2735*

—. Democracy. Foreign policy. Totalitarianism. 1960-76. *1924*

—. Foreign policy. 19c-20c. *1743*

—. Novels. USA. 1960-72. *1999*

—. Science and Society. Teachers. Values. Youth. 1920's-75. *1391*

Mass Transit *See also* Public Transportation; Subways.

—. Automobiles. Motoring, urban. North America. Travel. 1960-75. *2758*

—. Ontario. Public Utilities. Toronto Railway Company. 1891-1921. *2760*

Massachusetts *See also* New England; Northeastern or North Atlantic States.

—. Artists. Cleveland, Xenophon. New Brunswick. Stencils. 1839-99. *2379*

—. Diseases. Leprosy. New Brunswick. Social stigma. 1844-80. 1904-21. *2391*

—. Fellows family. Genealogy. Nova Scotia (Granville). 1635-1977. *2240*

—. Genealogy. Great Britain. Morris family. Nova Scotia. 18c-19c. *2242*

—. Maine. Newfoundland. Runestones. Vikings. 986-1121. *481*

Massachusetts (Boston). Atlantic Provinces. Economic conditions. Immigration. Kennedy, Albert J. 1910's. *2162*

—. Depressions. Emigration. Maritime Provinces. New England. 1860-1900. *2154*

—. New Brunswick (Saint John). Steamships. Trade. 1836-1945. *2390*

—. Nova Scotia (Halifax). Steamship lines. 1840-1917. *2287*

—. Nova Scotia (Yarmouth). Steamship services. Transportation. 1855-1971. *2288*

—. Ponzi, Charles (pseud. of Charles Bianchi). Securities. 1919-20. *1187*

Massachusetts (Cambridge). Harvard University. Leverett, John. Quebec Expedition. Speeches, Addresses, etc. 1711. *610*

Massachusetts (Chicopee). Chicopee Manufacturing Company. Immigration. Irish Americans. Mills. Nativism. 1830-75. *635*

Massachusetts (Fall River). Immigrants. Labor Unions and Organizations. Textile industry. 1890-1905. *2659*

Massachusetts (Gloucester). Acadians. Assimilation. Nova Scotia (Arichat region). 1850's-1900. *2364*

Massachusetts (Holyoke). French Canadians. Immigration. Proulx, Nicholas. Working Class. 1850-1900. *2600*

Massachusetts (Lowell). Mills, woolen and cotton. Textile Industry. Women. 1833-57. *2664*

Massachusetts (Nantucket Island). American Revolution. Friends, Society of. Whaling Industry and Trade. 1750's-1800. *733*

Massachusetts (Springfield). Cotton mills. French Canadians. Immigration. Statistics. 1870. *2607*

Massey Commission. Colleges and Universities. Federal Aid to Education. National Conference of Canadian Universities. 1951-66. *1476*

Massey-Harris plant. Industrial council. Ontario (Toronto). Public relations. 1919-29. *1188*

Mast policy, royal. Forests and Forestry. Great Britain. Kennebeck Purchase Company. New England. Wentworth, John. 1769-78. *718*

Material linkages. Manufactures. Quebec (Montreal). 1927-71. *2604*

Mathias, Philip. Economic Growth. Federal Government. Free trade. 1973. *1266*

Mathieu, Olivier-Elzéar. Anglophiles. Francophiles. Saskatchewan (Regina). 1905-30. *3035*

—. Catholic Church. Immigration. Manitoba. Regina Archdiocese. Saskatchewan. 1911-31. *2936*

Maungwudaus (George Henry). Catlin, George. Chippewa Indians. Europe. Ontario. Theater. 1840's. *450*

Maurras, Charles. Conservatism. France. French Canadians. Groulx, Lionel. Nationalism. 1910-40. *1141*

Maxwell, Thomas R. Assimilation. Choquette, Robert. French Canadians (review article). Joy, Richard. 18c-20c. 1970's. *218*

Mayflower (Trailing Arbutus). Nova Scotia. Provincial Flowers. 1834-1901. *2254*

Mayo, Bernard. Festschriften publications. Kniffen, Fred B. Morris, Richard B. Talman, James J. 1863-1974. *109*

Mayors. Armstrong, Frederick H. Mackenzie, William Lyon. Ontario (Toronto). 1835-37. 1967. *2854*

McCabe, James (and descendants). Irish Canadians. Nova Scotia (Pictou). Pennsylvania (Philadelphia). ca 1743-1917. *2306*

McCarthy, D'Alton. Catholic Church. Church Schools. Manitoba. Provincial legislatures. 1870-90. *931*

—. Ontario. Politics. Social reform. 1876-98. *1057*

McCaul, Charles Coursolles. Lawyers. 1883-1928. *1019*

McClellan, George B. (reminiscences). Alberta (Edmonton). Royal Canadian Mounted Police. 1932-63. *3135*

McClung, Nellie L. Feminism. Literature. Politics.
Reform. 1873-1930's. *1189*
McClung, Nellie (review article). Feminism.
1902-15. *1097*
McCulloch, Thomas. Dalhousie College. Missions
and Missionaries. Nova Scotia. Pictou
Academy. Presbyterian Church. ca 1803-42.
2215
—. Education. Nova Scotia. Pictou Grammar
School. 19c. *2337*
McCulloch, Thomas *(Letters of Mephibosheth
Stepsure)*. Literature. Nova Scotia.
Presbyterian Church. Satire. 1821-22. *2339*
McDonald, Alexander N. Contracts. Nova Scotia
(Sherbrooke). Shipbuilding. Sutherland, Peter.
1873-74. *2265*
McDonald, Donald. Immigrants. Millenarianism.
Prince Edward Island. Scottish Canadians.
ca 1828-67. *2209*
McDonald, Robert. Church of England. Indians.
Missions and Missionaries. Northwest
Territories. Yukon Territory. 1850's-1913.
3292
McDonnell Aircraft Corporation. F2H-3 aircraft.
Naval Air Forces. 1956-63. *1272*
McDonnell, John. Baldwin, William Warren.
Duels. Ontario (Upper Canada). 1812. *2842*
McDougall, John. Alberta (Calgary, Banff). Travel.
1873-1902. *3137*
—. Indians. Missions and Missionaries. Prairie
provinces. Wesleyan Methodist. 1860-1917.
386
McDowall, Robert James. Exiles. Loyalists.
Missions and Missionaries. Ontario (Upper
Canada). Reformed Dutch Church. 1790-1819.
747
McDowell, Eugene A. Theater (tours). USA.
1875-90. *1054*
McGavin Toastmaster Limited v. Ainscough et al.
(Canada, 1975). Collective bargaining. Strikes.
Supreme Court. 1975-77. *1329*
McGee, D'Arcy. Anglin, Timothy Warren.
Fenians. Irish Canadians. Political debates.
1863-68. *891*
McGill University. Medical licensing. Montreal
Medical Board. 1833-34. *2573*
McInnis, George (interview). British Columbia.
Lumber and Lumbering. Maine. Washington.
1894-1949. *3261*
McKenzie, "Steamboat Bill" (reminiscences).
Saskatchewan. Steamboats. Transportation,
Commercial. 1901-25. *3036*
McKim, Andrew. Nova Scotia. Politics. Provincial
Legislatures. 1784-1840. *2348*
McLachlan, Alexander. Ontario. Poetry. Radicals
and Radicalism. Social reform. Working class.
1818-96. *924*
McLean, W. J. (diary). Cree Indians. Fort Pitt.
Frenchman's Butte, Battle of. Indians.
Manitoba. 1885. *1003*
McLeod, Evelyn Slater (reminiscences). Alberta
(Stettler). Frontier and Pioneer Life. 1900's.
3139
McLeod, Finlay J. C. (reminiscences). Canadian
Pacific Railway. Construction crews. Manitoba
(Virden). Presbyterian Church. 1881-82.
1005
McLoughlin, John. Fort Vancouver. Fur trade.
Hudson's Bay Company. Pacific Northwest.
1825-60. *861*
McMahon, Patrick. Catholic Church. Irish
Canadians. Poor. Quebec (Quebec). St.
Bridget's Home. 1847-1972. *2541*
McMaster, Susan Moulton Fraser. Baptist.
Christian Biography. Ontario (Toronto).
1819-1916. *2750*
McMurray, William. Church of England. Clergy.
1810-94. *665*
—. Fort McMurray. Moberly, Henry John.
Trading posts. 1870's. *935*
McNab, Allan. Family Compact. Political reform.
1838-44. *825*
McNailly, John Thomas. Alberta (Calgary Diocese).
Catholic Church. French Canadians. Irish
Canadians. 1871-1952. *3095*
Measurements *See also* Methodology.
—. Port activity. Quebec. St. Lawrence River
(south shore). 1944-66. *2660*
Meat. Animal husbandry. Frontier. Prince
Rupert's Land. 18c-20c. *2942*
Meat packing industry. Saskatchewan. 1879-1973.
3032
Mechanics' Institutes. Libraries. Ontario
(Napanee). Social Classes. 1850-1900. *914*
Mechanization. Diffusion theories. Ontario.
Reaping. Technology. 1850-70. *2846*
Medical licensing. McGill University. Montreal
Medical Board. 1833-34. *2573*

Medical reform. Physicians. Quebec. 1940-70.
2614
—. Quebec. 1975. *2554*
Medical Research. Autopsies. Osler, William.
ca 1876-1900. *2552*
Medicine *See also* headings beginning with the word
medical; Hospitals; Military Medicine;
Pharmacy; Physicians.
Medicine and State *See also* Public Health.
—. Public Health. Quebec. Regional councils.
Social services. 1971-74. *2547*
Medicine (practice of) *See also* Diseases.
—. Adamson, John. Cholera cures, ineffective.
Nova Scotia (Halifax). 1834. *2219*
—. Anatomy, morbid. Dreams. Osler, William.
USA. 1872-1919. *908*
—. Chloroform. Fraser, James Daniel Bain.
Nova Scotia (Pictou). Pharmacy. 1807-69.
2247
—. Cholera. Quebec (Lower Canada). 1832.
770
—. Manitoba. Ross, Charlotte W. 1865-1916.
3009
—. Nova Scotia (Kentville). Sanatoriums.
Tuberculosis. 1904-78. *2284*
Medley, John (letters). Church of England. New
Brunswick (Fredericton). Oxford Movement.
Pusey, Edward Bouverie. ca 1840-44. *2389*
Meisel, John (review). Ethnic Groups. Politics.
Simeon, Richard (review). 1960-68. *1713*
Melnyk, George (reminiscences). Immigration.
Manitoba (Winnipeg). 1949. 1977. *2995*
Melville, Herman. Lectures. Quebec (Montreal).
1857. *2519*
Melyn, Cornelis. Fur trade. New England. Nova
Scotia. 1633-52. *569*
Memoirs. *See* Autobiography and Memoirs; also
individual names with the subdivisions
(autobiography) or (memoir) or (reminiscences).
Men. Economic Conditions. Unemployment.
USA. Women. 1950-73. *1533*
Mennonite Conference of 1970 (leaders). Church
and State. Social issues. Students. 1917-74.
1381
Mennonite history resources. Archives, public.
19c-1975. *39*
Mennonites. Alberta. Farming. Namaka Farm.
1920's-40's. *3121*
—. Alberta (Coaldale). Community organizations.
Germans, Russian. Social Change. 1920-76.
3145
—. Amish. Dukhobors. Hutterites. Molokans.
North America. ca 1650-1977. *184*
—. Atlantic Provinces. Settlement. 1950-70.
2168
—. Baerg, Anna (diary). Immigration. Russian
Revolution. 1917-23. *1171*
—. Brubacher brothers. Letters. Ontario.
Pennsylvania. 1817-46. *786*
—. Conference of Historic Peace Churches. World
War II. ca 1914-45. *1235*
—. Conservatism. Liberalism. Ontario (Waterloo
County). 1977. *2767*
—. *Der Bote* (newspaper). Germans, Russian.
Nazism. Saskatchewan. USSR. Völkisch
thought. 1917-39. *3077*
—. Eby, Ezra E. Immigration. Loyalists.
Pennsylvania. 18c-1835. *743*
—. Emigration. Epp, Johann (letter). North
America. Russia. 1875. *981*
—. Farmers. French Canadians. Kansas. Swedish
Americans. 1875-1925. *150*
—. Folk Art. Fraktur. Ontario (Waterloo
County). Weber, Anna. 1825-88. *2836*
—. Great Plains. Immigration. Manitoba. Russia.
1871-74. *994*
—. Immigration. Ukraine. 1922-23. *1173*
—. Indians. Manitoba (Red River Valley). Métis.
Saskatchewan River Valley. Settlement.
1869-95. *963*
—. Manitoba. 1870-1900. *3005*
—. Missions and Missionaries. USA. 1880-1910.
941
—. Ontario (Oxford, Waterloo Counties).
1839-1974. *2739*
—. Russian Canadians. Saskatchewan (Rosthern).
Settlement. 1891-1900. *1036*
—. Saskatchewan (Hague-Osler area). Settlement.
Social Change. 1895-1977. *3044*
—. Social Customs. Urbanization. USA. 1961-71.
1379
Mennonites, Bergthaler. Immigration. Manitoba.
Stoesz, David. Ukraine. 1872-76. *988*
Mennonites, Russian. Chippewa Indians.
Immigration. Manitoba. Métis. 1872-73.
990
—. Funk, John F. Manitoba. Settlement. 1873.
993

—. Immigrants. Manitoba. Russians. Shantz,
Jacob Y. 1873. *1024*
—. Immigration. Manitoba. Russians. 1873.
989
—. Immigration. Passenger lists. Quebec.
1874-80. *966*
—. Immigration. Saskatchewan (Rosthern). Social
conditions. 1923. *3052*
—. Manitoba. Settlement. 1870-80. *991*
Menominee Indians. Blackfoot Indians. Identity.
Indians. Militancy. 1950's-60's. *457*
Mental health. British Columbia (Kitsilano).
Community services. Politics. Psychiatry.
1973-74. *3237*
Mental Illness *See also* Psychiatry.
—. Asylums. New Brunswick. Nova Scotia.
1749-1900. *2159*
—. Catholic Church. General Hospital. Quebec.
1692-1845. *2543*
—. Psychiatry. Quebec. Sociology. 1717-1960.
2513
—. Riel, Louis. Saskatchewan (Regina). Treason.
Trials. Valade, François-Xavier (medical
report). 1885. *973*
Mentally handicapped. Nova Scotia. Organizations.
Social Reform. ca 1900-27. *2245*
Menzies, Archibald. Great Britain. Landscape
Painting. Nature. Vancouver, George. ca
1775-1800. *633*
Merchant Marine *See also* Ships.
—. Atlantic Provinces. Boardinghouses.
Government. Labor. Social reform. ca
1850's-90's. *916*
Merchants. Fur Trade. Quebec (Montreal). Social
Classes. 1750-75. *703*
—. Historiography. Manufacturing. 19c. 1975.
134
—. Taylor and Drury, Ltd. Yukon Territory.
1898-1924. *3342*
Mercier, Honoré. Jesuits. Land Tenure.
Legislation. Protestant Churches. Quebec.
1886. *2645*
Mercury poisoning. Ontario, northwestern.
Pollution. Regional government. 1970's.
2781
Mergers. British Columbia (Fraser River). Canning
industry. Labor. Salmon. 1885-1902. *3240*
Messianic Movements. North West Rebellion.
Prairie Provinces. Religion. Riel, Louis.
1869-85. *971*
Meteorites. Alberta. Blackfoot Indians. Cree
Indians. 1810-1973. *442*
Meteorology *See also* Climate; Cyclones; Droughts;
Hurricanes; Snow; Storms.
—. Alberta (Banff). Sanson, Norman Bethune
(biography). 1896-99. *3153*
Methodism. Bland, Salem. Theology. 1880-86.
1038
—. Coughlin, Lawrence. Newfoundland.
1765-1815. *2191*
—. Courtship. Field, Eliza. Great Britain
(London). Indians. Jones, Peter. New York.
1820's-33. *451*
—. Evangelism. United Church of Canada.
18c-20c. *85*
—. Missions and Missionaries. New York
Conference. 1766-1862. *677*
—. Social gospel movement. 1890-1914. *1089*
Methodist Church. Archives. Presbyterian Church.
United Church of Canada. 18c-1973. *233*
—. Cree Indians. Evans, James. Missions and
Missionaries. 1833-46. *651*
—. Evangelism. Holiness Movement Church.
Horner, Ralph Cecil. 1887-1921. *1064*
—. Evangelism. Holiness Movement Church.
Horner, Ralph Cecil. 1887-1921. *1065*
—. Frontier. Missions and Missionaries.
1840-1925. *950*
—. Nova Scotia (Springhill). Presbyterian Church.
St. Andrew's Wesley United Church of Canada.
1800-1976. *2233*
—. Regionalism. Trades and Labour Congress of
Canada. Two-party system. 1870-1919. *2916*
Methodist Episcopal Church. 1788-1812. *671*
—. Cromwell, James. Garrettson, Freeborn.
Missions and Missionaries. Nova Scotia. USA.
1785-1800. *2315*
Methodists, Primitive. Agricultural colony. Bee,
William. Saskatchewan (Grenfell). 1882.
949
Methodology *See also* Measurements; Models;
Quantitative Methods; Research.
—. Algonquin College Resource Centre.
Bibliography, regional. Ontario (Ottawa).
1974-78. *2142*
—. British Columbia (Vancouver). Ideology.
Manitoba (Winnipeg). Political Parties.
1967-69. *1727*

—. Business history. Naylor, R. T. (*A History of Canadian Business, 1867-1914*). 1867-1914. *933*
—. Census. Documents. Literacy. 1861. *852*
—. Census. Literacy. Ontario (Peel, Hamilton Counties). Social organization. 19c. *2822*
—. Census. New Brunswick (Saint John). Social organization. 1871. 1974. *2400*
—. Census. Population. Quebec (Quebec). 1795-1805. 1974-76. *2584*
—. Demography. Family reconstitution studies. Migration, Internal. Quebec (Laterrière). 1855-1970. *2474*
—. Employment. Families (low-income). Models. 1974. *1510*
—. Ethnic groups. Maps. North America. 1900-78. *1457*
—. Genealogy. Lewis, Waitsill (family). Nova Scotia (Yarmouth). 1976. *2212*
—. Land Tenure. Quebec (Saguenay County). 1840-1975. *2633*
—. Migration, Internal. Quebec (Saguenay region). 1842-1931. *2545*
—. Oral history. 1930's-70's. *1323*
—. Political participation. 1974. *1641*
—. Political Science. 1974. *1309*
—. Politics. Public opinion. 1970's. *1687*
—. Urban history. 1960's-70's. *224*
Métis. Alberta, northern. Indians. Jackson, Mary Percy. Physicians. 1929-70's. *3119*
—. Art. Chippewa Indians. Cree Indians. Prairie Provinces. 1750's-1850's. *357*
—. Assiniboia, Council of. French Canadians. Manitoba. 1860-71. *2910*
—. Bibliographies. Eskimos. Indians. 1975. *283*
—. Big Bear. North West Rebellion. Poundmaker. Trials. 1885. *948*
—. Catholic Church. Chippewa Indians. Hudson's Bay Company. Provencher, John N. (memoir). Quebec. Red River Settlement. 1812-36. *2948*
—. Children. Education. Fur trade. Hudson's Bay Company. 1820's-60's. *628*
—. Chippewa Indians. Immigration. Manitoba. Mennonites, Russian. 1872-73. *990*
—. Corbett, Griffiths Owen. Half-breeds (English). Manitoba. Red River Rebellion. 1863-70. *1014*
—. Education. Employment. Hudson Bay. Hudson's Bay Company. 1790's-1820's. *771*
—. Education. Eskimos. Indians. Northwest Territories (Mackenzie District). Whites. 1969-70. *3358*
—. Education. Federal government. Indians. 1940-70. *361*
—. Government commissions. Indians. Land claims. Prairie Provinces. 1885-1900. *396*
—. Indians. Manitoba (Red River Valley). Mennonites. Saskatchewan River Valley. Settlement. 1869-95. *963*
—. Indians. Smallpox. Traders. Vaccination program. 1837-38. *439*
—. Lindsay, James. Military Campaigns. Red River Expedition. 1869-70. *999*
—. Local Government. Manitoba (Assiniboia, Red River settlement). 1857-65. *2911*
—. Manitoba. Political theory. Red River Rebellion. Riel, Louis. 1869. *972*
—. Manitoba (Winnipeg). Minnesota (St. Paul). Prairies. Red River of the North. Trade. Trails. 19c. *976*
—. Nolin, Jean-Baptiste (and daughters). Prairie Provinces. Red River of the North. St. Boniface School. 1760-1840. *776*
—. Prairie Provinces. Religion. Riel, Louis (letter). Taché, Alexandre. 1880's. *974*
Metropolitan Areas *See also* Cities; Urban Renewal.
—. Autocovariance procedures. Ontario, southern. Population. 1871-1975. *2732*
—. City Government. Libraries. 1950-71. *1361*
Mexico. Bicycle industry. Labor. Production. USA. 1972-76. *1906*
—. Bilateral commissions. Judicial organizations, international. USA. 19c-1974. *262*
—. Boundaries. Environmental control. International Boundary and Water Commission. International Joint Commission. USA. 1973. *2053*
—. Civil rights. Law. USA. Violence. 18c-1974. *52*
—. Diplomatic relations. Foreign Policy. USA. 1945-74. *1860*
—. Foreign Relations. 1944-73. *1754*
—. Immigration. DeLaGarza, E. (Kika). Public Policy. USA. 1910-74. *1732*
—. International Trade (nontariff barriers). Tariff. USA. 1946-74. *1954*

—. Locomotives rosters. Railroads. USA. 1911-78. *48*
Meyer, Rudolf. Aristocracy. Estate ownership. France. Roffignac, Yves de. Saskatchewan (Eastern Assiniboia; Whitewood). 1885-1900. *982*
—. Aristocracy. France. Saskatchewan (Pipestone Creek, Whitewood). Settlement. 1880's. *985*
M'Grath, Michael. Devit, Charles. Nova Scotia (Halifax). Trials. Westmacott, John (murder of). 1816. *2243*
Michigan *See also* North Central States.
Michigan (Detroit). British North America. Fur Trade. Garrison towns. Military Camps and Forts. Quebec (Montreal). 1760-75. *637*
—. Seigniorialism, French. Social organization. 1701-1837. *583*
Michigan (Port Huron). Ontario (Sarnia). Railroad tunnels. St. Clair River. Transportation, Commercial. 1884-91. *108*
Micmac Indians. Acadia. Copper kettles. Mobility. Settlement. 17c. *424*
—. Art. Atlantic Provinces. 17c-1974. *420*
—. Baptists. Language. Missions and Missionaries. Nova Scotia. Rand, Silas Tertius. 1830-89. *422*
—. Bromley, Walter. Nova Scotia. Self-help. Urban poor. 1813-25. *2258*
—. Christianity. Cultural transmission. Maritime Provinces. Western civilization. 1970's. *344*
—. Christianization. Indian-White Relations. New Brunswick. Nova Scotia. 1803-60. *465*
—. Cultural ecology. European contact. 15c-18c. *423*
—. Diseases. Indians. Population. 16c-17c. *302*
—. France. Great Britain. Indian-White Relations. Prince Edward Island. 1763-1873. *468*
Middle Classes. Adult education. Halifax Mechanics' Institute. Nova Scotia. Working class. 1830's-40's. *2291*
—. Adult education. Libraries. Social Organization. Working class. 19c. *104*
—. Business. Civil service. Quebec. Technocracy. 1939-75. *2451*
—. Commerce. France. Fur trade. Great Britain. Quebec (Montreal). 1750-92. *702*
—. Consumers. Newspapers. Ombudsmen. 1970's. *1299*
—. Depressions. 1930's. *1201*
—. Federal government. Language policy. Modernization. Provincial government. Quebec. 1960-76. *2090*
—. Physical education and training. Sports. 1850-1900. *930*
—. Quebec. 1850-1914. *2442*
Middle powers. Australia. Germany. Political integration. South Africa. 1850-1900. *903*
Midland Continental Railroad. North Dakota. Railroads. Seiberling, Frank A. 1912-20. *2983*
Midwest. Alberta (Banff). Elites. Power, interorganizational. 1960's-70's. *3123*
—. Politics. Reciprocity. USA. 1909-11. *1110*
Migrant labor. Census. Construction. Irish Canadians. Quebec (Sherbrooke area). Railroads. 1851-53. *2520*
Migrants. Ethnic stigma. Impression management. Indian-White Relations. 1967-68. *371*
Migration *See also* Emigration; Immigration; Refugees.
—. Charbonneau, Hubert. Dechêne, Louise (review article). Family structure. Quebec. Vital Statistics. 1660-1713. 1974-75. *527*
—. Indians. USA. 1972. *407*
—. MacLeod, Norman. Nova Scotia (St. Ann's). Presbyterian Church. Scotland. ca 1800-50's. *2244*
Migration, Internal *See also* Geographic Mobility.
—. 1964-74. *1477*
—. Attitudes. Rural-Urban Studies. Urbanization. 1955-75. *1366*
—. Catholic Church. French Canadians. Parishes. Quebec (Compton County). Rural-Urban Studies. 1851-91. *2534*
—. Demography. Family reconstitution studies. Methodology. Quebec (Laterrière). 1855-1970. *2474*
—. Economic Conditions. USA. 1960's-70's. *1415*
—. Government policy. Immigration. 1896-1973. *99*
—. Labor. Lowry, Ira S. Models. Quebec. -1973. *2593*
—. Methodology. Quebec (Saguenay region). 1842-1931. *2545*
—. North West Rebellion. Prairie Provinces. 1885. *995*

Miles, Walter K. (and ancestors). British Columbia. Great Britain. 1602-1977. *3229*
Militancy. Blackfoot Indians. Identity. Indians. Menominee Indians. 1950's-60's. *457*
Military *See also* headings beginning with the words military and paramilitary; Aeronautics, Military; Air Warfare; Armaments; Armies; Artillery; Cavalry; Conscription, Military; Defense Policy; Logistics; Navies; Uniforms, Military; War.
—. American Revolution. Congress. Hazen, Moses. 1776-1803. *734*
—. American Revolution (antecedents). Georgia. Great Britain. Immigrants. Nova Scotia. 1765-75. *729*
—. Canals. Imperial funds (diversion). Ottawa-Rideau military canal. 1815-25. *799*
—. Caribbean Region. Garrison duty. Great Britain. 1914-45. *1131*
—. Civil War. Great Britain. Williams, William Fenwick. 1859-67. *881*
—. Economics. Foreign policy. Politics. 1950's-70's. *1856*
—. Land grants. Ontario (Upper Canada). Settlement. 1816-20. *788*
—. NATO. Political strategy. 1969. *1755*
—. Technology. Weapons. 1970-76. *1277*
Military Biography *See also* names of wars with the subdivision biography, e.g. World War II (biography).
—. Bradstreet, John. Great Britain. Louisbourg, Fortress of. Nova Scotia. 1739-74. *604*
Military Campaigns. Lindsay, James. Métis. Red River Expedition. 1869-70. *999*
Military Camps and Forts *See also* names of military camps and forts, e.g. Fort Apache; Fortification.
—. Alberta (Writing-On-Stone, Milk River). Indians. Law Enforcement. North West Mounted Police. 1887-1918. *957*
—. Architecture. France. Guardhouses. Louisbourg, Fortress of. Nova Scotia. 1713-68. *616*
—. Architecture. Martello towers. USA. 19c. *188*
—. British North America. Fur Trade. Garrison towns. Michigan (Detroit). Quebec (Montreal). 1760-75. *637*
—. Champlain, Samuel de. Maine. Monts, Sieur de. New Brunswick. St. Croix Island. 1603-05. *507*
—. Construction. France. Lime preparation. Louisbourg, Fortress of. Nova Scotia. 1725-58. *615*
—. Excavations. Gunflints. Louisbourg, Fortress of. Nova Scotia. 1720-60. *608*
—. Louisbourg, fortress of. Nova Scotia. Restorations. 1654-1745. 1928-73. *613*
Military Capability. Artillery. Martello towers. 1796-1871. *198*
Military Education *See also* names of service academies, e.g. US Military Academy, West Point, etc.; Military Camps and Forts.
—. Canadian Armed Forces Command and Staff College. Ontario (Toronto). 1966-74. *1312*
Military expeditions, English. Nova Scotia (Port Royal). Phips, William (journal). 1690. *611*
Military Finance. Great Britain. World War II. 1943-45. *1227*
Military General Staff. Casualty rates. Currie, Arthur. Hughes, Sam. World War I. 1914-30. *1156*
Military History *See also* Military Biography.
—. Amherst, Jeffrey. French and Indian War. Iroquois Indians. New France. Pontiac's Rebellion. 1760-65. *612*
Military installations. British colonial materials. Excavations. Newfoundland (Signal Hill National Historic Park). 1800-60. 1965-66. *2186*
Military Medicine. Alberta. North West Rebellion. Pennefather, John P. (reminiscences). Winnipeg Light Infantry. 1885. *1016*
Military museum (collection). Flags. North America. Volunteers. Yugoslavia (Belgrade). 1917-18. 1974. *1162*
Military Occupation. American Revolution. Attitudes. Carleton, Guy. Peasants. Quebec. 1775-76. *717*
Military operations. Europe. Politics. World War II. 1939-45. *1244*
Military planning. Attitudes. USA. 1776-1976. *178*
Military Recruitment *See also* Conscription, Military.
—. Crimean War. Great Britain. Howe, Joseph. USA. 1854-56. *867*

Military Service. British Columbia. Chinese. Japanese Canadians. World War II. 1939-45. *1242*

—. Cobbett, William. New Brunswick. 1785-91. *629*

—. French Canadians. World War II. 1939-45. *1228*

—. Political Campaigns. Voting and Voting Behavior. World War I. 1917. *1159*

Military service, British. Boer War. Patriotism. Socioeconomic characteristics. Volunteers. 1899-1902. *1099*

Military Strategy See also Logistics; Naval Strategy.

—. American Revolution. Gates, Horatio. 1777-80. *721*

—. Arctic. 1945-77. *3286*

—. Armies. Larsen, Lawrence W. (paper). North Dakota. 1919. 1975. *1157*

—. Atlantic region. Buchan, Alastair. Foreign Relations. Institute of Strategic Studies. 1958-75. *1913*

—. Defense policy. 1957-77. *1291*

—. Defense policy. Economic Conditions. Government. NATO. 1973-76. *1863*

—. Defense policy. Force, attitudes toward. 1970's. *1278*

—. Defense policy. North American Air Defense Command. USA. 1930's-70's. *1988*

—. Jackman, Alonzo. New York. Quebec. Travel. Vermont. 1838. *2443*

Military structure. Defense Policy. USA. 1963-70's. *2004*

Military Uniforms. See Uniforms, Military.

Militia. Defense Policy. Hartford Convention. New England. War of 1812. 1812-15. *757*

—. Labor disputes. Nova Scotia (Cape Breton Island). 1920's. *2298*

Millenarianism. Immigrants. McDonald, Donald. Prince Edward Island. Scottish Canadians. ca 1828-67. *2209*

Miller, Alfred J. Art (romantic, review article). Bartlett, William Henry. Indians. ca 1840-70. *659*

Mills. Chicopee Manufacturing Company. Immigration. Irish Americans. Massachusetts (Chicopee). Nativism. 1830-75. *635*

Mills, water-powered. 1607-1975. *183*

Mills (cotton, woolen). Massachusetts (Lowell). Textile Industry. Women. 1833-57. *2664*

—. Industry. Women. 1833-57. *2664*

Mina (Eskimo woman). Eskimos. Hudson Bay. Religion. 1940's-50's. *326*

Mineral Resources. Developing nations. Economic Policy. Mines. 1960-77. *1779*

—. Fur trade. Hudson's Bay Company. North America. 17c-20c. *258*

—. Industrialization. Mining. USA. 1700-1977. *208*

Mines. Developing nations. Economic Policy. Mineral Resources. 1960-77. *1779*

—. Natural Resources. Saskatchewan. 1960-74. *3064*

—. Ports. Quebec (Havre, Saint Pierre). 1948-73. *2628*

Mining See also specific types of mining, e.g. Silver Mining.

—. Alaska. Arctic. Scandinavia. USSR. 1917-78. *3288*

—. Assimilation. Immigration. Quebec. 1941-71. *2639*

—. Economic Conditions. Railroads. 1960's-70's. *1623*

—. Economic History. Quebec (Abitibi-Témiscamingue). 1885-1950. *2625*

—. Economic Theory. Vertical integration. 1960's-70's. *1513*

—. Industrialization. Mineral Resources. USA. 1700-1977. *208*

—. Ontario (Cobalt). Research. 20c. *2728*

Ministers and Ministries Act. Government Reorganization Act of 1971. Parliamentary system. Presidential politics. 1966-74. *2106*

Minnesota See also North Central States.

—. Nova Scotia. Petroglyphs. Scandinavians. West Virginia. 14c. *478*

Minnesota (Crookston). Lectures. Manitoba (Winnipeg). Twain, Mark. 1895. *2989*

Minnesota (Gentilly). Catholic Church. French Canadians. Settlement. Theillon, Elie. 1870's-1974. *946*

Minnesota (Portage Plains; Prospect). School districts. 1876-80. *3019*

Minnesota (St. Paul). Manitoba (Winnipeg). Métis. Prairies. Red River of the North. Trade. Trails. 19c. *976*

Minorities See also Discrimination; Ethnic Groups; Nationalism; Population; Racism; Segregation.

—. Aged. Sociology. Women. 1970's. *1339*

—. Alaska Land Settlement of 1971. Eskimos. Politics. 1960-73. *318*

—. Alberta. Immigration. Nativism. 1925-30. *3144*

—. British Columbia. Japanese communities. Public schools. 1900-72. *3191*

—. *Charte du Français* (proposed). French language. Quebec. 1913-77. *2503*

—. Economic issues. French-speakers. Quebec. Separatist Movements. 1976. *2689*

—. French Canadians. Social Organization. Ukrainian Canadians. 1970's. *1458*

—. Institutional completeness. Manitoba (Winnipeg). Segregation, residential. -1974. *2978*

—. Language. Official Language Act (Quebec, 1974). Quebec. 1750's-1974. *2476*

Minorities in Politics. Acadians. Assimilation. Emigration. New Brunswick (Moncton). 1871-1971. *2385*

—. Confederation. Creighton, D. G. English Canadians. French Canadians. Heintzman, Ralph. 1850's-90's. *922*

Minority government. Parliaments. 19c-20c. *53*

Minville, Esdras. *Action Nationale* (periodical). French Canadians. Quebec. 1933. *2688*

—. Arès, Richard. French tradition. Quebec. Tremblay Commission. 1953-56. *2676*

—. Bibliographies. Economic Theory. Quebec. 20c. *2467*

—. Catholic Church. French Canadians. Quebec. 1975. *2459*

—. École des Hautes Études Commerciales. Economics. Educators. Quebec (Montreal). 20c. *2457*

—. Economic development. Forests and Forestry. Multinational corporations. Quebec. USA. 1923-36. *2629*

—. Economic Theory. French Canadians. Quebec. 20c. *2586*

—. Economics. Periodicals. Quebec (Montreal). 1922-28. *2533*

Miron, Gaston. Poetry. Quebec. Sovereignty. 1969-74. *2470*

Missionary Society of the Canadian Church. China. Church of England. Scovil, G. C. Coster (reminiscences). 1946-47. *1262*

Missions and Missionaries See also Christian Biography.

—. Alaska (Metlakahtla). British Columbia. Duncan, William. Tsimshian Indians. 1857-1974. *373*

—. Alberta. Blackfoot Indians. Church of England. Cree Indians. Trivett, Samuel. 1878-91. *360*

—. Algonkin Indians. Historical Sites and Parks. Iroquois Indians. Quebec (Oka). Sulpicians. 1700's-1800's. *521*

—. Algonkin Indians. Indians. Maine. Maritime Provinces. Social change. 1610-1750. *516*

—. Anglican Communion. Cree Indians. Faries, Richard. Ontario (York Factory). 1896-1961. *379*

—. Anglican Communion. Manitoba (Red River). Wives. 1820-37. *462*

—. Arctic. Churches. Fur Trade. 20c. *3281*

—. Atlantic Provinces (review article). France. Historiography. New France. Politics. 1000-1770. 19c. *67*

—. Baptists. Language. Micmac Indians. Nova Scotia. Rand, Silas Tertius. 1830-89. *422*

—. Bible. Indians. Myths and Symbols. Pacific Northwest. 1830-50. *438*

—. British Columbia (Queen Charlotte Islands). Haida Indians. Protestantism. Settlement. Subsistence patterns. 1876-1920. *398*

—. Business. Federal Government. Indians (reservations). Ontario (Manitoulin Island). 1830-60. *350*

—. Catholic Church. Immigration. Sisters of Service. 1920-30. *2963*

—. Catholic Church. Indians. Louisiana. 18c-20c. *587*

—. China. Hurford, Grace Gibberd (reminiscences). Teaching. World War II. 1928-45. *1122*

—. Christianity. Sex roles. Women. 1815-99. *923*

—. Church Missionary Society. Church of England. Eskimos. Hudson's Bay Company. Northwest Territories (Baffin Island). Peck, E. J. Trade. 1894-1913. *340*

—. Church of England. Domestic and Foreign Missionary Society. Japan. 1883-1902. *932*

—. Church of England. Hudson's Bay Company. Hunter, James. 1844-64. *2946*

—. Church of England. Indians. McDonald, Robert. Northwest Territories. Yukon Territory. 1850's-1913. *3292*

—. Church of England. Indians. Ontario (Algoma, Huron). Wilson, Edward F. 1868-93. *432*

—. Church of England. Nova Scotia (Halifax). St. Paul's Church. Society for the Propagation of the Gospel. Tutty, William. 1749-52. *2359*

—. Church of England. Ontario (Moosonee). Vincent, Thomas. 1835-1910. *3296*

—. Church of England. Quebec (Three Rivers). Wood, Samuel. 1822-68. *658*

—. Church Schools. East Indians. Presbyterian Church. Trinidad and Tobago. 1868-1912. *2319*

—. Cree Indians. Evans, James. Methodist Church. 1833-46. *651*

—. Creek Indians. Manitoba (Camperville, Duck Bay). 1600-1938. *435*

—. Cromwell, James. Garrettson, Freeborn. Methodist Episcopal Church. Nova Scotia. USA. 1785-1800. *2315*

—. Dalhousie College. McCulloch, Thomas. Nova Scotia. Pictou Academy. Presbyterian Church. ca 1803-42. *2215*

—. Dukhobors. Galicians. Lake Geneva Mission. Presbyterian Church. Saskatchewan (Wakaw). 1903-42. *3027*

—. Education. Great Britain. Protestantism. Sudan Interior Mission. 1937-55. *197*

—. Episcopal Church, Protestant. Hudson's Bay Company. Indians. Pacific Northwest. 1825-75. *402*

—. Evans, James. Ontario (Lake Superior). Voyages. Wesleyan Methodist Church. 1837-38. *2810*

—. Exiles. Loyalists. McDowall, Robert James. Ontario (Upper Canada). Reformed Dutch Church. 1790-1819. *747*

—. Fort Frontenac. Indian-White Relations. Iroquois Indians. Quinte Mission. Sulpicians. 1665-80. *522*

—. Frontier. Methodist Church. 1840-1925. *950*

—. Indians. McDougall, John. Prairie provinces. Wesleyan Methodist. 1860-1917. *386*

—. MacGregor, James. Nova Scotia (Pictou). Presbyterian Church of Scotland. 1786-1830. *2343*

—. Mennonites. USA. 1880-1910. *941*

—. Methodism. New York Conference. 1766-1862. *677*

—. Nova Scotia. Raymond, Eliza Ruggles. Sierra Leone (Sherbro Island). Slaves. 1839-50. *2241*

Mississauga Indians. Chippewa Indians. Indians. 1650-1975. *452*

—. Fur trade. Indian-White Relations. Ramsay, David. 1760-1810. *686*

Mississippi Flyway. Government. Great Plains. Hunting. North Central States. Spring shooting issue. Waterfowl. 1887-1913. *906*

Mississippi River. Discovery and exploration. Environmental determinism. Natural resources. North America. St. Lawrence River. 17c-19c. *270*

—. Empire, establishment of. Federal government. St. Lawrence River. USA. 1760's-1860's. *631*

—. Forman, George. Lewis, Henry. Logging. Shipping. 1849-54. 1883. *2755*

Mississippi River Valley. Colonial Government. France. Louisiana Territory. New France. 1683-1762. *584*

—. Discovery and Exploration. France. Spain. 16c-17c. *588*

Missouri See also North Central States.

—. Athens (battle). Civil War. 1861. *834*

Mistassini, monastery of. Catholic Church. Cistercians. Quebec. Trappists. 1900-03. *2482*

Mitchell, Peter. Fishing. Foreign Relations. New England. 1866-70's. *1070*

Mitchell, W. O. Alberta. Fiction. Provincial consciousness. Ross, Sinclair. 20c. *3093*

Moberly, Henry John. Fort McMurray. McMurray, William. Trading posts. 1870's. *953*

Mobility. See Geographic Mobility; Social Mobility.

Models See also Methodology.

—. Agricultural expansion. Prairie Provinces. Settlement. 1870-1911. *1037*

—. Alberta (Calgary). Nationalism. Political ideologies. Regionalism. 1974. *2921*

—. Attitudes. Legislatures. Ontario. Political Parties. 1957-74. *2890*

—. British Columbia (Vancouver). Elections. Political parties. 1937-74. *3230*

—. Cultural cleavages. Occupational categories. Voting and Voting Behavior. 1965-71. *1470*
—. Employment. Families (low-income). Methodology. 1974. *1510*
—. European Economic Community. Foreign policy. USA. 1957-77. *1890*
—. Labor. Lowry, Ira S. Migration, Internal. Quebec. -1973. *2593*
—. Labor Unions and Organizations. 1911-70. *7*
—. Local Government. Quebec (Montreal). 1911-71. *2445*
—. Strikes. USA. 1900-71. *216*
Modernization *See also* Developing Nations; Economic Theory; Foreign Aid; Industrialization; Machinery; Social Change.
—. Cree Indians. Fertility. 1968. *441*
—. Federal government. Language policy. Middle Classes. Provincial government. Quebec. 1960-76. *2090*
—. Ontario. Quebec. Social change. 1950-1974. *2479*
—. Political Change. Quebec. Separatist Movements. 19c-1970's. *151*
Moffett, Samuel E. Americanization. Historiography. 1867-1974. *162*
Mohawk Indians. Alberta. Johnson, Pauline (Tekahionwake). Poetry. 1895-1913. *363*
Molden, John. Cannibalism tales. Fort Churchill. Fort York. Manitoba. Shipwrecks. 1833. *3012*
Molokans. Amish. Dukhobors. Hutterites. Mennonites. North America. ca 1650-1977. *184*
Monetary policy. Employment. Fiscal Policy. Income. Labor Unions and Organizations. 1975. *1624*
—. Investments. 1950-73. *1605*
Monetary systems. Economic Conditions. 1973. *1537*
—. French Canadians. Independence. Parti Québécois. Quebec. 1974. *2424*
Monopolies *See also* Antitrust; Capitalism; Corporation Law; Railroads.
—. Manufacturing. Multinational corporations. 1970's. *1757*
Monroe Doctrine. Diplomacy. Pacific Northwest. Russia. 1812-23. *657*
Monroe, James. Adams, John Quincy. Diplomacy. Fishing. Great Britain. Newfoundland banks. USA. 1815-18. *782*
—. Conquest (discouraged). Lyon, Matthew (letter). USA. War of 1812 (Antecedents). 1811. *756*
Mont Blanc (vessel). Disasters. *Imo* (vessel). Nova Scotia (Halifax). 1917. *2332*
Montana *See also* Western States.
—. Assiniboin Indians. Cree Indians. Prairie Provinces. Social organization. ca 1640-1913. *446*
—. Bighorn River. Discovery and Exploration. Indians. Wyoming. Prehistory-1965. *444*
—. Boundary Waters Treaty. British Columbia (Cabin Creek). Coal explorations. Ecology. USA. 1909. 1973-75. *2035*
—. Fire fighting. Forest fires. Great Idaho Fire. Idaho. 1910. *1082*
—. Indian Wars. Nez Percé Indians. Public sympathy. Settlers. 1877. *431*
Montana (Dune Buggy Site, 24RV1). Indians. Pottery. Prehistory. 1947-70's. *299*
Montreal Citizens' Movement. Drapeau, Jean. Quebec. 1957-76. *2649*
Montreal Medical Board. McGill University. Medical licensing. 1833-34. *2573*
Montreal Snowshoe Club. Quebec. Snowshoe clubs. 1840's-1900's. *2536*
Montreal Steamship Company. Great Britain (Liverpool). Industrial Insurance. Mutual Benefit Societies. 19c. *2662*
Montreal, University of, Melzack Collection. Libraries. 18c-. *6*
Monts, Sieur de. Champlain, Samuel de. Maine. Military Camps and Forts. New Brunswick. St. Croix Island. 1603-05. *507*
Monument setter. Boundaries. Fulford, Frederick M. J. (personal account). USA. 1908-12. *1091*
Monuments. Lobsticks. Trees. 1826-1973. *84*
Moodie, Susanna. Literature. National self-image. Social Classes. 1832-53. *670*
Moore, Steve. Imperialism (review article). Leftism. Nationalism. Wells, Debi. 1960's-70's. *1269*
Morality *See also* Ethics; Values.
—. Alienation. Hamilton, Pierce Stevens (memoirs). Social Conditions. 1826-93. *2335*

—. Catholics. Church History. Discipline, ecclesiastical. Prairie Provinces. 1900-30. *2907*
—. Historiography. New France. 17c-18c. *525*
Moreton, Andrew. *See* Defoe, Daniel.
Morgan, Daniel. American Revolution. Riflemen. ca 1735-1802. *719*
Morgan, J. P. Curtis, Edward S. Indians. Photographs. 1868-1952. *472*
Morice, Adrien-Gabriel. Historians. Saskatchewan, University of. ca 1900-38. *3049*
Morison, Samuel Eliot. Cabot, John. Day, John (letter). Newfoundland (Cape Bonavista). Voyages. 1497-98. *486*
Morison, Samuel Eliot (review article). Historians. Ocean Travel. Parkman, Francis. 1974. *485*
Morocco. Emigration. Jews. Quebec (Montreal). 1960's-70's. *2517*
Morris family. Genealogy. Great Britain. Massachusetts. Nova Scotia. 18c-19c. *2242*
Morris, Joe (interview). Canadian Labour Congress. Leadership. 1930's-78. *1527*
Morris, Richard B. Festschriften publications. Kniffen, Fred B. Mayo, Bernard. Talman, James J. 1863-1974. *109*
Morris, William. Church of England. Ontario (Kingston). Presbyterians. Queen's College. Scots. 1836-42. *2831*
Mortality *See also* Death and Dying.
—. Cemeteries. Frontier society. Ontario (Upper Canada, Midland District). 1783-1851. *749*
Mortgages. Homesteading and Homesteaders. Locusts. Manitoba. 1875-1941. *3002*
Morton, Bliss & Company. Canadian Pacific Railroad. Capital alliances. Railroads. St. Paul & Pacific Railroad. Stephen, George. USA. 1860-70's. *980*
Morton, Levi Parsons. Banking (international). France (Paris). Great Britain (London). USA. 1860's. *853*
Morton, Sydney (diary). Daily Life. Nova Scotia (Liverpool, Halifax). 1874. *2294*
Mosques. Muslims. USA. 1970. *1429*
Mothers. Alberta. Daughters. Oral history. Pioneers. 1890-1929. *1025*
Motherwell, W. R. Dairying. Government. Saskatchewan. Subsidies. Wilson, W. A. 1906-17. *3037*
Mount Allison University. Authors. Educators. New Brunswick (Sackville). Webster, John Clarence. 1882-1950. *2404*
Mount Allison University (Ralph Packard Bell Library). Libraries. New Brunswick (Sackville). 1970-73. *2394*
Mount Royal College (Learning Resource Center). Alberta (Calgary). Libraries (decentralization). 1973. *3142*
Mountain climbers. Alberta (Mount Alberta). Explorers. Hirohito, Emperor. Japanese. 1925-48. *2924*
—. Alpine Club of Canada. Himalayas. Pumori (mountain). 1977. *1260*
Mouvement National des Québécois. Quebec. St. John the Baptist Society. Separatist Movements. 1834-1972. *2692*
Movie palaces. Architecture. Capitol Theatre. Entertainment. Ontario (Ottawa). Vaudeville. 1920-70. *1138*
Movies. *See* Films.
Multiculturalism. Assimilation. Immigrants. Psychology. 1970's. *1424*
—. Bibliographies. Ethnic Groups. Public Policy. 1967-76. *98*
—. English Canadians. French Canadians. Quebec. 1970's. *1303*
—. Ethnic groups. French Canadians. Geographic space. Quebec. Regionalism. Urbanization. 1930-73. *2715*
—. Ethnic Groups. Public Policy. 1970's. *1494*
—. Haidasz, Stanley. Polish Canadians. 1975. *1412*
—. Roy, Camille. Royal Society of Canada. Speeches, Addresses, etc. 1929-78. *1414*
Multinational corporations. Alcan Aluminium, Ltd. Bauxite industry. Guyana. Nationalization. 1960-75. *1852*
—. British Columbia. Natural Resources. Provincial government. Social Classes. Towns, "instant". 1965-72. *3178*
—. Collective bargaining. Industrial relations. Labor Unions and Organizations (international). 1974. *1763*
—. Economic cooperation. Foreign Investments. USA. 1945-74. *1962*
—. Economic dependence. Foreign investments. USA. 1970's. *2060*

—. Economic development. Forests and Forestry. Minville, Esdras. Quebec. USA. 1923-36. *2629*
—. Federal Government. Foreign investments. 1972. *1874*
—. Federal Government. Labor Unions and Organizations. 1970's. *1268*
—. Federal government. USA. 1945-71. *2014*
—. Foreign investments. International Trade. 1973-76. *1895*
—. Foreign Investments. Oil Industry and Trade. Social organization. 1970's. *1819*
—. Foreign relations. Politics. UN. 1970's. *1868*
—. Foreign relations. USA. 1960's-70's. *2015*
—. France. Great Britain. 1960's-70's. *1850*
—. Industrialization. USA. 1879. 1961-74. *140*
— International Law. Labor Unions and Organizations (international). Latin America. North America. 1937-74. *1955*
—. Manufacturing. Monopolies. 1970's. *1757*
—. Natural resources. USA. 1950's-70's. *2003*
Municipal government. Alberta (Edmonton). City councillors. Decisionmaking. Voting and Voting Behavior. 1966-72. *3134*
Municipal limits. City Government. Quebec (Quebec). 1831-1972. *2426*
Municipalities, redistributing. Elections, federal. Political Parties. Quebec. Voting and Voting Behavior. 1968. *2422*
Munitions. *See* Armaments; Armaments Industry.
Munro, Alice. Country Life. Fiction. Ontario. South. 1940's-70's. *2869*
Murder. Farms. Nova Scotia (Cumberland County). 1838. *2349*
Murray, Joan. Art History (review article). British Columbia. Paintings. Reid, Dennis. 1778-1935. *3189*
Murray, Walter. Herzberg, Gerhard. Immigration policy. Scholars. 1935-37. *1212*
Museum of Anthropology. Archaeological exhibits. Artifacts. British Columbia, University of. 1947-70's. *3205*
Museums *See also* names of museums, e.g. American Museum of Natural History, etc.; Archives; Art Galleries and Museums; Libraries.
—. Alberta (Calgary). Glenbow Centre. Harvie, Eric L. 1954-76. *3100*
—. British Columbia Provincial Museum. 1978. *3190*
—. Oral history. 1970's. *1315*
Musgrave, Anthony. British Columbia. Colonial Government. Granville, George, 2d earl (letter). Great Britain. Seymour, Frederick (death). 1869. *3204*
Mushrooms. Jackson, Henry A. C. Naturalists. Painting. 1870's-1950's. *228*
Music *See also* Folk Songs; Radio.
—. 20c. *146*
—. Bibliographies. Indians. 20c. *354*
—. Bibliographies. Indians. Pacific Northwest. 1888-1976. *353*
—. Bricklin (automobile). New Brunswick. Popular culture. Russell, Charlie. Satire. 1970's. *2401*
—. Folk Songs. Patriotism. "Yankee Doodle" (song; origins). 1730-1820. *2295*
—. Ontario (Windsor). 1860's-1901. *2778*
Musicology. Densmore, Frances. Ethnology. Indians. 1918-57. *400*
Muslims. Mosques. USA. 1970. *1429*
Mutinies. France. King George's War. Louisbourg, Fortress of. Nova Scotia. 1744-45. *605*
Mutual Advisory Committee. Architecture. City planning. Ontario (London). Politics. Preservation. 1970-77. *2727*
Mutual Benefit Societies. Great Britain (Liverpool). Industrial Insurance. Montreal Steamship Company. 19c. *2662*
Myths and Symbols. Abnaki Indians, Western. Transformer figures. ca 1840-1976. *369*
—. Anthropology, Cultural. Pacific Northwest. Tsimshian Indians. Prehistory-20c. *456*
—. Bible. Indians. Missions and Missionaries. Pacific Northwest. 1830-50. *438*
—. Chippewa Indians. Grey Owl (Archie Belaney). Ontario. 1880-1938. *372*
—. Ghost ship. Nova Scotia (Mahone Bay). War of 1812. *Young Teazer* (vessel). 1812-1976. *764*
—. National characteristics. Poetry. 20c. *75*

N

Namaka Farm. Alberta. Farming. Mennonites. 1920's-40's. *3121*
Names *See also* Toponymy.
—. Cree Indians. Indians. Values. 20c. *355*
—. Birds. Indians. Mammals. 1973. *399*
Names, official. 1841-67. *824*
Names, Place. *See* Toponymy.
Nanabozho (mythical character). Chippewa Indians. Folklore. Indians. Ottawa Indians. 19c-20c. *397*
Nashwaak Miramichi Trail. New Brunswick (Fredericton). Tourism. Trails. 1973. *2406*
National Characteristics *See also* National Self-image; Nationalism.
—. Anti-Americanism. Attitudes. USA. 1972. *1969*
—. Foreign policy. 1973. *1737*
—. Foreign relations. Geography. USA. 19c-20c. *269*
—. Myths and Symbols. Poetry. 20c. *75*
—. Quebec. Separatist Movements. 1971-74. *2671*
—. Travel. 1799-1899. *44*
—. USA. 1776-1976. *147*
National characteristics, British. Great Britain. Textbooks. USA. 1880-1930. *14*
National Characteristics (US). French Canadians. 1837-1973. *2483*
National Conference of Canadian Universities. Colleges and Universities. Federal Aid to Education. Massey Commission. 1951-66. *1476*
National Conference on Canadian Culture and Ethnic Groups. Ethnic groups. 1973. *1356*
National Council of Women of Canada. Feminism. 1893-1929. *225*
National Democratic Party. British Columbia (northwest). Economic Growth. Natural Resources. 1973-74. *3270*
—. Co-operative Commonwealth Federation. Labor. Socialism. 1933-75. *1294*
National Development *See also* Economic Development.
—. Attitudes. Geographic Space. Language. 1776-1976. *56*
—. Canals. Geographic space. International Trade. Politics. Railroads. 1818-1930. *54*
National Farmers Union (convention, 1972). Farmers. Maoism. 1972-73. *1507*
National Film Board. Censorship. Films. Quebec. 1971. *1406*
National Gallery of Canada. Art (Wembley controversy). British Empire Exhibition (1923). Royal Canadian Academy. 1877-1933. *1170*
National identification. Anglophones. Political Attitudes. Quebec. Separatist Movements. 1970's. *2120*
National Institute for Arts and Crafts. Art. Chabert, Joseph. Education. Quebec (Montreal). Teachers. Working Class. 1861-94. *1053*
National Library of Canada. Bibliography, national. *Canadiana* (bibliography). 1950-77. *249*
—. Ethnic groups. Ethnic Serials Project. Newspapers. 18c-20c. *51*
—. Libraries. 1953-78. *244*
National Library of Canada (Library Documentation Centre). Libraries. 1970-73. *1488*
National Museum of Science and Technology. Markers. Surveying. 1765-19c. 1960-70. *129*
National Parks and Reserves *See also* Nature Conservation; Wildlife Conservation.
—. Alberta (Banff). Macdonald, John A. Natural resources. Tourism. 1885-1978. *1040*
—. Gold Rushes. Klondike Gold Rush Historic Park. Yukon Territory. 1897-98. 1974. *3324*
—. Nature Conservation. 1911-73. *159*
National Pensioners and Senior Citizens' Federation. Aged. 1954-73. *1570*
National Security *See also* Defense Policy.
—. External Affairs Department. Foreign relations. Skelton, O. D. 1925-41. *1120*
—. NATO. ca 1965-74. *1883*
National Self-image *See also* National Characteristics.
—. Anti-Communist movements. Anti-Semitism. Freedom of speech. Immigration. Ontario (Toronto). 1928-29. *2791*
—. Attitudes. Intellectual traditions. Science. Technology. 1970's. *1327*
—. Bilingualism. USA. 1760-1974. *1*
—. Continental dimension. Cultural environment. English Canadians. North America. 1840's-1960's. *210*

—. Economic integration. Foreign Relations. Sharp, Mitchell. USA. -1973. *2083*
—. Ethnicity. Regionalism. USA. 1974. *2146*
—. Foreign influences. Poland. Quebec. 1970's. *2675*
—. Foreign policy. USA. 18c-20c. *11*
—. Industrialization. Population. Utopias. 20c. *26*
—. Intellectual history. Nationalism. 1974. *145*
—. Literature. Moodie, Susanna. Social Classes. 1832-53. *670*
—. Ontario (Toronto). 1970. *1465*
National Trades and Labour Congress. Labor Unions and Organizations. Ontario (Kitchener). Quebec. Trades and Labour Congress of Canada. 1892-1902. *2655*
Nationalism *See also* Independence Movements; Minorities; Patriotism; Self-Determination; Separatist Movements.
—. 1967-74. *1293*
—. Acadians. Institutions. Nova Scotia. Social Organization. 1700's-1970. *2281*
—. Acculturation. French Canadians. New England. ca 1610-1975. *2704*
—. Airplanes, Military (training). China. Fraser, Douglas. Saskatchewan (Saskatoon). 1919-22. *1169*
—. Alberta (Calgary). Models. Political ideologies. Regionalism. 1974. *2921*
—. Americanism. Lemelin, Roger *(Les Plouffe)*. Quebec. 1938-45. *2722*
—. Anti-Americanism. Anti-Continentalism. Capitalism. 1960's-74. *2045*
—. Anti-Semitism. French Language Charter. Quebec. 1977. *2421*
—. Atlantic Provinces. Historiography. Regionalism. 19c-20c. *2160*
—. Belgium. Ethnicity. Quebec. Social Classes. 1970's. *2702*
—. Berger, Carl (review article). English Canadians. Historiography. 1900-76. *232*
—. Bibliographies. 1949-76. *46*
—. Biculturalism. Confederation, Fathers of. Diversity, doctrine of. 1860's-1970's. *154*
—. Bill C-58. Protectionism. *Reader's Digest* (periodical). Taxation. *Time* (periodical). 1922-76. *2017*
—. Britannic Idealism (concept). Imperialism. Parkin, George R. 1871-1922. *912*
—. Business community. Parti Québécois. Quebec. Working class. 1970's. *2690*
—. Carey, Henry C. Protectionism. Reciprocity Treaty, proposed. USA. 1871-76. *1060*
—. Castonguay, Claude (interview). Federalism. Quebec. 1917-73. *63*
—. Catholicism. French Canadians. Lévesque, Georges-Henri (personal account). Quebec. Youth movements. 1930's. *2700*
—. Children. USA. 1971-72. *1463*
—. Class struggle. Equality. French-speaking community. Intellectuals. Quebec. 1960's-70's. *2677*
—. Colleges and Universities. Historiography. 1810-1967. *165*
—. Congress. Jackson, John George. Republicanism. Virginia. War of 1812. 1813-17. *754*
—. Conservatism. France. French Canadians. Groulx, Lionel. Maurras, Charles. 1910-40. *1141*
—. Conservatism. LeSage, Simeon. Quebec. Riel, Louis. 1867-1909. *2717*
—. Constitutions. Supreme Court. USA. 1875-1973. *238*
—. Coubertin, Pierre de. Olympic Games. Quebec (Montreal). 1900-76. *2414*
—. Cultural traditions. 1960's-70's. *1330*
—. Culture. Economic independence. Foreign Relations. USA. 1948-75. *2081*
—. Defense policy. Foreign policy. 1971-75. *1857*
—. Economic Conditions. Interdependence. USA. ca 1910-73. *1990*
—. Economic Conditions. Social Classes. 1968-76. *1567*
—. Economic growth. Foreign investments. USA. 1961-74. *1987*
—. Economic Policy. Foreign policy. Trudeau, Pierre Elliott. 1968-78. *1772*
—. Economic rationality. 1900's-60's. *1126*
—. Economics. Popular Culture. USA. 1776-1976. *725*
—. Elections, provincial. Quebec. Social issues. 1973. *2099*
—. Empire Day celebrations. Great Britain. Imperialism. Ontario. Public Schools. 1890-1930's. *2864*

—. English Canadians. French Canadians. Laurendeau, André. Quebec. 1945-66. *2556*
—. English Canadians. Oil Industry and Trade. ca 1950-75. *1976*
—. Ethnic Groups. Identity. Regionalism. Students. 1960-77. *2915*
—. Foreign investments. Social Classes. USA. 1960's-70's. *2082*
—. Foreign Policy. French Canadians. Quebec. USA. 1945-76. *2044*
—. Foreign policy. Public opinion. 1972-75. *1875*
—. Foreign Relations. USA. 1945-75. *2037*
—. French Canadians. Groulx, Lionel. Historians. Nonviolence. Quebec. 1917-30. *489*
—. French Canadians. Independence Movements. Lévesque, René (views). Quebec. 1763-1976. *2701*
—. French Canadians. Official Language Act (Quebec, 1974). Quebec. USA. 1970's. *2577*
—. Higher education. Quebec. Symons report. 1970's. *1472*
—. Historical Society of Montreal. Lapierre, Eugène (obituary). Quebec. 1927-70's. *2450*
—. Immigration. Protestant churches. United Church of Canada. 1902-25. *1194*
—. Imperialism (review article). Leftism. Moore, Steve. Wells, Debi. 1960's-70's. *1269*
—. Indians. Nova Scotia (Cape Breton). Political socialization. Regionalism. Whites. 1860's-1970's. *2361*
—. Intellectual history. National Self-image. 1974. *145*
—. Leftism. Quebec. Social classes. 1970's. *2703*
—. National interest. Quebec. 1960's-70's. *2095*
—. Ontario. Publishers and Publishing. 1970-75. *2809*
—. Periodicals. Publishers and Publishing. Tariff. USA. 1920's. *1193*
—. Politics. Social change. 1957-75. *1720*
—. Public Opinion. USA. 1976. *1956*
—. Public Opinion. USA. 1976. *2019*
—. Publishers and Publishing. Royal Commission on Book Publishing. 1973. *1290*
—. Quebec. 1975. *1337*
—. Quebec. 1945-76. *2678*
—. Quebec. 1945-70. *2709*
—. Quebec. Separatist Movements. Socialism. USA. 1970's. *2021*
—. Students. USA. Values. 1967-71. *2051*
—. USA. 1976. *1259*
—. USA. 1960's-70's. *2054*
Nationalities *See also* names of specific national groups, e.g. Sudeten Germans, Ruthenians, Ibo, etc., Ethnic Groups.
— Professional activity. Social scientists. -1973. *1422*
Nationalization. Alcan Aluminium, Ltd. Bauxite industry. Guyana. Multinational corporations. 1960-75. *1852*
—. Borden, Robert. Railroads. 1915-19. *1154*
Nationhood. Government. Quebec. 1960-76. *2698*
Native Peoples' Caravan. Indians. Ontario (Ottawa). Political Protest. 1975. *463*
Nativism. Alberta. Immigration. Minorities. 1925-30. *3144*
—. Chicopee Manufacturing Company. Immigration. Irish Americans. Massachusetts (Chicopee). Mills. 1830-75. *635*
NATO. Committee on the Challenges of Modern Society. Environmentalism. Foreign Policy. USA. 1969-77. *1838*
—. Declaration of Atlantic Principles. 1974. *1862*
—. Declaration of Atlantic Principles. 1974. *1948*
—. Declaration of Atlantic Principles. USA. 1974. *1818*
—. Defense policy. Economic Conditions. Government. Military strategy. 1973-76. *1863*
—. Defense Policy. Foreign policy. North American Air Defense Command. USA. 1950's-70's. *1986*
—. Defense Policy. Peacekeeping Forces. Trudeau, Pierre Elliott. 1968-78. *1752*
—. Foreign Policy. Peacekeeping Forces. UN. 1956-77. *1861*
—. Military. Political strategy. 1969. *1755*
—. National Security. ca 1965-74. *1883*
Natural Gas *See also* Oil and Petroleum Products.
—. Arctic. Northwest Territories (Melville, King Christian Islands). Polar Gas Project. USA. 1972-75. *3355*
Natural History *See also* Botany; Geology.

—. Graham, Andrew. Hudson's Bay Company. Hutchins, Thomas. Plagiarism. 1770's-1815. *692*
Natural Resources *See also* Conservation of Natural Resources; Fishing; Forests and Forestry; Marine Resources; Mineral Resources; Power Resources; Soil Conservation.
—. Agriculture. Federalism. Forests and Forestry. Industrialization. Quebec. 20c. *2646*
—. Alberta. Canadian Shield. 1977. *273*
—. Alberta (Banff). Macdonald, John A. National Parks and Reserves. Tourism. 1885-1978. *1040*
—. Alberta (Banff). Resorts. Rocky Mountain Park. 1882-1909. *3117*
—. British Columbia. Multinational Corporations. Provincial government. Social Classes. Towns, "instant". 1965-72. *3178*
—. British Columbia (Gulf Islands). Economic development. Environment. 1858-1973. *3176*
—. British Columbia (northwest). Economic Growth. National Democratic Party. 1973-74. *3270*
—. British Columbia (Vancouver). Economic Growth. Population. 19c. *3223*
—. Coasting trade. Economic Growth. Employment. 1931-73. *1579*
—. Commodities. Economic Policy. International Organizations. USA. 1974-76. *1945*
—. Culture. Indians. Manitoba, southwestern. Pottery. Prehistory-18c. 1970's. *307*
—. Discovery and exploration. Environmental determinism. Mississippi River. North America. St. Lawrence River. 17c-19c. *270*
—. Economic Conditions. Foreign investments. 1950-75. *1903*
—. Economic prosperity. International Trade. 1950's-70's. *1833*
—. Economic Regulations. 1972-75. *1508*
—. Economics. Industrialization. 1950's-70's. *1765*
—. Foreign investments. Prince Edward Island. 1970's. *2205*
—. Foreign Investments. USA. 1920-55. *1125*
—. Foreign investments. USA. 1960's-70's. *1971*
—. Gill, Valentine. Nova Scotia. Smith, Titus. Surveying. 1800-15. *2271*
—. Iron mining. Newfoundland. Quebec (Fire Lake). SIDBEC (consortium). 1960's. *2622*
—. Mines. Saskatchewan. 1960-74. *3064*
—. Multinational corporations. USA. 1950's-70's. *2003*
Naturalists. Discovery and Exploration. Eskimo life. Hantzsch, Bernard. Northwest Territories (Baffin Island). 1910-11. *3314*
—. Jackson, Henry A. C. Mushrooms. Painting. 1870's-1950's. *228*
Nature *See also* Ecology.
—. 1893-1914. *264*
—. Great Britain. Landscape Painting. Menzies, Archibald. Vancouver, George. ca 1775-1800. *633*
Nature Conservation *See also* Wildlife Conservation.
—. National parks and Reserves. 1911-73. *159*
—. New York. Ontario. St. Lawrence Seaway. Thousand Islands. 19c-20c. *279*
Naval Air Forces. F2H-3 aircraft. McDonnell Aircraft Corporation. 1956-63. *1272*
Naval Bases. *See* Navy-Yards and Naval Stations.
Naval Battles *See* names of battles, e.g. Lake Erie (battle), etc.
Naval Construction. *See* Shipbuilding.
Naval Engineering. *See* Marine Engineering.
Naval expeditions. American Revolution. Amphibious operations. Marines. Nova Scotia. 1654-1798. *724*
Naval Recruiting and Enlistment. *See* Conscription, Military; Military Recruitment.
Naval Strategy. Great Britain. Halifax Citadel (fortress). Nova Scotia. 1825-60. *642*
Naval strength. 1790-1973. *3198*
Navies *See also* headings beginning with the word naval; Marine Engineering; Military; Navigation; Shipbuilding; Warships.
—. Arctic Ocean. Great Britain. Weavers. Whalers. 1818-25. *3300*
—. Civil War. Letters. Nova Scotia. Wade, Norman. 1859-62. *842*
—. Great Britain. Great Lakes. 1760-89. *680*
—. Great Britain. Nova Scotia (Halifax). War of 1812. 1795-1815. *760*
—. Puerto Rico (Culebra Island). Target ranges. USA. 1971-72. *2023*
Navigation *See also* Lighthouses; Navies; Shipbuilding.
—. Conservation of Natural Resources. Foreign Relations. Maritime Law. USA. 1975. *2052*
—. Great Lakes. Shipping. 1948-74. *2876*

—. Niagara Falls. Tatham, William. ca 1790-1819. *649*
—. St. Clair River. St. Lawrence Seaway. 1973. *1251*
Navy-yards and Naval Stations. British Columbia (Victoria). Nova Scotia (Halifax). Provincial capitals. 1749-1971. *2126*
Naylor, R. T. (*A History of Canadian Business, 1867-1914*). Business history. Methodology. 1867-1914. *933*
Naylor, R. T. (review article). Banks. Business. Industry. 1867-1914. *928*
Nazism. *Action Catholique* (newspaper). Catholic Church. Communist Parties and Movements. Quebec. 1917-39. *1411*
—. Anti-discrimination legislation. Anti-Semitism. 1930's. *1196*
—. *Der Bote* (newspaper). Germans, Russian. Mennonites. Saskatchewan. USSR. Völkisch thought. 1917-39. *3077*
—. Deutscher Bund Canada. German Canadians. Propaganda. 1934-39. *1216*
—. Deutscher Bund Canada. German Canadians. Saskatchewan. 1934-39. *1246*
Nebraska *See also* Western States.
—. Colorado. Daily Life. Frontier and Pioneer Life. Ouren, Hogan (reminiscences). 1861-66. *851*
Negroes *See also* Africans; Black Capitalism; Civil War; Confederate States of America; Discrimination; Race Relations; Racism.
—. Alberta. Homesteading and Homesteaders. Immigration. Race Relations. 1911-12. *3152*
—. Anderson, William J. House of Representatives. Political Leadership. Vermont (Montpelier, Shoreham). 1900-40's. *2565*
—. Antislavery Sentiments. Newspapers. Ontario. *Provincial Freeman* (newspaper). Shadd, Mary Ann. 1852-93. *1046*
—. Assimilation. British Columbia (Saltspring Island). Immigration. 1850-1900. *3211*
—. Attitudes. British officials. 1830-65. *668*
—. Bibb, Henry. Emigration. Separatism. USA. 1830-60. *858*
—. British Columbia. California. Discrimination. Gold Rushes. Race Relations. 1849-66. *846*
—. Consumers. 1970's. *1556*
—. Discrimination. Historiography. 1776-1976. *252*
—. Immigrants. Nova Scotia. 1776-1815. *640*
—. Immigration. Ohio (Cincinnati). Ontario (Wilberforce). 1829-56. *626*
—. Rapier, James Thomas. Refugees. 1856-64. *885*
—. Saskatchewan. Shadd, Alfred Schmitz. 1896-1915. *3070*
Neidhardt, W. S. Anglin, Timothy Warren. Baker, W. M. Fenians. Irish Canadians (review article). 19c. 1970's. *1073*
Neighborhoods. Boundaries. Ethnic Groups. Manitoba (Winnipeg; North End, St. Boniface). 19c-1978. *2977*
Neptune (vessel). Arctic. Federal Government. Sovereignty. 1903-04. *3294*
Netherlands. Aubert de la Chesnaye, Charles. Fur trade. 1695-98. *568*
—. Australia. Cabinet. Great Britain. Political recruitment. USA. 1940's-60's. *1666*
—. Cod. Fisheries. Newfoundland. 1589-1670. *570*
—. Discovery and Exploration. Great Britain. North America. Vancouver, George. 1778-98. *666*
—. New York. Trade. 1670-74. *567*
Neuberger, Richard. Columbia River Treaty. Foreign policy. USA. 1955-61. *2071*
Neutrality. British Columbia (Victoria). British Empire. Espionage. Spanish-American War. 1898. *1105*
—. British Commonwealth. Foreign Relations. Ireland. World War II. 1939-45. *1237*
Neville, Anthony. Frontier and Pioneer life. Neville, Harriet Johnson. Northwest Territories. 1882-1905. *3359*
Neville, Harriet Johnson. Frontier and Pioneer life. Neville, Anthony. Northwest Territories. 1882-1905. *3359*
New Brunswick *See also* Atlantic Provinces.
—. Acadians. Catholic Church. Discrimination. Irish. 1860-1900. *2402*
—. Acadians. Catholic Church. Irish Canadians. Politics. Quebec. Schools. Taxation. 1871-73. *1067*
—. American Revolution. Colonization. Loyalists. Saunders, John. Virginia. 1774-1834. *740*
—. Anglin, Timothy Warren. Catholic Church. Confederation. Fenians. 1866. *890*

—. Anglin, Timothy Warren. Catholic Church. Irish Canadians. Saint John *Freeman* (newspaper). 1849-83. *2373*
—. Anti-Americanism. Loyalist tradition. Political Attitudes. 1825-1914. *2375*
—. Anti-Catholicism. Pitts, Herman H. Religion in the Public Schools. 1871-90. *2388*
—. Arnold, Benedict. Arnold, Peggy. Great Britain. West Indies. 1781-1801. *2374*
—. Artists. Cleveland, Xenophon. Massachusetts. Stencils. 1839-99. *2379*
—. Asylums. Mental Illness. Nova Scotia. 1749-1900. *2159*
—. Autobiography and memoirs. Baptist Church. Crandall, Joseph. 1795-1810. *2378*
—. Bricklin (automobile). Music. Popular culture. Russell, Charlie. Satire. 1970's. *2401*
—. Census. Economic conditions. Social Conditions. 1861. *2377*
—. Champlain, Samuel de. Maine. Military Camps and Forts. Monts, Sieur de. St. Croix Island. 1603-05. *507*
—. Christianization. Indian-White Relations. Micmac Indians. Nova Scotia. 1803-60. *465*
—. Cobbett, William. Military Service. 1785-91. *629*
—. Cocagne Academy. Theal, George McCall (recollections). 1840-94. *2405*
—. Colebrook, William. Indians. Perley, Moses H. 1840's. *2408*
—. County Government. Local Government. Municipalities, rural. 1967-77. *2384*
—. Diseases. Leprosy. Massachusetts. Social stigma. 1844-80. 1904-21. *2391*
—. Economic Conditions. Employment. Nova Scotia. Rural Settlements. 1961-76. *2293*
—. Economic environment, bicultural. English. French. Worker attitudes. -1973. *2393*
—. Education. Socialism. Stuart, Henry Harvey. 1873-1952. *2380*
—. Forests and Forestry. Lumberers. Surveyors. 1820's-44. *2412*
—. France. French and Indian War. Great Britain. Restigouche River (battle). 1760. *592*
—. Fugitive Slaves. Land. Settlement. USA. 1815-36. *804*
—. Fundy National Park. Lumber industry. Settlement. 1820's-1976. *2383*
—. Hammer, Armand. Historical Sites and Parks. Roosevelt Campobello International Park. USA. 1959-74. *2077*
—. Literature. 18c-1977. *2382*
—. *Machault* (vessel). Pottery. Restigouche River (battle). 1760. *2376*
—. Newfoundland. Privateering. 1800-15. *759*
—. Parish boundaries. 1784-1861. *2413*
—. Politics. Satire. Street, Samuel Denny. 1802. *2409*
—. Shipbuilding. 1776-1890. *2372*
—. Travel. 1974. *2407*
New Brunswick (Fort Gaspereau). Excavations. Glassware. 1751-56. *2387*
New Brunswick (Fredericton). Church of England. Medley, John (letters). Oxford Movement. Pusey, Edward Bouverie. ca 1840-44. *2389*
—. Nashwaak Miramichi Trail. Tourism. Trails. 1973. *2406*
New Brunswick (Moncton). Acadians. Assimilation. Emigration. Minorities in Politics. 1871-1971. *2385*
—. Albert-Westmorland-Kent Regional Library. Libraries. 1911-73. *2398*
New Brunswick, northeastern. Acadians. Daily Life. Harley, William. Surveying. 1829. *2381*
New Brunswick (Northumberland County). Elections. Street, John Ambrose. Violence. 1842. *2403*
New Brunswick (Rimouski). Air Mail Service. Quebec (Montreal). 1920's-30's. *1179*
New Brunswick (Sackville). Authors. Educators. Mount Allison University. Webster, John Clarence. 1882-1950. *2404*
—. Libraries. Mount Allison University (Ralph Packard Bell Library). 1970-73. *2394*
New Brunswick (Saint John). Architecture, Victorian. Industrialization. Urban Renewal. 17c-1966. *2399*
—. Boosterism. Population. Railroads. 1851-80. *2410*
—. Catholic Church. Sisters of Charity of the Immaculate Conception. 1854-64. *2392*
—. Census. Methodology. Social organization. 1871. 1974. *2400*
—. Cholera. City Government. Epidemic. 1854. *2386*

—. Disaster relief. Fire. Nova Scotia. 1877. *2397*

—. Economic Development. Industrial Revolution. Railroads. Transportation. 1867-1911. *2395*

—. Economic Growth. Social Conditions. 19c. *2411*

—. Massachusetts (Boston). Steamships. Trade. 1836-1945. *2390*

New Brunswick, University of. International Programme for Loyalist Studies. Local history. MacNutt, W. Stewart (obituary). 1935-76. *2174*

New Brunswick (western). Humor. Social Customs. Wedding night pranks. 18c-1974. *2396*

New Deal. USA. 1930's. *1206*

New Democratic Party. Barret, David. British Columbia. Federal Government. 1959-75. *3195*

—. British Columbia. Elections, provincial. 1970-73. *3187*

—. British Columbia. Legislation. Public Policy. Social Democracy. 1972-75. *3241*

—. British Columbia. Political Indicators. Voting and Voting Behavior. 1968-74. *3212*

—. Communists. 1961-73. *1719*

—. Conservative Party. Elections. Liberal Party. 1972. *1675*

—. Cooperative Commonwealth Federation. Defense policy. 1932-75. *234*

—. Federal government. Parti Québécois. Quebec. Separatist Movements. 1960's-70's. *2102*

—. Liberal Party. Manitoba. Progressive Conservative Party. Voting and Voting Behavior. 1953-73. *3020*

New England *See also* individual states; Northeastern or North Atlantic States.

—. Abnaki Indians, Western. Quebec. Tufts, Henry. 1772-75. *368*

—. Acadia. France. Phips, William. War. 1689-1713. *597*

—. Acculturation. Bibliographies. French Americans. French Canadians. 1755-1973. *2566*

—. Acculturation. French Canadians. Nationalism. ca 1610-1975. *2704*

—. Ballads. French and Indian War. Quebec. Rogers' Rangers (retreat). 1759. *591*

—. Colonial Government. France. Great Britain. Nova Scotia (Canso, Cape Breton). 1710-21. *492*

—. Defense Policy. Hartford Convention. Militia. War of 1812. 1812-15. *757*

—. Depressions. Emigration. Maritime Provinces. Massachusetts (Boston). 1860-1900. *2154*

—. Durrell, Philip (and descendants). 17c-18c. *493*

—. Economic Conditions. King George's War. Louisbourg, fortress of. Nova Scotia. 1745-50. *607*

—. Fishing. Foreign Relations. Mitchell, Peter. 1866-70's. *1070*

—. Fishing industry. King William's War. Privateers. Queen Anne's War. Shipping. 1689-1713. *596*

—. Foreign Relations. USA. 1850's-1970's. *77*

—. Forests and Forestry. Great Britain. Kennebeck Purchase Company. Mast policy, royal. Wentworth, John. 1769-78. *718*

—. France. Great Britain. Nova Scotia (Canso). Territorial rivalry. 1710-21. *595*

—. French and Indian War. Rhetoric. War. 1754-60. *620*

—. French and Indian War. Rogers, Robert. 1755-60. *599*

—. Fur trade. Melyn, Cornelis. Nova Scotia. 1633-52. *569*

—. Nova Scotia (Yarmouth). Steamboats. 1839-89. *2325*

New France *See also* Louisiana; Nova Scotia; Quebec.

—. Amherst, Jeffrey. French and Indian War. Iroquois Indians. Military History. Pontiac's Rebellion. 1760-65. *612*

—. Architecture. Catholic Church. 1600-1760. *553*

—. Armies. Desertion. France. 1700-63. *530*

—. Atlantic Provinces (review article). France. Historiography. Missions and Missionaries. Politics. 1000-1770. 19c. *67*

—. Barbel, Marie-Anne. Business. Women. 18c. *575*

—. Clergy. Trade. 1627-1760. *563*

—. Colonial Government. France. Louisiana Territory. Mississippi River Valley. 1683-1762. *584*

—. Colonial Government. Frégault, Guy. Historiography. Rioux, Marcel. 1615-1763. 1957-60's. *491*

—. Colonial policy (review article). Eccles, William J. France. Seignelay, Marquis de. ca 1663-1701. 1962-64. *499*

—. Documents. Occupations. Social status. 1640's-1740's. *534*

—. Economic Conditions. Fur trade. Quebec. 1760-90. *574*

—. France. Huguenots. Protestantism. 1541-1760. *550*

—. Fur trade. Genealogy. Godbout, Archange. Population. Voyages. 1608-1763. *565*

—. Gosselin, Auguste-Honoré (review article). Laval, François de. School of Arts and Crafts of St. Joachim. 1668-1730. *535*

—. Historiography. Jesuits. Parkman, Francis. 17c. 1840's-60's. *518*

—. Historiography. Morality. 17c-18c. *525*

—. Intellectuals. Libraries. Royal intendants. 1663-1760. *555*

—. Production, mode of. Small producers. Social Classes. 17c-18c. *496*

—. School of Arts and Crafts of Saint Joachim. 1668-1715. *545*

New France (Notre Dame des Anges). Feudal law. Provost Court of Quebec. 1626-1750. *554*

New France (Sovereign Council). Catholic Church. Governors, provincial. Laval, François de. 1659-84. *546*

New Hampshire *See also* New England; Northeastern or North Atlantic States.

New Hampshire (Portland). Fabyan, Horace. Hotel trade. White Mountain Grand Hotel. 1807-81. *772*

New International Economic Order. Trudeau, Pierre Elliott. UN. 1968-78. *1909*

New World. Indians. Pottery. 4500-50 BC. *311*

New York *See also* Northeastern or North Atlantic States.

—. American Revolution. Business. Fort Niagara. 1775-83. *736*

—. Boats. Folklore. St. Lawrence River Skiff. 1860-1973. *133*

—. Courtship. Field, Eliza. Great Britain (London). Indians. Jones, Peter. Methodism. 1820's-33. *451*

—. Fur Trade. Hudson's Bay Company. Sutherland, James. 1751-97. *687*

—. Jackman, Alonzo. Military Strategy. Quebec. Travel. Vermont. 1838. *2443*

—. Nature Conservation. Ontario. St. Lawrence Seaway. Thousand Islands. 19c-20c. *279*

—. Netherlands. Trade. 1670-74. *567*

New York City. Anti-Canadianism. Civil War. Press. 1861-65. *864*

—. Confederate Army. Kennedy, Robert C. Saboteurs. 1861-65. *843*

—. Immigration. Jews. Vanger, Max. 1900-50. *1143*

New York Conference. Methodism. Missions and Missionaries. 1766-1862. *677*

New York (Ogdensburg). Lake Ontario. Ontario (Kingston). Steamboating. Transportation. 1815-70. *653*

New York (Taconic Mountains). Emmons, Ebenezer. Geology. Scientific Discoveries. 1840-1900. *277*

New York (Watertown). Children. Federal government. Ontario (Belleville). Political structures. Provincial government. 1977. *1423*

New Zealand. Australia. Government policy. Nonwhites. Race politics. South Africa. 1900-73. *1926*

Newfoundland *See also* Labrador.

—. Adams, John Quincy. Diplomacy. Fishing. Great Britain. Monroe, James. USA. 1815-18. *782*

—. Annexation. Confederation. Outports. Poverty. Social Customs. 1920-48. *2200*

—. Archives. Provincial government. 1825-1973. *2185*

—. Beothuk Indians. Indian-White Relations. 1500-1848. *466*

—. Beothuk Indians (review article). Howley, J. P. Indian-White Relations. Rowe, F. W. Prehistory-1830. 1977. *290*

—. Bishops. Catholic Church. Church of England. Liberal government. 1860-62. *2187*

—. Church of England. Clergy. Feild, Edward. Great Britain. 1826-44. *2190*

—. Church of England. Feild, Edward. Sects, Religious. 1765-1852. *2188*

—. Cod. Fisheries. Netherlands. 1589-1670. *570*

—. Convict transportation. Great Britain. Ireland. 1789. *2192*

—. Cook, James. Fisheries. Great Britain. 1763-67. *2203*

—. Coughlin, Lawrence. Methodism. 1765-1815. *2191*

—. Discovery and Exploration. Inscriptions. Ireland. Ogham alphabet. St. Lunaire boulder. ca 5c-1977. *487*

—. Economic conditions. Exports. Fishing. Foreign investments. 1600-1934. *2178*

—. Economic conditions. Fishing industry. 1880-1970. *2177*

—. Economic growth. Maritime Provinces. 1880-1940. *2151*

—. Economic Policy. Fishing Industry. International Trade. 1934-60's. *2175*

—. Fishing industry. Government. Political economy. 1949-75. *2179*

—. Fishing industry. Provincial government. 1972-77. *2196*

—. Fishing Rights. Great Britain. USA. 1905-12. *2184*

—. Fishing Rights. Labrador. Public Administration. Quebec. 1763-83. *735*

—. Geology. Great Britain. Jukes, Joseph Beete. Travel. 19c. *2181*

—. Great Britain. *Pegasus* (vessel). William IV (visit). 1786. *2193*

—. Irish Canadians. Politics. Religion. 19c. *2189*

—. Iron mining. Natural resources. Quebec (Fire Lake). SIDBEC (consortium). 1960's. *2622*

—. Liberal Party. Politics. Progressive Conservative Party. 1908-72. *2195*

—. Life-styles. Public identity. Sects, religious. Social Classes. 1949-75. *2183*

—. Maine. Massachusetts. Runestones. Vikings. 986-1121. *481*

—. New Brunswick. Privateering. 1800-15. *759*

—. Practical jokes. Sealers. 16c-1914. *2202*

Newfoundland (Avalon Peninsula). Calvert, George (1st Lord Baltimore). Catholic Church. Colonization. Religious Liberty. 1620's. *551*

—. Calvert, George (1st Lord Baltimore). Colonization. Great Britain. 1609-32. *2182*

Newfoundland (Calvert). Folk Songs. Sex roles. Social status. 1916-74. *2201*

Newfoundland (Cape Bonavista). Cabot, John. Day, John (letter). Morison, Samuel Eliot. Voyages. 1497-98. *486*

Newfoundland (Conception Bay; Bell Island). Economic History. Industrialization. Iron mining. Social History. 1870's-1966. *2199*

Newfoundland Fishermen, Food, and Allied Workers. Fishing industry. 1970-77. *2197*

Newfoundland (L'Anse aux Meadows). Discovery and Exploration. Excavations. Vikings. 1000. 1961-68. *480*

Newfoundland, Memorial University of (Maritime History Group). Indexing procedures. Shipping documents. 1863-1913. *2176*

Newfoundland Regional Library System. Libraries (circulation). 1942-68. *2198*

Newfoundland (Signal Hill National Historic Park). British colonial materials. Excavations. Military installations. 1800-60. 1965-66. *2186*

Newfoundland (St. John's). City government. Political Reform. 1888-92. *2180*

—. Elections. Political Reform. Representative government. 1815-32. *2194*

News. Canadian Broadcasting Corporation. Radio. USA. 1975-76. *2031*

News diffusion. Alberta (Calgary). Trudeau, Pierre Elliott. 1971. *1385*

News, European. Newspapers. Quebec. 1866-71. *2528*

News, foreign. Newspapers. Quebec. 1962-74. *2553*

—. Press. USA. 1974-76. *2042*

Newspapers *See also* Editors and Editing; Freedom of the Press; Journalism; Periodicals; Press; Reporters and Reporting.

—. Antislavery Sentiments. Negroes. Ontario. *Provincial Freeman* (newspaper). Shadd, Mary Ann. 1852-93. *1046*

—. Bibliographies. Editorials. French Canadians. Latin America. Quebec. 1959-73. *2433*

—. Catholic Church. Education (British, US). Ontario. 1851-1948. *2833*

—. Consumers. Middle classes. Ombudsmen. 1970's. *1299*

—. Domestic Policy. Foreign relations. Nova Scotia. USA. 1827-40. *2312*

—. Editorials. Elections. Foreign Relations. 1972-74. *1917*

—. Editorials. Political campaigns. 1972. *1722*

—. Enlightenment. Ideas, diffusion of. 1764-1810. *648*

—. Ethnic groups. Ethnic Serials Project. National Library of Canada. 18c-20c. *51*
—. Foreign policy. Press. ca 1970's. *1919*
—. French Canadians. Quebec (St. Francis District). Rebellion of 1837. 1823-45. *813*
—. Intergovernmental Relations. King, William Lyon Mackenzie. Public opinion. Taxation. 1945-46. *2119*
—. Lévesque, René. Parti Québécois. Provincial Government. Quebec (Montreal). 1976-77. *2423*
—. News, European. Quebec. 1866-71. *2528*
—. News, foreign. Quebec. 1962-74. *2553*
—. Political Parties. Saskatchewan. 1914-29. *3031*
—. Poverty. 1973. *1480*
—. Quebec. Strikes. 1977-78. *2574*
—. Radicals and Radicalism. 1870-1900. *940*
—. USA. 1963-70's. *2055*
Newsprint. Capitalists. Laurentide Company. Quebec. 1887-1928. *161*
—. Herty, Charles Holmes. Paper mills. Pine trees. Scientific Experiments and Research. Southeastern States. 1927-40. *1134*
Newsprint industry. Banking. International Power and Paper Company. USA. 1914-33. *1186*
Newton, William. Alberta (Edmonton). Church of England. 1875-1900. *983*
Nez Percé Indians. Great Plains. Horses (Appaloosa). 1670-1877. *411*
—. Idaho Territory. Indian Wars. MacDonald, Duncan. 1877. *418*
—. Indian Wars. Montana. Public sympathy. Settlers. 1877. *431*
Niagara Falls. Boundary Waters Treaty. Foreign Relations. USA. 1899-1911. *1088*
—. Electric power. Environment. Federal regulation. USA. 1895-1906. 1960's-70's. *2075*
—. Navigation. Tatham, William. ca 1790-1819. *649*
Nickerson, Vincent D. Artists. Great Lakes. Norton, Charles W. Ships. Sprague, Howard F. Whipple, Seth A. 1844-1901. *2861*
Nicol, A. Carnegie, Andrew. Libraries. Yukon Territory (Dawson). 1902-20's. *3340*
Nixon, Richard M. Political Speeches. 1970. *391*
Nobility *See also* Aristocracy.
—. Fishing company. France (Poitou; Les Sables d'Olonne). Huart, Christophle-Albert-Alberic d'. Louisbourg, Fortress of. Nova Scotia (Cape Breton Island). 1750-75. *560*
Nolin, Jean-Baptiste (and daughters). Métis. Prairie Provinces. Red River of the North. St. Boniface School. 1760-1840. *776*
Noncolonization principle. Alexander I (ukase). Foreign Relations. Great Britain. Pacific Northwest. Russo-American Convention of 1824. 1821-25. *627*
Nongovernmental subsystems. Foreign Relations. USA. 1775-1976. *185*
Nonviolence. French Canadians. Groulx, Lionel. Historians. Nationalism. Quebec. 1917-30. *489*
Nootka Sound controversy. British Columbia. Great Britain. Spain. Territorial rights. 1790. *691*
—. British Columbia (Vancouver). Diplomacy. France (Paris). Great Britain. Spain. 1789-90. *636*
—. British Columbia (Vancouver Island). *Columbia Rediviva* (vessel). Fourth of July. Kendrick, John. 1789. *647*
—. British Columbia (Vancouver Island). Cook, James. Discovery and Exploration. Great Britain. Spain. 1778-94. *695*
NORAD treaty. Economic interdependence. Foreign investments. Foreign policy. USA. 1970's. *1973*
Nordic area studies. Colleges and Universities. Libraries. 1970-73. *1343*
Normal school issue. Catholic Church. Discrimination. Prairie Provinces. 1884-1900. *2947*
Norman, E. Herbert. Communism. Congress. Espionage. USA. 1945-57. *2070*
Norman, E. Herbert (review article). Historians. Japan. 1940-77. *176*
North America. Acadians. Louisiana. 17c-20c. *580*
—. Africans. Asians. Indians. Racism. Whites. 1600-1900. *10*
—. Agricultural growth. Boserup, Ester. China. Russia. South. 18c-19c. *801*
—. Agriculture. Europe. Industrialization. Market economy. Peasant movements (colloquium). ca 1875-1975. *13*

—. Agriculture. Hutterites. Social Customs. Technology. 18c-20c. *2896*
—. Alexander I. Foreign policy. Pacific Area. Russian-American Company. 1799-1824. *678*
—. Amish. Dukhobors. Hutterites. Mennonites. Molokans. ca 1650-1977. *184*
—. Architecture. Europe. Subways. 1940's-70's. *1307*
—. Arctic. Discovery and Exploration. Finnie, Richard Sterling (account). Office of the Coordinator of Information. Stefansson, Vilhjalmur. 1931-62. *3302*
—. Art. Buffalo. Central America. Prehistory-20c. *265*
—. Artists. Clymer, John. West. 1960's-70's. *1460*
—. Atlantic Coast. Discovery and Exploration. Historical Sites and Parks. Vikings. 10c-14c. 20c. *483*
—. Automobiles. Mass transit. Motoring, urban. Travel. 1960-75. *2758*
—. Balance of power. Defense Policy. Quebec. Separatist Movements. 1970's. *1921*
—. Bethune, Angus. China (Canton). International Trade. North West Company. 1812-17. *802*
—. Bibliographies. Europe. Folk religion. 1900-74. *256*
—. Blakiston, Thomas Wright. British North American Exploring Expedition. Explorers. Ornithology. Palliser, John. 1857-91. *859*
—. Bonaparte, Jerome Napoleon. France. Travel. 1861. *839*
—. Botany. Douglas, David. Horticulture. Scientific Expeditions. 1823-34. *650*
—. Brendan, Saint. Discovery and Exploration. Ireland. Voyages. 500-85. 1976-77. *488*
—. Bureaucracies. Capitalism. Government. Institutions. Social change. 1750's-1850's. *656*
—. Catholic Church. Church and State. Europe, Western. Politics. 1870-1974. *246*
—. Climate. Environment. Indians. Settlement. Prehistory. 1956-78. *309*
—. Colleges and Universities. Publishers and Publishing. Scholarship. 1920's-70's. *206*
—. Colonialism. Cultural change. Fur trade. Indians. Prehistory-1900. *286*
—. Colonies. France. Great Britain. Historiography. Italy. 1663-1763. *598*
—. Colonization. France. Great Britain. 1670's-1760. *512*
—. Conference on the Historical Urbanization of North America. Urban history. 1973. *117*
—. Conservation of Natural Resources. International regulation. Pollution. Water quality. 1960's-74. *1982*
—. Continental dimension. Cultural environment. English Canadians. National Self-image. 1840's-1960's. *210*
—. Demography. Indians. 15c-1600. *298*
—. Discovery and exploration. Environmental determinism. Mississippi River. Natural resources. St. Lawrence River. 17c-19c. *270*
—. Discovery and Exploration. Forgeries. Vikings. Vinland map. 15c. 1957. *482*
—. Discovery and Exploration. Great Britain. Netherlands. Vancouver, George. 1778-98. *666*
—. Discovery and Exploration. Vikings. Voyages. 985-1975. *477*
—. Drug abuse programs. International cooperation. 1960's-74. *1417*
—. Emigration. Epp, Johann (letter). Mennonites. Russia. 1875. *981*
—. Energy supplies. 1960's-70's. *1908*
—. Ethnic groups. Maps. Methodology. 1900-78. *1457*
—. Ethnicity. Immigration. 1974. *1407*
—. Europe. Industrial plant size. 1963-67. *1609*
—. Europe. Physical achievement. Sports. 1740-1975. *131*
—. Exploration. Great Britain. Jameson, Robert. Northwest Passage. 1804-54. *689*
—. Family. Marriage. Sociology. Women. 1974. *1469*
—. Flags. Military museum (collection). Volunteers. Yugoslavia (Belgrade). 1917-18. 1974. *1162*
—. France. Legislation. Psychiatric care. Quebec. 1973. *2546*
—. Freedoms. Human rights. Race relations. 1973. *1478*
—. Fur trade. Hudson's Bay Company. Mineral Resources. 17c-20c. *258*
—. Immigrants. Occupations. Statistics. Women. 1964-71. *1516*
—. Indians. Sports. 16c-17c. *378*

—. International Law. Labor Unions and Organizations (international). Latin America. Multinational corporations. 1937-74. *1955*
—. Libraries. 1972. *1378*
—. Maps. 16c-18c. *498*
—. Psychoanalysis. Scientific Experiments and Research. Social Change. 1918-77. *9*
North American Air Defense Command. Defense Policy. Foreign policy. NATO. USA. 1950's-70's. *1986*
—. Defense policy. Military strategy. USA. 1930's-70's. *1988*
—. Foreign policy. 1973. *1991*
North American Water and Power Alliance. Ecology. USA. Water management. 1968-71. *1961*
North Central States *See also* individual states; Old Northwest.
—. Bibliographies. Lake Erie. Pollution. 1872-1965. *2730*
—. Brethren in Christ. Wesleyan Holiness. 1910-50. *1145*
—. Government. Great Plains. Hunting. Mississippi Flyway. Spring shooting issue. Waterfowl. 1887-1913. *906*
North Dakota *See also* Western States.
—. Armies. Larsen, Lawrence W. (paper). Military Strategy. 1919. 1975. *1157*
—. Army Corps of Engineers. Boundary protection. Sherrill, Clarence O. 1919. *1158*
—. Midland Continental Railroad. Railroads. Seiberling, Frank A. 1912-20. *2983*
North Land (vessel). Great Lakes. *North West* (vessel). Steamboats. 1888-1941. *937*
North West Company. Bethune, Angus. China (Canton). International Trade. North America. 1812-17. *802*
—. China. International Trade. 1784-1821. *783*
—. China market. Fur Trade. Oregon (Astoria). 1760's-1821. *785*
North West Rebellion. Alberta. Military Medicine. Pennefather, John P. (reminiscences). Winnipeg Light Infantry. 1885. *1016*
—. Alberta (Lac la Biche). Beaver Indians. Hudson's Bay Company. Pruden, Patrick. Trading posts. 1885. *1026*
—. Alberta (Lac la Biche). Erasmus, Peter. Faraud, Bishop. 1885. *1021*
—. Big Bear. Métis. Poundmaker. Trials. 1885. *948*
—. Messianic Movements. Prairie Provinces. Religion. Riel, Louis. 1869-85. *971*
—. Migration, Internal. Prairie Provinces. 1885. *995*
—. Nova Scotia (Halifax). Tupper, William Johnston (letters). 1885. *965*
—. Religious theory. Riel, Louis (letters). 1876-78. 1885. *970*
North West (vessel). Great Lakes. *North Land* (vessel). Steamboats. 1888-1941. *937*
Northeastern or North Atlantic States *See also* individual states; New England.
—. Birchbark. Containers. Indians. Prehistory-1978. *471*
—. Lake Champlain (battle). War of 1812. 1814. *758*
Northwest Coast Indians. Astronomy. British Columbia. Calendars. Indians. Prehistory. 1975. *303*
—. Bibliographies. Indians. 1975. *352*
Northwest Passage. Alaska. Anián, strait of. British Columbia. Cook, James. Discovery and Exploration. Voyages. 1778. *675*
—. Exploration. Great Britain. Jameson, Robert. North America. 1804-54. *689*
—. Explorers. Franklin, John. Hood, Robert (journal, paintings). 1819-22. *3308*
Northwest Territories. Anik Satellite. Communications. Satellites. 1972. *3287*
—. Arctic. Daily life. Hare Indians. Indians. Oil exploration. 1859-1974. *358*
—. Arctic. Discovery and Exploration. Fort Hope. Hudson's Bay Company. Rae, John. 1840's. *3298*
—. Arctic. Discovery and Exploration. Franklin, John. Hood, Robert (journal). 1819-21. *3309*
—. Arctic. Royal Canadian Mounted Police. 1890-1929. *3360*
—. Botany (specimens). Burke, Joseph. Hudson's Bay Company. Manitoba. Royal Botanic Gardens. 1843-45. *2922*
—. Business. Public finance. 1947-73. *3353*
—. Church of England. Indians. McDonald, Robert. Missions and Missionaries. Yukon Territory. 1850's-1913. *3292*
—. Development. 1976. *3291*
—. Economic Development. Political change. 19c-. *3352*

—. Economic Development. Public Opinion. Regionalism. 1970-73. *3277*
—. Economic Growth. 1970-74. *3275*
—. Educational Policy. Goggin, David James. Manitoba. Teaching. ca 1890's. *2904*
—. Food Supply. Fur trade. Hudson's Bay Company. Mackenzie River Valley. Winter. 19c. *3357*
—. Frontier and Pioneer life. Neville, Anthony. Neville, Harriet Johnson. 1882-1905. *3359*
—. Great Britain. Lefroy, John Henry (journals). Magnetic survey. Scientific Expeditions. 1843-44. *3306*
—. Indian-white relations. Social Organization. 1940-76. *416*
—. Law Enforcement. Prohibition. Royal Canadian Mounted Police. 1874-91. *984*
—. Mackenzie Valley Pipeline Inquiry. Oil Industry and Trade. Pipelines. 1976. *3343*
—. Parliamentary representation. 1870-87. *2935*
Northwest Territories (Aklavik). Eskimos. Masak (personal account). Socialization. 1930's. *324*
Northwest Territories (Baffin Island). Arctic. Discovery and Exploration. Hantzsch, Bernard. Trichinosis. 1911. *3316*
—. Church Missionary Society. Church of England. Eskimos. Hudson's Bay Company. Missions and Missionaries. Peck, E. J. Trade. 1894-1913. *340*
—. Colonization. Frobisher, Martin. Great Britain. Hall, Charles Francis. Pottery. 1578. 1862-1974. *513*
—. Discovery and Exploration. Eskimo life. Hantzsch, Bernard. Naturalists. 1910-11. *3314*
—. Discovery and Exploration. Hantzsch, Bernard. Soper, J. Dewey. 1929. *3317*
—. Entrepreneurs. Jackson, Walter John. ca 1875-1922. *3362*
—. Eskimos. Radio. Television. 1972-73. *321*
—. Eskimos. Social customs. Television. 1972-74. *320*
Northwest Territories (Baffin Island, Devon Island). Eskimos. Hudson's Bay Company. Russell, Chesley (account). Settlement. 1934-36. *332*
Northwest Territories (Baffin Island, Pangnirtung Pass). Explorers. Soper, J. Dewey (journal). 1925. *3318*
Northwest Territories (Baffin Island, Takuirbing Lake). Canoe trips. Frobisher Bay. Travel. 1973. *3320*
Northwest Territories (Baker Lake District). Douglas, W. O. (reminiscences). Quangwak (Eskimo). Royal Canadian Mounted Police. 1919-20's. *323*
Northwest Territories (Beechey Island). Arctic. Discovery and Exploration. Franklin, John. Great Britain. 1845-48. *3312*
Northwest Territories (Bylot Island). Discovery and Exploration. 1818-1977. *3311*
Northwest Territories (Chesterfield Inlet). Comer, George. Douglas, W. O. (reminiscences). *Finback* (whaler). Shipwrecks. 1919. *3351*
Northwest Territories (Dismal Lakes). 1820's-1978. *3345*
Northwest Territories (Ellesmere Island). Garlington, Ernest A. Greely, Adolphus W. Hazen, William B. Scientific Expeditions. 1881-83. *3303*
Northwest Territories (Frobisher Bay). Arctic. Explorers. Frobisher, Martin. Gold. Great Britain (London). 1570's. *3310*
—. Arctic. Waste disposal. Water supply. 1973. *3354*
—. Art. Eskimos. 1969. *316*
Northwest Territories (Great Bear Lake). Prehistory-1972. *3356*
Northwest Territories (Hudson Bay, Baffin Island). Eskimo life. Fur trade. Hudson's Bay Company. 1909-30's. *3348*
Northwest Territories (Mackenzie District). Education. Eskimos. Indians. Métis. Whites. 1969-70. *3358*
—. Fur trade. Indian-White Relations. Kutchin Indians, Eastern. Yukon Territory. 1800-60. *3285*
Northwest Territories (Mackenzie District, eastern). Chipewyan Indians. Cree Indians. Expansionism. Fur Trade. Indian-White Relations. Prairie Provinces. 1680's-18c. *476*
Northwest Territories (Mackenzie River). Amazon River. Americas (North and South). Environment. Rivers. 1977. *268*
—. *Norweta* (vessel). Travel. 1973. *3347*

Northwest Territories (Mackenzie River Delta). Alaska, western. Bahr, Andrew. Reindeer. 1928-34. *3295*
Northwest Territories (Mackenzie River region). Industrialization. 1970-75. *3349*
Northwest Territories (Mackenzie Valley). Canol Project. Oil Industry and Trade. Pipelines. Planning. World War II. 1942-45. *3274*
Northwest Territories (Marble Island). Hudson's Bay Company. *Perseverance* (vessel). Whaling Industry and Trade. 1866-67. 1892-97. *681*
Northwest Territories (Melville, King Christian Islands). Arctic. Natural gas. Polar Gas Project. USA. 1972-75. *3355*
Northwest Territories (Rae). Social Change. Thlingchadinne (Dog-rib) Indians. 1939. 1974. *380*
Northwest Territories (Roes Welcome Sound). Eskimo (Aivilik). Witchcraft. 1953-73. *327*
Northwest Territories (Southampton Island). Eskimos, Sadlermiut. Gibbons, Jimmy (interview). Housing. Marsh, Donald B. (reminiscences). ca 1900. *328*
Northwest Territories (Thelon River, Hornby Point). Adlard, Harold. Christian, Edgar. COSMOS (satellite). Hornby, John. 1926-27. 1976. *3346*
—. Adlard, Harold. Christian, Edgar. Dewar, Kenneth M. (reminiscences). Diaries. Hornby, John. 1928. *3350*
Northwestern International Yachting Association. British Columbia. Washington (Puget Sound area). Yacht racing, organized. 1870-1914. *3207*
Norton, Charles W. Artists. Great Lakes. Nickerson, Vincent D. Ships. Sprague, Howard F. Whipple, Seth A. 1844-1901. *2861*
Norton, John (interview). Brant, Joseph (Thayendanegea, Mohawk chief), interview. Iroquois Indians. 1801. *351*
Norway *See also* Scandinavia.
Norweta (vessel). Northwest Territories (Mackenzie River). Travel. 1973. *3347*
Nova Albion (location of). California. Discovery and Exploration. Drake, Francis. *Golden Hinde* (vessel). 1579. *505*
Nova Scotia *See also* Atlantic Provinces.
—. Acadians. Acculturation. Exiles. France. Great Britain. 18c. *606*
—. Acadians. Colonial Government. Great Britain. Land tenure. Oath of allegiance. 11c-1755. *594*
—. Acadians. Exiles. Great Britain. 1710-55. *614*
—. Acadians. Institutions. Nationalism. Social Organization. 1700's-1970. *2281*
—. Acadians. St. Lawrence, Gulf of. 1756-95. *622*
—. Adult education. Colonial Government. ca 1820-35. *2289*
—. Adult education. Educators. Howe, Joseph. 1827-66. *2290*
—. Adult education. Halifax Mechanics' Institute. Middle Classes. Working class. 1830's-40's. *2291*
—. Africa, West. American Revolution. Emigration. Fugitive slaves. Great Britain. 1776-1820. *737*
—. Akins, Thomas Beamish. Public Records. 1857-91. *2246*
—. Alabama. Alcohol. Florida. Pentz, Gabriel. Smuggling. 20c. *2249*
—. Alline, Henry. Charisma. 1776-83. *732*
—. American Revolution. Amphibious operations. Marines. Naval expeditions. 1654-1798. *724*
—. American Revolution. Bailey, Jacob. Church of England. Letters. 1784. *726*
—. American Revolution (antecedents). Georgia. Great Britain. Immigrants. Military. 1765-75. *729*
—. Antigonish Movement. Catholic Church. Rural Development. Social change. ca 1928-73. *2297*
—. Apple industry. Calkin(s) family. Halliburton, Robert Grant. Inglis, Charles. Starr family. 19c. *2279*
—. Apple industry. Crops. Genealogy. Prescott, Charles Ramage. 1772-1970's. *2280*
—. Apportionment. British North America Act (1867). 1971-72. *2336*
—. Architecture. France. Guardhouses. Louisbourg, Fortress of. Military Camps and Forts. 1713-68. *616*
—. Armstrong, E. H. Politics. 1923-24. *2367*
—. Asylums. Mental Illness. New Brunswick. 1749-1900. *2159*

—. Atlantic Coast. Blockade-running. Civil War. Letters. Wade, Norman. 1859-62. *841*
—. Atlantic Provinces. Bargaining rights. Fisheries. Legislation. 1975. *2351*
—. Automobiles. Legislation. 1899-1913. *2300*
—. Baptists. Language. Micmac Indians. Missions and Missionaries. Rand, Silas Tertius. 1830-89. *422*
—. Barracks. Historical Sites and Parks. Louisbourg, Fortress of. 1716-39. 1969. *590*
—. Belcher, Jonathan. Grand jury. Law. 1754. *2362*
—. Bell, Alexander Graham. Communications. Field, Cyrus. Fleming, Sandford. Gisborne, F. N. 1749-1964. *2260*
—. Bibliographies. 1974. *2370*
—. Bibliographies. Legislative Library. 1976. *2371*
—. Blockades. Civil War. Letters. Wade, Norman. 1861-62. *889*
—. Bradstreet, John. Great Britain. Louisbourg, Fortress of. Military Biography. 1739-74. *604*
—. Bromley, Walter. Micmac Indians. Self-help. Urban poor. 1813-25. *2258*
—. Buildings. Halifax Historic Properties. Restorations. 1825-1905. 1978. *2255*
—. Canals. Shubenacadie Canal. 1791-1974. *2270*
—. Canoe trip. MacKenzie, A. Stanley (journal). 1885. *2299*
—. Cary, James. Exiles. Great Britain. Jamaica. Loyalists. 1781-1804. *744*
—. Cattle disease. Ragwort weed. 1850-1910. *2299*
—. Champlain, Samuel de. L'Ordre de Bon Temps. Social Organizations. 1606-07. *543*
—. Chignecto Ship Railway (proposed). Construction. Ketchum, Henry George Clepper. 1888-91. *2353*
—. Christianization. Indian-White Relations. Micmac Indians. New Brunswick. 1803-60. *465*
—. Church of England. Loyalists. Society for the Propagation of the Gospel. 1787-1864. *751*
—. Civil War. Letters. Navies. Wade, Norman. 1859-62. *842*
—. Cobb, Sylvanus. Fundy, Bay of. Ships. Trade. *York* (vessel). 1755. *2163*
—. Cochran, William. Education. Enlightenment. 1789. *745*
—. Colleges and Universities. Dalhousie University. Mackenzie, Arthur Stanley. Stanley, Carleton. 1911-45. *2282*
—. Communications. Prehistory-1977. *2261*
—. Confederation. Doyle, Hastings. Federal government. Local government. 1867-68. *895*
—. Confederation. Howe, Joseph. 1832-69. *892*
—. Conservation of Natural Resources. Smith, Titus. Surveying. 1801. *2328*
—. Construction. France. Lime preparation. Louisbourg, Fortress of. Military Camps and Forts. 1725-58. *615*
—. Cricket (game). 19c. *2318*
—. Cromwell, James. Garrettson, Freeborn. Methodist Episcopal Church. Missions and Missionaries. USA. 1785-1800. *2315*
—. Daily life. Pioneers. 19c-1910. *2311*
—. Dalhousie College. McCulloch, Thomas. Missions and Missionaries. Pictou Academy. Presbyterian Church. ca 1803-42. *2215*
—. Disaster relief. Fire. New Brunswick (Saint John). 1877. *2397*
—. Domestic Policy. Foreign relations. Newspapers. USA. 1827-40. *2312*
—. Economic Conditions. Employment. New Brunswick. Rural Settlements. 1961-76. *2293*
—. Economic Conditions. King George's War. Louisbourg, fortress of. New England. 1745-50. *607*
—. Economic growth. Federal policy. Maritime Union Movement. Regional development. 1783-1974. *2167*
—. Education. McCulloch, Thomas. Pictou Grammar School. 19c. *2337*
—. Elections. Fielding, William Stevens. Liberal Party. 1891-96. *2313*
—. Excavations. Gunflints. Louisbourg, Fortress of. Military Camps and Forts. 1720-60. *608*
—. Fishing industry. Maritime Fishermen's Union. 1977. *2366*
—. Folklore. Oral tradition. 20c. *2357*
—. France. King George's War. Louisbourg, Fortress of. Mutinies. 1744-45. *605*
—. France. Langille family. 1718-1804. *2230*
—. Fur trade. Melyn, Cornelis. New England. 1633-52. *569*

—. Gardens. 1850-1900. *2345*

—. Genealogy. Great Britain. Massachusetts. Morris family. 18c-19c. *2242*

—. Genealogy. Harvie, John (and family). 1730-1945. *2276*

—. Germans. Immigrants. Protestants. 1749-52. *2259*

—. Gill, Valentine. Natural resources. Smith, Titus. Surveying. 1800-15. *2271*

—. Great Britain. Halifax Citadel (fortress). Naval Strategy. 1825-60. *642*

—. Great Britain. Public opinion. Reciprocity. Treaties. USA. 1846-54. *871*

—. Harris, Robert Edward. Supreme Court. Townshend, Charles James. 1887-1931. *2286*

—. Holy Ghost and Us Society. Sanford, Frank. Sects, Religious. Shipwrecks. 1910-48. *2333*

—. Immigrants. Negroes. 1776-1815. *640*

—. Indians. Public Policy. 1783-1871. *467*

—. Knollin, William Mortimer. Marshall, Samuel. Pioneers. Villiers, Charles E. 19c. *2309*

—. Lawson, Mary Jane Katzman. Literature. 1828-90. *2292*

—. Libraries. Strathbeg Reading Society. 1866-69. *2347*

—. Literature. McCulloch, Thomas (*Letters of Mephibosheth Stepsure*). Presbyterian Church. Satire. 1821-22. *2339*

—. Literature. Pictou Literature and Scientific Society. Science. 1834-54. *2248*

—. Louisbourg, fortress of. Military Camps and Forts. Restorations. 1654-1745. 1928-73. *613*

—. Mayflower (Trailing Arbutus). Provincial Flower. 1834-1901. *2254*

—. McKim, Andrew. Politics. Provincial Legislatures. 1784-1840. *2348*

—. Mentally retarded. Organizations. Social Reform. ca 1900-27. *2245*

—. Minnesota. Petroglyphs. Scandinavians. West Virginia. 14c. *478*

—. Missions and Missionaries. Raymond, Eliza Ruggles. Sierra Leone (Sherbro Island). Slaves. 1839-50. *2241*

—. Novels. Raddall, Thomas (memoirs; review article). 1913-75. *2238*

—. Sculpture. USA. Wilson, John A. 1877-1954. *2301*

—. Nova Scotia (Annapolis, Halifax). Harris, John. Provincial Government. Roads. 1816-30's. *2253*

Nova Scotia (Annapolis County; Wilmot Township). Burns family. Immigration. Ireland. 1764-20c. *2305*

Nova Scotia (Annapolis, Digby counties). Bear River. Bridges. 1853-66. *2323*

Nova Scotia (Arichat region). Acadians. Assimilation. Massachusetts (Gloucester). 1850's-1900. *2364*

Nova Scotia (Barrington). Doane, Elizabeth O. M. P. (memoirs). Payne, John Howard. 1715-98. *2224*

Nova Scotia (Bay of Fundy). *Chesapeake* (vessel). Civil War. Confederate States of America. 1863. *872*

Nova Scotia (Bay of Fundy, Londonderry). Boomtowns. Iron Industry. Steel industry. 1844-98. *2352*

Nova Scotia (Beaubassin). Acadian townsite. Excavations. Glassware. Settlement. ca 1670-1800's. *2274*

Nova Scotia (Beaver River, Chebogue). Genealogy. Raymond, Daniel (family). Raymond, Jonathan (family). 1772-1869. *2331*

Nova Scotia (Bedford). Fire Department. 1921-22. *2360*

Nova Scotia Board of Commissioners of Public Utilities. Gasoline Licensing Act (1934). Marketing. Provincial Government. 1960's-74. *2283*

Nova Scotia (Canso). France. Great Britain. New England. Territorial rivalry. 1710-21. *595*

Nova Scotia (Canso, Cape Breton Island). Colonial Government. France. Great Britain. New England. 1710-21. *492*

Nova Scotia (Canso Causeway, Cape Breton Island). Economic development. Harbors. 1955-73. *2320*

Nova Scotia (Cape Breton). Bournot, John (impressions). 1867. *2358*

—. Earthquakes. 1882. 1909. 1929. *278*

—. Indians. Nationalism. Political socialization. Regionalism. Whites. 1860's-1970's. *2361*

—. Marshall, John George. Roads. 1823-26. *2222*

Nova Scotia (Cape Breton Island). Architectural drawings. Fortification. Historical Sites and Parks. Louisbourg, Fortress of. 1707-58. *603*

—. British Empire Steel Corporation. Coal industry. Economic Development. 1910's-20's. *1175*

—. Buildings. Historical Sites and Parks. Louisbourg, Fortress of. 1713-58. *529*

—. Co-op development. Economic development. 1906-73. *2237*

—. Daily life. Historical Sites and Parks. Louisbourg, Fortress of. Social classes. 1713-50. *537*

—. Fishing company. France (Poitou; Les Sables d'Olonne). Huart, Christophle-Albert-Alberic d'. Louisbourg, Fortress of. Nobility. 1750-75. *560*

—. Historical Sites and Parks. Louisbourg, Fortress of. Restorations. 18c. 1961-75. *602*

—. Labor disputes. Militia. 1920's. *2298*

—. Louisbourg, Fortress of. Preservation. 1720-68. 1976. *619*

—. Loyalists. Settlers. 1784-1820. *748*

Nova Scotia (Cape Breton Island; Arichat). Genealogy. LaVache family. 1774-20c. *2365*

Nova Scotia (Cape Breton Island, Isle Royale). Fishing industry. Historical Sites and Parks. Louisbourg, Fortress of. 1705-50. *573*

Nova Scotia (Cape Breton Island; Port Hood Island). Bird, Lilah Smith (recollections). Daily Life. ca 1907-70. *2221*

Nova Scotia (Cape Sable Island). Barrington and Cape Island Steam Ferry Company. Ferries. 1847-1949. *2216*

Nova Scotia (Charlottetown, Pictou). *Fairy Queen* (vessel). Shipwrecks. 1853. *2170*

Nova Scotia (Chebogue). *Baltimore* (vessel). Buckler, Susannah. 1735. *2314*

Nova Scotia (Cornwallis). Genealogy. Walton, Jacob (identity). ca 1811-1914. *2252*

Nova Scotia (Cornwallis Township). Disciples of Christ. 1812-1910. *2251*

Nova Scotia (Cumberland County). Farms. Murder. 1838. *2349*

Nova Scotia (Dartmouth). Thompson, Catherine (death). 1846. *2263*

Nova Scotia (Digby County). Pioneers. Stehelin, Emile Charles Adolph (family). 1837-1918. *2324*

Nova Scotia (East Hants). Local Government. 1861-1923. *2363*

Nova Scotia, eastern. Antigonish Movement. Cooperatives. Economic Development. Social Classes. 1920's-30's. *2338*

Nova Scotia (Eastern shore). Gold. Roads. Travel. 19c. *2266*

Nova Scotia (Glenwood). Daily Life. Ricker, Helen S. (reminiscences). 1895-1909. *2334*

Nova Scotia (Granville). Banks, Joshua. Banks, Moses. Genealogy. 1739-1843. *2308*

—. Fellows family. Genealogy. Massachusetts. 1635-1977. *2240*

Nova Scotia (Guysborough). Business. Electric Power. 1927. *2268*

—. Children. Education. Welsh, Matthew. Wills. 19c. *2267*

Nova Scotia (Guysborough County). Diaries. Hurricanes. Marshall, John George. 1811. *2223*

Nova Scotia (Halifax). Actors and Actresses (American). Theater. 1768. *2213*

—. Adamson, John. Cholera cures, ineffective. Medicine (practice of). 1834. *2219*

—. Annan, Ebenezer (letters). Daily Life. Immigration. 1842. *2220*

—. Architecture. 1749-1973. *2239*

—. Architecture. Historical Sites and Parks. Waterfront. 1815-1973. *2229*

—. Armies. Great Britain. Kent, Duke of (Edward). Lyons, Charles (family). 1812-63. *2273*

—. British Columbia (Victoria). Navy-yards and Naval Stations. Provincial capitals. 1749-1971. *2126*

—. Census. 1838. *2327*

—. *Challenger* (vessel). Expedition. Honeyman, David. Oceanography. 1872-76. *2317*

—. Children. Orphan House. 1752-87. *2262*

—. Church of England. Missions and Missionaries. St. Paul's Church. Society for the Propagation of the Gospel. Tutty, William. 1749-52. *2359*

—. *Cobequid* (vessel). Rescue operations. Shipwrecks. 1914. *2322*

—. Containerization. Ports. 1971-73. *2296*

—. Devit, Charles. M'Grath, Michael. Trials. Westmacott, John (murder of). 1816. *2243*

—. Disasters. *Imo* (vessel). *Mont Blanc* (vessel). 1917. *2332*

—. Economic Growth. Urbanization. 1815-1914. *2356*

—. French and Indian War. Great Britain. Pringle, Henry (letters). 1757. *617*

—. Genealogy. Howe, John (and family). 18c-19c. *750*

—. Great Britain. Navies. War of 1812. 1795-1815. *760*

—. Great Pontack Inn. Inns, waterfront. 1754-1837. *2303*

—. Howe, Joseph. Journalism. *Novascotian* (newspaper). 1824-38. *828*

—. Howe, Joseph. Local Government. Political Corruption. Trials. 1835. *808*

—. Hugo, Adèle. 1863-66. *2278*

—. Hydroelectric power. Street railways. 1907-17. *2211*

—. Irish Canadians. Tobin, Thomas (and descendants). ca 1759-1936. *2329*

—. Massachusetts (Boston). Steamship lines. 1840-1917. *2287*

—. North West Rebellion. Tupper, William Johnston (letters). 1885. *965*

—. Political Participation. Sabatier, William. 1780-1826. *2256*

—. Riots. 1863. *2368*

—. Theater. 1816-19. *2214*

Nova Scotia (Halifax area). Colonization. Cornwallis, Edward. 1749-52. *2217*

Nova Scotia (Halifax, Liverpool). Daily Life. Morton, Sydney (diary). 1874. *2294*

Nova Scotia (Halifax, Lunenburg). Genealogy. West family. Wuest, Johann Wendel. 17c-20c. *2330*

Nova Scotia (Hants County). Genealogy. Weatherhead family. ca 1820-1946. *2272*

Nova Scotia (Herring Cove). Shipwrecks. *Tribune* (vessel). 1796-1968. *2326*

Nova Scotia (Kentville). Medicine (practice of). Sanatoriums. Tuberculosis. 1904-78. *2284*

Nova Scotia (King's County). Borden, Frederick W. Business. Family. Liberal Party. Parliaments. 1874-96. *2316*

Nova Scotia (Kingsport). Cox, Ebenezer. Shipbuilding. ca 1840-1915. *2250*

Nova Scotia (Lochaber). Howe, Joseph. Rural Development. 1795-1880. *2285*

Nova Scotia (Lockport). American Revolution. Fishing. Privateers. 18c. *720*

Nova Scotia (Lunenburg Township). Bachman, John Baptist (and descendants). 1752-1952. *2218*

Nova Scotia (Mahone Bay). Ghost ship. Myths and Symbols. War of 1812. *Young Teazer* (vessel). 1812-1976. *764*

Nova Scotia (Melville Island). 17c-1974. *2304*

Nova Scotia (New Glasgow). Political Campaigns. 1875-1926. *2350*

Nova Scotia (Pictou). Banking. 1872-85. *2232*

—. Chloroform. Fraser, James Daniel Bain. Medicine (practice of). Pharmacy. 1807-69. *2247*

—. Coal Mines and Mining. Disasters. 1832-1957. *2231*

—. Crerar family. Shipping. 1840's-50's. *2344*

—. Irish Canadians. McCabe, James (and descendants). Pennsylvania (Philadelphia). ca 1743-1917. *2306*

—. MacGregor, James. Missions and Missionaries. Presbyterian Church of Scotland. 1786-1830. *2343*

Nova Scotia (Pictou County). Albion mines. Coal Mines and Mining. 1767-1881. *2226*

—. Blair, Duncan Black. Gaelic language, Scots. Poetry. Scholars. Scotland. 1846-93. *2346*

—. British Columbia. Politics. Tupper, Charles Hibbert. 1882-1904. *2140*

—. Cabinet. Politics. Tupper, Charles H. 1882-1904. *2321*

—. Courts. Trials. 1813. *2341*

Nova Scotia (Pictou County; Stellarton). Bakewell, Robert. Coal Mines and Mining. Howe, Joseph. 1798-1881. *2227*

Nova Scotia (Pictou Harbor). *Hector* (vessel). Immigrants. Mackenzie, Alexander. Passenger lists. Scotland. 1773. 1883. *2302*

—. *Hector* (vessel). Immigrants. Scotland. Voyages. 1773. *2340*

Nova Scotia (Pictou Island). Daily Life. ca 1930-75. *2342*

Nova Scotia (Port Hood Island). *St. Lawrence* (vessel). Shipwrecks. 1780. *713*

Nova Scotia (Port Royal). Champlain, Samuel de. L'Ordre de Bon Temps. Social Organizations. 1606. *542*

—. Charles I. Colonization. France. Great Britain. Scotland. 1629-32. *501*

—. France. Immigration. Settlement. 1650-1755. *511*

—. Military expedition, English. Phips, William (journal). 1690. *611*

Nova Scotia (Sable Island). Colonization. Rescue stations. Shipwrecks. 1759-1801. *2235*

—. Lifesaving service. Wentworth, John. 1801. *2236*

Nova Scotia (Sherbrooke). Contracts. McDonald,. Alexander N. Shipbuilding. Sutherland, Peter. 1873-74. *2265*

Nova Scotia (Springhill). Clergy. Presbyterian Church. 1874-1925. *2234*

—. Methodist Church. Presbyterian Church. St. Andrew's Wesley United Church of Canada. 1800-1976. *2233*

Nova Scotia (St. Ann's). MacLeod, Norman. Migration. Presbyterian Church. Scotland. ca 1800-50's. *2244*

Nova Scotia (Terence Bay). Ancient, William J. *Atlantic* (vessel). Heroes. Shipwrecks. 1873. *2225*

Nova Scotia (Truro). Educators. Forrester, Alexander. ca 1848-69. *2277*

Nova Scotia (Upper Musquodoboit). Howe, Joseph. 1845-47. *2355*

Nova Scotia (Waverley). Gold Mines and Mining. 1860-1976. *2275*

Nova Scotia (Yarmouth). Economic Conditions. Great Awakening. Social Conditions. 1760's-70's. *2354*

—. Genealogy. Lewis, Waitsill (family). Methodology. 1976. *2212*

—. Investments. Ports. Shipping. 1840-89. *2210*

—. Massachusetts (Boston). Steamship services. Transportation. 1855-1971. *2288*

—. New England. Steamboats. 1839-89. *2325*

Nova Scotia (Yarmouth and Argyle). Grand Jurors' Book. Local government. 1814-51. *2310*

Nova Scotia. 19c-20c. *2307*

Novascotian (newspaper). Howe, Joseph. Journalism. Nova Scotia (Halifax). 1824-38. *828*

Novels. delaRoche, Mazo. Loyalist myth. USA. 1780's. 1920's-40's. *742*

—. Duncan, Sara Jeanette *(The Imperialist)*. Imperialism. 1902-04. *1109*

—. French Canadians. Literary characters. Ontario (Glengarry County). 1925-75. *2857*

—. French Canadians. Quebec. USA. 1960's-70's. *2074*

—. Great Britain. Lawrence, D. H. 1911-30. *1121*

—. Literary Criticism. Realism. 1920-30. *1176*

—. Mass Media. USA. 1960-72. *1999*

—. Nova Scotia. Raddall, Thomas (memoirs; review article). 1913-75. *2238*

—. Ontario (Glengarry County). Pioneers. 1815-1945. *2820*

Nuclear Arms *See also* Atomic Energy; Atomic Warfare.

—. Decisionmaking. Foreign policy. 1950's-60's. *1847*

—. Diplomacy. Pearson, Lester B. 1957-59. *1832*

—. Foreign Relations. Pearson, Lester B. USA. 1945. *2024*

Nuclear nonproliferation. 1957-78. *1876*

Nuclear Nonproliferation Treaty (1968). Government secrecy. India. Nuclear Science and Technology. 1968-70's. *1844*

Nuclear proliferation. Atomic energy. 1945-75. *1328*

Nuclear Science and Technology *See also* Atomic Energy.

—. Diplomacy. Great Britain. 1973-74. *1888*

—. Government secrecy. India. Nuclear Nonproliferation Treaty (1968). 1968-70's. *1844*

Nuechterlein, Donald E. (views). Foreign Policy. USA. 1972-78. *2028*

Nuyten, Edmund. Belgian families. Immigration. Manitoba (Winnipeg, East St. Boniface). Nuyten, Octavia. 1880-1914. *2991*

Nuyten, Octavia. Belgian families. Immigration. Manitoba (Winnipeg, East St. Boniface). Nuyten, Edmund. 1880-1914. *2991*

O

Oath of allegiance. Acadians. Colonial Government. Great Britain. Land tenure. Nova Scotia. 11c-1755. *594*

O'Beirne, Eugene Francis. Manitoba (Red River country). Travel. 1860's. *3015*

Obscenity. Law reform. 1966-73. *1382*

Occupational attainment. Colleges and Universities. Graduates. Ontario. Social mobility. Women. 1960-75. *2821*

Occupational Health Act (1972). Saskatchewan. Workmen's Compensation. 1972-73. *3034*

Occupational mobility. 19c-1970's. *73*

—. Executive Behavior. -1973. *1583*

Occupational segregation. Labor. Women. 1941-71. *1502*

Occupational structure. Ontario (Ottawa). 1870. *2751*

Occupations. Bilingualism. Puerto Rico. 1970. *2587*

—. Cultural cleavages. Models. Voting and Voting Behavior. 1965-71. *1470*

—. Documents. New France. Social status. 1640's-1740's. *534*

—. Elections (federal). Parliaments. Political candidates. 1974. *1657*

—. Engineers. Ethnic groups. Quebec. Values. -1974. *2559*

—. Ethnic Groups. Europe. Immigration. Ontario (Toronto). Social Status. 1940's-70's. *2814*

—. Ethnic groups. Ontario (London). 1871. *2744*

—. Immigrants. North America. Statistics. Women. 1964-71. *1516*

—. Labor. Quebec (Montreal). 1960's-70's. *1594*

—. Periodicals. Sex roles. Women. 1920's. *1195*

Ocean currents. Climate. Cultural development. Economic development. 1925-76. *3278*

Ocean Travel *See also* Ships; Voyages.

—. Historians. Morison, Samuel Eliot (review article). Parkman, Francis. 1974. *485*

Oceanography *See also* Marine Resources; Navigation.

—. *Challenger* (vessel). Expedition. Honeyman, David. Nova Scotia (Halifax). 1872-76. *2317*

Oceans *See also* names of oceans and seas, e.g. Atlantic Ocean; International Waters; Navigation; Storms.

—. International law. Jurisdiction. Space. 1945-73. *1797*

O'Connell, Martin. Immigration policy. Public opinion. 1975. *1376*

Odlum, Victor Wentworth. China. Diplomacy. 1943-46. *1877*

Office and Professional Employees International Union. Labor Unions and Organizations. White-collar employees. 1973. *1515*

Office de la construction du Québec. Construction industry. Labor. Quebec. 1960's-70's. *2647*

Office of the Coordinator of Information. Arctic. Discovery and Exploration. Finnie, Richard Sterling (account). North America. Stefansson, Vilhjalmur. 1931-62. *3302*

Official Language Act (Quebec, 1974). English language. French Quebec Movement. Quebec. 1974. *2460*

—. Federal government. Language equality. Quebec. 1960-76. *1438*

—. French Canadians. Nationalism. Quebec. USA. 1970's. *2577*

—. French language. Quebec. 1974. *2458*

—. French language. Quebec. 1974. *2465*

—. Language. Minorities. Quebec. 1750's-1974. *2476*

Ogden, Peter Skene. Discovery and Exploration. Fur Trade. Hudson's Bay Company. 1811-54. *688*

Ogelsby, J. C. M. Developing nations. Foreign Relations (review article). Ismael, T. Y. Lyon, P. V. USA. 1860's-1976. *239*

Ogham alphabet. Discovery and Exploration. Inscriptions. Ireland. Newfoundland. St. Lunaire boulder. ca 5c-1977. *487*

Ogilvie, William (field notes). Alberta. Indians. Surveying. 1878-79. *433*

Ohio *See also* North Central States.

—. Fort Meigs. Harrison, William Henry. Virginia (Petersburg). Volunteer Armies. War of 1812. 1812-13. *765*

Ohio (Cincinnati). Immigration. Negroes. Ontario (Wilberforce). 1829-56. *626*

Oil and Petroleum Products *See also* Oil Industry and Trade.

—. Alberta (Athabasca River). Bitumen. Syncrude oil Project. 1974-75. *3150*

—. Economic growth. Energy crisis. Quebec (Montreal). 1960-80. *2644*

—. Great Lakes. Ontario. St. Lawrence Seaway. Shipping. 1973. *1539*

Oil, Chemical, and Atomic Workers International Union. Consumers Cooperative Refineries Ltd. Co-op. Saskatchewan. 1934-73. *3074*

Oil exploration. Alberta. 1890's-1910's. *3099*

—. Arctic. Daily life. Hare Indians. Indians. Northwest Territories. 1859-1974. *358*

Oil Industry and Trade. Alaska pipeline. Economic competition. USA. 1973-75. *2041*

—. Alberta (Athabasca River). Syncrude oil project. USA. 1975. *2036*

—. Alberta (Calgary). Cattle Raising. Economic Conditions. 19c-20c. *3089*

—. Alberta (Fort McMurray). Great Canadian Oil Sands. Syncrude oil project. 1975. *3111*

—. Arab States. Economic Aid. International Trade. 1960's-70's. *1770*

—. Arctic. Decisionmaking. Technology. 1970's. *3284*

—. Canol Project. Foster, W. W. USA. War Department. 1942-45. *1219*

—. Canol Project. Northwest Territories (Mackenzie Valley). Pipelines. Planning. World War II. 1942-45. *3274*

—. Energy crisis. USA. 1947-48. *2032*

—. English Canadians. Nationalism. ca 1950-75. *1976*

—. Eskimos. Industrial expansion. Land use (control). Pollution. 1975. *338*

—. Federal policy. 1968-72. *3283*

—. Foreign Investments. Multinational corporations. Social organization. 1970's. *1819*

—. Great Lakes. Shipping. ca 1700-1974. *2076*

—. Land use planning. 1960's-70's. *3280*

—. Mackenzie Valley Pipeline Inquiry. Northwest Territories. Pipelines. 1976. *3343*

Oil rights. Alberta. Devolution. Federalism. Scotland. 1970's. *3118*

Oil sands. Alberta (Ft. McMurray). Draper, Tom. 1920's-30's. *3096*

—. Alberta (Ft. McMurray). Syncrude oil project. 1975. *3111*

Ojibwa Indians. Beardy, Q. P. Jackson. Indian-White Relations. Painting. 1944-75. *401*

Okanagan Indians. British Columbia. Saunas. 1973. *448*

Oklahoma *See also* South Central and Gulf States.

—. Blackfoot Indians. Dance. Indian Days. 19c-20c. *437*

—. Farmers. Grange. Saskatchewan. Socialism. Texas. 1900-45. *3083*

Old Northwest *See also* North Central States.

—. American Revolution. Great Britain. Great Lakes. Peace of Paris (1783). Shelburne, 2d Earl of (William Petty). 1783. *727*

Oliver, Adam. Business. Legislative investigations. Ontario (Ingersoll, Thunder Bay). Provincial Politics. 1820-85. *2763*

Olympic Games. Communist Party. Germany (Berlin). People's Olympic Games. Spain (Barcelona) 1936. *1302*

—. Coubertin, Pierre de. Nationalism. Quebec (Montreal). 1900-76. *2414*

—. Drapeau, Jean. Quebec (Montreal). Sports. 1970-76. *2521*

Ombudsmen *See also* Public Administration.

—. Alberta. Great Britain. Public Opinion. 1969-71. *3109*

—. Consumers. Middle classes. Newspapers. 1970's. *1299*

One Big Union. Alberta (Drumheller Valley). Labor disputes. United Mine Workers of America. 1919. *3163*

—. American Federation of Labor. Industrial Workers of the World. Washington. 1919. *1167*

—. Coal Mines and Mining. Labor Unions and Organizations. Saskatchewan. 1907-45. *3056*

—. Labor Unions and Organizations. Radicals and Radicalism. Socialism. 1917-19. *1149*

Onomastics. Bibliographies. Toponymy. USA. 1964-75. *203*

Ontario. Agricultural development. Deforestation. Ecology. 1880-1900. *275*

—. Agriculture. Political Attitudes. Quebec. Social change. 1850-1970. *2132*

—. Alienation. Socialization. Student activism. Western Ontario, University of. 1970. *2773*

—. Antilabor sentiments. Holmes Foundry. Immigrants. Strikes. 1935-40. *1210*

—. Antislavery Sentiments. Negroes. Newspapers. *Provincial Freeman* (newspaper). Shadd, Mary Ann. 1852-93. *1046*

—. Architecture. Rideau Canal. 1820's-1971. *2794*

—. Archives. Bishops. Catholic Church. Church History. Kingston, Archdiocese of. 1800-1966. *2847*

—. Art. Fraktur. German Canadians. 1976. *2741*

—. Artists. Chippewa Indians. Cree Indians. Indians. Legend painting. Manitoba. 1960's-70's. *470*

—. Attitudes. Legislatures. Models. Political Parties. 1957-74. *2890*

—. Beaudry Report. Ham Report. Industry. Quebec. Working Conditions. 1972-74. *1536*

—. Bilingual Education. French Canadians. Postsecondary schools. 1946-73. *1499*

—. Brown, George. Labor Unions and Organizations. Publishers and Publishing. Toronto *Globe* (newspaper). Toronto Typographical Union. 1843-72. *2893*

—. Brubacher brothers. Letters. Mennonites. Pennsylvania. 1817-46. *786*

—. Business History. Economic policy. Local Government. Property, private. 1898-1911. *1100*

—. California. *Design for Development* (Ontario, 1966). Regional planning. 1965-74. *2873*

—. Canoeing. Recreation. 1888-1914. *2738*

—. Catholic Church. Education (British, US). Newspapers. 1851-1948. *2833*

—. Catholics. Emigration (Scottish). Glengarry Highlanders. Great Britain. Macdonnell, Alexander. 1770's-1814. *805*

—. Catlin, George. Chippewa Indians. Europe. Maungwudaus (George Henry). Theater. 1840's. *450*

—. Children. Great Britain. Immigration. Poor. Press. Rye, Miss. 1865-1925. *2879*

—. Chippewa Indians. Grey Owl (Archie Belaney). Myths and Symbols. 1880-1938. *372*

—. Cities. Information Storage and Retrieval Systems. Public Records. 1974. *2859*

—. Collective bargaining. Crown Employees Collective Bargaining Act. Labor. Law. 1970-74. *2745*

—. Colleges and Universities. Employment. Social Status. 1960-71. *2787*

—. Colleges and Universities. Graduates. Occupational attainment. Social mobility. Women. 1960-75. *2821*

—. Colonization. Great Clay Belt. Quebec. 1900-30. *274*

—. Communications (international, theory of). Hecksher-Ohlin theory. Quebec. 1974. *2148*

—. Confederation. French Canadians. Provincial Government. Quebec. 1867-1937. *155*

—. Country Life. Fiction. Munro, Alice. South. 1940's-70's. *2869*

—. Courts. Rape. 19c. *676*

—. Cree Indians. Fort Albany. Henley House Massacres. Hudson's Bay Company. Woudbee (chief). 1750's. *348*

—. Cultural history. Protestantism. Victorian era. 1840's-1900. *913*

—. Curricula. Physical education and training. Public schools. Strathcona Trust fund. 1919-39. *1130*

—. Cyclones. Legislation. Sex Discrimination. Wages. Wages. 1946-71. *2777*

—. Davis, William. Politics. Quebec. Separatist Movements. 1976-77. *1280*

—. Demography. Peel County History Project. Population. Social History. 1840-80. 1973. *2770*

—. Diffusion theories. Mechanization. Reaping. Technology. 1850-70. *2846*

—. Discrimination, Educational. School attendance. Social Classes. Women. 1851-71. *2754*

—. Economic Conditions. Quebec. Social Change. Violence. 1963-73. *2127*

—. Economic development. Quebec. 1951-78. *2150*

—. Electric power. Manitoba. Public Utilities. 1905-30. *2138*

—. Empire Day celebrations. Great Britain. Imperialism. Nationalism. Public Schools. 1890-1930's. *2864*

—. Family. Feminism. Social reform. 1875-1900. *2830*

—. Family. Social Conditions. 1820-60. *2771*

—. Farmers. Inheritance. Land. 19c. *807*

—. Federal Government. Hepburn, Mitchell F. King, William Lyon Mackenzie. Lieutenant governors. Provincial government. 1937. *1208*

—. Fort George. Upper Canada. 1796-1969. *753*

—. Frederick House Massacre. Fur Trade. Hudson's Bay Company. Indian-White Relations. 1812-13. *2828*

—. Geographic mobility. Rural Settlements. Social mobility. 19c. *849*

—. Geography. Urban history. Prehistory-1976. *1317*

—. Government. Human rights agencies. Racism. 1973-77. *2790*

—. Great Lakes. Howell, William Maher (reminiscences). Pennsylvania (Erie). Quebec. St. Lawrence Seaway. Travel. 1928. *2131*

—. Great Lakes. Oil and Petroleum Products. St. Lawrence Seaway. Shipping. 1973. *1539*

—. Historians. Spragge, George Warburton (obituary). 1893-1976. *2731*

—. Iceland. Immigration. 1872-75. *2761*

—. Indian-White Relations. Schools. 1780-1841. *474*

—. Jarvis, Stinson. Psychic phenomena. Watkins, Kathleen ("Kit of the Mail"). 1885-95. *2891*

—. Liberal Party. Political participation. 1960's-70's. *2748*

—. Lime kilns. Pioneers. Technology. 1870-1917. *2850*

—. Manitoba. Winnipeg River. 1730's-1960's. *2122*

—. Mass transit. Public Utilities. Toronto Railway Company. 1891-1921. *2760*

—. McCarthy, D'Alton. Politics. Social reform. 1876-98. *1057*

—. McLachlan, Alexander. Poetry. Radicals and Radicalism. Social reform. Working class. 1818-96. *924*

—. Modernization. Quebec. Social change. 1950-1974. *2479*

—. Nationalism. Publishers and Publishing. 1970-75. *2809*

—. Nature Conservation. New York. St. Lawrence Seaway. Thousand Islands. 19c-20c. *279*

—. One-party dominant system. Opposition parties. Political Parties. Provincial Government. 1970-71. *2811*

—. Oral history. Theater. 1973-75. *2855*

—. Pharmaceutical education. Shuttleworth, Edward Buckingham. 1868-92. *2867*

—. Political participation. Students. Voluntary Associations. 1970. *2749*

—. Politics. Rolph, George. Rolph, John. Trials. 1825-30. *2843*

—. Population. Rural-Urban Studies. 1941-66. *2743*

—. Prohibition. Racism. Reform. 1890-1915. *2756*

—. Quantitative sources, utility of. Quebec. Transportation. Urban hierarchy. 1861-1901. *2137*

—. Queenston Heights (battle). Upper Canada. War of 1812. 1812. *766*

—. Rehabilitation services. Workmen's Compensation Board. 1973. *2780*

—. Rural Settlements. Social status. Women. 19c. *2729*

—. Short Hills raid. Trials. 1838-40. *818*

—. Tornadoes. 1792-1899. *2832*

Ontario (Algoma Diocese). Episcopal Church, Protestant. 1873-1973. *2880*

Ontario (Algoma, Huron). Church of England. Indians. Missions and Missionaries. Wilson, Edward F. 1868-93. *432*

Ontario (Ansonville). Jews. Kalter, Bella Briansky (reminiscences). Rural Settlements. 1929-40. *2800*

Ontario (Belleville). Children. Federal government. New York (Watertown). Political structures. Provincial government. 1977. *1423*

Ontario (Bruce County; Waterloo). Catholic Church. German Alsatians. Gravemarkers. Iron work. 1850-1910. *2837*

Ontario (Canada West). Agricultural journals. Animal husbandry. 1835-55. *792*

—. Attitudes. Immigration. Ireland. Potato famine. 1845-50. *797*

—. Cameron, John Hillyard. Conservatism. Political Leadership. 1854-56. *855*

Ontario (Casummit Lake). Frontier and Pioneer Life. Gold Mines and Mining. William, Eileen (recollections). 1930's. *2888*

Ontario (Charlton Island, James Bay). Excavations. Hudson's Bay Company. 1680's. 1972-73. *566*

Ontario (Cobalt). Mining. Research. 20c. *2728*

Ontario (Cobourg). Church of England. Clergy. Diocesan Theological Institute. Frontier and Pioneer Life. Strachan, John. 1840-55. *679*

Ontario (Craigmont). Corundum mining. 1900-13. *2812*

Ontario (Credit River Valley). Economic development. Population. 1820's-1976. *2824*

Ontario (Depot Harbour). Lake Huron (Georgian Bay). Lumber industry. Ports. 1900-28. *2742*

Ontario (Dunnville). Armour, John. Letters. 1829-81. *768*

Ontario (Ehwae). Indian Wars. Seneca Indians. 1640-42. *517*

Ontario (Essex County). Land. Speculation. 1790-1900. *777*

Ontario (Falconbridge-Sudbury). Pollution. Population. 1970-74. *2866*

Ontario (Georgian Bay). Canals. Public Finance. Railroads. 1850-1915. *925*

—. Lake Huron. Raguneau, Paul (letter). 1648. *589*

Ontario (Glengarry County). French Canadians. Literary characters. Novels. 1925-75. *2857*

—. Novels. Pioneers. 1815-1945. *2820*

Ontario (Grand River). Brant, Joseph (Thayendanegea, Mohawk chief). Indians. Iroquois Indians. 1742-1807. *440*

Ontario (Great Clay Belt). Colonization literature. Settlement. 1900-31. *2848*

Ontario (Guelph). Conservative Party. Drew, George. Political Campaigns. 1890-1925. *2736*

Ontario (Guelph area). Central Place System. Quantitative Methods. Urbanization. 1851-1970. *2753*

—. Urban development. 1824-1971. *2752*

Ontario (Haliburton, Victoria Counties). Political Campaigns. 1917. *2788*

Ontario (Hamilton). Business History. Marketing (wholesale). 1840-75. *2823*

—. Census. Household structure. 1851-71. *2759*

—. City Government. Pressure groups. Public Utilities. 1900-25. *2817*

—. Cooke, Willie. Custer, George A. Little Big Horn (battle). 1860's-70's. *2878*

—. Elites. Entrepreneurs. 1850's. *2801*

—. Family. Katz, Michael B. (review article). Social Classes. 1850-80. *2725*

—. Fuga, Francis J. Shrine of Our Lady of Klococov. Slovak Canadians. Uniates. 1952-77. *2895*

—. Industrialization. Public schools. Socialization. 19c. *2802*

—. Political parties. Socioeconomic groups. 1967-72. *2796*

Ontario (Hamilton; Westdale). Suburbs. 1911-51. *2883*

Ontario (Hamilton, Peel counties). Census. Literacy. Methodology. Social organization. 19c. *2822*

Ontario Historical Society. *Papers and Records* (periodical). 1899-1947. *2805*

Ontario (Holland Marsh). Ethnic groups. Rural settlements. 1930's-76. *2881*

Ontario (Ingersoll, Thunder Bay). Business. Legislative investigations. Oliver, Adam. Provincial Politics. 1820-85. *2763*

Ontario (Kenora, Anicinabe Park). Chippewa Indians. Indians. 1950's-74. *389*

Ontario (Kingston). Catholic Church. Church History. St. Mary's Cathedral of the Immaculate Conception. 1843-1973. *2765*

—. Catholic Church. Congregation of Notre Dame (Sisters). Religious education. Women. 1841-48. *2737*

—. Church of England. Morris, William. Presbyterians. Queen's College. Scots. 1836-42. *2831*

—. Collins Bay Penitentiary. Libraries. Prisons. Resocialization. 1963-73. *2851*

—. Lake Ontario. New York (Ogdensburg). Steamboating. Transportation. 1815-70. *653*

—. Political Leadership. Smith, Henry. 1830-70. *897*

Ontario (Kingston, Market Shoal). Excavations. Martello towers. 19c. 1972. *856*

Ontario (Kitchener). Elections, municipal and provincial. Urban Renewal. 1967-71. *2889*

—. Labor Unions and Organizations. National Trades and Labour Congress. Quebec. Trades and Labour Congress of Canada. 1892-1902. *2655*

Ontario (Lake of the Woods). Manitoba (Winnipeg). Water supply. 1912-75. *2997*

Ontario (Lake Ontario, Lake Erie). Welland Canal. 1967-73. *2856*

Ontario (Lake Superior). Evans, James. Missions and Missionaries. Voyages. Wesleyan Methodist Church. 1837-38. *2810*

Ontario (Lennox and Addington). Elections. Political Change. 1836. *823*

Ontario (London). Architecture. City planning. Mutual Advisory Committee. Politics. Preservation. 1970-77. *2727*

—. Bucke, Richard M. Whitman, Walt (interview). 1880. *1055*

—. Ethnic groups. Occupations. 1871. *2744*

—. Heritage Act (1975). Local Architectural Conservation Advisory Committee. Preservation. 1945-77. *2818*

—. Housing. Prices. Railroads. 1972. *1591*

Ontario (Long Branch). Aeronautics, Military. Royal Canadian Air Force (Flying School). 1915-16. *1153*

Ontario (Malden Township). Abstract Index to Deeds. Land. Law. 18c-1865. 1978. *778*

Ontario (Manitoulin). Agriculture and Government. Elections. Political Protest. 1914-18. *2775*

Ontario (Manitoulin Island). Business. Federal Government. Indians (reservations). Missions and Missionaries. 1830-60. *350*

—. Indian-White Relations. Violence. 1860-65. *410*

Ontario (Middlesex County). Crime and Criminals. Ethnicity. Illiteracy. Sex. Social Status. 1867-68. *1044*

—. Crime and Criminals. Quantitative Methods. 19c-20c. *74*

Ontario (Toronto). Clothing industries. Locational clustering. Publishers and Publishing. Quebec (Montreal). 1949-67. *1611*

Ontario (Moosonee). Church of England. Missions and Missionaries. Vincent, Thomas. 1835-1910. *3296*

Ontario (Napanee). Libraries. Mechanics' Institute movement. Social Classes. 1850-1900. *914*

Ontario, northern. Cadieux, Lorenzo (obituary). Jesuits. Scholarship. 1903-76. *2772*

—. Chippewa Indians. Cree Indians. Fishing. Indians. Lakes. 19c-1978. *341*

—. Railroads. Schools. 1922-28. *2865*

Ontario, northwestern. Mercury poisoning. Pollution. Regional government. 1970's. *2781*

—. Politics. 1908-76. *2887*

Ontario (Oakville). Beauty shop. Hair care. Harper, Martha Matilda. 1857-93. *2874*

Ontario (Orillia). Adolescence. Dependency. Employment. Frontier and Pioneer Life. Social change. 1861-71. *2769*

Ontario (Osceola). Dams. Energy crisis. Farms. Water power. 1902-05. *2813*

Ontario (Ottawa). Algonquin College Resource Centre. Bibliography, regional. Methodology. 1974-78. *2142*

—. Architecture. Capitol Theatre. Entertainment. Movie palaces. Vaudeville. 1920-70. *1138*

—. Archives. City Government. 19c-1976. *2886*

—. Art. Artifacts. Canadian Conservation Institute. Preservation. 1978. *31*

—. Boosterism. Capital, national. 1822-59. *865*

—. Catholic Church. D'Aquin, Marie Thomas. Joan of Arc Institute. Social Work. Women. 1903-19. *2746*

—. Church of England. Letters. Politics. Thompson, Annie Affleck. Thompson, John S. D. 1867-94. *1075*

—. Clays, sensitive. Geology. Soil Conservation. 1648-1971. *276*

—. Conservation movements. Federal Regulation. Lumber industry. "Robber Barons.". 1873-1914. *2774*

—. Economic Growth. Urbanization. 19c. *2872*

—. Indians. Native Peoples' Caravan. Political Protest. 1975. *463*

—. Occupational structure. 1870. *2751*

Ontario (Ottawa Diocese). Catholic Church. French Canadians. Guigues, Joseph-Eugène. 1848-74. *2747*

Ontario (Oxford, Waterloo Counties). Mennonites. 1839-1974. *2739*

Ontario (Peterborough). Botany. Traill, Catherine Parr. 1830's-99. *2819*

—. Colonial policy. Emigrant guides. Great Britain. Land grants (proposed). Traill, Catherine Parr. 19c. *869*

—. Labor Disputes. Textile Workers' Union of America. Tilco Plastics Strike (1965-67). 1965-70. *1610*

Ontario (Prince Rupert's Land). Daily life. Dufaut, J. (diary). Fur trade. Indians. XY Company. 1803-04. *2956*

Ontario (Queenston). 1780-1973. *2779*

Ontario reaction. Church and state. Elections (1890). Equal Rights Association. Quebec. 1885-95. *2827*

Ontario (Rideau Corridor). Architectural survey. -1880. 1969-74. *2793*

Ontario (Sandy Inlet, Lake Temagami). Camp Wanapitei. Paradis, Charles. Settlement. 1895-1970's. *2789*

Ontario (Sarnia). Michigan (Port Huron). Railroad tunnels. St. Clair River. Transportation, Commercial. 1884-91. *108*

Ontario (Sault Ste. Marie). Fishing. Indians. Trade. 17c-1920. *419*

—. Indians. Indian-White Relations. Schools. Shingwauk Industrial Home. Wawanosh Home for Indian Girls. Wilson, E. F. 1871-93. *475*

Ontario (Sault Ste. Marie, St. Joseph's Island). Archaeology (amateur). *Chicora* (vessel). Great Lakes. Scuba diving. 1961-62. *585*

Ontario (Silver Islet). Silver Mining. 1856-1922. *2868*

Ontario (Sioux Lookout Zone). Chippewa Indians. Cree Indians. Health services. 1900-73. *427*

Ontario, southern. Activity levels. Population. Spatial structure. 1941-71. *2733*

—. Autocovariance procedures. Metropolitan Areas. Population. 1871-1975. *2732*

—. Cities. Conservative Party. Voting and Voting Behavior. 1908-19. *2844*

—. Federal Government. Labor Disputes. Unemployment. 1901-20's. *89*

—. Friends, Society of. 19c. *2792*

Ontario (St. Catharines). Great Lakes. Shickluna, Louis. Shipbuilding. 1835-80. *2882*

Ontario (Sudbury). Inco, Ltd. Labor Disputes. 1977. *2816*

Ontario (Thorold). Bombings. Clan-na-Gael. Dillon, Luke. Irish Americans. Welland Canal. 1900-14. *1083*

Ontario (Thunder Bay). Businessmen. Voting and Voting Behavior. 1968-71. *2829*

Ontario (Toronto). Acculturation. Boardinghouses. Immigrants. Italian Canadians. 20c. *2782*

—. Acculturation. Immigrants. 1950's-70's. *2785*

—. Anti-Communist movements. Anti-Semitism. Freedom of speech. Immigration. National self-image. 1928-29. *2791*

—. Architects. 1834-90's. *2740*

—. Archives. Immigrants. Photographs. 1900-30. 1974. *2877*

—. Archives, City. 1959-73. *2797*

—. Armstrong, Frederick H. Mackenzie, William Lyon. Mayors. 1835-37. 1967. *2854*

—. Artisans. Construction. Labor Unions and Organizations. Politics. 1896-1914. *1103*

—. Arts programs. 1978. *2764*

—. Asian Canadians. Political Protest. 1970's. *2795*

—. Assimilation. Cultural autonomy. Italians. Mass media. 1970's. *2735*

—. Assimilation. Employment. Immigrants. Language training. 1968-70. *1625*

—. Assimilation. Immigrants. Macedonians. 1900-20. *2840*

—. Assimilation. Jews. Presbyterian Church. 1912-18. *2776*

—. Association of Commercial and Technical Employees. Canadian Labour Congress. Labor Reform. White-collar employees. 1972. *2731*

—. Baptist. Christian Biography. McMaster, Susan Moulton Fraser. 1819-1916. *2750*

—. Baptists. Fundamentalist-Modernist controversy. Jarvis Street Church. Religious factionalism. Social Classes. 1895-1934. *2762*

—. Behavior (aggressive). Hockey. Sports. Violence. 1972. *2862*

—. Bengough, John Wilson. City government. *Grip* (periodical). Political Reform. Protestantism. 1873-1910. *2807*

—. Book Industries and Trade. Copyright violations. Publishers and Publishing. Robertson, John Ross. 1877-90. *2815*

—. Business. Elites. Upper Canada Club. 1835-40. *812*

—. Canadian Armed Forces Command and Staff College. Military Education. 1966-74. *1312*

—. Canadian Catholic Historical Association. Catholic Church. 1933-73. *1318*

—. Catholic Church. Harris, William Richard (biography). 1846-1923. 1974. *2858*

—. Catholic Church. St. Basil's Seminary. Vatican Council II. 1962-67. *2806*

—. Catholic Church. Saints Cyril and Methodius Parish. Slovak Canadians. 1934-77. *2894*

—. Centre for Urban and Community Studies. Rural-Urban Studies. Urban history. 1965-78. *1352*

—. Chinese. Racism. 1881-1912. *2838*

—. Church and State. Church of England. King's College, York (charter). Scotland. Strachan, John. 1815-43. *625*

—. Church of England. Strachan, John. 1802-67. *2834*

—. City Government. Compensation, municipal. 1858-70. *2798*

—. City government. Political Corruption. Pressure Groups. Reform. 1890-1900. *2884*

—. City government. Progressivism. Wickett, Samuel Morley. 1900-15. *2885*

—. City planning. 1970's. *2804*

—. Class structure. Public schools. 1851. 1964-74. *1445*

—. Collective bargaining. Organizational Theory. Printing. 19c. *2892*

—. Consumer behavior. Population. Shopping centers. 1974. *2835*

—. Culture. Economic Growth. Urbanization. 1850-1914. *2863*

—. Discrimination. Economic Conditions. West Indians. 1977. *2768*

—. Discrimination, Employment. Immigrants. Social Status. West Indians. 1972. *2849*

—. Employment. Immigrants. Italians. 1885-1915. *2783*

—. Ethnic Groups. Europe. Immigration. Occupations. Social Status. 1940's-70's. *2814*

—. Ethnicity. Greek Canadians. Immigration. Private Schools. 1900-40. *2845*

—. Family. Italian Canadians. Social Mobility. 1935-60. *2870*

—. Feminism. Law Enforcement. Prostitution. Rape. 1975-78. *2825*

—. Fur Trade. La Jonquière, Marquis de. 1750-1887. *564*

—. Harbor Master. Marine Engineering. Richardson, Hugh. 1821-70. *2726*

—. Higgins, William (imprisonment). Political Corruption. 1834. *2853*

—. Immigrants. Macedonians. Urban history. 20c. *2786*

—. Immigrants. Stereotypes. Urban history. 19c-20c. *2784*

—. Immigration. Italian Canadians. Population. 1946-72. *2875*

—. Immigration. Macedonians. Social Conditions. 1900-30. *2841*

—. Immigration. Wages. 1971. *2871*

—. Industrial council. Massey-Harris plant. Public relations. 1919-29. *1188*

—. Industrialization. Knights of Labor. Knights of St. Crispin. Labor Unions and Organizations. 1856-90. *1050*

—. Labor Unions and Organizations. Production control. 1860-92. *2803*

—. National Self-image. 1970. *1465*

—. Social Status. Voting and Voting Behavior. 1971. *1662*

—. Urban Renewal. 1970-73. *2734*

Ontario (Toronto area). Children. Inequality (perceived). Public schools. Social Classes. Values. 1977. *1345*

Ontario (Upper Canada). Anti-Americanism. Rebellion of 1837. Sectarianism. 1837. *817*

—. Baldwin, William Warren. Duels. McDonnell, John. 1812. *2842*

—. Bell, George P. M. Business records. Depressions. Economic change. Rural Settlements. 1825-60. *672*

—. Bethune, Donald. Finance. Steamboat business. 19c. *837*

—. Burge family. Friendship. Letters. Simcoe family. 1790-1820. *669*

—. Church of England. Land endowment. Rolph, John. Strachan, John. Toronto, University of. 1820-70. *809*

—. Criminal Justice System. Prisons. Reform. 1835-50. *769*

—. Elementary education. 1810-45. *780*

—. Engineering. Keefer, Thomas Coltrin. Railroads. 1821-1915. *909*

—. Exiles. Loyalists. McDowall, Robert James. Missions and Missionaries. Reformed Dutch Church. 1790-1819. *747*

—. Fort George. 1796-1969. *753*

—. Frontier. Letters. Painting. Simcoe, Elizabeth. Values. 1790-1800. *638*

—. Governors. Great Britain. Head, Francis Bond. 1835. *667*

—. Gowan, Ogle. Immigration. Irish influence. Orangeism. Politics. 1830-33. *821*

—. Heir and Devisee Commission (2d, 1805). Land grants. 1800-45. *645*

—. History Teaching. Loyalism. Textbooks. 19c-20c. *741*

—. Intellectual history. Political theory. Reform. 1800-50. *832*

—. Land grants. Military. Settlement. 1816-20. *788*

—. Land speculation. Rural land occupation. Settlers. Townships. 1782-1851. *793*

—. Public Schools. Sports. Upper Classes (British). 1830-75. *852*

—. Queenston Heights (battle). War of 1812. 1812. *766*

—. Rural Development. Settlement. 1782-1851. *794*

—. Social control. Sunday schools. 19c. *643*

Ontario (Upper Canada, Midland District). Cemeteries. Frontier society. Mortality. 1783-1851. *749*

Ontario (Upper Canada; Toronto). Elites. Government. Simcoe, John Graves. Strachan, John. 1793-1818. *773*

Ontario (Upper Canada; York). Emigration. Great Britain (Sussex). Petworth Emigration Committee. 1830-40. *775*

Ontario Waffle. Socialist critiques (review article). 1973. *1487*

Ontario (Waterloo County). Conservatism. Liberalism. Mennonites. 1977. *2767*

—. Folk Art. Fraktur. Mennonites. Weber, Anna. 1825-88. *2836*

Ontario (Wentworth County). Family size. Rural-Urban Studies. Social Surveys. 1871. *2757*

Ontario (Wilberforce). Immigration. Negroes. Ohio (Cincinnati). 1829-56. *626*

Ontario (Windsor). Ford Motor Company of Canada. Labor Law. Rand formula. United Automobile Workers (Canadian Region). 1945-46. *1534*

—. Ford Motor Company of Canada. Labor Law. Rand formula. United Automobile Workers (Canadian Region). 1946. *1595*

—. Music. 1860's-1901. *2778*

Ontario (York Factory). Anglican Communion. Cree Indians. Faries, Richard. Missions and Missionaries. 1896-1961. *379*

Operation Crossroads Africa. Africa. Robinson, James H. Students. USA. 1958-73. *1749*

Ophthalmology. Eskimos. Eye diseases. 1974. *312*

Opposition parties. One-party dominant system. Ontario. Political Parties. Provincial Government. 1970-71. *2811*

Oral history. Academia. Archives. Journalism. 1960-75. *1311*

—. Alberta. Daughters. Mothers. Pioneers. 1890-1929. *1025*

—. Alberta. Rural Settlements. Women. 1890-1929. *3149*

—. Archives. Public Archives of Canada. 1976. *1265*

—. Art history. Bourassa, Napoléon. 1800-1930. *241*

—. Art history. Hill, Charles C. (account). 1975. *1400*

—. Biography. Crampton, Esmé (account). Dance. Lloyd, Gweneth. 1969-75. *1371*

—. Canadian Psychological Associations. Psychology. 1970-75. *1442*

—. Copyright laws. Oral Institute for Studies in Education. Publishers and Publishing. 1960's-75. *1313*

—. Daily life. Historiography. Popular thought. 20c. *1320*

—. Diefenbaker, John. Stursberg, Peter (reminiscences). 1957-75. *1264*

—. External Affairs Department (Historical Division). Videotaping. 1971-76. *1255*

—. Folklore. Kealey, James (and family). Quebec (Hull). 1974-75. *2492*

—. Foreign Policy. 1970-75. *1744*

—. Historiography. Working Class (review article). 20c. *103*

—. Methodology. 1930's-70's. *1323*

—. Museums. 1970's. *1315*

—. Ontario. Theater. 1973-75. *2855*

—. Ostry, Bernard (address). 1975-76. *1322*

—. USA. Videotapes. 1955-77. *164*

Oral Institute for Studies in Education. Copyright laws. Oral history. Publishers and Publishing. 1960's-75. *1313*

Oral tradition. British Columbia, southwestern. Indians. Lillooet Indians. Prehistory-1976. *289*

—. British Columbia, southwestern. Indians. Lillooet Indians. Prehistory-1976. *291*

—. Folklore. Nova Scotia. 20c. *2357*

Orange Order. Elections. Farmers. Political Attitudes. United Farmers of Ontario. 1920-25. *2839*

Orangeism. Gowan, Ogle. Immigration. Irish influence. Ontario (Upper Canada). Politics. 1830-33. *821*

Oregon. Boundary dispute. Diplomacy. Great Britain. Polk, James K. USA. 1845-46. *835*

Oregon (Astoria). China market. Fur Trade. North West Company. 1760's-1821. *785*

Organization and Methods Development. Civil Service Commission. 1946-76. *1660*

Organization of American States. Administrative structure. International law. Rio Treaty. San José resolution. 1945-75. *1892*

—. Americas (North and South). Indians. International law. UN. 19c-1974. *367*

Organizational Theory *See also* Public Administration.

—. Collective bargaining. Ontario (Toronto). Printing. 19c. *2892*

—. Political parties. 1960-70's. *1688*

Organizations *See also* specific organizations by name; Social Organizations; Societies; Voluntary Associations.

—. Immigration. Slovak Americans. 1890-1964. *112*

—. Mentally retarded. Nova Scotia. Social Reform. ca 1900-27. *2245*

Ormsby, Margaret. British Columbia. Cultural History. 1930's-74. *3234*

Ornithology. Blakiston, Thomas Wright. British North American Exploring Expedition. Explorers. North America. Palliser, John. 1857-91. *859*

—. Blakiston, Thomas Wright (letters). Saskatchewan River. 1857-59. *860*

Orphan House. Children. Nova Scotia (Halifax). 1752-87. *2262*

Osgood, Thaddeus. Evangelism. Religious Education. 1807-52. *673*

Osler, William. Anatomy, morbid. Dreams. Medicine (practice of). USA. 1872-1919. *908*

—. Autopsies. Medical Research. ca 1876-1900. *2552*

Ostry, Bernard (address). Oral history. 1975-76. *1322*

Ottawa Indians. Chippewa Indians. Folklore. Indians. Nanabozho (mythical character). 19c-20c. *397*

Ottawa-Rideau military canal. Canals. Imperial funds (diversion). Military. 1815-25. *799*

Otter, William. Internment operations. World War I. 1914-20. *1161*

Ouellet, Fernand. Agricultural crisis. Historiography. Paquet, Gilles. Quebec (Lower Canada). Wallot, J.-P. 1802-12. 1963-73. *789*

Ouimet, Marcel. Radio. 1939-75. *1441*

Ouren, Hogan (reminiscences). Colorado. Daily Life. Frontier and Pioneer Life. Nebraska. 1861-66. *851*

Outlaws. British Columbia (Quatsino Sound). Civil War. Quantrill, William Clarke. 1861-1907. *3226*

Outports. Annexation. Confederation. Newfoundland. Poverty. Social Customs. 1920-48. *2200*

Overland Journeys to the Pacific. Discovery and Exploration. Mackenzie, Alexander. Trade Routes. 1789-93. *2134*

Overtime. Employment. Fringe benefits (economic effects). 1957-67. *1552*

—. Employment. Labor cost, non-wage. 1973. *1566*

Oxford Movement. Church of England. Medley, John (letters). New Brunswick (Fredericton). Pusey, Edward Bouverie. ca 1840-44. *2389*

P

Pacey, Desmond. Editors and Editing. Grove, Frederick Philip (letters). Literature. 1912-48. 1976. *1135*

Pacific Area. Alaska. British Columbia. China (Macao). Cook, James. Fur trade. 1778-79. *784*

—. Alaska. Discovery and Exploration. Lapérouse, Jean François. Ledyard, John. Pacific Northwest. Russia (Siberia). 1778-1806. *652*

—. Alexander I. Foreign policy. North America. Russian-American Company. 1799-1824. *678*

—. Americas (North and South). Discovery and Exploration. Europe, Eastern. 16c-19c. *175*

—. California (San Francisco). Hudson's Bay Company. Ice trade. Russian-American Company. 1850's. *878*

—. Economic growth. Trade Regulations. 1970-73. *1830*

—. Economic organizations. Free Trade Area (proposed). International Trade. 1975. *1837*

—. Foreign policy. 1969-73. *1829*

Pacific Area (north). Defense Policy. Expansionism. Great Britain. 1850-1914. *919*

—. Diplomacy. Maritime Law. Territorial Waters. 1958-75. *1826*

—. Extinction, threatened. Hunting. Seals. USA. 1886-1910. *936*

Pacific Basin. Eskimos. Ethnology. Indians. Polynesians. Prehistory-1976. *285*

Pacific Northwest. Alaska. Discovery and Exploration. Lapérouse, Jean François. Ledyard, John. Pacific Area. Russia (Siberia). 1778-1806. *652*

—. Alexander I (ukase). Foreign Relations. Great Britain. Noncolonization principle. Russo-American Convention of 1824. 1821-25. *627*

—. Anthropology. Art. British Columbia. Duff, Wilson. 1950-76. *280*

—. Anthropology, Cultural. Myths and Symbols. Tsimshian Indians. Prehistory-20c. *456*

—. Baskets. Indians. Photographs. 1880's-1900's. 1978. *415*

—. Bible. Indians. Missions and Missionaries. Myths and Symbols. 1830-50. *438*

—. Bibliographies. British Columbia. Lumber and Lumbering. 1890's-1960's. *3221*

—. Bibliographies. Indians. Music. 1888-1976. *353*

—. British Columbia. Chinook jargon. 1830's-1976. *412*

—. British Columbia (Vancouver Island). Fishing rights. International Pacific Salmon Fisheries Commission. Salmon. Treaties. 1970's. *2018*

—. Buttons, Phoenix. Haiti. Indians. Trade. Uniforms, Military. 1812-30. 20c. *460*

—. Diplomacy. Monroe Doctrine. Russia. 1812-23. *657*

—. Episcopal Church, Protestant. Hudson's Bay Company. Indians. Missions and Missionaries. 1825-75. *402*

—. Firearms. Indians. 1774-1825. *382*

—. Fort Vancouver. Fur trade. Hudson's Bay Company. McLoughlin, John. 1825-60. *861*

—. Indians. -1973. *342*

Pacifism. Fairbairn, R. Edis. Protestantism. United Church of Canada. World War II. 1939. *1241*

Page Family. French Canadians. Genealogy. Quebec (Laprairie). 1763-1967. *2530*

Painting *See also* Landscape Painting.

—. Art Galleries and Museums (proposed). Légaré, Joseph. Quebec. 1824-1933. *2544*

—. Art History (review article). British Columbia. Murray, Joan. Reid, Dennis. 1778-1935. *3189*

—. Artists. Rand, Paul. 1930's-50's. *1118*

—. Beardy, Q. P. Jackson. Indian-White Relations. Ojibwa Indians. 1944-75. *401*

—. Birds. Discovery and Exploration. Hood, Robert. Saskatchewan River. 1819-21. *2928*

—. British Columbia. Carr, Emily. Forests and Forestry. Indians. 1904-45. *3260*

—. Carr, Emily. Indians. 1888-1972. *362*

—. Daily life. Great Lakes. Indians. Kane, Paul. 1845-46. *384*

—. Frontier. Letters. Ontario (Upper Canada). Simcoe, Elizabeth. Values. 1790-1800. *638*

—. Jackson, Henry A. C. Mushrooms. Naturalists. 1870's-1950's. *228*

—. Schoonover, Frank. Western States. 1899-1968. *2951*

Pakistan *See also* India.

—. Foreign Relations. 1973. *1733*

Palliser, John. Blakiston, Thomas Wright. British North American Exploring Expedition. Explorers. North America. Ornithology. 1857-91. *859*

Pan-American Union. Foreign Relations. Latin America. USA. World War II. 1939-44. *1239*

Paper Industry. Dubuc family papers. Quebec (Saguenay River, Lake St. John). 1892-1963. *2612*

Paper mills. Herty, Charles Holmes. Newsprint. Pine trees. Scientific Experiments and Research. Southeastern States. 1927-40. *1134*

Papers and Records (periodical). Ontario Historical Society. 1899-1947. *2805*

Papineau, Louis-Joseph. Act of Confederation (1867). Political Theory. Quebec, battle of. 1759-1867. *896*

—. Historiography. Politics. Quebec. Rebellion of 1837. Rumilly, Robert (review article). 1791-1871. 1934. 1977. *822*

Paquet, Gilles. Agricultural crisis. Historiography. Ouellet, Fernand. Quebec (Lower Canada). Wallot, J.-P. 1802-12. 1963-73. *789*

Paradis, Charles. Camp Wanapitei. Ontario (Sandy Inlet, Lake Temagami). Settlement. 1895-1970's. *2789*

Parent Commission. Educational Reform. Quebec. 1944-66. *2416*

Parent, Étienne. British Empire. Confederation. *Le Canadien* (newspaper). 1831-52. *830*
Paris, Treaty of (1783). Boundaries. Great Britain. Lake of the Woods. USA. 1755-1925. *723*
Parish registers. Catholic Church. Government. Quebec. 1539-1973. *526*
—. Catholic Church. Population. Quebec. 1616-1700. *540*
—. Population. Quebec. Statistics. 1621-99. *541*
Parishes. Catholic Church. French Canadians. Migration, Internal. Quebec (Compton County). Rural-Urban Studies. 1851-91. *2534*
—. New Brunswick. 1784-1861. *2413*
—. Quebec (Saint-Hyacinthe County). Regional complexity. Voting and Voting Behavior. 1867-86. *2555*
Parkin, Al (interview). British Columbia. Daily Life. Lumber camps. 1910's-30's. *3255*
Parkin, George R. Britannic Idealism (concept). Imperialism. Nationalism. 1871-1922. *912*
Parkman, Francis. Historians. Morison, Samuel Eliot (review article). Ocean Travel. 1974. *485*
—. Historiography. Jesuits. New France. 17c. 1840's-60's. *518*
Parliamentary representation. Northwest Territories. 1870-87. *2935*
Parliamentary system. Constitution of 1791. Quebec (Lower Canada). 1791. *710*
—. Government Reorganization Act of 1971. Ministers and Ministries Act. Presidential politics. 1966-74. *2106*
Parliament. Anglin, Timothy Warren. 1874-78. *1039*
—. Anti-Inflation Act. Supreme Court, Canada. 1975-76. *1685*
—. Apportionment. King, William Lyon Mackenzie. Saskatchewan (Prince Albert). 1925-35. *3038*
—. Borden, Frederick W. Business. Family. Liberal Party. Nova Scotia (King's County). 1874-96. *2316*
—. Bourassa, Henri. Progressives. 1926. *1182*
—. British North America Act (1867). Constitutional amendments. Great Britain. Trudeau, Pierre Elliott. 1867-1970's. *1249*
—. Brown, J. L. Liberal Party. Manitoba (Lisgar). Winkler, H. W. (career). 1926-53. *3021*
—. Elections. France. Language. Quebec. 1792-1810. *700*
—. Elections (federal). Occupations. Political candidates. 1974. *1657*
—. Federal Regulation. 1970's. *1659*
—. International Organizations. 1969-74. *1849*
—. Law. Political parties. 1920's-74. *1648*
—. Minority government. 19c-20c. *53*
—. Political Factions. 1858-1900. *907*
—. Political Parties. Ralliement des Creditistes. 1930's-71. *1700*
—. Television. 1970-73. *1673*
Parochial Schools. See Church Schools; Religious Education.
Parti Québécois. Business community. Nationalism. Quebec. Working class. 1970's. *2690*
—. Economic Conditions. French language. Politics. Quebec. Social Customs. 1973-78. *2696*
—. Economic independence. Quebec. USA. 1972-73. *1267*
—. Elections. Independence issue. Liberals. Quebec. 1973-76. *2707*
—. Elections. Labor Unions and Organizations. Quebec. 1970-77. *2591*
—. Elections. Quebec. 1973-76. *2693*
—. Elections. Quebec. 1976. *2695*
—. Elections, provincial. Jews. Quebec. Separatist Movements. 1976. *2721*
—. Federal government. New Democratic Party. Quebec. Separatist Movements. 1960's-70's. *2102*
—. Federal government. Provincial Government. Quebec. Social Change. 1960-77. *2420*
—. Federal Government. Quebec. Separatist Movements. 1976-77. *2112*
—. Foreign policy. Trudeau, Pierre Elliott. 1968-78. *1836*
—. Foreign Relations. Quebec. Separatist Movements. USA. 1973-77. *1993*
—. French Canadians. Independence. Monetary Systems. Quebec. 1974. *2424*
—. French Canadians. Liberal Party. 1978. *1716*
—. Lévesque, René. Newspapers. Provincial Government. Quebec (Montreal). 1976-77. *2423*
—. Lévesque, René. Quebec. Separatism. Trudeau, Pierre Elliott. 1970's. *2110*

—. Lévesque, René. Quebec. Separatist Movements. 1968-70's. *2713*
—. Political attitudes. Quebec. 1976-78. *2697*
—. Quebec. Self-determination. Sovereignty. 1970's. *2116*
—. Quebec. Separatist Movements. 1970's. *2107*
—. Quebec. Separatist Movements. 1973. *2720*
Parties, Political. See Political Parties.
Partisanship. Apportionment. British Columbia. Provincial Legislatures. 1952-78. *3199*
Pass Strike of 1932. Alberta. British Columbia. Coal Mines and Mining. Depressions. 1920's-30's. *1209*
Passamaquoddy Bay. Electric power. Energy. Fundy, Bay of. Tides. 1919-64. 1975. *115*
Passenger lists. *Hector* (vessel). Immigrants. Mackenzie, Alexander. Nova Scotia (Pictou Harbor). Scotland. 1773. 1883. *2302*
—. Immigration. Mennonites (Russian). Quebec. 1874-80. *966*
Pastoralism. Authors. 18c-19c. *259*
—. Grove, Frederick Phillip (writings). Literature. Technology. 1920-45. *38*
Patrick, William. Ecumenism. Presbyterian Church. 1900-11. *1085*
Patriote de l'Ouest (newspaper). Catholic Church. French language. Saskatchewan. 1910-41. *2929*
Patriote uprising. Rebellions. Vermont. 1837-38. *810*
Patriotism. Boer War. Military service, British. Socioeconomic characteristics. Volunteers. 1899-1902. *1099*
—. Folk Songs. Music. "Yankee Doodle" (song; origins). 1730-1820. *2295*
—. Literary growth, theories of. 1864-1914. *904*
Patronage. Agriculture Minister. Gardiner, James G. Liberal Party. 1935-57. *2959*
—. Bourassa, Robert. Liberal Party. Quebec. 1970-75. *2440*
—. Political parties. Quebec. 1944-72. *2439*
Payne, John Howard. Doane, Elizabeth O. M. P. (memoirs). Nova Scotia (Barrington). 1715-98. *2224*
Peace See also International Security; Pacifism.
Peace mission. Davis, Jefferson. Lincoln, Abraham. Virginia (Richmond). 1864. *838*
Peace of Paris (1783). American Revolution. Great Britain. Great Lakes. Old Northwest. Shelburne, 2d Earl of (William Petty). 1783. *727*
Peace River country. Alberta. Homesteading and Homesteaders. Ukrainians. Zahara, Dominka Roshko. 1900-30. *1034*
—. Pioneers. 1914-76. *3105*
Peacekeeping Forces. Africa, southern. Foreign Policy. Trudeau, Pierre Elliott. UN Conference on the Law of the Sea. 1968-78. *1775*
—. Defense Policy. NATO. Trudeau, Pierre Elliott. 1968-78. *1752*
—. Foreign Policy. NATO. UN. 1956-77. *1861*
—. International Commission for Supervision and Control. Vietnam War. 1954-73. *1774*
—. International Commission for Supervision and Control. Vietnam War. 1973. *1795*
—. International Commission for Supervision and Control. Vietnam War. 1973. *1938*
—. International Security. UN. 1975. *1823*
Peacetime. Anti-Inflation Act. Emergency powers. Supreme Court (Canada). Wages. 1976. *1607*
Pearkes, G. R. British Columbia. Conscription, Military. World War II. 1943-44. *3248*
Pearson, Lester B. 1897-1972. *1723*
—. 1936-72. *1915*
—. Cold War. Foreign Relations. 1948-57. *1821*
—. Commission on International Development. 1968-69. *1806*
—. Diplomacy. 1948-57. *1918*
—. Diplomacy. Great Britain. International meetings. USA. 1935-72. *1910*
—. Diplomacy. Korean War. Self-determination. UN. 1950-72. *1768*
—. Diplomacy. Nuclear Arms. 1957-59. *1832*
—. Diplomacy. St. Lawrence Seaway. USA. 1949-66. *1758*
—. Diplomacy. Suez crisis (1956). UN. 1956. *1873*
—. Diplomatic relations. Heeney, Arnold D. P. (memoirs). USA. 1897-1972. *1975*
—. Foreign Relations. 1948-57. *1855*
—. Foreign Relations. France. 1955-65. *1250*
—. Foreign Relations. Great Britain. 1936-72. *1791*
—. Foreign Relations. Nuclear arms. USA. 1945. *2024*
—. Great Britain. Heeney, Arnold D. P. (review article). USA. 1920's-70's. *1790*

—. Great Powers. Lie, Trygve. UN. 1946. *1738*
Pearson, William (reminiscences). Colonization. Real Estate. Saskatchewan. 1903-13. *1015*
Peasant movements (colloquium). Agriculture. Europe. Industrialization. Market economy. North America. ca 1875-1975. *13*
Peasants See also Farmers; Land Tenure; Working Class.
—. Agriculture. Capitalism. Quebec. 1600-1970's. *2595*
—. American Revolution. Attitudes. Carleton, Guy. Military Occupation. Quebec. 1775-76. *717*
Pêcheurs-Unis. Cooperatives. Fishing. Quebec (Gaspé Peninsula). World War II. 1939-48. *2638*
Peck, E. J. Church Missionary Society. Church of England. Eskimos. Hudson's Bay Company. Missions and Missionaries. Northwest Territories (Baffin Island). Trade. 1894-1913. *340*
Pedagogy. See Teaching.
Peel County History Project. Demography. Ontario. Population. Social History. 1840-80. 1973. *2770*
Pegasus (vessel). Great Britain. Newfoundland. William IV (visit). 1786. *2193*
Penal transportation. Durham, 1st Earl of. Political prisoners. Public opinion. 1835-50. *827*
Pennefather, John P. (reminiscences). Alberta. Military Medicine. North West Rebellion. Winnipeg Light Infantry. 1885. *1016*
Penner, Jacob. City Politics. Manitoba (Winnipeg). Webb, Ralph. 1919-34. *2993*
—. Manitoba (Winnipeg). Russia. Socialist movement. 1900-65. *2998*
Pennsylvania See also Northeastern or North Atlantic States.
—. Brubacher brothers. Letters. Mennonites. Ontario. 1817-46. *786*
—. Eby, Ezra E. Immigration. Loyalists. Mennonites. 18c-1835. *743*
Pennsylvania (Erie). Great Lakes. Howell, William Maher (reminiscences). Ontario. Quebec. St. Lawrence Seaway. Travel. 1928. *2131*
Pennsylvania (Lancaster County). Brethren in Christ. Engel, Jacob. Sects, Religious. 1775-1964. *250*
Pennsylvania (Philadelphia). American Revolution. Friends, Society of. Great Britain. Ireland. Relief funds. 1778-97. *739*
—. Irish Canadians. McCabe, James (and descendants). Nova Scotia (Pictou). ca 1743-1917. *2306*
Pensions See also Aged.
—. Aged. Labor Unions and Organizations. United Automobile Workers (Canadian Region). 1913. *1580*
—. Aged. Social security. -1973. *1505*
—. Houses, communal. 1971-73. *1297*
—. International Association of Machinists and Aerospace Workers. Social Security. 1968-73. *1618*
Pentecostal Assemblies of Canada. Purdie, James Eustace. Theological education. 1925-50. *1137*
Pentz, Gabriel. Alabama. Alcohol. Florida. Nova Scotia. Smuggling. 20c. *2249*
People's Olympic Games. Communist Party. Germany (Berlin). Olympic Games. Spain (Barcelona). 1936. *1202*
Pepperrell, William. British North America. Colonial Government. ca 1715-59. *601*
Periodicals See also Editors and Editing; Freedom of the Press; Newspapers; Press.
—. Economics. Minville, Esdras. Quebec (Montreal). 1922-28. *2533*
—. Fiction. Social Organization. 1930's-70's. *260*
—. Foreign investments. Income. Income Tax. Interest groups. USA. ca 1930-74. *2016*
—. Great Britain. India. Political science. 1970's. *1805*
—. Literature. Quebec. 20c. *2505*
—. Nationalism. Publishers and Publishing. Tariff. USA. 1920's. *1193*
—. Occupations. Sex roles. Women. 1920's. *1195*
Perley, Moses H. Colebrook, William. Indians. New Brunswick. 1840's. *2408*
Perry, Oliver Hazard. Dobbins, Daniel. Lake Erie (battle of). Madison, James. War of 1812. Warships. 1812-13. *762*
Persecution See also Anti-Semitism; Civil Rights; Religious Liberty.
—. Dukhobors. Immigration. Russia. Sects, religious. 1654-1902. *1033*

Perseverance (vessel). Hudson's Bay Company. Northwest Territories (Marble Island). Whaling Industry and Trade. 1866-67. 1892-97. *681*

Personal growth. Education. Income. Scandinavia. USA. 1975. *1450*

Personality. Eskimos, Inuit. Family. Values. 1974. *333*

—. Federal Government. Quebec. 1972-74. *2435*

Perspective Canada II (report). *Social Indicators, 1976* (report). USA. 1976. *1357*

Petroglyphs. Minnesota. Nova Scotia. Scandinavians. West Virginia. 14c. *478*

Petroleum. *See* Oil and Petroleum Products.

Petworth Emigration Committee. Emigration. Great Britain (Sussex). Ontario (Upper Canada, York). 1830-40. *775*

Pewaukee (vessel). Maritime history. Shipwrecks. *Two Friends* (vessel). Wisconsin (North Bay, Milwaukee). 1873-1913. *1048*

Peyto, Bill. Alberta. Banff Park. Explorers. Scientific expeditions. 1887-1933. *3092*

Pharmaceutical education. Ontario. Shuttleworth, Edward Buckingham. 1868-92. *2867*

Pharmacy *See also* Botany; Drug Abuse.

—. Chloroform. Fraser, James Daniel Bain. Medicine (practice of). Nova Scotia (Pictou). 1807-69. *2247*

Pharmacy, History of. American Institute of the History of Pharmacy. Canadian Academy of the History of Pharmacy. Stieb, Ernst W. (account). 1940's-70's. *2059*

Philanthropy *See also* Charities.

—. Sports. Strathcona, 1st Baron. 1870-1915. *938*

Philosophy *See also* Ethics.

—. Demers, Jerôme. Quebec. Science. Teaching. 1765-1835. *2502*

Phips, William. Acadia. France. New England. War. 1689-1713. *597*

Phips, William (journal). Military expedition, English. Nova Scotia (Port Royal). 1690. *611*

Phonographs. Cris Indians. Ethnomusicology. Leden, Christian. Songs. 1911. *387*

Photographs. Alberta. Harvests. Wheat. 1910-20. *3168*

—. Alberta (Edmonton). Sports. 1900's. *3170*

—. Archives. Immigrants. Ontario (Toronto). 1900-30. 1974. *2877*

—. Baskets. Indians. Pacific Northwest. 1880's-1900's. 1978. *415*

—. Bell, Alexander Graham. Deaf. Library of Congress, Gilbert J. Grosvenor Collection. 1870-1922. *2228*

—. Curtis, Edward S. Indians. 1892-1932. *403*

—. Curtis, Edward S. Indians. Morgan, J. P. 1868-1952. *472*

—. Lumber and Lumbering. Price, Vernon (interview). Quebec (Schyan River area). 1938-39. *2641*

Photography *See also* Films.

—. Agriculture. Alberta (Rosebud Creek). Biggs, Hugh Beynon. Ranches. 1892-1941. *3169*

—. Alberta. Boorne, W. Hanson. 1886-93. *3171*

—. Assiniboine and Saskatchewan Exploring Expedition. Discovery and Exploration. Hime, Humphrey Lloyd. Prairie Provinces. 1858. *863*

—. Geological surveys. 1858-97. *266*

—. Gold Rushes. Klondike Stampede. Restorations. Yukon Territory. 1897-98. 1970's. *3336*

Physical Education and Training *See also* Sports.

—. Borden, F. W. Strathcona Trust fund. ca 1900-10. *1104*

—. Curricula. Ontario. Public schools. Strathcona Trust fund. 1919-39. *1130*

—. Federal government. 1850-1972. *62*

—. Federal Government. Sports. 1909-54. *1144*

—. Middle classes. Sports. 1850-1900. *930*

—. Social sciences. 1970's. *1402*

Physical Geography *See also* Climate; Earthquakes; Oceans; Rivers.

—. British Columbia (Bridge River Valley). Economic conditions. Gold Mines and Mining. 19c-1970's. *3251*

—. Climate. Highway construction. Roads. 1949-73. *3297*

Physicians. Alberta, northern. Indians. Jackson, Mary Percy. Métis. 1929-70's. *3119*

—. Arctic. Explorers. Rae, John. 1835-93. *3315*

—. Europe (Eastern, Southern). Immigration. Legislation. Racism. 1920's. *1178*

—. Jews. Manitoba. 19c. *2994*

—. Medical reform. Quebec. 1940-70. *2614*

Pictou Academy. Dalhousie College. McCulloch, Thomas. Missions and Missionaries. Nova Scotia. Presbyterian Church. ca 1803-42. *2215*

Pictou Grammar School. Education. McCulloch, Thomas. Nova Scotia. 19c. *2337*

Pictou Literature and Scientific Society. Literature. Nova Scotia. Science. 1834-54. *2248*

Pietism. Great Plains. Prairie Radicals. 1890-1975. *2901*

Pinard, Maurice. Political Parties. Third parties. 1900-73. *1148*

Pinard, Maurice (review article). *Créditiste* movement. French Canada. Quebec. Stein, Michael (review article). 1971-74. *2447*

Pine trees. Herty, Charles Holmes. Newsprint. Paper mills. Scientific Experiments and Research. Southeastern States. 1927-40. *1134*

Pinheiro, Diogo (voyages). Baptista de Lima, Manuel C. (research). Discovery and Exploration. Pinheiro, Manoel (voyages). Portugal (Barcelos). 1521-98. *508*

Pinheiro, Manoel (voyages). Baptista de Lima, Manuel C. (research). Discovery and Exploration. Pinheiro, Diogo (voyages). Portugal (Barcelos). 1521-98. *508*

Pioneers *See also* Frontier and Pioneer Life; Homesteading and Homesteaders; Voyages.

—. Alberta. Daughters. Mothers. Oral history. 1890-1929. *1025*

—. Alberta (Lethbridge). Culture. Industry. Transportation. 1880's. *3104*

—. Arctic, northern. Greist, Mollie Ward. Women. ca 1850-1970's. *3344*

—. British Columbia (Lower Fraser Valley). Landscape, physical. Surveyors. 1859-90. *3235*

—. Cooking. Food. 1750-1850. *803*

—. Daily life. Nova Scotia. 19c-1910. *2311*

—. Jews. Manitoba (Winnipeg). 1860's-1975. *2969*

—. Knollin, William Mortimer. Marshall, Samuel. Nova Scotia. Villiers, Charles E. 19c. *2309*

—. Lime kilns. Ontario. Technology. 1870-1917. *2850*

—. Lowes, Ellen McFadden (diary). Manitoba (Elliott Settlement). 1882-83. *998*

—. Manitoba. Red River of the North. Sutherland, Catherine McPherson. 1814-71. *1028*

—. Nova Scotia (Digby County). Stehelin, Emile Charles Adolph (family). 1837-1918. *2324*

—. Novels. Ontario (Glengarry County). 1815-1945. *2820*

—. Peace River country. 1914-76. *3105*

—. Saskatchewan. Welsh. 1902-14. *3069*

—. Sibbald, Susan *(Memoirs)*. 1783-1866. *2766*

Pipelines. Canol Project. Northwest Territories (Mackenzie Valley). Oil Industry and Trade. Planning. World War II. 1942-45. *3274*

—. Mackenzie Valley Pipeline Inquiry. Northwest Territories. Oil Industry and Trade. 1976. *3343*

Pit houses. British Columbia (Victoria). Provincial Museum. Salish (Flathead) Indians. Shuswap Lake Park. 1972. *455*

Pitts, Herman H. Anti-Catholicism. New Brunswick. Religion in the Public Schools. 1871-90. *2388*

Place Names. *See* Toponymy.

Plagiarism. Graham, Andrew. Hudson's Bay Company. Hutchins, Thomas. Natural history. 1770's-1815. *692*

Plains Indians. Buffalo migrations. Fur trade. Prairie Provinces. 1770-1869. *429*

—. Family. Indians. Kin terminologies. Language. Social Organization. Prehistory-19c. *426*

Planning *See also* City Planning; Regional Planning; Urbanization.

—. British Columbia. Civil Defense. Emergencies. Provincial Government. 1951-76. *3233*

—. Canol Project. Northwest Territories (Mackenzie Valley). Oil Industry and Trade. Pipelines. World War II. 1942-45. *3274*

—. Counties. Health care services. Quebec. 1974. *2428*

—. Economic development. Social Conditions. Sweden. 20c. *1310*

—. External Affairs Department (Policy Analysis Group). Foreign Policy. 1969-77. *1889*

—. Foreign policy. World War II. 1943-45. *1238*

—. Hydroelectric power. Water. 1973. *1335*

Plessis, Joseph-Octave. Atlantic Provinces. Catholic Church. Diaries. Quebec Archdiocese. 1812-15. *2155*

Poetry. Alberta. Johnson, Pauline (Tekahionwake). Mohawk Indians. 1895-1913. *363*

—. Blair, Duncan Black. Gaelic language, Scots. Nova Scotia (Pictou County). Scholars. Scotland. 1846-93. *2346*

—. British Columbia. Engineering. Lumber and Lumbering. Railroads. Swanson, Robert (interview). 20c. *3273*

—. *Canadian Forum* (periodical). Depressions. 1929-39. *1213*

—. McLachlan, Alexander. Ontario. Radicals and Radicalism. Social reform. Working class. 1818-96. *924*

—. Miron, Gaston. Quebec. Sovereignty. 1969-74. *2470*

—. Myths and Symbols. National characteristics. 20c. *75*

Poets. Carman, William Bliss (letters). Guiney, Louise Imogen. 1887-98. *1045*

—. Chesterton, G. K. (lectures). Intellectuals. 1921. 1930. *1184*

Poland. Art. Cultural relations. Mass Media. USA. 1940-74. *1953*

—. Foreign influences. National self-identity. Quebec. 1970's. *2675*

Polar exploration. Arctic Ocean. Eskimos. Mackenzie Bay (Herschel Island). Whaling Industry and Trade. 1826-1972. *339*

Polar Gas Project. Arctic. Natural gas. Northwest Territories (Melville, King Christian Islands). USA. 1972-75. *3355*

Police *See also* Crime and Criminals; Criminal Law; Law Enforcement; Prisons.

—. Alberta. 1917-32. *3156*

—. Jurisdiction. Intergovernmental Relations. Law Enforcement. Legislation. 1970's. *1711*

—. Public Opinion. Royal North West Mounted Police. 1874-83. *1007*

—. Politics. Provincial Government. Royal Canadian Mounted Police. Saskatchewan. 1916-28. *3065*

Polish Canadians. 1945-70's. *1359*

—. Acculturation. Immigrants. 1945-75. *1436*

—. Ethnicity (review article). Portuguese Canadians. Scottish Canadians. 18c-20c. 1976. *201*

—. Haidasz, Stanley. Multiculturalism. 1975. *1412*

—. Immigration. 1900-65. *1419*

—. Slavic Languages. 20c. *1392*

Political Attitudes. Agriculture. Ontario. Quebec. Social change. 1850-1970. *2132*

—. Anglophones. National identification. Quebec. Separatist Movements. 1970's. *2120*

—. Anti-Americanism. Loyalist tradition. New Brunswick. 1825-1914. *2375*

—. Apathy. Puerto Rico. Voter registration. 1974-77. *1957*

—. Confederation. Derby, 15th Earl of. Great Britain. Head, Edmund Walker. Letters. 1858. *894*

—. Cultural membership. Ethnic Groups. Quebec. 1974. *2548*

—. Elections. Farmers. Orange Order. United Farmers of Ontario. 1920-25. *2839*

—. Family compact. Government, responsible. 19c. *831*

—. Foreign Relations. USA. 1975-76. *2020*

—. Independence Movements. Quebec. 1960's-70's. *2100*

—. Parti Québécois. Quebec. 1976-78. *2697*

Political autonomy. Economic progression. Education. Immigration. Professions. 1945-75. *1425*

Political Campaigns *See also* Campaign Finance; Elections; Political Speeches.

—. Boucherville, Charles Eugène Boucher de. Federalism. Joly, Henri-Gustave. Liberal Party. Provincial government. Quebec. 1878. *2452*

—. Conservative Party. Drew, George. Ontario (Guelph). 1890-1925. *2736*

—. Editorials. Federal systems. USA. 1972. *1715*

—. Editorials. Newspapers. 1972. *1722*

—. Military Service. Voting and Voting Behavior. World War I. 1917. *1159*

—. Nova Scotia (New Glasgow). 1875-1926. *2350*

—. Ontario (Haliburton, Victoria Counties). 1917. *2788*

Political candidates. Elections (federal). Occupations. Parliaments. 1974. *1657*

Political change. Economic Development. Northwest Territories. 19c-. *3352*

—. Elections. Ontario (Lennox and Addington). 1836. *823*

—. Ideas, History of. Social Change. 1780-1800. *795*

—. Modernization. Quebec. Separatist Movements. 19c-1970's. *151*
Political Commentary. Democrats (writings). Social thought. 19c. *235*
—. Great Britain. Social change. Socialism. Webb, Beatrice. Webb, Sidney James. 1911. *1090*
Political Corruption *See also* Elections; Lobbying; Political Reform.
—. City government. Manitoba (Winnipeg). Public Administration. Urbanization. 1884-85. *3013*
—. City government. Ontario (Toronto). Pressure Groups. Reform. 1890-1900. *2884*
—. Higgins, William (imprisonment). Ontario (Toronto). 1834. *2853*
—. Howe, Joseph. Local Government. Nova Scotia (Halifax). Trials. 1835. *808*
Political Crimes *See also* Political Corruption; Treason.
—. Churchill Forest Industry. Fraud. Manitoba. ca 1965-74. *2982*
Political Culture. 1885-1974. *1726*
—. Attitudes. Regionalism. 1965. *2143*
—. "Civility" (measured). Gouzenko, Igor. USA. 1953-54. *1941*
Political debates. Anglin, Timothy Warren. Fenians. Irish Canadians. McGee, D'Arcy. 1863-68. *891*
Political decisions. UN Security Council. 1976. *1822*
Political Economy *See also* Economics.
—. Fishing industry. Government. Newfoundland. 1949-75. *2179*
—. Social sciences. USA. 1920-70. *45*
Political Factions *See also* Interest Groups; Lobbying.
—. Bermuda. Education. Religion. 1800-1977. *136*
—. British West Indies. 1884-1921. *196*
—. Elections. Legislative Assembly. Propaganda. 1792. *708*
—. Parliaments. 1858-1900. *907*
Political geography. Behaviorism. Quebec (Saguenay County). Spatial perception. Territorialism. 1969-74. *2448*
Political Indicators. British Columbia. New Democratic Party. Voting and Voting Behavior. 1968-74. *3212*
Political Integration *See also* Confederation.
—. Australia. Germany. Middle powers. South Africa. 1850-1900. *903*
Political Leadership. Anderson, William J. House of Representatives. Negroes. Vermont (Montpelier, Shoreham). 1900-40's. *2565*
—. Autobiography and Memoirs (review article). Behavior. 1914-70. *1661*
—. Barber, James David. King, William Lyon Mackenzie. Prime ministers. 1920's-40's. 1972-76. *1147*
—. Black, Conrad. Duplessis, Maurice. Historiography. Quebec. Rumilly, Robert. 1936-59. *2684*
—. Business. Economic growth. Manitoba (Winnipeg). Urbanization. 1874-1914. *2968*
—. Cameron, John Hillyard. Conservatism. Ontario (Canada West). 1854-56. *855*
—. Coldwell, Major J. Farmer Labor party. Progressivism. Social Democracy. 1907-32. *2962*
—. Farmer Labor Party. Radicals and Radicalism. Saskatchewan. Socialism. 1932-34. *3048*
—. Governors-General. 1915-72. *66*
—. Ontario (Kingston). Smith, Henry. 1830-70. *897*
—. USA. Women's liberation. 1960-75. *1270*
Political Leadership (review article). Autobiography and Memoirs. Biography. 19c-20c. *242*
Political oppression. Colonial Government. Great Britain. Quebec (Lower Canada). USA. 1851. *697*
Political participation. 1975. *1724*
—. Age. Voting and Voting Behavior. 1968. *1650*
—. Alberta (Calgary). Woman's Canadian Club. 1911-20's. *3097*
—. Co-operative Commonwealth Federation. Saskatchewan. United Farmers of Canada. 1930-45. *3047*
—. Liberal Party. Ontario. 1960's-70's. *2748*
—. Methodology. 1974. *1641*
—. Nova Scotia (Halifax). Sabatier, William. 1780-1826. *2256*
—. Ontario. Students. Voluntary Associations. 1970. *2749*
—. Public employees. Public Service Employment Act, 1967. 1967-70's. *1640*
—. USA. 1973. *1681*

Political Parties *See also* names of political parties, e.g. Democratic Party, Republican Party, etc.; Campaign Finance; Elections; Political Campaigns; Third Parties.
—. 1975-77. *1631*
—. 1958-74. *1705*
—. Alberta. Farmers. Provincial Legislatures. 1920's-30's. *2944*
—. Alberta. Unity movement. 1935-45. *3148*
—. Attitudes. Legislatures. Models. Ontario. 1957-74. *2890*
—. British Columbia. Elections (federal). Voting and Voting Behavior. 1974. *3231*
—. British Columbia. Government. Socialism. 1972-75. *3214*
—. British Columbia. Social Classes. 1971-73. *3272*
—. British Columbia (Vancouver). Elections. Models. 1937-74. *3230*
—. British Columbia (Vancouver). Ideology. Manitoba (Winnipeg). Methodology. 1967-69. *1727*
—. Church and State. Prince Edward Island. Prince of Wales College Act (1860). School Boards. 1860-63. *2208*
—. Conservative Party. Diefenbaker, John. 1956-67. *1672*
—. Constituency service. Provincial legislatures. 1972. *1647*
—. Cooperative Commonwealth Federation. Saskatchewan. Socialism. 1928-44. *3067*
—. Elections. 1965. 1968. *1653*
—. Elections, federal. Municipalities, redistributing. Quebec. Voting and Voting Behavior. 1968. *2422*
—. Entropy concept. Information theory. Voting and Voting Behavior. 1962-69. *1683*
—. Law. Parliaments. 1920's-74. *1648*
—. Newspapers. Saskatchewan. 1914-29. *3031*
—. One-party dominant system. Ontario. Opposition parties. Provincial Government. 1970-71. *2811*
—. Ontario (Hamilton). Socioeconomic groups. 1967-72. *2796*
—. Organizational theory. 1960-70's. *1688*
—. Parliaments. Ralliement des Créditistes. 1930's-71. *1700*
—. Patronage. Quebec. 1944-72. *2439*
—. Pinard, Maurice (theories). Third parties. 1900-73. *1148*
—. Political Systems. Socialism. USA. 1846-1972. *128*
—. Provincial Legislatures. Social Conditions. 1950-70. *2996*
—. Regionalism. 1965-68. *1654*
—. Socialism. USA. 1776-1976. *148*
—. USA. Voting and Voting Behavior. 1948-74. *1730*
—. Voting and Voting Behavior. 1975. *1671*
—. Voting and Voting Behavior. 1926-72. *1714*
Political philosophy. Catholic Church. Lamarche, Gustave. Quebec. Separatist Movements. 1922-75. *2705*
Political power. English Canadians. French Canadians. Press. Quebec. 1864-67. *2572*
Political prisoners. Amnesty International. 1961-75. *1831*
—. Durham, 1st Earl of. Penal transportation. Public opinion. 1835-50. *827*
Political Protest *See also* Revolution; Riots; Youth Movements.
—. Agriculture and Government. Elections. Ontario (Manitoulin). 1914-18. *2775*
—. Alberta. Cities. Social Conditions. 1918-39. *3110*
—. Asian Canadians. Ontario (Toronto). 1970's. *2795*
—. Canadian Labour Congress. Federal government. Wages. 1976. *1563*
—. Economic opportunities. Social Classes. USA. 1960-74. *1365*
—. Folk music. Social change. Values. 1776-1976. *1377*
—. Government financing. Radicals and Radicalism. Social services. 1960's-70's. *1689*
—. Indians. Native Peoples' Caravan. Ontario (Ottawa). 1975. *463*
—. Jesuits' Estates Act. Protestants. 1880-90. *1058*
Political Recruitment. Alberta. Cities. Local Government. 1971. *3129*
—. Australia. Cabinet. Great Britain. Netherlands. USA. 1940's-60's. *1666*
Political Reform *See also* names of reform movements, e.g. Progressivism, etc.; Lobbying; Political Corruption.

—. Bengough, John Wilson. City government. *Grip* (periodical). Ontario (Toronto). Protestantism. 1873-1910. *2807*
—. Bureaucracies. Citizen participation. Great Britain. USA. 1973. *1667*
—. City government. 1890-1920. *158*
—. City Government. 1875-1976. *243*
—. City government. Newfoundland (St. John's). 1888-92. *2180*
—. Constitutional Law. Federalism. 1968-77. *2118*
—. Elections. Newfoundland (St. John's). Representative government. 1974. *2194*
—. Family Compact. McNab, Allan. 1838-44. *825*
—. Government effectiveness. Quebec National Assembly. 1964-75. *2444*
—. Local government. Manitoba (Winnipeg). Working class. 1873-1971. *2990*
—. Marxism. Quebec. Revolution. 1960-65. *2640*
Political Science *See also* Constitutional History; Constitutional Law; Democracy; Government; Imperialism; Law; Legislation; Nationalism; Politics; Public Administration; Revolution; Utopias.
—. Great Britain. India. Periodicals. 1970's. *1805*
—. Leisure. Politics. 1974. *1696*
—. Lobbying. Politics. 1975. *1651*
—. Methodology. 1974. *1309*
—. Research. Voting and Voting Behavior. 1967-75. *1655*
—. Sociology. Textbooks. 1970's. *1459*
—. USA. 1970's. *1473*
Political scientists. 1971. *1404*
—. Diplomats. Public Policy. 1970's. *1703*
Political socialization. Children, English- and French-Canadian. Government. Quebec. 1970-71. *2549*
—. Indians. Nationalism. Nova Scotia (Cape Breton). Regionalism. Whites. 1860's-1970's. *2361*
—. Religion. Voting and Voting Behavior. 1965. *1670*
Political Speeches. Nixon, Ricahrd M. 1970. *391*
Political stability. Centralization. Quebec. Separatist movements. 1960-75. *1695*
—. Democracy. Dissent. Quebec. 1960's-70's. *2489*
Political strategy. Military. NATO. 1969. *1755*
—. Methodist Church. Regionalism. Trades and Labour Congress of Canada. 1870-1919. *2916*
Political success. Campaign Finance. Manitoba. Quebec. Voting and Voting Behavior. 1975. *1728*
—. Council of Europe. Foreign relations. International law. 1965-70's. *1801*
Political systems. Air pollution. Sweden. USA. 1974. *1691*
—. Children. Federal government. New York (Watertown). Ontario (Belleville). Provincial government. 1977. *1423*
—. Federalism. French Canadians. 1763-1973. *690*
—. Federalism. Government, federal and provincial. 1867-1974. *219*
—. Interest groups. Quebec. 1970's. *2429*
—. Political Parties. Socialism. USA. 1846-1972. *128*
Political Theory *See also* kinds of political theory, e.g. Democracy; Political Science.
—. Act of Confederation (1867). Papineau, Louis-Joseph. Quebec, battle of. 1759-1867. *896*
—. Brougham, Henry Peter. Canadian Rebellion Losses Bill. Gladstone, William Ewart. Great Britain. 1849. *814*
—. Democracy. Humanism. MacPherson, C. B. Marxism. 1976. *1338*
—. Extraparliamentarism. 1840-1972. *186*
—. Intellectual history. Ontario (Upper Canada). Reform. 1800-50. *832*
—. Manitoba. Métis. Red River Rebellion. Riel, Louis. 1869. *972*
Political Violence. *See* Violence.
Politics *See also* headings beginning with the word political; City Politics; Elections; Geopolitics; Government; Intergovernmental Relations; Lobbying; Local Politics; Minorities in Politics.
—. Aberhart, William. Alberta. Economic reform. Radio. Religion. 1934-37. *3088*
—. Abolition Movement. Anderson, John. Foreign Relations. Great Britain. USA. 1860-61. *883*

—. Acadians. Catholic Church. Irish Canadians. New Brunswick. Quebec. Schools. Taxation. 1871-73. *1067*

—. Alaska Land Settlement of 1971. Eskimos. Minorities. 1960-73. *318*

—. Alberta. Kansas. Leedy, John Whitnah. Prairie radical. Radicals and Radicalism. 1880's-1935. *3087*

—. Archambeault, Louis. 1815-90. *898*

—. Architecture. City planning. Mutual Advisory Committee. Ontario (London). Preservation. 1970-77. *2727*

—. Armstrong, E. H. Nova Scotia. 1923-24. *2367*

—. Art. Language. Regionalism. 1978. *2123*

—. Artisans. Construction. Labor Unions and Organizations. Ontario (Toronto). 1896-1914. *1103*

—. Asian Canadians. British Columbia. Immigration. Racism. 1850-1914. *900*

—. Atlantic Provinces. Bibliographies. Economic development. Social classes. 1920's-70's. *2161*

—. Atlantic Provinces (review article). France. Historiography. Missions and Missionaries. New France. 1000-1770. 19c. *67*

—. Bible-reading. Catholic Church. Prince Edward Island. Protestants. Public Schools. 1856-60. *2207*

—. Blake, Edward (career). Psychological problems. 1850-1900. *926*

—. British Columbia. Labor Unions and Organizations. 1976. *3232*

—. British Columbia. Legislation. Provincial Government. 1977. *3238*

—. British Columbia. Nova Scotia (Pictou County). Tupper, Charles Hibbert. 1882-1904. *2140*

—. British Columbia (Kitsilano). Community services. Mental health. Psychiatry. 1973-74. *3237*

—. British Columbia (Vancouver). Fishing industry. Housing. Labor. 1970's. *3172*

—. Business. Legislative Investigations. Oliver, Adam. Ontario (Ingersoll, Thunder Bay). 1820-85. *2763*

—. Cabinet. Nova Scotia (Pictou County). Tupper, Charles H. 1882-1904. *2321*

—. Canals. Geographic space. International Trade. National Development. Railroads. 1818-1930. *54*

—. Catholic Church. Church and State. Europe, Western. North America. 1870-1974. *246*

—. Church of England. Letters. Ontario (Ottawa). Thompson, Annie Affleck. Thompson, John S. D. 1867-94. *1075*

—. Colleges and Universities. Public opinion. Students. 1974. *1432*

—. Conservatism. Hartz, Louis. Liberalism. Socialism. USA. 1955-78. *1668*

—. Co-operative Union of Canada. Labor Unions and Organizations. 1909-31. *1129*

—. Davis, William. Ontario. Quebec. Separatist Movements. 1976-77. *1280*

—. Economic Conditions. 1970's. *1314*

—. Economic conditions. Foreign Relations. USA. 1970's. *1995*

—. Economic Conditions. French language. Parti Québécois. Quebec. Social Customs. 1973-78. *2696*

—. Economic development. Energy. Public Policy. 1945-76. *1571*

—. Economics. Foreign policy. Military. 1950's-70's. *1856*

—. Economics. Foreign Relations. USA. 1945-74. *1253*

—. Ethnic Groups. Meisel, John (review). Simeon, Richard (review). 1960-68. *1713*

—. Europe. Military operations. World War II. 1939-45. *1244*

—. Feminism. Literature. McClung, Nellie L. Reform. 1873-1930's. *1189*

—. Fiscal policy. Inflation. 1945-75. *1596*

—. Foreign Relations. Interdependence. USA. 1960's-70's. *2002*

—. Foreign relations. Multinational corporations. UN. 1970's. *1868*

—. Government. Regionalism. 1974. *2144*

—. Government. Textbooks. 1607-1974. *1729*

—. Gowan, Ogle. Immigration. Irish influence. Ontario (Upper Canada). Orangeism. 1830-33. *821*

—. Historiography. Papineau, Louis-Joseph. Quebec. Rebellion of 1837. Rumilly, Robert (review article). 1791-1871. 1934. 1977. *822*

—. Housework. Wages. Women. 1970's. *1692*

—. Irish Canadians. Newfoundland. Religion. 19c. *2189*

—. King, William Lyon Mackenzie. Liberal Party. Quebec. 1919-50. *1132*

—. Law. Macdonald, Hugh John. 1870-1929. *921*

—. Leisure. Political Science. 1974. *1696*

—. Liberal Party. Manitoba. Railroads. Schools. 1870's-90's. *2987*

—. Liberal Party. Newfoundland. Progressive Conservative Party. 1908-72. *2195*

—. Lobbying. Political science. 1975. *1651*

—. Maritime provinces. Prairie Provinces. Provincial Government. 1910-27. *2125*

—. McCarthy, D'Alton. Ontario. Social reform. 1876-98. *1057*

—. McKim, Andrew. Nova Scotia. Provincial Legislatures. 1784-1840. *2348*

—. Methodology. Public opinion. 1970's. *1687*

—. Midwest. Reciprocity. USA. 1909-11. *1110*

—. Nationalism. Social change. 1957-75. *1720*

—. New Brunswick. Satire. Street, Samuel Denny. 1802. *2409*

—. Ontario. Rolph, George. Rolph, John. Trials. 1825-30. *2843*

—. Ontario, northwestern. 1908-76. *2887*

—. Police, provincial. Provincial Government. Royal Canadian Mounted Police. Saskatchewan. 1916-28. *3065*

—. Public employees. 1930's-70's. *1679*

Polk, James K. Boundary dispute. Diplomacy. Great Britain. Oregon. USA. 1845-46. *835*

Polls. *See* Public Opinion; Social Surveys.

Pollution *See also* Air Pollution; Marine Pollution; Water Pollution.

—. Bibliographies. Lake Erie. North Central States. 1872-1965. *2730*

—. Conservation of Natural Resources. International regulation. North America. Water quality. 1960's-74. *1982*

—. Economic Growth. Industry. Quebec (Saint-Georges Est, Chaudière River). Tourism. 1973. *2652*

—. Eskimos. Industrial expansion. Land use (control). Oil Industry and Trade. 1975. *338*

—. Great Lakes. Illinois (Chicago). Sewage disposal. 1890-1940. *1117*

—. Industry. Working Conditions. 1973. *1296*

—. Marine Resources. UN Conference on the Law of the Sea. 1974. *1902*

—. Mercury poisoning. Ontario, northwestern. Regional government. 1970's. *2781*

—. Ontario (Falconbridge-Sudbury). Population. 1970-74. *2866*

—. Technology. Wastes, solid. 1973. *1334*

Polynesians. Eskimos. Ethnology. Indians. Pacific Basin. Prehistory-1976. *285*

Pond, Peter. Explorers. 1773-90. *2909*

Pontiac's Rebellion. Amherst, Jeffrey. French and Indian War. Iroquois Indians. Military History. New France. 1760-65. *612*

Ponzi, Charles (pseud. of Charles Bianchi). Massachusetts (Boston). Securities. 1919-20. *1187*

Poor *See also* Poverty.

—. Catholic Church. Irish Canadians. McMahon, Patrick. Quebec (Quebec). St. Bridget's Home. 1847-1972. *2541*

—. Children. Great Britain. Immigration. Ontario. Press. Rye, Miss. 1865-1925. *2879*

—. Quebec National Assembly. Social Credit Party. Tribunicial function. 1970-75. *2511*

Poor Law Commissioners. Immigration. Ireland. Servants. Women. 1865. *888*

Popular Culture *See also* Daily Life; Folk Art; Social Conditions.

—. Americanization. USA. 1921-75. *1979*

—. Bricklin (automobile). Music. New Brunswick. Russell, Charlie. Satire. 1970's. *2401*

—. Daily life. Historiography. Oral history. 20c. *1320*

—. Economics. Nationalism. USA. 1776-1976. *725*

Popular movements. American Revolution. French Revolution. Ideology. 1775-1838. *819*

Population *See also* names of ethnic or racial groups, e.g. Jews, Negroes, etc.; Aged; Birth Control; Birth Rate; Census; Demography; Eugenics; Fertility; Migration, Internal; Mortality; Vital Statistics.

—. 1945-74. *1433*

—. 1966-71. *3276*

—. Activity levels. Ontario, southern. Spatial structure. 1941-71. *2733*

—. Aged. British Columbia (Vancouver, Victoria). Income. Taxation. 1951-74. *3196*

—. Alabama (Mobile). France (Paris). Iberville, Pierre Le Moyne d'. Immigration. Women. 1702-04. *582*

—. Alaska. Economic Growth. Greenland. Scandinavia. 1970's. *281*

—. Australia. Federal Policy. Immigration. 1967-75. *1466*

—. Autocovariance procedures. Metropolitan Areas. Ontario, southern. 1871-1975. *2732*

—. Boosterism. New Brunswick (Saint John). Railroads. 1851-80. *2410*

—. British Columbia (Vancouver). Economic Growth. Natural resources. 19c. *3223*

—. Catholic Church. Parish registers. Quebec. 1616-1700. *540*

—. Census. German Canadians. 1891-1931. *2898*

—. Census. Methodology. Quebec (Quebec). 1795-1805. 1974-76. *2584*

—. Children. Quebec (Quebec). 1951-71. *2508*

—. Cities. Quebec (Montreal). 18c. *510*

—. Construction. Contracts. Housing. Quebec (Quebec). 1810-20. *2596*

—. Consumer behavior. Ontario (Toronto). Shopping centers. 1974. *2835*

—. Demography. Ontario. Peel County History Project. Social History. 1840-80. 1973. *2770*

—. Demography. Trudel, Marcel (review article). 1663. 1973. *509*

—. Discrimination. Ethnic groups. Immigrants. Manitoba (Winnipeg). 1874-1974. *2967*

—. Diseases. Indians. Micmac Indians. 16c-17c. *302*

—. Economic development. Federal Regulation. Transportation. 1945-77. *1273*

—. Economic development. Ontario (Credit River Valley). 1820's-1976. *2730*

—. Emigration. 1961-71. *1413*

—. Equal opportunity. Hutterites. Leadership succession. Prairie Provinces. Social Organization. 1940's-70's. *2908*

—. Farmlands (preservation of). 1974. *1589*

—. Foreign policy. Immigration. Labor. Refugees. 1950's-70's. *1887*

—. French Canadians. 1604-1971. *2156*

—. Fur trade. Genealogy. Godbout, Archange. New France. Voyages. 1608-1763. *565*

—. Hydrographic regions. Quebec. Statistics. 1845-1971. *2488*

—. Immigration. Italian Canadians. Ontario (Toronto). 1946-72. *2875*

—. Immigration policy. 1945-76. *1395*

—. Industrialization. National Self-image. Utopias. 20c. *26*

—. Land. Social change. Westward Movement. 1850's-67. *850*

—. Land. Urbanization. 1970-74. *1483*

—. Language. Representation Act (1974). 1974. *2104*

—. Ontario. Rural-Urban Studies. 1941-66. *2743*

—. Ontario (Falconbridge-Sudbury). Pollution. 1970-74. *2866*

—. Parish records. Quebec. Statistics. 1621-99. *541*

—. Quebec. 1951-71. *2535*

—. Quebec (Saguenay region). Social mobility. 19c-20c. *2473*

—. Research. 17c. *514*

Populists. Alberta. Edwards, Robert C. "Bob". *Eye Opener* (newspaper). 1904-22. *3108*

Port Blakely Mill Company. Lumber and Lumbering. Washington (Bainbridge Island). 1888-1903. *2257*

Porter, John. Radicals and Radicalism. Social Classes. 1950-65. *1462*

Ports. Containerization. Nova Scotia (Halifax). 1971-73. *2296*

—. Containerization. Shipping. 1970's. *2072*

—. France. French and Indian War. Trade. 1750's-60's. *562*

—. Great Lakes. Quebec. St. Lawrence River (north shore). Shipping. 1937-70. *1565*

—. Investments. Nova Scotia (Yarmouth). Shipping. 1840-89. *2210*

—. Lake Huron (Georgian Bay). Lumber industry. Ontario (Depot Harbour). 1900-28. *2742*

—. Measurements. Quebec. St. Lawrence River (south shore). 1944-66. *2660*

—. Mines. Quebec (Havre, Saint Pierre). 1948-73. *2628*

—. Quebec (Three Rivers). St. Lawrence Seaway. Shipping. 1874-1972. *2608*

Portugal (Barcelos). Baptista de Lima, Manuel C. (research). Discovery and Exploration. Pinheiro, Diogo (voyages). Pinheiro, Manoel (voyages). 1521-98. *508*

Portuguese Canadians. Ethnicity (review article). Polish Canadians. Scottish Canadians. 18c-20c. 1976. *201*

Post offices. Architecture. Manitoba (Winnipeg). 1855-1974. *2979*

Potato famine. Attitudes. Immigration. Ireland. Ontario (Canada West). 1845-50. *797*

Potlatches. British Columbia (Port Simpson). Tsimshian Indians. 1788-1862. *393*

Pottery. Colonization. Frobisher, Martin. Great Britain. Hall, Charles Francis. Northwest Territories (Baffin Island). 1578. 1862-1974. *513*

—. Culture. Indians. Manitoba, southwestern. Natural Resources. Prehistory-18c. 1970's. *307*

—. Indians. Montana (Dune Buggy Site, 24RV1). Prehistory. 1947-70's. *299*

—. Indians. New World. 4500-50 BC. *311*

—. *Machault* (vessel). New Brunswick. Restigouche River (battle). 1760. *2376*

Potts, Jerry. Frontier and Pioneer Life. North West Mounted Police. ca 1860-96. *1006*

Poundmaker. Big Bear. Métis. North West Rebellion. Trials. 1885. *948*

Poverty *See also* Charities; Economic Conditions; Poor; Public Welfare.

—. 1946-71. *1553*

—. Annexation. Confederation. Newfoundland. Outports. Social Customs. 1920-48. *2200*

—. Charities. Cities. Unemployment. 1815-60. *2157*

—. Developing nations. Humanitarian attitudes. UN Security Council. 1970's. *1796*

—. Economic security. Families, low-income. Public Welfare. Quebec. Social Aid Act (1969). 1969-75. *2668*

—. Federal Policy. Guaranteed annual income. 1974. *1509*

—. France. Great Britain. Jews. Uruguay. 1975. *1389*

—. Newspapers. 1973. *1480*

—. Unemployment. Winter. 1815-60. *779*

Power. Alberta (Banff). Elites. Midwest. 1960's-70's. *3123*

—. British Columbia. Cooperative Commonwealth Federation (origins). Ideology. Socialists. 1919-32. *3271*

Power plants. Development. Saskatchewan (Churchill River). 1929-74. *3053*

Power Resources *See also* Energy; Fuel.

—. Energy resources. International Trade. USA. 1950's-73. *1992*

—. Foreign Relations. USA. 1973. *1984*

—. Public Policy. 1970's. *1284*

Practical jokes. Newfoundland. Sealers. 16c-1914. *2202*

Prairie Provinces *See also* Alberta; Manitoba; Saskatchewan.

—. Agricultural expansion. Models. Settlement. 1870-1911. *1037*

—. Agricultural expansion. Settlement. 1872-1930. *1012*

—. Agricultural Technology and Research. Steam tractors. Western States. 1890-1925. *2913*

—. Agriculture. Jews. Settlement. 1884-1920's. *2950*

—. Architecture. British Columbia Mills, Timber, and Trading Company. Canadian Bank of Commerce. 1904-22. *2926*

—. Art. Chippewa Indians. Cree Indians. Métis. 1750's-1850's. *357*

—. Assimilation. French Canadians. 1871-1975. *2897*

—. Assiniboin Indians. Cree Indians. Montana. Social organization. ca 1640-1913. *446*

—. Assiniboine and Saskatchewan Exploring Expedition. Discovery and Exploration. Hime, Humphrey Lloyd. Photography. 1858. *863*

—. Balladry. Ukrainian Canadians. 1900-74. *2934*

—. British Columbia. Homesteading and Homesteaders. Immigration. Scandinavian Canadians. 1850's-1970's. *1032*

—. Bryan, William Jennings. Fund-raising. Lectures. Young Men's Christian Association. 1909. *2953*

—. Buffalo migrations. Fur trade. Plains Indians. 1770-1869. *429*

—. Campbell, Thomas D. Droughts. Farm income. Great Plains. Wheat. 1915-1940. *2964*

—. Canadian Pacific Railway. Engineers, locomotive. Labor Unions and Organizations. Strikes. 1883. *1066*

—. Catholic Church. Discrimination. Normal school issue. 1884-1900. *2947*

—. Catholics. Church History. Discipline, ecclesiastical. Morality. 1900-30. *2907*

—. Cattle Raising. Western States. 1880's-1900. *968*

—. Chipewyan Indians. Cree Indians. Expansionism. Fur Trade. Indian-White Relations. Northwest Territories (Mackenzie District, eastern). 1680's-18c. *476*

—. Chipman, George. Editors and Editing. *Grain Growers' Guide* (periodical). Teaching. 1903-05. *2938*

—. Cooperatives. Maritime Provinces. 1900-55. *2136*

—. Country Life. Depressions. Fiction. Literary themes. 1930's. *2918*

—. Cree Indians. Maskipiton (identity). 1830's-50's. *443*

—. Drug Abuse. 1860's-1919. *2905*

—. Dry farming. Economic Conditions. Grain production. 1870-1930. *2943*

—. Equal opportunity. Hutterites. Leadership succession. Population. Social Organization. 1940's-70's. *2908*

—. Freight and Freightage. Leeson & Scott (firm). 1883-1909. *1027*

—. Galt, Elliott. Indians. Letters. Travel. 1879-80. *959*

—. Government commissions. Indians. Land claims. Métis. 1885-1900. *396*

—. Government policy. Settlement. USA. 1870-80. *1018*

—. Historiography. 1974. *2900*

—. Historiography. Land Settlement. 1880-1900. *2902*

—. Immigration. Settlement. Ukrainians. 1910-31. *2937*

—. Indians. McDougall, John. Missions and Missionaries. Wesleyan Methodist. 1860-1917. *386*

—. Indians. Public Opinion. Social Change. 1976. *2920*

—. Maritime provinces. Politics. Provincial Government. 1910-27. *2125*

—. Messianic Movements. North West Rebellion. Religion. Riel, Louis. 1869-85. *971*

—. Métis. Nolin, Jean-Baptiste (and daughters). Red River of the North. St. Boniface School. 1760-1840. *776*

—. Métis. Religion. Riel, Louis (letter). Taché, Alexandre. 1880's. *974*

—. Migration, Internal. North West Rebellion. 1885. *995*

—. Woman Suffrage. 1890's-1920's. *2958*

Prairie Radicals. Alberta. Kansas. Leedy, John Whitnah. Politics. Radicals and Radicalism. 1880's-1935. *3087*

—. Great Plains. Pietism. 1890-1975. *2901*

Prairie States. *See* Great Plains.

Prairies. Agricultural economy. Railroads. Urbanization. 1871-1916. *2957*

—. Great Britain. Public Opinion. Settlement. 1840's-1860's. *2939*

—. Manitoba (Winnipeg). Métis. Minnesota (St. Paul). Red River of the North. Trade. Trails. 19c. *976*

Premier Établissement de la Foy dans la Nouvelle France (book). Bernou, Claude. France. LeClercq, Crestien. Renaudot, Eusèbe. 1691. *548*

Presbyterian Church. Archives. Methodist Church. United Church of Canada. 18c-1973. *233*

—. Assimilation. Jews. Ontario (Toronto). 1912-18. *2776*

—. British Columbia (Bennett). St. Andrews Church, construction of. 1898. *3253*

—. Canadian Pacific Railway. Construction crews. Manitoba (Virden). McLeod, Finlay J. C. (reminiscences). 1881-82. *1005*

—. Church Schools. East Indians. Missions and Missionaries. Trinidad and Tobago. 1868-1912. *2319*

—. Clergy. Nova Scotia (Springhill). 1874-1925. *2234*

—. Dalhousie College. McCulloch, Thomas. Missions and Missionaries. Nova Scotia. Pictou Academy. ca 1803-42. *2215*

—. Dukhobors. Galicians. Lake Geneva Mission. Missions and Missionaries. Saskatchewan (Wakaw). 1903-42. *3027*

—. Ecumenism. Patrick, William. 1900-11. *1085*

—. Gold Rushes. Yukon Territory. 1897-1910. *3334*

—. Literature. McCulloch, Thomas (*Letters of Mephibosheth Stepsure*). Nova Scotia. Satire. 1821-22. *2339*

—. MacLeod, Norman. Migration. Nova Scotia (St. Ann's). Scotland. ca 1800-50's. *2244*

—. Methodist Church. Nova Scotia (Springhill). St. Andrew's Wesley United Church of Canada. 1800-1976. *2233*

—. United Church of Canada. 1925. *1185*

Presbyterian Church of Scotland. MacGregor, James. Missions and Missionaries. Nova Scotia (Pictou). 1786-1830. *2343*

Presbyterians. Church of England. Morris, William. Ontario (Kingston). Queen's College. Scots. 1836-42. *2831*

Prescott, Charles Ramage. Apple industry. Crops. Genealogy. Nova Scotia. 1772-1970's. *2280*

Preservation *See also* Restorations.

—. Architecture. City planning. Mutual Advisory Committee. Ontario (London). Politics. 1970-77. *2727*

—. Art. Artifacts. Canadian Conservation Institute. Ontario (Ottawa). 1978. *31*

—. British Columbia (Queen Charlotte Islands). Haida Indians. Totem poles. 1700's-1800's. 1957. *453*

—. Heritage Act (1975). Local Architectural Conservation Advisory Committee. Ontario (London). 1945-77. *2818*

—. Louisbourg, Fortress of. Nova Scotia (Cape Breton Island). 1720-68. 1976. *619*

Press *See also* Books; Editors and Editing; Journalism; Newspapers; Periodicals; Reporters and Reporting.

—. Abortion. Public opinion. Social Change. 1960's-74. *1375*

—. Act of Sexual Sterilization (Alberta, 1928). Alberta. Eugenics. Immigration. Woodsworth, James S. 1900-28. *2906*

—. Anti-Canadianism. Civil War. New York City. 1861-65. *864*

—. Children. Great Britain. Immigration. Ontario. Poor. Rye, Miss. 1865-1925. *2879*

—. Counter Culture. Great Britain. USA. 1957-72. *1475*

—. Economic relations. European Economic Community. Foreign policy. 1974-75. *1820*

—. English Canadians. French Canadians. Political power. Quebec. 1864-67. *2572*

—. External Affairs Department. Foreign policy. 1942-76. *1789*

—. Foreign News (flow). USA. 1974-76. *2042*

—. Foreign policy. Newspapers. ca 1970's. *1919*

—. Historiography. World War II (antecedents). 1938-39. *1236*

Pressure Groups *See also* Interest Groups.

—. City Government. Ontario (Hamilton). Public Utilities. 1900-25. *2817*

—. City government. Ontario (Toronto). Political Corruption. Reform. 1890-1900. *2884*

Pressure Groups (review article). Elites. Great Britain. USA. 1960's-70's. *1325*

Price control. Board of Commerce of Canada. Sugar refining industry. 1919-20. *1192*

—. Legislation. 1973. *1698*

Price stability. Economic policy. Employment. Inflation. 1954-72. *1965*

Price, Vernon (interview). Lumber and Lumbering. Photographs. Quebec (Schyan River area). 1938-39. *2641*

Prices *See also* Wages.

—. British Columbia. Government Enterprise. 1977. *3243*

—. Housing. Ontario (London). Railroads. 1972. *1591*

Prices and Incomes Commission. 1973. *1501*

Priestley, Raymond. Antarctic. Australia. Explorers. Great Britain. 1912-74. *3321*

Primary Education. *See* Elementary Education.

Prime ministers. Barber, James David. King, William Lyon Mackenzie. Political leadership. 1920's-40's. 1972-76. *1147*

—. Economic policy. Foreign relations. Trudeau, Pierre Elliott. USA. 1960's-70's. *2006*

—. Foreign policy. 1948-70's. *1930*

—. Genealogy. Ireland (Waterford). Thompson, John S. D. 1796-1903. *1056*

Primitivism. Frye, Northrop. Levi-Strauss, Claude. Shadbolt, Jack. 1977. *251*

Prince Albert (vessel). Arctic. Bellot, Joseph René. Franklin, John. Kennedy, William. Voyages. 1851. *3307*

Prince Edward Island. Bible-reading. Catholic Church. Politics. Protestants. Public Schools. 1856-60. *2207*

—. Church and State. Political Parties. Prince of Wales College Act (1860). School Boards. 1860-63. *2208*

—. Collective bargaining. Public Employees. Teachers. 1970-74. *2204*

—. Excavations. Fort Amherst. Glass. 1758-71. 1970's. *2206*

—. Foreign investments. Natural resources. 1970's. *2205*

—. France. Great Britain. Indian-White Relations. Micmac Indians. 1763-1873. *468*
—. Immigrants. McDonald, Donald. Millenarianism. Scottish Canadians. ca 1828-67. *2209*
Prince of Wales College Act (1860). Church and State. Political Parties. Prince Edward Island. School Boards. 1860-63. *2208*
Prince Rupert's Land. Animal husbandry. Frontier. Meat (sources). 18c-20c. *2942*
Pringle, Henry (letters). French and Indian War. Great Britain. Nova Scotia (Halifax). 1757. *617*
Printing *See also* Books.
—. Collective bargaining. Ontario (Toronto). Organizational Theory. 19c. *2892*
Prisons *See also* Crime and Criminals; Criminal Law; Police.
—. Collins Bay Penitentiary. Libraries. Ontario (Kingston). Resocialization. 1963-73. *2851*
—. Criminal Justice System. Ontario (Upper Canada). Reform. 1835-50. *769*
Privacy. Census. History. Research. 1918-77. *57*
Private enterprise. Electricity and Electronics. Qu'Appelle Flour Mill. Saskatchewan. 1906-27. *3081*
Private Schools *See also* Church Schools.
—. Ethnicity. Greek Canadians. Immigration. Ontario (Toronto). 1900-40. *2845* (Lockport). 18c. *720*
—. Fishing industry. King William's War. New England. Queen Anne's War. Shipping. 1689-1713. *596*
—. New Brunswick. Newfoundland. 1800-15. *759*
Proch, Don. Art. Ukrainian Canadians. 1970's. *1403*
Production control. Labor Unions and Organizations. Ontario (Toronto). 1860-92. *2803*
Production, mode of. New France. Small producers. Social Classes. 17c-18c. *496*
Productivity. Bicycle industry. Labor. Mexico. USA. 1972-76. *1906*
—. Competitiveness. Corporations. Wages. 1970-77. *1622*
Professional activity. Nationality. Social scientists. -1973. *1422*
Professionalism. Athletes. Hanlan, Edward "Ned". Sports. 1870's-80's. *1042*
—. Corporation Law. Quebec. 1840's-1970's. *2615*
—. Journalism. 1973. *1491*
—. Social Conditions. Sports. 1835-1909. *910*
Professionals. Collective bargaining. 1940's-70's. *1496*
Professions. Economic progression. Education. Immigration. Political autonomy. 1945-75. *1425*
Professors. Colleges and Universities. Labor Unions and Organizations. Quebec. 1972-74. *2417*
Progressive Conservative Party. *See* Conservative Party.
Progressives. Bourassa, Henri. Parliaments. 1926. *1182*
Progressivism. City government. Ontario (Toronto). Wickett, Samuel Morley. 1900-15. *2885*
—. Coldwell, Major J. Farmer Labor party. Political Leadership. Social Democracy. 1907-32. *2962*
—. Conservatism. Saskatchewan. 1920's. *3039*
Prohibition. Law Enforcement. Northwest Territories. Royal Canadian Mounted Police. 1874-91. *984*
—. Ontario. Racism. Reform. 1890-1915. *2756*
Proletariat. *See* Working class.
Propaganda *See also* Public Opinion.
—. Deutscher Bund Canada. German Canadians. Nazism. 1934-39. *1216*
—. Elections. Legislative Assembly. Political Factions. 1792. *708*
Property *See also* Income; Real Estate.
—. Auteuil, Denis-Joseph Ruette d' (estate). Inventories. Quebec. 1661-80. *528*
—. Business History. Economic policy. Local Government. Ontario. 1898-1911. *1100*
Property ownership. Cities. Employment. Ethnic Groups. Social Classes. 19c. *90*
Prostitution. Feminism. Law Enforcement. Ontario (Toronto). Rape. 1975-78. *2825*
Protectionism *See also* Tariff; Trade Regulations.
—. Bill C-58. Nationalism. *Reader's Digest* (periodical). Taxation. *Time* (periodical). 1922-76. *2017*
—. Carey, Henry C. Nationalism. Reciprocity Treaty, proposed. USA. 1871-75. *1060*

Protestant Churches *See also* names of churches, e.g. Methodist Church, etc.; Protestantism.
—. Asia. Colleges and Universities. USA. 1850-1971. *5*
—. Bibliographies. Historiography. 1825-1973. *130*
—. Immigration. Nationalism. United Church of Canada. 1902-25. *1194*
—. Jesuits. Land Tenure. Legislation. Mercier, Honoré. Quebec. 1886. *2645*
Protestant ethic. Elites. Ethnic values. Rationality. Senators. 1971. *1645*
Protestantism *See also* Evangelism.
—. Adolescence. Boys. USA. Young Men's Christian Association. 1870-1920. *927*
—. Bengough, John Wilson. City government. *Grip* (periodical). Ontario (Toronto). Political Reform. 1873-1910. *2807*
—. British Columbia (Queen Charlotte Islands). Haida Indians. Missions and Missionaries. Settlement. Subsistence patterns. 1876-1920. *398*
—. Catholic Church. Ethnic groups. Evangelists. Quebec (Lower Canada). Rebellion of 1837. 1766-1865. *811*
—. Cultural history. Ontario. Victorian era. 1840's-1900. *913*
—. Ecclesiastical authority. United Church of Canada. 1925-73. *1401*
—. Education. Great Britain. Missions and Missionaries. Sudan Interior Mission. 1937-55. *197*
—. Eucharistic worship. Religion. United Church of Canada. 1952-72. *1452*
—. Fairbairn, R. Edis. Pacifism. United Church of Canada. World War II. 1939. *1241*
—. Family. France. Quebec. Trade. 1740-60. *593*
—. France. Huguenots. New France. 1541-1760. *550*
—. Sweet, H. C. 1866-1960. *119*
Protestants. American Revolution. France. Settlement. USA. Whaling industry and Trade. 17c-20c. *1287*
—. Anti-Catholicism. Ku Klux Klan. Saskatchewan. 1927-30. *3033*
—. Bible-reading. Catholic Church. Politics. Prince Edward Island. Public Schools. 1856-60. *2207*
—. Burchard, Jedediah. Revivals. Social Conditions. Vermont. 1835-36. *815*
—. Germans. Immigrants. Nova Scotia. 1749-52. *2259*
—. Jesuits' Estates Act. Political Protest. 1880-90. *1058*
Proulx, Nicholas. French Canadians. Immigration. Massachusetts (Holyoke). Working Class. 1850-1900. *2600*
Provencher, John N. (memoir). Catholic Church. Chippewa Indians. Hudson's Bay Company. Métis. Quebec. Red River Settlement. 1812-36. *2948*
Provigo (corporation). Food industry. Quebec. 20c. *2620*
Provinces. Constitutional law. Licensing procedures. States. USA. 1970's. *2063*
—. Economic development. Federal government. States. USA. 1950's-70's. *2012*
Provincial capitals. British Columbia (Victoria). Navy-yards and Naval Stations. Nova Scotia (Halifax). 1749-1971. *2126*
Provincial Flowers. Mayflower (Trailing Arbutus). Nova Scotia. 1834-1901. *2254*
Provincial Freeman (newspaper). Antislavery Sentiments. Negroes. Newspapers. Ontario. Shadd, Mary Ann. 1852-93. *1046*
Provincial Government. Aberhart, William. Alberta. Bowen, John C. Social Credit Party. 1937-38. *3158*
—. Aberhart, William. Alberta. Ideology. Social Credit Party. Theology. 1935-43. *3106*
—. Agricultural policy. Elections. Quebec. 1960-73. *2601*
—. Alberta. Department of Social Services and Community Health. Social policy. 1970's. *3133*
—. Archives. Newfoundland. 1825-1973. *2185*
—. Atlantic Provinces. Economic interests. International Trade. USA. 1960's-70's. *2013*
—. Auditors General. Public Accounts committees. Public spending. 1970-75. *1694*
—. Boucherville, Charles Eugène Boucher de. Federalism. Joly, Henri-Gustave. Liberal Party. Political Campaigns. Quebec. 1878. *2452*
—. British Columbia. Civil Defense. Emergencies. Planning. 1951-76. *3233*
—. British Columbia. Indians. Land policies. 1875-80. *383*

—. British Columbia. Legislation. Politics. 1977. *3238*
—. British Columbia. Multinational Corporations. Natural Resources. Social Classes. Towns, "instant". 1965-72. *3178*
—. British Columbia (Vancouver). Law Enforcement. Riots (anti-Chinese). 1887. *3247*
—. Canada Assistance Plan. Federal government. Federalism. 1966. *1652*
—. Catholic Church. Church and State. Public Charities Act (1921). Quebec. Recessions. 1921-26. *2578*
—. Charpentier, Alfred. Confederation of Catholic Workers of Canada. Industrial Relations. Quebec. 1935-46. *2609*
—. Children. Federal government. New York (Watertown). Ontario (Belleville). Political structures. 1977. *1423*
—. Commission on Industrial Accidents. Industry. Quebec. Workmen's Compensation. 1890-1978. *2623*
—. Confederation. French Canadians. Ontario. Quebec. 1867-1937. *155*
—. Constitutions. Economic Regulations. Federal government. 1856-1975. *60*
—. Constitutions. Federal Government. Quebec. Separatist Movements. 1968-76. *2117*
—. Co-operative Commonwealth Federation. Manitoba. Social Democratic Party. Socialism. ca 1940. *3022*
—. Economic development. 1960's-70's. *2919*
—. Energy policy. Federal Government. Trudeau, Pierre Elliott. 1950-77. *2093*
—. Federal Government. 1940-74. *2113*
—. Federal Government. Hepburn, Mitchell F. King, William Lyon Mackenzie. Lieutenant governors. Ontario. 1937. *1208*
—. Federal government. Language policy. Middle Classes. Modernization. Quebec. 1960-76. *2090*
—. Federal government. Parti Québécois. Quebec. Social Change. 1960-77. *2420*
—. Federal Government. Public Employees. Regulatory agencies. 1974. *1639*
—. Federalism. Public Policy. 1867-1977. *30*
—. Fishing industry. Newfoundland. 1972-77. *2196*
—. Foreign policy. 1970's. *1866*
—. Foreign relations. Saskatchewan. 1963-78. *3057*
—. French Canadians. Lawyers. LeSage, Simeon. Quebec. 1835-1909. *2570*
—. French language. 19c-20c. *47*
—. Gardiner, James G. Saskatchewan. 1905. *3079*
—. Gasoline Licensing Act (1934). Marketing. Nova Scotia Board of Commissioners of Public Utilities. 1960's-74. *2283*
—. Harris, John. Nova Scotia (Halifax, Annapolis). Roads. 1816-30's. *2253*
—. Lévesque, René. Newspapers. Parti Québécois. Quebec (Montreal). 1976-77. *2423*
—. Local government. Public Finance. Quebec. 1960-73. *2418*
—. Lotteries. Public Finance. Quebec. 1970-73. *2603*
—. Maritime provinces. Politics. Prairie Provinces. 1910-27. *2125*
—. One-party dominant system. Ontario. Opposition parties. Political Parties. 1970-71. *2811*
—. Police, provincial. Politics. Royal Canadian Mounted Police. Saskatchewan. 1916-28. *3065*
—. Public administration. Quebec. 1867-1975. *2436*
—. Quebec. Securities Commission. Stocks and Bonds. 1970's. *2427*
—. Quebec. Separatist Movements. 1955-75. *2568*
—. Quebec. Social Reform. 1973. *2539*
Provincial Legislatures. Alberta. Farmers. Political parties. 1920's-30's. *2944*
—. Anderson, James T. M. Elections. Gardiner, James G. Saskatchewan (Estevan). 1929-30. *3078* —. Attitudes. Economic nationalism. Elites. Foreign investments. 1973-74. *2147*
—. Attitudes. Models. Ontario. Political parties. 1957-74. *2890*
—. Apportionment. British Columbia. Partisanship. 1952-78. *3199*
—. Catholic Church. Church Schools. Manitoba. McCarthy, D'Alton. 1870-90. *931*
—. Constituency service. Political parties. 1972. *1647*
—. McKim, Andrew. Nova Scotia. Politics. 1784-1840. *2348*

—. Political parties. Social Conditions. 1950-70. *2996*

Provincial Museum. British Columbia (Victoria). Pit houses. Salish (Flathead) Indians. Shuswap Lake Park. 1972. *455*

Provost Court of Quebec. Feudal law. New France (Notre Dame des Anges). 1626-1750. *554*

Pruden, Patrick. Alberta (Lac la Biche). Beaver Indians. Hudson's Bay Company. North West Rebellion. Trading posts. 1885. *1026*

Psychiatry See also Mental Illness; Psychology.

—. British Columbia (Kitsilano). Community services. Mental health. Politics. 1973-74. *3237*

—. France. Legislation. North America. Quebec. 1973. *2546*

—. Mental Illness. Quebec. Sociology. 1717-1960. *2513*

Psychic phenomena. Jarvis, Stinson. Ontario. Watkins, Kathleen ("Kit of the Mail"). 1885-95. *2891*

Psychoanalysis See also Psychology.

—. North America. Scientific Experiments and Research. Social Change. 1918-77. *9*

Psychohistory. Byng of Vimy, Julian Hedworth George (Viscount). King, William Lyon Mackenzie. 1919-26. *1174*

Psychological problems. Blake, Edward (career). Politics. 1850-1900. *926*

Psychology See also Behaviorism; Psychiatry; Psychoanalysis.

—. Assimilation. Immigrants. Multiculturalism. 1970's. *1424*

—. Canadian Psychological Associations. Oral history. 1970-75. *1442*

—. Historiography. 1977. *122*

Public Accounts committees. Auditors General. Provincial government. Public spending. 1970-75. *1694*

Public Administration See also Bureaucracies; Civil Service; Government.

—. City Government. Economic growth. Quebec (Montreal). Social Conditions. Urbanization. 1850-1914. *2441*

—. City government. Manitoba (Winnipeg). Political Corruption. Urbanization. 1884-85. *3013*

—. Communism. Europe, Eastern. Historiography. USA. USSR. ca 1850-1975. *1316*

—. Federal Government. 1940's-78. *1678*

—. Fishing Rights. Labrador. Newfoundland. Quebec. 1763-83. *735*

—. Provincial government. Quebec. 1867-1975. *2436*

Public Archives of Canada. Archives. Oral history. 1976. *1265*

—. Frontier College history project. 1974-75. *1282*

—. Maps. Research. Urban history. 1865-1905. *917*

Public Charities Act (1921). Catholic Church. Church and State. Provincial Government. Quebec. Recessions. 1921-26. *2578*

Public Employees See also Civil Service.

—. British Columbia Government Employees Union. Labor Unions and Organizations. 1944-73. *3228*

—. Canadian Union of Public Employees. Labor Unions and Organizations. MacMillan, John F. "Lofty". 1935-73. *1504*

—. Canadian Union of Public Employees. Sex discrimination. Women. 1975. *1617*

—. Collective bargaining. 1920-73. *118*

—. Collective bargaining. Federal Government. 1940's-60's. *1500*

—. Collective bargaining. Prince Edward Island. Teachers. 1970-74. *2204*

—. Collective bargaining. Quebec. 1964-72. *2602*

—. Collective bargaining. Quebec. 1966-75. *2632*

—. Collective bargaining. Wages. 1960-70's. *1538*

—. Conflict and Conflict Resolution. Federal Government. Labor Disputes. 1967-76. *1718*

—. Federal Government. Fiscal policy. 1950-. *1532*

—. Federal Government. Provincial Government. Regulatory agencies. 1974. *1639*

—. Labor Disputes. 1973. *1547*

—. Manitoba. 1974. *3016*

—. Political Participation. Public Service Employment Act, 1967. 1967-70's. *1640*

—. Politics. 1930's-70's. *1679*

Public Finance. Academic exchange programs. Canadian studies. Five-Year Cultural Plan. 1970's. *1798*

—. Adult education. Manpower training programs. 1967-77. *1699*

—. Business. Northwest Territories. 1947-73. *3353*

—. Canals. Ontario (Georgian Bay). Railroads. 1850-1915. *925*

—. Federal Government. Glassco Commission. 1960's-70's. *1717*

—. Local government. Provincial government. Quebec. 1960-73. *2418*

—. Lotteries. Provincial Government. Quebec. 1970-73. *2603*

—. Political Protest. Radicals and Radicalism. Social services. 1960's-70's. *1689*

Public Health See also Diseases; Drug Abuse; Epidemics; Hospitals; Pollution; Sanitation; Water Supply.

—. Medicine and State. Quebec. Regional councils. Social services. 1971-74. *2547*

—. Quebec. Sociology. ca 1850's-1970. *2494*

Public health services. British Columbia (Vancouver). Epidemics. Influenza. 1918-19. *3174*

Public housing. City Government. Quebec (Hull). 1968-74. *2456*

—. Consumers' satisfaction. 1974. *1587*

Public identity. Life-styles. Newfoundland. Sects, religious. Social Classes. 1949-75. *2183*

Public Opinion See also Propaganda; Public Relations.

—. Abortion. Press. Social Change. 1960's-74. *1375*

—. Alberta. Great Britain. Ombudsmen. 1969-71. *3109*

—. Alberta (Edmonton). Hutterites. Social distance. 1966-75. *3132*

—. Annexation. USA. 1956-71. *1970*

—. British Columbia. Evacuation, forced. Federal government. Japanese. World War II. 1937-42. *1247*

—. British Columbia. Great Britain. Immigration. 1919-30. *3250*

—. Business. Cooperative movement. Quebec. 1970's. *2643*

—. Colleges and Universities. Politics. Students. 1974. *1432*

—. Durham, 1st Earl of. Penal transportation. Political prisoners. 1835-50. *827*

—. Economic Development. Northwest Territories. Regionalism. 1970-73. *3277*

—. Elections, federal. Government, majority. Voting and Voting behavior. 1965-74. *1686*

—. Foreign Investments. Foreign policy. USA. 1973-75. *2010*

—. Foreign policy. Nationalism. 1972-75. *1875*

—. Foreign relations. USA. 1950's-73. *2050*

—. Government of Higher Education. 1975. *1485*

—. Great Britain. Nova Scotia. Reciprocity. Treaties. USA. 1846-54. *871*

—. Great Britain. Prairie settlement. 1840's-1860's. *2939*

—. Immigration policy. O'Connell, Martin. 1975. *1376*

—. Indians. Prairie Provinces. Social Change. 1976. *2020*

—. Intergovernmental Relations. King, William Lyon Mackenzie. Newspapers. Taxation. 1945-46. *2119*

—. International Trade. USA. 1960's-70's. *2001*

—. Labor disputes. 1940's-70's. *1590*

—. Methodology. Politics. 1970's. *1687*

—. Nationalism. USA. 1976. *1956*

—. Nationalism. USA. 1976. *2019*

—. Police. Royal North West Mounted Police. 1874-83. *1007*

Public ownership. Energy development. Imperial Oil Company. 1970's. *1841*

—. Energy resources. USA. 1970-73. *1286*

Public Policy. Antitrust. Corporations. 1889-1910. *1081*

—. Bibliographies. Ethnic Groups. Multiculturalism. 1967-76. *98*

—. Bill C-256. Businessmen. Communications. Federal Regulation. Manitoba (Winnipeg). 1971-72. *2971*

—. British Columbia. Legislation. New Democratic Party. Social Democracy. 1972-75. *3241*

—. Councillors. Local government. 1968-75. *1632*

—. Decisionmaking. 1950's-70's. *1680*

—. Decisionmaking. Federal government. 1970's. *1636*

—. Diplomats. Political scientists. 1970's. *1703*

—. Economic development. Energy. Politics. 1945-76. *1571*

—. Ethnic Groups. Multiculturalism. 1970's. *1494*

—. Federal government. French Canadians. Quebec. Separatist Movements. 1976. *1306*

—. Federalism. Provincial Government. 1867-1977. *30*

—. Foreign Relations. Scandinavia. Transgovernmental politics. USA. 1970's. *1771*

—. Immigration. 1967-75. *1812*

—. Immigration. DeLaGarza, E. (Kika). Mexico. USA. 1910-74. *1732*

—. Indians. Nova Scotia. 1783-1871. *467*

—. Interest groups. USA. 20c. *1704*

—. Power resources. 1970's. *1284*

—. Social scientists. 1973. *1710*

—. Social security. USA. 1935-75. *1428*

—. Socialism. 1945-72. *1646*

Public Records See also Archives.

—. Akins, Thomas Beamish. Nova Scotia. 1857-91. *2246*

—. Cities. Information Storage and Retrieval Systems. Ontario. 1974. *2859*

Public Relations See also Public Opinion; Publicity.

—. Anti-inflation program. Trudeau, Pierre Elliott. 1976. *1656*

—. Industrial council. Massey-Harris plant. Ontario (Toronto). 1919-29. *1188*

Public Schools See also High Schools; Rural Schools; Schools.

—. Anderson, James T. M. Anti-Catholicism. Saskatchewan. School Act (amended). Secularization. 1929-34. *3050*

—. Bible-reading. Catholic Church. Politics. Prince Edward Island. Protestants. 1856-60. *2207*

—. British Columbia. Japanese communities. Minorities. 1900-72. *3191*

—. British North America. Teaching. Women. 1845-75. *880*

—. Calonne, Abbot de (letters). Catholic Church. Clergy. 1819-20. *706*

—. Children. Immigration. Jews. Manitoba (Winnipeg). 1900-20. *3007*

—. Children. Inequality (perceived). Ontario (Toronto area). Social Classes. Values. 1977. *1345*

—. Class structure. Ontario (Toronto). 1851. 1964-74. *1445*

—. Community involvement. Libraries. 1973. *1396*

—. Curricula. Ontario. Physical education and training. Strathcona Trust fund. 1919-39. *1130*

—. Empire Day celebrations. Great Britain. Imperialism. Nationalism. Ontario. 1890-1930's. *2864*

—. Industrialization. Ontario (Hamilton). Socialization. 19c. *2802*

—. Sports. Upper Canada. Upper Classes (British). 1830-75. *2852*

Public sector. Collective bargaining. 1964-73. *1628*

Public Service Employment Act, 1967. Political Participation. Public employees. 1967-70's. *1640*

Public Service Staff Relations Act. Finkelman report. Labor Relations. 1965-74. *1542*

Public services. Agricultural commodities. Banking. Foreign Investments. Puerto Rico. 1800-1977. *180*

—. Sex discrimination. Women. 1870-1975. *213*

Public spending. Auditors General. Provincial government. Public Accounts committees. 1970-75. *1694*

Public sympathy. Indian Wars. Montana. Nez Percé Indians. Settlers. 1877. *431*

Public Transportation See also Subways.

—. Alberta (Calgary). Streetcars. 1907-50. *3141*

Public Utilities See also Corporation Law; Corporations; Electric Power; Railroads; Telegraph; Water Supply.

—. British Columbia. Victoria Gas Company. 1860's-90's. *3246*

—. City Government. Ontario (Hamilton). Pressure groups. 1900-25. *2817*

—. Electric power. Manitoba. Ontario. 1905-30. *2138*

—. Mass transit. Ontario. Toronto Railway Company. 1891-1921. *2760*

Public Welfare See also Charities; Children; Hospitals; Social Security; Social Work.

—. Economic security. Families, low-income. Poverty. Quebec. Social Aid Act (1969). 1969-75. *2668*

—. Manitoba. Social services. 1973. *3017*

Publications. Government. 1977. *189*

Publicity See also Propaganda; Public Relations.

—. Colonization (supposed). Defoe, Daniel. Hudson's Bay Company. Rupert's Land. Sergeant, Henry. 1680's. *502*
Publishers and Publishing *See also* Books; Copyright; Editors and Editing; Press; Printing.
—. 1974. *1350*
—. Beaverbrook, 1st Baron. British Empire. Free trade movement. Great Britain. 1900-31. *24*
—. Bibliographies. Feminism. 1968-76. *255*
—. Book Industries and Trade. Copyright Act (Canada, 1900). 1872-1900. *934*
—. Book Industries and Trade. Copyright violations. Ontario (Toronto). Robertson, John Ross. 1877-90. *2815*
—. Brown, George. Labor Unions and Organizations. Ontario. Toronto *Globe* (newspaper). Toronto Typographical Union. 1843-72. *2893*
—. Clothing industries. Locational clustering. Ontario (Toronto). Quebec (Montreal). 1949-67. *1611*
—. Colleges and Universities. North America. Scholarship. 1920's-70's. *206*
—. Copyright laws. Oral history. Oral Institute for Studies in Education. 1960's-75. *1313*
—. Government. 1791-1972. *81*
—. Nationalism. Ontario. 1970-75. *2809*
—. Nationalism. Periodicals. Tariff. USA. 1920's. *1193*
—. Nationalism. Royal Commission on Book Publishing. 1973. *1290*
Puerto Rico. Agricultural commodities. Banking. Foreign Investments. Public services. 1800-1977. *180*
—. Bilingualism. Occupations. 1970. *2587*
—. Political apathy. Voter registration. 1974-77. *1957*
Puerto Rico (Culebra Island). Navies. Target ranges. USA. 1971-72. *2023*
Pumori (mountain). Alpine Club of Canada. Himalayas. Mountain climbers. 1977. *1260*
Purdie, James Eustace. Pentecostal Assemblies of Canada. Theological education. 1925-50. *1137*
Pusey, Edward Bouverie. Church of England. Medley, John (letters). New Brunswick (Fredericton). Oxford Movement. ca 1840-44. *2389*

Q

Quakers. *See* Friends, Society of.
Quangwak (Eskimo). Douglas, W. O. (reminiscences). Northwest Territories (Baker Lake District). Royal Canadian Mounted Police. 1919-20's. *323*
Quantitative Methods *See also* Methodology.
—. Central Place System. Ontario (Guelph area). Urbanization. 1851-1970. *2753*
—. Crime and Criminals. Ontario (Middlesex County). 19c-20c. *74*
—. Exports. Quebec. Regional Planning. 1969. *1254*
—. Ontario. Quebec. Transportation. Urban hierarchy. 1861-1901. *2137*
Quantrill, William Clarke. British Columbia (Quatsino Sound). Civil War. Outlaws. 1861-1907. *3226*
Qu'Appelle Flour Mill. Electricity and Electronics. Private enterprise. Saskatchewan. 1906-27. *3081*
Quebec. Abnaki Indians, Western. New England. Tufts, Henry. 1772-75. *368*
—. Acadians. Catholic Church. Irish Canadians. New Brunswick. Politics. Schools. Taxation. 1871-73. *1067*
—. Acculturation. Cultural alienation. French-speakers. 1950-73. *2569*
—. Act of Quebec (1774). French language. Sovereignty. 1774-1974. *2673*
—. *Action Catholique* (newspaper). Catholic Church. Communist Parties and Movements. Nazism. 1917-39. *1411*
—. *Action Nationale* (periodical). French Canadians. Minville, Esdras. 1933. *2688*
—. Africa. Foreign relations. France. French-speaking nations. 1950's-70's. *1845*
—. Africa, French-speaking. Belgium. France. International cooperation. 1964-74. *2718*
—. Agnosticism. Catholic Church. Students. 1970-78. *2455*
—. Agricultural Cooperatives. Coopérative Fédérée de Québec. 1971-73. *2597*
—. Agricultural policy. Elections. Provincial government. 1960-73. *2601*

—. Agriculture. Capitalism. Peasants. 1600-1970's. *2595*
—. Agriculture. Federalism. Forests and Forestry. Industrialization. Natural resources. 20c. *2646*
—. Agriculture. Ontario. Political Attitudes. Social change. 1850-1970. *2132*
—. Alliance Laurentienne. Barbeau, Raymond. Guillemette, Pierre. Independence Movements. 1960's-75. *2674*
—. Alliance Laurentienne. Federalism. Separatism. 1957-70's. *2681*
—. American Federation of Labor. French Canadians. Gompers, Samuel. 1900-14. *2588*
—. American Revolution. Attitudes. Carleton, Guy. Military Occupation. Peasants. 1775-76. *717*
—. American Revolution. British Army. Carleton, Guy. Logistics. 1776. *714*
—. American Revolution. Economic Conditions. Great Britain. 1770's. *731*
—. Americanism. Lemelin, Roger (*Les Plouffe*). Nationalism. 1938-45. *2722*
—. Anglicization. Language. Social classes. 1971. *2461*
—. Anglophones. Language. 1830-1976. *2714*
—. Anglophones. National identification. Political Attitudes. Separatist Movements. 1970's. *2120*
—. Anti-Semitism. French Language Charter. Nationalism. 1977. *2421*
—. Archives. Bibliographies. Canadian Institute of Montreal. 1844-1900. *120*
—. Arctic. Berthe, Jean. Eskimos. Fur trade. Stevenson, A. (account). 1930's. *2663*
—. Arès, Richard. French tradition. Minville, Esdras. Tremblay Commission. 1953-56. *2676*
—. Art Galleries and Museums (proposed). Légaré, Joseph. Painting. 1824-1933. *2544*
—. Artifacts. Eskimos. Europeans. Labrador. Ungava Peninsula. ca 400-18c. *300*
—. Assimilation. Immigration. Mining. 1941-71. *2639*
—. Auteuil, Denis-Joseph Ruette d' (estate). Inventories. Property. 1661-80. *528*
—. Balance of power. Defense Policy. North America. Separatist Movements. 1970's. *1921*
—. Ballads. French and Indian War. New England. Rogers' Rangers (retreat). 1759. *591*
—. Balloons (hot air). Haddock, John A. LaMountain, John. USA. 1859. *845*
—. Beaudry Report. Ham Report. Industry. Ontario. Working Conditions. 1972-74. *1536*
—. Bélanger Report. Taxation. 1966-76. *2419*
—. Belgium. Ethnicity. Nationalism. Social Classes. 1970's. *2702*
—. Bergeron, Léandre (review article). Historiography. Marxism. 1970-75. *2618*
—. Bergson, Henri. Creativity. Federal government. Intergovernmental Relations. 1970's. *2109*
—. Bibliographies. Economic Theory. Minville, Esdras. 20c. *2467*
—. Bibliographies. Editorials. French Canadians. Latin America. Newspapers. 1959-73. *2433*
—. Bibliographies. Europe. Literary associations (French-language). USA. Voluntary associations. 1840-1900. *2524*
—. Biculturalism. English Canadians. Federalism. French Canadians. 20c. *1354*
—. Bilingual districts. Federal Policy. 1969-76. *2480*
—. Bilingualism. Gendron Report. Schools. 1973. *2504*
—. Black, Conrad. Duplessis, Maurice. Historiography. Political Leadership. Rumilly, Robert. 1936-59. *2684*
—. Boucherville, Charles Eugène Boucher de. Federalism. Joly, Henri-Gustave. Liberal Party. Political Campaigns. Provincial government. 1878. *2452*
—. Boundaries. Vermont. 1684-1933. *662*
—. Bourassa, Robert. Liberal Party. Political patronage. 1970-75. *2440*
—. British Empire. Catholic Church. Ideology. Imperialism. 19c-20c. *2560*
—. Business. Civil service. Middle Classes. Technocracy. 1939-75. *2451*
—. Business. Cooperative movement. Public opinion. 1970's. *2643*
—. Business community. Nationalism. Parti Québécois. Working class. 1970's. *2690*
—. Business education. Cultural alienation. USA. 1972. *2034*

—. Caisses Populaires Desjardins. Credit unions. 1912-73. *2598*
—. Campaign Finance. Manitoba. Political success. Voting and Voting Behavior. 1975. *1728*
—. Capital investment, American. Economic Policy. 1970's. *2067*
—. Capitalism. Economic Regulations. 1870-1900. *2650*
—. Capitalism. Revolution. USA. 1920-40. 1960's. *2431*
—. Capitalists. Laurentide Company. Newsprint. 1887-1928. *161*
—. Caribou. Wildlife Conservation. 20c. *267*
—. Castonguay, Claude (interview). Federalism. Nationalism. 1917-73. *63*
—. Catholic Church. Chippewa Indians. Hudson's Bay Company. Métis. Provencher, John N. (memoir). Red River Settlement. 1812-36. *2948*
—. Catholic Church. Church and State. 18c-20c. *2699*
—. Catholic Church. Church and State. Provincial Government. Public Charities Act (1921). Recessions. 1921-26. *2578*
—. Catholic Church. Cistercians. Mistassini, monastery of. Trappists. 1900-03. *2482*
—. Catholic Church. École Sociale Populaire. Labor unions and Organizations. Social Change. 1911-75. *2500*
—. Catholic Church. Educational system. French Canadians. Parent-youth conflict. Social change. 1960-70. *2516*
—. Catholic Church. Fédération Nationale Saint-Jean-Baptiste. Feminism. Gérin-Lajoie, Marie. 1907-33. *1128*
—. Catholic Church. French Canadians. Minville, Esdras. 1975. *2459*
—. Catholic Church. General Hospital. Mental Illness. 1692-1845. *2543*
—. Catholic Church. Government. Parish registers. 1539-1973. *526*
—. Catholic Church. Hospitals. Hôtel-Dieu. Indian-White Relations. 1635-98. *552*
—. Catholic Church. Ideas, History of. Laval, François de. 17c. *549*
—. Catholic Church. Lamarche, Gustave. Political philosophy. Separatist Movements. 1922-75. *2705*
—. Catholic Church. Parish registers. Population. 1616-1700. *540*
—. Catholicism. French Canadians. Lévesque, Georges-Henri (personal account). Nationalism. Youth movements. 1930's. *2700*
—. Censorship. Films. National Film Board. 1971. *1406*
—. Centralization. Political stability. Separatist movements. 1960-75. *1695*
—. Charbonneau, Hubert. Dechêne, Louise (review article). Family structure. Migration. Vital Statistics. 1660-1713. 1974-75. *527*
—. Charpentier, Alfred. Confederation of Catholic Workers of Canada. Industrial Relations. Provincial government. 1935-46. *2609*
—. *Charte du Français* (proposed). French language. Minorities. 1913-77. *2503*
—. Châteauguay (battle). War of 1812. 1813. *763*
—. Children, English- and French-Canadian. Government. Political socialization. 1970-71. *2549*
—. Church and state. Elections (1890). Equal Rights Association. Ontario reaction. 1885-95. *2827*
—. Church names, origin of. Religion. Toponymy. 1600-1925. *2557*
—. Civil Service. USA. Wages. 1970's. *2599*
—. Class struggle. Equality. French-speaking community. Intellectuals. Nationalism. 1960's-70's. *2677*
—. Class struggle. Socialists. 1970's. *2670*
—. Collective bargaining. Public employees. 1964-72. *2602*
—. Collective bargaining. Public Employees. 1966-75. *2632*
—. Colleges and Universities. French Canadians. Historiography. 1947-72. *2449*
—. Colleges and Universities. French Canadians. Sociology. 1960-74. *2499*
—. Colleges and Universities. Labor Unions and Organizations. Professors. 1972-74. *2417*
—. Colonization. Great Clay Belt. Ontario. 1900-30. *274*
—. Commission on Industrial Accidents. Industry. Provincial Government. Workmen's Compensation. 1890-1978. *2623*

—. Commonwealth (proposed). Federal Government. Separatist Movements. 1976-77. *2087*
—. Communications. St. Lawrence Seaway. 16c-20c. *2582*
—. Communications (international, theory of). Hecksher-Ohlin theory. Ontario. 1974. *2148*
—. Confederation. Federalism. 19c-20c. *2105*
—. Confederation. French Canadians. Ontario. Provincial Government. 1867-1937. *155*
—. Conflict management. Institutions. Regional autonomy. Separatist movements. South. 19c-1970. *2101*
—. Conscription, Military. Elections. King, William Lyon Mackenzie. Ligue pour la Défense du Canada. World War II. 1942-44. *1226*
—. Conservatism. LeSage, Simeon. Nationalism. Riel, Louis. 1867-1909. *2717*
—. Constitutional History. Great Britain. 1791-1814. *2694*
—. Constitutions. Economic Conditions. Separatist Movements. 1973. *2115*
—. Constitutions. Federal Government. Provincial Government. Separatist Movements. 1968-76. *2117*
—. Construction industry. Labor. Office de la construction du Québec. 1960's-70's. *2647*
—. Construction Industry Labour Relations Act. Labor relations. 1973. *2631*
—. Cooperativism. Syndicalism. 1972-77. *2648*
—. Corporation Law. Professionalism. 1840's-1970's. *2615*
—. Counties (regrouping of). Health care services. Regions, homogeneous. Socioeconomic development, planning of. 1974. *2428*
—. Craftsmen's associations. French Canadians. 17c-18c. *533*
—. Créditiste movement. French Canada. Pinard, Maurice (review article). Stein, Michael (review article). 1971-74. *2447*
—. Cultural identity. Regionalism. 1973. *2672*
—. Cultural membership. Ethnic Groups. Political attitudes. 1974. *2548*
—. Davis, William. Ontario. Politics. Separatist Movements. 1976-77. *1280*
—. Death and Dying. Social Classes. 1934-74. *2468*
—. deGaulle, Charles (attitudes). France. French Canadians. 1940-67. *2685*
—. Demers, Jerôme. Philosophy. Science. Teaching. 1765-1835. *2502*
—. Democracy. Dissent. Political stability. 1960's-70's. *2489*
—. Democratic Union Central. Labor Unions and Organizations. 1968-74. *2621*
—. Demography. French Canadians. Social Organization. 1974. *2481*
—. Demography. St. Lawrence River (St. Ignace, Dupas islands). Settlement. 1648-1913. *2486*
—. Desjardins cooperative movement. Government. Interest groups. 18c-1973. *2415*
—. Drapeau, Jean. Montreal Citizens' Movement. 1957-76. *2649*
—. Economic Conditions. Ethnic Groups. Industrialization. Labor law. 1865-88. *2627*
—. Economic Conditions. French language. Parti Québécois. Politics. Social Customs. 1973-78. *2696*
—. Economic Conditions. Fur trade. New France. 1760-90. *574*
—. Economic Conditions. Ontario. Social Change. Violence. 1963-73. *2127*
—. Economic Development. Emigration. French Canadians. 1837-1930. *2616*
—. Economic development. Forests and Forestry. Minville, Esdras. Multinational corporations. USA. 1923-36. *2629*
—. Economic development. Ontario. 1951-78. *2150*
—. Economic Development. USA. 1960-73. *1983*
—. Economic expansion. Federalism. Independence Movements. 1867-1973. *2085*
—. Economic Growth. 1974. *2656*
—. Economic growth. Elites. Ideology. Laval University. Social sciences. 1930's-70's. *2527*
—. Economic growth. Service activities. 1968-72. *2141*
—. Economic independence. Parti Québécois. USA. 1972-73. *1267*
—. Economic issues. French-speakers. Minorities. Separatist Movements. 1976. *2689*
—. Economic policy. 1974. *2667*
—. Economic Policy. Water use (theories). 1970's. *1324*
—. Economic power. French Canadians. Separatist movements. 1960's-70's. *2679*

—. Economic security. Families, low-income. Poverty. Public Welfare. Social Aid Act (1969). 1969-75. *2668*
—. Economic Theory. French Canadians. Minville, Esdras. 20c. *2586*
—. Educational Reform. Parent Commission. 1944-66. *2416*
—. Elections. 1867-86. *2425*
—. Elections. France. Language. Parliaments. 1792-1810. *700*
—. Elections. Independence issue. Liberals. Parti Québécois. 1973-76. *2707*
—. Elections. Labor Unions and Organizations. Parti Québécois. 1970-77. *2591*
—. Elections. Parti Québécois. 1973-76. *2693*
—. Elections. Parti Québécois. 1976. *2695*
—. Elections, federal. Municipalities, redistributing. Political Parties. Voting and Voting Behavior. 1968. *2422*
—. Elections, provincial. Jews. Parti Québécois. Separatist Movements. 1976. *2721*
—. Elections, provincial. Nationalism. Social issues. 1973. *2099*
—. Electricity and Electronics. Energy crisis. James Bay. 1960-70's. *1292*
—. Elites. Science. 1824-44. *2515*
—. Employers' groups. 1967-73. *2592*
—. Energy situation (consumption, price). Fuel. 1974-. *2432*
—. English Canadians. French Canadians. 17c-20c. *33*
—. English Canadians. French Canadians. Laurendeau, André. Nationalism. 1945-66. *2556*
—. English Canadians. French Canadians. Multiculturalism. 1970's. *1303*
—. English Canadians. French Canadians. Political power. Press. 1864-67. *2572*
—. English language. French Quebec Movement. Official Language Act (Quebec, 1974). 1974. *2460*
—. Environment. Indians. Labrador. Religion. Social organization. 17c-20c. *428*
—. Ethnic groups. French Canadians. Geographic space. Multiculturalism. Regionalism. Urbanization. 1930-73. *2715*
—. Ethnohistory. St. Lawrence estuary. 20c. *2491*
—. Europe. Separatist Movements. USA. 1977. *1920*
—. Europe, influence of. Ideas, History of. Social Classes. 1960-75. *2501*
—. Evangelism. Hospitals. Indians. 1633-1703. *539*
—. Exports. Quantitative methods. Regional Planning. 1969. *1254*
—. Family. France. Protestantism. Trade. 1740-60. *593*
—. Farm. Land use. Markets. 1908-71. *2661*
—. Federal government. Fiscal policy. Income. Income Tax. Inflation. Regional Government. 1970-74. *1573*
—. Federal government. French Canadians. Public Policy. Separatist Movements. 1976. *1306*
—. Federal government. Language equality. Official Language Act (Quebec, 1974). 1960-76. *1438*
—. Federal government. Language policy. Middle Classes. Modernization. Provincial government. 1960-76. *2090*
—. Federal government. New Democratic Party. Parti Québécois. Separatist Movements. 1960's-70's. *2102*
—. Federal government. Parti Québécois. Provincial Government. Social Change. 1960-77. *2420*
—. Federal Government. Parti Québécois. Separatist Movements. 1976-77. *2112*
—. Federal Government. Personnel management. 1972-74. *2435*
—. Federal Government. Separatist Movements. 1960-77. *2710*
—. Federal Regulation. Radio-Québec. Television. 1969-76. *2478*
—. Federalism. French Canadians. 1970's. *2103*
—. Federalism. French Canadians. Social Change. 1968-77. *2114*
—. Federalism. French Canadians. Sovereignty. Territorialization. 1760-1977. *167*
—. Federalism. Lamontagne, Maurice (views). Separatist Movements. 1867-1976. *2097*
—. Federalism. Separatist Movements. 1759-1977. *69*
—. Feudalism. 1774-1971. *16*
—. Fishing Rights. Labrador. Newfoundland. Public Administration. 1763-83. *735*

—. Food industry. Provigo (corporation). 20c. *2620*
—. Foreign influences. National self-identity. Poland. 1970's. *2675*
—. Foreign policy. 1977. *2706*
—. Foreign Policy. French Canadians. Nationalism. USA. 1945-76. *2044*
—. Foreign policy. Separatist Movements. 1690-1976. *2680*
—. Foreign Relations. France. 1967-75. *1952*
—. Foreign relations. France. 1763-1976. *2686*
—. Foreign relations. Independence. USA. 1950's-73. *2005*
—. Foreign Relations. Parti Québécois. Separatist Movements. USA. 1973-77. *1993*
—. Foreign relations. Separatist Movements. 1960-76. *2711*
—. France. Lamaletie, Jean-André. Trading circles. 1741-63. *561*
—. France. Legislation. North America. Psychiatric care. 1973. *2546*
—. France. Sociology. USA. 1970's. *2551*
—. French Canadians. Groulx, Lionel. Historians. Nationalism. Nonviolence. 1917-30. *489*
—. French Canadians. Historiography. 1660-1976. *495*
—. French Canadians. Hume, David (writings). Literature, moralistic. Luxury, concept of. 1849-1900. *2617*
—. French Canadians. Independence. Monetary Systems. Parti Québécois. 1974. *2424*
—. French Canadians. Independence Movements. Lévesque, René (views). Nationalism. 1763-1976. *2701*
—. French Canadians. Industry. 20c. *2665*
—. French Canadians. Industry. 1961-75. *2009*
—. French Canadians. Jews. Separatist movements. Social Conditions. 1976-77. *2723*
—. French Canadians. Lawyers. LeSage, Simeon. Provincial Government. 1835-1909. *2570*
—. French Canadians. Literacy. 1745-1899. *2507*
—. French Canadians. Nationalism. Official Language Act (Quebec, 1974). USA. 1970's. *2577*
—. French Canadians. Novels. USA. 1960's-70's. *2074*
—. French Canadians. Separatism. 1974-76. *2683*
—. French Canadians. Separatist Movements. 1774-1975. *2719*
—. French language. Linguistics. 1971. *2576*
—. French language. Official Language Act (Quebec, 1974). 1974. *2458*
—. French language. Official Language Act (Quebec, 1974). 1974. *2465*
—. French language. Regionalism. Social Customs. 1977. *2716*
—. French-speaking adults. Separatism. Social-class levels. 1968. *2682*
—. Galtung, Johan. Separatism. Social change. 1961-75. *2712*
—. Government. 20c. *2098*
—. Government. Nationhood. 1960-76. *2698*
—. Great Lakes. Howell, William Maher (reminiscences). Ontario. Pennsylvania (Erie). St. Lawrence Seaway. Travel. 1928. *2131*
—. Great Lakes. Ports. St. Lawrence River (north shore). Shipping. 1937-70. *1565*
—. Health services. Patient use (regional analysis). 1974. *2540*
—. Higher education. Nationalism. Symons report. 1970's. *1472*
—. Historical Society of Montreal. Lapierre, Eugène (obituary). Nationalism. 1927-70's. *2450*
—. Historiography. 1790-1890. 1950-78. *2453*
—. Historiography. Papineau, Louis-Joseph. Politics. Rebellion of 1837. Rumilly, Robert (review article). 1791-1871. 1934. 1977. *822*
—. Historiography. Social Credit. 1936-65. *2619*
—. Historiography. Working class. 1897-1974. *2611*
—. Hydrographic regions. Population. Statistics. 1845-1971. *2488*
—. Immigration. Mennonites (Russian). Passenger lists. 1874-80. *966*
—. Independence Movements. Political Attitudes. 1960's-70's. *2100*
—. Indian Affairs Department. Iroquois Indians. Law. St. Regis Reservation. 1876-1918. *459*
—. Industrialization. Urbanization. 1941-61. *2613*
—. Inflation. Strikes. 1974. *2624*
—. Institutions. Legitimacy. Radio-Québec. Television. 1969-74. *2477*

—. Interest groups. Political Systems. 1970's. *2429*

—. Jackman, Alonzo. Military Strategy. New York. Travel. Vermont. 1838. *2443*

—. Jesuits. Lacouture, Onésime. 1931-50. *2493*

—. Jesuits. Land Tenure. Legislation. Mercier, Honoré. Protestant Churches. 1886. *2645*

—. King, William Lyon Mackenzie. Liberal Party. Politics. 1919-50. *1132*

—. Labor. Lowry, Ira S. Migration, Internal. Models. -1973. *2593*

—. Labor movement. Vaillancourt, Philippe (account). 1936-76. *2589*

—. Labor Unions and Organizations. National Trades and Labour Congress. Ontario (Kitchener). Trades and Labour Congress of Canada. 1892-1902. *2655*

—. Language. Minorities. Official Language Act (Quebec, 1974). 1750's-1974. *2476*

—. Leftism. Nationalism. Social classes. 1970's. *2703*

—. Lévesque, René. Parti Québécois. Separatism. Trudeau, Pierre Elliott. 1970's. *2110*

—. Lévesque, René. Parti Québécois. Separatist Movements. 1968-70's. *2713*

—. Literature. Periodicals. 20c. *2505*

—. Local government. Provincial government. Public Finance. 1960-73. *2418*

—. Lotteries. Provincial Government. Public Finance. 1970-73. *2603*

—. Marxism. Political Reform. Revolution. 1960-65. *2640*

—. Measurements. Port activity. St. Lawrence River (south shore). 1944-66. *2660*

—. Medical licensing. McGill University. Montreal Medical Board. 1833-34. *2573*

—. Medical Reform. 1975. *2554*

—. Medical reform. Physicians. 1940-70. *2614*

—. Medicine and State. Public Health. Regional councils. Social services. 1971-74. *2547*

—. Mental Illness. Psychiatry. Sociology. 1717-1960. *2513*

—. Middle Classes. 1850-1914. *2442*

—. Miron, Gaston. Poetry. Sovereignty. 1969-74. *2470*

—. Modernization. Ontario. Social change. 1950-1974. *2479*

—. Modernization. Political Change. Separatist Movements. 19c-1970's. *151*

—. Montreal Snowshoe Club. Snowshoe clubs. 1840's-1900's. *2536*

—. Mouvement National des Québécois. St. John the Baptist Society. Separatist Movements. 1834-1972. *2692*

—. National Characteristics. Separatist Movements. 1971-74. *2671*

—. National interest. Nationalism. 1960's-70's. *2095*

—. Nationalism. 1975. *1337*

—. Nationalism. 1945-76. *2678*

—. Nationalism. 1945-70. *2709*

—. Nationalism. Separatist Movements. Socialism. USA. 1970's. *2021*

—. News, European. Newspapers. 1866-71. *2528*

—. News, foreign. Newspapers. 1962-74. *2553*

—. Newspapers. Strikes. 1977-78. *2574*

—. Ontario. Quantitative sources, utility of. Transportation. Urban hierarchy. 1861-1901. *2137*

—. Parish records. Population. Statistics. 1621-99. *541*

—. Parti Québécois. Political attitudes. 1976-78. *2697*

—. Parti Québécois. Self-determination. Sovereignty. 1970's. *2116*

—. Parti Québécois. Separatist Movements. 1970's. *2107*

—. Parti Québécois. Separatist Movements. 1973. *2720*

—. Patronage. Political parties. 1944-72. *2439*

—. Population. 1951-71. *2535*

—. Provincial government. Public administration. 1867-1975. *2436*

—. Provincial Government. Securities Commission. Stocks and Bonds. 1970's. *2427*

—. Provincial government. Separatist Movements. 1955-75. *2568*

—. Provincial Government. Social Reform. 1973. *2539*

—. Public Health. Sociology. ca 1850's-1970. *2494*

—. Recreation. 1606-1771. *544*

—. Referendum (possible). Separatist Movements. 1867-1976. *2086*

—. Self-determination. Separatist Movements. 1970-76. *2088*

—. Separatist Movements. ca 1970-74. *1321*

—. Separatist Movements. 1960's. *2094*

—. Sociology. 1822-1974. *2497*

Quebec (Abitibi County). Bridges. 1820-1950's. *2438*

Quebec (Abitibi-Témiscamingue). Economic History. Mining. 1885-1950. *2625*

Quebec Act. Historians. 1774. 1974. *696*

Quebec Archdiocese. Atlantic Provinces. Catholic Church. Diaries. Plessis, Joseph-Octave. 1812-15. *2155*

Quebec, battle of. Act of Confederation (1867). Papineau, Louis-Joseph. Political Theory. 1759-1867. *896*

—. British Library (Townshend archive). French and Indian War. Great Britain. Maps. 1759. *609*

—. French and Indian War. Wolfe, James. 1759. *621*

Quebec (Caughnawaga, Sault St. Louis). Indians. Women. 1852. *374*

Quebec (Chicoutimi). Europe. Flint. Gunflints. Indians. Travel. 17c. 20c. *349*

Quebec (Chicoutimi Basin). Catholic Church. Eudists. Industrialization. Working class. 1903-30. *2475*

Quebec (Compton County). Catholic Church. French Canadians. Migration, Internal. Parishes. Rural-Urban Studies. 1851-91. *2534*

Quebec (Drummond County). Drummond County Mechanics Institute. Farmers. Labor Unions and Organizations. 1856-90. *2537*

Quebec (Eastern Townships). Catholicism. Church History. Colonization. Settlement. 1800-60. *704*

Quebec (Eastmain River). Anderson, James. Hudson's Bay Company. Rivers. Whaling Industry and Trade. 1850's-70. *847*

Quebec Expedition. Harvard University. Leverett, John. Massachusetts (Cambridge). Speeches, Addresses, etc. 1711. *610*

Quebec (Fire Lake). Iron mining. Natural resources. Newfoundland. SIDBEC (consortium). 1960's. *2622*

Quebec (Gaspé). Catholic Church. Ross, François Xavier. Social Conditions. 1923-45. *2532*

Quebec (Gaspé Peninsula). Cooperatives. Fishing. Pêcheurs-Unis. World War II. 1939-48. *2638*

Quebec (Gatineau Valley). Farming. 1800-1975. *2651*

Quebec (Havre, Saint Pierre). Economic Growth. Roads. 1685-1973. *2626*

—. Mines. Ports. 1948-73. *2628*

Quebec (Hérbertville). Colonization. Industrialization. 1844-1900. *2657*

Quebec (Hérbertville, Lake Saint John). Catholic Church. Settlement. ca 1840-1900. *2558*

Quebec (Hull). City Government. Public housing. 1968-74. *2456*

—. Folklore. Kealey, James (and family). Oral history. 1974-75. *2492*

Quebec (James Bay). Acculturation. Cree Indians. Indian-White Relations. 1970's. *345*

Quebec (La Beauce County). Catholic Church. Devotions, popular. Shrines, roadside. Social customs. 1970's. *2514*

Quebec (Lac-Saint-Jean, Portneuf Counties). Catholic Church. Cults, Liturgical. Devotions, popular. 1970's. *2561*

Quebec (Laprairie). French Canadians. Genealogy. Page Family. 1763-1967. *2530*

Quebec (Laterrière). Demography. Family reconstitution studies. Methodology. Migration, Internal. 1855-1970. *2474*

—. Economic development. Family structure. Geographic mobility. 1851-1935. *2471*

Quebec (Laurentian Mountains). Skiing. 1900's-1975. *2518*

Quebec (Lower Canada). Agricultural crisis. Historiography. 1802-12. *806*

—. Agricultural crisis. Historiography. Ouellet, Fernand. Paquet, Gilles. Wallot, J.-P. 1802-12. 1963-73. *789*

—. American Revolution. French Canadians. French Revolution. Reform. 1773-1815. *712*

—. Bédard, Pierre (discourse). Dionne, Narcisse-Eutrope. Language, official. 1792-1809. 1909. *699*

—. Canada Company. Galt, John. Hibernia colony (proposed). Settlement. 1825-35. *774*

—. Catholic Church. Clergy. Craig, James Henry. French Canadian nationalism. Government repression. 1810. *711*

—. Catholic Church. Ethnic groups. Evangelists. Protestantism. Rebellion of 1837. 1766-1865. *811*

—. Cholera. Medicine (practice of). 1832. *770*

—. Colonial Government. Great Britain. Political oppression. USA. 1851. *697*

—. Commerce. International Trade. Social Classes. 1792-1812. *796*

—. Constitution of 1791. Parliamentary government. 1791. *710*

—. Economic Development. Government. Social classes. Ultramontanism. 19c. *698*

—. Education. French Canadians. Literary associations. Social Problems. 1840-67. *2526*

—. Legislative assembly. Voting and Voting Behavior. 1792-1814. *701*

Quebec (Lower Canada; Potton). Rebellion of 1837. Vermont. Woods, N. R. (letter). 1837-38. *816*

Quebec (Lower Town, Place Royale). Buildings. Restorations. 17c. 1975. *515*

Quebec (Magdalen Islands). 1534-1973. *2437*

Quebec (Montreal). Air Mail Service. New Brunswick (Rimouski). 1920's-30's. *1179*

—. Alcoholism. Cultural influences. Social performance. 1973. *1443*

—. Anticlericalism. Boycotts. *Canada-Revue* (newspaper). Catholic Church. Freedom of the press. 1890-94. *2484*

—. Archives. Radio. Radio Canada Archives. Television. 1959-75. *1351*

—. Archives, city. 1913-74. *2434*

—. Armenians. Immigration. 1900-66. *28*

—. Art. Chabert, Joseph. Education. National Institute for Arts and Crafts. Teachers. Working Class. 1861-94. *1053*

—. Banking (locations). Urbanization. 1966-71. *2654*

—. Bibliographies. Brouillette, Benoit. Geography. 1903-73. *2496*

—. Bishops. Church of England. Fulford, Francis. 1850-68. *874*

—. Bossism. Houde, Camillien. Local government. Martin, Médéric. 1923-29. *2446*

—. Bothwick, J. Douglas (*History and Biographical Gazetteer of Montreal to the Year 1892*). Elites. Social stratification. 19c. *2550*

—. British garrison. Great Britain. 1840's. *833*

—. British North America. Fur Garrison towns. Michigan (Detroit). Military Camps and Forts. 1760-75. *637*

—. Brotherhood of the Holy Family. Catholic Church. Chaumonot, Joseph-Marie-Pierre. Elites. Laval, François de. 1663-1760. *547*

—. Business. 1825. *2594*

—. Canadian Institute of Montreal. Social history. 1845-73. *2509*

—. Capitalism (commercial, industrial). Research Group on Montreal Society. Social History. 19c. *2642*

—. Career patterns. Entrepreneurial behaviour. Real estate agents, residential. -1974. *2634*

—. Catholic Church. France (Paris). Reading rooms. Social Customs. 19c. *2531*

—. Cavalry. Frontier. 1837-50. *820*

—. Cities. Population. 18c. *510*

—. City Government. Economic growth. Public Administration. Social Conditions. Urbanization. 1850-1914. *2441*

—. Clothing industries. Locational clustering. Ontario (Toronto). Publishers and Publishing. 1949-67. *1611*

—. Commerce. France. Fur trade. Great Britain. Middle classes. 1750-92. *702*

—. Coubertin, Pierre de. Nationalism. Olympic Games. 1900-76. *2414*

—. Counterintelligence (US). Gage, Lyman. Spanish-American War. Spy ring, Spanish. Wilkie, John. 1898. *1094*

—. Drapeau, Jean. Olympic Games. Sports. 1970-76. *2521*

—. École des Hautes Études Commerciales. Economics. Educators. Minville, Esdras. 20c. *2457*

—. Economic conditions. Industrial structure. 17c-1971. *2610*

—. Economic growth. Energy crisis. Oil and Petroleum Products. 1960-80. *2644*

—. Economic growth. Regional accounting. 1951-66. *2635*

—. Economics. Minville, Esdras. Periodicals. 1922-28. *2533*

—. Emigration. Jews. Morocco. 1960's-70's. *2517*

—. Engineers. Ethnic groups. Occupational preferences and values. -1974. *2559*

—. Frégault, Guy. Historiography. 17c. 1950-60. *490*

—. French Canadians. Richelieu Company. 1845-54. *2666*

—. Fur Trade. Merchants. Social Classes. 1750-75. *703*

—. Hasidism. Judaism. 1942-71. *2510*
—. Industrialization. Shoe industry. 1840-70. *2606*
—. International Ladies' Garment Workers' Union. 1937-77. *1512*
—. Labor. Occupations. 1960's-70's. *1594*
—. Lectures. Melville, Herman. 1857. *2519*
—. Lévesque, René. Newspapers. Parti Québécois. Provincial Government. 1976-77. *2423*
—. Local Government. Models. 1911-71. *2445*
—. Manufactures. Material linkages. 1927-71. *2604*
—. Recreation. Sports. 1840-95. *2538*
—. Strikes. Teamsters, International Brotherhood of. 1864. *2630*
Quebec National Assembly. Disadvantaged. Social Credit Party. Tribunicial function. 1970-75. *2511*
—. Government effectiveness. Political Reform. 1964-75. *2444*
Quebec (Nicolet, Three Rivers dioceses). Clergy. 1852-85. *2580*
Quebec (Oka). Algonkin Indians. Historical Sites and Parks. Iroquois Indians. Missions and Missionaries. Sulpicians. 1700's-1800's. *521*
Quebec (Orléans Island). Historical Sites and Parks. Urbanization. 1969-76. *2490*
Quebec (Ottawa River). Treadwell Trenches. 1800-34. *800*
Quebec (Quebec). Archives, city. 1924-70's. *2430*
—. Bourget, Ignace. Catholic Church. Colleges and Universities. Laval University. 1840's-50's. *2523*
—. Catholic Church. Irish Canadians. McMahon, Patrick. Poor. St. Bridget's Home. 1847-1972. *2541*
—. Census. Methodology. Population. 1795-1805. 1974-76. *2584*
—. Children. Population. 1951-71. *2508*
—. City Government. Municipal limits. 1831-1972. *2426*
—. Construction. Contracts. Housing. Population. 1810-20. *2596*
—. Demography. Ethnic groups. 1795-1805. *2512*
—. French Canadians. Grey, Albert Henry George, 4th Earl. 1903-06. *2691*
—. Generation conflict, basis. Identity. Social integration. 1968. *2487*
—. Howells, William Dean. Travel. 1871-72. *2454*
—. Institute of History. Laval University. 1947. *2571*
—. Urbanization. 1790-1840. *2522*
Quebec (Quebec; Lower Town). Alienation. Charities. Government. Social Problems. Working Class. 1896-1914. *2637*
Quebec (Rawdon). Demography. Francisation. Rural Settlements. 1791-1970. *2575*
Quebec (Rimouski). Action Catholique. Catholic Church. Courchesne, Georges. 1940-67. *2466*
Quebec (Saguenay). Bishops. Catholic Church. Chicoutimi, Séminaire de. Church History. 1873-1973. *2542*
—. Catholic Church. Chicoutimi, Petit-Séminaire de. Religious Education. Students. 1873-1930. *2562*
—. Economic Development. Settlement. 1840-1900. *2658*
Quebec (Saguenay County). Behaviorism. Political geography. Spatial perception. Territorialism. 1969-74. *2448*
—. Higher Education. Students. 1975. *2498*
—. Land Tenure. Methodology. 1840-1975. *2633*
Quebec (Saguenay region). Agriculture. Industry. Social Conditions. 1840-1972. *2472*
—. Higher Education. 1949-69. *2506*
—. Methodology. Migration, Internal. 1842-1931. *2545*
—. Population. Social mobility. 19c-20c. *2473*
Quebec (Saguenay River, Lake St. John). Dubuc family papers. Paper Industry. 1892-1963. *2612*
Quebec (Saint-Georges Est, Chaudière River). Economic Growth. Industry. Pollution. Tourism. 1973. *2652*
Quebec (Saint-Hyacinthe County). Parishes. Regional complexity. Voting and Voting Behavior. 1867-86. *2555*
Quebec (Schyan River area). Lumber and Lumbering. Photographs. Price, Vernon (interview). 1938-39. *2641*
Quebec (Shawinigan). Geography. Industrial decline. 1932-72. *2605*
Quebec (Sherbrooke). Bishops. Christian Biography. Church History. 1868-72. *2579*

—. Catholic Church. Church Finance. Economic Development. LaRocque, Paul. 1893-1926. *2636*
—. Emigration. Foreign Relations. France. Trappists. 1903-14. *2529*
Quebec (Sherbrooke area). Census. Construction. Irish Canadians. Migrant labor. Railroads. 1851-53. *2520*
Quebec (southern). Geography. Regional divisions. 1932-66. *2687*
Quebec (St. Constant). Canadian Railway Museum. Railroads. 1940's-77. *1305*
Quebec (St. Francis District). French Canadians. Newspapers. Rebellion of 1837. 1823-45. *813*
Quebec (St. Jérôme). Labor. Textile workers. 1974. *2590*
Quebec (Three Rivers). Church of England. Missions and Missionaries. Wood, Samuel. 1822-68. *658*
—. Ports. St. Lawrence Seaway. Shipping. 1874-1972. *2608*
Quebec (Ungava Peninsula). Excavations. Vikings. Prehistory. 1965. *479*
Quebec, University of. Centre de documentation en civilisation traditionelle. French Canadian identity. Séguin, Robert-Lionel (writings). 1959-75. *494*
Queen Anne's War. Fishing industry. King William's War. New England. Privateers. Shipping. 1689-1713. *596*
Queen, John. Local Government. Manitoba (Winnipeg). Socialism. Taxation. 1909-42. *2992*
Queen's College. Church of England. Morris, William. Ontario (Kingston). Presbyterians. Scots. 1836-42. *2831*
Queenston Heights (battle). Ontario. Upper Canada. War of 1812. 1812. *766*
Quinlan, Thomas A. (letters). Gold Rushes. Klondike Stampede. Yukon Territory. 1898-1904. *3337*
Quinte Mission. Fort Frontenac. Indian-White Relations. Iroquois Indians. Missions and Missionaries. Sulpicians. 1665-80. *522*

R

Race. Attitudes. English Canadians. Sex. Woman Suffrage. ca 1877-1918. *902*
—. Australia. Government policy. New Zealand. Nonwhites. South Africa. 1900-73. *1926*
Race Relations *See also* Acculturation; Discrimination; Emigration; Ethnology; Immigration; Indian-White Relations; Negroes.
—. Acculturation. Cree Indians. Eskimos (Inuit). 1970-74. *284*
—. Alberta. Homesteading and Homesteaders. Immigration. Negroes. 1911-12. *3152*
—. Assimilation. Ethnic groups. Europe. USA. 20c. *15*
—. Boxing. Langford, Sam ("Boston Tarbaby"). 1886-1956. *2369*
—. British Columbia. California. Discrimination. Gold Rushes. Negroes. 1849-66. *846*
—. British Columbia, University of. Japanese Canadians. World War II. 1939-42. *3177*
—. Economic conditions. Foreign policy. USA. Vietnam War. 1970's. *2078*
—. Freedoms. Human rights. North America. 1973. *1478*
—. Japanese Canadians. Relocation, forced. World War II. 1890's-1940's. *1245*
—. Semantics. -1973. *1437*
Racism. Adachi, Ken (review article). Immigration. Japanese Canadians. 1877-1976. *123*
—. Africans. Asians. Indians. North America. Whites. 1600-1900. *10*
—. Asian Canadians. British Columbia. Immigration. Politics. 1850-1914. *900*
—. Atomic Warfare. Diaries. King, William Lyon MacKenzie. 1921-48. *1139*
—. Brain drain. British West Indies. Immigration policy. 1946-77. *1742*
—. Chinese. Ontario (Toronto). 1881-1912. *2838*
—. Europe (Eastern, Southern). Immigration. Legislation. Physicians. 1920's. *1178*
—. Government. Human rights agencies. Ontario. 1973-74. *2790*
—. Ontario. Prohibition. Reform. 1890-1915. *2756*
Radcliffe, Mary. Clark, Septimus Alfred. Frontier and Pioneer Life. Great Britain. Letters. Saskatchewan (Regina). 1884-1909. *967*
Raddall, Thomas (memoirs; review article). Nova Scotia. Novels. 1913-75. *2238*

Radicals and Radicalism *See also* Leftism; Political Reform; Revolution; Social Reform.
—. Alberta. Kansas. Leedy, John Whitnah. Politics. Prairie radical. 1880's-1935. *3087*
—. Attitudes. Industrialization. Labor Unions and Organizations. Working class. 1897-1919. *2899*
—. Ethnic tension. Immigration policy. 1896-1919. *1079*
—. Farmer Labor Party. Political Leadership. Saskatchewan. Socialism. 1932-34. *3048*
—. Finns. Immigrants. Labor Unions and Organizations. USA. 1918-26. *1183*
—. Government financing. Political Protest. Social services. 1960's-70's. *1689*
—. Industrial Workers of the World. Labor Unions and Organizations. 1905-14. *2940*
—. Labor Unions and Organizations. One Big Union. Socialism. 1917-19. *1149*
—. McLachlan, Alexander. Ontario. Poetry. Social reform. Working class. 1818-96. *924*
—. Newspapers. 1870-1900. *940*
—. Porter, John. Social Classes. 1950-65. *1462*
—. Riel, Louis. 1870-85. *952*
Radio. 1975-76. *3282*
—. Aberhart, William. Alberta. Economic reform. Politics. Religion. 1934-37. *3088*
—. Canadian Broadcasting Corporation. Drama. Fink, Howard (account). 1940's-50's. 1976. *1386*
—. Canadian Broadcasting Corporation. News. USA. 1975-76. *2031*
—. Eskimos. Northwest Territories (Baffin Island). Television. 1972-73. *321*
—. Ouimet, Marcel. 1939-75. *1441*
Radio Canada Archives. Archives. Quebec (Montreal). Television. 1959-75. *1351*
Radio-Québec. Federal Regulation. Quebec. Television. 1969-76. *2478*
—. Institutions. Legitimacy. Quebec. Television. 1969-74. *2477*
Rae, John. Arctic. Discovery and Exploration. Fort Hope. Hudson's Bay Company. Northwest Territories. 1840's. *3298*
—. Arctic. Explorers. Physicians. 1835-93. *3315*
Rae, John (travel account). Explorers. 1861. *2952*
Raguneau, Paul (letter). Lake Huron. Ontario (Georgian Bay). 1648. *589*
Ragwort weed. Cattle disease. Nova Scotia. 1850-1910. *2299*
Railroad tunnels. Michigan (Port Huron). Ontario (Sarnia). St. Clair River. Transportation, Commercial. 1884-91. *108*
Railroads *See also* Freight and Freightage.
—. 1840's-50's. *854*
—. Agricultural economy. Prairies. Urbanization. 1871-1916. *2957*
—. Alaska. USSR. World War II. 1942-43. *1248*
—. Alberta (Athabasca Landing). Canadian Northern Railway. *Edmonton Bulletin* (newspaper). Villages. 1912-77. *3113*
—. Alberta (Edmonton). Bridges. Calgary and Edmonton Railway. City Government. 1910-13. *3112*
—. Alberta (Edmonton). Canadian Pacific Railway. Local Politics. 1891-1914. *955*
—. Architecture. Canadian National Railroad System. Saskatchewan. 1890-1970's. *3030*
—. Architecture. Canadian Pacific Railway. Saskatchewan. 20c. *3029*
—. Boosterism. New Brunswick (Saint John). Population. 1851-80. *2410*
—. Borden, Robert. Nationalization. 1915-19. *1154*
—. British Columbia. Engineering. Lumber and Lumbering. Poetry. Swanson, Robert (interview). 20c. *3273*
—. British Columbia Electric Railway. Management. 1890-1920. *3245*
—. Canadian Pacific Railroad. Capital alliances. Morton, Bliss & Company. St. Paul & Pacific Railroad. Stephen, George. USA. 1860-70's. *980*
—. Canadian Railway Labour Association. Employment. Technology. Working Conditions. 1973. *1620*
—. Canadian Railway Museum. Quebec (St. Constant). 1940's-77. *1305*
—. Canals. Geographic space. International Trade. National Development. Politics. 1818-1930. *54*
—. Canals. Ontario (Georgian Bay). Public Finance. 1850-1915. *925*

—. Census. Construction. Irish Canadians. Migrant labor. Quebec (Sherbrooke area). 1851-53. *2520*

—. Colonization companies. Economic growth. Saskatchewan (Yorkton). 1882-1905. *1002*

—. Communications (Transcontinental). Telegraph. Watkin, Edward. 1860-65. *884*

—. Economic Conditions. Mining. 1960's-70's. *1623*

—. Economic Development. Industrial Revolution. New Brunswick (Saint John). Transportation. 1867-1911. *2395*

—. Engineering. Keefer, Thomas Coltrin. Ontario (Upper Canada). 1821-1915. *909*

—. Farms. Immigrants. Manitoba (Brandon). Wheat. 1880-87. *961*

—. Foreign Investments. Great Britain. Hudson's Bay Company. International Financial Society. 1863. *840*

—. Fur trade. Saskatchewan (Grand Rapids). Saskatchewan River. Tramways. 1877-1909. *997*

—. Grand Trunk Railway. Strikes. 1896-1912. *1111*

—. Housing. Ontario (London). Prices. 1972. *1591*

—. Liberal Party. Manitoba. Politics. Schools. 1870's-90's. *2987*

—. Locomotives rosters. Mexico. USA. 1911-78. *48*

—. Midland Continental Railroad. North Dakota. Seiberling, Frank A. 1912-20. *2983*

—. Ontario, northern. Schools. 1922-28. *2865*

—. Ships. Tourism. Travel. Yukon Territory. 20c. *3329*

—. White Pass and Yukon Railway. ca 1900-73. *3326*

Railroads (review article). Canadian Northern Railway. Canadian Pacific Railway. 19c-20c. 1968-77. *915*

Ralliement des Creditistes. Parliaments. Political Parties. 1930's-71. *1700*

Ramsay, David. Fur trade. Indian-White Relations. Mississauga Indians. 1760-1810. *686*

Ranchers. Alberta. Cowboys. Farmers. Round-ups. 1911-19. *2932*

Ranching. Agriculture. Alberta (Rosebud Creek). Biggs, Hugh Beynon. Photography. 1892-1941. *3169*

—. Alberta. Godsal, F. W. South Fork Ranch. 1897. *3155*

—. Cattle Raising. Farming. Saskatchewan (southwestern). 1872-1974. *3072*

Rand formula. Ford Motor Company of Canada. Labor Law. Ontario (Windsor). United Automobile Workers (Canadian Region). 1945-46. *1534*

—. Ford Motor Company of Canada. Labor Law. Ontario (Windsor). United Automobile Workers (Canadian Region). 1946. *1595*

Rand, Paul. Artists. Painting. 1930's-50's. *1118*

Rand, Silas Tertius. Baptists. Language. Micmac Indians. Missions and Missionaries. Nova Scotia. 1830-89. *422*

Rape. Courts. Ontario. 19c. *676*

—. Feminism. Law Enforcement. Ontario (Toronto). Prostitution. 1975-78. *2825*

"Rapid" Indians. Atsina Indians. "Fall" Indians. Indians. Saskatchewan, southcentral. 18c. *405*

Rapier, James Thomas. Negroes. Refugees. 1856-64. *885*

Rapier, John H., Sr. Alabama (Florence). Freedmen. 1830-60. *886*

Rationality. Elites. Ethnic values. Protestant ethic. Senators. 1971. *1645*

Rations policies. Cree Indians. Crooked Lakes Reserves. Saskatchewan (Qu'Appelle Valley). Yellow Calf (chief). 1884. *343*

Raymond, Daniel (family). Genealogy. Nova Scotia (Beaver River, Chebogue). Raymond, Jonathan (family). 1772-1869. *2331*

Raymond, Eliza Ruggles. Missions and Missionaries. Nova Scotia. Sierra Leone (Sherbro Island). Slaves. 1839-50. *2241*

Raymond, Jonathan (family). Genealogy. Nova Scotia (Beaver River, Chebogue). Raymond, Daniel (family). 1772-1869. *2331*

Reader's Digest (periodical). Bill C-58. Nationalism. Protectionism. Taxation. *Time* (periodical). 1922-76. *2017*

Reading rooms. British Columbia (Victoria). Herre, W. F. Libraries. 1858-63. *3256*

—. Catholic Church. France (Paris). Quebec (Montreal). Social Customs. 19c. *2531*

Real Estate *See also* Land Tenure; Mortgages.

—. Cities. Foreign Investments. USA. 1960's-75. *1766*

—. City planning. Economic growth. Saskatchewan (Saskatoon). Yorath, J. C. 1909-13. *3061*

—. Colonization. Pearson, William (reminiscences). Saskatchewan. 1903-13. *1015*

—. Land. 1863-1973. *36*

Real estate agents. Career patterns. Entrepreneurial behaviour. Quebec (Montreal). -1974. *2634*

Realism. Literary Criticism. Novels. 1920-30. *1176*

Reaping. Diffusion theories. Mechanization. Ontario. Technology. 1850-70. *2846*

Reapportionment. *See* Apportionment.

Rebellion of 1837. Anti-Americanism. Ontario (Upper Canada). Sectarianism. 1837. *817*

—. Catholic Church. Ethnic groups. Evangelists. Protestantism. Quebec (Lower Canada). 1766-1865. *811*

—. French Canadians. Newspapers. Quebec (St. Francis District). 1823-45. *813*

—. Historiography. Papineau, Louis-Joseph. Politics. Quebec. Rumilly, Robert (review article). 1791-1871. 1934. 1977. *822*

—. Quebec (Lower Canada; Potton). Vermont. Woods, N. R. (letter). 1837-38. *816*

Rebellions *See also* particular mutinies, insurrections, and rebellions by name, e.g. North West Rebellion, Red River Rebellion; Political Protest; Revolution; Revolutionary Movements.

—. *Patriote* uprising. Vermont. 1837-38. *810*

Recessions *See also* Depressions.

—. Catholic Church. Church and State. Provincial Government. Public Charities Act (1921). Quebec. 1921-26. *2578*

Reciprocity. British Empire. International trade. Sovereignty. USA. 1909-11. *1107*

—. Brown, George. Congress. Diplomacy. USA. 1870-80. *1071*

—. Carey, Henry C. Nationalism. Protectionism. USA. 1871-75. *1060*

—. Great Britain. Nova Scotia. Public opinion. Treaties. USA. 1846-54. *871*

—. Midwest. Politics. USA. 1909-11. *1110*

Recreation *See also* Leisure; Resorts; Sports.

—. Alberta. Rocky Mountains. Skiing. 1920's-30's. *3131*

—. Alberta (Banff, Calgary). Urbanization. 1890. *3162*

—. Canoeing. 16c-20c. *157*

—. Canoeing. Ontario. 1888-1914. *2738*

—. Glass works. Living conditions. Manitoba (Beausejour). Working conditions. 1909-11. *3000*

—. Quebec. 1606-1771. *544*

—. Quebec (Montreal). Sports. 1840-95. *2538*

Red River Academy. Education. Manitoba (Winnipeg). 1820's-50's. *2973*

Red River Expedition. Lindsay, James. Métis. Military Campaigns. 1869-70. *999*

Red River of the North. Alberta (Cochrane). British American Ranche Company. Cattle Raising. Cochrane Ranch. 1881-1905. *1010*

—. Manitoba. Pioneers. Sutherland, Catherine McPherson. 1814-71. *1028*

—. Manitoba (Winnipeg). Métis. Minnesota (St. Paul). Prairies. Trade. Trails. 19c. *976*

—. Métis. Nolin, Jean-Baptiste (and daughters). Prairie Provinces. St. Boniface School. 1760-1840. *776*

Red River Rebellion. Canada First (group). Expansionism. Mair, Charles. Riel, Louis. 1869-70. *1009*

—. Corbett, Griffiths Owen. Half-breeds (English). Manitoba. Métis. 1863-70. *1014*

—. Manitoba. Métis. Political theory. Riel, Louis. 1869. *972*

Referendum. Quebec. Separatist Movements. 1867-1976. *2086*

Reform *See also* types of reform, e.g. Economic Reform, Political Reform, etc.; reform movements, e.g. Abolition Movements, Temperance Movements, etc.; Social Conditions; Social Problems; Utopias.

—. American Revolution. French Canadians. French Revolution. Quebec (Lower Canada). 1773-1815. *712*

—. Atlantic Provinces. Maritime Rights Movement. Regionalism. 1900-25. *2158*

—. City government. Ontario (Toronto). Political Corruption. Pressure Groups. 1890-1900. *2884*

—. Criminal Justice System. Ontario (Upper Canada). Prisons. 1835-50. *769*

—. Feminism. Literature. McClung, Nellie L. Politics. 1873-1930's. *1189*

—. Intellectual history. Ontario (Upper Canada). Political theory. 1800-50. *832*

—. Ontario. Prohibition. Racism. 1890-1915. *2756*

—. Sports. 1920-40. *1127*

Reformed Dutch Church. Exiles. Loyalists. McDowall, Robert James. Missions and Missionaries. Ontario (Upper Canada). 1790-1819. *747*

Refugees *See also* Asylum, Right of; Exiles.

—. Communism. Czechoslovakia. Jesuits. Religious communities, dissolution of. 1950. *1416*

—. Developing nations. Immigration policy. 1950's-70's. *1747*

—. Foreign policy. Immigration. Labor. Population. 1950's-70's. *1887*

—. Negroes. Rapier, James Thomas. 1856-64. *885*

Refuse pits. Excavations. Indians. Manitoba, southwestern (Site DgMg-15). ca 1480-1740. *306*

Regina Manifesto. Cooperative Commonwealth Federation. League for Social Reconstruction. Saskatchewan. Underhill, Frank. 1933. *2927*

Regional accounting. Economic growth. Quebec (Montreal). 1951-66. *2635*

Regional councils. Medicine and State. Public Health. Quebec. Social services. 1971-74. *2547*

Regional development. Economic growth. Federal policy. Maritime Union Movement. Nova Scotia. 1783-1974. *2167*

Regional divisions. Geography. Quebec (southern). 1932-66. *2687*

Regional Government. Council of Maritime Premiers. Maritime Provinces. 1971-76. *2164*

—. Federal government. Fiscal policy. Income. Income Tax. Inflation. Quebec. 1970-74. *1573*

—. Mercury poisoning. Ontario, northwestern. Pollution. 1970's. *2781*

Regional Planning *See also* City Planning; Social Surveys.

—. Alaska-British Columbia-Yukon Conferences. British Columbia. Economic development. Yukon Territory. 1930-64. *2133*

—. California. *Design for Development* (Ontario, 1966). Ontario. 1965-74. *2873*

—. Exports. Quantitative methods. Quebec. 1969. *1254*

Regionalism *See also* Political Integration.

—. Alberta. Fiction. Mitchell, W. O. Ross, Sinclair. 20c. *3093*

—. Alberta (Calgary). Models. Nationalism. Political ideologies. 1974. *2921*

—. Art. Language. Politics. 1978. *2123*

—. Atlantic Provinces. Historiography. Nationalism. 19c-20c. *2160*

—. Atlantic Provinces. Maritime Rights Movement. Reform. 1900-25. *2158*

—. Attitudes. Political culture. 1965. *2143*

—. Catholic Church. Geographic Space. 1615-1851. *3*

—. Communications. Ethnic groups. Geographic Space. Great Britain. 1976. *2139*

—. Conflict management. Institutions. Quebec. Separatist movements. South. 19c-1970. *2101*

—. Cultural identity. Quebec. 1973. *2672*

—. Economic Conditions. Federalism. 1960's-70's. *2096*

—. Economic Development. Northwest Territories. Public Opinion. 1970-73. *3277*

—. Economic Policy. Industry. 1965-75. *2129*

—. Ethnic groups. French Canadians. Geographic space. Multiculturalism. Quebec. Urbanization. 1930-73. *2715*

—. Ethnic Groups. Identity. Nationalism. Students. 1960-77. *2915*

—. Ethnicity. National self-identity. USA. 1974. *2146*

—. French language. Quebec. Social Customs. 1977. *2716*

—. Government. Politics. 1974. *2144*

—. Great Britain. 1969-77. *1762*

—. Indians. Nationalism. Nova Scotia (Cape Breton). Political socialization. Whites. 1860's-1970's. *2361*

—. Labor reform. Socialism. 1918-19. *2917*

—. Maritime provinces. 1960-74. *2135*

—. Maritime Provinces. Self-perception. 1911-72. *2153*

—. Methodist Church. Trades and Labour Congress of Canada. Two-party system. 1870-1919. *2916*

—. Political Parties. 1965-68. *1654*

Registered Trap Lines system. Fur Trade. Manitoba. Trapping. Wells, Harold. 1940-53. *3011*

Regression results (cross-section, time series). Labor. Unemployment. -1973. *1612*

Regulatory agencies. Federal Government. Provincial Government. Public Employees. 1974. *1639*

Rehabilitation. Canadian Labour Congress. Labor Unions and Organizations. 1973. *1584*

—. Ontario. Workmen's Compensation Board. 1973. *2780*

Reid, Dennis. Art History (review article). British Columbia. Murray, Joan. Paintings. 1778-1935. *3189*

Reindeer. Alaska, western. Bahr, Andrew. Northwest Territories (Mackenzie River Delta). 1928-34. *3295*

Relief Camp Workers Union. British Columbia (Vancouver). Depressions. Strikes. 1935. *3209*

Relief funds. American Revolution. Friends, Society of. Great Britain. Ireland. Pennsylvania (Philadelphia). 1778-97. *739*

Religion *See also* Christian Biography; Christianity; Church History; Clergy; Ecumenism; Missions and Missionaries; Revivals; Sects, Religious; Theology.

—. Aberhart, William. Alberta. Economic reform. Politics. Radio. 1934-37. *3088*

—. Bermuda. Education. Political Factions. 1800-1977. *136*

—. Church names, origin of. Quebec. Toponymy. 1600-1925. *2557*

—. Church of England. Tractarians. 1840-68. *857*

—. Communism. Czechoslovakia. Jesuits. Refugees. 1950. *1416*

—. Environment. Indians. Labrador. Quebec. Social organization. 17c-20c. *428*

—, Eskimos. Hudson Bay. Mina (Eskimo woman). 1940's-50's. *326*

—. Eucharistic worship. Protestantism. United Church of Canada. 1952-72. *1452*

—. Irish Canadians. Newfoundland. Politics. 19c. *2189*

—. Messianic Movements. North West Rebellion. Prairie Provinces. Riel, Louis. 1869-85. *971*

—. Métis. Prairie Provinces. Riel, Louis (letter). Taché, Alexandre. 1880's. *974*

—. North West Rebellion. Riel, Louis (letters). 1876-78. *970*

—. Political socialization. Voting and Voting Behavior. 1965. *1670*

Religion in the Public Schools. Anti-Catholicism. New Brunswick. Pitts, Herman H. 1871-90. *2388*

Religious Education *See also* Church Schools; Religion in the Public Schools; Theology.

—. Catholic Church. Chicoutimi, Petit-Séminaire de. Quebec (Saguenay). Students. 1873-1930. *2562*

—. Catholic Church. Congregation of Notre Dame (Sisters). Ontario (Kingston). Women. 1841-48. *2737*

—. Evangelism. Osgood, Thaddeus. 1807-52. *673*

—. Pentecostal Assemblies of Canada. Purdie, James Eustace. 1925-50. *1137*

Religious factionalism. Baptists. Fundamentalist-Modernist controversy. Jarvis Street Church. Ontario (Toronto). Social Classes. 1895-1934. *2762*

Religious Liberty *See also* Church and State.

—. Calvert, George (1st Lord Baltimore). Catholic Church. Colonization. Newfoundland (Avalon Peninsula). 1620's. *551*

Religious Persecution. *See* Persecution.

Religious Revivals. *See* Revivals.

Relocation, forced. British Columbia. Federal Government. Japanese Canadians. Public Opinion. World War II. 1937-42. *1247*

—. Japanese Canadians. Race Relations. World War II. 1890's-1940's. *1245*

Remote Housing Program. Housing (low-cost). Intergovernmental relations. Manitoba. 1968-70. *2988*

Renaudot, Eusèbe. Bernou, Claude. France. LeClercq, Crestien. *Premier Établissement de la Foy dans la Nouvelle France* (book). 1691. *548*

Reporters and Reporting *See also* Editors and Editing; Journalism; News; Press.

—. Landscape Painting. Lynn, Washington Frank. USA. 1860's-70's. *947*

Representation Act (1974). Language. Population. 1974. *2104*

Representative government. Elections. Newfoundland (St. John's). Political Reform. 1815-32. *2194*

Republicanism. Congress. Jackson, John George. Nationalism. Virginia. War of 1812. 1813-17. *754*

Rescue operations. Anderson, James. Arctic. Franklin, John. Iroquois Indians. Woodsmanship. 1855. *3305*

—. *Cobequid* (vessel). Nova Scotia (Halifax). Shipwrecks. 1914. *2322*

Rescue stations. Colonization. Nova Scotia (Sable Island). Shipwrecks. 1759-1801. *2235*

Research *See also* Methodology.

—. Bibliographies. Biculturalism. Bilingualism. 1964-67. *1340*

—. Bibliographies. City planning. 1890-1939. *237*

—. Building plans. Insurance. Land use atlases. Urban historians. 1696-1973. *86*

—. Buildings. 19c-20c. *19*

—. Census. History. Privacy. 1918-77. *57*

—. Census. Urbanization. 1950's-78. *1353*

—. Federal government. Social sciences. 1976. *1467*

—. Feminism. Sociology. 1600-1975. *49*

—. French Americans. Historiography. Vermont. 1609-1976. *2583*

—. Ideology. Sociology of knowledge. Women's studies. 1970's. *1430*

—. Industry. Market structure. 1973. *1545*

—. Maps. Public Archives of Canada. Urban history. Shipwrecks. 1865-1905. *917*

—. Mining. Ontario (Cobalt). 20c. *2728*

—. Political Science. Voting and Voting Behavior. 1967-75. *1655*

—. Population. 17c. *514*

Research Group on Montreal Society. Capitalism (commercial, industrial). Quebec (Montreal). Social History. 19c. *2642*

Resettlement. British Columbia (northern). Government relief. Homesteading and Homesteaders. 1940-42. *3192*

Resorts. Alberta (Banff). Natural Resources. Rocky Mountain Park. 1882-1909. *3117*

Restigouche River (battle). France. French and Indian War. Great Britain. New Brunswick. 1760. *592*

—. *Machault* (vessel). New Brunswick. Pottery. 1760. *2376*

Restorations *See also* Historical Sites and Parks; Preservation.

—. British Columbia. Fort Langley. Hudson's Bay Company. 1827-58. 1976-77. *3210*

—. Buildings. Halifax Historic Properties. Nova Scotia. 1825-1905. 1978. *2255*

—. Buildings. Quebec (Lower Town Place Royale). 17c. 1975. *515*

—. Gold Rushes. Klondike Stampede. Photography. Yukon Territory. 1897-98. 1970's. *3336*

—. Historical Sites and Parks. Louisbourg, Fortress of. Nova Scotia (Cape Breton Island). 18c. 1961-75. *602*

—. Louisbourg, fortress of. Military Camps and Forts. Nova Scotia. 1654-1745. 1928-73. *613*

Retirement, forced. 1970's. *1454*

Revenue sharing. 1975. *1598*

Revitalization movements. Ghost Dance. Indians. Social Organization. 1889. *359*

Revivalism. Gospel Temperance Movement. Rine, D.I.K. 1877-82. *1041*

Revivals *See also* Great Awakening.

—. Burchard, Jedediah. Protestants. Social Conditions. Vermont. 1835-36. *815*

Revolution *See also* specific revolutions by name, e.g. Glorious Revolution, French Revolution, etc.; American Revolution; Radicals and Radicalism; Rebellions; Riots.

—. Capitalism. Quebec. USA. 1920-40. 1960's. *2431*

—. Culture. USA. Violence. 1776-1976. *61*

—. Marxism. Political Reform. Quebec. 1960-65. *2640*

Rhetoric *See also* Lectures; Political Speeches.

—. French and Indian War. New England. War. 1754-60. *620*

—. Social action. Trudeau, Pierre Elliott. War Measures Act (Canada, 1914). 1970. *1301*

Rhode Island *See also* New England; Northeastern or North Atlantic States.

Rhodesia *See also* Africa, Southern.

—. Foreign Policy. International Trade. South Africa. 1960's-76. *1905*

Richardson, Hugh. Harbor Master. Marine Engineering. Ontario (Toronto). 1821-70. *2726*

Richelieu Company. French Canadians. Quebec (Montreal). 1845-54. *2666*

Ricker, Helen S. (reminiscences). Daily Life. Nova Scotia (Glenwood). 1895-1909. *2334*

Rideau Canal. Architecture. Ontario. 1820's-1971. *2794*

Ridings. Liberal Party. Voting and Voting Behavior. 1968. *1637*

Riel, Louis. Canada First (group). Expansionism. Mair, Charles. Red River Rebellion. 1869-70. *1009*

—. Citizenship. Great Britain. Treason. USA. 1885. *951*

—. Conservatism. LeSage, Simeon. Nationalism. Quebec. 1867-1909. *2717*

—. Manitoba. Métis. Political theory. Red River Rebellion. 1869. *972*

—. Mental Illness. Saskatchewan (Regina). Treason. Trials. Valade, François-Xavier (medical report). 1885. *973*

—. Messianic Movements. North West Rebellion. Prairie Provinces. Religion. 1869-85. *971*

—. Revolutionary Movements. 1870-85. *952*

Riel, Louis (letters). Métis. Prairie Provinces. Religion. Taché, Alexandre. 1880's. *974*

—. North West Rebellion. Religious theory. 1876-78. 1885. *970*

Riflemen. American Revolution. Morgan, Daniel. ca 1735-1802. *719*

Riley, Carroll. Civilization (review article). Diffusion theories. Geography. Gordon, Cyrus H. Transoceanic contacts. Prehistory-1492. *304*

Rine, D.I.K. Gospel Temperance Movement. Revivalism. 1877-82. *1041*

Ringed seals. Arctic. Hunting. Seals. Wildlife Conservation. 1966-73. *335*

Rio de la Plata. Schooners. Trade. Voyages. ca 1860-1914. *935*

Rio Treaty. Administrative structure. International law. Organization of American States. San José resolution. 1945-75. *1892*

Riots *See also* Strikes.

—. British Columbia (Vancouver). Chinese. Law Enforcement. Provincial government. 1887. *3247*

—. Nova Scotia (Halifax). 1863. *2368*

Rioux, Marcel. Colonial Government. Frégault, Guy. Historiography. New France. 1615-1763. 1957-60's. *491*

Rites and Ceremonies. Alberta. Blackfoot Indians. Manhood ceremonies. Shaw, P. C. (personal account). 1894. *447*

Ritual toasts. Alberta. Athabasca Pass. British Columbia. 1811-1974. *694*

Rivers *See also* Dams; Water Pollution.

—. Amazon River. Americas (North and South). Environment. Northwest Territories (Mackenzie River). 1977. *268*

—. Anderson, James. Hudson's Bay Company. Quebec (Eastmain River). Whaling Industry and Trade. 1850's-70. *847*

Roads *See also* Highway Engineering; Highways.

—. Alaska (Skagway). Brackett, George. Entrepreneurs. Gold Rushes. Yukon Territory. 1897-98. *3323*

—. Climate. Highway construction. Physical Geography. 1949-73. *3297*

—. Economic Growth. Quebec (Havre, Saint Pierre). 1685-1973. *2626*

—. Gold. Nova Scotia (Eastern shore). Travel. 19c. *2266*

—. Harris, John. Nova Scotia (Halifax, Annapolis). Provincial Government. 1816-30's. *2253*

—. Marshall, John George. Nova Scotia (Cape Breton). 1823-26. *2222*

Robertson, John Ross. Book Industries and Trade. Copyright violations. Ontario (Toronto). Publishers and Publishing. 1877-90. *2815*

Robertson, Norman Alexander. Economic Policy. Foreign Policy. 1929-68. *1234*

Robin, Martin (review article). British Columbia. Business History. Economic Development. Historiography. 19c-20c. 1974. *3244*

Robinson, James H. Africa. Operation Crossroads Africa. Students. USA. 1958-73. *1749*

Rocky Mountain House. Alberta (North Saskatchewan River). Fur Trade. 19c. *3101*

Rocky Mountain Park. Alberta (Banff). Natural Resources. Resorts. 1882-1909. *3117*

Rocky Mountains. Alberta. Recreation. Skiing. 1920's-30's. *3131*

—. Alberta. Tupper, William Johnston (letters). 1885. *964*

Roffignac, Yves de. Aristocracy. Estate ownership. France. Meyer, Rudolf. Saskatchewan (Eastern Assiniboia; Whitewood). 1885-1900. *982*

Rogers' Rangers (retreat). Ballads. French and Indian War. New England. Quebec. 1759. *591*

Rogers, Robert. French and Indian War. New England. 1755-60. *599*

Rogers, William A. Artists. Dakota Territory. Frontier and Pioneer Life. *Harper's Weekly* (periodical). 1878. *2976*

Rolph, George. Ontario. Politics. Rolph, John. Trials. 1825-30. *2843*

Rolph, John. Church of England. Land endowment. Ontario (Upper Canada). Strachan, John. Toronto, University of. 1820-70. *809*

—. Ontario. Politics. Rolph, George. Trials. 1825-30. *2843*

Roman Catholic Church. *See* Catholic Church.

Romanov, Vladmir Pavlovich. Arctic. Kruzenshtern, Ivan Fedorovich. Russia. Scientific Expeditions. USA. 1819-25. *3299*

Romanticism. Discovery and Exploration. Western history. 1540-1800. *579*

Roosevelt Campobello International Park. Hammer, Armand. Historical Sites and Parks. New Brunswick. USA. 1959-74. *2077*

Rosenberg Case. Espionage. Leftism. USA. 1940's-50's. *1682*

Ross, Charlotte W. Manitoba. Medicine (practice of). 1865-1916. *3009*

Ross, François Xavier. Catholic Church. Quebec (Gaspé). Social Conditions. 1923-45. *2532*

Ross, Sinclair. Alberta. Fiction. Mitchell, W. O. Provincial consciousness. 20c. *3093*

Round-ups. Alberta. Cowboys. Farmers. Ranchers. 1911-19. *2932*

Rowe, F. W. Beothuk Indians (review article). Howley, J. P. Indian-White Relations. Newfoundland. Prehistory-1830. 1977. *290*

Rowing. Courtney, Charles. Hanlan, Edward "Ned". 1870's-80's. *1043*

Roy, Camille. Pluralism. Royal Society of Canada. Speeches, Addresses, etc. 1929-78. *1414*

Royal Bank of Canada. Chile. Churches. Loans. South Africa. 1976. *1951*

Royal Botanic Gardens. Botany (specimens). Burke, Joseph. Hudson's Bay Company. Manitoba. Northwest Territories. 1843-45. *2922*

Royal Canadian Academy. Art (Wembley controversy). British Empire Exhibition (1923). National Gallery of Canada. 1877-1933. *1170*

Royal Canadian Air Force. Dieppe (air battle). Great Britain. Leigh-Mallory, Trafford. World War II. 1942. *1220*

Royal Canadian Air Force (Flying School). Aeronautics, Military. Ontario (Long Branch). 1915-16. *1153*

Royal Canadian Mounted Police. Adams, Ian (interview). Intelligence Service. 1960's-70's. *1731*

—. Alberta (Edmonton). McClellan, George B. (reminiscences). 1932-63. *3135*

—. Alberta (Writing-on-Stone, Milk River). Indiana. Law Enforcement. Military Camps and Forts. 1887-1918. *957*

—. Arctic. Northwest Territories. 1890-1929. *3360*

—. Armies. Indians. Settlement. USA. 1870-1900. *1008*

—. Civil rights. Internal security. 1970's. *1708*

—. Criminology. 1873-1973. *106*

—. Douglas, W. O. (reminiscences). Northwest Territories (Baker Lake District). Quangwak (Eskimo). 1919-20's. *323*

—. Dukhobors. Ethnic groups. Saskatchewan. Settlement. 1899-1909. *3028*

—. Fort Herchmer. Gold Rushes. Klondike Stampede. Yukon Territory (Dawson). 1896-1905. 1972-76. *3328*

—. Frontier and Pioneer Life. Manitoba (Red River region). Sitting Bull (chief). Walsh, James. 1873- 1905. *1030*

—. Frontier and Pioneer Life. Potts, Jerry. ca 1860-96. *1006*

—. Gold Rushes. Klondike Stampede. Yukon Territory. 1896-99. *3335*

—. Indians. 1873-85. *1011*

—. Law Enforcement. Manitoba. 1873-74. *2985*

—. Law Enforcement. Northwest Territories. Prohibition. 1874-91. *984*

—. Police. Public Opinion. 1874-83. *1007*

—. Police, provincial. Politics. Provincial Government. Saskatchewan. 1916-28. *3065*

—. Uniforms, Military. 1873-1900. *190*

Royal Commission of Inquiry into the Relations between Capital and Labour. Labor Reform. 1886-89. *1047*

Royal Commission on Book Publishing. Nationalism. Publishers and Publishing. 1973. *1290*

Royal Engineers. British Columbia. Economic Development. 1845-1910. *3266*

Royal Society of Canada. 19c-1973. *1279*

—. Great Britain. Hudson's Bay Company. Wegg, Samuel. 1753-1802. *682*

—. Pluralism. Roy, Camille. Speeches, Addresses, etc. 1929-78. *1414*

Royal Society of Canada (Letters and Social Sciences Section). Canadian studies. French civilization. 1952-72. *1344*

Rumania *See also* Europe, Eastern.

—. Bulgaria. Great Powers. Hungary. UN. 1947-55. *1927*

Rumanians. Alberta. Homesteading and Homesteaders. Kokotailo, Veronia. 1898- . *3165*

Rumilly, Robert. Black, Conrad. Duplessis, Maurice. Historiography. Political Leadership. Quebec. 1936-59. *2684*

Rumilly, Robert (review article). Historiography. Papineau, Louis-Joseph. Politics. Quebec. Rebellion of 1837. 1791-1871. 1934. 1977. *822*

Runestones. Maine. Massachusetts. Newfoundland. Vikings. 986-1121. *481*

Rupert's Land. Canoe trips. Discovery and Exploration. Tyrrell, Joseph Burr. 1893. *975*

—. Colonization (supposed). Defoe, Daniel. Hudson's Bay Company. Publicity. Sergeant, Henry. 1680's. *502*

Rural Development. Antigonish Movement. Catholic Church. Nova Scotia. Social change. ca 1928-73. *2297*

—. Howe, Joseph. Nova Scotia (Lochaber). 1795-1880. *2285*

—. Ontario (Upper Canada). Settlement. 1782-1851. *794*

Rural land occupation. Land speculation. Ontario (Upper Canada). Settlers. Townships. 1782-1851. *793*

Rural Life. *See* Country Life.

Rural Settlements *See also* Settlement; Villages.

—. Alberta. Oral history. Women. 1890-1929. *3149*

—. Ball, George P. M. Business records. Depressions. Economic change. Ontario (Upper Canada). 1825-60. *672*

—. Demography. Francisation. Quebec (Rawdon). 1791-1970. *2575*

—. Economic Conditions. Employment. New Brunswick. Nova Scotia. 1961-76. *2293*

—. Ethnic groups. Ontario (Holland Marsh). 1930's-76. *2881*

—. Geographic mobility. Ontario. Social mobility. 19c. *849*

—. Jews. Kalter, Bella Briansky (reminiscences). Ontario (Ansonville). 1929-40. *2800*

—. Ontario. Social status. Women. 19c. *2729*

Rural-Urban Studies. Attitudes. Migration, Internal. Urbanization. 1955-75. *1366*

—. Catholic Church. French Canadians. Migration, Internal. Parishes. Quebec (Compton County). 1851-91. *2534*

—. Centre for Urban and Community Studies. Ontario (Toronto). Urban history. 1965-78. *1352*

—. Family size. Ontario (Wentworth County). Social Surveys. 1871. *2757*

—. Geography. 1900-73. *138*

—. Ontario. Population. 1941-66. *2743*

—. Urbanization. 1955-75. *1362*

Russell, Charlie. Bricklin (automobile). Music. New Brunswick. Popular culture. Satire. 1970's. *2401*

Russell, Chesley (account). Eskimos. Hudson's Bay Company. Northwest Territories (Baffin Island, Devon Island). Settlement. 1934-36. *332*

Russia *See also* Poland; USSR.

—. Agricultural growth. Boserup, Ester. China. North America. South. 18c-19c. *801*

—. Arctic. Kruzenshtern, Ivan Fedorovich. Romanov, Vladmir Pavlovich. Scientific Expeditions. USA. 1819-25. *3299*

—. British Columbia. Daily life. Dukhobors. Immigration. 1880's-1976. *1035*

—. Business. California (Fort Bragg). Jews. Shafsky family. 1889-1976. *1077*

—. Diplomacy. Monroe Doctrine. Pacific Northwest. 1812-23. *657*

—. Dukhobors. Immigration. 1652-1908. *996*

—. Dukhobors. Immigration. Religious persecution. Sects, Religious. 1654-1902. *1033*

—. Education. Immigration. Jews. Segal, Beryl (reminiscences). USA. 1900-70's. *204*

—. Emigration. Epp, Johann (letter). Mennonites. North America. 1875. *981*

—. Galt, Alexander. Jews. Kaplun, Alter (family). Saskatchewan. Settlement. 1880's-90's. *945*

—. Great Plains. Immigration. Manitoba. Mennonites. 1871-74. *994*

—. Manitoba (Winnipeg). Penner, Jacob. Socialist movement. 1900-65. *2998*

Russia (Siberia). Alaska. Discovery and Exploration. Lapérouse, Jean François. Ledyard, John. Pacific Area. Pacific Northwest. 1778-1806. *652*

—. Alaska. Bernard, Joseph Francis. Coasts. Eskimos. Traders. 1903-29. *314*

Russian Canadians. British Columbia. Dukhobors. Saskatchewan. 1652-1976. *152*

—. Mennonites. Saskatchewan (Rosthern). Settlement. 1891-1900. *1036*

Russian Revolution. Baerg, Anna (diary). Immigration. Mennonites. 1917-23. *1171*

Russian-American Company. Alexander I. Foreign policy. North America. Pacific Area. 1799-1824. *678*

—. California (San Francisco). Hudson's Bay Company. Ice trade. Pacific Area. 1850's. *878*

Russians. Immigrants. Manitoba. Mennonites, Russian. Shantz, Jacob Y. 1873. *1024*

—. Immigration. Manitoba. Mennonites, Russian. 1873. *989*

Russo-American Convention of 1824. Alexander I (ukase). Foreign Relations. Great Britain. Noncolonization principle. Pacific Northwest. 1821-25. *627*

Rye, Miss. Children. Great Britain. Immigration. Ontario. Poor. Press. 1865-1925. *2879*

S

Sabatier, William. Nova Scotia (Halifax). Political Participation. 1780-1826. *2256*

Sabbath. Lord's Day Act (1906). Sports. Sunday. 1906-77. *200*

Saboteurs. Confederate Army. Kennedy, Robert C. New York City. 1861-65. *843*

Sacred pipe myth. Indians. Sioux Indians. Tipi covers. 1770-1975. *366*

St. Albans Raid. Civil War. Fenians (raid). Foreign Relations. USA. 1861-66. *887*

—. Confederate Army. Vermont. Young, Bennett H. 1864. *868*

St. Andrews Church. British Columbia (Bennett). Presbyterian Church. 1898. *3253*

St. Andrew's Wesley United Church of Canada. Methodist Church. Nova Scotia (Springhill). Presbyterian Church. 1800-1976. *2233*

St. Basil's Seminary. Catholic Church. Ontario (Toronto). Vatican Council II. 1962-67. *2806*

St. Boniface School. Métis. Nolin, Jean-Baptiste (and daughters). Prairie Provinces. Red River of the North. 1760-1840. *776*

St. Bridget's Home. Catholic Church. Irish Canadians. McMahon, Patrick. Poor. Quebec (Quebec). 1847-1972. *2541*

St. Clair River. Michigan (Port Huron). Ontario (Sarnia). Railroad tunnels. Transportation, Commercial. 1884-91. *108*

—. Navigation. St. Lawrence Seaway. 1973. *1251*

St. Croix Island. Champlain, Samuel de. Maine. Military Camps and Forts. Monts, Sieur de. New Brunswick. 1603-05. *507*

St John *Freeman* (newspaper). Anglin, Timothy Warren. Catholic Church. Irish Canadians. New Brunswick. 1849-83. *2373*

St. John, J. Hector. *See* Crèvecoeur, Michel.

St. John the Baptist Society. Mouvement National des Québécois. Quebec. Separatist Movements. 1834-1972. *2692*

St. Joseph's College (Alberta). Alberta (Edmonton). Catholic Church. Colleges and Universities. MacDonald, John Roderick. 1922-23. *3140*

St. Lawrence estuary. Ethnohistory. Quebec. 20c. *2491*

St. Lawrence, Gulf of. Acadians. Nova Scotia. 1756-95. *622*

St. Lawrence River. Discovery and exploration. Environmental determinism. Mississippi River. Natural resources. North America. 17c-19c. *270*

—. Empire, establishment of. Federal government. Mississippi River. USA. 1760's-1860's. *631*

St. Lawrence River (north shore). Great Lakes. Ports. Quebec. Shipping. 1937-70. *1565*

St. Lawrence River Skiff. Boats. Folklore. New York. 1860-1973. *133*

St. Lawrence River (south shore). Measurements. Port activity. Quebec. 1944-66. *2660*

St. Lawrence River (St. Ignace, Dupas islands). Demography. Quebec. Settlement. 1648-1973. *2486*
St. Lawrence Seaway. Canals. 1760-1973. *787*
—. Communications. Quebec. 16c-20c. *2582*
—. Diplomacy. Pearson, Lester B. USA. 1949-66. *1758*
—. Great Lakes. Howell, William Maher (reminiscences). Ontario. Pennsylvania (Erie). Quebec. Travel. 1928. *2131*
—. Great Lakes. Oil and Petroleum Products. Ontario. Shipping. 1973. *1539*
—. Nature Conservation. New York. Ontario. Thousand Islands. 19c-20c. *279*
—. Navigation. St. Clair River. 1973. *1251*
—. Ports. Quebec (Three Rivers). Shipping. 1874-1972. *2608*
St. Lawrence Seaway Treaty of 1932. Foreign Relations. Hoover, Herbert C. USA. 1932. *1204*
St. Lawrence Valley. Land Tenure. Manors. Social Classes. 1663-1840. 1840D 1800H. *538*
St. Lawrence (vessel). Nova Scotia (Port Hood Island). Shipwrecks. 1780. *713*
St. Lunaire boulder. Discovery and Exploration. Inscriptions. Ireland. Newfoundland. Ogham alphabet. ca 5c-1977. *487*
St. Mary's Cathedral of the Immaculate Conception. Catholic Church. Church History. Ontario (Kingston). 1843-1973. *2765*
St. Paul & Pacific Railroad. Canadian Pacific Railroad. Capital alliances. Morton, Bliss & Company. Railroads. Stephen, George. USA. 1860-70's. *980*
St. Paul's Church. Church of England. Missions and Missionaries. Nova Scotia (Halifax). Society for the Propagation of the Gospel. Tutty, William. 1749-52. *2359*
St. Regis Reservation. Indian Affairs Department. Iroquois Indians. Law. Quebec. 1876-1918. *459*
St. Thomas More College. Catholics. Colleges and Universities. Saskatchewan (Regina, Saskatoon). 1918-21. *3042*
Saints Cyril and Methodius Parish. Catholic Church. Ontario (Toronto). Slovak Canadians. 1934-77. *2894*
Salaries. *See* Wages.
Salish Indians. British Columbia (Victoria). Pit houses. Provincial Museum. Shuswap Lake Park. 1972. *455*
Salmon. Black Capitalism. British Columbia. Canning industry. Deas, John Sullivan. 1862-78. *3239*
—. British Columbia (Fraser River). Canning industry. Labor. Mergers. 1885-1902. *3240*
—. British Columbia (Vancouver Island). Fishing rights. International Pacific Salmon Fisheries Commission. Pacific Northwest. Treaties. 1910-8. *2018*
—. Fisheries. Hudson's Bay Company. Ungava Bay region. 1830's-1939. *2653*
Salvage. Alaska Steamship Company. British Columbia (Queen Charlotte Islands). *Kennecott* (vessel). Shipwrecks. 1923. *3181*
San José resolution. Administrative structure. International law. Organization of American States. Rio Treaty. 1945-75. *1892*
San Juan (vessel). Archives. Basques. Labrador (Red Bay). Shipwrecks. Spain. 1565. 1978. *558*
Sanatoriums. Medicine (practice of). Nova Scotia (Kentville). Tuberculosis. 1904-78. *2284*
Sanborn, Franklin Benjamin. Abolition Movement. Brown, John. Civil War (antecedents). Harpers Ferry (raid, 1859). 1854-60. *875*
Sanford, Frank. Holy Ghost and Us Society. Nova Scotia. Sects, Religious. Shipwrecks. 1910-48. *2333*
Sanitation *See also* Cemeteries; Pollution; Public Health; Water Supply.
—. British Columbia (Vancouver). Water supply. 1886-1976. *3180*
Sanson, Norman Bethune (biography). Alberta (Banff). Meteorology. 1896-99. *3153*
Saskatchewan *See also* Prairie Provinces.
—. Aeronautics. 1908-18. *3040*
—. Alberta. Cypress Hills Provincial Park. 1859-1973. *2914*
—. Anderson, James T. M. Anti-Catholicism. Public schools. School Act (amended). Secularization. 1929-34. *3050*
—. Anti-Catholicism. Elections (provincial). Ku Klux Klan. Separate school legislation. 1929. *3024*
—. Anti-Catholicism. Ku Klux Klan. Protestants. 1927-30. *3033*

—. Archaeology. Boulder configurations. Indians. Solstices. Sun Dance structures. Prehistory. 1975. *406*
—. Architecture. Canadian National Railroad System. Railroads. 1890-1970's. *3030*
—. Architecture. Canadian Pacific Railway. Railroads. 20c. *3029*
—. British Columbia. Dukhobors. Russian Canadians. 1652-1976. *152*
—. Buffalo bones. Industry. 1884-93. *3026*
—. Buildings. Cumberland House. Hearne, Samuel. 1794-1800's. *3075*
—. Business unionism. Labor relations. Social democracy. 1974-75. *3062*
—. Catholic Church. French language. *Patriote de l'Ouest* (newspaper). 1910-41. *2929*
—. Cemetery. Jews. 1975. *3055*
—. Chippewa Indians. Cree Indians. Fur Trade. Thanadelthur ("Slave Woman," Chippewa Indian). 1715-17. *577*
—. Coal Mines and Mining. Labor Unions and Organizations. One Big Union. 1907-45. *3056*
—. Colonization. Pearson, William (reminiscences). Real Estate. 1903-13. *1015*
—. Communalism. Dukhobors. 1904. *1001*
—. Communist Party. Cooperative Commonwealth Federation. Elections (provincial). 1930's. *3066*
—. Conservatism. Progressivism. 1920's. *3039*
—. Consumers Cooperative Refineries Ltd. Co-op. Oil, Chemical, and Atomic Workers International Union. 1934-73. *3074*
—. Cooperative Commonwealth Federation. League for Social Reconstruction. Regina Manifesto. Underhill, Frank. 1933. *2927*
—. Co-operative Commonwealth Federation. Political Participation. United Farmers of Canada. 1930-45. *3047*
—. Cooperative Commonwealth Federation. Political Parties. Socialism. 1928-44. *3067*
—. Cumberland House. Hudson's Bay Company. 1774-1974. *3063*
—. Dairying. Government. Motherwell, W. R. Subsidies. Wilson, W. A. 1906-17. *3037*
—. Davis, Thomas O. Elections. Liberal Party. 1896. *3046*
—. *Der Bote* (newspaper). Germans, Russian. Mennonites. Nazism. USSR. Völkisch thought. 1917-39. *3077*
—. Deutscher Bund Canada. German Canadians. Nazism. 1934-39. *1246*
—. Dukhobors. Ethnic groups. Royal Canadian Mounted Police. Settlement. 1899-1909. *3028*
—. Electricity and Electronics. Private enterprise. Qu'Appelle Flour Mill. 1906-27. *3081*
—. Environment. Saskatoon Environmental Society. 1970-77. *3068*
—. Farmer Labor Party. Political Leadership. Radicals and Radicalism. Socialism. 1932-34. *3048*
—. Farmers. Grange. Oklahoma. Socialism. Texas. 1900-45. *3083*
—. Fires, prairie. Fur trade. Hudson's Bay Company. Indians. 1790-1840. *461*
—. Foreign relations. Provincial government. 1963-78. *3057*
—. Galt, Alexander. Jews. Kaplun, Alter (family). Russia. Settlement. 1880's-90's. *945*
—. Gardiner, James G. Provincial Government. 1905. *3079*
—. Government. Land. Settlement. 1929-35. *3060*
—. Hunter, R. H. (reminiscences). Teaching. 1923-67. *2931*
—. Indians. Sioux Indians. 1880-1970. *404*
—. McKenzie, "Steamboat Bill" (reminiscences). Steamboats. Transportation, Commercial. 1901-25. *3036*
—. Meat packing industry. 1879-1973. *3032*
—. Mines. Natural Resources. 1960-74. *3064*
—. Negroes. Shadd, Alfred Schmitz. 1896-1915. *3070*
—. Newspapers. Political Parties. 1914-29. *3031*
—. Occupational Health Act (1972). Workmen's Compensation. 1972-73. *3034*
—. Pioneers. Welsh. 1902-14. *3069*
—. Police, provincial. Politics. Provincial Government. Royal Canadian Mounted Police. 1916-28. *3065*
—. Saskatoon Women Teachers' Association. Teachers. Women. 1918-70's. *3051*
Saskatchewan (Arelee). Country Life. Lambert, Augustine. Sketches. 1913-14. *3054*
Saskatchewan (Cannington). Settlement. Sports. 1882-1900. *1017*

Saskatchewan (Cannington Manor). Daily Life. Humphrys, James (and family). 1880's-1908. *986*
Saskatchewan (Chaplin, Duval). Goodwin, Theresa (reminiscences). Teaching. 1912-13. *3045*
Saskatchewan (Churchill River). Power plants, development of. 1929-74. *3053*
Saskatchewan (Eastern Assiniboia; Whitewood). Aristocracy. Estate ownership. France. Meyer, Rudolf. Roffignac, Yves de. 1885-1900. *982*
Saskatchewan (Esterhazy). Esterhazy, Paul O. d' (Johan Baptista Packh). Hungarian immigrants. 1831-1912. *3043*
Saskatchewan (Estevan). Anderson, James T. M. Elections. Gardiner, James G. Provincial Legislatures. 1929-30. *3078*
Saskatchewan (Estevan region). Coal. Environmental effects. Strip mining. 1850's-1975. *3071*
Saskatchewan (Beaver Lake). Cullity, Emmet K. (memoir). Gold Mines and Mining. 1915-27. *3041*
Saskatchewan Grain Growers' Association. Education. Farmers. ca 1918-25. *3082*
Saskatchewan (Grand Rapids). Fur trade. Railroads. Saskatchewan River. Tramways. 1877-1909. *997*
Saskatchewan (Grenfell). Agricultural colony. Bee, William. Methodists, Primitive. 1882. *949*
Saskatchewan (Hague-Osler area). Mennonites. Settlement. Social Change. 1895-1977. *3044*
Saskatchewan (Humboldt). Electric Power. Saskatchewan Power Corporation. 1907-29. *3080*
Saskatchewan (Ile-à-La-Crosse, Fort Chipewyan). Duels. ca 1815-16. *3025*
Saskatchewan (Loon River area). Deutscher Bund Canada. German Canadians. Immigration. 1929-39. *3076*
Saskatchewan (Pipestone Creek, Whitewood). Aristocracy. France. Meyer, Rudolf. Settlement. 1880's. *985*
Saskatchewan Power Corporation. Electric Power. Saskatchewan (Humboldt). 1907-29. *3080*
Saskatchewan (Prince Albert). Apportionment. King, William Lyon Mackenzie. Parliaments. 1925-35. *3038*
Saskatchewan (Qu'Appelle Valley). Cree Indians. Crooked Lakes Reserves. Rations policies. Yellow Calf (chief). 1884. *343*
Saskatchewan (Regina). Actors and Actresses. Theater. 1900-14. *3059*
—. Anglophiles. Francophiles. Mathieu, Olivier-Elzéar. 1905-30. *3035*
—. Clark, Septimus Alfred. Frontier and Pioneer Life. Great Britain. Letters. Radcliffe, Mary. 1884-1909. *967*
—. Copyright. *D'Oyle Carte* v. *Dennis et al.* (Canada, 1899). Theater. 1899-1900's. *3058*
—. Mental Illness. Riel, Louis. Treason. Trials. Valade, François-Xavier (medical report). 1885. *973*
Saskatchewan (Regina archdiocese). Catholic Church. Immigration. Manitoba. Mathieu, Olivier-Elzéar. 1911-31. *2936*
Saskatchewan (Regina, Saskatoon). Catholics. Colleges and Universities. St. Thomas More College. 1918-21. *3042*
Saskatchewan River. Birds. Discovery and Exploration. Hood, Robert. Painting. 1819-21. *2928*
—. Blakiston, Thomas Wright (letters). Ornithology. 1857-59. *860*
—. Fur trade. Railroads. Saskatchewan (Grand Rapids). Tramways. 1877-1909. *997*
Saskatchewan River Valley. Indians. Manitoba (Red River Valley). Mennonites. Métis. Settlement. 1869-95. *963*
Saskatchewan (Rosthern). Immigration. Mennonites, Russian. Social conditions. 1923. *3052*
—. Mennonites. Russian Canadians. Settlement. 1891-1900. *1036*
Saskatchewan (Saskatoon). 1882-1973. *3073*
—. Airplanes, Military (training). China. Fraser, Douglas. Nationalism. 1919-22. *1169*
—. City planning. Economic growth. Real estate. Yorath, J. C. 1909-13. *3061*
Saskatchewan, southcentral. Atsina Indians. "Fall" Indians. Indians. "Rapid" Indians. 18c. *405*
Saskatchewan, southwestern. Assiniboin Indians. Cypress Hills Massacre. Historiography. 1873. *978*
—. Cattle Raising. Farming. Ranching. 1872-1974. *3072*

Saskatchewan, University of. Historians. Morice, Adrien-Gabriel. ca 1900-38. *3049*

Saskatchewan (Wakaw). Dukhobors. Galicians. Lake Geneva Mission. Missions and Missionaries. Presbyterian Church. 1903-42. *3027*

Saskatchewan (Yorkton). Colonization companies. Economic growth. Railroads. 1882-1905. *1002*

Saskatoon Environmental Society. Environment. Saskatchewan. 1970-77. *3068*

Saskatoon Women Teachers' Association. Saskatchewan. Teachers. Women. 1918-70's. *3051*

Satellites. Anik Satellite. Communications. Northwest Territories. 1972. *3287*

—. Arctic. Eskimos. Federal government. Mass Media. 1972. *329*

Satire. Bricklin (automobile). Music. New Brunswick. Popular culture. Russell, Charlie. 1970's. *2401*

—. Literature. McCulloch, Thomas (*Letters of Mephibosheth Stepsure*). Nova Scotia. Presbyterian Church. 1821-22. *2339*

—. New Brunswick. Politics. Street, Samuel Denny. 1802. *2409*

Saunas. British Columbia. Okanagan Indians. 1973. *448*

Saunders, John. American Revolution. Colonization. Loyalists. New Brunswick. Virginia. 1774-1834. *740*

Scandinavia. Alaska. Arctic. Mining. USSR. 1917-78. *3288*

—. Alaska. Economic Growth. Greenland. Population. 1970's. *281*

—. Bibliographies. USA. 1972. *230*

—. Education. Income. Personal growth. USA. 1975. *1450*

—. Foreign Relations. Public Policy. Transgovernmental politics. USA. 1970's. *1771*

Scandinavian Canadians. British Columbia. Homesteading and Homesteaders. Immigration. Prairie Provinces. 1850's-1970's. *1032*

Scandinavians. Minnesota. Nova Scotia. Petroglyphs. West Virginia. 14c. *478*

Schiff, Jacob H. Galveston Plan. Immigration. Jews. USA. 1907-14. *905*

Scholars. Blair, Duncan Black. Gaelic language, Scots. Nova Scotia (Pictou County). Poetry. Scotland. 1846-93. *2346*

—. Herzberg, Gerhard. Immigration policy. Murray, Walter. 1935-37. *1212*

Scholarship. Cadieux, Lorenzo (obituary). Jesuits. Ontario, northern. 1903-76. *2772*

—. Colleges and Universities. North America. Publishers and Publishing. 1920's-70's. *206*

—. Folklore studies. Sociopolitical milieu. ca 1900-75. *88*

School Act (amended). Anderson, James T. M. Anti-Catholicism. Public schools. Saskatchewan. Secularization. 1929-34. *3050*

School attendance. Discrimination, Educational. Ontario. Social Classes. Women. 1851-71. *2754*

School Boards. Church and State. Political Parties. Prince Edward Island. Prince of Wales College Act (1860). 1860-63. *2208*

School districts. Minnesota (Portage Plains; Prospect). 1876-80. *3019*

School of Arts and Crafts of St. Joachim. Gosselin, Auguste-Honoré (review article). Laval, François de. New France. 1668-1730. *535*

—. New France. 1668-1715. *545*

Schools *See also* Church Schools; Colleges and Universities; Education; High Schools; Private Schools; Public Schools; Rural Schools; Students; Teaching.

—. Acadians. Catholic Church. Irish Canadians. New Brunswick. Politics. Quebec. Taxation. 1871-73. *1067*

—. Alberta (Edmonton). Homesteading and Homesteaders. Waugh School District. 1901-40's. *3166*

—. Anti-Catholicism. Elections (provincial). Ku Klux Klan. Saskatchewan. Schools. Segregation. 1929. *3024*

—. Bilingualism. Gendron Report. Quebec. 1973. *2504*

—. Boys. Charities. Great Britain. Hudson's Bay Company. 18c-19c. *684*

—. Indians. Indian-White Relations. Ontario (Sault Ste. Marie). Shingwauk Industrial Home. Wawanosh Home for Indian Girls. Wilson, E. F. 1871-93. *475*

—. Indian-White Relations. Ontario. 1780-1841. *474*

—. Liberal Party. Manitoba. Politics. Railroads. 1870's-90's. *2987*

—. Ontario, northern. Railroads. 1922-28. *2865*

Schooners. Rio de la Plata. Trade. Voyages. ca 1860-1914. *935*

Schoonover, Frank. Painting. Western States. 1899-1968. *2951*

Schwermann, Albert H. (reminiscences). Alberta (Edmonton, Mellowdale). Concordia College. Lutheran Church. USA. 1891-1976. *3147*

Science *See also* headings beginning with the word scientific; Astronomy; Botany; Ethnology; Geology; Natural History.

—. Attitudes. Intellectual traditions. National self-image. Technology. 1970's. *1327*

—. Demers, Jerôme. Philosophy. Quebec. Teaching. 1765-1835. *2502*

—. Elites. Quebec. 1824-44. *2515*

—. Literature. Nova Scotia. Pictou Literature and Scientific Society. 1834-54. *2248*

Science and Government *See also* Technology.

—. Accountability. Decisionmaking. Environment. Federal government. 1950's-70's. *1725*

Science and Society. Mass media. Teachers. Values. Youth. 1920's-75. *1391*

Scientific Discoveries. Emmons, Ebenezer. Geology. New York (Taconic Mountains). 1840-1900. *277*

Scientific Expeditions *See also* names of specific expeditions.

—. Alberta. Banff Park. Explorers. Peyto, Bill. 1887-1933. *3092*

—. Arctic. Kruzenshtern, Ivan Fedorovich. Romanov, Vladmir Pavlovich. Russia. USA. 1819-25. *3299*

—. Botany. Douglas, David. Horticulture. North America. 1823-34. *650*

—. *Challenger* (vessel). Honeyman, David. Nova Scotia (Halifax). Oceanography. 1872-76. *2317*

—. Eskimos. Geological Survey of Canada. Tyrrell, J. W. (travel diary). 1890's. *337*

—. Garlington, Ernest A. Greely, Adolphus W. Hazen, William B. Northwest Territories (Ellesmere Island). 1881-83. *3303*

—. Great Britain. Lefroy, John Henry (journals). Magnetic survey. Northwest Territories. 1843-44. *3306*

Scientific Experiments and Research. Climate. Ice caps. 1954-77. *271*

—. Herty, Charles Holmes. Newsprint. Paper mills. Pine trees. Southeastern States. 1927-40. *1134*

—. North America. Psychoanalysis. Social Change. 1918-77. *9*

Scientists *See also* names of individual scientists. Scotland. Alberta. Devolution. Federalism. Oil rights. 1970's. *3118*

—. Blair, Duncan Black. Gaelic language, Scots. Nova Scotia (Pictou County). Poetry. Scholars. 1846-93. *2346*

—. Canadian Railway Museum. Japan. *John Molson* (locomotive, replica). Locomotives. 1849. 1969. *877*

—. Charles I. Colonization. France. Great Britain. Nova Scotia (Port Royal). 1629-32. *501*

—. Church and State. Church of England. King's College, York (charter). Ontario (Toronto). Strachan, John. 1815-43. *625*

—. Dawson, John William. Grant, George Monro. Higher education. 19c. *2*

—. *Hector* (vessel). Immigrants. Mackenzie, Alexander. Nova Scotia (Pictou Harbor). Passenger lists. 1773. 1883. *2302*

—. *Hector* (vessel). Immigrants. Nova Scotia (Pictou Harbor). Voyages. 1773. *2340*

—. MacLeod, Norman. Migration. Nova Scotia (St. Ann's). Presbyterian Church. ca 1800-50's. *2244*

Scots. Church of England. Morris, William. Ontario (Kingston). Presbyterians. Queen's College. 1836-42. *2831*

Scottish Canadians. Ethnicity (review article). Polish Canadians. Portuguese Canadians. 18c-20c. 1976. *201*

—. Immigrants. McDonald, Donald. Millenarianism. Prince Edward Island. ca 1828-67. *2209*

Scovil, G. C. Coster (reminiscences). China. Church of England. Missionary Society of the Canadian Church. 1946-47. *1262*

Scuba diving. Archaeology (amateur). *Chicora* (vessel). Great Lakes. Ontario (Sault Ste. Marie, St. Joseph's Island). 1961-62. *585*

Sculpture *See also* Monuments.

—. Nova Scotia. USA. Wilson, John A. 1877-1954. *2301*

Sea otters. Fur trade. Japan. Wildlife Conservation. 18c-20c. *257*

Sealers. Newfoundland. Practical jokes. 16c-1914. *2202*

Seals. Arctic. Hunting. Ringed seals. Wildlife Conservation. 1966-73. *335*

—. Extinction, threatened. Hunting. Pacific Area (north). USA. 1886-1910. *936*

Secondary Education *See also* Adult Education; High Schools; Private Schools; Public Schools.

Sectarianism. Anti-Americanism. Ontario (Upper Canada). Rebellion of 1837. 1837. *817*

Sectionalism. British Columbia, University of. 1885-1910. *3202*

Sects, Religious. Brethren in Christ. Engel, Jacob. Pennsylvania (Lancaster County). 1775-1964. *250*

—. Church of England. Feild, Edward. Newfoundland. 1765-1852. *2188*

—. Dukhobors. Immigration. Religious persecution. Russia. 1654-1902. *1033*

—. Holy Ghost and Us Society. Nova Scotia. Sanford, Frank. Shipwrecks. 1910-48. *2333*

—. Life-styles. Newfoundland. Public identity. Social Classes. 1949-75. *2183*

Secularization. Anderson, James T. M. Anti-Catholicism. Public schools. Saskatchewan. School Act (amended). 1929-34. *3050*

Securities *See also* Investments; Mortgages; Stocks and Bonds.

—. Massachusetts (Boston). Ponzi, Charles (pseud. of Charles Bianchi). 1919-20. *1187*

Securities Commission. Provincial Government. Quebec. Stocks and Bonds. 1970's. *2427*

Segal, Beryl (reminiscences). Education. Immigration. Jews. Russia. USA. 1900-70's. *204*

Segregation *See also* Discrimination.

—. Anti-Catholicism. Elections (provincial). Ku Klux Klan. Saskatchewan. Schools. 1929. *3024*

Segregation, residential. Institutional completeness. Manitoba (Winnipeg). Minorities. -1974. *2978*

Séguin, Robert-Lionel (writings). Centre de documentation en civilisation traditionelle. French Canadian identity. Quebec, University of. 1959-75. *494*

Seiberling, Frank A. Midland Continental Railroad. North Dakota. Railroads. 1912-20. *2983*

Seignelay, Marquis de. Colonial policy (review article). Eccles, William J. France. New France. ca 1663-1701. 1962-64. *499*

Seigneurial system. Economic development. Land tenure. 1700-1854. *798*

—. Michigan (Detroit). Social organization. 1701-1837. *583*

Self-determination. Armies. Defense. International relations. 1970's. *1778*

—. Diplomacy. Korean War. Pearson, Lester B. UN. 1950-72. *1768*

—. Parti Québécois. Quebec. Sovereignty. 1970's. *2116*

—. Quebec. Separatist Movements. 1970-76. *2088*

Self-government. British Empire. Ellice, Edward. 1838-40. *826*

Self-help. Antigonish Movement. Cooperatives. Maritime Provinces. 1920's-40's. *2169*

—. Bromley, Walter. Micmac Indians. Nova Scotia. Urban poor. 1813-25. *2258*

Self-perception. Maritime Provinces. Regionalism. 1911-72. *2153*

Semantics. *See* Linguistics.

Senators. Elites. Ethnic values. Protestant ethic. Rationality. 1971. *1645*

—. Institutional orientations. Liberal democracy. 1970's. *1644*

Seneca Indians. Indian Wars. Ontario (Ehwae). 1640-42. *517*

Separatism. Alliance Laurentienne. Federalism. Quebec. 1957-70's. *2681*

—. Bibb, Henry. Emigration. Negroes. USA. 1830-60. *858*

—. French Canadians. Quebec. 1974-76. *2683*

—. French-speaking adults. Quebec. Social-class levels. 1968. *2682*

—. Galtung, Johan. Quebec. Social change. 1961-75. *2712*

—. Lévesque, René. Parti Québécois. Quebec. Trudeau, Pierre Elliott. 1970's. *2110*

Separatist Movements. Anglophones. National identification. Political Attitudes. Quebec. 1970's. *2120*

—. Balance of power. Defense Policy. North America. Quebec. 1970's. *1921*

—. Catholic Church. Lamarche, Gustave. Political philosophy. Quebec. 1922-75. *2705*
—. Centralization. Political stability. Quebec. 1960-75. *1695*
—. Conflict management. Institutions. Quebec. Regional autonomy. South. 19c-1970. *2101*
—. Constitutions. Economic Conditions. Quebec. 1973. *2115*
—. Constitutions. Federal Government. Provincial Government. Quebec. 1968-76. *2117*
—. Davis, William. Ontario. Politics. Quebec. 1976-77. *1280*
—. Economic issues. French-speakers. Minorities. Quebec. 1976. *2689*
—. Economic power. French Canadians. Quebec. 1960's-70's. *2679*
—. Elections, provincial. Jews. Parti Québécois. Quebec. 1976. *2721*
—. Europe. Quebec. USA. 1977. *1920*
—. Federal government. French Canadians. Public Policy. Quebec. 1976. *1306*
—. Federal government. New Democratic Party. Parti Québécois. Quebec. 1960's-70's. *2102*
—. Federal Government. Parti Québécois. Quebec. 1976-77. *2112*
—. Federal Government. Quebec. 1960-77. *2710*
—. Federal Government. Quebec. 1976-77. *2087*
—. Federalism. Lamontagne, Maurice (views). Quebec. 1867-1976. *2097*
—. Federalism. Quebec. 1759-1977. *69*
—. Foreign policy. Quebec. 1690-1976. *2680*
—. Foreign Relations. Parti Québécois. Quebec. USA. 1973-77. *1993*
—. Foreign relations. Quebec. 1960-76. *2711*
—. French Canadians. Jews. Quebec. Social Conditions. 1976-77. *2723*
—. French Canadians. Quebec. 1774-1975. *2719*
—. Lévesque, René. Parti Québécois. Quebec. 1968-70's. *2713*
. Modernization. Political Change. Quebec. 19c-1970's. *151*
—. Mouvement National des Québécois. Quebec. St. John the Baptist Society. 1834-1972. *2692*
—. National Characteristics. Quebec. 1971-74. *2671*
—. Nationalism. Quebec. Socialism. USA. 1970's. *2021*
—. Parti Québécois. Quebec. 1970's. *2107*
—. Parti Québécois. Quebec. 1973. *2720*
—. Provincial government. Quebec. 1955-75. *2568*
—. Quebec. ca 1970-74. *1321*
—. Quebec. 1960's. *2094*
—. Quebec. Referendum (possible). 1867-1976. *2086*
—. Quebec. Self-determination. 1970-76. *2088*
Sergeant, Henry. Colonization (supposed). Defoe, Daniel. Hudson's Bay Company. Publicity. Rupert's Land. 1680's. *502*
Serials. See Periodicals.
Servants. Immigration. Ireland. Poor Law Commissioners. Women. 1865. *888*
Service activities. Economic growth. Quebec. 1968-72. *2141*
Settlement See also Colonization; Frontier and Pioneer Life; Homesteading and Homesteaders; Pioneers; Resettlement; Rural Settlements.
—. Acadia. Copper kettles. Micmac Indians. Mobility. 17c. *424*
—. Acadian townsite. Excavations. Glassware. Nova Scotia (Beaubassin). ca 1670-1800's. *2274*
—. Acculturation. Immigration. Slovak Canadians. 1885-1970's. *113*
—. Agricultural expansion. Models. Prairie Provinces. 1870-1911. *1037*
—. Agricultural expansion. Prairie Provinces. 1872-1930. *1012*
. Agriculture. Jews. Prairie Provinces. 1884-1920's. *2950*
—. Alberta. Construction. Housing. Sod. Williams, Wesley. 1909. *1004*
—. Alberta (Lethbridge). Coal Mines and Mining. Galt, Alexander. Government. 1879-93. *960*
—. American Revolution. France. Protestants. USA. Whaling industry and Trade. 17c-20c. *1287*
—. American Revolution. Language. Loyalists. 1774-84. *746*
—. Aristocracy. France. Meyer, Rudolf. Saskatchewan (Pipestone Creek, Whitewood). 1880's. *985*
—. Armies. Indians. Royal Canadian Mounted Police. USA. 1870-1900. *1008*
—. Atlantic Provinces. Mennonites. 1950-70. *2168*

—. British Columbia (Queen Charlotte Islands). Haida Indians. Missions and Missionaries. Protestantism. Subsistence patterns. 1876-1920. *398*
—. Camp Wanapitei. Ontario (Sandy Inlet, Lake Temagami). Paradis, Charles. 1895-1970's. *2789*
—. Canada Company. Galt, John. Hibernia colony (proposed). Quebec (Lower Canada). 1825-35. *774*
—. Catholic Church. French Canadians. Minnesota (Gentilly). Theillon, Elie. 1870's-1974. *946*
—. Catholic Church. Quebec (Hébertville, Lake Saint John). ca 1840-1900. *2558*
—. Catholicism. Church History. Colonization. Quebec (Eastern Townships). 1800-60. *704*
—. City planning. Geographical studies. USA. 19c-20c. *127*
—. Climate. Environment. Indians. North America. Prehistory. 1956-78. *309*
—. Colonization literature. Ontario (Great Clay Belt). 1900-31. *2848*
—. Demography. Quebec. St. Lawrence River (St. Ignace, Dupas islands). 1648-1973. *2486*
—. Dukhobors. Ethnic groups. Royal Canadian Mounted Police. Saskatchewan. 1899-1909. *3028*
—. Economic Development. Quebec (Saguenay). 1840-1900. *2658*
—. Eskimos. Hudson's Bay Company. Northwest Territories (Baffin Island, Devon Island). Russell, Chesley (account). 1934-36. *332*
—. France. Immigration. Nova Scotia (Port Royal). 1650-1755. *511*
—. French Canadians. Manitoba. 1870-1920. *1013*
—. Fugitive Slaves. Land. New Brunswick. USA. 1815-36. *804*
—. Fundy National Park. Lumber industry. New Brunswick. 1820's-1976. *2383*
—. Funk, John F. Manitoba. Mennonites, Russian. 1873. *993*
—. Galt, Alexander. Jews. Kaplun, Alter (family). Russia. Saskatchewan. 1880's-90's. *945*
—. Government. Land. Saskatchewan. 1929-35. *3060*
—. Government policy. Prairie Provinces. USA. 1870-80. *1018*
—. Immigration. Prairie Provinces. Ukrainians. 1910-31. *2937*
—. Indians. Manitoba (Red River Valley). Mennonites. Métis. Saskatchewan River Valley. 1869-95. *963*
—. Jews. Manitoba (Bender Hamlet). 1910-49. *3001*
—. Land grants. Military. Ontario (Upper Canada). 1816-20. *788*
—. Manitoba. Mennonites, Russian. 1870-80. *991*
—. Mennonites. Russian Canadians. Saskatchewan (Rosthern). 1891-1900. *1036*
—. Mennonites. Saskatchewan (Hague-Osler area). Social Change. 1895-1977. *3044*
—. Ontario (Upper Canada). Rural Development. 1782-1851. *794*
—. Saskatchewan (Cannington). Sports. 1882-1900. *1017*
Settlers. Indian Wars. Montana. Nez Percé Indians. Public sympathy. 1877. *431*
—. Land speculation. Ontario (Upper Canada). Rural land occupation. Townships. 1782-1851. *793*
—. Loyalists. Nova Scotia (Cape Breton Island). 1784-1820. *748*
Sewage disposal. Great Lakes. Illinois (Chicago). Pollution. 1890-1940. *1117*
Seward, William H. Annexation. British Columbia. Foreign Policy. 1865-69. *3252*
Sex See also Men; Women.
—. Age. Unemployment. 1957-70. *1606*
—. Attitudes. English Canadians. Race. Woman Suffrage. ca 1877-1918. *902*
—. Colleges and Universities. Mate selection preferences. Students. USA. 1970's. *1482*
—. Crime and Criminals. Ethnicity. Illiteracy. Ontario (Middlesex County). Social Status. 1867-68. *1044*
Sex Discrimination. *Attorney General of Canada* v. *Lavell* (Canada, 1973). Indians. Lavell, Jeannette (Wikwemikong Indian). Supreme Court. Women. 1973-74. *413*
—. Canadian Union of Public Employees. Public Employees. Women. 1975. *1617*
—. Cyclones. Legislation. Ontario. Wages. Wages. 1946-71. *2777*
—. Educational system. Ideological structures. Sociology. Women. 1970's. *1474*

—. Ethnic groups. Indian-White Relations. 1972-73. *1420*
—. Public services. Women. 1870-1975. *213*
Sex roles. Christianity. Missions and Missionaries. Women. 1815-99. *923*
—. Folk Songs. Newfoundland (Calvert). Social status. 1916-74. *2201*
—. Occupations. Periodicals. Women. 1920's. *1195*
Seymour, Frederick (death). British Columbia. Colonial Government. Granville, George, 2d earl (letter). Great Britain. Musgrave, Anthony. 1869. *3204*
Shadbolt, Jack. Frye, Northrop. Levi-Strauss, Claude. Primitivism. 1977. *251*
Shadd, Alfred Schmitz. Negroes. Saskatchewan. 1896-1915. *3070*
Shadd, Mary Ann. Antislavery Sentiments. Negroes. Newspapers. Ontario. *Provincial Freeman* (newspaper). 1852-93. *1046*
Shafsky family. Business. California (Fort Bragg). Jews. Russia. 1889-1976. *1077*
Shantz, Jacob Y. Immigrants. Manitoba. Mennonites, Russian. Russians. 1873. *1024*
—. Immigration. Manitoba. Ukraine. 1870's. *992*
Sharp, Mitchell. Diplomacy. USSR. 1973. *1813*
—. Diplomacy. USSR. 1973. *1848*
—. Economic integration. Foreign Relations. National self-image. USA. -1973. *2083*
—. Foreign Policy. Gauvin, Michel (speech). International Commission for Supervision and Control. Vietnam War. 1973. *1950*
Sharples (family). Alberta, southern. Homesteading and Homesteaders. 1870's-1902. *3085*
Shaw, Flora. Gold rushes. Great Britain. Journalism. Klondike Stampede. *Times of London* (newspaper). Yukon Territory. 1898. *3341*
Shaw, P. C. (personal account). Alberta. Blackfoot Indians. Manhood ceremonies. Rites and Ceremonies. 1894. *447*
Shelburne, 2d Earl of (William Petty). American Revolution. Great Britain. Great Lakes. Old Northwest. Peace of Paris (1783). 1783. *727*
Sherrill, Clarence O. Army Corps of Engineers. Boundary protection. North Dakota. 1919. *1158*
Shickluna, Louis. Great Lakes. Ontario (St. Catharines). Shipbuilding. 1835-80. *2882*
Shingwauk Industrial Home. Indians. Indian-White Relations. Ontario (Sault Ste. Marie). Schools. Wawanosh Home for Indian Girls. Wilson, E. F. 1871-93. *475*
Shipbuilding. Contracts. McDonald, Alexander N. Nova Scotia (Sherbrooke). Sutherland, Peter. 1873-74. *2265*
—. Cox, Ebenezer. Nova Scotia (Kingsport). ca 1840-1915. *2250*
—. Great Lakes. Ontario (St. Catharines). Shickluna, Louis. 1835-80. *2882*
—. New Brunswick. 1776-1890. *2372*
Shipping See also Maritime Law; Merchant Marine.
—. Containerization. Ports. 1970's. *2072*
—. Crerar family. Nova Scotia (Pictou). 1840's-50's. *2344*
—. Fishing industry. King William's War. New England. Privateers. Queen Anne's War. 1689-1713. *596*
—. Forman, George. Lewis, Henry. Logging. Mississippi River. 1849-54. 1883. *2755*
—. Great Lakes. International Ship Masters Association. 1886-1977. *1087*
—. Great Lakes. Navigation. 1948-74. *2876*
—. Great Lakes. Oil and petroleum products. Ontario (St. Lawrence Seaway). 1973. *1539*
—. Great Lakes. Oil Industry and Trade. ca 1700-1974. *2076*
—. Great Lakes. Ports. Quebec. St. Lawrence River (north shore). 1937-70. *1565*
—. Great Lakes. Steamships. 1871-1976. *43*
—. Great Lakes Towing Company. 1899-1901. *2826*
—. Investments. Nova Scotia (Yarmouth). Ports. 1840-89. *2210*
—. Ports. Quebec (Three Rivers). St. Lawrence Seaway. 1874-1972. *2608*
Shipping documents. Indexing procedures. Newfoundland, Memorial University of (Maritime History Group). 1933. *2176*
Ships See also names of ships, e.g. Bounty (vessel); Boats; Merchant Marine; Navigation; Ocean Travel; Steamboats; Warships.
—. Artists. Great Lakes. Nickerson, Vincent D. Norton, Charles W. Sprague, Howard F. Whipple, Seth A. 1844-1901. *2861*

—. Cobb, Sylvanus. Fundy, Bay of. Nova Scotia. Trade. *York* (vessel). 1755. *2163*
—. Colonization. Commerce. 19c. *144*
—. Railroads. Tourism. Travel. Yukon Territory. 20c. *3329*
Shipwrecks. Alaska Steamship Company. British Columbia (Queen Charlotte Islands). *Kennecott* (vessel). Salvage. 1923. *3181*
—. Ancient, William J. *Atlantic* (vessel). Heroes. Nova Scotia (Terence Bay). 1873. *2225*
—. Archives. Basques. Labrador (Red Bay). *San Juan* (vessel). Spain. 1565. 1978. *558*
—. Cannibalism tales. Fort Churchill. Fort York. Manitoba. Molden, John. 1833. *3012*
—. *Cobequid* (vessel). Nova Scotia (Halifax). Rescue operations. 1914. *2322*
—. Colonization. Nova Scotia (Sable Island). Rescue stations. 1759-1801. *2235*
—. Comer, George. Douglas, W. O. (reminiscences). *Finback* (whaler). Northwest Territories (Chesterfield Inlet). 1919. *3351*
—. *Fairy Queen* (vessel). Nova Scotia (Charlottetown, Pictou). 1853. *2170*
—. Holy Ghost and Us Society. Nova Scotia. Sanford, Frank. Sects, Religious. 1910-48. *2333*
—. Lake Ontario. 1679-1890. *58*
—. Lake Superior. 1872-1919. *943*
—. Maritime history. *Pewaukee* (vessel). *Two Friends* (vessel). Wisconsin (North Bay, Milwaukee). 1873-1913. *1048*
—. Nova Scotia (Herring Cove). *Tribune* (vessel). 1796-1968. *2326*
—. Nova Scotia (Port Hood Island). *St. Lawrence* (vessel). 1780. *713*
Shoe industry. Industrialization. Quebec (Montreal). 1840-70. *2606*
Shopping centers. Consumer behavior. Ontario (Toronto). Population. 1974. *2835*
Short Hills raid. Ontario. Trials. 1838-40. *818*
Shrine of Our Lady of Klocočov. Fuga, Francis J. Ontario (Hamilton). Slovak Canadians. Uniates. 1952-77. *2895*
Shrines, roadside. Catholic Church. Devotions, popular. Quebec (La Beauce County). Social customs. 1970's. *2514*
Shubenacadie Canal. Canals. Nova Scotia. 1791-1974. *2270*
Shuswap Lake Park. British Columbia (Victoria). Pit houses. Provincial Museum. Salish (Flathead) Indians. 1972. *455*
Shuttleworth, Edward Buckingham. Ontario. Pharmaceutical education. 1868-92. *2867*
Sibbald, Susan *(Memoirs)*. Pioneers. 1783-1866. *2766*
SIDBEC (consortium). Iron mining. Natural resources. Newfoundland. Quebec (Fire Lake). 1960's. *2622*
Sierra Leone (Sherbro Island). Missions and Missionaries. Nova Scotia. Raymond, Eliza Ruggles. Slaves. 1839-50. *2241*
Sifton, Clifford. Acculturation. Federal Policy. Indians. 1896-1905. *395*
Silver Mining. Ontario (Silver Islet). 1856-1922. *2868*
Simard, Ovide-D. (personal account). Catholic Church. Chicoutimi, Séminaire de. Church and State. 1873-1973. *2563*
Simcoe, Elizabeth. Frontier. Letters. Ontario (Upper Canada). Painting. Values. 1790-1800. *638*
Simcoe family. Burge family. Friendship. Letters. Ontario (Upper Canada). 1790-1820. *669*
Simcoe, John Graves. Elites. Government. Ontario (Upper Canada; Toronto). Strachan, John. 1793-1818. *773*
Simeon, Richard (review). Ethnic Groups. Meisel, John (review). Politics. 1960-68. *1713*
Simpson, George. Character book. Hudson's Bay Company. 1832. *2960*
—. Discovery and Exploration. Hudson's Bay Company. 1787-1860. *639*
Sioux Indians. Indians. Sacred pipe myth. Tipi covers. 1770-1975. *366*
—. Indians. Saskatchewan. 1880-1970. *404*
—. Indians. Sitting Bull (chief). USA. 1876-81. *1049*
Sisters of Charity of the Immaculate Conception. Catholic Church. New Brunswick (Saint John). 1854-64. *2392*
Sisters of Service. Catholic Church. Immigration. Missions and Missionaries. 1920-30. *2963*
Sitting Bull (chief). Frontier and Pioneer Life. Manitoba (Red River region). North West Mounted Police. Walsh, James. 1873-1905. *1030*
—. Indians. Sioux Indians. USA. 1876-81. *1049*

Skelton, O. D. External Affairs Department. Foreign relations. National security. 1925-41. *1120*
Sketches. Country Life. Lambert, Augustine. Saskatchewan (Arelee). 1913-14. *3054*
Skiing. 1879-1935. *132*
—. 1860's-1975. *137*
—. Alberta. Recreation. Rocky Mountains. 1920's-30's. *3131*
—. Alberta (Banff). 1890-1940. *3130*
—. Quebec (Laurentian Mountains). 1900's-70's. *2518*
Slander. Attitudes. French Canadians. 1712-48. *531*
Slave trade, Indian. British Columbia. Great Britain. Gunboats. Indians. Liquor. 1860's. *390*
Slaves. Missions and Missionaries. Nova Scotia. Raymond, Eliza Ruggles. Sierra Leone (Sherbro Island). 1839-50. *2241*
Slavic Languages. Polish Canadians. 20c. *1392*
Sleep paralysis. Alaska. Eskimos. Prehistory-1976. *315*
Slovak Americans. Cultural heritage. Ethnic Groups. USA. 19c-20c. *1449*
—. Immigration. Organizations. 1890-1964. *112*
Slovak Canadians. 1950-77. *1308*
—. Acculturation. Immigration. Settlement. 1885-1970's. *113*
—. Catholic Church. Ontario (Toronto). Saints Cyril and Methodius Parish. 1934-77. *2894*
—. Catholic parishes. 1900-77. *114*
—. Fuga, Francis J. Ontario (Hamilton). Shrine of Our Lady of Klocočov. Uniates. 1952-77. *2895*
Slovak World Congress. Behuncik, Edward J. (speech). Canadian Slovak League. 1970-72. *1740*
Small producers. New France. Production, mode of. Social Classes. 17c-18c. *496*
Smallpox. Indians. Métis. Traders. Vaccination program. 1837-38. *439*
Smith, Adam. American Revolution. Great Britain. 1770-76. *728*
Smith, Goldwin. Intellectuals. 1875-1933. *911*
Smith, Henry. Ontario (Kingston). Political Leadership. 1830-70. *897*
Smith, Henry Moore. Crime and Criminals. 1812-35. *641*
Smith, Titus. Conservation of Natural Resources. Nova Scotia. Surveying. 1801. *2328*
—. Gill, Valentine. Natural resources. Nova Scotia. Surveying. 1800-15. *2271*
Smoot-Hawley Tariff. Foreign Relations. Hoover, Herbert C. USA. 1929-33. *1203*
Smuggling. Alabama. Alcohol. Florida. Nova Scotia. Pentz, Gabriel. 20c. *2249*
—. USA. War of 1812. 1812-15. *761*
Snow. Technology. 1975. *1275*
Snowmobiles. Ecology. 1950-74. *1276*
Snowshoe clubs. Montreal Snowshoe Club. Quebec. 1840's-1900's. *2536*
Social Aid Act (1969). Economic security. Families, low-income. Poverty. Public Welfare. Quebec. 1969-75. *2668*
Social Change See also Economic Growth; Industrialization; Modernization.
—. 1945-70's. *1367*
—. Abortion. Press. Public opinion. 1960's-74. *1375*
—. Adolescence. Dependency. Employment. Frontier and Pioneer Life. Ontario (Orillia). 1861-71. *2769*
—. Agriculture. Ontario. Political Attitudes. Quebec. 1850-1970. *2132*
—. Alberta (Coaldale). Community organizations. Germans, Russian. Mennonites. 1920-76. *3145*
—. Algonkin Indians. Indians. Maine. Maritime Provinces. Missions and Missionaries. 1610-1750. *516*
—. Antigonish Movement. Catholic Church. Nova Scotia. Rural Development. ca 1928-73. *2297*
—. Arctic. Colonization. Eskimos. 1930-60. *317*
—. British Columbia (Vancouver). Japanese community. 20c. *3262*
—. Bureaucracies. Capitalism. Government. Institutions. North America. 1750's-1850's. *656*
—. Catholic Church. École Sociale Populaire. Labor unions and Organizations. Quebec. 1911-75. *2500*
—. Catholic Church. Educational system. French Canadians. Parent-youth conflict. Quebec. 1960-70. *2516*

—. Economic Conditions. Ontario. Quebec. Violence. 1963-73. *2127*
—. Education (review article). Historiography. 19c-20c. *248*
—. Federal government. Parti Québécois. Provincial Government. Quebec. 1960-77. *2420*
—. Federalism. French Canadians. Quebec. 1968-77. *2114*
—. Folk music. Political protest. Values. 1776-1976. *1377*
—. Galtung, Johan. Quebec. Separatism. 1961-75. *2712*
—. Great Britain. Political Commentary. Socialism. Webb, Beatrice. Webb, Sidney James. 1911. *1090*
—. Ideas, History of. Political change. 1780-1800. *795*
—. Indians. Prairie Provinces. Public Opinion. 1976. *2920*
—. Land. Population. Westward Movement. 1850's-67. *850*
—. Mennonites. Saskatchewan (Hague-Osler area). Settlement. 1895-1977. *3044*
—. Modernization. Ontario. Quebec. 1950-1974. *2479*
—. Nationalism. Politics. 1957-75. *1720*
—. North America. Psychoanalysis. Scientific Experiments and Research. 1918-77. *9*
—. Northwest Territories (Rae). Thlingchadinne (Dog-rib) Indians. 1939. 1974. *380*
—. Women. 1700-1976. *1456*
Social Classes See also Aristocracy; Class Struggle; Elites; Middle Classes; Social Mobility; Social Status; Upper Classes; Working Class.
—. Anglicization. Language. Quebec. 1971. *2461*
—. Antigonish Movement. Cooperatives. Economic Development. Nova Scotia, eastern. 1920's-30's. *2338*
—. Atlantic Provinces. Bibliographies. Economic development. Politics. 1950's-70's. *2161*
—. Atlantic Provinces. Capital. Unemployment. 1972-77. *2172*
—. Baptists. Fundamentalist-Modernist controversy. Jarvis Street Church. Ontario (Toronto). Religious factionalism. 1895-1934. *2762*
—. Belgium. Ethnicity. Nationalism. Quebec. 1970's. *2702*
—. British Columbia. Multinational Corporations. Natural Resources. Provincial government. Towns, "instant". 1965-72. *3178*
—. British Columbia. Political Parties. 1971-73. *3272*
—. Children. Inequality (perceived). Ontario (Toronto area). Public schools. Values. 1977. *1345*
—. Cities. Employment. Ethnic Groups. Property ownership. 19c. *90*
—. Colonialism. French Canadians. Great Britain. 18c. *707*
—. Commerce. International Trade. Quebec (Lower Canada). 1792-1812. *796*
—. Daily life. Historical Sites and Parks. Louisbourg, Fortress of. Nova Scotia (Cape Breton Island). 1713-50. *537*
—. Death and Dying. Quebec. 1934-74. *2468*
—. Discrimination, Educational. Ontario. School attendance. Women. 1851-71. *2754*
—. Economic Conditions. Nationalism. 1968-76. *1567*
—. Economic Development. Government. Quebec (Lower Canada). Ultramontanism. 19c. *698*
—. Economic opportunities. Political Protest. USA. 1960-74. *1365*
—. Education. Immigrants. Labor. 1973. *2149*
—. Ethnic Groups. Manitoba (Winnipeg). Voting and Voting Behavior. 1941. *3014*
—. Ethnic Groups. Manitoba (Winnipeg). Voting and Voting Behavior. 1945-46. *3023*
—. Europe, influence of. Ideas, History of. Quebec. 1960-75. *2501*
—. Family. Katz, Michael B. (review article). Ontario (Hamilton). 1850-80. *2725*
—. Foreign investments. Nationalism. USA. 1960's-70's. *2082*
—. Francophones. Quebec. Separatism. 1968. *2682*
—. Fur Trade. Merchants. Quebec (Montreal). 1750-75. *703*
—. Land Tenure. Manors. St. Lawrence Valley. 1663-1840. 1840D 1800H. *538*
—. Leftism. Nationalism. Quebec. 1970's. *2703*
—. Libraries. Mechanics' Institute movement. Ontario (Napanee). 1850-1900. *914*
—. Life-styles. Newfoundland. Public identity. Sects, religious. 1949-75. *2183*

—. Literature. Moodie, Susanna. National
self-image. 1832-53. *670*
—. New France. Production, mode of. Small
producers. 17c-18c. *496*
—. Ontario (Hamilton). Political parties. 1967-72.
2796
—. Porter, John. Radicals and Radicalism.
1950-65. *1462*
—. Voting and Voting Behavior. 1975. *1319*
Social Conditions *See also* Cities; Counter Culture;
Country Life; Daily Life; Economic Conditions;
Family; Labor; Marriage; Migration, Internal;
Popular Culture; Social Classes; Social Mobility;
Social Problems; Social Reform; Social Surveys.
—. Acadians. Catholic Church. English
Canadians. Maritime Provinces. 1763-1977.
2171
—. Agriculture. Industry. Quebec (Saguenay
region). 1840-1972. *2472*
—. Alberta. Cities. Political protest. 1918-39.
3110
—. Alienation. Hamilton, Pierce Stevens
(memoirs). Morality. 1826-93. *2335*
—. Arctic. Eskimos. 1950-75. *325*
—. Birch, Arthur N. (letter). British Columbia
(New Westminster). Local government. 1864.
870
—. Burchard, Jedediah. Protestants. Revivals.
Vermont. 1835-36. *815*
—. Catholic Church. Quebec (Gaspé). Ross,
François Xavier. 1923-45. *2532*
—. Census. Economic conditions. New Brunswick.
1861. *2377*
—. City Government. Economic growth. Public
Administration. Quebec (Montreal).
Urbanization. 1850-1914. *2441*
—. Economic Conditions. Great Awakening.
Nova Scotia (Yarmouth). 1760's-70's. *2354*
—. Economic development. Planning. Sweden.
20c. *1310*
—. Economic Growth. New Brunswick (Saint
John). 19c. *2411*
—. English Canadians. National Self-Image.
North America. 1840's-1960's. *210*
—. Family. Ontario. 1820-60. *2771*
—. Folklore studies. Scholarship. ca 1900-75.
88
—. French Canadians. Jews. Quebec. Separatist
movements. 1976-77. *2723*
—. Glass works. Manitoba (Beause jour).
Recreation. Working Conditions. 1909-11.
3000
—. Health care programs. Legislative determinants.
1945-65. *1383*
—. Higher education. Labor market. 1960-74.
1446
—. Immigration. Macedonians. Ontario (Toronto).
1900-30. *2841*
—. Immigration. Mennonites, Russian.
Saskatchewan (Rosthern). 1923. *3052*
—. Political parties. Provincial Legislatures.
1950-70. *2996*
—. Professionalism, concept of. Sports. 1835-1909.
910
Social control. Ontario (Upper Canada). Sunday
schools. 19c. *643*
Social Credit League. Alberta. Elections,
provincial. Liberal Party. United Farmers of
Alberta. 1905-73. *3107*
Social Credit Party. Aberhart, William. Alberta.
Bowen, John C. Provincial Government.
1937-38. *3158*
—. Aberhart, William. Alberta. Ideology.
Provincial Government. Theology. 1935-43.
3106
—. Alberta. Gardiner, James G. Liberal Party.
1935-39. *3157*
—. British Columbia. Elections, provincial.
1952-53. *3193*
—. Disadvantaged. Quebec National Assembly.
Tribunicial function. 1970-75. *2511*
—. Historiography. Quebec. 1936-65. *2619*
Social customs. Acculturation. Drama. Indians.
1606-1974. *414*
—. Agriculture. Hutterites. North America.
Technology. 18c-20c. *2896*
—. Alcoholism. Behavior. Quebec (Montreal).
1973. *1443*
—. Annexation. Confederation. Newfoundland.
Outports. Poverty. 1920-48. *2200*
—. Automobiles. Conestoga wagons. Driving.
USA. 1755-20c. *174*
—. Catholic Church. Devotions, popular. Quebec
(La Beauce County). Shrines, roadside. 1970's.
2514
—. Catholic Church. France (Paris). Quebec
(Montreal). Reading rooms. 19c. *2531*

—. Economic Conditions. French language.
Parti Québécois. Politics. Quebec. 1973-78.
2696
—. English Canadians. French Canadians.
1922-76. *102*
—. Eskimos. Northwest Territories (Baffin Island).
Television. 1972-74. *320*
—. French Canadians. Manitoba. Vallee, Frank.
1970-74. *2970*
—. French language. Quebec. Regionalism.
1977. *2716*
—. Humor. New Brunswick (western). Wedding
night pranks. 18c-1974. *2396*
—. Mennonites. Urbanization. USA. 1961-71.
1379
—. Nationalism. 1960's-70's. *1330*
Social Democracy. British Columbia. Legislation.
New Democratic Party. Public Policy. 1972-75.
3241
—. Business unionism. Labor relations.
Saskatchewan. 1974-75. *3062*
—. Coldwell, Major J. Farmer Labor party.
Political Leadership. Progressivism. 1907-32.
2962
Social Democratic Party *See also* Marxism;
Socialism.
—. Co-operative Commonwealth Federation.
Manitoba. Provincial Government. Socialism.
ca 1940. *3022*
Social distance. Alberta (Edmonton). Hutterites.
Public Opinion. 1966-75. *3132*
Social gospel. Christian responsibility. Fiction.
Labor. 1890's. *1112*
—. Methodism. 1890-1914. *1089*
Social history. Canadian Institute of Montreal.
Quebec (Montreal). 1845-73. *2509*
—. Capitalism (commercial, industrial). Quebec
(Montreal). Research Group on Montreal
Society. 19c. *2642*
—. Demography. Ontario. Peel County History
Project. Population. 1840-80. 1973. *2770*
—. Economic History. Industrialization. Iron
mining. Newfoundland (Conception Bay; Bell
Island). 1870's-1966. *2199*
—. Interdisciplinary studies. 17c-20c. *166*
—. Juvenile Delinquency. Legislation. Marxism.
1870's-1970's. *76*
Social Indicators, 1976 (report). *Perspective Canada
II* (report). USA. 1976. *1357*
Social Insurance *See also* Health Insurance;
Pensions; Unemployment Insurance; Workmen's
Compensation.
Social integration. Generation conflict, basis.
Identity. Quebec (Quebec). 1968. *2487*
Social issues. Church and State. Mennonite
Conference of 1970 (leaders). Students.
1917-74. *1381*
—. Elections, provincial. Nationalism. Quebec.
1973. *2099*
Social mobility. Blau-Duncan model. Stratification.
1972. *1373*
—. Colleges and Universities. Graduates.
Occupational attainment. Ontario. Women.
1960-75. *2821*
—. Corporations. Upper classes. 1951-72. *1369*
—. Domestics. Social networks. West Indies
(Montserrat). Women. 1960's-75. *1935*
—. Elites. Management. 1880-85. 1905-10.
899
—. Family. Italian Canadians. Ontario (Toronto).
1935-60. *2870*
—. Geographic mobility. Ontario. Rural
Settlements. 19c. *849*
—. Population. Quebec (Saguenay region).
19c-20c. *2473*
Social networks. Domestics. Social Mobility.
West Indies (Montserrat). Women. 1960's-75.
1935
Social Organization. Acadians. Institutions.
Nationalism. Nova Scotia. 1700's-1970. *2281*
—. Adult education. Libraries. Middle classes.
Working class. 19c. *104*
—. Anthropology. Authority. Ecology. Eskimos,
Central. 1970's. *322*
—. Assiniboin Indians. Cree Indians. Montana.
Prairie Provinces. ca 1640-1913. *446*
—. Beruson, David J. (review article). General
Strike. Industrial relations. Manitoba
(Winnipeg). 1919. 1975. *1165*
—. Business. Elites. Institutions. Law. 19c-1974.
211
—. Census. Literacy. Methodology. Ontario (Peel,
Hamilton Counties). 19c. *2822*
—. Census. Methodology. New Brunswick (Saint
John). 1871. 1974. *2400*
—. Chesterton, G. K. (principles). 1973-75. *1405*
—. Colleges and Universities. Sociology (teaching
of). 1940-70. *1398*

—. Demography. French Canadians. Quebec.
1974. *2481*
—. Egalitarianism. Women. Prehistory-1977.
409
—. Environment. Indians. Labrador. Quebec.
Religion. 17c-20c. *428*
—. Equal opportunity. Hutterites. Leadership
succession. Population. Prairie Provinces.
1940's-70's. *2908*
—. Family. Indians. Kin terminologies.
Language. Plains Indians. Prehistory-19c.
426
—. Fiction. Periodicals. 1930's-70's. *260*
—. Foreign Investments. Multinational
corporations. Oil Industry and Trade. 1970's.
1819
—. French Canadians. Minorities. Ukrainian
Canadians. 1970's. *1458*
—. Ghost Dance. Indians. Revitalization
movements. 1889. *359*
—. Indian-white relations. Northwest Territories.
1940-76. *416*
—. Michigan (Detroit). Seigniorialism, French.
1701-1837. *583*
Social Organizations. Champlain, Samuel de.
L'Ordre de Bon Temps. Nova Scotia (Port
Royal). 1606. *542*
—. Champlain, Samuel de. L'Ordre de Bon Temps.
Nova Scotia. 1606-07. *543*
Social policy. Alberta. Department of Social
Services and Community Health. Provincial
Government. 1970's. *3133*
—. Federal government. Unemployment. 1918-21.
1190
—. Rhetoric. Trudeau, Pierre Elliott. War
Measures Act (Canada, 1914). 1970. *1301*
Social Problems *See also* Alcoholism; Charities;
Crime and Criminals; Divorce; Drug Abuse;
Emigration; Housing; Immigration; Juvenile
Delinquency; Migrant Labor; Prostitution;
Public Welfare; Race Relations; Unemployment.
—. Alberta (Calgary). City government. 1894-96.
3122
—. Alienation. Charities. Government. Quebec
(Quebec; Lower Town). Working Class.
1896-1914. *2637*
—. Colleges and universities. 1972. *1370*
—. Education. French Canadians. Literary
associations. Quebec (Lower Canada). 1840-67.
2526
Social Psychology *See also* Violence.
Social Reform *See also* names of reform movements,
e.g. Temperance Movements; Social Problems.
—. Anthropologists. 1974. *1388*
—. Atlantic Provinces. Boardinghouses.
Government. Labor. Merchant Marine. ca
1850's-90's. *916*
—. Family. Feminism. Ontario. 1875-1900.
2830
—. McCarthy, D'Alton. Ontario. Politics.
1876-98. *1057*
—. McLachlan, Alexander. Ontario. Poetry.
Radicals and Radicalism. Working class.
1818-96. *924*
—. Mentally retarded. Nova Scotia. Organizations.
ca 1900-27. *2245*
—. Provincial Government. Quebec. 1973. *2539*
—. Women's Liberation Movement. 1955-75.
1431
—. Women's Liberation Movement. Working class.
1975. *1540*
Social responsibility. Academic responsibility.
Canadian studies. Colleges and Universities.
1970's. *1360*
Social Sciences *See also* Economics; Political
Science; Social Change; Sociology.
—. Economic growth. Elites. Ideology. Laval
University. Quebec. 1930's-70's. *2527*
—. Federal government. Research. 1976. *1467*
—. Physical Education and Training. 1970's.
1402
—. Political economy. USA. 1920-70. *45*
Social scientists. Cities. -1974. *68*
—. Nationality. Professional activity. -1973.
1422
—. Public policy. 1973. *1710*
Social Security *See also* Pensions; Unemployment
Insurance.
—. Aged. Pensions. -1973. *1505*
—. International Association of Machinists and
Aerospace Workers. Pensions. 1968-73. *1618*
—. Marsh, Leonard *(Report)*. Socialism. Welfare
state. 1930-44. *1200*
—. Public Policy. USA. 1935-75. *1428*
Social services. Government financing. Political
Protest. Radicals and Radicalism. 1960's-70's.
1689
—. Manitoba. Public Welfare. 1973. *3017*

—. Medicine and State. Public Health. Quebec. Regional councils. 1971-74. *2547*

Social Services and Community Health Department. Alberta. Provincial Government. Public policy. 1970's. *3133*

Social Status. Attitudes. Ethnic Groups. 1968. *1374*

—. Bothwick, J. Douglas (*History and Biographical Gazetteer of Montreal to the Year 1892*). Elites. Quebec (Montreal. 19c. *2550*

—. Colleges and Universities. Employment. Ontario. 1960-71. *2787*

—. Crime and Criminals. Ethnicity. Illiteracy. Ontario (Middlesex County). Sex. 1867-68. *1044*

—. Discrimination, Employment. Immigrants. Ontario (Toronto). West Indians. 1972. *2849*

—. Documents. New France. Occupations. 1640's-1740's. *534*

—. Ethnic Groups. Europe. Immigration. Occupations. Ontario (Toronto). 1940's-70's. *2814*

—. Folk Songs. Newfoundland (Calvert). Sex roles. 1916-74. *2201*

—. Ontario. Rural Settlements. Women. 19c. *2729*

—. Ontario (Toronto). Voting and Voting Behavior. 1971. *1662*

Social stigmas. Diseases. Leprosy. Massachusetts. New Brunswick. 1844-80. 1904-21. *2391*

Social Structure. *See* Social Organization; Social Status.

Social Surveys *See also* Sociology.

—. Demography. Family size. 1945-74. *1355*

—. Family size. Ontario (Wentworth County). Rural-Urban Studies. 1871. *2757*

Social thought. Catholic Church. Gibbons, James. Knights of Labor. Taschereau, Elzéar-Alexandre. 1880's. *1068*

—. Catholic Church. Journalism. Somerville, Henry. 1915-53. *1115*

—. Democrats (writings). Political Commentary. 19c. *235*

Social Welfare. *See* Public Welfare.

Social Work *See also* Charities; Public Welfare.

—. Catholic Church. D'Aquin, Marie Thomas. Joan of Arc Institute. Ontario (Ottawa). Women. 1903-19. *2746*

Socialism *See also* Capitalism; Communism; Labor; Labor Unions and Organizations; Leftism; Maoism; Marxism; Pensions; Social Democratic Party; Syndicalism; Utopias.

—. British Columbia. Government. Political Parties. 1972-75. *3214*

—. Capitalism. Imperialism. Women. ca 1870-1975. *139*

—. Conservatism. Hartz, Louis. Liberalism. Politics. USA. 1955-78. *1668*

—. Co-operative Commonwealth Federation. Labor. National Democratic Party. 1933-75. *1294*

—. Co-operative Commonwealth Federation. Manitoba. Provincial Government. Social Democratic Party. ca 1940. *3022*

—. Cooperative Commonwealth Federation. Political Parties. Saskatchewan. 1928-44. *3067*

—. Education. New Brunswick. Stuart, Henry Harvey. 1873-1952. *2380*

—. Farmer Labor Party. Political Leadership. Radicals and Radicalism. Saskatchewan. 1932-34. *3048*

—. Farmers. Grange. Oklahoma. Saskatchewan. Texas. 1900-45. *3083*

—. Great Britain. Political Commentary. Social change. Webb, Beatrice. Webb, Sidney James. 1911. *1090*

—. Labor reform. Regionalism. 1918-19. *2917*

—. Labor Unions and Organizations. One Big Union. Radicals and Radicalism. 1917-19. *1149*

—. Local Government. Manitoba (Winnipeg). Queen, John. Taxation. 1909-42. *2992*

—. Manitoba (Winnipeg). Penner, Jacob. Russia. 1900-65. *2998*

—. Marsh, Leonard (*Report*). Social Security. Welfare state. 1930-44. *1200*

—. Nationalism. Quebec. Separatist Movements. USA. 1970's. *2021*

—. Political Parties. Political Systems. USA. 1846-1972. *128*

—. Political parties. USA. 1776-1976. *148*

—. Public policy. 1945-72. *1646*

Socialist critiques (review article). Ontario Waffle. 1973. *1487*

Socialists. British Columbia. Cooperative Commonwealth Federation (origins). Ideology. Power struggles. 1919-32. *3271*

—. Class struggle. Quebec. 1970's. *2670*

Socialization *See also* Political Socialization.

—. Alienation. Ontario. Student activism. Western Ontario, University of. 1970. *2773*

—. Collins Bay Penitentiary. Libraries. Ontario (Kingston). Prisons. 1963-73. *2851*

—. Eskimos. Masak (personal account). Northwest Territories (Aklavik). 1930's. *324*

—. Industrialization. Ontario (Hamilton). Public schools. 19c. *2802*

Societies *See also* names of individual societies; Cooperatives; Organizations.

—. Geography. Hudson's Bay Company. Wegg, Samuel. 1750-1800. *683*

Society for the Propagation of the Gospel. Church of England. Loyalists. Nova Scotia. 1787-1864. *751*

—. Church of England. Missions and Missionaries. Nova Scotia (Halifax). St. Paul's Church. Tutty, William. 1749-52. *2359*

Society of Jesus. *See* Jesuits.

Socioeconomic characteristics. Boer War. Military service, British. Patriotism. Volunteers. 1899-1902. *1099*

—. British Columbia. Indians (reservations). Urban Indians. 1971. *458*

Sociology *See also* Cities; Emigration; Family; Immigration; Labor; Marriage; Population; Race Relations; Social Classes; Social Conditions; Social Organization; Social Problems; Social Surveys.

—. Aged. Minority group concept. Women. 1970's. *1339*

—. Colleges and Universities. 1972. *1363*

—. Colleges and Universities. French Canadians. Quebec. 1960-74. *2499*

—. Colleges and Universities. Social organization. 1940-70. *1398*

—. Educational system. Ideological structures. Sex Discrimination. Women. 1970's. *1474*

—. Ethnic studies. Immigrant adjustment. 1960's-70's. *1409*

—. Family. Marriage. North America. Women. 1974. *1469*

—. Feminism. Research. 1600-1975. *49*

—. France. Quebec. USA. 1970's. *2551*

—. Hughes, Helen McGill. USA. Women. 1916-77. *96*

—. Lipset, Seymour Martin. USA. 1963-73. *1304*

—. Mental Illness. Psychiatry. Quebec. 1717-1960. *2513*

—. Political science. Textbooks. 1970's. *1459*

—. Public Health. Quebec. ca 1850's-1970. *2494*

—. Quebec. 1822-1974. *2497*

Sociology of knowledge. Ideology. Research. Women's studies. 1970's. *1430*

Sod. Alberta. Construction. Housing. Settlement. Williams, Wesley. 1909. *1004*

Soil Conservation. Clays, sensitive. Geology. Ontario (Ottawa). 1648-1971. *276*

Soldiers. *See* Military Service and other headings beginning with the word Military.

Solstices. Archaeology. Boulder configurations. Indians. Saskatchewan. Sun Dance structures. Prehistory. 1975. *406*

Somatology. *See* Anthropology, Physical.

Somerville, Henry. Catholic Church. Journalism. Social thought. 1915-53. *1115*

Songs *See also* Folk Songs.

—. Cris Indians. Ethnomusicology. Leden, Christian. Phonograph. 1911. *387*

Soper, J. Dewey. Discovery and Exploration. Hantzsch, Bernard. Northwest Territories (Baffin Island). 1929. *3317*

Soper, J. Dewey (journal). Explorers. Northwest Territories (Baffin Island, Pangnirtung Pass). 1925. *3318*

South *See also* individual states; South Central and Gulf States; Southeastern States.

—. Agricultural growth. Boserup, Ester. China. North America. Russia. 18c-19c. *801*

—. Conflict management. Institutions. Quebec. Regional autonomy. Separatist movements. 19c-1970. *2101*

—. Country Life. Fiction. Munro, Alice. Ontario. 1940's-70's. *2869*

South Africa. Australia. Germany. Middle powers. Political integration. 1850-1900. *903*

—. Australia. Government policy. New Zealand. Nonwhites. Race politics. 1900-73. *1926*

—. Chile. Churches. Loans. Royal Bank of Canada. 1976. *1951*

—. Foreign Policy. International Trade. Rhodesia. 1960's-70's. *1905*

South Central and Gulf States *See also* individual states.

—. Alliances. Chickasaw Indians. Choctaw Indians. France. Indians. Tonti, Henri de. 1702. *581*

South Dakota *See also* Western States.

—. Hutterites. Life-styles, alternative. 1874-1975. *977*

South Fork Ranch. Alberta. Godsal, F. W. Ranches. 1897. *3155*

Southeastern States *See also* individual states.

—. Herty, Charles Holmes. Newsprint. Paper mills. Pine trees. Scientific Experiments and Research. 1927-40. *1134*

Sovereignty. Act of Quebec (1774). French language. Quebec. 1774-1974. *2673*

—. Arctic. Federal Government. *Neptune* (vessel). 1903-04. *3294*

—. British Empire. International trade. Reciprocity. USA. 1909-11. *1107*

—. Federalism. French Canadians. Quebec. Territorialization. 1760-1977. *167*

—. Miron, Gaston. Poetry. Quebec. 1969-74. *2470*

—. Parti Québécois. Quebec. Self-determination. 1970's. *2116*

Soward, F. H. (account). Canadian Institute of International Affairs. Colleges and Universities. External Affairs Department. Foreign Policy. 1926-66. *217*

Space *See also* names of space vehicles and space projects, e.g. Mariner Project, etc.

—. International law. Oceans (national jurisdiction). 1945-73. *1797*

Spain. Archives. Basques. Labrador (Red Bay). *San Juan* (vessel). Shipwrecks. 1565. 1978. *558*

—. British Columbia. Great Britain. Nootka Sound controversy. Territorial rights. 1790. *691*

—. British Columbia (Vancouver). Diplomacy. France (Paris). Great Britain. Nootka Sound Controversy. 1789-90. *636*

—. British Columbia (Vancouver Island). Cook, James. Discovery and Exploration. Great Britain. Nootka Sound controversy. 1778-94. *695*

—. Discovery and Exploration. France. Mississippi River Valley. 16c-17c. *588*

Spain (Barcelona). Communist Party. Germany (Berlin). Olympic Games. People's Olympic Games. 1936. *1202*

Spanish-American War. British Columbia (Victoria). British Empire. Espionage. Neutrality. 1898. *1105*

—. Counterintelligence (US). Gage, Lyman. Quebec (Montreal). Spy ring, Spanish. Wilkie, John. 1898. *1094*

Spatial perception. Behaviorism. Political geography. Quebec (Saguenay County). Territorialism. 1969-74. *2448*

Spatial structure. Activity levels. Ontario, southern. Population. 1941-71. *2733*

Special Interest Groups. *See* Interest Groups; Pressure Groups; Political Factions.

Speeches, Addresses, etc. *See also* Lectures; Political Speeches.

—. Harvard University. Leverett, John. Massachusetts (Cambridge). Quebec Expedition. 1711. *610*

—. Pluralism. Roy, Camille. Royal Society of Canada. 1929-78. *1414*

Sports *See also* Physical Education and Training.

—. 1770-1900. *193*

—. 1900-20. *1123*

—. Alberta (Edmonton). Photographs. 1900's. *3170*

—. Athletes. Hanlan, Edward "Ned". Professionalism. 1870's-80's. *1042*

—. Behavior (aggressive). Hockey. Ontario (Toronto). Violence. 1972. *2862*

—. British Columbia. Depressions. Education Department (Recreational and Physical Education Branch). Youth. 1934-40. *3217*

—. Drapeau, Jean. Olympic Games. Quebec (Montreal). 1970-76. *2521*

—. Europe. North America. Physical achievement. 1740-1975. *131*

—. Federal Government. Government control. ca 1930-70. *1468*

—. Federal Government. Physical Education and Training. 1909-54. *1144*

—. Horse racing. 1830-65. *644*

—. Indians. North America. 16c-17c. *378*

—. Lacrosse. 1840-89. *153*

—. Lord's Day Act (1906). Sabbath (observation). Sunday. 1906-77. *200*

—. Middle classes. Physical education and training. 1850-1900. *930*

—. Philanthropy. Strathcona, 1st Baron. 1870-1915. *938*
—. Professionalism, concept of. Social Conditions. 1835-1909. *910*
—. Public Schools. Upper Canada. Upper Classes (British). 1830-75. *2852*
—. Quebec (Montreal). Recreation. 1840-95. *2538*
—. Reform. 1920-40. *1127*
—. Saskatchewan (Cannington). Settlement. 1882-1900. *1017*
Spragge, George Warburton (obituary). Historians. Ontario. 1893-1976. *2731*
Sprague, Howard F. Artists. Great Lakes. Nickerson, Vincent D. Norton, Charles W. Ships. Whipple, Seth A. 1844-1901. *2861*
Spring shooting issue. Government. Great Plains. Hunting. Mississippi Flyway. North Central States. Waterfowl. 1887-1913. *906*
Stairs, Denis (review article). Diplomacy. Korean War. USA. 1950-53. *1881*
Stanley, Carleton. Colleges and Universities. Dalhousie University. Mackenzie, Arthur Stanley. Nova Scotia. 1911-45. *2282*
Stark, John. American Revolution. Bennington (battle). Burgoyne, John. Vermont. 1777. *730*
Starr family. Apple industry. Calkin(s) family. Halliburton, Robert Grant. Inglis, Charles. Nova Scotia. 19c. *2279*
State Department. Commerce Department. Foreign policy. USA. 1927-41. *1124*
State-monopoly power. Labor unity. 1967-72. *1574*
States. Constitutional law. Licensing procedures. Provinces. USA. 1970's. *2063*
—. Economic development. Federal government. Provinces. USA. 1950's-70's. *2012*
Statistics *See also* Social Surveys; Vital Statistics.
—. Cotton mills. French Canadians. Immigration. Massachusetts (Springfield). 1870. *2607*
—. Economic Conditions. GNP. USA. 1960-69. *1530*
—. Hydrographic regions. Population. Quebec. 1845-1971. *2488*
—. Immigrants. North America. Occupations. Women. 1964-71. *1516*
—. Parish records. Population. Quebec. 1621-99. *541*
Statues. *See* Monuments; Sculpture.
Statute. *See* Law; Legislation.
Steam tractors. Agricultural Technology and Research. Prairie Provinces. Western States. 1890-1925. *2913*
Steamboat business. Bethune, Donald. Finance. Ontario (Upper Canada). 19c. *837*
Steamboats. Great Lakes. *North Land* (vessel). *North West* (vessel). 1888-1941. *937*
—. Lake Ontario. New York (Ogdensburg). Ontario (Kingston). Transportation. 1815-70. *653*
—. McKenzie, "Steamboat Bill" (reminiscences). Saskatchewan. Transportation, Commercial. 1901-25. *3036*
—. New England. Nova Scotia (Yarmouth). 1839-89. *2325*
Steamship lines. Massachusetts (Boston). Nova Scotia (Halifax). 1840-1917. *2287*
—. Massachusetts (Boston). Nova Scotia (Yarmouth). Transportation. 1855-1971. *2288*
Steamships. Great Lakes. Shipping. 1871-1976. *43*
—. Massachusetts (Boston). New Brunswick (Saint John). Trade. 1836-1945. *2390*
Steel Industry *See also* Iron Industry.
—. Boomtowns. Iron Industry. Nova Scotia (Bay of Fundy, Londonderry). 1844-98. *2352*
—. International Trade. 1973-80. *1767*
Stefansson, Vilhjalmur. Arctic. Discovery and Exploration. Finnie, Richard Sterling (account). North America. Office of the Coordinator of Information. 1931-62. *3302*
—. Arctic. Explorers. 1915-24. *3319*
Stehelin, Emile Charles Adolph (family). Nova Scotia (Digby County). Pioneers. 1837-1918. *2324*
Stein, Michael (review article). *Créditiste* movement. French Canada. Pinard, Maurice (review article). Quebec. 1971-74. *2447*
Stencils. Artists. Cleveland, Xenophon. Massachusetts. New Brunswick. 1839-99. *2379*
Stephen, George. Canadian Pacific Railroad. Capital alliances. Morton, Bliss & Company. Railroads. St. Paul & Pacific Railroad. USA. 1860-70's. *980*

Stereotypes. Immigrants. Ontario (Toronto). Urban history. 19c-20c. *2784*
Stevenson, A. (account). Arctic. 1973. *3361*
—. Arctic. Berthe, Jean. Eskimos. Fur trade. Quebec. 1930's. *2663*
Stevenson, Lionel. Duke University (Lionel Stevenson Collection). Letters. Literature. 1860's-1960's. *4*
Stieb, Ernst W. (account). American Institute of the History of Pharmacy. Canadian Academy of the History of Pharmacy. Pharmacy, History of. 1940's-70's. *2059*
Stocks and Bonds *See also* Corporations; Investments; Securities.
—. Provincial Government. Quebec. Securities Commission. 1970's. *2427*
Stoesz, David. Immigration. Manitoba. Mennonites, Bergthaler. Ukraine. 1872-76. *988*
Storms *See also* Cyclones; Hurricanes; Snow; Tornadoes.
—. Alberta. Cloud-seeding program. Hail damage. 1955-74. *3136*
Stoves. Cast Iron. VanNorman, Joseph. 1820-80's. *195*
Strachan, John. Church and State. Church of England. King's College, York (charter). Ontario (Toronto). Scotland. 1815-43. *625*
—. Church of England. Clergy. Diocesan Theological Institute. Frontier and Pioneer Life. Ontario (Cobourg). 1840-55. *679*
—. Church of England. Land endowment. Ontario (Upper Canada). Rolph, John. Toronto, University of. 1820-70. *809*
—. Church of England. Ontario (Toronto). 1802-67. *2834*
—. Elites. Government. Ontario (Upper Canada; Toronto). Simcoe, John Graves. 1793-1818. *773*
Strategy. *See* Military Strategy; Naval Strategy.
Strathbeg Reading Society. Libraries. Nova Scotia. 1866-69. *2347*
Strathcona Trust fund. Borden, F. W. Physical Education and Training. ca 1900-10. *1104*
—. Curricula. Ontario. Physical education and training. Public schools. 1919-39. *1130*
Strathcona, 1st Baron. Philanthropy. Sports. 1870-1915. *938*
Stratigraphy. Alberta (Calgary, Mona Lisa Site). Artifacts. Bison kill. ca 8080 BP. 1968-74. *310*
Street, John Ambrose. Elections. New Brunswick (Northumberland County). Violence. 1842. *2403*
Street, Samuel Denny. New Brunswick. Politics. Satire. 1802. *2409*
Street, William Warren. Crime and Criminals. Depression of 1857. Embezzlement. Land speculation. 1830-70. *2799*
Streetcars. Alberta (Calgary). Public Transportation. 1907-50. *3141*
—. Hydroelectric power. Nova Scotia (Halifax). 1907-17. *2211*
—. Manitoba (Winnipeg). Urbanization. 1881-1913. *3006*
Strikes *See also* Arbitration, Industrial; Collective Bargaining; General Strikes; Labor Unions and Organizations; Syndicalism.
—. Antilabor sentiments. Holmes Foundry. Immigrants. Ontario. 1935-40. *1210*
—. British Columbia (Vancouver). Depressions. Relief Camp Workers Union. 1935. *3209*
—. Canadian Pacific Railway. Engineers, locomotive. Labor Unions and Organizations. Prairie Provinces. 1883. *1066*
—. Collective bargaining. *McGavin Toastmaster Limited* v. *Ainscough et al.* (Canada, 1975). Supreme Court. 1975-77. *1529*
—. Grand Trunk Railway. Railroads. 1896-1912. *1111*
—. Inflation. Quebec. 1974. *2624*
—. Models. USA. 1900-71. *216*
—. Newspapers. Quebec. 1977-78. *2574*
—. Quebec (Montreal). Teamsters, International Brotherhood of. 1864. *2630*
Strip mining. Coal. Environmental effects. Saskatchewan (Estevan region). 1850's-1975. *3071*
Strong, Cyril. American Federation of Labor. Canadian Labour Congress. Labor Unions and Organizations. 1949-77. *1525*
Stuart, Henry Harvey. Education. New Brunswick. Socialism. 1873-1952. *2380*
Student activism. Alienation. Ontario. Socialization. Western Ontario, University of. 1970. *2773*
Students *See also* Colleges and Universities; Schools.

—. Africa. Operation Crossroads Africa. Robinson, James H. USA. 1958-73. *1749*
—. Agnosticism. Catholic Church. Quebec. 1970-78. *2455*
—. Anti-Confucius Campaign. China. 1973-74. *1783*
—. Business Administration. French Canadians. 1973. *2585*
—. Catholic Church. Chicoutimi, Petit-Séminaire de. Quebec (Saguenay). Religious Education. 1873-1930. *2562*
—. Church and State. Mennonite Conference of 1970 (leaders). Social issues. 1917-74. *1381*
—. Colleges and Universities. Mate selection preferences. Sex status. USA. 1970's. *1482*
—. Colleges and Universities. Politics. Public opinion. 1974. *1432*
—. Ethnic Groups. Identity. Nationalism. Regionalism. 1960-77. *2915*
—. Ethnic groups. Interpersonal Relations. -1973. *1435*
—. Ethnic identity. 1971. *1380*
—. Federal Aid to Education. Mobility. 1960-. *1421*
—. Higher Education. Quebec (Saguenay County). 1975. *2498*
—. Humor. Identification classes. *Vicarious superiority* theory. Windsor, University of. 1969-74. *2808*
—. Nationalism. USA. Values. 1967-71. *2051*
—. Ontario. Political participation. Voluntary Associations. 1970. *2749*
Stuermer, Herbert. Lutheran synods. 1922. *1191*
Stursberg, Peter (reminiscences). Diefenbaker, John. Oral history. 1957-75. *1264*
Subarctic. Anthropology. Archives. Indians. 1975. *347*
—. Athapascan Indians. Ethnographers. 1900-65. *449*
Subsidies. Dairying. Government. Motherwell, W. R. Saskatchewan. Wilson, W. A. 1906-17. *3037*
Subsistence patterns. British Columbia (Queen Charlotte Islands). Haida Indians. Missions and Missionaries. Protestantism. Settlement. 1876-1920. *398*
Suburbs. City planning. Environment. Housing. 1893-1930. *236*
—. Ontario (Hamilton; Westdale). 1911-51. *2883*
Subways *See also* Mass Transit.
—. Architecture. Europe. North America. 1940's-70's. *1307*
Sudan Interior Mission. Education. Great Britain. Missions and Missionaries. Protestantism. 1937-55. *197*
Suez crisis (1956). Diplomacy. Pearson, Lester D. UN. 1956. *1873*
Suffrage *See also* Voter Registration; Voting and Voting Behavior; Woman Suffrage.
—. Australia. Federalism. USA. 19c-20c. *179*
—. British Columbia. Chinese. Immigration. Japanese. 1935-49. *3220*
Sugar Agreement. British Commonwealth. Economic development. 1949-51. *1870*
Sugar refining industry. Board of Commerce of Canada. Price control. 1919-20. *1192*
Sulpicians. Algonkin Indians. Historical Sites and Parks. Iroquois Indians. Missions and Missionaries. Quebec (Oka). 1700's-1800's. *521*
—. Fort Frontenac. Indian-White Relations. Iroquois Indians. Missions and Missionaries. Quinte Mission. 1665-80. *522*
Sun Dance structures. Archaeology. Boulder configurations. Indians. Saskatchewan. Solstices. Prehistory. 1975. *406*
Sunday. Lord's Day Act (1906). Sabbath (observation). Sports. 1906-77. *200*
Sunday schools. Ontario (Upper Canada). Social control. 19c. *643*
Supermarkets. Cooprix supermarkets. 1960-73. *1551*
Supreme Court. Americanization. Criminal Law. Laskin, Bora. 1973-74. *2068*
—. Anti-Inflation Act. Emergency powers. Peacetime. Wages. 1976. *1607*
—. Anti-Inflation Act. Parliaments. 1975-76. *1685*
—. *Attorney General of Canada* v. *Lavell* (Canada, 1973). Indians. Lavell, Jeanette. Sex discrimination. 1973-74. *473*
—. Collective bargaining. *McGavin Toastmaster Limited* v. *Ainscough et al.* (Canada, 1975). Strikes. 1975-77. *1529*
—. Constitutions. Nationalism. USA. 1875-1973. *238*
—. Bill of Rights (Canada, 1958). Civil Rights. 1960-75. *2089*

—. Harris, Robert Edward. Nova Scotia. Townshend, Charles James. 1887-1931. *2286*
—. Judicial Process. 1875-1975. *125*
Survey of Canadian English. Dialects. Language. Youth. 1972. *1484*
Surveying. Acadians. Daily Life. Harley, William. New Brunswick, northeastern. 1829. *2381*
—. Alberta. Birney, Earle (reminiscences). Waterton Lakes National Park. 1921. *3098*
—. Alberta. Indians. Ogilvie, William (field notes). 1878-79. *433*
—. Conservation of Natural Resources. Nova Scotia. Smith, Titus. 1801. *2328*
—. Gill, Valentine. Natural resources. Nova Scotia. Smith, Titus. 1800-15. *2271*
—. Markers. National Museum of Science and Technology. 1765-19c. 1960-70. *129*
Surveyors. British Columbia (Lower Fraser Valley). Landscape, physical. Pioneers. 1859-90. *3235*
—. Forests and Forestry. Lumberers. New Brunswick. 1820's-44. *2412*
Sutherland, Catherine McPherson. Manitoba. Pioneers. Red River of the North. 1814-71. *1028*
Sutherland, James. Fur Trade. Hudson's Bay Company. New York. 1751-97. *687*
Sutherland, Peter. Contracts. McDonald, Alexander N. Nova Scotia (Sherbrooke). Shipbuilding. 1873-74. *2265*
Swanson, Robert (interview). British Columbia. Engineering. Lumber and Lumbering. Poetry. Railroads. 20c. *3273*
Sweden *See also* Scandinavia.
—. Air pollution. Political structures. USA. 1974. *1691*
—. Economic development. Planning. Social Conditions. 20c. *1310*
Swedish Americans. Banking. Illinois (Chicago). Immigration. 1892-1974. *1093*
—. Farmers. French Canadians. Kansas. Mennonites. 1875-1925. *150*
Sweet, H. C. Protestantism. 1866-1960. *119*
Symonds, Herbert. Church of England. Ecumenism. 1897-1921. *194*
Symons report. Art. Canadian studies. 1960's-77. *1495*
—. Canadian studies. Higher education. 1970's. *1368*
—. Higher education. 1950's-70's. *1490*
—. Higher education. Nationalism. Quebec. 1970's. *1472*
Syncrude oil Project. Alberta (Athabasca River). Bitumen. Oil and Petroleum Products. 1974-75. *3150*
—. Alberta (Athabasca River). Oil Industry and Trade. USA. 1975. *2036*
—. Alberta (Fort McMurray). Great Canadian Oil Sands. Oil Industry and Trade. 1975. *3111*
Syndicalism *See also* Communism; Labor Unions and Organizations; Socialism.
—. Canadian Seamen's Union. Communists. 1936-49. *1197*
—. Cooperativism. Quebec. 1972-77. *2648*
Synods. *See* Councils and Synods.

T

Taché, Alexandre. Métis. Prairie Provinces. Religion. Riel, Louis (letter). 1880's. *974*
Talman, James J. Festschriften publications. Kniffen, Fred B. Mayo, Bernard. Morris, Richard B. 1863-1974. *109*
Target ranges. Navies. Puerto Rico (Culebra Island). USA. 1971-72. *2023*
Tariff *See also* Economic Integration; Free Trade; Protectionism; Smuggling.
—. Borden, Robert. British Empire. Economic cooperation. 1912-18. *1151*
—. British Empire. Foreign relations. France. Treaties. 1901-09. *1106*
—. British Empire. Foster, George. Free trade policy. 1912-17. *1152*
—. Economic imperialism. USA. 1870-1945. *199*
—. Exports. Horst, Thomas (review article). Trade Regulations. USA. 1970's. *1882*
—. International Trade (nontariff barriers). Mexico. USA. 1946-74. *1954*
—. Nationalism. Periodicals. Publishers and Publishing. USA. 1920's. *1193*
Taschereau, Elzéar-Alexandre. Catholic Church. Gibbons, James. Knights of Labor. Social thought. 1880's. *1068*
—. Catholic Church. Knights of Labor. Labor Unions and Organizations. 1884-94. *1069*
Tatham, William. Navigation. Niagara Falls. ca 1790-1819. *649*

Taxation *See also* Income Tax; Inheritance; Tariff.
—. Acadians. Catholic Church. Irish Canadians. New Brunswick. Politics. Quebec. Schools. 1871-73. *1067*
—. Aged. British Columbia (Vancouver, Victoria). Income. Population. 1951-74. *3196*
—. Bélanger Report. Quebec. 1966-76. *2419*
—. Bill C-58. Nationalism. Protectionism. *Reader's Digest* (periodical). *Time* (periodical). 1922-76. *2017*
—. Bill of Incorporation (1873). City Government. Manitoba (Winnipeg). 1873. *2984*
—. Energy crisis. USA. 1973-75. *1643*
—. Federal government. Unemployment. Wealth distribution. 1977. *1635*
—. Germany. Great Britain. Land prices. 1890-1970's. *214*
—. Intergovernmental Relations. King, William Lyon Mackenzie. Newspapers. Public opinion. 1945-46. *2119*
—. Local Government. Manitoba (Winnipeg). Queen, John. Socialism. 1909-42. *2992*
Taylor and Drury, Ltd. Merchants. Yukon Territory. 1898-1924. *3342*
Teachers *See also* Educators; Professors; Teaching.
—. Arbitration, compulsory. British Columbia. 1937-73. *3257*
—. Art. Chabert, Joseph. Education. National Institute for Arts and Crafts. Quebec (Montreal). Working Class. 1861-94. *1053*
—. Collective bargaining. Prince Edward Island. Public Employees. 1970-74. *2204*
—. Historiography. 19c-20c. *23*
—. Mass media. Science and Society. Values. Youth. 1920's-75. *1391*
—. Saskatchewan. Saskatoon Women Teachers' Association. Women. 1918-70's. *3051*
Teaching *See also* Education; History Teaching; Schools; Teachers.
—. British North America. Public schools. Women. 1845-75. *880*
—. China. Hurford, Grace Gibberd (reminiscences). Missions and Missionaries. World War II. 1928-45. *1122*
—. Chipman, George. Editors and Editing. *Grain Growers' Guide* (periodical). Prairie Provinces. 1903-05. *2938*
—. Colleges and Universities. USA. 1973. *2009*
—. Curricula. Higher Education. Women's history. 1940-73. *1387*
—. Demers, Jerôme. Philosophy. Quebec. Science. 1765-1835. *2502*
—. Educational Policy. Goggin, David James. Manitoba. Northwest Territories. ca 1890's. *2904*
—. Goodwin, Theresa (reminiscences). Saskatchewan (Chaplin, Duval). 1912-13. *3045*
—. Hunter, R. H. (reminiscences). Saskatchewan. 1923-67. *2931*
Teamsters, International Brotherhood of. Quebec (Montreal). Strikes. 1864. *2630*
Technocracy. Business. Civil service. Middle Classes. Quebec. 1939-75. *2451*
Technology *See also* Agricultural Technology and Research; Engineering; Inventions; Machinery; Manufactures; Science; Science and Government; Science and Society.
—. Agriculture. Hutterites. North America. Social Customs. 18c-20c. *2896*
—. Arctic. Decisionmaking. Oil development. 1970's. *3284*
—. Assimilation. Ethnicity. USA. 20c. *1408*
—. Attitudes. Intellectual traditions. National self-image. Science. 1970's. *1327*
—. Canadian Railway Labour Association. Employment. Railroads. Working Conditions. 1973. *1620*
—. Diffusion theories. Mechanization. Ontario. Reaping. 1850-70. *2846*
—. Economic viability. USA. 1900's-70's. *121*
—. Grove, Frederick Phillip (writings). Literature. Pastoral ideal. 1920-45. *38*
—. Labor movement. 1970's. *1514*
—. Lime kilns. Ontario. Pioneers. 1870-1917. *2850*
—. Military. Weapons. 1970-76. *1277*
—. Pollution. Wastes, solid. 1973. *1334*
—. Snow. 1973. *1275*
Telegraph. Alberta. Cree Indians. Fuller, Richard. Hudson's Bay Company. Treaties. 1870's. *1020*
—. Communications (Transcontinental). Railroads. Watkin, Edward. 1860-65. *884*
Television. *All in the Family* (program). USA. 1972-73. *1479*
—. Archives. Quebec (Montreal). Radio. Radio Canada Archives. 1959-75. *1351*

—. Attitudes. USA. 1975-76. *2056*
—. Eskimos. Northwest Territories (Baffin Island). Radio. 1972-73. *321*
—. Eskimos. Northwest Territories (Baffin Island). Social customs. 1972-74. *320*
—. Eskimos. Values. 1976-77. *330*
—. Federal Regulation. 1959-76. *1901*
—. Federal Regulation. Quebec. Radio-Québec. 1969-76. *2478*
—. Films. 1960's-70's. *1348*
—. Institutions. Legitimacy. Quebec. Radio-Québec. 1969-74. *2477*
—. Parliaments. 1970-73. *1673*
Temperance Movements *See also* Alcoholism.
—. Gospel Temperance Movement. Revivalism. Rine, D.I.K. 1877-82. *1041*
Tennessee *See also* South Central and Gulf States.
Territorial government. Commissioners, territorial. Yukon Territory. 1897-1954. *3327*
—. Federalism. French Canadians. Quebec. Sovereignty. 1760-1977. *167*
Territorial rights. British Columbia. Great Britain. Nootka Sound controversy. Spain. 1790. *691*
Territorial rivalry. France. Great Britain. New England. Nova Scotia (Canso). 1710-21. *595*
Territorial Waters *See also* International Waters; Maritime Law.
—. Boundaries. Fishing. Foreign Relations. 1977. *1933*
—. Diplomacy. Maritime Law. Pacific Area, North. 1958-75. *1826*
—. Fishing. 1977. *1854*
Territorialism. Behaviorism. Political geography. Quebec (Saguenay County). Spatial perception. 1969-74. *2448*
Territorialization. Federalism. French Canadians. Quebec. Sovereignty. 1760-1977. *167*
Texas *See also* South Central and Gulf States.
—. Farmers. Grange. Oklahoma. Saskatchewan. Socialism. 1900-45. *3083*
Textbooks. Art. History. Illustrators. Jeffreys, Charles William. 1920's-50. *1119*
—. Government. Politics. 1607-1974. *1729*
—. Great Britain. National characteristics, British. USA. 1880-1930. *14*
—. History Teaching. Loyalism. Ontario (Upper Canada). 19c-20c. *741*
—. Political science. Sociology. 1970's. *1459*
Textile industry. Immigrants. Labor Unions and Organizations. Massachusetts (Fall River). 1890-1905. *2659*
—. Massachusetts (Lowell). Mills, woolen and cotton. Women. 1833-57. *2664*
Textile workers. Labor. Quebec (St. Jérôme). 1974. *2590*
Textile Workers' Union of America. Labor Disputes. Ontario (Peterborough). Tilco Plastics Strike (1965-67). 1965-70. *1610*
Thailand. Canadian International Development Agency. Higher Education. Manitoba, University of. 1964-74. *1911*
Thanadelthur ("Slave Woman," Chippewa Indian). Chippewa Indians. Cree Indians. Fur Trade. Saskatchewan. 1715-17. *577*
Thanksgiving. 1578-1863. *500*
—. Manitoba. 1763-1957. *41*
Theal, George McCall (recollections). Cocagne Academy. New Brunswick. 1840-94. *2405*
Theater *See also* Actors and Actresses; Drama; Films.
—. Actors and Actresses. Saskatchewan (Regina). 1900-14. *3059*
—. Actors and Actresses (American). Nova Scotia (Halifax). 1768. *2213*
—. Alberta (Edmonton). Cameron, Alexander W. 1906-13. *3143*
—. Catlin, George. Chippewa Indians. Europe. Maungwudaus (George Henry). Ontario. 1840's. *450*
—. Copyright. *D'Oyle Carte* v. *Dennis et al.* (Canada, 1899). Saskatchewan (Regina). 1899-1900's. *3058*
—. Nova Scotia (Halifax). 1816-19. *2214*
—. Ontario. Oral history. 1973-75. *2855*
Theater (tours). McDowell, Eugene A. USA. 1875-90. *1054*
Theillon, Elie. Catholic Church. French Canadians. Minnesota (Gentilly). Settlement. 1870's-1974. *946*
Theology *See also* Christianity; Ethics; Religion.
—. Aberhart, William. Alberta. Ideology. Provincial Government. Social Credit Party. 1935-43. *3106*
—. Bland, Salem. Methodism. 1880-86. *1038*

Theosophy. Art. Bucke, Richard M. *(Cosmic Consciousness).* Harris, Lawren. 1920's. *1181*

Theses *See also* Dissertations.
—. Bibliographies. British Columbia. 12c-20c. 1974. *3267*
—. Bibliographies. British Columbia. 1975. *3268*
—. Bibliographies. British Columbia. Essays. 1976. *3269*

Thetis (vessel). Arctic. Voyages. Whaling vessels (converted). 1881-1950. *3290*

"Third Option" policy. Economic independence. Europe, Western. 1970's. *1777*

Third parties. Pinard, Maurice (theories). Political Parties. 1900-73. *1148*

Third World. *See* Developing Nations.

Thistle, R. British Columbia (Prince Rupert). Coastal defense. Diaries. World War II. 1941-42. *1243*

Thlingchadinne Indians. Northwest Territories (Rae). Social Change. 1939. 1974. *380*

Thompson, Annie Affleck. Church of England. Letters. Ontario (Ottawa). Politics. Thompson, John S. D. 1867-94. *1075*

Thompson, Catherine (death). Nova Scotia (Dartmouth). 1846. *2263*

Thompson, John S. D. Church of England. Letters. Ontario (Ottawa). Politics. Thompson, Annie Affleck. 1867-94. *1075*
—. Genealogy. Ireland (Waterford). Prime Ministers. 1796-1903. *1056*

Thousand Islands. Nature Conservation. New York. Ontario. St. Lawrence Seaway. 19c-20c. *279*

Tides. Electric power. Energy. Fundy, Bay of. Passamaquoddy Bay. 1919-64. 1975. *115*

Tilco Plastics Strike (1965-67). Labor Disputes. Ontario (Peterborough). Textile Workers' Union of America. 1965-70. *1610*

Time (periodical). Bill C-58. Nationalism. Protectionism. *Reader's Digest* (periodical). Taxation. 1922-76. *2017*

Times of London (newspaper). Gold rushes. Great Britain. Journalism. Klondike Stampede. Shaw, Flora. Yukon Territory. 1898. *3341*

Tipi covers. Indians. Sacred pipe myth. Sioux Indians. 1770-1975. *366*

Tlingit Indians. Alaska. Artifacts. Emmons, George Thornton. Ethnology. 1852-1945. *417*
—. Alaska. Haida Indians. Indians. Tsimshian Indians. 1649-1973. *430*

Tobin, Thomas (and descendants). Irish Canadians. Nova Scotia (Halifax). ca 1759-1936. *2329*

Tonti, Henri de. Alliances. Chickasaw Indians. Choctaw Indians. France. Indians. South Central and Gulf States. 1702. *581*

Tools. Indians. Manitoba, southwestern. Weapons. ca 10,000 BC-1600 AD. *308*

Toponymy. Alberta (Calgary). Fort Brisbois. 1875-76. *3151*
—. Bibliographies. Onomastics. USA. 1964-75. *203*
—. Bibliographies. USA. 1971-74. *1263*
—. Canadian Permanent Commission on Geographic Names. 1973. *1336*
—. Church names, origin of. Quebec. Religion. 1600-1925. *2557*
—. Great Lakes. USA. 1534-1974. *50*

Tornadoes *See also* Cyclones; Storms.
—. Ontario. 1792-1899. *2832*

Toronto *Globe* (newspaper). Brown, George. Labor Unions and Organizations. Ontario. Publishers and Publishing. Toronto Typographical Union. 1843-72. *2893*

Toronto Railway Company. Mass transit. Ontario. Public Utilities. 1891-1921. *2760*

Toronto Typographical Union. Brown, George. Labor Unions and Organizations. Ontario. Publishers and Publishing. Toronto *Globe* (newspaper). 1843-72. *2893*

Toronto, University of. Church of England. Land endowment. Ontario (Upper Canada). Rolph, John. Strachan, John. 1820-70. *809*

Totalitarianism *See also* Communism; Nazism.
—. Democracy. Foreign policy. Mass media. 1960-76. *1924*

Totem poles. British Columbia (Anthony, Queen Charlotte Islands). Haida Indians. Prehistory-1795. *375*
—. British Columbia (Queen Charlotte Islands). Haida Indians. Preservation. 1700's-1800's. 1957. *453*

Tourism *See also* Resorts; Voyages.
—. Alberta (Banff). Macdonald, John A. National Parks and Reserves. Natural resources. 1885-1978. *1040*

—. Economic Growth. Industry. Pollution. Quebec (Saint-Georges Est, Chaudière River). 1973. *2652*
—. Nashwaak Miramichi Trail. New Brunswick (Fredericton). Trails. 1973. *2406*
—. Railroads. Ships. Travel. Yukon Territory. 20c. *3329*

Towns, "instant". British Columbia. Multinational Corporations. Natural Resources. Provincial government. Social Classes. 1965-72. *3178*

Townshend, Charles James. Harris, Robert Edward. Nova Scotia. Supreme Court. 1887-1931. *2286*

Townships. Land speculation. Ontario (Upper Canada). Rural land occupation. Settlers. 1782-1851. *793*

Tractarians. Church of England. Religion. 1840-68. *857*

Trade *See also* International Trade; Tariff.
—. Annexation. USA. 1911. *1084*
—. Bernard, Joseph-Fidèle (diary). Chukchi natives. Firearms. USSR. 1921-22. *1166*
—. Buttons, Phoenix. Haiti. Indians. Pacific Northwest. Uniforms, Military. 1812-30. 20c. *460*
—. Caldwell, Billy. Frontier and Pioneer Life. Great Britain. Great Lakes. Indians. 1797-1841. *365*
—. Church Missionary Society. Church of England. Eskimos. Hudson's Bay Company. Missions and Missionaries. Northwest Territories (Baffin Island). Peck, E. J. 1894-1913. *340*
—. Clergy. New France. 1627-1760. *563*
—. Cobb, Sylvanus. Fundy, Bay of. Nova Scotia. Ships. *York* (vessel) 1755. *2163*
—. Employment. Manufacturing. 1949-70. *2145*
—. Family. France. Protestantism. Quebec. 1740-60. *593*
—. Fishing. Indians. Ontario (Sault Ste. Marie). 17c-1920. *419*
—. France. French and Indian War. Ports. 1750's-60's. *562*
—. Fur trade. Hudson's Bay Company. Indians. 17c-18c. *576*
—. Manitoba (Winnipeg). Métis. Minnesota (St. Paul). Prairies. Red River of the North. Trails. 19c. *976*
—. Massachusetts (Boston). New Brunswick (Saint John). Steamships. 1836-1945. *2390*
—. Netherlands. New York. 1670-74. *567*
—. Rio de la Plata. Schooners. Voyages. ca 1860-1914. *935*

Trade Regulations *See also* Free Trade; Protectionism; Tariff.
—. Economic growth. Pacific Area. 1970-73. *1830*
—. Exports. Horst, Thomas (review article). Tariff. USA. 1970's. *1882*
—. Great Britain. Imperial Shipping Committee. International Trade. 1918-63. *20*

Trade Routes. Brigade Trail. British Columbia. Hudson's Bay Company. 1849-60. 1967-73. *3203*
—. Discovery and Exploration. Mackenzie, Alexander. Overland Journeys to the Pacific. 1789-93. *2134*

Trade Union Movements. *See* Labor Movement.

Trade Unions. *See* Labor Unions and Organizations.

Traders. Alaskan Coast. Bernard, Joseph Francis. Eskimos. Siberian Coast. 1903-29. *314*
—. Indians. Métis. Smallpox. Vaccination program. 1837-38. *439*

Trades and Labour Congress of Canada. Labor Unions and Organizations. National Trades and Labour Congress. Ontario (Kitchener). Quebec. 1892-1902. *2655*
—. Methodist Church. Regionalism. Two-party system. 1870-1919. *2916*

Trading circles. France. Lamaletie, Jean-André. Quebec. 1741-63. *561*

Trading posts. Alberta (Lac la Biche). Beaver Indians. Hudson's Bay Company. North West Rebellion. Pruden, Patrick. 1885. *1026*
—. Daily Life. Hudson's Bay Company. ca 1850. *862*
—. Fort McMurray. McMurray, William. Moberly, Henry John. 1870's. *953*

Traill, Catherine Parr. Botany. Ontario (Peterborough). 1830's-99. *2819*
—. Colonial policy. Emigrant guides. Great Britain. Land grants (proposed). Ontario (Peterborough). 19c. *869*

Trails. Manitoba (Winnipeg). Métis. Minnesota (St. Paul). Prairies. Red River of the North. Trade. 19c. *976*

—. Nashwaak Miramichi Trail. New Brunswick (Fredericton). Tourism. 1973. *2406*

Tramways. Fur trade. Railroads. Saskatchewan (Grand Rapids). Saskatchewan River. 1877-1909. *997*

Transformer figures. Abnaki Indians, Western. Myths and Symbols. ca 1840-1976. *369*

Transoceanic contacts. Civilization (review article). Diffusion theories. Geography. Gordon, Cyrus H. Riley, Carroll. Prehistory-1492. *304*

Transportation *See also* names of transportation vehicles, e.g. Automobiles, Ships, Buses, Trucks, Railroads, etc.; Aeronautics; Bridges; Canals; Commerce; Freight and Freightage; Mass Transit; Merchant Marine; Ocean Travel; Public Transportation; Roads; Shipping; Subways; Trade Routes.
—. Alberta (Lethbridge). Culture. Industry. Pioneers. 1880's. *3104*
—. Economic development. Federal Regulation. Population. 1945-77. *1273*
—. Economic Development. Industrial Revolution. New Brunswick (Saint John). Railroads. 1867-1911. *2395*
—. Lake Ontario. New York (Ogdensburg). Ontario (Kingston). Steamboating. 1815-70. *653*
—. Massachusetts (Boston). Nova Scotia (Yarmouth). Steamship services. 1855-1971. *2288*
—. Ontario. Quantitative sources, utility of. Quebec. Urban hierarchy. 1861-1901. *2137*

Transportation, Commercial. McKenzie, "Steamboat Bill" (reminiscences). Saskatchewan. Steamboats. 1901-25. *3036*
—. Michigan (Port Huron). Ontario (Sarnia). Railroad tunnels. St. Clair River. 1884-91. *108*

Trapping *See also* Fur Trade; Hunting.
—. Fur Trade. Manitoba. Registered Trap Lines system. Wells, Harold. 1940-53. *3011*

Trappists. Catholic Church. Cistercians. Mistassini, monastery of. Quebec. 1900-03. *2482*
—. Emigration. Foreign Relations. France. Quebec (Sherbrooke). 1903-14. *2529*

Travel *See also* Voyages.
—. Alberta (Calgary, Banff). McDougall, John. 1873-1902. *3137*
—. Automobiles. Mass transit. Motoring, urban. North America. 1960-75. *2758*
—. Bonaparte, Jerome Napoleon. France. North America. 1861. *839*
—. British North America. Droz, Pierre-Frédéric. Europe. Watchmakers. 1768-70. *685*
—. Canoe trips. Frobisher Bay. Northwest Territories (Baffin Island, Takuirbing Lake). 1973. *3320*
—. Disturnell, John *(The Great Lakes, or 'Inland Seas' of America).* Great Lakes. Handbooks. 1862. *882*
—. Europe. Flint. Gunflints. Indians. Quebec (Chicoutimi). 17c. 20c. *349*
—. Galt, Elliott. Indians. Letters. Prairie Provinces. 1879-80. *959*
—. Geology. Great Britain. Jukes, Joseph Beete. Newfoundland. 19c. *2181*
—. Gold. Nova Scotia (Eastern shore). Roads. 19c. *2266*
—. Great Lakes. Howell, William Maher (reminiscences). Ontario. Pennsylvania (Erie). Quebec. St. Lawrence Seaway. 1928. *2131*
—. Howells, William Dean. Quebec (Quebec). 1871-72. *2454*
—. Jackman, Alonzo. Military Strategy. New York. Quebec. Vermont. 1838. *2443*
—. Manitoba (Red River country). O'Beirne, Eugene Francis. 1860's. *3015*
—. National Characteristics. 1799-1899. *44*
—. New Brunswick. 1974. *2407*
—. Northwest Territories (Mackenzie River). *Norweta* (vessel). 1973. *3347*
—. Railroads. Ships. Tourism. Yukon Territory. 20c. *3329*

Travelers. Diplomacy. External Affairs Department. 1973-74. *1865*

Treadwell Trenches. Quebec (Ottawa River). 1800-34. *800*

Treason. Citizenship. Great Britain. Riel, Louis. USA. 1885. *951*
—. Mental Illness. Riel, Louis. Saskatchewan (Regina). Trials. Valade, François-Xavier (medical report). 1885. *973*

Treaties *See also* names of treaties, e.g. Utrecht, Treaty of (1713), Nazi-Soviet Pact; names beginning with Convention, Agreement, Protocol, etc.

—. Alberta. Cree Indians. Fuller, Richard. Hudson's Bay Company. Telegraph. 1870's. *1020*

—. British Columbia (Vancouver Island). Fishing rights. International Pacific Salmon Fisheries Commission. Pacific Northwest. Salmon. 1970's. *2018*

—. British Empire. Foreign relations. France. Tariff. 1901-09. *1106*

—. Economic Policy. European Economic Community. Foreign policy. 1958-76. *1891*

—. Great Britain. Nova Scotia. Public opinion. Reciprocity. USA. 1846-54. *871*

Treaty Seven. Centennial Celebrations. Great Britain. Indians. 1877-1977. *370*

Trees. Lobsticks. Monuments. 1826-1973. *84*

Tremblay Commission. Arès, Richard. French tradition. Minville, Esdras. Quebec. 1953-56. *2676*

Trials *See also* Crime and Criminals.

—. Big Bear. Métis. North West Rebellion. Poundmaker. 1885. *948*

—. Courts. Nova Scotia (Pictou County). 1813. *2341*

—. Devit, Charles. M'Grath, Michael. Nova Scotia (Halifax). Westmacott, John (murder of). 1816. *2243*

—. Fenians. Foreign Relations. Irish Americans. USA. 1865-70. *876*

—. Howe, Joseph. Local Government. Nova Scotia (Halifax). Political Corruption. 1835. *808*

—. Mental Illness. Riel, Louis. Saskatchewan (Regina). Treason. Valade, François-Xavier (medical report). 1885. *973*

—. Ontario. Politics. Rolph, George. Rolph, John. 1825-30. *2843*

—. Ontario. Short Hills raid. 1838-40. *818*

Tribune (vessel). Nova Scotia (Herring Cove). Shipwrecks. 1796-1968. *2326*

Trichinosis. Arctic. Discovery and Exploration. Hantzsch, Bernard. Northwest Territories (Baffin Island). 1911. *3316*

Trigger, Bruce G. France. Huron Indians. Indians (review article). Jaenen, Cornelius J. Values. 1600-60. 1976. *520*

Trinidad and Tobago. Church Schools. East Indians. Missions and Missionaries. Presbyterian Church. 1868-1912. *2319*

Tripartism. Attitudes. Business community. Canadian Labour Congress. Federal government. 1977. *1295*

Trivett, Samuel. Alberta. Blackfoot Indians. Church of England. Cree Indians. Missions and Missionaries. 1878-91. *360*

Trotskyism. Canadian League for Socialist Action. 1973. *2040*

Trudeau, Pierre Elliott. Africa, southern. Foreign Policy. Peacekeeping Forces. UN Conference on the Law of the Sea. 1968-78. *1775*

—. Alberta (Calgary). News diffusion. 1971. *1385*

—. Anti-inflation program. Public relations. 1976. *1656*

—. Asia. Foreign Policy. 1968-78. *1907*

—. Authority. Government. 1950's-70's. *2111*

—. British Commonwealth. Foreign Policy. 1970's. *1842*

—. British North America Act (1867). Constitutional amendments. Great Britain. Parliaments. 1867-1970's. *1249*

—. China. Diplomatic recognition. Foreign Relations. 1968-73. *1807*

—. China. Diplomatic trips. 1973. *1934*

—. Defense Policy. NATO. Peacekeeping Forces. 1968-78. *1752*

—. Developing Nations. Economic Aid. 1968-78. *1816*

—. Developing nations. Foreign policy. 1968-78. *1929*

—. Economic Policy. Foreign policy. Nationalism. 1968-78. *1772*

—. Economic policy. Foreign relations. Prime ministers. USA. 1960's-70's. *2006*

—. Elections. Liberal Government. 1968-72. *1638*

—. Energy policy. Federal Government. Provincial Government. 1950-77. *2093*

—. Europe. Foreign Policy. 1968-78. *1946*

—. European Economic Community. Foreign Relations. USA. 1968-74. *1922*

—. Ford, Gerald R. Foreign Relations. USA. 1974-76. *2064*

—. Foreign policy. 1968-74. *1787*

—. Foreign policy. 1968-78. *1815*

—. Foreign policy. 1968-78. *1923*

—. Foreign policy. 1968-78. *1940*

—. Foreign policy. Japan. 1968-78. *1880*

—. Foreign policy. Latin America. 1968-77. *1803*

—. Foreign Policy. Latin America. 1940-76. *1804*

—. Foreign Policy. Latin America. 1968-78. *1878*

—. Foreign policy. Parti Québécois. 1968-78. *1836*

—. Foreign Relations. USA. 1968-78. *2058*

—. International trade. Latin America. 1968-76. *1802*

—. Lévesque, René. Parti Québécois. Quebec. Separatism. 1970's. *2110*

—. New International Economic Order. UN. 1968-78. *1909*

—. Rhetoric. Social action. War Measures Act (Canada, 1914). 1970. *1301*

Trudel, Marcel (review article). Demography. Population. 1663. 1973. *509*

Tsimshian Indians. Alaska. Haida Indians. Indians. Tlingit Indians. 1649-1973. *430*

—. Alaska (Metlakahtla). British Columbia. Duncan, William. Missions and Missionaries. 1857-1974. *373*

—. Anthropology, Cultural. Myths and Symbols. Pacific Northwest. Prehistory-20c. *456*

—. Archaeological findings. British Columbia (Prince Rupert area). ca 3,000 BC. *297*

—. British Columbia (Port Simpson). Potlatches. 1788-1862. *393*

Tuberculosis. Medicine (practice of). Nova Scotia (Kentville). Sanatoriums. 1904-78. *2284*

Tufts, Henry. Abnaki Indians, Western. New England. Quebec. 1772-75. *368*

Tupper, Charles H. Cabinet. Nova Scotia (Pictou County). Politics. 1882-1904. *2321*

Tupper, Charles Hibbert. British Columbia. Nova Scotia (Pictou County). Politics. 1882-1904. *2140*

Tupper, William Johnston (letters). Alberta. Rocky Mountains. 1885. *964*

—. North West Rebellion. Nova Scotia (Halifax). 1885. *965*

Turner, Frederick Jackson. Australia (Victoria). California, northern. Frontier thesis. 1850-1900. *247*

Turnover rates. Labor Unions and Organizations (presidents). 1912-71. *27*

Tutty, William. Church of England. Missions and Missionaries. Nova Scotia (Halifax). St. Paul's Church. Society for the Propagation of the Gospel. 1749-52. *2359*

Twain, Mark. Cable, George Washington. Kentucky. Lectures. 1884-85. *1076*

—. Lectures. Manitoba (Winnipeg). Minnesota (Crookston). 1895. *2989*

Two Friends (vessel). Maritime history. *Pewaukee* (vessel). Shipwrecks. Wisconsin (North Bay, Milwaukee). 1873-1913. *1048*

Typography. *See* Printing.

Tyrrell, J. W. (travel diary). Eskimos. Expedition. Geological Survey of Canada. 1890's. *337*

Tyrrell, Joseph Burr. Canoe trips. Discovery and Exploration. Rupert's Land. 1893. *975*

U

Ukraine. Immigration. Manitoba. Mennonites, Bergthaler. Stoesz, David. 1872-76. *988*

—. Immigration. Manitoba. Shantz, Jacob Y. 1870's. *992*

—. Immigration. Mennonites. 1922-23. *1173*

Ukrainian Canadians. Alberta (Cardiff, Edmonton). Chaban, Teklia. Coal Mines and Mining. Labor Unions and Organizations. 1914-20's. *3164*

—. Art. Proch, Don. 1970's. *1403*

—. Balladry. Prairie provinces. 1900-74. *2934*

—. French Canadians. Minorities. Social Organization. 1970's. *1458*

Ukrainian Labour-Farmer Association. Alberta (Edmonton). Farmer's Union of Alberta. Kyforuk, Peter. Manitoba. 1912-30's. *2961*

Ukrainian studies. Manitoba. 1949-74. *2999*

Ukrainians. Alberta. Architecture. Assimilation. 1891-1970's. *3127*

—. Alberta. Homesteading and Homesteaders. Peace River country. Zahara, Dominka Roshko. 1900-30. *1034*

—. Alberta. Houses. 1890's-1915. *3128*

—. Folklore. Immigration. 1945-75. *2933*

—. Immigration. Prairie Provinces. Settlement. 1910-31. *2937*

Ultramontanism. Economic Development. Government. Quebec (Lower Canada). Social classes. 19c. *698*

UN. Americas (North and South). Indians. International law. Organization of American States. 19c-1974. *367*

—. Bulgaria. Great Powers. Hungary. Rumania. 1947-55. *1927*

—. Developing nations. International law. Violence. 1945-75. *1739*

—. Diplomacy. Korean War. Pearson, Lester B. Self-determination. 1950-72. *1768*

—. Diplomacy. Pearson, Lester B. Suez crisis (1956). 1956. *1873*

—. Foreign Policy. NATO. Peacekeeping Forces. 1956-77. *1861*

—. Foreign relations. Multinational corporations. Politics. 1970's. *1868*

—. Great Powers. Lie, Trygve. Pearson, Lester B. 1946. *1738*

—. International Security. Peacekeeping Forces. 1975. *1823*

—. Maritime law. USA. 1970's. *2022*

—. New International Economic Order. Trudeau, Pierre Elliott. 1968-78. *1909*

UN Conference on the Law of the Sea. Africa, southern. Foreign Policy. Peacekeeping Forces. Trudeau, Pierre Elliott. 1968-78. *1775*

—. Defense Policy. Maritime Law. 1977. *1764*

—. Marine Resources. Pollution. 1974. *1902*

UN General Assembly, 30th. Foreign policy. 1975. *1825*

UN Security Council. Developing nations. Humanitarian attitudes. Poverty. 1970's. *1796*

—. Political decisions. 1976. *1822*

Underdeveloped Nations. *See* Developing Nations.

Underhill, Frank. Cooperative Commonwealth Federation. League for Social Reconstruction. Regina Manifesto. Saskatchewan. 1933. *2927*

Unemployment *See also* Employment; Unemployment Insurance.

—. 1960-76. *1519*

—. 1970's. *1550*

—. Age. Sex. 1957-70. *1606*

—. Atlantic Provinces. Capital. Social classes. 1972-77. *2172*

—. Charities. Cities. Poverty. 1815-60. *2157*

—. Economic Conditions. 1975. *1518*

—. Economic Conditions. Men. USA. Women. 1950-73. *1533*

—. Economic Structure. 1971-74. *1528*

—. Federal Government. Labor Disputes. Ontario, southern. 1901-20's. *89*

—. Federal government. Social policy. 1918-21. *1190*

—. Federal government. Taxation. Wealth distribution. 1977. *1635*

—. Federal Policy. 1978. *1526*

—. Federal Policy. Immigration. 1950-77. *1410*

—. Industrialized Countries. USA. 1974-76. *1585*

—. Labor. Regression results (cross-section, time series). -1973. *1612*

—. Poverty. Winter. 1815-60. *779*

—. Youth. 1973. *1568*

Unemployment insurance. Canadian Labour Congress Executive Council. 1974-75. *1619*

—. Labor. 1953-73. *1576*

Ungava Bay region. Fisheries. Hudson's Bay Company. Salmon. 1830's-1939. *2653*

Ungava Peninsula. Artifacts. Eskimos. Europeans. Labrador. Quebec. ca 400-18c. *300*

Uniates. Fuga, Francis J. Ontario (Hamilton). Shrine of Our Lady of Klococov. Slovak Canadians. 1952-77. *2895*

Uniforms, Military. British North America. Great Britain. Indian Affairs Department. 1755-1823. *632*

—. Buttons, Phoenix. Haiti. Indians. Pacific Northwest. Trade. 1812-30. 20c. *460*

—. Canadian Voltiguer Regiment. Glengarry Light Infantry Fencible Regiment. War of 1812. 1812-16. *755*

—. Royal Canadian Mounted Police. 1873-1900. *190*

Union Steamship Company. British Columbia. Daily life. 1889-1959. *3185*

Union (USA 1861-65). *See* Civil War; also names of US Government agencies, bureaus, and departments, e.g., Bureau of Indian Affairs, War Department.

Unions. *See* Labor Unions and Organizations.

United Automobile Workers (Canadian Region). Aged. Labor Unions and Organizations. Pensions. 1973. *1580*

—. Ford Motor Company of Canada. Labor Law. Ontario (Windsor). Rand formula. 1945-46. *1534*

—. Ford Motor Company of Canada. Labor Law. Ontario (Windsor). Rand formula. 1946. *1595*

United Church of Canada. Archives. Methodist Church. Presbyterian Church. 18c-1973. *233*

—. Church History. Ecumenism. 1920-76. *29*

—. Ecclesiastical authority. Protestantism. 1925-73. *1401*

—. Eucharistic worship. Protestantism. Religion. 1952-72. *1452*

—. Evangelism. Methodism. 18c-20c. *85*

—. Fairbairn, R. Edis. Pacifism. Protestantism. World War II. 1939. *1241*

—. Immigration. Nationalism. Protestant churches. 1902-25. *1194*

—. Presbyterian Church. 1925. *1185*

United Farm Women of Alberta. Alberta. Depressions. Educational role. 1915-30. *3161*

United Farmers of Alberta. Alberta. Elections, provincial. Liberal Party. Social Credit League. 1905-73. *3107*

United Farmers of Canada. Co-operative Commonwealth Federation. Political Participation. Saskatchewan. 1930-45. *3047*

United Farmers of Ontario. Elections. Farmers. Orange Order. Political Attitudes. 1920-25. *2839*

United Mine Workers of America. Alberta (Drumheller Valley). Labor disputes. One Big Union. 1919. *3163*

United States. *See* entries beginning with the word American; states; regions, e.g. New England, Western States, etc.; British North America; also names of government agencies and departments, e.g., Bureau of Indian Affairs, State Department, etc.

Unity movement. Alberta. Political Parties. 1935-45. *3148*

Upper Canada Club. Business. Elites. Ontario (Toronto). 1835-40. *812*

Upper classes. Corporations. Social Mobility. 1951-72. *1369*

Upper Classes (British). Public Schools. Sports. Upper Canada. 1830-75. *2852*

Urban hierarchy. Ontario. Quantitative sources, utility of. Quebec. Transportation. 1861-1901. *2137*

Urban historians. Building plans. Insurance. Land use atlases. Research. 1696-1973. *86*

Urban history. Bibliographies. 19c-20c. *221*

—. Canadian Urban History Conference. 1977. *116*

—. Canadian Urban History Conference. 19c-20c. 1977. *220*

—. Centre for Urban and Community Studies. Ontario (Toronto). Rural-Urban Studies. 1965-78. *1352*

—. Conference on the Historical Urbanization of North America. North America. 1977. *117*

—. Geography. Ontario. Prehistory-1976. *1317*

—. Immigrants. Macedonians. Ontario (Toronto). 20c. *2786*

—. Immigrants. Ontario (Toronto). Stereotypes. 19c-20c. *2784*

—. Methodology. 1960's-70's. *224*

—. Maps. Public Archives of Canada. Research. 1865-1905. *917*

—. Western Canadian Urban History Conference (papers). 1974. *2954*

Urban Renewal *See also* Housing.

—. Architecture, Victorian. Industrialization. New Brunswick (Saint John). 17c-1966. *2399*

—. Elections, municipal and provincial. Ontario (Kitchener). 1967-71. *2889*

—. Ontario (Toronto). 1970-73. *2734*

Urbanization *See also* City Planning; Modernization; Rural-Urban Studies.

—. Agricultural economy. Prairies. Railroads. 1871-1916. *2957*

—. Agricultural Production. Climate. Energy shortages. Food supply. 1956-74. *1511*

—. Alberta. Bureaucratization. Criminal sentencing. Indians. 1973. *1663*

—. Alberta (Banff, Calgary). Recreation. 1890. *3162*

—. Attitudes. Migration, Internal. Rural-Urban Studies. 1955-75. *1366*

—. Banking (locations). Quebec (Montreal). 1966-71. *2654*

—. British Columbia (Vancouver). 1871-1974. *3242*

—. Business. Economic growth. Manitoba (Winnipeg). Political Leadership. 1874-1914. *2968*

—. Census. Research. 1950's-78. *1353*

—. Central Place System. Ontario (Guelph area). Quantitative Methods. 1851-1970. *2753*

—. City Government. Economic growth. Public Administration. Quebec (Montreal). Social Conditions. 1850-1914. *2441*

—. City government. Manitoba (Winnipeg). Political Corruption. Public Administration. 1884-85. *3013*

—. Culture. Economic Growth. Ontario (Toronto). 1850-1914. *2863*

—. Economic Growth. Nova Scotia (Halifax). 1815-1914. *2356*

—. Economic Growth. Ontario (Ottawa). 19c. *2872*

—. Ethnic groups. French Canadians. Geographic space. Multiculturalism. Quebec. Regionalism. 1930-73. *2715*

—. Historical Sites and Parks. Quebec (Orléans Island). 1969-76. *2490*

—. Historiography. 17c-1974. *222*

—. Industrialization. Quebec. 1941-61. *2613*

—. Land. Population. 1970-74. *1483*

—. Manitoba (Winnipeg). Streetcars. 1881-1913. *3006*

—. Mennonites. Social Customs. USA. 1961-71. *1379*

—. Ontario (Guelph Region). 1824-1971. *2752*

—. Quebec (Quebec). 1790-1840. *2522*

—. Rural-Urban Studies. 1955-75. *1362*

Uruguay. France. Great Britain. Jews. Poverty. 1975. *1389*

USSR *See also* Russia.

—. Alaska. Arctic. Mining. Scandinavia. 1917-78. *3288*

—. Alaska. Railroads. World War II. 1942-43. *1248*

—. Bernard, Joseph-Fidèle (diary). Chukchi natives. Firearms. Trade. 1921-22. *1166*

—. China. Developing nations. Foreign relations. USA. 1950-75. *1824*

—. China. Foreign Relations. International Trade. USA. 1969-72. *1853*

—. Cold War. Diplomacy. 1946-47. *1885*

—. Communism. Europe, Eastern. Historiography. Public administration. USA. ca 1850-1975. *1316*

—. *Der Bote* (newspaper). Germans, Russian. Mennonites. Nazism. Saskatchewan. Völkisch thought. 1917-39. *3077*

—. Detente. Foreign Policy. USA. 1947-75. *1925*

—. Diplomacy. Sharp, Mitchell. 1973. *1813*

—. Diplomacy. Sharp, Mitchell. 1973. *1848*

—. Foreign relations. USA. 1970-73. *1898*

—. Foreign Relations. Working class. 1917-73. *1944*

Utilities. *See* Public Utilities.

Utopias *See also* Communes.

—. British Columbia (Harmony Island). Finnish Americans. Kurikka, Matti. 1901-05. *3213*

—. Industrialization. National Self-image. Population. 20c. *26*

V

Vaccination program. Indians. Métis. Smallpox. Traders. 1837-38. *439*

Vaillancourt, Philippe (account). Labor movement. Quebec. 1936-76. *2589*

Valade, François-Xavier (medical report). Mental Illness. Riel, Louis. Saskatchewan (Regina). Treason. Trials. 1885. *973*

Vallee, Frank. French Canadians. Manitoba. Social Customs. 1970-74. *2970*

Values *See also* Attitudes; Public Opinion.

—. Children. Inequality (perceived). Ontario (Toronto area). Public schools. Social Classes. 1977. *1345*

—. Cree Indians. Indians. Names (assignation). 20c. *355*

—. Eskimos. Television. 1976-77. *330*

—. Eskimos, Inuit. Family. Personality. 1974. *333*

—. Folk music. Political protest. Social change. 1776-1976. *1377*

—. France. Huron Indians. Indians (review article). Jaenen, Cornelius J. Trigger, Bruce G. 1600-60. 1976. *520*

—. Frontier. Letters. Ontario (Upper Canada). Painting. Simcoe, Elizabeth. 1790-1800. *638*

—. Individualism. 1850-1914. *942*

—. Mass media. Science and Society. Teachers. Youth. 1920's-75. *1391*

—. Nationalism. Students. USA. 1967-71. *2051*

Vancouver City Archives. British Columbia. 19c-20c. *3227*

Vancouver, George. Discovery and Exploration. Great Britain. Netherlands. North America. 1778-98. *666*

—. Great Britain. Landscape Painting. Menzies, Archibald. Nature. ca 1775-1800. *633*

Vanger, Max. Immigration. Jews. New York City. 1900-50. *1143*

VanNorman, Joseph. Cast Iron. Stoves, cooking. 1820-80's. *195*

Vatican Council II. Catholic Church. Ontario (Toronto). St. Basil's Seminary. 1962-67. *2806*

Vaudeville. Architecture. Capitol Theatre. Entertainment. Movie palaces. Ontario (Ottawa). 1920-70. *1138*

Vermont *See also* New England; Northeastern or North Atlantic States.

—. American Revolution. Bennington (battle). Burgoyne, John. Stark, John. 1777. *730*

—. Boundaries. Great Britain. International Trade. 1763-1815. *630*

—. Boundaries. Quebec. 1684-1933. *662*

—. Burchard, Jedediah. Protestants. Revivals. Social Conditions. 1835-36. *815*

—. Confederate Army. St. Albans (raid). Young, Bennett H. 1864. *868*

—. French Americans. Historiography. Research. 1609-1976. *2583*

—. Jackman, Alonzo. Military Strategy. New York. Quebec. Travel. 1838. *2443*

—. *Patriote* uprising. Rebellions. 1837-38. *810*

—. Quebec (Lower Canada; Potton). Rebellion of 1837. Woods, N. R. (letter). 1837-38. *816*

Vermont Historical Society Library. Bibliographies. French Americans. French Canadians. 1609-1976. *504*

Vermont (Montpelier, Shoreham). Anderson, William J. House of Representatives. Negroes. Political Leadership. 1900-40's. *2565*

Vermont (Winooski). Assimilation. Catholic Church. French Americans. 1867-1900. *2469*

Versailles Treaty (Article X). Foreign Relations. Great Britain. Japan. 1919-21. *1168*

Vertical integration. Economic Theory. Mining. 1960's. *1513*

Victoria Gas Company. British Columbia. Public Utilities. 1860's-90's. *3246*

Videotaping. External Affairs Department (Historical Division). Oral history. 1971-76. *1255*

—. Oral History. USA. 1855-77. *164*

Vietnam. International assistance. USA. War damage repair agency. 1972. *1760*

Vietnam War. Economic conditions. Foreign policy. Race relations. USA. 1970's. *2078*

—. Foreign Policy. Gauvin, Michel (speech). International Commission for Supervision and Control. Sharp, Mitchell. 1973. *1950*

—. International Commission for Supervision and Control. Peacekeeping Forces. 1954-73. *1774*

—. International Commission for Supervision and Control. Peacekeeping Forces. 1973. *1795*

—. International Commission for Supervision and Control. Peacekeeping Forces. 1973. *1938*

—. Jews. USA. 1969-73. *1252*

Vikings. Atlantic Coast. Discovery and Exploration. Historical Sites and Parks. North America. 10c-14c. 20c. *483*

—. Discovery and Exploration. Excavations. Newfoundland (L'Anse aux Meadows). 1000. 1961-68. *480*

—. Discovery and Exploration. Forgeries. North America. Vinland map. 15c. 1957. *482*

—. Discovery and Exploration. North America. Voyages. 985-1975. *477*

—. Excavations. Quebec (Ungava Peninsula). Prehistory. 1965. *479*

—. Maine. Massachusetts. Newfoundland. Runestones. 986-1121. *481*

Villages *See also* Rural Settlements.

—. Alberta (Athabasca Landing). Canadian Northern Railway. *Edmonton Bulletin* (newspaper). Railroads. 1912-77. *3113*

Villiers, Charles E. Knollin, William Mortimer. Marshall, Samuel. Nova Scotia. Pioneers. 19c. *2309*

Vincent, Thomas. Church of England. Missions and Missionaries. Ontario (Moosonee). 1835-1910. *3296*

Vinland map. Discovery and Exploration. Forgeries. North America. Vikings. 15c. 1957. *482*

—. Discovery and Exploration. Geographical ideas, history of. Maps. 1974. *484*

Violence. Behavior (aggressive). Hockey. Ontario (Toronto). Sports. 1972. *2862*

—. Civil rights. Law. Mexico. USA. 18c-1974. *52*

—. Culture. Revolution. USA. 1776-1976. *61*

—. Developing nations. International law. UN. 1945-75. *1739*

—. Economic Conditions. Ontario. Quebec. Social Change. 1963-73. *2127*

—. Elections. New Brunswick (Northumberland County). Street, John Ambrose. 1842. *2403*

—. Federal government. 1869-1935. *231*

—. Indian-White Relations. Ontario (Manitoulin Island). 1860-65. *410*

Virginia *See also* Southeastern States.

—. American Revolution. Colonization. Loyalists. New Brunswick. Saunders, John. 1774-1834. *740*

—. Congress. Jackson, John George. Nationalism. Republicanism. War of 1812. 1813-17. *754*

Virginia (Petersburg). Fort Meigs. Harrison, William Henry. Ohio. Volunteer Armies. War of 1812. 1812-13. *765*

Virginia (Richmond). Davis, Jefferson. Lincoln, Abraham. Peace mission. 1864. *838*

Vital Statistics *See also* Birth Rate; Census; Mortality; Population.

—. Charbonneau, Hubert. Dechêne, Louise (review article). Family structure. Migration. Quebec. 1660-1713. 1974-75. *527*

Vocabulary. *See* Language.

—. British Columbia (southern). Fishing. 1975. *3201*

Völkisch thought. *Der Bote* (newspaper). Germans, Russian. Mennonites. Nazism. Saskatchewan. USSR. 1917-39. *3077*

Voluntary associations. Bibliographies. Europe. Literary associations (French-language). Quebec. USA. 1840-1900. *2524*

—. Canadian Institute of Longueuil. 1857-60. *2525*

—. Ontario. Political participation. Students. 1970. *2749*

Volunteer Armies *See also* Military Service.

—. 1945-76. *1283*

—. Fort Meigs. Harrison, William Henry. Ohio. Virginia (Petersburg). War of 1812. 1812-13. *765*

Volunteers. Boer War. Military service, British. Patriotism. Socioeconomic characteristics. 1899-1902. *1099*

—. Flags. Military museum (collection). North America. Yugoslavia (Belgrade). 1917-18. 1974. *1162*

Voter registration. Political apathy. Puerto Rico. 1974-77. *1957*

Voting and Voting Behavior *See also* Elections; Suffrage.

—. Accountability. Foreign policy. 1950's-74. *1872*

—. Age. Political Participation. 1968. *1650*

—. Alberta (Edmonton). City councillors. Decisionmaking. Municipal government. 1966-72. *3134*

—. British Columbia. Elections (federal). Political Parties. 1974. *3231*

—. British Columbia. New Democratic Party. Political Indicators. 1968-74. *3212*

—. British Columbia (Victoria). Elections (provincial). 1972. *3249*

—. Businessmen. Ontario (Thunder Bay). 1968-71. *2829*

—. Campaign Finance. Manitoba. Political success. Quebec. 1975. *1728*

—. Catholic Church. Macdonald, John. 1850's-91. *1059*

—. Cities. Conservative Party. Ontario, southern. 1908-19. *2844*

—. Cities. USA. 1952-68. *1649*

—. Cultural cleavages. Models. Occupational categories. 1965-71. *1470*

—. Elections (federal). 1974. *1702*

—. Elections, federal. Government, majority. Public Opinion. 1965-74. *1686*

—. Elections, federal. Municipalities, redistributing. Political Parties. Quebec. 1968. *2422*

—. Entropy concept. Information theory. Political Parties. 1962-69. *1683*

—. Ethnic Groups. Manitoba (Winnipeg). Social Classes. 1941. *3014*

—. Ethnic Groups. Manitoba (Winnipeg). Social Classes. 1945-46. *3023*

—. Legislative assembly. Quebec (Lower Canada). 1792-1814. *701*

—. Liberal Party. Manitoba. New Democratic Party. Progressive Conservative Party. 1953-73. *3020*

—. Liberal Party. Ridings. 1968. *1637*

—. Military Service. Political Campaigns. World War I. 1917. *1159*

—. Ontario (Toronto). Social Status. 1971. *1662*

—. Parishes. Quebec (Saint-Hyacinthe County). Regional complexity. 1867-86. *2555*

—. Political Parties. 1975. *1671*

—. Political Parties. 1926-72. *1714*

—. Political Parties. USA. 1948-74. *1730*

—. Political Science. Research. 1967-75. *1655*

—. Political socialization. Religion. 1965. *1670*

—. Social Classes. 1975. *1319*

Voyages *See also* Aeronautics; Explorers; Ocean Travel; Travel; Whaling Industry and Trade.

—. Alaska. Anián, strait of. British Columbia. Cook, James. Discovery and Exploration. Northwest Passage. 1778. *675*

—. Arctic. Bellot, Joseph René. Franklin, John. Kennedy, William. *Prince Albert* (vessel). 1851. *3307*

—. Arctic. *Thetis* (vessel). Whaling vessels (converted). 1881-1950. *3290*

—. Brendan, Saint. Discovery and Exploration. Ireland. North America. 500-85. 1976-77. *488*

—. Cabot, John. Day, John (letter). Morison, Samuel Eliot. Newfoundland (Cape Bonavista). 1497-98. *486*

—. Discovery and Exploration. North America. Vikings. 985-1975. *477*

—. Evans, James. Missions and Missionaries. Ontario (Lake Superior). Wesleyan Methodist Church. 1837-38. *2810*

—. Fur trade. Genealogy. Godbout, Archange. New France. Population. 1608-1763. *565*

—. *Hector* (vessel). Immigrants. Nova Scotia (Pictou Harbor). Scotland. 1773. *2340*

—. Rio de la Plata. Schooners. Trade. ca 1860-1914. *935*

W

Wade, Norman. Atlantic Coast. Blockade-running. Civil War. Letters. Nova Scotia. 1859-62. *841*

—. Blockades. Civil War. Letters. Nova Scotia. 1861-62. *889*

—. Civil War. Letters. Navies. Nova Scotia. 1859-62. *842*

Wages *See also* Prices.

—. 1971. *1613*

—. Anti-Inflation Act. Emergency powers. Peacetime. Supreme Court (Canada). 1976. *1607*

—. Anti-Inflation Board. Collective bargaining. Labor Unions and Organizations. 1975. *1630*

—. Canadian Labour Congress. Federal government. Political protest. 1976. *1563*

—. Civil Service. Quebec. USA. 1970's. *2599*

—. Collective bargaining. Public Employees. 1960-70's. *1538*

—. Competitiveness. Corporations. Productivity. 1970-77. *1622*

—. Cyclones. Legislation. Ontario. Sex Discrimination. Wages. 1946-71. *2777*

—. Cyclones. Legislation. Ontario. Sex Discrimination. Wages. 1946-71. *2777*

—. Economics. Employment. Immigration. 1970's. *1588*

—. Food costs. 1961-73. *1535*

—. Fringe benefits, cost of. Working Conditions. 1973. *1586*

—. Housework. Politics. Women. 1970's. *1692*

—. Immigration. Ontario (Toronto). 1971. *2871*

Wagner, William. Lutheran Church, Missouri Synod. Manitoba (Township Berlin). ca 1870. *1029*

Wakeham, William. Arctic islands. Discovery and Exploration. Hudson Strait (navigability). 1897. *3304*

Wallace, Dillon. Explorers. Hubbard, Leonidas. Labrador (northeast). 1903-05. *3313*

Wallot, J.-P. Agricultural crisis. Historiography. Ouellet, Fernand. Paquet, Gilles. Quebec (Lower Canada). 1802-12. 1963-73. *789*

Walsh, James. Frontier and Pioneer Life. Manitoba (Red River region). North West Mounted Police. Sitting Bull (chief). 1873-1905. *1030*

Walton, Jacob (identity). Genealogy. Nova Scotia (Cornwallis). ca 1811-1914. *2252*

Wann, Clyde. Airmail flights. Yukon Territory. 1927-35. *3330*

War *See also* names of wars, battles, etc., e.g. American Revolution, Gettysburg (battle), etc.; Civil War; International Law; Military; Military Strategy; Naval Strategy; Refugees.

—. Acadia. France. New England. Phips, William. 1689-1713. *597*

—. French and Indian War. New England. Rhetoric. 1754-60. *620*

War damage repair agency. International assistance. USA. Vietnam. 1972. *1760*

War Department. Canol Project. Foster, W. W. Oil Industry and Trade. USA. 1942-45. *1219*

War Measures Act (Canada, 1914). Rhetoric. Social action. Trudeau, Pierre Elliott. 1970. *1301*

War of 1812. American Revolution. USA. 1759-20c. *634*

—. Canadian Voltiguer Regiment. Glengarry Light Infantry Fencible Regiment. Uniforms, Military. 1812-16. *755*

—. Châteauguay (battle). Quebec. 1813. *763*

—. Congress. Jackson, John George. Nationalism. Republicanism. Virginia. 1813-17. *754*

—. Defense. Great Britain. USA. 1812-14. *767*

—. Defense Policy. Hartford Convention. Militia. New England. 1812-15. *757*

—. Dobbins, Daniel. Lake Erie (battle of). Madison, James. Perry, Oliver Hazard. Warships. 1812-13. *762*

—. Fort Meigs. Harrison, William Henry. Ohio. Virginia (Petersburg). Volunteer Armies. 1812-13. *765*

—. Ghost ship. Myths and Symbols. Nova Scotia (Mahone Bay). *Young Teazer* (vessel). 1812-1976. *764*

—. Great Britain. Navies. Nova Scotia (Halifax). 1795-1815. *760*

—. Lake Champlain (battle). Northeastern or North Atlantic States. 1814. *758*

—. Ontario. Queenston Heights (battle). Upper Canada. 1812. *766*

—. Smuggling. USA. 1812-15. *761*

War of 1812 (Antecedents). Conquest (discouraged). Lyon, Matthew (letter). Monroe, James. USA. 1811. *756*

War Office. Civil service. Committee of Imperial Defence. Defense policy. Great Britain. 1896-1914. *1092*

Warships. Dobbins, Daniel. Lake Erie (battle of). Madison, James. Perry, Oliver Hazard. War of 1812. 1812-13. *762*

Washington. American Federation of Labor. Industrial Workers of the World. One Big Union. 1919. *1167*

—. British Columbia. Lumber and Lumbering. Maine. McInnis, George (interview). 1894-1949. *3261*

Washington (Bainbridge Island). Lumber and Lumbering. Port Blakely Mill Company. 1888-1903. *2257*

Washington (Puget Sound area). British Columbia. Northwestern International Yachting Association. Yacht racing, organized. 1870-1914. *32C7*

Washington (Whatcom County). British Columbia. Foreign investments. Jurisdictional law. Land ownership. 1970's. *2047*

Waste disposal. Arctic. Northwest Territories (Frobisher Bay). Water supply. 1973. *3354*

Wastes, solid. Pollution. Technology. 1973. *1334*

Watchmakers. British North America. Droz, Pierre-Frédéric. Europe. Travel. 1768-70. *685*

Water *See also* Oceans; Rivers; Snow.

—. Hydroelectric power. Planning. 1973. *1335*

Water Conservation *See also* Water Supply.

—. Ecology. North American Water and Power Alliance. USA. 1968-71. *1961*

Water Pollution *See also* Water Supply.

—. 1960's-70's. *1300*

—. Conservation of Natural Resources. International regulation. North America. 1960's-74. *1982*

Water Supply *See also* Dams; Irrigation; Water Pollution.

—. Arctic. Northwest Territories (Frobisher Bay). Waste disposal. 1973. *3354*

—. British Columbia (Vancouver). Sanitation. 1886-1976. *3180*

—. Manitoba (Winnipeg). Ontario (Lake of the Woods). 1912-75. *2997*

—. USA. 1909-78. *143*

Water use (theories). Economic Policy. Quebec. 1970's. *1324*

Waterfowl. Government. Great Plains. Hunting. Mississippi Flyway. North Central States. Spring shooting issue. 1887-1913. *906*

Waterfront. Architecture. Historical Sites and Parks. Nova Scotia (Halifax). 1815-1973. *2229*

Waterpower *See also* Hydroelectric Power.

—. Dams. Energy crisis. Farms. Ontario (Osceola). 1902-05. *2813*

Waterton Lakes National Park. Alberta. Birney, Earle (reminiscences). Surveying. 1921. *3098*

Watkin, Edward. Communications (Transcontinental). Railroads. Telegraph. 1860-65. *884*

Watkins, Kathleen ("Kit of the Mail"). Jarvis, Stinson. Ontario. Psychic phenomena. 1885-95. *2891*

Waugh School District. Alberta (Edmonton). Homesteading and Homesteaders. Rural Schools. 1901-40's. *3166*

Wawanosh Home for Indian Girls. Indians. Indian-White Relations. Ontario (Sault Ste. Marie). Schools. Shingwauk Industrial Home. Wilson, E. F. 1871-93. *475*

Wealth distribution. Federal government. Taxation. Unemployment. 1977. *1635*

Weapons *See also* Armaments; Firearms; Ordnance.
—. Defense policy. 1976-78. *1285*
—. Indians. Manitoba, southwestern. Tools. ca 10,000 BC-1600 AD. *308*
—. Military. Technology. 1970-76. *1277*

Weather *See also* Climate; Snow; Storms.
—. Alberta (Medicine Hat). Beverly, James. 1899. *3103*

Weatherhead family. Genealogy. Nova Scotia (Hants County). ca 1820-1946. *2272*

Weavers. Arctic Ocean. Great Britain. Navies. Whalers. 1818-25. *3300*

Webb, Beatrice. Great Britain. Political Commentary. Social change. Socialism. Webb, Sidney James. 1911. *1090*

Webb, Ralph. City Politics. Manitoba (Winnipeg). Penner, Jacob. 1919-34. *2993*

Webb, Sidney James. Great Britain. Political Commentary. Social change. Socialism. Webb, Beatrice. 1911. *1090*

Weber, Anna. Folk Art. Fraktur. Mennonites. Ontario (Waterloo County). 1825-88. *2836*

Webster, John Clarence. Authors. Educators. Mount Allison University. New Brunswick (Sackville). 1882-1950. *2404*

Wedding night pranks. Humor. New Brunswick (western). Social Customs. 18c-1974. *2396*

Wegg, Samuel. Geography. Hudson's Bay Company. Societies. 1750-1800. *683*
—. Great Britain. Hudson's Bay Company. Royal Society of Canada. 1753-1802. *682*

Welfare. *See* Public Welfare.

Welfare state. Marsh, Leonard *(Report)*. Social Security. Socialism. 1930-44. *1200*

Welland Canal. Bombings. Clan-na-Gael. Dillon, Luke. Irish Americans. Ontario (Thorold). 1900-14. *1083*
—. Ontario (Lake Ontario, Lake Erie). 1967-73. *2856*

Wells, Debi. Imperialism (review article). Leftism. Moore, Steve. Nationalism. 1960's-70's. *1269*

Wells, Harold. Fur Trade. Manitoba. Registered Trap Lines system. Trapping. 1940-53. *3011*

Welsh. Pioneers. Saskatchewan. 1902-14. *3069*

Welsh, Matthew. Children. Education. Nova Scotia (Guysborough). Wills. 19c. *2267*

Wentworth, John. Forests and Forestry. Great Britain. Kennebeck Purchase Company. Mast policy, royal. New England. 1769-78. *718*
—. Lifesaving service. Nova Scotia (Sable Island). 1801. *2236*

Wesleyan Methodist Church. Evans, James. Missions and Missionaries. Ontario (Lake Superior). Voyages. 1837-38. *2810*
—. Indians. McDougall, John. Missions and Missionaries. Prairie provinces. 1860-1917. *386*

West family. Genealogy. Nova Scotia (Halifax, Lunenburg). Wuest, Johann Wendel. 17c-20c. *2330*

West Indians. Discrimination. Economic Conditions. Ontario (Toronto). 1977. *2768*
—. Discrimination, Employment. Immigrants. Ontario (Toronto). Social Status. 1972. *2849*

West Indies *See also* individual islands by name; British West Indies.
—. Arnold, Benedict, Arnold, Peggy. Great Britain. New Brunswick. 1781-1801. *2374*

West Indies (Montserrat). Domestics. Social Mobility. Social networks. Women. 1960's-75. *1935*

West Virginia *See also* Southeastern States.
—. Minnesota. Nova Scotia. Petroglyphs. Scandinavians. 14c. *478*

Western Canadian Urban History Conference (papers). Urban history. 1974. *2954*

Western civilization. Christianity. Cultural transmission. Maritime Provinces. Micmac Indians. 1970's. *344*

Western civilization (review article). Diffusion. Geography. Gordon, Cyrus H. Riley, Carroll. Transoceanic contacts. Prehistory-1492. *304*

Western history. Discovery and Exploration. Romanticism. 1540-1800. *579*

Western Nations *See also* Industrialized Countries.

—. Economic Conditions. Industry. 1969-71. *1561*

Western Ontario, University of. Alienation. Ontario. Socialization. Student activism. 1970. *2773*

Western Ontario, University of, D. B. Weldon Library (Hitchins Collection). Aeronautics (history). Archival Catalogs and Inventories. Hitchins, Fred H. 20c. *94*

Western Provinces *See also* British Columbia; Prairie provinces.
—. Artists. Clymer, John. North America. 1960's-70's. *1460*
—. Communications. Frontier and Pioneer Life. Hutterites. 1874-1977. *1022*
—. Explorers. France. 18c. *586*

Western States *See also* individual states.
—. Agricultural Technology and Research. Prairie Provinces. Steam tractors. 1890-1925. *2913*
—. Bibliographies. *Dissertation Abstracts*. 1973. *2903*
—. Bibliographies. Dissertations. 1974-75. *2955*
—. Cattle Raising. Prairie Provinces. 1880's-1900. *968*
—. Painting. Schoonover, Frank. 1899-1968. *2951*

Westmacott, John (murder of). Devit, Charles. M'Grath, Michael. Nova Scotia (Halifax). Trials. 1816. *2243*

Westward Movement *See also* Cowboys; Frontier and Pioneer Life; Overland Journeys to the Pacific; Pioneers.
—. Land. Population. Social change. 1850's-67. *850*

Whalers. Arctic Ocean. Great Britain. Navies. Weavers. 1818-25. *3300*

Whales, bowhead. Arctic. Whaling Industry and Trade. Wildlife Conservation. Prehistory-1976. *3293*

Whaling industry and Trade. American Revolution. France. Protestants. Settlement. USA. 17c-20c. *1287*
—. American Revolution. Friends, Society of. Massachusetts (Nantucket Island). 1750's-1800. *733*
—. Anderson, James. Hudson's Bay Company. Quebec (Eastmain River). Rivers. 1850's-70. *847*
—. Arctic. Whales, bowhead. Wildlife Conservation. Prehistory-1976. *3293*
—. Arctic Ocean. Eskimos. Mackenzie Bay (Herschel Island). Polar exploration. 1826-1972. *339*
—. Basques. Labrador. 16c. *557*
—. Hudson's Bay Company. Northwest Territories (Marble Island). *Perseverance* (vessel). 1866-67. 1892-97. *681*

Whaling vessels (converted). Arctic. *Thetis* (vessel). Voyages. 1881-1950. *3290*

Wheat. Alberta. Harvests. Photographs. 1910-20. *3168*
—. Campbell, Thomas D. Droughts. Farm income. Great Plains. Prairie Provinces. 1915-1940. *2964*
—. China. Foreign relations. 1970-77. *1817*
—. Economic competition. Great Britain. USA. 1900-14. *1102*
—. Farms. Immigrants. Manitoba (Brandon). Railroads. 1880-87. *961*
—. Income. 1901-11. 1966-75. *1096*

Whigs. Durham, 1st Earl of. Great Britain. 1838-40. *829*

Whipple, Seth A. Artists. Great Lakes. Nickerson, Vincent D. Norton, Charles W. Ships. Sprague, Howard F. 1844-1901. *2861*

Whiskey. Distilling industry. 1668-1976. *181*

White Mountain Grand Hotel. Fabyan, Horace. Hotel trade. New Hampshire (Portland). 1807-81. *772*

White Pass and Yukon Railway. Railroads. ca 1900-73. *3326*

White Pass Aviation. Air Lines. Alaska. Yukon Territory. 1934-40. *3331*

Whites. Africans. Asians. Indians. North America. Racism. 1600-1900. *10*
—. Education. Eskimos. Indians. Métis. Northwest Territories (Mackenzie District). 1969-70. *3358*
—. Indians. Nationalism. Nova Scotia (Cape Breton). Political socialization. Regionalism. 1860's-1970's. *2361*

Whitman, Walt (interview). Bucke, Richard M. Ontario (London). 1880. *1055*

Wickett, Samuel Morley. City government. Ontario (Toronto). Progressivism. 1900-15. *2885*

Wilde, Oscar ("The House Beautiful"). Lectures. USA. 1882. *1061*

Wildlife Conservation *See also* Forests and Forestry; Great Plains; National Parks and Reserves; Natural Resources.
—. Arctic. Hunting. Ringed seals. Seals. 1966-73. *335*
—. Arctic. Whales, bowhead. Whaling Industry and Trade. Prehistory-1976. *3293*
—. Birds, migratory. Federal government. International Migratory Bird Treaty (1916). USA. 1883-1917. *920*
—. Caribou. Quebec. 20c. *267*
—. Fur trade. Japan. Sea otters. 18c-20c. *257*

Wildlife diseases. Demography. Epidemics. Fur trade. Indians. 15c-18c. *425*

Wilkie, John. Counterintelligence (US). Gage, Lyman. Quebec (Montreal). Spanish-American War. Spy ring, Spanish. 1898. *1094*

William, Eileen (recollections). Frontier and Pioneer Life. Gold Mines and Mining. Ontario (Casummit Lake). 1930's. *2888*

William IV (visit). Great Britain. Newfoundland. *Pegasus* (vessel). 1786. *2193*

Williams, W. H. (travel account). Alberta (Calgary, Edmonton). 1881. *1031*

Williams, Wesley. Alberta. Construction. Housing. Settlement. Sod. 1909. *1004*

Williams, William Fenwick. Civil War. Great Britain. Military. 1859-67. *881*

Wills. Children. Education. Nova Scotia (Guysborough). Welsh, Matthew. 19c. *2267*

Willson, Thomas Leopold "Carbide". Calcium carbide, manufacture of. Electrochemistry. Inventions. 1860-1915. *939*

Wilson, E. F. Indians. Indian-White Relations. Ontario (Sault Ste. Marie). Schools. Shingwauk Industrial Home. Wawanosh Home for Indian Girls. 1871-93. *475*

Wilson, Edward F. Church of England. Indians. Missions and Missionaries. Ontario (Algoma, Huron). 1868-93. *432*

Wilson, John A. Nova Scotia. Sculpture. USA. 1877-1954. *2301*

Wilson, W. A. Dairying. Government. Motherwell, W. R. Saskatchewan. Subsidies. 1906-17. *3037*

Winchester, Alice. Folk Art (review article). Harper, Russell. Lipman, Jean. USA. 19c. *149*

Windsor, University of. Humor. Identification classes. Students. *Vicarious superiority theory*. 1969-74. *2808*

Winemaking *See also* Alcoholism.
—. 1867-1976. *192*

Winkler, H. W. (career). Brown, J. L. Liberal Party. Manitoba (Lisgar). Parliaments. 1926-53. *3021*

Winnipeg Electrical Street Railway Company. Hydroelectric plants. Manitoba (Winnipeg River; Pinawa Channel). 1903-51. *3010*

Winnipeg Light Infantry. Alberta. Manitoba. Military Medicine. North West Rebellion. Pennefather, John P. (reminiscences). 1885. *1016*

Winnipeg River. Manitoba. Ontario. 1730's-1960's. *2122*

Winter. Food Supply. Fur trade. Hudson's Bay Company. Mackenzie River Valley. Northwest Territories. 19c. *3357*
—. Heating. Housing. 1958-77. *2485*
—. Poverty. Unemployment. 1815-60. *779*

Wisconsin *See also* North Central States.

Wisconsin (North Bay, Milwaukee). Maritime history. *Pewaukee* (vessel). Shipwrecks. *Two Friends* (vessel). 1873-1913. *1048*

Wit and Humor. *See* Humor.

Witchcraft *See also* Folklore.
—. Eskimo (Aivilik). Northwest Territories (Roes Welcome Sound). 1953-73. *327*

Wolf Collar (shaman). Alberta. Blackfoot Indians. Indians. 1870-1928. *356*

Wolfe, James. French and Indian War. Quebec (Battle of). 1759. *621*

Woman Suffrage. Attitudes. English Canadians. Race. Sex. ca 1877-1918. *902*
—. Bourassa, Henri. Divorce. Feminism. 1913-25. *1142*
—. British North America Act of 1929. 1870's-1940's. *72*
—. English Canadians. Family. 1877-1918. *901*
—. Prairie Provinces. 1890's-1920's. *2958*

Woman's Canadian Club. Alberta (Calgary). Political Participation. 1911-20's. *3097*

Women *See also* Divorce; Family; Feminism;
Marriage; Prostitution; Sex Discrimination;
Woman Suffrage.
—. Aged. Minority group concept. Sociology.
1970's. *1339*
—. Alabama (Mobile). France (Paris). Iberville,
Pierre Le Moyne d'. Immigration. Population.
1702-04. *582*
—. Alaska. Gold Rushes. Klondike Stampede.
Yukon Territory. 1897-99. *3322*
—. Alberta. Oral history. Rural Settlements.
1890-1929. *3149*
—. Anglican Communion. Manitoba (Red River).
Missionary wives. 1820-37. *462*
—. Arctic, northern. Greist, Mollie Ward.
Pioneers. ca 1850-1970's. *3344*
—. *Attorney General of Canada* v. *Lavell* (Canada,
1973). Indians. Lavell, Jeannette
(Wikwemikong Indian). Sex Discrimination.
Supreme Court. 1973-74. *473*
—. Barbel, Marie-Anne. Business. New France.
18c. *575*
—. Bibliographies. Management. 1970-73. *1523*
—. British Columbia. Labor Unions and
Organizations. 1973. *3225*
—. British North America. Public schools.
Teaching. 1845-75. *880*
—. Canadian Labour Congress. Conference on
Equal Opportunity and Treatment for Women
Workers. Employment. Equal opportunity.
1978. *1558*
—. Canadian Union of Public Employees. Public
Employees. Sex discrimination. 1975. *1617*
—. Capitalism. Imperialism. Socialism. ca
1870-1975. *139*
—. Catholic Church. Congregation of Notre Dame
(Sisters). Ontario (Kingston). Religious
education. 1841-48. *2737*
—. Catholic Church. D'Aquin, Marie Thomas.
Joan of Arc Institute. Ontario (Ottawa). Social
Work. 1903-19. *2746*
—. Christianity. Missions and Missionaries. Sex
roles. 1815-99. *923*
—. Colleges and Universities. Graduates.
Occupational attainment. Ontario. Social
mobility. 1960-75. *2821*
—. Creighton, Donald. Family. Macdonald, John
A. (biography). 1843-91. *1063*
—. Diplomats. Equal employment. External
Affairs Department. 1909-75. *82*
—. Discrimination. International organizations.
1960's-70's. *1447*
—. Discrimination, Educational. Ontario. School
attendance. Social Classes. 1851-71. *2754*
—. Domestics. Social Mobility. Social networks.
West Indies (Montserrat). 1960's-75. *1935*
—. Economic Conditions. Men. Unemployment.
USA. 1950-73. *1533*
—. Educational system. Ideological structures.
Sex Discrimination. Sociology. 1970's. *1474*
—. Egalitarianism. Social Organization.
Prehistory-1977. *409*
—. Equality. 1966-76. *1349*
—. Family. Marriage. North America. Sociology.
1974. *1469*
—. Frontier and Pioneer Life. 1794-1899. *191*
—. Housework. Politics. Wages. 1970's. *1692*
—. Hughes, Helen McGill. Sociology. USA.
1916-77. *96*
—. Immigrants. North America. Occupations.
Statistics. 1964-71. *1516*
—. Immigration. Ireland. Poor Law
Commissioners. Servants. 1865. *888*
—. Indians. Quebec (Caughnawaga, Sault St.
Louis). 1852. *374*
—. International Ladies' Garment Workers' Union.
Labor Unions and Organizations. 1975. *1937*
—. Labor. Occupational segregation. 1941-71.
1502
—. Labor. World War II. 1942-46. *1240*
—. Labor law. 1951-71. *1544*
—. Massachusetts (Lowell). Mills, woolen and
cotton. Textile Industry. 1833-57. *2664*
—. Occupations. Periodicals. Sex roles. 1920's.
1195
—. Ontario. Rural Settlements. Social status.
19c. *2729*
—. Public services. Sex discrimination. 1870-1975.
213
—. Saskatchewan. Saskatoon Women Teachers'
Association. Teachers. 1918-70's. *3051*
—. Social Change. 1700-1976. *1456*
Women (review article). Labor. Marxism.
19c-1976. *71*
Women's history. 1945-75. *1341*
—. Curricula. Higher Education. Teaching.
1940-73. *1387*

Women's liberation. Political Leadership. USA.
1960-75. *1270*
Women's Liberation Movement. Social Reform.
1955-75. *1431*
—. Social Reform. Working class. 1975. *1540*
Women's rights. British Columbia Federation of
Labour. Labor Unions and Organizations.
1970-75. *3216*
Women's studies. Ideology. Research. Sociology of
knowledge. 1970's. *1430*
Wood *See also* Forests and Forestry; Lumber and
Lumbering; Wood Carving.
—. British Columbia (Queen Charlotte Islands).
Fishing gear. Haida Indians. Indians.
Prehistory. *287*
Wood carving. Architecture. Houses. Woodland,
George. 1867-1969. *2264*
Wood, Samuel. Church of England. Missions and
Missionaries. Quebec (Three Rivers). 1822-68.
658
Woodland, George. Architecture. Houses. Wood
carving. 1867-1969. *2264*
Woods, N. R. (letter). Quebec (Lower Canada;
Potton). Rebellion of 1837. Vermont. 1837-38.
816
Woodsmanship. Anderson, James. Arctic.
Expedition, search. Franklin, John. Iroquois
Indians. 1855. *3305*
Woodsworth, James S. Act of Sexual Sterilization
(Alberta, 1928). Alberta. Eugenics.
Immigration. Press. 1900-28. *2906*
Words. *See* Language; Lexicology.
Work ethic. Attitudes. Industrialization. Youth.
1950's-73. *1455*
Workers. *See* Labor; Working Class.
Working Class *See also* Labor; Peasants; Social
Classes.
—. Adult education. Halifax Mechanics' Institute.
Middle Classes. Nova Scotia. 1830's-40's.
2291
—. Adult education. Libraries. Middle classes.
Social Organization. 19c. *104*
—. Alienation. Charities. Government. Quebec
(Quebec; Lower Town). Social Problems.
1896-1914. *2637*
—. Art. Chabert, Joseph. Education. National
Institute for Arts and Crafts. Quebec
(Montreal). Teachers. 1861-94. *1053*
—. Attitudes. Industrialization. Labor Unions and
Organizations. Radicals and Radicalism.
1897-1919. *2899*
—. Business community. Nationalism. Parti
Québécois. Quebec. 1970's. *2690*
—. Catholic Church. Eudists. Industrialization.
Quebec (Chicoutimi Basin). 1903-30. *2475*
—. Foreign Relations. USSR. 1917-73. *1944*
—. French Canadians. Immigration.
Massachusetts (Holyoke). Proulx, Nicholas.
1850-1900. *2600*
—. Historiography. Quebec. 1897-1974. *2611*
—. Labor Unions and Organizations. 1845-75.
866
—. Local government. Manitoba (Winnipeg).
Political Reform. 1873-1971. *2990*
—. McLachlan, Alexander. Ontario. Poetry.
Radicals and Radicalism. Social reform.
1818-96. *924*
—. Social Reform. Women's Liberation Movement.
1975. *1540*
Working Class (review article). Historiography.
Oral history. 20c. *103*
Working Conditions. Accident prevention.
International Longshoremen's and
Warehousemen's Union. 1973. *1601*
—. Accident prevention. Management theories.
20c. *87*
—. Alienation. Automation. 1973. *1557*
—. Beaudry Report. Ham Report. Industry.
Ontario. Quebec. 1972-74. *1536*
—. Canadian Railway Labour Association.
Employment. Railroads. Technology. 1973.
1620
—. Diseases, industrial. 1970-73. *1578*
—. Fringe benefits, cost of. Wages. 1973. *1586*
—. Glass works. Living conditions. Manitoba
(Beausejour). Recreation. 1909-11. *3000*
—. Industry. Pollution. 1973. *1296*
Workmen's Compensation. Commission on
Industrial Accidents. Industry. Provincial
Government. Quebec. 1890-1978. *2623*
—. Occupational Health Act (1972). Saskatchewan.
1972-73. *3034*
Workmen's Compensation Board. Ontario.
Rehabilitation services. 1973. *2780*
World War I *See also* battles and campaigns by
name.
—. Agricultural production. Cereals. Farmers.
1911-21. *1164*

—. Aliens. Austrians. Internment camps.
1914-19. *1150*
—. Anglo-French divisions. Canadian
Expeditionary Force. Hughes, Samuel.
Imperialist sentiment. 1853-1921. *245*
—. Canadian Expeditionary Force, 41st Battalion.
French Canadians. 1914-15. *1160*
—. Casualty rates. Currie, Arthur. Hughes, Sam.
Military General Staff. 1914-30. *1156*
—. Internment operations. Otter, William.
1914-20. *1161*
—. Military Service. Political Campaigns. Voting
and Voting Behavior. 1917. *1159*
World War II *See also* battles and campaigns by
name.
—. Air Warfare. Army Air Corps. Beeson, Duane.
Idaho (Boise). 1941-45. *1222*
—. Alaska. Railroads. USSR. 1942-43. *1248*
—. Alaskan Highway. Highway Engineering.
Logistics. Yukon Territory. 1942-43. *3338*
—. Alberta, southern. British Columbia. Japanese
Canadians. 1941-45. *1233*
—. Aleutian campaign. USA. 1938-45. *1231*
—. Artillery. British Columbia. Coast defenses.
1862-1941. *1232*
—. Attitudes. Citizenship. Japanese. USA.
1941-58. *1261*
—. British Columbia. Chinese. Japanese
Canadians. Military Service. 1939-45. *1242*
—. British Columbia. Conscription, Military.
Pearkes, G. R. 1943-44. *3248*
—. British Columbia. Evacuation, forced. Federal
government. Japanese. Public opinion.
1937-42. *1247*
—. British Columbia (Prince Rupert). Coastal
defense. Diaries. Thistle, R. 1941-42. *1243*
—. British Columbia, University of. Japanese
Canadians. Race relations. 1939-42. *3177*
—. British Commonwealth. Foreign Relations.
Ireland. Neutrality. 1939-45. *1237*
—. Canol Project. Northwest Territories
(Mackenzie Valley). Oil Industry and Trade.
Pipelines. Planning. 1942-45. *3274*
—. China. Hurford, Grace Gibberd
(reminiscences). Missions and Missionaries.
Teaching. 1928-45. *1122*
—. Conference of Historic Peace Churches.
Mennonites. ca 1914-45. *1235*
—. Conscription, Military. Elections. King,
William Lyon Mackenzie. Ligue pour la
Défense du Canada. Quebec. 1942-44. *1226*
—. Cooperatives. Fishing. Pêcheurs-Unis. Quebec
(Gaspé Peninsula). 1939-48. *2638*
—. Dieppe (air battle). Great Britain.
Leigh-Mallory, Trafford. Royal Canadian Air
Force. 1942. *1220*
—. Europe. Military operations. Politics. 1939-45.
1244
—. Fairbairn, R. Edis. Pacifism. Protestantism.
United Church of Canada. 1939. *1241*
—. Foreign policy. Great Britain. USA. 1939-45.
1225
—. Foreign policy. Planning. 1943-45. *1238*
—. Foreign Relations. King, William Lyon
Mackenzie. USA. 1939-45. *1223*
—. Foreign Relations. Latin America.
Pan-American Union. USA. 1939-44. *1239*
—. French Canadians. Military Service. 1939-45.
1228
—. Great Britain. Hyde Park Declaration (1941).
USA. 1939-41. *1224*
—. Great Britain. Military Finance. 1943-45.
1227
—. Historiography. 1939-45. *1221*
—. Historiography. 1939-78. *1229*
—. Historiography. 1939-45. *1230*
—. Japanese Canadians. Race Relations.
Relocation, forced. 1890's-1940's. *1245*
—. Labor. Women. 1942-46. *1240*
World War II (antecedents). Historiography.
Press. 1938-39. *1236*
Woudbee (chief). Cree Indians. Fort Albany.
Henley House Massacres. Hudson's Bay
Company. Ontario. 1750's. *348*
Wrong, Hume (views). Foreign Relations. USA.
1927-51. *1146*
Wuest, Johann Wendel. Genealogy. Nova Scotia
(Halifax, Lunenburg). West family. 17c-20c.
2330
Wyoming *See also* Western States.
—. Bighorn River. Discovery and Exploration.
Indians. Montana. Prehistory-1965. *444*

X

XY Company. Daily life. Dufaut, J. (diary). Fur trade. Indians. Ontario (Prince Rupert's Land). 1803-04. *2956*

Y

Yacht racing, organized. British Columbia. Northwestern International Yachting Association. Washington (Puget Sound area). 1870-1914. *3207*

"Yankee Doodle" (song; origins). Folk Songs. Music. Patriotism. 1730-1820. *2295*

Yellow Calf (chief). Cree Indians. Crooked Lakes Reserves. Rations policies. Saskatchewan (Qu'Appelle Valley). 1884. *343*

Yorath, J. C. City planning. Economic growth. Real estate. Saskatchewan (Saskatoon). 1909-13. *3061*

York boats (prototypes). Henley House. Hudson's Bay Company. ca 1750's. *556*

York (vessel). Cobb, Sylvanus. Fundy, Bay of. Nova Scotia. Ships. Trade. 1755. *2163*

Young, Bennett H. Confederate Army. St. Albans (raid). Vermont. 1864. *868*

Young Men's Christian Association. Adolescence. Boys. Protestantism. USA. 1870-1920. *927*

—. Bryan, William Jennings. Fund-raising. Lectures. Prairie Provinces. 1909. *2953*

Young Teazer (vessel). Ghost ship. Myths and Symbols. Nova Scotia (Mahone Bay). War of 1812. 1812-1976. *764*

Youth *See also* Adolescence; Children; Youth Movements.

—. Attitudes. Industrialization. Work ethic. 1950's-73. *1455*

—. British Columbia. Depressions. Education Department (Recreational and Physical Education Branch). Sports. 1934-40. *3217*

—. Dialects. Language. Survey of Canadian English. 1972. *1484*

—. Mass media. Science and Society. Teachers. Values. 1920's-75. *1391*

—. Unemployment. 1973. *1568*

Youth movements. Catholicism. French Canadians. Lévesque, Georges-Henri (personal account). Nationalism. Quebec. 1930's. *2700*

Yugoslavia (Belgrade). Flags. Military museum (collection). North America. Volunteers. 1917-18. 1974. *1162*

Yukon Territory *See also* Northwest Territories.

—. Air Lines. Alaska. White Pass Aviation. 1934-40. *3331*

—. Airmail flights. Wann, Clyde. 1927-35. *3330*

—. Alaska. Gold Rushes. Klondike Stampede. Women. 1897-99. *3322*

—. Alaska Highway. British Columbia. Highways. 1974. *3325*

—. Alaska (Klukman). Discovery and Exploration. 1890. *3339*

—. Alaska (Skagway). Brackett, George. Entrepreneurs. Gold Rushes. Roads. 1897-98. *3323*

—. Alaska-British Columbia-Yukon Conferences. British Columbia. Economic development. Regional Planning. 1930-64. *2133*

—. Alaskan Highway. Highway Engineering. Logistics. World War II. 1942-43. *3338*

—. Bone tools. Indians. Man, presence of. ca 25,000 BC. *296*

—. Boomtowns. British Columbia (Bennett). Gold Rushes. 1896-99. *3183*

—. Church of England. Indians. McDonald, Robert. Missions and Missionaries. Northwest Territories. 1850's-1913. *3292*

—. Commissioners, territorial. Territorial government. 1897-1954. *3327*

—. Fur trade. Indian-White Relations. Kutchin Indians, Eastern. Northwest Territories (Mackenzie District). 1800-60. *3285*

—. Gold rushes. Great Britain. Journalism. Klondike Stampede. Shaw, Flora. *Times of London* (newspaper). 1898. *3341*

—. Gold Rushes. Klondike Gold Rush Historic Park. National Parks and Reserves. 1897-98. 1974. *3324*

—. Gold Rushes. Klondike Stampede. Photography. Restorations. 1897-98. 1970's. *3336*

—. Gold Rushes. Klondike Stampede. Quinlan, Thomas A. (letters). 1898-1904. *3337*

—. Gold Rushes. Klondike Stampede. Royal Canadian Mounted Police. 1896-99. *3335*

—. Gold Rushes. Presbyterian Church. 1897-1910. *3334*

—. Merchants. Taylor and Drury, Ltd. 1898-1924. *3342*

—. Railroads. Ships. Tourism. Travel. 20c. *3329*

Yukon Territory (Dawson). Alaska (Eagle). DeWolfe, Percy. Mail carrier. 1915-50. *3332*

—. Carnegie, Andrew. Libraries. Nicol, A. 1902-20's. *3340*

—. Fort Herchmer. Gold Rushes. Klondike Stampede. Royal Canadian Mounted Police. 1896-1905. 1972-76. *3328*

Yukon Territory (Klondike; Dawson City). Gold Rushes. 1898-1913. *3333*

Z

Zahara, Dominka Roshko. Alberta. Homesteading and Homesteaders. Peace River country. Ukrainians. 1900-30. *1034*

49th parallel. Boundaries. USA. 18c-19c. *661*

AUTHOR INDEX

A

Abu-Laban, Baha 1339
Abu-Laban, Sharon 1339
Acheson, Keith 1522
Acheson, T. W. 899
Achtenberg, Ben 3172
Adam, Judith 2724
Adams, Blaine 590
Adams, Doreen B. 312
Adams, George F. 341
Adams, George W. 1496
Adams, Samuel T. 312
Adamson, Christopher R. 1340
Aggarwal, Arjun P. 1497
Aird, Paul L. 1271
Ajao, Adenihun O. 3084
Alberts, Laurie 3322
Albinski, Henry S. 1631 2671
Albrecht-Carrie, Rene 1
Aleksandrov, Iu 1249
Alekseev, V. P. 313
Alessandri, Giuseppe 2672
Alexander, David 1498 2151
2175 2176 2177 2178
2179 2210
Ali, Mehrunnisa 1733
Allain, Mathé 578
Allaire, Georges 2455
Allaire, Yvan 2585
Allard, Jean-Louis 1499
Allen, James P. 2152
Allen, Patrick 2414
Allen, Richard 1038
Allen, Robert S. 623 624 753
Alper, Donald 3173
Altmeyer, George 264
Alwin, John A. 556 2122
Ames, Michael M. 280 342
Amody, Francis J. 1272
Anders, Leslie 834
Anderson, John C. 1500
Anderson, Michael 2725
Anderson, Stuart 835
Anderson, Terry L. 2964
Anderson, W. R. 477
Andrew, A. J. 1734
Andrew, Caroline 1632 2456
Andrews, Isabel 343
Andrews, Margaret W. 1341 3174
Angers, François-Albert 489
696 2085 2457 2458 2459
2460 2586 2673 2674 2675
Angle, John 2587
Angrave, James 2 625
Ankli, Robert E. 2964
Anton, F. R. 1501
Appavoo, Patricia J. 2123
Applebaum, Louis 1495
Appleblatt, Anthony 3024
April, Serge 1735
Aquilina, Gerald G. 1954
Archibald, Clinton 2415
Arès, Richard 3 1342 2461
2462 2463 2676
Argaez, C. 2372
Armitage, Christopher M. 4
Armstrong, Christopher 158
1078 1100 2211
Armstrong, Frederick H. 768
2726 2727
Armstrong, Gregory 1736
Armstrong, Hugh 1502
Armstrong, Pat 1502
Armstrong, Terence E. 281
Armstrong, Willis C. 1956
Arnold, A. J. 945 2965
Arnon, Ruth Soulé 5
Arroyo, Gilberto 1957
Arthur, Elizabeth 3025
Artibise, Alan F. J. 2966 2967 2968
Askey, Donald E. 1343
Astrachan, Anthony 2969
Atherton, Jay 3175
Aubéry, Pierre 2677
Audet, Louis-Philippe 1344 2416
Austin, Jack 1958
Auwarter, Ruth 2212

Avery, Donald 900 1079

B

Baar, Carl 1633
Baba, Vishwanath 1503
Babcock, Robert 2588
Babe, Robert E. 1634
Baboyant, Marie 6
Bacchi, Carol 901 902
Backeland, Lucille 2970
Baehre, Rainer 769
Baer, Hans A. 2896
Baily, Marilyn 626
Bain, George Sayers 7
Bains, Yashdip Singh 2213 2214
Baird, Frank, Jr. 2215
Baird, Ron 8
Bakan, David 9
Baker, Donald G. 10
Baker, Melvin 2180
Baker, William M. 890 891 1039 2373
Baldus, Bernd 1345
Baldwin, Alice Sharples 3085
Baldwin, Bob 1635
Baldwin, Doug 2728
Baldwin, John R. 1273
Ball, Rosemary R. 2729
Ballantyne, Janet 100
Ballard, Robert M. 2730
Balls, Herbert R. 1636
Balthazar, Louis 11 1737 1959 2678
Balueva, T. S. 313
Banks, Herbert Robertson 2216
Banks, Margaret A. 824 2731
Bannister, Geoffrey 2732 2733
Barclay, C. N. 2374
Baril, Evelyn 1023
Barker, G. 2734
Barkham, Selma 557 558 559
Barkley, Murray 12 2375
Barnds, William J. 1960
Barnett, Le Roy 3026
Barr, Brenton M. 3084
Barr, Lorna 1961
Barral, Pierre 13
Barratt, Glynn R. 1166 3298 3299 3300
Barrea, Jean 903
Barrett, F. A. 2464
Barros, James 1738
Barry, Mary J. 314
Barry, P. S. 1219 3274
Barsness, Larry 265
Barthe, Joseph-Guillaume 836
Barton, K. J. 2376
Baskerville, Peter 837
Bassett, T. D. Seymour 591
Bate, Peter 1346
Bates, David 1725
Bates, George T. 2217
Battiste, Marie 344
Battistelli, Fabrizio 2735
Battram, Shelley 2051
Bauckman, Frank A. 2218
Baudoux, Maurice 2897
Bauer, Charles 1504 1505 2589 2590
Bauer, George W. 345
Bauer, Julien 2591 2592
Baureiss, Gunter 3086
Bawtinhimer, R. E. 2736
Bayliss, Robert A. 2181
Bearss, Edwin C. 3323
Beattie, Judith 592
Beauchamp, Pierre 565
Beaudoin, Gerald 2086
Beaudry, Richard 2593
Beaupré, Viateur 2465
Beauregard, Ludger 1506
Beck, J. Murray 808 2153
Beck, Jeanne M. 1115
Becker, A. 2898 3027
Beckman, M. Dale 2923 2971
Beckman, Margaret 1347
Beckow, S. M. 904
Beeching, W. C. 1507
Beer, D. B. 825
Beesley, J. Alan 1739

Begg, Hugh M. 3176
Begnal, Calista 2737
Behuncik, Edward V. 1740
Beigie, Carl E. 1508
Belanger, Gerard 2417 2418
Bélanger, Marcel 2419
Bélanger, Noël 2466
Bella, Leslie 1040
Bellerose, Pierre-Paul 1509
Belliveau, J. E. 524
Belzile, Bertrand 1510
Bender, Elizabeth 981
Bendickson, Jamie 2738
Benjamin, Jacques 2420
Bennett, Peter H. 3324
Benoit, Virgil 946
Benson, J. 14
Bentley, C. Fred 1511
Bercuson, David Jay 1080
1149 1167 2899 2900
Berger, Thomas R. 3343
Bergeron, Gérard 1741
Bergeron, Gerard 2087
Bergeron, Michel 2545
Bergevin, André 2467
Bergey, Lorna L. 2739
Bergquist, Harold E. 627
Bergsten, C. Fred 1962
Berkes, Fikret 346
Berlin, Simon 1512
Bernal, Ignacio 1953
Bernard, Elaine 3177
Bernard, Jean-Paul 2594
Bernard, Jean-Thomas 1513
Bernier, Bernard 2595
Bernier, Jacques 2596
Berry, Glyn R. 1742
Berry, Virginia 947
Bertrand, Louis-Claude 2597 2598
Besner, Jacques 2597 2598
Bessette, Luc 2599
Best, Gary Dean 905
Beszedits, S. 2740
Betcherman, Lita-Rose 1196 2421
Betke, Carl 3028
Beveridge, James 1348
Bicha, Karel D. 906 2901 3087
Billette, André 2468
Bilodeau, Therese 2600
Bilson, Geoffrey 770 2219
Bingaman, Sandra Estlin 948
Birchall, Stella 2220
Bird, Florence 1349
Bird, Lilah Smith 713 2221
Bird, Michael 2741
Birrell, Andrew J. 266 1041
Bishop, Charles A. 347 348
Bisson, Michel 2535
Biswas, Asit K. 1274
Biswas, Margaret R. 1274
Bjarnason, Emil 1514
Black, J. B. 1743
Black, Mary Ellouise 2222 2223
Blain, Jean 490 491 525
Blais, André 1148 1632 2422 2456 2601
Blake, Donald E. 1637 1638 1655
Blakeley, Phyllis Ruth 2224 2225
Blanchard, Guy 2679
Blanchette, A. E. 1743 1744
Blanchette, Jean-François 349
Bleasdale, Ruth 350
Blishen, Bernard 1495
Blishen, Bernard R. 2149
Bliss, Edwin T. 2226 2227
Bliss, Michael 944 1081
Bloom, Joseph D. 315
Blow, David J. 2469
Boardman, Robert 1745
Bogina, Sh. A. 15
Bogusis, Ruth 51
Bohi, Charles W. 3029 3030
Bohne, Harald 1350
Boissonnault, Charles-Marie 907
Boisvert, Michel 2667
Boivin, Jean 2602
Bone, Robert M. 3275

Bone, Ronald 1515
Bonenfant, Claude 267
Bonenfant, Jean-Charles 16 1963
Bonenfant, Joseph 2470
Bonin, Bernard 17
Bonnichsen, Robson 296
Booy, Cass 2972
Borden, Charles E. 292
Bosher, J. F. 560 561 593
Bothwell, Robert 18 1198 1746
Bouchard, Gérard 526 2471
2472 2473 2474 2475
Bouchard, Lorne 316
Bouchard, Louis 2508
Bouchard, Randy 289
Boucher, Michel 2603
Boudreau, Joseph A. 1150 3088
Boulle, Pierre H. 562
Bourgault, Jacques 2423
Bourgeon, C. Y. 1351
Bourne, Charles S. 262
Bourne, Edward Gaylord 579
Bourne, L. S. 1352 1353
Boutet, Odina 1354 2424
Bowler, R. Arthur 714
Bowman, James S. 1805
Boyce, Douglas W. 351
Boyd, Josephine W. 3344
Boyd, Monica 1355 1516
Bracher, M. D. 1453
Brack, D. M. 1275
Bradbury, J. H. 3178
Bradley, Ian L. 352 353 354
Bradley, James G. 1082
Brannan, Beverly W. 2228
Brannigan, Colm J. 1083
Braroe, Eva Ejerhed 355
Braroe, Niels Winther 355
Brasser, Ted J. 356 357
Brazeau, J. A. R. 1747
Brecher, Irving 1748 1964
Bredin, Thomas F. 2973
Breen, David H. 2902 3089
Brennan, J. W. 3031
Breton, Albert 1517
Breton, Raymond 1356
Bridenthal, Renate 409
Brody, Hugh 317 318
Bronson, H. E. 3032
Brookes, Alan A. 2154 2162 2377
Brooks, G. W. S. 3179
Brooks, Stanley 2604
Brooks, W. H. 949 950
Brossard, Jacques 2088
Brouillette, Normand 2605
Brower, Charles N. 262
Brown, Bern Will 358
Brown, D. H. 951
Brown, Desmond H. 594
Brown, Jennifer 628 771
Brown, LaVerne 1749
Brown, Lorne 1116 1675
Brown, Malcolm C. 1518
Brown, Ronald 2742
Brown, Stephen W. 754
Brown, Wallace 629 715 738
Brown-John, C. Lloyd 1639 1640
Brozowski, R. 2743
Bruce, C. J. 1519
Brumgardt, John R. 838
Brummell, A. C. 2835
Brunet, Michel 2476
Brunet, Michele 3237
Brusegard, David A. 1357
Brynn, Edward 630
Brzezinski, Steven J. 1805
Buchanan, Carl J. 3090 3091
Buchignani, Norm 1358
Buckley, Suzann 1151 1152
Bucksar, Richard G. 3325 3326
Budakowska, Elżbieta 1359
Buetow, David 3320 3345
Buggey, Susan 19 2229
Buick, Glen 1750
Bulkley, P. B. 772
Bumsted, J. M. 1495 2378
Burbank, Garin 3083
Burchell, Howard B. 908

Burgess, Joanne 2606
Burke, Mike 1641
Burles, Gordon 3092
Burley, Kevin 2744
Burley, Kevin H. 20
Burnet, Jean 1356
Burns, R. J. 773
Burry, Shierlaw 2124
Bush, Edward F. 21 22 909
3327 3328
Butler, Richard W. 1276
Byers, G. 2230
Byers, R. B. 1277 1278 1751 1752
Byrne, Cyril 2155

C

Cabatoff, Kenneth 2477 2478
Cadieux, Marcel 1753
Caillois, Roger 319
Cain, Louis P. 1117 3180
Cairnie, James 3257
Cairns, Alan C. 1642 1729
Calam, John 23
Calderwood, William 3033
Caldwell, Gary 2479
Calkin, G. A. 1754
Calton, Jerry M. 24
Calvert, Robert A. 3083
Cameron, David 1360
Cameron, Donald 1675
Cameron, J. M. 774
Cameron, James M. 2231 2232
Cameron, Wendy 775
Campbell, Bertha J. 2233 2234
Campbell, Colin 1643 1644 1645
Campbell, H. C. 1361
Campbell, John P. 1220
Campbell, Lyall 2235 2236
Campbell, P. MacKenzie 2237
Campbell, Robert 268
Campeau, Lucien 545 546 563
Camu, Pierre 269
Carcassonne, Marcel 564
Careless, J. M. S. 631 1362
Carey, Betty 3181
Carey, Neil G. 3182
Carlson, Alvar W. 25
Carpenter, David C. 3093
Carpentier, Rene 1363
Carrier, Denis 1659
Carroll, Daniel B. 839
Carroll, Kenneth L. 739
Carroll, Michael P. 359
Carrothers, A. W. R. 1520
Carson, John 1755
Carter, David J. 360
Carter, Donald D. 2745
Carter, Joseph Cleveland 2379
Carter, Margaret 3183
Carter, Norman M. 3184
Carvalho, Joseph, III 2607
Castel, J.-G 1953
Casterline, Gail Farr 2903
Castonguay, Charles 1364 2480
Castonguay, Claude 1521
Caulais, Jacques 26
Caves, Richard E. 1756 1757
Caya, Marcel 2425
Cayouette, Gilles 3276
Cermakian, Jean 2608
Cestre, Gilbert 2426
Chaison, Gary N. 27
Chalmers, John W. 361 362
363 364 2904 3094
Champoux, Edouard 2487
Chandler, William M. 1646
Chant, John F. 1522
Chapdelaine, Jean 2680
Chapman, J. H. 1279
Chapman, James K. 2380
Chapman, Peter 3185
Chapman, Terry L. 2905 2906
Chaput, Donald 776
Charbonneau, Hubert 509 527
540 541 565
Charbonneau, Michel 2427

Chard, Donald F. 492 595 596 597
Charner, Ivan 2787 2821
Charron, Marguerite 2746
Chartrand, René 632 755
Cheda, Sherrill 1523
Chevrier, Bernard 1168
Chevrier, Lionel 1758
Chichekian, Garo 28
Ching, Donald 3034
Choquette, Robert 2747 2907 2974 3035 3095
Chossudovsky, Michel 1965
Chouinard, Denys 2609
Chouinard, Jean-Yves 2681
Christensen, Deanna 3036
Christenson, Gordon 262
Chung, Joseph H. 1524 2610
Church, G. C. 3037
Church, Glenn 2978
Clark, Arthur Hill 270
Clark, John 117 1525 1526 1527
Clark, Peter 2908
Clark, S. D. 1365 1366 1367
Clarke, Harold D. 1641 1647 1681 1702 2748 2749
Clarke, John 777 778
Clarke, Mary-Jane 1681
Clarkson, Stephen 1368
Classen, H. George 271
Claval, Paul 2481
Cleaver, Harry 1966
Clegg, Legrand H., II 293
Clement, Wallace 1369
Clements, Kendrick A. 1084
Clemson, Donovan 3186
Cleveland, John 3187
Cliche, Marie-Aimée 547
Clifford, N. K. 29 1085
Clifton, James A. 365
Coakley, Thomas M. 2182
Cockburn, Robert 2238
Codignola, Luca 598 952
Cody, Howard 30 1280
Cogswell, Dale 2381
Cogswell, Frederick 2382
Cohen, Anthony P. 2183
Cohen, Maxwell 262 1967
Coldevin, Gary O. 320 321
Cole, Douglas 282 633 1118 3188 3189 3258
Cole, Roland J. 1728
Collins, Lewis W. 2239
Colthart, J. M. 826
Comeau, Robert 1197 2611
Comfort, D. J. 953 3096
Common, Robert 3346
Comstock, Betsy 31
Conacher, J. B. 1281
Conant, Melvin A. 1968
Conkling, Robert 516
Connelly, Dolly 3347
Conrad, Glenn R. 580
Consentino, Frank 910 1042
Contandriopoulos, A. P. 2428
Cook, George L. 1086 1282
Cook, Ramsay 911
Cook, Terry 32 912
Cooke, Alan D. 2130
Cooke, Edgar D. 2909
Copithorne, M. D. 1759
Copland, A. Dudley 3348
Corbet, Elise A. 3097
Corbett, Beatrice 2750
Cordier, Andrew W. 1760
Cormier, Clement 2156
Corry, J. A. 33 1370
Corum, Charles Ronald 366
Corzyn, Jeni 3098
Cosentino, Frank 1043
Côté, André 2482 2612
Cotler, Irwin 2723
Cotnam, Jacques 2483
Cotton, Charles A. 1283
Cottrell, Philip L. 840
Coull, J. R. 1761
Coulton, Richard L. 294
Court, Thomas 3099
Courtney, John C. 1147 1648 3038
Courville, L. D. 3039
Cousineau, Jean-Michel 1528
Cousins, Leone Banks 841 842 2240 2241
Couve de Murville, Maurice 1250
Cowan, G. K. 2204

Cowley, George A. 34
Cox, Bruce 3349
Cox, Robert W. 35
Cox, Steven 336
Craig, A. W. 1762
Craig, G. M. 634 809
Crampton, Esmé 1371
Crane, David 1284
Cranmer, Valerie 1483
Crathorne, Ethel 2242
Creery, Tim 1916
Creighton, Edith 2243
Criddle, Percy 954
Crispo, John 1763
Critchley, W. Harriet 1285 1764
Crone, Ray H. 1169 3040
Crook, Rodney K. 1283
Cross, L. Doreen 2751
Crossin, Alan L. 2975
Crowley, Ronald W. 1372
Crowson, E. T. 740
Cuff, Robert D. 1224
Cullen, Dallas 1969
Cullity, Emmet K. 3041
Cumming, Peter A. 367
Cuneo, Carl J. 1373 1970 2682
Cunningham, O. Edward 843
Cunningham, Robert B. 1649
Currie, Donald 1286
Currie, Justice L. D. 2244
Curry, Richard John 599
Curry, Starr 2245
Curtis, James E. 73 1373 1374 1422 1650 2682
Cuthbertson, Brian C. 2246
Cuthbertson, Shirley 3190
Cutler, Maurice 36 1765 1766 1971 2205
Czarnocki, B. Dan 2479

D

Dack, W. L. 1767
Dagg, Michael A. 283
Dahlie, Jorgan 3191
Dahms, Frederic A. 2752 2753
Dalfen, Charles 1797
D'Allaire, Micheline 528
Daly, William G. 1583
Damas, David 322
Daniel, Forrest W. 2976
D'Aoust, Claude 1529
D'Aquino, Susan 1376
Daub, Mervin 1530
Davey, Ian E. 2754
Davies, Ivor 3277
Davis, Ann 1170
Davis, Douglas F. 1531
Davis, William E. 2755
Day, Douglas 2383
Day, Gordon M. 368 369
Day, J. C. 276
Day, John P. 955
Dayal, Rajeshwar 1768
Deans, B. 3354
Dearborn, David Curtis 493
Deaton, Rich 1532
DeBonville, Jean 2484
Decarie, M. G. 2756
Dechêne, Louise 510
Deffontaines, Pierre 2485
DeGoumois, Michel 1769
DeKoninck, Rodolphe 2486 2490
DellaValle, P. A. 1533
Delude-Clift, Camille 2487
DelVillar, Samuel I. 1954
Delvoie, L. A. 1770
Dempsey, Hugh A. 370 956 957 3100 3101 3102 3103
DenOtter, A. A. 958 959 960 3104
Denton, Frank T. 2757
Denton, Trevor 371
D'Entremont, Harley 2384
Deschênes, Gaston 37
DeSeve, Micheline 2429
Desjardins, Bertrand 565
Desmeules, Jean 2488
DesRosiers, Rachel 1632 2422 2456
Dessaules, Louis-Antoine 697 844
deValk, Alphonse 1375 3042

DeVilliers-Westfall, William E. 913
Devlin, T. P. 3192
deVries, John 1657
Dewar, Kenneth C. 38
Dewar, Kenneth M. 3350
Dewees, Donald N. 2758
Dick, Ernest J. 39
Dickerman, C. Robert 1771
Dickey, John Sloan 40
Dickinson, John A. 554
Dickson, Lovat 372
Diebold, William, Jr. 1772 2083
Dion, Gérard 1534 1972
Dion, Léon 1651 2429 2489
Dion, Marc 2490
Dionne, Georges 2643
Dirlik, Andre 1973
Dixon, Marlene 1270
Dmitriev, S. 1773
Dobell, Peter C. 1376 1974 1975 2683
Dobell, W. M. 1774 1775
Dobkin, Donald S. 2089
Dodds, Ronald 845 1153
Dodge, William 1535
Doerksen, A. D. "Tony" 41 961
Doern, G. Bruce 1536
Doig, Ivan 373
Dojcsak, G. V. 3043
Dominique, Richard 2491
Donahue, Jim 1377
Donner, Arthur 1568
Donneur, André P. 42 1776 1777
Dorge, Lionel 2910 2911
Dornfield, A. A. 43
Dosey, Herbert W. 1087
Doucet, Michael J. 2759 2760
Doucet, Paul 1976
Doucette, Laurel 2492
Douglas, W. A. B. 1221 1229 1778
Douglas, W. O. 323 3351
Doutre, Joseph 374
Dove, Jack 1378
Doyle, James 44
Doyle, John E. 635
Doyle-Frenière, Murielle 2430
Drache, Daniel 45
Drache, Hiram 2964
Drakos, Georges E. 1629
Dreisziger, N. F. 962 1088
Driedger, Leo 963 1379 1380 1381 2977 2978 3044
Drolet, Jean Claude 2493
Dubé, Jean-Claude 555
Dudley, Leonard 1537
Duff, Wilson 375
Duffy, Dennis 741 1119
Duffy, John J. 810 815
Dull, Jonathan R. 716
Duly, Leslie C. 46
Dumais, Alfred 2494
Dumais, François 2495
Dunbar, M. J. 3278
Dunlop, Allan C. 964 965 2247 2248
Dunn, Robert M., Jr. 1977 1978
Dunnigan, Brian Leigh 600
Dunton, Davidson 47 1979
Dunwiddie, Peter W. 376
DuPasquier, Thierry 1287
Duran, Elizabeth C. 377
Duran, James A., Jr. 377
Durand, Guy 2613
Durocher, René 2684
Durrell, Harold Clarke 493
Dussault, Gilles 2614 2615
Dwivedi, P. P. 1288
Dyck, Peter J. 1171
Dyck, Rand 1652

E

Eadie, James A. 914
Eagle, John A. 915 1154
Eastman, H. C. 1629
Easton, Alan 2249
Easton, Carol 3105
Eaton, E. L. 2250 2251 2252
Eayrs, James 1780
Eckhardt, Konstantine 1781

Edson, William D. 48
Edwards, Claude A. 1538
Edwards, Malcolm 846
Eichler, Margrit 49
Eisen, George 378
Elford, Jean 1251 1539 2761
Elkins, David J. 1653 1654 1655 1730 2143 3193
Elliott, David R. 3106
Elliott, Jean Leonard 284
Ellis, Frank H. 1155 1172
Ellis, Walter E. 2762
Ellis, William Donohue 50 272
Elsheikh, Farouk 7
Emery, George N. 1089 2763
England, Claire 1382
English, H. Edward 1782 1980
English, John 1746
Ens, Adolph 966
Epp, Frank H. 1173
Erideres, James S. 2912
Ervin, Linda 51
Esberey, J. E. 1147 1174
Essar, D. 967
Esselmont, Harriet A. E. 3194
Evans, Brian 1783
Evans, G. R. 2253
Evans, Howard V. 636
Evans, Simon M. 968
Everett, Robert 2607
Ewanchuk, Michael 969
Eyman, C. E. 295

F

Fahmy-Eid, Nadia 698
Fairchild, Byron 601
Fairweather, Gordon L. 52
Falaise, Noël 2496
Falardeau, Jean-Charles 2497
Falcone, David J. 53 1383
Falkner, Ann 1289
Farb, Judith 1252
Farb, Nathan 1252
Farid, Z. 1540
Faries, Richard 379
Farine, Avigdor 1384
Farr, Robin 1290
Farrell, David R. 637
Farrell, R. Barry 1981
Fathi, Asghar 1385
Faucher, Albert 54 2431 2616 2617 2618
Fauriol, Georges A. 1784
Faust, Richard 285
Feaver, George 1090
Fée, Art 2913
Feldman, Mark B. 1982
Fellows, Jo-Ann 742
Feltham, Ivan R. 1954
Ferguson, Norman 1541
Fergusson, C. B. 892 2254 2255 2256
Ferres, John 55
Fetherling, Doug 2764
Ficken, Robert E. 2257
Fidler, Dick 2040
Fidler, Vera 2914
Filion, Gérard 56 1983
Filion, Jacques 2685
Findlay, Peter C. 1340
Fingard, Judith 779 916 2157 2258 2259
Fink, Howard 1386
Finkelman, Jacob 1542
Finkle, Peter Z. R. 1785 1786
Finn, Ed 1543
Finn, Jean-Guy 2385
Finnie, Richard 380 3301 3302 3329
Fireman, Janet R. 1387
Fischer, David W. 3284
Fischer, Lawrence J. 3303
Fisher, A. D. 381
Fisher, Robin 382 383
Flaherty, David H. 57
Flanagan, Thomas 970 971 972 973 3107
Flanagan, Thomas E. 974
Fleischman, Harry 3195
Fleming, Louis B. 2083
Fleming, Roy F. 58 384
Flemming, Brian 1953
Fletcher, Frederick J. 1656
Fleurot, Jean 1787

Flynn, Louis J. 2765
Foggin, Peter M. 2498
Folinsbee, Robert E. 273
Fontaine, André 2686
Foran, Max 3108
Forbes, Ernest R. 59 2125 2158
Forbes, H. D. 1714
Forbis, R. G. 295
Forcese, Dennis 1657
Forsey, Eugene 60 893
Forster, Donald 1208
Fortier, John 602
Fortier, Margaret 603
Forward, Charles N. 2126 3196
Fournier, Marcel 2499
Fowler, Marian E. 638 2766
Fowler, R. M. 1984
Fowlie, W. D. 2260 2261
Fox, Annette Baker 1985 1986
Fox, M. F. 917
Francis, Daniel 847 2159 3304
Franck, Thomas M. 1788
Frank, David 1175
Frank, J. A. 2127
Fraser, Don 2979
Fraser, John D. 1658
Fraser, Nancy W. 1176
Fredette, Jean-Guy 2432
Freeman, Milton M. R. 1388
Freeman, Susan 1987
Freifeld, Sidney A. 1789
French, Alice 324
Frenette, Jean-Vianney 2687
Fretz, J. Winfield 2767
Frideres, James S. 385 2128 2768 2915 2970
Friedkin, Joseph F. 262
Friedler, Egon 1389
Friedmann, Karl A. 3109
Friesen, Gerald 2916 2917
Friesen, John W. 386
Friesen, Victor Carl 2918
Frigon, F. J. 2500
Frisch, Jack A. 3305
Frizzell, Alan 260
Fry, Bruce W. 608
Fry, Garry L. 1222
Frye, Northrop 61
Fuga, Olga 2980
Fulford, Frederick M. J. 1091
Fulford, Robert 1390
Fursova, L. N. 15

G

Gaffield, Chad 2769
Gagan, David 807 848 849 850 2770 2771 3359
Gage, Gene G. 1343
Gagné, Jacques 387
Gagnon, François-Marc 388
Gagnon, Gabriel 2619
Gagnon, Marcel-Aimé 2688
Gagnon, Serge 2501
Gainer, Walter D. 2129
Galarneau, Claude 2502
Galbraith, John S. 639
Gallagher, John 389
Galloway, Wilda 392
Garant, Patrice 1659
Gardner, C. James 1660
Garner, Joseph John 1790 1791
Garnier, Gérard 1792
Garon, Jean 2620
Garon-Audy, Muriel 2503
Garrad, Charles 517
Gartner, Gerry J. 2919
Gaskin, Fred 975
Gaster, Patricia 851
Gaudette, Gabriel 2621
Gaulin, André 2504
Gauvin, Lise 2505
Gauvin, Michel 1950
Gay, Daniel 2433
Gear, James L. 62
Gelardin, Richard D. 315
Gelber, Sylva 1544
Gellner, John 1291 1988
Genest, Jean 63 1292 1391 2622 2623
Genest, Jean-Guy 2506
Geoffrey, Bilson 2386
George, Benjamin 1177

George, P. M. 2773
George, Peter J. 2757
Gerace, Mary C. 1874
Gérin-Lajoie, Henri 2434
Gérin-Lajoie, Paul 1793
Gersman, Elinor Mondale 64
Gerson, Carole 918
Gervais, Gaetan 2772
Geschwender, James A. 2773
Gibbens, R. G. 65
Gibbins, Roger 2920 2921
Gibbons, Lillian 2981
Gibson, James A. 66 827
Gidney, R. D. 780
Gill, Don 2130
Gillespie, Alastair 1989
Gillis, Robert Peter 781 2774
Gilman, Carolyn 976
Gilmour, James M. 2604
Gilpin, Robert 1990
Gizycki, Horst von 977
Glazier, Kenneth M. 1293 2689
Globerman, Steven 1545
Glorieux, Guy 1546
Glover, R. 2922
Gluek, Alvin C., Jr. 2184
Godfrey, William G. 67 604
Godler, Zlata 1178
Goheen, Peter G. 68
Goldberg, Steve 69
Goldblatt, Murray 1794 1795
Goldenberg, Sheldon 2768 2915
Goldenberg, Shirley B. 1547
Goldman, Ralph M. 1661
Goldman, Robert K. 1954
Goldring, Philip 978
Golladay, V. Dennis 782
Gonick, Cy 70 389 1294 1295 1548 1549 1550 1675 2624 2690 2982
Gooch, John 1092
Good, W. S. 2923
Goodman, Eileen 1551
Goodman, Elizabeth B. 505
Goodwin, Clive E. 1296
Goodwin, Theresa 3045
Gordon, J. King 1796
Goresky, Dennis 2050
Gorham, Deborah 71 72
Gotlieb, Allan E. 1797 1953
Goudy, H. G. 3212
Gouett, Paul M. 2262
Gough, Barry M. 390 783 784 785 919 979 3197 3198
Goulding, Stuart D. 518
Gourd, Benoît-Beaudry 274 2625
Gow, James Iain 2435 2436
Goyder, John C. 73
Grabowski, Yvonne 1392
Graff, Harvey J. 74 852 1044
Graham, John W. 1798
Grainge, Jack W. 325
Granatstein, J. L. 1198 1223 1224 1225 1226 1227
Grant, Dorothy Metie 2263
Grant, Francis W. 2264 3279
Grant, H. Roger 2983 3029 3030
Grant, John N. 640 2265 2266
Grant, K. Gary 1037
Grant, Laurier C. 2267 2268
Grantmyre, Barbara 641 2269 2270 2271
Gravel, J. Yves 1228
Graves, Ross 2272
Gray, Colin S. 1991
Grayson, J. Paul 1662 3110
Grayson, L. M. 3110
Green, Chris 1528
Green, Janet 920
Green, L. C. 1799
Greenberg, Dolores 853 980
Greene, John P. 2185
Greenhous, Brereton 1221 1229 1230
Greening, W. E. 854
Greenough, John Joseph 642
Greenwood, E. Murray 699
Greenwood, Ted 1992
Greer, Allan 605 643 2507
Greer, David M. 3199
Gregg, Richard B. 391
Grenier, Manon 2508
Grenier, Raymond 1800

Grenier, Robert 558
Grenon, Jean-Yves 1801
Gridgeman, N. T. 506
Griezic, Foster 855 2775
Griffiths, Naomi 606
Grindstaff, Carl F. 392
Groffier, Ethel 1393
Gross, Leonard 743 786 981
Grumet, Robert Steven 393
Gruneir, Robert 2776
Guay, Donald 644
Guerin, Gilles 1594
Guest, Henry James 921
Guillemin, Jeanne 394
Guindon, Hubert 2090
Guitard, Michelle 982 2509
Gullion, Edmund 2083
Gunderson, Morley 2777
Gundy, H. Pearson 645 1045
Gutteridge, Don 75
Gutwirth, Jacques 2510
Guy, James John 1802 1803 1804
Gwyn, Julian 607

H

Haddad, Jay 2808
Haddrell, Glenn 1297
Hadwiger, Donald 3083
Haering, R. R. 646
Hagan, John 76 1663 1664
Hajjar, Sami G. 1805
Hall, D. J. 395 396 922 3046
Hall, Frank 2984 2985
Hall, Frederick A. 2778
Hallett, Mary E. 2691
Halliday, Hugh A. 2437 2626 2779
Halstead, John G. H. 1952
Hameed, Syed M. A. 1552
Hamel, J. M. 1665
Hamel, Jacques 2511 2692
Hamelin, Louis-Edmond 3276 3352 3353
Hamilton, Douglas F. 2780
Hamilton, Edward K. 1806
Hamilton, Raphael N. 548
Hamilton, Richard 1553 2693 2707
Hamilton, T. M. 608
Hamilton, William B. 77
Hamilton-Edwards, Gerald 2273
Hancock, Harold B. 1046
Hand, Wayland D. 1298
Hanham, Harold J. 78 79
Hannant, Larry 3111
Hannigan, John A. 1299
Hanrahan, James 80
Hansen, Dagny B. 647
Harbottle, Jeanne 3330 3331
Harbron, John D. 1807 1808
Harding, Jim 2781
Hardisty, A. Pamela 81
Hardy, Allison Taylor 82
Hardy, René 811
Hare, John 648 700 701 717 2512 2584 2694
Harington, C. R. 296
Harmon, Julius Frasch 478
Harney, Robert F. 83 2782 2783 2784 2785 2786
Harrington, Lyn 2438
Harrington, Richard 2438 3200
Harris, Barbara P. 3201
Harris, Donald A. 856
Harris, Jane E. 2274 2387
Harris, R. Cole 3202
Hart, Edward J. 2924
Hart, Simon 569
Hartland-Rowe, Richard 1300
Hartlen, John 2275
Hartmann, Norbert 1356
Harvey, Edward B. 2787 2821
Harvey, Fernand 1047 2513 2627
Harvey, Jacquelin 2628
Harvey, Pierre 2629
Harvey, Robert Paton 2276 2277 2278
Hatch, F. J. 1179 1231
Hatchard, Keith A. 2279 2280
Hatfield, H. R. 3203
Hatfield, Michael 2388

Hauser, Gerald A. 391
Hautecoeur, Jean-Paul 2281
Hawkins, Freda 1394 1395 1809 1810 1811 1812
Haworth, Kent M. 3204
Hawthorn, Audrey 3205
Hayball, Gwen 84
Haycock, Ken 1396
Haycock, R. 2788
Hayes, Alan L. 85
Hayes, F. Ronald 2282
Hayes, Saul 1397
Hayward, Robert J. 86
Headey, B. W. 1666
Headon, Christopher F. 857 923 2389
Heald, Henry F. 1813
Heap, James L. 1301
Heap, Margaret 2630
Hébert, Gérard 87 2631 2632
Hedley, R. Alan 1398
Heeney, Stephen 1814
Heinke, G. W. 3354
Heisler, John P. 787
Helbig, Alethea K. 397
Held, Robert 1815
Helleiner, F. M. 2789
Helleiner, G. K. 1816
Helmers, Henrik O. 2027
Hemstock, R. A. 3280
Henderson, John R. 398
Henderson, M. Carole 88
Hendrickson, James E. 3206
Hennessey, R. A. 1302
Henripin, Jacques 1399
Hensen, Steven 3306
Henson, Tom M. 2925
Herndon, G. Melvin 649
Hero, Alfred O., Jr. 1985 1993
Herold, David 485
Heron, Craig 89
Hershberg, Theodore 90
Hervouet, Gérard 1817
Hickerson, Harold 286
Hickey, Donald R. 756 757
Higginbotham, Jay 581 582
Hill, Charles C. 1400
Hill, Daniel G. 2790
Hillmer, Norman 1120 1180 1199
Hindle, Walter 3355
Hinds, Margery 326
Hines, Robert J. 1554
Hinz, Evelyn J. 1121
Hippler, Arthur E. 327
Hirthe, Walter M. 1048
Hitchman, James H. 3207
Hite, Roger W. 858
Hobbs, R. Gerald 1401
Hobler, Philip M. 287
Hochbaum, H. Albert 3281
Hockin, Thomas 1818
Hodgetts, J. E. 1667 2091
Hodgins, Bruce W. 1303
Hodgson, Maurice 3307
Hoffman, George 3047 3048
Hogan, Brian F. 91 92
Hohn, E. Otto 399
Holdsworth, Deryck 2926 2941 3235
Holli, Melvin G. 583
Hollick, Ann L. 1994
Holloway, Trevor 650
Holmes, Jean 2092
Holmes, John W. 93 1995
Holmgren, Eric J. 859 983 3112
Holsti, Kal J. 1996
Holtslander, Dale 3113
Hopkinson, Marvin W. 94
Horn, Michael 1200
Horn, Michiel 1201 2791 2927
Horowitz, Gad 1668
Horowitz, Irving Louis 1304
Horrall, Stan W. 984
Hostetler, John A. 184
Houde, Pierre 2633
Houde, Serge 3208
House, J. Douglas 1819 2634
Houston, C. Stuart 860 2928 3308 3309
Hovinen, Elizabeth 2792
Howard, Helen Addison 400
Howard, Peter 2083
Howard, Victor 3209
Howell, Maxwell L. 1402

Howell, William Maher 2131
Howes, Helen C. 1305
Hubbard, Jake T. W. 486
Hubbard, R. H. 95
Huber, Paul B. 2283
Hudon, Raymond 2439 2695
Hudson, Heather E. 3282
Hudson, J. P. 609
Huel, Raymond 2929 2930 3049 3050
Hughes, Helen McGill 96
Hughes, Kenneth 401 924 1403
Hull, W. H. N. 1404
Humphreys, Barbara A. 2793 2794
Humphreys, David 1820
Humphrys, Ruth 985 986
Hunt, Peter 1405
Hunter, R. H. 2931
Hunter, T. Murray 1232
Huot, John 2795
Hurford, Grace Gibberd 1122
Hurlburt, William H. 3114
Hurley, Jefferson 1406
Hurtubise, Pierre 549
Hussey, John A. 861 862
Hutch, Danny 2950 3001
Hutchinson, Gerald M. 651
Hutchison, Bruce 1306
Hutten, Joanna 2284
Huyda, R. 863
Hyatt, A. M. J. 1156
Hynes, Gisa I. 511
Hyson, Stewart 1669

I

Igartua, José 702 703
Ignatieff, George 1821 1822
Inglis, Alex I. 1823 1824 1997 2024
Inglis, R. E. 2285 2286
Inglis, Richard I. 297
Inkster, Anne Ellen 2986
Inkster, Tom H. 3210
Inman, Ivan D. 2932
Inness, Lorna 828
Irby, Charles C. 3211
Irvine, William P. 1670
Isaacson, John A. 1093
Isajiw, Wsevolod W. 1356 1407 1408
Isbister, John 2132
Iwaasa, David B. 1233

J

Jacek, Henry 2796
Jackman, Albert H. 288
Jackson, C. I. 97
Jackson, Donald 652
Jackson, James A. 2987
Jackson, Robin 98
Jacob, Paul 2514
Jacobs, Wilbur R. 298
Jacomy-Millette, Anne-Marie 1825
Jaenen, Cornelius J. 519 550
Jager, Elizabeth 1955
Jain, Harish C. 1554
Jamal, Muhammad 1503
James, R. Scott 2797
Jameson, Sheilagh S. 3115
Jamieson, Stuart M. 35
Jarrell, R. A. 2515
Jarvis, Eric 788 925 2798
Jeffreys-Jones, Rhodri 1094
Jelks, Edward B. 2186
Jenness, R. A. 99 1555
Jensen, Robert 1307
Jenson, Jane 1671 1672 1702 1730
Jessett, Thomas E. 402
Jessop, David 1095
Jobson, J. D. 1969
Johannson, P. R. 2133
Johansen, Peter W. 1673
Johnson, Ann M. 299
Johnson, Arthur H. 3116
Johnson, Arthur L. 653 2287 2288 2390
Johnson, Barbara 1826
Johnson, J. K. 812 2799
Johnson, John H. 1556
Johnson, John M. 1674

Johnson, Keith 1955
Johnson, Leo 1675
Johnson, Lionel 3356
Johnson, Paul E. 483
Johnson, Ronald C. 3117
Johnston, Richard 100
Johnstone, John W. C. 2516
Jones, David Charles 248
Jones, Frank E. 1409
Jones, Frederick 2187 2188 2189 2190
Jones, H. R. 1410
Jones, Howard 654
Jones, Kevin G. 240 1123
Jones, Paul 1512
Jones, Richard R. 1411
Jordan, David Herrera 262
Josephy, Alvin M., Jr. 403
Jouandet-Bernadet, Roland 2635
Joxe, Alain 1827
Joyner, Christopher C. 1049
Judd, D. A. W. 3283
Juneau, Pierre 1998

K

Kaiser, Leo M. 610
Kalisch, Philip A. 2391
Kalter, Bella Briansky 2800
Kapiszewski, Andrzej 1412
Kaplanoff, Mark D. 655
Karamanski, Theodore J. 3357
Kardonne, Rick 2517
Karr, Clarence G. 101 2160
Kashtan, William 1676 1677
Kasurak, Peter 1124
Kattan, Naim 102 1999
Katz, Brian 2000
Katz, Elliott 2518
Katz, Michael 2801
Katz, Michael B. 656 2802
Kaulback, Ruth E. 611
Kavic, Lorne 1828
Kaye, Barry 2942
Kealey, Gregory S. 103 1050 2161 2803
Keane, Patrick 104 105 2289 2290 2291
Keenleyside, T. A. 1829 1830 2001
Kehoe, Alice B. 404 405 406
Kehoe, Mary 1557 1558
Kehoe, Thomas F. 405 406
Keith, Robert F. 3284
Kellas, James G. 3118
Keller, Alan 758
Kelly, John J. 1413
Kelly, Kenneth 275
Kelly, Michael 2127
Kelly, Nora 106
Kelsey, Harry 612
Kempthorne, Marlene 1831
Kendall, John C. 107 864
Kenn, John M. 108
Kennedy, Albert J. 2162
Kennedy, Dorothy I. D. 289
Kennedy, Estella 2392
Kennedy, Frederick James 2519
Kennedy, John F. 1832
Kenney, Alice P. 109
Kenniff, Patrick 1659
Kenyon, Walter 566 3310
Keohane, Robert O. 2002
Kernaghan, Kenneth 1678 1679
Kernaghan, Lois Kathleen 2292
Kerri, James Nwannukwu 407 2988
Kershaw, Gordon E. 718
Kerstan, Reinhold J. 987
Kerwin, Larkin 1414
Kess, Joseph F. 3201
Kesteman, Jean-Pierre 813 2520
Ketchum, Richard M. 719
Kewley, Arthur E. 2191
Keyfitz, Nathan 1833
Keywan, Zonia 3119
Khripunov, I. 1834
Kidd, Bruce 1202 2521
Kierans, Eric 2003
Kiker, B. F. 1415
Kilbourn, William 2804

Killam, G. D. 110
Killan, Gerald 2805
Kinghorn, Norton D. 2989
Kinsman, Jeremy 1835
Kirby, M. J. L. 1680
Kirk-Greene, Anthony H. M. 111
Kirley, Kevin 2806
Kirschbaum, J. M. 112 113 114 1308 1416
Kirton, John J. 1836
Klassen, Henry C. 3120 3121 3122
Kleber, Louis C. 512
Kleindienst, Richard G. 1417
Kleinschmidt, Martha 115
Klement, Susan 1418
Kliman, M. L. 1559
Klingelhofer, Eric 513
Klippenstein, Lawrence 988 989 990 991 992 993
Klymasz, Robert B. 2933 2934
Knight, David B. 116 117 865
Knox, Bruce A. 894
Koch, Agnes 3123
Kochan, Thomas A. 1500
Koehler, Wallace C., Jr. 2093
Koenig, Daniel J. 3212 3272
Koerper, Phillip E. 1051
Koester, C. B. 2935
Koester, Mavis Addie 3124
Kojder, Apolonja Maria 3051
Kojima, Kiyoshi 1837
Kolehmainen, John I. 3213
Kontak, Walter J. 2169
Koonz, Claudia 409
Kopkind, Andrew 2696
Korey-Krzeczowski, George 1781
Kornberg, Allan 1681 2749
Kothari, Vinay 2393
Kottman, Richard N. 1203 1204 1205
Koulack, Esther 1682
Koyen, Kenneth 613
Kozlov, V. I. 15
Krahn, Cornelius 994
Kraszewski, Piotr 1419
Krause, Eric R. 529
Krause, Robert 1647 2748
Kravtsov, A. K. 1560
Krech, Shepard, III 3285
Kreider, Robert 3052
Kresl, Peter Karl 1125 1126
Kristianson, Gerry L. 3214
Kroeker, H. V. 1680
Kronenberg, Vernon 2004
Kuo, Chun-Yan 3358
Kupp, Jan 567 568 569 570
Kupsch, Walter O. 3053
Kuruvilla, P. K. 118
Kushner, Howard I. 657
Kutcher, Stan 2807
Kuyek, Joan 1540
Kuzminov, I. 1561
Kwavnick, David 1562 2094 2095
Kyba, Patrick 1838
Kydd, Ronald 119

L

LaBerge, Roy 1563
Labovitz, Sanford 1420 3123
LaBrèque, Marie-Paule 704
Lachance, André 530 531
Lacroix, Robert 1421
LaFave, Laurence F. 2808
Laforce, Ernest 705
Lagassé, Jean 408
Lahey, R. J. 551
Lai, Chuen-Yan David 1052 3215
Lalande, Gilles 2096
Lall, A. 2743
Lalonde, André N. 995 2936
Lambert, Augustine 3054
Lambert, James H. 658 2523
Lambert, Robert S. 744
Lambert, Ronald D. 1374 1422 1650 2809
Lamonde, Pierre 2667
Lamonde, Yvan 120 706 2524 2525 2526
Lamont, James 3311

Lamontagne, Maurice 121 2097 2527
Lance, J. M. 2428
Lander, Clara 3055
Landes, Ronald G. 1423
Landon, Fred 2810
Landon, Richard 659
Landry, Dollard 2293
Landry, Yves 541 660
Landy, Sarah 1424
Langan, Joy 3216
Langdon, Frank 1826
Langdon, Steven 866
Langevin, Jean 2486
Langley, James 1839
Lanphier, C. M. 1564
LaPalm, Loretta 552
Laperrière, Guy 2636
Laplante, Pierre 2590
Lapointe, Pierre-Louis 2528
Laponce, J. A. 1309 1683
Lappage, Ronald S. 1127 3217
Lapul, David 3125
Larivière-Derome, Céline 1053
LaRochelle, Pierre 2535
Larocque, Paul 2637 2638
LaRose, André 514 526
LaRose, Helen 3126
Larouche, Fernand 2639
Larouche, Viateur 1510
Larsen, H. K. 1310
Larsen, Lawrence H. 1157 1158
Laskin, Bora 1684
Lass, William E. 661
Lasserre, Jean-Claude 1565
Lates, Richard 662
Latouche, Daniel 2005 2098 2099 2640
Laudadio, Leonard 1566
Lauder, Brian 1181
Laux, Jeanne Kirk 1840
Lavallée, Jean-Guy 2529
Lavender, David 2134
Laver, A. Bryan 122
Lavigne, Marie 1128
LaViolette, Forrest E. 123
Lawrence, Joseph C. 3218
Lawrence, Robert G. 1054
Lawson, Robert F. 1425
Laxer, James 1841 2006
Layton, Jack 1567
Layton, Monique 3219
Lazar, Fred 1568
Lea, Sperry 2007
Leach, Richard H. 1253 1842 2008
Leacock, Eleanor 409
Lebel, Maurice 2009
LeBlanc, Lawrence J. 1843
Lederman, W. R. 124 125 1685
LeDuc, Lawrence 1641 1686 1702 1875 2001 2010 2100
LeDuc, Lawrence, Jr. 1687 2811
Lee, Carol F. 3220
Lee, James 2749
Lee, Thomas E. 479
Leechman, Douglas 663
Leefe, John 614 759 2163 2294
Leeke, James 2440
Lee-Whiting, Brenda 2641 2812 2813
Lefebvre, Jean-Jacques 126 2530
Légaré, Jacques 514 1426 1427
Legault, Albert 1844
Legebokoff, Peter P. 996
Léger, Jean-Marc 1845
Legget, Robert F. 800
LeGoff, Jean-Pierre 1569
LeGoff, T. J. A. 789 806
Lehr, John C. 2937 3127 3128
Leighton, Douglas 410
Leitch, Adelaide 411
Lejeunesse, Marcel 2531
Leman, Christopher 1428
LeMarquand, David 2011
Lemay, J. A. Leo 2295
Lemelin, Claude 1846
Lemieux, Denis 1659
Lemieux, Donald J. 584
Lemieux, Lucien 664

Lemieux, Pierre 2697
Lemieux, Vincent 1688 2698
LeMoignan, Michel 2532
Lemon, James T. 127
Lennards, J. 1356
Lentner, Howard H. 1847
Leon, Jeffrey 76 1664
LePan, Douglas 1234
Lerette, Jack L. 1570
LeRoy, Gregory 1450
Leroy, Vély 1629
Lessard, Claude 571
Létourneau, Firmin 2533
Letourneau, Rodger 997
Lévesque, Delmas 2699
Lévesque, Georges-Henri 2700
Lévesque, René 2701
Levine, David 2769
Levine, Marc V. 2101
Levitt, Joseph 1182 2102
Levy, David 1848
Levy, Gary 1849
Levy, Thomas A. 2012 2013
Levy, Thomas Allen 1996 2135
Lewis, Frank 1096
Leyton-Brown, David 1751 1850 2014 2020
Li, Peter S. 2814
Liebler, William F. 867
Lightbody, James 2990
Lillard, Charles 412 3221
Lindberg, Leon N. 1571
Lindsay, Charles S. 480 615 616
Lindsey, David 868
Lindsey, G. R. 3286
Linteau, Paul-André 2441 2442 2594 2642
Lipset, Seymour Martin 128
Lipsey, Richard G. 1572
Lischke-McNab, Ute 869
Lismer, Marjorie 413
Lister, Rota 414
Lithwick, N. H. 2103
Little, C. H. 2296
Little, J. I. 2534
Litvak, Isaiah A. 1851 1852 1853 2015 2016
Livermore, Carol 3332
Livermore, John Daniel 926
Lizee, Ruth Rose 1573
Lobb, Allan 415
Lochead, Richard 1311
Lochhead, Douglas 2815
Loftus, D. S. 3287
LoGalbo, John R. 2017
Logan, Roderick M. 2018
Loh, Wallace D. 2702
Lohnes, Barry J. 760
Lomas, A. A. 2164
Loney, Martin 1689
Long, J. Anthony 3129
Long, Janet E. 129
Lord, Gary T. 2443
Loree, Donald James 416
Lotz, Jim 1854 2297
Loudfoot, Raymonde 2991
Lovell, Emily Khalled 1429
Lovink, J. A. A. 1690
Low, Jean 417
Lowe, Mick 2816
Lowes, Ellen McFadden 998
Lozynsky, Artem 1055
Lucas, Glenn 130
Lucas, John 131
Lucas, Richard 2817
Lunardini, Rosemary 2536
Lund, Rolf T. 132 3130 3131
Lundqvist, Lennart J. 1691
Lunt, Richard 133
Luodesmeri, Varpu 1183
Lussier, Jean Jacques 172
Lutman, John H. 2818
Luxton, Meg 1002
Lyon, Peyton V. 1855 2019 2020 2083

M

MacCallum, Elizabeth 2819
MacDonald, Duncan 418
MacDonald, George F. 297
MacDonald, Graham A. 419
MacDonald, H. A. 1312
MacDonald, L. R. 134

MacDonald, Norbert 3222 3223
MacEachen, Allan J. 1856
Macgillivray, Don 2298
MacGillivray, Royce 2820
MacInnis, Joseph B. 3312
MacKay, Daniel S. C. 999
MacKenzie, A. A. 2299
Mackie, Marlene 1430 3132
MacKinnon, Neil 745
MacLachlan, Morag 3224
MacLaren, Alasdair 1857
MacLaren, George 420 2300 2301 2302
Maclean, Hugh D. 665
MacLean, Terrence D. 537
MacLeod, Alex 2444 2703
MacLeod, David 927
MacLeod, Malcolm 617
MacNutt, W. S. 746
MacPherson, C. B. 1338
MacPherson, G. R. I. 1129
MacPherson, Ian 2136 2165 2938
MacPherson, Kay 1431
Madansky, Albert 1728
Magee, Eleanor E. 2394
Maghami, Farhat Ghaem 1432
Magnuson, Bruce 1574 1575
Mahant, E. E. 1858
Maier, Charles R. 870 3204
Main, John 1313
Major, Marjorie 2303 2304
Makahonuk, Glen 3056
Maki, Dennis R. 1576
Mallory, J. R. 1729 2104 2105 2106
Malmgren, Harald B. 1859
Malo, Marie-Claire 2643
Maloof, George 135
Manning, Bayless 1860
Manning, Frank E. 136
Manor, F. S. 1314 1861 2021
Mansbridge, Stanley H. 3133
Mansvelt, A. 666
Manzl, H. F. 2822
Maranda, E. K. 421
Marble, Allan E. 750 1056 2305 2306 2307
Marchak, Patricia 3225 3272
Marcolin, Lorenzo 585
Marion, Jacques 1364
Marmor, Theodore R. 1577
Marple, David 2137
Marsden, Lorna R. 1433 2821
Marsh, Donald D. 320
Marsh, John 137
Marshall, C. J. 1862 1863
Marshall, J. Furber 2308
Marshall, J. H. 1519
Marshall, John U. 138 1434
Marshall, Mortimer Villiers 422 2309 2310
Marshall, Nancy 2808
Marshall, Vera G. 2311
Martens, Hildegard M. 1235
Martin, Anita Shilton 139
Martin, Calvin 423 424 425
Martin, Fernand 2644
Martin, Gary R. 3212
Martin, Ged 667 668 669 814 2192 2193 2939
Martin, Marlene 3212
Martyn, Howe 140
Massam, Bryan H. 2445
Masse, Jacqueline C. 1435
Massicotte, Guy 1236
Massicotte, Jean-Paul 571
Masson, Claude 2667
Masson, Jack K. 3134
Mastromatteo, Ernest 1578
Matejko, Alexander 1436
Matheson, Gwen 1097
Mathews, Robin 670
Matthews, Barry 300
Matthews, Keith 2194
Matthews, Ralph 2195
Matthews, Robert O. 1864
Maule, Christopher J. 1851 1852 2015 2016
Mauro, R. G. 3313
Maxwell, James A. 1693
Maxwell, Joseph A. 426
Maybee, J. R. 1865
Mays, H. J. 2822
Mays, Herbert 2770
Mays, Robert G. 329

McAndrew, William J. 1206
McCaffrey, Gordon 1579
McCalla, Douglas 790 928 2823
McClellan, George B. 3135
McClure, J. Derrick 1437
McCollom, Pat 3333
McComber, Marie 2612
McCook, James 141 1000
McCorkell, Edmund J. 1184
McCormack, A. Ross 2940
McCormack, Martin 3136
McCormick, P. L. 1001
McCracken, Jane 1002 1315
McCurdy, Earle 2196 2197
McDermott, John 3226
McDonald, Charles 1580
McDonald, R. H. 871 872 895 2312
McDonald, Virginia 142
McDonough, John 2796
McDougall, John 3137
McDowell, D. 2981
McEvoy, Fred 1237
McGahan, Elizabeth 2395
McGavin, Robert James 143
McGhee, Robert 487
McGinnis, J. P. Dickin 3138
McIlwraith, Thomas F. 791 2824
McInnes, Simon 1694
McInnis, Marvin 807
McIvor, R. Craig 1581
McKay, Ian 2161
McKechnie, R. N. 144
McKee, Bill 3227
McKenzie, Ann 792
McKiernan, F. Mark 2755
McKillop, A. B. 145 2992
McKillop, Brian 2993
McKinney, Wayne R. 427
McKinsey, Lauren S. 1695
McLaren, Angus 929
McLaren, Robert I. 3057
McLaughlin, K. M. 2313
McLean, Anne 2825
McLean, Bruce 3228
McLean, W. J. 1003
McLeod, Carol 720 2314
McLeod, Evelyn Slater 1004 3139
McLeod, Finlay J. C. 1005
McMenemy, John 2889
McMillan, Alan D. 301
McMillan, C. H. 1853
McMillan, Keith 146
McNab, David 869
McNairn, Norman A. 671 2315
McNally, Paul 532 2206
McNaught, Kenneth 147 148
McPherson, Hugo 149
McQuillan, D. Aidan 150
McRoberts, Kenneth 151 1438 2107
Meakin, Alexander C. 2826
Mealing, F. M. 152
Medovy, Harry 2994
Meekison, J. Peter 1866
Mégélas, Roger 1867
Mehmet, Ozay 1582
Meisel, John 1696
Mellos, Koula 1709
Melnyk, George 2995
Melzer, Ian 1714
Ménard, Camil 428
Menard, Johanne 2537
Meredith, Brian 1868
Metcalfe, Alan 153 930 2538
Metzger, Stanley D. 1954
Meunier, C. 2428
Meyer, B. 1533
Meyer, Larry L. 586 1006
M'Gonigle, R. Michael 1869
Mifflen, Jessie B. 2198
Migner, Robert Maurice 2446
Migué, Jean-Luc 1324 1439 1697
Miles, Edward J. 1440
Miles, P. 3288
Miles, Walter K. 3229
Millar, W. P. J. 672 673
Miller, Carman 1098 1099 2316
Miller, D. R. 2108
Miller, Fern 3230
Miller, J. R. 154 931 1057 1058 1059 2645 2827

Miller, Robert F. 1316
Miller, Virginia P. 302
Millman, T. R. 873 874 932
Mills, Edward 2926
Mills, Eric L. 2317
Mills, G. E. 2941
Mills, Thora McIlroy 3334
Milsten, Donald E. 2022
Minogue, K. R. 1338
Mintz, Max M. 721
Minville, Esdras 155 2646
Miquelon, Dale 572
Mireault, Réal 2647
Miron, Gaston 494
Mishler, William 1383
Mitchell, Betty L. 875
Mitchell, Elaine Allen 2828
Moir, John S. 747
Molot, Maureen Appel 2080
Monet, Jacques 156 495
Monière, Denis 496
Moodie, D. W. 429 497 2942
Moogk, Peter N. 533 534 535
    545
Moon, Robert 515
Moore, Christopher 573
Moore, Donald S. 1185
Moore, Larry F. 1583 1614
    1615
Moorhead, Thomas B. 1955
Moreau, Jean-Paul 1441
Morel, André 536
Morgan, E. C. 1007
Morgan, Lael 430
Morgan, Robert J. 537 748
Morin, Fernand 2648
Morin, Rosaire 2539
Morlan, Richard E. 296
Morley, John T. 3231
Morley, Terence 1698 3232
Morris, Joe 1584
Morris, R. N. 1564
Morrison, Ian 1699
Morrison, K. L. 2829
Morrison, Kenneth M. 520
Morrison, Monica 2396
Morrison, Rodney J. 1060
Morrison, W. R. 2830 3335
Morrow, Dan 1130
Morse, Eric W. 157
Morton, Desmond 1008 1159
    1160 1161
Morton, W. L. 1009
Moss, Robert 2318
Mount, Graeme S. 2023 2319
Moy, Joyanna 1585
Moynagh, Michael 1870
Muise, D. A. 2166
Muller, H. Nicholas, III 761
    810 815 816
Munro, Gordon R. 1871
Munro, John A. 2024
Munton, Don 1238 1872 2012
    2025
Murphy, Cornelius J., Jr.
    2026
Murray, D. R. 1239
Murray, David 1131
Murray, Donald 1700
Murray, Geoffrey 1873
Murray, J. Alex 1874 1875
    2001 2010 2027
Murricane, Kenneth 2604
Mutimer, Brian T. 1402
Myers, C. R. 1442
Myers, Rex C. 431

N

Naftel, William 1010
Nafziger, James A. R. 1953
Nappi, Carmine 1254
Naylor, R. Thomas 933 944
Naysmith, John 3289
Nearing, Peter 3140
Neary, Peter 900
Neary, Peter F. 2199
Neatby, H. Blair 1132
Neatby, Hilda 2831
Neatby, Leslie H. 3314
Negrete, J. C. 1443
Neidecker, John F. 674
Neidhardt, W. S. 876
Neill, Robin F., Jr. 2167
Nelles, H. V. 158 1100 2138
    2211
Nelson, J. G. 159

Nelson, Paul David 722
Neutell, Walter 160
Newark, Michael J. 2832
Newbound, I. D. C. 829
Newell, Dianne 3336
Newinger, Scott 3141
Newton, David 2320
Newton, Norman 303
Nguyen, Hung 2540
Nicholls, Robert V. V. 877
Nicholson, G. W. L. 1133
Nicholson, L. H. 1011
Nicholson, N. L. 723
Nihart, Brooke 724
Nikitiuk, Costia 3233
Niosi, Jorge 161
Nitkin, Nathaniel 481
Nitoburg, E. L. 15
Nixon, Joanne 392
Noble, Dennis L. 3290
Noble, John J. 1876
Nock, David 432
Noel, S. J. R. 162
Noppen, Luc 553
Norrie, Kenneth H. 1012
    1037 2943
Norris, Darrell A. 1317
Norris, John 675 3234
North, John 3142
North, M. 3235
Norton, William 793 794
Nossal, Frederick 1444
Nossal, Kim Richard 1877
Nourry, Louis 830
Nousiainen, Seppo 1586
Novogrodsky, Myra 1445
Nuechterlein, Donald E. 2028
Nye, Joseph S., Jr. 2002 2029

O

O'Brien, Kevin H. F. 1061
O'Connell, Robert J. 1953
O'Connell, Sheldon 330
O'Connor, D'Arcy 2649
Oden, Jack P. 1134
O'Driscoll, Dennis 2833
O'Farrell, John K. A. 1318
O'Flaherty, Patrick 2200
O'Gallagher, Marianna 2541
Ogden, R. Lynn 3236
Ogelsby, J. C. M. 1878
Ogilvie, William 433
Oglesby, Jack 1879
Ogmundson, Rick 1319 2996
Ohly, D. Christopher 262
Okuma, Tadayuki 1880
Oldham, Evelyn 434
Olive, David Allen 1955
Oliver, Michael K. 1340
Oliver, Peter 1320
Olling, R. D. 2944
Olsen, Ruth A. 676
Olsson, Harry R., Jr. 1953
O'Malley, Martin 2997
O'Neill, Daniel J. 1941
O'Neill, P. B. 3058 3059
O'Neill, Robert 1881
Onibokun, Adepoju G. 1587
Oppen, William A. 498
Orban, Edmond 2109 2704
Orfila, Alejandro 163
Orr, Dale 1882 2030
Orrell, John 3143
Ørvik, Nils 1883 3291
Osborne, Brian S. 749
Osmond, Oliver R. 2834
Ossenberg, Richard J. 1321
Ostenstad, W. L. 878
Ostman, Ronald E. 2031
Ostry, Bernard 164 1322 1323
Ostry, Sylvia 1446
Oswalt, Wendell H. 331
Ouellet, Fernand 165 166 538
    574

P

Packlington, Guy 3187
Padden, R. C. 304
Page, Donald M. 1238 1255
    1884 1885 2032 2033
Pageau, René 2705
Paillé, Michel P. 2584
Painchaud, Paul 167 1886
    1952 2706

Painchaud, Robert 1013
Palda, Kristian S. 1728
Palmer, Bryan D. 89
Palmer, Gwen 435
Palmer, Howard 168 3144
Paltiel, Freda L. 1447
Paltiel, Khayyam Z. 1701
    2415
Pammett, Jon H. 1702
Panitch, Leo 1487
Pannekoek, Frits 1014
Panting, Gerald E. 169
Panting, Gerry 2210
Papageorgiou, George J. 2835
Papineau, Louis-Joseph 896
Paquet, Gilles 795 796 806
Paquin, Michel 1324
Parai, Louis 1448
Paré, Marius 2542
Parenteau, Roland 2034 2139
Parizeau, Gérard 2650
Parker, George 934
Parker, Keith A. 2945
Parker, W. J. Lewis 935
Parks, J. G. M. 276
Parks, M. G. 1135
Parr, G. J. 797
Parry, Geraint 1325
Parson, Helen E. 2651
Passaris, Constantine 1588
    1887
Paterson, D. G. 936
Patterson, F. H. 2140 2321
Patterson, Graeme H. 831 832
Patterson, Nancy-Lou 2836
    2837
Patterson, R. S. 1136
Paučo, Joseph 1449
Paulston, Rolland G. 1450
Paupst, Kathy 2838
Peacock, Don 1888
Peake, Frank A. 2946 3292
Pearse, Charles R. 170
Pearson, G. A. H. 1889
Pearson, Geoffrey 1703
Pearson, Norman 1589
Pearson, Samuel C., Jr. 171
Pearson, William 1015
Peccei, Riccardo 1268
Peitchinis, Stephen G. 1590
Pennefather, John P. 1016
Pennefather, R. S. 2839
Penner, Norman 2110 2998
Penner, Peter 2168
Penner, Rita 966
Penney, J. 2734
Pentland, C. C. 1890
Pentland, Charles 1891
Percy, Michael 1566
Perry, Ruth B. 2322
Persky, Stan 463 3237 3238
Peterson, Hans J. 2035
Petroff, Lillian 2840 2841
Petryshyn, J. 1207
Phelan, Josephine 2842 2843
Phelps, Edward C. H. 2727
Philips, R. A. J. 1326
Phillips, Doris 2397
Phillips, Paul 798
Phinney, William R. 677
Pichette, Robert 172
Pick, Alfred 1892
Piédalue, Gilles 173 1186
Pierson, Ruth 1240
Pike, Robert 1451
Pilgrim, Donald G. 499
Pilisi, Paul 1893
Pinard, Maurice 1148 1553
    2693 2707
Pinch, Frank C. 1283
Pinczuk, J. R. 2999
Piotte, Jean-Marc 1337
Pirenne, J.-H 678
Piva, Michael J. 2844
Plamondon, Lilianne 575
Plato, W. R. 1452
Plumb, Louise 174
Plumptre, T. 1894
Plumstead, A. W. 618
Pluta, Leonard A. 2169
Pocius, Gerald L. 2201
Poel, Dale H. 1872
Poelzer, Irene A. 2947
Polèse, Mario 2141
Polisenský, Josef 175
Polyani, J. C. 1327
Polyzoi, Eleoussa 2845
Pomfret, Richard 2846

Ponting, J. Rick 2920
Pool, D. I. 1453
Poon, L. C. L. 1591
Porter, Glenn 1592
Porter, James 2934
Porter, John D. 521
Porter, John R. 2543 2544
Portes, Jacques 879 2708
Pothier, Bernard 592
Potvin, Claude 2398
Poulin, Antonio 2652
Pouyez, Christian 2545
Povolotskii, V. 1895
Powell, Margaret S. 203 1263
Powell, Robert Baden 2323
    2324 2325
Powell, T. J. D. 3060
Powell, William E. 1062
Power, Geoffrey 2653
Powles, Cyril 176
Pratt, Larry 2036
Preeg, Ernest H. 1896
Prentice, Alison 880
Presser, Carolynne 177
Presthus, Robert 1704
Preston, Adrian 881
Preston, Richard A. 178 2037
    2038
Preston, Richard J. 436
Price, Brian J. 2847
Price, Richard G. 1647 2748
Pringle, Jim 1454
Pritchard, James S. 522
Pritchett, Craig H. 1593
Proudfoot, Dan 619
Proulx, M. 1421
Provencher, John N. 2948
Proverbs, Trevor B. 3272
Pugh, Donald E. 2848
Pullen, Hugh Francis 2326
Punch, Terrence M. 750 1056
    2327 2328 2329 2330
Purdy, Harriet 3359
Purdy, J. D. 679

Q

Qualter, Terence H. 179
Quarter, Jack 1455
Quinlan, Thomas A. 3337

R

Racine, Jean-Bernard 2654
Raczka, Paul 437
Raeithel, Get 1456
Rainville, Jean-Marie 1594
Raitz, Karl B. 1457
Rakhmanny, Roman 1458
Ralston, H. Keith 3239
Ramcharan, Subhas 2849
Ramirez, Bruno C. 1101
Ramsey, Jarold 438
Rand, Ivan C. 1595
Randall, Stephen J. 180
Rankin, Ernest H., Sr. 882
Rannie, William F. 181
Rao, G. Lakshmana 1466
Rapprich, William F. 937
Raudzens, George K. 799
Rawlyk, G. A. 725
Ray, Arthur J. 429 439 576
    2949
Raymond, Ann 2331
Raymondis, L. M. 2546
Raynauld, André 1256 1596
Reaburn, Pauline 182 183
    2850
Reaburn, Ronald 182 2850
Read, Colin 817 818 1208
Reck, W. Emerson 500
Redekop, Calvin 184
Redekop, John H. 185 1459
Redmond, Gerald 938
Reed, Walt 1460
Rees, R. 3061
Rees, Ronald 1017 2399
Reese, Thomas 1643
Reeves, Randall 3293
Reeves, W. 2768
Reford, Robert W. 1328
Regeher, Ted D. 3145
Regenstreif, Peter 1705 1897
Reibel, Daniel B. 680
Reid, David J. 3240
Reid, John G. 501

Reid, Ronald F. 620
Reifschneider, John Charles
    3000
Reilly, Nolan 2161
Reinders, Robert C. 883
Remley, David A. 3338
Rempel, Henry David 2111
Renaud, François 2422 2547
Reschenthaler, G. B. 1597
Resnick, Philip 186 1337 3241
Reuber, Grant L. 2039
Reynolds, Arthur 1461
Rhodes, J. 2851
Rich, E. E. 187 502 503
Rich, Harvey 1462 1706
Richard, Bruce 1102
Richards, John 1598 3062
Richards, Mary Helen 3063
Richards, R. L. 3315
Richardson, Evelyn M. 2332
    2333
Richert, Jean Pierre 1463
    1464 2548 2549
Richmond, Anthony H. 1329
    1465 1466
Richtik, James 2950 3001
Richtik, James M. 1018
Ricker, Helen S. 2334
Riddell, John 2040
Riddell, W. A. 3064
Ridge, Alan D. 1019
Riegert, P. W. 3002
Rigby, G. Reginald 800
Rigin, Y. 1898 2041
Rinehart, James W. 1599
    2773
Ritchie, Charles 1899
Ritchie, Ronald S. 1900
Riverin, Bérard 2562
Rivett-Carnac, Charles 3360
Robardet, Patrick 2384
Robb, Andrew 46 884
Robert, Jean-Claude 2550
    2594
Roberts, Barbara 1063
Roberts, David 2400
Roberts, Terry 2852
Roberts, Wayne 1103
Robertson, D. F. 3065
Robertson, Gordon 1707
Robertson, Ian Ross 2207
    2208
Robinson, Gertrude Joch
    2042
Robinson, Helen Caister 440
Robinson, J. Lewis 3242
Robinson, Kenneth R. 1600
    1601 1602
Robinson, Willard B. 188
Rocher, Guy 2551
Rodin, Alvin E. 2552
Rogel, Jean-Pierre 2553
Rogers, A. Robert 1257
Rogers, William D. 1953
Rolland, Solange Chaput 2083
Romaniuk, A. 441
Romanow, Walter Ivan 1901
Romney, Paul 2853 2854
Romsa, G. 2743
Ronaghan, Allen 442 443
    1020
Rose, Frances 189
Rose, Joseph B. 27 1603 1604
Rosenberg, Neil V. 2401
Ross, Brian R. 1064 1065
    1137
Ross, Charles R. 262
Ross, David 190
Ross, W. Gillies 681 3294
Rossetto, Luigi 1258
Rostecki, Randy R. 3003
    3004
Rothwell, David R. 1241
Rotstein, Abraham 1259
Roueche, Leonard R. 3243
Rouillard, Jacques 2655
Rouslin, Virginia Watson 191
Rousseau, François 539
Rousseau, Henri-Paul 1605
Rovinsky, Robert T. 1343
Rowand, Evelyn 1021
Rowe, Ian 1260
Rowe, P. A. 192
Rowley, G. 3316
Rowley, Kent 2043
Roxborough, Henry 193
Roy, Jean-Louis 2044 2709

Roy, Jean-Yves 2554
Roy, Maurice 2508
Roy, Patricia E. 1242 3244
　3245 3246 3247
Roy, Raymond 514 540 541
Roy, Reginald H. 1243 3248
Royle, John C. 325
Rubin, Don 2855
Rubin, Julius 801
Rubinoff, Lionel 1330
Ruddell, Thiery 2522
Ruddick, Valley 1902
Rudé, George 819
Rudin, Ronald 2555
Ruff, Norman J. 3249
Ruggeri, Giuseppe C. 1606
Ruggle, Richard 194
Ruggles, Richard I. 682 683
　684
Russell, Chesley 332
Russell, Francis 1187
Russell, Hilary 802 1138
Russell, Loris S. 195 939
Russell, Peter H. 1607
Russell, Ruth B. 1760
Rutan, Gerard F. 1708 2045
　2046 2047
Rutherford, Paul 2335
Rutherford, Paul F. W. 940
Ryan, Claude 2556
Ryerson, Stanley B. 2447

S

Saban, Vera D. 444
Sabourin, Louis 2710 2711
Safarin, A. E. 1903
Saguin, André-Louis 2448
Sainsbury, George V. 2856
Saint-Germain, Maurice 2656
Salaff, Stephen 1139
Salter, Michael A. 542 543
Samardžić, Dragana 1162
Samaroo, Brinsley 196
Sancton, Andrew 2336
Sanderson, Lilian 197
Sanger, Clyde 1904
Sankoff, David 1709
Santos Hernández, Angel 587
Sarjeant, William A. S. 3068
Saul, John S. 1905
Saunders, Ivan J. 198
Sauter, John V. 1906
Savard, Pierre 2449 2557
Sawatzky, H. L. 3005
Sawula, Lorne W. 1104 1468
Sawyer, Tom 1973
Sayced, Khalid B. 1710
Saylor, Stanley G. 305
Saywell, William 1907
Schaafsma, Joseph 1608
Schaefer, Otto 333
Schanz, A. B. 3339
Schechter, Rebecca 803
Scheinberg, Stephen 199
Schelbert, Leo 685
Schenck, Ernest 2450
Scherer, F. M. 1609
Schlabach, Theron F. 941
Schledermann, Peter 334
Schlesier, Karl H. 523
Schlesinger, Benjamin 1469
Schneck, Rodney 1969
Schneer, Cecil J. 277
Schomp, Gerald 488
Schoonover, Cortlandt 2951
Schramm, Carl J. 2048
Schreiber, E. M. 1470
Schrodt, Barbara 200
Schroeter, Gerd 201 445
Schrumm, J. R. 3146
Schultz, J. A. 3250
Schwartz, Louis B. 1955
Schwartz, Mildred A. 1261
Schweninger, Loren 885 886
Schwermann, Albert H. 3147
Schwieder, Dorothy A. 1022
Scollard, Robert J. 2858
Scollie, F. Brent 2859
Scotland, James 2337
Scott, Anthony 202 2011 2049
Scott, Beverly 2142
Scott, Bruce 1188
Scott, John R. 2202
Scotter, George W. 3295
Scovil, G. C. Coster 1262
Seager, Allen 1209

Sealock, Richard B. 203 1263
Seastone, D. A. 1908
Seccombe, W. 2734
Secouman, R. James 2338
Segal, Beryl 204
Séguin, Normand 2558 2657
　2658
Séguin, Robert-Lionel 544
Seifert, Traudl 482
Sellekaerts, Willy 1965
Selwood, H. John 1023 3006
Senior, Elinor 820 833
Senior, H. 821
Serfaty, Meir 3148
Sewell, James P. 1909
Seymour, Edward E. 1610
Shack, Sybil 3007
Shantz, Jacob Y. 1024
Sharman, G. C. 1711
Sharman, V. 2339
Sharp, Mitchell 1916
Sharrock, Susan R. 446
Shaw, Edward C. 205
Shaw, P. C. 447
Sheehan, Bernard S. 1471
Sheffield, Edward F. 2860
Sherfield, Lord 1910
Sheriff, Peta 2559
Sherman, Ro 3339
Sherrard, William R. 2257
Sherrin, P. M. 1105
Sherwood, Roland H. 2340
　2341 2342 2343 2344
Shewchuk, Murphy 3251
Shi, David E. 3252
Shields, R. A. 1106 1107
Shimizu, Ronald 2796
Shugg, Roger W. 206
Sibert, C. Thomas 2861
Siegenthaler, David 726
Siemens, L. B. 1911
Siemens, Nettie 3008
Sigelman, Lee 1712
Sigler, John 2712
Sigler, John H. 2050
Silver, A. I. 2560
Silver, Marietta 2345
Silverman, Bernie I. 2051
Silverman, Elaine Leslau 1025
　3149
Silvia, Philip T., Jr. 2659
Simard, Jean Paul 2561 2562
Simard, Jean-Jacques 2451
Simard, Ovide-D 2563
Simard, Sylvain 2564
Simeon, Richard 2143 2144
Sims, A. G. 207
Sims, E. Leigh 306
Sinclair, D. M. 2346 2347
Sinclair, James M. 3253
Sinclair, Peter R. 3066 3067
Singer, Howard L. 2713
Sirois, Antoine 1472
Sismey, Eric D. 448
Skaggs, David C., Jr. 727
Skinner, Andrew S. 728
Skinner, Brian J. 208
Slack, B. 2660
Slemkó, Brian 3129
Slimman, Donald J. 2052
Slobodin, Richard 449
Small, A. Douglas 1912
Smart, Ian 1913
Smedresman, Peter S. 2053
Smiley, Donald V. 209 1473
　1713 2112 2113
Smith, Allan 210 942
Smith, Arnold 1914
Smith, Burton M. 2054
Smith, David 211
Smith, David E. 212
Smith, Denis 1303
Smith, Donald B. 450 451 452
　686 1140 1163
Smith, Dorothy Blakey 3254
Smith, Dorothy E. 1474
Smith, Elsie B. 2565
Smith, Helen Pollitt 3009
　3010 3011
Smith, Howie 3255
Smith, James F. 2170 2348
　2349 2350
Smith, Janet 213
Smith, Joel 1681
Smith, Michael D. 2862
Smith, Norman 1915 2083
Smith, Patrick 2796
Smith, Ralph 507

Smith, Roger S. 214
Smith, Shirlee A. 687
Smith, Shirley A. 3012
Smith, T. G. 335
Smith, W. I. 215
Smith, William 2661
Smyly, Carolyn 453 454
Smyly, John 453 454 455
Sniderman, Paul M. 1714
Snow, Duart 1210
Snow, Richard F. 762
Snyder, David 216
Snyder, Marsha 3296
Soames, Christopher 1916
Socwell, Clarence P. 688
Soderlund, Walter C. 1722
　1917
Solano Costa, Fernando 588
Solberg, Janet 1340
Solerlund, Walter C. 1715
Song, Sunmin 456
Soper, J. Dewey 3317 3318
Soroka, Lewis 2145
Sorrell, Richard S. 2566
Sorrentino, Constance 1585
Soward, F. H. 217 1211
Sparkes, Vernone M. 2042
　2055 2056
Spates, James L. 1475
Spector, David 1066 3013
Spencer, Stephen 2863
Spiess, Arthur 336
Spigelman, Martin S. 218
　1067 2402
Spindel, Donna J. 729
Spindler, George D. 457
Spindler, Louise S. 457
Spira, Thomas 46
Spragins, F. K. 3150
Spray, William A. 804 2403
Sproule-Jones, Mark 219
Spry, Irene M. 2952
Squires, J. Duane 730
Srebnik, Henry 1716
St. Claire, Denis E. 301
St. John, Edward S. 2857
St. John, Peter 2083
Stacey, C. P. 1244
Stager, David A. A. 1476
Stairs, Denis 1918 1919
Stammers, M. K. 2662
Stamp, Robert M. 2864 2865
Stanbury, W. T. 458
Stanley, George F. G. 1026
　2404 3151
St.-Arnaud, Pierre 2494
Starnes, John 1920
Stauffer, Anne Tholen 504
Steck, Warren F. 3068
Stedman, Charles 2057
Steed, Guy P. F. 1611
Steele, G. G. E. 1717
Stegner, Wallace 2146
Stein, Michael 2114 2714
Steinberg, Charles 2351
Stelter, Gilbert A. 220 221
　222 223 224
Stephens, David E. 2352 2353
Stethem, Nicholas 1921
Stevens, Geoffrey 1922
Stevens, Neil 2866
Stevenson, A. 2663 3361
Stevenson, Garth 2058 2147
Steward, Donald M. 1027
Stewart, Catharine McArthur
　731
Stewart, Gordon 732 2354
Stewart, Marianne C. 2748
Stewart, Nellie R. 2355
Stewart, William 1331
Stieb, Ernst W. 2059 2867
Stiff, John 2868
Stokes, Lawrence D. 1212
Stokesbury, James L. 621
Stone, Leroy O. 1477
Stone, Thomas 459
Story, Donald C. 1923
Stouffer, Allen P. 887
Stranges, John B. 2060
Strobridge, Truman R. 3290
Strong, Emory 460
Strong-Boag, Veronica 225
　1189
Strum, Harvey 2953
Struthers, J. R. 2869
Struthers, James 1190
Sturino, Franc 2870
Stursberg, Peter 1264

Subbarao, A. V. 1718
Sugimoto, Howard H. 1108
Sullivan, Clare D. 483
Sullivan, Richard F. 1332
Summers, Jack L. 190
Sunter, Ronald 805
Surlin, Stuart H. 1479
Sussman, Leonard R. 1478
　1924
Sutherland, David 2356
Suthren, Victor J. H. 763
　2061
Svacek, Victor 1338
Swaison, Donald 897
Swankey, Ben 1719
Swanson, Roger Frank 226
　1925 2062 2063 2064
　2065
Sweet, Jessie M. 689
Swidinsky, Robert 227 1612
Sylvain, Philippe 1068 1069
　2567
Syms, E. Leigh 307 308

T

Tallman, Richard S. 2357
Tallman, Ronald 1070
Tallman, Ronald D. 1071
Tanaka, June K. 1245
Tandon, B. B. 1613 2871
Tandon, K. K. 1613
Tanner, Dwight 764
Tanti, Spiro 3256
Tavernier, Yves 13
Taylor, George Rogers 733
Taylor, Hugh A. 1265
Taylor, John H. 116 2872
　2954
Taylor, K. W. 3014 3023
Taylor, Mimi Cazort 228
Taylor, Murray W. 2955
Teeple, Gary 1266 1720
Tegelberg, Laurie 1028
Tennyson, Brian D. 278 2358
　2405
Tepperman, Lorne 211 1072
Teschke, W. R. 1680
Tetrault, Gregory 3340
Teversham, J. 3235
Thakur, Ramesh C. 1928
Thapar, Romesh 1929
Theberge, C. B. 3319
Theberge, Henry 3319
Theriault, Leon 2171
Thériault, Yvon 2511
Thoman, Richard S. 2873
Thomas, C. E. 751 2359
Thomas, Clara 1109
Thomas, Gregory 461
Thomas, Lewis H. 3069
Thompson, Agnes L. 2664
Thompson, Arthur N. 462
Thompson, John H. 1164
Thompson, Katheryn M. 229
Thompson, Lee Briscoe 1213
Thompson, Mark 1614 1615
　3257
Thompson, Patricia T. 2228
Thomson, Colin A. 3070 3152
Thomson, Dale C. 2568
Thomson, Theresa E. 3153
Thorburn, Hugh 2115
Thordarson, Bruce 1930
Threinen, Norman J. 1029
　1191
Thure, Karen 2874
Tiblin, Mariann 230
Ticoll, David 463
Tiessen, Hugo 3071 3072 3073
Tippett, Maria 633 3258 3259
　3260
Tishkov, V. A. 707
Toh, Swee-Hin 1931
Tolson, Elsie Churchill 2360
Tomasi, Lydio F. 2875
Toner, Peter M. 1073
Torge, Janet 1512
Torrance, Judy 231
Torrelli, Maurice 1141
Toulouse, Jean-Marie 2585
Tousignant, Pierre 708 709
　710
Tovell, Freeman M. 1932

Traves, Thomas D. 1192
Travis, Paul D. 1110
Travis, Ralph 1933
Traynham, Earle C., Jr. 1415
Treddenick, J. M. 1267
Tremblay, Marc-Adélard 2116
　2569 2715 2716
Tremblay, Rodrigue 2665
Trent, John 2117
Trent, John E. 2118
Trépanier, Lise 898
Trépanier, Pierre 232 822 898
　2119 2452 2453 2570
　2717
Trevena, J. E. 3074
Trezise, Philip H. 1333 2066
　2083
Tribe, Verna 1345
Trimble, Paul E. 2876
Trofimenkoff, Susan Mann
　1142
Trooboff, Peter D. 2067
Troper, Harold 2784 2877
Trower, Peter 3261
Trudel, Marcel 2571
Trudel, Pierre 2572
Trueman, Stuart 2406 2407
Truman, Tom 1721
Tuck, J. H. 1111
Tuck, James 487
Tulchinsky, Gerald 2666
Tunis, B. R. 2573
Turcotte, Claude 1934
Turner, A. E. 3154
Turner, C. Frank 1030 2878
Turner, Wesley B. 888 2879
Turrittin, Jane Sawyer 1935
Tusseau, Jean-Pierre 1074
Tweed, Tommy 3015
Twiss, James 2890
Tyrrell, J. W. 337

U

Uhler, R. S. 1683
Ujimoto, K. Victor 3262
Ullman, Stephen H. 2361
Unrau, William E. 464
Upton, L. F. S. 290 465 466
　467 468 469 734 2408
Urquhart, G. M. 234
Usher, Peter J. 338
Usherwood, Stephen 3341

V

Vachon, G.-André 235
Vagts, Detlev 1955
Vaillancourt, François 2148
Vaillancourt, Pauline 2574
Valaskakis, Kimon 1939
Vanderberg, Richard D. 1620
Vanderbok, William G. 1712
Vandycke, Robert 2503
VanDyke, Vernon 1481
Vanger, Max 1143
VanKirk, Sylvia 577
VanLoon, Richard J. 1729
VanNus, W. 236 237
Vaugeois, Denis 2718
Vaughan, Frederick 238 2068
Veeman, Michele M. 1621
Veeman, Terrence S. 1621
Velez, Claudio 239
Vellathottam, T. George 240
Veltman, Calvin J. 2575 2576
　2577
Veltmeyer, Henry 2172
Verby, John 3320
Verma, Ravi P. 1329
Verney, Diana M. 690
Verney, Douglas V. 690
Vernon, Donald E. 3017
Vernon, Howard A. 2956
Vézina, Jean-P 2667
Vézina, Raymond 241
Vigneras, L.-A 508
Vigod, B. L. 2578
Villa-Arce, José 3156
Vincent, Thomas B. 2362
　2409
Vipond, Mary 1112 1193 1194
　1195
Voisey, Paul 2957 2958
Voisine, Nive 2579 2580
Volpe, John 2007

VonRiekhoff, Harald 1940
VonSchoenberg, Brigitte 2547

W

Wade, Mason 622
Wade, Norman 889
Wadley, W. 2880
Wagenberg, Ronald H. 1715
   1722 1917
Wagner, J. Richard 1941 2069
   2070 2071
Wagner, Jonathan F. 1246
   3076 3077
Wagner, Jonathan R. 1216
Waisglass, Harry J. 1942
Waite, P. B. 1075
Wakefield, Theodore D. 589
Wakil, S. Parvez 1482
Waldie, Ken 1622
Walker, Gerald 2881
Wallace, A. I. 3297
Wallace, C. M. 2410 2411
Wallace, Iain 1623 2072
Wallace, Lee A., Jr. 765
Wallace, Mrs. Ernest 2363
Wallis, Helen 484
Wallot, Jean-Pierre 711 712
   795 796 806
Walsh, Sam 2719 2720
Walsh, William D. 1624
Walton, Bruce 823
Warburton, T. Rennie 1398
   2149
Ward, E. Neville 1483
Ward, Norman 242 1729 1943
   2959 3078 3079 3157
   3158
Ward, W. Peter 1247

Warkentyne, H. J. 1484
Warner, Iris 339
Warner, John Anson 470
Warner, Malcolm 1268
Warnock, John 1269 1723
Warnock, John W. 2073
Warren, Iris 3342
Warwick, Peter 2882
Waterston, Elizabeth 2454
Watts, Ronald L. 1485
Wawrzysko, Aleksandra 2581
Weale, David 2209
Weaver, Bill 1076
Weaver, John C. 243 2883
   2884 2885 3159
Webb, Jonathan 1217
Webb, Paul 691
Webber, Alika 471
Webber, L. R. 1334
Wees, Ian 244
Weiermair, Klaus 1625
Weinberger, Caspar, Jr. 472
Weinfeld, Morton 1486 2721
Weir, John 1944
Weiss, Jonathan M. 2074
   2722
Welch, Edwin 2886
Welch, Susan 1724
Weller, G. R. 2887
Wells, E. H. 3339
Welsch, Erwin K. 230
Wendland, Wayne M. 309
Wertheim, Edward G. 1626
West, J. Thomas 1144
Whitaker, Reg 1487
White, Arthur 2075
White, Bruce M. 3323
White, Clinton O. 3080 3081
White, Gavin 340 3362
White, Graham 1148

White, Stephen A. 2364 2365
White, Walter L. 2811
Whitehouse, John R. W. 1627
Whiteley, Albert S. 2582
Whiteley, William H. 735
   2203
Whitfield, Carol 245 766
Whitney, Harriet E. 1113
   1114
Whittington, Michael S. 1729
Whynot, G. Keith 2076
Whyte, John D. 473
Whyte, John H. 246
Wilbur, J. R. H. 1218
Wilgat, T. 1335
Wilkinson, Ron 1336
Williams, C. Brian 1628
Williams, Glyndwr 692 2960
Williams, Linda K. 752
Williams, P. J. 3297
Williams, Rick 2366
Williams, Roger 1725
Williams, W. H. 1031
Williamson, David T. 3160
Williamson, Eileen 2888
Williamson, Norman J. 3018
   3019
Willoughby, William R. 2077
Wills, Morris W. 247
Wilson, Alan 2173
Wilson, Bruce 736
Wilson, J. Donald 248 474
   475
Wilson, John 1726 3020
Wilson, L. J. 3082 3161
Wilson, Leroy R. 1136
Wilson, Marion C. 249 1488
Wilson, Maureen 3263
Wilson, Michael 310
Wilson, V. Seymour 1489

Wilson, W. A. 2078
Winberg, Alan R. 1945
Winer, Stanley L. 2103
Winham, Gilbert R. 1649
Winkler, H. W. 3021
Winn, Conrad 2889 2890
Wionczek, Miguel S. 1955
Wise, S. F. 693
Wiseman, N. 3014
Wiseman, Nelson 3022 3023
Wisse, Ruth R. 2723
Wittlinger, Carlton O. 250
Wittlingern, Carlton O. 1145
Wolfe, Art 415
Wolff, Julius F., Jr. 943
Wollock, Jeffrey 2891
Wonders, William C. 694
   1032
Wong, George G. 1165
Wonnacott, R. J. 2079
Wood, C. E. D. 3162
Wood, G. N. 767
Woodcock, George 251 695
   1033
Woodman, Lyman L. 1248
Woods, John 1490
Woods, John G. 279
Woodward, Frances M. 3264
   3265 3266 3267 3268
   3269
Woodward, John 311
Woolfson, Peter 252 2583
Workman, Leslie J. 109
Woywitka, Anne B. 1034
   2961 3163 3164 3165
   3166
Wright, A. Jeffrey 2367
Wright, Charles 3321
Wright, Donald K. 1491
Wright, Gerald 253 254 1946

2080
Wright, Jeffrey 2368
Wright, N. J. R. 3288
Wrong, Hume 1146
Wukasch, Peter 1492
Wyn, Graeme 2412 2413

Y

Yaffe, Phyllis 255
Yankel, Reb 3270
Yerbury, J. C. 476
Yoder, Don 256
Yonge, C. M. 257
Young, Alexander 2369
Young, Christopher 2081
Young, John J. 3167
Young, Murray 2174
Young, R. A. 2120
Young, R. S. 258
Young, Walter D. 2962 3271
Yuzyk, Paul 1947 2121

Z

Zacher, Mark W. 1869
Zehr, Dan 1381
Zerker, Sally 2892 2893
Zezulka, J. M. 259
Ziegler, Suzanne 1493
Zielinska, Marie F. 1494
Zink, Ella 2963
Zipp, John F. 1727
Zureik, Elia T. 260
Zurlo, John A. 737

LIST OF PERIODICALS

A

Acadiensis: Journal of the History of the Atlantic Region [Canada]
Action Nationale [Canada]
Actualité Économique [Canada]
Aerospace Historian
Affari Esteri [Italy]
Agricultural History
Alabama Historical Quarterly
Alaska Journal (ceased pub 1980)
Alberta Historical Review (see Alberta History) [Canada]
Alberta History [Canada]
Albion
América Indígena [Mexico]
American Aviation Historical Society. Journal
American Behavioral Scientist
American Book Collector (ceased pub 1976)
American Economic Review
American Heritage
American Historical Review
American History Illustrated
American Indian Art Magazine
American Jewish Archives
American Jewish Historical Quarterly (see American Jewish History)
American Jewish History
American Journal of Economics and Sociology
American Journal of International Law
American Journal of Political Science
American Neptune
American Political Science Review
American Review of Canadian Studies
American Scandinavian Review (superseded by Scandinavian Review)
American Scholar
American Society of International Law. Proceedings (issues for 1970-73 appeared under the title American Journal of International Law)
American Sociological Review
American Speech
American West
Américas (Organization of American States)
Annales de Géographie [France]
Annales Historiques de la Révolution Française [France]
Annals of Iowa
Annals of Science [Great Britain]
Annals of the American Academy of Political and Social Science
Annals of the Association of American Geographers
Annals of Wyoming
Année Politique et Économique (ceased pub 1975) [France]
Archív Orientální [Czechoslovakia]
Archives [Great Britain]
Arctic [Canada]
Armed Forces and Society
Army Quarterly and Defence Journal [Great Britain]
Atlantic Community Quarterly
Australian Foreign Affairs Record [Australia]
Australian Journal of Politics and History [Australia]

B

BC Studies [Canada]
Beaver [Canada]
Behind the Headlines [Canada]
Black Scholar
British Journal of Educational Studies [Great Britain]
British Library Journal [Great Britain]
Bulletin de la Société de l'Histoire du Protestantisme Français [France]
Bulletin des Séances de l'Académie Royale des Sciences d'Outre-mer [Belgium]
Bulletin of the Atomic Scientists (briefly known as Science and Public Affairs)
Bulletin of the Committee on Archives of the United Church of Canada [Canada]
Bulletin of the History of Medicine
Bulletin of the Society for the Study of Labour History [Great Britain]
Bulletin of the United Church of Canada (see Bulletin of the Committee on Archives of the United Church of Canada) [Canada]
Business History [Great Britain]
Business History Review

C

Cahiers de Géographie de Québec [Canada]
Cahiers Internationaux d'Histoire Économique et Sociale [Italy]
California Historical Quarterly (see California History)
California History
Canada: An Historical Magazine (ceased pub 1976) [Canada]
Canadian Dimension [Canada]
Canadian Ethnic Studies = Études Ethniques au Canada [Canada]
Canadian Geographic [Canada]
Canadian Geographical Journal (see Canadian Geographic) [Canada]
Canadian Historic Sites [Canada]
Canadian Historical Association Historical Papers (see Historical Papers) [Canada]
Canadian Historical Review [Canada]
Canadian Journal of Economics and Political Science (see Canadian Journal of Political Science) [Canada]
Canadian Journal of History = Annales Canadiennes d'Histoire [Canada]
Canadian Journal of History of Sport = Revue Canadienne de l'Histoire des Sports [Canada]
Canadian Journal of History of Sport and Physical Education (see Canadian Journal of History of Sport) [Canada]
Canadian Journal of Political Science = Revue Canadienne de Science Politique [Canada]
Canadian Labour [Canada]
Canadian Library Journal [Canada]
Canadian Oral History Association Journal = Journal de la Société Canadienne d'Histoire Orale [Canada]
Canadian Public Administration = Administration Publique du Canada [Canada]
Canadian Review of American Studies [Canada]
Canadian Review of Sociology and Anthropology = Revue Canadienne de Sociologie et d'Anthropologie [Canada]
Canadian Review of Studies in Nationalism = Revue Canadienne des Études sur le Nationalisme [Canada]
Chesterton Review [Canada]
Chicago History
Chronicles of Oklahoma
Church History
Civil Liberties Review (ceased pub 1979)
Civil War History
Civil War Times Illustrated
College and Research Libraries
Columbia Journal of Transnational Law
Commentary
Communication Monographs
Communist Viewpoint [Canada]
Comparative Political Studies
Comparative Studies in Society and History [Great Britain]
Concordia Historical Institute Quarterly
Crisis
Cry California
Cultures [France]
Current History

D

Dalhousie Review [Canada]
Défense Nationale [France]
Delaware History
Diogenes [Italy]
Dissent

E

Economic Development and Cultural Change
Economic Geography
Encounter [Great Britain]
Encounter
Estudios del Departamento de Historia Moderna (IHE) [Spain]
Ethnicity
Ethnohistory
Études Françaises [Canada]
Études Internationales [Canada]
Explorations in Economic History

F

Fides et Historia
Florida Historical Quarterly
Foreign Affairs
Foreign Policy
Foundations: A Baptist Journal of History and Theology
Frankfurter Hefte [German Federal Republic]
Freedom at Issue
French Historical Studies
Frontiers

G

Gazette: International Journal for Mass Communication Studies [Netherlands]
Geographical Journal [Great Britain]
Geographical Review
Geography [Great Britain]
Government and Opposition [Great Britain]
Government Publications Review Part A: Research Articles

H

Halve Maen
Harvard Library Bulletin
Hawaiian Journal of History
Histoire Sociale (see Social History = Histoire Sociale) [Canada]
Historian
Historic Preservation
Historical Archaeology
Historical Journal of Massachusetts
Historical Journal of Western Massachusetts (see Historical Journal of Massachusetts)
Historical Magazine of the Protestant Episcopal Church
Historical Methods
Historical Methods Newsletter (see Historical Methods)
Historical New Hampshire
Historical Papers = Communications Historiques [Canada]
Historical Reflections = Réflexions Historiques [Canada]
Historische Zeitschrift [German Federal Republic]
History of Education Quarterly
History Teacher
History Today [Great Britain]
History Workshop Journal [Great Britain]
Hitotsubashi Ronsō [Japan]
Horizon
Human Organization
Humanities Association Review = Revue de l'Association des Humanités [Canada]
Huntington Library Quarterly

I

Idaho Yesterdays
India Quarterly: Journal of International Affairs [India]
Indian Historian (see Wasseje Indian Historian)
Indiana Social Studies Quarterly
Industrial and Labor Relations Review
Industrial Relations = Relations Industrielles [Canada]
Inland Seas
Inter-American Economic Affairs
International Affairs [Great Britain]
International Affairs [Union of Soviet Socialist Republic]
International Journal [Canada]
International Journal of Comparative Sociology [Canada]
International Migration Review
International Organization
International Perspectives
International Social Science Journal [France]
International Socialist Review
International Studies Quarterly
Isis
Italian Americana

J

Japan Interpreter [Japan]
Jednota Annual Furdek

Jewish Social Studies
Journal of American Folklore
Journal of American History
Journal of American Studies [Great Britain]
Journal of Black Studies
Journal of Business
Journal of Canadian Studies = Revue d'Études
    Canadiennes [Canada]
Journal of Church and State
Journal of Commonwealth and Comparative Politics
    [Great Britain]
Journal of Communication
Journal of Conflict Resolution
Journal of Contemporary History [Great Britain]
Journal of Economic History
Journal of Economic Literature
Journal of Educational Administration and History
    [Great Britain]
Journal of Ethnic Studies
Journal of Family History: Studies in Family,
    Kinship, and Demography
Journal of Forest History
Journal of Historical Geography
Journal of Imperial and Commonwealth History
    [Great Britain]
Journal of Interamerican Studies and World Affairs
Journal of Interdisciplinary History
Journal of Law & Economics
Journal of Modern History
Journal of Negro History
Journal of Political Economy
Journal of Politics
Journal of Popular Culture
Journal of Religion in Africa = Religion en Afrique
    [Netherlands]
Journal of Social History
Journal of Sport History
Journal of Studies on Alcohol
Journal of the American Institute of Planners (see
    Journal of
Journal of the American Planning Association
Journal of the Canadian Church Historical Society
    [Canada]
Journal of the Folklore Institute
Journal of the History of Medicine and Allied
    Sciences
Journal of the History of the Behavioral Sciences
Journal of the Illinois State Historical Society
Journal of the Royal United Services Institute for
    Defence Studies [Great Britain]
Journal of the Society for Army Historical Research
    [Great Britain]
Journal of the Society of Architectural Historians
Journal of the Society of Archivists [Great Britain]
Journal of the West
Journal of World Trade Law [Switzerland]
Journalism Quarterly
Judicature

K

Kansas Historical Quarterly (superseded by Kansas
    History)
Kultura i Społeczeństwo [Poland]
Kyklos [Switzerland]

L

Labour = Travailleur [Canada]
Land Economics
Law & Society Review
Library Quarterly
Library Review [Great Britain]
Lincoln Herald
Louisiana History
Louisiana Review = Revue de Louisiane

M

Manitoba Pageant (superseded by Manitoba History)
    [Canada]
Marine Corps Gazette
Mariner's Mirror [Great Britain]
Maritime History [Great Britain]
Marxist Perspectives
Maryland Historical Magazine
Massachusetts Review
Masterkey
Medical History [Great Britain]
Mennonite Historical Bulletin
Mennonite Life
Mennonite Quarterly Review
Methodist History
Michigan Academician
Midstream

Military Affairs
Military Collector and Historian
Military Review
Minnesota History
Mirovaia Ekonomika i Mezhdunarodnye Otnosheniia
    [Union of Soviet Socialist Republic]
Missionalia Hispanica [Spain]
Missouri Historical Review
Modernist Studies: Literature and Culture 1920-1940
    [Canada]
Montana: Magazine of Western History
Monthly Labor Review
Muslim World

N

Names
National Civic Review
Nautical Research Journal
Nebraska History
New England Historical and Genealogical Register
New England Quarterly
New Left Review [Great Britain]
New York Folklore Quarterly (superseded by New
    York Folklore)
New York History
New York University Journal of International Law
    and Politics
New-England Galaxy
New-York Historical Society Quarterly
Niagara Frontier
North Dakota History
North Dakota Quarterly
Notes and Records of the Royal Society of London
    [Great Britain]
Nova Scotia Historical Quarterly [Canada]
Nova Scotia Historical Society Collections [Canada]

O

Old-Time New England
Ontario History [Canada]
Oral History Review
Orbis
Oregon Historical Quarterly

P

Pacific Affairs [Canada]
Pacific Historical Review
Pacific Northwest Quarterly
Pacific Northwesterner
Paedagogica Historica [Belgium]
Pakistan Horizon [Pakistan]
Pakistan Library Bulletin [Pakistan]
Parliamentary Affairs [Great Britain]
Patterns of Prejudice [Great Britain]
Peace and Change
Peasant Studies
Peasant Studies Newsletter (see Peasant Studies)
Pennsylvania Magazine of History and Biography
Pharmacy in History
Philippine Journal of Public Administration
    [Philippines]
Phylon
Pioneer America
Plains Anthropologist
Plural Societies [Netherlands]
Polar Record [Great Britain]
Policy Studies Journal
Polish Review
Polish Western Affairs [Poland]
Political Science [New Zealand]
Political Science Review [India]
Political Studies [Great Britain]
Politique Étrangère [France]
Polity
Ponte [Italy]
Prairie Forum [Canada]
Present Tense
Presidential Studies Quarterly
Proceedings of the Academy of Political Science
Proceedings of the American Philosophical Society
Proceedings of the Annual Meeting of the Western
    Society for French History
Protée [Canada]
Przegląd Zachodni [Poland]
Public Administration [Great Britain]
Public Interest
Public Opinion Quarterly
Public Policy
Public Welfare
Publius

Q

Quarterly Journal of Studies on Alcohol (see Journal
    of Studies on Alcohol)
Quarterly Journal of the Library of Congress
Quarterly Review of Economics and Business
Queen's Quarterly [Canada]

R

Railroad History
Rassegna Italiana di Sociologia [Italy]
Reason
Recherche Sociale [France]
Recherches Sociographiques [Canada]
Register of the Kentucky Historical Society
Relations Industrielles (see Industrial Relations =
    Relations Industrielles) [Canada]
Review of Economics and Statistics
Review of Social Economy
Revista/Review Interamericana [Puerto Rico]
Revue de Louisiane-Louisiana Review (see Louisiana
    Review = Revue de Louisiane)
Revue de l'Université d'Ottawa (see University of
    Ottawa Quarterly = Revue de l'Université
    d'Ottawa) [Canada]
Revue d'Histoire de la Deuxième Guerre Mondiale
    [France]
Revue d'Histoire de l'Amérique Française [Canada]
Revue d'Histoire Économique et Sociale (suspended
    pub 1977) [France]
Revue Française d'Histoire d'Outre-mer [France]
Revue Internationale de Droit Comparé [France]
Revue Internationale d'Histoire de la Banque
    [Italy]
Rhode Island Jewish Historical Notes
Rivista Storica Italiana [Italy]
Rocky Mountain Social Science Journal (see Social
    Science Journal)
Round Table [Great Britain]

S

Saskatchewan History [Canada]
Scandinavian Review
Scandinavian Studies
Scholarly Publishing [Canada]
Scottish Geographical Magazine [Great Britain]
Serials Librarian
Sessions d'Étude: Société Canadienne d'Histoire de
    l'Église Catholique (published simultaneously in
    one volume with Study Sessions: Canadian
    Catholic Historical
Signs: Journal of Women in Culture and Society
Slavonic and East European Review [Great Britain]
Slovakia
Slovanský Přehled [Czechoslovakia]
Smithsonian
Social Forces
Social History = Histoire Sociale [Canada]
Social Problems
Social Science
Social Science Journal
Society
Sociological Inquiry
Sociological Quarterly
Sociological Review [Great Britain]
Sociology and Social Research
Sound Heritage [Canada]
South Atlantic Quarterly
South Carolina Historical Magazine
South Dakota History
Southern Economic Journal
Southern Folklore Quarterly
Southern Studies: An Interdisciplinary Journal of the
    South
Sovetskaia Etnografiia [Union of Soviet Socialist
    Republic]
Sovetskoe Gosudarstvo i Pravo [Union of Soviet
    Socialist Republic]
Special Libraries
Speech Monographs (see Communication
    Monographs)
Spiegel Historiael [Netherlands]
Strategy and Tactics
Studies in Comparative International Development
Study Sessions: Canadian Catholic Historical
    Association (published simultaneously in one
    volume with Sessions d'Étude: Société
    Canadienne d'Histoire de l'Église Catholique)
    [Canada]
Survival [Great Britain]
Swedish Pioneer Historical Quarterly
Swiss American Historical Society Newsletter
Synthesis

T

Teachers College Record
Teaching History: A Journal of Methods
Technology and Culture
Terrae Incognita
Transactions of the Historical and Scientific Society
    of Manitoba (superseded by Manitoba History)
    [Canada]
Transactions of the Royal Society of Canada =
    Mémoires de la Société Royale du Canada
    [Canada]
Turun Historiallinen Arkisto [Finland]

U

Ukrainian Quarterly
Ukrainian Review [Great Britain]
University of Ottawa Quarterly = Revue de

l'Université d'Ottawa [Canada]
University of Windsor Review [Canada]
Urban History Review = Revue d'Histoire Urbaine
    [Canada]
Urbanism Past and Present

V

Vermont History
Vesnik Vojnog Muzeja — Beograd [Yugoslavia]
Victorian Studies
Virginia Cavalcade
Virginia Magazine of History and Biography
Voprosy Istorii [Union of Soviet Socialist Republic]

W

Wasseje Indian Historian

West Virginia History
Western American Literature
Western Folklore
Western Historical Quarterly
Western Political Quarterly
Western States Jewish Historical Quarterly
Westways
William and Mary Quarterly
Working Papers for a New Society
World Affairs
World Marxist Review [Canada]
World Politics
World Today [Great Britain]
Worldview

Y

Yale University Library Gazette
Youth and Society

LIST OF ABSTRACTERS

A

Aimone, A. C.
Alvis, R.
Anderson, B. P.
Anderson, P. J.
Anstey, C.
Athey, L. L.
Atkins, L. R.

B

Bailey, E. C.
Barkan, E.
Barnard, R. S.
Bassett, T. D. S.
Bates, C.
Bauer, K. J.
Bauhs, T. H.
Beaber, P. A.
Beck, P. J.
Belles, A. G.
Billigmeier, J. C.
Blanc, A. E. Le
Blethen, H. T.
Bobango, G. J.
Bowers, D. E.
Bradford, J. C.
Brewster, D. E.
Broussard, J. H.
Brown, J.
Brown, L.
Burnett, B.
Buschen, J.
Butchart, R.
Butcher, K.

C

Calkin, H. L.
Cameron, D. D.
Campbell, E. R.
Casada, J. A.
Chan, L. B.
Chaput, D.
Chard, D. F.
Chard, E. A.
Churchill, E. A.
Cleyet, G. P.
Clive, A.
Coleman, P. J.
Collon, C.
Colwell, J. L.
Correia-Afonso, J.
Crapster, B. L.
Crowther, K. N. T.
Curtis, G. H.

D

Davis, G. H.
Davison, S. R.
Dean, D. M.
Dibert, M. D.
Dodd, D. B.
Driggs, O. T.

E

Egerton, F. N.
Elison, W. W.
Eminhizer, E. E.
Engler, D. J.
Evans, A. J.
Evans, H. M.

F

Falk, J. D.
Farmerie, S. A.
Fitzgerald, C. B.
Fox, G.
Frame, R. M., III.
Frank, S. H.
Franz, D. A.
Frederick, R. D.
Frenkley, N.
Frey, L.
Frey, M. L.
Fulton, R. T.

G

Gagnon, G. O.
Gammage, J. K.
Garland, A. N.
Gassner, J. S.
Genung, M.
Gibson, E.
Glasrud, B. A.
Grant, C. L.
Gunter, C. R.

H

Harahan, J. P.
Harrington, J. F.
Harrow, S.
Hartigan, F. X.
Harvey, K. A.
Heermans, D.
Held, C. H.
Herrick, J. M.
Hewlett, G. A.
Hively, W. R.
Hobson, W. K.
Hoffman, A.
Homan, G. D.
Hough, M.
Howell, R.
Hubbard, L. L.
Huff, A. E.
Human, V. L.
Hurt, R. D.
Hyslop, E. C.

I

Iklé, F. W.

J

Jacobsen, B.
Johnson, D. W.
Johnson, E. D.
Johnson, E. S.
Johnson, L. F.

K

Kamika, T.
Kaufman, M.
Kearns, W. A.
Kennedy, P. W.
Khan, R. O.
Kicklighter, J. A.
Kimmel, B.
Knafla, L. A.
Kubicek, R. V.

L

LaBue, B. J.
Larson, A. J.
LeBlanc, A. E.
Lederer, N.
Leedom, J. W.
Lewis, J. A.
Lifka, M. L.
Lokken, R. N.
Lovin, H. T.
Lowitt, R.

M

Mahood, H. R.
Marr, W. L.
Marshall, P. C.
Mattar, P. S. J.
McCarthy, J. M.
McDorman, K. S.
McGinnis, D.
McIntyre, W. D.
McKinney, G. B.
McLendon, E. M.
Miller, R. M.
Moen, N. W.
Moody, C.
Morrison, S. C.
Murdoch, D. H.
Murdock, E. C.
Mycue, D. J.
Myers, R. C.
Myres, S. L.

N

Neville, J. D.
Neville, R. G.
Nielson, D. G.
Niven, A. C.
Novitsky, A. W.

O

Oaks, R. F.
Ohrvall, O. W.
Olbrich, W. L.
Olson, C. W.
Osur, A. M.

P

Palais, E. S.
Panting, G. E.
Parker, H. M.
Patterson, S. L.
Patzwald, G. A.
Paul, B. J.
Paul, J. F.
Pergl, G. E.
Pickens, D. K.
Piersen, W. D.
Porter, B. S.
Powers, T. L.
Puffer, K. J.
Pusateri, C. J.

Q

Quéripel, S. R.

R

Reed, J. B.
Riles, R.
Ritter, R. V.
Rosenthal, F.
Rossi, G. J.

S

Samaraweera, V.
Sapper, N. G.
Schoenberg, P. E.
Schoonover, T. D.
Selleck, R. G.
Sevilla, S.
Shields, H. S.
Shipton, A. R.
Simmerman, T.
Sindermann, R. P.
Smith, C. O.
Smith, D. B.
Smith, D. L.
Smith, L. C.
Smith, L. D.
Smith, R. A.
Smith, S. R.
Smith, T. W.
Smoot, J. G.
Soff, H. G.
Spira, T.
Sprague, S. S.
Stickney, E. P.
Stoesen, A. R.
Street, J. B.
Street, N. J.
Sweetland, J. H.
Swiecicka-Ziemianek, M.
Szewczyk, M. W.

T

Tate, M. L.
Tennyson, B. D.
Thacker, J. W.
Thomas, J. R.
Travis, P.

U

Underwood, T. L.

V

Van Wyk, L. W.
Vance, M. M.
Verardo, D. R.

W

Walker, W. T.
Ward, H. M.
Watson, C. A.
Weltsch, R. E.
Wendel, T. H.
Wengenroth, U.
White, J. L.
Whitham, W. B.
Williams, J.
Williams, J. W.
Wilson, M. T.
Woodward, R. L.

Y

Yanchisin, D. A.
Yerburgh, M. R.
Yntema, S. G.

Z

Ziewacz, L. E.
Zornow, W. F.

LIST OF ABBREVIATIONS

A. .... Author-prepared Abstract
Acad. .... Academy, Academie, Academia
Agric. .... Agriculture, Agricultural
AIA .... Abstracts in Anthropology
Akad. .... Akademie
Am. .... America, American
Ann. .... Annals, Annales, Annual, Annali
Anthrop. .... Anthropology, Anthropological
Arch. .... Archives
Archaeol. .... Archaeology, Archaeological
Art. .... Article
Assoc. .... Association, Associate
Biblio. .... Bibliography, Bibliographical
Biog. .... Biography, Biographical
Bol. .... Boletim, Boletin
Bull. .... Bulletin
c. .... century (in index)
ca. .... circa
Can. .... Canada, Canadian, Canadien
Cent. .... Century
Coll. .... College
Com. .... Committee
Comm. .... Commission
Comp. .... Compiler
DAI. .... Dissertation Abstracts International
Dept. .... Department
Dir. .... Director, Direktor
Econ. .... Economy, Econom-.
Ed. .... Editor, Edition
Educ. .... Education, Educational
Geneal. .... Genealogy, Genealogical, Gencalogique
Grad. .... Graduate
Hist. .... History, Hist-.
IHE .... Indice Historico Espanol

Illus. .... Illustrated, Illustration
Inst. .... Institute, Institut-.
Int. .... International, Internacional, Internationaal,
                    Internationaux, Internazionale
J. .... Journal, Journal-prepared Abstract
Lib. .... Library, Libraries
Mag. .... Magazine
Mus. .... Museum, Musee, Museo
Nac. .... Nacional
Natl. .... National, Nationale
Naz. .... Nazionale
Phil. .... Philosophy, Philosophical
Photo. .... Photograph
Pol. .... Politics, Political, Politique, Politico
Pr. .... Press
Pres. .... President
Pro. .... Proceedings
Publ. .... Publishing, Publication
Q. .... Quarterly
Rev. .... Review, Revue, Revista, Revised
Riv. .... Rivista
Res. .... Research
RSA .... Romanian Scientific Abstracts
S. .... Staff-prepared Abstract
Sci. .... Science, Scientific
Secy. .... Secretary
Soc. .... Society, Societe, Sociedad, Societa
Sociol. .... Sociology, Sociological
Tr. .... Transactions
Transl. .... Translator, Translation
U. .... University, Universi-.
US .... United States
Vol. .... Volume
Y. .... Yearbook

Abbreviations also apply to feminine and plural forms.
Abbreviations not noted above are based on *Webster's Third New International Dictionary*
and the *United States Government Printing Office Style Manual*.

CAMROSE LUTHERAN COLLEGE
LIBRARY